THE ROUGH GUIDE TO
MALAYSIA
SINGAPORE & BRUNEI

This ninth edition updated by

Marco Ferrarese, Richard Lim, Simon Willmore and
Charles Young

ROUGH
GUIDES

Contents

OPPOSITE PYROPS CANDELARIA, GUNUNG MULU NATIONAL PARK **PREVIOUS PAGE** MOUNT KINABALU

Introduction to

Malaysia, Singapore and Brunei

Populated by a blend of Malays, Chinese, Indians and indigenous groups, Malaysia, Singapore and Brunei boast a rich cultural heritage, from a huge variety of annual festivals and wonderful cuisines, to traditional architecture and rural crafts. There's astonishing natural beauty to take in too, including gorgeous beaches and some of the world's oldest tropical rainforest, much of which is surprisingly accessible. Malaysia's national parks are superb for trekking and wildlife-watching, and sometimes for cave exploration and river rafting.

As part of the Malay archipelago, which stretches from Indonesia to the Philippines, Malaysia, Singapore and Brunei share not only similarities in their ethnic make-up but also part of their **history**. Each became an important port of call on the trade route between India and China, the two great markets of the early world, and later became important entrepôts for the Portuguese, Dutch and British empires. Malaysia has only existed in its present form since 1963, when the federation of the eleven Peninsula states was joined by Singapore and the two Bornean territories of Sarawak and Sabah. Singapore didn't last even two years inside Malaysia, becoming an independent city-state in 1965; Brunei chose to stay outside the federation and only became independent of the British in 1984.

Since then, Malaysia, Singapore and Brunei have been united in their **economic predominance** among Southeast Asian nations. While Brunei is locked into a paternalistic regime, using its considerable oil wealth to guarantee its citizens a respectable standard of living, Singapore has become a giant in commerce, having transformed itself from a strategic port. Malaysia, always competitive with its southern neighbour, is pursuing a similarly ambitious goal, to which end the country is investing heavily in new infrastructure, from highways to ports and factories.

Today, the dominant cultural force in the region is undoubtedly **Islam**, adopted by the

ABOVE PERHENTIAN ISLANDS **OPPOSITE** ORANG-UTAN, SEPILOK

Malays in the fourteenth century, though in Chinese-dominated Singapore, **Buddhism** and **Taoism** together hold sway among half the population. But it's the religious plurality – there are also sizeable Christian and Hindu minorities – that is so attractive, often providing surprising juxtapositions of mosques, temples and churches. Add the colour and verve of Chinese temples and street fairs, Indian festival days and everyday life in Malay kampungs (villages), as well as the indigenous traditions of Borneo, and it's easy to see why visitors are drawn into this celebration of ethnic diversity; indeed, despite some issues, both Malaysia and Singapore have something to teach the rest of the world when it comes to building successful multicultural societies.

Where to go

Malaysia's capital, **Kuala Lumpur** (usually referred to as KL), is the social and economic driving force of a nation eager to better itself, a fact reflected in the relentless proliferation of air-conditioned shopping malls, designer bars and restaurants in the city, and in the continuing sprawl of suburbia and industry around it. But KL is also firmly rooted in tradition, where the same Malay executives who wear suits to work dress in traditional clothes at festival times, and markets and food stalls are crowded in among high-rise hotels and bank towers, especially in older areas such as Chinatown and Little India.

Just a couple of hours' drive south of the capital lies the birthplace of Malay civilization, **Melaka**, its historical architecture and mellow atmosphere making it a must on anybody's itinerary. Much further up the **west coast**, the island of **Penang** was the site of the first British settlement in Malaysia. Its capital, **George Town**, still features beautifully restored

FACT FILE

- **Malaysia** is a federation of nine **sultanates**, plus the states of Penang, Melaka and, on the island of Borneo, Sabah and Sarawak.

- **Peninsular Malaysia**, where the federal capital Kuala Lumpur is located, and **East Malaysia**, the northern section of Borneo, are separated by more than 600km of the South China Sea.

- In terms of **population**, Malays make up just over half of Malaysia's 32 million people, ethnic Chinese around 22 percent, indigenous Orang Asli and Borneo tribes together 12 percent, and ethnic Indians 7 percent.

- Tiny **Singapore**, just 700 square kilometres in size, is a wealthy city-state cramming in 5.5 million inhabitants, including a sizeable minority of expats.

- Made up of two enclaves in eastern Sarawak, **Brunei** is nearly ten times the size of Singapore, but holds less than one tenth of the population.

- Both Malaysia and Singapore are British-style **parliamentary democracies**, the former with a ceremonial head of state known as the Yang di-Pertuan Agung (the post rotates among the sultans of the federation). Brunei is ruled by its **sultan**.

- The world's largest flower, **Rafflesia**, is a Malaysian rainforest plant measuring a metre across and smelling of rotten meat. It's named after the naturalist and founder of Singapore, Sir Stamford Raffles.

- Malaysia's **economy**, historically dominated by agriculture and mining, now features a healthy manufacturing sector, as does Singapore, where shipping and financial services are also key industries. Brunei profits handsomely from its reserves of oil and gas.

colonial buildings and a vibrant Chinatown district, and is, together with Melaka, recognized for its cultural and architectural diversity as a UNESCO World Heritage Site. The former hill station **Cameron Highlands** has lost most of its colonial atmosphere, but its cooler temperatures and lush countryside provide ample opportunities for walks, birdwatching, rounds of golf and cream teas. North of Penang, Malay, rather than Chinese, traditions hold sway at **Alor Star**, the last major town before the Thai border. This far north, the premier tourist destination is **Langkawi**, an island with international-style resorts and picture-postcard beaches.

The Peninsula's **east coast** is much more rural and relaxing, peppered with rustic villages and stunning islands such as **the Perhentians** and **Tioman**, busy with backpackers and package tourists alike. The state capitals of **Kota Bharu**, near the northeastern Thai border, and **Kuala Terengganu**, further south, still showcase something of the Malay traditions, craft production and performing arts.

Crossing the Peninsula's mountainous **interior** by road or rail allows you to venture into the majestic tropical rainforests of **Taman Negara**. The national park's four thousand square kilometres hold enough to keep you occupied for days: trails, salt-lick hides for animal-watching, aerial forest-canopy walkways, limestone caves and waterfalls. Here you may well also come across the **Orang Asli**, the Peninsula's indigenous peoples, a few of whom cling to a semi-nomadic lifestyle within the park.

Across the sea from the Peninsula lie the east Malaysian states of Sarawak and Sabah. For most travellers, their first taste of **Sarawak** comes at **Kuching**, the old colonial capital, and then the Iban **longhouses** of the Batang Ai river system. **Sibu**, much further north on the Rajang River, is the starting point for trips to less touristed Iban, Kayan and Kenyah longhouses. In the north, **Gunung Mulu National Park** is the principal

destination; many come here to climb up to view its extraordinary razor-sharp limestone pinnacles, though spectacular caves also burrow into the park's mountains. More remote still are the **Kelabit Highlands**, further east, where the mountain air is refreshingly cool and there are ample opportunities for extended treks.

More so than any other part of Malaysia, **Sabah** draws visitors with its wildlife. The state's surviving forests are well enough protected to host elephants, orang-utans, proboscis monkeys, hornbills and rare creatures such as the clouded leopard, while its southeastern islands, notably **Sipadan**, are home to some of the world's most cherished dive sites, which teem with stunning marine life. Perhaps the best-known attraction, though, is the 4095m granite peak of **Mount Kinabalu**, which needs no special gear or skills to hike up – though it's a pricey experience. The mountain is easily reached from the modern, lively capital Kota Kinabalu.

An easy entry-point for first-time visitors to Southeast Asia, **Singapore** is exceptionally safe, organized and accessible, thanks to its small size, excellent modern infrastructure

WILDLIFE

Peninsular Malaysia, Borneo and Singapore are a paradise for wildlife-spotters, harbouring over 600 types of birds and 200 mammal species – including Asian elephants, sun bears, tigers, tapirs, barking deer, gibbons, hornbills and pythons. Borneo's speciality is the **proboscis monkey**, so-called because of its bulbous, drooping nose. The island is also one of only two natural habitats (with Sumatra) for **orang-utans** – indeed, the name is Malay for "man of the forest". **Marine life** is equally diverse: divers can swim with white-tip sharks, clownfish and barracuda, not to mention green and hawksbill **turtles**, which drag themselves ashore in season to lay their eggs by night. Even cosmopolitan Singapore maintains a pocket of primary rainforest that's home to long-tailed macaques.

Author picks

Our authors have traversed every corner of Malaysia, Singapore and Brunei, from KL's shopping malls and Sarawak's longhouses to the jungles of Taman Negara and the summit of Mount Kinabalu. Here are some of their favourite experiences.

Wildlife-spotting Hornbills and long-tailed macaques are widespread, and you can see elephants at the Kinabatangan River (see p.434), proboscis monkeys at Bako (see p.339) and orang-utans at Sepilok (see p.431) and Semenggoh (see p.342).

Tastiest laksa Compare famous variations of the region's signature seafood soup in Penang (p.161), Singapore (p.543) and Kuching (p.331).

Shadow puppets Experience the magical Malay tradition of *wayang kulit* at Kota Bharu's Cultural Centre (p.224).

Amazing caves Sarawak has major cave systems which are both spectacular – especially at Gunung Mulu National Park (p.372) – and of archeological significance, as in the case of Niah (p.368).

Eccentric desserts Satisfy your sweet tooth with ABC – shaved ice drenched in condensed milk and luridly coloured fruit syrups (p.42).

Turtle beaches Stay up late to catch marine turtles laying their eggs at Sabah's Turtle Islands Park (see p.433)

Glittering cityscapes Admire the night lights from atop Menara KL (p.78) and *Marina Bay Sands'* SkyPark in Singapore (p.506).

Rowdiest festival You can't beat the crowds and slightly gory celebrations surrounding the Hindu festival of Thaipusam at KL's Batu Caves (p.106).

Bizarre blooms Discover the weird *Rafflesia* flower, whose scent mimics rotting meat, at the Royal Belum State Park (p.136), Gunung Gading (p.343) or Tambunan (p.447).

> Our author recommendations don't end here. We've flagged up our favourite places – a perfectly sited hotel, an atmospheric café, a special restaurant – throughout the guide, highlighted with the ★ symbol.

OPPOSITE ELEPHANTS **FROM TOP** ABC; SHADOW PUPPETS

SHOPHOUSES

A standard feature of local townscapes is rows of **shophouses** – two- or three-storey buildings traditionally containing a shop at street level, with residential quarters behind and above. For visitors, their most striking feature is that at ground level the front wall is usually set back from the street. This creates a so-called "**five-foot way**" overhung by the upper part of the house, which shelters pedestrians from the sun and pelting rain.

Shophouses were fusion architecture: facades have **Western** features such as shuttered windows and gables, while inside there might be an area open to the sky, in the manner of **Chinese** courtyard houses. Some, especially from the early part of the last century, are bedecked with columns, floral plaster motifs and beautiful tilework, while later properties feature simpler Art Deco touches. Sadly, shophouses went out of favour in the 1980s, and recent ones tend to be bland, functional affairs; older buildings, however, have won a new lease of life as swanky restaurants and boutique hotels.

and Western standards of hygiene – though prices are likewise at Western levels. The island has fascinating Chinese and Indian quarters, excellent historical museums and a smattering of colonial architecture as well as great shopping, all of which will keep you occupied for several days. Singapore also rightly holds a reputation as one of Asia's **gastronomic capitals**, where you can just as readily savour fantastic snacks at simple hawker stalls or an exquisite Chinese banquet in a swanky restaurant.

For those who venture into the tiny kingdom of **Brunei**, enveloped by Sarawak's two most northerly divisions, the capital **Bandar Seri Begawan** holds the entrancing Kampung Ayer, a sprawling stilt village built out over the Brunei River, plus a handful of interesting museums and mosques. In the sparsely populated Temburong district, you can visit unspoiled rainforest at the **Ulu Temburong National Park**, where abundant wildlife roams.

When to go

Temperatures vary little in Malaysia, Singapore and Brunei, hovering constantly at or just above 30°C by day, while humidity is high year-round. Showers occur year-round too, often in the mid-afternoon, though these short, sheeting downpours clear up as quickly as they arrive.

The major distinction in the seasons is marked by the arrival of the northeast monsoon (ushering in what is locally called the **rainy season**). This particularly affects the east coast of Peninsular Malaysia and the western end of Sarawak, with late November to mid-February seeing the heaviest rainfall. On the Peninsula's west coast and in Sabah, September and October are the wettest months. Monsoonal downpours can be heavy and prolonged, sometimes lasting two or three hours and prohibiting more or less all activity for the duration; boats to most islands in affected areas won't attempt the sea swell at the height of the rainy season. In mountainous areas like Cameron Highlands, the Kelabit Highlands and in the hill stations and upland national parks, you may experience more frequent rain as the high peaks gather clouds more or less permanently.

The **ideal time** to visit most of the region is between March and early October, when you will avoid the worst of the rains and there's less humidity, though both ends of this period can be characterized by a stifling lack of breezes. Despite the rains, the months of January and February are rewarding, and see a number of significant **festivals**, notably Chinese New Year and the Hindu celebration of Thaipusam. Visiting just after the rainy season can afford the best of both worlds, with verdant countryside and bountiful waterfalls, though there's still a clammy quality to the air. In late May and early June, a **rice harvest** festival takes place in both Sabah (where it's called Kaamatan) and Sarawak (Gawai). It's an excuse for extended merry-making, with much quaffing of rice wine, music and dancing – all best witnessed in longhouses, although Kota Kinabalu hosts more formal celebrations.

AVERAGE DAILY TEMPERATURES AND RAINFALL

	Jan	Feb	Mar	April	May	June	July	Aug	Sept	Oct	Nov	Dec
KOTA BHARU												
Max/min °C	29/22	30/23	31/23	32/24	33/24	32/24	32/23	32/23	32/23	31/23	29/23	29/23
Rain (mm)	163	60	99	81	114	132	157	168	195	286	651	603
KOTA KINABALU												
Max/min °C	30/23	30/23	31/23	32/24	32/24	31/24	31/24	31/24	31/23	31/23	31/23	31/23
Rain (mm)	153	63	71	124	218	311	277	256	314	334	296	241
KUALA LUMPUR												
Max/min °C	32/22	33/22	33/23	33/23	33/23	32/23	32/23	32/23	32/23	32/23	31/23	31/23
Rain (mm)	159	154	223	276	182	119	120	133	173	258	263	223
KUCHING												
Max/min °C	30/23	30/23	31/23	32/23	33/23	33/23	32/23	33/23	32/23	32/23	31/23	31/23
Rain (mm)	683	522	339	286	253	199	199	211	271	326	343	465
SINGAPORE												
Max/min °C	32/23	32/23	32/24	32/24	31/24	31/24	31/23	31/23	31/23	31/23	31/23	31/23
Rain (mm)	70	93	141	214	240	170	208	235	341	380	246	107

22

things not to miss

It's not possible to see everything that Malaysia, Singapore and Brunei have to offer in one trip – and we don't suggest you try. What follows is a selective taste, in no particular order, of their highlights: natural wonders, stunning buildings and colourful heritages. Each entry has a page reference to take you straight into the Guide, where you can find out more. Coloured numbers refer to chapters in the Guide section.

1

1 NIAH NATIONAL PARK Page 368
This compact park is the site of a cave system holding important archeological remains, and also offers the chance to see edible swiftlet nests being harvested at certain times of year.

2 GEORGE TOWN
Page 148
A bustling, Chinese-dominated town with historic temples, colonial-era mansions and a blossoming cultural scene.

3 LANGKAWI
Page 175
Luxurious resorts on sublime beaches pretty much sums up this west-coast island, close to the Thai border.

7

4 KAMPONG AYER
Page 459

Take a boat ride around this wooden village in the middle of the Brunei River.

5 TAMAN NEGARA
Page 191

Peninsular Malaysia's premier national park, Taman Negara is one of the world's oldest rainforests, with hides for wildlife-spotting, treetop walkways and many trekking options.

6 ADVENTURE TOURISM
Page 48

Whitewater rafting, caving and jungle trekking are among activities widely available in Malaysia.

7 SINGAPORE'S ARTS SCENE
Page 546

As befits the largest city in the region, Singapore offers a dynamic range of artistic activities – catch anything from Chinese street opera to indie rock gigs.

8 KELABIT HIGHLANDS
Page 378

These remote uplands offer excellent walks and hikes, plus encounters with friendly tribal communities along the way.

8

11

12

13 THE PETRONAS TOWERS
Page 74
KL's iconic towers not only hold your gaze from all angles but also house one of the city's best shopping malls.

14 THE KINABATANGAN RIVER
Page 434
Boat trips here are brilliant for spotting proboscis monkeys, hornbills and, if you're lucky, elephants and orang-utans.

15 MALIAU BASIN
Page 449
Billed as Sabah's "Lost World", this forest conservation area has excellent multi-day treks to remote waterfalls, plus decent wildlife-spotting opportunities.

16 TRADITIONAL CRAFTS
Page 51
Malaysia boasts a wide range of crafts, from batik and *songket* (brocade) to rattan baskets and *labu*, gourd-shaped ceramic jugs.

17 FOOD
Page 38
Simple stalls in markets and malls and on the street serve up mouthwatering noodles, snacks and desserts.

18

19

18 LONGHOUSES IN SARAWAK

Page 345

Large communal dwellings, home to members of indigenous tribes, are found along rivers and in remote mountain locations.

19 PROBOSCIS MONKEYS, BAKO

Page 339

These odd-looking creatures roam *kerangas* forest and mangrove swamps in the national park, not far from Kuching.

20 RAINFOREST MUSIC FESTIVAL

Page 338

Held annually near Kuching, this world music festival is an opportunity to see indigenous performers alongside musicians from across the globe.

21 MOUNT KINABALU

Page 417

Watch dawn over Borneo from the summit of one of Southeast Asia's highest peaks.

22 DIVING AT SIPADAN

Page 441

Off southeast Sabah, Sipadan and neighbouring islands are world-renowned for their dive sites and astonishing marine life.

Itineraries

Malaysia, Singapore and Brunei cover such a spread-out area that it would be impossible to see everything in one trip, but each of the following routes makes a great way to spend two or three weeks in the region. While the Peninsula Circuit is the most varied, you can head east to Borneo if you prefer an outdoor-focused option. Singapore is more of a long-weekend destination, but a stay here could easily be tacked onto a wider trip north up into Peninsular Malaysia.

PENINSULA CIRCUIT

For a straightforward taster of everything the region has to offer, try this three-week circuit.

❶ **Kuala Lumpur** Malaysia's capital offers shiny malls, showcase architecture and a mix of Muslim, Chinese and Hindu districts, with some of the best street food in the country. **See p.66**

❷ **Cameron Highlands** This former retreat for colonial administrators is now a rural idyll of tea plantations and forest walks. **See p.138**

❸ **Pangkor Island** Kick back at this low-key resort island that's a favourite with Malaysian families. **See p.125**

❹ **Penang** Packed with historic guildhalls and streets, eccentric temples, surprisingly wild gardens and its own national park. **See p.146**

❺ **Kota Bharu** One of the few places where you can see shadow-puppet performances of the Hindu epics. **See p.221**

❻ **Perhentian islands** Superb tropical hangouts with gorgeous beaches and splendid snorkelling and scuba diving. **See p.231**

❼ **Jungle Railway** This slow-moving commuter train chugs past languid towns, tiny kampungs and market gardens along the way. **See p.204**

❽ **Taman Negara** One of the world's oldest rainforests features superlative wildlife-spotting and jungle treks lasting up to a week or more. **See p.191**

SINGAPORE AND MELAKA

You can pack this round-up of the region's great food and centuries-old history into a week.

❶ **Little India, Singapore** Charismatic area of temples and shops selling gold and saris with the liveliest market in Singapore. **See p.490**

PENINSULA CIRCUIT

SINGAPORE AND MELAKA

THAILAND

PENINSULAR MALAYSIA

INDONESIA

SINGAPORE

❷ Chinatown, Singapore Amid the modern shophouses, restaurants and markets, don't miss the Buddha Tooth Relic Temple, full of dynamic statuary and the tooth itself. **See p.496**

❸ Night Safari, Singapore The highlight of Singapore Zoo's superbly displayed collection of native wildlife, the Night Safari section lets you see creatures such as tigers, leopards, elephants and rhinos. **See p.514**

❹ Bukit Timah, Singapore The last patch of real rainforest left in Singapore offers an easy, leech-free introduction to jungle trails and colourful birdlife. **See p.513**

❺ Eating, Singapore Indulge in one of the world's gastronomic capitals, with varied menus of Indian, Chinese and Malay dishes. **See p.536**

❻ Istana Kesultanan, Melaka An exquisite Malay palace, built without nails and founded during the fifteenth century. **See p.277**

❼ Baba-Nyonya Heritage Museum, Melaka An elegant row of traditional houses decorated with the tiles, lanterns and woodcarvings of the Chinese-Malay Peranakan culture, now – aside from its cuisine – virtually extinct. **See p.279**

❽ Bukit China, Melaka Hilltop covered in many crescent-shaped Chinese graves, some dating to the seventeenth century. **See p.281**

SARAWAK AND MT KINABALU

Allow at least three weeks for this adventurous trip into Malaysia's least-developed corners.

❶ Kuching Find your bearings in Sarawak's small, likeable capital: the museum's ethnological collection is worth a browse, and the Semenggoh orang-utan sanctuary makes a rewarding day-trip. **See p.321**

❷ Bako Sarawak's oldest national park, this small patch of well-preserved coastal forest is home to waterfalls, proboscis monkeys and bizarre pitcher plants. **See p.339**

❸ Batang Ai Take a boat through spectacular riverine forest in this often overlooked national park, and visit traditional longhouse communities such as Nanga Sumpa. **See p.345**

❹ Gunung Mulu National Park Offers jungle scenery, particularly on the three-day trek out to a clutch of limestone towers and a network of rugged caverns. **See p.372**

❺ Miri A stepping stone to the more remote corners of Sarawak and to Sabah. Don't miss the caves at Niah National Park, inhabited by humans over 40,000 years ago. **See p.362**

❻ Bario Set out on some demanding multiday trekking via remote Kelabit longhouses or up Mount Murud. **See p.380**

❼ Kota Kinabalu Sabah's capital has lively markets, a district of traditional houses built over the water and an interesting indigenous museum. **See p.393**

❽ Kinabalu Park This small reserve surrounds wind-seared Mount Kinabaulu, which hosts one of the toughest hikes in all of Malaysia. **See p.417**

SARAWAK AND MT KINABALU

BRUNEI

MALAYSIA

INDONESIA

TRISHAW

Basics

Getting there

Located at the heart of Southeast Asia, on the busy aviation corridor between Europe and Australasia, Malaysia and Singapore enjoy excellent international air links. Singapore is served by many more flights than Kuala Lumpur (KL), but can also be slightly more expensive to fly into. Of Malaysia's regional airports, those in Kota Kinabalu, Kuching and Penang have the most useful international connections, albeit chiefly with other East Asian cities. If you're heading to Brunei, you'll most likely have to stop over elsewhere in the region or in the Middle East.

During the **peak seasons** for travel to Southeast Asia – the Christmas/New Year period, typically from mid-December until early January, and July and August – prices can be fifty percent higher than at other times of year, though you can often avoid the steepest fares by booking well **in advance**. Fares also rise at weekends and around major local festivals, such as Islamic holidays and the Chinese New Year. Sample fares given here are for **round-trip** journeys and include taxes and current fuel surcharges. If you're thinking of visiting on a **package trip**, note that it's generally cheaper to book one after you've arrived than with a tour operator in your home country.

From the UK and Ireland

London Heathrow has daily **nonstop** flights to KL with Malaysia Airlines (W malaysiaairlines.com), and to Singapore with British Airways (W britishairways.com) and Singapore Airlines (W singaporeair.com). At the time of writing, the low-cost carrier Norwegian (W norwegian.com) had launched a competing nonstop Singapore flight from London Gatwick. From Manchester, Singapore Airlines departs several times a week nonstop to Singapore. On these routes, reckon on the journey time being twelve to thirteen hours. Flying with any other airline or from any other airport in the UK and Ireland involves a change of plane in Europe, the Middle East or elsewhere in Asia. The very best **fares** to KL or Singapore are around £450/€500 outside high season, with nonstop flights always commanding a premium.

From the US and Canada

In most cases the trip from North America, including a stopover, will take at least twenty hours if you fly the **transatlantic** route from the eastern seaboard, or nineteen hours minimum if you cross the **Pacific** from the west coast. It is, however, possible to fly nonstop from San Francisco to Singapore on Singapore Airlines (W singaporeair .com), and from Los Angeles to Singapore on United (W united.com), with trips lasting around seventeen hours. From Honolulu, there's also the option of flying with Scoot (W flyscoot.com), Singapore Airlines' low-cost-arm, to Singapore.

The quickest route isn't always the cheapest: it can sometimes cost less to fly westwards from the east coast, stopping off in Northeast Asia en route. **Fares** start at around US$800 or Can$1100 for flights from major US or Canadian airports on either coast.

Plenty of airlines operate to East Asia from major North American cities. If your target is Borneo, it's worth investigating connecting with one of the east Asian airlines – Kota Kinabalu, for example, has flights from Hong Kong, Shanghai and Seoul.

From Australia and New Zealand

Geographical proximity means there's a good range of flights from Australia and New Zealand into Malaysia, Singapore and Brunei, including a useful link between Melbourne and Borneo with Royal Brunei Airlines (W flyroyalbrunei.com). **Budget flights** include services from Australia to KL with AirAsia (W airasia.com) and Malindo Air (W malindoair.com), and to Singapore with Jetstar (W jetstar .com) and Scoot (W flyscoot.com), and from Christchurch in New Zealand to KL (AirAsia) and Singapore (Jetstar).

If you're flying from, say, Perth to Singapore or KL, expect **fares** to start at as little as Aus$450 return in low season, while Melbourne to Singapore will set you back at least Aus$550. Christchurch to KL or Singapore generally starts at NZ$1000 return.

From South Africa

The quickest way to reach Malaysia or Singapore from South Africa is to fly with **Singapore Airlines** (W singaporeair.com), which offers nonstop flights to Singapore from Cape Town (11hr) via Johannesburg; reckon on ten hours' flying time. That said, it's often cheaper to book a ticket that involves changing planes en route, usually in the Middle East. If you're lucky you may land a fare of around R8000 return, including taxes, though it's not uncommon to have to pay R1000–2000 more.

From elsewhere in Southeast Asia

Budget airlines make it easy to explore Malaysia, Singapore and Brunei as part of a wider trip through Southeast Asia. The most useful no-frills carriers for the three countries covered in this book are Malaysia's AirAsia (ⓦairasia.com), Firefly (ⓦfireflyz.com.my) and Malindo Air (ⓦmalindoair.com), and Singapore's Scoot (ⓦflyscoot.com) and Jetstar Asia (ⓦjetstar.com). Though fuel surcharges and taxes do take some of the shine off the fares, prices can still be good, especially if you book well in advance.

You can, of course, reach Malaysia or Singapore from their immediate neighbours by means other than flying. There are **road** connections from Thailand and from Kalimantan (Indonesian Borneo); **ferries** from Indonesia and from the southern Philippines, and **trains** from Thailand. Below is a round-up of the most popular routes.

From Thailand

A daily Special Express **train** service leaves Hualamphong station in Bangkok at 3.10pm on the 1000km journey south to the Malaysian border town of Padang Besar, where travellers can change for Malaysian ETS trains on the west-coast line (see p.32). The train calls at (among others) Hua Hin, Surat Thani and Hat Yai before reaching Padang Besar at 9am Thai time (10am Malaysian time). Also useful is the Thai rail service from Hat Yai across to Sungai Golok on the east coast of the Kra isthmus, close to the Malaysian border crossing at Rantau Panjang, from where buses run to Kota Bharu.

As regards **flights**, plenty of services connect Bangkok, Chiang Mai and Thai resorts with Malaysian airports and Singapore. Some are run by the low-cost airlines, while others are provided by Bangkok Airways (ⓦbangkokair.com) and Singapore Airlines subsidiary SilkAir (ⓦsilkair.com).

A few scheduled **ferry** services sail from the most southwesterly Thai town of Satun to the Malaysian west-coast town of Kuala Perlis (30min) and to the island of Langkawi (1hr 30min). If you're departing from Thailand by sea for Malaysia, ensure your passport is stamped at the immigration office at the pier to avoid problems with the Malaysian immigration officials when you arrive. Another option is the ferry from the southern Thai town of Ban Taba to the Malaysian town of Pengkalan Kubor, where frequent buses run to Kota Bharu, 20km away. Buses connect Ban Taba with the provincial capital, Narathiwat (1hr 30min).

The easiest **road** access from Thailand is via Hat Yai, from where buses, minivans and a few shared taxis run to Butterworth (4hr) and nearby George Town on Penang Island, with some buses continuing right to KL or Singapore. From the interior Thai town of Betong, there's a road across the border to the Malaysian town of Pengkalan Hulu, from where Route 67 leads west to Sungai Petani; share taxis serve the route. You can also get a taxi from Ban Taba for the few kilometres south to Kota Bharu.

From Indonesia

Plenty of **flights**, including many operated by the low-cost airlines, connect major airports in Java and Sumatra, plus Bali and Lombok, with Malaysia and Singapore. There's also a service between Manado in Sulawesi and Singapore with Singapore Airlines' subsidiary SilkAir (ⓦsilkair.com). As for Kalimantan, AirAsia (ⓦairasia.com) operates between Balikpapan and KL, and

---

THE EASTERN & ORIENTAL EXPRESS

Unlike some luxury trains in other parts of the world, the **Eastern & Oriental Express** (ⓦbelmond.com) isn't a re-creation of a classic colonial-era rail journey, but a sort of fantasy realization of how such a service might have looked had it existed in Southeast Asia. Employing 1970s Japanese rolling stock, given an elegant old-world cladding with wooden inlay work and featuring Thai and Malay motifs, the train travels between Bangkok and Singapore, with the option of starting or ending the trip in KL, at least monthly. En route there are extended stops at Kanchanaburi for a visit to the infamous bridge over the **River Kwai**, and at **Kuala Kangsar**. An observation deck at the rear of the train makes the most of the passing scenery. The trip doesn't come cheap, of course: the two-night Bangkok–KL segment costs around £2000/US$2600 per person in swish, en-suite Pullman accommodation, including meals – and alcohol costs extra.

Malaysia Airlines' subsidiary MASwings (Ⓦ maswings.com.my) operates between Pontianak and Kuching, and also between Tarakan and Tawau in southeastern Sabah.

It's possible to reach Sarawak from Kalimantan on just one **road route**, through the western border town of Entikong and onwards to Kuching. The bus trip from the western city of Pontianak to Entikong takes seven hours, crossing to the Sarawak border town of Tebedu; stay on the same bus for another three hours to reach Kuching.

As for **ferries**, Dumai, on the east coast of Sumatra, has a daily service to Melaka (2hr), with more sailings from Dumai and Tanjong Balai further south to Port Klang near Kuala Lumpur (3hr). There are also a few services from Bintan and Batam islands in the Riau archipelago (accessible by plane or boat from Sumatra or Jakarta) to Johor Bahru (30min) or Singapore (30min), and there's a minor ferry crossing from Tanjung Balai to Kukup (1hr), just southwest of Johor Bahru. Over in Borneo, ferries connect Tawau in Sabah with Nunakan (1hr) and Tarakan (3hr).

From the Philippines

A weekly ferry service operates between Zamboanga in the southern Philippines and Sandakan in Sabah, and Philippine budget airline Cebu Pacific (Ⓦcebupacificair.com) was considering launching a flight on the same route at the time of writing. Other low-cost **flights** include from Clark to KL and Kota Kinabalu (both AirAsia; Ⓦairasia.com), from Clark and Manila to Singapore (JetStar Asia; Ⓦjetstar.com), and from Boracay and Cebu to Singapore (Scoot; Ⓦflyscoot.com). Full-cost airlines provide additional links, including Manila to Bandar Seri Begawan (Royal Brunei Airlines; Ⓦflyroyalbrunei.com).

TRAVEL AGENTS AND TOUR OPERATORS

Adventure Alternative UK ☎ 028 7083 1258, Ⓦ adventurealternative.com. A superb range of off-the-beaten track Borneo tours.

Adventure World Australia ☎ 1300 295049, Ⓦ adventureworld .com.au; New Zealand ☎ 0800 238368, Ⓦ adventureworld.co.nz. Short Malaysia tours, covering cities and some wildlife areas.

Allways Dive Expedition Australia ☎ 1800 338239, Ⓦ allwaysdive.com.au. Dive holidays to the prime dive sites of Sabah.

Asia Classic Tours US ☎ 1800 717 7752, Ⓦ asiaclassictours.com. Malaysia tours, lasting ten days or more, taking in various parts of the country and sometimes Singapore, too.

Audley Travel US & Canada ☎ 1855 838 2120, UK ☎ 01993 838000, Ireland ☎ 1800 992198, Ⓦ audleytravel.com. Luxury tours concentrating on East Malaysia.

Bestway Tours US & Canada ☎ 1800 663 0844, Ⓦ bestway.com. A handful of cultural and wildlife tours featuring East Malaysia and Brunei, plus the peninsula and Singapore.

Borneo Tour Specialists Australia ☎ 07 3221 5777, Ⓦ borneo .com.au. Small-group, customizable tours of all of Borneo, covering wildlife, trekking and tribal culture.

Dive Adventures Australia ☎ 1300 657420, Ⓦ diveadventures .com.au. Sabah and Labuan dive packages.

Eastravel UK ☎ 01473 214305, Ⓦ eastravel.co.uk. Bespoke Malaysia trips.

Exodus Travels US ☎ 1844 227 9087, UK ☎ 020 3553 6240, Ⓦ adventurecenter.com. Several packages, mainly focused on East Malaysia, plus tailor-made trips.

Explore UK ☎ 01252 883618, Ⓦ explore.co.uk. A handful of Malaysia tours.

Explorient US ☎ 1800 785 1233, Ⓦ explorient.com. Malaysia and Singapore packages, including both city and jungle breaks.

Intrepid Travel US ☎ 1800 970 7299, Canada ☎ 1855 299 1211, UK ☎ 0808 274 5111, Australia ☎ 1300 854500, New Zealand ☎ 0800 600 610; Ⓦ intrepidtravel.com. Several Malaysia offerings, mainly focused on Borneo or taking in Thailand and Singapore as well.

Jade Tours Canada ☎ 1800 387 0387, Ⓦ jadetours.com. Borneo and Peninsular Malaysia trips.

Lee's Travel UK ☎ 0800 811 9888, Ⓦ leestravel.com. Far Eastern flight deals, including discounted Malaysia and Singapore Airlines tickets.

Namaste Travel UK ☎ 020 7725 6765, Ⓦ namaste.travel. Half a dozen varied Malaysia packages.

Pentravel South Africa ☎ 087 231 2000, Ⓦ pentravel.co.za. Flight deals plus city breaks that combine Singapore with Bangkok or Hong Kong.

Peregrine Adventures US ☎ 1855 832 4859, UK ☎ 020 7408 9021, Australia ☎ 1300 854455; Ⓦ peregrineadventures.com. Experienced operator with a handful of East Malaysia packages.

Premier Holidays UK ☎ 0844 493 7531, Ⓦ premierholidays .co.uk. Tours of East Malaysia, plus holidays in Peninsular Malaysia and Singapore.

Reef & Rainforest US ☎ 1800 794 9767, Ⓦ reefrainforest.com. Sabah dive packages based in resorts or a liveaboard.

Rex Air UK ☎ 020 7439 1898, Ⓦ rexair.co.uk. Specialist in discounted flights to the Far East, with a few package tours to boot.

Sayang Holidays US ☎ 1888 472 9264, Ⓦ sayangholidays .com. City- or resort-based Peninsular Malaysia and Singapore tours, plus Borneo.

STA Travel US ☎ 1800 781 4040, Ⓦ statravel.com; UK ☎ 0333 321 0099, Ⓦ statravel.co.uk; Australia ☎ 134782, Ⓦ statravel.com.au; New Zealand ☎ 0800 474400, Ⓦ statravel.co.nz; South Africa ☎ 0861 781781, Ⓦ statravel.co.za. Worldwide specialists in low-cost flights for students and under-26s; other customers also welcome.

Symbiosis UK ☎ 0845 123 2844, Ⓦ symbiosis-travel.com. Diving, trekking and longhouse stays in various Malaysian locations.

Tour East Canada ☎ 1877 578 8888, Ⓦ toureast.com. A couple of excursions throughout Malaysia, with the option of taking in Singapore, too.

ADDRESSES AND PLACE NAMES

Place names in Malaysia present something of a linguistic dilemma. **Road signage** is often in Malay only, and some colonial-era names have been deliberately changed to Malay ones, but since **English** is widely used in much of the country, local people are just as likely to say "Kinta River" as "Sungai Kinta", or talk of "Northam Road" in George Town rather than "Jalan Sultan Ahmad Shah", and so on. The Guide mostly uses English-language names, for simplicity. The Glossary includes Malay terms for geographical features like beaches, mountains and so forth (see p.601).

Trailfinders UK ☎ 020 7368 1200, ⓦ trailfinders.com; Ireland ☎ 01 677 7888, ⓦ trailfinders.ie. Flights and a few tours, including major Malaysian cities, Borneo and Singapore.
Travel Masters US ☎ 512 323 6961, ⓦ travel-masters.net. Dive packages at Sipadan, Mabul and Kapalai in Sabah.
USIT Ireland ☎ 01 602 1906, ⓦ usit.ie. Student and youth travel.

Visas and entry requirements

Nationals of the UK, Ireland, US, Canada, Australia, New Zealand and South Africa do not need visas in advance to stay in Malaysia, Singapore or Brunei, and it's easy to extend your permission to stay.

That said, check with the relevant embassy or consulate, as the rules on **visas** are complex and subject to change. Ensure that your passport is valid for at least six months from the date of your trip, and has several blank pages for entry stamps.

Malaysia

Upon arrival in **Malaysia**, citizens of Australia, Canada, the UK, Ireland, US, New Zealand and South Africa receive a passport stamp entitling them to a ninety-day stay. Visitors who enter via **Sarawak**, however, receive a thirty-day stamp.

It's straightforward to **extend** your permit through the Immigration Department, who have offices (listed in the Guide) in Kuala Lumpur and major towns; you can also find details of visa requirements for various nationalities on their website, ⓦ www.imi.gov.my. Visitors from the aforementioned countries can also cross into Singapore or Thailand and back to be granted a fresh Malaysia entry stamp.

Tourists travelling from the Peninsula to **East Malaysia** (Sarawak and Sabah) must be cleared again by immigration. Visitors to Sabah can remain as long as their original entry stamp is valid, but Sarawak maintains its own border controls – a condition of its joining the Federation in 1965 – which means you are always stamped in and given a thirty-day Sarawak visa even when arriving from other parts of Malaysia. For a full list of Malaysia's embassies and consulates, see ⓦ kln.gov.my.

MALAYSIA EMBASSIES AND CONSULATES

Australia 7 Perth Ave, Yarralumla, Canberra ☎ 02 6120 0300.
Brunei 61, Junction 336, Jalan Duta, Bandar Seri Begawan ☎ 02 381095.
Canada 60 Boteler St, Ottawa ☎ 613 241 5182.
Indonesia Jalan H.R. Rasuna Said, Kav. X/6, No. 1–3 Kuningan, Jakarta South ☎ 021 522 4947.
Ireland Shelbourne House, Level 3A–5A, Shelbourne Rd, Ballsbridge, Dublin ☎ 01 667 7280.
New Zealand 10 Washington Ave, Brooklyn, PO Box 9422, Wellington ☎ 04 385 2439.
Singapore 301 Jervois Rd ☎ 6235 0111.
South Africa 1007 Francis Baard St, Arcadia, Pretoria 0083 ☎ 012 342 5990.
Thailand 33–35 South Sathorn Rd, Bangkok 10120 ☎ 02 629 6800.
UK 52 Bedford Row, London ☎ 020 7242 4308.
US 3516 International Court, NW Washington DC ☎ 202 572 9700.

Singapore

Singapore reserves the term "visa" for permits that must be obtained in advance. Travellers from many countries, however, are granted a **visit pass** on arrival. Although the duration of the pass can vary at the discretion of immigration officials, citizens of the UK, Ireland, US, Canada, Australia, New Zealand and South Africa are usually given at least thirty days. There is a formal procedure for extending it, but it's usually much easier to simply do a day-trip by a bus to Johor Bahru just inside Malaysia and be given a fresh pass on returning to Singapore.

For details of nationalities that require visas, along with how to apply and how to extend a visit pass, see ⓦ ica.gov.sg. Full details of Singapore's embassies abroad are at ⓦ mfa.gov.sg.

SINGAPORE EMBASSIES AND CONSULATES

Australia 17 Forster Crescent, Yarralumla, Canberra, ACT 2600 ☎ 02 6271 2000.
Brunei 8 Junction 74, Jalan Subok, Bandar Seri Begawan ☎ 02 262741.
Indonesia Block X/4 Kav No. 2, Jalan H.R. Rasuna Said, Kuningan, Jakarta South ☎ 021 2995 0400.
Ireland 2 Ely Place Upper, Dublin ☎ 01 669 1700.
Malaysia 209 Jalan Tun Razak, Kuala Lumpur ☎ 03 2164 1013.
New Zealand 17 Kabul St, Khandallah, Wellington ☎ 04 470 0850.
South Africa 980–982 Francis Baard St, Pretoria ☎ 012 430 6035.
Thailand 129 South Sathorn Rd, Bangkok 10120 ☎ 02 348 6700.
UK 9 Wilton Crescent, Belgravia, London ☎ 020 7235 8315.
US 3501 International Place NW, Washington DC ☎ 202 537 3100.

Brunei

UK and US nationals are allowed to stay in **Brunei** for up to ninety days on arrival; Australian and New Zealand passport holders are granted thirty days; and Canadians get fourteen days. South African citizens need to apply for a visa in advance. Once in Brunei, extending your permission to stay is usually a formality; apply at the Immigration Department in Bandar Seri Begawan. For full details of Brunei's embassies, see Ⓦ mofat.gov.bn.

BRUNEI EMBASSIES AND CONSULATES

Australia 10 Beale Crescent, Deakin, Canberra ☎ 02 6285 4500.
Canada 395 Laurier Ave East, Ottawa ☎ 613 864 5654.
Indonesia 3 & 5 Jalan Patra Kuningan 9, Jakarta South ☎ 021 2911 0242.
Malaysia 2 Jalan Diplomatik 2/5, Putrajaya ☎ 03 8888 7777.
Singapore 325 Tanglin Rd ☎ 6733 9055.
South Africa c/o the embassy in Singapore.
Thailand 12 Soi Ekamai 2, 63 Sukhumvit Rd, Bangkok ☎ 02 714 7395.
UK 19–20 Belgrave Square, London ☎ 020 7581 0521.
US 3520 International Court NW, Washington DC ☎ 202 237 1838.

Customs allowances

Malaysia's duty-free allowances are 200 cigarettes or 225g of tobacco, and one litre of wine, spirits or liquor. Entering **Singapore** from anywhere other than Malaysia (with which there are no duty-free allowances), you can bring in up to three litres of alcohol duty-free; duty is payable on all tobacco.

Visitors to **Brunei** may bring in 200 cigarettes, 50 cigars or 250g of tobacco, and 60ml of perfume; non-Muslims over seventeen can also import two bottles of liquor and twelve cans of beer for personal consumption (any alcohol brought into the country must be declared upon arrival).

DRUGS: A WARNING

In Malaysia, Singapore and Brunei, the possession of **illegal drugs** – hard or soft – carries a hefty prison sentence or even the death penalty. If you are arrested for drugs offences you can expect **no mercy** from the authorities and little help from your consular representatives. The simple advice, therefore, is not to have anything whatsoever to do with drugs in any of these countries. Never agree to carry anything through customs for a third party.

Getting around

Public transport in Malaysia, Singapore and Brunei is reliable and inexpensive. Much of your travelling, particularly in Malaysia, will be by bus, minivan or, occasionally, long-distance shared taxi. Budget flights are a good option for hopping around the region, especially given that no ferries connect Peninsular and East Malaysia. The Peninsula's rail system is now partly upgraded, slashing journey times.

Sabah and **Sarawak** have their own travel peculiarities – in parts of Sarawak, for instance, you're reliant on boats or light aircraft. The chapters on Sarawak, Sabah, Brunei and Singapore contain specific information on their transport systems; the focus in this section is largely on Peninsular Malaysia.

The transport system is subject to heavy pressure during any nationwide **public holiday** (see p.56) – particularly Muslim festivals, the Chinese New Year, Deepavali, Christmas and New Year. A day or two before each festival, whole communities embark upon **balik kampung**, which literally means a return to the village (or hometown) to be with family. It's worth buying tickets at least one week in advance to travel at these times; if you're driving, steel yourself for more than the usual number of jams.

And finally, bear in mind that **chartering** transport – longboats, or cars with drivers – to reach some off-the-beaten-track national park or island is always pricey for what it is.

By bus

Malaysia's **bus network** is fairly comprehensive, at least in terms of serving major cities and towns. However, buses rarely stray off main roads to reach rural sites of the kind that tourists might want to get to – nature reserves, caves, hill resorts and so forth. In such instances, the best you can do is to ask the driver if you can get off at the start of the turning for your destination, after which you're left to your own devices.

Long-distance (express) buses

The **long-distance bus network** borders on the anarchic: a largish town can be served by a dozen or more express bus companies. **Timetabling** is a mess, too: every bus station has signs above a zillion ticket booths displaying a zillion routes and departure times, but these may be out of date, as may even the websites of the biggest bus companies. Given this, the route details in this Guide are a general indication of what you can expect; for specifics, you will need to call the bus company's local office (stations do not have central enquiry numbers) or ask in person.

At least the plethora of companies means you can often find **tickets** at the station for a bus heading to your destination within the next two hours. However, it can be worth booking a day in advance for specific departures or on routes where services are limited (in between, rather than along, the west and east coasts for example). **Online booking** is possible, either on the websites of the biggest operators or on recently launched umbrella websites (such as ⓦeasybook.com) representing multiple firms, but there is nothing as reliable as buying a ticket at the bus station itself.

Most intercity buses are comfortable, with **air conditioning** and curtains to screen out the blazing sun, though seats can be tightly packed.

BUS COMPANIES

A handful of well-established bus companies give reliable service in Peninsular Malaysia. The largest is **Transnasional** (ⓦtransnasional.com.my) and its slightly pricier subsidiary Plusliner (ⓦplusliner.com.my), whose services have the entire Peninsula pretty well covered. Among many competitors are **Sri Maju** (ⓦsrimaju.com) and **Konsortium Bas Ekspres** (ⓦkbes .com.my), both strong on the west coast.

There are rarely toilets on board, but longer journeys feature a rest stop every couple of hours, with a short meal stopover if needed. On a few plum routes, notably KL–Singapore and KL–Penang, additional **luxury** or "executive" coaches charge up to twice the regular fares and offer plush seats, greater legroom plus on-board movies.

Local buses

In addition to express buses, the Peninsula has a network of simple, somewhat sporadic **local buses** serving small towns on routes that can stretch up to 100km end to end. Local buses are organized at the **state level**, and this means that many services do not cross into adjacent states even when the same firm is active on both sides of the border. **Tickets**, usually bought on board from the driver or conductor, cost a few ringgit, reaching RM10 only on the longest routes. Note that services typically run only during **daylight hours**, winding down by 8pm if not earlier.

By train

For years, Malaysian trains were a laughing stock – antiquated and generally much slower than buses. Now, after belated investment, the trains are once again a competitive option in parts of the country, and even bigger changes are in the pipeline, with plans to build a high-speed rail link between Kuala Lumpur and Singapore by the mid-2020s as well as a new, metro-like shuttle service between Johor Bahru and Singapore.

The Peninsula's rail service is operated by **KTM** (short for Keretapi Tanah Melayu, literally "Trains of the Malay Land"; ☎03 2267 1200, ⓦktmb.com.my). Its network is shaped roughly like a Y, with the southern end anchored at Johor Bahru and the intersection, for historical reasons, at the small town of Gemas. The northwest branch links up with Thai track at the border town of Padang Besar via KL, Ipoh and Alor Setar; the northeast branch cuts up through the interior to terminate at Tumpat, beyond Kota Bharu on the east coast. KTM also runs a useful **Komuter** rail service in the Kuala Lumpur area (see p.86) and the northwest (see p.116).

Trains are at their best on the west-coast line, which is electrified and double-tracked right from Gemas up to Padang Besar, enabling the modern, fast (and thus much in demand) **Electric Train Service (ETS)** to run. The fly in the ointment is that although there were at least a dozen services north of KL daily at the time of research, services between KL and Gemas were still sparse. The ETS should eventually be extended all the way to Johor Bahru, possibly by 2020.

Intercity (*Antarabandar*) services make up the rest of the network, between Johor Bahru and the east via the interior. These remain backward and single-tracked, meaning a handful of slow, often basic, trains run in one direction each day – journeys can be mind-numbing and are often delayed. Even so, trains can still be the quickest way to reach some settlements here, and the **Jungle Railway** stretch is also entertaining in parts (see p.204). Unfortunately, there were no direct services between KL and the east coast at the time of research, although these may return in the near future; in the meantime, passengers from KL and the west coast need to change at Gemas for the east-coast line.

Seats and fares

ETS trains have no **seat classes**, but fares still vary depending on whether you travel on a "platinum" (faster, with fewer stops) or "gold" service; KL to Butterworth, for example, costs around RM80 in platinum (4hr), RM60 in gold (4hr 30min). On intercity trains, seats theoretically divide into premier (first), superior (second) and economy (third) class, although not all trains feature all three; **sleeper services** are limited to the overnight trains between Johor Bahru and Tumpat, and are also split into three theoretical classes. As an indication of fares, a seat from Johor Bahru all the way to Wakaf Bharu (near Kota Bharu) costs RM45, a sleeper berth just a few ringgit more.

Tickets and timetables

You can buy **tickets** at stations via KTM's website or their KTMB MobTicket app; for ETS trains, it's best to book at least a couple of days in advance.

Note that as KTM is continually upgrading and maintaining its lines, it has made frequent, often radical changes to its **timetables** and routes over the past few years – it's a good idea to check the latest details on the company's website before you travel.

By long-distance taxi

Long-distance taxis are fading away somewhat, but still run between some cities and towns, and are especially useful in Sabah. They can be a lot quicker than buses, but the snag is that they operate on a **shared** basis, so you have to wait for enough people to show up to fill the vehicle. In practice, you're unlikely to make much use of them

THE MALAYSIAN RAIL NETWORK

BANGKOK (Thai Railways)
Hat Yai (Thailand)
Padang Besar
Arau
Alor Setar
Gurun
Sungai Petani
Bukit Mertajam
Butterworth
Tumpat (Kelantan coast)
Parit Buntar
Wakaf Bharu (for Kota Bharu)
Bagan Serai
Taiping
Pasir Mas
Kuala Kangsar
Sungai Siput
Tanah Merah
Ipoh
Batu Gajah
(Kuala) Krai
Kampar
Dabong
Tapah Road
Gua Musang
Tanjung Malim
Kuala Lipis
Rawang
Sungai Buloh
Jerantut
Kuala Lumpur
KL SENTRAL
Bandar Tasik Selatan
Kuala Krau
Kajang
Seremban
Mentakab
Rembau
Pulau Sebang/Tampin
Triang
Bahau
Gemas
Segamat
Labis
Paloh
Kluang
Kulai
Kempas Bahru
Johor Bahru (JB Sentral)
SINGAPORE (Woodlands)

Malaysian long-distance rail services

Express Train Service (ETS)
KL Sentral to Ipoh
Gemas to Butterworth
Gemas to Padang Besar (mostly bypassing Butterworth)

Intercity (Antarabandar)
JB Sentral to Pulau Sebang/Tampin
JB Sentral to Tumpat
JB Sentral to Singapore

Thai Railways Special Express
Padang Besar to Bangkok

This map shows stations served by most express/intercity trains. There are also local services on stretches of the JB–Tumpat line, calling at minor stations. Komuter rail services in the KL and Butterworth areas are detailed in chapters 1 & 2

KERETA SAPU AND MINIVANS

In rural areas of Malaysia, notably in East Malaysia, private cars, minivans and (on rough roads) four-wheel-drives fill in handily for the lack of buses along certain routes. Sometimes called **kereta sapu** in Malay, or "taxis" as a shorthand, they may not be as ad hoc as they sound, even running at fixed times each day in some places.

Minivans also operate on a more formal level: travel agencies run them to take backpackers to destinations such as the Perhentians and Taman Negara, or just across the border to Hat Yai in Thailand.

unless you're travelling in a group or you want to travel to a destination that's off the beaten track. **Fares** usually work out at double the corresponding bus fare; official prices are usually chalked up on a board at the taxi rank or listed on a laminated tariff card (*senarai tambang*), which you can ask to see.

Some taxi operators assume any tourist who shows up will want to charter a taxi; if you want to use the taxi on a shared basis, say "*nak kongsi dengan orang lain*".

By ferry or boat

Regular **ferries** serve all the major islands, from Penang to Labuan off the coast of Sabah. Within Sarawak, there are scheduled boat services between Kuching and Sibu and up the Rejang River to Belaga. Vessels tend to be narrow, cramped affairs – imagine being inside an aircraft, only on water – and some may be no more than speedboats or motorized *penambang* (fishing craft). It's best to book in advance when there are only a few sailings each day; otherwise, just turn up and buy tickets at the jetty. Boat travel also often comes into play in **national parks** and in a few rural areas, where you may need to charter one to travel between coastal beaches or to reach remote upriver villages. Details are given in the text of the Guide where relevant.

By plane

It's easy to fly within Malaysia, Singapore and Brunei. Most state capitals have **airports** (though some have only one or two flights a day), and there

are also regional airports at Langkawi, Labuan, Redang and Tioman islands, and scattered around Sabah and Sarawak – for example, at Mulu for Mulu National Park. You can fly either with the established national airlines or with a variety of low-cost operators, though there may be little to choose between them pricewise if you book late.

Fares can be remarkably cheap, especially for early-morning or late-night departures, or when booked some way in advance. The ninety-minute flight from KL to Kuching, for example, can cost as little as RM100 one way including tax with a budget airline, though two or three times that is more typical. Note also that any trip involving Singapore or Brunei will be more expensive than the distance might suggest, as it will count as an international flight.

DOMESTIC AIRLINES AND ROUTES

AirAsia Ⓦ airasia.com. The airline that pioneered the local low-cost market offers a comprehensive service throughout Malaysia and also serves Singapore and Brunei.

Firefly Ⓦ fireflyz.com.my. Malaysia Airlines' discount subsidiary has some useful flights out of KL's Subang airport, Penang and Ipoh, serving other Peninsula cities and Singapore.

Jetstar Asia Ⓦ jetstar.com. Budget flights from Singapore to KL and Penang.

Malindo Air Ⓦ malindoair.com. Part-owned by the Indonesian budget airline Lion Air, this has a good range of flights throughout Peninsular Malaysia and also serves Singapore.

MASwings Ⓦ maswings.com.my. A subsidiary of Malaysia Airlines, MASwings operates on many routes, largely rural, within Borneo, often using nineteen-seater propeller-driven Twin Otter planes that are a lifeline for isolated communities.

Malaysia Airlines (MAS) Ⓦ malaysiaairlines.com. Flies between KL and many state capitals, plus Langkawi, Labuan, Singapore and Brunei.

Scoot Ⓦ flyscoot.com. Singapore's Airlines' low-cost wing serves major Peninsular destinations, plus Kuching, from Singapore.

SilkAir Ⓦ silkair.com. Singapore Airlines' non-budget subsidiary operates between Singapore and KL, Penang, Langkawi, Kuching and Kota Kinabalu.

By car

The roads in **Peninsular Malaysia** are good, making driving a viable prospect for tourists – though the cavalier local attitude to road rules takes some getting used to. It's mostly the same story in **East Malaysia** and **Brunei**, though here major towns tend to be linked by ordinary roads rather than wide highways. **Singapore** is in another league altogether, boasting modern highways and a built-in road-use charging system that talks to a black-box gizmo fitted in every car. All three countries **drive on the left**, and wearing seat belts

FARE COMPARISONS

Journey	By bus	By train	By plane
KL–Penang	RM45; 4hr 30min	RM22; 4hr (to Butterworth)	RM120; 45min
Ipoh–Johor Bahru	RM65; 8hr	RM80; 8hr	RM180; 1hr 20min

is compulsory in the front of the vehicle (and in the back too, in Singapore). To **rent a vehicle**, you must be 23 or over and will need to show a clean driving licence.

The rest of this section concentrates on **Malaysia**. For more on driving in Singapore and Brunei, see the respective chapters in the Guide.

Malaysian roads

Malaysian highways – called **expressways** and usually referred to by a number prefixed "E" – are a pleasure to drive; they're wide and well maintained, and feature convenient **rest stops** with toilets, shops and small food courts. In contrast, the streets of major cities can be a pain, regularly traffic-snarled, with patchy signposting and confusing one-way systems. Most cities and towns boast plenty of **car parks**, and even where you can't find one, there's usually no problem with parking in a lane or side street.

Speed limits are 110km per hour on expressways, 90km per hour on the narrower trunk and state roads, and 50km per hour in built-up areas. Whatever road you're on, keep to the speed limit; speed traps are not uncommon and fines hefty. If you are pulled up for a traffic offence, note that it's not unknown for Malaysian police to ask for a bribe,

which will set you back less than the fine. Never offer to bribe a police officer and think carefully before you give in to an invitation to do so.

All expressways are built and run by private concessions and as such attract **tolls**, generally around RM20 per 100km, though on some roads a flat fee is levied. At toll points (signed "Tol Plaza"), you can pay in cash (cashiers can dispense change) or by waving a stored-value **Touch 'n Go** card (W touchngo.com.my) in front of a sensor (see p.86). Get in the appropriate lane as you approach the toll points: some lanes are for certain types of vehicle only.

Once out on the roads, you'll rapidly become aware of the behaviour of quite a few Malaysian motorists, which their compatriots might term *gila* (Malay for "insane"). Swerving from lane to lane in the thick of the traffic, overtaking close to blind corners and careering downhill roads are not uncommon, as are tragic press accounts of pile-ups and road fatalities. Not for nothing does the exhortation *"pandu cermat"* (drive safely) appear on numerous highway signboards, though the message still isn't getting through.

If you're new to driving in Malaysia, the best approach is to take all of this with equanimity and drive conservatively; concede the right of way if

MALAY VOCABULARY FOR DRIVERS

The following list should help decipher road signage in Peninsular Malaysia and parts of Brunei, much of which is in Malay.

Utara	North	**Kawasan rehat**	Highway rest stop
Selatan	South		
Barat	West	**Kurangkan laju**	Reduce speed
Timur	East	**Lebuhraya**	Expressway /highway
Di belakang	Behind		
Di hadapan	Ahead	**Lencongan**	Detour
Awas	Caution	**Pembinaan di hadapan**	Road works ahead
Berhenti	Stop		
Beri laluan	Give way	**Pusat bandar/ bandaraya**	Town/city centre
Dilarang meletak kereta	No parking		
Dilarang memotong	No overtaking	**Simpang ke...**	Junction/ turning for...
Had laju/jam	Speed limit /per hour		
Ikut kiri/kanan	Keep left/right	**Zon had laju**	Zone where speed limit applies
Jalan sehala	One-way street		

you're not sure of the intentions of others. One confusing local habit is that some drivers flash their headlights to claim the **right of way** rather than concede it.

Car and bike rental

Car rental rates with the national chains start at around RM150 per day for a basic 1.2-litre Proton, although you may find better deals with local firms. The rate includes unlimited mileage and collision damage waiver insurance; the excess can be RM1500 or more, but can be reduced by paying a surcharge of up to ten percent on the daily rental rate. Both petrol and diesel cost around RM2.30 per litre at the time of writing.

Motorbike rental tends to be informal, usually offered by Malaysian guesthouses and shops in more touristy areas. Officially, you must be over 21 and have an appropriate driving licence, though it's unlikely you'll have to show the latter; you'll probably need to leave your passport as a deposit. Wearing helmets is compulsory. Rental costs around RM20 per day, while **bicycles**, useful in rural areas, can be rented for a few ringgit a day.

LOCAL CAR RENTAL AGENCIES

Hawk ☎ 03 5631 6488, ⓦ hawkrentacar.com.my.
Mayflower ☎ 1800 881 688, ⓦ mayflowercarrental.com.my.
Orix ☎ 03 9284 7799, ⓦ orixauto.com.my.

Transport in cities and towns

The companies that run local buses in each state also run city and town buses, serving urban centres and suburbs. Fares seldom exceed RM5, though schedules can be unfathomable to visitors (and even locals). KL also has an MRT and LRT metro system, plus local rail and monorail systems.

Outside the largest cities, **taxis** do not ply the streets looking for custom, so using one means heading to a taxi rank, typically outside big hotels and malls. Malaysian taxis are notorious for being **unmetered** except in a few big cities, notably KL, so it's worth asking locals what a fair price to your destination would be and haggling with the driver before you set off. At a few taxi ranks, notably at airports and train stations, you buy a voucher for your destination at a sensible price. In a few areas it can be worthwhile **chartering** a taxi for several hours, for example to reach a remote nature park and perhaps collect you when you're done; prices will depend on the area and your bargaining skills.

The good news for taxi users is that in a handful of big cities, you can now book a ride using the homegrown **Grab app** (ⓦ grab.com.my) as well as Uber (ⓦ uber.com). Grab is particularly useful: fares are distance-based and can work out a third cheaper than using an unmetered taxi, and drivers will pick you up from wherever you are.

Trishaws (bicycle rickshaws), seating two people, are seen less these days, but they're still part of the tourist scene in places like Melaka, Penang and Singapore. You're paying for an experience here, not transport as such; details are given in the relevant sections of the Guide.

Accommodation

Accommodation in Malaysia is good value: mid-range en-suite rooms can go for as little as RM120 (£22/US$30). Details of accommodation in Brunei and Singapore are given in the relevant chapters of the Guide.

The cheapest form of accommodation is offered by hostels, guesthouses and lodges, which usually have both dorms and simple private rooms, sharing bathrooms. These places exist only in well-touristed areas, whether urban or rural. Elsewhere, you'll need to rely on hotels, which range from world-class luxury affairs to austere concrete blocks with basic rooms.

Advance reservations are essential to be sure of securing a budget or mid-range room during major festivals or school breaks (see p.56). The East Asian accommodation specialist ⓦ agoda.com has a wide selection of hotels in all three countries. In addition to "conventional" accommodation, it's also possible to find apartments in cities using the likes of Airbnb (ⓦ airbnb.com).

Air conditioning is standard in all but the cheapest hotels, and is fairly common in guesthouses too. **Wi-fi** is practically standard, although a few (usually pricey) hotels charge extra for it – we have indicated where this is the case in the Guide. Baby cots are usually available only in more expensive places.

Guesthouses, hostels and lodges

The mainstay of the travellers' scene in Malaysia are **hostels** and **guesthouses** (also called backpackers or lodges – all these terms are somewhat interchangeable). These can range from basic affairs to smartly refurbished shophouses with satellite TVs and games consoles. Almost all offer **dorm beds**, starting at around RM20, though you can pay double that in fancy establishments. Basic double rooms are usually available for RM50 to RM100 a night, often with mere plywood partitions separating them from adjacent rooms. **Breakfast** is usually available – a simple self-service affair of coffee or tea and toast.

Hotels

Malaysia's **cheapest hotels** tend to cater for a local clientele and seldom need to be booked in advance. Showers and toilets may be shared and can be pretty basic, although most places have some en-suite rooms. Another consideration at cheap and even some mid-range hotels is the **noise** level, as doors and windows offer poor sound insulation. Note that some cheap hotels also function as brothels, especially those that allow rooms to be paid for by the hour.

Mid-range hotels can be better value. Prices start at around RM120 in cities, and less in rural areas and towns, for which you can expect air conditioning, en-suite facilities and relatively decent furnishings, as well as sometimes, a refrigerator, in-room safe and access to a restaurant.

High-end hotels are as comfortable as you might expect, and many have state-of-the-art facilities, including a swimming pool, spa and gym. Some may add a touch of class by incorporating grand extrapolations of kampung-style architecture, such as saddle-shaped roofs with woodcarving. Although rates can be as low as

> ## CHALETS
> Banish all thoughts of Alpine loveliness when it comes to Malaysian **chalets**: these are guesthouse and resort rooms in the form of little self-contained wooden or concrete cabins. They're mostly to be found in rural areas, especially at nature reserves and beaches. Chalets range from cramped, stuffy A-frames – sheds named for their steeply sloping roofs, sometimes with a tiny bathroom at the back – to luxury en-suite affairs with a veranda, sitting area, minibar and the like; prices vary accordingly.

RM250 per night, in big cities they can rocket above the RM400 mark.

In the major cities, look out for **boutique hotels**, usually set in refurbished shophouses or colonial-era office buildings. They are the most characterful places to stay, offering either retro-style décor or über-hip contemporary features – although never at budget prices.

Hotel **breakfasts**, where available, are either Asian/Western buffets with trays of noodles next to beans and eggs, or simpler affairs where you order off a menu. They're usually included in the rate except at four- and five-star places, where the spread is so elaborate that there are two room rates – with and without breakfast. In the Guide listings, we have indicated when breakfast is included in the price.

ACCOMMODATION PRICING AND TAXES

Many mid-range hotels in Malaysia have a published tariff or rack rate and a so-called **promotional rate**, generally around a third less. What's important to realize is that the promotional rate is the de facto price, applying all year except, perhaps, during peak periods such as important festivals. To be sure of getting the promotional rate, either book online or call in advance of your arrival.

Top-tier and some mid-range hotels, plus some hostels, have a different strategy: their online booking engines constantly adjust prices according to demand. This means the best rates usually go to those who book early, although some last-minute discounts may also pop up.

Note that mid-range and pricey hotels levy a **service charge** (usually ten percent) and that most hotels levy **GST** (six percent; see p.53). Unless otherwise stated, the accommodation prices **quoted in the reviews** in this Guide include such surcharges and are based on promotional rates or, at luxury hotels, typical rates.

Finally, there's the matter of the **tourism tax**. Introduced in 2017, it essentially requires foreigners to have to pay an additional RM10 per room per night. Naturally, this hits people staying in cheap hotels or in private rooms in hostels especially hard, though dorm occupants may find the tax is divided by the number of beds or even absorbed by the hostel owner. When booking online, if the tax isn't added you will probably have to pay it upon checking in.

Camping

There are few official opportunities for **camping** in Malaysia, perhaps because guesthouses are so reasonably priced, and because the heat and humidity, not to mention the copious insect population, not make camping something only strange foreigners would willingly do. Where there are **campsites**, typically in nature parks, they are either free to use or entail a nominal fee; facilities are basic and may not be well maintained. A few lodges and camps have tents and other equipment for rent, but you generally need to bring your own gear (see box, p.49).

If you go trekking in very remote regions, for example in the depths of Taman Negara and the Kelabit Highlands in Sarawak, camping is about your only option. Specialist tour operators or local guides can often provide gear.

Longhouses

A stay in a **longhouse**, de rigueur for many travellers visiting Sarawak (and also possible in Sabah), offers the chance to experience tribal community life, do a little trekking and try activities such as weaving and using a blowpipe. It used to be that visitors could simply turn up and ask the tuai rumah (headman) for a place to stay, paying only for meals and offering some gifts as an additional token of thanks. While some tourists still try to work things like this, these days most longhouse visits are invariably arranged through a **tour operator** and can therefore be a little pricey. Gawai (see p.48) is the most exciting time of year to stay.

More expensive packages put visitors up in their own section of the longhouse, equipped with proper beds and modern washing facilities; meals will be prepared separately rather than shared with the rest of the community. More basic trips generally have you sleeping on mats or in hammocks rather than beds, either in a large communal room or on the veranda, and the main washing facilities may well be the nearest river. For meals, the party will be divided up into smaller groups, and each will dine with a different family.

Homestays

In many rural areas especially, **homestay programmes** offer the chance to stay with a Malaysian family, paying for your bed and board. The arrangement is an appealing one on paper, giving you a chance to sample home cooking and local culture. In practice, however, hosts may not be able to speak much English, a situation that effectively cuts foreign guests off from them and the community. As a result, homestays often end up being used by Malaysian travellers rather than foreigners. Tourist offices can usually furnish a list of local homestays on request, but be sure to raise the above issues if pursuing the idea.

Food and drink

One of the best reasons to come to Malaysia and Singapore (even Brunei, to a lesser extent) is the food, comprising two of the world's most venerated cuisines, Chinese and Indian, and one of the most underrated – Malay. Even if you think you know two out of the three pretty well, be prepared to be surprised: Chinese food here boasts a lot of the provincial diversity that you don't find in the West's Cantonese-dominated Chinese restaurants, while Indian food is predominantly southern Indian, lighter and spicier than the cuisine of the north.

Furthermore, each of the three cuisines has acquired more than a few tricks from the other two – the Chinese here cook curries, for example – giving rise to some distinctive fusion food. Add to this cross-fertilization a host of regional variations and specialities, plus excellent seafood and unusual tropical produce, and the result can be a dazzling gastronomic experience.

None of this need be expensive. From the ubiquitous food stalls and cheap street diners called **kedai kopis**, the standard of cooking is high and food everywhere is remarkably good value. Basic noodle- or rice-based one-plate meals at a stall or kedai kopis rarely cost more than a few ringgit or Singapore dollars. Even a full meal with drinks in a fancy restaurant seldom runs to more than RM50 a head in Malaysia, though expect to pay Western prices at quite a few places in Singapore. The most renowned culinary centres are Singapore, George Town, KL, Melaka and Kota Bharu, although other towns have their own distinctive dishes too.

Food stalls and food courts

Some of the cheapest and most delicious food available in Malaysia and Singapore comes from **stalls**, traditionally wooden pushcarts on the roadside, surrounded by a few wobbly tables with stools. Most serve one or a few standard **noodle** and **rice dishes** or specialize in certain delicacies, from oyster omelettes to squid curry. One myth to bust immediately is the notion that you will get food poisoning eating at stalls or cheap diners. Standards of hygiene are usually good, and as most food is cooked to order (or, in the case of rice-with-toppings spreads, only on display for a few hours), it's generally pretty **safe**.

Many stalls are assembled into user-friendly **medan selera** (literally "appetite square") or **food courts**, also known as **hawker centres** in Singapore. Usually taking up a floor of an office building or shopping mall, or housed in open-sided market buildings, food courts feature stall lots with menus displayed and fixed tables, plus toilets. You generally don't have to sit close to the stall you're patronizing: find a free table, and the vendor will track you down when your food is ready (at some Singapore food centres you quote the table number when ordering). Play it by ear as to whether you pay when ordering, or when the food is delivered.

Stalls open at various times from morning to evening, with most closing well before midnight except in the big cities. During the Muslim fasting month of **Ramadan**, however, Muslim-run stalls don't open until mid-afternoon, though this is also when you can take advantage of the **pasar Ramadan**, afternoon food markets at which stalls sell masses of savouries and sweet treats to take away; tourist offices can tell you where one is taking place. Ramadan is also the time to stuff yourself at the massive fast-breaking buffets laid on by most major hotels.

EATING ETIQUETTE

Malays and Indians often eat with the **right hand**, using the palm as a scoop and the thumb to help push food into the mouth. **Chopsticks** are, of course, used for Chinese food, though note that a spoon is always used to help with rice, gravies and slippery food such as mushrooms or tofu, and that you don't pick up rice with chopsticks (unless you've a rice bowl, in which case you lift the bowl to your mouth and use the chopsticks as a sort of shovel). **Cutlery** is universally available; for local food, it's best to eat mainly with a spoon, using a fork to get food on to it.

Kedai kopis

Few downtown streets lack a **kedai kopis**, sometimes known as a *kopitiam* in Hokkien Chinese. Although both terms literally mean "coffee shop", a *kedai kopis* is actually an inexpensive diner rather than a café. Most serve noodle and rice dishes all day, often with a *campur*-style spread (see below) at lunchtime, sometimes in the evening too. Some *kedai kopis* function as miniature food markets, housing a handful of vendors – perhaps one offering curries and griddle breads, another doing a particular Chinese noodle dish, and so on.

Most *kedai kopis* open at 8am to serve breakfast, and don't shut until the early evening; a few stay open as late as 10pm. Culinary standards are seldom spectacular but are satisfying all the same, and you're unlikely to spend more than small change for a filling one-plate meal. In some Malaysian towns, particularly on the east coast, the Chinese-run *kedai kopis* are often the only places where you'll be able to get **alcohol**.

Restaurants, cafés and bakeries

Sophisticated **restaurants** only exist in the big cities. Don't expect a stiffly formal ambience, however – while some places can be sedate, the Chinese, especially, prefer restaurants to be noisy, sociable affairs. Where the pricier restaurants come into their own is for **international food** – anything from Vietnamese to Tex-Mex. The chief letdown is that the service can be amateurish, reflecting how novel this sort of dining experience is for many of the staff.

Most large Malaysian towns feature a few attempts at Western **cafés**, serving passable fries, sandwiches, burgers, shakes and so forth. It's also easy to find **bakeries**, which can offer a welcome change from the local rice-based diet – though don't be surprised to find chilli sardine buns and other Asian Western hybrids, or cakes with decidedly artificial fillings and colourings. For anything really decent in the café or bakery line, you'll need to be in a big city.

Cuisines

A convenient, cheap way to get acquainted with local dishes is to sample the spreads available at many *kedai kopis*, particularly at lunchtime. The concept is pretty much summed up by the Malay term **nasi campur** ("mixed rice"), though Chinese and Indian *kedai kopis*, too, offer these arrays of stir-fries, curries and other savouries in trays. As in a cafeteria, you tell the person behind the counter which items you want, and a helping of each will be piled atop a mound of rice. If you don't like plain rice, ask for it to be doused with gravy (*kuah* in Malay) from any stew on display.

Nasi campur is not haute cuisine – and that's precisely its attraction. Whether you have, say, *ikan kembong* (mackerel) deep-fried and served whole, or chicken pieces braised in soy sauce, or bean sprouts stir-fried with salted fish or shrimp, a *campur* spread is much closer to **home cooking** than anything served in formal restaurants.

Nasi campur and noodle dishes are meals in themselves, but otherwise eating is generally a **shared** experience – stir-fries and other dishes arrive in quick succession and everyone helps themselves to several servings of each, eaten with rice, as the meal progresses.

Breakfast can present a conundrum in small towns, where rice, *roti canai* and noodles may be all that's easily available. If you can't get used to the likes of rice porridge at dawn, you'll find that many a *kedai kopis* offers *roti bakar*, toast served with butter and **kaya**. The latter is a scrumptious sweet coconut curd jam, either orange or green, not unlike English lemon curd in that egg is a major ingredient.

Malay food

In its influences, **Malay cuisine** looks to the north and east, most obviously to China in the use of noodles and soy sauce, but also to neighbouring Thailand, with which it shares an affinity for such ingredients as lemongrass, the ginger-like galangal and fermented fish sauce (the Malay version, *budu*, is made from anchovies). But Malay food also draws on Indian and Middle East cooking in the use of spices, and in dishes such as *biriyani* rice. The resulting cuisine is both spicy and a little sweet. Naturally there's an emphasis on **local ingredients**: *santan* (coconut milk) lends a sweet, creamy undertone to many stews and curries, while *belacan*, a pungent fermented prawn paste (something of an acquired taste), is found in chilli condiments and sauces. **Herbs**, including curry and kaffir lime leaves, also play a prominent role.

The cuisine of the southern part of the Peninsula tends to be more *lemak* (rich) than further north, where the Thai influence is stronger and *tom yam* stews, spicy and sour (the latter by dint of lemongrass), are popular. The most famous Malay dish is arguably **satay** (see p.41), though it can be hard to find outside big cities. Also quintessentially Malay,

rendang is a dryish curry made by slow-cooking meat (usually beef) in coconut milk flavoured with galangal and a variety of herbs and spices.

For many visitors, one of the most striking things about Malay food is the bewildering array of **kuih-muih** (or just *kuih*), or sweets, on display at markets and street stalls. Often featuring coconut and sometimes *gula melaka* (palm-sugar molasses), *kuih* come in all shapes, sizes and colours (often artificial nowadays) – rainbow-hued layer cakes of rice flour are about the most extreme example.

Chinese food

The range of **Chinese cooking** available in Malaysia and Singapore represents a mouthwatering sweep through China's southeastern seaboard, reflecting the historical pattern of emigration from **Fujian**, **Guangzhou** and **Hainan Island** provinces. This diversity is evident in dishes served at hawker centres and *kopitiams*. Cantonese *char siew* (roast pork, given a reddish honey-based marinade) is frequently served over plain rice as a meal in itself, or as a garnish in noodle dishes such as *wonton mee* (*wonton* being Cantonese pork dumplings); also very common is Hainanese chicken rice, comprising steamed chicken accompanied by savoury rice cooked in chicken stock. Fujian province contributes dishes such as *hae mee*, yellow noodles in a rich prawn broth; *yong tau foo*, from the Hakka ethnic group on the border with Guangzhou, and comprising bean curd, fishballs and assorted vegetables, poached and served with broth and sweet dipping sauces; and *mee pok*, a Teochew (Chaozhou) dish featuring ribbon-like noodles with fishballs and a spicy dressing.

Restaurant dining tends to be dominated by **Cantonese** food. Menus can be formulaic, but the quality of cooking is usually high. Many Cantonese places also offer great **dim sum**, at which small servings of numerous savouries such as *siu mai* dumplings (of pork and prawn), crispy yam puffs and *chee cheong fun* (rice-flour rolls stuffed with pork and drenched in sweet sauce) are consumed. Traditionally, these would be served in bamboo steamers and ordered from waitress-wheeled trolleys, but these days you might well have to order from a menu.

Where available, take the opportunity to try **specialities** such as **steamboat**, a sort of fondue that involves dunking raw vegetables, meat and seafood into boiling broth to cook, or **chilli crab**, with a spicy tomato sauce. A humdrum but very commonplace stomach-filler is **pow**, steamed buns containing a savoury filling of *char siew* or chicken, or sometimes a sweet red bean paste.

SIX OF THE BEST

The dishes listed below are mostly easy to find, and many of these cut across ethnic boundaries as well, with each group modifying the recipe slightly to suit its cooking style.

Nasi lemak Rice fragrantly cooked in coconut milk and served with fried peanuts, tiny fried anchovies, cucumber, boiled egg and spicy *sambal*.

Roti canai Basically Indian paratha (indeed it's called *roti prata* in Singapore), a delicious griddle bread served with a curry sauce. It's ubiquitous, served up by Malay and Indian *kedai kopis* and stalls.

Nasi goreng Literally, fried rice, though not as in Chinese restaurants; Malay and Indian versions feature a little spice and chilli, along with the usual mix of vegetables plus shrimp, chicken and/or egg bits.

Char kuay teow A Hokkien Chinese dish of fried tagliatelle-style rice noodles, often darkly coated in soy sauce and garnished with egg, pork and prawns. The Singapore version is decidedly sweet. Malay *kuay teow goreng* is also available and tends to be spicier.

Satay A Malay dish of chicken, mutton or beef kebabs on bamboo sticks, marinated and barbecued. The meat is accompanied by cucumber, raw onion and *ketupat*, cubes of sticky rice steamed in a wrap of woven leaves. All are meant to be dipped in a spicy peanut sauce. Chinese pork satay also exists.

Laksa A spicy seafood noodle soup, Nyonya in origin. Singapore *laksa*, served with fishcake dumplings and beansprouts, is rich and a little sweet thanks to copious use of coconut milk, while Penang's *asam laksa* features flaked fish and a tamarind tang.

Nyonya food

Named after the word used to describe womenfolk of the Peranakan communities (see p.575), **Nyonya food** is a product of the melding of Penang, Melaka and Singapore cultures. A blend of Chinese and Malay cuisines, it can seem more Malay than Chinese thanks to its use of spices – except that pork is widely used.

Nyonya **popiah** (spring rolls) are very common: rather than being fried, the rolls are assembled by coating a steamed wrap with a sweet sauce made of palm sugar, then stuffed mainly with stir-fried *bangkwang*, a crunchy turnip-like vegetable. Another classic is **laksa**, noodles in a spicy soup with the distinctive *daun kesom* – a herb fittingly referred to in English as *laksa* leaf. Other well-known Nyonya dishes include **asam fish**, a spicy, sour fish stew featuring tamarind (the *asam* of the name), and **otak-otak**, fish mashed with coconut milk and chilli paste then put in a narrow banana-leaf envelope and steamed or barbecued.

Indian food

The classic southern Indian dish is the *dosai* or *thosai*, a thin rice-flour pancake. It's usually served accompanied by *sambar*, a thin vegetable and lentil curry; *rasam*, a tamarind broth; and perhaps small helpings of other curries. Also very common are *roti* griddle breads, plus the more substantial *murtabak*, thicker than a *roti* and stuffed with egg, onion and minced meat, with sweet banana versions

sometimes available. At lunchtime many South Indian cafés turn to serving *daun pisang* (literally, banana leaf) meals comprising rice heaped on a banana-leaf "platter" and small, replenishable heaps of various curries placed alongside. In some restaurants you'll find more substantial dishes such as the popular fish-head curry (don't be put off by the idea – the "cheeks" between the mouth and gills are packed with tasty flesh).

A notable aspect of the eating scene in Malaysia is the "**mamak**" *kedai kopis*, run by Muslims of South Indian descent (and easily distinguished from Hindu Tamil places by the framed Arabic inscriptions on the walls). *Mamak* establishments have become de facto meeting places for all creeds, being halal and open late, often round the clock. Foodwise, they're similar to other South Indian places, though with more emphasis on meat.

The food served in **North Indian** restaurants (found only in big cities), is richer, less fiery and more reliant on mutton and chicken. You'll commonly come across **tandoori** dishes – named after the clay oven in which the food is cooked – and in particular tandoori chicken, marinated in yoghurt and spices and then baked. Breads such as *nan* also tend to feature rather than rice.

Borneo cuisine

The diet of the indigenous groups living in settled communities in **East Malaysia** can be not dissimilar to Malay and Chinese cooking. In remoter regions,

SPECIAL DIETS

Malay food is, unfortunately, a tough nut to crack for **vegetarians**, as meat and seafood are well blended into the cuisine. Among the standard savoury dishes, vegetarians can only really handle *sayur lodeh* (a rich mixed-veg curry made with coconut milk), *tauhu goreng* (deep-fried tofu with a peanut dressing similar to satay sauce) and *acar* (pickles). Chinese and Indian eating places are the best bets, thanks to the dietary influence of Buddhism and Hinduism. Chinese restaurants can always whip up veg stir-fries to order, and many places now feature **Chinese vegetarian** cuisine (usually also good for **vegans**), using textured veg protein and gluten mock meats – often uncannily like the real thing, and delicious when done right.

Strict vegetarians will want to avoid **seafood derivatives** commonly used in cooking. This means eschewing dishes like *rojak* (containing fermented prawn paste) and the chilli dip called *sambal belacan* (containing *belacan*, the Malay answer to prawn paste). Oyster sauce, often used in Chinese stir-fries, can easily be substituted with soy sauce or just salt. Note also that the gravy served with **roti canai** often comes from a meat curry, though some places offer a lentil version, too.

If you need to **explain in Malay** that you're vegetarian, try saying "*saya hanya makan sayuran*" ("I only eat vegetables"). Even if the person taking your order speaks English, it can be useful to list the things you don't eat; in Malay you'd say, for example, "*saya tak mahu ayam dan ikan dan udang*" for "I don't want chicken or fish or prawn". Expect a few misunderstandings; the cook may leave out one thing on your proscribed list, only to put in another.

HALAL FOOD

Halal food doesn't just feature at Malay and *mamak* eating places. The catering at mid-range and top-tier Malaysian hotels is almost always halal (or at least "**pork-free**"), to the extent that you get turkey or beef "bacon" at breakfast. Of course, the pork-free billing doesn't equate to being halal, but many local Muslims are prepared to overlook this grey area.

In areas where the population is largely Muslim, such as **Kelantan** and **Terengganu**, halal or pork-free food is the norm, even at Chinese and Indian restaurants. In largely Chinese **Singapore**, most hawker centres have a row or two of Muslim stalls.

---

however, or at festival times, you may have an opportunity to sample indigenous cuisine. Villagers in **Sabah**'s Klias Peninsula and in **Brunei** still produce *ambuyat*, a gluey, sago-starch porridge; then there's the Lun Bawang speciality of *jaruk* – raw wild boar, fermented in a bamboo tube and definitely an acquired taste. Sabah's most famous dishes include *hinava*, raw fish pickled in lime juice. In **Sarawak**, Iban and Kelabit communities sometimes serve wild boar cooked on a spit or stewed, and served with rice (perhaps *lemang* – glutinous rice cooked in bamboo) and jungle ferns. River fish is a longhouse basic; the most easily available, tilapia, is usually grilled with pepper and herbs, or steamed in bamboo cylinders.

Desserts

Given the steamy climate, stalls offer a range of desserts that often revolve around **ice** milled down to something resembling slush. More jarringly, desserts often include ingredients such as **pulses**, **sticky rice** or even **yam** and **sweet potato**, all of which can be turned into a sweet stew or porridge.

At their best, local desserts are certainly a lot more interesting than most ice-cream sundaes ever get. Easy to find and worth trying is **eis kacang** (also known as *air batu campur* – "mixed ice" – or ABC), comprising a small helping of aduki beans, sweetcorn and bits of jelly, covered with a snowy mound doused in colourful syrups. Even better, though high in cholesterol, is **cendol**, luscious coconut milk sweetened with *gula melaka* and mixed with green threads of mung-bean-flour jelly. You'll even find delicious red-bean ice cream on sale, its flavour dominated by coconut milk rather than the beans.

Drinks

While **tap water** is generally safe to drink, **bottled water** is widely and cheaply available. Among freshly squeezed **juices**, watermelon, orange and carrot are pretty common, as is the faintly sappy but invigorating sugar cane, extracted by pressing the canes through mangles. Lychee and *longan* drinks can also be good, made with diluted tinned juices and served with some of the fruit at the bottom.

Sweetened soya milk in cartons or – much tastier – freshly made at stalls is another popular local choice, as is the refreshing, sweet *chin chow*, which looks like cola but is in fact made from a seaweed and comes with strands of seaweed jelly.

Tea (*teh*) and **coffee** (*kopi*) are as much national drinks as they are in the West, and locals adore them served **tarik**, literally "pulled" – which means frothing the drink by repeatedly pouring it between mugs in each hand. If ordered with milk, they'll come with a generous dollop of the sweetened condensed variety or sometimes evaporated milk (only large hotels and smarter Western-style cafés have regular milk). If you don't have a sweet tooth, either ask for your drink *kurang manis* ("lacking in sweetness"), in which case less condensed milk will be added, or have it black. Note that there can be even more intricacies involved when ordering drinks (see p.600).

Alcohol

Alcohol is not generally hard to find in **Malaysia**. Most big cities have a bar scene, though in Malaysian towns drinking is limited to non-Muslim eating places, food courts (drink stalls usually have beer and perhaps stout) and Chinese-run bars – sometimes little more than tarted-up *kedai kopis*, the walls plastered with posters of Hong Kong showbiz poppets. However, in strongly Muslim areas, particularly Kelantan and Terengganu, only a handful of establishments, usually Chinese, sell alcohol. **Brunei** is officially dry (see p.457), and different rules again apply for details of **Singapore** drinking (see p.543).

TROPICAL FRUIT

Markets throughout the region feature a delightful range of locally grown **fruit**, though modern agricultural practices are leading to a decline in some varieties. Below are some of the more unusual fruits to watch out for.

Bananas (pisang) Look out for the delicious *pisang mas*, small, straight, thin-skinned and aromatically sweet; *pisang rastali*, slightly bigger, with dark blotches on the skin and not quite so sweet, and green- and even red-skinned varieties.

Cempedak This smaller version of the *nangka* (see jackfruit, below) is normally deep-fried, enabling the seed, not unlike a new potato, to be eaten too.

Ciku Looks like an apple; varies from yellow to pinkish brown when ripe, with a soft, pulpy flesh.

Durian One of Southeast Asia's most popular fruits, durians are also, for many visitors, the most repugnant thanks to their smell. In season (May–Aug & Nov–Feb), they're the size of footballs and have a thick green skin covered with sharp spikes. Inside, rows of large seeds are coated with squidgy yellow-white flesh, whose flavour has been likened by some to vomit-flavoured custard.

Jackfruit Like a giant grenade, the jackfruit (*nangka*) grows up to 40cm long and has a coarse greenish-yellow exterior, enclosing large seeds whose sweet flesh has a powerful odour like overripe pineapple. The unripe fruit, stir-fried, is a bit like bamboo shoots.

Langsat Together with its sister fruit, the *duku*, this looks like a small, round potato, with juicy, segmented white flesh containing small, bitter seeds.

Longan Not unlike the lychee, this stone fruit has sweet, juicy translucent flesh inside a thin brown skin.

Mangosteen Mangosteens have a segmented white flesh with a sweet, slightly tart flavour. Be warned: the thick purple rind can stain clothes indelibly.

Pomelo Much grown in Perak, this pale green citrus fruit is slightly smaller than a soccer ball and, at its best, is juicier and sweeter than grapefruit. Slice away the rind with a knife, then separate and peel the giant segments with your hands.

Rambutan The shape and size of chicken eggs, rambutans have a soft, spiny exterior that gives them their name – *rambut* means "hair" in Malay. To get at the sweet translucent flesh coating the stone inside, simply make a small tear in the peel with your nails and twist open.

Salak Teardrop-shaped, the *salak* has a skin rather like a snake's and a bitter taste.

Soursop Inside the bumpy, muddy-green skin is smooth white flesh that Margaret Brooke, wife of Sarawak's second rajah, Charles, described as "tasting like cotton wool dipped in vinegar and sugar".

Starfruit Also called carambola, this yellow-green fruit, star-shaped in cross section, is said to be good for high blood pressure – though it can be insipid to taste.

Anchor and Tiger **beer** (lager) are locally produced and easily available, and you can get Western and Thai beers as well as the Chinese Tsingtao and various **stouts**, including Guinness. More upmarket restaurants and bars serve beer on draught, cocktails and (generally pricey) imported **wine**. In the longhouses of East Malaysia, you will probably be invited to sample *tuak* (Sarawak) or *tapai* (Sabah), a rice wine that can be potent or weak and as sickly as sweet sherry.

At a food court or *kopitiam*, a 330ml can of Tiger, say, will cost up to RM8, a 640ml bottle up to RM15 – slightly above what they sell for at a supermarket or convenience store. Proper bars may charge up to fifty percent more, except during **happy hour** (which could last from opening time until 8pm), when prices are sharply lower. While some bars open from lunchtime, most tend to open from early evening until the small hours.

Health

No inoculations are required for visiting Malaysia, Singapore or Brunei, although the immigration authorities may require a yellow-fever vaccination certificate if you have transited an endemic area, normally Africa or South America, within the preceding six days. Though levels of hygiene and medical care in Malaysia, Singapore and Brunei are higher than in much of Southeast Asia – with any luck, the most serious thing you'll go down with is an upset stomach – it's a wise precaution to visit your doctor no less than two months before you leave to check that you are up to date with your polio, typhoid, tetanus and hepatitis inoculations.

Heat problems

Travellers unused to tropical climates may suffer from sunburn and **dehydration**. The easiest way to avoid this is to restrict your exposure to the midday sun, use high-factor sun screens, wear sunglasses and a hat. You should also drink plenty of water and, if you do become dehydrated, keep up a regular intake of fluids. **Heat stroke** is more serious and can require hospitalization: its onset is indicated by a high temperature, dry red skin and a fast pulse.

Stomach problems

The most common complaint is a stomach problem, which can range from a mild dose of diarrhoea to full-blown dysentery. The majority of stomach bugs may be unpleasant, but are unthreatening; however, if you notice blood or mucus in your stools, then you may have amoebic or bacillary dysentery, in which case you should seek medical help.

Stomach bugs are usually transmitted by contaminated food and water, so steer clear of raw vegetables and shellfish, always wash unpeeled fruit, and stick to freshly cooked foods, avoiding anything reheated. However careful you are, food that's spicy or just different can sometimes upset your system, in which case, try to stick to relatively bland dishes and avoid fried food.

Tap water is drinkable in Singapore and in parts of Malaysia and Brunei, although in rural areas it's best to buy bottled water, which is widely available.

Air quality

In general, **air quality** is not a major health issue. However, the region is occasionally blanketed by what's locally called "the haze", most recently in 2015 when peat forest fires in Indonesia burned out of control for months. Schools had to be closed and major outdoor events were cancelled, while local people ventured out wearing surgical-style masks. If and when the haze returns (keep a close eye on the weather forecasts), people with respiratory problems should seek medical advice and try to avoid the worst-hit areas – or even postpone the trip.

Cuts, bites and stings

Wearing protective clothing when swimming, snorkelling or diving can help avoid sunburn and protect against any sea stings. **Sea lice**, minute creatures that cause painful though harmless bites are the most common hazard; more dangerous are **jellyfish**, whose stings must be doused with vinegar to deactivate the poison before you seek medical help.

Coral can also cause nasty cuts and grazes; any wounds should be cleaned and kept as dry as possible until properly healed. The only way to avoid well-camouflaged sea urchins and stone fish is by not stepping on the seabed: even thick-soled shoes don't provide total protection against their sharp spines, which can be removed by softening the skin by holding it over a steaming pan of water.

As for **mosquitoes**, you can best avoid being bitten by covering up as much as is practical, and applying repellent to exposed flesh. Note that most repellents sold locally are based on **citronella**; if you want one containing **DEET**, which some say is more effective, buy it at home as it's not sold locally.

Rural or beachside accommodation often features **mosquito nets**, and some places also provide slow-burning **mosquito coils** that generate a little smoke that can deter the insects.

For many people, the ubiquitous **leech** – whose bite is not actually harmful – is the most irritating aspect to jungle trekking (see below). Venomous **snakes** are not that common, and any that you might encounter will usually slink away. If you are unlucky enough to be bitten then remain still and call for an ambulance, or get someone else to summon help. If one of your limbs has been bitten, ideally a pressure bandage should also be applied to slow the spread of any venom.

Dengue fever, Zika and malaria

The main mosquito-borne disease to be aware of – and the chief reason to take measures to avoid being bitten (see p.44) – is **dengue fever**. It is caused by a virus spread by the *Aedes aegypti* mosquito (identifiable by the white markings on its legs) and outbreaks occur. A new vaccine, not widely available, is recommended only to prevent reinfection in those who have already had dengue. Symptoms include severe headaches, pain in the bones, fever and often a fine rash over the body. There's no specific treatment, just plenty of rest, an adequate fluid intake and painkillers when required.

The **Zika** virus is spread by the same mosquito species and a number of cases have been reported in Malaysia and Singapore. Symptoms are mild, flu-like and can involve rashes, but the infection can affect foetal development so pregnant women should postpone travelling or seek medical advice on the latest risks.

Although the risk of catching **malaria** is fairly low, you should consider taking antimalarial tablets if you think you might be staying in remote jungle areas of **Borneo** for some time. Bear in mind you have to start taking the tablets before you arrive in a malarial zone – ask your doctor for the latest advice.

Altitude sickness

Altitude sickness (or acute mountain sickness) can occur if you ascend above around 3500m. In Malaysia it's only likely to be relevant to those climbing **Mount Kinabalu** (4095m), and those affected usually report only mild symptoms at this altitude. Those symptoms include dizziness, headache, shortness of breath and nausea; severe cases can be life-threatening. Painkillers and other over-the-counter drugs may bring symptomatic relief in mild cases, but you must descend to lower altitude if symptoms drag on after a day or two or are severe.

Pharmacies, clinics and hospitals

Medical services in Malaysia, Singapore and Brunei are excellent; staff almost everywhere speak English and use up-to-date treatments. Details of pharmacies and hospitals are in the "Directory" sections of the Guide for cities and major towns.

COMBATING LEECHES

Leeches are gruesome but pretty harmless creatures, related to earthworms, which almost all trekkers will encounter – especially after rain, when you can rely upon them to come out. Slender, muscular tubes with teeth at one end, they lie dormant in rainforest leaf litter until, alerted by footfalls and body heat, they make strange, darting movements towards you, latching onto your boot, then climbing until they find a way through socks and trousers and onto your skin. Their bites are painless, so you may not notice you've been bitten until you see a growing red stain on your clothes – formed by the trickle of blood that continues for several minutes. That said, the bite of the larger, orange-striped tiger leech can hurt or be felt as a slight itching sensation.

If you see one beginning to bite, you can use your fingernail or a credit card to gently dislodge its head end. Otherwise salt or a quick dose of mosquito repellent will cause it to let go rapidly, as will scorching it with a cigarette lighter.

Of course it's best to **avoid being bitten** in the first place. Some nature guides recommend simply wearing open shoes and shorts, so that you can see any leeches – an approach that requires an advanced jungle mentality. Most people prefer, at the very least, to wear trousers tucked into their socks. Better still, tuck your trousers into **leech socks**. The size of Christmas stockings and made from calico, they have a string at the top that you tie tight at the knee; you can buy them in specialist stores and at some Malaysian nature parks. For an additional deterrent, spray socks and boots with insect repellent.

Pharmacies stock a wide range of medicines and health-related items, from contraceptives to contact lens solution; opening hours are the same as for other shops. The two big local chains are Watsons and Guardian, found in most towns. Only the largest pharmacies have **pharmacists**. If you need a **prescription drug**, you should see a doctor at a clinic, at whose discretion the clinic's own dispensary may be able to provide it. That said, in Malaysia at least, lax regulation means some pharmacies will sell such drugs over the counter.

Private **clinics** can be found even in small towns – your hotel or the local tourist office will be able to recommend one. In Malaysia a consultation costs around RM30, not including the cost of any treatment or medication; keep the receipts for insurance-claim purposes. Finally, the emergency department of each town's general hospital will see foreigners for a small fee, though obviously costs rise rapidly if continued treatment or overnight stays are necessary.

The media

Both Malaysia and Singapore boast plenty of newspapers, TV channels and radio stations serving up lively reportage of events, sports and entertainment, though don't expect to come across hard-hitting or healthily sceptical coverage of domestic politics. The major media organizations in each country are at least partly owned by the establishment; in Singapore, most newspapers have actually been herded into a conglomerate in which the state has a major stake.

Furthermore, the media are kept on their toes by a legal requirement that they must periodically renew their licence to publish. Thus the *Sarawak Tribune* was suspended indefinitely in 2006 after it reproduced the controversial Danish cartoons of the Prophet Muhammad; only in 2010 did it resume publication as the *New Sarawak Tribune*.

Given these circumstances, it's no surprise that the **Press Freedom Index** issued annually by the pressure group Reporters Without Borders, regularly puts Malaysia and Singapore in the bottom third of the world's nations. Brunei, also languishing low down in the table, has a much less well-developed media sector, and its newspapers are packed with anodyne stories about the latest deeds of the sultan and other royals.

Foreign newspapers and magazines are sold in the main cities, and international TV channels are available via satellite and cable. That said, issues of foreign magazines containing pieces that displease the authorities have occasionally been banned, while Singapore's leaders have a long history of winning defamation suits against foreign publications in the island's courts.

If this all seems a bleak picture, it should be said that coverage of Malaysia's opposition parties has increased since they have become more of a force to contend with in recent elections. Added to that, the advent of independent domestic **news websites** and **blogs** has been a breath of fresh air in both Malaysia and Singapore. It's also possible to turn up **YouTube** clips of discussion forums and interviews with activists, offering an alternative take on local issues.

Newspapers, magazines and online news

Both Malaysia and Singapore have English, Malay, Chinese and Tamil newspapers, while Brunei's papers appear in English and Malay. Though Malaysia's national dailies are available in towns in East Malaysia, locally published English-language papers such as the *Borneo Post* in Sarawak (Ⓦ theborneopost.com) and the *Daily Express* in Sabah (Ⓦ dailyexpress.com.my) are more popular there.

MALAYSIA

Aliran Monthly Ⓦ aliran.com. Campaigning magazine with an avowed pro-human-rights stance.

Free Malaysia Today Ⓦ freemalaysiatoday.com. Non-partisan coverage of Malaysian politics and society, with a dedicated East Malaysia section.

Malaysia Insight Ⓦ themalaysianinsight.com. Considered more moderate than some of its online counterparts, the *Insider* provides intelligent news and commentary.

Malaysiakini Ⓦ malaysiakini.com. Invigorating reportage and opinion with an anti-establishment slant.

New Straits Times Ⓦ nst.com.my. Closely linked to the UMNO party, this offshoot of Singapore's *Straits Times* was created after the island separated from the Federation.

Sarawak Report Ⓦ sarawakreport.org. Not a Malaysian site – it's run out of London – but worth a look for its hard-hitting coverage of issues such as logging, native peoples' rights and the probity of Sarawak's government.

The Star Ⓦ thestar.com.my. Founded by the MCA party, *The Star* is Malaysia's best-selling English daily and carries a broad range of local news, arts reviews and so forth.

SINGAPORE

The Online Citizen Ⓦ theonlinecitizen.com. An alternative and rather less sanguine view of Singapore affairs than you find in the island's mainstream media.

Straits Times Ⓦ straitstimes.com. This venerable broadsheet was founded in 1845, though sadly its pedigree isn't matched by the candour of its journalism; it's not bad on foreign news, however.

Today Ⓦ todayonline.com. A free online-only paper from the state-owned broadcaster Mediacorp, *Today* is generally less blandly pro-establishment than the *Straits Times* and carries worthwhile commentaries at the weekend.

TR Emeritus Ⓦ tremeritus.com. Formerly the Temasek Review, this website offers independent-minded reporting of the island's affairs.

BRUNEI

Borneo Bulletin Ⓦ borneobulletin.com.bn. Pleasant enough but hardly the most challenging of reads.

Television and radio

TV and radio in Malaysia, Singapore and Brunei are dominated by the state-owned broadcasters **RTM**, **Mediacorp** and **RTB** respectively, putting out programmes in several languages. Terrestrial **television** features an unexceptional mix of news, documentaries and dramas made locally and abroad, cookery and talk shows, Islamic discussions and so forth; **radio** is even less original and tends to be dominated by pop music and talk shows. Various foreign TV channels, including CNN, BBC World, National Geographic, ESPN Sports and Al-Jazeera (which has its East Asian base in KL), are available on cable and satellite in Malaysia, and on cable in Singapore (where ownership of satellite dishes is banned). Note that Malaysian broadcasts are easily picked up in Singapore, and Singapore broadcasts in southern Johor.

MALAYSIA

Cats FM Ⓦ catsfm.my. Kuching-based FM station offering music plus Sarawakian news; see the website for frequencies around the state.

RTM1 & RTM2 Ⓦ www.rtm.gov.my. Malaysia's staple state-owned TV channels, with some programming in English, Chinese and Tamil. News in English is broadcast on RTM2 at 8pm daily.

Traxxfm Ⓦ traxxfm.rtm.gov.my. Established RTM station with a mix of news and music in English, available on various frequencies around the country.

TV3 Ⓦ www.tv3.com.my. English and Malay news, drama and documentaries, plus some Chinese programmes. It's part of the same conglomerate as the *New Straits Times*.

SINGAPORE

BBC World Service Ⓦ bbcworldservice.com. 88.9FM, 24hr.

Channel News Asia Ⓦ channelnewsasia.com. Mediacorp's CNN-like diet of rolling TV news, via cable.

Channel 5 Ⓦ 5.mediacorptv.sg. The main terrestrial channel for English programming, with plenty of imported shows.

BRUNEI

Radio and Television Brunei (RTB) Ⓦ rtb.gov.bn. Locally made dramas, religious programmes and news, interspersed with dramas and soaps from as far afield as Korea.

Festivals

With so many ethnic groups and religions represented in Malaysia, Singapore and Brunei, you'll be unlucky if your trip doesn't coincide with some sort of festival. Religious celebrations range from exuberant family-oriented pageants to blood-curdlingly gory displays of devotion. Chinese religious festivals are the best times to catch free performances of Chinese opera, or wayang, featuring crashing cymbals, clanging gongs and stylized singing. Secular events might comprise a parade with a cast of thousands, or just a local market with a few cultural demonstrations laid on.

Bear in mind that the major festival periods may play havoc with even the best-planned travel itineraries, and that some festivals are also public holidays (see p.56).

A festival and events calendar

The dates of many festivals change annually according to the lunar calendar. The Islamic calendar in particular shifts forward relative to the Gregorian calendar by about ten days each year, so that, for example, a Muslim festival that happens in mid-April one year will be nearer the start of April the next. We've listed rough timings; actual dates can vary by a day or two in practice depending on the sighting of the new moon.

JANUARY & FEBRUARY

Ponggal (mid-Jan) A Tamil harvest and New Year festival held at the start of the Tamil month of Thai. *Ponggal* translates as "overflow", and the festival is celebrated by boiling sugar, rice and milk together in a new claypot over a wood fire till the mixture spills over, symbolizing plenty.

Thaipusam (late Jan/early Feb) Entranced Hindu penitents carry elaborate steel arches (*kavadi*), attached to their skin by hooks and skewers, to honour Lord Subramaniam. The biggest processions are at

Kuala Lumpur's Batu Caves and from Singapore's Sri Srinivasa Perumal Temple to the Chettiar Hindu Temple.

Chinese New Year (late Jan/early to mid-Feb) At which Chinese communities settle debts, visit friends and relatives and give children red envelopes (*hong bao/ang pao*) containing money; Chinese operas and lion- and dragon-dance troupes perform in the streets, while markets sell sausages and waxed ducks, pussy willow, chrysanthemums and mandarin oranges. Singapore and the major towns of west coast Malaysia see Chingay parades, featuring stilt-walkers, lion dancers and floats.

Chap Goh Mei (Feb) The fifteenth and climactic night of the Chinese New Year period, and a time for more feasting and firecrackers; women who throw an orange into the sea at this time are supposed to be granted a good husband.

Brunei National Day (Feb 23) The sultan and tens of thousands of Bruneians watch parades and fireworks at the Sultan Hassanal Bolkiah National Stadium, just outside Bandar Seri Begawan.

MARCH–MAY

Easter (March/April) Candlelit processions are held on Good Friday at churches.

Qing Ming (April) Ancestral graves are cleaned and restored, and offerings made by Chinese families at the beginning of the third lunar month, signifying the start of spring and a new farming year.

Ramadan (mid-May in 2018) Muslims spend the ninth month of the Islamic calendar fasting in the daytime, and breaking their fasts nightly with delicious Malay sweetmeats served at stalls outside mosques.

Vesak Day (May) Saffron-robed monks chant prayers at packed Buddhist temples, and devotees release caged birds to commemorate the Buddha's birth, enlightenment and attainment of Nirvana.

Kaamatan (May 30 & 31) The Kadazan/Dusun version of Sarawak's Iban *gawai* rice-harvest festival, Kaamatan is marked all over Sabah (and Labuan Island), most notably with week-long festivities at the Kadazan/Dusun Cultural Association in Kota Kinabalu.

JUNE–AUGUST

Hari Raya Puasa/Aidilfitri (June) Muslims celebrate the end of Ramadan by feasting and visiting family and friends; this is the only time the region's royal palaces are open to the public.

Gawai Dayak (June) Sarawak's people, especially the Iban and Bidayuh, celebrate the end of rice harvesting with extravagant longhouse feasts. Aim to be in a longhouse on the Rejang or Batang Ai rivers, or around Bau.

Feast of St Peter (June 24) Melaka's Eurasian community decorate their boats to honour the patron saint of fishermen.

Dragon Boat Festival (June/July) Rowing boats, bearing a dragon's head and tail, race in Penang, Melaka, Singapore and Kota Kinabalu, to commemorate a Chinese scholar who drowned himself in protest against political corruption.

George Town Festival (July/Aug) One of the best arts festivals in Malaysia sees the historic streets and buildings of Penang given over to music recitals, art exhibitions and the like, over a month.

Sultan of Brunei's Birthday (July 15) Starting with a speech by the

sultan on the padang, celebrations continue for two weeks with parades, lantern processions, traditional sports competitions and fireworks.

Singapore National Day (Aug 9) Singapore celebrates its independence with a huge show featuring military parades and fireworks.

Hari Raya Haji/Aidiladha (Aug) Muslims gather at mosques to honour those who have completed the hajj, or pilgrimage, to Mecca; goats are sacrificed and their meat given to the needy.

Festival of the Hungry Ghosts (late Aug) Held to appease the souls of the dead released from purgatory during the seventh lunar month. Chinese street operas are staged, and joss sticks, red candles and paper money are burnt outside Chinese homes.

Merdeka Day (Aug 31) Parades in KL's Merdeka Square and other cities mark the formation of the state of Malaysia.

SEPTEMBER–DECEMBER

Moon Cake Festival (Sept) Also known as the Mid-Autumn Festival, this is when Chinese people eat and exchange moon cakes, made from sesame and lotus seeds and sometimes stuffed with a duck egg. Essentially a harvest festival.

Yang di-Pertuan Agong's Birthday (Sept) Celebrates the birthday of Malaysia's king, elected every five years by the Peninsula's nine sultans from among their number.

Malaysia Day (Sept 16) Commemorates the establishment of Malaysia in 1963, when Singapore, Sabah and Sarawak joined with already-independent Malaya.

Navarathri (Sept–Oct) Hindu temples devote nine nights to classical dance and music in honour of the consorts of the Hindu gods, Shiva, Vishnu and Brahman.

Thimithi (Oct/Nov) Hindu firewalking ceremony in which devotees prove the strength of their faith by running across a pit of hot coals; best seen at the Sri Mariamman Temple in Singapore.

Deepavali (Oct/Nov) Also known as Diwali, this Hindu festival celebrates the victory of Light over Dark: oil lamps are lit outside homes to attract Lakshmi, the goddess of prosperity, and prayers are offered at all temples.

Christmas (Dec 25) Shopping centres in major cities compete to create the most spectacular Christmas decorations.

Sports and outdoor activities

With some of the world's oldest tropical rainforest and countless beaches and islands, Malaysia offers plenty of opportunities for trekking, snorkelling and scuba diving, and rafting, tubing, abseiling and paragliding – among others – are available in certain locations.

If you intend to take up any of these pursuits, check that they are covered by your insurance policy.

Watersports

The crystal-clear waters and abundant tropical fish and coral of Malaysia make snorkelling and diving a must for any underwater enthusiast. This is particularly true of the islands of southeast Sabah – Sipadan, Mabul and their neighbours boast some of the world's best dive sites – and the Peninsula's east coast, with islands like the **Perhentians**, **Redang**, **Kapas** and **Tioman**.

Dive shops offer all-inclusive, internationally recognized certification courses, ranging from a beginner's open-water course (around RM1300), right through to the dive-master certificate (RM2200). If you're already qualified, expect to pay at least RM150 for dive trips, although prices vary depending on the locality.

Most beachside guesthouses rent snorkelling equipment for around RM20 per day. Some popular **snorkelling** areas mark out lanes for motorboats with buoy lines – stay on the correct side of the line to avoid a nasty accident. If you're not sure where it's safe to swim or snorkel, always seek local advice. Never touch or walk on coral as this will cause irreparable damage – besides which, you risk treading on the armour-piercing spines of sea urchins, or a painful encounter with fire coral.

Jetskiing and **parasailing** are also on offer at many popular beaches. **Windsurfing**, however, has yet to take off except at a few, usually pricey, resorts, as well as at Cherating on the east coast, where the open bay and shallow waters provide near-perfect conditions during the northeast monsoon.

Whitewater rafting and tubing

Whitewater rafting has become a popular activity in Sabah, where there are several rivers in the vicinity of Kota Kinabalu that tour operators organize regular trips to, notably the Padas River. Opportunities for rafting in **Peninsular Malaysia** are limited and hard to reach, with the notable

---

CHECKLIST OF CAMPING AND TREKKING EQUIPMENT

As camping and trekking are not especially popular with Malaysians, you need to bring your own **gear** if possible – especially core items like tents and sleeping bags – or take your chances with locally sold products, which are generally inexpensive and sometimes correspondingly short-lived. Hiking boots and shoes may not be that easy to find, especially in larger sizes, though local people, including trekking guides, often swear by plain, slip-on **rubber shoes** (*kasut gatah*), sold everywhere. Available in sizes up to about 40 for just RM15, they are surprisingly versatile, offering a decent grip on the forest floor and suitable for fording streams as they can't soak up water. That said, you may find them less suitable for multiday trekking in difficult terrain.

There are small (and very expensive) "proper" outdoor gear stores in major cities; you might also be able to rent some of what you'll need on site, especially at Taman Negara, or have it supplied as part of a hiking package.

ESSENTIALS

Backpack
Breathable shirts/T-shirts
First-aid kit (basic)
Insect repellent
Lightweight, quick-drying trousers
Pocket knife
Poncho or rainproof coat

Sandals or rubber shoes (for wading through streams)
Sun block
Toilet paper
Toiletries
Torch (and/or head torch)
Trekking shoes/boots
Water bottle

OTHER USEFUL ITEMS

Binoculars
Compass
Emergency snack food
Fleece jacket (if at altitude)
Hat, cotton, with brim (for exposed terrain)
Heavy-duty refuse bag (to rainproof your pack)
Insulation mat

Leech socks
Lip balm
Mosquito net
Sewing kit
Sleeping bag
Sunglasses (UV protective)
Tent (if sleeping out)
Towel, small
Water purification tablets

exception of Gopeng (see p.124); here, it's best to go with an operator such as Nomad Adventure (ⓦnomadadventure.com) or River Bug (ⓦriverbug .asia). Prices vary depending on the location. A few nature parks also offer the chance to go **tubing** down jungle rivers.

Trekking

The majority of **treks** in Malaysia require forethought and preparation. In addition to the fierce sun if you're not in the jungle, the tropical climate can unleash torrential rain without warning, which rapidly affects the condition of trails or the height of rivers – what started out as a ten-hour trip can end up taking twice as long. That said, the time of year is not a hugely significant factor when planning a trek, although in the rainy season (Nov–Feb) trails can be slow going (or even closed for safety reasons) and the parks and adventure tours will be less busy.

Treks in national parks almost always require that you go in a group with a **guide**; solo travellers can usually join a group once there. Costs and conditions vary between parks; each park account in the Guide contains details, while tour operators in Kuala Lumpur, Kuching, Miri and Kota Kinabalu (listed throughout the relevant sections in the Guide) can also furnish information on conditions and options.

For inexperienced trekkers, **Taman Negara** is probably the best place to start, boasting a good range of walks, many of which can be done without a guide, while **Bako National Park** in southwest Sarawak offers fairly easy, day-long hikes. For more experienced walkers, other parks in Sarawak, especially **Mulu National Park**, should offer sufficient challenges for most tastes, while Sabah's **Maliau Basin** is at the demanding end of the scale. **Kinabalu Park** in Sabah is in a class of its own, the hike to the top of the mountain a demanding but highly rewarding combination of trekking and climbing. Equally challenging, although lesser in stature, is **Mount Trus Madi**, also in Sabah.

Culture and etiquette

Despite their obvious openness to influences from around the globe, Malaysia, Singapore and Brunei remain fairly conservative and conformist places.

Behaviour that departs from cultural norms – basically, anything that draws attention to the individuals concerned – is to be avoided.

Foreigners are generally cut some slack, but until you acquire some familiarity with where the limits lie, it's best to err on the side of caution. Get the balance right and you'll find locals helpful and welcoming, while respectful of your need for some privacy.

Dress

For both men and women, exposing lots of bare flesh is generally a no-no, and the degree to which you should **cover up** can seem surprisingly prim. Islamic tradition suffuses the dress code for locals, Muslim or otherwise, and dictates that both men and women should keep torsos covered; shirt sleeves, if short, should come down to the elbow (for women, long-sleeved tops are preferable), while shorts or skirts should extend down to the knee (long trousers are ideal). Figure-hugging clothes are often frowned upon, particularly for women. All of this said, dress codes are more liberal in most cities (especially Singapore), on the beach, and when doing sports or other activities.

Note that in Muslim tradition, the soles of **shoes** are considered unclean, having been in contact with the dirt of the street. Thus before entering any home (Muslim or otherwise), it's almost universal practice to remove footwear at the threshold or before stepping onto any carpeted or matted area.

Body language

Two things to **avoid** are public shows of affection (holding hands is OK, kissing is not) and drinking alcohol in the street, i.e. outside the confines of a bar or hawker centre. In a situation where you need to make a **complaint**, the most effective approach is not to raise your voice but to go out of your way to appear calm while stating your case.

As for body language, note that **touching someone's head**, be they Muslim or otherwise, is to be avoided as the head is considered sacred. Handshakes are fairly commonplace when meeting someone; Muslims often follow this by touching the palm of the right hand to their own chest. Some Muslims may be reluctant to shake hands with the opposite sex; however, in this case a smile, nod and that same right-hand-palm gesture will

THE STATUS OF MALAY WOMEN

Malay women are among the most **emancipated** in the Islamic world. They often attain prominent roles in business, academia and other areas of public life and are very much the lynchpin of the family.

Although the more conservative tide running through the Islamic world has had relatively little impact on this situation, many Malay women now wear a *tudung* (headscarf). Sometimes this merely indicates an acceptance of the trappings of the religion – it's not unusual to see Malay women at a gig or club partying away in headscarf, T-shirt and jeans.

suffice. Muslims and Indians also avoid using their left hand for human contact or eating.

Visiting places of worship

It's common to see various temples and mosques happily existing side by side, each providing a social as well as a religious focal point for the corresponding community. Some shrines are among the oldest structures you're likely to see in the region and are worth a look around.

In theory all **mosques** are open to visitors outside prayer times, though in conservative areas they may not welcome tourists. Male visitors should wear long trousers and a shirt or top with sleeves coming down to the elbows (long sleeves are even better); women will also have to don a long cloak and headdress, which is provided by most mosques. You'll be required to remove your shoes before entering. Most Chinese and Hindu **temples** are open from early morning to early evening; devotees go in when they like, to make offerings or to pray. Hindu temples also expect visitors to remove shoes.

Even if there are no signs barring **photography**, staff at some temples don't take kindly to it; if in doubt, ask.

Women travellers

Women who respect local customs and exercise common sense should have few problems travelling alone or with other women, though some Western women have been known to find the atmosphere in largely **Muslim areas**, such as Kelantan or Terengganu, off-putting. Arriving there from Thailand or from a more cosmopolitan part of Malaysia, you may be stared at or subjected to wolf-whistles or lewd gestures, even if you are dressed more conservatively than some local Chinese or Indian women. If it's any consolation, this sort of thing is quite random, and the reason local non-Muslim women might get away with a bit more is that there is an unspoken understanding as to how Malaysia's various communities can behave in public.

Shopping

Southeast Asia can offer bargain shopping, with electrical equipment, cameras and fabrics all selling at competitive prices. What's more, the region's ethnic diversity means a range of unusual souvenirs and handicrafts to choose from.

One point to be aware of is that a lot of the crafts on sale in Malaysia are in fact made elsewhere in the region, particularly in Indonesia. Worthwhile buys, especially domestically made ones, are highlighted throughout the Guide. Also be aware that prices in small outlets such as family-run shops tend to be negotiable, and **bargaining** is expected. Asking for the "best price" is always a good opening gambit; from there, it's a question of technique, though be realistic – shopkeepers will soon lose interest if you offer an unreasonably low price. If you buy any electrical goods, it can be worth ensuring you get an international guarantee, endorsed by the shop.

Fabrics

Batik cloth is made by applying hot wax to a piece of cloth with either a pen or a copper stamp; when the cloth is dyed, the wax resists the dye and a pattern appears, a process that can be repeated many times to build up colours. Note that some vendors try to pass off printed cloth as batik. Make sure the brightness of the pattern is equal on both sides – if it's obviously lighter on one side, it is likely the cloth is printed.

Batik is used to create shirts, skirts, bags and hats, as well as traditional **sarongs**. The exquisite gold-threaded brocade known as **songket**, used to make sarongs, headscarves and the like, is a big step up in price from batik; RM200 for a sarong-length of cloth is not uncommon, and prices soar for the finest pieces.

Unique to Sarawak is **pua kumbu** (in Iban, "blanket"), a textile whose complex designs are created using the *ikat* method of weaving (see p.327). The cloth is sold in longhouses as well as in some souvenir outlets. Sabah's tribes have their own woven fabrics, some of which are sold by Sabah Tourism's Kadaiku subsidiary (W kadaiku .com).

Woodcarving

Woodcarving skills, once employed to decorate the palaces and public buildings of the early sultans, are today used to make less exotic articles such as mirror frames. However, it's still possible to see statues and masks created by the Orang Asli. As animists, Orang Asli artists draw upon the natural world – animals, trees, fish, as well as more abstract elements like fire and water – for their imagery. Of particular interest are the carvings of the Mah Meri of Selangor, which are improvisations on the theme of *moyang*, literally "ancestor", the generic name for all spirit images. In Borneo, look out for tribal face masks and rectangular shields adorned with intricate motifs. It's also possible to buy hardwood blowpipes, though these are drilled rather than carved.

Metalwork

Of the wealth of metalwork on offer, **silverware** from Kelantan is among the finest and most-intricately designed; it's commonly used to make earrings, brooches and pendants, as well as more substantial pieces. Selangor is known for its **pewter** – a blend of tin, antimony and copper – which can be used in elegant vases, tankards and ornaments.

Other souvenirs

Rattan, cane, **bamboo** and *mengkuang* (pandanus) are traditionally used to make baskets, bird cages, mats, hats and shoulder bags. The best items make surprisingly impressive accessories, and in Borneo it's possible to find baskets and bags bearing traditional motifs, too. Another unusual raw material is **breadfruit bark**; in Sarawak it's pressed to produce a "cloth" that makes excellent hats and jackets, as well as a canvas for paintings.

Malay pastimes throw up some interesting purchases: leather *wayang kulit* (shadow play) **puppets**, portraying characters from Hindu legend, are attractive and light to carry; equally colourful but impractical to cart around are Malay **kites** (*wau*), which can be a couple of metres long.

> ## DUTY-FREE GOODS
> Malaysia has no duty on cameras, watches, cosmetics, perfumes or cigarettes. Labuan, Langkawi and Tioman are duty-free islands, which in practice means that goods there (including alcohol) can be a third cheaper than on the Malaysian mainland, though it's not as though a particularly impressive range of products is on sale. Duty-free products in Singapore include electronic and electrical goods, cosmetics, cameras, clocks, watches, jewellery, precious stones and metals.

Pottery, though sometimes mass-produced, can be a worthwhile decorative acquisition. Examples include the Malay *labu*, a gourd-like slender-necked water jug (it's made in, among other places, Perak) and Sarawak pots and jars bearing tribal motifs. Finally, it's possible to buy some fine examples of **beadwork** – from pricey Peranakan beaded slippers to Kelabit jackets from the northern highlands of Sarawak.

Travel essentials

Costs

Anyone entering Malaysia from Thailand will find that costs are noticeably higher. Travelling in a group naturally helps keep costs down. The region affords some savings for senior citizens, and an ISIC student card (W isic.org) might occasionally pay dividends.

Note that **bargaining** is routine throughout Malaysia and Singapore when buying stuff in markets or small shops, though you don't haggle for meals or accommodation.

Malaysia

In **Peninsular Malaysia** you can scrape by on £12/US$17/RM70 per day staying in dorms, eating at hawker stalls and getting around by bus. Double that and you'll be able to exist in relative comfort without worrying about occasionally treating yourself. Over in **East Malaysia**, everything tends to cost that little bit extra – partly due to archaic regulations that require imported goods to be sent via Peninsula ports rather than arriving directly; here, expect to spend about ten percent more. Of course, if you do any ticketed sightseeing or book tours – especially pricey to reach remote nature parks – then costs will shoot up, wherever you are.

Singapore and Brunei

Costs in **Singapore** are at Western levels, with a minimum budget of around £30/US$45/S$60 per day. Upgrading your lodgings to a private room in a guesthouse, eating one daily meal in a cheap restaurant, and having a beer or two could require £50/US$65/S$90 per day.

Like-for-like costs in **Brunei** are perhaps ten to twenty percent less than in Singapore, though note that budget accommodation in the capital is limited. Otherwise, costs can spiral as you'll have to rely on taxis or package trips to reach outlying places of interest, notably Ulu Temburong National Park.

Crime and personal safety

If you lose something in Malaysia, Singapore or Brunei, you're more likely to have someone run after you with it than run away. Nevertheless, don't become complacent, as petty crime is an issue in Malaysia at least. Sensible **precautions** include carrying your passport and other valuables in a concealed money belt, and using the safety deposit box provided by many guesthouses and hotels. Take a photocopy of the relevant pages of your passport, too, in case it's lost or stolen. If you have to report a crime, be sure to get a copy of the police report for insurance purposes.

It's worth stating here on no account should you have anything to do with **illegal drugs** of any description in Malaysia, Singapore and Brunei (see p.31).

> ### SALES TAXES AND SERVICE CHARGES
>
> Top-end and many mid-range hotels and restaurants in Malaysia and Singapore levy two surcharges: a **service charge** (usually ten percent) and a **goods and services tax** (GST; six percent in Malaysia, seven percent in Singapore). Always check if prices quoted – including those on online booking sites – include these charges (they are "nett" prices, in local parlance) or exclude them; the presence of "**++**" after a price indicates that you need to add them. GST also applies to goods sold in shops.

> ### EMERGENCY NUMBERS
>
> #### MALAYSIA
> Fire brigade ☎994
> Police/Ambulance ☎999
>
> #### SINGAPORE
> Fire Brigade/Ambulance ☎995
> Police ☎999
>
> #### BRUNEI
> Ambulance ☎991
> Fire Brigade ☎995
> Police ☎993

Malaysia

Pickpockets and **snatch-thieves** can be a problem in Malaysian cities, although violent crime is relatively rare; horrific incidents like the alcohol-fuelled murder of two British students in central Kuching in 2014 are quite out of the ordinary.

Restrictions on contact between people of the opposite sex (such as the offence of *khalwat*, or "close proximity") and eating in public during daylight hours in the Ramadan month apply to Muslims only.

Singapore

Singapore is known locally as a "fine city". Substantial **fines** can be levied to punish misdemeanours like littering, jaywalking – defined as crossing a main road within 50m of a designated pedestrian crossing – and so forth, though these penalties are seldom enforced as the populace has become compliant over the years. Bear in mind that **chewing gum** – despite what you may hear – is not illegal in Singapore. Although it isn't on sale there, on the grounds that used gum can foul the streets, you can bring in gum for your own consumption.

Electricity

Mains voltage in Malaysia, Singapore and Brunei is **230 volts**, so any equipment using 110 volts will need a converter. The plugs in all three countries have three square prongs like British ones.

Insurance

A typical travel insurance policy usually provides cover for the loss of bags, tickets and – up to a certain limit – cash or cheques, as well as cancellation or curtailment of your journey. Some policy premiums include dangerous sports; in Malaysia, for example, this can mean scuba diving, whitewater rafting or paragliding. Always ascertain whether medical coverage will be paid out as treatment proceeds or only after return home, and whether there's a 24-hour medical emergency number. When securing baggage cover, make sure that the per-article limit will cover your most valuable possession. If you need to make a claim, you should keep receipts for medicines and medical treatment, and in the event you have anything stolen, you must obtain an official statement from the police.

Internet

The explosion of smartphones and wi-fi has put paid to most Malaysian **internet** cafés. Those that still exist tend to be found in malls or in upstairs premises along central streets; they charge a few ringgit an hour to get online, but now make most of their money as gaming parlours. For details of internet access in Brunei and Singapore, see the relevant chapters of this Guide. Throughout, we have indicated whether accommodation, eating or drinking establishments have wi-fi using a symbol at the end of reviews.

If you like being online constantly, it's worth buying a local **SIM card** and getting a data plan with it (see p.57).

Laundry

Most Malaysian towns have laundries (*dobi*) where you can have clothes washed cheaply and quickly, according to weight (typically RM4 a kilo), picking them up later in the day or early the next day. Some hostels and guesthouses have washing machines that guests can use for a small charge. Coin-operated **launderettes** are becoming increasingly common, too, and are less tricky to use than might appear at first, with machines that dispense change and detergent. Dry-cleaning services are less common, though any hotel of a decent standard will be able to oblige.

LGBT+ travellers

Though Malaysia's largest cities, plus Singapore, have long had a discreet LGBT+ scene, its public profile was until recently still summed up by the old "don't ask, don't tell" maxim. However, cyberspace has helped galvanize LGBT+ people by providing a virtual refuge within which to socialize and campaign. Hitherto strait-laced **Singapore** now permits exploration of gay themes in the arts, hosts the hugely successful annual rally Pink Dot (see p.546) and for a time even played host to popular outdoor rave parties. Although the environment in **Malaysia** is always going to be more conservative, the Malaysian government has no obvious appetite, Islamically inspired or otherwise, to clamp down on the existing, limited LGBT+ nightlife.

For all the general loosening up over the years, it's very much a case of two steps forward and one step back, however. In 2007, following an extraordinary parliamentary debate, Singapore MPs finally agreed to repeal **colonial-era laws** criminalizing anal and oral sex, though they retained the injunction on such activity between men. The same colonial legislation remains on the statute book in Malaysia, and what LGBT+-related campaigning exists tends to be channelled into the relatively uncontentious issue of HIV and AIDS. Meanwhile, Singapore has consistently declined to give official recognition to its **gay lobby** group, People Like Us, and now bars tourists from attending Pink Dot (as well as multinational firms from sponsoring it). Needless to say, all this makes legal recognition of LGBT+ partnerships a distant prospect in either country.

This mixed picture shouldn't deter LGBT+ visitors from getting to know and enjoy the local scene, such as it is. A small number of LGBT+ establishments are reviewed in this Guide.

Living in Malaysia and Singapore

Opportunities for non-residents to find short-term **employment** in Malaysia and Singapore are few and far between. Helpers are often required in guesthouses; the wages for such tasks are low, but board and lodging are often included. On a more formal level, both Singapore and KL in particular hold large communities of skilled expats with work permits, secured by their employer. In Malaysia expats might still expect elevated salaries, but this perk is increasingly rare in Singapore, where pay is already at Western levels.

English-teaching qualifications are in demand by language schools in both countries, while qualified **diving instructors** can also find work in Malaysia. There are also a few **volunteer schemes**, mainly focusing on nature conservation fieldwork, though some require you to pay to join.

STUDY AND WORK PROGRAMMES

AFS Intercultural Programs ⓦ afs.org/countries/malaysia. Community service schemes in Malaysia.

Ape Malaysia ⓦ apemalaysia.com. Opportunities to do wildlife conservation work, and not just with orang-utans – they have projects at the Sun Bear Conservation Centre near Sandakan, for example.

Camp Borneo ⓦ campsinternational.com. Blurs the distinction between ecotourism and volunteering, with a range of trips that take in Sabah's top nature sights with stints spent doing conservation or community projects.

Fulbright Program ⓦ macee.org.my. Regular opportunities for US citizens to spend several months teaching English in rural Malaysia, without requiring teaching experience.

Turtle Conservation Society ⓦ turtleconservationsociety.org. my. Lists organizations offering volunteer conservation work schemes in Peninsular Malaysia.

Workaway ⓦ workaway.info. Voluntary work – maintenance, gardening, sometimes language teaching – at guesthouses, farms and even art galleries, in return for free or discounted accommodation.

Mail

Malaysia has a well-organized postal service operated by Pos Malaysia (☏ 1300 300 300, ⓦ pos. com.my), whose website details postage rates, express mail and courier (PosLaju) services and so forth. Expect airmail delivery to take one to two weeks depending on the destination.

In **Brunei**, post offices are open Monday to Thursday and Saturday between 8am and 4.30pm, while some may open part of Friday as well. Postal services in **Singapore** are detailed in the Singapore chapter of the Guide (see p.472).

Maps

Online mapping of Malaysia offered by the usual internet giants sometimes contains **inaccuracies**, especially when it comes to road names. The best printed maps of Malaysia are the city and regional maps published by the Johor Bahru-based World Express Mapping, although these are harder to find in bookshops than they once were. Most Malaysian **tourist offices** have their own free maps of the local area, but these are often of poor quality and offer little that the maps in this Guide don't already include. Whichever maps you use, be aware that the high rate of road construction and development in rural and urban areas alike means that maps can be a little out of date as soon as they appear. Singapore maps are covered in the Singapore chapter of this Guide (see p.527).

Money

Malaysia's currency is the **ringgit** (pronounced *ring-git* and abbreviated to "RM", and sometimes informally called "dollar"), divided into 100 sen. Notes come in RM5, RM10, RM20, RM50 and RM100 denominations. Coins are currently minted in 5 sen, 10 sen, 20 sen, 50 sen and RM1 denominations. At the time of research, the **exchange rate** was around RM4 to US$1 and RM5.40 to £1.

Singapore's currency is the **Singapore dollar**, written simply as $ (or S$ in this book to distinguish it from other dollars) and divided into 100 cents. Notes are issued in denominations of S$2, S$5, S$10, S$20, S$50 and S$100, with a couple of larger notes, rarely seen; coins come in denominations of 1, 5, 10, 20 and 50 cents, and S$1. At the time of research, the **exchange rate** was around S$1.80 to US$1, S$2 to £1. Confusingly, some coins in Singapore are very similar in size and appearance to some of their Malaysian counterparts, so it's best to keep them separate.

Brunei's currency, the **Brunei dollar**, is divided into 100 cents; you'll see it written as B$, or simply as $. The Brunei dollar has parity with the Singapore dollar and both are accepted by banks and larger businesses in either country. Notes come in B$1, B$5, B$10, B$50, B$100 and rare larger denominations; coins come in denominations of 1, 5, 10, 20 and 50 cents.

Banks

Major banks in **Malaysia** include Maybank, HSBC, Citibank, Standard Chartered, RHB and CIMB, most with ATMs; those of Maybank and HSBC, to name two, seldom have problems with foreign bank cards, but other banks' machines vary. In rural parts of Malaysia – for example, in the interior of Sabah or Sarawak, plus some coastal areas – banks can be scarce, so here it's a wise idea to carry a fair amount of cash, in smallish denominations.

Licensed **moneychangers**' kiosks, found in bigger towns all over the country, tend to open later than banks, until around 6pm; some open at weekends and until 9pm, too. Some hotels will exchange money at all hours. Exchange rates tend to be more generous at moneychangers, though anyone still depending on travellers' cheques should note that moneychangers don't generally exchange them.

Singapore banks are detailed in the relevant chapter of the Guide (see p.551). Banks represented in **Brunei** include the International Bank of Brunei, Citibank, Standard Chartered Bank and the Overseas Union Bank.

Plastic

Credit and debit cards are only accepted by larger businesses in Malaysia and Brunei – you won't, for example, be able to use your Visa card at a *kedai kopi*, though a café chain in a big city may well accept it. In Singapore many companies accept card payments, but small firms may only do so for larger payments.

Opening hours and public holidays

In **Malaysia**, shops are open daily from around 9.30am to 7pm, though outlets in shopping centres and malls are typically open later. Government offices tend to work Monday to Friday from 8am to 4.15pm or 9am to 5pm, with an hour off for lunch, except on Friday when the break lasts from 12.15 to 2.45pm (or 11.45 to 2pm in East Malaysia) to allow Muslims to attend prayers. Banking hours are generally Monday to Friday 9.30am to 4pm and Saturday 9.30 to 11.30am (closed on every first and third Saturday of the month), except in the states where Friday is the day off: Kedah, Perlis, Kelantan, Terengganu and to a lesser extent Johor. In these states, the working week runs from Sunday to Thursday, with Friday and Saturday as days off.

In **Singapore**, offices generally work Monday to Friday 8.30am to 5pm and sometimes on Saturday mornings. Shop hours vary, but malls are typically open from 10am to 10pm.

Brunei **banking hours** are Monday to Friday 9am to 3pm and Saturday 9 to 11am.

Opening hours for temples and mosques are given in the text of the Guide where they keep to a formal schedule (often not the case).

Public and school holidays

The list of public holiday dates (see below) is a guide only – government websites issue new lists for each year a few months in advance. Note that Muslim holidays (marked with an asterisk) move earlier by ten or eleven days each year, and that precise dates depend on the sighting of the new moon, which determines when each month of the Muslim calendar begins. Note also that each Malaysian state has its own additional holidays, which could be to do with its sultan's birthday or an Islamic (in states with a largely Muslim population) or tribal event, such as the *gawai* in June in Sarawak. Some holidays below are marked by special festivities (see p.47).

It pays to be aware of not just public holidays but also local **school holidays**, as Malaysian accommodation can be hard to come by during these periods. In Malaysia, schools get a week off in mid-March and late August, and two weeks off at the start of June, with a long break from mid-November to the end of the year. Singapore school breaks are almost identical, except that the June holiday lasts the whole month, and kids get a week off in early September rather than late August.

MALAYSIAN PUBLIC HOLIDAYS

Jan 1 New Year's Day
Jan/Feb Chinese New Year
May 1 Labour Day
May/June Vesak Day
May/June Hari Raya Aidilfitri*
Aug Hari Raya Haji*
Aug 31 National Day
Sept 9 Yang Dipertuan Agong's Birthday
Sept 16 Malaysia Day
Aug/Sept Awwal Muharram (the Muslim New Year)*
Oct/Nov Deepavali
Nov Birthday of the Prophet Muhammad*
Dec 25 Christmas

SINGAPORE PUBLIC HOLIDAYS

Note that Singapore has designated dates for Islamic festivals and does not adjust them to fit sightings of the new moon.
Jan 1 New Year's Day
Jan/Feb Chinese New Year
March/April Good Friday
May 1 Labour Day
May/June Vesak Day

May/June Hari Raya Puasa*
Aug 9 National Day
Aug Hari Raya Haji*
Oct/Nov Deepavali
Dec 25 Christmas

BRUNEI PUBLIC HOLIDAYS

Brunei observes the same Muslim festivals as Malaysia, plus New Year, Chinese New Year, Christmas and the following:

February 23 National Day
March/April Israk Mikraj (the night when the Prophet ascended to heaven)*
April/May First day of Ramadan*
May 31 Armed Forces' Day
May/June Anniversary of Revelation of the Koran*
July 15 Sultan's Birthday

Phones

Malaysia, Singapore and Brunei all have a comprehensive **mobile network**. There are many outlets selling mobiles (known locally as "hand phones"), even in the smallest of towns. If your own phone is unlocked and GSM compatible, you can use a local SIM card from phone shops and 7–Eleven stores. You can top up your balance at the same outlets; you either get a receipt with a pin number on it for you to dial and activate the recharge, or the shop staff will do this for you. It's worth looking out for low-priced SIMs aimed at

---

INTERNATIONAL CALLS

To make international calls to any of the countries below, dial your international access code (☎00 in Malaysia and Brunei, usually ☎001 in Singapore) then the relevant country code from the list, then the number (including any area code, but excluding any initial zero). From Singapore, you can call Malaysia by dialling ☎020, then the area code (omitting the initial zero), then the number.

IDD COUNTRY CODES

Australia ☎61
Brunei ☎673
Ireland ☎353
Malaysia ☎60
New Zealand ☎64
Singapore ☎65
South Africa ☎27
UK ☎44
US & Canada ☎1

---

tourists, loaded with a small amount of credit for voice calls and a data balance that should be good for a week or two of moderate online use.

Malaysia

The two big players in the **mobile phone** market are Maxis (which uses the Hotlink brand for its SIM cards; ☻hotlink.com.my) and Celcom (aka XPax; ☻celcom.com.my), with the smaller DiGi (☻digi.com.my) and Tune Talk (☻tunetalk.com/my) bringing up the rear. Cellular coverage in Peninsular Malaysia is fairly good, though expect it to be patchy or nonexistent in rural areas. Sabah and Sarawak coverage is variable, focusing on urban areas, major roads and populated river valleys. Tariffs can be complex, though you can expect calls made to other Malaysian numbers to cost no more than RM0.50 per minute.

Local calls from a landline are very cheap at just 10 sen for three minutes, but for long-distance calls, it can be more convenient to buy a **phonecard**, available from service stations, 7–Eleven outlets and newsagents. Your best bet is to use a card such as iTalk (☻tm.com.my; from RM10), which enables you to make discounted calls from the line in your hotel room as well as from payphones.

Singapore

Three companies, Singtel (☻singtel.com), Starhub (☻starhub.com) and M1 (☻m1.com.sg) dominate the mobile phone market in Singapore (and some also sell phonecards for surviving payphones). Their **SIM cards** (from S$10) are available from post offices and 7–Eleven stores, though note that your passport will be scanned as a form of registration of any SIM purchase. Two more things to note are that old **2G phones** do not work in Singapore, and that you pay not only to make mobile calls but also to receive them.

Local calls cost 10¢ per minute from a mobile (10¢ for three minutes from a payphone). The island has no area codes – the only time you'll punch more than eight digits for a local number is if you're dialling a toll-free (☎1800) or special-rate number. For directory enquiries, call ☎100 (☎104 for international enquiries).

Brunei

International calls can be made from cardphones. To call collect, substitute ☎01 for the usual ☎00 international code, then dial the number as though making an ordinary international call; this brings the number up on the operator's system.

OPERATOR AND DIRECTORY SERVICES

MALAYSIA

Business number online searches
ⓦyellowpages.com.my
Local directory enquiries ☎103
Operator-assisted calls (including international collect/reverse charge) ☎101

SINGAPORE

Business number online searches
ⓦyellowpages.com.sg
Local directory enquiries ☎100
Operator-assisted international calls ☎104

BRUNEI

Local directory enquiries ☎113

Phonecards start at $10 and can be bought from post offices. **SIM cards** can be obtained from outlets of the mobile provider DST Communications (ⓦdst.com.bn).

Time

For administrative convenience, Malaysia, Singapore and Brunei are all **eight hours** ahead of Universal Time (GMT), all year. This close to the equator, you can rely on dawn being around 6.30am in the Peninsula and Singapore, dusk at around 7.30pm; in Borneo both happen half an hour to an hour earlier. Not taking into account daylight saving time elsewhere, the three countries are two hours behind Sydney, thirteen hours ahead of US Eastern Standard Time and sixteen hours ahead of US Pacific Standard Time.

Tipping

Tipping is seldom necessary in Malaysia, Singapore and Brunei. That said, when eating out at a proper restaurant, it's customary to tip if a **service charge** isn't included, though you are never required to tip in *kedai kopis* or *kopitiams*. It's not necessary to tip taxi drivers either, unless they have gone out of their way to be helpful. Otherwise you might want to offer a modest tip to a hotel porter or hairdresser, or a tour guide who has been exceptional.

Tourist information

Most Malaysian state capitals have a tourist office run by the national agency **Tourism Malaysia** (ⓦtourism.gov.my) and may boast a second tourist office, sometimes called the **Tourism Information Centre**, run by the state government; details are given in the Guide. Where these state-level tourist offices exist, they are generally better informed than the local Tourism Malaysia branch.

Whichever tourist office you deal with, bear in mind that staff always have plenty of glossy brochures to hand out, but their practical knowledge can be patchy – reflecting the hopelessly incoherent way information circulates in Malaysia. To find out about out-of-the-way attractions, you may be better off contacting local accommodation – calling is best, as emails often elicit slow responses.

Singapore is another proposition altogether. A huge amount of generally reliable information on everything from bus times to museum exhibitions is available in print and online. Tourist information is put out by the **Singapore Tourism Board**, which has a comprehensive website (ⓦvisitsingapore .com), and operates several downtown **Visitor Centres**. Brunei's official tourism website is ⓦbruneitourism.travel.

Travellers with disabilities

Of the three countries covered in this guide, **Singapore** is the most accessible to travellers with disabilities; tax incentives are provided for developers who include disabled access features into new buildings. In contrast, Malaysia and Brunei make few provisions.

Across the region, life is made a lot easier if you can afford to stay in the more upmarket hotels, which usually have disabled provisions, and to shell out for taxis and the odd domestic flight. However, few tour operators in the region are similarly accommodating.

Singapore is certainly making a concerted effort to improve: the **MRT** metro system has lifts on most, if not all, of its stations, and many bus routes have wheelchair-accessible vehicles, though these operate only at certain times of day (see ⓦmytransport.sg for details). Most major **taxi** companies have accessible vehicles available to book, too.

In Malaysia, wheelchair users will have a hard time negotiating the uneven pavements in most towns and cities, and find it difficult to board buses, trains, ferries and the LRT system in Kuala Lumpur, although the new MRT is meant to be accessible. The situation is similar if not worse in

East Malaysia and Brunei, with little provision for disabled travellers.

CONTACTS FOR TRAVELLERS WITH DISABILITIES

Caring Fleet ⓦ caringfleet.com. Transport services in Singapore for people with disabilities.

Disabled People's Association Singapore ⓣ 6791 1134, ⓦ dpa.org.sg. Nonprofit organization whose website has an FAQ section for tourists, with details of accessible taxis and local buildings.

Handicaps Welfare Association ⓦ hwa.org.sg. Transport services for people with disabilities in Singapore.

Malaysian Confederation of the Disabled ⓣ 03 7931 9038. A member of Disabled Peoples International, working for equal opportunities for disabled people in Malaysia.

Silveray Transport Services ⓦ silveray.com.sg. Transport services for people with disabilities in Singapore; also tours within the city.

Travelling with children

Malaysia, Singapore and Brunei are child-friendly countries in which to travel. Disposable nappies and powdered milk are easy to find (fresh milk is sold in supermarkets), and bland Chinese soups and rice dishes, or bakery products, are ideal for children unaccustomed to spicy food. Many restaurants and the slicker *kedai kopis* have high chairs, though only upmarket hotels provide baby cots or a baby-sitting service. However, rooms in the cheaper hotels can usually be booked with an extra bed for little extra cost. Children under 12 get into many attractions for half the price and enjoy discounts on buses and trains.

Kuala Lumpur and around

KL SKYLINE

1

Kuala Lumpur and around

Founded at the head of the Klang Valley in the mid-nineteenth century, Kuala Lumpur – widely known as KL – has never had a coherent style. The earliest grand buildings around Merdeka Square, dating from the 1890s, are an eccentric fusion of influences from across the British Empire, now overshadowed by soaring modern landmarks (notably the Petronas Towers) that wouldn't be out of place in Hong Kong or New York. This melange extends to the people too, as you could spend a visit to KL simply soaking up its excitingly diverse Malay, Chinese and Indian cultures: the conversations heard on the street, the huge range of food and the profusion of onion-domed mosques, incense-infused Buddhist temples and colourful Hindu shrines.

A stay of a few days is enough to appreciate the best of KL's attractions, including the colonial core around **Merdeka Square** and the adjacent enclaves of **Chinatown** and **Little India**, plus, to the east, the restaurants, shops and nightlife of the so-called **Golden Triangle**, the modern heart of downtown KL. It can be equally rewarding just to take in the street life, in particular the boisterous **markets**, ranging from fish and vegetable stalls stuffed into alleyways, via clothes and accessories vendors, to stands selling cooked food of every shape and description. Indeed, the capital offers some of the most exciting **cuisines** in the country, not only in the street markets but also in a plethora of restaurants to suit all tastes and budgets.

KL's hinterland has a number of worthwhile sights, too, among them the rugged limestone **Batu Caves**, which contain the country's most sacred Hindu shrine; **Kuala Selangor** and its magical fireflies; and the hard-to-reach birding hotspot of **Fraser's Hill**.

Brief history

KL was founded in 1857 when the ruler of Selangor State, Rajah Abdullah, sent a party of Chinese to prospect for **tin** deposits around the junction of the Gombak and Klang rivers. The pioneers duly discovered rich deposits 6km from the confluence near **Ampang** (east of the present-day city centre), which grew into a staging post for Chinese mine labourers. Unusually, the settlement acquired the name Kuala Lumpur ("muddy confluence") rather than, as convention dictated, being named after the lesser of the two rivers – KL should, by rights, have been called "Kuala Gombak".

At first, KL was little more than a wooden shantytown; small steamers could approach within 30km along the Klang River, but the rest of the trip was either by shallow boat or through the jungle. Yet settlers poured in, seeking to tap the wealth

JALAN ALOR

Highlights

❶ Petronas Towers Come to gawp at these surprisingly serene twin structures, then browse in one of KL's best shopping malls just beneath. **See p.74**

❷ Menara KL Tower Forget the Petronas Towers' Skybridge – this is the place for bird's-eye views of KL in all its glory. **See p.78**

❸ Islamic Arts Museum One of the most sophisticated museums in the capital, documenting Muslim cultures through arts and crafts. **See p.79**

❹ Eating around Jalan Alor KL has excellent restaurants offering cuisines from around the world, but it's the street food, notably around

Jalan Alor, that's often the most memorable. **See p.95**

❺ Drinking in TREC KL is Malaysia's party capital, home to exceptional clubs like *Zouk* that draw big-name DJs. **See p.101**

❻ Shopping in KL's malls and markets Whether you prefer the bright lights of the state-of-the-art malls or the bustle of the city's endless street markets and bazaars, KL is a city made for bargain-hunting. **See p.102**

❼ Batu Caves Equal parts spiritual destination and theme park, these limestone caves on the edge of KL house a Hindu temple complex and offer subterranean adventures. **See p.107**

HIGHLIGHTS ARE MARKED ON THE MAP ON P.64

KUALA LUMPUR & AROUND

HIGHLIGHTS
1. Petronas Towers
2. Menara KL Tower
3. Islamic Arts Museum
4. Eating around Jalan Alor
5. Drinking in TREC
6. Shopping in KL's malls and markets
7. Batu Caves

---- KTM Railway

0   10
kilometres

N

GENTING HIGHLANDS

Mount Ulu Kali (1772m)

Mount Nuang (1493m)

Fraser's Hill (120km) & Ipoh (210km)

Cameron Highlands (200km) & Butterworth (350km)

Lumut (133km) & Ipoh (160km)

East Coast Highway & Jerantut (180km)

Johor Bahru (330km) & Singapore (350km)

Port Dickson (90km) & Melaka (150km)

KLIA (55km) & KLIA2 (57km)

Orang Asli Museum

Forest Research Institute of Malaysia

Batu Caves

Royal Selangor Visitor Centre

KUALA LUMPUR

Petaling Jaya

Shah Alam

Klang

Putrajaya

Sunway Lagoon

KUALA SELANGOR NATURE PARK

Kampung Kuantan

Bukit Melawati

Kuala Selangor

Batang Berjuntai

Batu Rotan

Baru Arang

Kuang

Meru

Kapar

Batu Enam

Port Klang

Telok Gong

Rawang

Serendah

S. Buloh

Kepong

Subang

Ulu Kelang

Kampung Lui

Ampang

Ulu Langat

Balakong

Serdang

Kajang

Semenyih

Beroga

S. Chua

Batu Tiga

S. Besi

Sedang

River Langat

River Klang

River Selangor

KARAK HIGHWAY

NORTH–SOUTH EXPRESSWAY

NEW KLANG VALLEY EXPRESSWAY

LEBUHRAYA PERSEKUTUAN

Ketam

Indonesia

of this unexplored region: British investors, Malay farmers, Chinese *towkays* (merchants) and labourers. The Chinese also formed two **secret societies**, the fierce rivalry between which restrained the township's growth until the influential former miner **Yap Ah Loy** was appointed as Kapitan Cina, or Chinese headman, in 1869. Ah Loy brought law and order to the frontier town by ruthlessly making an example of criminals, parading them through the streets on a first offence and executing them if they reoffended. He led the rebuilding of KL after it was razed during the **Selangor Civil War** (1867–74) and personally bore much of the cost of a second rebuilding after a devastating fire in 1881.

The British Resident of Selangor State, **Frank Swettenham**, had most of KL's remaining wooden huts demolished in the 1880s, and he imported **British architects** from India to design solid, grand edifices suitable for a new capital. By 1887 the city had five hundred brick buildings, and eight times that number in the early 1900s, by which time KL had also become capital of the **Federated Malay States**.

The early twentieth century

Development continued steadily in the first quarter of the twentieth century, during which time Indians mainly from Tamil Nadu swelled the population. Catastrophic floods in 1926 inspired a major engineering project that straightened the course of the Klang River, confining it within reinforced, raised banks. By the time the **Japanese invaded** the Peninsula in December 1941, the commercial zone around Chinatown had grown to eclipse the original colonial area, and the *towkays*, enriched by the rubber boom, were already installed in opulent townhouses along today's Jalan Tuanku Abdul Rahman and Jalan Ampang. While the city suffered little physical damage during World War II, the Japanese inflicted terrible brutality on their historic enemies, the Chinese – at least five thousand were killed in the first few weeks of the occupation alone – and sent thousands of Indians to Myanmar (Burma) to build the infamous railway; very few survived, as noted in Pierre Boulle's book, *The Bridge on the River Kwai*. At the same time, the Japanese ingratiated themselves with certain Malays by suggesting that loyalty to the occupiers would be rewarded with independence after the war.

Following the **Japanese surrender** in September 1945, the British found that nationalist demands had replaced the Malays' former acceptance of the colonizers, and many Chinese felt alienated by talk that a future Malay government would deny them full citizenship. The ensuing Communist-inspired **Emergency** (see p.563) left KL relatively unscathed, but the atmosphere in the city was tense. These issues finally came to a head in KL's May 1969 **race riots**, in which at least two hundred people lost their lives – though things calmed down rapidly after the imposition of a state of emergency.

Recent times

In 1974 KL was plucked from the bosom of Selangor State and designated **Wilayah Persekutuan** (Federal Territory), an administrative zone in its own right; **Shah Alam**, west along the Klang Valley, replaced it as Selangor's capital. After a period of consolidation, KL and the rest of the Klang Valley, including KL's satellite town of **Petaling Jaya**, became a thriving conurbation in the 1990s. That decade, and the early part of the new millennium, saw the realization of several huge infrastructural ventures that are part and parcel of local life today – KL's international **airport** and the **racetrack**, both at Sepang in the far south of Selangor; the **Petronas Towers** and the attendant **KLCC** shopping development; the various urban **rail systems** across the city; and **Putrajaya**, the government's administrative hub off to the south (though KL remains the legislative centre and seat of parliament). The transformation of swathes of KL and much of Selangor is less dramatic today, but still proceeds apace – not least in the ongoing extension of the **Klang Valley MRT rail network** – and concerns are being voiced over the potential strain on water resources and other environmental repercussions.

1

While KL is a noticeably sociable and safe place for visitors today, many Malaysians have mixed feelings about their capital. The city is second only to Singapore in regional economic clout, but it's undeniable that rapid development has bequeathed many featureless buildings, follies and terrible traffic snarls, which some locals tolerate only because KL offers them good money and experience before they retire to a cherished provincial village. Conversely, others feel that it has been their salvation, the one city in the country where they can explore their artistic or spiritual identity.

Kuala Lumpur

Rather than a discernible city centre, Kuala Lumpur has several hubs of activity. Close to the rivers' original "muddy confluence", the former **colonial district** and its distinctive architecture surrounds **Merdeka Square** – don't miss the informative **Textile Museum** here – with the busy tourist hub of **Chinatown** just southeast. In between the two lie the attractive **Jamek Mosque** and the craft cornucopia that is **Central Market**. Worthwhile forays can be made north to **Little India's** more locals-oriented shops and the altogether grittier **Chow Kit Market**.

Some 2km east, the **Golden Triangle** presents the city's modern face, with lively **Bukit Bintang** packed with upmarket hotels, restaurants and designer shopping malls. Overlooking it to the north are the tall, strikingly modernist **Petronas Towers**; visitors flock to the Skybridge here, though in fact the westerly **Menara KL Tower**, poking out of wooded Bukit Nanas, has better views.

Southwest of the centre – and tricky to reach on foot across one of KL's many pedestrian-unfriendly traffic flows – a clutch of worthwhile sights surrounds the green and airy **Lake Gardens**, notably **Masjid Negara**, one of the country's largest mosques, and the excellent **Islamic Arts Museum**. Below here, the **National Museum** is not as good as it could be, while **Brickfields** is another strongly Indian district, worth a peek for its day-to-day residential street life.

Colonial district

Pasar Seni or Masjid Jamek LRT; Kuala Lumpur KTM

The city's small **colonial district**, which developed around the confluence of the Gombak and Klang rivers in the 1880s, is the area of KL that best retains its historic character. At its heart on the west bank of the Klang, the beautifully tended open padang (field) of **Merdeka Square** is where on 31 August 1957, Malaysia's first prime minister, Tuanku Abdul Rahman, hauled down the British flag and declared *merdeka*, or independence. The 95m-high **flagpole** to the south is supposedly the tallest in the world, and the tiled square below is a popular spot for people to gather in the evenings.

KUALA LUMPUR'S MOORISH STYLE

KL's colonial look originated with **Charles Edwin Spooner**, the state engineer, and architect **Anthony Norman**, who in the 1890s fused a Neoclassical Renaissance style – then the standard for government buildings throughout the British Empire – with "Eastern" motifs, which were felt to be more appropriate for an Islamic country. This **Moorish style**, however, characterized by onion domes, cupolas, colonnades, arched windows and wedding-cake plasterwork, owed more to Indian Moghul architecture than wooden Malay structures. Buildings by Norman in this mould include the **Sultan Abdul Samad Building**, the Old Post Office next door, and the National Textile Museum further south. Norman was succeeded in 1903 by **A.B. Hubback**, who had lived in India and smoothly continued the Moorish theme in the **Jamek Mosque**, old Kuala Lumpur train station and elsewhere.

Royal Selangor Club

On the western side of Merdeka Square, the **Royal Selangor Club**, founded in 1884, was the British elite's favourite watering hole, popularly known as the "Spotted Dog" after a former Dalmatian mascot. It was here, on 30 November, 1938, that **Albert Gispert** and fellow drinkers at the club's *Hash House* bar organized a weekly cross-country run; thus the now international **Hash House Harriers** were born. The original KL group, respectfully regarded as the mother of all hashing groups, is still in existence (ⓦmotherhash.com). Closed to non-members, the club's history outweighs the appeal of its facade, an oversized 1970s mock-Tudor affair that replaced a 1910 structure built by A.B. Hubback after the original burned down.

To the north, the Anglican **St Mary's Cathedral** (1894), usually open in the daytime, welcomed the city's European inhabitants every Sunday before they retired to the club.

National Textile Museum

26 Jalan Sultan Hishamuddin • Daily 9am–6pm • Free • ☎ 03 2694 3457, ⓦ www.muziumtekstilnegara.gov.my

Housed in an elegant Moghul-Islamic building dating back to 1905, KL's **National Textile Museum** traces the trends and development of textiles that have characterized and shaped the lifestyles of the people of Malaysia. As there are **four galleries** on two floors, it takes more than an hour to do the fairly informative collection justice – though the highlights can be skimmed over in far less time.

On the ground floor, the **Pohon Budi Gallery** focuses on the evolution of textiles from prehistory to modern times and the different weaving techniques adopted in Malaysia. Displays include fine double *ikat* textiles, made with a technique introduced from India in the eighteenth century, along with traditional equipment and paraphernalia for weaving, embroidery, batik making and beadwork.

The adjacent **Pelangi Gallery** displays textiles from Malaysia's multiethnic communities, including Chinese and Baba Nyonya silk and brocades, the elaborate embroidered textiles of Sabah and handwoven *ikat* and *songket* of Sarawak. Look out for Sarawak's Iban *pua kumbu* blankets, decorated with motifs of crocodiles and wild plants.

Upstairs, the **Teluk Beranti Gallery** is dedicated to Malay textiles, especially iridescent *songket* and *limar* cloth, which incorporates fine gold thread into its patterns. There are several pieces of splendid *berayat*, or scripted cloths, with brocade woven into the design in Arabic.

The final **Ratna Sari Gallery** departs into ceremonial metalwork for jewellery and personal adornments, including finely chased filigree tobacco boxes, golden anklets worn by Malay and Peranakan women in the early nineteenth century, and a small case of flame-bladed *kris* daggers and Iban head-hunting machetes from Sarawak.

Jamek Mosque (Masjid Jamek)

Entrance on Jalan Tun Perak • Mon–Thurs, Sat & Sun 8.30am–12.30pm & 2.30–4pm, Fri 3–4pm • Free

East of Merdeka Square, across the river, Lebuh Pasar Besar connects the colonial district with the more frenetic life of the old commercial district. Just north of the river bridge is the **Jamek Mosque** (or more officially the Sultan Abdul Samad Jamek Mosque), on a promontory at the confluence of the Klang and Gombak rivers – pretty much where the first tin prospectors built their shacks in the 1850s. Part of the second great period of expansion in KL, the mosque was completed in 1909 by Hubback, its attractive pink brick walls and arched colonnades topped by oval cupolas and squat minarets. There's an intimacy here that's lacking at the modern, much larger Masjid Negara to the south, and the grounds, bordered by palms, are a pleasant place to sit and rest – though the best view of the mosque is from over the Klang at the base of the HSBC building on Jalan Benteng.

Map legend:

- M LRT Railway
- KTM Railway
- M Monorail
- M M Interchange

EATING
Contango 1

ACCOMMODATION
Carcosa Seri Negara 1
Grid 9 Hotel 3
Hotel Majestic 2

DRINKING AND NIGHTLIFE
The Roof 1

KLPac (5km), Sentul (7km) & E8 Highway
Titiwangsa Station (4km)

N

Pekeliling Bus Station
Vistana
Kompleks Damai

JALAN IPOH
JALAN LUMUT

JALAN PAHANG

Putra World Trade Centre

Putra Bus Station

SEE 'LITTLE INDIA & CHOW KIT' MAP FOR DETAIL

The Mall

PWRC

Chow Kit

JALAN PUTRA

CHOW KIT

Chow Kit Market

JALAN TYERS

Putra KTM Station

JALAN KUCHING

River Gombok

JLN 2
JLN 6
LRN 2
Jln Tiong Nam 1
JLN TIONG NAM

JLN HAJI TAIB

JLN KHUSEIN

Sultan Ismail

JALAN TUN ISMAIL

JALAN RAJA LAUT

JLN SIR AMAR

JALAN CERAK

JALAN TIN ISMAIL

JALAN KERJA AIR

JLN TAMINGSARI

JALAN SULTAN SALLAHUDDIN

PESARAN SULTAN SALAHUDDIN

PERKAR ANGANTUN

JALAN NISWALI

Bandaraya

JALAN ISFAHAN

JALAN DANG WANGI

LITTLE INDIA

JALAN MUNSHI ABDULLAH

Medan Tuanku

JALAN TUANKU ABDUL RAHMAN

JALAN SULTAN

JLN MEDAN TUANKU

Bank Negara KTM Station

JALAN RAJA LAUT

LOROENG GOMBAK

LEBUHRAYA MAHAMERU

JALAN TAMINGSARI

JALAN PARLIMEN

JALAN CENDERAWASIH

JALAN PARLIMEN

National Monument

JALAN BUKITAMAN

SEE 'COLONIAL DISTRICT AND CHINATOWN' MAP FOR DETAIL

MERDEKA SQUARE

Masjid Jamek

Jamek Mosque

JLN TUN

JALAN PERAK

JALAN GEREJA

JALAN SUKUT TUN

JALAN HANAS

E1 Highway via Jalan Buta & E1 (11.8km)

JALAN KEBUN BUNGA

JALAN CENDERAMULLA

Lake Gardens

Deer Park

Butterfly Park

Orchid and Hibiscus Gardens

JLN TUGU

JLN CENDERASARI

Masjid Negara

JALAN LEMBAH PERDANA

JALAN TEMBUSU

Tun Abdul Razak Memorial

Bird Park

Islamic Arts Museum

RMP Museum

JALAN PERDANA

LEBUH PASAR BESAR

JLN SULTAN HISHAMUDDIN

JLN KANANG

JALAN RAJA

JLN HANG KASTURI

JLN HANG LEKIR

JLN SULTAN

Pasar Seni

JLN SUL TAN MOHAMED

JLN BALAI POLIS

Chinwoo Stadium

JALAN DAMANSARA

JALAN PESARHAMAMERU

Lake Gardens

JALAN KEBUN BUNGA

National Planetarium

KTM

KL Train Station

JALAN KINABALU

Chan See Shu Yuen Maharajalela

JLN STADIUM

National Museum

JALAN TRAVERS (JALAN RAKYAT)

JLN SULTAN HISHAMUDDIN

JALAN SULTAN

JLN SULTAN ISMAIL

JLN SULTAN ISMAIL

JLN KG. ATIP

JALAN DAMANSARA

River Rang

JALAN HOSE

KL Sentral Train Station

BRICKFIELDS

0 ——— 1 kilometre

Pantai Medical Centre (5km)

Bangsar (5km), Midvalley Megamall (5km) & E1 Highway via E23

KUALA LUMPUR

Istana Budaya (2km)

National Library

General Hospital

River Bunus

JALAN TUN RAZAK

JLN TR. ISMAIL

JALAN RAJA MUDA

JLN H.J. YAHYA
SHEIKH AHMAD
JALAN MAHMOOD
JLN DATUK ABD. MALIK

JALAN HAMZAH

JALAN SEMARAK

JLN MAKTAB ENAM

JALAN RAJA UDA

JALAN RAJA BOT

JALAN DAUD

JALAN SALLEH

JALAN PESIARAN GURNEY

JALAN RAJA MAHMUD
L RAJA M. MUSA 6

KAMPUNG BAHRU

JALAN DAMAI

JALAN DAMAI

JLN MURNI

JALAN RAJA ALANG

L. RAJA M. MUSA 6
L. DAUD
L.KM MUSA (3)
L.KM MUSA

AMPANG ELEVATED HIGHWAY

JALAN AMAN

JLN D. ABD RAZAK
JALAN RAJA MUDA

JLN RAJA ALI
L. RAJA MAHADU

JALAN SUNGAI BAHARU

River Klang

JLN QWA LENG

JALAN YAP KWAN SENG

JLN SULTAN SULAIMAN

Malay Stalls

Ⓜ **Kampung Baru**

JALAN AMPANG

JALAN MAYANG

KLCC

Ⓜ **Ampang Park**

JALAN AMPANG

JALAN RAJA ABDULLAH

JLN CENDANA

Ⓜ **Dang Wangi**

R. Klang

Petronas Towers

Suria KLCC

Menara Maxis

KLCC

ⓘ **Malaysia Tourism Centre**

Ⓜ **Bukit Nanas**

JALAN SULTAN ISMAIL

JALAN P. RAMLEE

JALAN PINANG

KL Convention Centre & Aquarium

JALAN AMPANG

JALAN PERAK

PERSIARAN STONOR

Menara KL

JALAN PUNCHAK

JALAN BUKIT NANAS

JALAN TENGAH

Raja Chulan Ⓜ

JALAN KIA PENG

JALAN STONOR

JALAN EATON

JALAN RAJA CHULAN

JLN BUKIT CEYLON

JALAN CONLAY

JALAN PERSIARAN RAJA CHULAN

JALAN CEYLON

Pavilion KL

JALAN RAJA CHULAN

LORONG CEYLON

JLN BEDARA

CHANGKAT BUKIT BINTANG

LORONG IMBI

JALAN PUDU LAMA

JLN TINGKAL TUNG SHIN

JALAN ALOR

Bukit Bintang

JALN GADING GRENIER

JALAN JATI

JLN KEMUNING

PUDU

★ **Pudu Sentral Bus Station**

JALAN BUKIT BINTANG

WALTER

MYTHE

JALAN UTARA

JALAN DELIMA

Ⓜ **Plaza Rakyat**

JALAN GALLOWAY

BB Plaza

JALAN MELATI

Pasar Rakyat Bus Station ★

JALAN HANG JEBAT

JALAN ESELEN

Imbi Ⓜ

JLN EDOETEKE

JALAN BARAT

JALAN KAMPUNG

JALAN BARU

JALAN TUN RAZAK

JALAN HORLEY

JALAN SELATAN

Stadium Negar

JALAN STADIUM

JALAN EBERWEN

JALAN IMBI

CHANGKAT THAMBY DOLLAH

JALAN JAMPUNG PANDAN

JALAN SELATAN

SEE 'THE GOLDEN TRIANGLE' MAP FOR DETAIL

ⓂⓂ **Hang Tuah**

Merdeka Stadium

JALAN HANG TUAH

JALAN KENANGA

JALAN PUDU

JALAN SARAWAK

JLN MERLIMAU

JALAN BERNAM

JALAN 1/77C

JALAN DAVIS

MAHARAJALELA

JLN JALALA

JLN CHOO CHENG KHAY

JLN BUGIS

SMART TUNNEL

E2 Highway via E7 & E9

E2 Highway

Glen Eagles Hospital (2.3km)

1

THE COLONIAL DISTRICT & CHINATOWN

ACCOMMODATION	
Hotel 1915	2
5 Elements Hotel	8
Back Home	1
Birdnest Guesthouse 2	9
Hotel China Town 2	10
The Explorers Guesthouse	5
Geo Hotel	6
Raizzy's Guesthouse	11
Reggae Mansion	3
Swiss Inn	7
Winsin Hotel	4

EATING	
Bbun	6
Central Market Food Court	3
Lai Foong	4
Lokl Coffee Co.	2
Lucy in the Sky	10
Nam Heong	9

Old China Café	12
Penjaja Gallery	8
Purple Cane Tea House	11
Santa	1
Yusoof Dan Zakhir	5
Zuliani Corner	7

DRINKING AND NIGHTLIFE	
Reggae Bar	2
Rooftop Mansion	1

SHOPPING	
Heritage of the Orient	2
Junk Book Store	1
Kwong Yik Seng Crockery	3
Peter Hoe	5
Popular Bookshop	4

Central Market

Jalan Hang Kasturi • Daily 10am–9.30pm • ☎ 1300 228688, ⓦ centralmarket.com.my

The Art Deco **Central Market** is housed in a blue-and-white brick hangar, which was built in the 1920s as the capital's wet market. However, the butchers and fishmongers have long since left for places like Chow Kit and the back alleys of nearby Chinatown, and the market was converted in the mid-eighties into what's now known as **Pasar Seni** (which translates as "art market"). Most of the shops now sell souvenirs: Royal Selangor pewter, specialist antiques, Malay regional crafts, carvings and batiks, plus clothes, sarongs, silverware and T-shirts; there's also a decent food court upstairs. Most artists, in fact, have moved into the newer **Central Market**

Annexe immediately north, and the pavement in between is clogged with their enthusiastic – if unmemorable – canvases. Blatantly touristy, it is also enjoyable, with a lively atmosphere in the evenings.

Old Kuala Lumpur train station

Best reached south from Central Market along Jalan Tun Sambanthan, over the river and past the post office (Poslaju), then via the footbridge to the station

Old Kuala Lumpur train station, one of the city's best-known colonial buildings and now a stop on the KTM train lines, was completed in 1911 by A.B. Hubback. As with the Jamek Mosque, its meshing spires, minarets and arches reflect his inspiration from North Indian Islamic architecture. Inside, the main platforms sit under an airy, light vault of fine ironwork, reminiscent of Victorian stations in London.

Although the station is architecturally linked to similar-vintage buildings around Merdeka Square, feverish traffic makes it difficult to reach on foot from there. For the best view of the facade, you'll need to get across to the western side of Jalan Sultan Hishamuddin. Conveniently, a pedestrian subway links the station with the **KTM headquarters** opposite – yet another attractive Moorish structure designed by Hubback, finished around the same time as the station and actually more imposing than its counterpart. From the KTM headquarters it's a few minutes' walk to either Masjid Negara or the National Museum.

Chinatown and around

Pasar Seni LRT

Spreading out southeast from the Central Market, **Chinatown** was KL's original commercial kernel, dating from the arrival of the first traders in the 1860s. Bordered by Jalan Sultan to the east, Jalan Tun Perak to the north and Jalan Maharajalela to the south, the area had reached its current extent by the late nineteenth century, with southern Chinese shophouses, coffee shops and temples springing up along narrow streets such as Jalan Tun H.S. Lee and Jalan Petaling. Though the shophouses today are fairly workaday, it is encouraging that many period buildings are being refurbished in the face of recurrent threats of redevelopment; in 2011, public outcry saved a row of old shophouses on **Jalan Sultan** from demolition during construction of the ongoing Klang Valley railway.

Although Chinatown scores more on atmosphere than essential sights, it's a hub for **budget accommodation**, and holds a wealth of inexpensive places to shop, eat and go out, so it's likely you'll spend some time here.

Jalan Petaling

For locals and visitors alike, pedestrianized **Jalan Petaling** (still often called **Petaling Street**) is very much Chinatown's main draw. Home to brothels and gambling dens in KL's early years, these days it's a gauntlet of closely packed market stalls doing a roaring trade in clothing, watches and fake designer handbags, from late morning until well into the evening. Check goods thoroughly for workmanship – stitching especially – and bargain hard; in truth, you might find better deals in ordinary shops nearby. The narrow lanes parallel and either side of Petaling host grittier **wet markets** too, as well as a popular early morning bric-a-brac market, selling everything from old clothes to mobile phones.

Crossing Petaling at right angles, the eastern end of **Jalan Hang Lekir** hosts a slew of good, inexpensive restaurants and stalls selling *ba kwa* (slices of pork, given a sweet marinade and grilled), local fruits and molasses-like herbal brews in tureens.

Chan See Shu Yuen

Southern end of Jalan Petaling • Daily 8am–5pm • Free

The largest of Chinatown's numerous Chinese shrines, **Chan See Shu Yuen** was founded at the turn of the twentieth century. It's not actually a temple (though it looks like

1

one), but rather a clan hall for families with the very common name of Chan – also transliterated Chen and Tan. A classic of southern Chinese architecture, the eaves are decorated in a riot of three-dimensional ceramic friezes depicting events in Chinese history and mythology; inside the green walls are a series of courtyards and halls, with the inner shrine covered in scenes of lions, dragons and mythical creatures battling with warriors. Most engaging of all are the two gentleman figurines on the altar, representing ancestors of the clan or possibly their servants – and wearing Western top hats to indicate their link with the colonial past.

Sri Maha Mariamman Temple
Jalan Tun H.S. Lee • Daily 24hr • Free; small donation appreciated

Oddly perhaps, one of KL's main Hindu shrines, the **Sri Maha Mariamman Temple**, is located in the heart of Chinatown. The earliest shrine on the site was built in 1873 by Tamil immigrants, so this is the oldest Hindu temple in the city. It was named after the Hindu deity Mariamman, whose intercession was sought to provide protection against sickness and "unholy incidents". In the case of the Tamils, who had arrived to build the railways or work on the plantations, they needed all the solace they could find from the appalling rigours of their working life.

Significant rebuilding of the temple took place in the 1960s, when sculptors from India were commissioned to design idols to adorn the five tiers of the multicoloured, 22.9m-high gate tower – these now shine with gold embellishments, precious stones and exquisite Spanish and Italian tiles. Garland-makers sell their wares outside the entrance, while above it is a hectic profusion of Hindu gods, painted in realistic colours and frozen in dozens of scenes from the *Ramayana*.

During the Hindu **Thaipusam** festival, the temple's golden chariot is paraded through the streets on its route to the Batu Caves, on the city's northern edge (see p.107). The rest of the year, the chariot is kept in a large room in the temple; you might be able to persuade an attendant to unlock the door and let you take a peek.

Court Hill Ganesh Temple
9 Jalan Pudu Lama • Daily 6am–8.30pm • Free

East of the Maybank Building and hidden up a small lane, **Court Hill Ganesh Temple** is KL's second most important Hindu shrine, dating to 1897 and reputedly founded by a gardener – which may explain why there's a **tree** growing beside the building. As it is dedicated to the elephant-headed Lord Ganesh, who specializes in the removal of all obstacles to prosperity, peace and success, the temple was understandably popular with visitors on their way to KL's original law courts, which were once located nearby.

Jalan Tuanku Abdul Rahman and around
On foot from Chinatown, it takes around 45min to reach Chow Kit via Little India along Jalan TAR; the LRT, Monorail and buses also traverse the area

Running north from Chinatown, **Jalan Tuanku Abdul Rahman** – commonly abbreviated to **Jalan TAR** – brings you within reach of a series of small-scale, local neighbourhoods, which are somewhat unexpected in such a large city. First is **Little India**, a bustling commercial district renowned for its fabrics, especially saris and *songkets*, as well as jewellery. The clothing theme persists immediately west, where Gulati's Silk House and the SOGO department store stock everything from saris to brand-name outdoor gear. There are also some fine 1920s Neoclassical and Art Deco buildings, including the dove-grey **Coliseum Cinema**, screening Bollywood releases, and the adjacent **Coliseum Café** (at no. 98). Once a favourite watering hole with British rubber plantation owners, its interior can't have been decorated since Independence, and the clientele look of similar vintage. Drop in for the atmosphere and a cold beer rather than the food, which is nothing more than ordinary. Beyond here, **Chow Kit Market** is the place to find bargain clothing and local produce, while **Kampung Bahru**, off to the east of Jalan TAR, is a low-key enclave of Malay housing. There are no major sights, but a visit adds depth to KL's character, and all three have excellent eating opportunities.

Little India

Masjid Jamek or Bandaraya LRT

East off the lower end of Jalan TAR, **Little India** is still a commercial centre for KL's Indian community, though these days it's eclipsed by Brickfields (see p.82). Only a few steps north from the Masjid Jamek LRT station, **Jalan Melayu** holds Indian stores, some selling excellent *burfi* and other sweet confections; its name derives from the former Malay community here. Approaching **Jalan Masjid India**, you'll encounter a popular covered market, smaller but otherwise similar to Chinatown's Jalan Petaling. Further up is **Masjid India** itself, an Indian-influenced affair dating from the 1960s and tiled in cream and brown.

A few minutes further along the street, you'll come to a little square, to the right (east) of which you'll find plenty of *kedai kopis* and, come evening, street vendors selling food; turn off to the left to reach Lorong Tuanku Abdul Rahman, whose northern end is dominated by a **night market**, which gets going at around 6pm and is busiest at weekends. Mainly Malay-run, the stalls sell both food and eclectic bits and pieces, from T-shirts to trinkets. Just past here, Madras and Semua House are two huge haberdasheries, packed to their roofs with **Indian textiles**.

Chow Kit

Chow Kit Monorail or Sultan Ismail LRT

Chow Kit district, 1.5km north of Little India, is mostly known for the sprawling, busy **Chow Kit Market**, which fills the lanes east off Jalan TAR. It's one of KL's busiest, most in-your-face fresh produce markets, a tight, overcrowded grid of alleyways under low-slung awnings. Stalls sell everything fit to put in your mouth:

LITTLE INDIA & CHOW KIT

- Ⓜ LRT Railway
- Ⓜ KTM Railway
- Ⓜ Monorail

DRINKING AND NIGHTLIFE	
Coliseum Café	1

EATING	
Capital Café	3
Jai Hind	5
Kedai Makanan Sithique	1
Saravanaa Bhavan	4
Syed Bistro	2

ACCOMMODATION	
Crossroads Hotel	1
Hotel De' Grand Orchard	6
K Hotel	4
Palace Hotel	7
Premiera Hotel	3
Silka Maytower Hotel	5
Tune Hotel	2

1

bulk tropical fruits at bargain prices, live and prepared fish and poultry, hunks and haunches of various animals, and piles of fresh or dried vegetables and spices. Hawkers around the edge sell freshly cooked snacks too, many with a definite Indonesian slant.

Chow Kit is also a good place to buy **secondhand clothes** (sometimes called "*baju* bundle"). The best deals are west of Jalan TAR along Jalan Haji Taib, where you may chance upon items like Levi's 501s in reasonable condition and at prices that are almost too good to be true – starting from RM20 a pair. The market runs for much of the day and into the evening, but note that some locals prefer to give Chow Kit a wide berth after dark, as it's also something of a red-light area; even during the day, the area can be pretty sketchy.

Kampung Bahru
Kampung Baru LRT

If you've time on your hands and enjoy a wander, head 1km east from Chow Kit (along either Jalan Raja Bot or Jalan Raja Alang) into **Kampung Bahru**, one of Malaysia's several designated Malay reserve areas – land that only people whose ID defines them as ethnic Malays can own, and indeed with its own status in law, not under the direct control of the KL city council. Though the Petronas Towers are visible off to the south, Kampung Bahru's quiet lanes and painted wooden bungalows with gardens – not to mention chickens wandering the pavements – lend it a distinct village feel. Sadly, plans to "redevelop" the district may well involve wholesale demolitions.

Despite its proximity, you can't walk southeast to KLCC (Kuala Lumpur City Centre) from here, owing to the riverside expressway.

Golden Triangle

The heart of modern KL, the **Golden Triangle** is a sprawling area bounded to the north by **Jalan Ampang**, and to the west by Chinatown and the Klang River. Many visitors make a beeline for **KLCC**, a group of huge developments surrounding the focal KLCC Park, on a site once home to the Selangor Turf Club. The chief attractions here are the **Petronas Towers**, soaring above one of KL's best malls, **Suria KLCC**, and the city's glossy **aquarium**.

Further south, the Golden Triangle's other magnet is **Bukit Bintang** ("Star Hill"), home to upmarket and workaday malls, many of KL's best hotels and restaurants, and some engaging street life. East, **Kompleks Kraf** is the city's largest handicrafts gallery, while northwest lies **Bukit Nanas**, a forested hill where the **Menara KL** communications tower affords great views of the city.

Petronas Towers
Tues–Thurs, Sat & Sun 9am–9pm, Fri 9am–1pm & 2.30–9pm; tours 45min; last admission 8.30pm • RM85; 1000 passes/day issued online and at the base of Tower 2 from 8.30am onwards, often sold out by 11am • ☎ 03 2331 8080, ⦿ petronastwintowers.com.my

Very much the symbol of modern Malaysia, the twin columns of the **Petronas Towers** rise 451.9m above KL's downtown area, towering over the enormous **Suria KLCC mall** at their base. When they were completed in 1998, as the headquarters of the state-owned oil company Petronas, many questioned whether the US$1.6 billion price tag was an unwarranted drain on the Malaysian economy, but the tapering steel-clad structures (designed by the Argentinian architect Cesar Pelli) are a stunning piece of architecture. Despite a definite Art Deco feel, the unusual eight-pointed cross-sectional profile obviously draws on Islamic art, while the profusion of squares and circles on the interior walls symbolize harmony and strength. The project is also permeated by Chinese numerology, in that the towers have 88 floors and the postcode is 59088 – eight being a very auspicious number for the Chinese.

One tower was built by a Japanese team, the other by rivals from Korea; while the Japanese topped out first, the Koreans had the honour of engineering the **Skybridge**, which joins the towers at both the 41st and 42nd floors. The **views** of KL's sprawl from the Skybridge are pretty spectacular, thanks not least to the blue, glassy towers soaring either side of you – but they're not quite as good as from the **Observation Deck** on the 86th floor.

Aquaria KLCC

KLCC Complex, accessed by a long pedestrian underpass from Suria KLCC • Daily 10am–8pm; last admission 7pm; check website for feeding times • RM69; check website for shark scuba dives • ⓦ aquariaklcc.com

KL's **Aquaria KLCC** is housed within the sizeable **KL Convention Centre**, which sits on the southern edge of KLCC. It's expensive, and labelling is occasionally lost thanks to the muted lighting, but some sections are wonderful. Prime examples include the well-lit **Living Reef** tank, which is packed with multicoloured, multiform anemones and corals, and will help you make sense of the riches on view at the Perhentian Islands and elsewhere, and the **Flooded Forest** tank, with its pair of hefty, 2m-long Amazonian arapaima freshwater fish. It also holds electric eels, otters and even piranhas, but the *pièce de résistance* is the vast **Living Ocean** tank, which is traversed on a moving walkway through a transparent tunnel, replete with sand tiger sharks, octopuses and huge rays. There's a raised pedestrian walkway from here to Pavilion KL mall.

Bukit Bintang

Bukit Bintang Monorail

For tourists and locals alike, **Bukit Bintang** – the broad corridor either side of Jalan Bukit Bintang – is one of the best spots in town for a wander. There's a **mall** here to suit everyone: the gigantic, massively modern Pavilion KL, packed with international chains and designer outlets; posh Starhill Gallery, with an exclusive, snazzy Art Deco feel; the more modest Berjaya Times Square, Lot 10 mall and BB Plaza, and casual Farenheit 88; and the behemoth tech mall Low Yat. The southwestern end of Jalan Bukit Bintang is lined with royal palms and inexpensive clothing shops – and a few too many touts hissing "massage, nice lady, young lady" at passers-by – while the pavement around Lot 10 has evolved into a parade of smart cafés and shops, which is especially buzzing since the opening of the new MRT train station. By night the centre of attention, at least for dining, switches to nearby **Jalan Alor**, which boasts some great alfresco Chinese eating. Close by, Changkat Bukit Bintang and Tengkat Tong Shin hold even more excellent bars and restaurants, serving differing cuisines.

Kompleks Kraf

63 Jalan Conlay, south of KLCC • Daily 10am–6pm; museum daily 9am–5pm • RM5; batik-painting workshop RM15 • ⓣ 03 2162 7459, ⓦ kraftangan.gov.my

The sprawl of Malay Terengganu-style buildings housing **Kompleks Kraf** offers a good opportunity to see excellent examples of Malaysia's crafts in one place – including carved wooden boxes, modern textiles and woven baskets – and to do some serious souvenir shopping. Their small, well-presented **museum** is also worth a quick browse to explore the intricacies of the weaving, tie-dyeing and batik processes, *keris* casting and Malay kite construction. For a hands-on experience, try the batik-painting workshop, where you can make a handkerchief to take home.

Badan Warisan

2 Jalan Stonor • Mon–Sat 10am–5pm; guided tours Mon–Sat 11am & 3pm (45min) • Free; minimum donation for tours RM15 • ⓣ 03 2144 9273, ⓦ badanwarisan.org.my

Badan Warisan, Malaysia's architecture conservation trust, campaigns to preserve the rich heritage of shophouses, temples and colonial buildings that developers and many municipal authorities seem intent on destroying. It's housed close to Kompleks Kraf in a 1925 colonial mansion that contains a gift shop, good for books on local architecture, and hosts occasional temporary exhibitions, focusing on anything from colonial furniture to restoration work.

1

THE GOLDEN TRIANGLE

●SHOPPING	
Avenue K	1
Berjaya Times Square	11
House of Suzie Wong	7
Kinokuniya	3
Lot 10	8
Low Yat	10
Pavilion KL	5
Starhill Gallery	6
Sungei Wang Plaza	9
Suria KLCC	2
Times Bookstore	4

N

BUKIT NANAS FOREST RESERVE

Menara KL

BUKIT NANAS

Forestry Office

Maybank Building

Tung Shin Hospital

Pudu Sentral

Plaza Rakyat

CHINATOWN

Swiss Garden

Curry Houses

BUKIT BINTANG

Chinese Stalls

Low Yat

Imbi

Berjaya Times Square

Kampung Baru

British Council

Medan Tuanku

Asian Heritage Row

Dang Wangi

Bukit Nanas

Malaysia Tourism Centre

Saloma

Kompleks Antarabangsa

Raja Chulan

0   150
metres

Chinwoo Stadium

Stadium Negara

Merdeka Stadium

Hang Tuah

M — LRT Railway
M — Monorail

EATING

Acme Bar & Coffee (ABC)	4
Ben's	2
Cantaloupe	3
Din Tai Fung	8
Feeka	10
Hakka	7
Lot 10 Hutong	17
Luk Yu Tea House	15
The Magnificent Fish & Chips Bar	14
Marble 8 Steakhouse	1
Muar	20
Nagasari Curry House	11
Neroteca	9
Pinchos	12
Sao Nam	18
Shook!	15
Sushi Hinata	6
TG's Nasi Kandar	19
Thai Somtam Seafood	16
twenty.one	13
Zenzero	5

DRINKING AND NIGHTLIFE

Alexis Bistro Ampang	1
Beach Club	5
Blue Boy	13
Fuego	4
The Green Man	14
Havana	16
Healy Mac's	15
Heli Lounge	8
Hubba Hubba	10
Luna Bar	7
Marini's on 57	2
No Black Tie	11
Pisco Bar	12
Sky Bar	6
Taps	9
Zion	17
Zouk	3

ACCOMMODATION

Anggun Boutique Hotel	21	Hotel Maya	2	Sahabat Guesthouse	15
Classic Inn	25	The Mesui Hotel	8	Seri Bukit Ceylon	9
Dorms KL	19	Metro Hotel	24	Swiss Garden	23
Dorsett Regency	14	Myhotel	22	Traders Hotel	6
Fahrenheit Suites	17	Orange Pekoe Guesthouse	12	Travellers Palm Lodge	16
Fraser Place	5	Pacific Regency Hotel Suites	7	Tropical Guesthouse KL	20
Invito Hotel Suites	10	Rainforest Bed & Breakfast	11	Villa Samadhi	1
Mandarin Oriental	4	Renaissance	3	The Yard Boutique Hotel	18
Marriott	13				

1

In the grounds is the beautifully restored **Rumah Penghulu Abu Seman**, a traditional timber house that once belonged to a Malay chieftain. Moved here from Kedah, it can only be visited on a guided tour.

Bukit Nanas

The western side of the Golden Triangle is dominated by forested **Bukit Nanas** (Pineapple Hill), where you can follow an easy forty-minute **walking trail** from the Forestry Office on Jalan Raja Chulan (daily 9am–6pm; free map available) to Jalan Ampang, close to the Bukit Nanas Monorail station. There are big trees, bird's nest ferns, stands of bamboo and a few monkeys if you're lucky.

Just west of the hill, on Jalan Bukit Nanas, the fine collection of **colonial school buildings** includes the St John's Institution from 1904 and Convent Bukit Nanas School – still rated among KL's top academic institutions.

Menara KL

2 Jalan Punchak • Daily 9am–10pm; last entry 9.30pm • Observation deck RM52; sky deck RM105; combination ticket for all Menara KL attractions RM155 • ☎ 03 2020 5444, ⓦ menarakl.com.my • Take one of the free shuttles (every 15min) or walk 15min uphill from Jalan Puncak

At 421m, the **Menara KL** tower offers vistas east across the Petronas Towers to the blue peaks of the Titiwangsa Mountains, which mark the start of the Peninsula's interior, and west along the unmitigated urban sprawl of the Klang Valley. Dusk is an especially worthwhile time to visit, as the city lights up – as does the tower itself at hourly intervals after dark and for special occasions (green for Muslim festivals, purple for Deepavali and red for the Chinese New Year). Though free audioguides describe what can be seen in each direction, it's probably best to hold off visiting until you know KL well enough to be familiar with its general layout.

The **observation deck** sits at 276m inside in the bulbous portion of the tower, which was designed in the shape of a *gasing*, the Malay spinning top. Fixed binoculars (free) allow you to observe city life in minute detail. The **sky deck**, at 421m high, is open to the elements and makes for an even more bracing and impressive view.

Lake Gardens and around

Old Kuala Lumpur train station KTM

West of the colonial district, the **Lake Gardens** offer a pleasant escape from KL's more frenetic streets amid a humid, hilly spread of green. Near the sizeable, modern **Masjid Negara**, which fronts the area on Jalan Sultan Hishamuddin, a cool, white building contains the superb **Islamic Arts Museum**. Uphill lie the gardens themselves, complete with close-cropped lawns, a lake and a host of child-friendly attractions – including a Butterfly Park, a Bird Park, the **Royal Malaysia Police Museum** and the National Planetarium – while Malaysia's **National Museum** is just south via a walkway over Jalan Damansara. Although you could easily spend half a day strolling around, you should focus on the three museums if you're pushed for time.

The easiest **access** on foot is via Kuala Lumpur train station and the underpass to the KTM building (see p.71), from where you can edge around to the mosque – otherwise you have to risk crossing the usual furious traffic flows. As smaller roads run through the gardens, however, it's perhaps easiest to get here by taxi.

Masjid Negara

Jalan Sultan Hishamuddin • Mon–Wed, Sat & Sun 9am–6pm, Fri 2.45–6pm • ⓦ masjidnegara.gov.my

Opened in 1965, **Masjid Negara** (National Mosque) features an unusual theme: the 73m-high minaret resembles a folded umbrella, and the imposing blue 16-point dome looks like an open one. Surrounding it are paved courtyards and colonnades, all rectangles of white marble bisected by pools of water. The prayer hall can hold up to ten thousand worshippers, though size gives way to decorative prowess in its finely detailed stone archways and engravings of the Koran, inspired by Istanbul's Blue Mosque. To enter as a visitor (outside of prayer times), you must be properly dressed: robes can be borrowed for free at the mosque entrance.

Islamic Arts Museum

Jalan Lembah Perdana • Daily 10am–6pm • RM14 • ☎ 03 2274 2020, ⓦ iamm.org.my

The ultramodern **Islamic Arts Museum** is housed in an elegant open-plan building with gleaming marble floors. This well-documented collection is a real standout; allow around ninety minutes to do it justice, and bear in mind that there's an excellent on-site Middle Eastern restaurant (open Tuesday to Sunday during museum hours). If you're arriving by taxi, you may find that the driver will know only the museum's Malay name, which is Muzium Kesenian Islam – if that doesn't work, just ask for the Masjid Negara, which is just a short walk away.

Level 1

The **first level** begins with a large collection of dioramas of Muslim holy places, including that of the Great Mosque of Xi'an in central China that draws attention to the neglected subject of Islam in the Far East, a theme continued elsewhere on this level. In the **India gallery**, devoted to the Moghuls, look for an intricately carved wooden locking mechanism, designed to cloister the harem away from the rest of the world; the **China gallery** features porcelain and scroll paintings bearing Arabic calligraphy. Best of all is an impressive three-metre-high archway in the **Malay gallery**, once part of a house belonging to an Indonesian notable, with black, red and gold lacquering and a trelliswork of leaves as its main motif. An equally fine trunk below it was used as a travelling box by Terengganu royalty. Built of the much-prized *cengal* hardwood, it's decorated in red and gold and bears the names of Islam's revered first four caliphs.

Level 2

On the **second level**, richly embroidered textiles and marquetry back up unusual examples of Western European ceramic crockery, influenced by the Islamic world in their design – and sometimes produced for that market. Most interesting here is the terrace containing the museum's main **dome**, a blue-and-white affair with floral ornamentation. Built by Iranian craftsmen, it's the only one of several similar examples in the building that's intended to illustrate the exterior of a grand mosque. Finally, look out for the bizarre reversed dome ceiling, bulging downwards from above – it's the last thing you see as you make your way back to the foyer from the area containing the excellent **gift shop**.

Royal Malaysia Police Museum

5 Jalan Perdana • Tues–Thurs, Sat & Sun 10am–6pm, Fri 10am–noon & 3–6pm • Free • ☎ 03 2272 5689

The **Royal Malaysia Police Museum** (RMP) covers the vivid history of the Royal Malaysian Police force. Fascinating photographs include a shot of British officers and their local charges on patrol on buffaloes, around 1900. The museum also displays **weapons** confiscated from the Communists during the Emergency of the 1950s, including a vicious assortment of *parangs* and a curved, bladed implement known as a Sarawak or Iban axe, all presented in a jungle-themed exhibition space. Once you've had a look around, you can, if you're feeling energetic, continue up Jalan Perdana into the Lake Gardens or head up the flight of steps opposite the museum to the hill where the National Planetarium is located (see p.80).

Lake Gardens

KL's **Lake Gardens** (Taman Tasik Perdana) were laid out in the 1890s by the British state treasurer to Malaya, Alfred Venning. Not quite parkland or gardens in the usual sense, they're probably best seen as a pleasant setting for various attractions, all

1

connected by paths and sealed roads. If you're out this way in the afternoon, consider dropping into KL's most exclusive hotel, the colonial mansion **Carcosa Seri Negara** (see p.93), off to the west. Their oh-so-English **high tea** is a fitting reward for a hot day's wander around the gardens – as long as you don't mind dressing smartly (it can get hot on the verandah) and paying RM80 per head for the privilege.

Butterfly Park

Lake Gardens • Daily 9am–6pm • RM25 • ☎ 03 2693 4799, ⓦ klbutterflypark.com

The beautiful **Butterfly Park** is an unexpected delight. Enclosed in invisibly fine netting, this garden of tropical vines, shrubs and ferns nurtures 120 species of gorgeous butterflies – some with 15cm wingspans – flitting about amid the undergrowth and feed stations baited with pineapple and banana. There are also tranquil ponds full of giant koi carp, and a small but informative insect museum.

Bird Park

Lake Gardens • Daily 9am–6pm • RM67 • ☎ 03 2272 1010, ⓦ klbirdpark.com

Billed as the world's largest, KL's popular **Bird Park** features a well-designed network of ponds and streams underneath a huge mesh tent, all linked together by a looped walkway. There are free-flying egrets, storks, African starlings, nutmeg pigeons and parrots all over the place, and there's a flock of flamingoes living in one of the ponds, as well as cages of indigenous species that you might well encounter in Malaysia's wilder corners – hornbills, birds of prey such as the Brahminy kite, and the sizeable argus pheasant. Give yourself an hour and a half to look around and take in a show; the only real downside is the park's high cost, relative to any other attraction in town.

Orchid and Hibiscus Gardens

Lake Gardens • Daily 9am–6pm • Mon–Fri free, Sat & Sun RM1 • ☎ 03 2617 6000

If you're into tropical plants, you'll love the **Orchid and Hibiscus Gardens**. There are said to be more than eight hundred Malaysian orchids alone, all lining paved walkways in brightly coloured, formal arrangements. The hibiscus collection is laid out along terraces and includes Malaysia's national flower, the bright red *bunga raya*. There are also groves of South American **heliconias** in the gardens, which look a bit like ginger plants but with brightly coloured, strikingly shaped flowers.

Tun Abdul Razak Memorial

Lake Gardens • Tues–Thurs, Sat & Sun 9am–5.30pm, Fri9am–noon & 3–5.30pm • ☎ 03 2693 7141

The main road through the Lake Gardens weaves south past a field of deer to the **Tun Abdul Razak Memorial**, a house built for the second Malaysian prime minister. He's commemorated with assorted memorabilia inside, while his motorboat and golf trolley are ceremonially positioned outside. Behind here is the **lake** itself, which takes nearly an hour to walk around.

National Planetarium

Lake Gardens • Tues–Sun 9am–4.30pm • Free; planetarium shows RM12 • ☎ 03 2273 4301, ⓦ www.planetariumnegara.gov.my

Set on a forested hill east of the lake, the **National Planetarium** is reachable on foot using the steps opposite the RMP Museum (see p.79). Its blue dome and geometrically latticed walls make this an unlikely example of the city's Islamic-influenced architecture. The interior, admittedly a little gaudy, is full of insightful notes about space travel; there's a cutaway space capsule, a Viking rocket engine and spacesuits in glass cases, all lit up by blue lighting. The **Space Theatre** also shows an hourly film on various topics, not necessarily about space. Take the lift up to the top-floor **viewing platform** – it's a hidden gem of a lookout spot – for views stretching across the parks to KLCC and beyond. A **pedestrian bridge** runs south from the planetarium to the National Museum.

National Museum

Jalan Damansara • Daily 9am–6pm; free guided tours Mon–Sat 10–11am • RM5 • ☎ 03 2267 1111, ⓦ www.muziumnegara.gov.my •
KL train station; walk via the underpass to the KTM building, as there are no other crossings on Jalan Sultan Hishamuddin

Built in 1963, the **National Museum** (Muzium Negara) has a sweeping roof
characteristic of northern Malay architecture, and **four galleries** that focus perhaps a bit
too much on the Malay side of things, giving relatively little space to the Orang Asli,
Indians, Chinese and Europeans who have also left their mark on the nation's history
and culture. Despite this, the museum is definitely worth an hour, especially if you've
seen the Textile Museum's complementary exhibits.

On the first floor, **Gallery A** offers a stroll through prehistory, with human skeletal
remains from Kelantan that prove that settlers were present on the Peninsula around
6000 BC. **Gallery B** covers early Malay kingdoms, in particular the Melaka Sultanate,
with a particularly good collection of finely chased *kris* daggers and items recovered from
sunken Chinese trading vessels. The pace accelerates upstairs, where **Gallery C** covers the
colonial era, from reconstructions of Melaka's Portuguese fortifications to intricate models
of trading ships to a fine seventeenth-century German Bellarmine jug depicting a bearded
face – characteristic of such jugs – on the neck of the vessel. There's also ungenerous
coverage of the British "interference" in the Malay States, including a diorama of the
signing of the Pangkor Treaty (see p.559). Tin, the metal that opened up Malaysia to
development, dominates the final part of the gallery; mining equipment sits alongside
animal-shaped coinage – including a 30cm crocodile – once used in Selangor and Perak.

Gallery D parcels modern Malaysia into a triumphant photo parade of the nation's
founding fathers, of various races, whose names you see on street signs downtown
– though there's only cursory coverage of broader history, such as the Emergency
during the 1950s (see p.563). Finally, don't miss the open-air courtyard at the back,
which features an excellent run-down of the Peninsula's **indigenous groups**,
alongside fantastic totem-pole-like objects and grotesque face masks such as the
one-fanged *moyang melor*, which were used in rites of ancestor worship.

1

Brickfields and KL Sentral

KL Sentral LRT, KTM and Monorail

The laidback residential neighbourhood of **Brickfields**, 2km south of the city centre near **KL Sentral** station, was first settled by Tamils employed to build the railways, and named after the brickworks that lined the rail tracks. Even today, the area retains a strong South Indian presence along **Jalan Tun Sambanthan** – the main thoroughfare – especially the western stretch beyond the huge pink fountain marking the intersection with Jalan Travers; the road has flowers painted on it, buildings are pastel-hued, and Indian pop tunes blare out of sari shops and grocers. This is one of the city's corners to visit for local ambience rather than monumental sights, though there are two wonderful temples and the area is also home to some good places to eat (see p.97).

Sri Kandaswamy Temple

3 Lorong Scott • Mon–Thurs 5.30am–9pm, Fri–Sun 5.30am–9.30pm • ☎ 03 2274 2987, ⓦ srikandaswamykovil.org

The Hindu **Sri Kandaswamy Temple** was founded by the Sri Lankan Tamil community in the 1900s, though the present structure was consecrated in 1997. Its facade, a riot of brightly coloured statues reminiscent of Chinatown's Sri Maha Mariamman Temple, is all the more appealing for being little visited by tourists; just don't expect to find anyone who can explain the layout, which includes, in the far right corner of the entrance wall, a collection of nine garlanded deities representing the planets.

Thean Hou Temple

65 Persiaran Endah • Daily 8am–9pm • ☎ 03 2274 7088

A stone's throw southeast from Brickfields proper, the six-tiered **Thean Hou Temple** is dedicated to the Chinese sea goddess Mazu and affiliated with Buddhism, Taoism and Confucianism. Built by local Hainanese communities and opened in 1989, it remains one of the largest Chinese temples in South East Asia. The building is illuminated with hundreds of lanterns on the birthdays of goddesses Tian Hou, Kuan Yin and Mazu (all of whom have shrines inside along with Chinese zodiac symbology) and looks particularly good on Chinese New Year – it's spellbinding stuff.

ARRIVAL AND DEPARTURE | KUALA LUMPUR

KL's airports cover all major destinations across Malaysia, Singapore and Bandar Seri Begawan, as well as many Southeast Asian and international airports. If you're coming to KL by plane from anywhere outside of Southeast Asia, you'll arrive at KLIA, while regional flights will arrive at the low-cost terminal KLIA2 or at Subang Skypark, depending on the airline. If you're arriving by train, you'll stop at KL Sentral, the main station, while buses are likely to stop at TBS (Terminal Bersepadu Selatan), 12km south of the centre.

BY PLANE

Kuala Lumpur International Airport (KLIA; ☎ 03 8777 8888, ⓦ klia.com.my), the main long-haul airport, is some 50km south of KL and serves all major long-haul services. The arrivals hall contains a visitor centre (daily 8am–11pm; ☎ 03 8776 5647), a 24hr bureau de change, exchange facilities, and desks representing car rental outlets and KL's pricier hotels.

Kuala Lumpur International Airport 2 (KLIA 2; ☎ 03 8778 5540, ⓦ klia.com.my), just 2km north of KLIA, is used by budget airlines including AirAsia, Malindo Airways, Cebu Pacific and TigerAir, flying both domestic and international routes. Facilities include ATMs, a 24hr bureau de change and plenty of duty-free shops. KL's small second airport, Subang Skypark Sultan Abdul Aziz Shah Airport; ☎ 03 7842 2773,

---

KUALA LUMPUR INTERNATIONAL AIRPORT: IN-TOWN CHECK-IN

Passengers departing from KLIA with Malaysia Airlines, Cathay Pacific, Cathay Dragon, Emirates, Etihad Airlines or Malindo Air can check bags in up to 2hr before departure time at the KLIA Express ticket desks at KL Sentral station. It's a useful option if you have a late flight and don't want to lug your bags around all day after you check out of your accommodation.

1

ⓦ subangskypark.com), 25km west of the city, hosts only Firefly and Berjaya airlines at present, covering a few domestic destinations plus Singapore and Koh Samui in Thailand.

Destinations from KLIA and KLIA 2 Bintulu (1 daily; 1hr); Kota Kinabalu (13 daily; 1hr 30min); Johor (6 daily; 1hr); Kedah (3 daily; 1hr); Kelantan (8 daily; 1hr); Kuching (12 daily; 1hr 30min); Labuan (2 daily; 1hr 30min); Langkawi (10 daily; 1hr); Miri (4 daily; 1hr 30min); Penang (10 daily; 1hr); Sandakan (3 daily; 1hr 30min); Tawau (4 daily; 1hr 30min); Terengganu (4 daily; 1hr).

Destinations from Subang Skypark Johor Bahru (hourly; 1hr); Koh Samui (4 weekly; 2hr); Kota Bahru (hourly; 1hr); Kuala Terengganu (4 daily; 1hr); Langkawi (4 daily; 1hr); Penang (hourly; 1hr); Singapore (daily; 1hr).

ONWARD TRANSPORT FROM KLIA AND KLIA 2

An airport shuttle covers the short distance between KLIA and KLIA 2, so the transport options between the sister airports and the city centre are largely the same.

By train Two fast, convenient rail links (ⓦ kliaekspres.com) connect both KLIA and KLIA2 with downtown KL Sentral station: KLIA Transit (from KL Sentral daily 4.30am–midnight and from KLIA daily 5.30am–1am; every 20–30min in both directions; 40min; RM350), which stops three times along the way; and the nonstop KLIA Ekspres (from KL Sentral 5am–12.30am and from KLIA 5am–1am; every 15–20 min in both directions; 28min; RM55.

By bus Buses between KLIA and KL are much cheaper, if slower, than the trains. Services by Airport Coach (☏ 016 228 9070, ⓦ airportcoach.com.my) depart hourly around the clock for KL Sentral station (1hr; RM10 one-way, RM18 return), while Star Shuttle (☏ 03 4043 8811, ⓦ starwira .com) runs hourly to Pudu Sentral (UTC) bus station in Chinatown and hotels in Bukit Bintang (from KLIA 5am–2.15am, from Pudu Sentral 12.15am–11.15pm; 1hr 15min for both routes; RM10–18). There are also buses to Ipoh with Star Shuttle, and some to Melaka and Seremban; if you want to bypass KL and catch a bus to another part of the Peninsula, go to Terminal Bersepadu Selatan (see opposite).

By taxi The hour-long taxi ride to downtown KL costs between RM80–100, and you can buy a fixed-fare ticket from the counter near the arrivals exit. Alternatively, get a Grab or Uber (around RM75) to meet you at one of the airport doors.

ONWARD TRANSPORT FROM SUBANG SKYPARK

By train Until the Subang Jaya train line opens in 2018, the quickest way into town is to catch a taxi from the airport to Kelana Jaya LRT train station (30min; RM35) and then take the LRT to KL Sentral or Pasar Seni (35min).

By bus KL Airport shuttle coaches (ⓦ subangskypark.com) connect the airport to KLIA (daily 5am–11pm; hourly; RM10) and KL Sentral (daily 9am–9pm; hourly; RM10).

By taxi A taxi from Subang Skypark to the city centre will set you back about RM50 (40min); a Grab/Uber will cost around RM40.

BY TRAIN

Located just southwest of downtown KL, KL Sentral station is the main hub for the Peninsula's trains, and also for many of KL's local rail services. Inside, you'll find separate ticket counters for all train services, plus the various airport buses. By the north entrance near where the *Hilton* is located, there are also ATMs, left-luggage lockers (daily 8am–10.30pm; RM5/day; ☏ 012 395 6969) and taxi ticket counters for the rank outside. Fast ETS trains arrive at KL from Ipoh, Butterworth and the border town Padang Besar, as well as from the southern rail hub of Gemas, which has a slow connection with Johor Bahru, the interior and the east coast. For fares and timetables, see ⓦ ktmb.com.my. KTM Komuter trains connect KL Sentral with Port Klang, where ferries from Indonesia (see p.86) dock at the Asa Niaga terminal near the station, and with Seremban.

Destinations Alor Setar (5 daily; 4hr 30min–5hr); Butterworth (7 daily; 4hr 15min); Gemas (4 daily; 2hr 15min); Ipoh (every 1hr–1hr 30min; 2hr 30min); Kuala Kangsar (11 daily; 3hr); Padang Besar (5 daily; at least 5hr); Port Klang (every 15–30min; 1hr); Seremban (every 15–20min; 1hr 20min); Sungai Petani (5 daily; 4hr 15min); Taiping (11 daily; 3hr 15min).

ONWARD TRANSPORT

By train Pasar Seni station in Chinatown is just one stop from KL Sentral on the Kelana Jaya–Gombak LRT line (ⓦ myrapid.com.my). For Bukit Bintang, you need the Monorail which, in a minor planning lapse, is 200m away on Jalan Tun Sambathan – descend to street level on the southeast side of KL Sentral and follow a signed walkway.

By taxi There's a taxi rank on the northern side of KL Sentral station, open until around 1am. You can negotiate a price with the driver; a taxi to Chinatown should cost roughly RM12 and to Bukit Bintang no more than RM15.

BY BUS

To buy tickets, you'll generally need to turn up and speak to the various bus companies directly, though the larger ones such as Easybook (☏ 010 396 6688, ⓦ easybook.com) can also be contacted by phone.

PUDU SENTRAL

KL's most central long-distance bus station, Pudu Sentral (Puduraya), occupies a multistorey complex on Jalan Pudu, just east of Chinatown. It deals mainly with northbound traffic, with dozens of bus companies ensuring regular departures to most places. On the main passenger level are ATMs and food stalls, and there's also a

1

TRAVEL AGENTS AND TOUR OPERATORS

For advice on local **tours**, Perhentian trips, or packages to Taman Negara, either ask at your hotel or hostel, or visit Malaysia Tourism Centre (see p.88). Specific **Taman Negara** operators include NKS (☎03 2072 0336, ⓦ taman-negara-nks.com) and Han Travel (☎03 2031 0899, ⓦ han-travel.com), who both charge around RM350 per person for a three-day trip (see p.197). Kuala Lumpur Travel Tour (☎017 633 0062, ⓦ kualalumpurtraveltour.com), meanwhile, organizes plenty of private tours in and around the capital, including to the Blue Mosque, the country's largest, at Shah Alam.

bank upstairs. On arrival, exit the west side of the building for the short walk to Chinatown, or connect to Merdeka station on the Laluan Sungai Buloh (LBS) line #9; there's also an alley leading east to Plaza Rakyat LRT station on the Ampang #3 and Sri Petaling #4 lines. A useful pedestrian bridge crosses Jalan Pudu from the north side, from where Bukit Bintang's hostels are a 15min walk. Alternatively, reach Bukit Bintang aboard RapidKL bus #400, #401 or #508, all of which head east along Jalan Pudu and Jalan Imbi, then north up Jalan Sultan Ismail to the Lot 10 Mall. When departing from this bus station you'll need to check your ticket, as it will be marked with the departure bay in the basement – each of the bays is reached by a separate numbered staircase.

Destinations Alor Setar (hourly; 7hr 30min); Butterworth (hourly; 5hr 30min); Cameron Highlands (hourly; 4hr); Genting Highlands (every 30min; 1hr); Georgetown (hourly; 4hr); Hat Yai (2 daily; Thailand; 9hr); Ipoh (hourly; 3hr 30min); Kangar (8 daily; 7hr); Kuala Kangsar (6 daily; 2hr 30min); Kuala Perlis (8 daily; 8hr); Lumut (every 1hr 30min; 3hr 30min); Penang (every 30min; 5hr); Taiping (5 daily; 4hr 30min).

PEKELILING

Pekeliling bus station (sometimes known as Jalan Pekeliling), 3km northwest of central KL and just off Jalan Tun Razak, is used mainly by buses from Pahang including Taman Negara, along with some services to the Genting Highlands. The separate Titiwangsa stations on the Monorail and the LRT are just to the north.

Destinations Jerantut (for Taman Negara National Park; 6 daily; 3hr 30min); Kuala Lipis (10 daily; 4hr).

TERMINAL BERSEPADU SELATAN (TBS)

With mostly services to the south and east of KL, TBS (ⓦ tbsbts.com.my) is an important bus hub for the city, and the closest bus station to KLIA. It's 10km south of KL, next to Bandar Tasik Selatan LRT station, and is served by some airport shuttles (see opposite).

Destinations Alor Setar (2 daily; 4hr 40min); Butterworth (3 daily; 3hr 40min); Johor (every 30min; 5hr); Kuala Perlis (daily; 5hr 30min); Ipoh (5 daily; 3hr 30min); Kuantan (3 daily; 3hr); Lumut (3 daily; 3hr 15min); Melaka (every 30min; 2hr 30min); Penang (5 daily; 4hr 30min); Singapore (every 30min; 6hr); Sungai Petani (daily; 4hr).

OTHER BUS STATIONS

Old Kuala Lumpur train station Luxury buses from Kuala Lumpur train station serve destinations including Johor (every 30min; 5hr 30min), Melaka (every 30min; 3hr 30min) and Singapore (every 30min; 6hr).

Klang bus station Located in Chinatown just below Pasar Seni train station, the Klang bus station serves Port Klang (every 15min; 1hr 30min), but it's far quicker to make this journey aboard the KTM Komuter train to Pelabuhan Klang station.

Jalan Imbi Transtar (☎65 6292 9009, ⓦ transtar.travel) luxury buses to and from Singapore (4 daily; 6hr) arrive and leave from here. It's convenient, as it's practically in the heart of Bukit Bintang.

BY LONG-DISTANCE TAXI

Long-distance taxis leave from Pudu Sentral bus station; typical fares per vehicle are around RM340 to Cameron Highlands, RM450 to Kuala Tahan (the main entrance for Taman Negara) and RM550 to Kota Bharu or Kuala Terengganu.

BY CAR

Leaving KL by car onto the Peninsula's main highways is hampered by confusing road signage, one-way systems and countless express bypasses – this is only recommended for confident drivers.

E1 The North–South Expressway, northbound, is signed from Jalan Duta, which branches off Middle Ring Rd I west of the Lake Gardens. Major towns on the route include Tanjong Malim, Kuala Kangsar, Bukit Mertajam (for Penang Island) and Butterworth.

E2 The North–South Expressway, southbound, starts at Sungai Besi 2km south of Chinatown, and is most quickly reached using the long underground SMART tunnel on the eastern section of Jalan Tun Razak. This passes notable destinations like Seremban, Alor Gajah (for Melaka) and Yong Peng, on the way to Johor Bahru.

E8 To reach the E8 (Karak Highway), which is linked to the East Coast Highway to Kuantan, and Route 8 into the interior, get onto Jalan Tun Razak (or Jalan Raja Laut if starting from Chinatown) and head northwest to Jalan Ipoh; proceed up this for a short distance, then turn right onto Jalan Sentul and follow signs for the highway.

1

BY FERRY

The only ferries from the vicinity of KL are those from Port Klang to Dumai (Sumatra; daily 10.30am; 3hr 30min; RM110); check current schedules on ☎ 03 3167 7186. The port is on the KTM Komuter line to KL Sentral and Kuala Lumpur train stations.

GETTING AROUND

Downtown KL isn't that large, so it's tempting to do a lot of your exploring **on foot**, but it's likely you'll soon find yourself wilting thanks to the combined effects of humidity and traffic fumes from the vehicle-choked roads. Thankfully, the light rail transit (**LRT**) and mass rapid transit (**MRT**) lines and the **Monorail**, along with **KTM Komuter** train services and taxis, are efficient and inexpensive. The services did not always coordinate well, though much of this has been rectified with the recent RM10 billion extension project. The main governing body is **RapidKL** (⊛ myrapid.com.my), which runs the LRT, MRT and Monorail lines, plus many of the city's buses; its website includes network maps and details of monthly transport passes.

BY TRAIN

LRT AND MRT

The Klang Valley Integrated Transit System (daily 6am–midnight; every 5–10min) features three operational Light Rail Transit (LRT, ⊛ myrapid.com.my) lines and the planned three-line Mass Rapid Transit system (MRT, ⊛ mrt.com .my), which at the time of research was being opened stage by stage. The LRT network comprises the #3 Ampang Line, #4 Sri Petaling Line and #5 Kelana Jaya Line, which became a lot more user-friendly in 2017 with the line extension to Putra Heights. The Ampang and Sri Petaling lines both follow the route from the northern terminus at Sentul Timor to Chan Sow Lin in the south, before splitting off to Ampang to the east or Putra Heights to the southwest via Sri Petaling. For visitors, these lines are mainly of use for travel between Chinatown (Plaza Rakyat) and Little India (Masjid Jamek or Bandaraya) and Chow Kit Market (Sultan Ismail). The Kelana Jaya Line was the first fully automated and driverless rail link in the Klang Valley. The route starts at Gombak near the Batu Caves, passes through KL Sentral, Chinatown and the old colonial district (Pasar Seni or Masjid Jamek) and its former terminus at Kelana Jaya, before reaching Putra Heights. The first MRT service, the #9 Sungai Buloh–Kajang Line, has opened, and the #12 Sungai Buloh–Serdang–Putrajaya Line is set to follow by 2020. The feasibility of the third #13 Circle Line is still under review. The Sungai Buloh–Kajang Line is now easily the best option for travel between Bukit Bintang, Pasar Seni, Merdeka (for Plaza Rakyat) and Muzium Negara (for KL Sentral and the National Museum), and this service connects Sungai Buloh in the northwest with Kajang in the southeast. It will also serve the proposed Kuala Lumpur International Financial District (KLIFD) in the east of the city, from the Tun Razak Exchange (TRX) station.

MONORAIL

Trains on this elevated rail system (daily 6am–midnight; every 5–10min; RM1.20–2.50; ⊛ myrapid.com.my) have a noticeable tilt as they camber around bends. From the KL Sentral terminus (200m from the KL Sentral rail hub), the line at first heads east, through Brickfields and the southern edge of Chinatown, then swings north and west through Bukit Bintang and along Jalan Sultan Ismail, nearly reaching Jalan TAR before heading north through Chow Kit to terminate at Titiwangsa station on Jalan Tun Razak. There are interchanges with the LRT at Bukit Nanas (a 5min walk to Dang Wangi station) and at Hang Tuah.

KTM KOMUTER

Run by national rail operator KTM (⊛ ktmb.com.my), trains travel on two lines: one from Pulau Sebang/Tampin, north of Melaka, to Batu Caves via Seremban, the other from coastal Port Klang (Pelabuhan Klang in Malay) north to Tanjung Malim in Perak. Both of them connect downtown at four stations: Putra, near the Putra World Trade Centre; Bank Negara, near Little India; the Kuala Lumpur train station, in the colonial district; and KL Sentral. Trains run every 15–20min during the day, but only every 30min after 8pm. Tickets (up to RM10) can be purchased from the stations and automatic machines at the stops; return tickets cost double the one-way fare. Weekly and monthly

---

TOUCH 'N GO CARDS

As if literally named after KL's not-yet-realized dreams of a fully integrated transport system, the **Touch 'n Go card** (☎ 03 2714 8888, ⊛ touchngo.com.my) is a useful **stored-value card** that you simply touch across the sensors at KTM Kommuter, LRT and Monorail stations, and when you board RapidKL buses. You can also use it to pay Expressway tolls on the Peninsula, and in various car parks and fast-food joints around KL. Cards cost RM10.60 from many stations (look for the blue and yellow logo); ticket office staff at the same places can recharge them (RM10–500 at a time; cash only), as can 7-Eleven stores and highway toll stations (*plaza tol*). As the cards save time queuing, rather than save money, they're of most use if you are in the city a good deal or plan to drive yourself around the Peninsula.

KUALA LUMPUR TRANSPORT SYSTEM

Legend:
- 1 Seremban (KTM Komuter)
- 2 Port Klang (KTM Komuter)
- 3 Ampang (LRT)
- 4 Sri Petaling (LRT)
- 5 Kelana Jaya (LRT)
- 6 KLIA Ekspres (ERL)
- 7 KLIA Transit (ERL)
- 8 KL Sentral–Titiwangsa (Monorail)
- 9 Sungai Buloh–Kajang (MRT)
- ┼┼┼┼┼ Walk between stations
- ∞ Interchange station

passes for designated journeys are also available. Note that Komuter trains all have a central women-only carriage.

BY BUS

KL has a comprehensive city bus network, with Metrobus and RapidKL as the two main operators, but the lack of clearly marked terminuses and bus stops can make it baffling for outsiders to use. Services start up around 6am and begin winding down from 10pm onwards. Given KL's frequent traffic snarl-ups, do allow plenty of time for your journey. The small grid of streets around Pudu Sentral and Central Market (Pasar Seni station) is a hub of sorts;

buildings with key stops close by, including the Sinarkota Building, the Kotaraya Building and the Bangkok Bank, appear on our Chinatown map (see p.70). RapidKL (ⓦmyrapid.com.my) offers SMART7/Weekly and SMART30/Monthly passes for discounted rates, as well as Touch 'n Go (see p.86) that also work at car toll booths.

BY TAXI

KL taxis are cheap and convenient, though drivers used to be notorious for negotiating inflated prices rather than using the meter – a problem that has decreased drastically since the advent of competition from Grab and Uber. There are two ways to deal with this: ask if they use the meter before getting in, and flag down another cab if they don't; or buy a prepaid coupon for your journey from booths attached to designated cab ranks or at the airport. A few drivers don't speak much English, so you may want to have the address of your destination, or a well-known landmark nearby, written down in Malay. There are numerous taxi ranks around the city, usually close to bus stops and outside shopping malls and tourist attractions. Fares are generally low: in regular taxis the flagfall is RM3, and the tariff is 10 sen for every 150m travelled. This translates into just RM5–6 for a typical journey between Bukit Bintang and Chinatown, or RM7–8 for Bukit Bintang to KL Sentral or Chinatown to KLCC. Expect to pay a bit more for downtown journeys in the smarter (often blue) taxis; luggage in the boot is charged at RM1/bag. To book a taxi, which costs an extra couple of ringgit, call Sunlight Radio Taxis (☎03 9200 1166, ⓦsunlighttaxi.com).

INFORMATION

Bear in mind that, given the chaotic nature of KL city planning, **maps** and listings tend to go out of date fairly quickly; don't be surprised if roads, venues and buildings have sprung into existence or ceased to be.

Tourism Malaysia The national tourist board has branches across the city (ⓦtourism.gov.my), handing out brochures and general advice. You can also book accommodation, local tours and packages to Taman Negara and the like through in-house travel agents. The main office is at Malaysia Tourism Centre (MaTiC), 109 Jalan Ampang, not far from the Bukit Nanas Monorail stop (daily 8am–10pm; ☎03 9235 4900, ⓦmatic.gov.my); bus #B105 also runs here from Central Market in Chinatown. Other branches include: Sultan Abdul Samad Building on Jalan Raja (daily 9am–6pm; ☎03 2602 2014, ⓦtourismmalaysia.gov.my); KL Sentral Station, Level 1 (daily 9am–6pm; ☎03 2272 5823); KLIA international arrivals hall (daily 8am–11pm; ☎03 8776 5647); KLIA 2 (daily 8am–11pm; ☎03 8778 7080).

Listings To keep an ear to the ground on happenings around town, check out the monthly *Time Out KL* (ⓦtimeout.com/kuala-lumpur). Also worth a look is ⓦvisionkl.com, a handy repository of sights, restaurants, clubs and events.

TOURS

Food Tour Malaysia ☎013 227 1505, ⓦfoodtourmalaysia.com. Offers excellent "off the eaten track" and KL walking tours both during the day and in the evenings, which are perfect for getting acquainted with Malaysia's many cuisines. Tours start from RM250 and last around three hours.

Go KL City Bus ☎1 800 887723, ⓦgokl.com.my. There are free buses that stop off at major sights around the city (Mon–Fri 6am–11pm, Sat & Sun 7am–11pm; every 5–10min); you can use the services as often as you please, and hop on and off as many times as you fancy. You can pick up a detailed map at the tourist office, and board the bus right outside MaTiC on Jalan Ampang.

KL Hop-on Hop-off ☎1 800 885546, ⓦmyhoponhopoff.com. The KL Hop-on Hop-off bus service, which loops around a set circuit via a string of tourist sights (daily 9am–8pm; every 20–30min; unlimited-use day ticket RM55, 48hr RM95). Buses are open-top double-deckers, and audio commentaries are available in a handful of languages.

Kuala Lumpur City Hall Tours ☎03 2698 0332, ⓦwww.visitkl.gov.my. There are free Dataran Merdeka heritage tours that start at the Kuala Lumpur City Gallery (Mon, Wed & Sat 9am; 2hr 30min), as well as Little India walking tours from Vivekananda Ashram (Sat 9am; 2hr 30min). Plans for night walks around Masjid Jamek were also being finalized at the time of research.

ACCOMMODATION

While **Chinatown** has traditionally been the favourite location for budget travellers, with its surfeit of inexpensive places to sleep, eat, drink and shop, it faces growing competition from **Bukit Bintang**, a 15min walk east, where you'll find plenty of excellent guesthouses on and around Tengkat Tong Shin. Even though they're usually more expensive than in Chinatown, they're often better value – less cramped and noisy, with slicker facilities and self-service breakfasts included in the rate. Slightly further afield, more upscale hotels can be found along **Jalan Sultan Ismail** and **Jalan Ampang**, which, together with Bukit Bintang, form part of KL's **Golden Triangle**. All other parts of KL pale in comparison when it comes to accommodation, though **Little India** also features several mid-range options.

CHINATOWN AND AROUND

Chinatown's backpacker-oriented guesthouses are mostly concentrated either side of Jalan Petaling, alongside budget hotels offering simple rooms but with better facilities. Both are increasingly modern and efficiently run, though furnishings are minimal and the cheapest rooms are unlikely to have windows. Only the more upmarket places feature frills like swimming pools, though there is an ageing public pool nearby at the Chinwoo Stadium (see p.105).

HOTELS

Hotel 1915 49 Jalan Lebuh Ampang ☎03 2026 0043, ⓦhotel1915kl.com.my; map p.70. Just walking into the lobby of this hotel, located in a beautifully renovated building that dates back to 1915, is a welcome respite from the hubbub of Chinatown. The lobby features bare brick walls, black-and-white prints and Chinese stone sculptures and vases, while the contemporary rooms are equipped with modern amenities, en-suite facilities and in-room safes. 📶 RM118

5 Elements Hotel 243 Jalan Sultan ☎03 2031 6888, ⓦthe5elementshotel.com.my; map p.70. Rooms are clean and comfortable at this fourteen-storey hotel, which has great views of Chinatown and beyond; the twelfth- to fourteenth-floor rooms will set you back RM35 extra. Some rooms are in better shape than others, so it's wise to take a look at a couple before settling in. 📶 RM208

Hotel China Town 2 70–72 Jalan Petaling ☎03 2072 9933, ⓦhotelchinatown2.com; map p.70. Located on bustling Jalan Petaling in the heart of Chinatown, this decent hotel offers clean rooms with private baths at affordable prices, including some singles (RM80). 📶 RM110

Geo Hotel 7 Jalan Hang Kasturi ☎03 2032 2288, ⓦgeohotelkl.com; map p.70. Just a few steps from the Central Market, this great-value hotel offers well-kept, white a/c rooms with chocolate-coloured fittings and flat-screen TVs; the superior rooms (RM220) are just like the standards, but also include a fresh fruit basket. The premises are strictly non-smoking, except on the third floor where all rooms are smoking. The friendly staff are an added bonus. 📶 RM195

★**Hotel Majestic** Jalan Sultan Hishamuddin ☎03 2785 8000, ⓦmajestickl.com; map p.68. Opposite the old Moorish-style railway station, this hotel, a wonderfully restored 1930s building, houses exquisitely furnished suites with butler service (RM885), the fifteen-storey Art Deco Tower Wing with deluxe rooms and suites (RM745), along with a swimming pool and gym. Other facilities include a bar, spa, barber and screening room. 📶 RM540

Swiss Inn 62 Jalan Sultan ☎03 2072 3333, ⓦswissgarden.com; map p.70. A pleasant surprise in the heart of Chinatown, this clean, modern hotel has a range of inviting rooms spread out over seven colour-coded floors. Rooms have tasteful furnishings and crisp linen; the executive options (RM680) are brighter thanmthe windowless regular rooms. The coffee house offers a good view of the Petaling Street market. 📶 RM560

Winsin Hotel 1–3 Jalan Petaling ☎03 2031 5011, ⓦwinsinchinatownhotel.com.my; map p.70. This hotel is admittedly a bit dated, but the small rooms are modern and in good nick, with en-suite facilities and a/c, and livened up with Chinese paintings. It's well placed for Central Market, bang in the middle of the Petaling Street buzz. 📶 RM88

ACCOMMODATION ESSENTIALS

RATES

Thanks to an over-supply of rooms for much of the year, rates remain competitive in KL – a bed in a dorm can be had for as little as RM30, and it's seldom hard to find a simple double in a guesthouse with shared facilities for RM50/night, or RM80 if you need en-suite facilities and a/c. A good mid-range hotel room costs around RM150, while anything above RM250/night will be pretty luxurious. Check online or ask when booking about promotional rates or weekday hotel discounts; the prices here refer to weekend rates.

BOOKINGS

Although it's almost inconceivable that you'd be unable to find somewhere to stay in your price range here, it always makes sense to book ahead, especially during busy periods – July to August and November to December, plus school and public holidays. As well as individual accommodation websites, you can try ⓦhostelworld.com, ⓦairbnb.com or ⓦhostelbookers .com for hostels and guesthouses.

BREAKFAST

All high-end, international-brand hotels include breakfast in their rates, and this is usually a buffet spread featuring Asian and Western cuisine. Mid-range hotels and guesthouses tend to offer a more modest meal of toast or *nasi lemak* and a drink. For hostels, breakfast is rarely complimentary, but there is often an on-site café or *mamak* that offers discounts to residents.

1

HOSTELS AND GUESTHOUSES

★**Back Home** 30 Jalan Tun H.S. Lee ☎ 03 2022 0788, ⓦ backhome.com.my; map p.70. This leafy hostel features hardwood floors, bare brick walls and comfortable, modern rooms set around a courtyard with coffee tables, where guests are invited to socialize. Staff are friendly and there's an excellent café next door under the same management. ☞ Dorms RM60, doubles RM130

Birdnest Guesthouse 2 64 Jalan Hang Kasturi ☎ 012 694 7366, ⓦ birdnestghouse.com; map p.70. Friendly place dotted with birdcages (some made into quirky lamps) that the owner has picked up from various flea markets; the furniture is all recycled, and there's even a rooftop café. The little rooms, with fan or a/c units, feature polished hardwood floors, with most looking onto the interior courtyard; there are three-bed female and mixed dorms too. ☞ Dorms RM30, doubles RM80

The Explorers Guesthouse 128 & 130 Jalan Tun H.S. Lee ☎ 03 2022 2928, ⓦ theexplorersguesthouse.com; map p.70. An oasis of calm in the hubbub of Chinatown, this guesthouse features a pleasant communal area with a water feature, decorative fans, dangling dream-catchers and pebble tiles in the bathrooms. The rooms are on the smallish side but are kept immaculate, as are the bathrooms, and staff will happily advise on what to see and do in the area. ☞ Dorms RM35, doubles RM95

Raizzy's Guesthouse 165g Jalan Tun H.S. Lee ☎ 03 2022 0873, ⓦ raizzy.com; map p.70. Just a few steps from the Sri Maha Mariamman Temple, this friendly hostel offers small, darkish dorms (most are windowless or look onto the interior of the building), although the doubles are appealing enough and are a real bargain given the location. Guests are entitled to breakfast discounts at the *Lucy in the Sky* café next door. ☞ Dorms RM32, doubles RM78

★**Reggae Mansion** 53 Jalan Tun H.S Lee ☎ 03 2072 6877, ⓦ reggaemansionkl.com; map p.70. Located in a three-storey colonial-era block, this is a flashpacker hostel at its best, although it is a bit of a tourist-trail factory. The spick-and-span premises are kitted out with mock-Louis XIV armchairs and prints that depict life in a British stately home. Each dorm bed is equipped with a privacy curtain, reading lamp, power socket and under-bed lockers. There's even an in-house cinema, and the rooftop bar is one of the places to be for cheap backpacker boozing. ☞ Dorms RM48, doubles RM140

LITTLE INDIA AND CHOW KIT

Crossroads Hotel 1 Jalan Raja Muda Abdul Aziz ☎ 03 2698 7000, ⓦ crossroads-hotel.com; map p.73. A stone's throw away from Chow Kit's market, this excellent budget hotel offers immaculate rooms kitted out with dark furnishings, in a pleasant interior with bare brick walls and funky orange chairs at reception. The area of Chow Kit, however, is known for prostitution and it's also wise to watch your wallet at all times. Breakfast is an extra RM25. ☞ RM120

Hotel De' Grand Orchard 81–83 Medan Bunus ☎ 03 2691 2146, ⓦ hoteldegrandorchard.com; map p.73. Not to be confused with its sister hotel *Grand Orchard*, this budget place, just off Jalan Masjid India, features welcoming rooms with chocolate-brown furnishings, faux wooden floors and smallish, albeit very clean, bathrooms. Rates increase by RM25 over the weekends. ☞ RM120

K Hotel 142–146 Jalan TAR ☎ 03 2693 4246, ⓦ khotel .com.my; map p.73. Make your way past a yogurt shop on the ground floor and up to the bright red lobby of this recently renovated hotel. The carpeted rooms are smallish but sparklingly clean. ☞ RM168

Palace Hotel 40a Jalan Masjid India ☎ 03 2698 6122, ⓦ palacehotel.com.my; map p.73. The simple rooms at this 1960s-style hotel are decorated in beige and olive green and are a bit drab and dated, though all have a/c and the hotel is in a lively location. RM150

Premiera Hotel 232 Jalan TAR ☎ 03 2615 1000, ⓦ premiera.com.my; map p.73. In the heart of Little India and just a short walk from Chinatown, this is a great independent option offering spacious rooms with modern amenities, and wonderful views of the city from the higher floors. Note that 76 out of the hotel's 90 rooms are twins (RM275), so if you're after a double make sure you book ahead. ☞ RM325

Silka Maytower Hotel 7 Jalan Munshi Abdullah ☎ 03 2692 9298, ⓦ silkahotels.com/maytower; map p.73. This international-standard hotel, set over 32 floors, offers modern rooms and apartments with earthy tones, equipped with flat-screen TVs and safes; the deluxes (RM250) are more spacious, with sofas and bathtubs, and there are also two pools – one for adults, one for kids – on the eighth floor, along with a sauna and gym. ☞ Doubles RM220, studio suites RM339

Tune Hotel 316 Jalan TAR ☎ 03 2694 3301, ⓦ tunehotels.com; map p.73. AirAsia-supported no-frills hotel, which is usually quite cheap if you book early. The

---

THE BEST PLACES TO STAY IN KL

Best for views *Traders Hotel* (see p.91)
Best for luxury *Mandarin Oriental* (see p.91)
Best for colonial grandeur *Hotel Majestic* (see p.89)
Best for nightlife *Invito Hotel Suites* (see p.91)
Best hostel for parties *Reggae Mansion* (see above)
Best hostel for service *Dorms KL* (see p.92)

en-suite rooms are small and functional, with fans; you pay extra for a/c, towels, TV and the like if you want them, which can add RM45 to the basic rate. Lobby facilities amount to a couple of fast-food outlets and a convenience store. This is a hotel best booked online; the rate quoted here is for walk-ins. 🛜 RM125

THE GOLDEN TRIANGLE

Many of the Bukit Bintang guesthouses occupy nicely restored old shophouses, with small, comfortable rooms separated from each other by partitions. It's hard to go wrong with any of these, just as it's difficult to be badly disappointed with any of the Golden Triangle's upmarket hotels. The area also boasts excellent serviced apartments offering a lot more space than you'd get in a similarly priced hotel room.

HOTELS

★**Anggun Boutique Hotel** 7 & 9 Tengkat Tong Shin ☏ 03 2145 8003, ⓦ anggunkl.com; map p.76. This welcoming boutique hotel aims to recreate a Peranakan house from yesteryear, with rooms set around an airy central courtyard with a little fishpond and a lovely antique Chinese medicine cabinet. Some have four-poster beds, while the three suites have balconies overlooking the street; bathrooms feature beautiful Chinese sinks with lotus and fish motifs. 🛜 RM315

Dorsett Regency 172 Jalan Imbi ☏ 03 2716 1000, ⓦ dorsettregency.com; map p.76. Within a rather unappealing salmon-pink tower block lies this great-value mid-range hotel with modern rooms, some with superb views of the Petronas Towers; facilities include a small pool. The central location is a real plus – it's just a couple of minutes' walk from Starhill Gallery and Pavilion mall, while the bars and clubs of Changkat Bukit Bintang are a 15min walk away. 🛜 RM420

Fraser Place 10 Jalan Perak ☏ 03 2118 6288, ⓦ frasershospitality.com; map p.76. Right by the Petronas Towers and KLCC, *Fraser Place* offers stylish, excellent-value rooms between the ninth and thirtieth floors of a retail and office complex. All rooms feature floor-to-ceiling windows boasting wonderful city views, and facilities include a well-equipped gym and eighteenth-floor infinity swimming pool. 🛜 RM405

Invito Hotel Suites 1 Lorong Ceylon, Bukit Ceylon ☏ 02 2386 9288, ⓦ invitohotelsuites.com.my; map p.76. The elegantly furnished family rooms and studio suites feature modern designs and the higher floors boast terrific city views from the floor-to-ceiling windows. All rooms are equipped with kitchenettes, and there's a particularly inviting pool, well-equipped gym and comfy TV lounge, too. 🛜 RM420

Mandarin Oriental Kuala Lumpur City Centre (KLCC) ☏ 03 2380 8888, ⓦ mandarinoriental.com; map p.76. Enormous hotel – it only looks small by virtue of being conveniently next to the Twin Towers – that's as sumptuous as they come, with its own luxury spa, swimming pools, tennis courts and tiptop restaurants. Rooms are spacious and feature lovely KLCC Park or Petronas Tower views. 🛜 RM630

Marriott 183 Jalan Bukit Bintang ☏ 03 2715 9000, ⓦ marriott.com; map p.76. In the heart of Bukit Bintang and with direct access to chic Starhill Gallery from the lobby, this branch offers well-appointed rooms with modern amenities, a huge pool, spa facilities and well-equipped gym. 🛜 RM645

Hotel Maya 138 Jalan Ampang ☏ 03 2711 8866, ⓦ hotelmaya.com.my; map p.76. This stylish boutique hotel is sandwiched between two office blocks in the heart of KL's commercial district; the contemporary rooms with wooden floorboards feature modern amenities and floor-to-ceiling glass panels overlooking the city. There's an inviting hydrotherapy pool with massage jets, a welcome treat after a long day in the hustle and bustle of the capital, along with a gym and access to yoga classes. 🛜 RM371

★**The Mesui Hotel** 9 Jalan Mesui ☏ 03 2144 8188, ⓦ themesuihotel.com; map p.76. Located in a unique building with a design that reflects the 1970s – porthole windows and retro furnishings – this contemporary hotel offers tasteful rooms decorated with fun wall designs; "loft" rooms (RM146) are substantially larger than those in the entry-level "lush" category, but all are inviting and spick-and-span. 🛜 RM138

Metro Hotel 208 Jalan Pudu ☏ 03 2143 7001, ⓦ metrohotel.com.my; map p.76. This budget business hotel offers clean, carpeted rooms with crisp linen, just a few steps from Imbi monorail station and Berjaya Times Square. Breakfast is an extra RM20. 🛜 RM150

Myhotel 120 Jalan Pudu ☏ 03 2143 5000, ⓦ myhotels .com.my; map p.76. Budget business hotel, offering the usual value-conscious, low-frills rooms: trim modern furnishings, en-suite bathrooms and a/c, with little space for anything else. RM20 extra gets you a window. 🛜 RM130

Renaissance Junction of Jalan Sultan Ismail and Jalan Ampang ☏ 03 2162 2233, ⓦ marriott.com; map p.76. Part of the Marriott group, this sumptuous hotel overlooking the Petronas Towers features two wings with well-appointed rooms, an Olympic-sized swimming pool, spa and fitness centre, along with a number of dining outlets. 🛜 RM680

Swiss Garden 117 Jalan Pudu ☏ 03 2141 3333, ⓦ swissgarden.com; map p.76. This substantial modern hotel, which also features good-value serviced apartments (RM330), is conveniently located at the edge of Bukit Bintang and halfway to Chinatown. Facilities include satellite TV, a couple of restaurants plus a pool, gym and spa. 🛜 RM290

Traders Hotel Kuala Lumpur City Centre (KLCC) ☏ 03 2332 9888, ⓦ tradershotels.com; map p.76. This great four-star hotel offers direct access to Suria KLCC mall – hotel buggies shuttle customers across the park to the

1

mall. The well-appointed rooms feature modern amenities, and some have exceptional views of the Petronas Towers. The real draw is the hotel's *Sky Bar*, on the 33rd floor, which is one of the city's most popular bars with 360-degree views of the capital. The hotel has four food outlets, including a steakhouse. ☞ RM460

★**Villa Samadhi** 218 Jalan Ampang ☎03 2143 2300, ⓦvillasamadhi.com.my; map p.76. This luxurious villa has been converted into a sumptuous boutique hotel. The rooms, decorated with Asian furnishings, brim with individual character – the Sarang rooms feature their own private plunge pools, while the cosy Loft room, with its slanted ceiling, has its own shallow lap pool. Lower-ground floor rooms have direct access to the lagoon pool from their private balconies. ☞ RM900

The Yard Boutique Hotel Lot 623, 51d Jalan Tengkat Tong Shin ☎03 2110 2449, ⓦtheyard.com .my; map p.76. Calling this place a boutique hotel may be a bit of an overstatement – it's more of a very pleasant guesthouse, offering comfortable modern rooms set around a courtyard dripping with greenery and dotted with lanterns. The location, tucked away off Jalan Tengkat Tong Shin in the heart of Bukit Bintang, is a definite plus. ☞ RM180

HOSTELS AND GUESTHOUSES

Classic Inn 36 Jalan 1/77a, Changkat Thambi Dollah ☎03 2148 8648, ⓦclassicinn.com.my; map p.76. Don't be put off by the anonymous backstreet location, nor the word "inn"; this pleasant guesthouse with wooden corridors and little piles of decorative pebbles has modern en-suite rooms with a/c and TV, and there's a peaceful café area with rustic wooden stools. A sister building a few doors down offers backpacker accommodation with travellers' notes plastered over the walls; the dorms are probably the tiniest you will ever come across. ☞ Dorms RM50, doubles RM135

Dorms KL 5 Tengkat Tong Shin ☎03 2110 1221; map p.76. Modern backpacker place with funky interior mural, smart black and white decor and a buzzing communal space. It has an amazing location in between Jalan Alor and Bukit Bintang; the friendly and knowledgeable owners are also in charge of the neighbouring *TG's Nasi Kandar* restaurant and do food promotions. Dorms with bunk beds only. ☞ RM35

★**Orange Pekoe Guesthouse** 1-1 Jalan Angsoka, off Jalan Nagasari ☎03 2110 2000, ⓦorangepekoe.com .my; map p.76. This cosy guesthouse, on a quiet road just a couple of streets back from Changkat's throng of activity, has clean and cosy rooms with wicker baskets as bedside tables. There are splashes of greenery throughout, and a communal area with cable TV and DVDs. ☞ RM105

Rainforest Bed & Breakfast 27 Jalan Mesui ☎03 2145 3525, ⓦrainforestbnbhotel.com; map p.76. A welcoming place that creates a jungle lodge ambience with plenty of greenery complemented by tasteful wooden furniture. The clean and tidy rooms are all en suite, with TVs, and there are a couple of small dorms sleeping three. Really, it's more of a boutique hostel than a B&B, though breakfast is indeed included. ☞ Dorms RM35, doubles RM109

Sahabat Guesthouse 39 & 41 Jalan Sahabat, off Tengkat Tong Shin ☎03 2142 0689, ⓦsahabatguesthouse.com; map p.76. The fourteen rooms at this bright blue guesthouse, just a few steps away from Changkat's numerous bars, are named after spices. Each room is individually decorated with colourful wallpaper (stripes or rectangles) and has en-suite facilities. There's a little communal area where guests can socialize, and staff are always happy to help with suggestions on the area. ☞ RM109

Travellers Palm Lodge 10 Jalan Rembia ☎03 2145 4745, ⓦtravellerspalm-kl.com; map p.76. This gorgeous little guesthouse with seven rooms is located down a lane off Tengkat Tong Shin and fronted by two travellers' palms in the tiny front garden. The colour-coded rooms are on the smallish side, although they are secure – only guests have a front gate key. The smiley owner makes guests feel right at home. ☞ Dorms RM35, doubles RM90

Tropical Guesthouse KL 2 Tengkat Tong Shin ☎03 2141 1168, ⓦtropicalguesthousekl.blogspot.my; map p.76. A pleasant choice with leafy bamboo and pebble walkways leading to a myriad of cosy little rooms that are kept clean and tidy. Couples can opt for the two larger rooms that are interestingly named "sexy room" and "horny room" (RM120). ☞ RM80

SERVICED APARTMENTS

Fahrenheit Suites Fifth floor, Fahrenheit 88 Mall, 179 Jalan Bukit Bintang ☎03 2148 2686, ⓦfahrenheitsuites. com; map p.76. Modern serviced apartments, including some sleeping up to six, with their own pleasant lounge, kitchenette, plus use of swimming pool. Parking available. Occasional excellent online rates. ☞ RM360

Pacific Regency Hotel Suites KH Tower, Jalan Punchak, off Jalan P. Ramlee ☎03 2332 7777, ⓦpacific-regency.com; map p.76. Luxury apartments with kitchenettes, huge bathrooms, satellite TVs and, on the roof, a swimming pool and the excellent *Luna* bar (see p.99). Ample parking too. Check the website for promotional rates. ☞ RM400

Seri Bukit Ceylon 8 Lorong Ceylon ☎03 2055 8887, ⓦhotelabest-kl.com map p.76. Popular with executive types, these immaculate studio, one-, two and three-bed apartments in a well-located tower block are equipped with swish furnishings and satellite TV/DVD systems. Facilities include a rooftop pool and sauna, along with a gym, shop and restaurant. ☞ RM345

BRICKFIELDS AND KL SENTRAL

Hilton 3 Jalan Stesen Sentral ☎03 2264 2264, ⓦkuala-lumpur.hilton.com; map p.81. Overlooking the National Museum and just a few steps from KL Sentral, this stylish hotel with a lavish lobby offers rooms as modern and comfortable as you'd expect from this reputable international chain. Facilities include ten dining outlets; the trendy *Zeta Bar* hosts international live bands and resident DJs. ⓦ RM470

Le Meridien 2 Jalan Stesen Sentral ☎03 2263 7888, ⓦlemeridienkualalumpur.com; map p.81. This 35-storey business hotel houses contemporary rooms; most of them boast panoramic views. Facilities include a freeform outdoor swimming pool with deckchairs partly immersed in water, a gym, spa and a handful of restaurants serving international cuisine. ⓦ RM850

YMCA 95 Jalan Padang Belia ☎03 2274 1439, ⓦymcakl.com; map p.81. This institutional place has been here since 1931, though rooms have been recently upgraded and there are plenty of facilities including a café, laundry and even tennis courts (you'll need your own gear, though). Rates include breakfast. ⓦ RM99

FURTHER OUT

Carcosa Seri Negara Taman Tasik Perdana ☎03 2295 0888, ⓦshr.my; map p.68. Set in sixteen hectares of well-manicured grounds just west of the Lake Gardens, these two elegant, whitewashed colonial mansions, containing thirteen suites between them, date to 1904 – the management can truthfully boast "Queen Elizabeth slept here". If a night here is out of the question, consider donning smart-casual clothes and dropping in for their English cream tea (daily 3–6pm; RM80). ⓦ RM800

Grid 9 Hotel 9 Jalan Maharajalela ☎03 9226 2629, ⓦgrid9hotels.com; map p.68. This excellent flashpacker hostel has a young and funky feel, with a welcoming lounge area dotted with colourful beanbags, communal computers, a pool table and flat-screen TV. The modern dorm rooms have reading lamps and individual sockets, while private doubles have a/c, TV and en-suite facilities. Guests enjoy complimentary access to *Zouk* club (see p.99). ⓦ Dorms RM45, doubles RM135

EATING

Without doubt, a highlight of any visit to KL is the city's **food**. There are more opportunities to enjoy high-calibre cooking here, in assorted local and international styles, than anywhere else in the country, and whether you dine in a chic bistro-style restaurant or at a humble roadside stall, prices are almost always very reasonable. Despite plenty of scope for cosmopolitan, upmarket dining, eating for many locals is still fundamentally about Malay, Chinese and Indian **street food**. Stalls, whether on the street or collected into **food courts** (found in or close to major office blocks and shopping malls), are your best bets for inexpensive, satisfying meals, as are *kedai kopis*, though these are a little scarce in the Golden Triangle. The best-known food stalls are held in the same kind of reverence as a top-flight restaurant might be in a Western city, and people will travel across KL just to seek out a stall whose take on a particular dish is said to be better than anyone else's; if you find customers lining up to partake of some stall's spring rolls or *laksa*, it's a sure-fire indicator of quality. Ranging from small affairs in beautifully refurbished shophouses to banqueting halls in five-star hotels, KL's **restaurants** are an equally vital part of the food experience. Be aware, however, that price and decor are not a watertight indicator of consistency or quality, and that service can be unhurried, even in big hotels.

CHINATOWN AND AROUND

Superb food stalls in Chinatown serve up everything from rich yet subtle *bak kut teh* (pork-rib consommé) to cooling sweet treats like *cendol*. Foreign visitors can find it hard to get to grips with the smaller stalls, especially as some are signed only in Chinese or not at all. Still, for an excellent taster of how they operate, and of street food in general, try the *Tang City Food Court*. Otherwise, the area has plenty of *kedai kopis* and a few cheap or mid-priced restaurants, with some touristy places at the eastern end of Jalan Hang Lekir. You're not limited to Chinese food; the fringes of Chinatown, especially north of Jalan Hang Lekir and around the Central Market, feature plenty of restuarants and *mamaks*.

Bbun Lot 265 Jalan Hang Lekir ☎016 666 8704; map p.70. This stall stands out, with its sparkling shelves and neatly arrayed freshly baked buns and roti (RM3) that come in five types: stuffed with chocolate, coffee, chocolate lava, blueberry and durian – the perfect snack as you explore

Chinatown. They have home-made sorbet ice cream too, including mango and soursop (RM6.90). Daily 10am–10pm.

Central Market Food Court Jalan Hang Kasturi ☎016 555 9839, ⓦcentralmarket.com.my; map p.70. The Central Market has plenty of excellent outlets specializing in food from different corners of the Peninsula and beyond, from traditional Nyonya food (RM10) to Japanese crepes (RM8). Daily 10am–9.30pm.

Contango Hotel Majestic, Jalan Sultan Hishamuddin ☎03 2785 8000, ⓦmajestickl.com; map p.68. Within the *Majestic Hotel*, this contemporary restaurant features a lively open kitchen with an incredible selection of cuisines on offer: Indian, Chinese, Japanese and Western, including Italian and grilled dishes. The buffet (breakfast RM68; lunch RM95 weekdays, RM105 weekends; dinner RM115 weekdays, RM125 weekends) includes a delectable selection of desserts, and can feature a free flow of wine (just add RM60). Daily 6.30am–11am, noon–3pm & 6.30–10.30pm.

1

KUALA LUMPUR'S TOP RESTAURANTS AND CAFÉS

Best for curries *Nagasari Curry House* (see p.96)

Best for dumplings *Din Tai Fung* (see p.95)

Best for colonial atmosphere *Old China Café* (see below)

Best for luxury *Cantaloupe* (see p.95)

Best for coffee *Feeka* (see p.95)

Best for brunch *Acme Bar & Coffee* (see below)

Lai Foong 138 Jalan Tun H.S. Lee ☎ 03 2072 8123; map p.70. The six stalls at this historic *kopitiam* rustle up all manner of local delicacies including noodle and rice dishes – try the Hainanese beef noodle (RM8), flavoured with herbs and served with not only beef slices but also tripe. Daily 6.30am–9pm.

Lokl Coffee Co. 30 Jalan Tun H.S. Lee ☎ 03 2072 1188, ⓦ loklcoffee.com; map p.70. Small and welcoming café, under the same management as the *Back Home* hostel, which is a great spot for a mid-morning snack or light lunch (set lunch of soup and main RM27) as you explore Chinatown and Little India. The interior is cosy with wooden tables and bare brick walls, and the menu offers a selection of pastries as well as Western dishes including burgers (RM21). Daily 8am–6pm.

Lucy in the Sky 167 Jalan Tun H.S. Lee ☎ 03 2022 1526, ⓦ facebook.com/lucyintheskykl; map p.70. Located in a former warehouse, this café has pleasant staff and a minimalist interior, featuring bare brick walls and spotlights, and offers Western dishes including pastas (RM16), burgers (RM20) and all-day breakfasts such as French toast (RM20). Tues–Sun 8am–6pm.

Nam Heong 56 Jalan Sultan ☎ 03 2078 5879; map p.70. Original Hainanese chicken rice is rustled up in front of your very eyes as you enter this popular, spick-and-span restaurant, which attracts those in the know in Chinatown. A meal (the recipe of which won't have changed much in thirty years) will set you back about RM10. Daily 10am–3pm.

★ **Old China Café** 11 Jalan Balai Polis ☎ 03 2072 5915, ⓦ oldchina.com.my; map p.70. Wonderfully atmospheric café set in a pre-World War I shophouse with old-world charm; much of the decor, including the saloon-style swing doors at the entrance, is original and lovingly preserved. Must-trys include the classic Peranakan dish *pie tee* (RM8), rice flour cones stuffed with minced chicken and vegetables, and *ikan asam* (RM21), mackerel cooked in tamarind. Daily 11.30am–11pm.

Penjaja Gallery Jalan Tun H.S. Lee & Jalan Petaling; map p.70. It's worth heading into the alleyway that connects Jalan Petaling with Jalan Tun H.S. Lee to get a feel for life in Chinatown – vendors here display all manner of meats, vegetables and other foods, and there are a handful of great stalls where you can sample local dishes such as curry *laksa* (RM4) as a morning snack. Tues–Sun 7am–2pm.

Purple Cane Tea House Third floor, 6 Jalan Panggong ☎ 03 2072 1349; map p.70. This calm and peaceful retreat from Chinatown's hubbub serves a range of speciality Chinese teas. Customers are invited to remove their shoes before taking a seat at wooden benches or on cushions at low tables. Teas are ceremoniously served (RM5–20 depending on tea type), and the menu even features simmered black tea giant drumstick rice (RM12) as well as tea eggs (RM3.50), which, as the name suggests, have been boiled in tea. Daily 11am–7pm.

Santa 11 Jalan Tun H.S. Lee ☎ 019 269 9771; map p.70. This laidback restaurant hums with activity at lunchtime, when locals flock here for the freshly made *chapatti* (RM1.50) and *kimma mutton* (RM3), which are undoubtedly among the best in town. Mon–Fri 6.30am–6.30pm, Sat 6.30am–3pm.

Yusoof Dan Zakhir 44 Jalan Hang Kasturi ☎ 03 2026 8685; map p.70. Clean and friendly diner, offering tasty dishes including great *roti nan* with chicken tandoori (RM7), fish head curry (RM15) and *nasi biriyani* (RM9). Portions are generous and, inside, the piped Islamic music doesn't intrude as much as you'd think from the street. Daily 6am–11pm.

Zuliani Corner Jalan Hang Lekir & Jalan Tun H.S. Lee ☎ 010 287 2216; map p.70. Just across the road from Popular Bookshop (see p.103), this little stall churns out excellent Muslim Indian *rojak* (RM5) – fried dough fritters with potatoes, bean curd, egg and shredded cucumbers mixed with a sweet and spicy peanut sauce. Mon–Sat 9.30am–7pm.

THE GOLDEN TRIANGLE AND KAMPUNG BAHRU

Acme Bar & Coffee (ABC) Ground floor, The Troika, 19 Persiaran KLCC ☎ 03 2162 2288, ⓦ acmebarcoffee. com; map p.76. The interior of this stylish coffee house and restaurant is reminiscent of a warehouse, with floor-to-ceiling windows, low-hanging light bulbs and exposed pipe work. It's good for soups (RM25), salads (RM27), pastas (RM30) and other international favourites from salmon fillet to smoked duck breast, as well as all-day weekend brunches. There are sister restaurants in Pavilion and Bangsar. Mon–Thurs 11am–midnight, Fri 11am–1am, Sat 9.30am–1am, Sun 9.30am–midnight.

Ben's First floor, Suria KLCC mall ☎ 03 2163 1655, ⓦ thebiggroup.co; map p.76. Part of one of KL's most reputable F&B chains, this is a reliable choice serving international cuisine in a pleasant setting modelled after a Manhattan townhouse. The menu includes soups (RM16), salads (RM22), sandwiches (RM20) and pies (RM26), along with more substantial mains such as steak frites (RM65). Also has branches in Bangsar and Pavilion. Daily 10am–11pm.

Cantaloupe Level 23A, Tower B, The Troika, 19 Persiaran KLCC ☎03 2162 0886, ⓦtroikaskydining.com; map p.76. This swanky French restaurant, on the top floor of KL's swish Norman Foster building, offers fine dining and a bird's-eye view of the city. The popular Sunday lunch (RM150) is a favourite among well-heeled Malays and expats alike, with dishes changing seasonally – expect the likes of smoked duck and caramelized onion bread, roast chicken and sage anchovy butter, and soursop *jalousies*. Daily noon–2.30am & 6–10.30pm.

Din Tai Fung Level 6, Pavilion KL mall ☎03 2148 8292, ⓦdintaifung.com.my; map p.76. This superb Michelin-starred Taiwanese light-meal chain specializes in Shanghainese *xiao long bao* – little pork dumplings served in a bamboo steamer, eaten dipped in ginger vinegar. You can watch the chefs at work at the open kitchen, painstakingly cutting out and stuffing each dumpling with minced pork and shrimp (RM15.80/six pieces). Mon–Sat 10.30am–10pm, Sun 10am–10pm.

★**Feeka** 19 Jalan Mesui ☎03 2110 4599 ⓦasianagegroup.com; map p.76. Pleasant coffee house in a renovated shophouse, serving locally roasted beans and home-made pastries (RM7), as well as a smattering of light meals including omelettes (RM18) and French toast (RM17). It's a great spot to refuel for the morning after a long night out. Daily 8am–11pm.

★**Hakka** 6 Jalan Kia Peng ☎03 2143 1908; map p.76. Excellent open-air Chinese restaurant, with seating under twinkling fairy lights, serving top-notch Hakka cuisine. The seafood is particularly good, although there are plenty of other dishes on offer including vegetables and even ostrich. Mains from RM15. Daily noon–3pm & 6–11.30pm.

Lot 10 Hutong Basement, Lot 10 Mall, Jalan Bukit Bintang; map p.76. This evocative, modern take on heritage food, located in the basement of Lot 10 mall, offers a plethora of authentic Malay and Chinese meals. With over 900 dishes on offer, there's plenty of choice, from *hokkian mee* noodles to freshly made *siew bao*. A dish will set you back about RM12. Daily 10am–10pm.

Luk Yu Tea House Basement, Starhill Gallery, 181 Jalan Bukit Bintang ☎03 2782 3850, ⓦstarhillgallery.com; map p.76. Shaped like a teapot, this welcoming place is more of a restaurant than a teahouse, with excellent Hong Kong-style pork-free dim sum (RM10) and other Chinese favourites; needless to say, there are plenty of fine teas too, including silver needle jasmine and ginseng oolong. Mon–Sat noon–11pm, Sun 10am–10pm.

The Magnificent Fish & Chips Bar 28 Changkat Bukit Bintang ☎03 2142 7021; map p.76. This funky restaurant with British-inspired decor (take a look at the first floor, with Minis "crashed" into the wall) truly lives up to its name, with excellent battered fish and chips (RM22) served in newspaper wrappings – there are four types of fish to choose from, including Icelandic cod and barramundi. The menu, scribbled in chalk on blackboards, includes plenty of other British staples such as Guinness and steak pie (RM32) and full all-day English breakfasts (RM28), too. Daily 9am–3am.

Marble 8 Steakhouse 163 Jalan Binjai ☎03 2386 6030, ⓦmarble-8.com; map p.76. Exceptional upmarket steakhouse serving fine cuts of wet-aged Wagyu (RM358) and Black Angus (RM138) beef, with unparalleled views of the Twin Towers. The *Privé* lounge offers a fine collection of whiskies and cigars, and a selection of pre-or post-prandial cocktails. Mon–Fri & Sun noon–2.30pm & 7–11pm, Sat 7–11pm.

Muar 6g Tengkat Tong Shin ☎03 2144 2072; map p.76. This great restaurant in the heart of bustling Bukit Bintang offers a chance to try specialities from Muar, a little town that is renowned for its tasty variations of Chinese and Malay dishes. The menu includes the likes of butter *kalian* (RM11), deep-fried vegetables with butter and evaporated

JALAN ALOR: KL'S OUTDOOR FOOD HAVEN

Along with numerous restaurants, the Golden Triangle also boasts one of KL's best alfresco experiences in **Jalan Alor**. The street actually has a double layer of food outlets: the open-fronted restaurants that line the street, and the food stalls arranged in front of them. The food is predominantly Chinese, with a strong seafood bias – and some of the city's tastiest Hokkien noodles, comprising egg noodles fried in lard, seasoned with dark soy sauce and garnished with prawn, pork and fishcake slices, and greens – but there are plenty of Thai and Malaysian options too, plus fresh fruit and drink vendors. It all fires up from 6pm, and the stalls stay open well into the small hours. Some menus omit prices, so fix them when ordering to avoid nasty surprises when the bill arrives. Cheaper dining options are easy to find, but the experience is worth the extra spend; dishes cost RM8–25, and you can usually order small, medium or large portions.

1

milk, and crispy fried egg (RM7). Tues–Sun 11am–3pm & 6–10pm.

★**Nagasari Curry House** 17-1 Jalan Angsoka; map p.76. This no-frills curry house buzzes with customers and dishes out some of the best curries you'll find in the city; it offers a range of tasty North and South Indian dishes including tandoori chicken (RM9), chicken tikka (RM14.50) and vegetable banana-leaf curries (RM7.50). Daily 24hr.

Neroteca Unit G-1, Seri Bukit Ceylon, 8 Lorong Ceylon ☏03 2070 0530, ⓦneroteca.com; map p.76. This stylish Italian restaurant has floor-to-ceiling shelves lined with wine bottles, and a deli counter displaying meats and cheese. There's a wide selection of cold cuts and platters of antipasti, and it's a great spot for a boozy Sunday brunch. At RM98 (RM148 with unlimited – selected – wines and Prosecco) it doesn't come cheap, but you won't be leaving hungry. Sister venue *Nerovivo*, just around the corner, is a slightly more upmarket venue with some wonderful seafood on offer. Daily 11am–3pm & 6–11.30pm.

★**Pinchos** 18 Changkat Bukit Bintang ☏03 2145 8482, ⓦpinchoskl.com; map p.76. Authentic tapas and *pinchos* (RM11–26) are served at this bustling Spanish tapas bar, which gets packed in the evenings. The atmosphere is warm and cosy, with seating at the bar or at wooden tables, and service is friendly and efficient. The dates wrapped in bacon are to die for. Tues–Sun 5pm–3am.

Sao Nam 25 Tengkat Tong Shin ☏03 2144 1225, ⓦsaonam.com.my; map p.76. This welcoming Vietnamese restaurant continues to attract plenty of custom mainly thanks to the plethora of awards it has won in the past. The dishes are still very good, with the likes of deep-fried chicken spring rolls (RM21) and house speciality mangosteen and prawn salad (RM36), all served beneath wall posters extolling the collectivist life. Tues–Fri 12.30–2.30pm & 7.30–10.30pm.

Shook! Basement, Starhill Gallery 181 Jalan Bukit Bintang ☏03 2782 3875, ⓦstarhillgallery.com; map p.76. Attracting celebrities and moneyed Malaysians and expats, this interactive restaurant with four show kitchens offers Japanese, Chinese, Italian and Western grill dishes. There's an extensive wine list (the walk-in cellar holds more than three thousand bottles), and the daily live jazz adds a nice touch to the restaurant's already appealing ambience. The crunchy snow-white dancing prawn starter (lightly wok-fried prawns coated in a hot mayonnaise and honey-glazed walnut sauce; RM58) is an absolute must. Daily 6am–11pm.

Sushi Hinata A-01, St Mary Residence, 1 Jalan Tengah ☏03 2022 1349, ⓦshin-hinata.com; map p.76. Touted as one of the capital's best Japanese restaurants, this superb place specializes in sushi and fine cuts of sashimi. Ingredients are flown in from Japan, and dishes are expertly prepared by the experienced Japanese chef at the open counter. Mon–Sat noon–3pm & 6–11pm.

TG's Nasi Kandar 3 Tengkat Tong Shin, ☏03 2110 1221, map p.76. Offers simply the best naan breads in Bukit Bintang, within walking distance of Changkat. They also do a range of delicious north Indian specialities like chicken *kadai* (RM13) and a savoury pancake *murtabak* with meat and/or cheese (RM11), plus fresh juices (RM5) and a self-service curried vegetable (from RM4) counter. Daily 24hr.

Thai Somtam Seafood 88 Changkat Bukit Bintang ☏014 637 6583; map p.76. You climb up a flight of little steps to reach this unassuming Thai place, which rustles up some pretty tasty grub, including an exceptionally spicy papaya salad (RM12) and other tasty Thai specials such as green chicken curry (RM18). Daily 11am–11.30pm.

twenty.one 20–1 Changkat Bukit Bintang ☏03 2142 0021, ⓦdrbar.asia; map p.76. This trendy place is a restaurant, bar and club all in one. The modern European cuisine has an Asian touch and is top-notch, and the meal and drink lunch deal, including creamy salmon fettucini, is a steal (RM19). Cocktails (from just RM12) are enjoyed on the modish first-floor balcony that overlooks the hustle and bustle of Changkat Bukit Bintang. Mains from RM25. Daily noon–2am.

Zenzero A-09 Ground floor, St Mary Place, 1 Jalan Tengah ☏03 2022 3883, ⓦzenzero.com.my; map p.76. Understated casual-chic interior and refined cuisine, prepared by an experienced Italian chef. The menu changes seasonally and the wine list includes an excellent selection from Italy and beyond. Express lunch such as *crochetta di carne* and a drink is a bargain at RM30, and a la carte mains start from RM48. Mon–Fri & Sun noon–2.30pm & 6–11pm, Sat 6–11pm.

LITTLE INDIA, CHOW KIT AND BEYOND

Little India is a good area for both Indian and Malay food – inexpensive Indian restaurants and sweetmeat shops are ranged along Jalan Melayu, while in nearby Lorong Tuanku Abdul Rahman's *pasar malam* are quite a few Malay food stalls and Indian *kedai kopis*, and a useful food court opposite the *Palace Hotel* stays open late. A few truly venerable *kedai kopis*, some housed in equally impressive shophouses, can be found along hectic Jalan TAR, while there are more stalls, Malay and even Indonesian, around Chow Kit Market.

★**Capital Café** 213 Jalan TAR ☏03 2698 2884; map p.73. Locals flock to this endearing and enduring family-run *kedai kopis*, which first opened its doors in 1956 for morning *nasi lemak* (RM4) or toast with *kaya* (coconut jam) or honey (RM2.50); plenty of other dishes are offered at lunch, including beef *rendang* (RM5) and fried noodles (RM4), while the sizzling satay, said to be one of the best in town (ten sticks RM10) is available from 5pm. Mon–Fri 7am–8pm, Sat 10am–8pm.

Jai Hind 13 Jalan Melayu ☎03 2692 0041; map p.73. Friendly *kedai kopis* which, besides an impressively wide-ranging spread of curries and stir-fries, also has an extensive menu of North Indian savouries and sweets, as good as you'll get in smarter restaurants but at half the price. Around RM15–18 should be enough to see you full. Daily 8am–9pm.

Kedai Makanan Sithique 237 Jalan Tuanku Abdul Rahman; map p.73. One of a handful of popular *kedai kopis* specializing in *nasi kandar* with chicken (RM7) or fish (RM5); fluffy *roti canai* and *thosai* are made on the spot, along with pretty tasty *mee goreng* (RM4). Daily 7am–7.30pm.

Syed Bistro 57 Jalan Dang Wangi ⓦ syedbistro.com; map p.73. This laidback place proudly boasts they have "the one and only *biriyani*" and in all fairness it's pretty tasty – there's chicken (RM13), mutton (RM16) and lamb (RM25), as well as a selection of fiery curries and freshly baked *roti canai* to choose from. Daily 24hr.

BRICKFIELDS

★**Annalakshmi** Temple of Fine Arts, 116 Jalan Berhala ☎03 2272 3799, ⓦ annalakshmi.com.my; map p.81. This community-run South Indian vegetarian restaurant, with a warm and welcoming ethnic interior, offers a stupendous eat-all-you-want lunchtime buffet for RM16; in the evenings it's a la carte only, and the profits go to support various projects. There's a small, informal canteen in the car park beneath the building, where you pay what you feel the meal is worth. Smart-casual dress; no shorts, sports clothes or open shoes. Tues–Sun 11.30am–3pm & 6.30–10pm.

Gem 124 Jalan Tun Sambanthan ☎03 2260 1373; map p.81. Reliable, moderately smart restaurant serving South Indian chicken, mutton and seafood curries. The vegetarian thali costs around RM15. Conveniently close to the Monorail station. Daily 11.30am–11.30pm.

1

Saravanaa Bhavan 196 Jalan Tun Sambathan ☎ 03 2260 3755, ⓦ saravanabhavan.com; map p.81. One of a slightly eccentric Madras-based chain of vegetarian restaurants that's spread as far afield as London and New York. Concentrate on the South Indian dishes – *dosai, idli, uthapam* and so forth – and be warned that spicing can be incendiary. Inexpensive, with main courses under RM12. Daily 7.30am–11pm.

Sri Devi 9 Jalan Travers ☎ 03 2260 1553; map p.81. Widely reckoned to sell some of Brickfields' best Indian food, this little place does excellent banana-leaf curries from noon onwards and wonderful *dosai* (RM6) all day. Daily 7am–11pm.

BANGSAR BARU

The small grid of streets known as Bangsar Baru, 5km southwest of Chinatown, is one of several satellite suburbs known for smart restaurants and bars, as well as a very upcoming speakeasy culture. Bus #822 travels to Bangsar from the Sultan Mohamed terminal in Chinatown, via KL Sentral. Bangsar LRT station isn't convenient for Bangsar Baru, as it's some way downhill with busy highways to cross in between. A taxi from Chinatown shouldn't cost more than RM10.

Alexis Bistro 29 Jalan Telawi 3 ☎ 03 2284 2880, ⓦ alexis.com.my; map p.97. This sleek café, bistro and wine-bar is worth visiting for its delectable cakes alone (RM15), although the menu includes Asian and Western dishes, along with hearty breakfasts (RM32); it's popular among expats and well-heeled Malaysians, especially for live music. Daily 9am–2am.

La Bodega 16 Jalan Telawi 2 ☎ 03 2287 8318, ⓦ bodega.com.my; map p.97. This well-liked tapas chain attracts a loyal expat following for its tapas (from RM14), paella (RM35) and wine buffets (RM120); this branch is augmented by a lounge and deli that serves imported Spanish produce. Daily 10am–2am.

Mercat 51g Jalan Telawi 3 ☎ 03 2201 5288, ⓦ mercat .my; map p.97. Catalan gastro-bar with walls embellished with sketches of Barcelona's landmarks. Exceptional tapas include *patatas bravas* (creamy potato nuggets; RM22) and Catalan *fuet* (succulent pork salami; RM19), as well as more substantial mains including Iberico meatballs of minced pork and beef served with cuttlefish and peas (RM39). Tues–Fri 4–11pm, Sat & Sun 11am–11pm.

Rendez-vous 100 Lorong Maarof ☎ 03 2202 0206; map p.97. Another expat favourite, this restaurant serves authentic French food at very reasonable prices. The regularly changing menu includes the classics with an emphasis on seafood, such as a platter of oysters, langoustine, whelks, prawns, cockles, clams and winkles (around RM120). Tues–Sun noon–3pm & 6pm–1am.

Sri Nirwana Maju 43 Jalan Telawi 3 ☎ 03 2287 8445; map p.97. This hugely popular banana-leaf curry house with canteen decor stands out in the swanky Telawi area of Bangsar, and attracts crowds for its excellent dishes such as mutton *varuval* and fried squid (around RM9). Be prepared to queue. Daily 10am–2am.

WTF 98 Lorong Maarof ☎ 019 261 7070, ⓦ wtfrestaurants .com.my; map p.97. It actually stands for What Tasty Food, and so it is – this place serves excellent Indian vegetarian dishes, although there are also other cuisines to choose from including Chinese, Mexican and Italian. Mon–Thurs 11.30am–10pm, Fri–Sun 11.30am–11pm.

Yeast 24g Jalan Telawi 2 ☎ 03 2282 0118, ⓦ yeastbistronomy.com; map p.97. A boulangerie, bistro and bar all in one, this is a great spot for a morning coffee and croissant (RM4.50), home-made granola (RM16) or for more substantial dinners. The experienced French chef rustles up exceptional dishes including *boeuf bourguignon* (RM78) and steak tartare (RM55). Mon–Thurs & Sun 8am–10pm, Fri & Sat 8am–10.30pm.

DRINKING

KL's most fashionable **bars** and clubs are concentrated in the Golden Triangle, while Bangsar (see p.100) also plays host to a few slick bars. Only during Ramadan are both the bars (and clubs) distinctly quiet. Beer in KL costs around RM22 a pint (when available on draught; bottles and cans are more common), a couple of ringgit less during the **happy hours** that most places offer. Note that it's common for a sixteen-percent tax to be added to alcohol, so be prepared for a larger bill than you first thought.

CHINATOWN AND AROUND

Reggae Bar 158 Jalan Tun H.S. Lee, Chinatown ☎ 03 2041 8163; map p.70. No-frills bar that's very popular with backpackers, though a few locals drop by too. The walls are plastered with Bob Marley memorabilia, though the DJs do recognize that other reggae artists are available. Daily noon–2am.

Rooftop Mansion 53 Jalan Tun H.S. Lee, Chinatown ☎ 03 2072 6878; map p.70. Rooftop bar and chillout space with pool table on top of the *Reggae Mansion* hostel. As such

it's very popular with backpackers and expats; the cocktails are vicious and thus very popular. Daily noon–2am.

LITTLE INDIA, CHOW KIT AND BEYOND

Coliseum Café 98–100 & 102 Jalan TAR ☎ 03 2692 6270, ⓦ coliseum1921.com; map p.73. Endearingly antiquated – or creakingly ancient – the bar here has a rich history (it was established in 1921) and a relaxed atmosphere; some of the furnishings date back to the 1920s, although the original tables and stools didn't make it to the present day. Sip a Gunner A (the bar's signature cocktail of ginger beer, ginger ale and angostura bitters; RM10.50) and imagine the planters and colonial administrators of yesteryear who once gathered here to quench their thirst. Daily 10am–10pm.

THE GOLDEN TRIANGLE AND KAMPUNG BAHRU

Fuego Level 23A, Tower B, the Troika, 19 Persiaran KLCC ☎ 03 2162 0886, ☎ troikaskydining.com; map p.76. As you'd expect from a 23rd-floor location, this tapas bar with open-air seating boasts stunning views of the cityscape; it's a great spot for a sundowner as you watch the sun set over the Twin Towers – the views don't get much better than this. Daily 6.30pm–1am.

The Green Man 40 Changkat Bukit Bintang ☎ 03 2141 9924, ☎ greenman.com.my; map p.76. This small, likeable venue serves good traditional pub grub, including pork pies and bangers and mash, washed down with a refreshing pint (RM25) or jug (RM50) of lager. It gets particularly busy when there's football or rugby on TV. Daily 1pm–2am.

Healy Mac's 38 Changkat Bukit Bintang ☎ 03 2144 5778, ☎ healymacs.com; map p.76. Quintessential Irish pub in the middle of Changkat with good Guinness and cocktails (RM25). The quiz on Monday nights is usually a raucous and entertaining affair that's popular with Westerners and locals alike, and all major sports matches are shown on the multiple TV screens. It has sister branches on Jalan P Ramlee, Mont Kiara and beyond. Daily 1pm–3am.

Heli Lounge Level 34, Menara KH, 1 Jalan Sultan Ismail ☎ 03 2110 5034; map p.76. Hidden gem turned talk of the town, this aeronautics-themed venue features an active helipad that becomes a sprawling rooftop bar in the evenings and is perhaps the best place to watch the sunset over KL. Expect good cocktails (from RM25) and happy hour promotions, but be prepared to queue if you stay beyond 9pm. Daily 6pm–10pm.

Hubba Hubba Ground floor, Invito Hotel Suites, 1 Lorong Ceylon ☎ 017 786 7611; map p.76. This large restaurant and bar, with high ceilings and a warehouse-style feel, offers great Western and Asian dishes including Japanese, Malay and Indian, plus early breakfasts and day-long happy hours, and rustles up some great cocktails (RM25). On Thurs, Fri and Sat nights at 10pm DJs spin house, commercial and R&B tracks. Mon–Wed & Sun 6am–1am, Thurs–Sat 6am–3am.

Luna Bar Level 34, Pacific Regency Hotel Suites, KH Tower, Jalan Punchak, off Jalan P. Ramlee ☎ 03 2332 7777, ☎ luna.my; map p.76. This gorgeous rooftop poolside venue plays loungey sounds, affords breathtaking views of KL's skyline and serves cocktails from RM22. On the same floor is *Cristallo di Luna*, a sparkling restaurant with Italian influence and tasty mains such as confit chicken

KUALA LUMPUR'S BEST PLACES TO DRINK

Best for views *Heli Lounge* (see below)
Best bar with rooftop pool *Luna Bar* (see below)
Best hotel bar *Sky Bar* (see below)
Best for high-class opulence *Marini's* (see below)
Best Irish pub *Healy Mac's* (see below)
Best for international live music *Alexis Bistro* (see p.101)
Best for jazz *No Black Tie* (see p.101)
Best for old-school tunes *Havana* (see p.101)
Best for craft beer *Taps* (see below)
Best for whisky and cigars *The Roof* (see p.101)
Best club *Zouk* (see p.101)

(RM47). Mon–Thurs & Sun 10am–1am, Fri & Sat 10am–3am.

Marini's on 57 Seventh floor, Petronas Tower 3 ☎ 03 2161 2880, ☎ marinis57.com; map p.76. As you'd expect, the capital's highest rooftop bar boasts spectacular views of the city and close-ups of the Petronas Towers. Here, too, award-winning mixologists shake up classic and signature cocktails such as the White Dame (RM38), with bourbon, cointreau, grapefruit juice, lemon, honey and egg white. Smart attire (trousers for gents) only, or you will be refused entry. Mon–Thurs & Sun 5pm–1.30am, Fri & Sat 5pm–3am.

Pisco Bar 29 Jalan Mesui ☎ 03 2142 2900, ☎ piscobarkl.com; map p.76. A range of excellent Peruvian/Spanish tapas (RM24) are to be had at this trendy nightlife spot, where pisco sours (RM28) are the drink of choice. Walls are adorned with blown-up photographs of pop icons and other celebs, while upturned buckets serve as bar lamps. Tues–Sun 5pm–1am, Fri & Sat 5pm–3am.

Sky Bar Level 33, Traders Hotel, KLCC ☎ 03 2332 9888, ☎ shangri-la.com; map p.76. One of the capital's most renowned bars offers the chance to sip cocktails (RM35) at the poolside while taking in exceptional views of the city from the 33rd floor. The bar hosts themed events nights (check the website) and guest DJs on Saturday nights spin an eclectic mix, from EDM to R&B. Mon–Thurs & Sun 10am–1am, Fri & Sat 10am–3am.

Taps A-0-3 One Residency, 1 Jalan Nagasari ☎ 03 2110 1560, ☎ tapsbeerbar.my; map p.76. The best, if not only, place to enjoy craft beer in Kuala Lumpur. There's a regularly rotating selection of beers from Belgium, the UK, France and beyond – the staff claim to have served the best part of 1000 unique beers since opening. Live music on Thursday to Saturday, often the talented house band playing classic rock,

1

KL'S SPEAKEASY CULTURE

In many ways surprisingly relevant for a still conservative Muslim country, the recent rapid rise of **speakeasy bars** in Greater KL has caught the attention of well-off Chinese locals and Western visitors, and has attracted superstar bartenders from Japan, Hong Kong and Europe to Malaysia.

Some of the first venues were concentrated around the still derelict (from the outside) shophouses in the south end of **Chinatown**, where swanky surroundings and plush furnishing lurk behind worn walls and dark windows. Increasingly, posh upmarket suburbs such as **Damansara** and **Mont Kiara** are stashing away trendy venues behind bookcases in stairwells or above newsagents. By their very nature, speakeasy bars may not be around for more than a season, but the ones below have, so far, lasted at least a year and show no signs of closing.

Omakase + Appreciate Jalan Ampang, Bukit Bintang. Behind an inconspicuous ventilation cupboard door in the basement of the Bangunan Ming Annexe building near Masjid Jamek, this intimate space has a regularly changing cocktail menu, designed by founders Shawn and Karl. If you can't decide what to order, let the knowledgeable staff know and they'll invent a cocktail just for you. Tues–Sat 8pm–2am.
PS150 150 Jalan Petaling, Chinatown ☎03 2022 2888. Hidden down a dark back alley not too far from Petaling Street, this bar's setting is as dark as the building's history – it's a former brothel. Drinks

designed by Angel Ng, who is well known in the industry, include the Pandan Flip (RM38) with rum and coconut and Red Poison Princess (RM90 for two) with absinthe, tequila and mezcal. Tues–Sat 8pm–2am.
Tate Intermark Mall, 348 Jalan Tun Razak ☎03 216 2367. Operated by the same chain as *Ben's* and one of the first speakeasies in the city, this darkly lit gentleman's club-inspired space has a pool table, cigar selection and innovative cocktails by the barrel-load. Walk towards the back of the ground floor of the Intermark building and look for a plain white wall on the left with a black diagonal line – push the wall and *voilà*! Tues–Sat 8pm–1am.

and surprisingly good food including Beer Bites (from RM15). Mon–Sat 5pm–1am, Sun 12pm–1am.

BANGSAR
Mantra Bangsar Village 2, 2 Jalan Telawi 1 ☎03 7344 8299, ⓦmantrabarkl.com; map p.97. On the rooftop of a shopping centre, this venue is where young expats and Chinese Malaysians go to see and be seen. The music ranges from house to heavier dance later in the evening,

and there's a huge balcony space, which looks back towards Bukit Bintang, plus innovative cocktails (RM35) and whiskey. Mon–Sat 5pm–1am.
Ronnie Q's 32 Jalan Telawi 2 ☎03 2282 0722; map p.97. The focus at this watering hole, with its four TVs and a projector, is very much on sport – not just soccer but also cricket and rugby. Offers plenty of drinks including Guinness (RM28/pint) and Tiger beer (RM22/pint). Mon–Thurs 4pm–1am, Fri–Sun noon–1am.

NIGHTLIFE

If the drinking scene seems to tick over healthily enough, KL's **clubbing** scene appears surprisingly buoyant for its size (although as with the bars, things are quiet during Ramadan). KL's clubland largely focuses around the junction of Jalan Tuz Razak – home of newly renovated superclub *Zouk* and the purpose-built entertainment hub TREC (see p.101) – and Jalan P. Ramlee in the Golden Triangle, although venues are also springing up around Asian Heritage Row on Jalan Doraisamy, near Medan Tuanku Monorail station. The music policy at each venue tends to change with alarming frequency, but as a rule weekends feature more serious dance sounds, while weekdays offer retro hits and fairly accessible R&B. To keep up with the latest news, including which big-name DJs might be in town, check out the Friday **club listings** in the *Star* newspaper, *Juice* magazine (ⓦjuiceonline.com) or the clubs' own websites. The usual cover charge of around RM40–70 rises if well-known DJs are playing. Unfortunately, **live music** in KL is much less happening than in Singapore, partly because of Malaysia's old reputation as a centre for music piracy, which has caused many international bands to choose not to play here in the past. Religious conservatives have also protested when the likes of Avril Lavigne, Selena Gomez and Gwen Stefani have performed. Consequently, most concerts tend to involve safe big-name pop, soul or country artists, plus occasional indie bands. That said, KL has a few small venues where local English-language singer-songwriters and bands get to strut their stuff, and shows by Malay pop stars and old-school rockers are occasionally publicized in the press.

CLUBS
Beach Club 924 Jalan P. Ramlee, Golden Triangle ☎03 2170 6666, ⓦbeachclubcafe.com; map p.76. Established

venue with a somewhat clichéd thatched-tropical-hut theme, with towering coconut trees and an aquarium full of baby sharks. The mix of commercial chart and house sounds does pull in the punters most nights of the week, although it is something of a meat market. Daily noon–3am.

Blue Boy 50 Jalan Sultan Ismail, on a small lane off the main street, Golden Triangle ☎014 661 6447; map p.76. Kuala Lumpur's chief gay venue is a bit of a dive but still attracts a large local and foreign crowd to its bar and dance area – though beware the odd hustler. Daily 8pm–3am.

Havana Changkat Bukit Bintang, Golden Triangle ☎03 2142 7170, ⓦhavanakl.com; map p.76. Located just above the bustling steak-and-grill restaurant of the same name, this place has been attracting punters for over two decades. At weekends locals and expats alike hang out over beers and stomp about to old school and retro hits. There's also a lounge and rooftop terrace bar for those who want to natter away over a few drinks. Fri & Sat 10am–2am.

The Roof 1 First Ave, Bandar Utama, Petaling Jaya ☎012 691 0628, ⓦtheroof.com.my; map p.68. This large entertainment hub in Petaling Jaya to the west of the centre hosts five nightlife outlets in one, including a bar on a grassed helipad with brilliant 360-degree views, a sports bar with darts, and a whiskey and cigar lounge. The gastro-lounge has great cocktails and opens for lunch, and the late-night club (Wed–Sat 10pm–3am) hosts international DJs and live music gigs, and is often packed with KL's younger party crowd. Daily 1pm–1am.

Zion 31 Changkat Bukit Bintang ☎012 209 7300, ⓦfacebook.com/ZionClubKL; map p.76. The closest you will get to a late-night club in Bukit Bintang without

venturing out to entertainment hub TREC (see box, p.000). Expect pumping house sounds, with regular focus on afrobeat DJs, and a dressed-to-the-nines clientele. Daily 6pm–5am.

Zouk 113 Jalan Ampang ☎03 2171 1997, ⓦzoukclub .com.my; map p.76. This offshoot of one of Singapore's top clubs has become a mainstay of the KL scene and recently relocated to a swanky new venue in TREC (see box, p.000). The whopping thirteen rooms here spin an eclectic range of music, including a smidgeon of indie. There's even a slide from one room to another for VIP guests to use. Cover charge is around RM60 according to the night, but is often free before 1am for tourists. Tues–Sat 10pm–7am.

LIVE MUSIC VENUES

Alexis Bistro Ampang Great Eastern Mall, 303 Jalan Ampang, Golden Triangle ☎03 4260 2288, ⓦalexis.com .my; map p.76. Under the same management as *Alexis Bistro* in Bangsar and elsewhere, this upmarket bistro and wine bar hosts excellent local and international jazz acts on Friday and Saturday nights at 10pm. Mon–Thurs 11am–midnight, Fri & Sat 11am–2am, Sun 10am–midnight.

★ **No Black Tie** 17 Jalan Mesui, Golden Triangle ☎03 2142 3737, ⓦnoblacktie.com.my; map p.76. The venue of choice for discerning music lovers, this great jazz and gastro-bar hosts regular jazz, classical blues and folk sets, as well as international poetry readings. Pricey tapas (concert dinner from RM160) and cocktails (RM32) can be enjoyed in the performance/dining area while you watch the show. Mon–Sat 7pm–1am.

ENTERTAINMENT

The modest local **performing arts** scene is split between KL and its satellite town Petaling Jaya, which, with its complex system of numbered roads that even residents don't understand, is best accessed by taxi. **Theatre** is probably the strongest suit, with concerts, musicals and so forth throughout the year, by local as well as international performers and troupes. There's also a dedicated community of people working in the visual arts. For **listings**, check the national press and *Time Out* (ⓦtimeout.com/kuala-lumpur). Kakiseni (ⓦkakiseni.com) is also worth consulting, not only for listings but also for an intelligent look at how the performing arts can find a balance with the Asian and Muslim values that hold sway in Malaysia.

THEATRE AND CLASSICAL MUSIC

Aside from the Actors Studio (see p.102), other drama companies worth making time for include the Five Arts Centre (ⓦfiveartscentre.org) and the satirical Instant Café (ⓦinstantcafetheatre.com). There are two

home-grown orchestras, namely the Malaysian Philharmonic Orchestra (ⓦmpo.com.my) and the Dama Orchestra (ⓦdamaorchestra.com), the latter specializing in Chinese classical music and musicals. Keep an eye on the press for news of international recitals. Besides the

TREC – MALAYSIA'S ENTERTAINMENT HUB

As part of a KL's Tourism Master Plan 2015–2025, entertainment district **TREC** was opened up in August 2015 with the relaunch of clubbing institution *Zouk*. The space became the first entertainment enclave in KL to be granted a **5am license** (much to the surprise of some punters). Bar chains that have already established themselves in other parts of Malaysia, including *Mango's* and *Friendscino*, have also made an appearance, and also been joined by new ventures such as *Donkey* and *Crow* pubs and *Le Noir* nightclub, with the aim of capturing the hearts and wallets of the population in the immediate vicinity.

1

venues listed here, there are occasional concerts at the KL Convention Centre and also at out-of-town resorts such as Genting Highlands.

Actors Studio ☎03 2142 2009, ⓦ theactorsstudio .com.my. The most prominent of KL's theatre companies, this studio mounts several productions each year, ranging from Malaysianized versions of foreign classics to works by local playwrights, and has been instrumental in the creation and running of one of the city's more impressive independent arts centres, KLPac (see below).

Dewan Filharmonik Level 2, Tower 2, Petronas Towers, Golden Triangle box office ☎03 2051 7007, ⓦ mpo.com.my. The home of the Malaysian Philharmonic, this venue also hosts concerts by other performers, not just in the classical domain. The box office is on the ground floor, Tower 2, and is open Tues–Sat 10.30am–6.30pm.

Istana Budaya (National Theatre) Jalan Tun Razak, east of the junction with Jalan Pahang and south of Titiwangsa Gardens, Titiwangsa ☎03 4026 5555, ⓦ istanabudaya.gov.my. Besides providing a spacious modern home for the National Theatre Company and the National Symphony Orchestra, this venue sees performances by visiting international orchestras and also stages pop concerts, plays and ballets. Just over 1km from Titiwangsa (LRT/Monorail) or Chow Kit (Monorail) stations.

KL Performing Arts Centre Jalan Strachan, off Jalan Ipoh, Sentul ☎03 4047 9000, ⓦ klpac.org. A joint project of the stalwart Actors Studio company and the construction conglomerate that's redeveloping the area, the KL Performing Arts Centre (KLPac) is housed in a former rail depot revamped to look like a Frank Lloyd Wright doodle. It hosts jazz, indie and dance events plus, of course, plays by various companies. The location couldn't be more awkward, in the depths of the old Sentul Raya Golf Club and cut off from the nearby Sentul Komuter station by the rail line, which you can't cross safely without a big detour. Getting here and back is by far easiest by taxi or Grab/Uber.

Panggung Bandaraya Sultan Abdul Samad Building, Jalan Tuanku Abdul Rahman, Colonial District ☎03 2602 3335, ⓦ dbkl.gov.my. Occasional performances of Malay drama (*bangsawan*) take place in this historic theatre with a Moorish facade.

CULTURAL SHOWS

Traditional dance can be seen at the cultural shows put on by the Malaysian Tourism Centre and by a couple of restaurant theatres, though what's on offer is inevitably touristy. Indian dance is better catered for, thanks to the Temple of Fine Arts.

Malaysia Tourism Centre (MaTiC) 109 Jalan Ampang, Golden Triangle ☎03 2164 3929, ⓦ matic.gov.my. Produces 45-minute dance shows, featuring performers from Borneo as well as the Peninsula, from Mon–Sat at 3pm (RM9).

Saloma Next to MaTiC, Jalan Ampang, Golden Triangle ☎03 2161 0122, ⓦ saloma.com.my. This place offers tiffin set lunches (RM25/person, minimum two), and an evening buffet (RM100) with a performance of traditional dance (daily 8.30–9.30pm), supposedly focusing on different states of the Federation each night. Daily 11am–10pm.

Temple of Fine Arts 116 Jalan Berhala, Brickfields ☎03 2274 3709, ⓦ tfa.org.my. Community-run cultural centre set up to preserve Tamil culture by promoting dance, theatre, folk, classical music and craft-making. Probably the best place in KL to see traditional Indian dance.

CINEMA

Coliseum Cinema Jalan TAR, Little India. As a total contrast to the main chains, this cinema is worth a trip for its 1930s Art Deco character, even if Bollywood and Chinese kung fu films aren't your thing.

Golden Screen Cinemas Third floor, Mid Valley Megamall, Mid Valley City ⓦ gsc.com.my. Cinema chain with branches also in Pavilion KL and Berjaya Times Square in Bukit Bintang; their Mid Valley Megamall screen is your best bet for occasional foreign art-house films. RM12–50.

TGV Suria KLCC mall, Golden Triangle ⓦ tgv.com.my. A conveniently located multiplex. Tickets range from RM12–50, depending on the time and film.

SHOPPING

There's no city in Malaysia where **consumerism** is as in-your-face as KL. The **malls** of the Golden Triangle are draws for youths and yuppies alike, while street markets attract everyone, offering goods of all sorts. Jalan Petaling in Chinatown (see p.71) is where you'll find fake watches and leather goods; some of these have started to creep into the **covered market** on Jalan Masjid India and the nearby Lorong Tuanku Abdul Rahman *pasar malam* (see p.73), but their mainstays remain clothes and fabrics, plus a few eccentricities such as herbal tonics. Chow Kit Market (see p.73) has some clothing bargains but little else of interest to tourists except photo opportunities. A great just-out-of-town **flea market** for knick-knacks and general bric-a-brac happens every weekend inside the Amcorp Mall in Petaling Jaya, close to Taman Jaya station on the LRT.

ANTIQUES

Antiques can be extremely expensive in Southeast Asia, and are often fake; the dealers listed below are sound but even experts can be fooled, so don't fork out unless you know what you're doing. The biggest market is for Chinese and Peranakan (Nyonya) porcelain, woodcarvings and artefacts, though there are also some Malaysian and Asian specialists in town.

Heritage of the Orient Ground floor, Central Market, Chinatown ☎03 2274 6443; map p.70. Select range of genuine antiques from Tibet, China and Central Asia, plus a few pieces from Sarawak. Pricey. Daily 10am–8pm.

House of Suzie Wong Fourth floor, Lot 10 Mall, 50 Jalan Sultan Ismail, Bukit Bintang, ☎03 2143 3220; map p.76. Interesting, eclectic range of antiques and collectibles from mainland China and Tibet, including furniture and carpets; high quality but reasonable prices. Daily 10am–10pm.

Madame Butterfly Second floor, Mid Valley Megamall, Mid Valley City ☎03 2282 8088; map p.68. Antiques and antique-style arts and crafts; best for gemstone jewellery and Nyonya porcelain. Daily 10am–10pm.

Tomlinson Collection 30 Jalan Telawi 5, Bangsar ☎03 2283 2196, ⓦtomlinson-collection.com; map p.97. One of Asia's leading antique specialists showcasing a fine selection of classic Ming style Chinese furniture in prized woods, as well as Khmer sculptures, fine porcelain, Chinese robes and textiles and terracotta Han, Tung and Ming figurines. Daily 11am–6pm.

BOOKS AND MUSIC

The larger KL bookshops are pretty impressive, divided into Chinese-, English- and Malay-language sections, and carrying a good range of publications. They tend to be strong in literature about Malaysia and the rest of Southeast Asia – everything from historical monographs and classics-in-translation, to Manga, cookbooks and coffee-table tomes on architecture and garden design. Unfortunately, as this country has long been famous for rampant piracy, the music shops are nothing to write home about.

Junk Book Store 78 Jalan T.S. Lee, Chinatown ☎03 2078 3822, ⓦjunkbookstore.com; map p.70. Ancient establishment, jammed to its dusty rafters with secondhand books, most in English, covering every conceivable topic from pulp fiction to gardening. Mon–Fri 8.30am–5pm, Sat 8.30am–5pm.

Kinokuniya Fourth floor, Suria KLCC mall, Golden Triangle ☎03 2164 8133, ⓦmalaysia.kinokuniya.com; map p.76. Huge and efficient Japanese chain, with the broadest selection of books in KL. Daily 10am–10pm.

MPH Lower ground floor, Mid Valley Megamall ☎03 2938 3818, ⓦmphonline.com; map p.68. This veteran survivor of the local book trade is resting on its laurels somewhat, though it still carries a decent mix of novels and nonfiction titles. They also have smaller outlets at Nu Sentral mall in KL Sentral and at the Bangsar Village mall. Daily 10am–10pm.

Popular Bookshop Second floor, Avenue K, KLCC ☎03 2161 2364, ⓦpopular.com.my; map p.76. Stationer-style bookshop, worth checking out for maps, paperbacks

and cookbooks before heading further afield. Daily 10am–10pm.

Rock Corner First floor, The Gardens, Mid Valley City mall ☎03 2201 4893; map p.68. Bravely independent music retailer, good for hard-to-find rock and indie CDs. Daily 10am–10pm.

Times Bookstore Sixth floor, Pavilion KL mall, Golden Triangle ☎03 2148 8813, ⓦtimesbookstores.com.my; map p.76. Large, well-organized member of the Singapore-based chain. Also sells stationery and gifts. Daily 10am–10pm.

HANDICRAFTS

KL is a good place to stock up on handicrafts, though they tend to be available a little more cheaply in the provincial areas where they originate, and some here might even have been imported from overseas. For a broad range – everything from Royal Selangor pewter models of the Petronas Towers to bright batik, tribal textiles and original paintings or sculptures – visit Chinatown's Central Market and Kompleks Kraf.

Kwong Yik Seng Crockery 144 Jalan Tun H.S. Lee, Chinatown ☎03 2078 3620; map p.70. Hand-carved wooden Chinese cake moulds, Nyonya *pie tee* moulds, intricately decorated tea sets and stacks of modern pink-and-green Nyonya porcelain (at almost antique prices, however). They'll generally bargain a little. Mon–Sat 9am–5pm.

Peter Hoe First floor, The Row KL, Jalan Doraisamy, Chow Kit ☎03 2026 0711; map p.70. Moved from its old home in the Lee Rubber Building, this well-established brand's new shop sells a range of arty-crafty soft furnishings, knick-knacks, textile bags and so forth, with a Southeast Asian flavour. There's also a pleasant café within the shop. Daily 10am–7pm.

MALLS

Locals and visitors alike come to KL's shopping malls to seek refuge from the heat as much as to shop; for local young people, the malls are also important places to socialize. Mostly located outside the old centre, particularly in the Golden Triangle, the malls divide into two categories – gargantuan affairs in the manner of Western malls, featuring international chains and designer names, and smaller, denser Southeast Asian-style complexes, basically indoor bazaars with row upon row of tiny independent retailers. The simpler malls tend to be much more popular than their more sophisticated, pricier counterparts, and can be atmospheric places to wander. Many malls house a supermarket or department store of one sort or another.

BUKIT BINTANG

Berjaya Times Square Jalan Imbi, opposite the Monorail's Imbi stop ⓦtimessquarekl.com; map p.76.

1

Enormous mall with several shops and even an indoor theme park plus entertainment attractions, though not as buzzing as it really ought to be considering its size, and living somewhat in the shadow of Pavilion KL and Suria KLCC. Daily 10am–10pm.

Lot 10 Bintang Walk ⓦlot10.com.my; map p.76. Specializes in designer clothes and accessories with many Western brands such as H&M. Daily 10am–10pm.

Low Yat Off Jalan Bukit Bintang ⓦplazalowyat.com; map p.76. The best place in KL for electronic and digital purchases, from laptops to cameras. Daily 10am–10pm.

Pavilion KL Between Jalan Bukit Bintang and Jalan Raja Chulan ⓦpavilion-kl.com; map p.76. One of the very largest malls in the city – and that's saying something – with a parade of big-name designer outlets on Jalan Bukit Bintang. There are branches of Singaporean department stores and Malaysia's own Parkson chain, present here in an especially upmarket version. There's also a *Times* bookshop, GSC cinema and a plethora of eating and nightlife outlets. Daily 10am–10pm.

Starhill Gallery Next to the Marriott, Bintang Walk ⓦstarhillgallery.com; map p.76. Expect more designer names than is healthy, orbiting a suitably grand atrium. Just as noteworthy is the maze of top-notch restaurants and bars in the basement of the building. Daily 10am–10pm.

Sungei Wang Plaza Jalan Sultan Ismail ⓦsungeiwang.com; map p.76. KL's first mall offers everything from clothes to a Giant brand supermarket to souvenirs and consumer electronics, all of which is generally keenly priced. Daily 10am–10pm.

KLCC

Avenue K 156 Jalan Ampang ⓦavenuek.com.my; map p.76. Worth a look if you're into designer outlets but a bit staid for shopping. However, there are a couple of cracking restaurants on the upper floor such as *Samba Brazilian Steakhouse*, whose balcony looks towards the Petronas Towers. Daily 10am–10pm.

Suria KLCC At the base of the Petronas Towers ⓦsuriaklcc.com.my; map p.76. A mall so large it's subdivided into sub-malls for ease of reference, Suria KLCC's oval atriums are home to UK department store Marks & Spencer, Isetan and Cold Storage supermarkets, plus numerous restaurants, the Petrosains science museum (ⓦpetrosains.com.my) and a TGV multiplex cinema. Daily 10am–10pm.

BANGSAR AND MID VALLEY CITY

Bangsar Shopping Centre 285 Jalan Maarof, Bangsar ⓦbsc.com.my; map p.97. This is an upmarket affair, and a good place to have a suit made, buy gifts or just find some food from home that you miss. Plenty of restaurants and coffee shops to boot. Daily 10am–10pm.

Bangsar Village and Village II Bangsar Baru ⓦbangsarvillage.com; map p.97. The boutiques tend to play second fiddle to the restaurants in these two malls, joined by a bridge above street level. Shopping highlights include an MPH bookshop and the Country Farm Organics (ⓦcountryfarmorganics.com) supermarket, selling organic produce and even eco-friendly detergent – the likes of which you'll hardly see on sale anywhere else in the country. Daily 10am–10pm.

Mid Valley Megamall and Gardens Mall Off Jalan Syed Putra, 2km south of Brickfields ⓦmidvalley.com .my; map p.68. The sprawling Mid Valley Megamall certainly gives Suria KLCC a run for its money; come here for the Carrefour hypermarket, the Jusco and Metrojaya department stores, the MPH bookshop, the GSC cinema and the usual plethora of family restaurants and outlets selling everything from cosmetics to computers. The newer, adjacent Gardens Mall has sprung up alongside, joined by a bridge from Level 2, home to designer labels and the Singapore-based department store Robinsons. Both malls are easy to reach, as the KTM Mid Valley Komuter station is close by. Daily 10am–10pm.

OUTDOOR GEAR

Lafuma Ground floor 16 Jalan Telawi, Bangsar Baru ☎03 2287 1118, ⓦlafuma.com.my; map p.97. Also known as Yellow Stone, this small but serious outdoor shop features hiking boots, waterproofs, sleeping bags, water purifiers, camping stoves, packs, water bottles, tents, trekking clothing and accessories. They can also organize trekking guides in Peninsular Malaysia, Mount Kinabalu and beyond. Daily 11am–9pm.

Ufl Outdoors 26 Jalan Telawi 5, Bangsar Baru ☎03 2282 5721, ⓦufl.com.my; map p.97. Good for small, low-tech essentials – seam sealer, plastic water bottles, small nylon bags – plus sleeping bags and even basic tents. Some decent snorkelling, gymnastics and even archery gear, too. Daily 10am–8.30pm.

DIRECTORY

Banks and exchange Banks with ATMs are located throughout KL; Maybank is usually your best bet for foreign exchange – there are several branches across the centre of town. You may get better rates from official moneychangers, which can be found in shopping malls and in and around transport hubs.

Casino The casino at Genting Highlands (ⓦrwgenting.com) attracts both vacationing locals and tourists as it offers several resorts, a theme park and shopping malls. It's 30km out of town, best reached via the Karak Highway (E8); express buses head there from Pudu Sentral and Pekeliling bus stations, and there are also share taxis from Pudu Station.

Cultural centres Alliance Française, 15 Lorong Gurney (📞 03 2694 7880, 🌐 alliancefrancaise.org.my); British Council, West Block, Wisma Selangor Dredging, Jalan Ampangm next to the *Maya* hotel (📞 03 2723 7900, 🌐 britishcouncil.my); Goethe-Institut, suite 06-07, sixth floor, 374 Jalan Tun Razak (📞 03 2164 2011, 🌐 goethe.de).

Embassies and consulates Australia, 6 Jalan Yap Kwan Seng (📞 03 2146 5555, 🌐 malaysia.embassy.gov.au); Brunei, 19-01 Tingkat 19, Menara Tan & Tan, Jalan Tun Razak (📞 06 7387 16001, 🌐 mofat.gov.bn); Cambodia, 46 Jalan U Thant (📞 03 4257 1150, 🌐 camemb.mys.mfa.gov.kh); Canada, seventeenth floor, Menara Tan & Tan, 207 Jalan Tun Razak (📞 03 2718 3333, 🌐 canadainternational.gc.ca); China, Plaza OSK, 25 Jalan Ampang (📞 03 2164 5250, 🌐 my.china-embassy.org); India, 1 Jalan Mont Kiara (📞 03 6205 2350, 🌐 indianhighcommission.com.my); Indonesia, 233 Jalan Tun Razak (📞 03 2116 4016, 🌐 kbrikualalumpur.org); Ireland, The Amp Walk, 218 Jalan Ampang (📞 03 2161 2963, 🌐 embassyofireland.my); Japan, 11 Persiaran Stonor (📞 03 2177 2600, 🌐 my.emb-japan.go.jp); Laos, Jalan Damai and Jalan Mesra (📞 03 2148 7059); Netherlands, The Amp Walk, 218 Jalan Ampang (📞 03 21686200, 🌐 nederlandwereldwijd.nl); New Zealand, Level 21, Menara IMC, 8 Jalan Sultan Ismail (📞 03 2078 2533, 🌐 mfat.govt.nz); Philippines, 1 Changkat Kia Peng (📞 03 2148 4233, 🌐 philembassykl.org.my); Singapore, 209 Jalan Tun Razak (📞 03 2161 6277, 🌐 mfa.gov.sg/kualalumpur); South Africa, Menara HLA, 3 Jalan Kia Peng (📞 03 2170 2400, 🌐 www.dirco.gov.za/malaysia); South Korea, 9 & 11 Jalan Nipah, off Jalan Ampang (📞 03 4251 2336, 🌐 mys.mofa.go.kr); Thailand, 206 Jalan Ampang (📞 03 2145 8004, 🌐 thalembassy.org/kualalumpur); UK, Level 27 Menara Binjai, 2 Jalan Binjai (📞 03 2170 2200, 🌐 gov.uk/world/organisations/british-high-commission-kuala-lumpur); US, 376 Jalan Tun Razak (📞 03 2168 5000, 🌐 my.usembassy.gov); Vietnam, 4 Persiaran Stonor (📞 03 2148 4534, 🌐 vietnameseembassy.org).

Emergencies Police and ambulance 📞 999, fire and rescue 📞 994.

Hospitals and clinics General Hospital, Jalan Pahang (📞 03 2615 5555, 🌐 hkl.gov.my); Gleneagles Hospital, Jalan Ampang (📞 03 4141 3000, 🌐 gleneagleskl.com.my); Pantai Medical Centre, 8 Jalan Bukit Pantai (📞 03 2296 0888, 🌐 pantai.com.my); Tung Shin Hospital, 102 Jalan Pudu (📞 03 2037 2288, 🌐 tungshin.com.my).

Left luggage Luggage can be stored for a few ringgit per day at KL Sentral station and Pudu Sentral bus station (look out for a couple of counters at the back of the passenger level). At KLIA, the service costs RM15–30/day depending on the size of the bags.

Police KL has its own 24-hour Tourist Police station, where you can report stolen property for insurance claims, within the same complex as MATIC tourist office at MTC, 109 Jalan Ampang (📞 03 9235 4999).

Post office The General Post Office is just south of the Dayabumi Complex on Jalan Sultan Hishamuddin (Mon–Fri 8.15am–5pm; 📞 03 2267 2267); poste restante/general delivery mail comes here. A post office with extended hours can be found at Suria KLCC (daily 10am–6pm).

Rock climbing Guide Pro (📞 03 4821 5708, 🌐 theguideproshop.com) runs excursions for novices or experienced climbers to sites around Batu Caves and Bukit Tabur. Trips cost RM1750–3250/person, guides and all equipment supplied; hotel pick-ups upon request at extra cost.

Sports facilities Public sports facilities in downtown KL are limited. The most convenient pool is at Chinwoo Stadium, uphill south off Jalan Hang Jebat in Chinatown (Mon–Fri 2–8pm, Sat & Sun 9am–8pm; RM4.30 weekdays; RM5.30 weekends). The pool is well maintained but the showers and changing facilities are basic, and baggy swimwear is not allowed (men can purchase appropriate swimming trunks if required). Private health clubs, with gyms and other facilities, include Fitness First (🌐 fitnessfirst.com.my), with central locations at Avenue K mall, Jalan Ampang, next to the KLCC LRT station. The TPC Kuala Lumpur golf club (formerly Kuala Lumpur Golf & Country Club) is at Bukit Kiara, 8km west of the city centre (daily 7am–10pm; 📞 03 2011 9188, 🌐 tpckl.com).

Visa extensions The Immigration Office is at Kompleks Kementerian, Dalam Negeri, 69 Jalan Sri Hartamas 1 (Mon–Fri 7.30am–5pm, counter closes at 4pm; 📞 03 6205 7400, 🌐 www.imi.gov.my).

Around Kuala Lumpur

The most obvious attraction worthy of an excursion from KL is 13km north, where limestone peaks rise up from the forest at the Hindu shrine of **Batu Caves**, one of Malaysia's main tourist destinations. Nearby, the **Forest Research Institute of Malaysia** (FRIM) encompasses a small but surprisingly thick portion of primary rainforest, where you can see birds and a few animals within an hour of downtown KL.

Further northwest of KL, the quiet town of **Kuala Selangor** offers the chance to observe the nightly dance of **fireflies**, while northeast, **Fraser's Hill** is one of Malaysia's many hill stations, set up in colonial times to allow government officials an escape from lowland heat. The most surreal day-trip you can make from KL is to the very Chinese

1

fishing village on **Ketam Island**, off the coast near southwesterly Port Klang, which hardly feels like Malaysia at all.

Batu Caves and Ketam Island are easy to reach on **public transport**, but you'll need a rental car or taxi to reach FRIM. About the only package trip widely offered by KL's accommodation and tour agents goes to see the fireflies; you can do this on public transport, but it's bit of a slog and really requires an overnight stay at Kuala Selangor.

Forest Research Institute of Malaysia

16km northwest of KL • Daily 5am–7.30pm • Free • ☎ 03 6279 7000, ⓦ frim.gov.my • KMT Komuter train to Kepong station (20min), then taxi for the final 5km (10min)

The **Forest Research Institute of Malaysia** (FRIM) sits amid a fifteen-square-kilometre reserve of rainforest and parkland, threaded with sealed roads and walking trails. It's a popular spot for weekend picnics, appealing to birdwatchers, joggers and anyone after some greenery and fresh air, but sadly its main attraction, the canopy walkway, was closed permanently in 2017 due to concerns over safety and the health of the trees that supported it. A couple of hours here is plenty of time for a walk around, and this makes a good warm-up for wilder affairs at Taman Negara (see p.191); for a full day out you could always continue to the Batu Caves and Orang Asli Museum (see p.108).

Taxis can drop you off at the gates; once there, pick up a **map** and follow the main road 1km into the park, past open woodland and rolling lawns, to the **One Stop Centre** for advice. A small **museum** nearby, which is strongly biased towards the timber industry, gives thumbnail sketches of the different types of tropical forests and the commercial uses of various woods.

For a good walk, follow the clear Rover **walking track** past the mosque and uphill into the forest; there are some huge trees, birds and butterflies here, and a single-plank suspension bridge across a deep gully – you may also see monkeys, if you're lucky. You'll also have the option of joining up with a couple of other trails along the way, which will bring you back to the One Stop Centre in around ninety minutes.

THAIPUSAM AT THE BATU CAVES

The most important festival in the Malaysian Hindu calendar (along with Deepavali), **Thaipusam** honours the Hindu deity Lord Subramaniam. It's held during the full moon in the month of "Thai" (which in the Gregorian calendar always falls between mid-January and mid-February), when huge crowds arrive at the Batu Caves. Originally intended to be a day of penance for past sins, it has now become a major tourist attraction, attracting Malaysians and foreigners alike each year.

The start of Thaipusam is marked by the departure at dawn, from KL's Sri Maha Mariamman Temple, of a **golden chariot** bearing a statue of Subramaniam. Thousands of devotees follow on foot as it makes its seven-hour procession to the caves. As part of their penance – and in a trance-like state – devotees carry numerous types of **kavadi** ("burdens" in Tamil), the most popular being milk jugs decorated with peacock feathers placed on top of the head, which are often connected to the penitents' flesh by hooks. Others wear wooden frames with sharp protruding spikes, which are carried on the back and hooked into the skin, while trident-shaped skewers are placed through some devotees' tongues and cheeks. This rather grisly procession has its origins in India, where most of Lord Subramaniam's temples were situated on high ridges that pilgrims would walk up, carrying heavy pitchers or pots. At Batu Caves, the climb up to the main chamber expresses the idea that you cannot reach God without expending effort.

Once at the caves, the Subramaniam statue is placed in a tent before being carried up to the **Temple Cave**, where devotees participate in ceremonies and rituals to Subramaniam and Ganesh. Things climax with a celebration for Rama, which involves milk from the kavadi vessels being spilt as an offering; incense and camphor are burned as the bearers unload their devotional burdens.

Extra buses run to the caves during Thaipusam – make sure you get there early (around 7am) for a good view. Numerous vendors sell food and drink, but it's a good idea to take water and snacks with you, as the size of the crowd is horrendous.

Sunway Lagoon

15km southwest of KL • Adult RM170, child RM140 • ☎03 5639 0000, ⓦsunwaylagoon.com • KTM Komuter line from KL Sentral to Setia Jaya (hourly; 25min) then a taxi (5min; RM10)

Though it's not a must-see, **Sunway Lagoon** is Malaysia's most famous, and one of Asia's most popular, water parks, and is certainly worth a visit if you're spending a few weeks in KL. One of its main draws, the Vuvuzela ride, sees participants boarding a chute from an eleven-storey-high tower and plummeting into a huge horn-shaped waterslide. It's not all about slides and pools, however, as there's a total of ninety attractions, and the site also includes an amusement park, wildlife park and the Lost Lagoon, Asia's first Nickelodeon-themed attraction. The *Sunway Resort Hotel & Spa* is also based on site, which is handy if you find yourself too worn out to return to KL at the end of the day.

Putrajaya

30km south of KL • KLIA Transit from KL Sentral to Putrajaya/Cyberjaya (every 30min; 20min) then a taxi (10min; RM10) to Dataran Putrajaya

Though it's generally viewed as a soulless admin hub, the city of **PUTRAJAYA** does in fact have some seriously impressive architecture and a wealth of gorgeous green areas, so it's more than suitable for an enjoyable daytrip from KL. The city is the Federal Government's administrative centre, though the main sights for tourists include the bright pink **Putra Mosque** at Putra Square and the nearby **Tuanku Mizan Zainal Abidin Mosque**, plus the **Botanical Gardens** and **Putrajaya Wetlands Park**. The enormous lake, popular for watersports, is also well worthy of a wander or a bike ride (there is bicycle rental desk inside the Botanical Gardens), and you can take in the Millennium Monument along the way – inspired by the Washington Monument in Washington DC, it is 68m tall and depicts various milestones in Malaysia's history.

Botanical Gardens

Persiaran Sultan Sallahuddin Abdul Aziz Shah • Free • Daily 7am–6pm • ☎ 03 2615 8188, ⓦ ppj.gov.my

Putrajaya's **Botanical Gardens** house a wealth of beautifully maintained green spaces and structures, including a Moroccan pavilion with exquisite *zellige* (Moroccan mosaics), the Sun Garden with its enormous sundial and the short but worthwhile canopy walk. Avoid visiting in the middle of the day, as it'll be unbearably humid. The views out across the lake to the Putra Mosque and beyond are fabulous. Look out for the *Putrajaya Seafood Restaurant* (daily 11am–9pm; ☎03 8889 1188, ⓦpcs .my) on the shore of the lake, which is a good place to settle down at sunset for a decent dinner and a visual treat.

Putrajaya Wetlands Park

Persiaran Persekutuan • Tues–Fri 9am–5pm, Sat & Sun 8.30am–5.30pm • Free • ☎ 03 8887 7774, ⓦ ppj.gov.my

Constructed in 1998, the two-square-kilometre Putrajaya Wetlands Park transformed an oil palm plantation into a thriving ecosystem – the first man-made wetland in Malaysia and the largest constructed freshwater wetland in the region. The site has a few informational displays at the Interpretive Centre, but the main draw here is the flamingo lake, where you can spot egrets and cinnamon bitterns.

Batu Caves

13km north of KL on Jalan Batu Caves, roughly midway between the junctions with Jalan Ipoh and the E8 • Free • KTM Komuter train from KL Sentral to Batu Caves (every 15–30min; 30min)

The **Batu Caves** sit right on the northern edge of Greater KL, where forested limestone thumbs poke out of a ridge of hills in the suburb of Gombak. In 1891, ten years after the caves were brought into the limelight by American explorer William Hornaby, local Indian dignitaries convinced the British administration that the caves were ideal places in which to worship (probably because their geography was reminiscent of the sacred

1

THE FRIM–BATU CAVES–ORANG ASLI MUSEUM CIRCUIT

The proximity of FRIM, the Orang Asli Museum and the Batu Caves to **Middle Ring Road II** (also known as Jalan Batu Caves) makes it feasible for drivers to visit all three in a day. From KL, either take the E8 highway, which intersects Jalan Batu Caves, or use Jalan Ipoh, which starts at Chow Kit and meets Jalan Batu Caves 4km west of the E8. FRIM is west of Jalan Ipoh, the Orang Asli Museum close to the E8, and the caves are in between the two.

Unfortunately, no buses connect the three, but you could use taxis or Grab/Uber to reach FRIM (RM15) and the Orang Asli Museum (RM20) from Batu Caves.

Himalayas). Soon ever-increasing numbers of devotees were visiting the caves to pray at the shrine established here to Lord Murugan, also known as **Lord Subramaniam**; later the temple complex was expanded to include a shrine to the elephant-headed deity **Ganesh**. Although the caves are always packed with visitors, by far the most atmospheric way to visit is to join the thousands of devotees attending the annual three-day **Thaipusam festival** in late January or early February (see box, p.106).

Arriving at the site, you can't miss the immense staircase leading up into the limestone crags, and the gigantic golden statue of **Lord Murugan**, the Hindu god of war, to one side; it's claimed to be the tallest such statue in the world. A number of minor temples stand at ground level, but most visitors head straight up the 272 steps to the caves, pausing only to catch their breath or take photos of the marauding macaques who make their presence all too known.

Ramayana Cave

Daily 8am–7pm · RM5

A minute's walk west of the Lord Murugan statue, past a blue 15m statue of Hanuman, lies the elaborately decorated and vividly illuminated **Ramayana Cave**, which depicts the story of the life of Lord Rama. The tale includes Rama's fight to rescue his wife Sita from Ravana, the demon king; one of the focal points of the temple is an enormous statue of a sleeping Kumbhakarna, brother of Ravana and a famous warrior in the battle. As the cave is still a relatively recent addition – the temple was only consecrated in 2001 – it's much less busy than the main cave complex, though it's perhaps more impressive thanks to its intricate carvings and absorbing storyline.

Dark Cave

Tues–Sun 9.30am–5pm · **Educational tour** Tues–Fri 10am–5pm, Sat & Sun 10.30am–5.30pm; 45min · RM35, child RM25 · **Adventure tour** Sat & Sun, check website for times; 3–4hr; minimum group size 10 (aged 12 and above) · RM80; book at least a week ahead · ☎03 6186 7011 🌐darkcavemalaysia.com

Three-quarters of the way up the steps to the Batu Caves – at step 204, to be precise – a turning on the left leads to a vast side cavern known as the **Dark Cave**, which can only be visited on a guided tour. Here a 2km-long passageway opens into seven chambers populated by a large range of insects, the rare trapdoor spider (thought to be unique to the caves) and at least three types of **bats**, which can be distinguished by their calls. Take the Educational Tour for a walkthrough of the cave's history and limestone formations, including several towering **flow stones**, or sign up to the Adventure Tour to climb and crawl through narrow passageways.

Subramaniam Swamy Temple

Daily 8am–7pm · Free

At the top of the main staircase, there's a clear view through to the **Subramaniam Swamy Temple**, devoted to Lord Subramaniam and another deity, Rama. It's set deep in a cave (known today as **Temple Cave**) that's around 100m high and 80m long, the walls of which are lined with idols representing the six lives of Lord Subramaniam. In a chamber at the back, a statue of Rama, adorned with silver jewellery and a silk sarong, is said to watch over the wellbeing of all immigrants. If you want to look closely at this inner sanctum, the temple staff will mark a small red dot on your forehead, giving you the spiritual right to enter.

Royal Selangor Visitor Centre

11km northeast of central KL on Jalan Usahawan 6, Setapak Jaya • Daily 9am–5pm • Free • ☎ 03 4145 6000, ⊛ royalselangor.com • LRT Kelana Jaya line from Dang Wangi to Wangsa Maju (every 20min; 25min), then a taxi (5min; RM5).

Pewter is something of a souvenir cliché in Malaysia, though the platters, mugs and other objects found in the **Royal Selangor Visitor Centre** still make elegant gifts. You wouldn't have been able to call this place a visitor centre a few years ago, but following a revamp it now offers the whole package, with exhibits on the origins of pewter and smithing, hands-on craft workshops and free guided tours. If you're tempted to buy something but don't fancy carrying it back from Setapak Jaya, the centre also has stores in Pavilion, Bangsar and Suria KLCC malls.

Orang Asli Museum

20km north of KL on Jalan Pahang Lama, Gombak • Mon–Thurs & Sat 9am–5pm • Free • ☎ 03 6189 2117, ⊛ jakoa.gov.my • Best to take a taxi, Grab or Uber (35min; RM30)

Run by the government's Department for Orang Asli Development, the **Orang Asli Museum** aims to present a portrait of the various groups of Orang Asli, former nomadic hunter-gatherers in the jungle who are now largely resident in rural settlements. A large map of the Peninsula in the foyer makes it clear that the Orang Asli can be found, in varying numbers, in just about every state, and that surprises some visitors, who see little sign of them during their travels. Besides collections of the fishing nets, guns and blowpipes the Orang Asli use as part of their traditional lives, the museum also has photographs of Orang Asli press-ganged by the Malay and British military to fight Communist guerrillas in the 1950s. Other displays describe the changes forced more recently on the Orang Asli – some positive, like the development of health and school networks, others less encouraging, like the erosion of the family system as young men drift off to look for seasonal work.

Hidden in an annexe to the rear of the building, examples of traditional handicrafts include the **head carvings** made by the Mah Meri tribe from the swampy region on the borders of Selangor and Negeri Sembilan, and the Jah Hut from the slopes of Gunung Benom in central Pehang. Around 50cm high, the carvings show stylized, fierce facial expressions, and are fashioned from a strong, heavy hardwood. They still have religious significance – the most common image used, the *moyang*, represents the spirit of the ancestors.

Kuala Selangor

70km northwest of KL • Buses to Kuala Selangor leave from KL's Pudu Sentral station daily every 30min (2hr); the last bus back leaves at 7.45pm

Coastal **KUALA SELANGOR** lies close to the junction of routes 5 and 54 on the banks of the Selangor River. A former royal town, today it's a small, sleepy affair; the chief reason visitors continue to come here is to see the river's **fireflies**, which glow spectacularly in the early evening.

This natural spectacle appeared at one stage to be in terminal decline: the fireflies' mangrove habitat was rapidly being cleared away, and the river was becoming more and more polluted. Government intervention seems to have stabilized things, and you stand a reasonable chance of enjoying a decent light show, **weather** permitting – the flies don't perform in rain. It's easiest to see Selangor's highlights on an evening firefly **package tour** from KL, though you can visit independently if you're prepared to stay overnight.

1

Fort Altingsburg
Daily 9am–4.30pm • Free

All that remains of Kuala Selangor's glorious past are the remnants of two forts overlooking the town. The largest, **Fort Altingsburg**, recalls an era when this part of the country changed hands, bloodily, on several occasions. Originally called Fort Melawati, Altingsberg was built by local people during the reign of Sultan Ibrahim of Selangor in the eighteenth century, and later captured by the Dutch (who renamed it) as part of an attempt to wrestle the tin trade from the sultans. The fortress was partly destroyed during local skirmishes in the Selangor Civil War (1867–73). Within its grounds is a cannon, reputed to be from the Dutch era, and a rock used for executions. **Bukit Melawati**, the hill on which the fort is based, also holds a **lighthouse** and a British colonial resthouse, and has hundreds of (mostly) friendly monkeys on the hunt for fruit.

Kuala Selangor Nature Park
Below Fort Altingsburg • Daily 9am–5pm • RM4 • ☎ 03 3289 2294 • The park is a 500m walk from Bukit Melawati (follow signs for Taman Alam); you can also get here on the buses that run up Route 5 from Klang – ask to be let off at the park, and you'll be dropped at a petrol station, from where the park is 200m up Jalan Klinik

The **Kuala Selangor Nature Park**, which encompasses mud flats, mangroves and a small patch of forest, is host to around 150 species of birds, with thirty more migratory species passing through, as well as silverleaf monkeys, which live in the forest, and crabs and fish in the mangroves. Clearly marked trails take between 30min and 1hr 30min to walk.

ACCOMMODATION AND EATING   **KUALA SELANGOR**

Firefly Park Resort Jalan Haji Omar, Kampung Bukit Belimbing ☎ 03 3260 1208. Slick accommodation with simple, modern, a/c en-suite chalets for four. There's a BBQ area and Chinese seafood restaurant, with breakfast upon request (weekends only; RM50). Rates drop by up to RM50 Mon–Thurs. RM190

Firefly Villa 1 Jalan Sungai Gulang-Gulang (SGG) 5/4, Tanjong Karang ⓦ fireflyvilla.com. Twelve km north of town, this pleasant place has four en-suite rooms set around a quiet pool area amid palm and banana trees. The friendly owners are keen to share their knowledge of the area, and provide hearty breakfasts each morning. RM398

Nature Park Chalets Taman Alam, Kuala Selangor Nature Park ☎ 03 3289 2294. A mix of basic chalet and hostel accommodation. Book in advance, as school groups can fill the place up. There's nowhere to eat nearby, so it's best to bring everything you think you'll need. Dorms RM35, chalets RM50

Jetty Seafood Restaurant Pasir Penambang off Jalan Feri Lama. Situated amid a group of similar waterside seafood restaurants, this one stands out for its bright red seating and fresh seafood, including crab in a variety of sauces (RM100/kg). Mains from RM19.

Ketam Island
50km west of KL • From KL Sentral, take a KTM Komuter train to Klang (1hr 15min); boats to Pulau Ketam Village via Sungai Lima leave from Klang's Terminal Penumpang South Port, opposite the train station

The moment you set foot aboard ferries to **KETAM ISLAND** (Crab Island), you'll find yourself in a kind of parallel universe: this is Chinese day-tripper land, with videos of Chinese karaoke clips and soap operas blaring from the on-board screens. The majority of Ketam's five thousand inhabitants are Teochew and Hokkien Chinese, who traditionally live almost entirely by fishing from their low, flat, mangrove-encrusted island. Every house is built on stilts above the sand, and practically every street is a concrete walkway or boardwalk raised in the same fashion. Aside from the chance to eat tasty, inexpensive seafood, you'd visit Ketam mainly for a slightly surreal break from KL's pace, and a couple of good places to stay if you like peace and quiet.

From the jetty, walk past the mosque towards Jalan Tepi Sungai and Jalan Besar, which are lined with grocers, general stores, and stalls and restaurants selling **seafood** – including, of course, crab. Beyond a shop selling Buddhist paraphernalia is a central square, where you'll find the **Hock Leng Temple**, as well as a small grotto containing a representation of Kwan Yin, the Goddess of Mercy, looking decidedly Madonna-like with

1

FIREFLY TRIPS

Kuala Selangor's **fireflies**, known as *kelip-kelip* in Malay, are actually 6mm-long beetles of a kind found between India and Papua New Guinea. During the day, the fireflies rest on blades of grass or in palm trees behind the river's mangrove swamps, and after sunset they move to the mangroves themselves, the males attracting mates with **synchronized flashes** of light at a rate of three bursts per second. Females flash back at males to indicate interest and initiate mating. Typically, the most successful males are those that flash brightest and fly fastest.

Boats leave on 30min firefly-spotting trips from two locations several kilometres from town: **Bukit Belimbing**, where you'll find fibreglass boats run by *Firefly Park Resort*, on the north bank across the river bridge (daily 7.40–10.30pm; RM25/person); and **Kampung Kuantan**, where you can hop on a manually steered wooden boat from the south bank (daily 7.30–11.30pm; RM50/ four-person boat). There are no buses to either of the jetties, so taxis from Kuala Selangor get away with pretty steep prices – expect the ride to cost at least RM20. It's important to remain quiet when watching the firefly display and not to use flash photography, as it scares the insects away.

It's possible to take firefly tours all the way from KL with Han Travel (ⓦ han-travel.com) for RM190 per person, or you can combine the fireflies trip with a **tour** that takes in the Batu Caves, a batik factory, a pewter factory, and a chocolate outlet for RM450, or RM300 per person for groups of two or more, including return transport, all fees and a seafood dinner.

a halo of red electric lights. Beyond, you'll come to a residential area of concrete and wooden houses, nearly all with their front doors left wide open. There's lots of refuse littering the mud flats beneath unfortunately, but you'll still get to see plenty of shrines outside the homes as well as netting containing seafood that's been left out to dry.

ARRIVAL AND TOURS

KETAM ISLAND

By ferry Ferries (every 45min; 45min; RM8) depart Klang Mon–Fri 8.45am–6.30pm, Sat 8.45am–7.10pm and return Mon–Fri 8.45am–6.30pm, Sat 8.45am–6pm.

By tour Not far from the jetty, Greenway (ⓟ 012 322 5331, ⓦ greenway2u.com) offers packages including daytime fishing trips (RM90/person) and an overnight stay at a floating fish farm (RM60/person, minimum three people).

ACCOMMODATION AND EATING

Hotel Sea Lion S3 Jalan Merdeka ⓟ 03 3110 4121, ⓦ sealion.com.my. Near the jetty, in a distinctive yellow and white building, this simple establishment has a nice deck overlooking the water. The cheapest rooms are windowless with fans, while the others have a/c and a bit more space. You can book good-value packages here, such as one night's

accommodation, one evening meal and a fishing trip from RM98. RM58

Restoran Seng Huat On the main street. This place is similar to other places to eat nearby, but is just that little bit livelier. It offers excellent seafood omelettes, prawns, crab, noodles soups and generic stir-fries. Around RM18 should be enough to leave you stuffed. Daily 8am–8pm.

Fraser's Hill

98km northeast of KL

Set 1500m up in the forested Titiwangsa mountains, the collection of colonial bungalows comprising **FRASER'S HILL** was established after World War I as one of Malaysia's earliest **hill stations**, a retreat for administrators seeking relief from the torrid lowland climate. Though less visited than the much larger Cameron Highlands to the north, Fraser's Hill boasts excellent **nature trails** and superb **birdwatching**; some 250 species have been recorded here, and the Fraser's Hill International Bird Race each June (ⓦ pkbf.org.my) sees teams competing to clock up as many as possible within a day. Even if you don't have the slightest interest in twitching, the hill remains a good getaway from the heat and hubbub of KL, and at weekends (when accommodation prices shoot up) it draws families from as far away as Singapore.

Sprawling amid a handful of wooded slopes, the hill station focuses on a T-junction at the south end of a **golf course**. *Puncak Inn* (see p.113) is located here, along with a

1

> ## COMMUNISTS ON THE HILL
>
> During the Emergency in the 1950s, the mountainous jungle at Fraser's Hill provided perfect cover for some of the Communist guerrillas' secret camps, from where they launched strikes on British-owned plantations and neighbouring towns.
>
> If you approach Fraser's Hill via Kuala Kubu Bharu (known as KKB), due north of KL, roughly halfway up you'll see a sign, "Emergency Historical Site", marking the spot where **Sir Henry Gurney**, the British High Commissioner for Malaya at the height of the communist insurgency in 1951, was ambushed and killed. The guerrillas hadn't known how important their quarry was: their aim had been only to steal guns, ammunition and food, but when Gurney strode towards them demanding that they put down their weapons, they opened fire.

distinctive **clock tower**, a post office and a bank, and the roads and trails head off in all directions from here to clusters of hidden bungalows and cabins.

Trails

The easiest targets for a stroll are **Allan's Water**, a small lake less than 1km from the clock tower, and **Jeriau Waterfall**, 4km north via *Ye Olde Smokehouse* (see opposite), where the convincing English country decor and **cream teas** (daily 3–6pm) are a strong inducement to pause for a breather. Another good walk involves taking Jalan Lady Guillemard east to the loop road, Jalan Girdle; this leads to the most remote section of the hill station, bordering **Ulu Tramin Forest Reserve**, though completing the entire circle only takes around ninety minutes.

Even most of the **longer trails** can be covered in less than two hours; indeed it would only take a couple of days to cover them all. Signage, however, can be spotty – it's best to talk to the tourist office about your route before you set out, and consider hiring a guide. The trails can get slippery in wet weather, so be sure to wear proper footgear; leeches (see p.45) have also been known to be a problem.

The **Hemmant trail** begins on Jalan Genting close to the mosque, and snakes along the edge of the golf course just within the jungle. At its far end, you can turn left and either walk on to Jalan Lady Maxwell, or continue as far as the Bishop's House, where you can pick up the **Bishop's trail** en route to the **Maxwell trail**, at which point you can either leave the trail by turning right up the hill and returning to town via Jalan Lady Maxwell, or continue another hour until it reaches Jalan Quarry.

ARRIVAL AND DEPARTURE   FRASER'S HILL

By car Fraser's Hill is reached by a single-lane road that branches off Route 55, which connects Kuala Kubu Bharu (KKB, on Route 1) and Raub (Route 8) at a spot called the Gap. In theory, this road takes summit-bound traffic only, while downhill traffic uses a road that joins the KKB–Raub road 1km northeast. When either one is closed by landslips, however, traffic alternates hourly in each direction on the other. The entire journey to or from KL

typically takes 2hr or so. There is no fuel station at Fraser's Hill, so be sure to fill up in KL.

By train and taxi Catch a Komuter train (blue Seremban line north) from KL to Kuala Kubu Bharu (KKB; 1hr 15min); note that not all trains stop off at KKB, so make sure you ask before boarding. From KKB, you'll have to take a taxi to Fraser's Hill (45min; RM60) – it might be better to simply take a Grab or Uber from the centre of KL (RM100).

INFORMATION

Banks There is a small branch of Maybank at the *Shahzan Inn*, where you can change money (Mon–Thurs 9.15am–4.30pm, Fri 9.15am–4pm); there is also an ATM, although it only accepts local cards.

Tourist information The tourist office is based inside the *Puncak Inn* at the centre of the hill station (daily

8am–11pm; ☎ 09 362 2007, ⓦ pkbf.gov.my); they can provide maps, advise on current trail conditions and put you in touch with local guides. For up-to-date information on hotel and guesthouse accommodation plus the local attractions and a handy rundown of all the trails, check ⓦ fraserhill.info.

ACCOMMODATION

Accommodation in Fraser's Hill is mostly motel-like and geared towards families and groups, though some **bungalows** – here either detached single-storey houses or small apartment blocks – are also available. Always book in advance, and expect rates quoted here to rise by as much as fifty percent at weekends and during holidays.

★**Puncak Inn** Jalan Gap ☎09 362 2007, ⓦpkbf .gov.my. The block of this tourist-office-run hotel is not the most inspiring in town, but this is one of the best places to stay in Fraser's Hill, featuring neat and tidy rooms with flowery curtains, heating and en-suite facilities. There is free wi-fi at reception, but not in the rooms. RM125

Shahzan Inn Jalan Lady Gullemard ☎09 362 2300, ⓦshahzaninn-fraserhill.com. Located in a large white concrete block, this bland hotel consists of tiers of rooms ascending a terraced hillside. Rooms are a bit dated and don't have much personality, although they are spacious

and pretty comfortable, and either look onto the garden or the town's golf course. RM200

★**Ye Olde Smokehouse** Jalan Jeriau ☎09 362 2226, ⓦthesmokehouse.my. Founded in 1937 as a resort for British servicemen who fought in World War I, this stereotypical English country inn offers fireside chairs and spacious rooms with four-poster beds, guaranteed to make the cool nights pass all the more blissfully. There's a good restaurant, too (see below). Rates drop by around thirty percent on weekdays (though it still doesn't hurt to ask about discounts on weekends) and include a full English breakfast. RM320

EATING

Fraser's Hill doesn't offer much choice for eating: aside from the two restaurants here, there's a central **food court** offering a mix of Malay, Indian and Chinese staples for about RM8 per dish.

Scott Restaurant 2 Jalan Genting ☎09 362 2118. Under the same management as *Ye Olde Smokehouse*, this pleasant restaurant is reminiscent of a British country pub, with a cosy fireplace, wooden tables and chintzy sofas. Food can also be enjoyed on the little patio-cum-garden at the front of the building. The menu offers British classics including fish and chips (RM20), and there are some Asian dishes too, such as Thai green curry with chicken (RM18). Daily 11am–10pm.

Ye Olde Smokehouse Jalan Jeriau ☎09 362 2226, ⓦthesmokehouse.my. This quaint hill resort is the

epitome of British country living, with its charming conservatory and log fire lit on colder days. English afternoon tea (daily 3–6pm) is served in the garden, and includes freshly baked scones and home-made strawberry jam. The restaurant menu features traditional British staples such as roast beef and Yorkshire pudding (RM65) and chicken and mushroom pie (RM50). Things are fairly informal during the day, but it's best not to turn up in a T-shirt and shorts in the evening. Daily noon–9.30pm.

The west coast

LANGKAWI

The west coast

It was on the west coast that the British got their first toehold in the Malay Peninsula, and long exposure to colonial influence has made it in many ways the most historical, multicultural and well-developed part of Malaysia today. Nowhere epitomizes this better than the island of Penang, whose capital, George Town, is arguably the most endearing city in the country, a fascinating conglomeration of century-old temples, museums and shophouses that set the backdrop to a modern and thriving art and café scene. Aside from Penang, the west coast's other major attraction is Langkawi, an island best known for its pricey resort hotels, although it also has plenty of budget places to stay along its southwestern beaches. The only other significant island off this coast, Pangkor, pales in comparison, but offers a more down-to-earth seaside experience.

Over on the mainland, the largest city is **Ipoh**, an excellent base for visiting **Cameron Highlands** (also easily reached from Kuala Lumpur), once a British hill station and still a popular refuge from the stifling heat of the plains. Ipoh's hinterland encompasses a number of attractions, including opportunities to take in Malay royal architecture or indulge in a spot of **white-water rafting**. Points of interest thin out inland, but it is possible to see the rainforest at the **Ulu Muda Eco Park** and the **Royal Belum State Park**, both bordering Thailand, and explore Malaysia's newest World Heritage Site, the archeologically important **Lenggong Valley** – though all are tricky to reach without your own transport.

GETTING AROUND   THE WEST COAST

By plane Penang has frequent flights to and from many other Malaysian and Southeast Asian cities, notably Singapore. Flights from KL, Singapore and Kuching, among others, serve Langkawi.

By car The west coast's major artery is the North–South Expressway (also referred to as "NSE", and north of KL, as the E1). Access to the east coast is mainly via Route 76, which links up with Route 4 (the East–West Highway) to Kelantan state in the northeast.

By bus Frequent express buses link the west coast with KL, the south and Singapore, and the east coast.

By train The West Coast Line operates frequent ETS (Electric Train Service) metre-gauge fast trains between Padang Besar on the Malaysia–Thai border and Gemas in Negeri Sembilan, where the line connects with the East Coast Line to Kota Bharu. Most trains stop at all major destinations, including Alor Star, Butterworth, Taiping, Kuala Kangsar, Ipoh and Kuala Lumpur. There are also two convenient and cheaper KTM Komuter services between Butterworth and Padang Besar, and Bukit Mertajam (15min from Butterworth) to Taiping and Padang Rengas (for Kuala Kangsar).

By boat Langkawi is linked with southern Thailand by ferry, and there are also boat services between Langkawi and Penang, Kuala Kedah and Kuala Perlis.

Perak

Perak is still an unsung part of the country, but deserves to be more than just a pleasant corridor between the capital and the well-oiled tourist facilities of Penang and Langkawi.

PANGKOR ISLAND

Highlights

❶ Ipoh Fast-gentrifying mining city of old, surrounded by intriguing attractions including cave temples and the bizarre Kellie's Castle. **See p.119**

❷ Gopeng This former mining town packs in history, nature, caving and excellent white-water rafting. **See p.124**

❸ Pangkor Island Laidback tropical island with some of the best beaches on the west coast. **See p.125**

❹ Taiping Traditional town with tranquil gardens and a mini hill station; Malaysia's largest mangrove reserve lies nearby. **See p.131**

❺ Royal Belum State Park Bordering Thailand, this unexpectedly fine nature reserve is a great place to spot *Rafflesia* flowers. **See p.136**

❻ Cameron Highlands Cool down amid the tea plantations and jungle trails of this former colonial hill station. **See p.138**

❼ George Town In Penang's capital, rows of old shophouses, elaborate temples and clan houses perfectly set the scene for an eclectic art and café culture. **See p.148**

❽ Langkawi This upmarket resort island on the Thai border features white-sand beaches and a cable car over the forested interior. **See p.175**

HIGHLIGHTS ARE MARKED ON THE MAP ON P.118

THE WEST COAST

THAILAND

Hat Yai
Wang Kelian
Kelam Cave
Padang Besar
Kaki Bukit
Sadao
Satun
Dano
PERLIS
Bukit
Kangar Kayu Hitam
Arau
Changlun
Langkawi
Kuala Perlis
Jitra
E1
Kedah River
Pedu Lake
Tuba
Kuala Kedah
Alor Star
Naka
Muda Lake
ULU MUDA ECO PARK
Dayang Bunting
PULAU PAYAR MARINE PARK
Gubir
KEDAH
Sik

Mount Jerai (1217m)
Gurun
Bujang Valley
Bedong
Pengkalan Hulu
Betong
ROYAL BELUM STATE PARK
Sungai Petani
E67
Kota Bharu
Temenggor Lake
Batu Ferringhi
George Town
Butterworth
E1
E15
Kulim
Ayer Itam
Snake Temple
Bukit Mertajam
Gerik
TEMENGGOR FOREST RESERVE
KELANTAN
Penang
PENANG
130
Batu Kawan
Selama
76
BANJARAN TITIWANGSA
A6
Lenggong Valley
Musang Cave
Lata Kekabu
Lenggong
PERAK
Raban Lake
Raub & Kuala Lipis
1
Maxwell Hill (Bukit Larut)
Kuala Sepetang
Taiping
185
MATANG MANGROVE FOREST RESERVE
Kuala Kangsar
Kinta River
Kampung Raja
60
Ipoh
Mount Brinchang (2032m)
Simpang Pulai
Brinchang
72
Kellie's Castle
Tanah Rata
CAMERON HIGHLANDS
Batu Gajah
Gopeng
Ringlet
Mount Bujang (1771m)
Perak River
5
1
E1
59
Mount Beremban (2075m)
Pangkor
70
Tapah Road
Tapah
PAHANG
Lumut
5
Bidor
Teluk Intan
58
Slim River
Fraser's Hill
E1
The Gap
Sungai Besar
Tanjung Malim
55
K. Kubu Bharu
STRAIT OF MALACCA
5
SELANGOR
Selangor River
E2 Johor Bharu & Singapore

HIGHLIGHTS

1. Ipoh
2. Gopeng
3. Pangkor Island
4. Taiping
5. Royal Belum State Park
6. Cameron Highlands
7. George Town
8. Langkawi

0   50
kilometres

N

The state's topography is surprisingly diverse – monotonous coastal plains of mangrove and oil palm giving way inland to jagged limestone hills and the Titiwangsa mountain range – and so, in fact, are its attractions, not least its history. This was where the British began branching out from the Straits Settlements to open up the rest of the Peninsula, and consequently Perak's towns have relatively deep roots and more than a veneer of prosperity. Much of that wealth was founded on tin – a little ironic given that *perak* is Malay for "silver". Malaysia was the world's biggest tin producer as recently as the 1970s, but a collapse in prices in the mid-1980s led to the country turning away from the metal. The old mining centres now offer inducements to visit that are anything but obviously linked to mining: grand Malay buildings at **Kuala Kangsar**, lush gardens and hill hiking at **Taiping**, and **white-water rafting** at **Gopeng**. One hub for all these is the state capital, **Ipoh**, a likeable city with colonial architecture, a widely respected food scene and unique cave temples. In contrast are the laid-back resort island of **Pangkor** (Perak's most mainstream draw) and the **Royal Belum State Park** in the interior, which is an excellent place to spot stinky *Rafflesia* blooms. The most overlooked attraction is the UNESCO World Heritage Site at **Lenggong Valley**, also in the interior, with two clusters of archeological sites spanning 1.83 million years, and the oldest evidence of hominids outside of Africa.

Ipoh and around

IPOH was founded on the back of the great tin rush that kicked off in the 1880s, when major deposits were found in the area. The new settlement was sited at the highest navigable point on the **Kinta River**, a tributary of the Perak River – the Peninsula's second longest river – so was well placed for the ores to be collected for export. In common with the rest of the state, the city has seen a mini-exodus with the decline in mining, but in recent years people have been returning to invest in their hometown. Some half a million live here, making Ipoh the third-largest city in the country, its centre an architectural snapshot of how the tin boom helped create the diverse Malaysia of today, with the bonus of nearby sights such as outlying **Chinese cave temples**, set in dramatic surroundings, and the eccentric, anachronistic ruin of **Kellie's Castle**. With excellent places to stay and eat, Ipoh is also a good springboard for the rest of Perak and Cameron Highlands.

Old town

Ipoh began on the west bank of the Kinta, an area still known as the **old town**. The padang and the colonial core lie in the northwest, the centrepiece being the grand **train station**, another Anglo-Moorish effort by A.B. Hubback (see p.66), completed in 1917. A plaque at the front of the station marks the spot where an old specimen of an upas tree (*pokok ipoh*) used to stand, until it collapsed in 2017. Once abundant in the area, the upas – which gave the city its name – produces a toxic sap that the Orang Asli used on blowpipe darts. Opposite the station and nearly as handsome is the old **City Hall** (another Hubback creation), restored but used only for receptions and functions. Just east, the elegant **Birch Memorial Clock Tower**, commemorating the first British Resident of Perak (see p.559), takes some of the sting out of the jarringly ugly 1960s **Masjid Negeri** nearby on Jalan Sultan Iskandar.

Chinatown

South of the colonial area is what might be deemed Ipoh's historic **Chinatown**, a tight grid of streets lined with pastel-coloured shophouses that are starting to gentrify as new cafés and restaurants spring up. Amid the still-mainly-Chinese shops selling dried goods and textiles, look out for narrow **Panglima Lane**, which was nicknamed Concubine Lane, as this back alley was where wealthy merchants kept their mistresses; and for dying trades – Lau Hooi Kee, for example, is a maker of **bamboo blinds** on a lane just north of Jalan Sultan Iskandar.

2

SHOPPING

Gerbang Malam Night Market	5
Guan Heong Biscuits	6
Ipoh Parade Shopping Mall	4
Kong Heng Artisan Market	1
Memory Lane Flea Market	3
Novel Hut	2

CENTRAL IPOH

ACCOMMODATION			EATING				DRINKING	
1981 Guest House	4		Artisan Handmade Bread	6	Lou Wong (Old Town)	3	Bricks & Barrels	1
27@ Concubine Lane	3		Foh San	5	Nam Heong	10	Sinhalese Bar	2
Bedrock Hotel	5		Haji Yahaya	8	Plan B	1		
Container Hotel	2		Kong Heng	2	Sin Yoon Long	9		
Sekeping Kong Heng	1		Lou Wong (New Town)	7	Thin Hei	4		

There are some worthwhile **museums**, too: Art Deco **Han Chin Pet Soo** shophouse, on Jalan Bijeh Timah, houses a reconstruction of a former mining tycoon's club; book a tour online (1hr 30min; RM10; wipohworld.org). And on Lorong Panglima, gallery **Yasmin At Kong Heng** (Sat & Sun 10am–4pm; free; wfacebook.com/yasminatkongheng) commemorates the legacy of legendary Malaysian film director Yasmin Ahmad, a voice for liberal and multicultural values.

New town

The tin boom had been under way for barely a decade when the cramped, wooden old town was devastated by fire in 1892. It underlined the pressing need for Ipoh to expand across the river, where hundreds of new shophouses were built on land once devoted to pig farms. But the tin price had slumped by the time this **new town** was completed in 1909, and the buildings remained vacant for some time – only to pick up when, in a smart move, the old town's brothels were moved here.

Today there's little sense of a transition upon crossing the Kinta, except that the new town has some modern high-rises, almost totally absent in the old town. The only sight here is the pretty blue-and-white **Panglima Kinta mosque**, close to the river and named after a prominent line of local Malay chieftains.

Chinese cave temples

Ipoh's sprawling suburbs and noisy outer roads are overlooked by craggy limestone peaks, some riddled with **caves** where Chinese workers established popular shrines. On the Kuala Kangsar Road, 6km north of Ipoh, **Perak Tong Temple** (daily roughly 7.30am–5pm; free; bus #35 from Medan Kidd) has a huge first chamber dominated by a 15m-high golden statue of the Buddha. At the back, a steep flight of 385 steps climbs up to a sort of balcony, with views over the Kinta valley. **Sam Poh Tong Temple** (daily roughly 7.30am–3pm; free; bus #66 to Kampar or #T34 from Medan Kidd) starts small but opens in a beautiful tropical garden with turtle pond and a bright red-and-yellow pagoda encased by four lush limestone walls. Next to it, smaller **Ling Sen Tong** and **Nam Then Tong temples** have quirky and colourful statues, including characters from *Journey to the West*. From here it's 1.7km north off the main road and right into a housing area to **Kek Look Tong** (daily roughly 7.30am–5pm; free). The massive cave entrance filled with statues and huge stalagmites leads to a large landscaped garden, bizarrely spoilt by a red-and-white transmission tower.

Kellie's Castle

Kinta Kelas Rubber Estate, 12km south of Ipoh • Mon–Thurs 9am–5pm, Sat & Sun 9am–5.30pm • RM10 • ☎ 05 365 3381 • Taxi from Ipoh about RM50 return including a wait while you look around; alternatively, take Perak Transit #T36 or #T35a from Medan Kidd to Batu Gajah (30min), from where you can either walk the remaining 4km on the clearly signposted A8 road or take a taxi (around RM7)

Kellie's Castle symbolizes the prosperity achieved by many enterprising foreigners in the rubber and tin industries in the early 1900s. One of these was **William Kellie Smith**, a Scot who celebrated his success – and the birth of a long-desired son – by designing this extraordinary mansion. A flu epidemic in 1920 killed many of the Tamil workers; when work resumed, Smith embarked on a trip to Britain but fell ill and died in Portugal, and the building was never completed.

Far from being a ruin, however, the mansion is a sort of tropical palace in apricot-coloured bricks, with a rectangular, off-centre tower. It incorporates a lift (the first in the Peninsula), underground tunnels only rediscovered in 2003, and rows of arched colonnades in Moorish style. Heavily influenced by Indian culture, Smith imported many of the bricks from Chennai (Madras) and even constructed an adjacent **Hindu temple** in thanks for the birth of his son.

ARRIVAL AND DEPARTURE | IPOH

Ipoh's compact **centre** has two major thoroughfares: Jalan Sultan Idris Shah, taking eastbound traffic, and westbound Jalan Sultan Iskandar. The **suburbs** are anything but compact, and the main bus station, Terminal Aman Jaya, is far north of the centre.

BY PLANE

Sultan Azlan Shah airport The airport is 5km southeast of the centre (☎ 05 318 8202, ⊕ipoh.airport-authority.com). In theory, Perak Transit Bus #T37 and #T30 connect Terminal Aman Jaya to the airport and Medan Kidd bus station hourly from 6am–9pm (30min); in reality, these buses to stop at the airport roughly every 2hr, and only until 6.30pm. A taxi into the centre costs around RM20.

Destinations Johor Bahru (1–2 daily; 1hr 20min); Singapore (2 daily; 1hr 30min).

BY TRAIN

Train station Ipoh station is on Jalan Panglima Bukit Gantang Wahab, at the western end of the centre (☎05 254 7987). A trip from any central hotel should cost RM10.

Destinations Alor Star (5 daily; 2hr 30min); Butterworth (7 daily; 2hr); Gemas (4 daily; 4hr 30min); Kuala Kangsar (11 daily; 30min); Kuala Lumpur (every 1hr–1hr 30min; 2hr 30min); Padang Besar (5 daily; 2hr 50min); Sungai Petani (5 daily; 1hr 50min); Seremban (4 daily; 3hr 30min); Taiping (11 daily; 50min).

2

BY BUS

Ipoh's main bus station, Terminal Aman Jaya, is nearly 10km north of the centre. From here, hourly Perak Transit (ⓦperaktransit.com.my) buses #T37 and #T30a run to Medan Kidd bus station (40min), a 10min walk south of the train station in the centre, where local buses service Perak's satellite towns and the airport. Note that most services dwindle after 6.30pm.

Medan Kidd destinations Cameron Highlands (4 daily; 2hr 30min); Gopeng (#T34; every 1hr 30min; 45min); Kuala Kangsar (#35; every 20–30min; 1hr 15min);

Taiping (every 45min; 1hr 45min).

Terminal Aman Jaya destinations Alor Star (8 daily; 3hr 30min); Butterworth (at least 8 daily; 2hr 30min); Cameron Highlands (every 2hr; 2hr); Johor Bharu (4 daily; 8hr); Kangar (5 daily; 4hr); KLIA/KLIA2 (8 daily; 4hr); Kota Bharu (2 daily; 8hr); Kuala Lumpur (hourly; 3hr 30min); Kuala Perlis (3 daily; 3hr 45min); Kuantan (3 daily; 8hr); Lenggong (hourly; 1hr 45min); Lumut (8 daily; 1hr 15min); Melaka (at least 6 daily; 5hr); Penang (every 2hr; 2hr 30min); Seremban (several daily; 4hr); Singapore (4 daily; 9hr 30min); Taiping (hourly; 1hr 30min); Sungai Petani (4 daily; 3hr).

GETTING AROUND

By taxi Uber (ⓦuber.com) and Grab (ⓦgrab.com/my) are available in Ipoh and better value than regular taxis, which

park opposite the Medan Kidd bus station. To book one, call ☎05 254 0251.

INFORMATION

Tourist office Ipoh City Council runs an information centre at Jalan Tun Sambanthan, by the Padang (Mon–Thurs 8am–1pm & 2–5pm, Fri 8am–12.15pm &

2.45–5pm; ☎05 208 3155). Although staff dispense brochures liberally, their practical knowledge is variable and they may not keep to their opening hours.

ACCOMMODATION

1981 Guest House 26 Jalan Market ☎010 965 6991, ⓦfacebook.com/1981GuestHouse; map p.120. Right in the heart of the old town, this spick-and-span hostel has nice wooden floors and three big dorms – mixed, male and female – with mosquito nets and personal lockers. Free computers and self-service washing machine available. Cheaper if booked online. ☞ Dorms RM25

★**27@Concubine Lane** 26 Jalan Market ☎012 221 3202, ⓦfacebook.com/IpohConcubineLane; map p.120. Only three a/c rooms and a mezzanine for groups up to seven (RM30/person) are available in this old-town shophouse, immaculately restored by British resident Big John without altering a single original fitting. It's also a vintage haven, full of Malaysian memorabilia for sale. ☞ RM100

Bedrock Hotel 13–15 Jalan Che Tak ☎05 241 3031;

map p.120. *Bedrock* offers ten stylish and larger-than-life en-suite rooms, with Nespresso machines and Coway water purifiers, housed in a dark-hued boutique hotel with a unique Chinese Scholar's Rock theme. ☞ RM220

Container Hotel 89–91 Jalan Sultan Yusuf ☎05 243 3311, ⓦchgworld.com; map p.120. This two-storey industrial-chic hotel, with a quirky, futuristic theme and indoor slide, offers immaculate personal capsules (singles and queens). ☞ RM65

Sekeping Kong Heng 75 Jalan Panglima ☎05 241 8977, ⓦsekeping.com; map p.120. Once a hostel for travelling troupes of Chinese opera performers, *Sekeping Kong Heng* seeded the old town's gentrification when it was artfully restored in shabby-chic style. Rooms are charming, and the new wing next door boosts a swimming pool overlooking the old town. ☞ RM220

EATING

Although most of Ipoh's incredible range of restaurants and bars are in the burgeoning **suburbs**, there's a reasonable choice in the low-key centre as well. The numerous *kopitiam* joints of the **old town** are pretty foolproof for decent, cheap meals, though few are open at night.

Artisan Handmade Bread 27 Jalan Market ☎05 253 8558, ⓦfacebook.com/ArtisanHandmadeBread; map p.120. If you've tired of local food, come here for a taste of excellent Italian- and French-styled bread, including sourdough, wheat and rye varieties, and other European mains like chicken hash and *croque madame*. Vegetarian-friendly, too. A meal will set you back about RM30. Daily 9.30am–6pm.

★**Foh San** 51 Jalan Leong Sin Nam ☎05 254 0308, ⓦfohsan.com.my; map p.120. On two open-sided floors,

this palatial restaurant is a fun place to come for a *dim sum* breakfast – order from counters packed with dumplings, *pow*, steamed sticky rice, custard tarts and other morsels. Some dishes are cooked to order, especially from noon when the lunch menu kicks in. Breakfast RM20. Daily except Tues 6.30am–2.30pm.

Haji Yahaya Jalan Dato Onn Jaafar, a 2min walk south of the UTC market complex; map p.120. Marvellous Malay joint serving fried chicken and fish, curries, stews, noodles and rice, all for less than RM10 per plate – choose from *nasi kunyit* (turmeric rice) or even the purplish Kelantan-style *nasi kerabu*. Daily 7.30am–8pm.

Kong Heng Jalan Bandar Timah ☎012 227 2745; map p.120. Popular old-town, old-school *kopitiam*, where the stalls excel at any number of things: *rojak*, *laksa*, *chee cheong fun* (Cantonese noodle rolls in a savoury sauce, with optional pork filling; RM5). You may have to queue for a table at lunchtime. Mon, Tues & Thurs–Sun 7.30am–4pm.

Lou Wong New Town: 49 Jalan Yau Tet Shin; Old Town: 69 Jalan Bandar Timah ☎05 254 4199; map p.120. Ipoh residents wax lyrical over – of all things – local bean sprouts, supposedly plumper, crunchier and sweeter than any elsewhere in the country. The favoured way to have them is stir-fried, with a separate plate of steamed sliced chicken and a bowl of noodles – and *Lou Wong* is the most popular of a cluster of restaurants serving it (around RM15). Branches in both the old and new towns. Daily 10.30am–11pm.

Nam Heong 2 Jalan Bandar Timah ☎012 588 8766; map p.120. A no-frills local institution packed with Chinese customers who come here for the delicious white coffee (RM1.50), egg tarts, *chee chong fun* and freshly baked Portuguese egg tarts. Daily 6.30am–5pm.

★**Plan B** 75 Jalan Panglima ☎05 249 8286, ⊛thebiggroup.co/plan-b; map p.120. Part of *Sekeping Kong Heng* hotel, this glossy restaurant/café revels in high ceilings and glass panelling. It's especially busy at weekends, when people come for brunch (around RM30), but just as worthwhile are the fusion-inspired mains, excellent pastries and cakes, and the decent selection of beers, ciders and wines. Mon–Thurs & Sun 9am–10pm, Fri & Sat 9am–midnight.

Sin Yoon Loong 17 Jalan Bandar Timah ☎05 241 4601; map p.120. The *kopitiam* that popularized Ipoh's quintessential white coffee still dishes up hearty Chinese delicacies such as chicken rice and barbecue pork (4.50RM), curry or mushroom *chee cheong fun* (RM4) and toasted bread with kaya (coconut jam). Daily 6.30am–5pm.

Thin Hei 22 Jalan Dass ☎05 253 7388; map p.120. The best bet in town for vegetarians, serving up Chinese stir-fries and lots of fake soy/gluten "meats", including an excellent spicy mock-mutton. Around RM15 for a meal with drinks. Daily 11am–2.30pm & 6–9.30pm.

DRINKING

Bricks & Barrels 28–30 Jalan Lau Ek Ching ☎05 253 8558, ⊛facebook.com/BricksAndBarrels; map p.120. The city centre's pioneer bar, where the decor is themed around exposed-brick walls and beer barrels, offers a wide range of draught beers. Bench seating ensures everyone can have a convivial chinwag, and there's live music most nights from 10pm. Mon–Thurs & Sun 4pm–1am, Fri & Sat 4pm–2am.

★**Sinhalese Bar** 2 Jalan Bijeh Timah ☎05 241 2235; map p.120. There's no better place in the old town for a drink than this boxy institution, opened in the 1930s, with saloon-style doors, lace curtains and what look like bathroom tiles on the walls. Come for cheap, cold beer to a backdrop of Tamil pop music and the whirring of fans overhead. Daily noon–10pm.

SHOPPING

MARKETS
Gerbang Malam Night Market Jalan Dato Tahwil Azar; map p.120. This market sells a bit of everything from clothes to trinkets, and it's all dirt-cheap. Daily 6pm–midnight.

Kong Heng Artisan Market Jalan Panglima ⊛bit .ly/HongHeng; map p.120. A old-town market offering handmade crafts and trendy trinkets. Daily 10am–5pm.

Memory Lane Flea Market Jalan Lim Bo Seng; map p.120. Full of memorabilia, this morning market is a treasure trove for those looking for bargain antiques. Sun 6am–1pm.

MALLS
Ipoh Parade Shopping Mall Eastern end of Jalan Sultan Idris Shah ⊛ipoh.parade.com.my; map p.120. One downtown mall worth browsing for its many shops and restaurant chains, and a Cineplex. Daily 10am–10pm.

BOOKSHOPS
Novel Hut 87 Jalan Abdul Jalil ☎05 253 6284, ⊛bit.ly/ NovelHut; map p.120. Good selection of new and secondhand books and magazines. Daily 9am–7pm.

GIFTS
Guan Heong Biscuits 160 Jalan Sultan Iskandar ☎017 573 6277, ⊛guanheong.com; map p.120. Century-old traditional Chinese shop, good for chicken floss and lotus-paste biscuits. Daily 9am–7pm.

DIRECTORY

Banks There are Maybank and Bank Muamalat ATMs on Jalan Sultan Idris Shah.
Hospital Jalan Hospital (☎05 208 5000, ⊛hrpb.moh .gov.my).
Police Jalan Panglima Bukit Gantang Wahab, south of the train station (☎05 245 1562).
Visa extensions The Immigration Department is on the third floor of the UTC market complex on Jalan Laxamana (☎05 241 3524).

Gopeng

On Route 1, some 20km southeast of Ipoh, **GOPENG** was one of the first of the Kinta Valley rubber and tin boomtowns. Today it's a charming village set around a compact central square, and backed by a swathe of forest.

Gopeng draws visitors for the nearby **Gaharu Tea Valley** (daily 9am–6pm; RM10; ⌨gaharu.com.my), about 3km east of the town centre along Jalan Sungai Itek and best approached by car. This impressive, though touristy, agarwood tea plantation is encased by an odd 3m-high replica of the Great Wall of China. The **white-water rafting** down the **Kampar River** (rated Grade I–III depending on how rainy it's been) is also a draw, with a cluster of accommodation close by.

Although it's possible to see Gopeng on a day-trip, many visitors stay at least a night, combining rafting with a jungle hike or a visit to the nearby **caves** of **Tempurung** (☎012 529 2426, ⌨gtoc.asia) and **Kandu**, featuring the longest (90m) in-cave zipline in Asia.

Gopeng Heritage House and Gopeng Museum

House 6 Jalan Sungai Itek, main square • Sat & Sun 9.30am–3pm • **Museum** 28 Jalan Eu Kong, main square • Mon, Tues & Fri–Sun 9.30am–3pm • Entry free, but donation expected • ☎012 598 7857

Gopeng Heritage House, a beautiful three-storey wooden shophouse with a charming café, all choreographically furnished in the way of old, offers a feel for the town's past. On the opposite side of the main square, the exhibits at **Gopeng Museum** tell a lot about the impact of tin and rubber on local history.

ARRIVAL AND ACTIVITIES

By bus Bus #66 from Ipoh's Medan Kidd bus station drops you on Jalan Pasar in the heart of the old town. Although you could attempt to trudge to the river (where all the rafting operators and accommodation are) from here, far better to arrange for your hotel or tour company to collect you. Alternatively, take a Kampar-bound bus from Medan Kidd station and get off at the Sungai Itek junction along Road 1 (look out for the Nomad Adventure signboard), from where it's about 2km to the river. Gopeng's small long-distance bus station, in walking distance from the Heritage House, has useful connections to Kuala Lumpur and the south; hopping on a bus from here can save you backtracking 30km to Terminal Aman Jaya in Ipoh.

Destinations Ipoh (every 1hr 30min; 45min); Johor Bahru (5 daily; 9hr); KLIA/KLIA2 (several daily; 4hr); Kuala Lumpur (9 daily; 3hr); Kuantan (2 daily; 7hr); Melaka (2 daily; 5hr); Seremban (2 daily; 5hr); Singapore (5 daily; 10hr).

Activities Most visitors come on combined accommodation/activity deals, for which it's best to book in advance. Nomad Adventures (☎016 201 1219, ⌨nomadadventure.com), Gopeng's first and most established operator, is recommended. Book ahead to organize pick up in town, as their headquarters are 7km away next to the river. Rafting will cost around RM165 for a 4–5hr trip; a full-day package (RM265) adds a second activity (which otherwise costs RM65/person, minimum five people), such as a visit to one of the caves, or abseiling down a waterfall. From Nomad Adventures, it's a 2km walk to Tempurung Cave, with paths branching off to the riverside and into the surrounding jungle.

ACCOMMODATION

Gopeng's hotels are, inconveniently, 7km away in the river valley, reached by an informally signed narrow country road via Kampung Sungai Itek. If you are not driving, your accommodation should be able to pick you up in Gopeng town, connected to Ipoh by regular buses, or you can catch a taxi/Uber from Ipoh.

Adeline Along Jalan Sungai Itek, before Kampung Ulu Geruntum ☎05 359 2833, ⌨adelinevilla.com. Superbly run by a sociable hairdresser-turned-hotelier, *Adeline* offers slick timber-and-glass solar-powered "villas", with a/c and en-suite rooms and dorms, alongside a "rest house" complex of shared-bathroom dorms in bamboo and rattan buildings. Everyone eats together in the restaurant, where meals can be basic or fancy depending on the chef's mood. You can add on rafting and other activities, or go for a package. Rates are full board per person. Dorms RM105, doubles RM275

★**Nomad Earth Camp** Off Route 1, roughly 2km inland along Jalan Hussin ☎016 201 1219, ⌨nomadadventure.com. Nomad Adventure's headquarters offers a collection of eco-friendly en-suite chalets, simple treehouses and dorms next to the river. Meals are consumed in a convivial common area, next to which are the shared bathrooms. Groups can rent out full units. Rates include dinner and breakfast, and are per person. Dorms/treehouses RM59, chalets RM89

Pangkor and Lumut

The laidback island of **Pangkor**, barely 10km long, is known to every student of Malaysian history as the place where the **Pangkor Treaty** was signed, leading to the creation of the Resident system by which the British gradually brought every sultanate in the Peninsula under their wing (see p.559). Now it's a popular, affordable weekend beach retreat for families, taking advantage of the ease of getting here from cities like KL and Ipoh: there are frequent ferries from **LUMUT**, a small port and naval base 80km southwest of Ipoh.

Visitors mostly stay on the beaches of the island's west coast, at **Pasir Bogak** or **Teluk Nipah**. The islanders are concentrated in a town and villages on the east coast,

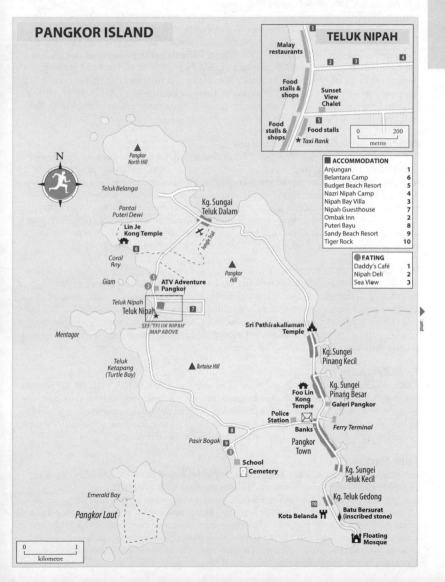

PANGKOR ISLAND

TELUK NIPAH

Malay restaurants

Food stalls & shops

Sunset View Chalet

Food stalls & shops

Food stalls

★ Taxi Rank

0   200
metres

■ ACCOMMODATION

Anjungan	1
Belantara Camp	6
Budget Beach Resort	5
Nazri Nipah Camp	4
Nipah Bay Villa	3
Nipah Guesthouse	7
Ombak Inn	2
Puteri Bayu	8
Sandy Beach Resort	9
Tiger Rock	10

● EATING

Daddy's Café	1
Nipah Deli	2
Sea View	3

Pangkor North Hill

Teluk Belanga

Pantai Puteri Dewi

Lin Je Kong Temple

Coral Bay

Giam

Teluk Nipah

Mentagor

Teluk Ketapang (Turtle Bay)

Kg. Sungai Teluk Dalam

Jungle Trail

Pangkor Hill

ATV Adventure Pangkor

SEE 'TELUK NIPAH' MAP ABOVE

Tortoise Hill

Sri Pathirakaliaman Temple

Kg. Sungei Pinang Kecil

Kg. Sungei Pinang Besar

Foo Lin Kong Temple

Galeri Pangkor

Police Station

Banks

Ferry Terminal

Pangkor Town

Pasir Bogak

School

Cemetery

Kg. Sungei Teluk Kecil

Kg. Teluk Gedong

Emerald Bay

Pangkor Laut

Kota Belanda

Batu Bersurat (inscribed stone)

Floating Mosque

Lumut

0   1
kilometre

2

and the interior is hilly and forested. Things are pretty quiet except during holidays and the annual Hindu festival of **Thaipusam**, centred on the Sri Pathirakaliaman Temple in the east coast village of **Sungai Pinang Kecil**. There's also a community-run **arts festival** with outdoor film screenings and concerts (Sept; ⓦpangkorislandfestival.com).

Pangkor Town and around

Ferries from Lumut dock at **PANGKOR TOWN**, the island's principal settlement. The town has a few shops, banks and places to stay, but most people get straight on a minibus taxi to one of the beaches.

Just a couple of minutes' walk east of the jetty, **Galeri Pangkor** (daily 9am–5pm; free) is a small museum with nineteenth-century photos of the Pangkor Treaty signatories, a few fish traps and pieces of Chinese porcelain. From the terrace, you can survey the boats docked at wooden wharves in **Kampung Sungai Pinang Besar**, then descend to the mainly Malay village itself and take a signed road 1km inland to **Foo Lin Kong**. Renovated in 2016, this Taoist complex is a riot of red and gold decorations and bright sculptures of animals – real and imaginary. There's a semi-wild garden behind, with a fishpond inhabited by enormous arapaima, and a miniature version of the Great Wall of China snaking up the hillside above.

Kampung Teluk Gedong and around

The wooden stilt houses at **Kampung Teluk Gedong** stand 1.5km south of Pangkor Town along the coastal road. Set back from the road is **Kota Belanda**, or Dutch fort, founded in 1670 to store tin supplies from Perak and keep a check on piracy in the Straits. Destroyed twenty years later, it was rebuilt in 1743 but abandoned again in 1748; the half-built structure you see today is a recent reconstruction. About 100m south, **Batu Bersurat** is a huge granite boulder under a canopy. Look here for carvings of the Dutch East India Company logo, an intertwined "VOC", and a **tiger** – a warning after a Dutch child was taken by one while playing nearby in 1743.

Pasir Bogak

It's just 2km from Pangkor Town to the west coast and the southern end of **Pasir Bogak**, one of the island's two main tourist beaches. This initial stretch is as busy as Pangkor gets, clustered with mid-range resorts popular with Malaysian Chinese. The beach itself is a lovely 2km arc of sand, looking out over a placid bay to the much smaller, privately owned **Pangkor Laut island**, and largely tranquil even though there is accommodation scattered across its length.

Teluk Ketapang

Around 2km north of Pasir Bogak and 1km south of Teluk Nipah is **TELUK KETAPANG** ("Turtle Bay"), named after the leatherback turtles that once nested here. The beach is worth a look, wide and attractively backed by forested hills, and quieter than it ought to be – perhaps because there are no facilities apart from a jetty and a lookout tower, or because a certain amount of debris can wash up on a bad day.

Teluk Nipah

In complete contrast to Pasir Bogak, **TELUK NIPAH** beach has a more Malay character and plenty of budget places to stay. It's also teeming with **hornbills**; every day at 6.30pm, they come in droves for a feeding session at *Sunset View Chalet* (ⓦsunsetviewchalet.com). The beach is slightly narrower than at Bogak, especially at its north end – the busiest part of the strip – where the embanked road and a profusion of stalls encroach; at high tide there's barely sand to stroll on without the water rushing around your ankles. Views over the bay are beautiful at sunset, with hunchbacked **Mentagor Island** rising darkly against the dusk.

The northern extension of Teluk Nipah, sometimes called **Coral Bay**, is a quieter, pleasant cove with a couple of eating places right on the beach, making this a great spot for a sundowner. Amid the rocks at its far end is a bizarre shrine, **Lin Je Kong**, replete with concrete toadstools and animal statues, including Mickey Mouse.

ARRIVAL AND INFORMATION

By bus Lumut's bus station is 100m from the ferry terminal.
Destinations Alor Setar (at least 2 daily; 3hr 30min); Butterworth (7 daily; 2hr 30min); Ipoh (Perak Roadways buses to Medan Kidd: every 1hr 30min–2hr; 2hr); Ipoh (Amanjaya; 3 daily; 1hr 15min); Johor Bahru (at least 5 daily; 9hr); Melaka (3 daily; 5hr 30min); KLIA (5 daily; 5hr); Kota Bharu (3 daily; 9hr 30min); Kuala Kangsar (2 daily; 2hr); Kuala Lumpur (hourly; 4hr); Kuala Perlis (1 daily at 7.30am; 4hr 30min); Kuala Terengganu (at least 3 daily; 6hr); Kuantan (at least 1 daily; 9hr); Penang (1 daily at 3pm; 3hr); Seremban (2 daily; 5hr); Singapore (at least 5 daily; 10hr); Sungai Petani (at least 2 daily; 3hr); Taiping (3 daily; 1hr 10min).

PANGKOR AND LUMUT

By ferry Ferries run between Lumut and Pangkor Town daily from around 7am to 8.30pm (every 45min; 35min; RM14 return), calling at the village of Sungai Pinang Kecil en route. The Lumut ferry terminal has three ATMs, with a moneychanger and food court close by.
By taxi Lumut's taxi rank is outside the bus station. A cab from Ipoh costs RM150 (1hr 30min).
Tourist office None on Pangkor itself; in Lumut, Tourism Malaysia occupies a traditionally styled wooden building close to the ferry terminal (Mon–Thurs, Sat & Sun roughly 9am–12.30pm & 1.30–5.30pm, Fri 9am–noon & 3–5.30pm; ☎05 683 4057).

GETTING AROUND

An 18km coast road, steep in places, loops around Pangkor, cutting inland only between Pangkor Town and Pasir Bogak. There are no buses.

By minibus taxi Pink minibus taxis park outside Pangkor's ferry terminal and at the southern end of both Pasir Bogak and Teluk Nipah. A sign at the ferry terminal displays fares, for up to four passengers: from RM10 to Pasir

Bogak (2km) to RM70 for a 2hr, round-island circuit.
By bicycle/motorbike Renting a motorbike in Pangkor Town or via your hotel costs RM40–50/day; some guesthouses have bikes to rent at RM10–15/day.

ACCOMMODATION

Pangkor has plenty of accommodation, all rather hit-and-miss. Most budget places are at **Teluk Nipah**, which has a bustling neighbourhood feel and is cluttered with cheap restaurants and shops. Mid-range hotels, meanwhile are concentrated at **Pasir Bogak**, which is more upmarket and more dispersed, with few shops and restaurants outside the resorts (It can be worth taking a full-board package). The rates we quote here are typical outside holidays and weekends, when prices can rise by ten to fifty percent depending on the establishment.

PASIR BOGAK
Puteri Bayu 300m inland from the beach along the

main road ☎05 685 1929, ⓦputeribayu.com; map p.125. Pleasant complex of not-bad rooms and some quite

---

PANGKOR WATERSPORTS AND ACTIVITIES

Malaysian holidaymakers at Pangkor are particularly keen on **banana boat** rides, with four people being towed around one of the bays astride an elongated float, culminating in an obligatory dunking at the end (RM15). Rides on other bizarrely shaped floats are available too, as is **jetskiing** (RM60 for two; 15min). Much more worthwhile than any of these is a 45-minute **island-hopping tour** (negotiable RM150–250 for a group of up to four; make sure operators have a license and insurance), taking you out to Mentagor, Pangkor Laut and other islets for views of odd rock formations, after which you can swim and snorkel (no time limit – just arrange to be collected). For serious **fishing** or **snorkelling**, you'll need to charter a boat out to the Sembilan Islands, well west of Pangkor, costing at least RM1500. You can book all of the above with Happy Island (☎012 414 1749), based in Pasir Bogak.

You can also ride all-terrain vehicles (ATVs) from Teluk Nipah along the Bukit Merah trail, a jungle path that goes beyond the airport strip and ends close to Teluk Dalam. **ATV Adventure Pangkor** (from RM80/person; ☎011 2746 0251, ⓦfacebook.com/ATVAdventurePangkor) at the northern end of Teluk Nipah is a reliable operator.

2

attractive chalets. Breakfast included. 🛜 Doubles <u>RM140</u>, chalets <u>RM250</u>

Sandy Beach Resort Off the right end of Pasir Bogak's access road ☎05 685 3027, 🌐pangkorsandybeach.com; map p.125. Low-key buildings curling around a snazzy freeform pool. Rooms have all the customary conveniences, including fridges and safes, but are a little plain for the rate, which includes breakfast. 🛜 <u>RM210</u>

TELUK NIPAH

Anjungan North end of Teluk Nipah ☎05 685 1500, 🌐anjunganresortpangkor.com; map p.125. The only mid-range resort in Teluk Nipah, comprising four-storey buildings surrounding a boat-shaped pool, with a popular restaurant. The rooms are comfortable enough, if rather plain; still, the overall tone is relaxed and the place is competently run. 🛜 <u>RM160</u>

★Belantara Camp North end of Teluk Nipah; map p.125. Superbly chilled beach campsite for bliss-seekers. They provide four-man tents or you can bring your own, and there are basic toilets, a wooden bar and tables under a charming umbrella of branches where you can barbecue your food. No electricity, just candlelight. 🛜 Camping pitch <u>RM10</u>, 4-man tent <u>RM50</u>

Budget Beach Resort Southernmost turning off the main road ☎05 685 3529, 🌐budgetbeachresort.com; map p.125. The densely packed chalets here aren't anything special at first sight, but they are in above-average condition, each with balcony and bathroom, and helpful staff keep the whole place shipshape. A sound choice. 🛜 <u>RM80</u>

Nazri Nipah Camp Second turning off the main road ☎0111 142 8907, ✉nazrinipahcamp@gmail.com; map p.125. Laid back to a fault, with slightly frayed fan

chalets and poky A-frames, some with bathrooms, around a pleasant communal garden area. A/c chalets are available too. 🛜 Dorms <u>RM25</u>, A-frames <u>RM40</u>, chalets <u>RM60</u>

Nipah Bay Villa Second turning off the main road ☎05 685 2198, 🌐pulaupangkornipahbayvilla .blogspot.com; map p.125. Behind the shaded restaurant at the front is a tall, institutional block of rooms as well as rather better chalets, all with a/c, TV and bathroom. 🛜 Doubles <u>RM90</u>, chalets <u>RM130</u>

★Nipah Guesthouse Southernmost turning off the main road ☎017 506 9259, 🌐facebook.com/Nipah .Guesthouse; map p.125. This wonderful guesthouse has four spick-and-span A-framed huts surrounding a pleasant pool area with loungers, and a cluster of mini-apartments for families. The included breakfast consists of a continental buffet in the breezy dining area, where guests are encouraged to rustle up eggs and pancakes themselves. 🛜 <u>RM120</u>

Ombak Inn Southernmost turning off the main road ☎05 685 5223, 🌐ombakinnchalet.com; map p.125. Like a little kampung in the woods, this is a homely collection of chalets in grounds overgrown with bougainvillea. Rooms have a/c, TV and slightly cramped bathrooms. 🛜 <u>RM100</u>

ELSEWHERE

Tiger Rock Inland of Kota Belanda ☎019 574 7183, 🌐tigerrock.info; map p.125. *Tiger Rock* is almost a mini country estate, but set in the tropics. There's a huge, wooden main house and various other buildings, all in colonial-era styles, lovingly decorated by the owner, artist Rebecca Duckett-Wilkinson. There's a total of eight tasteful rooms, a beautiful infinity pool facing a wild jungle slope, and a tennis court. Wi-fi in the lobby only. Full-board double plus round-island trip 🛜 <u>RM1400</u>

EATING

There are few restaurants but plenty of street stalls on **Teluk Nipah's main road**, mostly dishing up simple Malay food and snacks such as BBQ sweetcorn and *lempeng pisang* (a banana and coconut pancake grilled inside a banana-leaf wrapping). At **Pasir Bogak**, a few stalls cluster on the road to the *Sea View* hotel, but most visitors eat at their resort.

PASIR BOGAK

★Sea View Sea View Hotel, Pasir Bogak ☎05 685 1605; map p.125. With tables on a beachside verandah, this perennially popular restaurant has an all-round menu of Chinese food (RM12–30) – try standbys like tangy chicken in lemon sauce or the curry fish with *asam* (tamarind) – plus Western mains and snacks including black pepper steak (RM40). Daily 7am–11pm.

TELUK NIPAH

★Daddy's Café A 5min walk north from Teluk Nipah ☎011 5984173, 🌐bit.ly/DaddysCafe; map p.125. This beachside restaurant-bar has tables on the sand

overlooking the bay, a nice setting for a candlelit dinner. The menu covers a range of Western dishes, including steak and fish and chips, but the jumbo grilled prawns are spectacular. Beer is frosty-cold. Mains from RM30. Daily 11am–11pm.

Nipah Deli Teluk Nipah, before Daddy's Café ☎05 685 1416, 🌐facebook.com/NipahDeli; map p.125. The Chinese resident chef here makes his steamboat spicy – and delicious. Other menu items include hot-off-the-wok, unusual green-curry chicken noodles, Nyonya seafood *laksa* and seafood-based rice dishes (all RM12–18). Vegan and vegetarian versions on request. Daily roughly 12.30–10pm.

Kuala Kangsar

A bustling country town, **KUALA KANGSAR** is Perak's **royal seat**, playing a similar role opposite Ipoh as Pekan on the east coast (see p.263) does for Kuantan, Pahang's capital. For Malaysians, Kuala Kangsar is best known as a centre for the production of **labu** – water pitchers with a pumpkin-shaped base (*labu* means "gourd" in Malay), excellent as souvenirs – and as the home of the **Malay College**. Founded in 1905 as a British-style boarding school, it began educating the most promising or well-connected Malay boys, thus bringing the community least involved in the colonial project into the Western intellectual fold; many of its students have gone on to achieve greatness in Malaysian public life, notably the prominent opposition politician and former deputy prime minister, Anwar Ibrahim. For visitors, the town is worthwhile for its royal and Islamic buildings, although note that the most interesting of these, the **Perak Royal Museum**, seems eternally closed, pending long-term repairs.

Royal quarter

What passes for the town's **royal quarter** is **Bukit Chandan**, the hilly area south of the little Kangsar River, spanned by a road bridge close to the golden-topped clock tower in the town centre. The most prominent sight is the hilltop **Sultan Azlan Shah Gallery**, a colonially styled former palace containing daft regalia and ephemera pertaining to the Perak royals (Mon–Thurs, Sat & Sun 10am–5pm, Fri 10am–12.15pm & 2.45–5pm; RM4; ☎05 777 5362). Some 500m beyond, **Masjid Ubudiah** sports a splendid array of golden onion domes amid a thicket of striped minarets.

Perak Royal Museum

Closed at the time of writing

Around 1km beyond Masjid Ubudiah, past the marble 1930s **Istana Iskandariah**, the sultan's palace, lies the former palace, the **Istana Kenangan**. Now the **Perak Royal Museum**, it was built in the 1920s as a modest temporary residence while the present palace was being finished, and is of interest not for its exhibits but as a beautiful example of a traditional Malay mansion. Fashioned from wood without a single nail being used, the house is adorned with friezes and geometric-patterned panels. Sadly, it was closed for long-term repairs at the time of writing; ask at local tourist offices to find out whether it has reopened.

2

ANTHONY BURGESS'S HERITAGE

It's little-known that British writer Anthony Burgess, author of *A Clockwork Orange* (1962), taught in Kuala Kangsar from 1954 to 1956. His debut novel *Time for a Tiger* (1956), first in his *Malayan Trilogy*, is set in **Kuala Hantu**, a fictional Kuala Kangsar. Some of the locations described in the book still exist today: besides the **Malay College** there's the **Idris Club** (now a social club), the watering hole where protagonist Victor Crabbe – and possibly Burgess himself – would drink himself silly. A twenty-minute walk southeast of the Malay College is a girl's school, **SMK Raja Perempuan Kelsom**, formerly the **King's Pavilion**, where Burgess and his wife lived.

Sayong

Head east from the clock tower and you come almost immediately to the **estuary** of the **Kangsar** and the wide **Perak River** that the town is named for. Visible on the east bank of the latter is the village of **Sayong**, where the production and sale of *labu* is a major cottage industry. Boats shuttle across the river sporadically for a nominal sum; once across you can ask around for the location of *labu* makers, no more than a fifteen-minute walk away.

ARRIVAL AND INFORMATION   KUALA KANGSAR

The town centre is on the north bank of the Kangsar River. Although Route 1 runs through town, skirting the train station, the historic main street is Jalan Kangsar.

By train The station (☎05 776 1094) is on the outskirts, a 20min walk from the clock tower. Note that Padang Rengas station, 12.5km west of Kuala Kangsar, is the terminus of the KTM Komuter service to Butterworth (via Bukit Mertajam). Destinations Alor Star (5 daily; 2hr); Butterworth (ETS 7 daily, every 1–2hr from Padang Rengas via Bukit Mertajam; 1hr 10min); Ipoh (11 daily; 30min); Gemas (4 daily; 5hr); Kuala Lumpur (11 daily; 3hr); Padang Besar (5 daily; 2hr 20min); Seremban (4 daily; 4hr); Sungai Petani (5 daily; 1hr 25min); Taiping (11 daily; 20min).

By bus The bus station is on Jalan Bendahara, a few minutes' walk from Jalan Kangsar; it's served mainly by local buses, although some express buses call here too.
Destinations Butterworth (at least 4 daily; 1hr 30min); Ipoh (#35; every 20–30min; 1hr 15min); Kota Bharu (2 daily; 7hr); KLIA/KLIA2 (2 daily; 4hr 40min); Kuala Lumpur (several daily; 3hr 30min); Lenggong (#99; every 90min; 75min); Lumut (2 daily; 2hr); Sungai Petani (2 daily; 2hr 45min); Taiping (every 45min; 1hr).

Tourist office The tourist office, by the clock tower, has plenty of leaflets (Tues–Thurs & Sat 9am–1pm & 2–6pm, Fri 9am–12.30pm & 3–6pm, Sun 9am–1pm; ☎05 777 7717).

ACCOMMODATION

★**The Shop** 1 Persiaran Seri Delima, about 1km east of the train station, up a side road to the right ☎05 777 3288, ⓦfacebook.com/TheShopHotel; map p.129. Kuala Kangsar's first boutique hotel has its own hipster café, where young locals sit on vintage chairs, surrounded by exposed brick. Upstairs is a series of retro-chic en-suite rooms, most with windows. The rooms are quite small, but in this town at this price, you can't ask for more. 🛜 **RM88**

EATING

If you're in Kuala Kangsar at the weekend, consider checking out the wide range of sweet and savoury snacks available at the **night market** around the main market off Jalan Kangsar (Fri 4.30–8pm), and at the **craft market** close to the jetty (Sat & Sun 7.30am–noon).

Laksa Pak Ngah Restaurant: Jalan Dato Sagor, behind Tsung Wah secondary school; food truck: along Persiaran Sungai Perak, 50m before the craft market ☎05 775 7986, ⓦbit.ly/LaksaPakNgah; map p.129. This mini chain started dishing up their signature *laksa* (RM5) in 1955, before independence, and when Anthony Burgess was still in town. The main outlet is quite a hike from the centre, but they now also have some food trucks, one of which is near the craft market. Mon, Tues & Thurs–Sun 9am–7pm.

Pusat Makanan Kuala Kangsar Behind the Store mall; map p.129. This breezy food court, by the river, is an ideal escape from the stifling heat; sip iced *kopis* and eat cheap *char koay teow*, *nasi goreng* and other Malay and Chinese staples (all RM8 or less) under the shade of giant trees. Daily 8am–10pm.

Yat Lai Jalan Kangsar ☎05 776 6369; map p.129. Also signed *Yut Loy*, this is a gloriously antiquated, Chinese-owned, Malay-run *kedai kopi* – look out for the ancient notice from the days when Malay was still written in Arabic script, imploring people not to spit or beg. It's famous nationwide for its signature *char siew pow* (steamed pork buns), served from

2.30pm; they also serve, sometimes glacially slowly, simple rice and noodle dishes, plus attempts at steak and scrambled egg. Hardly anything over RM10. Mon–Sat 9am–6pm.

SHOPPING

Craft market Close to the jetty; map p.129. Kuala Kangsar isn't a bad place to buy crafts and souvenirs. Here you'll find a good range of basketry, wickerwork (including

bags), some textiles and of course the obligatory *labu* – a 20cm-tall specimen will set you back just RM20. Daily 9am–7pm.

2

Taiping and around

Set against the mist-laden Bintang Hills, **TAIPING** is one of few big towns in Malaysia with a Chinese name – one that means "everlasting peace", though it's somewhat ironic given the **clan wars** here between rival Cantonese and Hakka factions during the town's early days. Relaxed and mostly low-rise, it doesn't look like it was once one of the most important towns in the Peninsula. Yet the great **tin boom** in the second half of the nineteenth century, to which Taiping owes its existence, meant that by the 1890s it was in a race with Kuala Lumpur to be chosen as capital of the newly constituted Federated Malay States. Taiping evidently lost. Within a few years it suffered a second ignominy as Ipoh outgrew it, usurping even its role as state capital in 1937.

TAIPING

N

0 — 100 metres

Ling Nam Temple
Prisoners' Handicraft Store
Perak Museum
All Saints' Church
Prison
JLN TAMING SARI
JLN AIR TERJUN
Kamunting Faya Express Bus Terminal (7km)
Taiping War Cemetery (1km); Coronation Pool (1.2km); Maxwell Hill (Bukit Larut) (1.5km) & ■ (2km)
JLN ISTANA LARUT
JALAN KELAB LAMA
Police Station
JALAN SULTAN MANSOR
Zoo
Lake Gardens
JLN WIZMUL HUDA
LORONG KING EDWARD
JLN KEMUNTING
JLN PADANG BOLA
JALAN ALANG AHMAD
Padang
District Office
JLN PASAR
King Edward VII School
Antong Coffee Mill
JLN STESEN
JLN BARRACK
JALAN ONG SAIK
JLN LIM TEONG CHYE
JLN MANJOIKA
JLN LIM TEONG CHYE
Boat and bike Rental
OLD JALAN SULTAN
JALAN TAMAN TASIK
Old House Museum
Guardian Pharmacy
Clocktower
JLN KOTA
JLN KELAB LINA
JLN TUPAI
JLN MAHARAJA LELA
JLN ABDULLAH
JLN PASAR
JLN YUSOF
JALAMAN PASAR
JLN LIM HYE PIN
Taiping KTM Train Station
Central Market
Taxis
Taiping Bus Hub
Jalan Iskandar
JLN ISKANDAR
JLN IDRIS
Matang Mangrove Forest Reserve (16km)
JALAN STESEN
Watsons Pharmacy
Konsortium Tickets
JLN PANGGUNG WAYANG
Local Bus Station
JLN CONVENT
JALAN MASJID
Mosque
Penang & Ipoh

DRINKING
Atrium	1
Sky Bar	2

ACCOMMODATION
Flemington	3
Legend Inn	5
Louis Hotel	4
Sentosa Villa	1
Sojourn Beds & Cafe	2

EATING
Larut Matang Food Court	4
Prima	1
Sri Annapoorana Curry House	3
Taman Tasik Food Court	2

SHOPPING
Kapitan Antiques House	1
Taiping Mall	2

2

Today's Taiping is a discreetly prosperous affair, regarded as a desirable place to retire. Few foreign visitors come, which is a pity as it's one of the nicest provincial towns to relax in for a day or two. As you'd expect from its Chinese heritage, much of **central Taiping** comprises old shophouses, some being restored, centred on an unusual old **market** housed inside two huge, century-old wooden hangars. In addition to its **museums** there's the 1933 **Antong Coffee Mill**, the oldest coffee factory in the country, and the house where Sun Yat-sen stayed when he visited Taiping. The green **Lake Gardens** on the eastern edge of town, and the nearby former hill retreat of **Maxwell Hill (Bukit Larut)** and the lush **Matang Mangrove Forest Reserve** are also worth exploring.

Old House Museum

2a Medan Pasar • RM5 • Ask the owner at Kapitan's Antique House for the key

The **Old House Museum** nicely evokes how a well-to-do Taiping family might have lived decades ago. Beautifully carved screens and altars figure prominently downstairs at this late nineteenth-century timber shophouse, where there's also a rustic kitchen at the back with a heavy granite pestle and mortar of the sort once used to pound chillies and spices.

Antong Coffee Mill

8a Jalan Assam Kumbang, under the flyover next to the train station • Daily 8.30am–5.30pm • Free • ☎ 014 900 0055, ⓦ antongcoffeemill.com.my

The oldest coffee factory in Malaysia, opened in 1933, **Antong Coffee Mill** still uses traditional wood-fire roasting techniques. You can sample a wide variety of brews, but the main reason to come here is visiting the enterprise's office, set in the historical house where founding father of the Republic of China, Sun Yat-sen, stayed with his Hong Kong-born concubine, Chen Chui Fen. Look out for the exquisite original Peranakan woodcarvings on the partition walls.

All Saints' Church

Jalan Taming Sari

Founded in 1887, **All Saints' Church** is the oldest Anglican church in what would become the Federated Malay States. It's built in a lightweight English Gothic style – though the roof is tiled in very Malaysian wooden shingles – and is also noteworthy for having one of the very few pipe organs in the country. The tiny churchyard contains the graves of some of the earliest British and Australian settlers.

Perak Museum

Jalan Taming Sari • Daily 9am–6pm • RM5 • ☎ 05 807 2057

Housed in a purpose-built colonial building, the state-run **Perak Museum** is another Taiping "first" – it's the oldest museum in the Malay Peninsula, opened in 1883 at the instigation of the Resident Hugh Low. The three collections portray Malaysia's anthropology, zoology and local history, with displays of stuffed local fauna, as well as an extensive collection of ancient weapons and Orang Asli implements and ornaments. Incidentally, the grim, grey wall opposite the museum is the outside of Taiping's **prison**, built in 1879 and used by the Japanese during World War II.

Lake Gardens

Pedal boats can be rented from the gardens' south side Mon–Thurs 10am–7.30pm, Fri–Sun 9am–7.30pm • From RM12/15min

Taiping's extensive **Lake Gardens**, at the eastern edge of the centre, were created in 1880 when Hugh Low decided that the mess left by two tin mines should be landscaped and turned into a park. Today it's an inviting expanse of lawns, clumps of bamboo and mature trees covered in moss and ferns. At the time of writing, works were underway to turn part of it into **botanic gardens**. The view from the town side is particularly impressive on bright evenings, when the gardens seem to merge with the sunlit forested hills to the east, though the goofy duck-shaped **pedal boats** can mar the most meticulously composed photos.

Taiping Zoo and Night Safari

Zoo Daily 8.30am–6pm • RM16 • **Night safari** Daily 8–11pm (Sat til midnight) • RM20 • ☎ 05 808 6577, ⓦ zootaiping.gov.my

A big magnet for Malaysian visitors, the **zoo** on the Lake Gardens' far side houses plenty of local wildlife, including *siamang* (a type of gibbon), civets, orangutan, tigers, elephants and bearded pigs. It also boasts the **Night Safari** – a modest copy of Singapore's – showcasing nocturnal animals.

Taiping War Cemetery

On the Bukit Larut Rd, 1.2km from the start of the Lake Gardens • Open access • ⓦ bit.ly/TaipingWarCemetery

A serene memorial to the casualties of World War II, the Taiping **War Cemetery** contains the graves of 866 men, more than five hundred of whom are unidentified. Split in two by the road, it's divided between Hindu and Muslim Indians on one side and Christian British and Australians on the other.

Maxwell Hill (Bukit Larut)

Land Rovers 8.30am, 10.30am, 12.30pm & 2.30pm • 35min • RM10 return • ☎ 05 807 7241 • Summit Rd begins 1.5km beyond the Lake Gardens – turn right at the Coronation Pool for Ranger Station; Rapid Kamunting Bus #20A/B shuttles between the Hab Bus on Jalan Iskandar and Jalan Air Terjun

Bukit Larut, still widely known by its colonial-era name, **Maxwell Hill**, is Malaysia's smallest and oldest hill station, its summit a mere 6km east of Taiping as the crow flies. The climate is wonderfully cool; when it isn't raining – this is one of the wettest places in the country – you can be treated to good views down to the coast. Local visitors prefer to ride the Land Rovers up and down, but the long, often steep hike up offers the chance to do some **birdwatching** or spot unusual **pig-tailed macaques** (the name makes sense when you come across one) which live in the forests lower down.

Walking to the summit

The **summit road** (10km to the top) twists and turns round some 72 terrifying bends; walking, allow at least three hours up, two hours down if you only take short breathers. About halfway up, the Tea Garden House, once part of an extensive tea estate but now little more than a shelter, makes an ideal rest stop, with a view of Taiping and the mirror-like waters of the gardens visible below. The main **hill station area** (1036m) has a few minor trails and circuits in the vicinity. Ambitious walkers continue a further 3km through groves of evergreens to the 1250m-high summit of **Mount Hijau**, although it's as well to seek advice from the rangers if you want to attempt this.

ACTIVITIES   MAXWELL HILL (BUKIT LARUT)

ATV tours It's possible to ride ATVs from the Lake Gardens up the hill to a waterfall, have lunch and return (RM150), or camp overnight (RM250/person, minimum six). ATV

Adventure Park Larut (☎012 210 4761, ⓦbit.ly/ ATVAdventurePark) is an established and reliable operator.

ACCOMMODATION

The Nest ☎012 239 5569, ⓦbit.ly/TheNestBL. You can now stay at a refurbished 130-year-old bungalow flanked by virgin rainforest, with four rooms hosting a

maximum of twelve people. Reserve at least two weeks in advance by phone. Full board per person RM130

Matang Mangrove Forest Reserve

16km west of Taiping, 2km before Kuala Sepetang (Port Weld) • Daily 9am–5pm • RM15 • ☎ 05 858 1762 • Bus #77 from Taiping bus station (every 1hr 20min) to Kuala Sepetang

More than a century old, the **Matang Mangrove Forest Reserve** is Peninsular Malaysia's largest surviving spread of mangrove, most of which has been extensively cleared for

2

development or for **charcoal production** (still practised, sustainably, in the nearby town of **Kuala Sepetang**). After the 2004 Indian Ocean tsunami, local interest in the mangroves increased; the trees' mesh of aerial support roots can absorb some of the force of tsunamis, and thus protect coastlines. They're also breeding grounds for small marine creatures, from fiddler crabs to mudskippers and archerfish. Extensive **boardwalks** at the reserve lead through a forest of tall, thin trunks and mangrove ferns; keep your eyes peeled for dusky-leaf monkeys.

ARRIVAL AND INFORMATION

TAIPING AND AROUND

By train Taiping station is on Jalan Stesen, just north of the centre (☎ 05 807 2591). There are frequent ETS services to points south and KL, and cheaper KTM Komuter trains to Butterworth.

Destinations Alor Star (5 daily; 1hr 40min); Butterworth (ETS 7 daily, Komuter every 2hr via Bukit Mertajam; 45min); Gemas (4 daily; 5hr 20min); Ipoh (11 daily; 50min); Kuala Kangsar (11 daily; 20min); Kuala Lumpur (11 daily; 3hr 15min); Padang Besar (ETS 5 daily, Komuter every 2hr; 2hr); Seremban (4 daily; 4hr 20min); Sungai Petani (5 daily; 1hr).

By local bus The local station in Taiping is off Jalan Masjid.

Destinations Ipoh (every 45min; 1hr 45min); Kamunting (#10A/B; every 40min; 30min); Kuala Kangsar (every 45min; 1hr); Kuala Sepetang (#77; every 1hr 20min; 30min).

By express bus The nearest express bus station to Taiping is Kamunting Raya Express Bus Terminal, 7km north, in the industrial town of Kamunting; confusingly, some bus firms advertise services for Taiping when they mean this station. Rapid Kamunting buses #10A/B run between Taiping's train station and the Kamunting Long Distance Bus Terminal; a taxi costs RM15. You can buy tickets for one bus company, Konsortium, in Taiping at its office on Jalan Panggung Wayang across from the bus station.

Destinations Butterworth (hourly; 1hr 15min); Johor Bahru (several daily; 8hr 30min); Kota Bharu (every 2 days; 6hr); Kuala Lumpur (hourly; 3hr 30min); Penang (several daily; 1hr 30min); Singapore (3 daily; 9hr 30min).

Tourist office Run by volunteers, inside the old clock tower on Jalan Kota (Mon–Sat 10am–5pm; ☎ 05 805 3245).

GETTING AROUND

Although Taiping is built on a grid layout, it's easy to lose your bearings thanks to patchy street signage (note that many of the north–south streets change their name across Jalan Kota). **Jalan Taming Sari** is the main street, busy by day but dead at night.

By bus Rapid Taiping Buses 20A/20B leave every 40min 6am–10pm from the bus hub on Jalan Iskandar, stopping at the Taiping KTM Station, the Perak Museum, Maxwell Hill's foothills, the Taiping Zoo and the Lake Gardens. Buses 10A/10B shuttle passengers between Jalan Iskandar and the Kamunting Raya Express Bus Terminal, stopping at both Kamunting and Taiping KTM Stations.

By taxi Taxis await next to the bus hub on Jalan Iskandar. A trip to Maxwell Hill costs around RM15, and RM10 to the Lake Gardens.

By bike The pedal-boat rental outlet at the Lake Gardens also rents bikes (RM15/4hr) – useful, given how scattered some of the town's sights are.

By motorbike You can rent motorbikes for RM10/hr or RM50/day from Jeffrey Ong (☎ 016 238 6067).

ACCOMMODATION

Flemington Jalan Samanea Saman ☎ 05 820 7777, ⓦ flemingtonhotel.com.my; map p.131. A modern hotel with a rooftop pool offering great views out over the Lake Gardens and east to the mountains (pricier rooms also have good vistas). The rooms could be a little more distinctive for the price, although breakfast is thrown in. ☞ RM168

Legend Inn 2 Jalan Long Jaafar ☎ 05 806 0000, ⓦ legendinn.com; map p.131. The best of the mid-range hotels in the centre, and convenient for local buses. An extra RM10 or so per head pays for the buffet breakfast in the coffee house. ☞ RM118

Louis Hotel 129 Jalan Pasar ☎ 05 808 2333, ⓦ louishotel.com.my; map p.131. This four-storey boutique hotel next to the old market has pleasant en-suite rooms with full facilities – hairdryers, safety boxes and

ironing boards. Great value, despite the somewhat boxy toilets. ☞ RM98

Sentosa Villa In the Taman Sentosa residential estate off the Bukit Larut Rd, 2km from the Lake Gardens ☎ 05 805 1000, ⓦ sentosa-villa.com; map p.131. The reward for staying this far from town is being in a sort of back-to-nature motel, the buildings styled like jumbo treehouses in a leafy compound with a stream-fed pool to swim in and ducks and geese waddling around. There's a café where you can buy breakfast. ☞ Doubles RM138, villas RM208

★ **Sojourn Beds & Cafe** 54 Jalan Kota ☎ 012 464 3434, ⓦ facebook.com/SojournBC; map p.131. Taiping earned another first with this top-notch backpacker hostel. Renovated from a central shophouse that's walking distance to most sights, *Sojourn* is lovingly tendered by a local-Aussie team of backpacking aficionados. Their enthusiasm seeps into the many well-thought-out details – such as free desktop computers for guest use – and the spotless rooms and dorms (all with shared bathrooms). Simple breakfast included. 🛜 Dorms RM35, doubles RM85

EATING

Larut Matang Food Court Jalan Panggung Wayang; map p.131. This food court is divided into halal (basically Malay) and non-halal (Chinese) halves. Try the local fish-egg *char koay teow* (RM 4.5) at Stall 78, and the impressive "snow mountain" *ais kacang*, a pyramid of ice and syrup (RM4). Daily: Malay 9am–11pm, Chinese 7am–10pm.

Prima Jalan Kota, opposite Jalan Maneksha; map p.131. Two *kopitiam*-type places on opposite street corners, with tables out on the street come evening, *Prima* runs the gamut of Malaysian hawker food: *laksa*, *rojak*, *nasi lemak* and more, plus some Western options too. Meals RM8–20. Daily 8am–11pm.

Sri Annapoorana Curry House Corner of Jalan Taming Sari and Jalan Yusof; map p.131. The friendliest eating place in Taiping's Indian quarter, with *roti* and *thosai* made to order, noodles, more substantial meals (around RM10) with or without meat, plus starchy South Indian breakfasts like *pongal* – almost a lightly spiced risotto. Mon–Sat 7.30am–8pm, Sun 7.30am–3pm.

Taman Tasik Food Court Western side of the Lake Gardens; map p.131. Excellent, inexpensive Chinese food (mains RM5–10), including seafood noodles, rice with chicken *rendang* and, more unusually, century-egg porridge (rice gruel with gelatinous pickled eggs). Locals rate the stalls on the outside edge, facing the gardens, as the best. Daily 24hr.

DRINKING

★**Atrium** 36 Jalan Kota ☎ 05 807 6624, 🌐 bit.ly/ AtriumTaipei; map p.131. Housed in the splendid 1896 Shun Tak clan hall, this hip bistro offers a fusion menu of Asian and Western dishes; it's also the most atmospheric spot for a beer in town. Live bands on most weekends.

Mon–Sat 10am–12.30am.

Sky Bar Top of Flemington Hotel; map p.131. Set on the Flemington's terrace, this is a good place for a sundowner as the light changes over the mountains and the Lake Gardens. Daily 8am–2am.

Lenggong Valley

The one-horse town of **LENGGONG**, 77km north of Ipoh in the midst of Perak's jungle, hosts Malaysia's lesser-known fourth UNESCO World Heritage site. Inscribed in 2012, the town's open-air and cave sites span from the Palaeolithic to the Neolithic and Bronze Age up to 1700 years ago. Hand axes found in nearby **Bukit Bunuh**, the site of a meteorite impact from 1.83 million years ago, are among the oldest outside Africa, and suggest that the Lenggong Valley was an extremely early site of hominids' presence in Southeast Asia. Both this and nearby **Bukit Jawa**'s workshop site, with tools dating back to 200,000 BC to 100,000 BC, are open to the public and are best visited with your own set of wheels. A tour should include stops at **Lata Kekabu**, 7km south of Lenggong off Route 76, a 50m-high waterfall, passing over three consecutive rock pools; and at **Tasik Raban**, 5km further south, a shimmering man-made lake popular with local holidaymakers.

Lenggong Valley Archaeological Gallery

Signed off Route 76, 6km south of Lenggong town near the village of Kota Tampan • Daily 9am–5pm • Free • ☎ 05 767 9700 • Board a Kuala Kangsar-bound bus and get off at the turnoff on the main road, then walk the 2km to the site; alternatively, try to find an unofficial taxi in Lenggong – Soon Lee Hotel may help

The main focus of the **Lenggong Valley Archaeological Gallery** is on 10,000 year-old **Perak Man**, Southeast Asia's most complete early human skeleton. His bones appear jumbled and inscrutable to the untrained eye, although it has deformities that indicate he had a congenital disease. He was buried in a cave called **Gua Gunung Runtuh**, 4km north of Lenggong, together with shells and tools, making him one of few known examples of ancient people with disabilities given a ceremonial burial; archaeologists believe he was considered a shaman by his community.

By bus The bus station is by the central market off Jalan Besar, Lenggong's main road, where you will find everything from ATMs to grocery shops, a post office and a hospital. Some Kuala Lumpur buses leave from Dataran Lenggong, a parking lot along Route 76, 1.5km north of Lenggong's bus stand.

Destinations Ipoh (7 daily; 1hr 30min); Johor Bharu (via Kuala Lumpur; daily at 10am; 8hr); Kuala Kangsar (hourly till 6.15pm; 45min); Kuala Lumpur (3 daily; 4hr); Gerik (roughly every 2hr; some continue to Betong, in Thailand; 1hr).

By car Lenggong is on Route 76, between Kuala Kangsar and Gerik. From the E1, exit at Kuala Kangsar toll and proceed north. A more interesting rural route from Penang goes through Road 136 between Kulim and Selama, in Kedah, before joining road A6, which connects to Route 76 about 7km north of the Lenggong turnoff.

Tours Lenggong Valley Archaeological Gallery can arrange free guided tours to the burial site and other caves by appointment (Mon–Fri 9am–5pm; donations welcome; you must have your own transport). Apply at least one week in advance by contacting the museum director, Mr Sanjit (☎ 013 419 0401; ✉ tengah@heritage.gov.my).

ACCOMMODATION AND EATING

Chat Sook Back Lane West, 10m to the right of the bus station ☎ 012 598 1733, ⓦ bit.ly/ChatSook. Try Lenggong's famous fish balls and riverfish belly, cooked in sweet-and-sour sauce and garlic, at this no-frills place that set the standard for most to follow. A meal won't set you back more than RM40. Daily 8am–noon & 6pm–10pm.

★ **Loh Dee** Jalan Besar. Look for the signboard over a red metallic awning to try juicy char siew-covered *wan tan mee*, roasted over charcoal, a rarity nationwide. Come very early for breakfast, and you will still fight for a table with dozens of hungry locals. Daily 7am–noon.

Permaculture Perak On a remote hill south of Lenggong, only reachable by 4WD ⓦ permacultureperak.com. A one-of-a-kind off-grid farm built by a Czech named Ladia, who collects guests from Lenggong by arrangement. It's rustic but not overly so: the guests' farmhouse has proper bedrooms and cold showers, and there's solar power and even wi-fi. You share the compound with various goats; diversions include swimming in a stream full of tiny fish, and wooded trails further uphill. Minimum two nights. Full board per person 🛜 **RM165**

Soon Lee Hotel 31 Jalan Besar ☎ 014 327 6204, ⓦ facebook.com/SoonLeeHotel. Basic yet clean en-suite rooms, in the heart of town. Amiable owners Mr. Ng and Pinky Mok are a fountain of local knowledge. 🛜 **RM70**

Royal Belum State Park

Perak's last outpost before Kelantan is the underrated **Royal Belum State Park**, a pocket of rainforest and lakeland snuggled up against a Thai national park across the border. The lake here, **Temenggor**, was created in the 1970s as a hydropower project, although locals say it was also intended to frustrate infiltration by Communist insurgents from the Emergency days (see p.563), who had taken refuge in Thailand. Whatever the truth of that, the park itself and the adjoining Temenggor forest reserve to the south offer an excellent taste of Malaysian nature: the area is home to all ten of the country's indigenous **hornbill** species, plus the odd elephant, gaur and other wildlife. **Rafflesia** flowers bloom year-round, too.

Visitors reach the park via the **Banding jetty** on the western edge, just off Route 4. Some 40km away on Route 76 is the nearest town, **Gerik** (or Grik), which is 65km east of Butterworth and 95km north of Ipoh as the crow flies.

By bus and taxi Local buses from Ipoh head to Gerik via Lenggong (5 daily; 3hr), from where a taxi to the jetty costs RM55. Express buses travelling between Penang (or other west coast cities) and Kota Bharu should call at Gerik and may be able to drop you at the access road for the jetty.

By car From Penang, take the E15/Route 67 to just before Kupang, where you turn right on to a minor road that eventually links up with Route 4 near Gerik. From points south, join Route 76 at the Kuala Kangsar exit on the North–South Expressway.

By boat Without a permit, you can still see some of the park by chartering a boat at the Banding jetty (RM30/person/hr or around 200RM/hr for the whole boat).

Permits To access the park, visitors need to apply for permits (RM10) at least a week in advance and through a licensed operator. In practice, given that travellers must also hire guides and a boat to enter the reserve, the easiest way to come is on a pricey package (from RM965 for 3 days/2 nights, including full board, accommodation and one day in the reserve) offered by the resorts.

ACCOMMODATION

Privately run lodges and houseboats are outside the park in the **Temenggor** reserve. Book a week in advance so they can sort out your park permits.

Belum Eco Resort Temenggor forest reserve ☎ 05 281 0834, ⊛ belumecoresort.com.my. Affordable, well-run place with simple chalets that have built-in showers, although toilets are shared. There's also a Malay-style houseboat that sleeps up to six. Packages include boat rides, kayaking, trekking to salt licks and a visit to an Orang Asli community. Three days full board including activities and permits, per person ☎ RM590

Belum Rainforest Resort Temenggor forest reserve ☎ 05 791 6800, ⊛ belumresort.com. The slickest accommodation in the area, offering big-city creature comforts and style in a range of spacious rooms and chalets. They price activities separately: a day's worth of boat rides and trekking can cost more than a night's stay. Breakfast included. ☎ RM490

Cameron Highlands

On the western fringes of Pahang state, **CAMERON HIGHLANDS** take its name from William Cameron, a colonial surveyor who stumbled across the area in 1885, though not until forty years later did civil servant Sir George Maxwell propose it be turned into what would become the Peninsula's largest hill station. Indian planters, Chinese vegetable farmers and wealthy landowners in search of a weekend retreat flocked in, establishing **tea plantations** and leaving a swathe of what can only be called mock-mock-Tudor buildings in their wake.

The Camerons remain one of the most publicized attractions in Malaysia, although very much trading on past glories. Don't come expecting the pastoral idyll of the brochures.

TEA PLANTATIONS

The countless cups of *teh tarik* served up daily in Malaysia are likely to be made with home-grown **tea**, which is – no pun intended – a bit of a mixed bag. Some people think local tea simply doesn't taste very good, although the stuff served up at food courts and *kedai kopis* is usually so swamped with condensed milk that it's impossible to tell what the underlying taste is. Even if it doesn't float your boat, tea is such a feature of Cameron Highlands that it would be perverse not to visit a plantation during your stay: all have **teahouses** with views over the terraces, some with **tours** that give a glimpse of the production process. Despite the romantic imagery used on packaging, the **handpicking** of tea leaves is giving way to mechanical pruning, often by migrant workers. At the factory, the leaves are withered and partly dried by alternate blasts of hot and cold air, then rolled by machine to release more moisture for the all-important process of **fermentation**. The soggy mass is eventually heated to 90°C to halt the process; finally, the leaves are graded by shaking them through meshes of different grades.

PLANTATIONS

Most tour operators organize half-day visits for RM25/person.

Bharat 4.5km south of Tanah Rata ☎ 05 491 1133, ⊛ bharattea.com.my. Two teahouses, though no tours. Daily 8.30am–6pm.
Boh Near Habu, 6km southeast of Tanah Rata, 7km off the main road ☎ 05 493 1324, ⊛ boh.com.my. Boh's biggest plantation in Cameron Highlands has impressive views, a café and a colonial-era factory, open for free tours. Tues–Sun 9am–4.30pm.
Sungai Palas 6km north of Brinchang ☎ 05 496 1363, ⊛ boh.com.my. Boh's most visited northern branch has an observation deck with café and offers not just the usual cursory free tour but also a worthwhile tea-tasting tour (9am, 11am & 1pm; 45min; RM35), on which you get a proper introduction to tea production, with a chance to taste various brews at the end, along with scones. The 11am session is best, as this is when the tea tends to arrive for processing. Call in advance as tours may be cancelled during periods of low harvest. Tues–Sun 9am–4.30pm.

CAMERON HIGHLANDS

Mount Irau (2110m)

Mount Brinchang (2032m)

Sungai Palas Boh Tea Estate

Butterfly Farm

Kea Farm

Rose Centre

Lavender Garden (4km) & (10km) & Lojing Highlands

ROUTE 59

Time Tunnel Museum

Army Quarters

Big Red Strawberry Farm

Brinchang

Sam Poh Temple

Path 1

Path 2

Orang Asli Village

Mount Perdah (1576m)

Weather Station

Arcadia Cottage

All Souls Church

Path 3

Path 6

Path 10

Mount Jasar (1696m)

Path 10

TAMAN SEDIA

Rain Shelter

Path 5

Path 3

Mount Beremban (1847m)

Tan's Camella Garden

Tanah Rata

Path 4

Parit Waterfall

Path 7

MARDI

Haiwan

Path 8

Mentiga Hill (1563m)

Robinson Waterfall

Path 9

Path 8a

Power Station

Bharat Tea Estate

Boh Tea Estate

Bharat Tea Estate

ROUTE 59

Gunong Emas Tea Estate

Habu Power Station

Raub & Kuala Lipis

Ringlet

Tapah

EATING
The Smokehouse — 1

ACCOMMODATION
Planters Country Hotel (Bala's) — 3
Lakehouse — 4
Moonriver Lodge — 1
The Smokehouse Hotel — 2

0 — 1
kilometre

2

2

This is a major agroindustrial area, producing not only tea but also flowers, vegetables and fruit that are exotic for Malaysia (notably **strawberries**), much of it under unsightly plastic. What's more, it gets packed out during weekends, holidays and school breaks, when there can be long tailbacks on the main road, and then there's the din of building work wherever hotels and holiday apartments are springing up. Many from the Camerons bemoan the commercialization, but as ever in Malaysia, the real problem is the haphazard and unsustainable way in which it happens. (If you want to know more about the **environmental challenges** facing the area, contact the local campaigning group REACH: ⓦ reach.org.my). All that said, many visitors have a perfectly pleasant time here. Lying more than 1000m above sea level, the area offers **cool relief** from the sultriness of just about everywhere else in the country, which is the main reason locals visit. Throw in forest hikes and tea plantations, and you have promising ingredients for a short break.

The Camerons' 700 square kilometres are threaded by the twisty **Route 59**, linking all the main towns and officially called Jalan Besar (or just "main road"), where it becomes a town's main street. The towns themselves are mundane concrete affairs, although plenty of buildings sport a webbing of dark lines in homage to that ersatz half-timbered look. A three-night stay is an attractive option, allowing two full days for treks and seeing a tea plantation and other minor sights. Although it never really gets cold, have a warm sweater to hand for nights. Hikers should also have waterproofs for the frequent showers or storms (local general stores sell plastic ponchos for just a few ringgit) and footwear that can cope with slippery, muddy conditions.

Tanah Rata

Some 1400m above sea level, **TANAH RATA** is both the Camerons' biggest town and the least spoiled. With plenty of places to stay and eat along or just off the 500m-long main road (officially **Jalan Besar**), it's the ideal base for visitors, although there are no sights except perhaps the delightfully wild **Tan's Camellia Garden**, brimming with lilies, agapanthus and pitcher plants.

Brinchang

BRINCHANG is a scruffy town some 5km north from Tanah Rata via the main road, although walkers can use a shortcut around the golf course (see p.143). With something resembling a town square, it's denser and more built up than Tanah Rata, but in its favour it has a **market** just uphill from the centre – the first of several on the road north – which morphs in the afternoon as one set of stalls is replaced by another, forming a *pasar malam*.

Time Tunnel

A 15min walk northeast of Brinchang's centre on Route 59 • Daily 9am–6pm • RM5 • ☎ 05 491 4481

On the edge of town, the quirky **Time Tunnel** is part of one of the area's many "self-plucking" strawberry farms. It serves as a museum of Malaysian ephemera, worth a quick look to see just how much the country has changed over the past few decades. The best section is the evocation of a simple 1950s domestic interior, although for no obvious reason it has a colonial poster of the time announcing the creation of a Home Guard to combat the "bandits", as the British were wont to refer to the Communists during the Emergency. Elsewhere, you can gaze at vintage photos of a once-bucolic Camerons and weep.

North of Brinchang

The area **north of Brinchang** is Cameron Highlands at its most intensively farmed; head up on a bus from Ipoh or Penang and you'll see the plastic tunnels off the Simpang

TANAH RATA

▲ Brinchang

MARUI, Robinson Waterfall, Hospital & Path 5, 7, 8, 9 ▲

Watson's Pharmacy

Century Pines Resort

59

Police

JALAN MASJID

PERSIARAN DAYANG INDAH

JALAN TENGKOLOK

JALAN LARIGGAK MERCU

JALAN BESAR (MAIN ROAD)

Tanah Rata Park

Bus Station & Taxis

P

Food Court

Shops

Market

Clinic

PERSIARAN CAMELLIA 3

EVO

@ Internet Point

Laundry

Eco Cameron

PERSIARAN CAMELLIA 4

Maybank

JALAN CAMELLIA

Food Court

Food Stalls

Cameron Fair Shopping Mall

JALAN MENTIGI

JALAN CANATIONV

JALAN GEREJA

JALAN GEREJA

59

Tan's Camellia Garden

Path 10

3

1

1 1

2 2

1

4

9

7

5

6

▲ Ringlet

▼ E (300m)

■ ACCOMMODATION	
Arundina	7
Bird's Nest	3
Cameronian Inn	5
Father's Guest House	6
Gerard's Place	4
Heritage	2
Kang Travellers Lodge (Daniel's Lodge)	1
The Mentigi Bungalow	8

● EATING	
Barracks Café	3
Bunga Suria	2
Mayflower	4
Singh Chapati	1

■ DRINKING	
Jungle Bar	1
Travellers Bistro & Pub	2

0   100   metres

2

Pulai Road even before it joins Route 59 at Kampung Raja. The Camerons' two highest peaks, Irau and Brinchang (see box, p.144), are here too, as is the Sungai Palas tea estate and a couple of minor attractions locals make a beeline for. Three kilometres from Brinchang is the **Butterfly Farm**, home to other insects and snakes too (daily 8am–6pm; RM5; ⓦcameronbutterflyfarm.com.my), and, slightly further on, the **Rose Centre** (daily 8am–6pm; RM5; ☏05 496 2988), a garden and nursery featuring a kitsch nursery-rhyme shoe house. Even more popular – cars double-park on the road close by, causing tedious jams – is the **Lavender Garden**, some 9km from Brinchang just beyond Tringkap (Mon–Thurs 9am–6pm, Fri–Sun 9am–7pm; RM5; ☏05 496 1208, ⓦcameronlavender.com). The sizeable nursery is home to lavender and other plants, while the shop sells lavender-scented gifts and lavender-themed food.

Lojing Highlands

10km east of Kampung Raja on Route 185 • Self drive or catch a taxi from Tanah Rata's bus stand (RM80/one-way)

Technically in Kelantan but more like a northern extension of Cameron Highlands, the **LOJING HIGHLANDS** are a lesser known, virtually unvisited part of the Titiwangsa Range. The fact that busloads of tourists haven't arrived here yet, however, doesn't mean that farmers haven't. The place has a couple of perks, primarily one well-organized eco-farmstay (see p.145), and the chance to see the elusive *Rafflesia* plant, almost ubiquitous in this region.

ARRIVAL AND DEPARTURE   CAMERON HIGHLANDS

By bus Cameron Highlands' main bus station is at the east end of Tanah Rata, and is used by both local Perak Transit and express buses. Backpacker minivans also operate to and from the Highlands.

Destinations Butterworth (5 daily; 4hr); Hat Yay (1 daily at 8am; 8hr); Ipoh (7 daily; 2hr); KLIA/KLIA2 (3 daily; 5hr); Kuala Lumpur (at least 9 daily; 4hr); Lumut (8 daily; 3hr 45min); Penang (7 daily; 5hr); Perhentian Islands (2 daily; 7hr); Raub (3 daily; 3hr 30min); Singapore (2 daily; 10hr); Taman Negara (1 daily; 5hr).

By car The Camerons can be easily reached off the E1, the North–South Expressway; use the exits at Tapah (if

arriving from the south) or Simpang Pulai near Ipoh (from the north). If coming from Tapah, stop at Lata Iskandar, a waterfall 25km south of Ringlet. The Simpang Pulai Rd meets Route 59 at Kampung Raja before continuing to Musang Cave and Route 8 to Kota Bharu. A minor road links up with Route 8 via Sungai Koyan in the heart of the Pahang interior, connecting Ringlet on Route 59 with Raub and Kuala Lipis. Remember to top up your tanks: there is only one petrol station in Brinchang and one 200m west of Simpang Pulai. After these, it's either 55km away in Simpang Pulai, or 80km away in Musang Cave.

GETTING AROUND

By bus Local services from Tanah Rata's bus station run north to Kampung Raja via Brinchang (every 2hr 6.30am–6.30pm) and south to Tapah via Ringlet (two in each direction daily).

By taxi Taxis park next to Tanah Rata's bus station (☏05 491 2355) and on the main road in Brinchang. A taxi

between Tanah Rata and Brinchang costs around RM10; to charter a taxi for excursions, expect to pay RM25/hr, minimum 3hr. Fares for intercity charter are clearly written at the taxi park in Tanah Rata.

By motorbike Renting motorbikes is increasingly popular; it's RM50/8hr and RM30/4hr from Tanah Rata's bus station, and around RM80/day from most guesthouses.

On foot You can easily walk directly between Tanah Rata and Brinchang (40min) via Taman Sedia, the Malay village in the little depression in between. Signs on Route 59 outside both towns point the way to the village, the walk taking you past the Anglican All Souls' Church and skirting the golf course.

INFORMATION AND TOURS

Pahang Tourism used to run a tourist office at the western end of Tanah Rata, now occupied by a **tour agency** that still advertises itself as an information point – as does just about every other tour agency in town. The only reason to deal with an agency is if you want to arrange a guided **trek** or a taste-of-everything day **tour** (from RM96). The standard ingredients for the latter include a drive up Mount Brinchang to see the mossy forest, visits to a tea plantation and an Orang Asli settlement (although the latter might be modern and charmless), and a foray to find *Rafflesia* flowers if in bloom.

TOUR AGENTS
Cameron Secrets Father's Guesthouse, Tanah Rata (see below) ⓦ cameronsecrets.com.
CS Travel & Tours 47 Jalan Besar, Tanah Rata

ⓣ 05 491 1200, ⓦ cstravel.com.my.
Eco Cameron 72A Jalan Persiaran Camellia, Tanah Rata ⓣ 05 491 5388, ⓦ ecocameron.com.

ACCOMMODATION

Both Tanah Rata and Brinchang have a fair amount of mid-range **accommodation**, although the former's hotels tend to be better run. Tanah Rata is also where you find most of the Camerons' budget **guesthouses**; all have hot water. Some places also have **apartments** to rent, listed on their websites. The rates given below rise by ten to fifty percent at weekends, and can double during school breaks and public holidays, when it's best to book ahead.

TANAH RATA
Arundina 17A Jalan Mentigi, behind the Hillview Inn ⓣ 05 491 1129, ⓦ arundina.com; map p.141. Twelve spick and span en-suite rooms with hardwood floors housed in a converted fifteen-year-old bungalow. The garden filled with tropical flowers is atmospheric, but at this price range the simple (included) DIY breakfast could be improved. ⓦ RM180

Bird's Nest 1 Jalan Perdah ⓣ 05 491 4375, ⓦ birdsnesthotel.com.my; map p.141. The mundane grey exterior of this five-storey block is unpromising, but inside is a modern hotel with slick rooms as well as a Sarawakian Orang Ulu-style mural in the lobby. Terrific value midweek, but best avoided during school-break weekends, when rates almost treble. ⓦ RM82.50

Cameronian Inn 16 Jalan Mentigi ⓣ 05 491 1327, ⓦ thecameronianinn.com; map p.141. This guesthouse serves up scones and offers plain but airy dorms and doubles (some en suite) in spotless bungalows, surrounded by a bougainvillea trellis and small garden. Classier family rooms are in the new wing. ⓦ Dorms RM25, doubles RM60

Father's Guest House 4 Jalan Mentigi ⓣ 016 566 1111, ⓦ fathersguesthouse.net; map p.141. *Father's* is the best-run budget guesthouse in the Camerons, and the best-informed on trekking. Occupying a modern house with a small garden, they offer a range of pleasant rooms and a dorm; a new annexed wing has slightly better rooms, all en suite and with a/c, and most with balconies. ⓦ Dorms RM30, doubles RM70

★ **Gerard's Place** C9 Block Carnation, opposite the Heritage Hotel, 10min walk from Tanah Rata ⓣ 016 566 1111, ⓦ gerardsplace.com; map p.141. Run by Gerard of *Father's* and his lovely family, this sleek B&B in a quiet block of flats has only eight rooms, most en suite, set around a homey TV lounge, with a leafy terrace out back. Free coffee and tea are provided 24hr, as well as a simple breakfast, and possibly the best information on treks in the area. ⓦ RM88

Heritage Jalan Gereja ⓣ 05 491 3888, ⓦ heritage.com. my; map p.141. A 10min uphill walk from town, this hotel is the closest Tanah Rata has to a resort-style complex, with "heritage" dating all the way back to the 1990s. Besides tidy, unexceptional rooms, it has a choice of restaurants plus indoor recreational facilities, such as snooker, for those inevitable wet spells. Breakfast included. ⓦ RM406

Kang Travellers Lodge (Daniel's Lodge) 9 Lorong Perdah ⓣ 05 491 5823, ⓦ kangholiday.com; map p.141. Not the friendliest place but certainly laid-back, *Kang's* guesthouse is a worthy standby with a relaxing patio plus its own little bar right at the back. Choose between the large upstairs dorm and institutional rooms, some with attached bathroom. ⓦ Dorms RM16, doubles RM50

The Mentigi Bungalow Jalan Mentigi, 5min walk uphill from Father's Guesthouse ⓣ 05 491 5598, ⓦ mentigi.com; map p.141. This recent mid-range hotel, set on top of a hill has smart and spacious rooms with balconies overlooking the town and, sadly, a construction site. There's a homey lounge with TV and a quiet garden outside. ⓦ RM138

2

WALKING IN CAMERON HIGHLANDS

A network of **walking trails** makes it possible to take in Cameron Highlands' forests, packed with ferns, pitcher plants, orchids, thick moss and even *Rafflesia*. But despite the presence of mammals such as sun bears, you're unlikely to see interesting fauna other than insects and the odd wild pig.

Unfortunately, the trails are often poorly marked and maintained, and seem to have little immunity from being bulldozed to make way for development. The account below should be treated as a snapshot and is certainly not meant to provide turn-by-turn directions. *Father's Guest House* in Tanah Rata is a good place to get current trail information, and produces maps that mention lots of useful landmarks as well as wrong turns to avoid on each trail. It is also one of several tour operators offering guided treks – again, a good option given the state of the trails.

If **hiking independently**, tell staff at your accommodation where you intend to go and when you expect to be back. On longer hikes, take warm clothing and ample water. If you do get lost and can get a cellular signal, call your accommodation for them to alert the authorities.

TRAILS

The paths here are numbered according to local convention. Timings are one-way, for people going at an average pace. Note that at the time of writing, paths 9, 9B and 10 were **not recommended**, as several solo hikers had been assaulted and mugged here. Go in a group, or stick to the other paths. Some sections require a **permit** from the Forestry Department (W forestry.gov.my); ask your guesthouse to obtain one, or risk a RM300 fine.

Path 1 (2hr 30min) The trail to Mount Brinchang's summit (2000m) was closed for conservation at the time of research. You can still walk the trail from just north of Brinchang's street market – look for a track opposite the police headquarters – until the boardwalk through the ethereal Mossy Forest, where the trees are covered in a spongy, soft coat of green. But to climb further, you must get a permit. There is a road – the highest in Peninsular Malaysia – up to the forest, so you can cheat by taking a taxi up from Brinchang (RM15) and walking down. The road begins close to Kea Farm, passing a turning for the Sungai Palas tea estate.

Path 2 (1hr 30min) Starting just before the Sam Poh Temple below Brinchang, it's not clearly marked and is often a bit of a scramble. The route undulates severely and eventually joins Path 3.

BETWEEN TANAH RATA AND BRINCHANG

Planters Country Hotel Route 59, about 1km north of Tanah Rata ❶05 491 1660, W balaschalet.com; map p.139. Also known by its old name, *Bala's*, this former colonial school still oozes old-world charm, doing a passable impression of English cottages with the lushest gardens imaginable, complete with country-pub-style dining room and a lounge with chintzy sofas. It's a bargain, if you can cope with the slightly wayward management. Free lifts to and from town. 🛜 RM140

★**The Smokehouse Hotel** Route 59, midway between Tanah Rata and Brinchang ❶05 491 1215, W thesmokehouse.com.my/ch.htm; map p.139. If ever a 1930s building could capture that mythical English country look, it's this one. Long the classiest place to stay in the Camerons, it boasts fifteen individually decorated suites, some with four-poster beds, others more modern in feel, as well as some more affordable rooms. Throw in the leaded windows, roast-beef meals (see p.146) and private garden with immaculate lawns, and you could pretend it's Surrey. Full English breakfast included. 🛜 RM400

BRINCHANG

Parkland 45 Jalan Besar ❶05 491 1299, W parkland .com.my; map p.142. The friendly *Parkland* has uncluttered rooms that are good value midweek. The snag is that there's no lift, although you can pay fifteen percent more to stay at their more upmarket *Express* branch next door. Online bookings get discounted rates. 🛜 RM110

Pop Ash 24 Jalan Besar ❶05 491 1666, ✉ hotelpopash@gmail.com; map p.142. For the price, this is a good-value hotel; rooms are en suite and smart, though tiny. The cheapest are windowless, but then the townscape doesn't exactly tempt you to pay fifty percent extra for one with a view. 🛜 RM60

Rosa Pasadena 1 Bandar Baru Brinchang ❶05 491 2288, W hotelrosapsdn.com.my; map p.142. Gargantuan hotel packing in more than a hundred rooms which, though slightly tatty, are quite comfortable and bigger than average, plus there are two restaurants. Breakfast included. 🛜 RM160

★ **Snooze** 4 Jalan Besar ❶014 669 0108, W facebook .com/SnoozeCH; map p.142. *Snooze* is a boutiquey homestay on two floors, with thirteen en-suite rooms.

Path 3 (2hr 30min) Starts at Arcadia Cottage southeast of the golf course, crossing streams and climbing quite steeply to reach the peak of Mount Beremban (1841m). Once at the top, you can retrace your steps, or head down via paths 5, 7 or 8.

Path 4 (20min) Paved in stretches and well marked, this walk starts south of the golf course and goes past Parit Waterfall, then on to the Forestry Office (Pejabat Hutan), where a sealed path leads back to the main road.

Path 5 (1hr) Branches off from Path 3 at the rain shelter – a little gazebo – and ends up at the Malaysian Agriculture Research and Development Institute (MARDI). From here the road, Persiaran Dayang Indah, takes you into Tanah Rata just north of the bus station.

Path 6 (2hr) From the Forestry Office on Path 4, this branches away to the rain shelter.

Path 7 (2hr) Starts near MARDI and climbs steeply to Mount Beremban; an arduous and overgrown hike better done as a descent from Path 3.

Path 8 (2hr 30min) Another route to Mount Beremban. From Tanah Rata, head up Persiaran Dayang Indah, ignore the MARDI turning on the left, and then turn right up a paved path for Robinson Waterfall. Just before the waterfall, turn left and you're on Path 8. Even more taxing than Path 7.

Path 9 As Path 8 initially, except that you head all the way to Robinson Waterfall (20min). You then descend to the access road to the Boh tea plantation, although there's a choice of routes. **Path 9B** (45min) is the direct, steep option via the hydropower station, where you may have to ask staff to let you through to the Boh road. **Path 9A** (1hr) curls away from it and descends more gently, though note that the last part is overgrown, so many people turn right here on to an easier trail to a vegetable farm, after which the track joins the path down to the Boh Road.

Path 10 (3hr) Beginning at the back of Tan's Camellia Garden in Tanah Rata (see p.140), this involves a fairly strenuous climb to Mount Jasar (1696m). It's best to turn back here, as the original path to Route 59 no longer has a clear exit .

Mount Irau (sometimes called **Path 14**; 6hr) The demanding ascent of Irau, the Highlands' highest peak (2110m), requires asking a permit at least one month before the climb. The trail commences at the end of Mount Brinchang's Mossy Forest walkway (take a taxi up rather than attempting this as an extension of Path 1). You return the way you came. It's best not to go alone, and an early start is advisable, as people often get lost when the light fades in the late afternoon.

Everything is well set for traveller comfort, from the common lounge areas equipped with couches, writing desks and TVs, to the cute choice of bedsheets and wall coatings – part of which are plastered with guests' praise and comments. 📶 RM88

RINGLET

Lakehouse Ringlet 15km south of Tanah Rata ☎05 495 6152, ⓦlakehouse-cameron.com; map p.139. With your own transport, it's worth staying at this retro boutique hotel in Ringlet. Stone fireplaces and old-fashioned furniture meet plasma-screen TVs in the rooms; there's a suitably pub-like restaurant and bar, and a reading lounge, too. Breakfast included. 📶 RM600

LOJING HIGHLANDS

★**Moonriver Lodge** 12km east of Kampung Raja ☎016 550 3107, ⓦmoonriverlodge.com; map p.139. Next to a vegetable farm on a lush hillside, *Moonriver Lodge* is a relaxed cluster of wooden buildings, connected by walk paths and flanked by manicured tropical gardens and ponds. They have futon-style dorm beds, simple doubles or bunks, each wing with its own shared bathrooms. Pay for kitchen usage and bring provisions, or buy meals cooked on site (RM15–35/person). Multi-day packages include hiking activities; check the website for details. 📶 RM85 per person

EATING

Two things sum up Cameron Highlands cuisine – **steamboats** (see p.40) and **scones**. The former is highly popular with locals, with RM25/head as the going rate; many restaurants still heat the stock using old-fashioned charcoal vessels with a central chimney. Plenty of hotels and even curry houses bake fine scones as part of their take on English cream teas – if only they weren't marred by the artificially pink local strawberry jam and "cream" with the colour and consistency of toothpaste.

TANAH RATA

★ **Barracks Café** 1 Jalan Gereja, ☎05 491 5823,

ⓦfacebook.com/TheBarracksCafe; map p.141. Quirky yet original, and housed in the original zinc barracks used by the British army during World War II, this café sits just downhill from the school once used as a military hospital by the Japanese. The outdoor seating area, in a manicured garden, is very pleasant, and the menu appealing: besides tea and scones, there are curries, chicken chops, breadbowl curries, cakes and mocktails. A meal will set you back around RM50, coffee and cakes around RM30. Tues–Fri 7pm–midnight, Sat & Sun noon–10pm.

Bunga Suria Persiaran Camellia 3 ☏ 05 491 4666; map p.141. Cheap and cheerful South Indian establishment, good for *thosai*, self-service *nasi campur*, great samosas and banana *lassi*, and local breakfasts like half-boiled eggs and *kaya* toast. Daily 8am–10pm.

Mayflower 22 Jalan Besar, opposite Cameron Fair shopping mall ☏ 05 491 1793; map p.141. This authentically tatty and boisterous old timer serves the best-value steamboats in town (RM25/person), along with hearty portions of juicy noodles. Packed and happening on most nights. Daily 8pm–10pm.

Singh Chapati Bangunan Brij Court, opposite Bird's Nest Hotel ☏ 017 578 6454; map p.141. Excellent Punjabi food, somewhat expensive for the category (RM10 for veggie curry), but always freshly made. Long waits are

accompanied by Indian MTV, constantly blaring from the cable TV. Daily 1–9.30pm.

BETWEEN TANAH RATA AND BRINCHANG

The Smokehouse Route 59, between Tanah Rata and Brinchang ☏ 05 491 1215; map p.139. If you feel a visit to the Camerons isn't complete without pukka English food, head here for roasts (beef Wellington RM95; duck and lamb are available too) or cream teas (with quality jam and cream; 11am–6pm; RM30). They also do a full breakfast (until 11am; RM55) – and this is one of the very few pricey hotels left in Malaysia that still serves pork bacon and sausages. There's an atmospheric pub section, too (from 6.30pm). Daily 7.30am–11pm.

BRINCHANG

Cameron Organic Jalan Angsana ☏ 05 491 4807; map p.142. Down-to-earth place popular for its steamboats which, unusually, come with either chicken or vegetable stock, and really do use organic local produce. Around RM30 for a meal. Daily 11am–9pm.

OK Tuck 26 Jalan Besar ☏ 05 491 2380; map p.142. Busy Chinese restaurant with an extensive menu, including excellent black vinegar sparerib and fried prawns. Mains around RM10. Daily 11am–9pm.

DRINKING

TANAH RATA

Jungle Bar Kang Travellers Lodge (Daniel's Lodge), 9 Lorong Perdah ☏ 05 491 5823, ⓦ kangholiday.com; map p.141. With a pool table and fireplace, this backpackers' watering hole is a great hangout when busy, although it can be dead some nights – perhaps because it's so discreetly tucked away at the back of the guesthouse.

Daily roughly 7pm–midnight.

Travellers Bistro & Pub 68a Persiaran Camellia 3 ☏ 05 491 3666, ⓦ facebook.com/TravellersBistroPub; map p.141. Tanah Rata's sole attempt to emulate a city bar doesn't exactly nail it, but it still attracts a (predominantly Western) crowd to compare travel stories over imported beers. Daily 10am–1am.

DIRECTORY

TANAH RATA

Banks It's easy to find banks with ATMs on and just off the main road in both Tanah Rata and Brinchang.

Hospital Persiaran Dayang Indah (☏ 05 491 1966). Dr Ayob also runs a clinic on the main road (☏ 05 491 1654).

Pharmacy There's a branch of Watsons just a 5min walk from the centre of Tanah Rata, beyond the *Century Pines Resort*.

Police The police station is on Jalan Besar (☏ 05 491 1222).

Penang

In the far northwest of Peninsular Malaysia, **PENANG** is the most ambiguously named part of the country: depending on context, the moniker may refer to the **island** (Pulau Pinang in Malay; *pinang* is what Malays call the betel-nut palm), or the state (the island plus a chunk of mainland opposite, around the town of Butterworth), or even just the state capital – properly **George Town**. This was where the British established their first port on the Peninsula in the late eighteenth century, laying the foundations for the George Town of today, a fascinating blend of colonial, Indian, Malay and – especially – Chinese and Peranakan heritage. (At forty percent of the total population, Penang has the highest proportion of Chinese residents than any

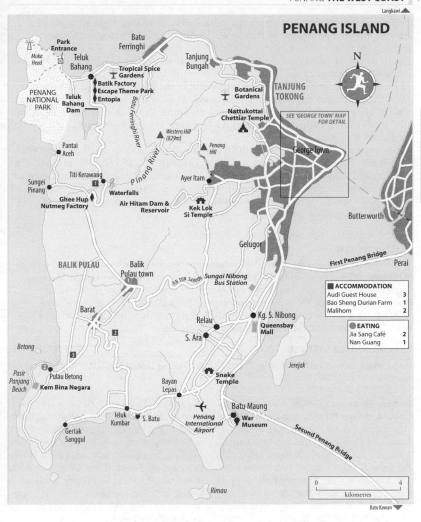

Langkawi

PENANG ISLAND

N

2

Muka Head

Park Entrance

Teluk Bahang

Batu Ferringhi

Tropical Spice Gardens
Batik Factory
Escape Theme Park
Entopia

Tanjung Bungah

PENANG NATIONAL PARK

Teluk Bahang Dam

Botanical Gardens

TANJUNG TOKONG

Nattukottai Chettiar Temple

SEE 'GEORGE TOWN' MAP FOR DETAIL

George Town

Pantai Aceh

Western Hill (829m)

Penang Hill

Titi Kerawang

Ayer Itam

Sungei Pinang

Waterfalls

Ghee Hup Nutmeg Factory

Air Hitam Dam & Reservoir

Kek Lok Si Temple

Butterworth

Gelugor

First Penang Bridge

Perai

BALIK PULAU

Balik Pulau town

JLN TUN SARDON

Sungai Nibong Bus Station

Barat

Relau

Kg. S. Nibong

Queensbay Mall

Betong

S. Ara

Jerejak

■ ACCOMMODATION
Audi Guest House   3
Bao Sheng Durian Farm   1
Malihom   2

● EATING
Jia Sang Café   2
Nan Guang   1

Pasir Panjang Beach

Pulau Betong

Kem Bina Negara

Snake Temple

Gertak Sanggul

Teluk Kumbar

S. Batu

Bayan Lepas

Penang International Airport

Batu Maung

War Museum

Second Penang Bridge

Rimau

0   4
kilometres

Batu Kawan

Peninsular state.) The city has seen a renaissance since its central old quarter, along with that of Melaka (see p.274), were jointly made a UNESCO World Heritage Site in 2008, and makes a wonderful base to see all of Penang. Elsewhere on the 285-square-kilometre island are a coastal national park where you might see **nesting turtles**, a couple of unusual temples and a rather overdeveloped beach at **Batu Ferringhi**.

Brief history

Penang Island was ruled by the **sultans of Kedah** until the late eighteenth century. But increasing harassment by Thai and Burmese raiding parties encouraged Sultan Abdullah to seek help from **Francis Light**, a British "country trader" searching for a regional trading base to counter the Dutch presence in Sumatra. A deal was struck: Light would provide military aid through the **British East India Company** and the sultan would receive 30,000 Spanish dollars a year. There was one snag – the East India Company's Governor-General, **Charles Cornwallis**, refused to get involved.

Concealing the full facts from both the sultan and Cornwallis, Light went ahead anyway and took **possession** of Penang on 11 August 1786, then spent five years assuring the sultan that the matter was being referred to London. The sultan finally caught on but failed to evict the British, ending up with a modest annuity and no role in the island's government.

Penang thus became the **first British settlement** in the Malay Peninsula. Within two years, the population had reached ten thousand, swollen largely by Indian and Chinese traders. Light was made superintendent and, renaming the place Prince of Wales Island after the British heir apparent, declared it a **free port**. George Town took its name from the British king, George III.

For a brief time all looked rosy, with George Town proclaimed capital of the **Straits Settlements** (incorporating Melaka and Singapore) in 1826. But Singapore, founded in 1819, would soon overtake George Town in every respect. Post-independence, even as Penang as a whole generally prospered through manufacturing, George Town itself had languished – which, ironically, helped preserve its historic core, rendering it ripe for UNESCO recognition (see p.151).

Butterworth

Some 70km north of Taiping and 40km south of Sungai Petani, the industrial port of **BUTTERWORTH** is home to **Penang Sentral**, the transport hub of northwest Malaysia. There's no need to linger, but with some time between connections, check out **Butterworth Art Walk**, an interesting attempt to keep up with George Town's artsy rebrand. It's a narrow lane 1.8km north of the ferry terminal, beside the Dewan Dato Haji Ahmad Badawi Field, and right next to hotel *Lodge 18*.

ARRIVAL AND DEPARTURE   **BUTTERWORTH**

The bus station, ferry pier and train station are in a cluster, called **Penang Sentral** (☎ 04 331 2796, ⊛ penangsentral .com.my).

By train Besides fast ETS trains, there's also a KTM Komuter service up to Padang Besar, for Thailand. Komuter trains also run from the next stop, Bukit Mertajam, to Taiping and Padang Rengas (12km from Kuala Kangsar). Destinations Alor Star (hourly; 1hr 10min); Ipoh (7 daily; 2hr); Gemas (2 daily; 6hr 30min); Kuala Kangsar (ETS 7 daily, Komuter every 2hr; 1hr 10min); Kuala Lumpur (7 daily; 4hr 15min); Padang Besar (hourly; 1hr 45min); Seremban (2 daily; 5hr 30min); Sungai Petani (hourly; 35min); Taiping (7 daily; 50min).

By bus Tickets for bus journeys from Butterworth can be bought at the stations or through agents at George Town's KOMTAR building (see p.156). Destinations Alor Star (hourly; 1hr 30min); Cameron Highlands (4 daily; 4hr 30min); Hat Yai (Thailand; 5 daily; 4hr); Ipoh (9 daily; 2hr 30min); Johor Bahru (several daily; 10hr); Kangar (several daily; 2hr 15min); Kota Bharu (at least 2 daily; 6hr 30min); KLIA/KLIA2 (3 daily with a change at Kamunting; 7hr); Kuala Besut (for Perhentian islands; daily at 9.30pm; 7hr); Kuala Kangsar (4 daily; 2hr 45min); Kuala Lumpur (at least hourly; 5hr); Kuala Perlis (4 daily; 3hr); Kuala Terengganu (1 daily; 8hr); Kuantan (4 daily; 9hr); Lumut (for Pangkor; at least 4 daily; 4hr); Melaka (several daily; 8hr); Padang Besar (2 daily; 3hr); Seremban (6 daily; 6hr); Singapore (several daily; 11hr); Sungai Petani (several daily; 45min); Taiping (Kamunting bus station; hourly; 1hr 15min).

By ferry The ferry to George Town costs just RM1.20. Destinations George Town (every 20min–1hr, 6am–12.30am; 20min).

By taxi If catching a taxi across to Penang Island (around RM40), check whether the bridge toll is included in the fare.

George Town

Visiting **GEORGE TOWN** in 1879, stalwart Victorian traveller **Isabella Bird** called it "a brilliant place under a brilliant sky", a description that's hard to improve. Filling a triangular cape at the island's northeastern corner is George Town's centre, the UNESCO-listed core of which is essentially the area south and east of Lebuh Farquhar,

GEORGE TOWN'S CAT SHUTTLE

George Town's centre is served by the **CAT shuttle bus** (also signed as #5; daily 6am–11.40pm; every 15–30min; free), which can be useful, especially if you're flagging in the heat. Operated by Rapid Penang, it sets off from the Pengkalan Weld terminal, heading north to Little India and the colonial district, then Lebuh Muntri. It then turns southwest along Jalan Penang to the KOMTAR building, meandering in the vicinity before returning east via Lebuh Carnarvon, Jalan Masjid Kapitan Keling and the colonial district to the bus terminal.

2

Love Lane and Lebuh Melayu. It's a surprisingly harmonious maze of lanes lined with **shophouses** in various states of repair, and liberally sprinkled with religious buildings, impressive **clan associations** or *kongsi* – a blend of Chinese welfare organization, social club and temple (see p.575) and other monuments. The obvious comparison is with Singapore, but it's as if the same ingredients have created an altogether mellower dish, without the slickness, crowds and incessant din of its former Straits Settlements partner. If time is short, make a point of seeing the **Khoo Kongsi** and **Cheong Fatt Tze mansion**; otherwise simply enjoy the relaxed pace and stroll at will.

The main arteries are **Jalan Penang**, **Jalan Masjid Kapitan Kling** and **Lebuh Pantai**, which run roughly west–east, along with traffic-clogged **Lebuh Chulia**, which runs northwest–southeast. Note that parts of Lebuh Chulia and Jalan Penang are distinctly

2

seedy at night. George Town's northern fringes and the rugged, forested hills of the island's centre are home to a few interesting **temples** and the attractive **Botanic Gardens**.

Colonial district

Clustered around historic **Fort Cornwallis** are a motley collection of colonial buildings, including the former Town and City halls, St George's Church and some of George Town's oldest and most prestigious schools. A useful landmark, at the eastern end of Lebuh Pantai (Beach Street) and close to the tourist offices, is the graceful Moorish-style **clock tower**, with onion-dome roof and scalloped Arabesque windows. Presented in 1897 to mark Queen Victoria's Diamond Jubilee, it's 60ft (20m) high, a foot for each year of her reign.

Fort Cornwallis

Entrance in the northwest of the site, via the Padang · Daily 9am–10pm · RM20

At the very eastern tip of the island, overpriced **Fort Cornwallis** marks the spot where Francis Light landed to take possession of Penang on 16 July 1786. The fort, named after Lord Charles Cornwallis, Governor-General of India, dates from 20 years later. Square in shape with redoubts at each corner, it's all a bit forlorn nowadays, the mildewed, lightly vegetated brickwork conveying little sense of history. The **statue** of Light by the entrance was cast in 1936 for the 150th anniversary of the founding of Penang, his features copied from a portrait of his son, Colonel William Light, founder of Adelaide in Australia. (Francis Light's **grave** is in the cemetery on Jalan Sultan Ahmad Shah, 1km west). Inside the walls, look for the early nineteenth-century chapel, powder magazine and bronze **Sri Rambai cannon**, sited in the northwest corner – local belief was that infertile women could conceive by laying flowers in its barrel.

Padang Kota Lama

The expanse of green that borders Fort Cornwallis, the **Padang Kota Lama**, was once the favourite promenade of the island's colonial administrators. The **Esplanade** here offers a vista of mainland hills and, to the left, the distant high-rise apartments of Tanjung Tokong in the northwest. Bordering the padang are a slew of grand buildings, including the early nineteenth-century **Dewan Undangan Negeri** (State Legislative Hall) to the south and, to the west, the yellow-and-white old **town hall** (1879) and the more ornate but less attractive former **city hall** (1903).

Penang Museum

57 Macalister Rd · Daily except Fri 9am–5pm · RM1 · ☎ 04 226 1462, ⓦ penangmuseum.gov.my

The **Penang Museum** is a worthwhile introduction to life on the island. Among the memorabilia are rickshaws, Peranakan furniture, clothing and ceramics, faded black-and-white photographs of early Penang's Chinese millionaires, and a panoramic photograph of George Town taken in the 1870s (note how many buildings survive to this day).

St George's Church

1 Lebuh Farquhar · Mon–Thurs 10am–noon & 2–4pm, Fri 2–4pm, Sat 10am–noon; visitors may be allowed in at other times if no services are in progress · Free · ☎ 04 261 2739

As simple and unpretentious as anything built in Neoclassical style in Asia can be, **St George's Church** is one of Penang's oldest buildings, having been completed in 1818 by the East India Company using convict labour. Its construction marked the arrival of the Anglican Church in Southeast Asia, and early congregations must have found the airy interior a welcome reprieve from the heat.

Eastern & Oriental Hotel (E&O)

10 Lebuh Farquhar · ⓦ eohotels.com

Though a little overshadowed by its recently added annexe, the **Eastern & Oriental Hotel** – built in 1885 by the Armenian Sarkies brothers, who also launched Singapore's even

UNESCO AND GEORGE TOWN

It might be hard to believe today, but George Town was in a bad way as the new millennium arrived. This was a classic case of inner-city decay: the centre, its shophouses shabby and unloved, was a place to make a hasty exit from once the day's work was done.

Then came the idea of putting George Town forward for consideration as a **UNESCO World Heritage Site**. So it would become, though not in the form Penangites envisaged. George Town was perhaps too Chinese a city in the context of the country's politics, and Malaysia wound up lobbying for a joint ticket comprising George Town and Melaka, the other former British Straits Settlements' port in Malaysia (see p.274). It was this two-headed entity that was honoured as a single World Heritage Site in 2008. Watershed elections that same year saw, among other surprises, Penang taken over by the opposition. Suddenly the state was being run along pragmatic, less racially focused lines, and had a UNESCO listing to boot. The scene was set for the city's regeneration.

The results are obvious for anyone to see. Properties all over the centre are being restored, some as boutique hotels and slick restaurants; young people are back in George Town, lounging in wannabe hipster cafés or cycling around checking out street art (see p.154); and the city has a real sense of its own heritage and creativity, celebrated in a slew of festivals and cultural events (see p.162).

However, as gentrification compels old businesses and community organizations to relocate, conservation groups are worried that George Town is losing its **intangible heritage** – a key ingredient in the UNESCO listing. Rapid social change is also an important factor, of course, and it may be that even with principled management, central George Town could one day become like Singapore's Chinatown: immaculate, thriving, but with little sense of deep-rooted neighbourhoods and traditions.

more famous *Raffles Hotel* – still epitomizes colonial elegance. Behind the grand, waterfront facade is an interior of cool marble floors, airy, dark timber and plasterwork, with a domed ceiling crowning the lobby; Rudyard Kipling, Somerset Maugham and Herman Hesse were among the guests, taking tiffin on the terrace and enjoying the sea breeze. If the hotel rates are beyond your budget, get a peek by treating yourself at its *Sarkies* restaurant.

House of Yeap Chor Ee

4 Lebuh Penang • Mon–Fri 10am–6pm • RM13 including written guide • ☏ 04 261 0190, ⓦ houseyce.com

The **House of Yeap Chor Ee**, a southern Chinese merchant who made his fortune becoming a sugar magnate and a banker, nestles within George Town's historical **business district**, dominated by the banks of Lebuh Pantai. Look for it next to the bright yellow former Chinese Chamber of Commerce building. Slicker than most of the country's state-owned museums, it's a privately run museum. Many of the artefacts are transplants from the vast mansion that Yeap Chor Ee later acquired on Jalan Sultan Ahmad Shah.

Peranakan Mansion

29 Lebuh Gereja • Daily 9.30am–5pm • RM20 • ☏ 04 264 2929, ⓦ pinangperanakanmansion.com.my

A sprinkling of Peranakan restaurants aside, George Town's one nod to Baba-Nyonya culture (see p.575) is a museum, the **Peranakan Mansion**. Painted pastel green, the house was built in the 1890s for Kapitan Cina Chung Keng Kwee, a Penang personality and secret society leader. Chinese wooden doors, gorgeous inlaid furniture and carved screens are everywhere, alongside more European touches including florid glass light fittings. The **display cases** are full of trinkets and heirlooms: green-and-pink Chinese-made porcelain painted with phoenixes and peonies, snuffboxes, embroideries and shoes. Upstairs, a **bedroom** with a four-poster bed has been left pretty much intact. There's also a section devoted to traditional **jewellery**, an adjoining shrine holding ancestral tablets, and a small **gift shop** selling Peranakan-themed souvenirs.

2

● **EATING**

China House	15
Jawi House	14
Kassim Mustafa	13
Line Clear	4
The Mugshot	7
Nasi Padang Minang	2
Penang Road 55 Tahun Cendol	12
Red Garden Food Paradise	1
Roti Canai Transfer Road	3
Sri Ananda Bahwan	9/10
Swimming Cat Café	5
Tai Tong	11
Toh Soon Café	6
Woodlands	8

● **SHOPPING**

41 Living Story	1
Chowrasta Market	4
Gerakbudaya	5
Jonathan Yun Sculptural Jewellery	9
Kedai Songkok	7
Occupy Beach Street	3
Prangin Mall	11
Rozana's Batik	10
Sam's Batik House	2
Shop Howard	8
Tropical Spice Garden – in the City	6

LEBUH FARQUHAR

JALAN SULTAN AHMAD SHAH

Grave of Captain Light

St. Francis Xavier Church

Cheong Fatt Tze Mansion

Red Garden

LEBUH LEITH

UPPER PENANG ROAD

JALAN SRI BAHARI

JALAN A.S. MANSOOR

JALAN ARIFFIN

TRANSFER RD

JALAN ARGYLL

LEBUH CLARKE

JALAN D. KOYAH

JALAN PENANG

LEBUH MUNTRI

24hr Laundry

Bengali Mosque

Hainan Temple

La Belle

JALAN HUTTON

JALAN DINDING

LORONG POPUS

LORONG AMOY

HUTTON LANE

JALAN KEDAH

LEBUH DICKENS

Mydin Supermarket

Police Headquarters

Campbell Street Archway

G+C Laundry

JALAN KG. MALABAR

LEBUH CHULIA

Air Asia

JALAN BURMA

JALAN PHEE CHEN

CHOWRASTA ST.

LEBUH TAMIL

LEBUH CAMPBELL

Chowrasta Market

JALAN PINTAL TALI

CARNAVON

LORONG MADRAS

JLN ONG CHONG KENG

KINTA

LEBUH KENG KWEE

LEBUH KIMBERLEY

LEBUH CINTRA

JALAN PINTAL TALI (ROPE WALK)

PESARA CLAIMANT

Syed Alatas Mansion

JALAN MACALISTER

LORONG KINTA

JALAN TALIPON

JALAN KUALA KANGSAR

JALAN S. UJONG

Police Station

JALAN KG.

Taxi Stand ★

JALAN PENANG

JALAN DR. LIM CHWEE LEONG

JALAN RIA

GTWHI (George Town World Heritage Incorporated)

Armenian Park

LORONG CARNAVON

KOMTAR

Ong Kongsi

Express Bus Stop

JALAN MAXWELL

JLN. CHEONG FATT ZE

LEBUH CARNARVON

LEBUH MELAYU

LORONG CARNAVON

LIMBIT

LORONG TOH

The Top@KOMTAR

ICT Digital Mall

Prangin Mall

Prangin Mall

LEBUH TEK SOON

LEBUH PRANGIN

LORONG IKAN

JALAN MACALISTER

JALAN DATO' KERAMAT

Gama Dept. Store

Penang House of Music

1st Avenue Shopping Mall

JALAN MAGAZINE

PERANGIN

JALAN TRANG

JALAN GURDWARA

LEBUH NOORDIN

JLN JAWA LAMA

Hin Bus Depot

JALAN TIMAH

LEBUH PRESGRAVE

LEBUH MCNAIR

JALAN C.Y. CHOY

● **STREET ART**

Boy on the Chair	6	The Lucky Cat Pyramid	11
Bruce Lee Kicks a Cat	4	Teach You to Speak	
Cat and Mouse	9	Hokkien	3
Indian Man on a Boat	2	Two Kids on a Bicycle	7
Kids on a Swing	8	Man on a Motorbike and	
Kids Playing Basketball	10	Kid with Dinosaur	5
Kung-Fu Girl	1		

GEORGE TOWN COLONIAL DISTRICT

0   100
metres

2

Swettenham Pier (Ferries to Langkawi)

Butterworth

Eastern & Oriental Hotel 1

LEBUH LEITH

LEBUH FARQUHAR

JALAN TUN SYED SHEH BARAKBAH

Esplanade

GREEN HALL

JALAN PADANG KOTA LAMA

BARAKBAH

Penang Art Gallery

Old City Hall

Dewan Sri Pinang

Old Town Hall

Padang Kota Lama

Fort Cornwallis

Supreme Court

LEBUH FARQUHAR

LEBUH LIGHT

House of Yeap Chor Ee

Dewan Undangan Negeri

JALAN T. S. S.

Penang Tourist Assoc. & TDC

LOVE LANE (LRG CINTA)

LORONG ARGUS

LORONG STEWART

St George's Church

LEBUH PITTI

LEBUH KING

LEBUH BISHOP

Clocktower

Police

Immigration Office

LORONG CHULIA

LEBUH KLANG

Goddess of Mercy Temple (Kuan Yin Teng)

LEBUH PENANG

Standard Chartered Bank

LORONG PASAR

LRG MUDA

LEBUH GEREJA (CHURCH STREET)

Penang Heritage Trust

Penang Global Tourism Office 3

LEBUH DOWNING

HSBC

Kapitan Keling Mosque (Masjid Kapitan Keling)

JALAN MASJID KAPITAN KELING

LEBUH QUEEN

LEBUH CHINA

Peranakan Mansion

The Whiteaways Arcade

LEBUH SECK CHUAN

Sri Mahamariamman Temple Moneychangers

Han Jiang Temple

PASAR (MARKET STREET)

LORONG CHE EM

LEBUH PANTAI

GAT LEBUH GEREJA

JLN BUCKINGHAM

LRG SECK CHUAN

GAT LEBUH CHINA

Wisma Kastam

Mor Hun Club

KOLAM

LEBUH AH QUEE

Sun Yat-sen Museum

LRG SOO JONG

Kew Leong Tong Lim

LEBUH CHULIA

MPP Bus Station

GAT LEBUH PASAR

PENGKALAN WELD

Yep Temple

LEBUH CANNON

Cheah Kongsi

LEBUH ARMENIAN

Yeoh Kongsi

LESUH ACEH

Hock Teng Cheng Sin Temple

CANNON SQUARE

Khoo Kongsi

STEP BY STEP LANE

Masjid Melayu

Penang Tourist Guides Association

LEBUH PANTAI

LEBUH ARMENIAN

LORONG TOH AKA

LEBUH VICTORIA

Rapid Penang Local Bus Station & Taxi Stand

N

Pengkalan Weld Ferry Terminal

LEBUH ACHEH

PENGKALAN WELD

LEBUH MELAYU

Chew Jetty

Chinese Clan Jetties

Lee Jetty

Tan Jetty

DRINKING & NIGHTLIFE

Hong Kong Bar	3
Good Friends Club	7
Magazine 63	6
Mish Mash	4
Narrow Marrow	4
Soundmaker	5
Three Sixty Degree Sky Bar	1

ACCOMMODATION

23 Love Lane	6	Hutton Lodge	8
The Blue Mansion	2	Jawi Peranakan Mansion	3
Chew Jetty Homestay	20	Old Penang Guest House	9
China Tiger Studio		Penaga Hotel	7
Apartments	14	Red Inn	5
Chulia Mansion	10	Ren I Tang	12
Le Dream	17	Roommates Penang	11
Eastern & Oriental		Ryokan	4
(E&O) Hotel	1	Sinkeh	19
East Indies Mansion	15	Spices Hotel &	
The Frame Guest House	13	Spices by the Park	18
House of Journey	16		

2

Jalan Masjid Kapitan Kling

For some locals, **Jalan Masjid Kapitan Kling** will always be **Pitt Street**, named after William Pitt the Younger, British prime minister when Francis Light founded Penang. It's also nicknamed the **Street of Harmony**, as, if you include the compound of St George's Church at its eastern end, it's home to places of worship representing all of Malaysia's major faiths.

Goddess of Mercy Temple (Kuan Yin Teng)

Jalan Masjid Kapitan Kling, close to the start of Lebuh China • Daily 7am–7pm • Free

The oldest and liveliest of George Town's Chinese temples, **Goddess of Mercy Temple (Kuan Yin Teng)** is a down-to-earth granite hall dating to 1801, and where dragon-carved pillars and wooden roof beams are blackened by incense smoke. As Kuan Yin is the goddess of mercy, the temple is perpetually jammed with devotees, mostly beggars down on their luck and women praying for children, grandchildren and safe childbirth. The huge bronze bell in the first hall is rung by those who have made a donation; the flagstone forecourt features performances of **Chinese opera** during festivals.

Sri Mahamariamman Temple

Lebuh Queen, with a second entrance on Jalan Masjid Kapitan Kling • Daily 8am–noon & 4–9pm • Free

The **Sri Mahamariamman Temple**, founded in 1833, is the chief sight in George Town's small but characterful **Little India**, centred on Lebuh Pasar. Recently renovated, its pale green and red entrance tower is a riot of sculpted deities, among which four **swans** represent incarnations of the goddess Mariamman.

Kapitan Keling Mosque (Masjid Kapitan Keling)

Western end of Jalan Masjid Kapitan Kling • Mon, Sat & Sun 1–5pm, Fri 3–5pm • Free

The oldest and largest mosque in Penang, **Kapitan Keling Mosque (Masjid Kapitan Keling)** dates back to 1801, when Indian Muslim migrants built a mosque here on land granted them by the East India Company. *Keling* is an old term – now regarded as derogatory – said to originate from the sound of clinking chains tied on the legs of British colonial Indian slaves – and Kapitan Keling was one Cauder Mohudeen, a successful businessman appointed by the East India Company to speak for the community. The present mosque was refashioned in Anglo-Moorish style at the start of

---

GEORGE TOWN'S STREET ART

Street art is a recent phenomenon in George Town but has already become a big draw for local visitors, who wander around the centre tracking down the murals and cartoons executed in steel wire on shophouse walls. The **wire pieces** – some fifty of them – were commissioned in 2009 from KL studio **Sculpture at Work** as a whimsical way of marking out the UNESCO-listed parts of the city.

In 2012, Lithuanian artist Ernest Zacharevic sketched a series of mural installations entitled **Mirrors of George Town** for the George Town Festival. Ever since, Penang has taken off as one of Southeast Asia's street art capitals. In 2013, Zacharevic's piece depicting two children on a bicycle was selected by *The Guardian* as among the best street art in the world, consolidating the position of the city's murals as a tourist draw. In the wake of George Town's success, Zacharevic has sketched walls as far as Ipoh, Kuala Lumpur, Johor Bahru and Singapore.

As well as Zacharevic's pieces, George Town hosts work by local and international artists such as Kenji Chan (Sandakan), Fritilidea (KL), Rone (Melbourne), Elle (New York) and Julia Volchkova (Russia). You'll spot their art as you walk around town (see map, p.152)

The gallery **Hin Bus Depot** (31A Jalan Gurdwara; daily 11am–8pm; ⓦhinbusdepot.com) has long promoted street art in Penang, and today is still the best place to meet local artists and creative types, who organize rotating art exhibitions and the weekly **Sunday pop-up market** (ⓦfacebook .com/HinPopup). Also lookout for **13 Armenian Street** (1st floor, 13 Lebuh Armenian; Mon–Sat 10am–6pm; ☎04 251 9463), an artists studio and gallery hosting workshops on a regular basis.

the last century, and its dark onion domes, arched portico and minaret are especially attractive at night, when the whole place is subtly lit.

Lebuh Armenian (Armenian Street)

Short and curved at one end, **Lebuh Armenian (Armenian Street)** offers good value for visitors, packing in a number of minor sights along its highly gentrified length, including at its southern end the popular *Two Kids on Bicycle* street art. The narrow house at the street's northern end is the **Syed Alatas mansion**, which is undergoing a second restoration; the house is named after a merchant and arms dealer from Aceh, in northern Sumatra, who lived here in the 1870s.

Mor Hun Club

122 Lebuh Armenian • Puppet and opera house Tues–Sun 10am–6pm • RM10; puppet shows (1hr) around RM25, including museum entry • ☎ 04 262 0377, ⓦ facebook.com/TeochewPuppetAndOpera)

The **Mor Hun Club** is one of George Town's surviving traditional social clubs, its entrance distinguished by colourful tilework and gorgeously carved gilt doors; walk past at night and you may hear the clacking of a game of mahjong from the upstairs windows. Downstairs is the **Teochew Puppet & Opera House** with displays on Chinese opera and metal rod puppetry, only preserved in Penang. Try to catch one of their occasional **puppet shows**, with some English explanations.

Sun Yat-sen Museum

120 Lebuh Armenian • Museum Tues–Sat 9am–5pm, Sun 1–5pm • RM5 • ☎ 04 262 0123

The **Sun Yat-sen Museum**, located in a beautifully restored shophouse, offers a permanent exhibition and guided tour of the Penang base of one of Asia's most important historical personalities, Sun Yat-sen. He led the revolution that overthrew the last Chinese emperor, drawing on support from the overseas Chinese.

Yap Kongsi

Corner of Lebuh Armenian and Lebuh Cannon • Daily 8am–6pm • Free • ☎ 04 261 0679

It's hard to imagine two more contrasting shrines than the pair that make up the most obvious sight on Lebuh Armenian, the **Yap Kongsi**. On the left of the clan house compound is the conventionally styled **Ciji Temple** (also called **Choo Chee Keong**), its roof photogenically bedecked with dragons; next door, built in the 1920s on land furnished by the tycoon Yeap Chor Ee, the green-and-white **Yap Temple** looks like a European-style villa and holds the clan's ancestral tablets.

Hock Teik Cheng Sin Temple

57 Lebuh Armenian • No fixed times • Free

Just south of the corner with Lebuh Cannon, a passageway beneath a Chinese facade gives access to the gaudy, two-storey **Hock Teik Cheng Sin Temple**, with altars on both levels. It's dedicated to **Tua Peh Kong**, sometimes described as the god of prosperity and one of the most popular Chinese deities in Malaysia – many cities have at least one Tua Peh Kong shrine. In the mid-nineteenth century the temple and surrounding area was a stronghold of the Kean Teik secret society, which became embroiled in the Penang Riots of 1867. For nine days, George Town was shaken by gang fights around Armenian, Church and Chulia streets, where the groups were holed up. A bricked-up passageway can still be seen that once allowed a surreptitious escape to the street or to the Khoo Kongsi compound.

Khoo Kongsi

18 Cannon Square • Daily 9am–5pm • RM10 • ☎ 04 261 4609, ⓦ khookongsi.com.my

Khoo Kongsi is the best known of Penang's clan associations, and no wonder: this is practically a gated community in its own right, reached by an alleyway off Lebuh

Cannon. It brings you into an overpoweringly gaudy complex that includes shrines, opera stage, ancestral hall and residences. The *kongsi* represents Khoos from a particular village in southern China; one such was Khoo Thean Teik, the ringleader of the Kean Teik secret society during the Penang Riots, although he later rehabilitated himself and became a very wealthy pillar of local society.

The two-storey **main building** looks ready to collapse under the weight of the multicoloured ceramic sculptures, woodcarvings and shining gold leaf adorning its roof. Finished in 1906, this is a lesser version of an even more extravagant original that had just burned down – some say destroyed by jealous deities, angered by its ostentation.

The building opposite was the **opera stage**, beside which is the slightly incongruous administration building, a colonial-styled affair which houses some ancestral tablets. A former kitchen next to the main building is now a little **museum** explaining the evolution of the complex.

Chinese clan jetties
Pengkalan Weld

They're not as atmospheric as the water villages at Pulau Ketam near Kuala Lumpur or in the capital of Brunei, but the seven **Chinese clan jetties** of George Town still make for a good wander. Communities of stilt houses built over the water, they were set up by Chinese immigrants before George Town properly got going, and are so named because six of them are inhabited by individual clans whose roots are in specific villages in Fujian province, southeast China. The houses are connected by wooden boardwalks and dotted with temples. The **Chew jetty**, smack in the middle, is the largest and, as the target of most tourists, drowning in tacky souvenir shops; best to try one of the other jetties, though do be sensitive in this cramped residential environment – it's not ideal for loud conversations and incessant photography.

Cheong Fatt Tze Mansion
14 Lebuh Leith • Compulsory tours: daily 11am, 2pm & 3.30pm; 1hr • RM16 • ☎ 04 262 0006, ⓦ cheongfatttzemansion.com

Leith Street was once lined by a gaggle of villas belonging to Hakka Chinese tycoons, one such being the **Cheong Fatt Tze Mansion**, the local home of a nineteenth century Dutch East Indies tycoon, and a splendid example of Penang's eclectic late nineteenth-century house design. Now trading mainly as *The Blue Mansion* hotel (see p.159), it's broadly southern Chinese in form, with good-luck motifs and complex decorative mouldings along the tiled roof, though its **arches** and **shutters** are definitely European touches, as are the Art Nouveau stained glass and the sweeping interior staircase, even if the delicate iron tracery and balconies might owe a nod to wooden Malay verandas.

KOMTAR
the Top@KOMTAR Daily 10am–10pm • RM98 till 6pm; RM118 after 6pm with glass of wine and snacks, RM138 with dinner • ☎ 04 262 3800, ⓦ thetop.com.my • Penang House of Music Daily 11am–7pm • RM30 • ☎ 04 370 6675, ⓦ penanghouseofmusic.com

George Town's most prominent landmark, the **Kompleks Tun Abdul Razak** (**KOMTAR**) is a 68-storey cylindrical tower at the western end of the city centre. It languished for years, only partially filled with local government offices and malls clustered beneath and around it, and serving mainly as a transport hub. In 2015, three new levels were added to the existing 65, increasing the structure's height to 249m. Rebranded as **the Top@ KOMTAR**, the extension has a 360-degree panoramic observatory, several restaurants and, at the very top, a bistro next to the open-air glass **Rainbow Skywalk**, Southeast Asia's first thrilling walk into the clouds. Plans are afoot to decorate one side of the tower with a 230m-tall, 13m-wide mural – the world's biggest – by early 2018.

Among Komtar's other (forgettable) theme-park-styled attractions and museums, don't miss **Penang House of Music**, on the fourth floor of ICT Digital Mall, next to

Pranging Mall. The exhibits in this interactive museum span Penang's rich pop-music history from the 1940s to the 1960s. Their performance space has live jazz and other musical events and workshops.

Thai Temple

Lorong Burma, in the Pulau Tikus area on the northern edge of town • Daily 7am–5.30pm • Free • Bus #101, #103 or #304; get off on Jalan Kelawei

The Buddhist **Thai Temple** (Wat Chaiya Mangkalaram) dates to the 1900s and is noticeably very different to the Chinese equivalents elsewhere in Penang. Brightly painted, it has flame-edged eaves and a huge gilded pagoda, all soft curves. The main hall's entrance is flanked by *nagas* – fierce serpents painted gold and bright green – and guarded by two hefty demons weilding swords. The aircraft-hangar-like interior is a stark contrast to the exterior; in it lies a 33m-long **reclining Buddha** statue, draped in a gold sarong and with his aura flaming about him.

Burmese Temple

Lorong Burma, Pulau Tikus • Daily 8am–5pm • Free • ☎ 04 226 9575 • Bus #101, #103 or #304; get off on Jalan Kelawei

The guardians of the **Burmese Temple** (Dharmikarama Temple) are two snarling white and gold lions, with scales, claws and fiery trim. The Buddha inside stands, smiling mysteriously into the gloom, one oversized white hand pointing up, and one down. The grounds are a bit nicer than those over the road at Wat Chaiya Mangkalaram, with more greenery and less concrete, and a few naturalistically painted statues.

Nattukottai Chettiar Temple

Jalan Kebun Bunga • Daily 7am–noon & 4–9pm • Free • ☎ 04 227 1322 • Bus #10 from Pengkalan Weld

The **Nattukottai Chettiar Temple** (more formally the **Arulmigu Thandayuthapani Temple**) is the focus of the riotous three-day Hindu **Thaipusam** festival, in honour of Lord Subramanian (January or February). One of the crowning moments is the arrival of a silver chariot carrying the statue of Lord Murugan, and a golden chariot, introduced in 2017 to carry the statue's spear. The temple itself has an unusual wooden colonnaded walkway with exquisite pictorial tiles, leading up to the inner sanctum, where a life-sized solid-silver peacock bows its head to the deity, Lord Subramanian.

Botanic Gardens

Jalan Kebun Bunga, 6km west of central George Town • Daily 5am–8pm • Free • ☎ 04 226 4401, ⓦ botanicalgardens.penang.gov.my • Bus #10 (every 45min; 45min)

Dating to 1884, George Town's **Botanical Gardens** boast extensive lawns, a stream and little jungly waterfall, and several (rather paltry) plant houses. It's often packed with groups of exercising Malaysians, who storm around the circuit trail.

You can walk to **Penang Hill** (see p.166) from here using the so-called jeep track, but it's a tough uphill hike (3hr) – better to head down this way. A much easier hike just outside the gardens begins at the circular Chinese **moon gate arch** easily spotted on the main road; from here a wooded trail leads uphill, with views back over George Town. Most people head back down once they've reached the signed "Station 3" (allow 30min to get here).

ARRIVAL AND DEPARTURE   **GEORGE TOWN**

Unless you're on a plane or ferry, you'll reach or leave Penang island by one of two mammoth bridges linking it with the mainland part of the state: the 14km **Penang Bridge** (from Seberang Prai, just south of Butterworth) and the 24km **Second Penang Bridge** (from Batu Kawan, 15km south of Butterworth).

BY PLANE
Penang International Airport One of the busiest in the country, the airport (ⓦ penangairport.com), 19km south of George Town at Bayan Lepas, has two tourist information

counters (daily: Tourism Malaysia 8am–10pm; Penang Global Tourism 9am–5pm), a few ATMs and car rental kiosks. Buses #401 and #401E (both every 30min) run from outside the building to the terminal at Pengkalan Weld

2

(1hr) via the KOMTAR building in the west of the city centre (see below); bus #102 (hourly) also serves KOMTAR and then heads out to the beach at Batu Ferringhi. Uber and Grab are popular in Penang, and have the best rates from the airport and George Town. The airport operates a coupon system for unmetered taxis (around RM40, or RM60 in the small hours) – buy a ticket from inside the airport building. **Destinations** Johor Bahru (2 daily; 1hr 10min); Kota Bharu (daily; 1hr); Kota Kinabalu (1–2 daily; 2hr 45min); Kuala Lumpur (KLIA: 22 daily; Subang: 20 daily; 1hr); Kuantan (3 weekly; 1hr 15min); Kuching (1–2 daily; 2hr); Langkawi (3 daily; 35min); Melaka (1 daily; 1hr 20min); Singapore (at least 12 daily; 1hr 25min).

BY TRAIN

Penang's train station is in Butterworth (see p.148). From here, you can either catch an Uber or a cab to George Town (20min; around RM30) or follow the signed footbridge to the ferry. There is also a ticket office at George Town's ferry terminal (Mon–Thurs, Sat & Sun 10am–2pm & 3–5pm, Fri 10am–1pm & 3–5pm).

BY BUS

You don't have to buy bus tickets from the relevant terminal: there are bus company kiosks on the ground floor of the Prangin Mall close to the KOMTAR building, and informal travel agents on Lebuh Chulia plus some hostels sell train, bus and Langkawi ferry tickets.

Express bus station At Sungai Nibong, 8km southwest of George Town on Jalan Sultan Azlan Shah, the express bus station is served by several local buses, including #102 (for the airport, the KOMTAR building and Batu Ferringhi; hourly), plus #307 and #401 (both serve KOMTAR and the Pengkalan Weld terminal; every 30–45min). A taxi into town costs about RM25. Departures from the bus station often head first to Butterworth, although a few

southbound buses bypass it. In general, though, Butterworth still has more frequent services and a wider range of destinations, so it may pay to catch the ferry to the mainland and pick up a bus there.

Backpacker minibuses Run by tour agencies, minivan shuttles serving the east coast, Cameron Highlands and southern Thailand, among other destinations, pick up and drop passengers at hostels and the Prangin Mall, with tickets sold at both of these. The journey across the border to Hat Yai, for example, costs around RM35.

BY FERRY

Butterworth Ferries shuttle between Butterworth and Pengkalan Weld (daily 5.40am–12.30am; every 20min–1hr; 20min; RM1.20 to George Town, free to Butterworth), docking at a terminal close to the local bus station at the end of Chulia Street.

Langkawi Langkawi ferries use the Swettenham Pier, just east of Fort Cornwallis, with tickets available from a cluster of agencies just outside, by the clock tower. There are daily departures at 8.30am and 2pm (2hr 45min; RM67 including port fees); the earlier of these also calls at the Pulau Payar Marine Park, making it possible to do (expensive) day-trips there with dive operators such as East Marine (see box, p.179). Check the latest schedules and prices at ⓦ langkawi -ferry.com and buy tickets at least a day in advance.

BY CAR

Driving to George Town Whichever bridge you use, tolls are payable only on the journey over from the mainland (Penang Bridge RM7, Second Penang Bridge RM8.50) and only using a local Touch 'N Go Card (ⓦ touchngo.com.my) – you won't be able to go through the turnpike without one. Arriving on the island, bear right (north) up the coast for George Town. There's a reasonably central car park in the KOMTAR building on Jalan Penang.

GETTING AROUND

By bus Rapid Penang (ⓦ rapidpg.com.my) operates buses across Penang state. Many island routes originate at their station on Pengkalan Weld, with a station beneath the KOMTAR building serving as a secondary hub. The website gives a breakdown of routes, operating times (daily roughly 6am–9.30pm, although some services wind down much earlier or later) and frequencies (every 15min–1hr depending on the route). Fares climb with distance from RM1.40 (any trip within George Town) to RM4 in four steps; the airport to George Town, say, is RM2.70. A seven-day pass, Rapid Passport, offers unlimited travel for RM30 and is available at the bus station, KOMTAR and the Penang Global Tourism tourist office (see p.159). Remember that drivers don't give change. The overpriced double-decker Hop-On Hop-Off (RM40/24hr, RM74/48hr; ⓦ myhoponhopoff.com/pg)

plies a city route (13 stops) and a beach route (15 stops), connecting all major tourist sites.

By taxi It's more convenient to use Uber or Grab, as taxi drivers don't use their meters and tend to overcharge, but there are ranks on Pengkalan Weld, on Penang Rd near the *Cititel* hotel, and on Jalan Dr Lim Chwee Long, around the Prangin Mall – a trip to across town will be around RM15, out to Penang Hill or Batu Ferringhi about RM30. To book a taxi in advance, call Penang Taxi Drivers Association ☎ 04 262 5721.

By trishaw The humble trishaw (*beca*) clings on in George Town, mainly for the benefit of tourists. You'll find the vehicles parked up on Lebuh Penang at the corner with Lebuh Muntri, and on Lebuh Armenian close to the Yap Kongsi, among other places. An hour's pedal around the old town starts at RM35.

By bike Bike sharing system LinkBike (ⓦ linkbike.my) has 25 docking stations scattered around George Town, Straits Quay and Queensbay. Packages start at RM2/day; download the app, purchase credit and scan the QR code to get your bike. Some guesthouses and shops rent bicycles out for around RM20/half day.

By motorbike Most guesthouses in Chulia St have motorbikes for rent, starting at around RM35/day.

By car Hawk, at the airport (ⓣ 04 227 9440, ⓦ hawkrentacar.com.my); Hertz, 38 Lebuh Farquhar (ⓣ 04 263 5914); La Belle, 48 Lebuh Leith (ⓣ 016 416 0617, ⓦ facebook.com/LaBelleCar); Mayflower, at the airport (ⓣ 04 641 1191, ⓦ mayflowercarrental .com.my).

INFORMATION AND TOURS

Penang Global Tourism Ground floor, The Whiteaways Arcade, Lebuh Pantai ⓣ 04 263 1166, ⓦ mypenang .gov.my; map p.152. Penang state's tourist office can provide maps and leaflets on various aspects of local history and culture, some of which can be downloaded from their website, where you can also get e-coupon twenty percent discounts for several tours and many of George Town's hit-and-miss museums. Mon–Fri 9am–5pm, Sat 9am–3pm, Sun 9am–1pm.

Tourism Malaysia 10 Jalan Tun Syed Shah Barakbah ⓣ 04 262 2093; map.152. Close to Fort Cornwallis, this is one of the more knowledgeable Tourism Malaysia offices. Mon–Fri 8am–5pm.

Tour guides If you have a special interest in, for example, architecture or history, or want to get off the beaten track, it can be worth engaging a professional guide at the Penang Tourist Guides Association (7 Lebuh Cannon; Tues–Sun; ⓣ 04 261 4461, ⓦ ptga.my).

ACCOMMODATION

There's such a vast choice of hotels and guesthouses in **George Town** that there's little reason to base yourself further afield. That said, it's feasible to stay at the Batu Ferringhi beach or Balik Pulau and see George Town on day-trips.

HOTELS

★**23 Love Lane** 23 Love Lane ⓣ 04 262 1323, ⓦ 23lovelane.com; map p.152. Step through the square gateway hung with lanterns and it immediately feels like you've arrived at a private villa. Set around a lush garden of frangipani trees are ten spacious rooms, eclectically done out in snazzy hues. Besides doubles, there's also a two-level family unit and a glorious three-bedroom shophouse. Breakfast and afternoon tea included. 🛜 **RM500**

The Blue Mansion 14 Lebuh Leith ⓣ 04 262 0006, ⓦ cheongfatttzemansion.com; map p.152. An expensive choice, but there are few more characterful places to stay in Penang. Cheong Fatt Tze's former villa (see p.156) now offers eighteen stylish suites plus a swimming pool, spa, reading room and its own restaurant and bar. Noise from the adjacent *Red Garden* food court can be a little annoying at night, though. Breakfast included. 🛜 **RM1000**

Chulia Mansion 139 Chulia St ⓣ 04 261 8788, ⓦ chuliamansion.com; map p.152. If you must stay on busy Chulia St, this tall, refurbished concrete hotel is a reliable option, with good-value rooms and a sheltered rooftop with open-air bar and a free jacuzzi. They also serve free-flowing wine, coffee, tea and ice cream to guests. 🛜 **RM168**

Le Dream 139 Jalan Pintal Tali ⓣ 04 251 9370, ⓦ ledreamhotel.com; map p.152. The snazziest in an endless series of central George Town's gentrifying refurbishments, *Le Dream* has an attractive neo-noir decor and smart rooms with Japanese-style bathrooms. A perk is the panoramic rooftop with bar and mini

swimming pool, great for sunsets and city views. On the ground floor, upmarket restaurant *Le Vie* is popular for French-fusion mains and inch-thick Aussie-style ribeye steaks. 🛜 **RM400**

★**Eastern & Oriental (E&O) Hotel** 10 Lebuh Farquhar ⓣ 04 222 2000, ⓦ eohotels.com; map p.152. Some rooms at Penang's historic hotel (see p.150) are set in the original colonial building, while many more are in a fifteen-storey newer wing. But you'll pay hardly much more to stay in the former, where you can immerse yourself in what feels like a period mansion right on the seafront. The new wing has an infinity pool, and the original wing has a pool within a couple of metres of the sea. Breakfast included. 🛜 **RM860**

East Indies Mansion 25 Lebuh China ⓣ 04 261 8025, ⓦ eastindieshotel.com; map p.152. Converted from a recently restored private residence, this boutiquey hotel was once a tycoon's home set around two adjacent Chinese courtyards. Some of the ten suites have mezzanines (with an extra queen bed) and a pretty spiral staircase. Breakfast is extra, but there's a huge kitchen and dining hall for guest's use. 🛜 **RM180**

Jawi Peranakan Mansion 153 Jalan Hutton ⓣ 04 261 8888, ⓦ georgetownheritage.com/jawi-peranakan-mansion; map p.152. The latest in architect Chris Ong's heritage boutique hotel collection conjures a legacy of opulent Muslim-Indian colonial traders. The eight mansion rooms and six family suites, some with elevated wooden mezzanines, maintain the mansion's original fittings, accompanied by a drizzle of authentic touches sourced directly from South India. Breakfast included. 🛜 **RM400**

2

Penaga Hotel Corner of Jalan Hutton & Lebuh Clarke ☎04 291 3201, ⊛hotelpenaga.com; map p.152. A block of 45 elegant rooms and several family villas set around a pool and garden in walking distance to all the main sites. Each of the spacious and well naturally lit suites has a unique design, warm wooden floors and original beams. *Penaga* also runs an artist residency programme, and guests are invited to socialize with whoever is working in-house at the moment. Breakfast costs RM28. 🛜 RM430

★**Ren I Tang** 82a Lebuh Penang (entrance on Lebuh China) ☎04 250 8383, ⊛renitang.com; map p.152. This imposing three-storey colonial building originally housed a Chinese apothecary, its name now given to the mid-range hotel that has emerged following a splendid conversion – although they've deliberately retained a herbalist's shop downstairs. There's a vast range of rooms, including a family unit, a self-contained apartment and assorted doubles, some with distressed paintwork for that aged look. Note that there's no lift, but they can winch your luggage to the top floor, on request. Breakfast included. 🛜 RM220

Sinkeh 105 Lebuh Melayu ☎04 261 3966, ⊛sinkeh .com; map p.152. Nine rooms in a lovely nineteenth-century house, reimagined by an award-winning architect. The rooms are compact and modern, with attached bathrooms and a/c, and a courtyard for socializing. *Sinkeh* also houses Reka Arts Space, which hosts small-scale theatre performances. 🛜 RM280

Spices Hotel and Spices by the Park 29 Lebuh China ☎04 263 3580, ⊛spiceshotel.com; map p.152. Tucked in behind Armenian Park, *Spices Hotel* feels more like an upmarket guesthouse. The rooms are large, with high ceilings and tall windows, and believe it or not, there's a living Bodhi tree uprooting on the premises. If it's full, ask to stay next door at, *Spices by the Park*, where the six delightful rooms are set above a little bistro, with a tiny rooftop to peek out over the Acheh mosque's minaret. 🛜 *Spices* RM175, *Spices by the Park* RM140

HOSTELS AND GUESTHOUSES

Chew Jetty Homestay 59a Chew Jetty ☎013 438 1217, ⊛mychewjetty.com; map p.152. One of the families at the old clan jetties offers a/c rooms in their house, with shared facilities; it's a good opportunity to mingle with the community and wake to the sight of the sun rising over the mainland. Breakfast included. 🛜 RM168

★**China Tiger Studio Apartments** 29 Lebuh China ☎04 263 3580, ⊛chinatiger.info; map p.152. Two five-person apartments, right in the hustle of Little India, yet perfectly insulated for quiet. The bright colours, quilted blankets and wall decorations by Penang-based visual artist and owner Rebecca Duckett-Wilkinson truly make you feel at home in Penang. Apartment 🛜 RM500

The Frame Guest House 168 Lebuh Chulia ☎04 263 8807, ⊛theframeguesthouse.com; map p.152. Another in a series of cookie-cutter industrial shabby-chic George Town guesthouses, which are so popular with young flashpackers. Rooms have all the bells and whistles the standard demands, but lack distinctive character. This said, the long and airy common kitchen is a nice touch. 🛜 Dorms RM33, doubles RM85

House of Journey 47 Lorong Seckchuan ☎04 263 3580, ⊛houseofjourney.wordpress.com; map p.152. Inspiring backpacker hostel with large and airy dorms, a sociable vibe, and hundreds of comments and travel tips scribbled on the walls. The hairdryers and individual mirrors in the shared bathrooms are a welcome touch in this price category. 🛜 Dorms RM34

★**Hutton Lodge** 17 Jalan Hutton ☎04 263 6003, ⊛huttonlodge.com; map p.152. It calls itself a budget hotel, but operates more like an informal guesthouse with a dorm and a wide range of plainly furnished rooms, singles and doubles, some en suite. What gives it a proper homely feel is that it occupies a detached two-storey former mansion that's perhaps 100 years old, although what you see now was largely rebuilt after a major fire in 2003. Breakfast included; good value. 🛜 Dorms RM32, doubles RM90

Old Penang Guest House 53 Love Lane ☎04 263 8805, ⊛oldpenang.com; map p.152. One of the better restored shophouses, with a range of a/c rooms and two dorms. The sheets are crisp and clean, there's a relaxing airy lounge with plasma TV, and staff are helpful. Light breakfast included. 🛜 Dorms RM25, doubles RM80

Red Inn 55 Love Lane ☎04 261 3931, ⊛redinnpenang. com; map p.152. A nicely converted shophouse with polished wooden floors, although the dorms are basic and unremarkable. They also have branches in the vicinity with double rooms as well as dorms. Perhaps the best feature is the generous breakfast – staff go out to buy noodles and *roti canai*. 🛜 Dorms RM30, doubles RM90

Roommates Penangg 17b Lorong Chulia ☎04 261 1567, ⊛bit.ly/RoommatesPenang; map p.152. This tiny hostel has just two eight-bed dorms, and feels all the homelier for it. They're cosy, too, with privacy curtains and built-in lights for each bunk bed. 🛜 RM32

Ryokan 62 Lebuh Muntri ☎04 250 0287, ⊛myryokan.com; map p.152. Despite naming itself after a certain class of traditional inns in Japan, there's not much that's Japanese about *Ryokan* other than perhaps a fascination with slickness and modernity. Popular with budget-conscious locals, the place certainly goes all out for the flashpacker vote, with individual power points, lights and lockers for every dorm bed, and breakfasts that stretch to sausage and egg. They have en-suite rooms, too, and a bar. 🛜 Dorms RM30, doubles RM140

EATING

Despite lacking the glitz of KL's eating scene, Penang has earned a solid international reputation as the jewel in Asia's street-food crown. Rightly or not, people the world over come to relish local specialities such as **asam laksa**, a rendition of *laksa* with the tang of tamarind; and **nasi kandar**, Muslim–Indian curries served with rice. The latter is ubiquitous in Malaysia now, of course, but originated, so the story goes, with Penang street vendors who carried their dishes in pots hanging from a shoulder pole (*kandar*).

RESTAURANTS AND CAFÉS

★**China House** 153 & 155 Lebuh Pantai, with another entrance at 183b Lebuh Victoria ☎04 263 7299, ⓦ chinahouse.com.my; map p.152. This café-restaurant-gallery led the charge of Western-style venues setting up shop in George Town . It's famed for its enormous range of luscious cakes – more than two dozen at any time, including their signature tiramisu – though it also serves great meals (pies, pasta, etc) and breakfasts. Reckon on RM12 for cake, RM20 for breakfast, RM35 for a main course, not including drinks. Mon–Thurs 9am–midnight, Fri–Sun 9am–1am.

★**Jawi House** 85 Lebuh Armenian ☎04 261 3680, ⓦ jawihouse.com; map p.152. A celebration of the Jawi Peranakan culinary heritage, cultivated by Middle Eastern and northern Indian spice traders who came to Penang and married local Malay women. Try specialities such as herbal *lemuni* rice, Jawi *biriyani*, or the highly recommended house signature *bamieh* – spice-rich tomato and lamb stew served with crusted Bengali bread. Count on RM30 for a meal, excluding drinks. Daily except Tues 11am–10pm.

Kassim Mustafa 12 Lebuh Chulia, at Lebuh Penang ⓦ kassimmustafa.com.my; map p.152. Filling half a block with green and yellow frontage, *Kassim* is a pretty standard Mamak joint, probably the slickest place in town for *nasi kandar* (around RM5). Daily 24hr.

Line Clear In an alleyway by 177 Jalan Penang, ☎04 261 4440; map p.152. The origins of the name are lost, although it may have been a cry related to cleaning drains or settling the bill. What isn't in doubt is the decades-long popularity of the *nasi kandar* in this unprepossessing joint. Meals rarely exceed RM10. Daily 24hr.

★**The Mugshot** 302 Lebuh Chulia ☎12 405 6276, ⓦ facebook.com/TheMugshotCafePenang; map p.152. This little café does excellent sesame bagels, baked in their own wood-fired oven. Wash them down with excellent coffee or freshly squeezed juice; there's also homemade yoghurt in exotic flavours such as jackfruit and *gula melaka* (palm molasses). The artisan bakery next door is run by the same people, offering focaccia, poppy seed bloomers and the like. Daily 8am–midnight.

★**Nasi Padang Minang** 92 Transfer Rd; map p.152. A feast of tangy Padang food cooked by Indonesian residents and housed in a Chinese *kopitiam*. Take your own rice and dishes, and elbow your way to a table, as it's always packed with local workers on lunch break. The *ikan sumbat* (deep fried fish stuffed with shallots; RM8) is recommended. Daily 11am–6pm.

Sri Ananda Bahwan 53 & 55 Lebuh Penang ☎04 264 4204; map p.152. Popular Indian cheapie with two outlets churning out the usual range of starchy, spicy breakfasts, *thosai* and curries, none of them more than RM10. The one on the corner with Lebuh China serves meat, the other doesn't. Daily 7am–11pm.

Swimming Cat Café 15 Lebuh Queen; map p.152. Artsy café fitted with potted plants and cute primary school desks and chairs, with a good mix of alternative tunes, coffee (RM6) and light snacks such as pizzas and Japanese-style titbits (around RM15), as well as an impressive selection of hipster magazines. Wed–Fri 3pm–10pm, Sat–Sun 11am–8pm.

★**Tai Tong** 45 Lebuh Cintra ☎04 263 6625, ⓦ facebook.com/TaiTongRestaurant; map p.152. This dim sum restaurant has plastic chairs, wall fans and utilitarian metal trolleys groaning with food. The dim sum – until 11.30am and all evening – is excellent, including standards such as yam puffs and prawn dumplings; at lunchtime and at night the kitchen does à la carte orders, with dishes such as victory chicken (crisply roasted) and veg stir-fries. RM30 without drinks. Daily 7am–2.30pm & 7–10.30pm.

Woodlands 60 Lebuh Penang ☎04 263 9764; map p.152. Run by two brothers, this a/c place is a tad smarter than the other Indian veg places in the area, and the cooking is a cut above, too. Come here for the usual banana-leaf meals, *thosai* and South Indian snacks, plus North Indian dishes such as *malai kofta* (cheesy potato dumplings in a creamy sauce). RM15, excluding drinks. Daily 8.30am–10pm.

FOOD COURTS

New Lane Hawker Centre Lorong Baru; map p.149. An alternative to touristy Gurney Drive, yet increasingly popular with foreigners, New Lane's cluster of open-air hawker stalls has a bit of everything Penang is famous for, all within walking distance of town. Mon, Tues & Thurs–Sun 4pm–11pm.

Red Garden Food Paradise 20 Lebuh Leith ☎12 421 6767, ⓦ redgarden-food.com; map p.152. Touristy and thus regarded as a bit suspect by locals, nonetheless this food court offers an excellent range of hawker dishes, even stretching to Japanese and Filipino cuisine. If you're feeling flush, order some spicy fish, prawn or crab dishes from the

2

East Coast Grill Seafood outlet, which prices by weight. Mon–Fri 5pm–midnight, later at weekends.

STREET STALLS

Penang Road 55 Tahun Cendol Lebuh Keng Kwee 🕿 017 581 9091; map p.152. Penang's quintessential ice-and-sugar-based sweets, *cendol* and *ais kacang* (RM2.50), have been dished up here for fifty-odd years. Daily 8am–5.30pm.

Roti Canai Transfer Road Transfer Rd, between Jalan Hutton and Jalan Koyah; map p.152. Sit at the roadside among chatty locals to enjoy Penang's *roti canai, mamak*-style at this eighty-year-strong powerhouse. Famous for *roti* and curry, frothy *kopi*, and boiled eggs on *roti bakar* – toasted bread smeared with coconut jam and butter. Daily 6.30am–1pm.

Toh Soon Café Off 184 Campbell St 🕿 017 427 9327; map p.152. Tucked up a side lane full of tables under a metal awning, this street-side *kopitiam* is perfect for coffees and all-day breakfast of roti bakar with *kaya* and boiled eggs. Penang's chief minister, Lim Guan Eng is a regular. Constantly packed, but worth the wait. Mon–Sat 8am–6.30pm.

DRINKING AND NIGHTLIFE

Besides our selection, the pedestrianized eastern end of Jalan Penang, aka **Upper Penang Rd**, has two rows of cookie-cutter pubs and a few dance clubs. Several discos also line **Beach and Chulia St** – expect trendy techno and R&B, and a predominantly well-heeled Chinese crowd. **Nagore Square**, a 10min walk from Chulia St up Hutton Rd, is a more interesting entertainment strip, packed with open-air bars, restaurants, cafés and a largely local crowd. The middle part of **Chulia St** and down along Love Lane and Muntri St has turned, for better or worse, into a blander version of Bangkok's Khaosan Rd.

A YEAR OF PENANG FESTIVALS

For its size, Penang hosts an impressive number of **cultural events**, from religious celebrations to international arts festivals. Timing your visit with one of these can be the highlight of any trip; keep up with schedules on Penang Tourism's website (📶 visitpenang.gov.my).

JANUARY–APRIL

Thaipusam (Jan–Feb) Devotees carry *kavadi* from George Town to the Waterfall Hilltop temple.

Chinese New Year (Jan–Feb) Celebrated with fervour in George Town, with lion dances and fireworks, especially on the ninth day at the Clan Jetties on Weld Quay.

Chap Goh Meh (Jan–Feb) On the fifteenth day of Chinese New Year, unmarried girls throw oranges into the sea, traditionally an auspicious omen to get a good husband.

Penang Hot Air Balloon Fiesta (Feb) Huge hot-air balloons fill up the sky at Padang Polo in George Town, close to the Botanical Gardens.

MAY–AUGUST

George Town World Heritage Site Celebration (7–9 July) Three days of cultural events and pop-up stages to celebrate George Town's UNESCO status (📶 facebook.com/ GeorgeTownCelebrations).

George Town Festival (weekends in Aug) A month-long celebration packed with local and international art, music, drama, film and dance – most of it free of charge (📶 georgetownfestival.com).

Hungry Ghost Festival (Aug–Sep) Quirky Chinese religious festival celebrated with pop-up stages to appease the return of demanding dead ancestors.

SEPTEMBER–DECEMBER

Nine Emperor Gods (Sep–Oct) A parade of chariots to welcome the arrival of the Taoist gods, with some light acts of self-injury.

Mid-Autumn Festival (Sep–Oct) Chinese festival celebrated eating moon cakes, which were used in ancient China to carry secret messages.

Deepavali (Nov) The Indian festival of lights enlivens the streets of Little India, George Town.

George Town Literary Festival (last weekend of Nov) Increasingly significant Southeast Asian literary event (📶 georgetownlitfest.com).

Penang Island Jazz Festival (early December) Annual summit of international jazz musicians and fans, held at Batu Ferringhi (📶 penangjazz.com).

Penang International Dragon Boat Festival (Dec) Dragon boats from all over Asia race on Teluk Bahang.

BARS

Hong Kong Bar 371 Lebuh Chulia ☎ 04 261 9796; map p.152. You can't miss this Chinese-run dive, adorned with military insignia –if you're over forty, this will feel like a haven compared with other venues on Chulia. Daily 2pm–midnight.

Good Friends Club 31a Jalan Gurdwara, right next to Hin Bus Depot ☎ 016 452 9250, ☺ facebook.com/ GoodFriendsClubPenang; map p.152. Packed with local artists and hipsters, this shabby-chic hole in the wall has a tiny, dimly lit backroom filled with low tables. The bar out front serves beers, rums and fries, and more chairs spill on the kerb under a bright-pink neon sign – you can't miss it. Mon & Wed–Sun 7pm–1am.

Mish Mash 24 Muntri St ☎ 017 536 5128, ☺ facebook .com/MishmMashPg; map p.152. Fairly upmarket bar with a large menu of not-so-cheap cocktails (from RM30), an obsession with whisky, a good selection of tobacco and cigars, and a largely local crowd. Tues–Sun 5pm–midnight.

★ **Narrow Marrow** 252a Lebuh Carnarvon ☎ 016 553 6647, ☺ narrowmarrow.com; map p.152. The favoured den of Penang creatives, *Narrow Marrow* is a long and indeed narrow converted shophouse, cleverly decorated with second-hand furniture and installations from recycled items by the owners, artist Jamie and architect Alvin. There are nutmeg sodas and unusual mojitos made with palm rice wine, plus tasty meals such as lamb curries with Bengali bread. Fri–Sun 2pm–1am.

Seventy7 34 Jalan Nagore, off Jalan Burma ☎ 04 226 2067, ☺ seventy7cafe.com; map p.149. A 10min walk from KOMTAR, Penang's main LGBT venue is a friendly affair in a chic refurbished shophouse, drawing a crowd of mainly twenty- and thirty-somethings. Mon–Thurs & Sun 6.30pm–1am, Fri & Sat 6.30pm–3am.

Three Sixty Degree Sky Bar Bayview Hotel, 25a Lebuh Farquhar ☎ 04 261 3540, ☺ 360rooftop.com .my; map p.152. This open space around the *Bayview* revolving restaurant is a good spot for cocktails, Nyonya snacks and a bird's-eye view of the *E&O Hotel*, St George's Church and the dimly lit expanses of shophouses, dwarfed by the cylindrical KOMTAR building and more modest towers beyond the conservation zone. Daily 4pm–1am.

CLUBS

Magazine 63 63 Jalan Magazine ☎ 016 469 0164, ☺ facebook.com/magazineM63; map p.152. Hidden behind a wooden partition inside an apparently empty corner shophouse, George Town's first speakeasy relies on the element of surprise. Once you push the right wooden panel, the glamorous interior, fitted like an old Chinese opium den, complete with smartly attired waiters, will take you back a couple centuries. Alas, the overpriced cocktails (from RM20) won't, but the well-choreographed concept is a mark above the competition. DJs play most nights. Reservations recommended. Daily 7pm–3am.

Soundmaker Second floor, 62 Pengkalan Weld ☎ 017 428 7327, ☺ facebook.com/SoundmakerStudio; map p.152. One of a rare breed in Malaysia, *Soundmaker* is a countercultural rock venue specializing in indie, punk, metal and so forth, with the occasional shot of hip-hop for good measure. Check their website for a list of gigs. Thurs–Sun 5pm–1am.

SHOPPING

George Town has a mixture of old shops selling traditional goods, cheap-and-cheerful touristy outlets, and several pricier galleries and souvenir shops, generally rather chichi.

MARKETS

Chowrasta Market Jalan Chowrasta; map p.152. Even if it now looks like a shopping mall, Chowrasta is one of the city's oldest markets, mainly selling produce, although there are some secondhand book stalls upstairs. Proceedings spill over colourfully into Jalan Kuala Kangsar behind; note too the traditional spring-roll-wrap maker on Jalan Chowrasta. Daily 7.30am–noon.

Occupy Beach Street Lebuh Pantai ☺ facebook.com/ OccupyBeachStreet; map p.152. Not a market as such, but there are craft and other stalls amid the general weekly merrymaking when the street becomes pedestrianized for buskers, dancers and other groups. Sun 7am–1pm.

MALLS

Prangin Mall Jalan Dr Lim Chwee Leong ☺ prangin-mall .com; map p.152. The most popular of the malls around KOMTAR, unpretentious Prangin proves yet again that in Malaysia upmarket isn't usually best. There's something for everyone – a Parkson department store, a supermarket, bargain clothes shops, electronics and phone shops (fourth floor) and a food court (fifth floor). Daily 10am–10pm.

BOOKSHOP

Gerakbudaya 78 Jalan Masjid Kapitan Kling ☎ 04 261 0282, ☺ gerakbudayapenang.com; map p.152. The best bookshop in town is a radical upstart with hard-to-find titles on Malaysian society and politics, Asian-focused coffee-table books, as well as English paperbacks. A great starting point to find out about George Town's many art events, too. Daily 11am–8pm.

CLOTHES, TEXTILES AND SHOES

Kedai Songkok Corner of Chulia St & Lebuh King; map p.152. The last remaining traditional Malay skullcap artisan in Penang still makes *songkoks* to order. Daily 9am–8pm.

2

Rozana's Batik 81b Lebuh Aceh ☎014 247 5347, ☜bit.ly/RozanasBatik; map p.152. Small, family-run shop specializing in hand-painted textiles on cotton or silk, with some clothing available to buy. They also run walk-in batik classes (2hr; RM50). Daily 11.30am–6pm.

Sam's Batik House 183 & 185 Jalan Penang ☜samsbatikhouse.com; map p.152. This shop has mounds of slightly garish batik and silk, including tops and dresses galore; there's more like this a few doors south at the Penang Bazaar. Daily 10am–6pm.

SOUVENIRS, CURIOS AND GIFTS

41 Living Story 41 Love Lane ☎04 261 1970, ☜facebook .com/41LivingStory; map p.152. Two floors of classic Asian trinkets, from Hong Kong-style China Girl posters, to batiks,

cutesy wallets and handbags. Daily 10am–6pm.

Jonathan Yun Sculptural Jewellery 152 Jalan Masjid Kapitan Keling ☎04 263 1152, ☜jonathanyunjewelry. com; map p.152. Bespoke pieces of fine jewellery, mainly in silver, that draw on Straits Chinese patterns and motifs by award-winning artist Jonathan Yun.

Shop Howard 154 Jalan Masjid Kapitan Keling ☎04 261 1970, ☜studiohoward.com; map p.152. Run by local shutterbug Howard Tan, this place sells artsy pictures and hip collectables. Mon–Sat 12pm–6pm.

Tropical Spice Garden – in the City 29 Lebuh China ☎012 412 1744, ☜bit.ly/TropicalSpiceGarden; map p.152. Packets of tropical spices, batik, rattan-woven handbags and essences. Mon–Fri 10.30am–4.30pm, Sat 10am–6pm.

DIRECTORY

Banks and exchange The major banks are on Lebuh Pantai, with ATMs also located on Jalan Penang and at the KOMTAR development; moneychangers are easily found on Jalan Masjid Kapitan Kling and elsewhere.

Consulates Australia, YMCA, 211 Jalan Macalister (☎04 226 7285); Indonesia, 467 Jalan Burma (☎04 227 4686); Thailand, 1 Jalan Tuanku Abdul Rahman (☎04 226 8029); UK, Suite 9-04, Menara Zurich, 170 Jalan Argyll (☎04 227 5336).

Hospitals General Hospital, Jalan Residensi (☎04 222 5333); Gleneagles, 1 Jalan Pangkor (☎04 222 9111).

Internet access The island's Wireless@Penang service offers free wi-fi at malls, the KOMTAR building, the ferry terminal and even a few sights, including the top of Penang Hill. When connecting for the first time, you'll need to

register: just type in an arbitrary twelve-digit number in response to the question about your ID card/MyKad – you won't need it again.

Pharmacies Guardian and Watsons both have branches at KOMTAR and the Prangin Mall (both daily 10am–10pm).

Police The police headquarters is on Jalan Penang; emergencies ☎999.

Post office The General Post Office is on Lebuh Downing, with a branch at KOMTAR and one at Jalan Buckingham (all Mon–Fri 8.30am–5pm, Sat 8.30am–1pm).

Visa extensions The immigration office (Pejabat Imigresen) is on the corner of Lebuh Pantai and Lebuh Light (Mon–Thurs 7.30am–1pm & 2–5.30pm, Fri 7.30am–12.15pm & 2.45–5.30pm; ☎04 250 3410).

Ayer Itam (Air Hitam) and around

6km west of George Town • Bus #201, 203, 204 or #502 (45min)

The town of **AYER ITAM** amounts to little more than a 100m-long bottleneck, with the traffic squeezed between shops and the canvas awnings of a busy wet market. There are three reasons to visit: **Kek Lok Si**, a ludicrously overbuilt hilltop Buddhist complex; the colonial-era retreat of **Penang Hill** to the north; and the best-known *laksa* stall on the island. You could easily do all three, arriving at lunchtime for *laksa*, then spending a couple of hours at Kek Lok Si before heading up Penang Hill for views of the island lighting up at dusk.

Kek Lok Si

A 5min walk west from Jalan Pasar • Daily roughly 8.30am–6pm; Sky Lift shuts at 5.30pm • Free; climbing the steps to the top or using the Sky Lift costs RM2 • ☎04 828 3317 • From the market bus stop on Jalan Pasar, follow the road towards the temple and look out for a passageway on the left lined with trinket stalls; from here, steps ascend to the temple forecourt

Supposedly the largest Buddhist temple in Malaysia, **Kek Lok Si** was founded by the abbot of George Town's Kuan Yin Teng in the 1890s, when the initial bout of construction was bankrolled by Cheong Fatt Tze and other local tycoons. Today, the hill sprouts all sorts of fantastic shrines and pagodas, linked by multiple flights of steps, and bedecked with flags, lanterns and statues. The best time to visit is during Chinese New Year, when thousands of red lanterns and multicoloured LEDs illuminate the temple at night.

OPPOSITE FUNICULAR RAILWAY, PENANG HILL >

The two most prominent features of the temple are the white, seven-tier wedding-cake assemblage that is the **Ten Thousand Buddhas Pagoda**, capped by a golden Burmese stupa; and a 30m-high bronze statue of the goddess of mercy, **Kuan Yin**, sheltered from the elements by an open-sided pavilion, its pillars wreathed in carved dragons. Both can be reached either on foot (193 steps) or using the **Sky Lift**, a sort of glass-sided funicular compartment that glides up and down the 45-degree slope.

Penang Hill

Jalan Stesen Bukit Bendera • Funicular: every 15min from 6.30am (5min); last service down at 11pm • RM15 one-way, RM30 return • ☎ 04 828 8880, ⓦ penanghill.gov.my • Bus #204 from George Town; a 20min walk from Air Hitam and 25min from Kek Lok Si – turn left at the roundabout signed "Bukit Bendera"

Once called Flagstaff Hill, when it was a retreat for British administrators, **Penang Hill** is now a mixed bag of gardens, woodland, shrines and colonial houses in various states of repair. The bus drops you at the foot of the hill close to the lower funicular station, where signs point the way to the **Bats Cave Temple**, worth a quick look for its colony of bats in a cave shrine at the back; they're regarded as auspicious because part of the Chinese term for "bat" sounds like the word for "luck". The **funicular**, a modern version of the original, built in 1923, can whisk you to the summit in just over five minutes. From here there's a great vista of the cape of George Town and across the straits to Butterworth.

For a decent couple of hours' **hike**, follow the main summit road round counterclockwise, heading towards the start of the path to Tiger Hill, then veer left on to Moniot Road. From here you can eventually join Viaduct Road, from where there are various routes back up to the summit. The sketch map on the leaflet given out with funicular tickets shows the options.

The Habitat

Mon, Tues & Thurs–Sun 9.30am–6pm • RM50 • ☎ 04 826 767, ⓦ thehabitat.my

Scattered around the hilltop park are a multicoloured Hindu temple, a mosque, an overpriced food court and numerous forgettable tourist traps. Worth visiting instead is **the Habitat**, an educational 1.6km guided hiking trail snaking along the course of an old British irrigation channel set above Penang Hill's best-conserved slope. The Habitat also operates a 230m-long **Canopy Walk**, still under construction at the time of writing, and **Curtis Crest Treetop Walk**, Penang's highest, boasting 360-degree views that stretch all the way to Mount Jerai in Kedah.

EATING AND DRINKING   AYER ITAM

Bellevue Hotel Summit of Penang Hill ☎ 04 227 4006. Set in a dreary 1960s building, *Bellevue* is no colonial haven. Its saving grace is the terrace restaurant, which has good views, cream teas and highly regarded – though undeniably pricey – steamboat (RM66 for two people). Daily 7am–9pm.

David Brown's Restaurant and Tea Terraces On its own mound 100m from the upper funicular station, Penang Hill ☎ 04 828 8337, ⓦ penanghillco.com.my. A very English menu of cream teas, pies and steaks, plus a roast of the day and an excellent wine list, all in a smart country-pub-like setting – or as close to it as a house perched on a

tropical hilltop can get. A few tables are set out on the immaculate lawn, and there's a separate *Sky Terrace* section for drinks and snacks. Tea and scones costs RM28, and beef Wellington will set you back RM90 – when it's available. Daily: restaurant 11am–9pm; Sky Terrace 9am–9pm.

★ **Pasar Air Itam Laksa** Jalan Pasar, Ayer Itam, where the bus sets down. Look for a small stall backed by a big red sign, and you'll find what many rate as the best *asam laksa* in Penang, costing just RM3. The sauce is salty, sour and thick with *heh koh* prawn paste, all topped off with rice noodles, shredded vegetables, pounded fish and a handful of fresh herbs. Daily morning to mid-afternoon.

Northwest Penang

An 18km-long road runs along Penang's northern coast, squeezed for much of the way between the sea and forests inland. The main settlement here, the dull beach resort of **Batu Ferringhi**, remains moderately popular as an alternative base to

George Town and has a frequent bus service to the city, but frankly you're not missing much if you simply shoot through to the **Tropical Spice Garden** or the coastal jungle of **Penang National Park** at **Teluk Bahang**, in the island's northwest corner. There's also a small clutch of minor sights along the road south of Teluk Bahang, en route to Balik Pulau.

Batu Ferringhi

Bus #101 from Pengkalan Weld/KOMTAR (every 20–30min) or #102 from the airport/KOMTAR (hourly)

To look at it now, you wouldn't think that **BATU FERRINGHI** was the standard-bearer for Penang tourism during the long years when George Town was in the doldrums. These days it distinctly plays second fiddle, thanks as much to ugly overdevelopment as George Town's successes.

Its centrepiece is some 2km of **beach**, not too narrow but with sand that, disappointingly, is the colour of milky tea. The whole beach is publicly accessible: either stride through the hotel compounds to reach it or, in the unlikely event staff are obstructive, use the path lined by beach-gear stalls that begins roughly opposite the McDonald's at the start of the strip. All that said, the beach still makes for a nice contrast with George Town and is decent enough for **watersports**, with multiple firms competing for custom. For a general look, turn up in the late afternoon when the beach starts to get busy, and perhaps linger for an evening meal when the road comes alive with stalls selling batik, T-shirts and fake designer watches.

Tropical Spice Garden

Lone Crag Villa, Jalan Teluk Bahang • **Garden** Daily 9am–6pm (last entry 5.15pm) • RM29 with audioguide; RM49 on guided tour (daily 9am, 11am & 1.30pm) • **Cooking classes** Tues–Sun 9am–1pm • RM235/person; book one day in advance • ☎ 04 881 1210, ⓦ tropicalspicegarden.com • Bus #101 or #102

Between Batu Ferringhi and Teluk Bahang, the delightful **Tropical Spice Garden** has turned an abandoned rubber plantation into a cornucopia of herbs, spices and decorative flora, all set in a stylishly landscaped gully and shaded by former plantation trees. Three easy circuit trails loop between waterfalls and streams and introduce you to the plants and their commercial, culinary and traditional uses. There are **cookery classes**, a gift shop selling spices and products, and annexed Thai **restaurant** *Tree Monkey*, with a terrace overlooking nearby Monkey Beach – perfect for sunsets.

Teluk Bahang Road

Escape Tues–Sun 10am–6pm • RM83 • ☎ 04 881 1106, ⓦ escape.my • **Entopia** Daily 9am–7pm, last entry 5.30pm • RM65 • ☎ 04 885 1253, ⓦ entopia.com • Bus #101 or #102 both make a short detour here

Once it reaches the small town of **Teluk Bahang**, the **road** veers south and inland, passing two minor sights within the first kilometre before continuing to Balik Pulau. The first is **Escape** theme park, a series of obstacle-course-type challenges including zip lines and climbing ropes. Right next to it is **Entopia**, a two-storey indoor landscaped

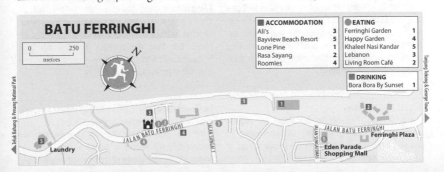

BATU FERRINGHI

0 _____ 250
metres

ACCOMMODATION		EATING	
Ali's	3	Ferringhi Garden	1
Bayview Beach Resort	5	Happy Garden	4
Lone Pine	1	Khaleel Nasi Kandar	5
Rasa Sayang	2	Lebanon	3
Roomles	4	Living Room Café	2

DRINKING	
Bora Bora By Sunset	1

Teluk Bahang & Penang National Park

Tanjung Tokong & George Town

JALAN BATU FERRINGHI
JALAN SUNGAI
JALAN BATU FERRINGHI
Ferringhi Plaza
Laundry
Eden Parade Shopping Mall

park home to 15,000-odd free-flying butterflies, 200 species of plants, and all manner of frogs, snakes, stick insects and scorpions.

Penang National Park

At the end of a small coastal road 1.5km beyond the centre of Teluk Bahang • **Park office** Mon–Fri 8am–5pm, Sat & Sun 8am–6pm • **Canopy walkway** Mon–Wed, Sat & Sun 10am–4pm • Free • **Nature guides** RM250/half-day guided trek for up to five people • ☎ 04 881 4788 • **Boat rides** RM50–60/boat one-way to Monkey Beach, RM100 to Kerachut • ☎ 04 881 3530, ⓦ bit.ly/PenangNationalPark • Bus #101 calls at the park (1hr from George Town) before doubling back to terminate at Teluk Bahang; bus #102 terminates at Teluk Bahang

2

PENANG NATIONAL PARK tends to fly under visitors' radar, but it's likeable all the same, a hilly chunk of old-growth forest, pandanus and mangroves. The trails lead to a handful of secluded, undeveloped **beaches**, where marine **turtles** nest throughout the year; the park also has some resident dusty-leaf monkeys in addition to the predictable long-tailed macaques.

At time of research, the **canopy walkway** was closed for maintenance. There are also two main trails, generally easy to follow, though steep and eroded in places. At the end of the initial 500m boardwalk, turn right for the 4.7km route to the **Muka Head Lighthouse**, where you might see sea eagles, passing **Monkey Beach** (3.4km), a good spot for a swim. Turn left for **Kerachut Beach** (3.4km), a cove with one of the only two meromictic lakes in the world (two layers of fresh and sea water that never mix), and a turtle hatchery at the far end; **Teluk Kampi** (4.9km) is yet another secluded beach.

At the park entrance is a booth staffed by **nature guides**, where you can book guided treks and buy useful gear. If you're short on time, talk to the various **boat operators** opposite the park entrance; they offer surprisingly cheap rides to the beaches.

ACCOMMODATION

NORTHWEST PENANG

BATU FERRINGHI

Ali's 53 & 54b Jalan Batu Ferringhi ☎ 04 881 1316; map p.167. The best of a series of beachfront guesthouses, *Ali* has bland, old-fashioned a/c rooms, some en suite, in a two-storey brick building surrounding a courtyard packed with pot plants. ☎ RM80

Bayview Beach Resort Western end of Batu Ferringhi ☎ 04 886 1111, ⓦ bbr.bayviewhotels.com; map p.167. Rooms are arrayed around the impressive pyramid atrium at this reasonably priced hotel, with tennis courts and two swimming pools. Booking weeks in advance might bring discounts. ☎ RM375

Lone Pine 97 Jalan Batu Ferringhi ☎ 04 886 8686, ⓦ lonepinehotel.com; map p.167. Now run by George Town's *Eastern & Oriental*, this boutique hotel was founded as a humble lodge in 1948. Completely renovated and extended since, it now comprises what might as well be a swanky apartment building behind the original, low-rise block with shuttered windows next to a well-tended sea-facing garden. The rooms are bright and contemporary, complemented by a spa, pool and several restaurants. Book online for discounts. ☎ RM465

Roomies Fourth floor of the block opposite the Parkroyal Hotel, Jalan Batu Ferringhi ☎ 04 881 1344, ⓦ roomiespenang.com; map p.167. The slickest guesthouse on the strip, with flashpacker capsule-style bunk beds plus two rooms, one sleeping three, the other a double with its own bathroom. ☎ Dorms RM40, double RM200

★**Shangri-La Rasa Sayang** Batu Ferringhi ☎ 04 888 8888, ⓦ shangri-la.com; map p.167. One of the very first resorts at Batu Ferringhi is still recommendable today, a lush, sprawling complex topped by Malay-style roofs and with an excellent freeform pool. There's a garden wing for the hoi polloi and, for a premium of at least twenty percent, a boutique "Rasa" wing with its own pool, along with free cocktails and afternoon tea. ☎ RM900

PENANG NATIONAL PARK

Campsites Penang National Park ☎ 04 881 3530, ⓦ wildlife.gov.my. There are campsites at Monkey and Kerachut beaches, though bear in mind that either is a 75min trek from the entrance. Kerachut has basic bathrooms and a kitchen, but wherever you stay, bring your own tent, stove and kitchenware. **Free**

EATING

BATU FERRINGHI

Eating in Batu Ferringhi is dominated by slightly overpriced restaurants, including an assortment of Middle Eastern places catering to the steady stream of Saudi and Gulf tourists.

Ferringhi Garden 34a, b & c & 43d Jalan Batu Ferringhi ☎ 04 881 1193, ⓦ ferringhigarden.com.my; map p.167. The most elegant of the strip's restaurants, the outdoor tables drowning in potted orchids, ferns and pitcher plants, with plenty of stylish wood panelling and screens inside. There are two parts to the place: the *Coffee Garden*, serving light meals and snacks by day, and the main restaurant, with a more ambitious menu of Western/ fusion dishes. Mains from RM30. Daily: Coffee Garden 8am–6pm; restaurant 4pm–midnight.

Happy Garden Western end of Batu Ferringhi ☎ 016 490 3543; map p.167. *Happy Garden* looks more like a residential bungalow, in a lovely garden planted with bougainvillea, than a Hainanese restaurant. There's plenty of seafood on the menu, plus predictable Western-inspired dishes such as chicken chop (RM15). Breakfasts include oats, pancakes or sausage and egg. Daily 9am–2.30pm & 6–10.30pm.

Khaleel Nasi Kandar Ground floor, towards the rear of the Eden Parade Shopping Centre ☎ 016 501 7324; map p.167. A fine place to escape inflated prices and get your daily curry, *roti* and *teh tarik* fix – the food is genuinely above par, too, and meals rarely exceed RM10 per person. Daily 24hr.

Lebanon 190a Jalan Batu Ferringhi ☎ 04 881 3228; map p.167. Middling among the Arabic restaurants in terms of price and quality. The mainstays are, unsurprisingly, kebabs (RM30) and meze (RM10), with curries and pizza for conservative local palates. Daily 2pm–12.30am.

Living Room Café 43c Batu Ferringhi ☎ 012 589 9136, ⓦ facebook.com/LivingRoom11100; map p.167. This informal place majors on Nyonya and other local cuisines, offering a limited number of dishes and doing them right. Locals tend to go for the beef *rendang*, although you can also take your pick from Western mains such as burgers and barbecued ribs. Around RM45, excluding drinks. Daily except Weds 10am–3pm & 6–10pm.

DRINKING

Bora Bora By Sunset 415 Jalan Batu Ferringhi ☎ 04 885 1313, ⓦ facebook.com/BoraBoraBySunset; map p.167. Fairly standard beach bar and restaurant with tables out on the sand and in the bar area under an *atap* roof. Food ranges from pizza to Malaysian staples (RM10–15); it's not haute cuisine, but the sunset compensates. Mon–Thurs & Sun noon–1am, Fri & Sat noon–3am.

Snake Temple

Jalan Sultan Azlan Shah, close to the airport • Daily 6am–7pm • Free • ☎ 04 643 7273 • Bus #102 from KOMTAR or #401 or #401E from George Town's Pengkalan Weld

Visible from the airport road, Penang's **Snake Temple** is a bright Buddhist affair, its forecourt guarded by two stone lions. Inside, the front altar – along with strategically placed shrubs in other halls – is draped in poisonous **green pit vipers** which, legend has it, mysteriously appeared upon completion of the temple in 1850. Pit vipers are naturally lethargic, but even so it's hard to account for quite how dozy the temple's specimens are – though you'd best not poke them to see if they're real.

Penang War Museum

Batu Maung • Daily 9am–6pm • RM35 • ☎ 04 626 5142 • ⓦ facebook.com/PenangWarMuseum • Bus #302

The **Penang War Museum** stands on the site of a 1930s British military fortress. You climb the hill to an area of bunkers, forts, underground tunnels and an observation tower, all designed to defend the position from a naval attack; unfortunately for the British, the Japanese stormed it from inland. The fort became a prison, abandoned after the war partly because it was believed to be haunted by those tortured to death here. It was recovered from the undergrowth and opened as a private museum during the 1980s.

Balik Pulau

Stretching from the lower end of Teluk Bahang all the way to Pulau Betong in the far south, off-the-radar **BALIK PULAU** (literally "back of the island") roughly comprises one third of western Penang. It's by far the least developed part of the state, a paddy-field strewn coastal plain encased between the Andaman Sea and Penang Hill's western flanks, covered in viridian exotic fruit plantations, primarily coconut, banana, the endemic **nutmeg**, and the much prized, yet very smelly, **durian**. Roughly in the middle, Balik Pulau town is a 250m-long main street lined by old buildings, some recently tinted by Russian mural artist Julia Volchkova; though only **Fong Silversmith**, on the

2

corner near the roundabout, is especially compelling. Its charming owner has been turning out simple, attractive jewellery for decades. At the other end of town there's a nineteenth-century convent and the **Sacred Heart Church**, a pale grey and cream tin-sided structure dating to 1854.

Balik Pulau is best experienced outside the town, pedalling through streams and paddies on a bicycle, or enjoying the fishing villages and beach at Pulau Betong, Penang's southwest corner, which also includes an islet of the same name. **Pantai Pasir Panjang** is one of the island's best and quieter beaches, on Penang's far southwestern headland, right in front of military base Kem Rimba Negara; watch out for the strong surf here. Uninhabited atoll Pulau Betong lies just north across the water; swimming here is prohibited, but it's a good spot for angling (Ah Keat can organise boat transfers; ☎012 560 0201).

ARRIVAL AND GETTING AROUND   BALIK PULAU

By bus Bus #401, #401E or #502 runs to Balik Pulau Bus Hub (a 5min walk to the town's main strip) from George Town (#502 via Ayer Itam is the most direct service). It's also possible to catch the #501 from Teluk Bahang, hopping on and off en route to the sites. Bus #503 connects the Balik Pulau Bus Hub to Pulau Betong.

By bike Two reliable operators organize half and full-day

bicycle tours (RM60–99/person, including return transfers from George Town). Explore Balik Pulau (☎016 452 2100, ⓦexplorebalikpulau.com.my) arrange tours in Balik Pulau's central area of Sungai Burong, while Audi Penang (☎012 499 9099, ⓦaudipenang.com) organize tours in the Pulau Betong area. Audi Penang also rent bikes for RM20/day.

ACCOMMODATION

Audi Guest House 609 Jalan Pulau Betong, bus #503 stops nearby ☎04 866 2569, ⓦaudipenang.com; map p.147. Charming Malay wooden kampung house, 6km from Pasir Panjang beach. Guests stay in fan dorms or simple tatami-style a/c rooms (sleeping up to seven; whole rooms are booked out) with spacious balconies overlooking the peaceful countryside. This is also Audi Penang's headquarters, where you can rent bicycles or join tours. Breakfast costs an additional RM5. ☞ Dorms RM20, triples RM90

Bao Sheng Durian Farm Along the Balik Pulau–Teluk Bahang main road, close to Titi Kerawang waterfall ☎012 401 0800, ⓦdurian.com.my; map p.147. Wake up and smell the durian in these two storeys of interconnected glass box rooms and private villas (RM50 extra) set around swimming pools on the slope of a durian farm. Mr "Durian" Seng, a true devotee of the spiky fruit,

offers stay-and-eat packages in harvest season that include dinner, breakfast, and two durian tastings (RM300). Staying here off-season is no less charming, with good views over Penang and frequent burning-pink sunsets. Breakfast included; dinner RM60 extra. ☞ RM90

★Malihom Up a steep hill off the main Balik Pulau–Teluk Kumbar main road ☎04 261 0190, ⓦmalihom .com; map p.147. Pure high-class seclusion atop a private hill estate, with sweeping views over Penang's southeastern coast. The eight imported Thai wooden rice barns with en-suite bathrooms – some featuring sunken bathtubs with panoramic views, great for sunsets – are intimately clustered around the pool and restaurant-lobby. *Malihom*'s private 2km hiking trail passes through tropical fruit farms and woodland. Stays include one free transfer from the bottom of the hill. Wi-fi in the lobby. ☞ RM540, full board RM900

EATING

Jia Sang Café 321 Mk 7 Pulau Betong, right at the village junction to Pantai Pasir Panjang ☎019 746 8465; map p.147. A popular no-frills *kampung* seafood restaurant dishing up fresh catch straight from the fish market nearby. You can bring in your own fish (about RM30–50), which the chef will cook for you in lemongrass or homemade Thai-style sauce for RM12–20. Gets very

busy on weekends. Daily noon–6.30pm.

Nan Guang 67 Jalan Balik Pulau; map p.147. The pineapple-tinged *asam laksa* and Thai curried *laksa* (RM4) at this down-at-heel *kopitiam* in Balik Pulau town have people lining up some time before they start serving to make sure they get a bowl. Mon, Tues & Thurs–Sun 11am–late afternoon.

Kedah and Perlis

The far northwest of Peninsular Malaysia is taken up by the states of Kedah and Perlis, which, in common with the northeast, were historically part of the Siamese sphere of influence. British rule this far north, in marked contrast to Penang and Perak, was relatively brief, kicking off in 1909 when the region was ceded to them by the Thais, who briefly reclaimed it during World War II courtesy of another treaty, this time with the invading Japanese.

Kedah has long been billed as the Peninsula's *jelapang padi*, or rice bowl, and its landscape remains largely a mosaic of lustrous paddy fields. By far the best-known part of the state is the popular resort island of **Langkawi**, with good air links as well as ferry connections with Penang, Kuala Kedah, Kuala Perlis and southern Thailand. The mainland is easily bypassed, then, and the rewards for passing through are low-key, chiefly the **Ulu Muda Eco Reserve**, the odd **archeological remains** near the town of **Sungai Petani**, and the mosque-strewn capital, **Alor Star**. **Perlis**, Malaysia's smallest state – at just 800 square km, it's ten percent larger than Singapore – is also the greenest and least visited. **Kelam Cave**, in a national park straddling the Thai border, is worth slowing down for between transport connections.

2

Sungai Petani and around

On the north bank of the Petani River, **SUNGAI PETANI** is the most populous town in Kedah, with bustling suburbs and industrial areas that thrive on its location in Penang's hinterland (Butterworth is just 35km away). There's nothing to see in the old town centre other than the Art Deco King George V **clock tower** on the main street, but the town is the jumping-off point for anyone travelling to the **Bujang Valley** archeological site by public transport.

Bujang Valley (Merbok Museum/Lembah Bujang)

15km northwest of Sungai Petani, 2km from Merbok's main street along a signed lane • Daily 9am–7pm • Free • ☎ 04 457 2005 • Alor Star-bound Maraliner buses from Sungai Petani's local bus station stop in Merbok (hourly; 45min), or charter a taxi (around RM50 return, with a 1hr wait)

Just outside the town of **Merbok**, the **Bujang Valley** site commemorates a significant Hindu-Buddhist kingdom that flourished here for hundreds of years, possibly from as early as the second century. That said, there's not very much to see; a brief visit of an hour or two is ample. First impressions are that you've arrived at the most surreal attraction in Malaysia, where a team of bricklayers has run riot on a landscaped hillside. What you're looking at are in fact the low, stepped remains of *candi* (temples) from various locations nearby, reassembled here in an unnaturally tight cluster.

The centrepiece, **Candi Bukit Batu Pahat**, is a 27m-long granite structure that was not moved but restored *in situ*; the other *candi* are much smaller, some made of what look like worn, crimson-tinged brick, others suspiciously pristine. The on-site **museum** explains, somewhat incoherently, what little is known about the Bujang Valley kingdom, and how pre-war excavations brought its existence back to light. There are also some interesting finds from the various *candi*, including pots, gems and stone carvings of deities.

ARRIVAL AND INFORMATION

SUNGAI PETANI

Sungai Petani lies on Route 1, which doubles up as the main street.

By train A couple of blocks south of the clock tower, a bridge up and over the railway line leads east to the train station (☎ 04 421 0703).

Destinations Alor Star (hourly; 40min); Arau (hourly; 1hr); Ipoh (7 daily; 2hr); Kuala Kangsar (7 daily; 1hr 25min); Kuala Lumpur (7 daily; 4hr 20min); Taiping (7 daily; 1hr).

By bus The long-distance bus station is opposite the train station, in the UTC Building. The local bus station and taxi stand is on Jalan Petri, a further block south of the clock tower.

Destinations Alor Star (every 45min–1hr; 1hr 30min); Butterworth (RapidPenang Bus EB60; every 45min 6am–9pm; 45min); Ipoh (almost hourly; 4hr); Jerantut (for

Taman Negara; 1 daily at 9.30pm; 8hr); Johor Bahru (at least 5 daily, all departing after 9pm; 10hr); Kota Bharu (2 daily at 11am and 8pm; 6hr); Kuala Besut (for Perhentian Islands; 1 daily at 10.50pm; 9hr); Kuala Kangsar (2 daily; 3hr); Kuala Lumpur (hourly; 5hr); Kuala Terengganu (2 daily; 5hr 30min); Kuantan (5 daily; 10hr); Lumut (for Pangkor; 3 daily; 4hr 30min); Melaka (4 daily; 7hr); Mersing (for Pulau Tioman; 1 daily at 10.15pm; 12hr); Seremban (3 daily; 5hr 30min); Singapore (4 daily; 10hr30min); Sik (en route to Ulu Muda; several daily; 2hr).

ACCOMMODATION AND EATING

There's no reason to stay in Sungai Petani unless you want to catch an early connection to Lembah Bujang. Eat at the Malay and Chinese stalls in food courts just north of Jalan Petri.

M Season Boutique Hotel 119 Jalan Masjid ☏ 04 424 2133, ⌨ mseasonhotel.com.my. Don't get turned off by the 80s bright-pink exterior – the rooms here really stand up to the "boutique" moniker: plush mattresses, sparkling en-suite bathrooms and all the amenities you could hope for, for a fraction of the price you'd expect. However, some rooms are windowless, and breakfast is not included. Walk one block west of the local bus station and beyond the Cayman complex; *M Season* is on the right at the end of the road. ☏ **RM80**

Alor Star

A largely Malay town, conservative in feel, **ALOR STAR** (Alor Setar), Kedah's transport hub, is remarkably sleepy for a state capital, especially at night. Clustered around the padang are several historic buildings, including a prominent mosque and former **sultan's palace**, providing enough architectural and cultural interest that you might want to pause here for half a day en route to or from Langkawi, the Thai border or Ulu Muda Eco Park. **Orientation** is simple: the padang forms the heart of town, with the commercial centre to the east and what passes for Chinatown to the west across Route 1.

Padang

Alor Star's **padang** and the open space on its north side are dotted with a mishmash of buildings, some associated with Kedah's ruling house. Within the padang itself, the long white-stucco **Balai Seni Negeri** is a courthouse-turned-gallery showcasing local artists (daily 9am–5pm; free). The curious octagonal tower topped by a yellow onion dome, on the western side of the open space, is the **Balai Nobat**, housing sacred instruments played only during royal ceremonies. At the north end is the low, Neoclassical facade of the former **High Court**, now the **Galeri Sultan Abdul Halim**, showcasing assorted royal regalia (Mon–Thurs & Sun 10am–5pm; RM2). The most refined building here, though, is the **Masjid Zahir** just across Jalan Pekan Melayu, which succeeds admirably despite being a mishmash of Moorish arches, a Turkish pencil minaret and weighty black bulbous domes.

Istana Balai Besar

The history of the padang's most important building, the elegant **Istana Balai Besar** (Royal Audience Hall), mirrors that of the town. Founded in 1735, it was badly damaged in 1770 by the Bugis (seafaring raiders from Sulawesi in Indonesia), and later by Thai armies in 1821. The present, late nineteenth-century version has a Malay multilayered shingle roof, supported by colonial-style iron columns and eave decorations, alongside a very European-influenced flowing staircase. One of its first functions was to host the **marriages** of Sultan Abdul Hamid's five eldest children in 1904: the celebrations lasted three months, and the cost bankrupted Kedah – forty buffaloes had to be slaughtered to feed the crowds each day.

Kedah Royal Museum (Muzium Diraja)

Behind the Balai Besar, northeast of the padang • Mon, Sat & Sun 9am–5pm, Fri 9am–12.30pm & 2.30–5pm • Free

Guarded by a motley collection of bronze cannon (some stamped with the "VOC" of the Dutch East India Company), the **Kedah Royal Museum** was once the royal palace. Squat and compact, dating to 1930, it must have made a fairly modest palace, and though the cases of ceremonial *keris* daggers, silver dinner services, gold anklets and brass betel sets hint at wealth, there's no feeling of splendid indulgence – indeed, many exhibits (including a pair of binoculars used by one sultan on safari in Africa) are decidedly mundane.

Alor Setar Tower (Menara Alor Setar)

Route 1, north of the padang • Daily 10am–10pm • RM16 • ⓦ menaraalorsetar.com.my/en

A mini-version of KL's similar Menara Tower, **Alor Setar Tower (Menara Alor Setar)** is a 165m-tall communications tower with an observation platform halfway up. Come here for views of pancake-flat paddy fields pierced by distant limestone outcrops, and the mostly low-rise, unprepossessing town below.

State Museum (Muzium Negeri)

Jalan Lebuhraya Darulaman (Route 1), 2km north of the centre • Mon–Thurs, Sat & Sun 9am–5pm, Fri 9am–12.30pm & 2.30–5pm • Free • ⓦ kedahmuseum.gov.my • Any bus from Pekan Rabu bound for Shahab Perdana

The **State Museum (Muzium Negeri)** fills you in on Kedah's traditions and history, including background to the archeological finds at the Bujang Valley (see p.171). One noteworthy exhibit is the *bunga mas dan perak* ("the gold and silver flowers"), a pair of 1m-tall "trees", one in gold, one in silver – in the past, the Malay rulers would have despatched such items in tribute to their Thai overlords.

Pekan Rabu

Jalan Tunku Ibrahim

Pekan Rabu is the town's main market, three concrete floors of preserved, fresh and cooked food, clothes, handicrafts and household necessities, plus local farm produce. Look for stalls selling **dodol durian** (a sort of black, gooey jam made from the fruit) and "durian cake", a plain mix of pulp and palm sugar.

Tun Mahathir House (Rumah Kelahiran Mahathir)

18 Lorong Kilang Ais, southwest of the padang • Tues–Thurs 10am–5.30pm, Fri 10am–noon & 3–5.30pm • Free

The life of the local doctor who became the most powerful Malaysian prime minister of modern times, Mahathir Mohamad, is documented at his birthplace and family home, **Tun Mahathir House (Rumah Kelahiran Mahathir)**, now a museum. Even if you're not interested in the brash former premier, it's worth dropping by to get an idea of what a traditional middle-class Malay home looked like in the middle of the last century.

ARRIVAL AND INFORMATION   ALOR STAR

By plane The Sultan Abdul Halim Airport is 11km north of town, accessible by the hourly Kepala Batas bus from the express bus station, or by taxi (around RM25).

Destinations Kuala Lumpur (KLIA2; 4–5 daily; 1hr); Kuala Lumpur (Subang; 8 daily; 1hr).

By train The station is centrally located, just southeast of the centre on Jalan Stesyen (☎04 731 4045).

Destinations Arau (hourly; 20min); Butterworth (hourly; 1hr 50min); Gemas (3 daily; 7hr 30min–8hr); Ipoh (5 daily; 2hr 30min); Kuala Kangsar (5 daily; 2hr 50min); Kuala Lumpur (5 daily; 4hr 30min–5hr); Seremban (3 daily; 6hr 30min–7hr); Sungai Petani (hourly; 30min); Taiping (5 daily; 1hr 30min).

By local bus A small number of firms, including HBR, MARA and Cityliner, run local buses to most parts of the state (daily 6am–8pm). They all use a central bus stop – with no ticket office or timetables – on the north side of Jalan Tunku Ibrahim, opposite the Pekan Rabu market. Some long-distance buses also call here en route to/from Shahab Perdana.

Destinations Kangar (hourly; 1hr 15min); Kuala Kedah (1–2 hourly; 20min); Naka (for the Ulu Muda Eco Park; hourly; 2hr); Sungai Petani (#2; every 45min–1hr; 1hr 30min).

By long-distance bus Long-distance buses use the Shahab Perdana station, annoyingly far away at 5km northwest of the centre, connected to town by local bus #2 and taxis (RM10). Some express buses pass through town

first, setting passengers down at Pekan Rabu; some northbound local buses pass through Shahab Perdana en route to their destination.

Destinations Butterworth (8 daily; 2hr); Ipoh (10 daily; 4hr); Johor Bahru (4 daily; 12hr); Kota Bharu (daily at 10am and 10pm; 5hr); Kuala Kangsar (4 daily; 4hr); Kuala Kedah (every 30min; 15min); Kuala Lumpur (hourly; 6hr); Kuala Terengganu (2 daily; 8hr 30min); Kuantan (2 daily at 8.45am and 9.30pm; 9hr); Lumut (5 daily; 4hr 30min); Melaka (8 daily; 7hr); Mersing (for Pulau Tioman; daily at 8.45pm; 12hr); Penang (3 daily; 2hr 30min); Seremban (at least 2 daily; 6hr); Singapore (3 daily; 13hr); Taiping (daily at 9.45pm; 3hr 30min).

By ferry Langkawi ferries (☎04 762 6295, ⌨langkawi-ferry.com) dock at Kuala Kedah, 12km west of town. Local buses drop off and pick up on the main road outside the ferry terminal; a taxi costs around RM20.

Destinations Langkawi (Kuah; 14 daily, 7am–7pm; 1hr 45min; RM23).

By taxi Taxis can be found around Pekan Rabu. A ride to the main Thai border crossing at Bukit Kayu Hitam costs RM55 (45min).

Tourist office Tourism Malaysia occupies a yellow building behind the 1930s former courthouse on Jalan Raja (Mon–Wed, Sat & Sun 8am–5pm, Thurs 8am–3.30pm; ☎04 730 1322).

ACCOMMODATION

With mainland Kedah seeing few visitors, Alor Setar's selection of hotels is quite dreary.

Miramar 46 Jalan Putra ☎04 733 8144; map p.172. One of the better cheapies, the *Miramar* is a low-rise concrete block with dull but more than adequate a/c en-suite rooms, nicely located for the eating places elsewhere on the street. ☞ **RM70**

★**New Regent** 1536 Jalan Sultan Badlishah ☎04 731 5000, ⌨bit.ly/newregent; map p.172. It's rare to see a modest facelift successfully transform an ageing hotel, giving the atrium a light, airy feel and imbuing the rooms with touches of contemporary style. Nothing lavish but cosy and good value. ☞ **RM132**

EATING

Alor Star's **Chinatown (Pekan Cina)**, along a quiet bend of the Kedah River south of the Masjid Zahir, hasn't remained immune to street art and café gentrification, and is the best part of town for eating and drinking. At night, while the rest of the centre shuts down, the food courts around Jalan Putra and Jalan Cheah Toon Lok buzz with cheap Chinese street stalls.

★**Caffè Diem** 44 Jalan Penjara Lama ☎04 730 8895, ⌨facebook.com/DiemCaffe; map p.172. This

award-winning restored double-storey shophouse is a recent addition to Chinatown's hipster scene. Three original

Kedah wooden fishermen boats dangle from the ceiling over exposed brick walls, maroon tiles and marble-topped wooden, retro-chic tables. Besides coffee and cakes (about RM10), there's a wide array of pastas and burgers alongside Malaysian staples. A meal will set you back RM30. Daily noon–midnight.

Nasi Kandar Salam Jalan Putra, close to Jalan Menanti; map p.172. Friendly joint with a lunchtime *biriyani* offering in addition to the usual *nasi kandar* curries, plus *roti canai* and tandoori chicken, all for less than RM10. Daily 24hr.

Parrot Espresso 95 Pekan Cina ☎016 400 3333; map p.172. This tiny shophouse, with just a couple of tables

and sofas as well as a delightful veranda over the Kedah River, is Alor Star's attempt to imitate George Town's Western-style cafés. The coffee is more than tolerable, as are the cream cakes (from RM10), but it's the views of Masjid Zahir soaring over the river that make it really worth a visit. Bottled beers and ciders available too. Daily noon–midnight.

Viet Café 89 Pekan Cina ☎017 550 4713; map p.172. Sharing the veranda with *Parrot Espresso* is this Mekong-inspired restaurant serving Vietnamese, Thai and Chinese dishes in a better-than-average dining hall. A meal costs about RM30. Mon–Thurs 11am–3pm & 5.30pm–11pm, Fri–Sun 11am–11pm.

Ulu Muda Eco Park

Tucked up against the Thai border and enclosing three lakes, **Ulu Muda Eco Park** has similarities with Perak's Royal Belum. However, this isn't a state-level park, but a mere forest reserve which, in the context of Malaysia, confers little protection – indeed, logging remains an issue in an area that is, for now, still rich in **wildlife**. Due to its remoteness, the only practical way to see the park is on a pricey **package trip**, but the rewards can be substantial. Thick with salt licks that lure animals, the park offers a reasonable chance of encountering **elephants** and **wild boar**, as well as reptiles and birds, including the rare **spotted leopard** and, between May and September, the **plain-pouched hornbill**.

The park is accessed by boat from **Gubir**, not much more than a jetty 75km east of Alor Star; a two-hour sampan ride from here lands you at the only accommodation, **Earth Lodge**. Hiking tracks link the lodge to limestone caves, hot springs (which many animals visit early in the morning or at night, when the temperatures drop) and wildlife hides.

ARRIVAL AND DEPARTURE   ULU MUDA ECO PARK

By bus and taxi The closest you can get to Gubir by public bus is either Sik, 30km southwest (buses from Sungai Petani), or Naka, 25km northwest (buses from Alor Star). From either of these, you'll need to find a taxi (most likely, just a local with a car); expect to pay RM50.

By car From Alor Star, take Route 175/K8 through Langgar and on up the K11 to Kuala Nerang, where you turn southeast for Gubir. From Butterworth, take the North South Expressway and exit at Gurun, taking route K10 to Sik, where you turn on to Route K8 to Gubir.

ACCOMMODATION

Earth Lodge Kuala Labua, inside the park ☎019 442 8926, ⊛earthlodgemalaysia.com. Newly renovated cabins, managed by two committed conservationists. Book

at least two weeks in advance. Rates here are per person for a three-day package including full board, boat rides, various activities and park permits. Dorms RM900, doubles RM1100

Langkawi

Situated 30km off the coast, just south of the Thai border, **LANGKAWI** is, at 500 square kilometres, the largest of an archipelago of mostly uninhabited islands. Once a haven for pirates, the island is now home to some of the priciest resorts in the country, taking advantage of **beaches** that are among the best on the west coast. Thankfully there's relatively little high-density development, and there is a sprinkling of budget and mid-range accommodation at two beaches, **Tengah** and **Cenang**. The island is also popular with international yachties for its **marinas**, which are relatively cheap – and Langkawi's **duty/GST-free status** means beer is ridiculously cheap. Many diversions are on offer beyond lazing around on the sand, including taking a **mangrove cruise** after

2

LANGKAWI

Kuala Perlis

Kuala Kedah

Satun

5

0 kilometres

Pulau Payar Marine Park & Penang

Chorong

Timon

372m

Bumbun

Tiloi

Teluk Apau

420m

Tuba

Laggun

285m

Kisap River

Kg. Penerah

Jetty

Kuah

Doyang Bunting

285m

Tanjung Dendang

Cave of Bats

Kilim Geoforest Jetty

Gua Cerita

117m

Tanjung Rhu

Kisap

Cave of Legends

1

Telaga Air Panas

Durian Perangin Waterfall

Mount Raya (881m)

Hospital

Singa Besar Island

2

Padang Lalang

Air Hangat Village

Lubuk Semilang

Kota Mahsuri

Langkawi Golf Club

Pasir

Gusing

Black Sand Beach

Teluk Ewa

Kg. Ulu Melaka

Padang River

Kedawang

Underwater World

SEE 'CENANG AND TENGAH BEACHES' MAP

Pasir Tengkorak

Padang Matsirat

Helioutpost

Cenang

Tengah

Tepor

China River

Els Golf Club

Pantai Datai

3

4

Mount Machinchang (700m)

Telaga Tujuh

Perdana Horse Stables
Langkawi Cable Car

Umgawa Zipline Eco Adventures
Oriental Village

Skytrex Adventure

6

Kuala Teriang

Rebak Besar

Pantai Kok

5

N

sea eagles, snorkelling or scuba diving at the **Pulau Payar Marine Park** to the south, and riding the terrific **Langkawi Cable Car** and adventurous **zipline** over the interior forests to the top of **Mount Machinchang**.

Langkawi is sufficiently far north that, as at Phuket and other west-coast Thai resorts, the **southwest monsoon** can have some bite. From May to August, rainy days can be more frequent here than elsewhere in Malaysia, with a dampening effect on the crowds and room rates.

Kuah

If you fly in, chances are that you'll never glimpse Langkawi's forgettable main town, **KUAH**, in the southeast of the island; indeed visitors off the ferries stay barely long enough to use the ATMs at the boat terminal and find a taxi to their accommodation. Just north of the ferry terminal, a separate section of the waterfront is home to **Dataran Lang** or Eagle Square, graced by the town's only landmark: an enormous sculpture of a sea eagle (*lang* being a contraction of *helang*, Malay for "eagle").

Cenang Beach

Around 18km west from Kuah, **Cenang Beach** is Langkawi at its most built-up, a 2km stretch that has seen an orgy of seemingly unrestrained get-rich-quick development in recent years, packing in numerous places to stay and eat as well as duty-free shopping malls. Whatever you think of the strip, you'll almost certainly warm to the beach – Langkawi's most popular – a long, broad strip of fine-white sand. There may be **jellyfish** in the water, so take local advice about swimming.

Laman Padi Rice Garden and Museum

At the northern end of Cenang Beach, opposite Meritus Pelangi Beach • Daily 10am–6pm • Free • ☎ 04 955 4312

The **Laman Padi Rice Garden and Museum** is home to an interesting collection of artefacts, photos and tools showing the history of rice cultivation in Langkawi and Kedah. There is a **Paddy Gallery**, a floating rice garden, and a viewing deck over a pretty, multi-tiered rooftop rice terrace. Things get more exciting at the **Herb Garden** and **Garden of Variety**, where you can don a straw hat and have a go at rice farming.

Underwater World

On the headland at the southern end of Cenang Beach • Daily 10am–6pm (public and school holidays 9.30am–6.30pm) • RM46 • ☎ 04 955 6100

Although their Coco Valley duty-free emporium seems to be a significant reason for the enterprise, **Underwater World** is actually a substantial aquarium, with more than a hundred tanks housing thousands of marine and freshwater fish. The highlight is the obligatory walk-through tunnel where sharks, turtles and hundreds of other sea creatures swim around and above you. There are also penguin and seal sections, with daily feeding sessions.

Tengah Beach

In contrast to Cenang, **Tengah Beach** still has something of a rural feel, although development is slowly catching up here, as new hotels and restaurants continue to sprout up on both sides of the road. The beach is slightly shorter than Cenang and not quite as pleasant, with coarser sand and occasionally rough surf. All this means, of course, that there are fewer people about, which can be a bonus.

Pantai Kok and around

North up the coast from Cenang Beach, beyond the **airport**, is **Pantai Kok**, another of Langkawi's well-known beaches, with a handful of resorts scattered on or near it. Just inland are two major sights: the **Langkawi Cable Car**, the only one of the island's man-made attractions that ranks as essential, and the cascades at **Telaga Tujuh**.

2

CENANG AND TENGAH BEACHES

▼ Island-Hopping Tour Jetties (700m)

Langkawi Cable Car

Oriental Village • **Cable car** Daily 9.30am–7pm • RM55 return, RM50 extra to jump the queue; glass-bottomed gondola RM105; Skyglide and Skybridge RM15, or walking up RM5 • ☎ 04 959 4225, ⓦ panoramalangkawi.com • **SkyTrail** RM200/person for the complete ascent and return by SkyCab • ☎ 019 590 2300, ⓦ junglewalla.com

Much of Langkawi's northwest is untouched rainforest atop low peaks of mixed sandstone and shale, one of which is **Mount Machinchang** (710m). At its foot, the tourist-trap theme park Oriental Village is the lower terminus of the magnificent **Langkawi Cable Car** up the mountain. With a 42-degree incline, the ride is not only the steepest of its kind, but also boasts the longest free span for a mono-cable car: a thrilling 950m long, great for eagle-spotting. Return trips are sold as package combos that include entrance to the Oriental Village's other hit-and-miss attractions, such as 360-degree 3D cinema **Skydome**; dinosaur-themed, tram-simulator **Skyrex**; and the **3D Art Museum** – be prepared to fend off local selfie sticks. You can also ride a **glass-bottomed gondola** for full-views of the broccoli-head rainforest underneath your feet.

Upon reaching **Middle Station** at an elevation of 650m, choose between taking the **Skyglide** and walking the 900m to the **Top Station**, where a 125m-long **SkyBridge** spans a deep valley and gives a spectacular view over the Andaman Sea – not for those with a fear of heights. Keen hikers may consider walking the **SkyTrail** from Middle (900m; 45min), or even Base to Top Station (2.2km; 6–8hr return, with lunch and sightseeing breaks).

Seven Wells Waterfall (Telaga Tujuh)

About 1.5km beyond the Langkawi Cable Car turning, the main road terminates at the entrance to the **Seven Wells Waterfall (Telaga Tujuh)**, where a cascading freshwater stream has eroded the rock to form several pools down a slope. During the rainy season, the slipperiness of the

LANGKAWI TOURS AND ACTIVITIES

Operators based at Cenang Beach and elsewhere offer a wide range of activities around Langkawi, perhaps the most popular being mangrove cruises and island-hopping trips. The price for non-beach activities often includes free pick-up from Cenang or Tengah beaches.

The standard itinerary for **island-hopping boat trips** (4hr; RM45/person) takes in forested Pregnant Maiden Island (Pulau Dayang Bunting), whose crater lake is good for swimming, Singa Besar for eagle feeding, and Beras Basah for beach and clear water. For something more luxurious, firms such as Crystal Yacht (Ⓦcrystalyacht.com) and Tropical Charters (Ⓦtropicalcharters.com.my) offer sunset cruises with drinks and a barbecue dinner for around RM260 per head.

If it's **wildlife** you're after, your best bets are Junglewalla (from RM180; ☎019 590 2300, Ⓦjunglewalla.com), run by expert naturalist Irshad Mobarak, and Dev's Adventure Tours (RM140–250; ☎019 494 9193, Ⓦlangkawi-nature.com). Both companies offer numerous excursions including cycling trips, birding tours, kayaking through mangroves and evening jungle treks, during which you might spot the bizarre flying lemur (colugo) – something like a cross between a fruit bat and a squirrel.

MANGROVE AND SEA SAFARIS

The Langkawi archipelago is a member of the Global Geoparks Network, a UNESCO-endorsed initiative to protect and promote "geological heritage of international significance". In Langkawi's case (Ⓦlangkawigeopark.com.my), that geology includes **karst** landscapes, and it's the limestone crags and peaks that add a special flavour to local **mangrove cruises**. In fact the mangroves themselves often play a mere supporting role, as these trips also involve a visit to a bat cave, a fish farm and **eagle-feeding** sessions.

Trips set off from the jetties at Tanjung Rhu (see p.180) and the Kilim Geoforest Park (see p.180) when enough people show up to fill them (RM110/4hr); ideally turn up at 9 or 10am, although you can haggle to charter a boat privately (RM400/eight people). These cruises are essentially unguided as the fee just pays for the ride; for a professionally guided trip by boat or kayak (RM980/five people for a private boat or RM170/person), with a restaurant meal along the way, try Dev's Adventure Tours (see above). Dev's also run the naturalist-guided **Sea Safari** (RM200/person, maximum eight people), an eco-adventure cruise through the lesser-visited southwestern islets of Langkawi's archipelago that includes jungle hiking and swimming at a secluded beach.

WATERSPORTS, SNORKELLING AND DIVING

On the beach, several watersports operators charge about RM120/180 for **parasailing** on the beach or around their bay, or RM180 for half an hour on a **jet ski**, among other activities. It's even possible to do an island-hopping tour by jet ski (3hr; from RM600/person; Ⓦmegawatersports.com).

Pulau Payar Marine Park is the place to head for **snorkelling and scuba diving**; south of Langkawi, it features seasonally clear water and colourful fish life including giant potato cod and blacktip reef sharks. A well-established operator is East Marine (diving day-trips RM390, or RM250 to snorkel; same prices for day-trips out of Penang; Ⓦeastmarine.com.my), though agents in Cenang Beach have cheaper deals.

moss covering the rock in between the pools helps you slide from one pool to another, before the fast-flowing water disappears over the cliff to form the 90m-high waterfall visible from below – it's only the depth of the water in the last pool that prevents you from shooting off the end. Legend as it that mountain fairies created the *sintuk*, a climbing plant with enormous pods, that grows around these pools; the locals use it as a hair wash, said to rinse away bad luck. The walk to the pools from the car park takes about 45 minutes, the last stage of which involves a steep 200m-high climb up from the inevitable cluster of souvenir stalls at the base of the hill. From the pools, you can climb further up to the top of the waterfall, where an ugly looking red metallic bridge offers unparalleled views over the Geopark and the Andaman Sea.

2

Umgawa Zipline Eco Adventures

Seven Wells Waterfall's Parking Lot • Daily 7am–7pm • Jungle Flight (1hr) RM199; Big Waterfall Adventure RM499 (2hr 30min) • ☏ 013 343 8900, ⓦ umgawa.com

Langkawi's newest attraction, **Umgawa Zipline Eco Adventures** is also the island's first zipline eco-tour. The twelve zips, of up to 200m in length, send visitors soaring over the Machinchang Cambrian Geoforest Park, offering a bird's – and monkey's – eye view of the Seven Wells Waterfall and the Andaman Sea. The experience doesn't come cheap, but security standards are world-class and the guides are all English speaking and well trained in spotting fauna and flora.

Skytrex Adventure

Opposite the Danna resort • Daily 9am–5pm, last entry 3pm • RM50–70 depending on the obstacle course • ☏ 019 280 5679, ⓦ skytrex-adventure.com

Skytrex Adventure sounds a discordant note amid the manicured resorts of Pantai Kok, and that's no bad thing. Here you can challenge yourself on three obstacle courses of varying levels of toughness, each taking two to three hours – expect lots of net and rope bridges and the odd spot of abseiling.

Black Sand Beach

Around halfway along Langkawi's north coast, **Black Sand Beach** (Pantai Pasir Hitam) is actually pale grey – said to have been caused by ash, after locals torched their rice fields during a war with the Thais in the eighteenth century. It's a pleasant place to pull up, with little craft hauled up on the gently sloping shoreline.

Tanjung Rhu

Langkawi's northernmost road runs to the tip of **Tanjung Rhu**, a 4km-long promontory fringed in casuarina trees, where you can join a **mangrove** cruise from the jetty. There's a good **beach**, sheltered and overlooking several islets – one of which, **Chabang**, can be reached on foot at low tide. Be sure to check tide times to avoid being stranded or swimming the 500m back to shore.

Kilim Geoforest Park

Taking up the northeastern part of the island, **Kilim Geoforest Park** showcases contorted limestone formations, some forested, others starkly beautiful, interspersed with valleys where mangroves thrive. There are no trails, however; most visitors make a beeline for the **jetty** to sign up for a **mangrove boat** trip or **kayaking**. If you don't fancy either, you can simply survey the mangroves from a boardwalk, which ends at a cave populated by bats.

Mount Raya

Summit lookout tower daily 9am–6.30pm • RM10

Reached off a road through the centre of the island, **Mount Raya** (881m) is Langkawi's highest point. It also happens to be driveable, although if you plan to head up in a rental vehicle, check with the agent that it can cope with the steep, twisting 7km access road. Once at the top, you're rewarded with views down over jungle to the coast that can rival those from the cable car. This is also one promising place on the island to spot **hornbills**.

ARRIVAL AND DEPARTURE   **LANGKAWI**

Langkawi's excellent travel links with other parts of Malaysia, as well as with Singapore and southern Thailand, mean you don't have to return the way you arrived. Various **agents** at Cenang and Tengah beaches can assist with onward travel, including combined boat-and-van transfers to Thailand.

By plane Langkawi Airport is on the west coast at Padang Matsirat, 20km by road from Kuah and only 5km from Cenang Beach. There's a tourist information point and a taxi counter where you buy a coupon for your destination; the fare to Tengah or Cenang beaches, say, is around RM25.

Destinations Johor Bahru (1 daily; 1hr15min); Kuala Lumpur (KLIA: hourly; 1hr; Subang: 3–5 daily; 1hr); Kuching (4 weekly; 2hr 10min); Penang (3–4 daily; 35min); Singapore (1–2 daily; 1hr 30min).

By ferry At the southeastern edge of Kuah, Langkawi's ferry terminal feels like a shopping mall with piers out the back. There are ATMs inside the building, while at the front is a separate building housing a tourist office and booths selling ferry tickets (schedules for most routes at ⓦ langkawi-ferry.com). It's worth booking Penang tickets

a day in advance. To get to Koh Lipe, Thailand, in low season, buy a ferry and minivan combo ticket via Satun and Pak Bara at Kuah's Ferry Terminal. Taxis from Langkawi's ferry terminal should be around RM30 to Cenang or Tengah beaches, RM40 to Tanjung Rhu and RM45 to Pantai Kok.
Destinations Koh Lipe (Thailand; 1 daily; 1hr 20min); Kuala Kedah (14 daily; 1hr 30min; RM23); Kuala Perlis (14 daily; 1hr; RM18); Penang (daily at 8.30am and 2pm; 3hr; RM70); Satun (Thailand; daily at 9am and 3.30pm; 1hr 15min; RM35).

GETTING AROUND

Langkawi has a reasonable network of country roads, with a veritable expressway between Kuah and Cenang Beach. Unfortunately, there are no buses, so you'll be using taxis at some point or renting a vehicle. As the island is barely 25km across at its widest point, even a comprehensive tour is unlikely to cover more than 100km.

By taxi Langkawi has some Uber and Grab drivers – try these apps first for the best fares. Taxis have set fares from the airport, ferry terminal and taxi stands, which can be found at *McDonald's* next to Underwater World at Cenang Beach and *Tropical Resort* at Tengah Beach, among other places. If you think you're being overcharged, ask to see the official tariff sheet or check with tourist offices. For journeys that start elsewhere, you may need to haggle.

Vehicle rental Some car rental agents at Cenang soundly undercut the usual chains on price, but Kuah's ferry terminal is by far the best place for cheap rental vehicles. Don't be afraid to negotiate, and remember that a day should be counted as 24hr, not the date. A basic Malaysian-built Perodua will set you back around RM70/day. Scooters and two-strokes motorbikes will cost around RM35/day. Note that rates can rise by fifty percent or even double over busy holiday periods, at which time the chains may not be such a bad deal.

INFORMATION

Tourism Malaysia Both the counters at the airport (daily 9am–10pm; ⓣ 04 955 7155) and at the back of the small building fronting the ferry terminal (daily 9am–5pm; ⓣ 04 966 0494) have leaflets covering tours and activities and can help with practical advice on taxi fares and sightseeing.

LADA The authority that manages Langkawi runs a centralized tourist information website of varying usefulness (ⓦ naturallylangkawi.my). Check also (ⓦ langkawi-info.com) for best of listicles and tour information.

ACCOMMODATION

Practically all the worthwhile cheap places to stay are at Cenang Beach, all of the upmarket resorts are elsewhere, and you'll find a few mid-range options at **Tengah** and **Cenang**. If it's a toss-up between the last two, choose Cenang for buzz, cheap food and ready access to shops; Tengah if you'd prefer to pay a bit more for food and lodging in leafier surroundings. As ever, book a few days ahead over holiday periods, when rates can rise by ten to fifty percent above those listed below.

CENANG BEACH
AB Motel Jalan Pantai Cenang ⓣ 04 955 1300, ⓦ abmotel.weebly.com; map p.178. This beachside motel isn't much to look at, but it's well established and popular. All rooms are a/c and en suite, some in the main block, others in single-storey rows. 🛜 **RM100**
★**Bon Ton/Temple Tree** Coast road 2km north of Cenang Beach ⓣ 04 955 1688, ⓦ bontonresort.com.my and ⓦ templetree.com.my; map p.178. Adjacent resorts run by the same team and both comprising vintage timber houses from all over the country that have been dismantled and rebuilt here using a harmonious mixture of period and contemporary fittings. *Bon Ton* is a collection of fine Malay kampung houses; *Temple Tree* features some quite substantial buildings from towns or plantations. Both have

their own restaurants and pools, and *Bon Ton* overlooks a lagoon rich in birdlife. Every house is priced differently depending on how many it sleeps. Breakfast included. 🛜 *Bon Ton* **RM750**, *Temple Tree* **RM800**
Casa del Mar Northern end of Jalan Pantai Cenang ⓣ 04 955 2388, ⓦ casadelmar-langkawi.com; map p.178. With buildings in a terracotta hue, creating a faintly Moroccan feel, this boutique resort succeeds in screening out the general hubbub of the strip. It's slightly overpriced, but does boast spacious rooms and suites, a spa, beachside pool and two restaurants. Breakfast included. 🛜 **RM855**
Gecko Guesthouse Off Jalan Pantai Cenang ⓣ 019 428 3801, ⓦ bit.ly/GeckoGuesthouse; map p.178. Pioneer rustic budget accommodation in kampung-style chalets as well as a boring concrete block, all set in a shady garden

2

teeming with backpackers and their LCD screens. Paying a little extra will get you en suite, even a/c. 📶 Dorms RM25, doubles RM50

Kampung Guest House 25 Jalan Madrasah, off Jalan Pantai Cenang ☎017 425 3302, 🌐kampongguesthouse @gmail.com; map p.178. New, well-staffed guesthouse for those on a budget. There's one dorm and six simple yet clean and inviting fan rooms, mostly en suite, all with small verandas. The only thing missing is breakfast. 📶 Dorm RM20, doubles RM60

Langkapuri Inn Jalan Pantai Cenang ☎04 955 1202; map p.178. A motel-like collection of slightly faded rooms with tiled interiors, tiny balconies and satellite TV, comfortable enough but in need of a refresh. Breakfast included. 📶 RM170

★**Langkawi Dormitorio** Unit 5, 1556 Jalan Pantai Cenang, to the right of Underwater World ☎017 2362587, 🌐facebook.com/LgkDormitorio; map p.178. A good central choice, 2min walk from the beach, with clean and airy dorms with individual pods and private bathrooms, or bigger, luminous family rooms that are ideal for groups travelling together. Minimum stay two nights. 📶 Dorms RM50

Meritus Pelangi Beach Jalan Pantai Cenang ☎04 952 8888, 🌐meritushotels.com; map p.178. Top-notch resort with two-storey chalets, echoing traditional Malay architecture, in expansive gardens. There's a pool, spa, tennis and squash courts, and several restaurants. 📶 RM1600

Sweet Monkey Backpacker 1556 Jalan Pantai Cenang, in the block to the right of Underwater World ☎017 4921135; map p.178. This sociable dorm-only hostel is a reliable choice in central Cenang, with mixed and female rooms. Besides providing useful information, a kitchenette and a relaxing, reggae-themed common living room, they offer discounted island-hopping tours and *muay thai* lessons with Malaysian trainers (Tues & Sun 5–7pm; RM30), as well as scooter and car rental. 📶 Dorms RM25

TENGAH BEACH

Frangipani Jalan Teluk Baru ☎04 952 0000, 🌐frangipanilangkawi.com; map p.178. A sprawling complex of buildings with roofs shaped like those of traditional Malay houses. There are rooms in two-storey buildings and a selection of "beach villas" (bungalows), as well as a spa, gym and jacuzzi. One of the two pools is salt water – odd, when the beach is just a minute away. Book directly on their website for the best deals. Breakfast included. 📶 Doubles RM500, villas RM630

★**Lot 33 Boutique Hotel** Jalan Pantai Tengah, right next to the Turkish Bazaar ☎04 952 3652, 🌐bit.ly/ Lot33Hotel; map p.178. New Mekong-inspired glitzy boutique hotel in a leafy double-storey house filled with

Buddha statues and Balinese-styled bamboo handicrafts. The seven rooms here are all huge, with jacuzzis, sofas, LCD screens, and balconies. The swimming pool is hidden at the back, shaded by a tall wall of vegetation, and there's an equally classy Chinese-style seafood restaurant at the front where you can have your complimentary breakfast. 📶 RM550

Tropical Resort Jalan Teluk Baru ☎04 955 4075, 🌐tropicalresortlangkawi.com; map p.178. Just a 2min walk from the beach along a leafy path, this resort has a series of bungalows, each containing modern, blandly furnished rooms facing in different directions. Good value; breakfast included. 📶 RM300

NORTHWEST

Andaman Teluk Datai ☎04 959 1088, 🌐theandaman .com; map p.176. This substantial place offers chic rooms set in rainforest above one of Langkawi's best beaches, where hornbills are often seen. The unusual feature here is the coral nursery, set up following the discovery of a nearby reef damaged by the 2004 Indian Ocean tsunami. Now the resort rehabilitates coral in its own pool, where guests can take part in guided snorkelling sessions. Breakfast included. 📶 RM820

Berjaya Langkawi Pantai Kok ☎04 959 1888, 🌐berjayahotel.com; map p.176. The resort for the hoi polloi, better value than much of the competition, with some newly refurbished chalets set inland among the trees or out over the sea. Facilities include watersports, tennis and the obligatory pool and spa. Breakfast included. 📶 RM880

The Danna Pantai Kok ☎04 959 3288, 🌐thedanna .com; map p.176. Generically grand, this place has a glut of marble and high ceilings, but it scores highly with its Olympic-sized infinity pool that's right by the beach, and its large, slick rooms overlooking the leafy courtyard, marina or ocean. Breakfast included. Book online for big discounts. 📶 RM1700

The Datai Teluk Datai ☎04 950 0500, 🌐thedatai .com; map p.176. On the gloriously secluded Datai Beach, this is the quintessential luxury retreat, with self-contained mini-villas embedded in the woods or out on the beach, some with their own paddling pool or jacuzzi, as well as less extortionately priced rooms in the main building. Facilities include two pools, a Malay-style spa, watersports and use of the adjacent golf course. Breakfast Included. 📶 RM1800

TANJUNG RHU

Four Seasons Resort Langkawi Tanjung Rhu ☎04 950 8888, 🌐fourseasons.com; map p.176. Close to the karst formations of Langkawi's northeast, this phenomenally expensive retreat doesn't so much have rooms as mini-apartments taking up a whole floor of their

two-storey pavilions, as well as self-contained villas, all with outdoor showers in addition to their bathroom. Breakfast included. Apartments ⬥ **RM3309**
Tanjung Rhu Resort Tanjung Rhu ☎ 04 959 1033, ⬥ tanjungrhu.com.my; map p.176. Well-designed

rooms – all billed as suites and featuring wooden floors, teak furnishings and balconies – set this resort apart. Facilities include two pools, tennis courts and a spa, and they run their own short mangrove trips. Breakfast included. ⬥ **RM1100**

EATING

The eating scene on Langkawi is predictably cosmopolitan and, away from the resorts, tends to focus on mid-range restaurants, although there are stalls and snack places to be found, especially at Cenang Beach.

CENANG BEACH

My French Factory Jalan Pantai Cenang, across from Underwater World ☎ 04 955 5196, ⬥ facebook.com/MyFrenchFactoryLangkawi; map p.178. A husband-wife team runs this tiny and friendly creperie, the first on Langkawi, serving up delicious salty or sweet options (from RM7). Most items can be ordered gluten-free. Mon–Thurs, Sat & Sun 11am–11pm.

★ **Orkid Ria** North end of the beach ☎ 04 955 4128; map p.178. Popular alfresco Chinese place specializing in fresh seafood, grilled, steamed, fried or however you want it. Huge tiger prawns, lobster and whole crab, all sold by weight (be careful not to over-order and risk a large bill), are some of the best you'll find in town. Around RM40 without drinks, more if you go for lots of seafood. Daily 11am–3pm & 6–11pm.

Red Tomato Jalan Pantai Cenang, across from Underwater World ☎ 04 955 40 55, ⬥ redtomato.com.my; map p.178. Middle-of-the-road, touristy restaurant easily spotted by virtue of the fuchsia VW Beetle usually parked outside (but don't confuse it with the *Red Sky* restaurant close by). Come here for Western cooked breakfasts (RM12) and a largely Italian menu of pizza and pasta meals (RM22). Daily 9am–10.30pm.

★ **Yasmin** Jalan Pantai Cenang, across from Orkid Ria ☎ 019 449 5081; map p.178. Many residents claim that this small Syrian-owned restaurant makes the best Middle Eastern food on the island. From creamy hummus and fresh *tabbouleh* to BBQ kebab sets (about RM18) and cheaper backpacker-tailored *shawarma* (RM10), falafel and *shish taouk*, the jovial chefs masterfully reproduce their region's flavours. Daily noon–midnight.

TENGAH BEACH

Cactus South end of the beach, across from Holiday

Villa Resort ☎ 012 477 3098; map p.178. Humble yet popular open-air restaurant adorned with international customers' autographed T-shirts, and offering a wide selection of cheap Asian and Western breakfast favourites (about RM15 per set), coffees, tea and juices. Daily 8am–1pm & 4pm–1am.

Hummingbird Café North end of the beach ☎ 04 955 2152, ⬥ facebook.com/HummingbirdLgk; map p.178. This cutesy, female-run café, guarded by a rubber dinosaur and tiger, specializes in all-day breakfasts, including baguette sandwiches (from RM15), yogurt smoothies, cold-pressed juices and the usual espressos and mochas. Mon & Wed–Sun 9am–6pm.

La Chocolatine North end of the beach ☎ 04 955 8891; map p.178. Tiny French-owned café with pastries – croissants, *millefeuilles*, etc – crepes, quiche and sandwiches, complemented (or not) by Edith Piaf over the speakers. It's all acceptable enough for breakfast, but still a welcome change if you're fed up with *roti canai*. Coffee and cake will set you back around RM25. Daily 9am–6pm.

Unkaizan Far southern end of the beach ☎ 04 955 4118, ⬥ unkaizan.com; map p.178. Up a jungly slope is this hidden gem of a Japanese restaurant where you can dine out on the terrace or indoors. The range of sushi and sashimi offerings is impressive (around RM60), although the set meals – chicken cutlet or tempura with rice, soup and pickles, say – are better value at around RM45. There's Japanese ice cream, too. Daily 6–11pm.

Yam-Yam Café South end of the beach ☎ 012 6164417, ⬥ yamyamlangkawi@gmail.com; map p.178. With an original Italian espresso machine, this Malaysian–Dutch-run café mixes European and Asian home-style cuisine, and is perfect for breakfast or a casual lunch (around RM30). The non-dairy smoothies, especially the berry blast, are great on a hot day. Mon & Wed–Sun 9am–10.30pm.

DRINKING AND NIGHTLIFE

Langkawi has a more pragmatic attitude to **alcohol** than anywhere else in the four overwhelmingly Malay states of the north: many restaurants are licensed, and then of course there are the duty-free outlets where you can buy cheap spirits and beer – a can of Tiger is only RM2.

Bam-Boo-Ba End of Sunba Block, Jalan Teluk Baru ☎ 0125660254, ⬥ facebook.com/BamBooBaLoungeBar; map p.178. A lively horseshoe-shaped sports bar with tables

spilling out front on the kerb. Kick off the night here munching on burgers (RM19) and pizzas (RM26). Their "buy two drink three" cocktail happy hour (daily 5–9pm; from

2

RM16) always packs a good crowd. Tues–Sun 5pm–1am.

★**The Cliff** Over the water at the south end of Cenang Beach ☎04 953 3228, ⓦtheclifflangkawi.com; map p.178. One of the priciest standalone restaurants in Cenang, *The Cliff* majors on fusion cooking (mostly spicy seafood; mains around RM50), but it's the little bar that stands out. Get here around 6pm, park yourself at one of the few beachside seats and watch parasails darting across the sea, silhouetted against a scarlet sky. Daily noon–11pm.

★**Kalut Bar** Cenang Beach, behind Casa del Mar ☎012 259 4836, ⓦfacebook.com/KalutBar; map p.178. Trendy beach shack without the scruff, set behind rows of colourful beanbags slung on the sand out front. The perk here is the daily fire juggling shows, starting after sunset and going on throughout the night, with an eclectic soundtrack of anything from R&B to reggae, trance and pop. Prime Aussie beef burgers (RM20), happy hour,

"cheeky buckets" and free shots for ladies on Wed evenings all make it popular. Mon & Tues 4pm–1am, Wed–Sun 11am–1am.

Sunba Retro Bar Slightly inland from Tengah Beach ☎04 953 1801, ⓦsungroup-langkawi.com; map p.178. Part of a modern complex but decked out in wood to simulate an old kampung house, this is a relaxed bar with pretensions of being a proper club. There's a live band most nights, otherwise DJs spin mainly mainstream oldies and some dance sounds. Daily 11pm–4am.

Thirstday Cenang Beach, access via Orkid Ria's dining hall ☎017 515 5395, ⓔthirstdaybarandrestaurant@ gmail.com; map p.178. Mid-range, beachside outdoor bar and restaurant serving 35 different cocktails (from RM20), good pizzas, pastas (about RM20) and Malaysian staples. The tables face a pretty stretch of beach – an ideal spot for sundowners. Daily 11am–1am.

SHOPPING

Langkawi's **duty-free status** can draw in even those not normally obsessed with cheap alcohol and cigarettes – don't be surprised if at some point you find yourself among the hordes at the **malls around Underwater World**, grabbing armfuls of beer, imported chocolates and the like. The **Cenang Mall**, also on the main drag, is a more orthodox and underwhelming shopping complex, best for branches of Western fast food and coffee chains.

DIRECTORY

Banks and exchange There are ATMs at Cenang Mall, the Zon duty-free mall, Underwater World (all at Cenang Beach), the airport and the ferry terminal. Cenang Mall also has a Maybank foreign-exchange counter.

Hospital The island's main hospital is on the main road (Jalan Padang Matsirat) midway between Kuah and Cenang Beach (☎04 966 3333). There's also Klinik Mahsuri,

a clinic at Tengah Beach, next to Hummingbird Café (daily 8am–1pm, 2pm–7pm & 8pm–10pm).

Internet Wi-Fi@Langkawi is a free service available in certain spots on Cenang Beach's main street, at the ferry terminal and elsewhere, though not necessarily reliable.

Pharmacies Guardian has an outlet at Cenang Mall.

Kangar and around

As the fastest road to and from Thailand passes through Kedah rather than **Perlis**, it's easy to bypass the latter state completely. The few travellers who end up here do so to access Langkawi using convenient transport hub **Kuala Perlis**, or on visa runs to or from Penang via the border post at **Padang Besar**, which is much quieter than at Bukit Kayu Hitam in Kedah. Unremarkable **KANGAR**, Perlis's capital, sits immediately north of little **Sungai Perlis**. About 10km east of Kangar, **ARAU** is the least interesting of all Malaysia's royal towns; from the main road you can peek at the istana, looking like a small European stately home except that it sports two golden domes.

Kelam Cave

Daily 8am–5pm • RM1; camping license RM2 • Bus T11 from Kangar to Padang Besar stops very close to the park; taxis charge RM60 return, including a 1hr wait

From Kangar, it's about 30km north to **Kelam Cave**, a 370m-long limestone tunnel that leads to a forest park at the foot of the Nakawan Range near **Kaki Bukit** village. You can camp at the nearby Hutan Hujan Hujan campsite.

Wang Kelian

Nine kilometres north of Kelam Cave, over a mountain pass, is ghost town **Wang Kelian**, once home to a thriving border market which closed down after the discovery of immigrant Rohingya workers' mass graves in 2015. The village is the entrance to the small state park of **Taman Negara Perlis** (☎04 945 7898) and an unorthodox **border crossing** to Satun, in Thailand, where boats depart for Koh Lipe. It's best to come here with your own transportation.

ARRIVAL AND DEPARTURE

Train station In the centre of Arau, off Road 176 (☎04 986 1225).

Destinations Alor Star (7 daily; 20min); Butterworth (almost hourly; 1hr 30min); Ipoh (7 daily; 2hr 50min); Kuala Kangsar (7 daily; 2hr 15min); Kuala Lumpur (7 daily; 5hr); Sungai Petani (hourly; 50min); Taiping (7 daily; 2hr).

By bus Express and local services use the long-distance bus station on Jalan Bukit Lagi in Kangar, just south of the river. Kuala Perlis' bus station has connections to all over the country; it's a 5min walk from the ferry terminal: turn left from the jetty, then right once you come to what's obviously a main street.

Destinations from Kangar bus station Alor Star (local bus T14; 12 daily; 1hr 15min); Butterworth/Penang (at least 3 daily; 2hr 30min); Changlun (for Thailand border at Bukit Kayu Hitam; local bus T10; 12 daily; 1hr); Ipoh (3 daily; 4hr 30min); Johor Bahru (2 daily; 12–13hr); Kaki Bukit (local bus T11; 10 daily; 45min); Kota Bharu (daily at 9am and 9pm; 6hr 30min); Kuala Kangsar (3 daily; 3hr); Kuala Lumpur (almost hourly; 7hr); Kuala Perlis (local bus T12; 10 daily; 30 min); Kuala Terengganu (2 daily; 8hr); Kuantan (1 daily; 10hr); Melaka (8 daily; 11hr); Padang Besar (local bus T11; 10 daily; 1hr); Singapore (3 daily; 13hr).

Destinations from Kuala Perlis bus station Alor Star (hourly; 1hr 15min); Ipoh (5 daily; 5hr); Johor Bahru (4 daily; 11hr); Kota Bharu (daily at 8pm; 7hr); Kuala Besut (for Perhentian Islands; daily at 8pm; 8hr); Kuala Lumpur (almost hourly; 7hr); Kuala Terengganu (daily at 7.30pm; 7hr); Lumut (5 daily; 5hr 30min); Melaka (daily at 9am and 9.30pm; 8hr).

By ferry Langkawi ferries (☎ langkawi-ferry.com) dock at Kuala Perlis (☎ 016 418 2539), 15km west of Kangar.

KANGAR AND AROUND

Destination Langkawi (14 daily; 1hr; RM18).

TO THAILAND

The three border crossings (daily 6am–10pm) in this area are: Padang Besar, 30km north of Kangar, where the rail line enters Thailand; Bukit Kayu Hitam in Kedah, 30km northeast of Kangar as the crow flies; and Wang Kelian, 9km north of Kelam Cave. Bukit Kayu Hitam is overwhelmingly more popular, as it's on the North–South Expressway. Bear in mind that, since 2017, international travellers are only allowed two overland entries to Thailand per calendar year, and you may be asked to produce ten thousand Thai baht in cash as proof of sufficient funds for your stay in Thailand.

By train KTM operates a cheap and convenient hourly service between Padang Besar and Butterworth. At Padang Besar, change to one of the two daily services (9.55am and 3.40pm) to Hat Yai in Thailand, clearing immigration directly on the platform before train departure. Otherwise, exit the station and walk 500m to Malaysian immigration, before proceeding 1km to the Thai checkpoint. You can catch onward bus or train connections from the Thai side of Padang Besar, where minivans to Hat Yai (50 Thai baht) await.

By bus There are no buses through to Thailand, although tour-agency minivans service the Hat Yai route (you can book a place on ☎ 016 673 8082). From Kangar, it's also possible to take local bus T11 or charter a taxi to Padang Besar (RM50), where you have to get off before the border and cover the 2km to the Thai border post on foot or by motorbike taxi.

ACCOMMODATION AND EATING

Hutan Hujan Hujan Kelam Cave forest park ☎ 019 358 6838. Well-equipped campsite in a superb location surrounded by huge trees right at the foot of the Nakawan range. Staff provide tents, four meals per day and a set of activities that includes hiking in the surrounding hills. Toilets are basic yet clean, and when it rains the tents are pitched under the protection of Malay-style open-sided hall. Camping with full board, per person RM35

Kedai Khuan Bee Kaki Bukit's main junction ☎ 04 945 7673. Friendly Chinese *kopitiam* famous for its strong coffee, handmade giant pork *pao* (steamed buns; RM4) and breakfast titbits. Daily 7am–7pm.

The interior

CANOPY WALKWAY, TAMAN NEGARA

The interior

Peninsular Malaysia's interior comprises a vast swathe of territory, stretching northeast of Kuala Lumpur all the way up to Kota Bharu on the east coast. Until relatively recent times, this was a remote region of steep, limestone peaks with knife-edge ridges and luxuriant valleys inhabited by Orang Asli groups. Colonial administrator Hugh Clifford described the terrain in the 1880s as "smothered in deep, damp forest, threaded across a network of streams and rivers". Indeed, rivers were the sole means of transportation until prospectors and planters opened the interior up through the twentieth century; roads and a railway arrived, helping to establish the towns of Temerloh, Gua Musang and Kuala Lipis.

Much of the interior has now been logged, settled and tamed, though Clifford's deep, damp forests survive in the dense chunk of undeveloped jungle that is **Taman Negara** (literally "National Park"). Gazetted as Malaysia's **first national park** in 1925 and covering 4343 square kilometres, Taman Negara forms the largest tract of rainforest in Peninsular Malaysia; it contains some of the **oldest rainforest** in the world, which has evolved over 130 million years as a home for a fabulous array of wildlife. Some of the Peninsula's 1500 **Batek** Orang Asli live here too, many as hunter-gatherers; the park authorities generally turn a blind eye to their hunting game.

Reached via the transport nexus of **Jerantut**, Taman Negara's main entry point, the riverside town of **Kuala Tahan** is the trailhead for jungle hikes. With so much to see here, it's easy to overlook the rest of the region, but outside the park you can ride the Jungle Railway north through the interior, touching on lesser known sections of the wilds – caves and waterfalls at **Kenong Rimba State Park** and **Kota Gelanggi Cave Complex**; remoter areas of Taman Negara at **Merapoh** and **Kuala Koh**; the ancient Hakka settlement of **Kampung Pulai**; and more forest, waterfalls and views at **Gunung Stong State Park**.

GETTING AROUND

THE INTERIOR

By bus Buses along Route 8 and the East Coast Highway can get you within range of all the main sights, but remoter corners require the help of your own vehicle, taxis or local tour operators.

By car Route 8, the interior's main artery, runs for 500km from Bentong near KL to Kota Bharu. It's a well-maintained road, though not a multi-lane highway, so expect to be periodically slowed behind ponderous lorries. The quickest way to reach Route 8 from KL is the E8 (Karak Highway), which careers northeast from KL through the foothills of the Genting Highlands. Expect a few thrilling, cambered descents – and be warned that there are often nasty accidents.

The Orang Asli p.191
Planning a visit to Taman Negara p.193
The Kuala Gandah elephant sanctuary p.196
Taman Negara packages p.197
Kuala Tahan activities p.198

Picking up trekking gear and supplies p.199
Hiking from Kuala Tahan p.201
Kuala Tahan hides (blinds) p.202
The Jungle Railway p.204

GUNUNG STONG STATE PARK

Highlights

❶ **Kota Gelanggi Cave Complex** Right outside Jerantut, these little-visited caves make for the perfect prelude to – or conclusion from – Taman Negara. **See p.193**

❷ **Taman Negara via Kuala Tahan** The Peninsula's largest and oldest nature reserve offers river trips, hikes and wildlife spotting amid a swathe of ancient rainforest, best visited via the park headquarters at Kuala Tahan. **See p.195**

❸ **Kenong Rimba State Park** A barely developed reserve adjoining Taman Negara,

offering its own trekking and animal spotting opportunities. **See p.206**

❹ **Kampung Pulai** Discover Malaysia's oldest Kuan Yin temple in this riverside Chinese Hakka village, set amid rubber plantations and limestone karsts. **See p.212**

❺ **Gunung Stong State Park** In the interior of Kelantan state, Mount Stong boasts a picturesque waterfall, good mountain trekking and a marvellous jungle camp. **See p.214**

HIGHLIGHTS ARE MARKED ON THE MAP ON P.190

THE ORANG ASLI

The twentieth-century spread of the timber, rubber and palm oil industries through the interior had a huge impact upon the region's **Orang Asli**, who were traditionally nomadic peoples living by hunting and slash-and-burn agriculture. These days many have been forced to settle down, existing at the fringes of the cash economy. The mountain-dwelling **Temiar**, for instance, trade in forest products such as herbal medicines and, increasingly, **timber** (though their logging activities are minimal compared with those of the State Forestry Department and private companies). Some **Batek** do still live fairly traditional lives at Taman Negara, where you might meet shy groups walking in single file along trails, or come across their temporary vine and forest brush shelters in jungle clearings.

However, three-quarters of Orang Asli peoples (including many local Batek, **Senoi** and **Semang**) live below the poverty line, compared to less than a tenth of the population as a whole. That fact makes it all the harder for them to confront the many forces, from planning agencies to Christian and Muslim groups, who seek to influence their destiny. The issue of **land rights** is among their gravest problems, for while the country's Aboriginal People's Act has led to the creation of Orang Asli reserves, at the same time many Asli traditional areas have been gazetted as state land, rendering the inhabitants there, at best, tolerated guests of the government.

3

Taman Negara: Kuala Tahan

The main gateway to Taman Negara, the town of **Kuala Tahan**, 250km northeast of KL, is where you'll find the **national park headquarters** and the pick of its visitor facilities. It's also the place to get your bearings and seek advice before crossing the Tembeling River and heading into the forest: well-marked **trails** include an easy boardwalk stroll to a popular **canopy walkway**; tougher day-treks out to waterfalls and hides overlooking salt licks in the jungle (for which you'll need to hire guides); or the seven-day return ascent of **Mount Tahan**, Peninsular Malaysia's highest peak, involving steep climbs and river crossings. Activities other than hiking include river swimming, low-key rafting and angling.

Listening to the sounds of the birds, insects and other animals, marvelling at the sheer size of the trees and peering into the tangled understorey of flowering lianas, luminous fungi and giant bamboo are memorable experiences. However, keep your expectations of spotting **wildlife** – particularly big game – low, as these days it's very rare to encounter any, even on the park's remotest trails.

Kuala Tahan is reached via the service town of **Jerantut**, or – increasingly – directly on minibuses from Cameron Highlands or the Pulau Perhentian jetty at Kuala Besut. It's also possible to enter Taman Negara further north at **Merapoh** (see p.210) and **Kuala Koh** (see p.213) – or even to hike to either from Kuala Tahan in a week-long traverse of the park. Both require more effort to reach and have fewer facilities, but they're also less crowded than Kuala Tahan – though not necessarily easier places to see wildlife.

Jerantut

In tranquil **JERANTUT**, 70km south of Kuala Tahan, road, rail and river converge on a small grid of streets. Activity revolves around the main artery **Jalan Besar**, 200m east of the **train station**. The **Tembeling Jetty**, a short taxi ride north, sees traffic upriver to Kuala Tahan. For most, Jerantut is just somewhere to find last-minute supplies and top up with **cash**, as there are no banks at Kuala Tahan. However, it's worth lingering for an enjoyable half-day visiting the **Kota Gelanggi Cave Complex**, and if you're here on a Saturday, try some of the cheap local food at the bustling **night market** (5–10.30pm) next to the new bus station.

3

TAMAN NEGARA

N

0   10
kilometres

Dungun

Kuala Berang

Dungun River

768m

742m

Kuala Terengganu

580m

Mount Padang (1320m)

Mount Gajah Terum (1571m)

Mount Mandi Angin (Mount Chedah) (1480m)

Mount Besar (742m)

Tanjung Mentong

Kenyir Lake

Mount Bewek (947m)

Mount Gagau (1376m)

Mount Beldai (854m)

Kuala Chamir
Aur

Tembeling River

Mount Dutong (1063m)

Kg. Landang

Pettang River

Melinau River

Kuala Klapor

Kenyiam River

Mount Penumpu (1096m)

Kuala Perkai

Kuala Keniam
Kepayang Besar
Bumbun Kumbang
Kuala Trenggan

Abai Waterfall

Tekal River

64 & Jerantut

Lebir River

Kuala Koh

Perkal Lodge

Park HQ

Mount Warisan

Kuala Tahan

Sungai Tiang Airstrip

1508

Koh River

Mount Perlis (1279m)

Trenggan River
Kuala Teku

Putih Camp
Melantai Camp
Lata Berkoh

Telinga Cave

Kuala Atok

Kg. Kemara

Four Steps Waterfall

Wray's Camp

Tahan River

Kemah Yong

Guling

Rentis Tenor Trail

Tembeling Jetty

Kg. Geno

G.Tahan Trail

Tenor River

Gendang Hill (570m)

Arring River

Relai River

Chiku River

Simpang Aring

Mount Tahan (2187m)
Mount Gedong (2065m)

Mount Lubu Kechau (1946m)

Padang Camp

Tumpat Cave

Hulu Kelir Hill (773m)

Atok River

Jerantut

Kota Bharu

Peningat Hill (715m)

Siput Cave

Batu Lompat

Kechau River

KENONG RIMBA

Mount Kesong (580m)

Jelai River

Kota Bharu

Kuala Juram

Jurdih River

Menara
Bukit Seraya

Mount Rabong Sinting (1539m)

Bumbun Rimau

Gajah Cave

Kg. Toh

Tujoh Hill (867m)

Kuala Lipis

Dabong

Gua Musang

Merapoh

Tanum River

Padang Tengku

Cameron Highlands

PLANNING A VISIT TO TAMAN NEGARA

Given that tropical rainforest is always sodden, the **driest** time of year is between February and mid-October, with the **peak tourist season** roughly from May to August – make sure you book ahead. Mid-November to mid-January is extremely **wet**, and movement within the park can be restricted as paths are submerged and rivers flood. Usually, however, most of the park's **trails** require no more than an average level of fitness, though of course longer trails require some stamina. Some essential **camping and trekking gear** is available to buy at Jerantut (see p.195), or to rent at Kuala Tahan, but take your own if possible.

Campsites are scattered through the park; they have absolutely no facilities at all, though most are close to rivers where you can wash. There's a small fee for hides and campsites (see below), payable at the national park office, where you can also reserve bunks in hides.

To **budget** for your trip, remember that for any trek involving overnighting in the forest (other than in a hide close to a park office or accessible by boat), you must hire a guide. It's generally more cost-effective to arrange guides through external operators than through the park headquarters, although the latter may be preferable if you would like a guide with a particular area of expertise. The fees for guides and boat excursions are the only substantial outlays you'll face, as inexpensive accommodation, eating and transport options are easy to find.

FEES AND CHARGES

The following fees apply to all sections of Taman Negara:

Park entry	RM1/person
Camping permit	RM1/person/night
Photography Permit	RM5/camera
Fishing licence (for Kenyam only)	RM10/rod
Use of hides or fishing lodges	RM5/person
Guide hire	RM180–250/day, plus RM60 for overnight

GETTING AROUND THE PARK

If you simply need to **cross the river** from Kuala Tahan, you can take one of the small wooden boats (daily dawn–11pm; RM1) that cross on demand from Kuala Tahan's floating restaurants to the jetty below the resort and national park headquarters. Put your fare in the tin by the ferryman.

Aside from trekking, **wooden longboats** seating four to ten people are the only way to get around Taman Negara from Kuala Tahan; you can use them like a taxi service to reach distant trekking trails, or speed your return journey after a long hike. Boats might wait for you or, more likely, return at an agreed time; don't expect them to hang around indefinitely if you are late. Book through the national park office; prices are the same for single or return trips.

Destination	Cost	Destination	Cost
Blau/Yong hides	RM80	Lata Berkoh	RM160
Canopy walkway	RM60	Lubok Lesong	RM100
Kuala Keniam	RM350/450	Nusa Camp	RM90
Kuala Trenggan	RM120	Tabing/Cegar Anjing hides	RM60

Kota Gelanggi Cave Complex

10km east of Jerantut's city centre, along the main road to Maran • Daily 9am–5.30pm • RM5; guides RM45/person, minimum four people

Most travellers zip from Jerantut to Taman Negara, neglecting this remarkable limestone cave complex. A handful of the ten or so caves, including **Tongkat**, Terang Bulan and **Balai**, are scattered along the paved road that starts from the park's entrance. You will need a guide to hike further into the jungle to **Elephant's Head Cave**, a small tunnel that leads to the tiny **Portrait Cave**. The curious rock formation on the upper right-hand side of the rock face here resembles a female figure in the pose of Leonardo da Vinci's *Mona Lisa*. Hiking for another fifteen minutes brings you to a clearing with six empty archaeological digs and the entrance to **Wind Cave**, taking its name from its gale-battered upper chamber. Once inside, you reach the last two hollows, **Elephant** and **Wedding Cave** (Gua Sanding). It's actually a single hall divided into two chambers, each with its own rock formation shaped in the guise of an elephant, and of two human figures seated

JERANTUT

EATING
RS Café	1
Restoran Wan	
Chai Kok	2
Sayed Mohd. Aziz	3

ACCOMMODATION
Chong Heng Backpackers'	5
Greenleaf Travellers' Inn	2
Sakura Castle Inn	3
Sri Emas	4
WAU Hotel & Café	1

next to each other. From March to October, the sunlight that comes in through the huge hole in the chambers' ceiling casts spectacular light beams on the cave floor.

You can visit Kota Gelanggi independently, but hiring a guide from the **NKS** office on Jalan Besar in Jerantut saves you the hassle of organizing transportation and finding the park's elusive ticket seller.

ARRIVAL AND DEPARTURE   JERANTUT

By train Jerantut is on the Jungle Railway (see box, p.204) but both daily departures – south to Johor Bahru, at 2.21am, and north to Tumpat, at 4.23am – travel through the scenic jungle sections in the dead of night.

Destinations Dabong (1 daily; 5hr 20min); Gua Musang (1 daily; 3hr 20min); Johor Bahru (1 daily; 8hr 30min); Kuala Lipis (1 daily; 1hr 30min); Gemas (for Kuala Lumpur; 1 daily; 4hr 20min); Wakaf Bharu (for Kota Bharu; 1 daily; 8hr).

By bus The new bus station is a 5min walk northwest of the Keris roundabout at the upper end of Jalan Besar. To catch the daily 6.30pm bus to Ipoh, Butterworth, Alor Star and Kangar you must travel first to Jengka Sentral and change bus there. For Tembeling Jetty, take a bus towards Kuala Lipis and ask to

be let off near the jetty, or use the backpacker minivans leaving from NKS Café (RM10/person). NKS also runs daily departures to Cameron Highlands (60RM) and Kuala Besut jetty for the Perhentian islands (RM70).

Destinations Jengka (7 daily; 1hr); Kota Bharu (1 daily at 9.30pm; 8hr); Kuala Lipis (3 daily; 1hr 30min); Kuala Lumpur (hourly 7am–7pm; 3hr 30min); Kuala Tahan (3 daily 8am, 1pm & 5pm; 1hr 45min); Kuala Terengganu (Mon at 5pm, Thurs at 8.30am & 5pm, Fri–Sun at 7.30pm; 3hr 10min); Kuantan (2–3 daily; 3hr).

By taxi Taxis from the bus station run to Tembeling Jetty (RM26), Kuala Tahan (RM70) and various east coast destinations; it's RM200 to Kuantan, or RM440 to Kota Bharu.

By boat Boating up to Kuala Tahan on the muddy Tembeling River in motorized ten-seater sampans is an essential part of the Taman Negara experience, though you may prefer to take the faster return trip downstream. Boats to Kuala Tahan (daily at 2pm; 2hr 30min; RM45 one-way) depart from Tembeling Jetty, 17km north of Jerantut; catch NKS minivan (RM10) or taxi (RM30). Tickets can be purchased at NKS in Jerantut or the NKS and Han Travel desks at the jetty.

ACCOMMODATION

Chong Heng Backpackers' Jalan Besar ☎013 963 6019; map p.194. This simple hostel, in a converted 1930s shophouse, is a little scruffier than it used to be. Nonetheless, the partitioned rooms and shared facilities are decent, and the owner, Tan, is a great source of information on the area. No wi-fi. RM20

Greenleaf Travellers' Inn Jalan Diwangsa ☎09 267 2131, ⌨greenleaf-tamannegara.com; map p.194. A homely backpackers' place, with dorm beds and a variety of unexciting rooms with a/c and shared bathrooms. They also run package tours into the park, and non-guests can shower and get online for RM3/person. 🛜 Dorms RM15, doubles RM35

★ **Sakura Castle Inn** S1 & S2 Jalan Bomba ☎09 266 6200; map p.194. Over the road from the post office, this reliable mid-range option has spacious and clean a/c en-suite rooms in a central location. The best value in Jerantut. 🛜 RM60

Sri Emas 46 Jalan Besar ☎09 266 4499, ⌨taman-negara-nks.com; map p.194. Part of the NKS empire, *Sri Emas* offers dorms (actually just shared twin rooms) and simple and cheap private rooms with fan or a/c, some en suite and with TV. Everything's well run, with laundry service and wi-fi (lobby only), but most rooms were in dire need of a repaint at the time of research. 🛜 Dorms RM15, doubles RM35

WAU Hotel & Café Pusat Perniagaan Sungai Jan ☎09 260 2255, ⌨wauhotels.com; map p.194. The closest Jerantut comes to a boutique hotel, *WAU* has fourteen squeaky-clean, modern en-suite rooms with TVs, plus a café in the lobby. It's a 15min walk from the bus station: walk 500m east, take the third road on the left, and continue straight for another 600m. 🛜 RM65

EATING

During the day, open-air **food courts** serve inexpensive pan-Asian dishes either side of the train station access road. To stock up on supplies for the park, try Aktif supermarket on Jalan Diwangsa.

RS Café Jalan Stesen ☎09 266 1230; map p.194. This cool little Chinese-run café serves up the standard range of noodle and rice dishes (RM5–8), with ice-based desserts and a range of beers on tap (from RM9). Daily 2pm–1am.

Restoran Wan Chai Kok Jalan Stesen ☎019 911 5720; map p.194. Local Chinese restaurant specializing in Pahang's river fish, such as the popular *ikan patin*, *gahak* and *baung* (RM75–95/kg). Closed every other Thurs. Daily 5pm–12.30am.

Sayed Mohd. Aziz Jalan Besar; map p.194. Decent *roti canai*, curries and *nasi lemak*, all for under RM10. Daily breakfast & dinner.

DIRECTORY

Banks There are banks with ATMs along Jalan Tahan and Jalan Dulang 1.

Camping and hiking gear Numerous stores on Jalan Diwangsa sell day packs, rubber shoes, canvas track shoes and flashlights; check the quality before buying, especially stitching and straps on packs.

Pharmacy Jalan Tahan holds two well-stocked pharmacies.

Kuala Tahan

Around 70km north of Jerantut, **KUALA TAHAN** is a knot of guesthouses and floating restaurants facing a solid green wall of jungle across the turbid, 50m-wide **Tembeling River**. As a base, it has many virtues: reasonable transport connections, plenty of accommodation, a few stores selling (and renting) basics, and even mobile coverage, though there are **no banks or ATMs**. Most importantly, the **national park headquarters** – where you can pick up information, register and pay park fees – is a quick ferry ride over the river at the start of the park's **hiking trails**. Take a torch when wandering around the village after dark, as **electricity** can be flaky.

ARRIVAL AND DEPARTURE   KUALA TAHAN

By bus Buses drop at a roadside shelter on the edge of Kuala Tahan, a 5min walk from the river. Buses return to Jerantut three times a day (10am, 3pm & 6.30pm; 1hr 45min).

KUALA TAHAN

■ ACCOMMODATION
Abot Guesthouse	7
Durian Chalet	3
Han Rainforest Resort	8
I Am Wild Travellers	2
Mahseer Chalet	4
Mutiara Taman Negara Resort	1
Rainbow Guesthouse	5
Tahan Guesthouse	6
Xcape Resort	9

● EATING
Family	2
Mama Chop	3
Seri Mutiara	1

By minibus Several tour operators run minibuses between Kuala Tahan and regional tourist destinations. Prices vary little between operators, usually with a single morning departure. Destinations George Town (9hr; RM130); Ipoh (7hr30min; RM120); Jerantut (1hr 30min; RM25); Kota Bharu (8hr; RM100); Kuala Besut (for Perhentian islands; 7hr; RM95 or RM165 including boat ticket); Kuala Lumpur (5hr; RM75); Mersing (for Tioman Island; 8hr; RM95); Tanah Rata (for Cameron Highlands; 6hr; RM85).

By boat Arriving boats deposit passengers at the park jetty, where steps lead up to the sprawling *Mutiara Taman Negara Resort* and park headquarters, or among the floating restaurants on the shingle beach opposite, with Kuala Tahan village on the bank above. Tickets downstream to Tembeling (1 daily 9am; RM45) can be purchased the day before your journey at the Han Travel (*Mama Chop Restaurant*) or NKS (*Wan Café*) jetties. Once at the Tembeling Jetty, catch a bus, minibus (RM10) or taxi (RM30) to Jerantut.

THE KUALA GANDAH ELEPHANT SANCTUARY

One attraction in the southern interior worth making a diversion for is the **Kuala Gandah Elephant Conservation Centre** (daily 8am–1pm & 2.30–4.30pm; donations appreciated; ☎ 013 908 8207, ⓦ bit.ly/KualaGanda). Here, staff from the Wildlife Department care for elephants being relocated to reserves from areas of habitat destruction, or which had to be sedated while *mengamuk* – a Malay term that would be untranslatable were it not the origin of the English word "amok". The best time to turn up is 2pm (2.45pm on Fri), when for a couple of hours visitors have the chance to get hands-on with the elephants, feeding or bathing them. Numbers are limited for bathing, though it's possible to book your spot (RM30 guide fee/group, plus RM10/participant) up to three days in advance. The centre gets very crowded on weekends and holidays – visit midweek if possible.

If you're **driving** from KL via Route E8 (east), turn north at **Lanchang**, about 70km along, for the twenty-minute drive to the sanctuary. **Day-trips** are offered from Kuala Lumpur by NKS (ⓦ taman-negara-nks.com) and Han Travel (ⓦ taman-negara.com); and **from Jerantut** through Greenleaf Holidays (RM160/person; ⓦ greenleaf-tamannegara.com).

TAMAN NEGARA PACKAGES

Besides a few short trails looping around the park headquarters, going anywhere beyond Bukit Indah requires hiring a guide, and thus many visitors prefer booking themselves on a convenient **package trip**. These typically comprise two or three nights at Kuala Tahan with a range of accommodation and meal options, and possibly activities such as walks and boat excursions as well; expect to pay upwards of RM350/person.

The most established operators, **NKS** (Ⓦtaman-negara-nks.com) and **Han Travel** (Ⓦtaman-negara.com), have offices in KL, Jerantut and at the Tembeling Jetty. Both have dedicated restaurants in Kuala Tahan, and NKS also runs the *Sri Emas Hotel* in Jerantut. Jerantut-based agents include **Danz Travel** (Ⓦdanzecoresort.com) and **Greenleaf Holidays** (Ⓦgreenleaf-tamannegara.com).

If you're using one of the expensive but convenient minibus **transfers** to Kuala Tahan, your journey will typically feature a stop at the tour company offices. Despite what you may be told, there's no need to book park accommodation or day-trips through the same company; simply shop around once you've arrived or call ahead.

3

By car The road to Kuala Tahan, Route 1508, branches north off Route 64 10km east of Jerantut. From KL, leave the East Coast Highway at Temerloh, heading up Route 98 for Jerantut, then pick up Route 64 eastwards for the Kuala Tahan Road. From Kuantan, pick up Route 64 at Maran.

INFORMATION

National Park Headquarters Stopping here, just north of the main park jetty, is an essential first port of call to pay the nominal entry fee, pick up a map and check the latest trail conditions (Mon–Thurs, Sat & Sun 8am–6pm, Fri 8am–noon & 3–6pm; ☎09 266 1122, Ⓦwildlife.gov.my). You can also book hides and activity packages, charter boats and hire guides. Make sure you check the whiteboard, where the odd sightings of interesting creatures are listed; there are about fifty tigers in Taman Negara, with some three or four sightings per year, usually deep in the forest (many national park staff have never seen one).

Guides If you have a specialist interest, call the headquarters a week in advance to see if a guide with matching knowledge can be arranged. Trained by the Wildlife Department, the guides are generally better on fauna than flora, though many are experts on neither. They know the trails, but may fall short when it comes to more general skills, such as offering support in the event of a mishap.

ACCOMMODATION

Almost all accommodation is in the village of Kuala Tahan itself, with the exception of the *Mutiara* resort on the opposite bank. Book in advance, especially during the peak season (May–Aug). Should you wish to **overnight in the forest**, the best option is to use one of five **hides** (see box, p.202); these sleep up to twelve people in bare wooden bunks (bring your own bedding), and some have tank water and toilets.

Abot Guesthouse At the top of the hill from the bus stop ☎017 916 9616, Ⓦfacebook.com/AbotGH; map p.196. Low-set house with ten cosy en-suite rooms in two blocks, all with a/c. Light sleepers should avoid rooms facing the road from the bus stop. 🛜 **RM90**

★ **Durian Chalet** A 5min walk past Tahan Guesthouse, down a steep hill and through a small stand of rubber trees ☎012 9496 630; map p.196. Double rooms and chalets with mosquito nets and shack-like bathrooms, clustered around a pretty hillside garden with a teeming fishpond – a great place to get away from it all. Breakfast available (extra). Doubles 🛜 **RM40**, chalets **RM50**

Han Rainforest Resort 300m down the road from X-Cape Resort ☎09 266 7888, Ⓦhan-rainforestresort.com; map p.196. Han Tours' efforts to accommodate both backpackers and package tourists under the same roof produced this one-size-fits-all concrete monster. There are three sections: a budget block with dorms and doubles, a zone with spacious yet cookie-cutter standards (RM180), and a wing with superior en-suites (RM250). The airy common area packs a lot of travellers, busy enjoying Kuala Tahan's fastest wi-fi. Dorms 🛜 **RM35**, doubles **RM90**

I Am Wild Travellers On the river road ☎016 989 3588, Ⓦfacebook.com/IAmWildTravellers; map p.196. Newly refurbished backpacker place with twenty-odd beds in fan rooms overlooking the river, all with plush mattresses, free wi-fi and hot showers. The hostel runs its own treks, tours and onward minivan transport. The balcony is a popular evening hangout, with occasional live music. 🛜 Dorms **RM25**

Mahseer Chalet Walk left from the main view deck and beyond the kindergarten ☎019 383 2633, Ⓦfacebook.com/MahseerChalet; map p.196. Good

3

value rooms and dorms in chalets set around an open-air cafeteria facing the quieter bend of the river. Breakfast included. 🛜 Dorms RM25, doubles RM90

★**Mutiara Taman Negara Resort** In front of the national park headquarters, across the river from Kuala Tahan ☏ 09 266 2200, 🌐 mutiaratamannegara.com; map p.196. Busy three-star resort occupying a strip of land between the river and forest, mostly comprising a/c chalets with spacious bathrooms, woven bamboo walls, cane furniture and jungle or river views. There's also an expensive, institutional dorm with bunk beds. Boat transfers to and from Tembeling can be arranged for a fee. Buffet breakfast included. 🛜 Dorm RM80, chalets RM340

Rainbow Guesthouse Next to Mahseer Chalet ☏ 017 9115 473; map p.196. A handful of homely and clean rainbow-coloured en-suite twins and doubles, set inside a Malay household, that offer a relaxing peek into Kuala Tahan's daily life. 🛜 RM80

★**Tahan Guesthouse** By the mosque ☏ 017 970 2025;

map p.196. This 20-year-old stalwart is a well-kept two-storey affair, brightly painted with wildlife murals, and set in a relaxing child-friendly garden where hornbills come to snag fruit. Accommodation comprises en-suite twins and doubles, all fan-cooled with mosquito nets and squat toilets; the double rooms have small balconies. The only downside is the morning call to prayer from the mosque at 5.30am. Walk uphill from the bus stop, following the main road for about 50m; turn right after the mini market, continue past the police station, and it's 3min along on the right. RM40

Xcape Resort Just south of Kuala Tahan ☏ 09 266 1111, 🌐 xcapetamannegara.com; map p.196. One of a handful of incongruous developments in this area, *Xcape* offers a pool, regimented rows of chalets with characterless but comfortable rooms – featuring a/c, TV, fridge and modern bathroom – and Kuala Tahan's cleanest and best-value four-person dorms. That said, the dorms are way out at the back of a field, an off-putting trek from the wi-fi-equipped lobby. Breakfast is RM30 extra. 🛜 Dorms RM30, chalets RM240

EATING

Most visitors gravitate towards the row of ten or so floating, glorified **kedai kopis** moored beside the shingle beach. Opening around 8am and not closing until well into the evening, the restaurants offer the usual rice and noodle dishes, plus

---

KUALA TAHAN ACTIVITIES

Most people who are in the park for just a few days sign up for various **activity packages** offered through Kuala Tahan guesthouses and tour operators. Many operators work together – you might book onto one company's trip, only to find yourself tagging along with another (often larger) group – if in doubt, clarify before you book.

SHORT TRIPS

Night jungle walks (1hr 30min; RM30). Easy and, despite being crowded and taking place along the park's most heavily used paths, can turn up everything from tapirs to scorpions; the sharp-eyed guides invariably spot camouflaged creatures you'd otherwise miss. Bring a torch.
Night safaris (2hr; RM45). These actually take place outside the park; you're driven around a plantation in a 4WD, and may get to see leopard cats, wild pigs, civets and the occasional snake.
Orang Asli village visit (2hr; RM45). Shows you how to use a blowpipe and fire-making using sticks at a semi-permanent Batek encampment; very touristy, but interesting too.

RIVER TRIPS AND FISHING

Rapids shooting trips (2hr; RM40). Taking place a few kilometres upstream, these are fairly tame, designed to appeal to families rather than hard-core rafters; you'll ride this stretch anyway if you catch a boat back from Kuala Trenggan (see p.202).
Night river safaris (2hr; RM60). Trips are run on a tamer stretch of water, where you often see larger animals along the riverside.
Fishing The most popular area is along the Keniam River, northeast of Kuala Tahan, where you can hope to catch catfish or snakehead; all fish must be returned. The very basic *Perkai Fishing Lodge*, around 2hr upstream from Kuala Tahan, is a popular base; a boat there costs RM480, and 2D/3N packages including transport, guide and meals RM1500.

LONGER TRIPS

Guided forest walks The best operators arrange for you to stay overnight at a hide – Bumbun Kumbang is a favourite (see p.202) or cave; you usually make your way down to the river on the second day and catch a boat back to Kuala Tahan. Prices depend on numbers, duration and destination, but expect to pay at least RM200/person for an all-inclusive two-day, one-night trip.

PICKING UP TREKKING GEAR AND SUPPLIES

CAMPING AND TREKKING GEAR
Mat Leon's floating store (daily 9am–6pm) rents out well-worn sleeping bags and mats, canvas jungle boots, tents, mosquito nets, backpacks, flashlights and gas stoves. **Minimarts** around town sell torches, batteries, rubber ankle boots and day packs; a few places near the bus stop sell dry bags.

SUPPLIES
Kuala Tahan's **minimarts** (roughly daily 8am–10pm) sell water, biscuits and snacks, tinned sardines, soft drinks, ice cream, insect repellent and toothpaste. Across the river, the only store is a pricey one attached to the *Mutiara Taman Negara Resort*.

Western travellers' favourites including pancakes, sandwiches and milk shakes. The establishments we review are the most popular, but other places often serve similar food at lower cost. If you're in need of a drink, you could try the bar in the *Xcape Resort* car park; alcohol is also served at the *Seri Mutiara*.

3

Family On the river; map p. 196. With its view of the river, bamboo blinds and potted orchids, it's easy to see why this place is constantly packed with tourists. They don't like solo diners, however, especially in the evening, and staff can be quite abrupt. Mains RM10. Daily 8am–2pm & 6–9pm.

Mama Chop On the river; map p. 196. Housing the Han Travel headquarters means that *Mama Chop* has a captive audience of visitors waiting to begin tours, enabling them to charge high prices for average food and lacklustre service. Though it's open all day, it can be hard to get served outside main meal times. Mains around RM10. Daily 8am–9pm.

★Seri Mutiara Beside the Mutiara resort ☏09 266 2200, ⓦmutiarahotels.com; map p. 196. This smart, open-sided dining room in the jungle is well worth a splurge if you've been out in the wilds for a few days. The menu is geared to Taman Negara's better-heeled Malay and Western guests – pizza, *nasi lemak*, prawn *sambal*, T-bone steak, *rendang* – and the relatively steep prices reflect this, though a coffee and slice of black forest gateau will set you back RM40 or so. Around RM85/100 for a full meal. Daily 8am–2pm & 6–9pm.

Day treks

Cross the river and turn right at the national park headquarters, and you're at the start of most of the **hiking trails** that spread into the park. Popular and easy places to visit close to the park headquarters include **Bukit Teresek**; the **canopy walkway**, where you can observe treetop jungle life close up; and the waterfall at **Lata Berkoh** (following the first part of the trail there is a good way to kill a couple of spare hours). You could feasibly tackle two, perhaps three, of these in a day, and none of them require a guide.

Bukit Teresek
2.5km one-way from the park headquarters; 1hr

Although it's the most heavily used trail in the park, the route to the summit of **Bukit Teresek** (342m) is an excellent starter trek, taking about an hour in each direction along a boardwalk. Heading northeast away from the river, the trail passes an impressive stand of **giant bamboo** before ascending Bukit Teresek itself via a steep series of fibreglass **steps**; if you haven't already noticed the sauna-like conditions, you will now. The clanking of your shoes against the fibreglass is enough to scare off most wildlife, so content yourself with the promise of views – though the clearing at the top is partially screened by trees. Continue along the hilltop for another fifteen minutes to reach the so-called **second view**, where on clear days you can get marvellous vistas north over the valley to 2187m-high **Mount Tahan** (see p.205) and smaller Mount Gedong. Return the way you came and the canopy walkway will be just 300m to the south along a clearly marked path, or make the more challenging descent from the second view to the side of the Tahan River, from where you can loop back to the park headquarters (3km; 1hr 30min).

Canopy walkway

Mon–Thurs, Sat & Sun 9.30am–3.00pm, Fri 9am–noon; closed during rain or if lightning is likely; numbers are limited, so waits possible • RM5

About thirty-minute walk from the national park office along the boardwalk, the **canopy walkway** is one of Taman Negara's highlights – though it's better for views down over the canopy to the Tembeling River than wildlife spotting. You climb a sturdy wooden tower and step out, 30m above the forest floor, onto a 330m-long swaying aluminium bridge, anchored to some suitably placed, 250-year-old *tualang* trees. Animals you may well see include the grey-banded leaf monkey, with a call that sounds like a rattling tin can, and the white-eyed dusky leaf monkey, with its deep, nasal "ha-haw" cry. At the end, you return to terra firma by another wooden stairwell.

Bukit Indah

3.5km from the park headquarters; 2hr

The route to **Bukit Indah** follows the boardwalk as far as the canopy walkway, before continuing along a rougher trail towards Kuala Trenggan and Bumbun Kumbang. After about 3km you'll see a signposted path leading to a 500m scramble. Use the fixed ropes to haul yourself up to the top of Bukit Indah, and enjoy views over the Tembeling River.

Kemah Keladong

5km from the park headquarters; 3hr

In the quiet **Kemah Keladong** area, 5km downriver from Kuala Tahan on the far side of the Tembeling River, trails link the Blau and Yong **hides** with a **campsite** at Kemah Keladong. They can be tackled either by catching a boat to drop-off points for the hides (15–20min), or by crossing by sampan to a trailhead just up the Tahan River from Kuala Tahan and hiking – in which case, allow a full day for the return trip. A major attraction of this route used to be **Telinga Cave**, but the cave – home to thousands of tiny **roundleaf bats** – has been off-limits since a roof collapse in 2013.

HIKING FROM KUALA TAHAN

The shortest hiking trails from Kuala Tahan are clearly signposted and easy to follow, but to go any distance beyond Bukit Indah, hiring a guide is compulsory. Exposed to the elements and the passage of migrating elephant herds, the trails quickly deteriorate into slippery tangles of roots and leaf litter. If you're moderately fit, the hiking **time estimates** given out by the park authorities (and in the text of this Guide) are pretty reliable; expect to average 2km/hour.

Even on the very simple day hikes, you should **inform** park staff of your plans so they know where to look if you get into difficulty. You won't be able to phone for help, as the mobile phone signal dies out just a little way from Kuala Tahan. Perhaps the most important advice is to **know your limitations** and not run out of time. Slipping and sliding along in the dark is no fun and can be dangerous – thus, if you start hiking **after 4pm**, you will still need a guide even before Bukit Indah.

Don't be paranoid about encountering large **wildlife** – in fact, you could count yourself very lucky if you do, as most animals don't hang around after they hear you coming. Unfortunately, there's almost no way you can avoid getting bitten by a few **leeches**, whose numbers increase dramatically after rain; there are a few general guidelines, however, on keeping them at bay (see p.45).

3

From the turn-off to Telinga Cave the trail continues for another 2km through beautiful tall forest, past the **Yong** and **Blau hides**, to where the trail divides. North is the track to Kemah Rentis (see p.206), while southeast it's just 500m to the tranquil **Kemah Keladong campsite** on the terraced bank of the Yong River. With an early start, it's possible to reach this point, have a swim in the river and get back before dusk.

Lata Berkoh

8.5km; 4hr from the park headquarters; a guide is compulsory if not travelling directly by boat • Return boat trip RM160

Most visitors catch a boat (at least in one direction) to the roaring rapids of **Lata Berkoh**, around 8.5km up the Tahan River; the return trip is a long way to walk in a day, and if water levels are high you may face a swim across the river near the end.

The trail from the park headquarters leads gently downhill. About fifteen minutes on is an excellent swimming spot, **Lubok Simpon**, a deep pool in the Tahan River next to a pebbled beach. After another 2km you pass the turning for **Bumbun Tabing** and then, 5km from the park headquarters, the **Lubok Lesong** campsite. The route to the waterfall veers west from the main trail, crossing gullies and steep ridges before reaching the river, which must be forded. The final part of the trail runs up the west side of the Tahan River, passing the simple **Berkoh Lodge**, a small shelter in a clearing and a **campsite** before reaching the falls.

The **waterfall** itself drops into a deep pool with surprisingly clear water for swimming (tread carefully around the large rocks on the river bed). You can picnic here, too, overlooking the swirling water. Keep eyes peeled for kingfishers with their yellow-and-red wings and white beaks; large grey-and-green fish eagles; and, on the rocks, camouflaged monitor lizards.

Overnight trips

There are a number of possible guided **overnight trips**. The 24km-long, two-to three-day trail northeast of Kuala Tahan to **Kuala Keniam** involves overnighting in the jungle, either at **Bumbun Kumbang** or one of several **caves**, with the chance of seeing large animals, after which you could organize a **boat** back to base, rather than having to retrace your steps. If you're pushed for time or simply not so dedicated, hiking as far as Bumbun Kumbang (12km), staying the night there, then taking the alternative return trail – or again, catching a boat – is an excellent compromise. Note that you need to arrange any **boat transfers** before you head out, and that **guides** are compulsory.

KUALA TAHAN HIDES (BLINDS)

Spending a night in one of the park's **hides** (known as **bumbuns**) doesn't guarantee sightings of large mammals, especially in the dry season when the **salt licks** – where plant-eating animals come to supplement their mineral intake – are often so waterless that there's little reason for deer, tapir, elephant, leopard or seladang to visit, but it's an experience you're unlikely to forget. It's best to go in a group and take turns keeping watch, listening hard and occasionally shining a **torch** at the salt lick – if an animal is present its eyes will reflect brightly in the beam.

Kuala Tahan's five hides are covered in the hiking trail accounts in this Guide. We have also listed details of costs and time-saving boat rides to/from the hides (see box, p.193).

Trails to Bumbun Kumbang

10–12km from the park headquarters; 5–7hr hike, depending on route • Boat to Kuala Tahan (45min) RM120

Both the two **trails to Bumbun Kumbang** are fairly damp and muddy. The longer, flatter, easier route initially follows the Lata Berkoh Trail (see p.201), then arcs northeast to the narrow **Trenggan River** – which has to be waded across, and may be impassable after heavy rain – beyond which you're just 1km from the hide.

The tougher, more direct route follows the Tembeling River upstream past the Bukit Indah turn-off (see p.200), crossing numerous **creeks**, each involving a steep, slippery descent and clamber up the far side. Eventually things settle down, and you will see a permanent settlement of the **Batek** people after crossing the small Trenggan River **bridge**. The path seems to peter out on the far side, but keep going and you soon come to a definite junction. Turn left and Bumbun Kumbang is a thirty-minute walk; right, and it's 1km to **Kuala Trenggan**, where some broken-down wooden cabins overlook the confluence of the Tembeling and Trenggan rivers.

Bumbun Kumbang

Book bunks through the park headquarters

Raised high off the ground on concrete posts, the **Bumbun Kumbang** hide sits at the edge of a clearing, about 200m from a natural **salt lick** that attracts animals at wetter times of the year. As always, seeing anything is down to luck, though scan the muddy trails nearby and you'll often find three-toed tapir prints. Carrying binoculars and a powerful torch is a good idea.

Bumbun Kumbang to Kuala Keniam

8km one-way, 4–5hr

The superb hike between Bumbun Kumbang and Kuala Keniam forms the basis of most tour operators' shortest overnight treks, and combines the real possibility of seeing **elephants** with visits to three **caves**, one of which is big enough for an army to camp in. The trail is slow going, even in drier conditions, with innumerable streams to wade through, hills to circumvent and trees blocking the path. Most groups take two days, typically hiking this route in reverse and overnighting at **Kempayang Besar**.

Limestone caves

From Bumbun Kumbang, it takes around three hours on a boggy trail before you enter limestone cave country, first reaching **Kepayang Kecil**. A line of fig trees here drops a curtain of roots down the rock, behind which lies a small chamber, with a slightly larger one to the right, containing stalactites and stalagmites. A short way on is much larger **Kepayang Besar**, where the huge chamber at the eastern side of the outcrop makes an excellent place to spend the night, especially as you can dispense with tents. Despite its popularity with trekkers (on public holidays, the cave can see upwards of a hundred people overnighting here), civets and leopard cats are often seen after dark.

3

THE JUNGLE RAILWAY

Riding the scenic **Jungle Railway** used to be one of Peninsular Malaysia's highlights and the best way to reach or leave Taman Negara. Sadly, in December 2014 the route – officially the less romantic "Sektor Timur–Selatan" (East–South Route) – was damaged by severe floods. Since resuming in 2016, the limited services are no longer convenient either for seeing the jungle or reaching Taman Negara.

Nonetheless, the Jungle Railway maintains great historical significance: it took indentured Tamil labourers eight years to build the line's 500km-long section from **Gemas**, southeast of KL, to **Tumpat**, on the northeast coast near Kota Bharu. The first section from Gemas to Kuala Lipis opened in 1920, with the full extent of the line following in 1931. Initially it was used exclusively for freight – tin and rubber, and later oil palm – until a passenger service, originally known as the "Golden Blowpipe", opened in 1938. At the time of writing, only two daily **overnight trains** make the complete 700km journey between Johor Bahru and Kota Bharu, travelling mostly in the dead of night. Southbound ERT27 leaves Wakaf Bharu at 6.18pm, stops in Jerantut at 2.21am, and reaches Kota Bharu at 11.10am. Northbound ERT26 leaves Johor Bahru at 7pm, stops in Jerantut at 4.23am, and arrives in Wakaf Bharu at 12.37pm. The northbound train is the best option for jungle views, as it travels for six hours in daylight between Merapoh and Wakaf Bharu – arguably the most pristine sector of the line. Note that by virtue of its existence, the line doesn't pass through virgin jungle; much of the route is flanked by regrowth forest and belukar woodland, as well as plantations of rubber, pepper and oil palm. None of this is to detract from the fact that as a way to encounter **rural life**, a ride on the jungle train can't be beaten, giving you the chance to take in backwater scenery in the company of cheroot-smoking old men in sarongs, and fast-talking women hauling kids, poultry and vegetables to and from the nearest market.

The best way to reach **Jerantut from Taman Negara** via some jungle views is to catch southbound train SH57 from Wakaf Bharu (2.19pm), alight at Gua Musang (8.30pm), and immediately board the connecting train to Kuala Lipis (arrival 11.07pm). Continue by bus to Jerantut the next day.

Buy **tickets** at the station (you shouldn't need to book in advance except on express services during school holidays) or through KTM's website (ⓦ www.ktmb.com.my) and Easybook (ⓦ easybook.com). Don't expect luxury: the Jungle Railway's rolling stock is worn and fairly ordinary, with several classes of simple sleepers and seats available on all routes. Check current schedules at KTM's website before you set off.

Fifteen minutes north are **Luas Cave** and more impressive **Daun Menari Cave** ("Cave of the Dancing Leaves"), a breezy chamber inhabited by thousands of roundleaf bats.

Kuala Keniam

Once beyond the limestone band, the rest of the route to **Kuala Keniam** passes through a meranti forest of tall, straight trees with distinctive reddish-brown bark, much prized as timber. Finally, you reach the river at Kuala Keniam, where there's a **campsite** and **jetty** for boats back to Kuala Tahan (RM300).

Longer trails

For the two major **long-distance hiking trails** at Taman Negara, you'll need to hire guides and bring full camping and trekking gear, including food, cooking equipment and water-purifying tablets. The four-day **Mount Tahan Trail**, undoubtedly the toughest in the park, culminates in the ascent of Peninsular Malaysia's highest peak, after which you have to hike out again, perhaps via the alternative, shorter trail to Merapoh (see p.210); you'll definitely need sleeping bags for a couple of nights spent at altitude. The other option is the three-to-four-day **Tenor Trail**, a lasso-shaped trek leading west from Kuala Tahan to Telinga Cave, then northwest to the campsite on the Tenor River. Either way, expect to see plenty of jungle, and to get soaked during river crossings and rain; allow a day extra either side of the trek to sort out arrangements.

Mount Tahan Trail
55km one-way, nine-day return from Kuala Tahan • Book in advance

To the Batek Orang Asli, **Mount Tahan** – Peninsular Malaysia's highest peak at 2187m – is the Forbidden Mountain, its summit the home of a vast monkey, who stands guard over magic stones. Though the Batek rarely venture beyond the foothills, ascending Mount Tahan is the highlight of any adventurous visitor's stay in Taman Negara. Although hundreds complete the trail every year, the sense of individual achievement after tackling the innumerable river crossings, steep hills and nights camping in the jungle – let alone the arduous ascent – is supreme.

Days 1–2
The **first day** involves an easy six-hour walk from Kuala Tahan to **Melantai**, the campsite on the east bank of the Tahan River, not far from Lata Berkoh. On the **second day** more ground is covered, the route taking eight hours and crossing 27 hills, including a long trudge up Bukit Malang ("Unlucky Hill"). This section culminates at **Mount Rajah** (576m), before descending to the Puteh River, a tiny tributary of the Tahan. Before the campsite at **Kuala Teku** you'll ford the Tahan half a dozen times.

   If you're really enjoying the hike, consider a two-day detour from Kuala Teku to **Four-Steps Waterfall**, east of Mount Tahan. The trail up to it follows the course of the Tahan River for eight hours, right to the foot of the 30m-high falls.

Day 3
The **third day** on the trail to Mount Tahan sees you climb from 168m to 1100m in seven hours of steady, unrelenting legwork, leaving you on a ridge. Prominent among the large trees here is *seraya*, with a reddish-brown trunk, though as the ridge runs west these are replaced by montane oak forest, where **elephant tracks** are common. The night is spent at the Mount Tahan base camp, **Wray's Camp**, named after the leader of the first team to climb the mountain in 1905.

Day 4: to the summit
Day four involves six hours of hard climbing along steep gullies, ending up at **Padang Camp**, on the Tangga Lima Belas Ridge, sited on a plateau sheltered by tall trees. The summit is now only two and a half hours away, through open, hilly ground with knee-high plants, exposed rocks and peaty streams. The trail follows a ridge and soon reaches **Mount Tahan's summit**; provided it's clear, there's a stupendous view of around 50km in all directions. Weather conditions up here can't be relied upon, however: the **moss forest**, which dominates above 1500m, is often shrouded in cloud.

On from the summit
Most hikers make a straight return trip, spending the **fifth night** back at the padang, the **sixth** at the Puteh River, and reaching Kuala Tahan late on **day seven**. It's also possible to continue westwards from the mountain for a further two days, completing a **traverse** of the park and exiting Taman Negara at **Merapoh**. For more information about this route, contact a Merapoh-based tour operator (see p.211).

Tenor Trail
30km circuit from Kuala Tahan; 3–4 days

Shorter and not as tough as the hike to Mount Tahan, the mostly low-lying **Tenor Trail** is more likely to be flooded out during extra-wet conditions, but is otherwise an extremely satisfying trek, with a few easy ascents to viewpoints along the way.

Day 1
On **day one**, initially the **Tenor Trail** follows the track southwest from Kuala Tahan to Telinga Cave and the Yong hide (see p.200), before bearing northwest along the small

Yong River and reaching the campsite at **Kemah Yong**, around 10km from the start.

A side trail from here ascends **Bukit Guling Gendang** (570m), a steep hour-and-a-half climb best undertaken in the morning. Towards the summit the terrain changes from lowland tropical to montane forest, where tall conifer trees allow light to penetrate to the forest floor and **squirrels** predominate, with the black giant and cream giant the main species. From the top, views reach north to Mount Tahan, west to Siput Cave and beyond that to Bukit Peningat (713m), the highest limestone outcrop in Peninsular Malaysia.

Day 2

From Kemah Yong campsite, the main trail continues on **day two** into the upper catchment of the Yong River, then over a low saddle into the catchment of the **Rentis River**. The path narrows through thick forest alongside the river, crossing it several times, until it joins the **Tenor River** three hours later, marked by a remote and beautiful riverside clearing, **Kemah Rentis**, where you camp, roughly at the halfway point.

Day 3

You can make it back to Kuala Tahan in one day from Kemah Rentis, though many people take it easy and rest up in one of the campsites along the way. Following the river downstream through undulating terrain on **day three** brings you first to rapids at **Lata Keitiah**, beyond which there's a campsite at **Kemah Lameh**. You're now in lowland open forest where walking is fairly easy; after four hours the trail leads to **Bumbun Cegar Anjing** (another possible overnight stop) from where it's a final 3km to Kuala Tahan.

North through the interior

North of Jerantut, Route 8 and the parallel **Jungle Railway** run around 350km to Kota Bharu, up on the east coast. Head this way if you want to spend time among the region's abundant forests and limestone hills at **Kenong Rimba State Park**, reach the alternative entrances to Taman Negara at **Merapoh** and **Kuala Koh**, or trek along forested waterfall trails at **Gunung Stong State Park**. Settlements along the way – including relatively substantial **Gua Musang** and **Kuala Lipis** – are more jumping-off points for nearby sections of wilds, rather than destinations in their own right. For a change from jungle trekking, experience southern Kelantan's unique Chinese culture at limestone-strewn **Kampung Pulai**, one of the oldest Hakka settlements in Malaysia.

ESSENTIALS
NORTH THROUGH THE INTERIOR

Banks The only regional banks are at Kuala Lipis and Gua Musang, though there is an ATM in Dabong, near Mount Stong.

Climate Conditions are damp throughout the year, though driest from April to Sept; you'll need to check in advance about access if heading here during the wet season (Nov–Jan).

Kenong Rimba State Park

Covering 128 square kilometres and backing onto the remote southwestern corner of Taman Negara, **Kenong Rimba State Park** offers jungle trails, riverside camping, mammal-spotting and excellent birdwatching, plus the likelihood of crossing paths with the nomadic **Batek** people. You can see the main sights in **five days**, on a 50km-long **loop** through the park past a series of caves, the seven-step **Lata Kenong waterfall** and limestone outcrops with **rock-climbing** potential. If you've only time for a brief visit, explore the **caves** strung out along the main trail, stop overnight at the Mount Kesong campsite and retrace your steps the following day.

The park is far less developed than the area around Kuala Tahan, and trails quickly get overgrown – arranging a **tour** from Kuala Lipis, or at least a guide, is

KENONG RIMBA
STATE PARK

mandatory to access the reserve. Make sure you bring everything you'll need with you.

ARRIVAL AND TOURS KENONG RIMBA STATE PARK

TRAVELLING INDEPENDENTLY

By boat Kenong Rimba lies about 20km east of Kuala Lipis; the nearest village is Kuala Kenong, from where you can get a boat to the trailhead at Tanjung Kiara. All boats are by arrangement only, through your guide or an agent. Kuala Kenong to the Tanjung Kiara jetty costs RM10/person.

TOURS

Though it's possible to explore Kenong Rimba independently, it's much easier to visit on a tour from Kuala Lipis; guides, transport, meals and accommodation (in cabins or tents) are all part of the deal.

Appu's Jungle Treks First floor of the building opposite the Kuala Lipis train station; access on Jalan Besar ☎017 947 1520, ✉jungleappu@yahoo.com. Appu has been exploring Kenong Rimba since the 1990s, and organizes budget hiking and camping trips in the park. Die-hards can make a six-to-seven-day circuit with him, on which the trekking can be quite tough, despite short daily distances. Expect to pay RM80/person/day (minimum four people) including food, plus RM150 return/group to cover transport, and RM15 for the park entry fee.

Kiara Holidays Level 4, Centrepoint Complex, Kuala Lipis ☎09 312 2777, ⓦcentrepointhotel.com.my/pkiaraholidays.html. Don't be put off by their threadbare office or the shabby building; the friendly staff can arrange packages from RM328/person including transfers, meals and accommodation in tents. Rafting also available.

ACCOMMODATION AND EATING

To **camp** in the park costs RM5 per person per night; the most established campsite is at **Mount Kesong**, about 2hr in from the entrance, with the popular **Kenong campsite** another 5hr north of here at Lata Kenong waterfall. Some **chalets** are available, but your guide must book them through the Forestry Department at least one month before your visit, and their quality is not guaranteed.

Kuala Lipis

It's hard to believe that **KUALA LIPIS**, 50km northwest of Jerantut, was the state capital of **Pahang** from 1898 to 1955. Today, it's a sleepy, inconsequential place, situated at the confluence of the Lipis and Jelai rivers and surrounded by rolling hills and plantations. There are a few mementos from colonial days – many associated with the veteran administrator, **Sir Hugh Clifford** (the Pahang Resident 1896–1905), plus plenty of shops and places to eat, but Kuala Lipis's biggest draw is access to the relatively unvisited rainforest trails at nearby **Kenong Rimba State Park**.

Old town

Kuala Lipis started life as a **trading centre** for *gaharu* (a fragrant aloe wood used to make joss sticks) and other jungle products, collected by the Semiar and traded with Chinese *towkays*. The remnants of these origins survive in the **old town**, a busy grid of pastel-coloured **shophouses** squeezed between the railway and the Jelai River, where the jetty and steps still stand, though goods no longer arrive and depart by river. Overlooking the river to the west, the small, tin-roofed **Masjid Negeri**, dating from 1888, was reputedly founded by a trader from Yemen.

Pahang Club

Jalan Pahang Club

Incongruously hidden behind the huge new **hospital**, the **Pahang Club** dates to 1907. It's an archetypal tropical colonial building, a sprawling structure of whitewashed timber with black trim and wrap-around verandah, raised slightly off the ground on stumps as protection against damp and termites – which, given the lean on the building, clearly hasn't been entirely successful, and the club has fallen into disuse.

Lipis District Office

Kuala Lipis was chosen as a headquarters for the colonial government despite the town's relative isolation – the trip upriver from Singapore took more than two weeks, and there was no road out until the 1890s – though minor **tin deposits** brought short-lived prosperity. These boom days led to the construction of the surprisingly large **Lipis District Office**, which overlooks Kuala Lipis from a hilltop 1km southeast of town; a solid crimson-and-white Edwardian edifice, it now serves as local government offices.

Clifford School

Below the District Office, at the back of green playing fields, **Clifford School** was built in 1913 and part-funded by Hugh Clifford; the original buildings are at the far end of the compound, visible from Jalan Pahang Club. The school is still one of a select group where the country's leaders and royalty are educated – though these days it's equally well known for being the alma mater of Malaysia's biggest-selling female pop star, Siti Nurhaliza.

Bukit Residen

A small rise just south of town is crowned by **Bukit Residen**, a graceful two-storey house built in the 1890s as Hugh Clifford's residence. Clifford arrived in Malaysia in 1883, aged seventeen, and worked his way up through the colonial administration, serving in Malaysia, Sri Lanka and West Africa before ending his career as the Malaya High Commissioner in 1930. The house's associations are more interesting than the building itself – it's now the *Government Rest House* – though it does enjoy great views over the surrounding hills.

ARRIVAL AND INFORMATION   **KUALA LIPIS**

By train Kuala Lipis's 1926 train station is right in the old town (ticket office daily 9am–4.30pm; ☏ 09 312 1341), on the Jungle Railway line. Check ⓦ www.ktmb.com.my for the latest.

Destinations Dabong (1 daily at 5.37am; 4hr); Gua Musang via Merapoh (1 daily at 3am & 1.30pm; 2hr); Jerantut (1 daily at 1.16am; 1hr 30min); Johor Bahru (1 daily; 9hr); Kuala Lumpur (change at Gemas; 1 daily at 1.16am; 9hr); Wakaf Bharu (for Kota Bharu, change at Gua Musang; 1 daily at 3am & 1.30pm; 8hr).

By bus The main bus station, Terminal Anggerik, sits 1km north of the centre; cross the river, head up the hill and turn right into the small cluster of shops, where you'll see the open-sided barn of a station.

Destinations Jerantut (3 daily; 1hr 30min); Kuala Lumpur (hourly 6.30am–6.30pm; 4hr); Kota Bharu (via Gua Musang; 1 daily at 11.30am; 5hr 30min); Kuantan (2 daily; 6hr); Sungai Koyan (for Cameron Highlands; 4 daily; 2hr).

Bank There's a Maybank with ATM on Jalan Besar.

Laundry A same-day laundry service is available on Jalan Jelai.

ACCOMMODATION

Bestari 42–43 Lorong BBKL, just north of town ☏ 09 312 6626; map p.209. A 5min walk from the bus station on the opposite side of the main road, this modern, motel-like affair, owned by the Hotel Jelai group, is popular with travelling business people; they take credit cards and the

spacious en-suite rooms all have cable TV and a/c. ☏ **RM100**

★**Hotel London** 82 Jalan Besar ☏ 09 312 1618; map p.209. Beyond the dull facade, the orange-painted interiors of the *London* impress with an array of freshly renovated yet tiny rooms, and modern dorms with private curtains. This is the closest Kuala Lipis gets to a backpacker joint. ☞ Dorms RM30, doubles RM48

Jelai Hillview 7 Jalan Bukit Bius ☎ 09 312 3598, ⓦ hoteljelai.com/lipis-hillview-index; map p.209. The second branch of this franchise hotel feels smarter than its predecessor on the riverside, offering a series of decent en-suite rooms that are good value for the price. Book ahead; they're often full. ☞ RM60

Lipis Plaza Komplex Taipan Jalan Benta-Lipis ☎ 09 312 5521, ⓦ lipisplaza.com; map p.209. Spacious but rather plain rooms in a modern complex at the base of Bukit Residen. Rates include breakfast. ☞ RM100

Poly Star 5 Jalan Bukit Bius ☎ 09 312 3225; map p.209. Not as well looked after as it used to be, the rooms here are smallish, with basic furnishings, attached bathrooms and a/c. Not much English is spoken. ☞ RM58

Residen Inn (Government Rest House) Bukit Residen ☎ 09 312 2788; map p.209. Hugh Clifford's former home (see p.209) is now a rather odd guesthouse with an abandoned museum on the ground floor and fifteen vast en-suite rooms in dire need of renovation. The on-site Thai restaurant has good-value set menus. A taxi from town will cost around RM10. RM100

EATING

The area around the taxi stand holds a few despondent Malay stalls, but there's more atmosphere to be had in the bustling **kedai kopis** that line the covered arcade between Jalan Besar and Jalan Jelai. There's also a **night market** with plenty of food from 3pm every Fri in the purpose-built Kompleks Melati next to the bus station, a 15min walk from the old town. For **trekking supplies**, if you can't find what you need along Jalan Besar, head south of the tracks to the **Aktif supermarket** on the ground floor of the Centrepoint Complex – a shoddy, graffiti-covered block awaiting redevelopment.

Restoran Pak Boh Recipe Overlooking town from the north bank of the river, near the Bestari Hotel ☎ 09 312 6082; map p.209. In a great setting over the river, this place has a jungle theme with rattan decor, potted palms and water misters. The food – from staples such as noodle soup and chicken chop 'n' chips, through to beef stew with medicinal herbs – is adequate but rather overpriced. Mains RM10–25. Daily 11.30am–11.30pm.

★**Selvamalar** 94 Jalan Besar ☎ 09 312 2422; map p.209. A terrific, friendly Tamil curry house with the usual spread of fiery food for around RM10, as well as *roti canai, nasi lemak* and *mee goreng* at breakfast; go for lunch over dinner, as they often run out of the tastiest curries come evening. Daily 6.30am–8pm.

Merapoh

The tiny market town of **MERAPOH**, served by road and rail 80km north of Kuala Lipis, marks a 7km-long access road east to **Taman Negara's western entrance**, officially known as **Sungai Relau**. This is the only part of Taman Negara where a proper vehicle road runs deep into the park, providing access to the trails – most famously that to **Mount Tahan** (see p.205). There's not much point in turning up here with your own car, however, as the 14km-long park road is closed to private vehicles, and all trails – even the easiest strolls around the park's headquarters – require hiring a guide. What might make it worth stumping up for guide fees and official transportation is the chance of seeing elephants, as well as leopard cats, civets, otters and banting – a mix of buffalo and seladang. A new **tree-top walk** should open here by 2020.

Into the park

RM1, RM5 camera fee • ☎ 09 915 0214, ⓦ wildlife.gov.my

Beyond the park office and picnic ground, cross the little Relau River via a small **bridge** and you'll come to the narrow surfaced road that undulates through the jungle. Several trails lead off the initial few kilometres, including **Rentis Gajah** ("Elephant Trail"), leading south off the road to Gajah Cave, though you can't hike here independently; allow four hours for the return trip from the gate, plus an hour exploring.

Driving a few kilometres along the jeep track will take you to the 12m-high, red Menara Bukit Seraya, an **observation tower** with views of forested ridges and valleys to the north, and, on a clear day, east to Mount Tahan. Some 2km beyond Bukit Seraya is Air Terjun Sungai Kelam, a pretty **waterfall** in a secluded woodland setting.

The road ends at **Kuala Juram**, where trees overhang the Juram River, a stretch of which teems with *kelah* (mahseer), and where it's possible to kayak and fish. The suspension bridge over the river here is the gateway to the Mount Tahan mountain trail.

ARRIVAL AND DEPARTURE   **MERAPOH**

By bus There's no bus station, but the daily bus between Kuala Lipis or Kuala Lumpur and Gua Musang can drop you off; local tour operators can also deliver/collect from Gua Musang, just 30min north (RM15–20/person one way).

By train Merapoh train station is just west of Route 8. There is no local transport between the station and the park; if you can't get a ride, you can walk it: it takes 2hr to walk the rolling 7km through oil palm plantations.

Destinations Dabong (1 daily at 7.15am; 2hr 30min); Gua Musang (3 daily; 40min); Kuala Lipis (3 daily; 2hr); Johor Bahru (1 daily at 11.26pm; 10hr 30min); Wakaf Bharu (for Kota Bharu; 1 daily at 7.15am; 5hr 15min).

TOURS AND GUIDES

Guides cost RM24/person/day (minimum five people) or RM100 per jeep. The park headquarters quotes RM150/day per guide for a maximum of twelve people; agencies are slightly more expensive. The four-day trek from Merapoh up Mount Tahan and back costs RM950; a week-long traverse of the park between Merapoh and Kuala Tahan costs RM1400.

Merapoh Adventure Along the main road leading to the access road, ☏09 912 2321 or ☏019 372 1812, �ⓌFacebook.com/merapohadventure. Reliable local operator offering a wide range of tours, from multi-day caving explorations (RM190–RM420), canoeing and fishing inside and outside Taman Negara, and the five-day to a week-long Mount Tahan hike. All prices include permits and insurance. They can also arrange accommodation in private homes where you can use the kitchen, an ideal option for self-catering groups (from RM30/person per day).

Relau Agency Merapoh ☏017 915 3034. This established operator organizes tours and local transport. Trekking guides cost RM180/day for groups of up to eight, plus RM80/night per group for overnight stays. Fees include RM10/person for the ride between Merapoh and

the park gates; and RM65/person for a night safari (minimum four people). Their drivers tend to speak little English, but park staff should be able to smooth communication once you've arrived.

SGI Outdoor 200m towards the park from Merapoh down the access road ☏09 912 1443, Ⓦnatureguidemerapoh.webs.com. This operation arranges accommodation in Merapoh, plus tours and transport into the park; they also run multi-day caving trips in the surrounding area (from RM89/day; add RM30 for insurance). Tents (RM10) and sleeping bags (RM5) are available to rent from their welcoming offices; there's also a decent range of gear (including boots and waterproofs) for sale. As for Relau Agency, trekking guides cost RM180/day for groups of up to eight, plus RM80/night for overnight stays.

ACCOMMODATION AND EATING

It makes sense to base yourself 7km away in Merapoh to use the clutch of guesthouses and *kedai kopis* along the main road, as food and accommodation options are very limited in this part of Taman Negara. If camping at the park headquarters, you'll need to bring all your own food and cooking gear.

Park Headquarters ☏09 915 0214, Ⓦtamannegara-sungairelau.com. For the time being, accommodation at the park is limited to a campsite equipped with toilets, showers and a covered seating area for dining. Camping per person RM1.

Speleo Inn Merapoh, not far from Route 8 ☏09 912 1443. Simple bunk-bed dorms run by SGI Outdoor, housed in a well-maintained block. Book ahead, especially during school holidays, as it's often used by student groups. Dorms RM35

Gua Musang

GUA MUSANG ("Civet Cave"), 30km from Merapoh, is a former logging town strung thinly along a stretch of Route 8. A 100m-wide knot of scruffy buildings and shops surrounds the old **train station**, while a **new satellite town** coalesces 3km south. This being Kelantan, the Malay accent here displays a distinctive twang, and alcohol is available only at a few shops run by Chinese residents.

Gua Musang is fairly close to the **Taman Negara entrances** at Merapoh (see opposite) and Kuala Koh (see p.213). Time spent between connections can be filled with a day-trip to **Kampung Pulai** (see p.212) or exploring the **caves** that riddle a mass of limestone that looms over the train tracks. Note that the path up to the caves is steep, crumbling and very overgrown, and particularly difficult after rain – it's best attempted with a local guide (RM20).

GUA MUSANG

EATING
Kak Zah Restoran   2
Kedai Makan Mana Lagi   1
Under the Tree   3

ACCOMMODATION
Gua Idaman   3
Mines Inn Hotel   1
My Home Hotel   4
Welcome Inn GM   2

Main Bus Station (2km), Merapoh & Kuala Lipis

ARRIVAL AND INFORMATION   GUA MUSANG

Route 8, between the old and new parts of town. A taxi to the old town or bus station costs RM10.

Destinations Dabong (2 daily at 5.22am & 3.52pm; 2hr 20min); Gemas (for Kuala Lumpur; 1 daily at 10.53pm; 7hr 20min); Kuala Lipis (2 daily at 10.05 am & 8.36pm; 2hr 30min); Merapoh (2 daily at 10.05am & 8.36pm; 30min); Johor Bahru (1 daily at 10.53pm; 12hr); Wakaf Bharu (for Kota Bharu; 2 daily at 5.22am & 3.52pm; 5hr 20min).

By bus Gua Musang's main bus station is 2.5km south of the train station in the new town. There are no direct buses to Cameron Highlands; take the train to to Kuala Lipis and then a bus to Sungai Koyan, from where three daily departures reach Tanah Rata.

Destinations Kota Bharu (3 daily; 3hr); Kuala Lumpur (5 daily; 5hr).

Banks There are several banks with ATMs on Route 8 near the train station.

By train The new train station sits astride the Jungle Railway's tracks 400m south of its predecessor, just off

Supplies Stores along Jalan Besar sell everything from food to batteries and umbrellas.

ACCOMMODATION

Gua Idaman 400m west of the station ☎ 09 912 0081; map above. This place is close to the train station, but has largely windowless and slightly musty rooms, each with TV and a tiny bathroom. Little English spoken. ☎ RM60

Mines Inn Hotel Jalan Persiaran Raya ☎ 09 912 1339, ✉ minesinnhotel@gmail.com; map above. This simple hotel packs in twenty-odd clean, simple en-suite rooms that easily beat the competition along Route 8. ☎ RM80

My Home Hotel Jalan Persiaran Raya ☎ 09 912 3191, ⊕ myhomehotel.com.my; map above. Part of a nationwide chain, this hotel has dismissive staff and clean but poky a/c rooms. ☎ RM60

★ **Welcome Inn GM** PT 2870 Jalan Cengai, about 2km walk northwest of the new train station along the main road ☎ 09 912 2912, ⊕ bit.ly/WelcomeInnGM; map above. Not central but next to a supermarket in a new area of town, this is Gua Musang's best-value hotel, with squeaky clean and airy en-suite a/c rooms (some windowless). Contact them in advance for a free pick-up from either the bus or train station. ☎ RM75

EATING

Kak Zah Restoran Jalan Besar ☎ 013 268 1942, ⊕ facebook.com/KakZahRestoran; map above. One of Gua Musang's most appreciated Malay restaurants serves an array of local curries and dishes, of which *nasi kerabu*, the quintessential Kelantanese blue-coloured rice served with crackers, dried fish and fried chicken, is highly recommended. Daily 7am–2pm.

Kedai Makan Mana Lagi Jalan Besar; map above. Open-air Malay food court that's festooned with coloured lights in the evening. Food has a Thai twist, as is often the case in Kelantan; even the humble fried *kangkung* with squid has a lemongrass kick to it. A good range of *tom yam* and *kerabu*-style dishes for around RM10, plus seafood, including house speciality *ikan tiga rasa* – though none of the staff can explain what the three flavours of the name derive from. Daily 5pm–late.

★ **Under the Tree** Jalan Tepi Sungai Chindai, 200m west of the old train station ☎ 013 746 1338; map above. With outdoor tables that spill under an umbrella of low-hanging tree branches, this *kopitiam* serves up Chinese noodles (RM5), *kopi* and breakfast titbits. And in tune with the town's multi-ethnic mix, there's a food court on the other side of the tree to satisfy any Malay food craving. Daily 7am–2pm & 6pm–10pm.

Kampung Pulai

KAMPUNG PULAI, 8km south of Gua Musang, may be southern Kelantan's best-kept secret. This traditional Hakka village lies in a beautiful riverside setting, where lush greenery is punctuated by karst formations rising dramatically from the earth. The Hakka first came here around six hundred years ago in search of gold. The continued prevalence of Hakka traditions today can be attributed to the village's isolation: the first tarred road to Gua Musang only arrived in 1988.

Life in Kampung Pulai revolves around the **Water and Moon Temple**, dedicated to goddess of mercy Kuan Yin, and said to be more than 400 years old. The centrepiece is an extremely rare Ming Dynasty painting of Kuan Yin as a maiden, brought here from China by the early settlers. On the nineteenth day of the second month of the Chinese lunar calendar, Kampung Pulai celebrates the goddess's birthday: the village fills up with devotees from all over Southeast Asia, rituals and parades are held in the main square, and free vegetarian food is served in the community hall next to the temple.

Princess Hill

Daily 9am–7pm • Ask for the guardian at the Water and Moon Temple for the key

From the courtyard outside the shrine, a suspension bridge crosses the **Galas River** joining a path to the foot of **Princess Hill**, a limestone karst housing a set of ancient meditation caves and a shrine with a statue of Kuan Yin carved out of a giant stalagmite. From the two viewing platforms at the top, the sunset views over the Galas River, snaking quietly through a carpet of untamed green jungle, are superb.

ARRIVAL AND INFORMATION | KAMPUNG PULAI

By taxi There is no public transport between Gua Musang and Kampung Pulai. Taxis from Gua Musang's bus station charge RM20–30 each way.

By car From Gua Musang's bus station, turn right towards the hospital and then left at the main junction with Road D29. From here, it's a short drive along the D241.

ACCOMMODATION AND EATING

There's a series of inexpensive Malay restaurants along **Road D241**, all serving the usual Kelantanese staples – a mix of zesty Malay food with southern Thai influences, such as *tom yum* and *nasi kerabu*.

Chinese noodle corner store Next to the temple square, facing the river. This Chinese *kopitiam* dishes up a wide selection of cheap noodles (RM4) and breakfast titbits. Note that it doesn't have an official name. The karaoke bar next door is the place to go for a beer. Daily 7am–4pm, closed every other Tues

★ **Pulai Holiday Village** 1km before the turn off to the Water and Moon Temple ☎ 016 921 6652, ⍟ pulai .org. Pulai's only guesthouse has two blocks of smart en-suite rooms next to a secluded rubber estate. The older block, all decked out in wood, has slightly simpler but more picturesque rooms next to a private limestone cave, which you can explore at your leisure. Ample parking space available. 🛜 RM55

Kuala Koh

With its jungle trails, boat trips and canopy walkway, **Kuala Koh**, Taman Negara's northern entrance, 85km east of Gua Musang, sounds like the ideal alternative to touristy Kuala Tahan. On the ground, however, the experience is dramatically different: a lack of visitors, coupled with poor maintenance of both the canopy walkway and the trails after the 2014 floods, have left the place in a mess. At the time of writing, the canopy walkway was closed, pending repairs, and accommodation was only available in a campsite. Given that expensive private transport is the only way to get here, and guides are compulsory to venture anywhere beyond the bridge at the park's headquarters, it's strongly recommended that you contact the office (call rather than rely on the infrequently updated website) to enquire about the state of trails and facilities before you set off on a potentially disappointing journey.

Canopy walkway

Closed at time of research but usually open Mon–Thurs, Sat & Sun 9.30am–12.30pm & 2.30–4.30pm, Fri 9.30am–noon & 3.30–4.30pm; closed during rain or if lightning is likely • RM5

Walk through park headquarters to reach the **suspension bridge** that leads over the Lebir River into the forest; turn left on the far side and it's 100m to the **canopy walkway**. The walkway is 20m up, over partially cleared forest with bamboo and barbed rattan palms below; from the top you can expect to see birds, insects and occasional troupes of monkeys.

Forest trails

Beyond the canopy walkway, several kilometres of **trails** weave through the forest and along the river. All hikes require arranging a guide in advance (see below), either through the park headquarters or a tour operator. During the day, **listen** for wildlife – the zithering of cicadas, whooshing of hornbill wings, and staccato rustle of lizards amid the leaf litter. Pick of the routes are the **Rentis Ara** ("Fig Trail"), a 3km circuit, and the 1.5km-long **Rentis Bumbun**, ending at a pole-frame **hide** overlooking a salt lick – somewhere to sit still for an hour and see what turns up.

On the river

A pleasant **river trip** heads up the Lebir for half an hour to **Kuala Pertang**, passing a few sandy banks where you can camp, swim or fish; the river is home to *ikan kelah* and other freshwater denizens. The ride takes you under the overhanging boughs of leaning neram trees, some hung with the leafy tresses of **tiger orchids**, among the world's largest orchid species. You can also go **tubing** along the river, being carried downstream on an inflated rubber ring, or arrange a trip to a semi-permanent **Batek camp**, two hours upstream.

ARRIVAL AND INFORMATION   KUALA KOH

By car Driving, turn off Route 8 at Simpang Aring (40km east of Gua Musang) and follow signs along a sealed but windy road through the Felda Aring oil palm plantation, looking out for plantation vehicles, before turning off onto an access road for the last 15km. The road passes an Orang Asli village just before entering the park, with the headquarters a short drive further on above the confluence of the Lebir and Koh rivers.
By taxi Taxis from Gua Musang charge a negotiable

RM200 each way
Park office Staff at the park office (☎017 900 9522, ⊚taman-negara-koh.blogspot.my) can give you a photocopied schematic map of Kuala Koh, and accept payment of the nominal entry (RM1) and photography (RM5) fees. Book guides and all river activities here too: tubing on the river costs RM25 each (minimum four people), while an hour-long guided night walk, when you might see slow loris and civets, is RM40.

ACCOMMODATION

Camping The only way to stay within the park is to camp. Keep in mind that you'll have to bring everything you'll need, including food, cutlery, plates and a stove, with you. Camping per pitch RM5.

Gunung Stong State Park

Around 70km north of Gua Musang, **Gunung Stong State Park** (otherwise known as **Jelawang Jungle**) is based around 1420m-high **Mount Stong**, a prominent, forested granite mountain 7km outside the small rail township of **DABONG**. Current train schedules make it a great day stop, with a short but tough hike up through lush forest to a series of **waterfalls** and plunge pools, where you can have a swim and catch a late afternoon train out. However, it's also worth staying **overnight** on the mountainside for the magical sunrise views. Before heading to the park, you could also spend a few hours exploring the **Gua Ikan complex**, a system of five caves connected by an underground stream, roughly 3km out of Dabong. It's possible to visit independently, but hire a guide when the water level is high, when the main path becomes hard to to follow.

Air Terjun Jelawang
Daily 8am–10pm

The access road from Dabong ends at the foot of the mountain, where you buy your entry ticket. From the gate, follow a path that crosses a rickety suspension bridge into the forest, where the paving quickly gives way to a muddy path, tangled with tree roots but perfectly clear. This is extremely steep, with ropes and chains to help you up the worst bits – fortunately the gritty mud gives a decent grip. After about 1km, you'll reach a ramshackle pavilion where a side trail leads sharply down 300m to a pretty spot near the foot of the largest cascade.

As you continue along the main trail, *Baha's Camp* (see below) sits a sweaty 1.5km further up the hillside on the riverbank between the first and second tiers of **Air Terjun Jelawang**, also known as Lata Jelawang, Peninsular Malaysia's **highest waterfall**, which cascades a total of 540m down a bald granite rock face in seven steps. There's a pool that's great for swimming and a wonderful viewpoint – if you stay overnight, this is where you'll want to be at dawn to watch the **sunrise** over a sea of cotton wool clouds blanketing the plains. Do take care, though; the rocks are slick and a Singaporean student slipped to his death here in 2013.

Mountain trails
Baha's Camp is the trailhead for the **Elephant Trek**, which follows the main path up the mountain for two hours to the top of Mount Stong, before winding along the ridge and crossing over onto neighbouring **Mount Ayam** (1500m). Although it's possible to return to *Baha's* the same day, it's recommended to **camp** for the night on top of Mount Ayam – you'll need warm clothing and a good sleeping bag. Elephants are sometimes seen here, and there's a chance of encountering **tapir** and **deer** in the early morning or early evening.

ARRIVAL AND INFORMATION · GUNUNG STONG STATE PARK

By train It's feasible to come on a day-trip, visit the caves and the falls and have a swim, if you arrive at Dabong on an early train from either direction, and leave the same evening (timetables on ⓦ www.ktmb.com.my). Ask at Dabong station for a lift (RM15 from the train station to the caves; RM20 from the train station to the park's entrance).
Destinations Gemas (for Kuala Lumpur; 1 daily; 9hr); Gua Musang (3 daily; 2hr 10min); Jerantut (1 daily; 4hr 50min); Johor Bahru (1 daily; 14hr); Kuala Lipis (1 daily; 4hr 20min);
Merapoh (1 daily; 2hr 20min); Wakaf Bharu (for Kota Bharu; 4 daily; 3hr 40min).
By car Dabong is just off Route 66, 70km north of Gua Musang; it's 40km west of the Sam River and Route 8. From Penang/Kedah and points north, follow the E4 to Jeli, then take the Route 66 turning and head south for 53km to the Dabong turning. Cross the river and drive north for 7km, before taking the signed road to the mountain that ends at the park gates.
Admission fee RM15.

ACCOMMODATION AND EATING

Simple meals are available from the restaurant at the **park gates** (daily 8am–7pm). Meals at *Baha's Camp* are by arrangement only. There are several *kedai kopis* around Dabong train station, but the closest place to buy supplies is Gua Musang.

Baha's Camp Inside the forest, 1hr 30min from the park gates, by the waterfall ☎ 012 968 1554. A superb – if extremely basic – place to stay, with tents scattered around a jungle clearing. There's no electricity or running water, unless you count the nearby waterfall, and you might find yourself sharing the tent with some of the smaller forest creatures. If you can't contact the camp in advance (they're sometimes out of range), bring your own tent just in case their own are full, as well as your own food – they should be able to cook it for you. Four-person tent RM20
Park Headquarters ☎ 019 335 5167. The cluster of chalets at the foot of the mountain was being restored at the time of writing, and will be in operation by early 2018. It's a great place to stay if you don't want to rough it up, or if you arrive at the park late. Budget travellers can opt to bunk at a basic campsite, and there's a restaurant. Camping per two-man tent RM10, chalets RM50
★ **Rose House** Down from the road bridge across the railway, Dabong ☎ 013 960 6789, ⓦ facebook.com/Rose.House.Dabong. With six rooms in two rose-pink blocks, this guesthouse is a great place to recuperate after a trip into the mountains. Clean rooms have fans, a/c and bathrooms, and the friendly owner may throw in *nasi kerabu* for breakfast. RM80

The east coast

TRADITIONAL KITE MAKER, TERENGGANU

The east coast

The 400km-long stretch from the northeastern corner of the Peninsula to Kuantan, roughly halfway down the east coast, draws visitors for two major reasons: the beaches and islands, and traditional Malay culture. Islands such as the Perhentians, Redang and Kapas offer great opportunities for diving and snorkelling; further south, the backpackers' coastal enclave of Cherating is a deservedly popular place simply to kick back for a few days. Among the cities, vibrant Kota Bharu, close to the Thai border, stands out for its opportunities to access Malay crafts and performing arts.

The east coast displays a different cultural legacy to the more populous, commercial western seaboard, from which it is separated by the mountainous, jungled interior. For hundreds of years, the Malay rulers of the northern states of **Kelantan** and **Terengganu** were vassals of the Thai kingdom of **Ayutthaya**, suffering repeated invasions as well as the unruly squabbles of their own princes. Nevertheless, the Malays enjoyed a great deal of autonomy, and both states remained free of British control until 1909. Only in 1931 did the railway arrive in Kelantan; previously, the journey from KL involved thirteen river crossings. In 1941 Kelantan saw the landing of the first Japanese troops, facilitated by the Thai government – who were rewarded by being given control over Kelantan once more from 1943 until 1945.

   While immigrants poured into the tin and rubber towns of the west during the twentieth century, the east remained rural. As a result, Kelantan and Terengganu remain very much **Malay heartland** states. There's a rustic feel to the area, the economy being largely based on agriculture and fishing, with the obvious exception of Terengganu's petroleum industry.

   The country's religious opposition party, **PAS**, which was born in Kelantan in the middle of the last century, has governed its home state since 1990. For foreign visitors, the political backdrop distils down to the simple truth that the **social climate** of Kelantan and Terengganu is more obviously **conservative** than elsewhere in Malaysia: **alcohol** is harder to obtain than in other states; most restaurants, whatever cuisine they serve, are **halal**; and **dress** – for both men and women – needs to be circumspect, except at well-touristed beaches. You will also find that **English** is less understood in Kelantan and Terengganu than in most other parts of the Peninsula.

GETTING AROUND   THE EAST COAST

While **flights** to Kota Bharu or Kuala Terengganu can be useful time-savers, road access to the east coast has really opened up with the development of the East Coast Expressway (E8). The expressway arrives on the coast just north of Kuantan, reducing the drive from KL to a 3hr whizz, then runs north to just west of Kuala Terengganu; the road is planned to reach Kota Bharu by 2020.

GREEN TURTLE, PERHENTIAN ISLANDS

Highlights

❶ **Kota Bharu** One of the Peninsula's most appealing cities, home to Malay crafts, traditional art forms and a popular night food market, with Buddhist temples within easy reach. See p.221

❷ **Perhentian Islands** Two of the most enticing islands the Peninsula has to offer, with excellent snorkelling and accommodation ranging from backpacker chalets to slick resorts. See p.231

❸ **Kapas Island** A delightful little island with decent sands and opportunities for snorkelling and kayaking – perfect for a couple of days' relaxation. See p.251

❹ **Cherating** Chill by the beach, watch fireflies or just enjoy the amiable, low-key nightlife in this long-established travellers' hangout. See p.255

❺ **Pekan** An appealingly quiet royal town, with a scattering of palaces, impeccable kampung houses and a newly renovated museum housed in a colonial building. See p.263

HIGHLIGHTS ARE MARKED ON THE MAP ON P.220

By bus The express buses that ply the east coast's **main roads** are convenient for trips between the major towns, but if you're heading anywhere else often the only option is to take one of the slower, local buses that serve the smaller stops.

By car In addition to the E8 and East Coast Highway, the region's old backbone roads remain intact: the coast road (called Route 3 between Kuala Terengganu and Kuantan)

and its shadow 10–20km inland (Route 14 south of Kuala Terengganu, Route 3 to the north). Unsurprisingly, the coast road, connecting a string of laidback towns and fishing kampungs, is the most interesting.

By train The only rail service is the atmospheric "Jungle Railway" through the interior (see p.204) to Tumpat, near Kota Bharu.

THE EAST COAST

0 _____ 50
kilometres

HIGHLIGHTS

1 Kota Bharu
2 Perhentian Islands
3 Kapas Island
4 Cherating
5 Pekan

THE EAST COAST IN THE OFF-SEASON

Many visitors give the east coast a wide berth during the **northeast monsoon**, which sets in during late October and continues until February. It's true that heavy rains and sea swells put paid to most boat services to the islands at this time, and most beach accommodation, whether on the mainland or offshore, is shut anyway. The rains will, however, usually be interspersed with good sunny spells, just as the so-called dry season can bring its share of torrential downpours. With luck, and a flexible schedule, you will find boats heading sporadically to and from the islands during the monsoon; some island accommodation opens year-round, although you should contact places in advance to be sure. While diving and snorkelling aren't great at this time of year, due to reduced visibility, the east coast comes into its own for **surfing** and **windsurfing**, with Cherating the prime destination. Away from the beaches, there's always reasonable sightseeing in Kota Bharu and Kuala Terengganu – just be prepared to take lengthy refuge in cafés or malls when yet another thunderstorm breaks.

Kota Bharu

The capital of Kelantan, **KOTA BHARU**, sits at the very northeastern corner of the Peninsula, on the east bank of the broad, muddy Kelantan River. Many visitors arrive across the nearby Thai border, and for most the city is simply a half-decent place to rest and get their Malaysian bearings. To breeze through Kota Bharu and the rest of Kelantan, however, would be to gloss over one of the country's most culturally fascinating states.

Kelantan has historically been a crucible for **Malay culture**, fostering art forms that drew on influences from around Southeast Asia and as far away as India. Kota Bharu is the ideal place to witness the region's distinctive heritage, on show at its **Cultural Centre** and in the various **cottage industries** that thrive in its hinterland – among them kite-making, batik printing and woodcarving. The city also boasts its share of historical buildings, now largely **museums**, plus some excellent **markets** and numerous **Buddhist temples** in the surrounding countryside.

The city centre is compact, with most of the **markets**, many of the **banks** and the biggest stores between Jalan Hospital and Jalan Pintu Pong, a few blocks north.

Around Padang Merdeka

West of the main markets, close to the river, the quiet oasis of **Padang Merdeka** marks Kota Bharu's historical centre. It was here that the British displayed the body of the defeated Tok Janggut (Father Beard), a peasant spiritual leader who spearheaded a revolt against colonial land taxes and tenancy regulations in 1915. Today the main attractions are a handful of historic buildings, several of which have been converted into **museums**.

One of the most obvious landmarks is the **Sultan Ismail Petra Arch**, beyond which is the **Istana Balai Besar** – a mid-nineteenth-century palace, closed to the public but still used for ceremonial functions – and the squat former **State Treasury**.

Istana Jahar

North of Sultan Ismail Petra Arch, Jalan Sultan • Mon–Wed, Sat & Sun 8.30am–4.45pm, Thurs 8.30am–3.30pm • RM4 • ☎ 09 748 2266

The well-preserved **Istana Jahar** was built in 1887 with a timber portico and pillars painted a regal shade of yellow. In 1911 Sultan Muhammad IV added an Italian marble floor and two wrought-iron spiral staircases. The palace now houses an exhibition on **royal ceremonies**, which can be seen in an hour (although you may want to linger on the breezy first-floor veranda). Rites illustrated include *istiadat pijak tanah*, a ceremony that marked the point when young royals – aged between five and seven years – were allowed to set foot on soil for the first time.

KOTA BHARU

▲ Kampung Laut   ▲ Tokong Mek (2km), 1 (5km) & PCB (9km)

Clock Tower
Padang Merdeka
Istana Batu
Istana Jahar
Medan Selera (night food market)
State Treasury
Central Market
Bazaar Buluh Kubu
Bird Singing Contests
Local Bus Station
Taxis
SEE MAP BELOW FOR DETAILS
Clock Tower
State Museum
Stadium
General Hospital
Immigration Office
Police
Cultural Centre (Gelanggang Seni)
Istana Kota Lama
KB Permai
KB Mall
Arulmigu Subramaniyar Siva Temple
Masjid Langgar
Tesco   Tesco Bus Station

Kelantan River

Wakaf Bharu (5km) & Tumpat (17km)

Thai Consulate (55m), Doremi Travel and Tours (5km) & Airport (8km)

JALAN POST OFFICE LAMA
JALAN SULTAN ZAINAB
JALAN PADANG GARONG
JALAN MAHMOOD
JALAN KEBUN SULTAN
JALAN PENGKALAN CHEPA
JALAN ABDUL KADIR ADABI
JALAN HOSPITAL
JALAN BELAKANG STADIUM
JALAN BAYAM
JALAN SULTAN IBRAHIM
JALAN TENGKU ZAINAB
JALAN HAMZAH
JALAN KOTA BHARU - PENGKALAN KUBOR
JALAN SULTAN YAHYA PETRA
JALAN SULTAN YAHYA PETRA

N

0   200
metres

ACCOMMODATION
Pasir Belanda	1
Perdana	3
Renaissance	4
Zeck's Travellers' Inn	2

SHOPPING
KB Mall	1

CENTRAL KOTA BHARU

Kampung Kraftangan

War Memorial Museum
Masjid Negeri
Islamic Museum
Istana Batu
Medan Selera (night food market)
Clock Tower
Padang Merdeka
Istana Jahar
Istana Balai Besar
Sultan Ismail Petra Arch
Maybank Forex
International Islamic Information Centre
State Treasury
Central Market
Bazaar Buluh Kubu
Pelangi Mall (closed)
Riverside restaurants
Local Bus Station
Guardian Pharmacy
Express Bus Ticket Booths
Radio Tower
HSBC
Taxis
Clock Tower

JALAN ISTANA SERI AKAR
JALAN ISTANA
JALAN HILIR KOTA
JALAN MAHMAD
JALAN TENGKU BESAR
JALAN BELAKANG ISTANA
JALAN KEBUN SULTAN
JALAN POST OFFICE LAMA
JALAN BULUH KUBU
JALAN PINTU PONG
JALAN SRI CEMERLANG
JALAN SULTANAH ZAINAB
JALAN PADANG GARONG
JALAN BULUH KUBU
JLN PARIT DALAM
JALAN DATO PERDANA
JALAN KEBUN SULTAN
JALAN TEMENGGONG
JALAN HILIR PASAR
JALAN PENGKALAN CHEPA
JALAN CHE SU
JALAN CHE SU
JALAN ISMAIL
JALAN DATO PATI
JALAN DOCTOR
JALAN MAJU

N

0   100
metres

EATING
Arnold Cycling Cafe	4
Cikgu	1
Medan	2
Muhibah	7
Shan Sri Dewi	6
Tang Ah Juan	5
Warisan Nasi Kukus	3

SHOPPING
Bazaar Buluh Kubu	3
Central market	4
Friday street market	6
Mydin	2
Parkson	5

ACCOMMODATION
Crown Garden	7
Crystal Lodge	10
Habib	11
Ideal Travellers' House	6
KB Backpackers	9
My Place Guesthouse	8
Royal Guest	5

The **weapons gallery**, in a separate building just behind the palace, features an exhibit devoted to the *kris*, a dagger that has important symbolic value to Malays (see box, p.245).

Istana Batu
North of Istana Jahar, Jalan Istana • Mon–Wed, Sat & Sun 8.30am–4.45pm, Thurs 8.30am–3.30pm • RM4 • ☎ 09 748 2266

An incongruous 1930s villa, **Istana Batu** was built as a wedding present for Muhammad IV's grandson. One of the first concrete constructions in the state (its name means "stone palace"), today it functions as the **Kelantan Royal Museum**.

Several rooms remain as they were when the royal family moved out, and a brief wander through is worthwhile if only to survey the tat that royals the world over seem to accumulate. Here it includes – among other treasures – tiger-skin rugs, a glass revolver and piles of imported crockery.

Kampung Kraftangan
Opposite Istana Batu, Jalan Hilir Kota • Mon–Thurs, Sat & Sun 8.30am–4.45pm • Free

In the **Kampung Kraftangan** (Handicraft Village), gift shops sell everything from tacky souvenirs to silverware, rattan baskets and other local products. You can try your hand at batik at Zecsman Design (classes from RM50; ☎ 012 929 2822), and the complex is home to two branches of the excellent *Cikgu* restaurant (see p.229).

Handicraft Museum
Mon–Thurs, Sat & Sun 8.30am–4.45pm • RM4 • ☎ 09 744 3949

The small **Handicraft Museum** upstairs in Kampung Kraftangan is worth a few minutes of your time; it displays traditional craft items including silverware, woven pandan, bamboo and rattan objects, woodcarving and *songket* (textiles woven with gold thread).

Masjid Negeri
Jalan Sultan • Permission required from International Islamic Information Centre on Jalan Sultanah Zainab (Mon–Thurs, Sat & Sun 10am–6pm; ☎ 09 747 7824) • Free

The white **Masjid Negeri**, on the northern side of the padang, was completed in the late 1920s. Once you have permission and are inside the mosque – each gender sticking to their respective prayer halls – male visitors should keep an eye out for the enormous drum (*bedok*) that once summoned the faithful to prayer. The small and rather dull **Islamic Museum** is housed in a mint-green villa immediately west of the mosque.

THE MARKETS OF KOTA BHARU

Kota Bharu has a fine array of **markets**, reflecting its role as state capital and as a centre for Malay culture and handicrafts. There is also an excellent nightly **food market** (see p.229).

Bazaar Buluh Kubu West of the central market. Though lacking in atmosphere, this market does have a good range of batik, *songket* and other crafts on sale. Daily 9am–6pm.

Central market East of the historical centre. Kota Bharu's humming central market, Pasar Besar Siti Khadijah, is one of the city's focal points, and aptly named after the Prophet Mohamed's entrepreneurial first wife as most of its traders are women. The main building, an octagonal hall, has a perspex roof casting a soft light over the patchwork of the main trading floor – a mass of fruit, vegetables and textiles. The whole scene is worth contemplating at length from the upper levels, especially when it's busy in the mornings. Trading continues east of here in an extension to the original market; some brilliant first-floor food stalls make it a great place to sample Kelantanese flavours. Daily 8am–6pm.

Friday street market Jalan Ismail, south of Jalan Hulu Pasar. A visit to the informal, morning-only Friday market is recommended as a way to witness the rustic heart of Kelantan laid bare, as traders and shoppers pour in from the surrounding kampungs on their weekend day out in the city. Fri 8am–noon.

4

War Memorial Museum

Jalan Sultan • Mon–Wed, Sat & Sun 8.30am–4.45pm, Thurs 8.30am–3.30pm • RM4 • 09 748 2266

In a solid yellow building that once housed the Mercantile Bank of India, the **War Memorial Museum** commemorates the fact that Japanese troops first set foot in Malaya on Kelantan's beaches. They captured the entire state in December 1941, and Singapore fell just two months later. During the occupation, the bank was the local base for the Japanese secret police.

While the war artefacts are desultory (fragments of ordnance, ration pouches and the like), the accompanying text gives insight into the swiftness of the Japanese advance – aided by their use of bicycles – and the British collapse. The exhibition downstairs also covers the years leading up to independence, while upstairs there's an exhibit on Kelantan's peacetime history, the walls covered with fading photographs of colonial administrators.

State Museum

Jalan Hospital • Mon–Wed, Sat & Sun 9am–4.45pm, Thurs 8.30am–3.30pm • RM4

Much of the ground floor of Kelantan's **State Museum** is used for temporary exhibits, although it also includes a "time tunnel", where old photographs of locations in the city are paired with contemporary images taken of the same spots. It's fascinating to see what has – and hasn't – changed. The upper floor focuses on traditional local pastimes, with displays of kites, spinning tops, *wayang kulit* puppets and various musical instruments.

Cultural Centre

Jalan Mahmood • Feb–Oct Mon 3.30pm, Wed 3.30pm & 9pm, Sat 3.30pm & 9pm; closed during Ramadan • Free

A high point of any visit to Kota Bharu, the excellent **Cultural Centre** (Gelanggang Seni) holds demonstrations of Kelantan's cultural and recreational activities. Each day's session is different; check with the state tourist office if you have a particular interest. Performances might include a combination of *gasing* (spinning tops), *pencak silat* (martial arts), *rebana ubi* (giant drums), *kertok* (smaller drums formed from coconuts) and *congkak* (a game involving the strategic movement of seeds around the holes on a wooden board). Best of all, Wednesday evenings see **wayang kulit** (traditional shadow puppetry) performances from 9–11pm.

Craft workshops

Most of Kota Bharu's **craft workshops** lie on the road to **PCB** , the uninspiring beach 11km north of the city. As they are quite spread out, the best way to see a variety of workshops (including kite-making, batik and more) is on a tour, arranged either via your accommodation or through the state tourist office. Half-day tours cost RM80–125 per person, and often require a minimum of two people. The workshops listed here are not on the way to PCB, and are easier to visit independently.

K.B. Permai

5406 Jalan Sultanah Zainab, near Jalan Hamzah intersection • Mon–Thurs, Sat & Sun 9am–6pm • 09 748 5661

Kelantanese **silverware** is well known throughout the Peninsula. At the **K.B. Permai** workshop, you can watch artisans shaping silver wire into fine filigree, and producing items such as embossed gongs and jewellery, and you can buy pieces here, or at their retail outlet in Kampung Kraftangan (see p.223), at much keener prices than in Kuala Lumpur, starting at around RM30 for small jewellery pieces.

THE PERFORMING ARTS IN KELANTAN

Kelantan has a rich artistic tradition, boasting two costumed dance/drama forms, **mak yong** and the Thai-influenced **menora**. Even more striking is **wayang kulit**, shadow puppetry, traditionally staged on a dais screened from the audience by a large sheet and illuminated from behind. The cast consists of a set of stencils made of hide and cut into silhouettes of the various characters; these are manipulated against the screen by a sole puppeteer, who also improvises all the dialogue. Reflecting India's historic influence in the region, the tales are taken from the Hindu epic, the *Ramayana*. In the past, *wayang kulit* functioned as a sort of kampung soap opera, serializing *Ramayana* instalments nightly during the months after the rice harvest. Performances are gripping affairs, with a hypnotic soundtrack provided by an ensemble of drums, gongs and the oboe-like *serunai*, whose players are seated behind the puppeteer.

Sadly, all three of the above traditional arts have been **banned** in Kelantan since the 1990s by the PAS-led state government. PAS has cited issues of public morality, which could mean they object to the fact that both *mak yong* and *menora* can involve an element of cross-dressing. PAS also objects to the non-Islamic nature of these performances, since they involve folk tales or Hindu mythology. Finally, the party also has a problem with the **spiritualism** permeating these arts. A *wayang kulit* performance begins with a *buka panggung* ceremony, in which the puppeteer readies the stage by reciting mantras and making offerings of food to the spirits, while *mak yong* can be staged for an individual as part of a folk-healing tradition called *main puteri*, in which the performers enter a trance to remove a spirit believed to be affecting that person.

Whatever the reasons for the ban, it has effectively deprived a generation of Kelantanese of their own traditions. A mere handful of *wayang kulit* troupes survive, performing outside Kelantan or, thanks to one **concession** from PAS, for the benefit of the largely tourist audience at Kota Bharu's Cultural Centre. On a brighter note, all three forms mentioned here are being passed on to a new generation outside their home state, at the National Academy of Arts, Culture and Heritage in KL (ⓦ aswara.edu.my), which occasionally stages performances.

Pak Yusoff workshop

Kampung Laut • Boat (RM2) from the jetty close to the Ridel Hotel • ☎ 012 340 6498

A *wayang kulit* **puppeteer** who also makes the tools of his trade, **Pak Yusoff** can be visited in Kampung Laut on the west bank of the Kelantan River. His workshop, to the right of the pier as you get off the boat, holds examples of his distinctive translucent puppets. Though it has become a well-worn stop on the tourist trail as it's the most easily accessible workshop from town, it's still a great excuse to take the atmospheric ferry ride across the river.

Buddhist temples

Tours (arranged via state tourist office or your guesthouse) RM65–80/person; 4–5hrs, including visit to nearby craft workshops

The area **north of Kota Bharu** is dotted with **Buddhist temples**, many decorated with a striking combination of Thai and Chinese motifs. The temples can be visited using buses bound for the Thai border at **Pengkalan Kubor**. It's a slow process, getting from one to the next on public transport (though it can also be done using local taxis); if you're pushed for time it's best to take a tour from the state tourist office or your guesthouse. The temples are especially worth visiting during **Vesak Day**, the festival (usually in May) celebrating the Buddha's birthday.

Wat Pracacinaram

Kampung Kulim, just outside Wakaf Bharu, on the road to Cabang Empat • Bus #19 or #27

The highly conspicuous main building of **Wat Pracacinaram** has an elaborate triple-layered roof decorated in gold, sapphire and red. The temple offers a herbal **steam bath** – with separate facilities for men and women – for RM5.

AROUND KOTA BHARU

Wat Phothivihan
Kampung Jambu • Bus #19 or #27; get off at Cabang Empat then walk 3.5km

The 40m-long reclining Buddha at **Wat Phothivihan** is the largest in Malaysia. The rather bland plaster statue was made by the monks themselves and contains ashes of the deceased who have been laid to rest here. Refreshments are available from *kedai kopis* inside the temple grounds.

Wat Machimmaram
Kampung Jubakar, 7km north of Cabang Empat • Bus #27

Topped by a 30m-high bronze-tiled seated Buddha, **Wat Machimmaram** contains bas-reliefs that depict the graphic punishments of hell – the corrupt are, for example, doomed to have molten tin poured into their mouths, while meat eaters are shown reincarnated as pigs on the carving block. Thai **massages** (RM40; ☎011 1931 5752) are available in a separate block.

Wat Mai Suwankiri
Around 4.5km southeast of Tumpat • Bus #43 stops outside the temple and #19 stops 500m away

The most striking construction at **Wat Mai Suwankiri** is a shrine built in the shape of a dragon boat, surrounded by a narrow moat to give the impression that it is afloat. The main temple hall is crowned by an elongated standing Buddha, its gorgeous interior decorated with hundreds of golden plaques.

Suri Island

Taxi to Kuala Besar (20–30min; RM25) then boat (15–20min; RM2); alternatively #43 bus to Jeti Kok Majid (1hr) then boat (40min; RM10/person, or RM50/boat)

One of many small riverine islands north of Kota Bharu, **Suri Island** is home to around five hundred people. Getting there is half the fun, requiring a trip down the tea-coloured Kelantan River in a motorized sampan, and the island itself has some pleasant paths for walking and a well-developed **homestay** programme (see p.229).

There are two ways to reach Suri from Kota Bharu. The most common route goes via **Kuala Besar** (not to be confused with Kuala Besut in Terengganu). While the second route, via **Jeti Kok Majid**, an hour's bus ride from the city centre, is considerably more scenic, it's also more time-consuming. If you're staying on the island, contact the homestay organizer in advance to arrange transport.

Arriving at Suri, you'll spot a boatyard next to the jetty where they mend traditional wooden craft. There's also a simple **café** or two for refreshments. From here you can head inland along a path lined with coconut trees.

ARRIVAL AND DEPARTURE

KOTA BHARU

BY PLANE

Sultan Ismail Petra airport The airport lies 9km northeast of the centre. The #9 bus runs between town and airport until 7pm. Official airport taxis (pre-paid at the counter before you exit customs) cost RM30 to get into town and RM93 to the Perhentians jetty at Kuala Besut. MAS (☎09 771 4700), Malindo (☎09 771 5082) and AirAsia (☎09 774 1421) offer a dozen flights between them between Kota Bharu and KL, while Firefly (☎09 774 1377) also has a couple of daily flights to Penang.

BY TRAIN

Train station The nearest station is 7km away in Wakaf Bharu (☎09 719 6986), a 20min ride on bus #19 (daytime only) from the local bus station – watch for the late-afternoon rush hour – or a RM20 taxi journey. Check the latest schedules at ⊛ www.ktmb.com.my. Change at Johor Bahru for Singapore, and at Gemas for Kuala Lumpur.
Destinations Dabong (4 daily; 2hr 45min–3hr 20min); Gemas (6am daily; 12hr); Gua Musang (3 daily; 4hr 35min–6hr 25min); Jerantut (6.16pm daily; 8hr); Johor Bahru (6pm daily; 14hr 40min); Kuala Lipis (6pm daily; 7hr 15min); Merapoh (6pm daily; 4hr).

BY BUS

Express bus station (aka Tesco Bus Station) Close to the eponymous supermarket, near the Kelantan River bridge on the southern edge of town; a RM10–15 taxi ride from the centre. Express bus tickets, including Perdana Express, can be purchased from a row of cabins just south of the local bus station on Jalan Doktor. Note that using Transnasional long-distance buses, which arrive and depart from the local bus station, is much more convenient, though a smidgen more expensive. Most long distance services leave between 8–10am and 8–10pm.
Destinations Alor Setar (10am & 10pm daily; 7–8hr); Butterworth (4 daily; 7hr); Gua Musang (3 daily; 3hr); Ipoh

(4 daily; 5hr); Johor Bahru (4 daily; 12hr); Kuala Kangsar (3 daily; 6hr 30min); Kuala Lumpur (12 daily; 8hr); Kuala Terengganu (12 daily; 3hr); Kuantan (10 daily; 7hr); Melaka (3 daily; 10hr 30min); Mersing (3 daily; 9hr 30min); Penang (3 daily; 7hr 15min); Seremban (3 daily; 10hr).

Local bus station Off Jalan Doktor in the town centre. Used by Cityliner buses running to places within or just outside Kelantan – notably Wakaf Bharu (#19 or #27, for trains), the Thai border crossings at Rantau Panjang (#29) and Pengkalan Kubor (#27 and #43), and Kuala Besut (#639, for the Perhentians; 7am, 9pm, 11am, 1pm & 5pm daily; 2hr). It is also used by Transnasional long-distance buses.
Destinations Alor Setar (9.30am & 9.30pm daily; 7–8hr); Butterworth (9.45am & 9.30pm daily; 7hr); Gua Musang (3 daily; 3hr); Ipoh (9.30am & 9.30pm daily; 5hr); Johor Bahru (3 daily; 12hr); Kuala Kangsar (9.30am & 9.30pm daily; 6hr 30min); Kuala Lumpur (10 daily; 8hr); Kuala Terengganu (5 daily; 3hr); Kuantan (7 daily; 7hr); Melaka (8.30pm daily; 10hr 30min); Mersing (1 daily; 9hr 30min); Penang (9.45am & 10pm daily; 8hr); Seremban (9.45am & 9.15pm daily; 10hr); Singapore (8pm daily; 13hr).

BY TAXI OR MINIVAN

Long-distance taxis Taxis depart from a yard on Jalan Doktor, south of the local bus station. A taxi to Kuala Besut will set you back RM60. Call ☎09 748 1386 to book. Note that you can no longer reach the Cameron Highlands and Taman Negara from Kota Bharu; minibuses to these destinations are now only available from Gua Musang or Kuala Besut.

TO THAILAND

There are two road crossings into Thailand – and none by rail – on the east coast. The closest large Thai town to either is Narathiwat, served by buses to other parts of southern Thailand and flights to Bangkok. Although the security

4

situation in southern Thailand has improved slightly in recent years, it's worth checking online for the current situation – at the time of writing, Western governments were still advising against travelling this way from Thailand. Visas for Thailand can be obtained from the consulate in Kota Bharu (see p.230) if required. Note that Thailand is one hour behind Malaysia.

Rantau Panjang The recommended crossing is at Rantau Panjang (daily 8am–9pm), 45km southwest of Kota Bharu; get there by local bus #29 (every 30min, 6.45am–6.30pm; 1hr–1hr 30min) or taxi (RM40;

45min). From Sungai Kolok, a short walk across the border on the Thai side, trains run to Bangkok, via Hat Yai and Surat Thani (11.30am & 2.20pm; 20–22hr; ⓦrailway.co.th), and frequent buses head to Hat Yai (hourly; 6am–4pm; 4hr).

Pengkalan Kubor The other crossing – slower to get through and with worse transport links – is at Pengkalan Kubor (daily around 8am–7pm), 25km northwest of Kota Bharu; take local bus #19, #27 or #43 (30min), or a taxi (RM30) then a car ferry (RM5). The small town of Tak Bai stands on the Thai side.

GETTING AROUND

By bus Red Cityliner buses serve most parts of the city and its environs in daylight hours. Useful routes include #10, which runs to PCB from Kampung Kraftangan.

By taxi Local taxis wait in the same yard as long-distance taxis. Drivers don't use meters, so agree the price before you leave. Journeys within the centre typically cost RM10. Most accommodations can call for private taxis, which are half the price of those hailed in

the street. Taxis can also be arranged by the hour for around RM30–35/hr.

By trishaw A few tourist-oriented trishaws can be found around the central market for short hops within the centre; agree fares, usually RM5–10, in advance.

Car rental Hawk (☎013 924 2455, ⓦhawkrentacar.com. my) and J&W (☎09 773 7312, ⓦjwcarental.com) have offices at the airport.

INFORMATION AND TOURS

Tourist information The state tourist office (Mon–Wed & Sun 8am–5pm, Thurs 8am–3.30pm; ☎09 748 5534, ⓦtic.kelantan.gov.my) on Jalan Sultan Ibrahim can tell you about festivals and give you a timetable of events at the Cultural Centre. The Tourism Malaysia office (Mon–Wed & Sun 8am–5pm, Thurs 8am–3.30pm; ☎09 747 7554) is at Kampung Kraftangan, Seksyen 20,

northwest of the central market.

Tours Doremi Travel & Tours (☎09 774 7458), or any of the town's backpacker hostels (especially *Zeck's*) can arrange city and craft tours, as well as the popular firefly tour along the Pengkalan River (8.30pm; 1hr; RM20/person). Roselan Hanafiah, based at the state tourist office, can also put together craft workshop tours (4–5hr; RM125/person).

ACCOMMODATION

Kota Bharu has an excellent range of accommodation. Budget travellers will appreciate the good-value if occasionally scruffy **guesthouses**, many of which can arrange tickets for onward travel and offer packages to Taman Negara via Kuala Koh and Stong State Park (see p.214).

HOTELS

Crown Garden 302 & 303 Jalan Kebun Sultan ☎09 743 2228, ⓦcrowngardenhotel.com; map p.222. At the upper end of the city's accommodation options, this 88-room hotel has marble floors and striking modern decor plus a seventh-floor bar. The cheapest rooms are cramped but still nicely appointed, and price includes a breakfast buffet. ☏ <u>RM150</u>

Crystal Lodge 124 Jalan Che Su ☎609 747 0888, ⓦcrystallodge.my; map p.222. Sleek mid-range hotel, with a café-restaurant, parking and satellite TV. The compact single (RM129) and superior single (RM159) rooms are good value, though the standard doubles and windowless twins are a bit disappointing. Breakfast included. ☏ <u>RM169</u>

Habib Lot 1159–1162, Jalan Maju ☎09 747 4788, ⓦhabibhotel.com.my; map p.222. Friendly, centrally located and a solid mid-range choice, featuring squeaky

clean rooms with flat-screen TVs. Deluxe rooms (RM190) are more spacious but otherwise identical to their cheaper counterparts. Price includes (a somewhat limited) breakfast. ☏ <u>RM160</u>

Perdana Jalan Mahmood ☎09 745 8888, ⓦhotelperdanakotabharu.com; map p.222. This Malaysian-owned five-star hotel is divided into two wings, "classic" and "executive", with slightly higher prices in the latter; both have the same comfortable rooms and psychedelic carpets. The multiple food outlets are alcohol-free. Breakfast included. ☏ <u>RM288</u>

Renaissance Jalan Sultan Yahya Petra ☎09 746 2233, ⓦmarriott.com; map p.222. Some of the 298 rooms in Kota Bharu's first five-star hotel enjoy great views over the city, though it now needs a bit of renovation. Facilities include two restaurants, a gorgeous semi-outdoor pool, spa and a 24-hour gym. You'll save around a third if you book from the website. ☏ <u>RM306</u>

4

Royal Guest House Lot 440–443 Jalan Hilir Kota ☎ 09 743 0008, ⓦ royalguesthse.com; map p.222. Despite its far-from-regal exterior, this conveniently central 45-room hotel is comparatively stylish inside, though the rooms are very brown and some are quite dark. It also offers a multi-cuisine restaurant as well as room service, though the proximity to the mosque (which occasionally broadcasts day-long sermons) may not suit light sleepers. Breakfast included. ⓦ RM140

GUESTHOUSES

Ideal Travellers' House 3954 f & g Jalan Kebun Sultan ☎ 09 744 2246; map p.222. The oldest guesthouse in town, somewhat worn but great value; most rooms have a fan and shared bathroom, but the three a/c rooms have private bathrooms, hot water and balconies. Friendly owner Kang offers temple tours (3hr; RM90) and sells both beer and Perhentian taxi/boat tickets. ⓦ RM30

KB Backpackers Lodge First floor, 1872d Jalan Padang Garong ☎ 019 944 5222, ⓔ backpackerslodge2@yahoo .co.uk; map p.222. Friendly travellers' haunt with private rooms, a bare-bones dorm and small library. Knowledgeable staff can arrange transfers, excursions, and city tours (RM80) as well as rent bikes (RM25/day). Not to be confused with the run-down *KB Backpacker Inn* across the road. ⓦ Dorms RM15, doubles RM35

★ **My Place Guesthouse** 4340 Jalan Kebun Sultan ☎ 013 901 1463, ⓔ myplacekb@yahoo.com; map p.222. Good backpacker option with appealing common areas, free tea and toast, and a movie room. The seven partitioned bedrooms are small but decent, all with shared bathrooms; a new site with larger rooms down the road should open in 2018. Owner Deen arranges city

tours (RM80) and trips to Taman Negara (two nights, RM450). ⓦ RM35

★ **Pasir Belanda** Jalan PCB, Banggol district, 5km north of the city ☎ 09 747 7046, ⓦ pasirbelanda. com; map p.222. This rural Dutch-run establishment consists of seven traditionally styled chalets, set in an immaculate garden with a swimming pool overlooking a creek. Activities include batik (RM35) and Malay cookery lessons (RM60), and they offer kayak and bike rental. Catch #10 bus to Banggol mosque, then follow signs 1.5km east, or take a RM20 taxi. Two-night minimum stay. ⓦ RM160

Zeck's Travellers' Inn Off Jalan Sri Cemerlang ☎ 09 743 1613, ⓔ zecktravellers@yahoo.com; map p.222. Friendly Malay guesthouse in a quiet residential area, with dorms and simple rooms with fan or a/c, some with private bathrooms. Tours and ticket booking are available, and bird-singing contests are held nearby on Friday and Saturday mornings. Dorms ⓦ RM15, doubles RM35

HOMESTAYS

KB homestay programme Various locations. Roselan Hanafiah, at the state tourist office, can arrange for visitors to stay with a local family whose members are expert in a particular craft. The price given here is per night, based on a standard two-night package for two people including all meals and activities. RM555

Pantai Suri homestay programme Suri Island ☎ 013 900 8820, ⓦ homestaypantaisuri.blogspot.com. Contact Fadhila Hanim, the programme coordinator to stay in one of the participating homes; conditions can be fairly basic. You can pay per night (including all meals) or for a two-night package (RM280) that may include fishing, crab catching and *kuih sepit* (wafer snack) making. RM150

EATING

Kota Bharu has plenty of **restaurants** dotted around the centre, plus some excellent food options at the main market and the nightly **Medan Selera** (night food market). The Chinese places on Jalan Kebun Sultan are among the few restaurants that aren't halal, and are your best bet for **alcohol**. Otherwise, the rather unexciting *Golden City* (Mon–Fri & Sun 4pm–midnight), next to *Pizza Hut* on Jalan Padang Garong, is the city's sole bar. For a good spot to watch the sun set over the river, head for the line of restaurants behind the closed Pelangi Mall.

Arnold Cycling Cafe Jalan Kebun Sultan ☎ 09 744 6888; map p.222. Everything a modern traveller wants from a café, with good a/c, plug sockets, strong wi-fi, decent coffee (RM8–18) and a range of delicious pastries (RM10–15). Despite the name, the only thing cycling-related is the bike hung on the wall. Daily 9am–midnight

★ **Cikgu** Kampung Kraftangan ☎ 019 940 6066; map p.222. Busy self-service lunch place, offering the classic Malay meal *nasi ulam* (a rice salad with blanched vegetables and herbs – some of them incredibly bitter). Dishes like fried chicken, vegetable curry and *asam*

pedas ikan patin (catfish in spicy sauce) are laid out alongside rice and *ulam*. If you're feeling brave, have the dip made of *tempoyak* (fermented durian) and *budu* (fermented fish sauce). Cheap (around RM8 for a filling meal) and best enjoyed with a group. Mon–Thurs, Sat & Sun 11.30am–4.30pm.

Medan Selera (night food market) Off Jalan Pintu Pong; map p.222. The few dozen stalls on the field here offer a great range of *murtabak* (savoury stuffed pancakes) as well as Kelantanese specialities such as *nasi kerabu* (rice tinted blue, traditionally using flower petals, and typically served with fish curry). Wash your meal down with *sup ekor* (oxtail soup) or *sup tulang* (made from beef bones), and round it off by sampling the colourful *kuih* (sweets). Almost everything costs RM1–5. Daily 6pm–midnight.

Muhibah Jalan Pintu Pong ☎ 09 744 3668; map p.222. Excellent, inexpensive vegetarian establishment. Downstairs a bakery café serves pastries and ice-blended shakes; the upstairs restaurant puts on a great veggie *nasi campur* spread (RM6–7), as well as à la carte dishes like "chicken" *rendang* (RM8) and other Chinese and Malay favourites using the Chinese-style textured tofu instead of meat. Daily: restaurant 10am–9pm; bakery 8.30am–10pm.

Shan Sri Dewi Jalan Kebun Sultan ☎ 09 746 2980; map p.222. Top-notch Malaysian-Indian *kedai kopi*, popular with locals but often with a scattering of foreigners, serving excellent banana-leaf *thalis* (from RM5–12) as well as snacks such as *roti canai*, *masala dosa*, *idly* and *vada* (RM2–4.50). Daily 7.30am–8.30pm.

Tang Ah Juan 4343 Jalan Kebun Sultan ☎ 012 983 2788; map p.222. Very popular with the local Chinese, this fairly basic diner with plastic tables and chairs in the heart of Chinatown serves a very decent Chaozhou-style Cantonese *nasi campur* for RM5–8; it also serves beer (RM18). Mon–Wed & Fri–Sun 9am–6pm.

★**Warisan Nasi Kukus** Jalan Kebun Sultan; map p.222. In front of the 7-11, this once humble pushcart operation is very popular, renowned for fresh *sambal* fish, okra curry, *ikan bakar* (grilled fish) and the like for around RM6–8 a helping. Your preferred toppings will be poured over steamed rice (*nasi kukus*), on a newspaper that's folded into a cone and wrapped for you to take away or eat at their plastic tables. Daily 6pm–late.

White House Jalan Sultanah Zainab ☎ 09 748 4119; map p.222. No grand mansion (though next to one) but a ramshackle bungalow housing a *kedai kopi* that's a city institution. The trademark dish is humble *telur setengah masak* – soft-boiled eggs cracked into a saucer, seasoned with soy sauce and white pepper (RM3), and delicious scooped up with *roti bakar* (buttered toast). Washed down with *teh* or *kopi tarik*, it's great for breakfast or a late snack. Daily 8am–1pm & 9pm–1am.

SHOPPING

In addition to its **markets**, Kota Bharu is also a good place to buy Malay **handicrafts**, with most of the workshops located outside town.

KB Mall Jalan Hamzah ☎ 09 747 6622; ⓦ mallofmalaysia.com.my; map p.222. For general shopping, this mall is useful, housing the huge Pacific supermarket, several branded clothing stores, Western food chains, a branch of Watsons pharmacy and plenty more besides. Daily 10am–10.30pm.

Mydin Jalan Pintu Pong; map p.222. Useful supermarket selling essentials. Daily 9am–10.30pm.

Parkson Jalan Parit Dalam; map p.222. A department store that includes a branch of the Giant supermarket. Daily 10am–10pm.

DIRECTORY

Hospital Jalan Hospital ☎ 09 745 2000.

Left luggage At the local bus station (daily 8am–8pm, Fri closed 12.30–2pm; RM2/day).

Pharmacies Central pharmacies include Guardian on Jalan Padang Garong and Watsons in KB Mall.

Police Jalan Sultan Ibrahim (☎ 09 748 5522).

Thai visas Many nationalities can get a visa at the border. Otherwise, visas can be obtained in advance from the Thai Consulate, 4426 Jalan Pengkalan Chepa (Mon–Thurs & Sun 9am–noon & 2–3.30pm; ☎ 09 743 0640); they have been known to refuse entry to people in shorts, so dress smartly.

Visa extensions At the Pejabat Imigresen (Immigration Department), Wisma Persekutuan, Jalan Bayam (Mon–Thurs & Sun 8am–4pm; ☎ 09 748 2120). Take bus #11 or #639; a taxi will cost RM10–15.

From Kota Bharu to Kuala Terengganu

Though there are a few resorts by the shore, plus some interesting villages and wildlife in the **Setiu Wetlands**, few travellers linger on the coast south of Kota Bharu; most are simply waiting for a boat from **Kuala Besut** (for the Perhentian Islands) or **Merang** (to Redang or Lang Tengah islands; not to be confused with Marang further south). Whether you're staying or passing through, get money before you set out; there are **no ATMs** on any of the islands, or near the jetty in Kuala Besut, though some hotels accept cards, and you might be able to get a cash advance (at punitive rates).

Kuala Besut

The only reason to visit the mainland town of **KUALA BESUT** is to catch a boat to the Perhentian Islands. Kuala Besut comprises a few lanes lined with **hotel offices** and **travel agencies** selling Perhentians packages and boat tickets at similar prices, with most of the action concentrated between the peach-coloured **boat terminal** complex and the **express bus and taxi station**.

ARRIVAL AND DEPARTURE KUALA BESUT

By bus There are express buses to KL and Penang directly from Kuala Besut Express bus station, but for other destinations you'll need to take a taxi (RM30–40; 30min) to the closest transport hub, Jerteh. However, coming from Kota Bharu, Cityliner bus #639 from the local bus station on Jalan Doktor will drop you at the jetty. S.P. Bumi runs a slow, sweaty bus service between the express bus station and Kuala Terengganu via Merang.
Destinations Kota Bharu (5 daily; 2hr); Kuala Lumpur (8 daily; 8hr); Kuala Terengganu (5 daily; 3hr); Penang (8am & 9pm daily; 8hr).
By taxi The taxi stand is next to the bus station, but drivers will also swoop on new arrivals from the islands.

Destinations Jerteh (RM20); Kota Bharu (RM68; RM75 to airport); Kuala Terengganu (RM130); Marang (RM150); Merang (RM85).
By minibus Several travel agents arrange minibuses to a handful of major destinations, including Cameron Highlands (RM60), Penang (RM70) and Taman Negara (RM80); all depart 10am.
By boat Boats sail from Kuala Besut Jetty to the Perhentians several times a day, leaving when full (daily 7am–5.30pm; 30min; RM35 one way). Operators usually sell open-return tickets (RM70), with boats returning to Kuala Besut at 8am, noon and 4pm. Boat service is regular from March to October; at other times sailings are much reduced.

ACCOMMODATION AND EATING

Nan Hotel Down the lane opposite the boat terminal ☎ 09 697 4892. Among Kuala Besut's cheaper rooms, all in decent condition. A couple of rooms have a/c and TV, while the most expensive (RM130) even has hot water. There are plenty of other options along the same street. RM55
Restoran Seafood Lucky Just north of the jetty on Jalan Besar ☎ 013 997 9354. This place opens extra early for breakfast, offering dishes such as *nasi ayam* (RM6) and noodles throughout the day, but it's the more expensive fresh seafood served later on that attracts most people. Daily 5am–10pm.

Samudera 200m north of the jetty on Jalan Besar ☎ 09 697 9326, ⓦ kekal-samudera.com. The 28 candy-coloured a/c rooms here are spacious, comfortable and reasonably good value, and it's certainly a step up from the other guesthouses near the jetty. RM112
T'Cafe Near the bus ticket offices ☎ 09 697 8777. Deservedly popular *kopi kedai* dishing up *roti canai* and *nasi dagang* (RM2–4) for breakfast, with variations on the rice-and-noodle theme and *kerabu* salads (RM6–8) to keep you going for the rest of the day. Daily 7am–10pm.

The Perhentian Islands

The name **Perhentian Islands** (Pulau Perhentian) actually covers two islands, **Perhentian Besar** and **Perhentian Kecil** (Big Island and Small Island are sometimes used instead, though Suitcase Island and Backpack Island might be more accurate descriptions). Both are textbook tropical paradises, which retain considerable appeal despite having been developed for tourism. The essentials of any idyllic island holiday – fantastic sandy beaches, great **snorkelling** and **diving** – are all in place. Both islands have jungly hills in their interior, with paths for **walking** and opportunities to spot flying foxes, monkeys and monitor lizards. All this is capped by a refreshingly laidback atmosphere that can make it difficult to tear yourself away.

For many years, large-scale development on the Perhentians was kept to a minimum. This was just as well, given that both islands have several **turtle nesting** sites, active from April to early August – the only organized viewing is through the *Bubbles* resort (see p.238) – and that the impact of the existing resorts on the environment is far from negligible. Shortages of **water**, for example, can be a hassle during peak season. The state government's attitude towards development has loosened in recent years, however, and a few larger resorts have been completed, with more in the works – particularly on

Perhentian Kecil. **Alcohol** is sold openly at restaurants and bars on both islands, and there's even a modest party scene at Long Beach.

ARRIVAL AND DEPARTURE THE PERHENTIAN ISLANDS

By boat All access to the Perhentians is from the mainland town of Kuala Besut (see p.231); boats depart several times a day (usually when full), regularly from March to October, with reduced sailings at other times. All will drop you at the bay of your choice, though at beaches without a jetty you may have to transfer to a smaller boat. The day before your departure, staff at your accommodation will arrange for you to be picked up, with boats usually leaving at 8am, noon and 4pm.

GETTING AROUND

By water-taxi Small speedboats operate a so-called water-taxi service around the Perhentians. Fares start at RM10 per person for a journey between adjacent bays – rocky obstructions often preclude walking – rising to RM25 to travel from one side of Besar to the other, or RM15 from one island to the other. Prices are clearly displayed in front of each water-taxi stand, with little room for bargaining, and it's usually possible to rustle up a boatman within a few minutes. The exception to this is after dark, when water-taxis can become scarce and you may have to pay double the usual fare. If you simply need to get to the next beach, you may be able to use a footpath instead (after dark a torch is essential).

ACCOMMODATION

Perhentian Kecil caters largely to the backpacker scene, and much of its accommodation is in low-priced chalets and resorts, many with restricted electricity supply. The construction of several **mid-range resorts**, however, has brought the same families, package tourists and better-heeled independent travellers that have traditionally gravitated to Perhentian Besar. Book in advance for the **peak season** – roughly June until the end of August – and at weekends, or you may have trouble getting a room. Many mid-range places offer full-board packages, typically for three days and two nights, and include boat transfers and some snorkelling or diving. B&B deals are also available, and unless you're on one of the more remote beaches, there's no shortage of places to eat. Outside peak season rates fall by at least a quarter. Many resorts begin closing in late October, sometimes earlier, and don't open again until February or March, but for a truly isolated island experience a few places stay open during the northeast monsoon. Note that both internet and 3/4G services are almost unusable on the islands, especially during the peak season, as there simply isn't enough bandwidth for either, and many places no longer bother with wi-fi due to the associated hassle. If you do have internet access, however, note that it generally works best between 2–8am.

Perhentian Kecil

The small island of **Perhentian Kecil** has something to please most people. If you're looking for a laidback backpacker scene with the odd beach party, you've come to the right place, but several mid-range resorts cater for those who need a comfortable bed after a day snorkelling. The most popular beaches, **Coral Bay** and **Long Beach**, are only ten minutes' walk apart, along a woodland footpath.

Long Beach

For many visitors, east-facing **Long Beach**, boasting a wide stretch of glistening-white, deep, soft sand, is the prime attraction of Perhentian Kecil. The pretty beach is possibly over-busy, far from litter free, and lacks a view of the sunset, but somehow that really doesn't matter: the light gently fades away, leaving the illumination from the beach restaurants (and their Bob Marley or dance music playlists) to dominate the senses. Come nightfall there's a genuinely infectious buzz – in peak season expect pop-up bars and a party vibe on the beach.

Coral Bay and the west coast

While west-facing **Coral Bay** has become significantly more developed since the building of its huge and ugly jetty, it remains quieter and more relaxed than Long Beach. It also has sheltered waters, which make it a better bet than its eastern rival during the northeast monsoon, plus good snorkelling and sunset views, if you can ignore the jetty.

ACCOMMODATION						
Abdul's Chalet	28	Ecoteer Community House	19	Oh La La	1	
B'First Chalets	32	Ewan's Place	11	Ombak Dive Resort	12	
Bayu Dive Lodge	33	Fauna Beach	30	Panorama	2	
Bintang View	5	Flora Bay & Flora Bay 2	29/31	Perhentian Island Resort	21	
Bubbles	34	Lemon Grass	6	Reef Chalets	23	
Bubu Resort	17	Mama's Chalet	25	Senja Bay Resort	14	
Butterfly	15	Mari Mari	20	Shari-La Island Resort	10	
Chempaka	8	Matahari	3	Sunrise	4	
Coral View	22	Maya Chalet	13	Tropicana Inn & Tivoli Backpackers	9	
D'Rock Garden	7	Mira Beach Chalet	18	Tunabay Island Resort	27	
D'Lagoon	16	New Cocohut	26	Watercolours Paradise Resort	24	

EATING	
Chillout Café	3
Ewan's Café	2
Rainforest Campground and Café	4
World Café	1

DRINKING	
Monkey Bar	1

A couple of quieter and more secluded beaches lie south of Coral Bay, with accommodation in rustic campsites or guesthouses reached along a shady coastal footpath. **Mira Beach** has just one backpacker hangout, while **Petani Beach** has two resorts awkwardly jammed into its eastern end, and two smaller guesthouses enjoying the remaining stretch of beach.

ACCOMMODATION   PERHENTIAN KECIL

Room rates on Perhentian Kecil – particularly on **Long Beach** – are rather fluid, varying from day to day with demand. Most of the cheaper accommodations are pretty poor value and badly maintained, mainly due to the scarcity of rooms during high season, so don't expect too much for your money – booking ahead is also highly recommended. The prices

---

PERHENTIANS DOS AND DON'TS

• Do bring more than enough **cash** – there are no banks or ATMs. Only mid-range places accept plastic for accommodation and food, often with a small surcharge. Several places offer cash advances for a significant fee.

• Do bring mosquito repellent.

• Don't leave **valuables**, even clothes, unattended on the beach – whether crowded or deserted – while you swim or snorkel. Thieves can appear seemingly from nowhere on snatch-and-grab raids, a particular problem on Perhentian Kecil. Also be aware thieves sometimes enter rooms, so keep your valuables with you if possible, and make sure your room is completely secured before you go out.

• Do **swim with care**: look out for boat lanes, marked by strings of buoys, and stay on the correct side to avoid being wiped out by a speedboat. Note also that Long Beach can have a significant **undertow** from February to April and in October; a few people get swept out every year and have to be rescued.

• Do be mindful of volleyball nets and sharp-pronged boat **anchors** sticking out of the sand as you walk along the beach at night – particularly if you're looking up at the stars.

• Don't touch the **coral** or disturb **marine life** when you snorkel or dive.

---

quoted here are at the higher end of the range for each property; ask about discounts if you visit midweek or either side of the July–August peak. Almost all accommodations now have attached dive shops, and rooms are much better value as part of a dive package. Due to the scarcity of rooms during high season there are now several places to camp, with campsites on Long Beach at the *Chillout Café* and at *Awatif* next door, as well as at the *Rainforest Campground and Café* between Coral Bay and Mira Beach

4

LONG BEACH

If you would rather a good night's sleep than party, don't stay anywhere near the beach.

★ **Bintang View** A short walk uphill from the beach ☎ 019 309 2145; map p.233. Run by a friendly Malay-Irish couple. Not the fanciest of chalets, but well-kept and very homely. Some of the fan-cooled chalets have en-suite bathrooms, while cheaper cabins lack power sockets and share facilities in a separate block. Electricity 7pm–7am. RM80

Bubu Resort Long Beach ☎ 016 260 3547, reservations ☎ 03 2142 6688, ⓦ buburesort.com; map p.233. With a motel-like complex of en-suite a/c rooms at one end of Long Beach, and a clutch of deluxe villas at the other, plus two spas and three restaurants (including the only Japanese), *Bubu* dominates the upper end of Perhentian Kecil's accommodation. The rooms and villas are perfectly nice, but it jars a little here. ⓦ Doubles RM871, villas RM1100

Chempaka End of the beach ☎ 013 697 7604; map p.233. This tucked-away place has a mishmash of run-down A-frames, and better en-suite chalets in a longhouse-type block around a pleasant garden. Electricity 7pm–7am. A-frames RM80, chalets RM120

★ **D'Rock Garden Resort** On the beach's southern headland ☎ 03 8920 2922, ⓦ rockgardenchalet.com; map p.233. A prime location on the hill overlooking the beach, the standard fan rooms with shared bathrooms are basic, but clean and pretty good value (a sea view will cost

RM90 extra, though) while the better a/c rooms are all en suite and have views of the sea (RM230), though hot water costs a staggering RM100 extra. There's 24hr electricity and wi-fi in the restaurant, which boasts the best views of the beach around. ⓦ RM60

Lemon Grass Long Beach ☎ 019 938 3893; map p.233. Splintery but sound chalets with fans, hammocks and mosquito nets; bathrooms in a separate shack. Three sea-view rooms are available for RM120. There's sporadic electricity and a two-night minimum stay in peak season. RM70

Matahari Set back from Long Beach ☎ 019 914 2883, ⓦ mataharichalet.com; map p.233. A hotel of two halves, with a collection of wooden chalets (fan and newer a/c ones) and A-frames, with an incongruous two-storey concrete dorm and fan room block – the dorms are pretty grubby, however. The largely en-suite chalets are a little rough around the edges, but pretty good value and popular. Both are accessed down a footpath that runs over a smelly creek. Electricity 6.30pm–9am & noon-3pm. Dorms RM30, chalets RM90

Oh La La Long Beach, ☎ 019 331 9624, ⓦ ohlalaperhentian.com; map p.233. European-run dive resort with ten simple wood-partitioned fan rooms, and a dorm, all with shared bathrooms. It's above one bar and beside another, however, so is quite noisy at night. There's a pleasant communal balcony with hammocks; most people staying here are doing dive courses as room prices are halved if you're doing one. ⓦ Dorms RM40, doubles RM80

Panorama Set back from Long Beach ☏ 019 960 8630; ⓦ panoramaperhentianisland.com; map p.233. Overpriced chalets with fans or a/c, plus better-value dorms, all set around a messy hillside garden. There's a popular restaurant plus a dive shop; they offer all-inclusive diving packages. High-season rates often include one free meal. Electricity 11am–4.30pm & 6.30pm–8am. ⓦ Dorms RM50, chalets RM120

Sunrise Long Beach ☏ 017 930 9053; map p.233. In the thick of things on the top floor of the two-storey block of shops in the middle of the beach. Ten-person dorms and fan-cooled rooms are a bit grotty but okay for just sleeping and understandably popular with those on a tight budget. Dorms RM20, doubles RM100

Tropicana Inn & Tivoli Backpackers Midway between Long Beach and Coral Bay ☏ 09 691 8888; map p.233. A compact development with 160 rooms in neat whitewashed bungalows, with budget and more upmarket (RM300) sections that share a reception. The good-value fan rooms and dorms (min. 3 nights) are the stars here, being bright and far cleaner than their equivalents on Long Beach. ⓦ Dorms RM30, doubles RM80

CORAL BAY

Butterfly At the end of Coral Bay ☏ 012 966 4232; map p.233. The tucked away, budget chalets strung out on the hill on the headland here are run-down but charming, popular with long-term guests including dive masters. The further you get from reception, the better the sea views become. Electricity 7pm–7am. RM70

Ewan's Place Just behind Coral Bay ☏ 014 817 8303; map p.233. A great choice if you don't mind being a couple of minutes from the beach, with clean and tidy rooms set around a scrubby clearing. The en-suite chalets are nicely maintained, with mosquito nets and *almost* 24hr electricity. Friendly owner Ewan also runs the on-site café, which has wi-fi. ⓦ RM90

Maya Chalet Coral Bay ☏ 019 990 2561; map p.233. En-suite fan chalets around a garden compound, with electricity 7pm–7am and a premium for sea-view rooms (RM170). They allow camping in the garden and can rent you a tent for RM10/day, as well as organizing popular snorkelling trips. Camping RM10, chalets RM50

Ombak Dive Resort Coral Bay ☏ 09 691 1002, ⓦ ombak.my; map p.233. A modern multistorey complex, *Ombak* has 24 fan and a/c rooms (RM100 extra)

4

SNORKELLING AND DIVING AROUND THE PERHENTIANS

Outside the monsoon, the waters around the Perhentians are superb with gentle currents and visibility up to 20m (although sea lice can sometimes be an irritant, inflicting unpleasant but harmless stings). A **snorkelling** foray around the rocks at the ends of most bays turns up an astonishing array of brightly coloured fish, including blacktip reef sharks, and an occasional turtle. The seas around the islands belong to a national park and the coral is protected, although as elsewhere in the region it suffered bleaching due to high sea temperatures in 2010, though patches of live coral still remain.

If you just want to explore around the main beaches, then snorkels and masks can be rented (RM15–20/day) from accommodation, dive shops or shacks on the main beaches – most places can also arrange **snorkelling trips** to undeveloped coves for around RM35–60 per person including gear. Many travellers recommend the trips operated by *Maya Guesthouse* (☏ 019 222 9257) on Coral Beach; like most operators, though, they often take very large groups. Typical itineraries include Turtle Point (between the islands), Shark Point, Romantic Beach and the lighthouse; lunch, normally in the village on Perhentian Kecil, costs extra.

Some very good **dive sites** lie a short boat ride offshore, including the Pinnacle (or Temple of the Sea), T3 and Sugar Wreck (a boat that sank while carrying a cargo of sugar). Several of the islands' numerous dive shops organize night dives on the "Vietnamese" Wreck (actually a 1976 US landing craft, Advanced Open Water qualification required). In addition to fun dives (RM75–80), the shops also offer **courses**, including Open Water (around RM1000), Advanced Open Water (around RM950) and the introductory Discover Scuba Diving (around RM250–300); a handful, including Flora Bay Divers, also offer specialist facilities such as Nitrox. Most places teach **PADI courses**, although Alu Alu (Perhentian Besar; ☏ 09 691 1650, ⓦ alualudivers .com) offers both PADI and SSI.

RECOMMENDED DIVE SHOPS

Bubbles Dive Resort Tanjung Tukas ☏ 012 983 8038, ⓦ bubblesdc.com.

Flora Bay Divers Flora Bay ☏ 09 691 9266, ⓦ florabaydivers.com.

Quiver Dive Team Coral Bay ☏ 09 691 1755, ⓦ quiver-perhentian.com.

Turtle Bay Divers Long Beach and Perhentian Besar Main Beach ☏ 019 669 0028, ⓦ turtlebaydivers.com.

awkwardly shoehorned behind their popular seafront restaurant and dive shop. All have en-suite bathrooms, some with balconies too, though they're only decent value if you take a dive package. � **RM265**

Senja Bay Resort Coral Bay ☎019 283 0802, ⓦsenjabay.com; map p.233. This complex of en-suite chalets, built on a hillside and connected by decking, contains quite spacious and well-maintained rooms. There's also a restaurant and dive shop; snorkelling and diving packages are available. Breakfast included, and there's 24-hour electricity. ⓦ **RM169**

Shari-La Island Resort Northern end of Coral Bay ☎09 691 1500, ⓦshari-la.com; map p.233. Fairly upmarket resort with dozens of chalets spread out over a well-manicured hillside and overlooking its own private beach. The rooms are pretty good value for the island, though the cheapest are a bit small and have no hot water. ⓦ **RM159**

THE REST OF THE ISLAND

★**D'Lagoon** Teluk Kerma ☎019 985 7089, ⓦdlagoon .my; map p.233. Nestling in a secluded cove at the island's northeastern tip (which is also one of the island's best snorkelling sites), this friendly, family-run place makes for a great escape. Accommodation includes a dorm, fan-cooled, en-suite cabins, and an a/c treehouse (RM170). It's a long walk to the cove, but a water-taxi costs just RM10/person from Long Beach. Dive shop on site, as well as a

short zipline. ⓦ Dorms **RM25**, cabins **RM100**

Ecoteer Community House Kampung Pasir Hantu ⓦecoteerresponsibletravel.com; map p.233. Staying in the islands' sole village gives a very different island experience, helping with marine conservation and research, and other eco-projects, while getting to know the community. Accommodation is in mixed dorms near the community house, with the weekly price dropping the longer you stay. Prices include the transfer from the mainland, meals, a minimum of eight dives a week, and a snorkel tour. Since the research is underwater, you'll need to do a PADI course if you don't already have a licence. Minimum two week package **RM3500**

★**Mari Mari** Petani Beach ☎012 998 1145; map p.233. The five rooms at this quirky guesthouse have been lovingly constructed from flotsam and jetsam, making it a great spot to live out your desert island dreams. Two rooms share bathroom facilities, while three have their own open-air bathroom (RM120). They serve up local food (RM20–50), or you can go to the restaurant at the swanky resort at the other end of the beach. Open year-round. **RM80**

Mira Beach Chalet Mira Beach ☎016 643 6406; map p.233. A range of rustic chalets clustered in an beautiful, isolated cove, a 20min walk south of Coral Bay. Despite a recent hike in prices and slightly chaotic management, it's still a backpacker favourite. Most of the nine rooms share bathroom facilities. Snorkelling trips RM40–55, and there's a small restaurant. Electricity noon–3pm & 7pm–7am. **RM130**

EATING AND DRINKING

Most places to **eat** are connected to accommodation – they're fine but rarely very exciting – we've listed the ones worth seeking out below. For nightlife, most people drink at guesthouse bars such as at *Oh La La*, or the *Monkey Bar* before decamping to the south of the beach where *Beach Bar* (one of many pop up bars here) has a fire show from 9pm; expect quite a party atmosphere. Coral Bay's only real bar is the pricey *Ombak Café*; beers sold from coolers on the beach can be taken into most restaurants.

LONG BEACH

Chillout Café Long Beach ☎017 979 2950; map p.233. Towards the north of a beach, this laidback café serves some great breakfast sets (RM14–22) along with pancakes (RM9–14), local-style meals (RM15–18) and a fair stab at pizza (RM18–30). They also have a local crafts shop and a campsite (two person tent RM50), though no wi-fi. Daily 8am–11pm.

Monkey Bar Long Beach; map p.233. One of only a handful of permanent bars on the beach, this is one of the places where people start the evening; sit by the bar or lounge around in a hammock or on the beach out front. Beers go for RM10 while a small bottle of "monkey juice" (twenty percent alcohol) costs RM40. Live music at weekends. It also has a dive shop and backpacker accommodation. Daily 6pm–around 2am.

World Café Long Beach ☎09 697 8888, ⓦbuburesort .com.my; map p.233. This good-looking beach restaurant

serves tasty but pricey Western food, from sandwiches (RM35–40) and pasta (RM50–60) to grilled lobster (RM185), with a buffet breakfast (RM55) every morning. Daily 7.30–10pm.

CORAL BAY

★**Ewan's Café** On the path between Coral Bay and Long Beach; map p.233. Superfriendly owner Ewan ("Ee-wan") serves tasty, well-presented and great-value Malay dishes in his large and airy wooden restaurant tucked away just behind the beach. Pick a main ingredient – chicken/beef (RM14), veg (RM9) or prawn (RM18) – then select a cooking style and/or sauce. Also does some pretty good Western standards such as burgers and sandwiches (RM6.50–9). Wi-fi. Daily 8am–10.30pm.

Rainforest Campground and Café Between Coral Bay and Mira Beach ☎012 308 0525; map p.233. On a quiet bay a 5min walk north of Mira Beach, *Rainforest* serves hot drinks, beers, juices and simple Malaysian food and breakfasts (RM10–15) in a Robinson Crusoe-esque environment, the floor covered with coral, the walls hung with fishing nets – it's a great place to break the coastal walk. There's a campsite attached (two-person tent), handy if you can't bring yourself to leave. Daily 9am–9pm.

Perhentian Besar

The larger of the two islands, **Perhentian Besar**, has a more grown-up atmosphere. Although it holds a few relatively cheap options in addition to the mid-range resorts, it doesn't have the backpacker scene or nightlife of its neighbour. On the other hand, the beaches remain relaxed, despite some nearly continuous strings of development.

Western shore

The chain of attractive beaches on the **western shore** facing Perhentian Kecil are separated by rocks, though the southernmost ones are best avoided unless you like boats zipping past every few minutes, and the vibe gets better the further north you go. At high tide most **beaches** can be accessed along concrete walkways, with the notable exception of the path between *Mama's* and *Cozy Chalet*, which is essentially a fifteen-minute jungle trek – a boat taxi may be preferable, especially if you're carrying luggage. Most beaches are lined with resorts, but in a pleasingly organic way; the main beach has a good vibe after dark when the restaurants get busy. At the northern end of the main strip, the *Perhentian Island Resort* sits alone on one of the best stretches of sand, Teluk Pauh.

Flora Bay and the south coast

Flora Bay (Teluk Dalam) is less cramped than the western shore. Although it is home to several of the larger resorts, there are also some family-run businesses. The beach isn't the best on the island, especially when the tide is out, but it's more relaxed than the west coast ones. Further east, *Bubbles* resort sits on its own beach, only accessible by boat.

From the western shore, a steep **trail** (1km; 30min) to Flora Bay begins just past the second jetty south of *Abdul's*, behind the Teluk Keke beach restaurant. Another, prettier trail links Flora Bay with the *Perhentian Island Resort* (1.5km; 40min), starting behind the island's waterworks in Flora Bay.

Three Coves Bay

For the finest beaches on the Perhentians, take a water-taxi to **Three Coves Bay** (also known as Turtle Bay or Teluk Tiga Ruang) on the north of the island, a stunning chain of three beaches with crystal-clear waters, separated from the western shore by rocky outcrops. It's a great spot to spend the day, so get your boatman's telephone number or arrange a pick-up time for the return trip. This area also provides a secluded haven for green and hawksbill **turtles** to lay their eggs and as such may be off-limits during nesting season.

| ACCOMMODATION | PERHENTIAN BESAR |

WESTERN SHORE

Coral View Northern main beach ☎ 09 691 1700, ⓦ coralviewislandresort.com; map p.233. A range of wood-panelled rooms, mainly in steep-roofed chalets with small attached bathrooms. They're connected by walkways through a pleasant garden, and the standard rooms in particular are good value. There's a restaurant, dive shop, minimart, batik shop, library and foreign currency exchange. ☎ RM149

Mama's Chalet Northern main beach ☎ 013 369 6232, ⓦ mamaschalet.com.my; map p.233. Prim, very decent chalets along a narrow stretch of beach, including a few

sea-facing ones with multicoloured fanlights. All rooms have private facilities, and there's a popular restaurant. Wi-fi available in restaurant only. ☎ RM100

New Cocohut Southern main beach ☎ 09 697 7988, ⓦ perhentianislandcocohut.com; map p.233. Friendly Chinese-run establishment with modern en-suite chalets; the same management also runs *Cozy Chalet* resort, with similar but more spacious chalets ranged over a nearby hillside (RM230–340). All have a/c, TV and fridge; the more expensive ones have sea views, and there's a popular restaurant. Rates include breakfast and are discounted by a quarter either side of peak season. ☎ RM280

Perhentian Island Resort Teluk Pauh ☎ 09 691 1112 or ☎ 03 2144 8532, ⓦ perhentianislandresort.net; map p.233. Set on a very appealing stretch of beach, this resort – known as *PIR* – has a veritable campus of bungalows and chalets, all spacious and boasting modern furnishings and verandas. There's even a swimming pool, tennis court and spa. 🛜 RM580

★ **Reef Chalets** Northern main beach ☎ 013 981 6762; map p.233. A semicircle of a/c chalets with hints of traditional Malay architecture in the design and spotless bathrooms. The interiors are simple, most rooms with mosquito nets and pleasant verandas, and the garden setting is very attractive. 🛜 RM140

★ **Tunabay Island Resort** Southern main beach ☎ 09 690 2902, ⓦ tunabay.com.my; map p.233. This slickly managed collection of chalets gets it just right, combining the comforts of a mid-range city hotel (including beach towels for guests) with a cool informality that's perfect for a laidback beach holiday. The bar and restaurant are deservedly popular. Breakfast included. 🛜 RM318

Watercolours Paradise Resort Northern main beach ☎ 019 981 1852, ⓦ impiani.com; map p.233. This resort offers en-suite chalet rooms with fans and small verandas though no power sockets. There's also a well-run dive shop and a busy restaurant (7.30am–10pm). Note that a RM20 surcharge is levied on school and public holidays. RM100

FLORA BAY AND THE SOUTH COAST

★ **B'First Chalets** Flora Bay ☎ 014 534 2114, ⓔ b'firstchalet@yahoo.com; map p.233. This row of six concrete buildings is nothing special, but the large, clean fan rooms are good value and its friendly, family-run

environment is far more pleasant than any of the resorts or hotels There's a typical beach café at the front, and all-day electricity, but no wi-fi. RM60

Bayu Dive Lodge Flora Bay ☎ 09 691 1650, ⓦ bayudivelodge.com; map p.233. You don't have to be a diver to stay in the friendly guesthouse linked to the Alu-Alu dive shop. There's a large range of rooms arranged compactly in a lush garden, including sea-view cottages (RM270), chalets and terraced fan rooms. Cottages are designed along traditional Malaysian lines, while other room categories are more standard. RM120

★ **Bubbles** Tanjung Tukas ☎ 019 599 9628, ⓦ bubblesdc.com; map p.233. A RM10 boat ride from Flora Bay, this family-friendly resort has a beach to itself, and combines isolation with good facilities including a dive shop and in-house zoologist who looks after the resort's turtle hatchery. Rooms cost RM64 extra on Friday and Saturday nights. 24hr electricity. RM340

Fauna Beach Flora Bay ☎ 019 978 2254, ⓔ d.fauna @yahoo.com; map p.233. Some of these 35 pleasant, unremarkable chalets are fan-cooled, and a couple of them enjoy Perhentian Besar's cheapest sea views (RM80). The remainder have a/c (RM90 extra), but are shabby and overpriced. RM65

Flora Bay & Flora Bay 2 Flora Bay ☎ 09 691 1666, ⓦ florabayresort.com; map p.233. En-suite accommodation ranging from inexpensive fan rooms to beachfront chalets, including some overpriced a/c units (RM170). *Flora Bay*, with its garden of frangipanis and oleanders, is marginally preferable; its counterpart (where the fan rooms are located) features utilitarian two-storey blocks. Breakfast costs RM30–35 extra and there's a good dive shop attached. RM70

EATING AND DRINKING

Almost all Besar's places to eat are affiliated with resorts. Most of the best options are on the **western shore**: you can't go far wrong at *New Cocohut* for Chinese food, *Mama's Chalet* for Malay or *Watercolours* for pizza. The food on **Flora Bay** is generally less interesting, with a few open-air restaurants serving Western and Asian standards plus the odd barbecue. As for drinking, it's largely a matter of choosing one of the **resort bars** that serves beer.

Mandalika Flora Bay ☎ 019 983 7690; map p.233. With an extensive menu that ranges from *roti canai* (RM4) to Malay style fish and chips (RM15), good sandwiches (RM10–20) and a nightly barbecue, this cool beach shack is a good way to escape expensive resort food. Owner Halim's sister runs *Nia Cafe* (south of the Marine Park Offices on Main Beach) along the same lines. No alcohol. Daily 7am–11pm.

Tuna Café Tunabay Island Resort, southern main beach ☎ 09 691 1800, ⓦ tunabay.com.my; map p.233. One of the most adventurous kitchens on the islands, serving pasta and salads (RM10–28) plus more expensive seafood, and evening barbecues (RM35–75) with wine by the glass (RM20) or bottle (from RM70). Daily 7.15–10am & 4pm–midnight.

Setiu Wetlands

As a breeding ground for the painted terrapin and green turtle, the **Setiu Wetlands**, between Kuala Besut and Merang, have been a focus for WWF projects since the

OPPOSITE BEACH ON PERHENTIAN BESAR ISLAND >

early 1990s, but even now they attract only a trickle of tourists. Both the main settlements hereabouts, namely **Penarik**, on the T1 coastal road, and **Mangkok**, 4km to the north, are small villages with poor transport connections, so the easiest way to explore is on a tour organized by an operator in Kuala Terengganu (see below).

Pewanis

Pink House, Kampung Mangkok • Mon–Thurs & Sun 8.30am–5pm • ☎ 013 997 1195, but note that little English is spoken so you may need to get a Malay speaker to call for you

The **Pewanis** community project improves the financial position of local women, while working with the WWF on environmental projects. With advance notice, visitors can learn how to make banana chip snacks, help plant mangrove trees or take part in kite-making sessions. Staff can arrange bicycle rental and organize trips to the nearby turtle hatchery.

ARRIVAL AND DEPARTURE   SETIU WETLANDS

By taxi Public transport is limited, so if you don't come on a tour it's best to rent a car or take a taxi (RM80 from Kuala Terengganu).
By bus Buses between Kuala Besut and Kuala Terengganu (4 daily) can drop you at the turning for Mangkok, and you can walk the 3km from there.

Tours By far the best option is to come on an organized tour. Ping Anchorage (see p.247), for example, can arrange a trip including a visit to Pewanis, a turtle hatchery and a man raising *ayam serama* (chickens bred for competitions, which sell for up to a staggering RM8000 each).

ACCOMMODATION AND EATING

The women of Pewanis have started a homestay scheme (full board RM100/person) and the area has a couple of places to stay, including a stunning **resort**. There are few notable places to **eat** other than at accommodation or roadside *kedai kopis* – look out for local speciality *ikan celup tebung* (battered fish).

Pandan Laut 4km south of Penarik on Pantai Rhu Sepuluh ☎ 013 681 2495, ⊛ pandanlaut.com. Set in a leafy site, the seventeen aged but tidy rooms range from a decent A-frame through wooden chalets to a vast family suite. You'll need to take your meals elsewhere, but turtle watching is free and they can arrange snorkelling day-trips to Redang Island (RM120/person). A-frames RM50, chalets RM100
★**Terrapuri Heritage Village** Kampung Mangkok

☎ 09 624 5020, ⊛ terrapuri.com. A labour of love for the owner of Ping Anchorage travel agency, this site, sandwiched between wetlands and beach, features 29 traditional wooden buildings that have been saved from neglect elsewhere in Terengganu and carefully reconstructed. Staff can arrange day-trips or you can lounge by the pool; there's also a spa. Breakfast included. RM639

Merang

Most travellers who make it to **MERANG**, on the coastal road just south of the Sungai Merang creek, only glimpse the back of the village on their way to the jetty. The **beach**, accessible along a couple of side roads, is not exceptional, there's reasonable swimming and memorable views of the islands offshore – from left to right, the Perhentians, Lang Tengah, Redang and finally Bidung Laut, now uninhabited but once the site of a refugee camp for Vietnamese boat people.

ARRIVAL AND DEPARTURE   MERANG

By bus S.P. Bumi's buses between Kuala Besut and Kuala Terengganu (4 daily) stop close to Merang's school.
By taxi A taxi to Merang costs around RM90 from Kuala Besut, RM80 from Kuala Terengganu.
By boat Jetties for the resorts on Redang and Lang Tengah line the riverside, 500m walk from the bus stop (walk towards and past the traffic lights). Most packages include boat transfers, but tickets are also available from

the boatmen. In peak season Nurul Boat Services (☎ 012 952 3307, ⊛ boattoredang.com) runs hourly return services to Redang Island (9am–3pm; RM50) and one to Lang Tengah Island (timing varies; RM80). They also do snorkelling trips to both islands which cost RM700–900 for up to ten people (9am–3pm; snorkelling equipment RM15/person; lunch not included) so you can save money by staying on the mainland.

ACCOMMODATION AND EATING

This quiet stretch of coast has a limited amount of beachfront accommodation, with one or two peeling resorts 4km south of the jetty, near Kampung Rhu Tapai. Merang's **dining scene** is limited to a handful of stalls near the jetty, and a few *kedai kopis* on the road to Kuala Terengganu.

Kembara Resort 474 Pantai Peranginan ☎ 09 653 1770, ⓦ kembararesort.tripod.com. A little run-down but the only budget accommodation in Merang, set in a large well-shaded garden; follow signs down a side road from the bus stop then turn right. The rooms, a mix of cabins and two single-sex dorms, some with a/c, are popular with groups – call ahead before lugging your bags out here. Dorms RM35, cabins RM140

Redang Island

Beautiful **Redang Island** is geared primarily toward visitors on resort-based scuba diving package trips. Don't expect a quiet island getaway; at weekends and school holidays, bars along the main beach have music or karaoke until midnight.

A **kampung** has been built inland for the two-thousand-strong fishing community who formerly lived in a traditional floating village here, which was removed in 2001 to make way for a jetty and other tourist developments. The highlight of the social calendar, April's **candat sotong** festival celebrates a pastime popular all along the east coast of the Peninsula, catching squid using small hand-held lures with hooks on one end.

Snorkelling and diving

For most visitors, the chief attraction of Redang is the abundant marine life. The **reefs** have endured a lot over recent decades, including a mid-1970s attack by the crown-of-thorns starfish, and silt deposition caused by development. More recently the coral has suffered from bleaching due to high water temperatures. Thankfully, coral reefs have remarkable properties for self-renewal, and Redang's marine environment appears to have stabilized.

Conservation has certainly been helped by the designation of the Redang archipelago as one of Malaysia's **marine parks**, and by the regulation of activities such as spear-fishing, trawling and watersports. The best **snorkelling** is off the southern coast around the islets of Pinang and Ekor Tibu; the larger resorts take endless boats stuffed with tourists – and bags of fish food – to the main sites, so find a smaller group if you can. **Diving** is also excellent, with most sites off Redang's eastern shore – almost every resort has its own dive shop. Snorkelling day-trips are also available from Merang and Pandan Laut (see opposite).

ARRIVAL AND DEPARTURE   REDANG ISLAND

Regular transport to Redang only runs between **March** and **October**, when the resorts are open. A conservation fee of RM5 covers three days' stay, and is included in your accommodation price.

By boat Most packages include a boat ticket to Redang. Departures are from Merang (RM90 return), or Kuala Terengganu's Shahbandar jetty (RM110 return); check with your accommodation.

ACCOMMODATION

Most of Redang's accommodation is on the island's **eastern shore**, on Pasir Panjang (Long Beach), the adjacent Shark Bay or, just to the south, Teluk Kalong. Pasir Panjang has a particularly gorgeous stretch of fine white sand; Teluk Kalong's beach is narrower and pebbly in places, but inviting nonetheless. Unless otherwise noted, the resorts have en-suite, a/c rooms and their own restaurants. Many also have dive shops and offer diving-specific packages.

Rates Given that packages tend to be the cheapest way to visit, reviews here include the price per night of a basic two-night full-board package for two people, which typically includes buffet meals, a couple of snorkelling trips (but not equipment rental) and transfers. Rates shown do not include typical weekend/holiday surcharges of RM25–100/person; expect discounts of around 25 percent at the start or end of the season.

PASIR PANJANG/SHARK BAY

Coral Redang Pasir Panjang ☎09 630 7110, ⓦcoralredang.com.my. Located at the quieter end of the beach, this place has more character than most others on Redang. Rooms are arranged in quaint two-storey buildings, and there's a small swimming pool with a poolside bar. The food isn't great, so you may prefer the B&B option over the full board package. Scuba diving is an additional RM200/person. B&B RM385, full board RM685

Laguna Redang Shark Bay ☎09 630 7888, ⓦlagunaredang.com.my. Huge, luxurious establishment, with more than two hundred rooms and a large free-form pool, famous within Asia as the location of the Hong Kong comedy movie *Summer Holiday* (1999). A wide range of packages and rooms, all very comfortable and well equipped. Activities include snorkelling, canoe rental, archery and massage. Wi-fi only available for a fee, in the lobby. ⓦ RM638

Redang Beach Resort Shark Bay ☎09 623 8188, ⓦredang.com.my. This is a sizeable collection of two-storey attractive wooden units with comfortable rooms, some of which have been recently remodelled. There's a tiny swimming pool and nightly entertainment, should

you need either. RM539

Redang Lagoon Chalet Pasir Panjang ☎09 666 5020, ⓦredanglagoon.com. While the wooden chalets – arranged in two long rows – are nothing special, this is still good value, and is particularly popular with Malay families. RM340

Redang Reef Shark Bay ☎09 630 6181, ⓦredangreefresort.com.my. Perched on the headland at the southern end of Shark Bay, reached by a long wooden walkway, this good-value resort is less luxurious than its neighbours, with simply furnished rooms and a bar overlooking the sea. RM400

TELUK KALONG

Redang Kalong Teluk Kalong ☎03 7960 7163 (KL), ⓦredangkalong.com. While this peaceful beach isn't quite as nice as Pasir Panjang, its only resort is popular nonetheless. Many of the 39 basic and rather sparsely furnished rooms offer sea views, and the five-star IDC "Divers' Den" dive centre gets rave reviews. RM420

FLORA BAY

The Taaras Beach & Spa Resort Flora Bay ☎09 221 3997, ⓦthetaaras.com. Formerly known as the *Berjaya*, this luxury resort is a cut above the rest in terms of service, facilities and prices, with golf buggies to help you get between the well-appointed rooms, spa, restaurants, dive shop, swimming pools and tennis courts. RM960

Lang Tengah Island

Although **Lang Tengah Island** (Pulau Lang Tengah) is largely a package destination, it holds just a handful of spread-out places to stay and therefore offers a lower-key experience than its near-neighbour Redang Island. As well as attractive and quiet beaches, there's some good **snorkelling**, including a patch of blue coral (*Heliopora coerulea*) offshore from the *Sari Pacifica*. All the resorts, with the exception of *Lang Sari*, have **dive shops**.

Turtles lay their eggs on certain beaches; staff at *D'Coconut Lagoon* wake guests if any are spotted during the night on nearby Turtle Beach.

ARRIVAL AND DEPARTURE   LANG TENGAH ISLAND

By boat Most people visit on packages, which usually includes boat transfers (and the RM5 per visitor conservation charge) from Merang. though *Lang Sari*

charge RM120 return on top of the listed price. Most boats leave before 10am, but afternoon charters are possible (contact resorts for details).

ACCOMMODATION

Lang Tengah holds just four resorts, all of which can get very busy at weekends and public holidays (when prices rise by RM30–100 per person). The **full-board prices** listed below are per night, based on two people sharing on a two-night package (which includes boat transfers and a daily snorkelling trip, though not gear).

D'Coconut Lagoon Lang Tengah Island ☎03 4252 6686, ⓦdcoconutlagoon.com. Split into two wings a couple of minutes' walk apart. All rooms have a/c and hot showers; those in the much nicer west wing are

more expensive (around RM100 more) than those in the east wing, quoted here. The resort gives out a very handy sketch map of the island. B&B RM280, full board RM465

Lang Sari Resort Lang Tengah Island ☎ 03 2181 8370, ⓦ saripacificalangtengah.com. This resort offering private accommodation in individual villas has some sea-view rooms pretty much on the beach (with good coral just offshore) and very friendly staff, though the whole place is in need of renovation. RM645

Sari Pacifica Lang Tengah Island ☎ 09 690 0300, ⓦ saripacificaredangisland.com. Set on a lovely bit of beach and decorated in a traditional yet modern style; the cheaper rooms are far from luxurious, but the more expensive ones are worth the extra (an additional RM100), though all have a jacuzzi bath in the bathroom. RM554

Summer Bay Resort Lang Tengah Island ☎ 09 623 9911, ⓦ summerbayresort.com.my. Packages at this resort, with simple, wood-panelled, en-suite rooms in two-storey blocks, though the more expensive rooms are much more luxurious. The resort also has the only minimart on the island. RM976

Kuala Terengganu

After a long spell as an important port trading with the Chinese, **KUALA TERENGGANU** (the capital of Terengganu state) had by the late nineteenth century been eclipsed by the rise of Singapore and other new ports in the Melaka Strait. Following the transfer of Terengganu from Siamese to British control in the early twentieth century, the state became the last in the Peninsula to take a British Adviser, in 1919. It continued to languish as a rural state with, unusually, most of its settlements at river mouths rather than on the lower reaches of rivers, as elsewhere in Peninsular Malaysia.

The discovery of oil in the 1980s transformed its fortunes; modern Kuala Terengganu is even more of a hotchpotch than most Malaysian cities, the remnants of its constituent kampungs sprinkled with oil-funded showpieces and construction sites. There is, nevertheless, a certain **austerity** about Terengganu state that's noticeable in Kuala Terengganu. It lacks the commercial buzz of Kuantan or even Kota Bharu, partly because oil revenues have barely trickled down to ordinary people but also because in some respects the state is more conservative and inward-looking than neighbouring Kelantan.

Many visitors use the city simply as a transit point for Terengganu's best-known attractions – the pleasant **beaches** that line most of the coastline, and glorious **islands** including the Perhentians, Redang, Lang Tengah and Kapas. Using the city as a base, you can also venture inland to the lake of **Tasik Kenyir**. Even in itself Kuala Terengganu holds enough to reward a day or two's sightseeing, in particular the **old town** with its lively **Central Market** and the adjacent historic **Chinatown**; the **State Museum**, among the best of such complexes in Malaysia; and **Duyong Island**, where the city's maritime heritage just about survives.

4

Old town

Kuala Terengganu's compact centre is built on a semicircular parcel of land that bulges north into the mouth of the Terengganu River, which flows past the western half of the city, where the **old town** is located. The eastern half of the city is flanked by the South China Sea, with ongoing land reclamation rapidly altering the shoreline.

Bukit Puteri

Mon–Thurs, Sat & Sun 9am–5pm, Fri 9am–noon & 3–5pm • RM1 • ☎ 09 622 1444

A lovely little park with mature trees and chirruping cicadas, the steep hillock of **Bukit Puteri** ("Princess Hill") is crowned by a white tower that still serves as a lighthouse. You can access the hill via the escalators at the Bazaar Warisan (Heritage Bazaar) on Jalan Sultan Zainal Abidin.

Wide-ranging views take in the Terengganu River and the bell-shaped roofs of the blindingly white **Masjid Zainal Abidin** just to the south. Relics of the hill's time as an early nineteenth-century stronghold include a fort, its bricks once bound with honey (although it's now concrete), and several cannons imported from Spain and Portugal.

KUALA TERENGGANU

SOUTH CHINA SEA

Pantai Batu Buruk (1.3km)

Tourist Office, 4 (7.5km) & Cendering (8km)

3 (3km)

Sultan Mahmud Bridge (3km), Terengganu State Museum (3.5km) & Airport (10km)

Redang Island

Terengganu River

Duyong Island

CHINATOWN

Taman Shahbandar

Friday Market

Friday Market

Central Market

Bazaar Warisan

Istana Maziah

Bukit Puteri

Masjid Zainal Abidin

Bus Station

Taxis

Banks

Food Stalls

Food Court

Teck Soon Heritage House

Ho Ann Temple

Peranakan Photo Gallery

Chinatown Arch

The Guardian Store

Watsons Pharmacy

Guardian Pharmacy

Stadium

Police

Wisma Darul Iman

Wisma Persekutuan

Masjid Negeri

Ferries

N

0   200
metres

Streets
Jalan Sultan Zainal Abidin
Jalan Kampung Dalam
Jalan Ladang Sekolah
Jalan Sultan Sulaiman
Jalan Sultan Ismail
Jalan Kampung Kolam
Jalan Sultan Mahmud
Jalan Panji Alam
Jalan Pejabat
Jalan Pusara
Jalan Sultan Omar
Jalan Pejabat
Jalan Sultan Zainal Abidin
Jalan Petani
Jalan Sultan Sulaiman
Jalan Masjid Abidin
Jalan Dato' Isaac
Jalan Tok Lam
Jalan Kota
Jalan Tok Lam
Jalan Syed Hussin
Jalan Masjid Abidin
Jalan Banggol
Jalan Sultan Ismail
Jalan Kampung Cina
Jalan Air Jernih
Jalan Kota
Jalan Balik Bukit
Jalan Engku Sar
Jalan Kemajuan
Jalan Haji Mat Zaikey

ACCOMMODATION
Awi's Yellow House	10
Grand Continental	1
KT Beach Resort	5
KT Mutiara	9
Ming Paragon	7
Primula Beach Resort	8
Sentral	3
Suite 18 Boutique Hotel	3
Tanjong Vista	6
YT Midtown	4

● EATING
Asia Signature	2
Golden Dragon	5
Madam Bee's Kitchen	3
Star Anise	1
Vinum Exchange	6
Vegan Recipe	4

● SHOPPING
Abu Bakar bin Mohammed Amin	3
Emporium Hock Kee Seng	1
Noor Arfa	4
Wanisma Craft	2

Central Market

Daily 6am–5pm

Close to the lacklustre Bazaar Warisan with its assorted batik shops and jewellers, the ground floor of the much more rewarding **Central Market** (Pasar Payang) is occupied by a thriving wet market. Look out for stalls selling *keropok* (dried fish paste) and Malay confections in just about every conceivable hue. The upper floors comprise a maze of food stalls and outlets selling batik, *songket* and brassware.

Chinatown

Reached via Jalan Kampung Cina, south of the central market, Kuala Terengganu's **Chinatown** was established in the eighteenth century, when the trading links between Terengganu and China drew in early Chinese settlers. The main street is lined with pastel-coloured **shophouses**, one of the finest examples of which, the sky-blue **Teck Soon Heritage House**, is occasionally open to the public as a museum. Further south, the **Peranakan Photo Gallery** (daily 9am–5pm; free) displays black-and-white photographs showing the town's development. Nearby, the photogenic **Ho Ann Temple** (daily 7.30am–7.30pm; free) is dedicated to Mazu, the Goddess of the Sea. The current complex was reconstructed in 2010 after its predecessor burned down, but the temple has occupied the same spot since the late eighteenth century. A useful leaflet, *Chinatown Heritage Trail*, is available from the state tourist office.

Terengganu State Museum

4

Bukit Losong, 6km west of town centre • Mon–Thurs, Sat & Sun 9am–5pm, Fri 9am–noon & 3–5pm • RM15 • ☎ 09 632 1200, ⓦ museum.terengganu.gov.my • Bas bandar service from city centre (C-02; 45min) or RM30 taxi ride (one way)

Arriving at the **Terengganu State Museum**, you might think you've strayed into *Gulliver's Travels*. Visitors are confronted by a series of buildings modelled on the archetypal Terengganu village house, but absolutely Brobdingnagian in scale. Along with being Malaysia's biggest state museum, the buildings also house one of the country's best collections.

The ground floor of the **main building** holds exquisite fabrics from around Southeast Asia, while the next floor up displays various crafts. The top floor details the history of Terengganu. The **Petronas Oil Gallery**, in the building to the left, is sporadically interesting but predictably skewed. Behind it, the old-fashioned **Islamic Gallery** displays fine examples of Koranic calligraphy.

THE KRIS

The **kris** (or *keris*) occupies a treasured position in Malay culture, a symbol of manhood and honour believed to harbour protective spirits. Traditionally, all young men crossing the barrier of puberty receive one that remains with them for the rest of their lives, tucked into the folds of a sarong; for an enemy to relieve someone of a *kris* is tantamount to stripping him of his virility. In the past, some weapons were reputed to have magical powers, able to fly from their owners' hand to seek out and kill an enemy.

The *kris* itself is intended to deliver a horizontal thrust rather than the more usual downward stab. When a sultan executed a treacherous subject, he did so by sliding a long *kris* through his windpipe, just above the collarbone, thereby inflicting a swift – though bloody – death. The distinguishing feature of the dagger is the hilt, shaped like the butt of a gun to facilitate a sure grip. The hilt can also be used to inflict a damaging blow to the head in combat, especially if there isn't time to unsheathe the weapon.

The daggers can be highly decorative: the iron blade is often embellished with fingerprint patterns or the body of a snake, while the hilt can be made from ivory, wood or metal. Hilt designs usually take the form of birds' heads.

BOAT-BUILDING ON DUYONG ISLAND

Historically, the boatyards of Duyong Island produced **schooners** that ranged from humble fishing craft to the hulking *perahu besar*, up to 30m in length. These days however, motorized, modern alternatives to the old-fashioned wooden boats, the increasing cost of timber, and the lure of other careers have all contributed to a steep decline in this traditional industry. Salvation for the handful of boatyards that remain has come from overseas, as clients from around the world place orders for all manner of bespoke craft.

The shipwrights of Duyong Island use the *pasat* technique that uses neither metal nails nor set plans. For hulls, their preferred material is **cengal**, a wood whose toughness and imperviousness to termite attack make it prized not only for boats but also the best kampung houses. After the hull planking is fastened with strong hardwood pegs, a special sealant – derived from the bark of swampland trees, and resistant to rot – is applied. Unusually, the frame is fitted afterwards, giving the whole structure strength and flexibility. As construction takes place in **dry docks**, the finished boats have to be manoeuvred on rollers into the water, an effort that often requires local villagers to pitch in.

Allow time to see the rest of the site. Beside the river are two examples of the **sailing boats** for which Kuala Terengganu is famed – unique blends of European ships and Chinese junks. The small **Seafaring Gallery** and larger **Fisheries and Marine Park Gallery** are close by, as is a collection of smaller, beautifully decorated fishing boats. Five old timber buildings have been disassembled and reconstructed within the grounds. Among them, the **Istana Tengku Long** was originally built in 1888 entirely without nails, which to Malays signify death because of their use in coffins.

Duyong Island

Very sporadic water-taxis from moorings north of the Central Market; better to take a taxi (RM15)

The proud home of a venerable **boat-building** tradition, **Duyong Island** (Pulau Duyong or "Mermaid Island") was once two islets in the Terengganu River; they were joined by reclamation to form what you see today. Although the northern end of Duyong was levelled to build a resort and a prestigious **yacht club**, the southeastern side of the island is essentially still a rustic kampung that's great for an hour's stroll.

If you want to visit one of the three surviving **boatyards**, ask around for directions or enquire at *Awi's Yellow House* (see p.247). One boatyard is owned by Awi, while several others are close to the Sultan Mahmud bridge on the island's eastern shore.

ARRIVAL AND DEPARTURE   KUALA TERENGGANU

By plane The airport is 14km north of the city; a prepaid taxi into the centre costs RM30. MAS (☎09 662 6600, ⓦmalaysiaairlines.com) and AirAsia (☎09 667 1017, ⓦairasia.com), both with offices at the airport, fly to KLIA, and Firefly (☎09 667 5377, ⓦfireflyz.com.my) operates 3 daily flights to the capital's Subang airport.

By bus The spacious, modern bus station, smack in the centre on Jalan Masjid Abidin, is used by intercity and local buses.

Destinations Alor Setar (9.30pm daily; 9hr); Batu Pahat (3 daily; 8hr); Butterworth (9.30am & 9.30pm daily; 8hr 30min); Cherating (6 daily; 3hr 30min); Dungun (8 daily; 2hr); Johor Bahru (9 daily; 9hr); Kangar (9.30pm daily; 10hr); Kemaman/Chukai (7 daily; 2hr 30min); Kota Bharu (10 daily; 3hr 40min); Kuala Besut (8 daily; 3hr);

Kuala Lumpur (30 daily; 6hr 30min); Kuantan (20 daily; 3hr 15min); Marang (hourly until 5pm; 30min); Melaka (4 daily; 7hr 30min); Merang (4 daily; 1hr); Mersing (5 daily; 6hr 30min); Muar (3 daily; 8hr); Pekan (3 daily; 4hr); Rantau Abang (8 daily; 1hr 30min); Segamat (4 daily; 6hr); Seremban (4 daily, 7hr); Singapore (9am & 9pm daily; 11hr 40min); Sungai Petani (9.30pm daily; 8hr 25min).

By taxi Long-distance taxis depart for destinations across the Peninsula from outside an office (☎06 626 5150) just south of the bus station. The fare to Kota Bharu is around RM180, and it's RM160 to Kuantan.

By boat The Shahbandar jetty on the seafront is used by a few resort boats to Redang Island, with a public boat leaving at 9am and returning at 1pm (RM110).

GETTING AROUND

By bas bandar Besides the city's standard bus services, an hourly "heritage bus" (bas bandar) service runs a hop-on, hop-off route to the main attractions. There are two different routes, each starting at the main bus station before going on to destinations including the State Museum (C-02) and Noor Arfa (C-01). Enquire at tourist offices for schedules and fares.

By taxi Taxis are easily found near the bus station or around the Central Market; you'd be lucky to flag one down in the street.

By trishaw Trishaws can be found near the Central Market, charging around RM30–50/hr.

By car Car rental is available from booths in the airport arrivals hall (from RM120/day).

INFORMATION

Tourist information The state tourist office is next to the GPO on Jalan Sultan Zainal Abidin (Mon–Wed & Sun 8am–5pm, Thurs 8am–3pm; ☎09 622 1553, ✉tourism.terengganu.gov.my). The Tourism Malaysia office is a little way south on Jalan Kampung Daik (Mon–Wed & Sun 8am–5pm, Thurs 8am–3.30pm; ☎09 630 9433). Ask at either about homestays in the city and its surroundings.

Travel agents Ping Anchorage Travel and Tours, 77a Jalan Sultan Sulaiman (daily 8.30am–7pm; ☎09 626 2020, ✉pinganchorage.com.my), is efficient and well organized (if pricey), offering packages throughout the east coast and the interior. They also run the brilliant *Terrapuri Heritage Village* north of the city (see p.240).

ACCOMMODATION

CITY CENTRE AND BEACH

Grand Continental Jalan Sultan Zainal Abidin ☎09 625 1888, ✉ghihotels.com; map p.244. The fanciest place in town when it opened in 1997, this chain hotel is showing its age despite recent renovations. However, the spacious rooms have marbled bathrooms and satellite TV, and there's a gym, Western restaurant, pool and coffee shop. Breakfast included. RM269

KT Beach Resort 548e Jalan Sultan Zainal Abidin ☎09 631 5555, ✉ktbeachresort.wordpress.com; map p.244. This old-school hotel no longer enjoys a beachside position, thanks to ongoing land reclamation. The a/c rooms are squeaky clean if unexciting, and they also manage some surprisingly appealing, fully furnished apartments in the residential block across from the *Tian Kee* restaurant. Doubles RM95, apartments RM200

KT Mutiara 67 Jalan Sultan Ismail ☎09 622 2655; map p.244. While some fittings look worn and dated, these are comfortable rooms for a decent price. Some have no windows, though at least they're quieter. It also has a pleasant courtyard garden and discounts available midweek. RM78

Ming Paragon 219e Jalan Sultan Zainal Abidin ☎09 631 9966, ✉mingstarhotel.com; map p.244. The deluxe room (RM188) has a computer and complimentary minibar (no alcohol), but even the cheapest standard rooms have flat-screen TV, hairdryer, iron and kettle – all they're missing is windows, for which you have to pay extra (RM168). Breakfast included, and there's a spa. RM98

Primula Beach Resort Jalan Persinggahan ☎09 622 2100, ✉primulahotels.com; map p.244. Behind the ugly facade is a decent 246-room hotel complete with pool, gym and two restaurants with a grand marbled lobby with a sea view. The a/c rooms are spacious and well kept. while the "Superior" rooms on the ground floor of an older block have patio doors leading to the beach. Ample parking, and free shuttle into the centre. Breakfast included. RM285

Sentral 28 Jalan Tok Lam ☎09 622 0318, ✉travel@redang.com.my; map p.244. Part of the *Redang Beach Resort* group, this centrally located hotel has a range of bright, attractive, en-suite rooms at equally attractive prices. All fifty have a/c, though some lack windows. RM79

★ **Suite 18 Boutique Hotel** 71 Jalan Kampung Cina ☎09 631 2288, ✉suite18boutiquehotel@gmail.com; map p.244. The only accommodation in Chinatown, this converted 1890's shop has retained some of its original features, with stylish and well-equipped (though small) en-suite, a/c rooms (most without windows), and three dorms. They also rent bikes (RM25/day) and there's a pleasant garden out back. Dorms RM35, doubles RM118

Tanjong Vista 132d Jalan Sultan Zainal Abidin ☎09 631 9988, ✉hoteltanjongvista.com.my; map p.244. The logo and uniforms may be bright pink but the rooms in this business hotel are tastefully furnished and good value. The small semi-outdoor swimming pool on the fourth floor has views of the beach and sea; there's also a small gym. Breakfast included. RM215

YT Midtown 30 Jalan Tok Lam ☎09 622 3088, ✉hotelytmidtown.com.my; map p.244. While this convenient central hotel is neither fancy nor flashy, it does stand out for its comfortable beds and reasonable prices. All rooms have big TVs, a/c and en suite, breakfast is included and there's a car park. RM108

DUYONG ISLAND

★ **Awi's Yellow House** Duyong Island ☎017 984 0337; map p.244. You'll need to ask for directions to reach this delightful no-frills timber complex, which sits on stilts over the water. Accommodation is in thatched-roof huts with mosquito nets; some have private bathrooms. There's also a kitchen, and kayaks (RM10/day) available to rent; Awi's small boatyard is nearby. RM35

EATING AND DRINKING

Terengganu's signature dish, **nasi dagang**, consists of slightly sticky rice, steamed with a little coconut milk and chopped shallots, and often served with fish curry for breakfast. Other key dishes include **laksam** (rolled rice noodles in a thick fish and coconut milk gravy) and **keropok** – dried fish paste, served *lekor* (long and chewy), *losong* (steamed) or *keping* (crispy). There are a few decent **Malay restaurants**, and the Malay stalls at the Central Market, as well as just south of the junction of Jalan Sultan Ismail and Jalan Tok Lam, are worth trying. Chinatown is the obvious focus for **Chinese food** – especially after dark, when many other areas are quiet – with a hawker centre along Jalan Kampung Tiong 1 and several excellent restaurants on the main street. Chinatown is also your best bet for finding **alcohol** in this largely dry city.

Asia Signature Jalan Sultan Zainal Abidin ☏ 09 620 5421; map p.244. This bright, airy café is handy if you find yourself east of the town centre. The menu ranges from chicken *rendang* to *keropok* (RM5.60–11.20) and dim sum (the salted egg buns, RM6.90, come recommended) and they also offer vegetarian versions of a few Malay classics, including a tasty *nasi lemak* (RM6.800) and a smattering of Western dishes (RM16–25). Daily noon–3pm & 6–9.30pm.

★ **Golden Dragon** Jalan Kampung Cina ☏ 09 622 3034; map p.244. One of the most established and popular Chinese restaurants in Chinatown, with a great *nasi campur* at lunchtime (RM8–10), and reliable seafood (RM5–12/100g; try the steamed fish) and other stir-fried dishes (RM8–15) in the evening. Portions are substantial. Daily 9.30am–3pm & 6.15–9.30pm.

★ **Madam Bee's Kitchen** 177 Jalan Kampung Cina ☏ 012 988 7495; map p.244. Specializing in Terengganu Peranakan dishes, this is the place to come to try local Malay and Chinese dishes, including *nasi kerabu* (RM8.90) and Terengganu *loh mee* (egg noodles in thick gravy with chicken and crab; RM7.90). Very popular so expect to wait for a table at lunchtime. Mon, Tues & Thurs–Sun 9.30am–5.30pm.

Star Anise 82 Jalan Kampung Cina ☏ 017 664 2368; map p.244. Head to this funky café for excellent coffee, locally grown tea (from RM7), and a slice of cake (RM10). Outdoor seating on a quiet side street and plenty of decorative touches make this one of the nicest spots to take a break in Chinatown. Daily noon–midnight.

Vegan Recipe Jalan Kampung Cina ☏ 012 922 2332; map p.244. Not a common sight in Malaysia, this fully vegan café does a good line in tasty and well-presented Malaysian and Chinese rice and noodle dishes (RM5.50–13.90) served in clean, modern surroundings. The rendang rice is particularly nice. Daily 8.30am–9.30pm.

Vinum Exchange 221 Jalan Kampung Cina ☏ 011 1697 1433; map p.244. With one wall covered by racks of spirits, pork chops (RM20.20) on the menu and tinted glass in the windows, this bar feels downright subversive in straight-laced KT. Lavazza coffee (espresso RM5) and pastries are served in the daytime, but crowds congregate in the evening for beer and wine (from RM11.50). Daily 11am–11pm.

SHOPPING

Emporium Hock Kee Seng Jalan Sultan Zainal Abidin; map p.244. Small shopping complex good for everyday purchases. Like the Store in Chinatown, this is more of a general emporium and supermarket. Daily 10am–10pm.

Noor Arfa Cendering Industrial Area, 7km south of the city ☏ 09 617 9700, Ⓦ noor-arfa.com.my; map p.244. Large showroom with a more extensive choice of batik than the shops on Jalan Sultan Zainal Abidin, and occasional demonstrations. Take the *bas bandar* service to Cendering. Mon–Thurs & Sat 9am–7pm.

ARTS AND CRAFTS WORKSHOPS

Like neighbouring Kelantan, Terengganu is renowned for its **handicrafts**. At several places in and around the city, visitors can watch craftspeople at work and buy their products.

Abu Bakar bin Mohammed Amin 500m west of Jalan Panji Alam, 1406 Lorong Saga in Pasir Panjang ☏ 09 622 7968; map p.244. Watch the making of the *kris*, a two-edged dagger, and its decorated wooden sheath. On S.P. Bumi local bus route; get off at Sekolah Kebangsaan Pasir Panjang. By appointment only.

Wanisma Craft Near junction of Jalan Sultan Zainal Abidin and Kampung Ladang Sekolah ☏ 019 622 3311, Ⓦ wanisma.com; map p.244. Local artisans have long been known for their brassware, working in a "white brass" alloy unique to the state. Containing at least forty percent zinc, with added nickel to make it less yellow, white brass is used for decorative items such as candlesticks. They have a largish shop selling metalware and batik and at their nearby workshop you can watch craftsmen using the traditional "lost wax" technique to make brass objects. Mon–Thurs & Sun 10am–6pm.

DIRECTORY

Hospitals and clinics The Hospital Sultanah Nur Zahirah is 1km southeast of the centre on Jalan Sultan Mahmud (☎09 621 2121). There are plenty of privately run walk-in clinics and the odd dentist's surgery along Jalan Tok Lam, some staying open well into the evening.
Left luggage At the bus station (daily 8am–10pm; RM3/2hr; ☎019 920 9679).

Pharmacy There are branches of Watsons and Guardian on Jalan Sultan Ismail.
Police The main police station is on Jalan Sultan Ismail (☎09 624 6222).
Visa extensions The Immigration Department is in Wisma Persekutuan on Jalan Sultan Ismail (Mon–Wed & Sun 7.30am–5pm, Thurs 7.30am–4pm; ☎09 622 1424).

Tasik Kenyir

More than three hundred square kilometres in area, **Tasik Kenyir** (Lake Kenyir) was created in 1985 by the building of the Kenyir hydroelectric dam across the Terengganu River. Much touted locally as a back-to-nature experience, the lake offers scope for **fishing**, waterborne excursions and wildlife-spotting – **elephants** are even glimpsed on the shore from time to time, thanks to the Department of Wildlife's policy of transporting wild elephants to the **Kenyir Elephant Conservation Village** (KECV; ⓦkecv.com.my; RM100) from elsewhere in the country. It's possible to swim in **waterfalls** on the periphery, while at the lake's southern end you can visit the limestone **Bewah and Taat caves**. The lake is also Terengganu's gateway to Taman Negara, thanks to the park entrance at **Tanjung Mentong** that has recently received a much-needed renovation.

Sadly, due to poor transport connections and the fact that the attractions are so scattered, Tasik Kenyir remains something of a half-baked proposition. The government is in the process of jollying the lake up, creating – among other things – several botanical gardens and an aviary as well as a soon-to-open **duty-free island**. What impact these will have remains to be seen, but for now, a lack of accommodation adds to the difficulty of visiting. Unless you plan to stay at the upmarket, easily accessible *Lake Kenyir Resort*, your best bet is to book through a travel agent in Kuala Terengganu. If you do arrive independently you can book trips on a per-person basis from the resort, while the packages from the main jetty are aimed at groups, so – for example – a trip to **Kelah fish sanctuary** costs RM450 for the whole boat, plus an RM15 per person entry fee.

ARRIVAL AND DEPARTURE   TASIK KENYIR

The jetty in the northeast of the lake, **Pangkalan Gawi**, can be reached by road and serves as the focal point for arrivals; a handful of tour operators have desks at the jetty and can arrange day-trips.

By bus No buses run to the lake from Kuala Terengganu, though there's a service all the way from KL: the Tasik Kenyir Express (☎09 822 2176, ⓦtasikkenyir.com.my) leaves from Terminal Bersepadu Selatan bus station (daily 9am & 9pm; 6–7hr).
By taxi A taxi to the jetty costs around RM100 from Kuala Terengganu or RM120 from the airport.

INFORMATION

Tourist office At the Gawi jetty (daily 8am–5pm; ☎09 626 7788, ⓦkenyirlake.com). Staff can hand out leaflets and advice, but cannot book you onto any tours – for that, speak to the companies with desks at the jetty or go to *Lake Kenyir Resort*.
Tours Most accommodation and packages are set up for groups of over eight people; the best bet for independent travellers is on a one-day tour from Kuala Terengganu with Ping Anchorage (see p.247; 6hr; RM295/person; min 2 people). Alternatively, if you're staying at the lake, you can arrange one of the various one-day boat trips (usually 5hr 30min; RM120–600 for up to eight people) from Kenyir Natural Holidays (☎011 1996 6276, ✉noraslinaabdulwahab@gmail.com) at the main jetty. Gawi-based local guide Kamarul (☎019 984 6012) can also help if you want something tailor-made.

4

ACCOMMODATION

A more economic option than the resort below is a homestay, which can be arranged through the tourist office or Kenyir Natural Holidays.

Lake Kenyir Resort 1.5km from Gawi Jetty ☎ 09 666 8888, ⓦ lakekenyir.com. This elegant collection of buildings, with Terengganu-style pitched roofs, is the swankiest accommodation at Tasik Kenyir, and currently undergoing much-needed refurbishment, so the price given here is indicative only. Numerous tours and activities are available. ATM on site. RM350

Marang

The coastal village of **MARANG**, 17km south of Kuala Terengganu and not to be confused with Merang further north, is only visited by tourists as the departure point for the delightful islands of **Kapas** and **Gemia**, just 6km offshore. The islands have no banks or ATMs, so this is your last chance to withdraw money – there are a couple of ATMs opposite the mosque and around 400m from the jetty, though note they often run out of money by the end of the weekend.

MARANG map: Kuala Terengganu (17km); Police Station; JALAN BATU MERAH; OLD FISHING VILLAGE; ROUTE 3; Supermarket; ATMs; Market; Minimart; Masjid Sultanah Nur Zahirah; Shops; Masjid Lama; Boat Services; JALAN BANDAR MARANG; Tasik Kenyir (65km); ROUTE 3; Marang River; Petronas Petrol Station; Rantau Abang (45km); Kapas Island & Gemia Island

ACCOMMODATION: Kamal Guest House 1; Marang Guest House 2; Hotel Seri Malaysia 3

EATING: Mak Su Yam 2; Marang Waterfront 1

0 — 200 metres

ARRIVAL AND DEPARTURE   MARANG

By bus Local buses run between Kuala Terengganu and Marang roughly hourly until 5pm (30min). It's also possible to reach Marang on the long-distance Kuantan–Kuala Terengganu buses that travel the coast road. To move on from Marang you can flag down a local bus, although southbound services go no further than Dungun or Kemaman. To catch an express bus further afield you'll need to make arrangements in Kuala Terengganu.

By taxi Chartering a taxi between Kuala Terengganu and Marang costs around RM50.

By boat The two main boat operators for the trip to Kapas and Gemia islands, MGH (☎ 016 922 5454, ⓦ pulaukapas.com) and Suria Link (☎ 019 983 9454), have their offices side by side at Marang's jetty. Both offer the same deal – RM20 one way or RM40 return – and can book accommodation. Boats usually run every 2hrs from 9am–5pm, though cease from Nov–Jan when all the accommodation on Kapas is closed. Tell the boatman which resort you're staying at and they'll drop you on the nearest beach (you may have to wade a short distance), though it's generally easiest just to get off at the main jetty.

ACCOMMODATION

Hotel Seri Malaysia 3964 Kampung Paya ☎ 09 618 2889, ⓦ serimalaysia.com.my; map left This modern block up a switchback driveway is Marang's most upmarket accommodation but poor value, with neat, if bland, rooms and a tiny swimming pool. The higher floors have views across to Kapas Island. Breakfast included, wi-fi in lobby only. 🛜 RM138

Marang Guest House Bukit Batu Merah, 1367 & 1368 Kampung Paya ☎ 09 618 1976; map opposite. The rustic wooden cabins here are careworn but have pleasant porches and are a good choice if you're on a tight budget. Its location at the top of the hill means it gets a nice sea breeze. Only a/c rooms have Western toilets (RM10 extra). 🛜 **RM60**

EATING AND DRINKING

Marang's best **waterside dining** is at the *Marang Waterfront*, a basic food court opposite the main market, where a handful of stalls do a roaring trade in *roti canai* and *nasi goreng* until well into the evening.

Mak Su Yam Marang ☎ 017 9873141; map opposite. Convenient for the jetty, at the top of a short flight of steps, this is a simple place with an inexpensive (RM6–7) *nasi campur* spread. Fine if you just want to fill up while waiting for transport. Mon–Thurs, Sat & Sun 7am–6pm.

Kapas Island

Diminutive **Kapas Island** (Pulau Kapas), less than half an hour from Marang by speedboat, boasts arcs of sandy beach the colour of pale brown sugar, and aquamarine waters that visibly teem with fish. It's a very appealing little island with a laidback charm, emphasized by the friendly approach of the best of the resorts. Just offshore, the even smaller **Gemia Island** (Pulau Gemia) is the site of just one resort. In theory it's possible to visit Kapas as a day-trip, by catching an early boat out and returning late in the afternoon, but this means dealing with the midday heat – and besides, it's really worth staying for at least a night or two.

The only **season** when things are not quite so idyllic is from June to August, particularly at the weekends, when the island can get pretty busy. The rest of the time it's a great place to do very little for a few days; the one notable highlight in the slim social calendar is the annual Kapas–Marang **swimathon** in April. During the northeast monsoon the island basically closes down.

A couple of marked trails make it possible to **hike** to the undeveloped eastern side of Kapas, ending up at the pebbly (and sadly far from litter-free) **Berakit Beach**, where you can take a dip. The longer but more interesting route (1.5km) starts close to *Kapas Turtle Valley*, the shorter (1km) from behind *Kapas Island Resort*, running alongside a stream for most of the way. You can combine them to take a circular route; both include steep sections close to Berakit. Bring plenty of water and use insect repellent, and avoid being in the forest after 5pm when the mosquitoes come out in force. The paths can be very slippery after rain.

■ ACCOMMODATION	
Captain's Longhouse	8
Gem Island Resort and Spa	1
Harmony Campsite	2
Kapas Beach Chalet (KBC)	4
Kapas Island Resort	6
Kapas Turtle Valley	9
Longsha Campsite	7
Pak Ya Sea View Chalet	5
Qimi Private Bay	3

● EATING	
Koko	1

KAPAS ISLAND

SNORKELLING AND DIVING AROUND KAPAS ISLAND

Snorkelling is of course a draw on Kapas; most places to stay can rent out gear (from RM15), or arrange a boat trip out to a choice site (from RM35). Visibility is best between May and August, but jellyfish can be a nuisance in June and July. Some of the most popular snorkelling spots are around rocky **Gemia Island**. If you're just renting equipment then try the rocks at the edges of the beaches beyond *Qimi Chalet* and the campsite.

Diving isn't generally considered to be as good as on the Perhentians or Redang, but there are opportunities for it, particularly on the eastern side of the island. Popular sites include Berakit Reef, Octopus Reef and Coral Garden. Blacktip reef sharks are regularly seen, and you can find turtles at Coral Garden and near *Kapas Turtle Valley*. There's only one **dive shop**, Aqua Sport (☎ 014 508 2185, ⓦ aquasportdiver.com.my), which offers PADI open water courses (RM1400) as well as regular dives (RM130).

ARRIVAL AND INFORMATION
KAPAS ISLAND

By boat Boats to Kapas leave from Marang (see p.250), return boats to Marang run every couple of hours from 9.30am–5.30pm; inform your accommodation when you want to leave and they'll arrange it for you.

Conservation fee As Kapas is a designated marine park, a conservation fee of RM5 applies for a stay of up to three days, though there isn't always an official present to collect it.

ACCOMMODATION AND EATING

For such a tiny island, Kapas has a surprising range of accommodation. Some mid-range places levy surcharges of twenty percent or more at weekends and during holidays, and all close down from November to February. Wi-fi is only available from the community wi-fi station by the jetty, which can reach up to 200m away.

KAPAS ISLAND

★**Captain's Longhouse** Southwestern shore ☎ 012 377 0214; map p.251. This rustic elevated longhouse of dark timber has seven decent fan rooms and a large, rather bohemian open dorm. All beds have mosquito nets and shared facilities. The driftwood beach-hut bar gives the impression that someone was shipwrecked here but made the best of it. Pretty over-priced but pretty cool. Dorm RM50, doubles RM100

Longsha Campsite Southwestern shore ☎ 017 965 2966; map p.251. Located at the more laidback end of the beach, this campsite has a mess of two-person tents (mattresses RM10 extra), a kitchen for guests to use and copious amounts of hammocks overlooking the beach. There's another, more isolated but similarly-priced campsite called *Harmony Campsite* on Long Beach. Both are popular with large student/youth groups. RM50

Kapas Beach Chalet (KBC) Western shore ☎ 012 288 2008; map p.251. Decent A-frame chalets plus small dorms and more basic rooms in a long bungalow on the main site, as well as a/c rooms by their *Lazy Islander Lounge* restaurant next door; all are en suite. The restaurant is good and along with the *Captain's Longhouse*, the best backpacker hangout on Kapas. Snorkelling equipment is free for guests. Dorms RM25, doubles RM50, chalets RM90

Kapas Island Resort Western shore ☎ 019 912 4557, ⓦ kapasislandresort.com; map p.251. Neat but badly-maintained Malay-style a/c bungalows, all en suite and with more character than most, set in an unkempt garden near the jetty. Western and Malay food is served in an airy but unpopular restaurant. A sea view will cost you RM70 extra and they also have an a/c dorm. Breakfast included. 🛜 Dorm RM50, bungalows RM130

★**Kapas Turtle Valley** Southwestern shore ☎ 013 354 3650, ⓦ kapasturtlevalley.com; map p.251. Marvellously low-key family resort, run by a Dutch couple and set on a secluded cove a short but steep walk from the western shore – boats from Marang can drop you off here. It has just eight chalets, including two for families (RM205), featuring four-poster beds and swish bathrooms; the Western menu in the restaurant is sophisticated if pricey, and includes a decent range of wines. There's a two-night minimum stay, and booking is essential. Breakfast included. RM200

Pak Ya Sea View Chalet Western shore ☎ 019 960 3130; map p.251. Seven tidy A-frames behind a low protective wall on the beach, all with double beds, fans, lino floors and small but clean bathrooms. The beach café is quite popular and serves the usual gamut of Malay rice/noodle dishes and local specialities. 🛜 RM80

Qimi Private Bay Qimi Bay Beach ☎ 017 917 5744; map p.251. Comfortable chalets ranged across a slope, the most expensive (RM350) with sea-facing balcony and open-air bathroom; the cheaper fan ones are nicely decorated but much more basic. The restaurant is quite pricdy and it can take a while for the food to arrive at your table on the sand, but it's worth the wait – you'll need to reserve by 4pm. RM100

GEMIA ISLAND

Gem Island Resort and Spa Southeastern tip ☎ 09 612 5110, ⊛ gemisland.com.my; map p.251. This quiet spot is the only resort on Gemia, with chalets on stilts; the cheapest are in a long block, with better views away from the restaurant. Turtles land to lay eggs and the resort is involved in their conservation; facilities include a spa, small swimming pool and restaurant. A surcharge of RM90 is applied at weekends and during school holidays. Two-night full-board package for two per night RM880

EATING

Each guesthouse has its own **restaurant**, but it's worth seeking out *Koko*, the only standalone restaurant of note. The most popular backpacker places are the restaurant at *Pak Ya Sea View Chalet* and *JT Café*, right next to the jetty, both of which have good, reasonably priced local food, and a strong wi-fi signal.

Koko Western shore, Kapas; map p.251. Serves up great local food in a breezy beachfront dining area – rice with veg, chicken, beef, squid or fish and a choice of sauces costs RM16–25. Very good, but a little expensive and dishes emerge very slowly from the kitchen. There's also a bar. Daily 8am–10pm.

Southern Terengganu

The stretch of **southern Terengganu** between Marang and the Pahang border offers fairly slim pickings for travellers. Pleasant **beaches** are the main draw, any of which make a good break during a drive along the coast road, though facilities at most amount to a mere straggle of food stalls.

4

Rantau Abang

Little more than a handful of guesthouses strung out along a dusty road 40km south of Marang, **RANTAU ABANG** used to reap a rich reward as one of a handful of places in the world where the giant **leatherback turtle** came to lay its eggs. No longer, thanks to overfishing, pollution and poaching – at the time of writing, the last officially recorded leatherback nesting was in 2010, though locals claim two or three a year still come. In the meantime, Rantau Abang has drifted into relative obscurity. It's still a pleasant enough way station though, offering a beach with fine, though plastic strewn, sand and superb 180-degree views of blue-green sea.

Turtle Conservation and Information Centre

Mon–Thurs & Sun 8am–5pm • Free • ☎ 09 844 4169

The **Turtle Conservation and Information Centre**, or *Hentian Penyu*, holds informative, if dry, displays on turtle biology and conservation, plus a paddling pool full of hatchlings. If you want to spot nesting turtles, your best bets are elsewhere (see p.258).

ARRIVAL AND DEPARTURE   RANTAU ABANG

By bus Buses stop on the main road close to the Turtle Conservation and Information Centre. Local services from Kuala Terengganu, Marang and Dungun pass through Rantau Abang every 30min–1hr (8am–6pm) and are most regular in the mornings.

By taxi Ask at your accommodation about long-distance taxis to Kuala Terengganu (RM70) or Dungun (RM40).

ACCOMMODATION AND EATING

The decline in tourism means that most places are now geared up for student groups and team-building sessions. The exception is the luxurious *Tanjong Jara Resort*, just south of Rantau Abang. Few accommodation options in Rantau Abang serve **food** other than for groups, but a handful of simple places to eat lie within walking distance.

Dahimah's Guesthouse 1km south of information centre ☎ 017 955 8455, ✉ dahimahs@hotmail.com. Located between the main road and a pretty lagoon, and run by Dahimah – originally from the UK – and her Malay husband. Accommodation ranges from simple fan doubles to huge family rooms with TV, a/c and hot water (RM140). 📶 RM35

Tanjong Jara Resort 4km south of Rantau Abang ☎ 09 845 1100, ⓦ tanjongjararesort.com. One of the priciest east coast resorts, a complex of timber pavilions and houses almost fit for a sultan. Traditional treatments are on offer in the spa, and there's a diving and watersports centre. Activities range from waterfall treks and trips to Tasik Kenyir to cooking classes. ⓦ RM880

Dungun to the Pahang border

Driving south from **Dungun to the Pahang border** takes you through the heartland of Terengganu's oil industry, with refineries lining both side of Route 3 around the town of **Paka**. Most of the towns have little to detain tourists, but there are a few upmarket resorts along the coast.

Dungun

The backwater town of **DUNGUN** straggles for 9km along the coast south of Tanjong Jara. The bus station lies towards the northern end of town in a largely Chinese neighbourhood, with a handful of shophouses and a night market each Thursday. The only reason to stop here is because it's a **transport hub**; there's a taxi stand next to the bus station, with an ATM a few blocks north.

Tenggol Island

Further from the mainland than the popular islands further north, **Tenggol Island** (Pulau Tenggol; reached by boat from Dungun) is correspondingly less developed. While the few visitors who venture out here have to make do with rather run-down accommodation, there's beautiful, unspoiled scenery and arguably the best **diving** and snorkelling on the east coast. It's possible to arrange a diving trip from the mainland through *Tanjong Jara* resort (see above).

Ma'Daerah Turtle Sanctuary

Kerteh, 12km south of Paka • ☎ 09 844 4169

Near the town of **Kertih**, on the road south of Paka, is the **Ma'Daerah Turtle Sanctuary**, with an information centre and hatchery on a quiet beach where green turtles lay their eggs. It's possible to volunteer here during the May to September hatching season.

Kemaman and Chukai

The southernmost settlement of significance in Terengganu is the fusion of **Kemaman** and neighbouring **Chukai**. The town, home of a major port, holds little attraction for visitors, but its two bus stations (Geliga Bus Station for express buses, and the local bus station in town) are useful, and it has the closest **banks** and ATMs to Cherating.

ARRIVAL AND DEPARTURE · DUNGUN TO THE PAHANG BORDER

By plane Both Malindo Air and Malaysian Air have services between Kuala Lumpur and Kerteh (3 daily; 1hr).
By bus You may need to change at Dungun or Kemaman/Chukai if you are using local buses to travel the coast (7am–6pm roughly hourly).

By boat Speedboats run from Dungun to Tenggol Island (45min); transfers are normally included in accommodation packages.

ACCOMMODATION

The **resorts** along the coast are largely aimed at business travellers, so look for weekend discounts. Those on Tenggol are only open from February to November, and only when there are guests, so it is essential to book ahead.

DUNGUN

Pen'U Cottage Kompleks Perniagaan, Sura Gate ☎ 09 845 8333. Located 1.5km south of the bus station down a quiet side street towards the beach, this semi-homestay has small but clean rooms, all with a/c and bathrooms. There's a kitchen available for guest use. ⓦ RM80

TENGGOL ISLAND

Tenggol Coral Beach Resort Pulau Tenggol ☏ 012 784 7357, ⓦ tenggol.com.my. Pleasant, spacious rooms are linked by sandy paths facing Teluk Air Tawar ("Freshwater Bay") in the largest of Tenggol's three resorts. Rates given here are per night on the basis of two people sharing a two-night all-inclusive snorkelling package; the diving equivalent, including five dives, costs around double. RM1130

Cherating

At first it can be hard to discern the enduring appeal of **CHERATING**, a laidback village 45km north of Kuantan. Its heyday as a tourist destination is clearly over; for proof you only need to see the former tourist office – now a karaoke lounge – at one end of **Cherating Lama** (the old town), and the closed cultural centre at the other end. Many locals have long since moved out to the new settlement of **Cherating Baru**, 4km to the south. What's more, the **beach** is pleasant but hardly the best on the coast – it's best suited to windsurfing and kitesurfing (March to September), and **surfing** during the northeastern monsoon (October to December).

Nevertheless, at its best, Cherating Lama is still an appealing little travellers' community, chilled out yet warm-spirited, a place to share quality time with old companions and – chances are – to end up with a whole bunch of new acquaintances too. Local entrepreneurs have devised an array of **activities** to keep

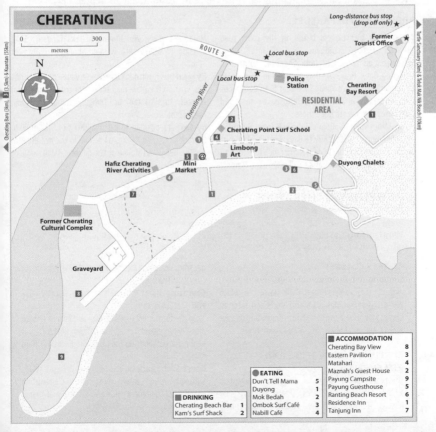

CHERATING

0 — 300 metres

N

ROUTE 3

Cherating River

Local bus stop

Long-distance bus stop (drop off only) ★

Former Tourist Office

Local bus stop ★

Police Station

RESIDENTIAL AREA

Cherating Bay Resort

Cherating Point Surf School

Limbong Art

Hafiz Cherating River Activities

Mini Market

@

Duyong Chalets

Former Cherating Cultural Complex

Graveyard

Cherating Baru (3km) ◀ B (3.5km) & Kuantan (55km)

Turtle Sanctuary (2km) & Teluk Mak Nik Beach (10km) ▶

4

■ ACCOMMODATION	
Cherating Bay View	8
Eastern Pavilion	3
Matahari	4
Maznah's Guest House	2
Payung Campsite	9
Payung Guesthouse	5
Ranting Beach Resort	6
Residence Inn	1
Tanjung Inn	7

● EATING	
Don't Tell Mama	5
Duyong	1
Mok Bedah	2
Ombok Surf Café	3
Nabill Café	4

■ DRINKING	
Cherating Beach Bar	1
Kam's Surf Shack	2

tourists coming, and it's well worth giving it a few days. Along the coast are a series of mid-range resorts that draw in families looking for a comfortable seaside break.

Cherating beach

No trip to Cherating would be complete without time spent on the **beach**. While the shelter of the bay ensures calm waters, jellyfish and currents are occasionally a problem, and it's best to avoid swimming at low tide, when the sea recedes 100m or more. The headland obliterates any sunrise views, but in good weather it's still worth taking a dawn stroll on the beach, when only a few fishing boats disturb the stillness.

Turtle sanctuary

3.5km east of Cherating village • Information centre Tues–Sun 9am–5pm • Free • ☎ 09 581 9087

Around the rocky headland at the eastern end of the bay sits Cherating's **turtle sanctuary** (signed from Route 3 as Santuari Penyu). Once a handy place to watch green and Hoxby turtles nesting on the beach, the development at *Club Med* nearby has caused the turtles to nest further north at Kemaman's Teluk Mak Nik Beach. Today the information centre has displays about the creatures, plus a few holding tanks at the back where you can see hatchlings and juveniles in season (May to September).

4

ARRIVAL AND DEPARTURE	CHERATING

By express bus Express buses on the coast road between Kuala Terengganu and Kuantan drop passengers on request at both Cherating Lama and Cherating Baru. However, they won't stop to pick up passengers, so reserve ahead for a seat from Geliga bus station near Chukai when you want to leave – taxis and local buses going north head there.

Destinations Ipoh (6.30pm daily; 7hr); Johor Bahru (4 daily; 6hr 30min); Kota Bharu (4 daily; 6hr); Kuala Besut (4 daily); Kuala Lumpur (14 daily; 4hr); Kuala Terengganu (6 daily; 5hr 30min); Kuantan (2 daily; 1hr–1hr 30min); Marang (6 daily; 2hr 30min); Melaka (2 daily; 5hr); Mersing (2 daily; 4hr); Rantau Abang (6 daily; 1hr 30min).

By local bus If you don't have a reservation on an express bus, wait on the main road for one of the sporadic local services to Kuantan or Dungun (roughly hourly; 7am–6pm).

By taxi It's possible to catch a taxi from Kuantan to Cherating (45 min; RM80), while one to the nearest ATM and the Geliga bus station at Chukai costs RM40 single or RM60 return.

ACTIVITIES IN CHERATING

During the northeast monsoon – and especially mid-October to early January, when the waves are good and the rain is not too bad – **surfing** is the big attraction in Cherating. **Windsurfing** and kitesurfing are possible throughout the year, weather allowing, while there's also a range of **activities** and organized tours (see opposite).

CRAFTS CLASSES

Limbong Art Cherating Lama ☎ 017 950 1281, ✉ umilimbong@gmail.com. Batik classes, in which you get your own designs onto T-shirts and sarongs. Classes take around two to six hours, depending on your project, and cost RM30–180. Daily 10am–10pm.

SURFING, WINDSURFING AND KITESURFING

There are only a couple of dedicated watersports schools, though surfboards (RM50–70/day) and lessons (RM100–120) are available from many guesthouses and cafés, the best being *Ombok* or *Cherating Beach Bar*.

Cherating Point Between Mazna's Guest House and Matahari ☎ 012 933 7590, ⓦ cheratingpoint .com. Surfboard rental (RM70/day) and lessons (90min plus 90min board rental after; from RM120), plus beginners' packages (including accommodation) from RM589. Daily Nov–June.

Kam's Surf Shack On the beach ☎ 017 362 4839. Surfing lessons in season; windsurfing and kitesurfing lessons, and equipment rental are available year-round. Mon, Tues & Thurs–Sun 9am–9pm.

TOUR OPERATORS AND GUIDES

Agencies along the main drag can book bus tickets and other travel arrangements, such as transfers to Taman Negara or islands off the east coast. All agencies and most guesthouses offer a range of **tours**, the selection and prices being similar wherever you go; night-time turtle-watching (RM60–70 including transport), firefly-watching (RM30–35; 1hr) and morning snorkelling trips to Snake Island (RM60–70; 2hr 30min) are the most popular options.

Hafiz Cherating River Activities Lot 1156, Cherating Lama ☏017 978 9256; map p.255. A self-taught expert on fireflies, Hafiz has developed a method of attracting the insects. The effect, as seen on evening excursions, is magical, although the trips have become very busy; many other agencies book guests onto his trips. Snorkelling, fishing and kayak rental also available.

Pak Su Cherating Lama ☏013 906 4828. Licensed nature guide, Pak Su, specializes in taking people to see turtles nesting on Teluk Mak Nik Beach (RM60). He works extensively with the Fisheries Department, buying turtle eggs from locals to prevent them ending up in the market.

ACCOMMODATION

The best places to stay are those by the river or towards the southern end of the beach as they have the **best vibe**, with the northern end of the beach now marred by the enormously expensive *Royale Chulan Cherating* resort, which has somewhat blotted the landscape. Prices can drop by up to twenty percent on weekdays (weekend prices shown below), with further **discounts** available during the northeast monsoon.

CHERATING LAMA

Cherating Bay View Cherating Lama ☏09 581 9248, ⓦcheratingbayviewresort.com; map p.255. At the quieter end of the bay, this complex has a range of a/c chalets, the cheapest of them around a greenish swimming pool. While the standard seafront chalets lack the modern fixtures and fittings of the deluxe options, they actually have better sea views. ☏ RM106

Matahari Cherating Lama ☏017 924 7465; map p.255. A mishmash of units, from spartan A-frames to larger chalets, all arranged around a pleasant grassy area. Toilets and showers are in a separate block; while a few rooms have private bathrooms (RM50), only one has a/c (RM120). There's a communal kitchen. ☏ RM30

Maznah's Guest House Cherating Lama ☏09 581 9307, ⓦmaznahguesthouse.blogspot.com; map p.255. Lovely family-run place with basic A-frames that share facilities, but you can hardly complain for the price. The spotless en-suite chalets are also good value, but the a/c ones are overpriced (RM150). Price includes breakfast and all day hot drinks. ☏ A-frames RM35, chalets RM50

★**Payung Guesthouse** Cherating Lama ☏019 917 1934, ⓦpayung-guesthouse.com; map p.255. A deservedly popular collection of ten no-frills chalets set in a small, very tidy garden, with a jetty at the back overlooking the river. All are en suite, with fan and mosquito net; most have double beds. Family-run and friendly, they also organize good-value trips, book buses and rent bikes (RM20/day). They are connected to the *Payung Campsite*, peacefully located between the middle of the beach and the river, which rents two-person tents for RM20 (mattress RM5 extra). ☏ RM60

Ranting Beach Resort Cherating Lama ☏09 581 9068; map p.255. Spacious, well-kept garden rooms, plus pricier beach chalets; good views compensate for the generally uninspiring decor – some have breezy verandas. All options are en suite, some with a/c and TV. ☏ Doubles RM140, chalets RM200

Residence Inn Cherating Lama ☏09 581 9333 ⓦric.my; map p.255. If you prefer resort-style accommodation but want to stay in Cherating Lama, then this complex of 138 tidy en-suite rooms is the place to come. The more expensive rooms in the old block are arranged around a children's swimming pool while the cheaper ones in the new block are quieter. Breakfast included. ☏ RM260

★**Tanjung Inn** Cherating Lama ☏09 581 9081, ⓦtanjunginn.com; map p.255. Timber-built en-suite accommodation, ranging from tents and simple fan chalets to brilliant traditionally styled kampung houses boasting a/c, four-poster beds and slate-tiled bathrooms with hot, which are set around two large ponds in a peaceful, pretty garden. The more basic fan rooms overlook the beach, and the glamping site is on the lagoon behind. ☏ Tents RM70, chalets RM106, kampung houses RM180

CHERATING BARU

Eastern Pavilion Cherating Baru ☏09 581 9500, ⓦeasternpavilion.com; map p.255. Twelve luxurious villas in traditional kampung houses from different Malaysian states. All have one or two beautifully appointed bedrooms, lounge and private outdoor jacuzzis; there's also a spa. This rate is for the cheapest turtle watching package, which includes breakfast. ☏ RM528

4

MARINE TURTLES

While four types of marine turtle lay their eggs on Malaysia's east coast, for years the sight of the largest – the giant, critically endangered **leatherback turtle** – was the star attraction, drawing visitors to Rantau Abang in Terengganu. In fact all other kinds of marine turtle – **green** (nesting sites include the Perhentians, Redang Island, Cherating, Penarik and the Turtle Islands National Park in Sabah), **hawksbill** (Redang Island, Turtle Islands National Park, Tioman Island and Padang Kemunting near Melaka), **olive ridley** (rarely seen), and **Kemp's ridley** and **loggerhead** (neither of which nest in Malaysia) – are also at risk.

Harmful fishing methods, such as the use of **trawl nets**, kill thousands of marine turtles each year, and help explain the dramatic reduction in leatherbacks nesting on the Terengganu coast. In 1956, more than ten thousand were recorded; in 2000, just three; in 2002, there were no sightings of leatherbacks in Rantau Abang for the first time since records began; by 2005, leatherback, hawksbill and olive ridley statistics in Terengganu were all at zero, and green turtle figures were significantly down. On the rare occasions when a leatherback turns up – there was a lone turtle in 2010 – their eggs often fail to hatch. This is probably because of the increasing rarity of male–female turtle encounters.

With a very meagre survival rate among hatchlings under ordinary conditions, any human pressure on turtle populations has drastic consequences for their survival. For the Chinese in Malaysia and Singapore, turtle soup is a classic delicacy, and while Malays eschew turtle meat, they do consume **turtle eggs**, which look like ping-pong balls and are sold at markets throughout the east coast. Their collection is licensed at certain sites, but there's no guarantee that anything on sale was collected legally. There appears to be no political will to outlaw this traditional food, a sad irony given Malaysia's general turtle conservation efforts: in many places, hatcheries pay licensed collectors for eggs rather than see them go to markets. At least the deliberate slaughter of turtles for their shells, once fashioned into bowls and earrings, has been banned since 1992.

TURTLE SPOTTING AND CONSERVATION

Nowadays, humans are excluded from various designated **sanctuaries** for nesting turtles. At these sites the eggs are dug up immediately after the turtle has laid them and reburied in sealed-off **hatcheries** on the beach. Burying the eggs in sand of the correct temperature is crucial as warm sand produces more females, while cooler sand favours males. When the hatchlings emerge, they are released at the top of the beach and their scurry to the sea is supervised to ensure their safe progress.

There are several officially sanctioned opportunities to watch nesting turtles on the east coast beaches and islands, including at Cherating, Perhentian Besar and Tioman Island (at Juara Beach). It is also possible to volunteer at turtle sites such as Ma'Daerah (see p.254). Be sure to avoid "turtle releasing" activities, however.

EATING AND DRINKING

Cherating Lama has a string of inexpensive **restaurants**, many emphasizing seafood including the *lala* – a sort of clam, which turns up in various sauces – but a couple of places also offer decent Western food. *Kedai kopis* across from the *Payung Guesthouse* serve reasonable Malay cuisine, with *roti canai* in the morning and *nasi campur* later in the day.

★ **Don't Tell Mama** Cherating Lama ☎ 019 996 1723; map p.255. Open year-round, the beachside *Don't Tell Mama* is a great place to chill out with a beer (from RM10) and one of their excellent giant cheeseburgers (RM25), enjoying the relaxed playlist from a hammock/lounge chair or while playing with the dogs. The other, mostly Western dishes (RM6–20), such as pasta, are also good. Food served until 10pm. Mon & Wed–Sun 6pm–1am.

Duyong Cherating Lama ☎ 09 581 9578; map p.255. A popular old faithful, this large, airy place overlooking the river offers excellent Chinese and Thai dishes (RM6–20), plus a few Western standbys such as lamb chop (RM20) and steak (RM25). Veggie dishes can be cooked to order. Mon, Tues & Thurs–Sun 11am–11pm.

Kam's Surf Shack Cherating Lama ☎ 017 362 4839; map p.255. Owned by a pair of local brothers, this simple, open-sided beach bar serves up cold beer (RM12), simple Western and Malay food (RM6–20), a constant stream of reggae, and watersports lessons. Mon, Tues & Thurs–Sun 6am–midnight.

Cherating Beach Bar Cherating Lama ☎017 674 7015; map p.255. In a great spot in the middle of the beach, this atmospheric bar built partly from driftwood – often called *Mazlan's* after the very laidback owner – serves up cold beer (from RM10), cocktails (from RM15) and simple snacks, though you're also welcome to make use of the barbecue. Daily noon–late.

Mok Bedah Cherating Lama ☎019 907 3842; map p.255. If you're after an authentic local breakfast, try this family-run place, serving a great *nasi campur* spread from a horseshoe-shaped counter, using *nasi dadang* (rice with coconut) or *nasi minyak* (heavily spiced rice mixed with yoghurt), all for RM7–8. Daily 7–10am.

Nabill Café Cherating Lama ☎019 985 3302; map p.255. Locals come here for their great *ikan bakar* (prices start from RM5.50/100g), but if they've run out of fresh fish you can choose from a range of Chinese, Malay, Thai and Western dishes, including a long list of rice- and noodle-based standards (all RM4–12). Daily 6pm–1am.

Ombok Surf Café Cherating Lama ☎09 581 9274; map p.255. Run by ecologically-minded Malaysian surfers, this very hip and funkily-decorated café serves up a mix of local and Western food, including satisfying breakfasts, pasta and sandwiches (all RM7–18) as well as espresso coffees and smoothies (RM6–12). They also can arrange surf boards and lessons, and have a small gallery, with evening musical jam sessions during high season. April–Nov daily 9am–5pm; Dec–March 8.30am–9.30pm or later.

Kuantan

The state capital of Pahang since 1955, **KUANTAN** is an undistinguished agglomeration of concrete buildings around an older core of shophouses close to the Kuantan River. While there's very little by way of historical or cultural interest in the city itself, Kuantan can be a breath of fresh air after a sojourn in Kelantan or Terengganu – it's closer in feel to the west coast cities than to Kuala Terengganu or Kota Bharu. If you're arriving from elsewhere in the country, however, Kuantan can seem mundane. With the creation of the **East Coast Highway** to Pelabuhan Kuantan, the port 40km north of the city, it's easy to bypass Kuantan altogether if you're travelling between KL and the east coast.

If Kuantan has a focus of sorts, it's the **padang**. The city's oldest streets, between there and the river, hold quite a few hotels and restaurants. The best reason to hang around for a night or two, though, is to take a day-trip to the cave temple of **Gua Charas** or the royal town of **Pekan**.

Masjid Negeri

Northeastern edge of the padang • Mon–Thurs, Sat & Sun 10am–noon, 3–4pm & 5.30–6pm • Free

The town's main sight, the **Masjid Negeri**, was built in 1991, with a pastel exterior like a piece of fine Wedgewood – green for Islam, blue for peace and white for purity. It's distinctly Turkish in appearance, thanks to the pencil minarets at all four corners of the sturdy square prayer hall, topped with a looming central dome. Non-Muslims can visit outside of prayer times: men should wear long trousers, while women are advised to cover their hair and dress modestly.

Pahang Arts Museum

Northeastern edge of the padang • Mon–Fri 9am–5pm • Free

Housed in a lovely old British colonial administration building from 1910, the new **Pahang Arts Museum** features six galleries of Islamic art and calligraphy, traditional east coast crafts such as shadow puppets, and musical instruments. It also has a gallery of abstract art, in addition to four abstract sculptures in the gardens depicting *raja sariman* (a Malaysian martial art), which are full of energy and movement. Temporary exhibits of international and local artists are also hosted here, and there are historic photos of the local people throughout.

EATING

Akob Patin House	8
Bombay Hamid Bros	9
Chan Poh	5
Jelita	3
Kula Cakes	7
Lila Wadi Barbecue	2
Sara Thai Kitchen	4
Tjantek Art Bistro	6
Ye Mi Won	1

ACCOMMODATION

Grand Darul Makmur Hotel	7
Hyatt Regency	4
Makmur Guesthouse	5
Megaview	9
Mista Reggae	3
Orchid	6
Seasons View	8
Swiss Garden Resort	2
Zenith	1

DRINKING

Country Ranch Pub	1

Esplanade

Boat trips depart Mon, Tues & Thurs–Sun 11am, 1pm, 3pm & 6pm, 8pm night cruises by advance booking only • RM38 • ☎ 011 2575 8033

Down by the river, starting at the *Megaview Hotel*, an **esplanade** clings to the banks of the Kuantan River. Early evening is a good time to take a stroll, to see fishing boats returning with the day's catch and perhaps the occasional red eagle swooping on its prey. A small **night market** sets up here each evening (6–10pm) and boat trips depart from the jetty at the southwest end of the promenade.

Teluk Chempedak

5km east of centre following Jalan Besar, which becomes Jalan Teluk Sisek then Jalan Teluk Chempedak • Bus #200 from local bus station (daily 6am–11pm every 20–30min; 30min); taxis RM25

Around the corner from a wooded headland, on an east-facing stretch of coast, **Teluk Chempedak** has long been a popular evening and weekend hangout for families and young people. The sands of the bay are encouragingly white, although undertows can render the sea off-limits (watch out for red flags). There is an appealing liveliness about the place, quite at variance from the langourous mood on the otherwise better sands of rural Terengganu. Bars, fast-food chains and restaurants line the main road as you arrive, before you reach the *Hyatt*, and there are more places to eat on the promenade.

ARRIVAL AND DEPARTURE KUANTAN

By plane Sultan Ahmad Shah airport is 15km west of town, 20min (RM35) by taxi. KL flights (3 daily; 45min) are operated by MAS (☎09 538 5430); Singapore flights (daily; 1hr) are with Firefly (☎09 538 2911).

By express bus Express buses depart from the lower level of Kuantan's modern Terminal Sentral bus station, 7.5km northwest of downtown Kuantan. It's a RM20 taxi ride, or you can take the #303 bus.

Destinations Alor Setar (3 daily; 10hr); Butterworth (6 daily; 9hr); Dungun via Cherating (9 daily; 2hr); Ipoh (4 daily; 6hr); Jerantut (4 daily; 3hr); Johor Bahru (31 daily; 5hr 30min); Kota Bharu (13 daily; 6hr); Kuala Lipis (2 daily; 6hr); Kuala Lumpur (every 30min–1hr; 4–5hr);

Kuala Terengganu (14 daily; 4–5hr); Melaka (3 daily; 4hr); Mersing (7 daily; 2-3hr); Seremban (10 daily; 6–7hr); Singapore (4 daily; 6hr 30min).

By local bus The local bus station is on Jalan Stadium, with regular #303 buses to the Terminal Sentral bus station (every 20–30min), Pekan, Sungai Lembing and Teluk Chempedak.

By taxi Local taxis can be found near the mosque; long-distance taxis arrive and depart from Terminal Sentral. Call ☎09 572 9892 to book.

By car For car rental, Avis (☎09 539 8768, ⓦavis.com), Hertz (☎09 538 4848, ⓦsimedarbycarrental.com) and Mayflower (☎09 538 4490, ⓦmayflowercarrental.com.my) are all at the airport.

INFORMATION

Tourist offices Tourism Pahang, the state tourism office (Mon–Thurs 9am–1pm & 2–5pm, Fri 9am–1pm & 2.45pm–5pm; ☎09 568 1623, ⓦpahangtourism.org.my), is at 33 ICT Hub, Jalan Putra Square 4, just south of the East

Coast Mall, with the Tourism Malaysia office just a few doors north (Mon–Thurs 8am–1pm & 2–5pm, Fri 8am–12.15pm & 2.45–5pm; ☎09 567 7112).

ACCOMMODATION

There's no shortage of places to stay in Kuantan, and you can also stay out of town at **Teluk Chempedak** or pleasant **Balok Beach**. For details of **homestays**, pick up the well-produced *Homestay Pahang* booklet from the state tourist office or visit ⓦgo2homestay.com.

CENTRAL KUANTAN

Grand Darul Makmur Hotel Lorong Gambut, off Jalan Beserah ☎09 511 8888, ⓦgdmhotel.com.my; map opposite. This slick, central four-star hotel offers spacious rooms, several food outlets, a fitness centre and a pool complete with waterfall. The upper rooms in the twelve-storey Tower Block also provide great views. Breakfast included. 🛜 RM290

Makmur Guesthouse Jalan Pasar Baru ☎09 514 1363; map opposite. The best of the cheapies close to the bus station, although that isn't saying a lot; fan rooms with shared facilities as well as a/c en-suite rooms (RM50), all simple and fairly shabby. 🛜 RM30

Mista Reggae House Jalan Mahkota ☎016 922 2864; map opposite. A decent backpacker option near the main mosque, this funky café has some of the cheapest beds around in their twelve-person dorm upstairs, as well as a few cheap fan rooms. The café has decent Western food, there's a rooftop chill-out area, and they also rent bikes (RM10/day), as well as organize tours. 🛜 Dorm RM15, doubles RM30

Orchid Jalan Merdeka ☎09 515 5570; map opposite. Despite the unpromising steps up to reception, the rooms in

this quirky backstreet Chinese hotel – while in need of a lick of paint – are decent for the price and come with a/c. 🛜 RM45

Seasons View A22 Lorong Haji Abdul Rahman 1 ☎09 516 2828, ⓦseasonsview-kuantan.com; map opposite. A self-proclaimed "oasis of gracious hospitality", the rooms here are not exactly luxurious but they're immaculate and easy to recommend for the price, though a window and breakfast both cost RM10 extra. 🛜 RM88

TELUK CHEMPEDAK

Hyatt Regency ☎09 518 1234, ⓦkuantan.regency .hyatt.com; map opposite. A long-established (though recently refurbished) beach retreat for well-heeled folk from KL and Singapore, with two swimming pools, a gym, tennis and squash courts, childcare facilities, multiple restaurants and a bar in a converted ship. Breakfast included. 🛜 RM435

BALOK BEACH

Some 15km north of Kuantan, Balok Beach can be reached by taxi (around RM30) or on the #600 bus from the local bus station (45min).

4

Swiss Garden Resort ☎ 09 548 8288, �🌐 swissgarden .com; map p.260. Balconied rooms overlooking a landscaped garden or the South China Sea, plus a free-form swimming pool, spa and several restaurants. A large range of activity packages are available for adults and children. Prices rise by around RM70–100 on weekends. 📶 __RM290__

EATING AND DRINKING

Laidback **kedai kopis** dot the streets west and south of the padang, while the area around Berjaya Megamall is packed with cafés and **mamak** joints. For inexpensive **Malay** food, try the places on and around the northern end of Jalan Haji Abdul Aziz or the area around the Central Market. International chain restaurants can be found at the East Coast Mall. Teluk Chempedak also holds plenty of eating choices, including many on the seafront, some open until as late as 2am. The **nightlife** in Teluk Chempedak is more lively than that in town, revolving around a handful of bars on the main road just before the beach.

CENTRAL KUANTAN

★**Akob Patin House** Lorong Tun Ismail ☎ 019 987 4463; map p.260. The signature ingredient at this humble place is *patin* (silver catfish), served at lunchtime as *ikan patin tempoyak* (RM20/30) – with chilli, tamarind and fermented durian – it's surprisingly tasty. Mon–Sat 8am–5pm.

Bombay Hamid Bros Jalan Teluk Sisek ☎ 09 513 1945; map p.260. Outstanding Indian food in a stylish a/c interior, serving very tasty banana leaf *thalis* (RM7–14.50) either side of midday, and various Indian snacks (RM1.05–5) and their highly-recommended *biriyanis* (RM6.50–30) at other times. Daily 7am–10pm.

Chan Poh 52 Jalan Bukit Ubi; map p.260. A good place for inexpensive dim sum, this earthy, no-frills place has a wide range of plates on display (RM3–6) for you to choose from, which are then steamed for you. Beer from RM8. Daily 6am–midnight.

Jelita Jalan Haji Abdul Aziz; map p.260. Essentially a posh-looking metal hangar housing several food outlets, the star attraction among which is a branch of *Satay Zul*, Kuantan's best-loved satay house (daily 5–11pm), offering beef, chicken, *kambing* (goat), *rusa* (venison) and even *perut* (stomach) at around 90sen to RM1.50 a stick. Other stalls offer rice, noodles and doner kebabs. Mon–Sat 7.30am–midnight.

Lila Wadi Barbecue Jalan Teluk Sisek ☎ 012 664 4054, �🌐 lilawadi.com.my; map p.260. This great spot serves Japanese-style barbecue that's self-cooked cooked at your table; you choose a main ingredient – beef, chicken or seafood – and receive a "set" (minimum two people; RM35–40) that includes side dishes. Leave space for a slice of their excellent cheesecake, which is so popular that *Lila Wadi* has opened a spin-off cake shop, *Kula Cakes*, on Jalan Taman. Tues–Thurs

12.30–3pm & 5–11.30pm, Fri–Sun 4pm–midnight.

Sara Thai Kitchen Jalan Gambut ☎ 012 937 9322; map p.260. Thai food seems to be particularly popular in Kuantan, and this busy restaurant – part of a small chain with another branch on Jalan Besar – is one of several places specializing in dishes like green curry, *tom yam* (RM7–8 for a small bowl) and mango salad. Daily 1–11pm.

★**Tjantek Art Bistro** 46 Jalan Besar ☎ 09 516 4144, ⒲ tjantek.blogspot.com; map p.260. With soft lighting, chilled music and vintage artwork plastering the walls, this is one of Kuantan's most atmospheric dining spots. The pasta dishes are great, as are the sandwiches and salads (all RM15–20) and the steak (RM40). There's no alcohol, but locals head here for their fresh juices and punches. Mon–Sat 5pm–1am.

★**Ye Mi Won** 236 Jalan Teluk Sisek; map p.260. A little way out of the centre, this traditional Korean family-run restaurant is as good as you'll find anywhere, laying out an excellent spread of homemade *banchan* (side dishes) and *kimchi* with the barbecued *samgyeopsal* (pork belly), *bulgogogi* (marinated beef) and *galbi sal* (beef ribs). It' not cheap, however, with a meal for two coming in at around RM100 with drinks; the soups are slightly cheaper at around RM25–35, and there are lunch sets for RM17–25. Daily 11am–10pm.

TELUK CHEMPEDAK

Country Ranch Pub 41 Teluk Chempedak ☎ 09 560 5717; map p.260. If you're a fan of English football you'll certainly find a talking point here – it's been owned by a string of Liverpool supporters. More of a straightforward pub than some of its neighbours, with a free pool, sport on the TV, occasional live music, and no karaoke. Daily 5pm–midnight.

DIRECTORY

Cinemas Two Golden Screen Cinemas (Berjaya Megamall and East Coast Mall; ⒲ gsc.com.my) show some English-language films, as does Lotus Five-Star cinema in the Teruntum Complex (☎ 09 515 6881).

Hospital Hospital Tengku Ampuan Afzan (☎ 09 513 3333) is on Jalan Besar; the private Kuantan Medical Centre is next to the Berjaya Megamall (☎ 09 514 2828, ⒲ kmc .tdmberhad.com.my).

Shops Popular malls include the Berjaya Megamall on Jalan Tun Ismail, Kuantan Parade on Jalan Penjara, and the East Coast Mall. Hamid Bros (Mon–Sat 9am–9pm, Sun 10am–3pm) on Jalan Haji Abdul Aziz has a limited range of English-language books, plus maps of Malaysia; a better selection is available at the Berjaya Megamall branch of Popular Bookstore (daily 10am–10pm).

Visa extensions The immigration office is out near the express bus station at Kompleks KDN, Bandar Indera Mahkota (Mon–Fri 7.30am–1pm & 2–5.30pm; ☏ 09 573 2200); take bus #302 from the local bus station.

Gua Charas

25km northwest of Kuantan on Route C4 • RM2 donation • Local bus #500 to Pekan Panching (30min) then 4km walk, or taxi from Kuantan (RM100 including waiting)

One of the great limestone outcrops close to Kuantan is home to **Gua Charas**, a **cave temple** that can be visited as a leisurely day-trip: if you charter a taxi from Kuantan then you can also visit the nearby Pandan River **waterfall**, where you can splash around in various pools. If you're taking the bus then you start at **Panching** village, where a sign to the cave points down a track through oil palm plantations. It's a long, hot 4km walk, so take plenty of water with you, though you may be able to hitch a lift from devotees.

Once you've reached the outer temple and paid your donation, you're faced with a steep climb to the cave temple itself. Halfway up, a flight of metal steps leads to the entrance of the main cave. The cave has been redeveloped to make it safer for worshippers to get inside, and concrete paths make access much easier than previously, though detract slightly from the atmosphere. Inside the echoing cavern, brightly illuminated shrines gleam from gloomy corners, guiding you past a phallic shrine dedicated to the Hindu god **Shiva** to the oldest shrine deep in the cave. Here a 9m-long reclining **Buddha** is almost dwarfed by its giant surroundings.

4

Sungai Lembing

42km northwest of Kuantan on Route C4 • **Muzium Sungai Lembing** daily 9am–6pm • RM5 • ⓦ sungailembingmines.com.my • **The Tin Mines Tunnels** daily 9am–12.30pm & 2–5pm • RM31.80 • Local bus #500 (roughly hourly 6.20am–7.20pm; 1hr)

The small town of **SUNGAI LEMBING** retains an old-fangled, unhurried feel that's fading from the likes of Kuala Lipis and Pekan. Once the richest tin mining town in Pahang, the now sleepy town sits in a lush valley with steep forested hills on both sides, its main road planted with banyans and lined with 1920s **shophouses**. At the end of the main street is a **padang**, flanked by a dark timber building, once the **staff clubhouse** of the Pahang Consolidated Company Limited (PCCL), which ran the nearby mines from 1905 until tin prices collapsed in the mid-1980s.

The history of the town and the PCCL are explored in the **Muzium Sungai Lembing** crowning the hill beyond the padang, formerly accommodation for PCCL's top managers. **The Tin Mines Tunnels** (some of the longest and deepest in the world) can also be toured, with a replica train taking you the first 100m, followed by recreations of working life for the old miners. Beyond the museum are several excellent **hikes** around the valley, the most popular of which is the 45-minute-long walk up **Panorama Hill**, signposted from the town. Sungai Lembing is popular with domestic tourists, who flock here on weekends for a hit of nostalgia so it's better to come on a weekday, when you'll find plentiful accommodation and few other visitors. Hiring a bike on the main street is also a good idea as there are several well-marked cycling routes through the surrounding countryside.

Pekan

Nearly 50km south of Kuantan lies the royal town of **PEKAN**, whose name literally means "small town". State capital of Pahang until 1898, Pekan still retains a measure of its charm and tranquillity, although this has been challenged in recent years with the growth of its modern centre. This is thanks in no small part – so locals say – to the fact that the town's MP is none other than prime minister Najib Tun Razak. Still, the town is definitely a worthwhile day-trip from Kuantan: you'll find unusually spruce **kampung houses** with pretty gardens, a few **museums** and a few wooden former **royal residences**.

Muzium Sultan Abu Bakar

Jalan Sultan Ahmad • Tues–Thurs, Sat & Sun 9.30am–5pm, Fri 9.30am–12.15pm & 2.45–5pm • RM15; Waterfront Gallery free • ☎ 09 422 1371

At the edge of the commercial area, Jalan Sultan Ahmad faces the languid riverfront and holds the **Muzium Sultan Abu Bakar** – the State Museum of Pahang. It's housed in a well-proportioned Straits colonial building that has variously served as the sultan's istana, the centre of British administration, and the headquarters of the Japanese army during the occupation.

You'll need to take your shoes off to pad around the galleries, which cover a wide range of topics, from Sultan Abu Bakar's predilection for polo to the Orang Asli. Displays are nicely designed but poorly lit, and content is thin in places – the most informative gallery is dedicated to Pahang's traditional arts and crafts. The open-air **Watercraft Gallery** (set to reopen in 2018 after refurbishment), part of the state museum but just across the river, houses a good selection of decorative boats that once plied Pahang's rivers and coast, the centrepiece being a boxy white houseboat built for Sultan Abu Bakar in the 1950s.

The palaces

At the intersection of Jalan Sultan Abu Bakar and Jalan Sri Terentang, an archway built to resemble elephants' tusks marks the way to the royal quarter of the town. The white timber building on the corner, once the **Istana Putih**, is now a centre for Koranic recitation. A few minutes' walk south, the squat **Istana Mangga Tunggal** is painted a dark blue. Continue and turn left at the archway to reach the expansive walled grounds of the **Istana Abu Bakar** – the gate flanked by a pair of fighter jets – current home of the royal family and closed to the public. The other side of the road holds some attractively colourful kampung houses. Follow the walls, and after nearly ten minutes you'll come to a vast **polo field**, home to a polo club founded in 1926.

South of the padang sits **Istana Leban Tunggal**, an unusual wooden porticoed building with two octagonal towers crowned with yellow cupolas. Sadly, the 1935 palace, once the only one of Pekan's istanas open to the public, is now locked up, its gardens slowly returning to the jungle.

ARRIVAL AND INFORMATION

PEKAN

By bus Cream-coloured rapid Kuantan bus #400 departs every 20–30min from Kuantan's local bus station for the hour-long journey to Pekan. If your main interest is the palaces, ask to be let off at the "Daulat Tuanku" arch on Jalan Sultan Abu Bakar, before the UFO-like water tower. Pekan's own bus station is in the modern centre, east of the padang. You'll need to head to Kuantan for most long-distance destinations.

Destinations Kota Bharu via Kuala Terengganu (4 daily; 7hr); Kuantan (every 20–30min; 50min); Johor Bharu (5 daily; 5hr 10min).

By taxi Taxis (☎ 09 422 2211) depart from close to the bus station, with fixed fares to Kuantan (RM60), Tasik Chini (RM80) and other destinations.

ACCOMMODATION AND EATING

The streets around the padang hold several places to **eat**, including a small row of stalls selling juice and snacks, with parasols providing a welcome break from the sun.

Chief's Rest House Jalan Istana Permai ☎ 09 422 6941; map p.264. Occupying a spacious 1929 timber bungalow, and not unlike some of the istanas, this resthouse has nine high-ceilinged rooms, some with four-poster beds and bamboo blinds, with a/c and TV, as well as a dorm. Booking is essential; it's a popular place, in a town with few alternatives. 🛜 Dorm RM30, doubles RM55

Farouk Maju 1 Jalan Engku Muda Mansor; map p.264. As well as a decent *nasi campur* spread (RM7–10), this typical *mamak* restaurant serves tasty and cheap *biriyani* (RM9–9.50), curries (RM4.50–9) and various Indian snacks such as *roti*, *poori*, *dosa* and *naan* (RM1–2.80) to a constant stream of locals. Daily 24hr.

4

The south

MELAKA

5

The south

The south of the Malay Peninsula, below Kuala Lumpur and Kuantan, holds some of the country's most historically and culturally significant towns. Foremost among these is the west coast city of Melaka, founded in the fifteenth century and ushering in a Malay "golden age" under the Melaka Sultanate. For all its enduring influence, though, the sultanate was short-lived and its fall to the Portuguese early in the sixteenth century marked the start of centuries of colonial involvement in Malaysia. Today Melaka fascinates visitors with its historical buildings and cultural blend, including the Peranakan community (also called Baba-Nyonya), which grew from the intermarriage of early Chinese immigrant traders and Malay women.

Melaka is not, however, the only place in the region with historical resonance. Between KL and Melaka, what is now the state of Negeri Sembilan is where the intrepid **Minangkabau** tribes from Sumatra settled, making their mark with architecture that can still be seen in **Seremban** and **Sri Menanti**. Both lie just over an hour south of the capital by road. Continuing down the west coast on the train line or the North–South Expressway (NSE), travellers soon reach the tip of the Peninsula and the thriving border city of **Johor Bahru** (JB) which dates back only to 1855. Beyond it, over the Straits of Johor, lies Singapore.

Visitors tend to avoid the mountainous interior, where the road network is poor, but Route 3 on the east coast is a good deal more varied than the NSE, and winds for 300km through oil-palm country and past pleasant beaches. The biggest attractions along the east coast are **Tioman** and the other islands of the **Seribuat Archipelago**; they are havens for divers, snorkellers and anyone else in search of white sandy beaches, clear water and a tranquil atmosphere. Back on the Peninsula, and accessible from either east or west coast, the **Endau Rompin National Park** is a more rugged and less visited alternative to Taman Negara.

Negeri Sembilan

During the fifteenth century, the **Minangkabau** tribes from Sumatra established themselves in what is now the Malay state of **Negeri Sembilan**. While the modern-day capital is **Seremban**, 70km south of Kuala Lumpur, the cultural heart of the state lies 30km east in the royal town of **Sri Menanti**. Both towns showcase traditional Minangkabau architecture, with its distinctive, saddle-shaped roofs.

Brief history

The modern state of Negeri Sembilan is based on an old confederacy of nine districts (hence its name – *sembilan* is Malay for "nine"). By the middle of the nineteenth century, the thriving **tin trade** and British control over the area were well established, with colonial authority administered from Sungai Ujong (today's Seremban). Rival

The Minangkabau p.273
Getting from Johor Bahru to Singapore p.294

Snorkelling and diving around Tioman Island p.299
Sandflies p.308

TIOMAN ISLAND

Highlights

❶ Minangkabau architecture The spectacular and distinctive architecture of this ancient Sumatran tribe survives in Sri Menanti and Seremban. **See p.273**

❷ Melaka The UNESCO World Heritage Site of Melaka has Portuguese, Dutch and British colonial buildings as well as unique Peranakan ancestral homes and some of Malaysia's best food. **See p.274**

❸ Johor Bahru It may still be gritty by Malaysian standards, but this border city is smartening itself up with a combination of

major public projects and small-scale entrepreneurship. **See p.291**

❹ Tioman Island Palm-fringed, scenic and with great diving, this island is understandably popular but retains a laidback feel. **See p.298**

❺ Seribuat Archipelago Tioman attracts all the attention, but the other islands of the Seribuat Archipelago offer even better beaches. **See p.309**

❻ Endau Rompin National Park A little-visited lush tropical rainforest, rich with rare species of flora and fauna. **See p.310**

HIGHLIGHTS ARE MARKED ON THE MAP ON P.270

THE SOUTH

HIGHLIGHTS

1 Minangkabau architecture
2 Melaka
3 Johor Bahru
4 Tioman Island
5 Seribuat Archipelago
6 Endau Rompin National Park

Malay and Minangkabau groups fought several wars for control over the mining and transport of tin, with Chinese secret societies (triads) manipulating the situation to gain local influence, before a treaty was eventually signed in 1895.

Seremban

An hour south of the capital and just twenty minutes from KL International Airport, the bustling town of **SEREMBAN** is often overlooked by passing tourists. It is, however, the access point for **Sri Menanti** and has good examples of Minangkabau architecture at the **Taman Seni Budaya Negeri** museum complex.

Lake Garden and around

The area around the **Lake Garden** – more lake than garden – holds the most appeal. Heading north alongside it you pass the **Craft Complex** (Kompleks Kraf; daily 9am–6pm), a good place to view and buy handmade ceramics and textiles. Nearby is the white-stuccoed former **State Library** (Perbadanan Perpustakaan Awam; daily 9am–5pm) – built as the centre of colonial administration – with its graceful columns and portico. Beyond the black-and-gilt wrought-iron gates of the Istana (closed to the public), just north, a left turn leads to the **State Secretariat**, whose architecture (such as the layered, buffalo-horn roof) reflects the Minangkabau tradition.

Taman Seni Budaya Negeri

Near North–South Expressway, 3km northwest of the centre • Daily 10am–6pm • Free • ☎ 06 763 1149 ⓦ lmns.ns.gov.my • Bus from Terminal 1 (every 30min; 10–15min); taxi from the centre RM10

Although the small museum at the centre of the **Taman Seni Budaya Negeri** (State Arts and Culture Park) is unlikely to hold your attention for long, two reconstructed buildings in the grounds provide a good introduction to the principles of Minangkabau architecture. The 20m-long **Istana Ampang Tinggi** was built as a royal residence in the mid-nineteenth century. The interior of the veranda, where male guests were entertained, displays a wealth of exuberant and intricate leaf carvings, with a pair of unusual heavy timber doors. The other building was used for formal state events and also bears elaborate carving on the exterior.

ARRIVAL AND INFORMATION

SEREMBAN

By train Seremban's train station, just south of the centre, has regular Komuter connections from KL Sentral and the old Kuala Lumpur station.

Destinations Alor Star (3 daily; 7hr 30min–8hr); Butterworth (2 daily; 5hr 30min); Gemas (4 daily; 1hr); Ipoh (4 daily; 3hr 30min); Kuala Kangsar (4 daily; 5hr); Kuala Lumpur (every 30min; 1hr 30min); Padang Besar (3 daily; 8hr).

By bus The bus station is just across the river west of the town centre on Jalan Sungai Ujong, connected to the handy Terminal 1 Shopping Centre (daily 10am–10pm) that houses a myriad of shops as well as a Golden Screen Cinema.

Destinations Alor Setar (2 daily; 8hr); Butterworth (3 daily; 5hr); Gua Musang (2 daily; 8hr); Hat Yai (Thailand; 3 daily; 10hr); Ipoh (3 daily; 5hr); Johor Bahru (every 1.5hr, 4hr); KLIA & KLIA2 (hourly; 1hr); Kota Bharu (2 daily; 8hr); Kuala Lumpur (every 10min; 1hr); Kuala Pilah (hourly; 45min); Kuala Terengganu (2 daily; 8hr); Kuantan (1 daily; 4hr 30min); Melaka (hourly; 1hr 15min); Mersing (1 daily; 6hr); Singapore (4 daily, 5hr).

By taxi A taxi or Grab / Uber from KL Sentral's taxi station costs around RM120.

Information Tourism Malaysia, Seremban Plaza, Jalan Dato' Muda Linggi (Mon–Fri 8am–5pm; ☎06 762 2388) about 3km east of the centre.

ACCOMMODATION

★**The Dusun** Kampung Kolam Air, Mukim Pantai ⓦ thedusun.com.my; map p.272. This wonderful orchard retreat, 15km northeast of Seremban, offers accommodation in six classic kampung-style units dotted amid mangosteen, mango, durian and orange trees in twelve acres of land. Most units are open-fronted with unobstructed views of the rainforest, and each is equipped with kitchenette and BBQ sets. Note that meals are only available upon request, well in advance, so you should bring your own food. Facilities include two inviting saltwater pools and a deer park; staff organize jungle treks and bird walks. Rates include breakfast. Online bookings only. ☎ RM400

5

SEREMBAN

EATING
Beef Noodle Stall	1
Chai Hong	2

ACCOMMODATION
The Dusun	2
Royale Chulan	3
Sun Lun Yik Hotel	1

Royale Chulan Jalan Dato' A.S. Dawood ☏ 06 766 6666, ⓦ royalechulan-seremban.com; map above. This large establishment is Seremban's most upmarket option; rooms are spacious and comfortable, if a bit dated. Good facilities, including a large swimming pool, gym and tennis court. 📶 RM270

Sun Lun Yik Hotel 19 Jalan Tun Dr Ismail ☏ 06 7635 572, ⓦ www.sunlunyik.com; map above. A lovely heritage-style hotel offering nine immaculate rooms, opening onto a hallway lined with local art. There's also an airy lounge area with marble tables and wooden stools. 📶 Dorms RM34, family room RM139

EATING, DRINKING AND NIGHTLIFE

There's no shortage of **places to eat** in the town centre; Seremban is known for its *pao* (Chinese steamed buns) and crab dishes. **Nightlife** focuses on the Taman AST area west of the centre, particularly in the new **Era Square** development, connected to the bus station.

Beef Noodle Stall Lot 748, upper floor of Pasar Besar (main market); map above. It's a little out of the way, but the fantastic (and cheap) noodles here are a local favourite – make sure you get here early. Miraculously, the stall managed to survive a serious fire that devasted much of Pasar Besar in 2017. Mon & Wed–Sun 8.30am–1.30pm.

Chai Hong 50 Jalan Kapitan Tam Yeong ☏ 06 762 4357; map above. Locals will tell you this place makes the best chicken rice they've ever tasted, even though it's among the most expensive at RM18. Customers can opt for an "economy set" (RM6). Service is lethargic, but it's well worth the wait. Mon & Wed–Sun 11am–6pm.

Sri Menanti

The former royal capital of Negeri Sembilan, **SRI MENANTI**, is set in a lush, mountainous landscape 30km east of Seremban. The only reason to visit is to see a jewel of Minangkabau architecture, the **Istana Lama**. As you look for it, don't be misled by the sign for the **Istana Besar**, the current royal palace, which is topped by a bright blue roof.

Istana Lama

Daily 10am–6pm • Free • ⓦ lmns.ns.gov.my

A timber palace set in geometric gardens, the splendid **Istana Lama** was the seat of the Minangkabau rulers (see box below). The sacking of Sri Menanti during the Sungai Ujong tin wars destroyed the original palace; today's four-storey version was designed and built in 1902 by two Malay master craftsmen, using no nails or screws. Until 1931, the building was used as a royal residence. Its tower, which once held the treasury and royal archives, offers a lovely view and can be reached by ladder from the sultan's private rooms. At its apex is a forked projection of a type known as "open scissors", now very rarely seen.

The whole rectangular building is raised nearly 2m off the ground by 99 pillars, 26 of which have been carved in low relief with complex foliated designs. Though the main doors and windows are plain, a long external veranda is covered with a design of leaves and branches known as *awan larat*, or "driving clouds". Above the front porch is the most elaborate decoration, a pair of Chinese-style creatures with lions' heads, horses' legs and long feathery tails.

ARRIVAL AND DEPARTURE   SRI MENANTI

By bus From Seremban, take a bus for the 45min journey to Kuala Pilah, then either wait for an infrequent local bus to Sri Menanti, or take a taxi (10 min; RM20).
By taxi A cab from Seremban costs RM80 (45min).

THE MINANGKABAU

The **Minangkabau people**, whose cultural heartland is in the mountainous region of western Sumatra (Indonesia), established a community in Malaysia in the early fifteenth century. As they had no written language until the arrival of Islam, knowledge of their origins is somewhat sketchy; their own oral accounts trace their ancestry to Alexander the Great, while the *Sejarah Melayu*, or Malay Annals, tells of a mysterious leader, Nila Pahlawan, whose son, Sanq Nila Utama, is said to have founded Singapore – originally "Singapura", Sanskrit for Lion City – after he saw a "lion" (more likely a Malayan tiger) in Temasek.

In early times the Minangkabau were ruled in Sumatra by their own overlords or rajahs, though political centralization never really rivalled the role of the strongly autonomous *nagari* (Sumatran for village). Each *nagari* was made up of numerous **matrilineal clans** (*suku*), whose members were descended from a common female ancestor and lived in a shared ancestral home. The household was also in control of ancestral property, which was passed down the maternal line. The *sumando* (husband) stayed in his wife's house at night but was a constituent member of his clan house, where most of his day was spent. Although the house and clan name belonged to the woman, and women dominated the domestic sphere, political and ceremonial power was in the hands of men; it was the *mamak* (mother's brother) who took responsibility for the continued prosperity of the lineage.

When and why the Minangkabau initially emigrated to what is now **Negeri Sembilan** in Malaysia is uncertain. Their subsequent history is closely bound up with that of Melaka and Johor, with the Minangkabau frequently called upon to supplement the armies of ambitious Malay princes and sultans. Evidence of intermarriage with the region's predominant tribal group, the Sakai, suggests some acceptance by the Malays of the matrilineal system. What is certain is that the Minangkabau were a political force to be reckoned with, aided by their reputation for supernatural powers. Today, the Minangkabau are very much integrated with the Malays, and their dialect is almost indistinguishable from standard Bahasa Melayu.

5

ACCOMMODATION

Sri Menanti Resort Kampung Buyau, next to the Istana Lama ☎ 06 497 0049. Twenty-six reasonable double rooms and chalets in Sri Menanti's only real accommodation option. There's also a pleasant pool where you can cool off. It doesn't hurt to ask about discounts. 📶 Doubles RM169, chalets RM205

Melaka

When Penang was known only for its oysters and Singapore was just a fishing village, the influence of **MELAKA** (formerly spelled "Malacca") already extended beyond the Peninsula. Political and cultural life flourished in this trading centre under the auspices of the **Melaka Sultanate**, founded early in the fifteenth century, and helped to define what it means to be Malay.

The city subsequently suffered neglect from colonial rulers and fared little better after Independence, but in some ways this added to its faded charm. Recent years, though, have seen such developments as a land reclamation project that created the Taman Melaka Raya district and, in 2008, the gaining of UNESCO World Heritage Site status jointly with Penang. The latter has helped to encourage the development of a new wave of guesthouses and restoration projects, but has also brought some less welcome tourism schemes. Melaka remains, nevertheless, an undoubted highlight of any Malaysian itinerary.

Brief history

Melaka has its roots in the fourteenth-century struggles between Java and the Thai kingdom of Ayuthaya for control of the Malay Peninsula. The *Sejarah Melayu* (Malay Annals) records that when the Sumatran prince **Paramesvara** could no longer tolerate subservience to Java, he fled to the island of Temasek (later renamed Singapore), where he set himself up as ruler. The Javanese subsequently forced him to flee north to Bertam, where he was welcomed by the local community. While his son, Iskandar Shah, was out hunting near modern-day Melaka Hill, a mouse deer turned on the pursuing hunting dogs, driving them into the sea. Taking this courageous act to be a good omen, Shah asked his father to build a new settlement there and named it after the *melaka* tree (*Phyllanthus emblica*) under which he had been sitting.

A trading centre

Under its sultans, Melaka rapidly became a wealthy and cosmopolitan market town, trading spices and textiles with Indonesia and India. This meteoric rise was initially assisted by its powerful neighbours Ayuthaya and Java, both of which made good use of its trading facilities, but they soon found that they had a serious rival as Melaka started a campaign of **territorial expansion**.

By the reign of its last ruler, Sultan Mahmud Shah (1488–1530), Melaka's territory included the west coast of the Peninsula as far as Perak, the whole of Pahang, Singapore and most of east coast Sumatra. Culturally, too, Melaka was supreme – its sophisticated language, literature, hierarchical court structure and dances were all benchmarks in the Malay world.

The colonial era

It took a sea change in Europe to end Melaka's supremacy. The Portuguese were seeking to extend their influence in Asia by dominating ports in the region and, led by Alfonso de Albuquerque, conquered Melaka in 1511. They maintained their hold for the next 130 years, introducing Catholicism to the region through the efforts of the Jesuit missionary **St Francis Xavier**, after whom the main church in town is named.

The formation of the Vereenigde Oostindische Compagnie (VOC), or **Dutch East India Company**, in 1602 spelled the end of Portuguese rule. The primary objective was

CENTRAL MELAKA

Bus Station (2.7km)

KAMPUNG MORTEN
1
Villa Sentosa
Shore Sky Tower
Footbridge

Bus Station (2.7km)

St Peter's Church

Stadium

N

Melaka River Pirates Park

JALAN HANG TUA

JALAN TAN CHAY YAN

JALAN KUBU

JALAN MASJID

JALAN PORTUGIS

JALAN KAMPUNG HULU

Masjid Kampung Hulu

Melaka River

JALAN MUNSHI ABDULLAH

JALAN MUNSHI ABDULLAH

JALAN KEE ANN

Madam King's Dept. Store

JALAN BUNGA RAYA PANTAI

LITTLE INDIA

JALAN KG JAWA

JALAN BUNGA RAYA PANTAI

JALAN BENDAHARA

Chinese Food Stalls

● SHOPPING
Artist Gallery   3
Joe's Design   4
Malaqa House   2
Wah Aik Shoemaker   1

■ DRINKING & NIGHTLIFE
Discovery Café   3
Exodus Lounge   2
The Irish Harp   1

Weekend Karaoke Stage

Cheng Hoon Teng Temple

Straits Chinese Jewellery Museum

JALAN TOKONG

JALAN HANG JEBAT (JONKER WALK)

CHINATOWN

JALAN HANG KASTURI

JALAN TUN TAN CHENG LOCK

JALAN HANG LEKIR

JALAN HANG LEKIU

Masjid Kampung Kling

Sri Poyyatha Vinayagar Temple

JALAN TUKANG EMAS

JALAN KAMPUNG KUL

JALAN KG PANTAI

Footbridge

JALAN KG PANTAI

LORONG HANG JEBAT

Baba-Nyonya Heritage Museum

Cheng Ho Cultural Museum

8 Heeren Street

Upriver boat trips

JALAN LAKSAMANA

JALAN BUKIT CHINA

Public Bank

JALAN TEMENGGONG

Bukit China (500m)

JALAN BANDA KABA

Food Court

Gurudwara Sahib Malacca

JALAN LAKSAMANA S

JALAN KOTA LAKSAMANA

Muzium Beliah Malaysia

DUTCH SQUARE

Christ Church

St Francis Xavier's Church

JALAN GEREJA

Waterwheel

Bastion

Maritime Museum

Boat Trips

Jetty for Dumai (Sumatra)

Melaka River

Stadthuys

Democratic Government Museum

Dutch Graveyard

JLN CHAN KOON CHENG

Police Station

Swimming Pool

BUKIT ST PAUL

St Paul's Church

JALAN KOTA

JALAN STANA

Forbidden Garden

Istana Kesultanan

Islamic Museum

Muzium Rakyat

Porta de Santiago

JALAN PARAMESWARA

Independence Memorial Museum

Portuguese Settlement (2km)

Taming Sari Revolving Tower

Duck Tours Office

PLAZA MAHKOTA

JALAN PM 2

JALAN PM 8

JALAN PM 3

JALAN PM 4

Newton Culture Food Village

Dataran Pahlawan Melaka Mega Mall

JALAN MERDEKA

Mahkota Parade Shopping Centre

Hatten Square

JALAN TAMAN MELAKA RAYA

Maybank

TAMAN MELAKA RAYA

Masjid Selat Melaka (2.5km)

0   400 metres

■ ACCOMMODATION
45 Lekiu	5	Jalan-Jalan	10	Rooftop Guest House	8
Casa del Rio	18	Jonker Boutique Hotel	3	Shore Hotel & Residences	1
Courtyard @ Heeren	14	Layang Layang	13		
Emily Travellers Home	20	The Majestic	2	Singgah de Jonker	11
Hotel Equatorial	19	The Opposite Place	7	The Stable	15
Fenix Inn	21	Hotel Puri	9	Tang House Hotel	4
Hangout @ Jonker	17	River View Guest House	6	Wayfarer Guest House	12
Heeren House	16				

● EATING
Baboon House	15	Eat at 18 Café	3	Low Yong Moh	4	Pak Putra	18
Café 1511	13	Eleven Bistro & Restaurant	7	Lung Ann Refreshments	11	River View Café	2
Calanthe Art Café	16	Hakka Zhan	19	Mods Café	1	Selvam	14
Capitol Satay	17	Jonker 88	5	Nancy's Kitchen	8	Teo Soon Loong Chan	10
The Daily Fix Café	9	Limau Limau	6	Ola Lavanderia Café	12	Veggie Planet	20

5

5

trade rather than religious conversion, but due to their high taxes the Dutch relied ever more on force to maintain their position in the Straits.

Weakened by French threats to their trading posts in the Indies, the Dutch handed Melaka over to the **British East India Company** on August 15, 1795. Yet the colony continued a decline that hastened when the free-trade port of Singapore was established in 1819. The British wanted Penang to be the main west coast settlement but attempted to revitalize Melaka, introducing progressive agricultural and mining concerns. They invested in new hospitals, schools and a train line, but only when a Chinese entrepreneur, Tan Chay Yan, began to plant **rubber** were Melaka's financial problems alleviated for a time. After World War I, even this commodity faced mixed fortunes – when the **Japanese occupied** Melaka in 1942, they found a town exhausted by the interwar depression.

Modern Melaka

Whatever damage was wrought during its centuries of colonial mismanagement, nothing can take away the enduring influence of Melaka's contribution to Malay culture. Taken together with the long-standing Chinese presence – with intermarriage fostering the Peranakan (or Baba-Nyonya) community (see p.575) – and the European colonial influences, Melaka has a fascinating heritage that understandably appeals to tourists.

To the cynical eye, though, there's something about the modern centre of Melaka that smacks of slapdash "preservation", apparent in the brick-red paint wash that covers everything around **Dutch Square**. The UNESCO listing has, in some respects, not exactly helped. As landowners have scented money and rents have skyrocketed, long-established businesses have been forced out and replaced by shops aimed at the tourist dollar. Ill-fated and incongruous tourism projects have included a RM15.9-million monorail north of the centre that memorably broke down on its first day – it turned out that it couldn't operate in the rain. Talk of reviving it continues, but with little sign of action.

It's not all bad news, though. The renewal of the riverside has been particularly welcome, and hopefully any further regeneration will continue to breathe life into the historical core, rather than turning it into a theme-park version of itself.

Colonial centre

The heart of Melaka's colonial centre is **Dutch Square**, dominated by the **Stadthuys**; beyond that lie **Bukit St Paul (St Paul's Hill)** and numerous museums. The square is one of the oldest surviving parts of the city, although two of its main features date from much later times: the marble fountain was built in 1904 to commemorate Queen Victoria's Diamond Jubilee, while the clock tower was erected in 1886 in honour of Tan Beng Swee, a rich Chinese merchant. Rather older are the ruins of the **Bastion of Fredrick Hendrick**, where you can see the alignment of the old Portuguese defensive wall.

Stadthuys

Dutch Square • Daily 9am–5.30pm • RM10 • ⓦ perzim.gov.my

The sturdy red **Stadthuys**, presiding over the entire south side of Dutch Square, is not a single building but a collection of structures dating from between 1660 and 1700; one now houses the **Museum of Ethnography**. The complex was used as a town hall throughout the Dutch and British administrations and the wide, monumental interior staircases, together with the high windows, are typical of seventeenth-century Dutch municipal buildings.

It's worth visiting mostly for the buildings themselves: the Museum of Ethnography displays an array of Malay and Chinese ceramics, weaponry, musical instruments and the like, plus a few dioramas and countless paintings depicting Melakan history. Several other **smaller museums** lurk behind the main buildings although they are mostly aimed at domestic visitors, covering topics such as the Malaysian education system.

Christ Church

Mon–Sat 9am–4.30pm; services Sun 8.30am (English), 10.30am (Mandarin) & 4.30pm (Malay) • Free

Christ Church was built in 1753 to commemorate the centenary of the Dutch occupation of Melaka, making it the oldest functioning Protestant church in Malaysia. The simple design, with neither aisles nor chancel, is typically Dutch; the porch and vestry were nineteenth-century afterthoughts. The cool, whitewashed interior has decorative fanlights high up on the walls and elaborate, 200-year-old hand-carved pews, while the roof features heavy timber beams each cut from a single tree. The plaques on the walls tell a sorry tale of early deaths in epidemics.

Dutch Graveyard

East of Christ Church, along Jalan Kota

Although the overgrown **Dutch Graveyard** was first used in the late seventeenth century, when the VOC was still in control (hence the name), British graves easily outnumber those of their predecessors. The tall column towards the centre of the tiny cemetery is a memorial to two of the many officers killed in the Naning War in 1831, a costly conflict which saw the nearby Naning region incorporated into Melaka's territory under the British.

Istana Kesultanan

Daily 9am–5.30pm • RM10 • ☎ 06 282 7464, ⚐ perzim.gov.my

The **Istana Kesultanan** (Sultan's Palace) has played a central role in Malaysian history, although the current dark-timber palace is a contemporary reconstruction of the original fifteenth-century building. In the best Malay architectural tradition, its multilayered, sharply sloping roofs contain no nails. It was here that the administrative duties of the state were carried out, and also where the sultan resided when in the city (he mostly lived further upriver at Bertam, safe from attacks on Melaka). Remove your shoes to ascend the wide staircase to the ground floor, where you'll find a cultural museum housing several dioramas of scenes from Malay court life.

Porta de Santiago

At the time they conquered Melaka, the Portuguese used the forced labour of fifteen hundred slaves to construct the mighty **A Famosa** fort, completed in 1511. The Dutch East India Company later used the fort as its headquarters, but the British demolished it at the start of the nineteenth century when they relocated to Penang. All that's left today is a single gate, the crumbling **Porta de Santiago**, which was only saved thanks to a last-minute intervention from Sir Stamford Raffles, the founder of modern Singapore.

St Paul's Church

St Paul's Hill • Reached by climbing the steps behind the Porta de Santiago • Free

On the summit of St Paul's Hill (**Bukit St Paul**), and now no more than a roofless shell, **St Paul's Church** was constructed in 1521 by the Portuguese as Our Lady of the Mount. **St Francis Xavier** visited the church between 1545 and 1552, and his body was brought here for burial after his death in 1553, before being exhumed and transferred to its final resting place in Goa (India) the following year. The Dutch Calvinists changed the denomination of the church when they took over in 1641, renaming it St Paul's Church, and it remained in use until the construction of Christ Church at the foot of the hill. The British found St Paul's more useful for military than for religious purposes, storing their gunpowder here during successive

5

wars. The 20-minute climb to the church is worth it, if only for the wonderful views over Melaka towards the sea.

Muzium Rakyat
Jalan Kota • Sat–Thurs 9am–5.30pm, Fri 9am–12.15pm & 2.45–5.30pm • RM5 • ⓦ perzim.gov.my

The **Muzium Rakyat** (People's Museum) is the most interesting of the museums that you pass as you skirt west around the base of St Paul's Hill from Porta de Santiago. Its ground and first floors house exhibits on such topics as the construction and competitive use of spinning tops. The third floor contains the much more interesting – and at times gruesome – **Museum of Enduring Beauty** (Mon–Fri 9am–5pm). Taking "endure" in the sense of "to suffer", the exhibits show how people around the world have sought to alter their appearance: head deformation, dental mutilations, tattooing, scarification, corsetry and foot-binding and the like. The fourth floor is home to the Kite Museum, which speaks for itself.

Maritime Museum
Quayside • Daily 9am–5.30pm • RM5 • ⓦ perzim.gov.my

The main part of the **Maritime Museum** (Muzeum Samudera) is housed in a towering replica of a Portuguese cargo ship, the *Flor de la Mar*, which sank in 1511 carrying treasure plundered from Melaka. Inside its hull, model ships, information boards and paintings chart the settlement's maritime history from the time of the Malay Sultanate to the arrival of the British in the eighteenth century.

It feels a little disjointed, rather than telling a single story, but there are some interesting facts in there. The same cannot be said of the drab displays across the road in the other section of the museum; the Royal Malaysian Navy patrol craft in the gardens is, however, popular with kids.

Taming Sari Revolving Tower
Jalan Merdaka • Daily 10am–11pm • RM23

You can't miss the 80m-tall **Taming Sari Revolving Tower**, which offers a great (if relatively expensive for a five-minute tour) 360-degree view of the city and the sea. Its construction so close to the colonial district in 2008 was controversial, but it has nevertheless proved to be a popular attraction, with big queues at the weekend. Duck Tour tickets are sold next door (see p.283).

Chinatown

Melaka owed a great deal of its nineteenth-century economic recovery to its Chinese community: it was one Tan Chay Yan who first planted rubber here, and a Chinese immigrant called Tan Kim Seng established what became the great Straits Steam Ship Company. Most of these entrepreneurs settled in what became known as **Chinatown**, across the river from the colonial district. For many visitors, it's the most interesting part of town.

Jalan Hang Jebat
Night market Fri–Sun 7pm–midnight

Chinatown's main street, **Jalan Hang Jebat** – popularly known as Jonker Street or Jonker Walk – runs parallel to Jalan Tun Tan Cheng Lock. It was formerly known for its antiques, but these days most shops sell souvenirs and cheap handicrafts. Still, its bars and restaurants continue to make it a centre of tourist activity.

The street is closed to traffic on weekend evenings for the **Jonker Walk Night Market**, when shops stay open late and the street is lined with vendors. Although very popular and often considered a must-do by visitors, it's nothing special by Malaysian street market standards – in particular, anyone looking for good street food is likely to come away disappointed.

5

Cheng Ho Cultural Museum

51 Lorong Hang Jebat • Daily 9am–6pm • RM20 • ☎ 06 283 1135, ⍟ chengho.org/museum

Dedicated to the life of Chinese Admiral **Cheng Ho** (also spelled Zheng He), who visited Melaka several times on his epic travels across Asia, the Middle East and Africa in the early fifteenth century, the **Cheng Ho Cultural Museum** provides an insight into early fifteenth-century Melaka, as well as trading and seafaring during the Ming Dynasty. Exhibits include a model of Cheng Ho's treasure ship and various navigational instruments; there's also a teahouse on the premises.

Jalan Tun Tan Cheng Lock

The elegant townhouses that line **Jalan Tun Tan Cheng Lock**, formerly Heeren Street, are the ancestral homes of the Baba-Nyonya community. The wealthiest and most successful of these merchants built long, narrow-fronted houses, minimizing the "window tax" by incorporating internal courtyards designed for ventilation and the collection of rainwater.

Several of the houses are now open to the public as shops, hotels and restaurants. You can't enter the **Chee Ancestral House** at no. 117, but it's worth checking out the exterior: an imperious Dutch building of pale green stucco topped by a gold dome, it's home to one of Melaka's wealthiest families. No less fascinating is the abandoned and overgrown property at no. 125, which once must have looked similarly impressive.

8 Heeren Street

8 Jalan Tun Tan Cheng Lock • Daily 11am–4pm • Free (donations welcome) • ☎ 06 281 1507 ⍟ badanwarisanmalaysia.org/visit-us/no-8-heeren-street

Make time for a visit to the model conservation project at **8 Heeren Street**, where you can see how the building (dating from the 1790s) has been used and modified over the years. Printed information gives background on topics such as building materials and techniques, while the knowledgeable staff are happy to answer questions. Some commercial restoration projects in Melaka introduce inauthentic elements in the name of "heritage", but here the history of the building is laid bare.

Baba & Nyonya Heritage Museum

48 & 50 Jalan Tan Tun Cheng Lock • Mon–Thurs 10am–1pm & 2–4pm; Sat-Sun 10am–1pm & 2–5pm • RM16 • ☎ 06 283 1273, ⍟ babanyonyamuseum.com

An amalgam of three adjacent houses belonging to a single family, the **Baba & Nyonya Heritage Museum** is an eclectic and ornate blend of Chinese and classical European architectural styles. Connected by a common covered footway, decorated with hand-painted tiles, each front entrance has an outer swing door of elaborately carved teak, while a heavier internal door provides extra security at night. Two red lanterns, one bearing the household name, the other messages of good luck, hang either side of the doorway, framed by heavy Greco-Roman columns.

The upper level of the building is the most eye-catching: a canopy of Chinese tiles over the porch frames the shuttered windows, with their glass protected by intricate wrought-iron grilles. The eaves and fascias are covered in painted floral designs. Inside, the homes are filled with gold-leaf fittings, blackwood furniture inlaid with mother-of-pearl, delicately carved lacquer screens and Victorian chandeliers. The guided tours, included in the entry price, add a great deal to the experience, revealing much about the Baba-Nyonyas themselves.

Straits Chinese Jewellery Museum

108 Jalan Tan Tun Cheng Lock • Daily 10am–5pm • RM15 • ☎ 06 281 9763 ⍟ straitschinesejewellerymuseum.com

The **Straits Chinese Jewellery Museum** displays a beautiful collection of Peranakan jewellery with Chinese, Malay and Indo-European designs and motifs. Nyonya traditionally kept their hair very long, tied up during the day in a tightly coiled bun

5

known as *sanggul*, held in place by three gold, silver or diamond hairpins; examples of these are on display. Look out too for the gold anklets, Indian in inspiration, worn by younger women before the turn of the twentieth century. The museum also showcases elaborate tobacco boxes, traditionally made for decorative or ceremonial purposes and often festooned with implements made of precious metals such as silver and gold.

Jalan Tukang Emas

Jalan Tukang Emas (Goldsmith Street), continuing on from Jalan Tokong, is sometimes known as "Harmony Street" in reference to its buildings from different religions. A short way east from Jalan Hang Jebat, **Cheng Hoon Teng temple** – dedicated to the goddess of mercy – is reputed to be the oldest Chinese temple in the country. A little further along, the 1748 **Masjid Kampung Kling** displays an unusual blend of styles: the minaret looks like a pagoda, there are English and Portuguese glazed tiles, and a Victorian chandelier hangs over a pulpit carved with Hindu and Chinese designs. Next door, the Hindu **Sri Poyyatha Vinayagar Temple** also has a minaret, decorated with red cows, and dates back to the 1780s.

Masjid Kampung Hulu

Jalan Kampung Hulu • Daily 5am–10pm

Thought to be the oldest mosque in Malaysia that remains in its original location, **Masjid Kampung Hulu** was constructed around 1728 in typical Melakan style. It's a large structure, surmounted by numerous pyramid-shaped roofs with red Chinese tiles, and has more than a hint of pagoda in its white minaret. Such architecture has its origins in Sumatra, perhaps brought over by the Minangkabau (see p.273) who settled in nearby Negeri Sembilan.

Northeast of the centre

From Christ Church, Jalan Laksamana leads north past the church of **St Francis Xavier**, a twin-towered, nineteenth-century, neo-Gothic structure. Further up from here on Jalan Bendahara you pass through the centre of Melaka's tumbledown **Little India**, a rather higgledy-piggledy line of incense and saree shops interspersed with a few eating houses.

Riverside walk

Melaka River Pirates Park Daily 5pm–midnight • Entry free; RM5/ride • ☎ 06 288 1100

The redevelopment of Melaka's **riverside** has been a real success story, encouraging the opening of guesthouses and cafés where once there were dilapidated buildings. It's a pleasant 1.5km walk from Dutch Square to Kampung Morten (see below), and almost the whole stretch is illuminated at night. On the west side you'll find the **Melaka River Pirates Park**; not exactly in keeping with Melaka's heritage feel, this neon-lit entertainment park – which includes a ferris wheel and a pirate ship – should keep children occupied for an hour or two, but closes on rainy days.

St Peter's Church

Just north of the Jalan Bendahara and Jalan Munshi Abdullah crossroads • Daily 7.30am–1pm • Free

The oldest Roman Catholic church in Malaysia, **St Peter's Church** was built by a Dutch convert in 1710 as a gift to the Portuguese Catholics, and has an impressive wooden, barrel-vaulted ceiling. The church really comes into its own at Easter as the centre of the Catholic community's celebrations.

Kampung Morten

The village of **Kampung Morten**, named after the British district officer who donated RM10,000 to buy the land, is a surprising find so close to the heart of Melaka. The wooden **stilt houses** here are distinctively Melakan, with their long, rectangular living rooms and kitchens, and narrow verandas approached by ornamental steps. It's easiest to explore on foot, and the riverside walk to get here is part of the experience.

Villa Sentosa
Daily 9.30am–6pm • Donation expected • ☎ 06 282 3988

The **Villa Sentosa**, with its miniature kampung house and mini-lighthouse, is a 90-year-old family home that now functions as a museum. The owner will gladly show you their artefacts, old family photographs and heirlooms, and there are a number of interesting newspaper articles on the wall near the entrance showing the news of the day from the 1930s.

Shore Sky Tower
Jalan Persisiran Bunga Raya • Daily 10.30am–10pm • RM25 • ☎ 06 288 3833 ⓦ theshoremelaka.com

One of Melaka's newest attractions and the tallest man-made structure in the city, the Shore Sky Tower provides unrivalled views of the area (billed as "50km in every direction") from the 43nd floor of the Shore Hotel and Residences. A visit starts with a walk along a stylish glass deck that's suspended above the hotel restaurant space, and which winds around to a staircase leading to a huge open rooftop where free telescopes allow for sight spotting. For the brave, the Sky Deck, projecting out beyond the building, has a glass floor so you can see the traffic moving down the road 140m beneath your feet.

Bukit China

East of the colonial heart of Melaka, **Bukit China** is the ancestral burial ground of the town's Chinese community – it's said to be the oldest and largest such graveyard outside China. Although Chinese contacts with the Malay Peninsula probably began in the first century BC, formal commercial relations were only established when the Ming Emperor Yung-Lo sent his envoy Admiral Cheng Ho here in 1409. Today, Bukit China is more an inner-city park than burial ground, where you're likely to encounter locals jogging, practising martial arts or simply admiring the view.

Sam Poh Kong temple
At the foot of Bukit China, at the eastern end of Jalan Temenggong

The **Sam Poh Kong temple** is a working temple dedicated to Admiral Cheng Ho. Accounts are vague as to the arrival of the first Chinese settlers, though it's said that on the marriage of Sultan Mansur Shah (1458–77) to the daughter of the emperor, Princess Hang Liu, the five hundred nobles who accompanied her stayed to set up home on Bukit China. It was supposedly these early Chinese settlers who dug the **Sultan's Well** behind the temple.

Portuguese settlement
Taxi or Grab/ Uber (RM20) from Dutch Square or Jalan Merdeka (15min)

The road east of Jalan Taman Melaka Raya leads, after about 3km, to Melaka's **Portuguese settlement**; turn right into Jalan Albuquerque, clearly signposted off the main road, and you enter its heart. Today you're likely to recognize the descendants of the original Portuguese settlers only by hearing their language, **Kristang**, a blend of Malay and old Portuguese. Note too the many Portuguese street names, including Fernandez, Rodriguez and Dominguez.

Medan Portugis
You could almost be forgiven for thinking that the whitewashed **Medan Portugis** (Portuguese Square), at the end of the road into the Portuguese settlement, is a

5

remnant from colonial times. In fact, it dates only from 1985, but the local restaurateurs make an effort to conjure up a Portuguese atmosphere even if the food is Malay in character. A three-day fiesta – the feast of St Pedro – starts on June 29 every year, with traditional Portuguese food, live music and dancing. Just beyond the square is a row of waterfront seafood restaurants.

Masjid Selat Melaka, the Floating Mosque

Jalan Baiduri 8, Taxi or Grab/ Uber (RM25) from Dutch Square or Jalan Merdeka (15min)

A little out of town, on Malacca Island, is the beautiful "Floating Mosque" – so-called because of its construction (which cost RM10 million) on stilts above the Strait of Malacca. Although rarely open to foreigners, especially during times of prayer, make sure you pay a visit just before sunset. From the entrance, follow the waterfront to the left and around to the makeshift "viewing platform" to see the sun set into the sea behind the mosque as the building's neon lights come on; it's spellbinding (and nowhere near as gaudy as it sounds).

ARRIVAL AND DEPARTURE   MELAKA

By plane Melaka's airport (☎06 317 5860 ⓦmalaysiaairports.com.my) is 10km north of the city centre and serves flights from Lion Air, Sky Aviation and Firefly. At the time of writing, the only domestic flights available are from and to Penang (1 weekly; 1hr). Irregular buses connect the airport to Melaka Sentral (every 30min; 40min), from where you'll have to change and catch a bus to the historical centre (every 30min; 20–30min). A taxi from the airport to the city centre is about RM35.

By train Pulau Sebang/Tampin train station, with Komuter trains to KL, 38km north of Melaka (☎06 441 1034), is connected by irregular buses to Melaka Sentral, although the journey can take up to 1hr 30min as the bus stops frequently; it's much more convenient to catch a taxi (40min; RM80). Destinations Alor Star (3 daily; 6hr 30min); Butterworth (2 daily; 6hr); Gemas (for Jungle Railway; ETS 4 daily, intercity 2 daily; 35min); Ipoh (4 daily; 4hr 30min); Johor Bahru (2 daily; 5hr); Kuala Lumpur (ETS 4 daily, Komuter 12 daily; 1hr 50min); Seremban (ETS 4 daily, Komuter 12 daily; 30min).

By bus Melaka's bus station, Melaka Sentral, is just under 4km north of the centre, at the corner of Jalan Panglima Awang and Jalan Tun Razak, close to a large Tesco supermarket. The #17 bus (every 30min; 20–30min) from the domestic part of the station stops off at the Clock House as well as at Jalan Kabu at the western end of Jalan Hang Jebat; a taxi will cost RM25 (15min). Transnasional

(ⓦtransnasional.com.my) operates buses from Melaka Sentral (12 daily; 3hr) to KLIA and KLIA 2, with four daily services also departing from Mahkota Medical Centre, close to the Mahkota Parade Shopping Centre.

Destinations Alor Star (4 daily; 7hr); Butterworth (6 daily; 6hr); Ipoh (5 daily; 4hr); Johor Bahru (hourly 8am–8pm; 3hr); Kluang (11 daily; 2hr); Kota Bahru (2 daily; 10hr); KLIA/ KLIA 2 (hourly 8am–8pm; 2hr); Kuala Lumpur (hourly 5am–10pm; 3hr); Kuala Terengganu (daily; 7hr); Kuantan (daily; 5hr); Mersing (5 daily; 4hr); Singapore (hourly 7.30am–7pm; 4hr).

By ferry From the jetty on Jalan Quayside, ferries head to Dumai in Sumatra (daily, 10am; 2hr 30min; RM110 one way (children RM55) or RM170 return (children RM85) plus RM20 port tax). For information and tickets, best bought a day in advance, contact Tunas Rupat Follow Me Express at G29, Jalan PM10, Plaza Mahkota (☎06 283 2506, ⓦtunasrupat. com).

By car Melaka's streets are very narrow and the one-way system is awkward, so drivers should park at the first opportunity and get around the city by foot, bus, trishaw or taxi. You'll have to display a coupon (1 day/RM5), which can be bought from the booth by the Taming Sari Tower. One local car rental operator is Hawk, 34 Jalan Laksamana (Mon– Fri 8am–5.30pm; ☎06 283 7878, ⓦhawkrentacar.com.my).

GETTING AROUND

By bus There are several useful routes for visitors, departing from Melaka Sentral: #17 runs through the historical centre to Taman Melaka Raya and stops off at the entrance of the Portuguese Settlement.

By taxi or trishaw For longer journeys, taxis or the colourful disco trishaws are the best bet. Both cost roughly the same, and you can book trishaws for tours (see below). You should be able to get a trishaw around the Dutch

Square or in front of the Taming Sari Revolving Tower; there's a taxi rank by the Mahkota Parade. Note that a commission system operates between Melaka's taxi drivers and some guesthouses; if you know where you want to go, don't necessarily believe a driver who tells you that the place is full.

On foot Most places of interest lie within the compact historical centre, and so are best visited on foot.

INFORMATION AND TOURS

Tourist information The helpful Tourism Malaysia office is on the ground floor of Bangunan Surau Warisan Dunia on Dutch Square (daily 9am–6pm; ☎06 283 6220; ⒲tourismmalaysia.gov.my). There is a state tourist office at Melaka Sentral bus station (daily 9am–5.30pm; ☎06 288 1340).

Duck Tours The Duck Tour uses an amphibious vehicle to explore Melaka on land and water. The main ticket office is by the Taming Sari Revolving Tower (daily 9am–6.30pm; 1hr; RM42; ☎06 292 5595 , ⒲melakaducktours.com.my).

Trishaw tours A sightseeing tour by trishaw, covering the major sights, should cost RM50/hr for two people.

Boat trips Boat trips up the river by Melaka River Cruise (☎06 286 1531, ⒲melakarivercruise.my) set off from the jetty behind the Maritime Museum (daily 9am–11pm; Mon–Thurs RM15.90; Fri–Sun RM21.20). Offering a good way to see the restored riverside area, the boat stops at numerous points along the river, taking you past the old Dutch quarter of red-roofed godowns (warehouses) as far as Kampung Morten.

ACCOMMODATION

Melaka has a huge selection of **hotels** and guesthouses, including many that are good value and well kept, and a scattering of lovely boutique properties; there are even a couple of highly recommended **apartments**. Book ahead for Friday and Saturday nights, as Melaka is a popular weekend break destination – rates rise by as much as RM100.

HOTELS AND GUESTHOUSES

Casa del Rio 88 Jalan Kota Laksamana ☎06 289 6888, ⒲casadelrio-melaka.com; map p.275. This resort-style riverfront complex offers spacious well-appointed rooms with balconies, some with river views. The excellent restaurant (open to non-guests) serves traditional sweet and savoury Nyonya dishes at high tea (noon–4pm; RM48), served in pretty tiffin boxes. ☎ **RM600**

★**Courtyard @ Heeren** 91 Jalan Tun Tan Cheng Lock ☎06 281 0088, ⒲courtyardatheeren.com; map p.275. The lobby of this boutique hotel sets the tone, with a soothing water feature, original marble floors, and the owner's collection of antique wooden furniture. The welcoming rooms offer a delightful mix of old and new, with intricately carved bedsteads and flat-screen TVs, while the deluxe rooms feature heritage design with four-poster wooden beds and replica period tiles. Prices increase by RM60–70 over the weekends. ☎ **RM200**

★**Emily Travellers Home** /1 Jalan Parameswara ☎016 925 8902; map p.275. A real backpacker gem near Taman Melaka Raya, which feels a world apart from the bustling streets of Melaka. Step over the threshold into an oasis of greenery, where cats, a friendly pet rabbit and even a duck roam free. Rooms are simple but welcoming with shared bath – those on the first floor are in better nick. There are also a couple of cottages with private bathroom. ☎ Doubles **RM80**, cottages **RM95**

Hotel Equatorial Bandar Hilir ☎06 282 8333, ⒲equatorial.com; map p.275. With 496 well-appointed rooms and suites set over 22 floors, this is one of Melaka's largest hotels. Facilities include a tennis court, fitness centre, four interconnected swimming pools, two restaurants and four cafés. ☎ **RM320**

Fenix Inn 156 Jalan Merdaka, Taman Melaka Raya ☎06 281 5511, ⒲fenixinn.com; map p.275. A decent budget choice with comfortable, practical, good-value rooms. It's a short walk to the historical centre, and there

are plenty of shopping malls just close by. Rates rise by RM30 over the weekends. ☎ **RM158**

Hangout @ Jonker 19 & 21 Lorong Hang Jebat ☎06 282 8318; map p.275. This spotless flashpackers' place features modern, vibrantly coloured rooms with cable TV, a/c and private bathrooms, set over four floors in the heart of town. There's a kitchen and lounge area with communal computers. ☎ **RM150**

Heeren House 1 Jalan Tun Tan Cheng Lock ☎06 281 4241, ⒲heerenhouse.com; map p.275. Formerly a warehouse, a coffee shop, a family home and eventually a guesthouse, this is a pleasant choice right in the historical centre, offering spacious rooms with colonial and Peranakan furniture – some could do with a splash of paint here and there. Weekend surcharge RM20. ☎ **RM159**

Jalan-Jalan 8 Jalan Tukang Emas ☎06 283 3937; map p.275. This excellent backpacker hangout is so popular that it now occupies two non-connected buildings. The main building has the reception and the livelier common area, while the other has a/c. There's a large ten-bed dorm, as well as a six-bed and a female-only dorm sleeping four. Free coffee and tea, and bike rental at RM10/day. ☎ Dorms **RM22**, singles **RM39**, doubles **RM80**

★**Jonker Boutique Hotel** 84 Jalan Tokong ☎06 282 5151, ⒲jonkerboutiquehotel.com; map p.275. Housed in a three-storey Art Deco building, the spacious rooms at this welcoming boutique hotel feature beautiful teak flooring and high ceilings. The central location, just a stone's throw from Jonker Walk, is a plus. Rates rise by RM50 at the weekend. ☎ **RM217**

Layang Layang 26 Jalan Tukang Besi ☎06 292 2722, ⒲layanglayangmelaka.com; map p.275. A lovely guesthouse with clean, welcoming rooms with parquet floors, set around a peaceful courtyard with a fishpond. The communal area is dotted with trinkets, including a guitar, the odd lantern and wooden giraffes; there are board games, too. ☎ **RM89**

5

★**The Majestic** 188 Jalan Bunga Raya ☎06 2891, ⓦwww.majesticmalacca.com; map p.275. Located in a beautiful 1920s colonial mansion, the inviting rooms and suites (RM2200) at this luxurious hotel feature polished timber floors, teakwood fittings and indulgent roll-top baths. The excellent spa offers therapies based on the healing heritage of the Peranakans, descendants of Chinese immigrants who intermarried with Malays; the restaurant offers traditional Nyonya cuisine, which combines Chinese cooking methods with Malay ingredients and spices. 📶 RM700

★**The Opposite Place** 18 Jalan Hang Lekiu ☎016 274 9686, ⓦopposite-place.com; map p.275. In a beautifully refurbished pre-World War II building, this boutique guesthouse features two sleek, individually designed suites – Opposite West has a living area with antique wooden furniture and a voyeuristic bathroom, while Opposite East has open-brick walls, hardwood floors and mock period armchairs. *Eat at 18 Café* downstairs (see p.285) serves excellent breakfast. Prices increase to RM699 on weekends. 📶 RM599

Hotel Puri 118 Jalan Tun Tan Cheng Lock ☎06 282 5588, ⓦhotelpuri.com; map p.275. Set in a beautifully restored Peranakan shophouse with a large foyer with polished marble floors, the rooms here are contemporary and stylish with hints of red and teak. The *Galeri Café*, open to non-guests, serves Peranakan and Western dishes to the soothing sound of the courtyard fountain. 📶 RM235

★ **River View Guest House** 94 & 96 Jalan Kampong Pantai ☎012 327 7746 or ☎012 380 7211, ⓦriverviewguesthouse.blogspot.my; map p.275. This guesthouse, with a three-bed mixed-sex dorm and doubles (all with fan and a/c) with shared bath, is full of character; the owners even bake cakes and pies for guests in the afternoons. The leafy terrace, with wonderful views over the river, makes a perfect spot to unwind at sunset. 📶 Dorms RM24, doubles RM70

Rooftop Guest House 39 Jalan Kampong Pantai ☎012 380 7211 or ☎012 327 7746, ⓔrooftopguesthouse@yahoo.com; map p.275. Opened by the owners of the *River View*, this well-run guesthouse has a small four-bed dorm with lockers and doubles with shared and private bath. The actual rooftop is leafy and calm, the common area has a couple of sofas and there's book exchange, too. Families and large groups should consider the *River View House*, a self-catered apartment owned by the same friendly couple, with two doubles and a master room with king-sized bed (RM450). 📶 Dorm RM25, doubles with shared bath RM58, en-suite doubles RM88

Shore Hotel & Residences 193 Jalan Persisiran Bunga Raya ☎06 2828 200, ⓦtheshorehotelmelaka.com;

map p.275. Part of Melaka's newest skyscraper development in the centre of town, this hotel has large rooms and suites (RM390) and apartments (RM420) in white with wooden finishes. Facilities include sauna, steam room and pool, and numerous restaurants including the *SkyDeli* underneath the Sky Tower. 📶 RM380

Singgah de Jonker 112 Lorong Hang Jebat ☎06 281 3623; map p.275. This B&B features clean, freshly painted a/c rooms with sturdy wooden beds and crisp linen in a historical building (note the original wall calligraphy) with some rooms overlooking the river, interior courtyard or the street. All have shared bathroom, and there's also a large attic dorm sleeping eight (groups only; RM200). Breakfast is served by the river and there's a small terrace with lovely views for soaking up the atmosphere. 📶 RM110

Tang House Hotel 78 Jalan Tokong ☎06 283 3969, ⓦtanghouse.com.my; map p.275. This welcoming family-run guesthouse features very simple rooms with mattresses on the floor, as well as newly built a/c rooms that are a steal; great rates for single travellers (RM35), too. The nearby Jonker Walk karaoke stage means it can get noisy on weekend evenings. 📶 Basic doubles from RM55, a/c doubles RM120

Wayfarer Guest House 104 Lorong Hang Jebat ☎012 723 0875, ⓦwayfarermelaka.com; map p.275. Formerly a rubber trading house, this airy guesthouse offers spacious well-appointed a/c rooms with hardwood floors; room 6 (RM180) has lovely views over the river and the Church of St Francis, while the large duplex room (RM240) features a double bed and two twins on the mezzanine. Prices increase by up to RM50 over the weekends. 📶 RM130

APARTMENTS

★**45 Lekiu** 45 Jalan Lekiu ☎012 698 4917, ⓦ45lekiu.com; map p.275. This wonderfully restored Art Deco building is today a stylish two-floor apartment featuring bare-brick walls and sleek dark furnishings. There's a small yet inviting pool and a terrace with panoramic views over the city's rooftops. Prices increase to RM1499 at weekends. 📶 RM1299

★**The Stable** D Jalan Hang Kasturi ☎012 623 4459, ⓦthestablemalacca.com; map p.275. A former stable that dates back to the sixteenth-century Dutch occupation, this trendy little apartment features original wooden beams, exposed brick walls and beautiful Peranakan tiles. The bedroom, on the first floor, has stylish black furnishings, while the ground-floor living area is decorated with paintings depicting city life of yesteryear. Prices increase to RM480 at weekends. 📶 RM380

EATING

Melaka offers excellent dining, especially in **Chinatown**, where new and established restaurants, bars and cafés compete for the hungry tourists and locals. **Taman Melaka Raya** is fast catching up; it's also worth trying the area aound **Jalan Kota Laksamana** southwest of Chinatown. For seafood, you could try the row of near-identical restaurants on the waterfront just beyond the Medan Portugis in the **Portuguese settlement**, where you can choose from the day's catch from around 7pm. Don't miss the chance to sample **Nyonya cuisine**; the emphasis is on spicy dishes, using sour ingredients like tamarind, tempered by sweeter, creamy coconut milk. One particularly unusual ingredient is *buah keluak*, a nut that contains hydrogen cyanide (prussic acid), but which is harmless once cooked.

★**Baboon House** 89 Jalan Tun Tan Cheng Lock; map p.275. Artist and owner Roger displays his artworks and funky installations at this lovely art-café (he even made the tables) with a courtyard dripping with greenery. The menu features seven types of burgers, made with chicken, lamb, beef or pork and served on home-made buns. Don't forget to check out the pretty gardens at the back. Mon & Wed–Sun 10am–6pm.

Café 1511 52 Jalan Tun Tan Cheng Lock ☏ 06 286 0150; map p.275. This pleasant little café was formerly the servants' quarter of what is now the Baba-Nyonya Heritage Museum next door. The marble tables and wooden stools lend the place historical character and add to the building's charm. The cuisine is mainly Nyonya and Malay, with dishes such as *otak-otak* fish cakes (RM6), a range of curries (RM16) and a sprinkling of Western dishes. Mon–Wed & Fri–Sun 9am–7pm.

Calanthe Art Café 11 Jalan Hang Kasturi ☏ 06 292 2960; map p.275. Jam-packed with odds and ends from vinyl discs to recycled condensed milk tins, this laidback café is a great spot for a morning coffee (there are thirteen types, one from each Malaysian state) or a bite for lunch; the Baba chef rustles up a mean *laksa* (RM11) and *ponteh chicken* (drumstick cooked with palm sugar and potatoes; RM10). The water feature, wicker chairs and soothing background tunes add to the place's easy-going atmosphere. Mon–Wed & Fri–Sun 9am–11pm.

★**Capitol Satay** Lorong Bukit Cina; map p.275. Experience the Melaka version of hotpot – satay *celup* – at this lively café, where you take your pick of assorted fish, meat and vegetables skewered on sticks and cook them in a spicy peanut sauce before eating. It's cheap – RM1 per stick – and delicious, so there are often queues of up to an hour; a sign out front warns customers to beware of similarly named imitators. Tues–Sun 5pm–midnight.

The Daily Fix Café 55 Jalan Hang Jebat ☏ 013 667 1788; map p.275. Not too obvious to spot, as it's located at the back of a shop, this relaxed café offers excellent home-made goodies including pancakes with maple syrup or honey (RM10), and plenty of home-baked cakes including cheesecake (RM13) and brownies (RM11). Wash them down with a refreshing lemongrass drink (RM5). Mon & Wed–Sun 8.30am–9.30pm.

★**Eat at 18 Café** 18 Jalan Hang Lekiu ☏ 06 281 4679, ⓦ eat18.com; map p.275. Healthy, wholesome dishes are lovingly prepared at this little gem of a café, featuring open brick walls, chandeliers, books and artworks. Delicious home-made organic bread accompanies most dishes, from grilled salmon with salad (RM32) to fresh roast chicken leg

(RM30). Breakfasts are excellent, too, and there are sweet treats throughout the day such as home-made cheesecake (RM14) and meringues with Häagen-Dazs ice cream and strawberry jam (RM14). Mon & Wed–Sun 8.30am–6pm.

Eleven Bistro & Restaurant 11 Jalan Hang Lekir ☏ 06 282 0011, ⓦ elevenbistro.com.my; map p.275. This pleasant bistro serves a great mix of Portuguese and Malay dishes such as salted egg crab (RM40) and Portuguese *sambal* prawns cooked with spicy chilli paste (RM27). It's also a good spot to grab a cocktail – in the evenings it morphs into a bar, with a house DJ after 10pm. Mon–Thurs 10am–2am, Fri–Sun 10am–3am.

Hakka Zhan 76 Jalan Laksamana 5 ☏ 017 225 8373; map p.275. Genuine Hakka cuisine is served at this Chinese place just a short walk south of the historical centre, with a scarlet a/c interior featuring dangling Chinese lamps. Among the best sellers are *hakka* mutton (RM25) and *hakka yong tau foo* (RM12), vegetables stuffed with pork paste. Tues–Sun 11am–2pm & 5.30–9pm.

Jonker 88 88 Jalan Hang Jebat ☏ 019 669 5959, ⓦ jonker88.com; map p.275. This well-established restaurant is renowned for its tasty *laksa* (RM9), which comes in three main varieties: sour-spicy, coconut spicy or a mix of the two. The *baba cendol* (RM5), a popular Malaysian dessert made with coconut milk, jelly noodles, palm sugar and shaved ice, is a sweet tooth's delight. Mon–Thurs & Sun 9.30am–5pm, Fri & Sat 9.30am–9pm.

Limau Limau 9 Jalan Hang Lekiu ☏ 012 609 9088; map p.275. This itsy-bitsy café, playing mellow background tunes and with wooden stools lining the bar, serves great freshly squeezed juices (try the pineapple and passion fruit; RM12) and light lunches including toasted focaccia sandwiches (RM13) and lasagne (RM21). There's also a cosy room upstairs featuring mismatched furniture and a motley range of lamps. Mon & Thurs–Sun 9am–5pm.

Low Yong Moh 32 Jalan Tukang Emas; map p.275. This excellent little place just opposite the mosque rustles up outstanding prawn, pork and fish dim sum (from RM3) steamed in front of your very eyes; the buns stuffed with pork (RM2) are also a real winner. Mon & Wed–Sun 5.30am–1pm.

Lung Ann Refreshments 91 Lorong Hang Jebat; map p.275. This buzzing café and restaurant functions as a popular noodle stall in the morning, a hugely popular chicken satay hangout in the afternoons and a café throughout the day. The delicious *kaya* toast (with coconut jam) is worth trying for breakfast (RM2), the duck noodles (RM6) and fish ball noodles (RM6) are a real hit, and the crowds are drawn in the afternoons for the sizzling charcoal

5

satay (RM1/stick) traditionally dipped in a peanut and pineapple sauce. Mon–Wed & Fri–Sun 8am–5pm.

Mods Café 14 Jalan Tukang Emas ☎012 756 4441; map p.275. The decor of this café takes its inspiration from 1960s British mod culture; the emphasis is on coffees, roasted and brewed on the premises, served from a bright orange VW camper van. It's a cool place to hang out over a coffee (RM8) and cake (RM11). Mon & Tues, Thurs–Sun 10am–6pm.

Nancy's Kitchen 7 Jalan Hang Lekir ☎06 283 6099, ⒲eatatnancyskit.com; map p.275. One of the best places to try Nyonya food, including the signature chicken candlenut (chicken served with a creamy candlenut sauce; RM13) or the prawn or fish fillet with coconut milk (RM18). There's also a little store at the back when you can buy Nyonya ingredients. Mon & Wed–Sun 11am–9pm.

Ola Lavanderia Café 25 Jalan Tukang Besi ☎012 612 6665, ⒲olalavanderiacafe.com; map p.275. This cosy little café with a minimalist design doubles as a laundry. It's a great spot to grab a morning coffee (RM5) and a freshly baked croissant (RM6) as you wait for your washing (RM5/kg); there's wi-fi, too. Light Western meals are served, including chicken and mushroom pies (RM7), Caesar salads (RM11) and all-day breakfast (RM11). Daily 9am–5pm.

★**Pak Putra** 56 & 58 Jalan Kota Laksamana ☎5012 601 5876; map p.275. Staggeringly good tandoori chicken (RM8) is the main draw here, although all the dishes are exceptional, from the mutton *rogan josh* (RM10) to the chicken curries (RM9), accompanied by fluffy *nan* (RM20) that is prepared in front of you. It gets very busy around 7–9pm on weekend evenings – make sure you arrive early. Daily 5.30pm–1am, closed every other Mon.

River View Café 82 Jalan Kampong Pantai ☎012 327 7746; map p.275. Under the same management as the nearby *River View Guesthouse*, this laidback café mainly catering to backpackers offers great *nasi lemak kukus* with beef *rendang* (rice steamed in coconut cream served with chilli paste, boiled egg, fried anchovies, ground nuts and Nyonya pickles; RM134), as well as good old comfort food like fish and chips (RM14), club sandwiches (RM13) and all-day breakfasts (8am–3pm; RM9). Daily 9am–10pm.

Selvam 2 Jalan Temenggong ☎06 281 9223; map p.275. Consistently good Indian restaurant serving set meal banana leaf curries (RM5) with rice, three types of vegetables and poppadums, and your choice of chicken, lamb, fish or seafood (RM6) at very reasonable prices. Daily 7am–10pm.

Teo Soon Loong Chan 42 & 44 Jalan KPKS 1 ☎06 288 0209; map p.275. This bustling Chinese restaurant is one of the best in town, serving traditional Teochew cuisine from southern China; the oyster noodles (RM14) and yam pudding (made with yam paste and sugar; RM9) both sell like hot cakes. Service can be annoyingly slow when it's busy. Tues–Sun 12–2.30pm & 6–9.30pm.

★**Veggie Planet** 41 Jalan Melaka Raya 8, Taman Melaka Raya ☎06 292 2819, ⒲veggieplanet.com.my; map p.275. Excellent, child-friendly, vegetarian café serving healthy organic dishes in a peaceful leafy interior. The Nyonya curry (RM156), made with cashew nuts instead of coconut cream, is a must, as is the *hoi lok feng* (RM14), a beautifully presented dish of brown rice with cabbage, beans, radish, ground nuts and other greens, accompanied by a healthy basil soup. Daily 9am–10pm.

DRINKING AND NIGHTLIFE

Melaka's **nightlife** is no great shakes; most places tend to shut at around 1am. Cafés and bars spill into Jalan Hang Lekir, the liveliest street in **Chinatown**; more places are also opening up along the revitalized riverfront, and **Taman Melaka Raya** also holds some lively places for a drink, along with numerous seedy karaoke bars.

Discovery Café 3 Jalan Bunga Raya ☎06 292 5606; map p.275. This riverside café hosts local live bands daily at 9pm – expect old school music with some recent pop songs thrown in. Beers RM12, local dishes RM11. They also organize evening bike tours (RM50; 3hr). Daily 9am–midnight.

Exodus Lounge 4 Jalan Hang Lekir; map p.275. It's debatable whether Melaka really needed a reggae bar, but this place has blazed the trail as the first in town. As the

evening progresses, though, the music generally turns to more commercial R&B, with some old school and dance thrown in. Happy hour 6–9pm. Mon–Thurs 6.30pm–3am, Fri–Sun 6pm–3.30am.

The Irish Harp 3 Jalan Hang Lekir; map p.275. Under the same management as the *Exodus Lounge*, this pub features the latest sports fixtures on the big screen and hosts live bands from Indonesia; Thurs–Sun 7pm–midnight. Mon & Wed–Sun 4pm–3am.

SHOPPING

Melaka's Chinatown was once famed for its **antiques**, but these days you'll find few bargains. If the item you're thinking of buying is a genuine antique rather than a modern reproduction, check that it can be exported legally and fill in an official clearance form; the dealer should provide you with this. For more general shopping there are plenty of options along Jalan Bunga Raya and Jalan Munshi Abdullah; the **malls** – including Dataran Pahlawan, Mahkota Parade and Hatten Square – are concentrated in the south of the centre.

Artist Gallery 49 Jalan Tun Tan Cheng Lock ☎ 06 281 2112, ⊕ thamsiewinn.com; map p.275. This family-run gallery offers arts and crafts, including limited-edition prints, hand-crafted Chinese "chops" (seals for documents), impressionist watercolours and pencil sketches. Daily 10am–6pm, sometimes closed Wed.

Joe's Design 6 Jalan Tun Tan Cheng Lock ☎ 06 281 2960; map p.275. Joe Ng, a Melaka native, produces handmade artisan jewellery which is rather more interesting and imaginative than most of Melaka's mass-produced handicrafts. Daily 9am–7pm.

Malaqa House 70 Jalan Tun Tan Cheng Lock ☎06 281 4770; map p.275. It describes itself as a museum but it's actually a shop and much of what is on sale – mostly furniture – is exquisite. Well worth a visit. Daily 10am–6pm.

Wah Aik Shoemaker 92 Jalan Tun Tan Cheng Lock ☎06 284 9726, ⊕ wahaikshoemakermelaka.webs. com; map p.275. This store was long renowned for making silk shoes, known as "lotus feet shoes," for the cruel Chinese tradition of foot binding. With the practice no longer legal, the shoes are lined up in the window as slightly macabre souvenirs at RM95/pair. Daily 9am–5.30pm.

DIRECTORY

Banks Banks include Maybank at 227 Jalan Melaka Raya 6, Public Bank at 60-68 Jalan Laksamana and HSBC, north of the centre at 777 Jalan Hang Tuah.

Cinema The Golden Screen Cinema on the top floor of Dataran Pahlawan Melaka Megamall shows English-language films.

Hospital Hospital Besar Melaka (General Hospital) is in the north of town on Jalan Mufti Haji Khalil (☎06 282 2344, ⊕hmelaka.moh.gov.my). The well-equipped Mahkota Medical Centre is at 3 Mahkota Melaka, Jalan Merdeka (☎06 285 2999, ⊕mahkotamedical.com).

Police The police station is on Jalan Merdeka, near the Maritime Museum (☎ 06 284 2222).

Post office There is a post office branch on Jalan Laksamana just a few steps from Christ Church, while the GPO (☎01 3455 6108) is inconveniently situated on the way to Ayer Keroh on Jalan Bukit Baru (both Mon–Fri 8.30am–5.30pm, Sat 8.30am–1pm).

Sport There's a public swimming pool (☎06 223 8796, ⊕mbmb.gov.my) in the shadow of the Taming Sari Revolving Tower on Jalan Kota.

Visa extensions The immigration office is out in Ayer Keroh, on floors 1–3 of Blok Pentadbiran, Kompleks Kementerian Dalam Negeri, Jalan Seri Negeri (Mon–Fri 7.30am–5pm; ☎ 06 232 2662).

Around Melaka

While there's more than enough to keep you occupied in Melaka, there are also a few popular getaways within day-trip distance. These include several opportunities to see animals: the tranquil coastal village of **Padang Kemunting** is a hatching site for hawksbill turtles, while **Ayer Keroh** has several wildlife parks and cultural attractions. Alternatively, the nearby island **Besar** provides an opportunity to feel some sand between your toes, even if the sea is fairly polluted.

Padang Kemunting Turtle Conservation and Information Centre

24km up the coast northwest of Melaka • Tues–Sat 9am–4pm • Free • ☎ 01 9644 3925 • Drive north towards Klebang Besar and proceed to Sungai Udang and then on to Masjid Tanah; from here take the junction to Padang Kemunting, commonly also referred to as Pengkalan Balak; or take a Panorama bus from Melaka Sentral to Masjid Tanah (every 30min; 1hr 30min), then taxi 8km (RM10–20); or taxi or Grab / Uber from Melaka Sentral (RM80)

Padang Kemunting is one of the last nesting areas of the hawksbill turtle and the painted terrapin in south Malaysia. Although open all year, it's only worth visiting the **turtle centre** during hatchling season (March–Sept). It's a friendly place with lots of information, including an introductory video about the turtle population of Melaka.

ACCOMMODATION AND EATING   PADANG KEMUNTING

There are a handful of places to stay near the sanctuary, plus several Malay **seafood restaurants** along the shore and a couple of convenience stores.

Ismah Beach Resort Next door to Padang Kemunting Turtle Sanctuary ☎ 06 384 8141, ⊕ismahresort.com. This simple resort has a restaurant and swimming pool, and is very close to the turtle centre; if the turtles appear at night, the centre can let you know by prior arrangement. 📶 RM138

5

Ayer Keroh

Despite its position adjacent to the North–South Expressway, 14km north of Melaka, **AYER KEROH** is a leafy recreational area with numerous attractions and a handful of places to stay. Although it's much cheaper to visit by bus, the attractions are quite spread out across both sides of the expressway so if you plan to visit several then it's better to rent a car or charter a taxi for the duration of the trip.

In addition to the attractions listed separately below, there are several others, including the **Botanical Gardens** (daily 24hr; free), an area of woodland set aside for walking and picnicking; the **Melaka Zoo** (Mon–Fri 9am–6pm, Sat, Sun and eve of holidays 9am–6pm & 8–11pm; RM23.70), Malaysia's oldest and second largest, but much in need of renovation; and the **World's Bees Museum** (daily 9am–6pm; free), which has exhibitions and provides honey tasting.

Taman Mini Malaysia & ASEAN

Lebuh Ayer Keroh • Daily 9am–5pm, cultural shows Mon–Thur 11am & 2.30pm, Fri–Sun 11am, 2.30pm & 4pm (30min) • RM22.50 • ☎ 06 234 9988, ⓦ minimalaysiaasean.com.my • Bus #19 from Melaka Sentral (hourly; 45min) drops you off at the Melaka Zoo, from where it's a short walk; taxi from Melaka RM3–45 (20–30min)

Ayer Keroh's most interesting attraction, **Taman Mini Malaysia & ASEAN**, holds full-sized reconstructions of typical houses from all thirteen Malay states and the other members of the Association of Southeast Asian Nations. Some buildings have displays inside and sell food, drink and souvenirs; cultural shows are also staged at the park's open-air arena.

Melaka Wonderland

Lebuh Ayer Keroh, Hang Tuah Jaya • Tues–Fri 11am–7pm, Sat & Sun 9am–7pm • Mon–Fri RM33.20, children RM26.05, Sat & Sun RM37.90, children RM32 • ☎ 06 231 3333, ⓦ melakawonderland.com.my

The **Melaka Wonderland** water park can provide a welcome break on a hot day. Attractions include the Tornado Chaser (where you start in a giant bowl before passing through a darkened tunnel and into a pool) and a wide range of twisting and straight slides, as well as more sedate swimming pools. The place is quiet on weekdays outside school holidays.

ARRIVAL AND INFORMATION   AYER KEROH

By bus Town bus #19 (hourly; 45min) from Melaka Sentral.

By taxi A taxi from Melaka costs RM35–45, Grab and Uber slightly less.

ACCOMMODATION AND EATING

INB Resort Lot 3169 Sempang Padang Keladi, Lebuh Ayer Keroh ☎ 06 553 3022, ⓦ inbresort.hotels.net. my. An affordable option, 15–20min on foot from Taman Mini Malaysia & ASEAN. With comfortable rooms in pink concrete buildings arrayed around a pool, it's very popular with local families. Breakfast is only served at the weekend, but there's a small place to eat outside. 🛜 RM120

Philea 2940 Jalan Ayer Keroh, off Jalan Plaza Tol ☎ 06 233 3399, ⓦ phileahotel.com. The stylish cabins at this site, built from Russian pine logs and with stone in the bathrooms, make great use of natural materials – although this does mean that ground-floor rooms can be a bit noisy. There's a spa, sauna and gym; the two Royal Villas have their own swimming pools. Doubles RM675, Royal Villas 🛜 RM6500

Besar Island

If you're looking for a beach getaway and don't have time to go further afield, then **BESAR ISLAND** ("Big Island", though in reality it covers just 16 square kilometres) may fit the bill. The island's beaches and hilly scenery are pleasant, although the waters are fairly polluted. Located 5km off the coast of Melaka, Besar Island was known as the burial ground of passing Muslim traders and missionaries; as a result, locals – particularly Indian Muslims – see the island as a holy place and visitors are asked to behave accordingly.

OPPOSITE KOTA TINGGI WATERFALL >

5

ARRIVAL AND DEPARTURE   BESAR ISLAND

By ferry Two jetties southeast of Melaka have boats to the island; neither is on bus routes, and a taxi to either should cost RM35. The Anjung Batu jetty sees regular ferries (6 daily, starting 8.30am, last boat back 7pm; RM11 (children RM8) return), while the Pengkalan Pernu jetty in Umbai has boats only on request (RM100 one way for up to five people).

ACCOMMODATION AND EATING

D'Puteri Besar Island ☎06 295 5899, ⓦdputeriresortpulaubesar.blogspot.com. You are unlikely to want to spend much time in your room, but fortunately the island's only resort – simple cabins with cold water and either fan or a/c – is right on the beach. They also have a campsite (you'll need your own tent). Camping per tent RM30, fan doubles RM115, a/c doubles RM145

From Melaka to Johor Bahru

The journey from Melaka southeast along **Route 5** to Johor Bahru covers just over 200km. The first 45km, as far as the town of **Muar**, passes through verdant countryside dotted with neatly kept timber stilt houses in some of Malaysia's prettiest kampungs. Further south, the towns of Batu Pahat and Pontian Kecil hold scant interest (the former, slightly inland, has a reputation as a red-light resort for Singaporeans). If you want to stop anywhere else before Johor Bahru and Singapore, aim instead for **Kukup**, right at the southern end of the west coast and terrific for seafood.

To get to Johor Bahru in a hurry, skip scenic Route 5 and use the **North–South Expressway** instead. From Melaka, you can head north to the expressway via Ayer Keroh; it's also straightforward to join the expressway from Muar (take the Bukit Pasir road for about 20km).

Muar

Also known as Bandar Maharani, the old port town of **MUAR** is a calm and elegant place that attracts few tourists but should reward a day's exploration. Legend has it that Paramesvara, the fifteenth-century founder of Melaka, fled here from Singapore to establish his kingdom on the southern bank of the Muar River, before being persuaded to choose Melaka. The town later became an important port in the Johor empire (see p.292), as well as a centre for the sentimental Malay folk-pop called **ghazal music**, and its **dialect** is considered the purest Bahasa Malaysia in the Peninsula.

Today, Muar's commercial centre looks like any other, with Chinese shophouses and *kedai kopis* lining its streets. Turn right out of the **bus station**, however, following the river as the road turns into Jalan Peteri, and you'll find Muar's **Neoclassical colonial buildings**. The Custom House and Government Offices (Bangunan Sultan Abu Bakar) are on your right, and the District Police Office and Courthouse on your left; they still have an air of confidence and prosperity dating back to the town's days as a British administrative centre. Completed in 1930, the graceful **Masjid Jamek Sultan Ibrahim** successfully combines Western and Moorish styles of architecture. Further along Jalan Petri you'll pass a jetty on your right, from where irregular **river cruises** depart.

ARRIVAL AND DEPARTURE   MUAR

By bus The bus station, on Jalan Maharani, is served by buses from Melaka's Sentral station (every 30min; 1hr 30min).

By taxi A taxi from Melaka costs around RM70–85 one way (1hr).

ACCOMMODATION

Hotel Leewa 75 Jalan Arab ☎06 952 1605. Fairly basic rooms but pleasant and helpful staff, and it's in a decent location; there's also a friendly cat that occasionally comes to play. RM65

Streetview Hotel 11 & 13 Jalan Ali ☎ 06 953 7088, ⓦ streetviewhotel.com.my. One of the town's best hotels, in a beautiful colonial building, featuring clean and comfortable a/c rooms. There are two more properties in the same chain, *Riverview* and *Townview*, both with equally well-kept rooms. 🛜 RM120

EATING

Muar has a good reputation for its **coffee** and its **food**, particularly *otak-otak* (fish dumplings) and *mee bandung* (see opposite). Another local speciality is satay (particularly satay *perut*, made from intestines) for breakfast.

Bentayan Hawker Centre Jalan Bentayan. Located at the end of the street, he stalls here – some of which have been operating for decades – serve up a wide range of dishes (RM6) including Muar's famous colourful steamed rice cakes, dim sum, *otak-otak* and much more. Daily 5.30am–11.30pm.

Wah San 69a Jalan Abdullah. Up to 30kg of noodles are produced every day; the speciality is *mee bandung* (noodles, beansprouts, egg, beef and tofu served in a sauce made from prawn, chillies and beef soup; RM5), which has been selling since 1961, and is regarded as the best in town. Daily 7am–5pm; closed alternate Thursdays.

Kukup

The small fishing community of **KUKUP**, 60km southwest of Johor Bahru and 20km south of Pontian Kecil along Route 5, is a regular stop for the Singapore package-tour trade. Busloads of tourists arrive to see the old stilt houses built over the murky river and to sample Kukup's real attraction, the **seafood**: the town's single tumbledown street is packed with restaurants.

ARRIVAL AND DEPARTURE   KUKUP

By bus and taxi If you are travelling from Johor Bahru, there are no direct buses, so you need to catch a bus to Pontian Kecil (every 15min; 1hr) and then take a taxi (RM30).

By ferry The jetty at Kukup remains a little-known exit point from Malaysia to Indonesia. Ferries operated by Penaga Timur (☎ 07 241 4477, ⓦ paj.com.my) run to Tanjung Balai on Karimun island (hourly; 1hr; RM60).

ACCOMMODATION

Kukup is a small and compact town, and most travellers only stay for a few hours. If you do choose to overnight, you will easily find a bed; virtually all the **houses** double as basic guesthouses and restaurants. Accommodation is normally for groups of eight or more, but with a bit of bargaining you may well be able to persuade them otherwise – most people would rather their rooms didn't go empty. Expect to pay about RM80 including meals.

Tanjung Piai Resort 1km north of Kukup towards Pontian Kecil ☎ 012 767 0699, ⓦ tanjungpiai-resort. blogspot.my. This string of large wooden buildings stands on concrete stilts at the edge of the mangrove swamps. The resort commands a dramatic vista of the ships coming to and from Singapore, and has a decent seafood restaurant, but is generally in need of repair. Prices rise by about fifty percent at weekends. 🛜 RM140

EATING

New Kukup Seafood Restaurant 1 Kukup Laut ☎ 07 696 0216. You are spoiled for choice for seafood restaurants in Kukup, but this large waterfront restaurant – complete with hanging lanterns – is one of the beter ones. It serves some excellent Chinese-style seafood dishes – fresh crayfish, crab, baby squid and cuttlefish are accompanied by stir-fried vegetables including pak choi, bean sprouts and green tea shoots. A full meal will set you back about RM25. Daily 10am–9pm.

Johor Bahru

The southernmost Malaysian city of any size, **JOHOR BAHRU** – or simply **JB** – is the main gateway into **Singapore**, linked to the city-state by a **causeway** carrying a road, a railway, and the pipes through which Singapore imports its fresh water. Every day around one hundred thousand vehicles travel across the causeway (the newer **second**

5

crossing from Geylang Patah, 20km west of JB, is much less used because of its higher tolls), and the ensuing traffic, noise and smog affects most of downtown.

The city has been moulded by its proximity to Singapore, for better or for worse – it has the air of both a border town and a boom town. The vast majority of visitors are **day-trippers**, many drawn by the cheap shopping and the duty-free zone to the east of the city centre. JB's environs are also being transformed by **Iskandar Malaysia**, a vast Singapore-backed project to create essentially a new city west of the existing one. It boasts industrial zones, universities, leisure facilities (notably Legoland Malaysia), and a glut of expensive property developments.

Brief history

Johor Bahru stands with Melaka as one of the country's most historic sites. Chased from its seat of power by the Portuguese in 1511, the Melakan court decamped to the Riau Archipelago, south of modern Singapore, before upping sticks again in the 1530s and shifting to the upper reaches of the Johor River. There they endured a century of offensives by both the Portuguese and the Acehnese of northern Sumatra.

Stability was finally achieved by courting the friendship of the Dutch in the 1640s, and the kingdom of Johor blossomed into a thriving trading entrepôt. By the end of the century, though, the rule of the tyrannical and decadent **Sultan Mahmud** had halted Johor's pre-eminence among the Malay kingdoms, and piracy was causing a decline in trade. In 1699, Sultan Mahmud was assassinated by his own nobles while returning from prayers. With the Melaka-Johor dynasty finally over, successive power struggles crippled the kingdom.

Immigration of the Bugis peoples to Johor eventually eclipsed the power of the sultans, and though the Bugis were finally chased out by the Dutch in 1784, the kingdom was a shadow of its former self. The Johor-Riau empire – and the Malay world – was split in two, with the Strait of Malacca forming the dividing line, following the Anglo-Dutch Treaty of 1824. As links with the court in Riau faded, Sultan Ibrahim assumed power, amassing a fortune based upon hefty profits culled from plantations. He established his administrative headquarters in the fishing village of Tanjung Puteri, which his son Abu Bakar – widely regarded as the father of modern Johor – later renamed Johor Bahru ("New Johor").

Downtown

JB is a sprawling city, and many of the administrative offices have been moved out of the centre to **Kota Iskandar** in the west. Most places of interest to visitors, though, are still **downtown** or close to the **waterfront** near the Singapore causeway. The downtown area blends the scruffy with the modern: the claustrophobic alleys of the sprawling market are within a few paces of thoroughly contemporary shopping malls such as **City Square**. Close by, the huge **CIQ** (Customs, Immigration and Quarantine) complex – built to streamline travel between JB and Singapore – includes **JB Sentral** station, combining bus and train terminals.

Arguably the most interesting part of the area, though, is on and around **Jalan Tan Hiok Nee** and **Jalan Dhoby**. Formerly quite seedy, these streets have been tidied up and are now at the centre of a vibrant shopping and dining scene.

Sri Mariamman Temple

Jalan Tun Abdul Razak, south of City Square, ⊛ rajamariammanjb.com

The **Sri Mariamman Temple** lends a welcome splash of colour to JB's cityscape. Underneath its *gopuram*, and beyond the two gatekeepers on horseback who guard the temple, stand vividly depicted figures from the Hindu pantheon. Shops outside the temple sell Bollywood movies and garlands of flowers used in worship, while on the street you can have your fortune told using cowrie shells.

Around the seafront

The views across to Singapore from the **seafront**, just a short walk from Sri Mariamman Temple, are doubly impressive after the cramped streets of the city centre. Several interesting attractions lie on or around Jalan Ibrahim, while just north of here is the fortress-like **Sultan Ibrahim Building**; formerly the home of the state government, which has been moved west to Kota Iskandar, the building is eventually scheduled to become a museum.

Chinese Heritage Museum

42 Jalan Ibrahim • Tues–Sun 9am–5pm • RM5 • ☎ 07 224 9633, ⊛ jb-tionghua.org.my

As the name suggests, the **Chinese Heritage Museum** focuses on the Chinese contribution to the founding and development of Johor Bahru, and specifically on the production of gambier (a tropical shrub traditionally used in leather tanning and textile dyeing) and pepper, both of which were the economic lifeline of the Chinese community in the nineteenth century.

Royal Abu Bakar Museum

Jalan Tun Dr Ismail, the western continuation of Jalan Ibrahim • Sun–Thurs 9am–5pm • US$7 (converted to ringgit) • ☎ 07 223 0222, ⊛ johor.attractionsinmalaysia.com/Royal-Abu-Bakar-Museum.php

Heading west along the waterfront you soon reach the Istana Besar, the former residence of Johor's royal family, which now functions as the **Royal Abu Bakar Museum**,

5

although the Grand Palace is still occasionally used for state and royal ceremonies. Ornate golden lamps line the path to the Istana, a magnificent building with chalk-white walls and a low, blue roof, set on a hillock overlooking the Johor Straits.

Masjid Abu Bakar
5min walk west of Royal Abu Bakar Museum • Daily 8am–5pm, closes Fri noon–3pm for prayers • ☎ 07 223 4935

The four rounded towers of the **Masjid Abu Bakar** make it the most elegant building in town. Completed in 1900 under the orders of Sultan Abu Bakar, the mosque is largely based on colonial Victorian architecture, although also incorporates Moorish and Malay elements. The grand mosque can accommodate up to two thousand worshippers.

Danga Bay
5km west of centre • ☎ 07 233 3888, ⓦ dangabay.com • Taxi RM18

A key component of the Iskandar Malaysia development project, the waterfront **Danga Bay** complex includes several restaurants, stalls offering outdoor dining, a stage for live performances and even a beach bar (on an unappealing scrap of sand). It's a popular spot in the evenings and at the weekend.

Legoland
7 Jalan Legoland, 23km west of the centre centre • Daily 10am–5pm • ☎ 07 597 8888, ⓦ legoland.com.my • Taxi RM30

Billed as "Malaysia's first international theme park", the Legoland Malaysia Resort, about a half-hour drive west from the centre of the city, features more than 70 attractions, rides and shows. Split up into six zones – Technic, Kingdoms, Imagination,

---

GETTING FROM JOHOR BAHRU TO SINGAPORE

There are several ways to head into Singapore from Johor Bahru.

BY TRAIN

The most obvious but currently least sensible route would be to use the **train** from JB Sentral; the problem being that this only takes you to Singapore's Woodlands station just across the causeway, and it's another's hour's journey to reach the city centre. This may change soon, as talks are currently underway for a Johor Bahru–Singapore Rapid Transit System Link. This is likely to be between Johor's Southern Integrated Gateway at Bukit Chagar, which interchanges with the KTM Intercity services at JB Sentral, and Republic Polytechnic in Singapore, which will soon connect with Woodlands North MRT Station on Singapore's upcoming Thomson-East Coast MRT Line. An initial engineering study was completed in 2014 and indications were that the line could be completed by 2019, but a target of 2024 now seems more likely.

BY BUS

It is far easier to get to downtown Singapore by bus. Starting from **Larkin bus station**, north of town, you can catch SBS #170X or #170 (daily 5am–midnight), or the faster yellow Causeway Link #CW1 and #CW2 services. All buses then proceed to the **CIQ** (Customs, Immigration and Quarantine) complex; at this point you need to get off the bus and clear customs, before getting on another to complete the journey to Singapore (take your luggage off the bus, keep your ticket and get on the same type of bus on the other side). If you're already in downtown Johor Bahru, simply board the bus at **JB Sentral**, which is part of the CIQ complex, and complete immigration formalities before you buy your ticket.

Once through customs, the Causeway Link buses run nonstop to Kranji MRT (#CW1) or Queen Street (#CW2); the SBS services go to Kranji MRT, with the #170 continuing to Little India and terminating at Queen Street, near Bugis MRT. There are also Transtar buses to **Changi Airport** from Larkin (hourly; 1hr 20min).

BY TAXI

It is also possible to reach downtown Singapore by **taxi** – which costs RM30 per person or RM70 for the whole vehicle – from outside JB Sentral station.

Land of Adventure, Lego City and Miniland – children engage in battle and solve puzzles to save the brick-shaped folk from their enemies. There's also an on-site water park and the *Legoland Hotel*, where the rooms take their interior design motif from the theme park, including knights, pirates and adventurers.

ARRIVAL AND DEPARTURE

JOHOR BAHRU

By plane Senai Airport (☎07 599 4500, ⓦsenaiairport.com) is 28km north of the city. Taxis to the city centre cost RM45; bus #333 travels to Larkin bus station (45min), while the white Causeway Link airport shuttle bus (ⓦcausewaylink.com.my) serves JB Sentral (45min). SkyBus offers a bus service (ⓦskybus.com.my) to major hotels including *Tune Hotel*.

Destinations Ipoh (daily; 1hr 20min); Kota Kinabalu (2 daily; 2hr 20min); Kuala Lumpur (6 daily; 45min); Kuching (4 daily; 1hr 30min); Miri (daily; 2hr); Penang (4 daily; 1hr); Sibu (daily; 1hr 40min).

By train JB Sentral train station is part of the JB Sentral terminal on Jalan Tun Abdul Razak, just across the road from CIQ (Customs, Immigration, and Quarantine complex).

Destinations Bekok (for Endau Rompin National Park; 4 daily; 3hr); Gemas (for northbound ETS trains; 4 daily; 4hr 30min); Jerantut (daily; 9hr 30min); Kuala Lipis (1 daily; 10hr 30min); Pulau Sebang/Tampin (near Melaka and for Komuter trains to KL; 2 daily; 5hr); Wakaf Bharu (for Kota Bharu; daily; 18hr); Singapore (Woodlands; several daily; 5min).

By long-distance bus Larkin bus station, on Jalan Geruda, 5km north of the centre (RM15 by taxi), is used by most long-distance services. If you don't want to go there for a ticket, try the row of bus company offices running along the side of the

Merlin Tower building in the city centre.

Destinations Alor Star (4 daily; 10hr); Batu Pahat (every 15min; 2hr); Butterworth (8 daily; 12hr); Dungun (2 daily; 9hr); Hap Chai (Thailand; daily; 12hr); Ipoh (8 daily; 7hr); Klang (6 daily; 4hr 30min); Kota Bharu (3 daily; 9hr); Kuala Lumpur (every 30min; 5hr); Kuala Perlis (2 daily; 12hr); Kuala Terengganu (4 daily; 8hr); Kuantan (4 daily; 6hr); Melaka (every 30min; 3hr 30min); Mersing (10 daily; 2hr 30min); Muar (every 30min; 3hr); Segamat (hourly; 3hr); Seremban (hourly; 3hr); Singapore (every 10min; 1hr).

By local bus Buses heading east start from the JB Sentral combined bus and train terminal; local buses heading west run from around City Square.

By ferry Ferries from Tanjung Pinang (3 daily; 2hr 30min; RM86) and Batam Island (hourly 7.15am–5.45pm; 2hr; RM69) in Indonesia arrive at ferry terminal, part of the Berjaya Waterfront Hotel complex 4km east of central JB; book tickets on ⓦberjayawaterfront.com.my. Fuel taxes and seaport charges will be applicable.

By taxi Taxis are available at JB Sentral station. Share taxis to Singapore charge RM70/vehicle (45min).

Car rental Avis, 15 Jalan Dato Abdullah Tahir (☎07 331 7644, ⓦavis.com); Hertz is based in Menara Ansar at 65 Jalan Trus (☎07 223 7520, ⓦhertz.com) or at the airport.

INFORMATION

Banks and exchange The main shopping centres hold ATMs and currency exchanges. There's also an HSBC on Jalan Bukit Timbalan; in JB Sentral there's a 24hr moneychanger at the main entrance.

Tourist information JOTIC (Johor Tourist Information Centre, Sun–Thurs 8am–1pm & 2–5pm; ☎07 222 3590, ⓦtourism.gov.my) has branches at Senai Airport, JB Sentral and CIQ.

ACCOMMODATION

JB's manufacturing boom means the city attracts more business travellers than tourists, so **hotel** prices tend to be on the high side. The city's budget and mid-range hotels are mostly just outside the city centre; some of the cheapest (not listed here) double as brothels.

Berjaya Waterfront 88, Jalan Ibrahim Sultan ☎07 221 9999, ⓦberjayahotel.com; map p.292. Enormous waterfront property with indoor spa and outdoor pool that stretches out into the Strait. The rooms are a little tired but the common areas are spick and span – and, thanks to its position near the ferry terminal, the property is basically its own duty-free zone, so the hotel bars and mini nightclub with live band have some of the cheapest hotel drinks in Malaysia. ⓦ RM212

Bliss Boutique Hotel 50 Jalan Jaya, Taman Maju Jaya ☎07 332 7188, ⓦblissboutiquehotel.com; map p.292. Boutique hotel may be a slight overstatement – the decor

is pretty kitsch, with cheesy love statements decorating the bedroom walls, but it is great value and just a few steps away from *Chez Papa*, one of JB's best international restaurants. ⓦ RM140

Renaissance 2 Jalan Permas 11, Bandar Baru Permas Jaya ☎07 381 3333, ⓦmarriott.co.uk/hotels/travel/jhbbr-renaissance-johor-bahru-hotel; map p.292. Located just ten minutes from the Singapore–Malaysia border, this five-star hotel offers modern, tastefully furnished rooms and state of the art facilities, including an outdoor swimming pool, spa, fitness centre and business centre. ⓦ RM400

5

Tune Hotel Danga Bay, Jalan Skudai ☎07 962 5888, ⓦtunehotels.com; map p.292. This popular chain of budget hotels offers modern, clean and practical rooms, with add-ons such as TV and a/c. There's also a good-value restaurant, computers for guests' use and a shuttle bus from Senai airport (RM8) that drops you off at the hotel door. ☎ RM88

Zoom Inn Unit 7, 8 & 9, Block 7, Danga Bay, Jalan Skudai ☎07 237 9323, ⓦzoominn.com.my; map p.292. Don't be fooled by the slightly drab exterior – this hotel in Danga Bay is a pleasant surprise. Rooms are neat and welcoming with quirky colourful wall drawings and modern bathrooms; there's also a small convenience store on the ground floor. ☎ RM125

EATING

There are scores of great international **restaurants** in JB, and some good street food on offer. The most interesting little cafés and restaurants are to the west of Jalan Segget, which also has its own **night market**.

FOOD MARKETS AND MALLS

Meldrum Walk Night Market Meldrum Walk; map p.292. Colourful and vibrant night market with a mouthwatering array. Try the local speciality *mee rebus* – noodles in a thick sauce garnished with bean curd, sliced egg, green chillies and shallots. Daily 6pm–midnight.

Stulang Laut Hawker Stalls Jalan Stulang Laut; map p.292. Vietnamese, Korean, Thai and other cuisines mingle together on this corner near the duty-free zone, with seafood the common theme binding them. The buzzy atmosphere contrasts nicely with the peaceful view across the sea. Daily 6pm–midnight.

Taman Sentosa Hawker Stalls Jalan Sutera; map p.292. A popular night food market where Chinese stalls line one side of the street and Malay places sit side by side on the other. Plenty of dishes on offer including prawn *mee* and *bak kut teh* (about RM7). Tues–Sun 6pm–midnight.

RESTAURANTS AND CAFÉS

Carabao 16 Jalan Dato Abdullah Tahir ☎07 335 9333, ⓦcarabaorestaurant.com; map p.292. The setting of JB's only proper Thai restaurant is particularly pleasant, with seating in an airy open-fronted area featuring natural materials and decorated with hanging lanterns, draped scarves and shell wind chimes singing in the breeze. The extensive menu includes a range of fish dishes (fried,

steamed or curried; RM15), as well as seafood (RM17), chicken (RM16) and sweet and sour beef (RM17). Daily noon–3pm & 6pm–1am.

★**Chez Papa** 38 & 40 Jalan Jaya, Taman Maju Jaya ☎07 333 4988, ⓦchezpapa.com.my; map p.292. This French bistro and wine bar offers traditional home cooking in a particularly welcoming interior that bursts with character; customers can sit at the bar lined with dangling wine bottle lamps, or at rustic wooden tables. There's a particular emphasis on hearty stews, and the menu includes French classics such as a dozen *escargots de Bourgogne* (RM42), *foie gras* (RM82) and mussels (RM24). Good selection of wines from France and beyond. Mon–Sat 6pm–midnight.

Hiap Joo Bakery & Biscuit Factory 13 Jln Tan Hiok Nee ☎07 223 1703; map p.292. Opened in 1919, this historic bakery is one of the very few in the country that bakes in a wood-fired oven. The coconut buns (RM34) and the banana cake (RM9) are the real winners. Mon–Sat 7am–5.30pm.

Roost Juice & Bar 9 Jalan Dhoby ⓦroostjuicebar .blogspot.sg; map p.292. This quirky little café and restaurant in the heart of JB features mismatched vintage furniture and exudes a shabby-chic feel. The international menu includes Western dishes such as fish and chips (RM14.90) and Malay favourites like *nasi lemak* (RM9), nicely washed down with a freshly made juice (RM78). Daily 10am–midnight.

SHOPPING

Although JB has plenty of Western-style shopping malls, it's much more enjoyable to explore the **boutiques** around Jalan Tan Hiok Nee and Jalan Dhoby.

The Girl Next Door Above Roost Juice & Bar, 9 Jalan Dhoby ☎07 222 4178; map p.292. Also known as TGND, this is typical of the boutiques in this area, with a young and enthusiastic owner Beverly selling mostly vintage clothes and shoes but also other bits and pieces which take her fancy; there's also a hairdressing section. Mon–Sat 1pm–midnight.

Jaro 18 Jalan Sungei Chat ☎07 224 5632, ⓦjaro .org.my; map p.292. The Johor Area Rehabilitation

Organisation (JARO) shop features handicrafts and artworks made by people with disabilities. Among the products on display are rattan baskets, picture frames and handmade cane furniture. Buying products here ensures the workers continue to have a source of employment, while also preserving traditional craft-making skills that have been passed down for generations. Mon–Thurs & Sun 8am–5pm.

The east coast

Without the patronage of neighbouring Singapore, the area around Johor Bahru would have quietly nodded off into a peaceful slumber. Most people heading to the **east coast** beat a hasty path along Route 3 to **Mersing**, a dusty little town that is the departure point for boats to **Tioman Island**.

Mersing

The industrious little fishing port of **MERSING**, 130km north of Johor Bahru, lies on the languid Mersing River. It serves as the main gateway to **Tioman Island** and most of the smaller islands of the **Seribuat Archipelago**.

ARRIVAL AND DEPARTURE

By boat Mersing is the main departure point for Tioman Island and most of the other islands of the Seribuat Archipelago, although boats to Sibu Island leave from Tanjung Leman (see p.309). At the jetty there's a secure car park (RM10/day), while there and in the R&R Plaza nearby, assorted booths and offices represent various islands, boats and resorts. Tioman Ferry (☎ 01 3465 1623, ⱳ tiomanferry. com) offers online booking.

By bus Buses normally stop at the bus station on the western edge of town, and also at the R&R Plaza beside the jetty. The overight bus from KI will arrive at around 5am in the morning, so if you're moving on to Tioman you may have to find a mamak to rest in for most of the morning. If you're leaving Mersing, for most destinations there is no need to walk to the bus station; buy tickets from SS International (☎ 03 7728 4789, ⱳ ssinternational.

MERSING

ACCOMMODATION
Embassy Hotel	3
Fishing Bay Resort	1
Sweet Hotel	4
Timotel	2

EATING
Loke Tien Yuen	2
Mersing Seafood Restaurant	3
Syed Ali	1

com.my) on Jalan Abu Bakar by the jetty. They will make sure the bus picks you up at the plaza. Leaving by bus in peak season can be problematic; many are full. Buy express bus tickets in advance, at the station or from a resort or travel agency.

Destinations Alor Star (1 daily; 12hr); Butterworth (1 daily; 9hr); Cherating (4 daily; 4hr 30min); Endau (hourly; 45min); Ipoh (1 daily; 8hr); Johor Bahru (9 daily; 2hr 30min); Kluang (5 daily; 1hr 30min); Kota Bahru (2 daily; 8hr); Kota Tinggi (hourly; 2hr); Kuala Lumpur (8 daily; 6hr); Kuala Perlis (1 daily; 12hr); Kuala Terengganu (5 daily, 9hr 30min); Kuantan (5 daily; 3hr 30min); Melaka (3 daily; 5hr 30min); Muar (3 daily; 5hr); Pengkalan Kubor (daily; 10hr); Singapore (5 daily; 4hr).

By taxi Taxis can be picked up either at the main bus station or at the jetty.

INFORMATION

Tourist information Mersing's neat new tourist office is at Jalan Abu Bakar on the way to the ferry port (METIC; Mon–Fri 8am–5pm; ☏ 07 798 1979).

Travel agents Numerous agents, operators and resort offices in and around the jetty complex deal primarily with Tioman and the Seribuat Archipelago. Hotel Mersing Travel & Tours, 7 Jalan Abu Bakar (☏ 01 3465 1623, ⊛ hotelmersing. com), also organize full-day tailor-made island-hopping trips (from RM150/person; minimum six people), and trips to Endau Rompin National Park (see p.310).

ACCOMMODATION

Embassy Hotel 2 Jalan Ismail ☏ 07 799 3545; map p.297. A rather soulless three-storey orange hotel building in the centre of town, featuring a selection of adequate rooms that will do the trick for the night if you're on a tight budget. **RM71**

Fishing Bay Resort 15km north of Mersing ☏ 07 799 6753, ✉ fishingbbr@yahoo.com.sg; map p.297. This good-value place has neat bungalows and rooms set around a beachside garden and small pool, and a restaurant serving excellent local and Thai food. Kayaks are available for a trip to Batu Gajah Island, just offshore. A taxi costs RM40 one-way, or ask about transfers. Weekend rates rise by almost fifty percent. **RM69**

Sweet Hotel 5 Jalan Jemaluang ☏ 07 799 2228; map p.297. A short walk from the bus station, this friendly hotel is the safest mid-range bet in town; the clean, a/c rooms, all with TV and hot water, feature pleasant touches like mounted fabrics. 🛜 **RM90**

Timotel 839 Jalan Endau ☏ 07 799 5888, ⊛ timotel. com.my; map p.297. Just across the bridge, Mersing's best hotel offers 44 spacious carpeted rooms with wicker chairs and large beds. The hotel seems to have changed little since opening two decades ago, although a few modern touches have been added, including in-room kettles and wi-fi throughout. 🛜 **RM260**

EATING

Mersing is a good place to **eat** out, with seafood unsurprisingly topping the menu. The **market** serves the popular local breakfast dish *nasi dagang*: glutinous rice cooked in coconut milk, served with *sambal* and fish curry.

Loke Tien Yuen 55 Jalan Abu Bakar; map p.297. The oldest and friendliest Chinese restaurant in town with a small, reliable menu. The sweet and sour pork is particularly good. Around RM7/dish; seafood around RM30. Daily 12.30pm–11pm.

Mersing Seafood Restaurant 56 Jalan Ismail ☏ 07 799 2550; map p.297. Great seafood dishes prepared Szechuan or Cantonese style in a slightly kitsch a/c interior, though some can be pricey; among the best sellers are deep-fried squid with salted egg yolk (RM14/piece), BBQ squid (RM15) and fried prawns with butter and coconut (RM16). Daily 11.30am–2.30pm & 5.30–10.30pm; closes on Wed every fortnight.

Syed Ali 72–73 Jalan Sulaiman ☏ 07 799 6336; map p.297. This bustling place just a short walk from the jetty offers a good selection of tasty Indian and local grub that is considered by most to be the best in town. A meal will set you back about RM8. Daily 24hr.

Tioman Island

Shaped like a giant apostrophe, located in the South China Sea 54km northeast of Mersing, **TIOMAN ISLAND** is the largest of the 64 volcanic islands that form the **Seribuat Archipelago**. Ever since the 1970s – when *Time* magazine ranked Tioman as one of the world's ten most beautiful islands – sun worshippers and divers have been flocking to its palm-fringed shores, in search of the mythical Bali H'ai (the island in the Hollywood musical *South Pacific*, which was filmed on Tioman).

It could be argued that this popularity, and its **duty-free** status, have dented the romantic isolation that once made the island so desirable. Tioman Island does, however, display a remarkable resilience – and in part due to the lack of a decent road network, the greater part of the island retains something of its intimate, village atmosphere. Anyone in search of unspoiled beaches is likely to be disappointed, though superb exceptions do exist; divers and snorkellers will find plenty to enjoy, and there are also opportunities to take jungle hikes in the largely untouched interior.

Accommodation possibilities range from international-standard resorts to simple beachfront A-frames; it takes time and money to get from one beach to another, so choose your destination carefully. During the **monsoon**, from November to February/March, the whole island winds down dramatically; many places close until at least mid-January. July and August are the busiest months, when prices increase and accommodation is best booked in advance; visibility for divers is also at its lowest during these months.

SNORKELLING AND DIVING AROUND TIOMAN ISLAND

The waters around Tioman boast abundant **marine life**. Many nearby islets provide excellent opportunities for **snorkelling**, and most of the hotel operations offer **day-trips**; prices start at RM75, including equipment. The relatively healthy coral and huge biodiversity in these temperate waters also make for great **diving, in areas well away from the ferry routes**. Dive centres offer a full range of PADI certificates, from a four-day Open Water course (around RM1000), through to the Dive Master (RM3200) and instructor qualifications. For the already qualified, a boat dive costs around RM110 per person. The **dive sites** listed below are the most popular on the west coast, where most people dive.

DIVE SHOPS

B&J Diving Centre Air Batang ☎09 419 1218, ⓦdivetioman.com; map p.302. Well-established shop with a second branch in Salang (☎09 419 5555).
Blue Heaven Divers Air Batang ☎09 419 1413, ⓦblueheavendivers.com; map p.302. Offers a good-value Open Water package that last 3–4 days (RM1100).
Eco-Divers Air Batang ☎09 419 12794, ⓦeco-divers.net; map p.302. Close to the jetty and with friendly staff. Half-day Discover Scuba courses from RM200; Open Water RM1100.
Freedive Tioman Tekek ⓦfreedive-earth.com

/school-location/malaysia; map p.302. The island's first freediving school, offering introduction, beginner and advanced courses, including Apnea Total Freediver.
Ray's Dive Adventure Air Batang ☎019 330 8062, ⓦraysdive.com; map p.302. Small but highly experienced outfit at Air Batang offering a range of courses; contact for prices.
Tioman Dive Centre Tekek ☎09 419 1228, ⓦtioman-dive-centre.com; map p.302. A reliable outfit on Tekek, with night dives that start from RM90 (excluding kit rental).

DIVE SITES

Golden Reef (typical depth 10–20m). 15min off the northwestern coast; boulders provide a breeding ground for marine life, and produce many soft and hard corals. Known for nudibranchs and other macro life.
Chebeh Island (15–30m). In the northwestern waters, this is a massive volcanic labyrinth of caves and channels. Napoleon fish, triggerfish and turtles are present in abundance.
Labas Island (5–20m). South of Tulai Island, this island has numerous tunnels and caves that provide a home for pufferfish, stingrays and moray eels.
Sawadee wrecks (25–30m). Two wooden Thai fishing boats just offshore from Tekek airport attract scorpionfish and juvenile barracuda, as well as more common marine life.
Tiger Reef (10–25m). Deservedly the most popular site, southwest of Tulai between Labas and Sepoi islands. Yellow-tail snappers, trevally and tuna, spectacular soft coral and gorgonian fans.
Tokong Magicienne (Magicienne Rock) (10–25m). Due north of Tioman, this colourful, sponge-layered coral pinnacle is a feeding station for larger fish – silver snappers, golden-striped trevally, jacks and groupers.

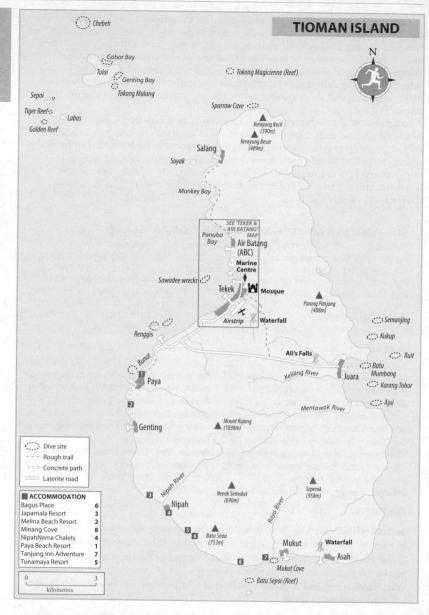

TIOMAN ISLAND

N

- Chebeh
- Gabor Bay
- Tulai
- Genting Bay
- Tokong Malang
- Sepoi
- Tiger Reef
- Labas
- Golden Reef
- Tokong Magicienne (Reef)
- Sparrow Cave
- Kerayung Kecil (390m)
- Salang
- Kerayung Besar (409m)
- Soyak
- Monkey Bay
- SEE 'TEKEK & AIR BATANG' MAP
- Panuba Bay
- Air Batang (ABC)
- Marine Centre
- Sawadee wrecks
- Tekek
- Mosque
- Parang Panjang (488m)
- Airstrip
- Waterfall
- Semanjing
- Kukup
- Renggis
- Ali's Falls
- Ruit
- Bunut
- Juara
- Batu Mumbang
- Paya
- Keliling River
- Karang Tohor
- Genting
- Mentawak River
- Ajui
- Mount Kajang (1038m)
- Nipah River
- Nenek Semukut (690m)
- Seperok (958m)
- Nipah
- Roya River
- Batu Sirau (753m)
- Mukut
- Waterfall
- Asah
- Mukut Cove
- Batu Sepoi (Reef)

- - - - - Dive site
- - - - - Rough trail
- - - - - Concrete path
- - - - - Laterite road

■ ACCOMMODATION

Bagus Place	6
Japamala Resort	3
Melina Beach Resort	2
Minang Cove	8
NipahNema Chalets	4
Paya Beach Resort	1
Tanjung Inn Adventure	7
Tunamaya Resort	5

0 ———— 3
kilometres

ARRIVAL AND DEPARTURE

TIOMAN ISLAND

By boat Blue Water Express (☏ 07 799 4811) has services from Mersing (2hr; RM35) to the island, with boats stopping off at Genting, Paya, Tekek, ABC and Sabang (in that order); note that when leaving the island, once the boats fills up, they travel directly to the mainland without picking up passengers at the remaining stops (although they always stop at Tekek, the main port). There are also ferries from Tanjung Gemok ferry terminal (1 daily; 2hr; RM35), about 40km north of Mersing. Allow extra time if you need to catch a flight from the mainland, as the boat services are not entirely reliable and dictated by the tide. Boats are also often full, especially in high season, when ferries get booked up days or even weeks in advance. Tickets can be booked online with Tioman Ferry (ⓦ tiomanferry.com) for a small fee; check the website for the latest schedules. Note that there is also an Tioman area

entry fee of RM25, payable when buying your ferry ticket. **By plane** *Tunamaya Resort* has a private eight-seater service from JB's Senai airport (1hr) and KL's Subang Airport; the flights can be booked over the phone or via their website (☎07 798 8108, ⓦcareluxuryhotels.com/tunamaya-tioman).

GETTING AROUND

On foot The best-connected stretch is on the west coast, between Tekek and Salang. A road runs from the *Berjaya* resort in the south, up through Tekek village and as far as the headland at the northern end of the bay, but it's an exposed and uninteresting walk – about 30min from the village to the headland. You're better off paying RM20 for a taxi from Tekek to the Marine Park Centre, from where steps lead over the headland to Air Batang. A narrow concrete path runs the length of the beach to the point where a jungle trail sets off to Penuba Bay, Monkey Beach and Salang. Other coastal trails include one that connects Genting with Paya, while you can walk across the island from Tekek to Juara (see p.307).

By bicycle Bicycle rental is a good option, but remember you'll have to carry the bike over the headlands at some point. The road to Juara is only for the resilient. Outlets in Tekek and Air Batang offer bikes from RM10/hr or RM30/day. **By 4WD** Only 4WD vehicles can safely drive the steep route between Tekek and Juara.

By boat The rented boats (known as water-taxis) that travel along the shore are very expensive by Malaysian standards, ranging from RM30 for the hop between ABC and Tekek up to RM150 between ABC and Juara. To save money you can join the Mersing ferry as it makes its scheduled stops, if there's room, although they will still charge you a fair bit (RM20–35/person).

INFORMATION

Banks and exchange Be sure to change money in Mersing before you head out to Tioman, where the exchange rates are lousy; the only ATM on Tioman is the Bank Simpanan Nasional in Tekek, opposite the airport.

Tourist information There is no official information office on Tioman, despite the fact that many agencies tout themselves as tourist information points – your best bet is to ask your hotel or guesthouse for information.

Tekek

The main settlement on Tioman, **TEKEK**, doesn't make a great first impression. The area around the airport, marina and public jetty has been rapidly developed, while coming from Air Batang you first pass a long stretch of deserted waterfront promenade. South of the marina, though, things start to get much better. Not only are there a handful of good resorts, but the beach is also attractive and has a dive shop as well as one of the island's best bars. Further south still is the high-end *Berjaya* resort.

Marine Park Centre

North of the main jetty, at the very end of the bay • Sat–Thurs 8am–1pm & 2–5pm, Fri 8am–12.15pm & 2.45–5pm • Free • ☎ 03 8886 1111

The hefty concrete jetty and dazzlingly blue roofs of the government-sponsored **Marine Park Centre** make it hard to miss. Set up to protect the island's coral and marine life, and to patrol the fishing in its waters, the centre also contains an aquarium and displays about marine conservation.

ARRIVAL AND INFORMATION   TEKEK

By plane and boat Whether you fly or come by boat, you're close enough to walk to most of the resorts within Tekek, although the *Berjaya* is too far and offers a transfer.

Services in and around the terminal complex next to the airstrip include an ATM, moneychangers, duty-free shops and an internet café.

ACCOMMODATION

Berjaya Tioman Resort Just south of Tekek ☎ 09 419 1000, ⓦ berjayahotel.com; map p.302. This village-sized complex at the end of Tekek Beach has a couple of great restaurants – including a gorgeous Thai place just

off the beach – plus two pools, tennis courts, and facilities for watersports, golf and jungle trekking. Some of the rooms are looking tired but a huge renovation programme has already begun and is due to finish by

5

ACCOMMODATION

ABC Chalet	3
Bamboo Hill Chalets	2
Berjaya Tioman Resort	15
Cheers	12
Coral Reef	13
Johan's	5
Mawar Beach Chalets	7
Mokhtar's Place	10
My Friend's Place	9
Nazri's II	4
Nazri's Place	11
Panuba Inn Resort	1
South Pacific	6
Swiss Cottage Beach Resort	14
YP Chalet	8

EATING

Warong Syahirah	1

DRINKING

B&J Beach Bar	2
Hallo Bar	1
Sunset Bar	3
Tioman Cabana	4

- - - Rough trail
= = Concrete path
===== Laterite road

**TEKEK &
AIR BATANG (ABC)**

2021; enquire about staying in one of the 40 recently refurbished rooms. 🛜 RM350

Cheers Tekek ☎013 931 1425; map left. Just a few hundred metres inland, this decent budget choice offers simple fan doubles aimed at backpackers, plus a/c rooms with hot showers giving onto a pleasant leafy garden with potted plants. Fish and meat barbecues can be rustled up upon request (RM35/person; minimum six people). Bike (RM10/hr) and motorbike (RM15/hr) rental, too. 🛜 Fan RM60, a/c RM120

Coral Reef Tekek ☎09 419 1868 or ☎013 357 8326, ✉info@coralreeftioman.com; map left. The crumbling fan rooms you walk past if coming from the main road are definitely worth a miss (overpriced and rather grotty), but the deluxe beachside rooms are a big step up, with decorative stone work on the walls, kettles, hot showers and hammocks slung between the trees just outside the rooms. 🛜 Garden doubles RM130, deluxe doubles RM220

★**Swiss Cottage Beach Resort** Tekek 🌐swiss -cottage-tioman.com; map left. Tekek's best all-round choice is a real winner – the clean and welcoming rooms feature tasteful individual furnishings, from pretty chests to sturdy wooden wardrobes. Fan-cooled bungalow rooms are in a shady beachside spot ensuring they don't get too warm, and the resort is located on a wonderful stretch of beach. The friendly, helpful owners can organize snorkelling trips, hikes to waterfalls and jungle tours. 🛜 Fan RM170, a/c RM250

EATING AND DRINKING

★**Tioman Cabana** Tekek Beach; map left. This quirky beach bar bursts with character, with its worn-out stools, mismatched wicker chairs, flags from the world over and a rusty anchor. It's a great spot to unwind over a drink or two, and the food's good too – including burgers (RM18) and local dishes including chicken fried rice (RM11) and curries (RM18). Daily 1.30pm–midnight.

Warong Syahirah Tekek village; map left. The cook at this friendly and popular roadside place fires up the barbecue at around 6pm, after which you'll find chicken, crab, squid, stingray and barracuda all on the menu (meal for two RM100). Daily 4.30–10.30pm.

Air Batang (ABC)

Despite its ever-increasing popularity, **AIR BATANG**, 2km north of Tekek from jetty to jetty, retains a sleepy charm and rivals Juara (which admittedly has a better beach) in its appeal for budget travellers. Larger than Salang or Juara, less developed than Tekek and well connected by boat services, Air Batang (or **ABC** as it's often called), is a happy medium as far as many visitors are concerned. What development there is has been sympathetically done and relatively low-key, and there's still a definite sense of community.

A jetty divides the bay roughly in half; the **beach** is better at the southern end of the bay, where there are fewer rocks, though the shallow northern end is safer for children. The cement path that runs the length of the beach is interrupted by little wooden bridges over streams and overhung with greenery; stretches are unlit at night. Between the guesthouses, a few small shops sell essentials such as shorts, T-shirts, sun cream and toiletries. Like the guesthouses they also arrange snorkelling trips and boat taxis.

A fifteen-minute **trail** leads over the headland to the north. After an initial scramble, it flattens out into an easy walk and ends up at **Panuba Bay**, a secluded cove that holds just one resort and a quiet little beach, and offers some of the best snorkelling on the island. From Panuba Bay, it's an hour's walk to **Monkey Beach** and then a further 45 minutes to Salang. Heading south instead from ABC, steps lead over the headland to **Tekek**.

ARRIVAL AND DEPARTURE   AIR BATANG (ABC)

By boat Ferries from the mainland stop off at Air Batang along with other major stops including Genting and Tekek.

There are also private taxi boats that connect the island's main beaches.

ACCOMMODATION

As you get off the boat, a helpful signpost indicates the numerous **places to stay** in the bay. All but the most basic A-frames have fans and their own bathrooms, and mosquito nets are usually provided. The pricier options should have hot showers. Some places charge significantly more at peak times, such as during school holidays.

ABC Chalet At the far northern end of the bay ☎ 013 922 0263, ⊚ abctioman.com; map opposite. A little quieter than most, due to its location, this is one of the area's best options, with chalets set in a garden. The cheapest are fair for the price, while the a/c doubles have great views, kettles and hot showers. ☞ Fan RM80, a/c RM160

★ **Bamboo Hill Chalets** On the northern headland of Air Batang ☎ 019 952 4392, ⊚ bamboohillchalets.com; map opposite. Six beautiful wooden chalets perch on the headland, all with wonderful sea views. All rooms are fan only, although the location means there's a nice breeze anyway. The cosy reception area has a book exchange. ☞ RM130

Johan's Just north of the jetty ☎ 09 419 1359, ⊚ johansresort.blogspot.com; map opposite. A pleasant spot with chalets dotted around a leafy slope offering fan and larger a/c doubles, plus a four-bed fan dorm nestled at the top of the hillside. They arrange snorkelling trips (RM95), as well as trips round the island (RM150). Dorm RM15, fan doubles RM60, a/c doubles RM90

Mawar Beach Chalets Just south of the jetty ☎ 013 9315 5695, ⊚ mawarbeach.weebly.com; map opposite. Simple chalets with smallish rooms and verandas; the cheapest use fans. The service is very friendly and the restaurant serves local dishes that are among the best in ABC. Fan doubles RM30, a/c doubles RM100

Mokhtar's Place South of the jetty ☎ 019 700 7541; map opposite. The rust-coloured chalets are clean and airy with little porches, although they face inwards, rather than out to sea. Staff can book buses on the mainland, snorkelling and fishing trips and water-taxis. ☞ RM60

My Friend's Place South of the jetty ☎ 019 419 1150; map opposite. A series of basic rooms lining a straggly

grassy area; the rooms for an additional RM15 are in better shape, and there's a stretch of beach just a stone's throw away. The occasional BBQs are stellar; ask the staff when the next one will be. ☞ Fan doubles RM50, a/c doubles RM130

Nazri's II Northern end of Air Batang ☎ 019 767 7496; map opposite. Owned by the same family as *Nazri's Place*, below, this outfit boasts cottages dotted around a pleasant garden area with swings and shaded by palm trees. ☞ Fan cottages RM75, a/c cottages RM150

Nazri's Place Southern end of the bay ☎ 016 362 3120 or ☎ 013 980 6072, ⊚ nazrisplace.net; map opposite. Clean a/c rooms in a series of red blocks that look onto a large courtyard. The rooms are some of the best on the beach, and often get booked up in advance. ☞ RM150

Panuba Inn Resort Panuba Bay ☎ 09 419 1424, ⊚ panubainnresort.com; map opposite. Set on stilts, these chalets and a dive shop enjoy fantastic views out to sea. This is the only accommodation at Panuba Bay, so unless you scramble over the unlit headland you have to eat in the run-of-the-mill restaurant every night. A water-taxi from ABC to the resort costs RM10 during the day. Attractive two-night packages including accommodation, meals, ferry tickets and snorkelling from RM415. ☞ RM115

South Pacific Close to the jetty ☎ 01 9708 5647; map opposite. Clean chalets with attached bathrooms and mozzie nets; those right on the beach are good value. There are also a few modern spacious chalets with hot showers and a/c; the beach just opposite is very rocky, though, so you're best off walking further south if you want to have a swim. ☞ Standard chalets RM50, a/c chalets RM120

YP Chalet South of the jetty ☎ 01 9419 1018; map

5

opposite. A basic place on this part of the island, with simple fan rooms that are very worn around the edges. It's best to scope out some of the other places first, but if you're on a very tight budget *YP* may be the answer, and it's a popular choice for scuba divers 🛜 **RM50**

EATING, DRINKING AND NIGHTLIFE

Most chalets have their own, generally unadventurous, **restaurants**, open to non-residents. Menus tend to reflect Western tastes and feature a lot of fish. Air Batang is the only place on the island with significant **nightlife**; there are a handful of laidback beach bars open until the early hours. Most have a **happy hour**, usually from around 5–7pm.

B&J Beach Bar Opposite B&J Diving Centre; map p.302. A real diver hangout, which generally kicks off at about 7pm when divers have returned to shore, ready to share their underwater tales. A nice little spot to socialize over a beer (RM7) and meet other travellers. Daily 6pm–midnight.
Hallo Bar Northern end of Air Batang; map p.302. Lively beach bar where you can enjoy drinks in one of the breezy

cabañas on stilts that stretch out into the sea. Three beers cost RM12 during happy hour. Daily 6pm–late.
★ **Sunset Bar** Southern end of the beach; map p.302. The most popular bar on the beach, this laidback place is a great spot for a sundowner. They shake up excellent mojitos (RM10) and offer tasty pizzas (RM22), too. Daily 6pm–late.

Salang and around

Just over 4km north of Air Batang, **SALANG** is a smaller bay with a pretty stretch of beach at its southern end by the jetty. The bay has seen a lot of development, but it still retains its own charm. The southern end of the beach is the more scenic; swimming can be an ordeal at the northern end due to the sharp rocks and coral. Just off the southern headland a small island, **Soyak**, has a pretty reef for snorkelling. There are also several dive shops.

A rough trail takes you over the headland to the south for the 45-minute scramble to **Monkey Bay**. There are few monkeys around these days, but the well-hidden cove is more than adequate compensation. Walkers can carry on to **Panuba Bay** (which will take about 1hr) and Air Batang.

ARRIVAL AND DEPARTURE

SALANG

By boat Ferries from the mainland stop off at Salang, along with other major stops including Genting and Tekek,

and is also served by served by private taxi boats (as is Monkey Bay).

ACCOMMODATION

Ella's Place Northern end of the bay ☎ 09 419 5004; map below. This place brims with character and oozes a

mellow vibe, with its chaos of potted plants, dangling buoys, small fishpond, and hammocks slung between palm trees. The little restaurant serves a handful of dishes for breakfast, including omelettes and pancakes (both RM5). Fan rooms are pretty simple, while the larger a/c rooms all sleep three. 🛜 Fan doubles **RM80**, a/c triples **RM90**
Puteri Salang Inn Set back at the southern end of the beach ☎ 01 7715 1706; map left. Offers seventeen pretty chalets, mostly A-frames, are set around a carefully landscaped garden with hammocks – the most peaceful spot in Salang. The cheaper rooms are pretty simple, but the friendly staff make up for it, and there's all-day tea and coffee, and a book exchange. 🛜 Fan doubles **RM50**, a/c doubles **RM120**
Salang Pusaka Resort ☎ 09 419 5034, 🌐 salangpusakaresorttioman.blogspot.my; map left. Set back from the beach, most of the

■ ACCOMMODATION	
Ella's Place	1
Puteri Salang Inn	3
Salang Pusaka Resort	2
Salang Sayang Resort	4

● EATING	
Mini White House Café	1
Salang Dreams	2

SALANG

Dive Asia
Salang Beach Mini Market
Police
B&J Diving Centre
Salang Complex
Azmi Dive
Monkey Beach

0   200
metres

chalets here give onto a spacious verdant garden. All rooms have a/c, and the basic rooms are pretty good value overall – some are in better shape than others, so it's wise to look at a few before settling in. 🛜 Basic a/c doubles RM140, standard a/c doubles RM180, family suites RM240

Salang Sayang Resort Southern end of the beach 📞 09 419 5020, 🌐 salangsayangresorts.webs.com;

map opposite. At the southern end of the beach, this place offers a range of accommodation, from garden and seafront fan rooms to larger a/c hillside chalets on "banana hill", from where there are lovely views over the bay. The attached restaurant serves a range of Malay dishes, and a nightly BBQ kicks off at 7pm. There are deckchairs for guests' use, too (RM10 for non-guests). 🛜 Fan doubles RM100, a/c doubles RM120

EATING AND DRINKING

Mini White House Café 📞 019 729 9563; map opposite. Sizzling prawns and squid form the basis of the nightly seafood BBQ (RM70 for two) at this laidback restaurant – you'll probably smell the grilled seafood as you make your way up the beach. Their *tom yam* soup (RM10) is also a bestseller. Daily 6–10.30pm.

Salang Dreams Close to the jetty 📞 019 790 0655; map opposite. The first place you see as you walk down the jetty, this laidback restaurant serves a range of Malay and Western dishes that are among the best on Salang, from local curries (RM8) to burgers and fries (RM15). Mon–Thurs & Sun 9am–5pm & 7–11pm, Fri 9am–noon & 3–11pm.

Paya

Just 5km south of Tekek, the pristine stretch of beach in **PAYA**, only accessible by private boat transfer from Genting, has been developed but still seems peaceful when compared to Genting a little further south. **Jungle walks** are worth exploring here, where the island's greenery is at its most lush. The thirty-minute trail north to Bunut ends up at a fantastic deserted beach. From here it's a hot 45-minute walk through the golf course to the *Berjaya Tioman Beach Resort* and a further half-hour to Tekek.

ACCOMMODATION   PAYA

Melina Beach Resort Between Paya and Genting 📞 09 419 7080, 🌐 melinabeachresort.com; map p.300. Appealing resort with its own beach, but accessible on foot from both Paya and Genting, which gives you more eating options. There's a good range of rooms, from the cheapest garden-view rooms with bunks (and sleeping four) to suites overlooking the forest canopy. 🛜 Garden-view rooms RM395, beachfront chalets RM650

Paya Beach Resort Northern end of Paya Bay 📞 07 799 1432, 🌐 payabeach.com; map p.300. Paya's best-value accommodation, with comfortable red-roofed chalets plus a restaurant, dive shop, swimming pool and spa. There's good snorkelling just in front of the resort, and staff can arrange excursions further afield, such as canoeing, trekking and adventure safaris. Two-night minimum stay in peak season. 🛜 RM310

Genting

Usually the first stop for boats from the mainland, **GENTING** has been very heavily developed, especially around the jetty. Its beach is not as appealing as its neighbours', and as a result doesn't attract as many travellers – sadly it's often littered especially by the jetty, although there's a nice stretch to the north by *Dumba Bay Resort*, and towards the southern end too. On the plus side, there are several dive shops and the beach is usually very quiet during the week.

ARRIVAL AND DEPARTURE   GENTING

By boat Genting is the first port of call for ferries from Mersing; from here, private water-taxis take passengers to other beaches around the island.

ACCOMMODATION AND EATING

Dumba Bay Resort 📞 09 419 7008 or 📞 019 764 2792, 🌐 dumbabayresort.com. This laidback place offers basic sea-facing chalets, although they are just on the main pathway, which means they can get quite noisy at night as

mopeds scoot past. The draw is the pleasant stretch of beach with picnic tables and the odd hammock. Nightly fish and seafood BBQs, too. 🛜 RM150

★**Impiana Inn** 📞 09 419 7705, 🌐 impianinn.com.

5

Highly popular with divers, and for good reason: the rooms are the best in Genting and the common areas are well kept. The deluxe rooms with TV are worth the extra RM20 – they are attractively furnished with sturdy wooden beds and the slightly aging bathrooms are kept nice and clean. A couple of attractive wooden garden pavilions make a pleasant spot to unwind and read a book. 🛜 RM160

Sun Beach Resort ☎ 09 419 7069, �🌐 sunbeachresort .com.my. Genting's widest range of rooms: the deluxe are mostly on the hillside; the cheaper ones on the beach. Overall, they are relatively clean, but take a look before deciding. 🛜 Fan-cooled budget chalets RM315, standard rooms RM345, deluxe rooms RM365

DRINKING

Bar Rumah Northern end of the beach. A surprisingly good little beach bar, serving beer and cocktails from a shack on the main path. There are chairs, hammocks and even a table (with attached chairs) suspended from a palm tree. Daily 6pm–late.

South of Genting

The area **south of Genting** is home to a number of upmarket resorts on private stretches of beach, which tend to be busiest at the weekend and on holidays and are reachable only by private boat transfer from Genting. The exception is **Nipah**, which has a couple of laid-back places and is accessible by water-taxi from Genting.

Nipah

There's no jetty, so access is by water-taxi from Genting (RM30)

Located on the southwest coast, **NIPAH** is the closest you'll get to an idyllic yet affordable backpacker beach hideaway on the island. There is good **snorkelling** around a nearby islet, and although there's no proper dive shop, the local accommodation options can make arrangements (expect to pay around RM150 for two dives, plus RM90 for equipment rental). They also offer kayak rental and jungle trekking. Don't turn up at Nipah without having first made a booking.

Mukut

Private taxi boats take passengers to Mukut from different points around Tioman

Lying in the shadow of granite outcrops, the ramshackle little fishing village of **MUKUT** is shrouded by dense forest. It's a peaceful and friendly spot to unwind, with a fine beach, though note that locals are unused to Western sunbathing habits and frown upon the open consumption of alcohol.

One good reason to stay here is to hike up **Bukit Nenek Semukut**, whose twin peaks are known as the "dragon's horns"; guides can be arranged at *Tanjung Inn Adventure* (RM80/person).

ACCOMMODATION   SOUTH OF GENTING

NIPAH AND AROUND

★ **Bagus Place** South of Nipah ☎ 03 4270 1502, �🌐 bagusplace.com; map p.300. This peaceful resort offers accommodation in unique chalets – the *Tree House* features an airy living space built around a sturdy tree trunk, while the *Boat House* offers accommodation in a mock boat with a sun deck. Popular with couples and honeymooners. 🛜 Full board for two RM1010

★ **Japamala Resort & Spa** On its own beach just north of Nipah ☎ 07 419 7777, �🌐 japamalaresorts .com; map p.300. This eco-luxe resort offers thirteen Malay village-style villas and chalets tucked away amid lush tropical rainforest. No trees were felled in building the resort – the villas were built with reclaimed timber around their natural landscape. 🛜 RM750

NipahNema Chalets Nipah ☎ 010 781 1036, �🌐 nipahnema.com; map p.300. Welcoming, eco-friendly place offering five huts made from wood and bamboo in a lush tropical setting a short walk from the beach; rooms are en suite and all have balconies with hammocks. There's a small restaurant and bar serving great international cuisine, as well as nightly riverside BBQs and beach campfires. 🛜 RM120

Tunamaya Resort On its own stretch of beach south of Nipah ☎ 07 798 8108, ⌨ careluxuryhotels.com/ tunamaya-tioman; map p.300. This pleasant upmarket resort, with wonderful views of the twin peaks, features more than fifty villas set on both sides of a small leafy stream that is atmospherically lit up in the evenings. The well-appointed rooms feature modern amenities and there's an inviting swimming pool and spa. The restaurant serves great Asian dishes, with weekend seafood BBQs. The resort's private plane flies to and from Johor Bahru and Kuala Lumpur (see p.301). 🌐 **RM930**

MUKUT AND AROUND

Minang Cove Standing alone on the southern end of the island, west of Mukut ☎ 07 799 7372; map p.300.

The rooms at this delightful resort are not the classiest around, but the location and service raise it well above the average. Excellent snorkelling, and they also arrange round-island trips. 🌐 Half-board for two **RM530**

Tanjung Inn Adventure At the far western end of Mukut Cove ☎ 013 293 1619; map p.300. Overlooking a small patch of beach, this place feels semi-abandoned unless a group of hikers is staying – but once you find manager Uncle Sam, you'll receive a warm welcome. Rooms are simple, with cold showers. 🌐 **RM60**

Juara

With Tioman's western shore now extensively developed, those eager for a hideaway often head for **JUARA**. The only east coast settlement, it's a quiet and peaceful kampung with two excellent beaches – **Juara Beach**, aka **Barok Beach**, where you arrive from Tekek, and Mentawak Beach just south. The sand is cleaner and less crowded than on the other side of the island, and Juara is altogether more laidback – even than Air Batang.

The beaches here do, however, have a reputation for harbouring **sandflies** (see box, p.308), so take what precautions you can. The bay, facing out to the open sea, is also susceptible to bad weather. The constant sea breeze keeps the water choppy; it attracts **surfers** from November to March, with 3m-plus waves in February. The beach break is good for beginners, while more experienced surfers favour the point at the southern end of Mentawak.

A popular, clearly marked 45-minute walk leads from the south beach to a small **waterfall** with a big freshwater pond that's good for swimming. Someone from the *Beach Shack* will take you for RM15 per person.

Juara Turtle Project

Mentawak Beach • Tours (15– 30min) daily 10am–5pm • Minimum donation RM10 • ☎ 09 419 3244, 🌐 juaraturtleproject.com

The southern beach is home to the **Juara Turtle Project**, whose work takes several forms. They collect eggs from the eastern beaches, then hatch and release turtles, and also campaign for greater protection, with a small Visitor Centre to raise awareness. Volunteers are welcome to get involved for a payment of RM120 per day for a minimum of four days, which includes accommodation, breakfast and lunch.

ARRIVAL AND INFORMATION
JUARA

By road A road starting just before the *Berjaya Tioman Beach, Golf & Spa Resort* (see p.301) has given 4WD vehicles easy access to Juara, costing RM150/car or RM40/person for four people for the 30min journey (you'll need to bargain hard). If you've booked a place to stay, the hotel staff will probably be able to organize transport for you from Tekek, which is likely to work out cheaper than sorting it yourself. Regular cars will struggle with the steep roads, but it's theoretically possible by motorbike or mountain bike (don't undertake either lightly). Several guesthouses in Juara can arrange transport back to Tekek.

On foot You can also reach Juara on foot through the jungle. The steep trek from Tekek takes about 2hr 30min, not counting rest stops, and is definitely not

JUARA

Cafés & Mini-Mart
Jetty
Mini Market
Scuba Amigo

N

0   200
metres

ACCOMMODATION

1511 Coconut Grove	8
Beach Shack	7
Bushman Square Chalets	6
Juara Beach	2
Mutiara	4
Rainbow Chalets	5
Riverview	1
Santai Bistro & Chalet	3

▼ **7** (50m), South Bay, **8** (750m) & Juara Turtle Project (900m)

5

recommended if you have luggage. Don't walk the less appealing vehicle road, and carry plenty of water. Starting as a concrete path a 5min walk away from the airstrip, the trail soon becomes rocky, running uphill with intermittent sections of concrete steps. After an hour or so you reach the highest point, and the route then tapers off into a smooth, downhill path, eventually joining the main road. There's a waterfall just off the main road that's a good spot for a refreshing dip; it's easy to miss – keep your eyes peeled for the little wooden hut on your right. Look carefully and you will see the words "waterfall" lightly inscribed on the side of the hut. It's just a couple of minutes' walk from there.

Information desk An unofficial information desk (daily 9am–6pm) by the jetty rents out motorbikes (RM30/day) and snorkelling equipment (RM10/day for mask and snorkel, RM10 for fins), and arranges full-day boat tours from RM100.

ACCOMMODATION AND EATING

★**1511 Coconut Grove** Mentawak Beach ☏ 010 766 4089; map p.307. This pleasant resort offers inviting chalets just a short walk from the beach; while along the seafront a couple of viewing towers have recently been converted into duplex rooms (RM700). Rates include breakfast and, unusually for the island, there's wi-fi throughout. 📶 **RM350**

★**Beach Shack** Mentawak Beach ☏ 012 696 1093, ✉ izanhussain2@yahoo.com; map p.307. Ozzie/Malay-run place with a relaxed backpacker vibe, offering accommodation in simple colourful A-frame chalets along the beach; there's also an a/c deluxe room, made of recycled timber, with great sea views, plus a café and book exchange. 📶 A-frame chalets **RM50**, a/c sea-view room. Open all year. **RM150**

Bushman Square Chalets End of the northern bay ☏ 09 419 3109 or ☏ 013 781 0005, ✉ matbushman @hotmail.com; map p.307. This friendly and easy-going option offers a handful of simple but gorgeous chalets at the northern end of the beach; all are clean, with hot water. There are a couple of a/c rooms, and meals can be cooked upon request. 📶 Fan doubles **RM60**, a/c doubles **RM85**

Juara Beach Close to the jetty ☏ 09 419 3188 or ☏ 013 771 1137; map p.307. This Chinese-run place is a good choice if you're looking for a/c and hot showers, and there's also an excellent Chinese restaurant. Spacious rooms, set around a verdant garden, all feature TV and fridge, and rates include breakfast. 📶 Standard doubles **RM120**, deluxe doubles **RM170**

Mutiara Near the jetty ☏ 09 419 3161, 🌐 juaramutiararesort.com; map p.307. Some of the rooms here are set on the beach, while others look onto a well-kept garden with palm trees and benches outside each room. There's a mini-market on-site and they can arrange fishing trips. Open all year. 📶 Fan doubles **RM90**, a/c doubles **RM160**

Rainbow Chalets South of the jetty ☏ 012 989 8572 or ☏ 09 419 3140, ✉ rainbow.chalets@ymail.com; map p.307. Brightly painted in pastel shades, these chalets are on a pleasant stretch of beach, with their own bathrooms and mosquito nets. There are basic fan rooms on offer as well as more spacious a/c doubles with hot showers. They can organize a taxi service from Tekek from RM30/person (RM40 after 6pm). 📶 Fan doubles **RM60**, a/c doubles **RM100**

Riverview North end of the bay ☏ 09 419 3168, 🌐 tioman-riverview.com; map p.307. Run by a friendly English woman, Julie, this place offers three types of rooms; the breezy and well-kept Indonesian kampung-style huts facing the river are a great choice, as are the sea-view chalets. The basic huts, the same price as the river views, are a bit dated and run-down. All rooms have fan and cold water only; there's a billiards table in the communal area. Kayak rental RM30/day. 📶 Small chalets **RM120**, large chalets **RM150**

Santai Bistro & Chalet Near the jetty ☏ 013 333 3670; map p.307. This is the first place you see when arriving by car from Tekek, and it provides a very decent option with clean and pleasant rooms (all with a/c and hot water) decorated with more care than usual for Tioman, and named after different types of fish and seafood. Some face the beach, while others open onto a garden area, and there's a good restaurant serving Malay dishes. 📶 **RM150**

SANDFLIES

Sandflies can be a real problem throughout the Seribuat Archipelago, including on Tioman Island. These little pests, looking like tiny fruit flies with black bodies and white wings, suck blood and cause an extremely itchy lump, which may become a nasty blister if scratched. The effectiveness of various treatments and deterrents is much debated; the general feeling is that, short of dousing yourself all over with insect repellent, covering up completely or hiding out in the sea all day long, there's not much you can do. You may find that Tiger Balm, available at any pharmacy, can reduce the maddening itch and help you sleep. If you are able to take them, antihistamines also provide some relief.

Seribuat Archipelago: the other islands

Tioman Island may be the best known and most visited of the 64 volcanic islands in the **SERIBUAT ARCHIPELAGO**, but a handful of other accessible islands hold beaches and opportunities for seclusion that outstrip those of their larger rival. For archetypal azure waters and table-salt sand, three in particular stand out: **Sibu**, **Besar** and **Rawa**. There are, however, a few resorts on other islands; Aur, for example, is popular among Singapore-based scuba divers. The tourist office in Mersing (see p.298) can advise on the various options. Wi-Fi is supplied at most accommodation; however, the signal is unreliable, even in upmarket places, especially when the weather is poor.

Sibu Island

Closest to the mainland, accessible from the village of Tanjung Leman, 30km south of Mersing, **SIBU ISLAND** is actually a cluster of four islands that are collectively the most popular after Tioman. Most resorts are on **Sibu Besar**, which, although not as scenically interesting as some of its neighbours, does have butterflies and huge monitor lizards. The sand here is yellower and the current more turbulent than at some others; most of the coves have good diving spots with offshore coral.

Besar Island

Long, narrow **BESAR ISLAND**, (not to be confused with the island of the same name off Melaka) is about 13km from Mersing and measures 4km by 1km. It holds several resorts and sets of chalets, but you're likely to have the place pretty much to yourself outside weekends and public holidays.

Rawa Island

The tiny island of **RAWA ISLAND**, just 16km (a thirty-minute boat ride) from Mersing, holds a glorious stretch of fine, sugary-sanded beach. The only sure way to get there is by resort-owned speedboat, booked in advance, but if you're lucky then the Tioman-bound ferry might make a stop (on request).

Tengah Island

Approximately 16km from Mersing, **TENGAH ISLAND** has a 3km circumference with eight powdery white sand beaches. The island was the setting for Swedish reality TV show *Expedition Robinson*, the predecessor of the world-famous *Survivor* series. The private island is today home to only one resort.

ARRIVAL AND DEPARTURE — SERIBUAT ARCHIPELAGO: THE OTHER ISLANDS

By resort transfer People staying on the islands normally have to take a boat from Mersing supplied by the resort they are staying at. Note that Sibu is reached by resort boats from Tanjung Leman, a tiny coastal village 30km south of Mersing.

ACCOMMODATION AND EATING

Except where noted, resorts operate on package deals, and the prices given in the reviews below are for two people for one night; subsequent nights may be cheaper. All resorts offer watersports facilities, and most have dive shops, too.

SIBU ISLAND

Rimba Beach Resort ☎ 01 2710 6855, ⟨w⟩ resortmalaysia. com. Friendly resort and spa with rustic, welcoming rooms on a lovely stretch of beach dotted with palm trees. There's an unspoilt reef just by the shore, which means you'll spot plenty of fish as you snorkel or dive. The tasty food is all home-made. Call ahead to book transfers from Singapore (RM160 return). ⟨wifi⟩ **RM600**

5

Sea Gypsy Village Resort East coast ☎ 019 753 4250, ⓦ siburesort.com. Set in well-manicured grounds in a 5-acre jungle clearing, this family-friendly resort offers accommodation in traditional Malay-style wooden chalets and A-frames (RM220); all are sea facing and feature private verandas. There are complimentary kids' clubs (6–10pm) and buckets of kids' activities throughout the day (extra charge), as well as plenty of activities including sailing. 📶 <u>RM260</u>

BESAR ISLAND

Aseania Island Resort Middle of the bay, west-facing beach ☎ 07 797 0057, ⓦ aseaniapulaubesar.com. Set on an appealing stretch of sand, with decent chalets, a swimming pool and good service – a great place to relax. 📶 Full board per couple <u>RM570</u>

★**Mirage Island Resort** Just south of the jetty, west-facing beach ☎ 019 789 6355, ⓦ mirageislandresort.com.my. This is a great choice for its friendly service, well-appointed chalets and reasonable prices. Cheaper rooms are A-frames, but still clean and comfortable. Rates include breakfast; all-inclusive

packages are also available. 📶 Three-day package for a couple in an A-frame with speed boat transfer <u>RM445</u>

RAWA ISLAND

Rawa Island Resort West-facing beach ☎ 07 799 1204, ⓦ rawaislandresort.com. Sumptuous resort and spa with wooden chalets equipped with a/c and hot showers, and there's kayaking, snorkelling and scuba diving. Rates include boat transfers, and decrease to RM1050 after the first night. 📶 Full board per couple <u>RM1250</u>

TENGAH ISLAND

Batu Batu ☎ 017 755 2813, ⓦ batubatu.com.my. This luxurious private island resort, built in the style of a kampung village, comprises 22 villas sprinkled around lush grounds. Being the only resort means that guests have all the island's beaches to themselves – it's a wonderful spot to relax, and the resort welcomes families with young children – the Turtle Watch Camp with be especially popular. There are one or two scheduled boat trips to the resort each day. 📶 Full board per couple <u>RM1300</u>

Endau Rompin National Park

One of the few remaining areas of lowland tropical rainforest left in Peninsular Malaysia, the **ENDAU ROMPIN NATIONAL PARK** covers 870 square kilometres. Despite its rich **flora and fauna**, prized by conservationists, the area has only been adequately protected from logging since 1989. There's plenty on offer for nature lovers, from gentle **trekking** to more strenuous **mountain climbing** and **rafting**; for the moment, its trails remain refreshingly untrampled.

Surrounding the headwaters of the lengthy Endau River, and sitting astride the Johor–Pahang state border, the region was shaped by volcanic eruptions more than 150 million years ago. The force of the explosions sent up huge clouds of ash, creating the quartz crystal ignimbrite that's still very much in evidence along the park's trails and rivers, its glassy shards glinting in the light. Endau Rompin's steeply sloped mountains level out into sandstone plateaus, and the park is watered by three **river systems** based around the main tributaries of the Marong, Jasin and Endau rivers, reaching out to the south and east.

Visiting the park

As it can be hard to arrange transport, most people come on one- or two-night **tours**, although day-trips can be organized from Mersing. The **best time** to visit is between March and October, while the paths are dry and the rivers calm. Take loose-fitting, lightweight cotton clothing that dries quickly – even in the dry season you're bound to get wet from crossing rivers – and helps to protect you from scratches and bites. Waterproofs will come in handy, and you'll need tons of insect repellent.

ARRIVAL AND DEPARTURE   ENDAU ROMPIN NATIONAL PARK

ENTRY POINTS

The park has three entry points: one from the west at Selai via Bekok (Johor), and two from the east, at Kuala Kinchin via Kuala Rompin (Pahang) and Kampung Peta

via Kahang (Johor). The best is Kampung Peta, where more activities are available; the least interesting, Kuala Kinchin, is often used for one-night tours, but is not recommended as you don't get enough time to get into the jungle proper. The useful Tourism Johor (☎07 922 2875, ⓦtourism.johor.my) office is at GPS coordinates Latitude 2.420260, Longitude 103.2611191, and would be a good place to start your planning.

ON TOURS

While it is possible, if tricky, to visit under your own steam, most visitors come on tours that include transport. Mersing (see p.297) is the best place to approach from the east; ask agents in KL for the western Selai entry. Tour Malaysia (☎019 336 6679, ⓦtourmalaysia.com.my) charges RM900 for two people for a one-night trip staying in Merekek, which includes all fees, transport to and from the park office near Bekok (2.5hr from Mersing) and accommodation.

ARRIVING INDEPENDENTLY

Kampung Peta Approaching from the south on the North–South Expressway, take the Ayer Hitam exit and continue straight through Kluang to Kahang town (1hr from Mersing); the park's administrative office is located here, at 11 Tingkat Bawah, Jalan Bawal 1 (☎07 788 2812), where you'll have to register and pay the RM20 entrance fee – given 48 hours' notice, they can help organize 4WD transport into the park. From here continue 5km east, turn north at the park sign and follow logging tracks for 48km (2hr; 4WD is strongly advised) until you reach the Visitor's Complex at Kampung Peta (daily 8am–5pm, registration ends 3pm). There are fan dorms (RM25) and chalets (RM90) here. A licensed guide will cost RM250/day. You can also catch a boat (return trip RM150/boat, or RM25/person – minimum five) to Kuala Jasin, where there are basic A-frame chalets.

Kuala Kinchin From Kuala Rompin in Pahang, a road runs through paddy fields 20km to Selandang; continue another 15km to Kuala Kinchin (gate open 9am–5pm), on the park boundary. Although a 4WD is not required, there's no public transport; a taxi to the park entrance from Kuala Rompin costs RM150. Contact the Forestry Department in Kuala Rompin (☎09 414 5204, ⓦforestry.gov.my).

Selai Catch a train to Bekok from JB Sentral, then rent a 4WD to get to the park entrance. By road from the west, exit the North–South Expressway at Yong Peng and head for Chaah in Segamat (20min). After Chaah, follow signs for Bekok (15min) then Sungai Bantang (another 7km). Go past the Sungai Bantang turn-off and carry on for 20km, through an oil-palm estate and past several resettled Orang Asli villages. There is a Visitor Centre at Selai (daily 8am–5pm; ☎07 922 2875).

Sarawak

PROBOSCIS MONKEY, BAKO NATIONAL PARK

Sarawak

6

With its beguiling tribal cultures and jungled highlands, Sarawak would seem to epitomize what Borneo is all about. By far the largest state in Malaysia, it packs in a host of national parks that showcase everything from coastal swamp forest to vast cave systems, and help preserve some of the world's richest and most diverse ecosystems. There are numerous opportunities for short or extended treks both inside and outside these protected areas, and it's also possible to visit remote longhouse communities, some of which can only be reached by venturing far upriver.

For all its attractions, however, Sarawak is not quite the paradise it might seem on paper. The state encapsulates the bitter dichotomy between development and conservation more clearly than anywhere else in Malaysia. Many of its forests have been degraded by **logging** or cleared for oil palm, putting wildlife and the traditional lifestyles of tribal communities under severe pressure. The state government has repeatedly won electoral mandates for its policies, but critics complain it has opened up Sarawak's resources to corporate exploitation in a way that's at best not transparent and at worst mired in corruption. While much of this may have little practical impact on visitors as they travel through, it's good to be aware that the changes you will see throughout the state have a subtext in the ongoing struggle for Sarawak's soul (see p.580).

The lie of the land is complex on many levels, not least **demographically**. Malays and Chinese each make up almost a quarter of Sarawak's almost two and a half million people, but indigenous tribal peoples account for nearly half that figure. They're sometimes subdivided under three broad headings, though it's nowadays much more common to refer to the tribes by name. The largest tribe by far, the **Iban**, constitute nearly thirty percent of Sarawak's population. They, along with the Muslim **Melanau** and other tribes, comprise the so-called **Sea Dyaks**, a slightly odd name given that these groups historically lived along river valleys. Then there are the **Land Dyaks**, who live up in the hills; chief among them are the **Bidayuh** of southwestern Sarawak, representing almost a tenth of the population. Finally, the **Orang Ulu** include disparate groups of the northern interior such as the **Berawan**, **Kenyah**, **Kelabit**, **Kayan** and the traditionally nomadic **Penan**. They're grouped together in that they live in the "ulu" or upriver regions of this part of the state.

While this cultural mosaic is a huge highlight of Sarawak, social and economic change, along with widespread conversion to **Christianity**, mean that the old ways are fast dying out. Classic multidoored **longhouses** do survive and can be superb places to

Highlights

❶ Kuching One of Malaysia's most endearingly chilled-out cities, with a pretty waterfront, reasonable museums and great food. **See p.321**

❷ Santubong Peninsula Lovely beaches hosting resort hotels and an impressive folk museum, all beneath the slopes of Mount Santubong. **See p.335**

❸ Bako National Park This beautiful reserve has good trekking and sublime sea views and is home to proboscis monkeys. **See p.339**

❹ Tanjung Datu National Park Little-visited national park on the Indonesian border featuring jungles and beaches, with

homestays available at nearby Malay kampungs. **See p.344**

❺ Niah National Park The superb caves here are not only a natural wonder, easily explored on foot, but also a workplace for men collecting edible swiftlet nests. **See p.368**

❻ Gunung Mulu National Park Sarawak's top attraction, with astonishing caves and a popular three-day trek to see the shard-like Pinnacles. **See p.372**

❼ Kelabit Highlands Trek to remote communities dotted around this cool upland backwater. **See p.378**

HIGHLIGHTS ARE MARKED ON THE MAP ON P.316

visit, and some peoples do still subsist semi-nomadically in the forest, but you'd be hard-pushed to find any Orang Ulu aged under fifty still sporting, say, the once-prized distended earlobes that previous generations developed by wearing heavy earrings. Meanwhile, there's no shortage of indigenous people pursuing careers in Sarawak's cities, and the future of indigenous languages appears under threat as Malay and English dominate the majority of state-run education.

AROUND KUCHING

HIGHLIGHTS

1 Kuching
2 Santubong Peninsula
3 Bako National Park
4 Tanjung Datu National Park
5 Niah National Park
6 Gunung Mulu National Park
7 Kelabit Highlands

For visitors, the most popular attractions are concentrated at either end of the state. In the southwest, **Kuching**, the understated, attractive capital, makes a perfect base to explore the superb **Bako National Park**, with its wild shoreline of mangrove swamp and hinterland of *kerangas* bush teeming with proboscis monkeys. The Kuching area also packs in lesser national parks, an **orang-utan** sanctuary and substantial **caves**. Although Sarawak is not noted for its **beaches**, there are beautiful ones in Bako and decent options nearer Kuching

6

at the family-friendly resorts of Santubong. A handful of **longhouses** are also worth visiting, notably south of Kuching at **Batang Ai** and around **Sibu.**

In terms of pulling power, Bako is exceeded only by **Gunung Mulu National Park** ("Mulu" to locals) in the far northeast. Most tourists fly in, either making the short hop from nearby **Miri**, Sarawak's second city, or direct from Kuching, to trek to the park's limestone Pinnacles and see its extraordinary caves. Miri itself, though a bland affair that thrives on the proceeds of Sarawak's oil and gas industry, has good accommodation and is the hub for Twin Otter flights to interior settlements, most notably **Bario** and **Ba'Kelalan** in the **Kelabit Highlands**. Here, close to the Indonesian border, you can undertake extended treks through jungled and mountainous terrain, overnighting in Kelabit villages. Other Twin Otter flights head to settlements in the upper reaches of the **Baram** river system, from where it's possible to reach isolated **Penan villages** offering homestays and yet more treks. Another major draw, visitable on a day-trip from Miri, is **Niah National Park**, its extensive caves a site of major archeological significance as well as a centre for the harvesting of swiftlet nests and bat guano.

Visitors who overland between Kuching and Miri tend to breeze through central Sarawak, but the region is worth considering for the state's most accessible river journey – the popular route along the **Batang Rejang**. The boat ride, beginning at the city of **Sibu**, is its own reward for making it up to nondescript Rejang towns such as **Kapit** and **Belaga**, though it's possible to arrange longhouse trips from either. Also noteworthy in this region is **Bintulu**, a coastal oil town like Miri that's conveniently placed for the beachside forests of **Similajau National Park**.

Brief history

Cave-dwelling **hunter-gatherers** were living in Sarawak forty thousand years ago. Their isolation ended when the first trading boats arrived from Sumatra and Java around 3000 BC, exchanging cloth and pottery for jungle produce. By the thirteenth century Chinese merchants were dominant, bartering beads and porcelain with the coastal Melanau people for bezoar stones (from the gall bladders of monkeys) and birds' nests, both considered aphrodisiacs. In time, the traders were forced to deal with the rising power of the Malay sultans including the Sultan of Brunei. Meanwhile, Sarawak was attracting interest from Europe; the Dutch and English established short-lived trading posts near Kuching in the seventeenth century, to obtain pepper and other spices.

With the decline of the Brunei sultanate, civil war erupted early in the eighteenth century. Local rulers feuded, while piracy threatened to destroy what was left of the trade in spices, animals and minerals. In addition, the indigenous groups' predilection

---

SARAWAK PLACE NAMES

As you travel through Sarawak, you'll notice certain terms cropping up repeatedly in the names of places, longhouses and other features. You'll seldom encounter them elsewhere in Malaysia, so it pays to know what they mean:

Batang "Trunk" or "strip"; used before a river name, it denotes that the river is the central member of a system of rivers.

Long "Confluence"; used in town names in the same way as the Malay "Kuala".

Nanga "Longhouse" in Iban; many longhouses are named "Nanga" followed by the name of the river they are next to.

Pa or **Pa'** In the Kelabit Highlands – denotes a village.

Rumah "House" in Malay; some longhouses are named "Rumah" followed by the name of the headman (if there's a change of headman, the longhouse name follows suit).

Ulu From the Malay *hulu*, meaning "upriver"; when used before the name of a river, it indicates the region surrounding the headwaters of that river – for example, the Ulu Ai is the upriver part of the Ai River and its tributaries there.

for **head-hunting** had led to a number of deaths among the traders and the sultan's officials, and violent territorial confrontations between powerful tribes were increasing.

The White Rajahs

Just when matters were at their most explosive, the Englishman **James Brooke** took an interest in the area. A former soldier, he helped the Sultan of Brunei quell a rebellion by miners and, as a reward, demanded sovereignty over the area around Kuching. The weakened sultan had little choice but to relinquish control of the awkward territory and in 1841 James Brooke was installed as the first White Rajah of Sarawak. He had essentially created a new kingdom, not formally part of the British Empire.

Brooke built a network of small **forts** – many are now museums – to repel pirates or tribal warring parties. He also sent officials into the malarial swamps and mountainous interior to make contact with the Orang Ulu. But his administration was not without its troubles. In one incident his men killed dozens of marauding tribesmen, while in 1857 Hakka Chinese **gold-miners**, based in Bau near Kuching, retaliated against his attempts to eliminate their trade in opium and suppress their secret societies. When they attacked Kuching, Brooke got away by the skin of his teeth. His nephew, **Charles Brooke**, assembled a massive force of warrior tribesmen and followed the miners; in the ensuing battle over a thousand Chinese were killed.

In 1863 Charles Brooke took over and continued to acquire territory from the Sultan of Brunei. River valleys were bought for a few thousand pounds, the local tribes either persuaded to enter into deals or crushed if they resisted. The sultan's territory had shrunk so much it was now surrounded on all three sides by Brooke's Sarawak, establishing the geographical boundaries that still define Brunei today.

Charles was succeeded by his son, **Vyner Brooke**, who consolidated his father's gains. However, the **Japanese occupation** of World War II effectively put an end to his control. Vyner escaped, but most of his officials were interned and some executed. Upon his return in 1946, he was compelled to cede Sarawak to the British government. The Brooke dynasty was effectively at an end, and a last link with its past was severed in 2011 when Vyner's nephew **Anthony Brooke**, his designated successor who had briefly run Sarawak before World War II while Vyner was in the UK, died.

To the present

With Malaysian independence in 1957, attempts were made to include Sarawak, Sabah and Brunei, but Brunei declined at the last minute to join the present-day **Federation of Malaysia**, inaugurated in 1963. Sarawak's inclusion was opposed by Indonesia, and the **Konfrontasi** broke out, with Indonesia arming communist guerrillas inside Sarawak. The insurgency continued for three years until Malaysian troops, aided by the British, put it down. To this day, many inhabitants of the interior remain displaced.

Since then, Sarawak has developed apace with the rest of Malaysia, though at considerable cost to the **environment**, with up to ninety percent of its primary rainforests having been logged. Politically, the state today is closely identified with the policies of **Taib Mahmud**, a Melanau, who was chief minister from 1981 to 2014, and who to an extent oversaw a time of infrastructural and economic growth, yet also passed laws that gave him control of the logging industry during that time. The support of his PBB party and allied parties has helped prop up the ruling coalition in general elections, and the PBB is often viewed as a proxy for UMNO. Sarawak is the only state where Malaysia's main Malay party has no presence.

There are signs of a backlash, however, brought on perhaps by the rising cost of living, economic disparity, and allegations from international environmental groups as well as Taib's opponents and the Malaysian media, that Sarawak's administration is tainted by **corruption** – the list of allegations is far too long to include here, but an internet search will return dozens of examples including damning leaked US embassy cables published by Wikileaks in 2011. In 2014, Taib resigned as chief minister (a role taken over by

6

Adenan Satem, his former brother-in-law) to become **Governor of Sarawak,** although many feel that Taib is still a big influence in the government.

The 2016 local elections saw the PBB claw back the swing to the opposition that took place in the 2011 election – ironically enough, given what is happening to the state's natural resources, with the continued help of rural voters. Much of this may have to do with the fact that rural areas in support of the PBB have seen much more infrastructure development in recent years than those that supported opposition parties.

Taib's main environmental legacy is the project to construct twelve hydroelectric dams in the state, of which only the **Bakun** and **Murum** dams have so far been commissioned and neither of which is generating to full capacity due to lack of demand. The **Baram Dam** was all set for construction but local and international oppostion to the project, which would have displaced over twenty thousand mainly Penan people, saw the plan shelved in 2015. Construction has already started on the newest dam, Baleh.

ARRIVAL AND DEPARTURE   SARAWAK

By plane It's easy enough to fly into Kuching, Miri, Bintulu or Sibu from the Peninsula, and there are also decent connections with Sabah, Brunei and Singapore; Malaysia Airlines, AirAsia, Firefly, MASwings and SilkAir provide a comprehensive service between them. There are also flights from Pontianak in Indonesian Kalimantan to Kuching, operated by AirAsia. Note that Sarawak has its own immigration controls, so you will be stamped in and out even if flying between here and the other states of Malaysia.

By boat There's a boat from Labuan island, off the Sabah coast, to Lawas.

By bus A handful of buses connect Bandar Seri Begawan and Miri, and Kota Kinabalu and Miri via Lawas. The only official border crossing between Kalimantan and Sarawak is at Entikong/Tebedu (daily, roughly 6am–6pm), 100km south of Kuching by road; it's used by frequent buses plying between Pontianak and Kuching and all the way to Miri. However, there may be another once the latest section of the Pan-Borneo Highway is completed to Telak Melano, on the Indonesian border near Sematan, in 2019.

GETTING AROUND

Sarawak covers pretty much the same area as England or the state of Mississippi, but with much of the state wild and thinly populated, there's not that much ground to cover unless you wish to visit remote communities or the interior's national parks, such as Mulu. As ever, it's essential to book **public transport** at least a week in advance if you want to travel around the time of a major festival, notably the two-day *gawai* harvest festival at the start of June, when huge numbers of indigenous people return to their original longhouses.

By plane Flying is a useful timesaver between Kuching and Miri, and to reach Mulu from either Kuching, Miri. and Kota Kinabalu. However, the most memorable flights are on the tiny Twin Otter planes (see p.371), connecting the interior with Bario and Ba'Kelalan.

By bus Numerous buses ply the trunk road between Kuching and Miri, though thanks to slow-moving trucks journeys take a little longer than distances might suggest. Buses operated by MTC (w mtcmiri.com) and Biaramas/ Bus Asia (no relation of AirAsia; w ba.my) are a cut above the rest in terms of comfort. Fares are reasonable – Kuching to Sibu, for example, costs RM50–55 one way (7hr). Local bus services also radiate from the main cities, in daylight hours only.

By boat The only scheduled boat services you're likely to catch are those between Kuching and Sibu, and express boats along the Rejang River.

By taxi On some routes, buses are supplemented by *kereta sapu* (see p.34); any "taxis" mentioned in small towns here

will usually be of this type. Useful in rural areas, such share taxi services are generally reliable though, of course, their operators are neither licensed nor insured. Prices are comparable to bus fares, unless you're in a 4WD (see opposite). Uber is available in Miri and Kuching, while other smaller cities only have Grab.

By car Sarawak's road network is simplicity itself. Given that signage is adequate and drivers' behaviour a little less manic than in the Peninsula, renting a car is worth considering. The state's one and only trunk road, part of the so-called Pan-Borneo Highway, runs between Kuching and Miri, via Sibu and Bintulu, and on into Brunei. It's a dual carriageway only as far east as the turning for Sri Aman, a 3hr drive from Kuching; beyond that it becomes little more than a two-lane country road. The coastal highway between Bintulu and Miri is also mostly a two-lane affair. Unlike its counterpart, it holds few facilities or settlements; if you intend to use it, fill up beforehand and set off in plenty of time to arrive before nightfall.

By longboat or 4WD Finally, in remote areas, you might need to charter a longboat for a river trip or a 4WD to gain access to the network of rough logging roads that have begun to supplant boat travel. As always in Malaysia, getting off the beaten track isn't cheap unless you're travelling in a small group – ideally of four people. Chartering a longboat for a 2hr trip might cost RM200–250 for two or three passengers (depending on luggage), assuming you can get hold of a boatman at all, while four passengers might pay the driver up to RM200 to go 100km in a 4WD. Details are given in the text where relevant, but unless you're on a budget it's often more worthwhile to pay a tour operator to arrange things.

Hitchhiking Although we don't recommend it in general, for male travellers and couples, hitching can significantly reduce your travel costs and help you meet Sarawak people. It's also possible to hitch along logging tracks, though be prepared to spend the night at a basic jungle rest stop if you don't find a ride.

6

Southwestern Sarawak

Visitors flying in from Peninsular Malaysia or Singapore are treated to a spellbinding view of muddy rivers snaking their way through the jungle beneath lush peaks. It not only just about sums up Borneo, but also sets the tone for what the southwest of Sarawak has in store. The area is home to several of Sarawak's national parks, notably **Bako**, with its proboscis monkeys and excellent trekking. It's also a good place to get a grounding in Borneo's tribal cultures, which you can do at the museums in the likeable state capital **Kuching**. Among other top draws are the orang-utans of the **Semenggoh Wildlife Rehabilitation Centre** and the **Sarawak Cultural Village**, a brilliant collection of tribal houses near the beaches of Damai. You can also see a proper longhouse at **Annah Rais**, or head east to the edges of **Batang Ai National Park**, home to many Iban communities, though they're very much maintained purely for the tourists, and whose inhabitants seem a bit sick of hanging around already.

Kuching

KUCHING, the state's oldest, largest city, is the perfect gateway to Sarawak. This is one of Malaysia's most charming and laidback cities, revelling in a picturesque setting on the Sarawak River, with Mount Santubong looming on the western horizon. Despite central high-rises, much of the recent development has been confined to the bland but burgeoning suburbs, and the historical core remains appealingly sleepy and human in scale, its colonial architecture redolent of a bygone era. Kuching's blend of contradictions – of commerce alongside a sedate pace of life, of fashionable cafés rubbing shoulders with old-fangled *kedai kopis* – makes it an appealing place to chill out for several days while exploring sights such as the **Sarawak Museum**, showcasing the state's ethnological heritage, and making excursions to the numerous national parks and other sights in the vicinity.

Most of Kuching lies on the south bank of the river, its core an easily walkable warren of crowded lanes. The area sandwiched between Jalan Courthouse to the west, Jalan Wayang to the east and Reservoir Park to the south, usually referred to as **old Kuching**, includes several colonial churches and administrative buildings. **Chinatown** occupies the same general area, incorporating what were once the main shopping streets of Main Bazaar, facing the river, and Carpenter Street, and Chinese businesses and restaurants also dominate Jalan Padungan to the east. The traditional **Malay district** is dominated by the domes of the **Masjid Negeri**, with several Malay kampungs north of the river too. The Chinese and Malays together make up nearly two-thirds of Kuching's population of just over 700,000, though there are also substantial communities of Bidayuh and Iban.

Brief history

When **James Brooke** came up the river in 1841, he arrived at a village known as Sarawak, on a small stream called Sungai Mata Kuching ("Cat's Eye"), adjoining the

6

KUCHING

SHOPPING
Bricks & Earthenware Factory	7
Greek's Outgear Discovery	3
The Museum	2
Plaza Merdika	4
Sarakraf	6
Sarawak Craft Council	1
Spring Mall	8
Ting & Ting	5

Sarawak General Hospital (1km), Jalan Penrissen Regional Express Terminal (7.7km), Airport (7.7km), & 7 (7.8km)

main river; he probably shortened the stream's name, which came to refer to the fast-expanding settlement. However, a much-repeated tale has it that the first rajah pointed to the village and asked its name. The Malay locals, thinking Brooke was pointing to a cat, replied – reasonably enough – "kuching" ("cat"; which explains the city's obsession with cat memorabilia). Either way, in 1872 Charles Brooke officially changed the settlement's name from Sarawak to Kuching.

Until the 1920s, the capital was largely confined to the south bank of the Sarawak River, stretching only from the Chinese heartland around Jalan Temple, east of today's centre, to the Malay kampung around the mosque to the west. On the north bank, activity revolved around the fort and a few dozen houses reserved for British officials. The prewar **rubber boom** financed the town's expansion, with tree-lined Jalan Padungan, running east from Chinatown, becoming one of its smartest streets. Kuching escaped relatively lightly during World War II, since Japanese bombing raids largely focused on destroying the oil wells in northern Sarawak.

Orchid Garden (200m) & Astana (600m)

JALAN LITERKAR DUN

Sarawak State
Assembly
Building

Fort Margherita/
Brooke Gallery

KAMPUNG
BOYAN

KAMPUNG
GERSIK

KAMPUNG
SOURABAYA
ULU

Boardwalk

Sampan Jetty

Sarawak River

Borneo
Adventure

Paradesa
Borneo

Waterfront

MAIN BAZAAR

Hong San
Temple

Bako Buses

Grand
Margharita
Hotel

Sarawak
Plaza

Chinese
History
Museum

JALAN TUNKU ABDUL RAHMAN

JLN EWE HAI

Medan
Pelita

Hilton

Tun Jugah Mall/
Tan Jugah Foundation
Gallery

JALAN ABELL

JALAN CHAN CHIN ANN

JLN TEMPLE

JALAN BORNEO

Bus Asia Ticketing
Counter Terminal

JALAN
PADUNGAN UTARA

Petanak
Market

JALAN WAYANG

Tua Pek
Kong

UTC
Centre

JLN PADUNGAN

JALAN PETANAK

Borneo
Headhunter

JLN

GREEN HILL

JALAN PADUNGAN

MASwings

JLN ABELL UTARA

Ting & Ting
Supermarket

Hills
Mall

JALAN BUKIT

MATA KUCHING

JALAN SONGTHIAN CHEOK

Rugby
Field

JALAN ABELL

JALAN MATHIE

Adventure
Alternative
Borneo

JLN TABUAN

Royal
Brunei

JALAN PADUNGAN

Chinese
Archway

Cat
Statue

JALAN BAN HOCK

JALAN BAN HOCK

JALAN JASHOR

JALAN CENTRAL TIMUR

LORONG PARK

JALAN TABUAN

JALAN TAN SRI ONG KEE HUI

CPH Travel '50m', 💧 (400m), Municipal Pool (900m), & Pending Wharf

6

■ DRINKING	
Culture Club	1
Junk/Backstage Bar	2
Monkee Bar	3
Ruai Café & Bar	4

■ ACCOMMODATION	
Hotel 48	11
Basaga Holiday Residences	14
Batik Boutique Hotel	9
Fairview	13
Grand Margherita	3
Kuching Waterfront Lodge	1
Kuching Hilton	8
The Limetree	10
The Marian Boutique Lodging House	7
Singgahsana Lodge	6
Telang Usan	12
Threehouse	5
The Waterfront Hotel	4
Wojia Lodge	2

● EATING			
Annuar	17	The Granery	9
Aroma Cafe	16	Hong Kong Noodle House	10
Bismillah Café	3		
Bing!	13	James Brooke Bistro and Café	6
Bla Bla Bla	15		
Black Bean Coffee	5	Junk	14
Bombay Spices	19	My Village Baruk	1
Carpenter Street stalls	2	Pincho Loco	7
Ceylonese Restaurant	11	Top Spot Food Court	12
the.Dyak	20	Zhun San Yen	8
Indah Café & Art Space	4	Zinc	18

14 (400m), Sarakraf Pavilion (700m), 20 (1km) & 8 (1.5km)

In recent decades, the city sprawled south and port facilities and warehouses in the centre closed as new shipping terminals and industrial estates were created downriver, to the northeast. Robbed of waterborne traffic, downtown's **riverside** was reinvented in the 1990s with partial success as a leafy, pedestrianized recreation area, its quaint panoramas spoiled only by the bizarre oversized hulk of the State Assembly building, completed in 2009 on the north bank, currently being joined to the south bank via a rather funky new bridge.

Kuching waterfront

Beginning along Jalan Gambier and continuing for just over 1km until it peters out close to the *Grand Margherita* hotel, Kuching's central **waterfront** is where most visitors begin exploring the city – almost everything of interest is within 500m of this esplanade. Sporting the odd fountain and several fast food kiosks, it has a somewhat sanitized feel, but a sprinkling of whitewashed colonial buildings, tranquil river views

6

and the shophouses of Main Bazaar and Jalan Gambier make for a worthwhile wander.

For views alone, the best time to turn up is around 6pm on a fine day, when you'll be treated within an hour to a fiery **sunset** behind Mount Serapi (one of the peaks of Kubah National Park), casting an orange glow over city and river. To get an aerial view, head up to the cinema on the top floor of the colourful Medan Pelita building on Lebuh Temple, where a large balcony offers a fine vista over old Kuching. It's possible to do an expensive sunset river trip, marketed as the **Sarawak River Cruise** (daily 5.30pm, from the jetty near the Sarawak Steamship Company building; 1hr 30min; RM65; ☎082 240 366, ⓦsarawakrivercruise.com), but the views are little better than those from dry land.

Along the Main Bazaar

The fast-gentrifying **Main Bazaar** is home to a few of guesthouses and tour agencies, plus a rash of souvenir shops and a gallery, the odd attempt at a posh café, and a handful of more traditional shops. At its junction with Jalan Tun Haji Openg lies the **Old Courthouse** that used to house many of the region's tourist facilities but has been now rented out to an assortment of high-end restaurants . Built in 1874, and sporting impressive Romanesque columns, the complex is fronted by the **Charles Brooke Memorial**, a 6m-high granite obelisk erected in 1924. Stone figures at its base represent the state's Chinese, Malay, Dayak and Orang Ulu communities.

Diagonally across, on the waterfront itself, the single-turreted **Square Tower** is all that's left of a fortress built in 1879. An earlier wooden construction burned during the 1857 gold-miners' rebellion. The trio of compact 1930s buildings next door, once belonging to the **Sarawak Steamship Company**, now house the so-called waterfront bazaar, a disappointing collection of souvenir outlets; you're better off checking out the touristy shophouses opposite.

Chinese History Museum

Eastern end of the Main Bazaar • Mon–Fri 9am–4.30pm, Sat & Sun 10am–4pm • Free; no photography allowed • ☎ 082 231520

The squat, pale orangey-pink **Chinese History Museum** was built in the 1910s as a courthouse for the Chinese community, after which it became the Chinese Chamber of Commerce. It's a source of pride to the local Chinese in a country where state-run museums often snub traditions that aren't Malay or tribal. While the artefacts are modest, apart from the half-sized – but depressingly large, given that it is made of ivory – carving of an emperor and empress, the museum gives a decent account of how nineteenth-century Chinese migrants opened up western Sarawak to agriculture and mining.

Around the Padang

Jalan Tun Abang Haji Openg leads away from the riverfront past a smattering of colonial buildings just beyond the courthouse complex and close to the **Padang**. Unfortunately the area's character has been diluted by the brash Plaza Merdeka mall and hotel just north of the Padang, though it doesn't totally steal the thunder of Kuching's grandest building, the Neoclassical central **post office** on the street's east side. That said, the street is so narrow that you can't get far back enough to enjoy a decent face-on view of the ornamental columns and a huge pediment, completed in 1931.

Sarawak Craft Council

Round Tower, Jalan Tun Abang Haji Openg • Mon–Fri 8.30am–1pm & 2–4.30pm • Free • ☎ 082 245652, ⓦ sarawakhandicraft.com.my

Unlike the Square Tower, the **Round Tower** is not the shape its name would suggest – it actually has two roundish towers on either side of a flat facade. Built in the 1880s as a fort, it's now used by the **Sarawak Craft Council**, formed to preserve and promote traditional skills in art forms such as weaving and beading, with an excellent showroom where all products are labelled with the part of Sarawak where they were made.

Textile Museum

Beside the Round Tower, Jalan Tun Haji Openg • Daily 9am–4.30pm • Free • ⓦ museum.sarawak.gov.my

"A piece of New Orleans transplanted to Kuching" is how the tourist office describes the ornate building with shuttered windows beside the Round Tower. They advisedly didn't say "literally", for it was originally built here in the early twentieth century as a hospital. The handsome restored structure certainly catches the eye, unlike the low-key signs announcing its present-day role as the city's **Textile Museum**, presenting Borneo costumes and artefacts across the centuries – headdresses, belts, traditional woven fabrics known as *pua kumbu*. Worthwhile though the collection is, it's less well presented than the Iban weaving at the gallery of the Tun Jugah Foundation (see p.327).

St Thomas's Cathedral and the Bishop's House

Jalan Tun Haji Openg • Mon–Sat 8am–5pm (though hours can vary) & services on Sun • Free

On a hillock off the east side of Jalan Tun Haji Openg, the Anglican **St Thomas's Cathedral** is a tidy, plain 1950s edifice, one of a cluster of colonial churches and mission schools hereabouts. Only the vaguely mock-Tudor **Bishop's House**, built in 1849, which is still the Anglican bishop's residence and the oldest surviving building in the city, is worth a look, though the inside is not usually open to the public; reach it by turning left off Jalan McDougall and walking uphill for a couple of minutes.

Chinatown

East of the Old Courthouse complex, a gaudy Chinese archway marks the entrance to Kuching's historic **Chinatown** via **Carpenter Street** (the name is still used rather than the Malay "Jalan Carpenter"), which becomes Jalan Ewe Hai at its eastern end. Truth be told, the district's Chinese flavour is somewhat diluted by a rash of bars these days, but a few old-fashioned *kopitiams*, herbalists and snack shops still dot the shophouses of Carpenter Street and the tiny lanes running off it, and a handful of well-maintained temples merit a peek, the largest being **Tua Pek Kong** on Lebuh Temple, at the district's eastern end. Tua Pek Kong, one explanation has it, is a sort of patron saint of Chinese communities in Southeast Asia; temples throughout Malaysia and Singapore bear his name. Raised behind a gaudy retaining wall, Kuching's version was built in the mid-eighteenth century, though a rather plastic restoration has left it slightly charmless; you may find the Siang Ti (Northern Deity) temple on Carpenter Street and the Hong San (Phoenix Hill) temple on Jalan Ewe Hai more atmospheric. Any of these temples may play host to theatrical or musical performances during **festivals**, especially Chinese New Year.

Ethnology Museum

Jalan Tun Abang Haji Openg • Mon–Fri 9am–4.45pm, Sat & Sun 10am–4pm; 1hr guided tour Fri 9.30am • Free • ☎ 082 244232, ⓦ museum.sarawak.gov.my

Borneo's oldest museum and housed in a lovely nineteenth-century faux Normandy townhouse set in lush grounds, the **Ethnology Museum** used to be regarded locally as one of the country's finest museums, thanks largely to its former curator, **Tom Harrisson** (1911–76). Best remembered for discovering a 39,000-year-old skull at Niah in 1957, which led to a reappraisal of the origins of early man in Southeast Asia, he also frequently visited tribal peoples to collect the artefacts that comprise the museum's biggest attraction. The main "old wing" of the museum is currently under renovation and will not be reopened until 2020, though it's likely Harrisson's hoard will still make up the bulk of the collection. The "new" wing next door is still open in the meantime, and contains an interesting exhibition of Sarawak history and culture.

Islamic Museum

Mon–Fri 9am–4.45pm, Sat & Sun 10am–4pm • Free • ☎ 082 244232, ⓦ museum.sarawak.gov.my

Just southwest of the Sarawak Museum's new wing, a former Malay college and religious school houses the **Islamic Museum**. Seven galleries in its cool, tiled interior

6

hold unexpectedly fine examples of Islamic art and displays on architecture, coinage and textiles, which are all set around a pleasant central courtyard garden.

West of the centre

The pocket of town immediately west of the Padang has a noticeably Islamic feel, with the golden-domed **Masjid Negeri** (Kuching Mosque; Mon–Thurs, Sat & Sun 9am–3pm, closed at prayer-times) atop a hillock at its heart and nearby streets packed with Malay and Indian Muslim *kedai kopis*. The most colourful approach to the area is via pedestrianized **Jalan India**, named for the Indian coolies who arrived in the early twentieth century to work at Kuching's port; today it's packed with market stalls selling cheap shoes, clothing and household items. The mosque aside, the only specific sight is a popular **weekend market**, further southwest.

Sunday market

Just north of the Tun Abdul Rahman Bridge at Medan Niaga Satok • Sat mid-afternoon until late, Sun early morning until noon • City Public Link buses #K5 and #K7 leave every 30min or so from Jalan Mosque bus park office or it's probably quicker to walk; head to Masjid Negeri, then down Jalan Haji Taha and under the flyover at Jalan Kulas, turning right into Jalan Satok at the second flyover, then follow Jalan Satok until it crosses the bridge

Variously known as the **Sunday market** or night market, the weekend market on Medan Niaga Satok is not quite the spectacle it used to be when it was in the street – but for once, that's no bad thing. The bush meat trade of years gone by has been halted by better environmental enforcement; these days the most exotic thing you might see on sale are edible sago grubs, which live on thorny sago palms in the jungle. However, the market is certainly colourful and frenetic, selling a good range of snacks as well as a few tribal souvenirs, jungle products including wild honey, and local vegetables such as the ubiquitous fern tops.

Sama Jaya Nature Reserve

Jalan Setia Raja, 8km southwest of the Padang • Daily 6am–6pm • Free • ☎ 082 368528

Little-known to anyone other than from the joggers that frequent it, the **Sama Jaya Nature Reserve** is the closest you'll get to real wildlife in the city. Despite being entirely surrounded by the city, the reserve is home to both a boisterous troop of short-tailed macaques and a wide range of birds. Most people come here to use the jogging trail, though there are also four short nature trails that give you a bit of an experience of the jungle (if you can ignore the hum of traffic). Here you'll also find the **Sarawak Forestry accommodation booking office** (see p.329), and a couple of tiny tree-related museums, though you'll have to ask for the keys at the office if you want to look inside.

SARAWAK'S CERAMIC JARS

The status and wealth of members of Sarawak's indigenous tribes depended on how many **ceramic jars** they possessed, and you can still see impressive models in longhouses as well as in the Ethnology Museum. Ranging from tiny, elegantly detailed bowls to much larger vessels, more than 1m in height, the jars were used for such purposes as storage, brewing rice wine and making payments – dowries and fines for adultery and divorce settlements. The most valuable jars were only used for ceremonies like the Gawai Kenyalang (the rite of passage for a mature man of means, involving the recitation of stories by the longhouse bard), or for funerary purposes. When a member of the Kelabit people died, the corpse was packed into a jar in a foetal position to await rebirth from the jar, its "womb". The Berawan did the same, and as decomposition took place, the liquid from the body was drained through a bamboo pipe, leaving the individual's bones or clothing to be placed in a canister and hoisted onto an ossuary above the river bank. It's said that the jars can also be used to foretell the future, and can summon spirits through the sounds they emit when struck.

East of the centre

Downtown Kuching's commercial district, east of Chinatown, is home to most of the city's modern hotels, a handful of ordinary shopping malls and several banks. The easiest way to get there is to follow Jalan Tuanku Abdul Rahman, the continuation of Main Bazaar, east until it swings away from the river at the *Grand Margherita* hotel to join the area's other main thoroughfare, **Jalan Padungan**. This road feels like a natural extension of Chinatown, its shophouses still home to several largely Chinese restaurants and *kopitiams*, though Western-style cafés and bars have made their presence felt too.

The archway by the major gyratory further east on Jalan Padungan has a certain notoriety as the site of Kuching's original **cat statue**, a tacky 1.5m-high white-plaster effigy, paw raised in welcome. Though the location isn't at all prepossessing, the statue was regarded as a city icon for many years, so much so that more cat statues have since appeared elsewhere on Jalan Padungan and in other parts of town.

Tun Jugah Foundation gallery

Level 4 (via lift), Tun Jugah mall, 18 Jalan Tuanku Abdul Rahman • Mon–Fri 9am–noon & 1–4.30pm • ☎ 082 239672, ⓦ tunjugahfoundation.org.my

The excellent modern **Tun Jugah Foundation gallery**, the showcase for a charity set up to honour a long-serving Iban politician who died in 1981, showcases fine Iban weaving – around a dozen examples of **pua kumbu** cloth, wall-mounted or framed in sliding panels. The geometrical patterns are fascinating but bafflingly abstract to the untrained eye, though once you read the labelling you might be able to make out the animal and other motifs. Most are in shades of reddish brown and black, the colour applied through *ikat* (tie-dyeing) with a base brown pigment traditionally made from the bark of the *engkudu* tree (*Morinda citrifolia*); vegetable indigos are added on top, yielding black in areas already dyed brown. The depth of colour depends on the type of yarn and the number of times it's dipped in the dyes.

In a large **teaching room**, the arts of weaving are passed on to a new generation of local women, not just Iban; you may be able to sit in on some classes or talk to the instructors or participants. An additional side gallery is devoted to **beads**, as used in the jewellery of the Iban and other tribes, and featuring examples in semiprecious stone and snazzy multicoloured glass.

The north bank

Orchid Garden 150m north of the Astana • Tues–Sun 9.30am–5.30pm • Free • ☎ 082 370141

The leafy far side of the Sarawak River, views of which are the major part of the waterfront's appeal, is currently being redeveloped with the construction of the new S-shaped Golden Bridge and a riverside walk past the two important colonial buildings here, the **Astana** (closed to the public) and **Fort Margherita**, which holds a small museum. The shoreline, however, is dominated by the outlandish **State Assembly Building** (also called the DUN Building), a sort of giant espresso maker crossed with a spaceship that locals disdain as a waste of taxpayers' money. Still, it is worth crossing the water to look back at downtown Kuching and perhaps to wander through the Malay kampungs.

The **orchid garden,** just up the road from the State Assembly Building, is home to around one hundred orchid species, which mostly bloom from late October to late December. **Sampans** shuttle across the river all day and into the evening, leaving when full from four small jetties along the waterfront (RM0.50 before 10pm, RM1 after 10pm); ideally you should depart from the jetty more or less opposite where you want to go, though once the bridge is finished this way of travelling may well disappear.

Fort Margherita/Brooke Gallery

600m east of the Astana • Mon–Fri 9am–4.45pm, Sat & Sun 10am–4pm • RM20 • ☎ 016 310 1880, ⓦ brookegallery.org

Dwarfed by the State Assembly Building, **Fort Margherita** is one of the best examples of the Brookes' system of fortifications, and named after James's wife Margaret – she must

6

have been quite a woman, as one of Oscar Wilde's fairy tales, *The Young King*, is also dedicated to her. It's a fine sturdy building, well preserved, too, since it never saw any action. The interior contains the three floors of the **Brooke Gallery**, explaining his extraordinary life and works as well as their effect on the iniginous peoples. You can also visit the grassy courtyard, where the small antique cannons still point out, and the execution room on the ramparts, containing a hanging bag of "laughing" skulls.

Malay kampungs

Quite a few **Malay kampungs** are visible on the north bank from downtown Kuching; the cluster of three east of Fort Margherita are the most visited. The obvious target is **Kampung Boyan**, marked out by its waterside food court with its twin-humped roof, though the mixture of traditional clapboard dwellings and more modern houses is not particularly atmospheric. Look out for the local cottage industry, the manufacture of multicoloured *kek lapis* (layer cake); street traders all along Main Bazaar hawk examples. If you come in the evening, consider dining at *My Village Baruk* (see p.332), a fine Malay restaurant.

ARRIVAL AND DEPARTURE   KUCHING

BY PLANE

KUCHING INTERNATIONAL AIRPORT

The airport (☎082 454242, ⊛kuchingairportonline.com) is 12km south of the city. AirAsia, Malaysia Airlines, Malindo Air and MASwings all have ticket offices in the departure terminal.

Facilities There's a small Tourism Malaysia desk (generally daily 9am–10pm) in the baggage hall, though the tourist office (see opposite) is much better. The arrivals hall also holds car rental agencies, ATMs and a foreign exchange counter.

Getting into town At least one booth in the airport sells coupons for the taxi ride into town, which will cost you around RM26. Alternatively if you walk to the main road beyond the car park (about 2km), you can cross at the lights where there is a bus stop heading north, and you can flag down any local bus (6am–8pm; 25min), all of which end up at one of the stops in the Kuching mosque area – ask here for which buses head out to the airport too.

Destinations Bintulu (5 daily; 55min); Johor Bahru (3–4 daily; 1hr 25min); Kota Kinabalu (4 daily; 1hr 25min); Kuala Lumpur (22 daily; 1hr 45min); Miri (6–7 daily; 1hr); Mukah (3 daily; 1hr); Mulu (Mon, Wed, Thurs & Sat; 1hr 30min); Pontianak (11.45am daily; 45min); Sibu (6 daily; 40min); Singapore (3-4 daily; 1hr 20min).

BY BUS

If you're leaving by bus, and want to avoid trekking out to the new bus station to buy a ticket in advance – advisable

around the time of a festival – it's useful to travel with Biaramas/BusAsia, which has a ticket office just off Jalan Padungan.

KUCHING SENTRAL REGIONAL EXPRESS BUS TERMINAL

All the bus companies arrive and depart from Kuching's long-distance bus station, 6.5km south of the centre on Jalan Tun Ahmad Zaidi Adruce.

Getting into town Taxi drivers may attempt to charge R50 to take you to the city centre, and are unlikely to be bargained below RM30 – those figures double between midnight and 6am. Alternatively, take a Grab/Uber or cross the main road and flag down any bus for RM1 – all will take you to the centre, most likely to one of the stops in the Kuching mosque area.

Destinations Bintulu (every 20min–1hr; 11hr); Miri (10 daily, most after 2pm; 15hr); Mukah (3 daily; 9hr); Pontianak (Indonesia; 8am & 11am daily; 8hr 45min); Sarikei (9 daily; 5hr 30min–6hr 30min); Sibu (7 daily; 8hr); Sri Aman (20 daily; 4hr).

BY BOAT

Ferries Express Bahagia (☎082 410076 or ☎016 896 6235) operates passenger ferries to and from Sibu (daily 8.30am; 4hr 30min; RM45), via Sarikei on the coast, using the Pending terminal 6km east of the centre. A taxi to the terminal from town costs RM30. It's advised to arrive an hour before departure.

GETTING AROUND

By city bus and minivan You're unlikely to use Kuching's city buses in the easily walkable downtown area, where bus stops offer practically no information or labelling. Also, while some services run two or three times per hour, many only go a few times a day, and local buses have in any case been in flux

for years; ask at the Visitors' Information Centre (see opposite) for the latest schedules. All buses operate between dawn and dusk only, and most start out from the area just east of Masjid Negeri, where cramped minivans shadow many bus routes. Minivans leave when full – avoid if you value comfort.

By local bus Most bus services that start and end inside Kuching are run by Rapid Kuching (red vehicles) or City Public Link (largely green vehicles). Both firms, along with the Sarawak Transport Company (green and cream buses) and some minor operators, also provide handy services out into Kuching's hinterland; details are given in the relevant accounts.

By taxi There are taxi ranks near the mosque and in front of hotels along Jalan Tuanku Abdul Rahman; alternatively, try Kuching Taxi (☎082 480000) or T&T (☎082 343343). Downtown journeys should cost RM15–20; double that between midnight and 6am.

By motorbike A couple of guesthouses along Jalan Carpenter rent motorbikes, but the best deals are to be had from Ah Hui Motor (☎082 240508), who rent 110cc bikes from RM30/day or RM175/week, and you need to show a licence.

By bike Paredesa and CPH Travel (see below) are the only places currently renting bikes, with bikes costing an an outrageous RM50/day. CPH also organizes bike tours of Kuching and the surrounding kampungs (see below).

By car Kuching Holidays (☎082 463318, ⓦkuchingholidays.com) at the airport; Flexi (☎082 452200, ⓦflexicarrental.com) at the airport and at Lot 7050, Jalan Sekama; Hertz at the airport (☎082 450740). Prices start at around RM100/day.

INFORMATION

Visitors' Information Centre The state's tourism office is in the Old Courthouse complex at the western edge of the waterfront (daily 9am–6pm; ☎082 410944, ⓦsarawaktourism.com). Staff are knowledgeable about Kuching and its environs as well as the rest of Sarawak.

Sarawak Forestry Corporation Located some way out of the centre at the Sama Jaya Nature Reserve (see p.326; Mon–Fri 8am–5pm; ☎082 248088, ⓦsarawakforestry .com). it takes bookings for accommodation at many national parks, though not Mulu. The friendly and knowledgeable staff can also tell you where *Rafflesia* flowers (see p.586) are blooming, though in theory all information and accommodation bookings (ⓦebooking .sarawak.gov.my) are online; this is a great place to work out which parks would be best for you (and see monkeys).

Newspapers and Magazines English-language newspapers such as the *Borneo Post*, *New Sarawak Tribune* and *The Star* (which has a separate Sarawak edition) detail cultural and other happenings in town and around the state. There's also a local lifestyle magazine called *Kuching In & Out* (ⓦkuchinginandout.com), which features not only a comprehensive listings section with maps, but also articles on tourism and culture; print copies are available free from hotels, restaurants and bars.

Guides Kuching is the ideal place to engage the services of a licensed guide through the Sarawak Tourist Guides Association (☎0168675296, ⓔsktgasecretary@gmail .com, FAO Abang Azahari or Edwin Lim). Guides are experienced, speak good English and have expert knowledge. Although they cannot by law arrange a package (you'll have to book everything yourself), they can help arrange visits – sometimes more cheaply than a tour agency – to longhouses, parks or other points of interest that are otherwise hard to reach or have few amenities. You will need to give them at least one week's notice. If you have a group, this is by far the best way to organize trips, especially to-off-the-beaten path destinations.

TOUR OPERATORS

Sarawak's tour operators come into their own for **longhouse stays**, typically around the Batang Ai area, and other trips off the beaten track – which could mean the less touristy national parks or a foray into an *ulu* area where local contacts are needed to ensure transport and accommodation. That said, if you're an experienced traveller, many of these destinations are perfectly easy to visit by organizing yourself using this Guide – and considerably cheaper, especially if you travel with companions.

★Adventure Alternative Borneo Lot 37, Jalan Tabuan ☎082 842000, ⓦadventurealternativeborneo .com. By far the best choice for interesting, off-the-beaten-track tours at reasonable prices. This British-run outfit also has top ethical credentials, not only putting half their profits back into the communities they work in, but also treating them with a lot more respect than some of the larger agencies. They go to many locations in southern Sarawak that nobody else goes to, with some excellent trips to remote Iban longhouses and wildlife spotting in the area between Simujang and Sri Aman.

Borneo Adventure 55 Main Bazaar ☎082 245175, ⓦborneoadventure.com. Award-winning, pioneering operation, particularly good on longhouse stays. Its jungle lodge along the Batang Ai at Nanga Sumpa (see p.347), is probably the best of the three companies that go to the region; prices for three days/two nights start at RM1588.

CPH Travel 70 Jalan Padungan ☎082 243708, ⓦcphtravel.com.my. Especially good on boat trips, for example to the mouth of the Santubong River (RM160; 4hr) to spot Irrawaddy dolphins (see p.336), though they also do longhouse tours on the Lemanak River from RM583 (two days, one night).

Kuching Caving ☎012 886 2347, ⓦkuchingcaving .com. Knowledgeable day tours (RM275–425) to little-visited limestone cave systems near Serian, southeast of

6

Kuching. All you need is a reasonable level of fitness; gloves, helmets and helmet-mounted lamps are provided, while boots and other gear can be rented if they're not included. Prices are for a minimum of two people and get cheaper with groups over five. Two-day trips may feature accommodation in Bidayuh villages.

Paredesa Borneo 1 Jalan Wayang ☎ 082 238801, ⓦ paradesaborneo.com. Offers a great one-day bike tours of Kuching (RM96–116), as well as one- and two-day

kayaking, biking and trekking tours – or a combination of all three – out in the wild.

The Rucksack Rainforest Kayaking ☎ 013 804 8338, ⓦ rainforestkayaking.com. Superb kayaking day-trips down a tributary of the Sarawak River, taking in a couple of Bidayuh villages and bizarrely shaped limestone hills. Packages start at RM188 including a riverside picnic, photo CD, and transfers; pricier trips include side visits to the Annah Rais longhouse

ACCOMMODATION

There's plenty of choice when it comes to places to stay. **Guesthouses** are clustered in and around Chinatown (especially Carpenter Street); they all have pretty similar rooms and prices (though most are without en-suite bathrooms), and include a "simple breakfast" which invariably turns out to be toast and jam. Most **hotels** are in the commercial district to the east, although it's not as atmospheric as staying near Carpenter Street. To stay at or near the **beach**, consider the Santubong Peninsula, a 30min bus ride west (see p.336). As ever, you should book ahead to stay during a major **festival** – a month ahead if you plan to be here over the weekend of June's Rainforest Music Festival (see p.338).

GUESTHOUSES, HOSTELS AND B&BS

Hotel 48 13 & 14 Jalan Greenhill ☎ 082 521016; map p.322. Very clean, inexpensive but large a/c rooms and dorms. There's not a great deal of character, but it's efficiently run and fantastic value. The cheapest doubles are fairly spartan (though some have windows), but you'll have to pay RM70 if you want a bathroom. Close to lots of places to eat and drink. ⏶ Dorms RM22, doubles RM43

Fairview 6 Jalan Taman Budaya ☎ 082 240017, ⓦ fairview.com.my; map p.322. This family-run guesthouse – a rare thing in Kuching – has assorted a/c, en-suite rooms. It's fraying slightly at the edges, but it's hospitable and set amid the lushest of gardens. On the downside, traffic can be noisy and Jalan Reservoir, the shortest route to Chinatown, is badly lit and eerie at night. Rates drop by a third Sept–May. ⏶ RM90

Kuching Waterfront Lodge 15 Main Bazaar ☎ 082 231111, ⓦ kuchingwaterfrontlodge.com; map p.322. Atmospheric and cosy lodge housed in a refurbished shophouse done out like a Chinese mansion with floor tiles, wooden beams and a chandelier in the foyer. Rooms are less slick and occasionally a bit tatty, but all are en suite, with a/c and TV, and some even have four-poster beds. ⏶ RM115

Singgahsana Lodge 3 Lorong Temple ☎ 082 429277, ⓦ singgahsana.com; map p.322. Behind the unprepossessing orange and yellow facade is a warren of rooms, all in bright colours, with a spacious central lounge featuring rattan lamps. Impeccably run and deservedly popular, it also has a tour agency and rooftop bar. All rooms – from the ten-person dorms (both female-only and mixed) to en-suite doubles and shared-bathroom family rooms – have a/c. ⏶ Dorms RM34, doubles RM125

★**Threehouse** 51 Upper China St. ☎ 082 423499, ⓦ threehousebnb.com; map p.322. Run by noted Iban tattoo artist Ernesto Kalum and his Swedish partner, *Threehouse* impresses with well-maintained, cosy six-bed fan

dorms and a/c doubles, decorated in bright colours in a kind of 1970s-tribal fusion. ⏶ Dorms RM22, doubles RM70

★**Wojia Lodge** 17 Main Bazaar ☎ 082 251776, ⓦ wojialodge.com; map p.322. The name means "my house" in Mandarin and the place does try to be homely, its spacious lounge featuring floor matting and a large sofa, and although nothing is terribly fancy (even the river view), it's comfortable, and it has a good smoking area. There's an a/c dorm, plus singles and doubles, some of which are a/c, though these mostly lack windows. ⏶ Dorms RM30, doubles RM49

HOTELS

Basaga Holiday Residences Jalan Tabuan, nearly 2km south of the centre ☎ 082 417069, ⓦ basaga.com; map p.322. Take one disused school built around a colonial mansion, apply a large dose of design expertise, and the result is this charming complex where you can only just tell the sleek rooms were once classrooms and dorms. Choose from rooms in the old house, or facing the swimming pool or the back garden (the latter have outdoor showers). The distance from town is a drag, but they have a convivial restaurant and bar with a central open-air dining area shaded by a great old tree. Rates include breakfast, and airport pick-up if you book directly. ⏶ RM186

★**Batik Boutique Hotel** 38 Jalan Padungan ☎ 082 422845, ⓦ batikboutiquehotel.com; map p.322. This boutique hotel has some of the classiest and cosiest rooms in town. Though not eye-poppingly stunning, all the funkily decorated rooms boast silk bedding, an iPod dock and a terrazzo bath or overhead rain shower, and there's also a decent Western restaurant, a small lobby bar and a courtyard. Rates include breakfast. ⏶ RM201

Grand Margherita Jalan Tuanku Abdul Rahman ☎ 082 423111, ⓦ grandmargherita.com; map p.322. Swanky top-end affair, with Cantonese restaurant, river-facing pool, and shuttle services to many local attractions and the airport. It's also pretty child-friendly, with a children's pool, playground and babysitting service. Rates on Fri & Sat can fall by RM50 or so. 🛜 RM215

Kuching Hilton Jalan Tuanku Abdul Rahman ☎ 082 223888, 🖥 kuching.hilton.com; map p.322. As well organized as you'd expect a *Hilton* to be, with many large, modern rooms, boasting comfortable beds; those on upper floors have great views. There is also a pool (with bar), mini-gym and six cafés and restaurants, but you may have to pay for in-room wi-fi. 🛜 RM297

The Limetree Jalan Abell ☎ 082 414600, 🖥 limetreehotel.com.my; map p.322. Though lacking any character, this is a reliable and clean mid-range option. The *Limetree* boasts modern rooms with stylish minimalist decor, including some jumbo-sized executive suites (from RM200), and a pleasant rooftop bar. Non-smoking throughout, and rates include breakfast. 🛜 RM167

★ **The Marian Boutique Lodging House 23, Lebuh Wayang** ☎ 082 252777, 🖥 themarian.com.my; map p.322. Housed in an old girls' school on a hill overlooking the main bazaar, this newly opened heritage boutique hotel has retained many of the 1885 building's original features. The forty-odd rooms (named after previous headmistresses) have the dark timber or tiled floors, with faux nineteenth-century decor but modern fittings. Also has a pool and a very good Western restaurant. 🛜 RM170

Telang Usan Off Jalan Ban Hock ☎ 082 415588, 🖥 telangusan.com; map p.322. Now in its fourth decade, this pioneering hotel is Kayan-owned, hence the swirly Orang Ulu motifs in its decor. The rooms are comfortable enough; on the downside, reaching the waterfront requires you to head south to Jalan Ban Hock and double back. Rates include breakfast. 🛜 RM130

The Waterfront Hotel 68 Jalan Tun Abang Haji Openg ☎ 082 227227, 🖥 thewaterfrontkuching.com; map p.322. Perched on top of Plaza Merdika, this high-rise, high-end hotel is far better located and has better views than those in the commercial district, and for a much better price. Decor of both rooms and public areas is "artrageous", painted in bright colours with artwork on the walls, and the hotel also boasts a pool, gym and restaurant. 🛜 RM188

EATING

Kuching's lively and dynamic **eating** scene offers opportunities to sample indigenous dishes as well as international cuisine. Popular **local dishes** include *manok pansoh* (or *ayam pansoh*), a Bidayuh/Iban dish of chicken and tapioca leaves stewed in bamboo tubes; *umai*, Sarawak's answer to sashimi – raw fish or prawn shreds mixed with chilli and lime juice; *ambal*, delicious rubbery little clams, usually curried; and, as greens, the ubiquitous fern tops *paku* and *midin*. And of course Sarawak has its own variants of common Malaysian dishes, notably *laksa* – the Sarawakian variety uses rice vermicelli and is usually served in the morning – and *kuay teow*, often prepared in a tangy tomato gravy (outside the state people add a little vinegar to get the same sourness). Many top-end restaurants close for several days over the Gawai festival, when staff return to their "hometown" longhouses or jungle villages.

HAWKERS, FOOD COURTS AND KEDAI KOPIS

Bismillah Café Jalan Khoo Hung Yeang ☎ 082 415803; map p.322. This little Malay place does a good range of rice and noodle dishes, plus *roti* and curries, at mostly RM4–5 – its location makes it the best place to fill up before catching a bus. Daily 7am–3pm.

★ **Carpenter Street stalls** Opposite Siang Ti temple; map p.322. A tiny, venerable clutch of Chinese-run stalls where the highlight is the Sarawak *laksa* (RM7–15) plus other popular favourites such as chicken rice (RM7) and *kueh chap* (pork and pig offal in broth; RM8.50). As ever, stalls keep their own time; don't expect to find *laksa* after late afternoon. Daily early–late.

★ **Top Spot Food Court** Jalan Padungan; map p.322. Forget the unpromising location – atop a blue multistorey car park topped with a giant plastic prawn – this is a great place, featuring a dozen large stalls focusing on seafood. Sit near a stall you like the look of and they'll present you with their menu; try *ambal*, or crab and prawns done with garlic or chilli, or *oh jian* – the Sarawak version of this oyster omelette is like an enormous bowl-shaped crêpe. No pork served. Not super-pricey – one seafood dish plus veg and other things to share should cost RM30/head upwards, excluding alcohol. Daily 5–11pm.

CAFÉS

Bing! 84 Jalan Padungan ☎ 082 421880, 🖥 bingcoffee .com; map p.322. Kuching's plushest, slickest independent café chain, with a stylish a/c interior and prices to match – you'll pay at least RM16 for coffee and, say, a brownie. Serves Illy coffee, has a smoking terrace, and free wi-fi. Daily 10am–midnight.

Black Bean Coffee 87 Carpenter St ☎ 082 420290; map p.322. This tiny café and shop serves coffee grown in Sarawak and parts of Indonesia, made using *robusta* and the little-known *liberica* beans – certainly worth a try, though some people find it bitter or even "burnt". A takeaway cappuccino blended from either type of bean costs around RM5.50, and they also sell beans – though beans can also be bought (and ground) at a convenience store on Main Bazaar for RM8–25/kg. Mon–Sat 9am–6pm.

★ **Indah Café & Art Space** 33 Upper China St. ☎ 012 388 6535; map p.322. Funky little café just off Carpenter

6

Street, this small, friendly place serves great espresso coffees (RM5–8), outstanding cakes (including lime cheesecake and their famous fruity "messy affair") as well as local dishes, sandwiches and a vegan menu (all dishes RM5–11). They also have a small gallery for local artists and a couple of rooms (RM75), plus they run yoga classes (Sun; RM25), day-long cookery classes and village tours (both RM150), and art and batik workshops upstairs. Daily 8am–5pm.

RESTAURANTS

Annuar BBQ Steamoat Close to the Telang Usan hotel, off Jalan Ban Hock, ☎019 886 7900; map p.322. Among the best places in town for steamboat; for RM18/ person you get unlimited helpings from their spread of seafood, meat and other ingredients, which you then cook yourself at the outdoor tables. Their slogan is "you cannot go home if you are not full". Daily 6–11pm.

★**Aroma Café** Jalan Tabuan ☎082 417163; map p.322. This simple Bidayuh-run restaurant, on the ground floor of a dreary commercial block, is a fine place to sample tribal dishes such as *umai*, *ayam pansoh* and *midin* with garlic. Best value is the popular lunchtime *campur*-style spread (Mon–Fri 11.30am–1.30pm; RM5–7), but going à la carte is unlikely to cost more than RM15/person with soft drinks. Mon–Sat 7am–11pm.

Bla Bla Bla... 27 Jalan Tabuan ☎082 233944; map p.322. Designer touches such as Oriental water features set the tone at this fusion restaurant where you can savour Chinese-style renditions of un-Chinese ingredients such as salmon, ostrich and lamb, and round off your meal with cheesecake (RM10). Their speciality is a tangy *midin* salad (RM22), but many main courses will set you back double that. Mon & Wed–Sun 6–11.30pm.

Bombay Spices Lot 62, Lorang 4, Jalan Nanas ☎016 700 8807; map p.322. One of the best curry houses in town, serving excellent and authentic North Indian food. It's a little difficult to find unless you take a taxi – it's about 2km out from the centre just off Jalan Tun Ahmad Zaidi Adruce. The tandoori items are the speciality (including a fine chicken tikka masala), with great *nan* bread, and you can sit inside the a/c interior or outside if you want to smoke. Veg mains RM6–15, non-veg RM10–16. Daily 10am–10pm.

Ceylonese Restaurant Jalan Greenhill ☎082 231391; map p.322. Open, spacious and clean restaurant with outdoor seating, serving a range of cuisines, from Sri Lankan *biriyanis* (RM5–16) and curries (RM8–10) to North Indian tandoori dishes (RM8–15) and filling *nan* (after 1pm; RM3–12) – the chef's special *nan* with cheese and meat is perfect for pre- or post-drinking. Also has a range of local Malay and Chinese standards. Daily 8am–11.30pm.

★**the.Dyak** GF, Panovel Commercial Complex, Jalan Simpang Tiga, almost 3km south of the centre ☎082 234068; map p.322. Tribal food (and beautiful decor) meets haute cuisine at this popular high-class Dayak restaurant that serves jungle foods such as *jani tunu* (chargrilled pork longhouse style) – they also cater for vegetarians and vegans with the tasty *ubi randau* (a type of fern), among others. Dishes are impeccably presented and you can eat either in the stylish a/c interior or outside. Vegetable mains are RM12–15, meat dishes RM22–25. They also serve *tuak laki stambak Ulu* (RM90/bottle), the best *tuak* you're likely to encounter, which compares well with quality European-style wines, and made to a traditional (and secret) family recipe. Mon–Sat noon–8.30pm.

The Granery Marian Boutique Lodging House, 23 Lebuh Wayang ☎011 2508 9321, ✆abellhotel.com; map p.322. Housed in a high-ceilinged, stylishly restored 1920's grain warehouse, this well run bar-restaurant isn't cheap but serves up very good Western favourites such as burgers (RM28–32), pizza (RM24–28), and meats such as steak, lamb shank, and sausages (RM38–62), plus desserts like pineapple-vodka crumble (RM15). It's also got a decent bar with imported draft and bottled beers, and live acoustic lounge music at weekends. Daily 7am–11pm.

Hong Kong Noodle House 95–98 Jalan Padungan ☎082 421622; map p.322. Inexpensive Cantonese restaurant serving familiar Chinese dishes in clean, bright surroundings. All the items on the long menu of noodle dishes are RM6–7, and you can get meat with rice (such as duck or sweet and sour pork) for the same price. For something more sophisticated, they have fish head curry (RM10–25) or pork belly in spicy sauce (RM15), plus soups such as crab meat and sweetcorn, and hot and sour (RM12–28). Daily 9am–9pm.

James Brooke Bistro and Café Waterfront, near the Hilton; map p.322. It's very touristy, but this open-sided, greenery-surrounded building offers nice views, even if the food – a mixture of Western and local standards such as Sarawak *laksa* (RM10) – is nothing special and the prices on the high side (mains from RM20). Unusually for this class of restaurant, they don't take plastic. Daily 10.30am–11pm.

Junk 80 Jalan Wayang ☎082 259450; map p.322. Part of the labyrinthine *Backstage Bar* this place has the same higgledy-piggeldy junk-store look, serving hearty and good-quality plates of Western cuisine, such as lamb shank, steak, fish'n'chips and other standards. Mains RM25–68. Mon & Wed–Sun 6–11pm.

★**My Village Baruk** Kampung Boyan, down the lane from the jetty and then to the right ☎082 448970; map p.322. Here's that rare thing, an excellent Malay restaurant in interesting surroundings – a two-storey wooden building decorated with drapes and lanterns and meant to recall a *baruk*, or Bidayuh roundhouse. Nasi ayam *penyet* – chicken tenderized by pummelling and then grilled – is the speciality, but they also grill mussels and fish, plus (off-menu) *ayam pansoh*, emptied gloopily from bamboo tubes, and *nasi goreng dabai*, rice fried with the locally grown olive-like *dabai* fruit, when available. Most dishes around RM10. Service can be slow at busy times. Daily 4.30pm–midnight.

Pincho Loco 94 Jalan Ewe Hai ☎082 232833; map p.322. This chic, Barcelona-style tapas bar has a tile-decorated interior, black tablecloths and authentic Spanish food – all masterminded by the Catalan chef from *Zinc*. Great *bocadillos* (RM15), *patas bravas* and other typical tapas (RM10–15), plus pizzas (RM15–25) and an decent Spanish wine list. Mon, Tues & Thurs–Sun noon–3pm & 6–10.30pm.

Zhun San Yen Jalan Chan Chin Ann, ☎016 898 8367; map p.322. The best of a handful of Chinese vegetarian places in the area, this is a cafeteria-like place where you can choose from a spread of two dozen stir-fries and soups (noodles dominate at breakfast). A meal with soft drinks

seldom comes to more than RM10. Mon–Fri 8am–6pm, Sat 9am–3pm.

★**Zinc** 38 Jalan Tabuan ☎082 258000; map p.322. Smart and convivial, this well-run and stylish restaurant's Catalan chef uses many imported ingredients to create delicious Mediterranean cuisine, such as imaginatively topped thin crust pizzas (including a *laksa* variety), paella and risotto, plus a variety of main salads and even suckling pig. Expect to pay at least RM40–50/head for a meal before drinks. They also serve a range of tapas and have a decent wine list and other imported booze. Housed in a restored 100-year-old shophouse, it has bags of charm and also has a pleasant terrace bar, popular with the after-work crowd. Mon, Tues & Thurs–Sun noon–3pm & 6–10.30pm.

DRINKING AND NIGHTLIFE

Kuching's **drinking** scene is pretty good in a low-key kind of way. Venues are intimate for the most part, and the locals are very approachable. Carpenter Street is now clogged with bars, all of which are pretty similar, catering to both tourists and locals, though they seem to open and close with alarming rapidity. For a city with a sizeable middle class, the entertainment on offer is surprisingly meagre, however, though *Culture Club* has nightly shows of tribal music and dancing. The Rainforest Music Festival is the highlight of the cultural year (see box, p.338), but otherwise a lack of performance venues means there's not that much on apart from bar bands and DJs. To find out what's on, check out *Kuching In & Out* (⊛ kuchinginandout. com).

Culture Club 18 Jalan Green Hill ☎016 800 0155; map p.322. Currently the largest performance venue in the city, this large, mainstream a/c bar features daily Dyak music and dance perfomances from 8–9pm (till 10pm on weekends) followed by cover bands and DJs until 2am. They have a wide range of beers on tap as well as more pricey cocktails. Daily 4pm–2am.

Junk/Backstage Bar 80 Jalan Wayang ☎082 259450; map p.322. The tiny *Junk* bar feels like an extension of the restaurant, whereas *Backstage* has its own look, festooned with Chinese lanterns. Both draw in a suave clientele, especially for the live music and DJs on Fri & Sat night and there's draught Heineken (RM19) and Hoegaarden (RM23) on offer, among other imported beers and spirits. Mon–Fri & Sun 6pm–midnight, Sat 6pm–2am.

Monkee Bar Jalan Song Thian Cheok ☎082 410588; map p.322. Cosy and low-lit foreign-owned bar décorated with Dyak and Iban woodcarvings and dedicated to the orang-utan rehabilitation centre at Matang – half of profits

are donated there. Fun and friendly, they serve a large range of imported beers (RM6.50–20) as well as wine, cocktails and of course local *tuak*. Daily 3pm–3am.

★**Ruai** Café & Bar Jalan Ban Hock. 282 Yun Phin Building, off Jalan Padungan ☎013 826 1147; map p.322. On its sixth location (so check before you go), this simple but excellent Iban-run community chill-out joint features tribal decor and antique artifacts on the inside and a terrace on the pavement outside festooned with jungle plants, with a couple of live music sessions a month at weekends. A Tiger beer costs RM7 and they also serve home-made *tuak*, not just regular rice wine (RM30/bottle) but also varieties they've concocted from fruits such as apple or dragon fruit (RM5 more). For the adventurous, there's also *langkan*, a surprisingly smooth yet potent scorpion liquor, and there's even a barber's inside, if you need a shave (RM10). Happy hour 4–7pm. Daily 4pm–2.30am.

SHOPPING

Although Kuching offers the best **shopping** in Sarawak, that's not always obvious from a stroll around downtown, which is mostly devoid of huge modern malls. There are certainly more souvenir shops than anywhere else in Sarawak; outlets along Main Bazaar sell tribal textiles, pottery, rattan mats, locally grown pepper and so forth. As ever, however, their handicrafts may well have been made abroad – especially in Indonesian Kalimantan. The listings here concentrate on places selling domestically made items; the Sarawak Craft Council is the obvious place to start. If you're heading out to longhouses, you may prefer to defer buying crafts until you get there, though what you'll be offered will probably vary considerably in quality.

ARTS AND CRAFTS

Bricks & Earthenware Factory 5th mile, Jalan Penrissen (just past the airport) ☎082 451540; map

p.322. Kuching has a cottage industry producing Chinese ceramics with tribal influences, and this is probably the best of the potteries. Watch the potters in action at the

6

wheel and firing kilns, and buy wares ranging from huge pots to coffee mugs or vases. Take Rapid Kuching bus #3a or #6, or STC bus #K3 or #K6. Daily 8am–6pm.

The Museum 94 Main Bazaar ☎ 082 550190; map p.322. This café-shop sells paintings by famed local artist Ramsey Ong, whose excellent and somewhat abstract, highly-textured paintings of Sarawakian nature and tribal peoples go for RM200–20,000. At the cheaper end, there's also postcards of his work (RM2), as well as bead and silver jewellery. Daily 9am-6pm.

Sarakraf 78 Jalan Tabuan ☎ 082 232771; map p.322. Locally produced high-quality (and pricey) crafts, near Sarawak Plaza, with a decent stock of baskets, woodcarvings, ceramics and other items, some made to their own designs. Daily 10.30am–10.00pm.

Sarawak Craft Council Round Tower, Jalan Tun Abang Haji Openg; map p.322. The Craft Council's shop showcases some of the best crafts made in the state, labelled by area of origin. Here you'll find beaded necklaces, hats made from breadfruit-tree bark and bags woven from *bemban* reeds, all costing several tens of ringgit, and the sun hats of the Orang Ulu, shaped like giant mushroom caps and sold for several hundred ringgit. Mon–Fri 8.30am–1pm & 2–4.30pm.

CAMPING GEAR

Greek's Outgear Discovery Second floor, Sarawak Plaza, Jalan Tuanku Abdul Rahman ☎ 082 235205; map p.322. This oddly named store sells a range of high-end rucksacks, waterproofs, tents and so forth. Daily 10.30am–9pm.

MALLS AND SUPERMARKETS

Plaza Merdika 88 Jalan Tun Haji Openg ⓦ plazamerdeka.com; map p.322. The biggest and best of the downtown malls, with a good range of foreign and domestic shops and food outlets, including a Parkson department store, a decent supermarket, and pharmacies. Daily 10am–10pm.

Spring Mall 3km south of the centre, Jalan Simpang Tiga ⓦ thespring.com.my; map p.322. Kuching's biggest, busiest mall holds a Parkson department store, a supermarket and outlets selling electronic gadgets, clothes, household items and so forth. Buses #K8 and #K11 come here from the centre. Daily 10am–10pm.

Ting & Ting Jalan Tabuan; map p.322. This well-established supermarket is a convenient (though pricey) place to buy cheese and pork products as well as other imported food and drinks. Mon–Sat 9am–9pm.

DIRECTORY

Consulates Australia (honourary), E39 Level 2, Taman Sri Sarawak Mall, Jalan Tunku Abdul Rahman (☎ 082 230777); Indonesia, 21 Lot 16557, Block 11, Jalan Sutong (☎ 082 241734); New Zealand, Lot 8679, Section 64, Pending Commercial Centre, off Jalan Pendingi (☎ 082 482177); UK, The English Language Centre, Fortune Land Business Centre, 2 ½ Miles, Jalan Rock (☎ 082 250950).

Cookery classes At the Bumbu cookery class, 57 Carpenter St (9am–1pm & 2.30–6.30pm; ☎ 019 879 1050,

ⓔ bumbucookingclass@hotmail.com), you'll learn how to cook a four-course indigenous meal of local dishes – meat, veg, dessert and cut fruit, with ingredients bought on a shopping trip to the local market – and you get to eat the results afterwards (minimum class size is two; RM150; book at least 24hr ahead).

Hospitals The main state-run hospital is the Sarawak General Hospital, 2km south of the centre off Jalan Tun Abang Haji Openg (☎ 082 276666). You can also try the private clinics

---

IBAN TATTOOS

For the Iban, **tattooing** is not just a form of ornamentation, but also an indication of personal wealth and other achievements. Many designs are used, from a simple circular outline for the shoulder, chest or outer side of the wrists, to more elaborate motifs (highly stylized dogs, scorpions or crabs) for the inner and outer thigh. The two most important places for tattoos are the hand and the throat. The tattooing process starts with a carved design on a block of wood that's smeared with ink and pressed to the skin; the resulting outline is then punctured with needles dipped in dark ink, made from sugar-cane juice, water and soot. For the actual tattooing a hammer-like instrument with two or three needles protruding from its head is used. These are dipped in ink and the hammer is then placed against the skin and tapped repeatedly with a wooden block.

Kuching has become a magnet for people wanting to have a Bornean tattoo, and guesthouses may be able to introduce you to practitioners. The leading light of the scene, however, is the Iban artist and musician Ernesto Kalum, whose studio, **Borneo Headhunter**, is upstairs at 47 Jalan Wayang (best to make appointments two weeks in advance; ☎ 019 856 6317, ⓦ borneoheadhunter.com). He offers traditional motifs done either the traditional way (from RM900) or by machine (as in any Western tattoo parlour; from RM450), and can also do modern designs (always by machine).

at the Timberland Medical Centre at the southern end of Jalan Rock (☎ 082 234466, ⊕ timberlandmedical.com).

Laundry My Express, at the eastern end of Carpenter St at 11 Jalan Wayang (wash RM5–7, dry RM5; 24hr).

Massage The Alternative Therapy Centre in the basement of Sarawak Plaza offers excellent massage from blind people at very reasonable prices (RM30 for 1hr; daily 10am–7pm).

Pharmacy All of the shopping centres have either a Watsons, a Guardian, or both.

Police Jalan Khoo Hun Yeang, opposite the Padang Merdeka (☎ 082 241222).

Post office The main post office is on Jalan Tun Haji Openg (Mon–Sat 8am–6pm, Sun 10am–1pm).

Visa extensions Immigration Office, first floor, Bangunan Sultan Iskandar, Jalan Simpang Tiga (Mon–Fri 8am–noon & 2–4.30pm; ☎ 082 245661). Get there by 3pm to have your application processed on the day.

Around Kuching

One joy of visiting Kuching is the sheer number of potential excursions within the vicinity, including several worthy of an overnight stay. Within an hour's bus ride north are the beaches and resorts of the **Santubong Peninsula**, also known as **Damai** after the beach area at its tip. Nearby is the **Sarawak Cultural Village**, a showpiece community where model longhouses are staffed by guides from each ethnic group. **Bako** is the essential national park to visit nearby, but there's also decent trekking at **Kubah National Park**.

South of Kuching, the main attractions are the orang-utans at the **Semenggoh Wildlife Centre** and the easily accessible Bidayuh longhouse at **Annah Rais**. Sarawak's remote western edge draws a trickle of visitors who mainly head to the **Gunung Gading National Park** to see *Rafflesia* blooms, though the beaches at **Sematan** and near **Lundu**, and the stunning **Tanjung Datu National Park**, further west, are also worthwhile.

Unless otherwise stated, all **buses** mentioned below are local services leaving from the area east of Kuching mosque.

Santubong Peninsula

Cut off from Kuching by the Santubong River to the south, the **Santubong Peninsula** has been inhabited since prehistoric times. Excavation in the 1960s and 1970s found tens of thousands of artefacts, including digging implements, across six neighbouring sites; they dated back to 3000 BC, when the Indian/Javanese Empire extended here, though little of any ancient civilization can be seen today.

Dominated by the 810m **Mount Santubong**, the area is dotted with oddly shaped geological formations amid patches of thick forest. The mountain is a **national park** (with the entrance 1km south of Damai Central; ☎ 082 367100) and the well-marked, moderately taxing trek to the top takes five to six hours return, with rope ladders to help where things get steep; if you're lucky you might see hornbills, or proboscis and silver leaf monkeys. There's also a shorter marked path past a small waterfall that takes just 45 minutes. Oddly, there is no charge to enter the park here, though if you enter via the privately-owned *Permai Rainforest Resort* you will be charged RM8.

However, most visitors prefer to venture out to the **beaches** of **Damai**, 35km from Kuching at the Peninsula's northwest tip, or the excellent if pricey folk museum nearby, the **Sarawak Cultural Village**. Since the 1980s, stretches of the river and coastline have been developed as retreats for tourists and city-weary locals, though thankfully the resorts have left the tranquil, almost lonesome, nature of the area largely undisturbed. There are also two low-key villages, **Buntal** and **Kampung Santubong**.

Sarawak Cultural Village

33km north of Kuching • Daily 9am–5pm; cultural shows 11.30am & 4pm • RM63.60; day-tours from Kuching around RM120 • ☎ 082 846411, ⊕ scv.com.my

After crossing onto the peninsula from Buntal, the main road continues west and then north past several resorts, ending at the modern leisure development of Damai Central. Not far from the end, the **Sarawak Cultural Village** features seven authentically styled, if rather too perfect, tribal dwellings of timber and thatch, close to a central lake, with

6

SPOTTING SANTUBONG WILDLIFE

The mouth of the Santubong River is a promising spot to see the rare **Irrawaddy dolphin**. With a rounded snout rather than a beak, these marine mammals live in brackish coastal waters and river deltas, as well as in fresh water further upriver – for example, along the Mekong in Indochina, where the population is dwindling. In fact the dolphin is considered vulnerable in many habitats due to human activity – they may get snared in nets or see their range whittled away by barrages, for example.

Several tour operators can take you on dolphin-spotting cruises, though the specialist is **CPH Travel** (see p.329), which has its own launch; their trips leave in the late afternoon, taking you along the Santubong River in search of proboscis monkeys and fireflies as well as dolphins (3hr 30min; RM180). The odds of spotting dolphins aren't great during the rainy season if seas are rough; the rest of the time you have a fair chance of seeing them, though not necessarily close up.

---

the jungle escarpment of Mount Santubong looming dramatically behind. As folk museums go, it's worth the steep price of admission and doesn't feel forced; in fact, many of the staff you see kitted out in traditional finery live on site, and the place has become a community in itself.

Arguably the most impressive dwelling is the massive **Orang Ulu longhouse**, raised almost impossibly high off the ground, though the Melanau "tall house" also grabs the eye, with windows on two levels. You'll also see Iban and Bidayuh longhouses, a refreshingly simple Penan lean-to shelter, and – mundane by comparison – a Chinese kampung house and a formal Malay house in a style that only someone of status could have afforded to build.

Despite being out of context, the twice-daily 45-minute cultural shows are worth catching, striking the right balance between entertainment and education, and demonstrations of activities such as weaving, sago-processing and blowpipe-making are staged throughout the day.

Damai Beach

While the pleasant stretches of beige sand at Damai have individual names, such as Teluk Bandung and Teluk Penyuk, most people simply refer to the area as **Damai Beach**. The beaches don't belong to the resorts, though resort staff may levy a small fee if you try to access them via their compounds. One way to avoid this is to head to **Damai Central**, the shopping development opposite the Cultural Village, from where a path leads down to the beach. It's also possible to arrange activities in the area, such as trekking in the nearby **Kuching Wetland National Park** (which also has a birdwatching tower) or kayaking along the coast – you can arrange these at the *Permai Rainforest Resort* (see p.338).

ARRIVAL AND DEPARTURE   SANTUBONG PENINSULA

Transport from Kuching Private shuttles leave from the *Grand Margherita* hotel for Damai and the Cultural Village (every 2hr; RM20 each-way), and some Kuching guesthouses can arrange transport for the same price. Otherwise, unreliable minibuses (RM10) leave when full from opposite the food stalls in the Kuching bus station area, near the mosque (and take a while to get there as they visit many of the villages on the way), while a taxi should cost RM100 one way.

ACCOMMODATION

Campsite Next to Damai Beach ☎ 012 856 6557. You can rent a two-person tent here or pitch your own – though you'll have to make do with Damai Central's bathrooms. Site only RM31, two-person tent RM51

★ **Damai Beach Resort** Teluk Bandung beach, Damai, 1km north of Damai Central ☎ 082 846200, ⓦ damaibeachresort.com. The rooms are mostly modern and not all that special, but the lovely freeform pool set back from the beach sets the tone beautifully at this huge complex, all the more homely for being one of the area's oldest resorts. Rooms near the reception and in the blocks stacked up on the lush hillside behind are cheaper, though you might feel like splashing out on a *baruk* suite (RM572), built to look like a Bidayuh roundhouse with a conical roof.

OPPOSITE TUA PEK KONG TEMPLE, SIBU >

6

There's also a spa plus a couple of restaurants and a bar, and staff can organize guided jungle walks (RM5) and other activities. Rates include breakfast. 🛜 RM280

BB Bunkers Damai Central ☎ 082 846835, 🌐 bbbunkers.com. The only budget accommodation in town, this vast, somewhat industrial thirty-bed dorm has single beds downstairs, with somewhat more private raised double beds upstairs with curtains. There's a/c, all beds are comfortable and have their own power sockets, but there are only three toilets and one shower. 🛜 Singles RM60, doubles RM100

Nanga Damai 2km from Santubong village, right of the road as you head north ☎ 019 887 1017, 🌐 nangadamai.com. Not a longhouse, as *nanga* might suggest, but a swish six-room "boutique homestay" in a substantial, beautifully decorated modern house. Good value, with rates including breakfast. They also have a dorm. Note that there's a two-night stay minimum and no under-14s. 🛜 Dorm RM80, doubles RM200

Permai Rainforest Resort Keep going north after Damai Central then follow the boardwalk ☎ 082 846487, 🌐 permairainforest.com. You could come to this place to laze by the beach, but the emphasis is on being active – they offer kayaking, Santubong climbs and even an obstacle course. Guests stay in individual en-suite cabins, mostly sleeping up to six and good value if you're in a group of three or more (a/c RM30 extra), or two-person treehouses and they also have a small campsite. Quite cheekily, they'll charge you RM8 to enter and use their jungle paths and access the two pretty, small beaches along here, despite the fact that the whole place is built within the national park. Rates include breakfast but activities cost extra. 🛜 Camping per person with own tent RM10, treehouses RM385, cabins RM480

★**The Village House** Kampung Santubong, 30m down the track to the beach from Santubong crossroads ☎ 082 846166, 🌐 villagehouse.com.my. This gorgeous timber-built development features en-suite rooms set around a long, narrow swimming pool. Many have four-poster beds, but otherwise the decor is elegant without being over the top. They also have two of the slickest six-bed dorms you'll ever see, each with its own bathroom. The restaurant serves Western, local and fusion food. No under-12s. Rates include breakfast. 🛜 Dorms RM123, doubles RM334

EATING

In addition to the places listed below, there's likely to be food available at your accommodation, or you can head for the inexpensive (if unexciting) stalls at Damai Central's food court.

Budaya Sarawak Cultural Village ☎ 082 846411. Authentic tribal cooking, with dishes from all over Sarawak served in an ethnic setting. The set menus (RM26.50/37.10) are very good for a taster of a diverse range of dishes, and include *mamok pansoh*, chicken and rice cooked in bamboo in the firepit. You can eat at the restaurant without paying the entrance fee if you ask at the ticket office. The same menu is also served at a higher price at the the outside

D'Sea restaurant (until 9.30pm) on Damai beach, which also has a big seafood menu. Daily 9am–5pm.

Escobar Bar and Grill Damai Central ☎ 082 846039. This place by the beach offers Western bar food such as burgers and meat/fish with chips, (not so good) pasta, and a few Indian and Malay dishes. Mains mostly RM17–33. It's a great place to watch the sunset, especially with a bottle of their *tuak* (RM33). Daily 11am–11pm.

THE RAINFOREST MUSIC FESTIVAL

Since 1998, the Sarawak Cultural Village has been home to the annual **Rainforest Music Festival** (day tickets RM147, three-day pass RM410; 🌐 rwmf.net), usually held during July. It would be hard to find a more appropriate and evocative setting for a major world music event, with the Village's beautiful tribal homes not far from the stages and Mount Santubong the perfect backdrop.

While the event attracts performers from across the globe, it's especially worthwhile for the opportunity to watch indigenous Bornean musicians – some of whom can seem decidedly exotic even to city-dwelling Sarawakian youth, never mind audiences from further afield. With some noted performers having died since the festival was first staged, the sense that many traditions are living on borrowed time makes the chance to glimpse *sape* players (pronounced *sap-ay*, the *sape* is the Orang Ulu lute, shaped like a longboat), gong ensembles and the like that much more valuable (especially if you catch them in the intimate confines of a workshop). Favourites have included Tuku Kame, led by the flautist Narawi Rashidi (who is also head of the Village's Heritage Resource Centre) and featuring charismatic electric *sape* player Jerry Kamit. Beds are hard to come by in Damai and Kuching over the period, so book accommodation early. During the festival City Link provide a late-running shuttle bus between Damai and Kuching until 1.30am.

Bako National Park

East of the Santubong Peninsula, and no further away from Kuching, a second peninsula is occupied by the fabulous **BAKO NATIONAL PARK**, named for its location at the mouth of the Bako River. Sarawak's oldest national park (once a timber reserve, it attained its current, fully protected status in 1957), it's also among its most memorable. Its steep coastal cliffs, offering huge vistas over the South China Sea, are thrillingly different from the rest of the predominantly flat and muddy Sarawak coastline, and there are opportunities to spot proboscis monkeys, swim in jungle streams or at isolated sandy coves, and hike through terrain that takes in rainforest, mangrove and *kerangas* (see below), with pitcher plants easily visible on some trails.

Bako is such a gem that trying to pack it all into one day is not ideal, though you can make a go of it if you set out early from Kuching and pay a boatman at the park to take you out to a remote beach, then walk back to the park headquarters; this gives you a good taste of the park without having to do a trek in both directions. A stay of at least one night is still preferable, though, and there's a range of accommodation to choose from – this also gives you the chance to see many of the park's nocturnal animals.

Note that the entire eastern side of the park (east of the Tajor Waterfall) is **closed for path renovation** with no date set as to its completion.

Inside the park

First impressions of Bako, the coastal forest and craggy outcrops you see as you head here by boat, don't begin to do justice to its riches. The park boasts a multitude of different types of **vegetation**, including peat bog, scrub and mangrove; most trails run through a mixture of primary dipterocarp forest and *kerangas*, an Iban term referring to soil too poor to support rice, and now used to mean a type of woodland on poor soil characterized by fairly sparse, small trees and scrub, plus insect-eating plants such as pitcher plants. The *kerangas* stems from the unusual, largely infertile **sandstone** geology of the peninsula, eroded down to produce striking honeycomb weathering on some trails, and contorted rock arches rising from the sea. As for fauna, **proboscis monkeys**

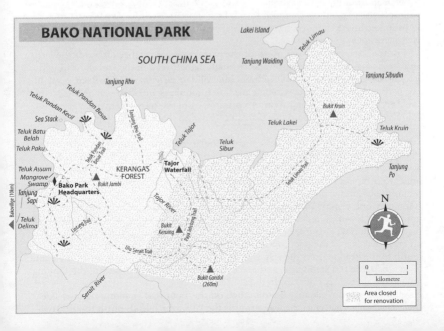

6

VISITING SARAWAK'S NATIONAL PARKS

Sarawak's two dozen or so **national parks** vary enormously, not just in terms of terrain and habitats – some boast accommodation for various budgets, well-marked trails and other amenities, while many others have nothing more than a ranger post and require a minor expedition to reach. All are managed by the state-owned **Sarawak Forestry Corporation** (W sarawakforestry.com) with the notable exception of Mulu, where tourist facilities have been privatized. You can pick up information about park conditions and accommodation at Sarawak Forestry's offices at the Sama Jaya Nature reserve on the outskirts of Kuching (see p.329) and at the desk inside the Sarawak Tourist Office in Miri (see p.365). Informal accommodation bookings can be made by calling the park concerned, while the Kuching office can confirm reservations with payment up front, and you can now also make reservations online at W ebooking.sarawak.gov.my. Almost all parks have well-organized **campsites** (RM5/person), usually covered, with bathrooms and cooking facilities, as well as a basic canteen nearby.

Guides can be engaged at just a few parks for around RM100–200/day, depending on their level of experiencee and English ability. Many, but not all, know about the local wildlife. Knowledgeable, licensed guides for parks in the Kuching area can be contacted through the Tourist Guide Association (see p.329).

---

are top of most visitors' lists; there's a good chance of seeing them not far from the park headquarters itself, though silverleaf monkeys tend to be harder to spot. Less exotically, monitor lizards and assorted snakes are sometimes seen, along with bearded pigs (a group have even made themselves at home close to the park cafeteria) and the usual assortment of creepy-crawlies, best spotted on a guided night walk.

No special equipment is needed, but pay particular attention to **sun protection** – it's amazing how you can be walking through a jungle glade one minute and in baking hot *kerangas* the next.

The trails

A free map from the park headquarters shows the **trails**, colour-coded and waymarked with splashes of paint on trees and rocks. Park staff can advise on what you can expect to complete in the time you have available, or whether to take a boat ride as a short cut (see opposite).

Most trails start from a spot north of the park headquarters, back towards the jetty and reached by a series of boardwalks through mangrove. You then ascend through steepish jungle, with the option of branching off left early on to **Teluk Paku**, a small, not particularly attractive cove where proboscis monkeys are often seen. Most people carry on to reach the **Padang** about 45 minutes from the start – here not a grassy colonial town square, but a rocky plateau of *kerangas* that's another hangout for proboscis monkeys.

At the Padang you're on the park's most popular trail, the looping **Lintang** trail that leads alternately through jungled slopes and *kerangas* via occasional stretches of boardwalk, and returns to the park headquarters from the south. Taking around four hours to complete if you don't pause frequently to rest or take photos, it can get monotonous after a while.

You may find it more interesting to branch off the Lintang trail at a clearly marked point only a few minutes' walk along the Padang. This two-hour side trail heads east to the **Tajor Waterfall**; a couple of low cascades in a jungled stream, the waterfall itself is no great shakes, but the pool just down from it is good for a swim. From here you can return to the headquarters the way you came, or continue east and south along a much bigger loop, the **Ulu Serait trail**, and returning along the southern part of the Lintang trail; allow at least six hours to do this.

Even more worthwhile may be to branch off the Tajor trail at another signed side trail, less than a quarter of the way towards the falls, which leads north towards two beautiful **beaches**, Teluk Pandan Kecil and Teluk Pandan Besar. Curiously, semi-dry stream beds seem to serve as the trail in some sections, eventually bringing you to viewpoints with superb views of the beaches and the South China Sea. The Pandan Kecil viewpoint also features bizarre hexagonal sandstone formations in the ground, where iron-rich rock has eroded less than the surrounding material. The steep descent to Pandan Kecil (15min) is rewarded with a swim at a secluded cove with whitish sand; unfortunately, no path leads down to Pandan Besar.

Other possible treks include heading to the remote Teluk Limau or Teluk Kruin beaches at the park's eastern end, taking at least eight hours (you'll probably want to travel one way by boat), or hikes off the main trails up to hills such as Bukit Gondol (260m) for great views.

ARRIVAL AND DEPARTURE — BAKO NATIONAL PARK

By bus Reaching the park from Kuching is straightforward: Rapid Kuching's red bus #1 heads east to Bako village roughly hourly from Jalan Khoo Hun Yeang, close to the Masjid Negeri, from 7am–5pm (1hr) with return buses running 6.30am–5.30pm. It stops en route at the Old Courthouse complex and along Jalan Tuanku Abdul Rahman, though given the lack of signage at bus stops, be sure to ask other commuters if the bus will call where you hope to flag it down. The bus stops at the Bako boat terminal for onward travel to the park.

By boat At the Bako boat terminal you can buy your park permit (see below), register, and board a park-bound boat (25min; RM40 return). They leave when full, from early morning until 3.30pm; last boat back is 4.30pm.

INFORMATION

Park HQ Just a few minutes' walk from the jetty, where you can pick up a simple park map, hire a green-jacketed official guide (RM100–200/day for up to 8 people, depending on English ability) or book to go on a guided night walk (8pm; 1hr 30min; RM20), which takes you south along the Lintang trail to spot insects, spiders and, with luck, nocturnal mammals and birds.

Information Centre Close to the Park HQ, the excellent information centre holds displays on the park's geology and history, and plenty of photographs to help you get a handle on the plants and animals you may see on the trails.

Admission Park permits, which you buy from the Bako boat terminal, cost RM20; a day-tour from Kuching (including admission) costs around RM280.

Contact details ☏ 082 370434, ⊛ sarawakforestry.com.

GETTING AROUND

By boat Saving time by using a boat to reach one of Bako's beaches is well worth considering; park staff can give an idea of the going rate, though you'll still have to negotiate with the boatmen at the jetty once you've signed in at the headquarters. The longest journey possible, out to Teluk Kruin (currently only accessible by boat), costs around RM250 one way for a group of five, but you're more likely to make the short hop to a popular beach such as Teluk Paku (around RM20) or Teluk Pandan Kecil (around RM40); prices are per person and boats leave when full.

ACCOMMODATION AND EATING

It's much cheaper to buy provisions in town before you arrive than to eat at the park's sole café, though note that cooking is not allowed inside any of the accommodation.

Bako National Park accommodation ☏ 082 478011, ⊛ sarawakforestry.com. The park's accommodations include a campsite; a recently renovated hostel with four-bed dorms; forest lodges, which are a little worn, where the three-bedded rooms share facilities; and en-suite doubles. Best are the newer a/c chalets, with two bedrooms that sleep up to six. Camping RM5, dorms RM15, en-suite doubles RM50, lodge rooms RM100, chalets RM225

Kubah National Park

Some 20km west of Kuching, **Kubah National Park** is a rainforest reserve considered one of the world's richest sites for **palm** species: of the 95 types found, including coconut, sago and many rattans, eighteen are endemic to the region. Look out too for giant squirrels, which are the bigger than a cat.

Three modest peaks, **Selang**, **Sendok** and **Serapi**, emerge out of the lush forest; they're crisscrossed by trails, waterfalls and streams. Marked hikes include the three-hour **Raya**

6

Trail, a good walk to catch sight of the palms, and the **Waterfall Trail**, a ninety-minute uphill hike to impressive, split-level falls. Kubah's best views, however, come on the three-hour **Mount Serapi (Summit) Trail** – from the top of the peak, you can take in Kuching and much of southwestern Sarawak.

Also within the park is **Matang Wildlife Centre**, where injured, sick or orphaned wild animals such as orang-utans, gibbons and hornbills are rehabilitated before being returned to the wild. There are many foreign volunteers working here, but it's fairly underfunded so you may find the conditions and state of the animals distressing – if you want to help with funding or volunteering, visit the *Monkee Bar* in Kuching (see p.333).

ARRIVAL AND INFORMATION   KUBAH NATIONAL PARK

By bus City Public Link bus #K21 runs to Kubah from Kuching (every 3hr – check timetable with the tourist office; 30–40min).

Admission The RM20 entrance ticket includes the wildlife centre.
Contact details ☎ 082 845033, ⊕ sarawakforestry.com.

ACCOMMODATION AND EATING

Kubah National Park accommodation ☎ 082 370422, ⊕ sarawakforestry.com. The park offers accommodation in either a hostel or a two-bedroom lodge. There's no canteen, or anywhere to eat nearby, so bring supplies to cook meals yourself. Dorms RM15, lodges RM150

Semenggoh Wildlife Centre

Off Sarawak's main trunk road, 25km south of Kuching • Feeding times daily 9am & 3pm • RM10; a day-tour from Kuching costs around RM80 • ☎ 082 442180 • City Public Link bus #K6 (45min) leaves Kuching to coincide with feeding times (8am & 2pm), and returns shortly after (10pm & 4pm); it stops by the ticket office on the main road, a 1.5km walk from the centre along an undulating access road

The first forest reserve in the state, the **Semenggoh Wildlife Rehabilitation Centre** was set aside by Vyner Brooke in 1920. Today it's a sort of open zoo in a surviving pocket of forest, where tourists flock to watch orang-utans being fed fruit by rangers, who have names for all of them. How many you're likely to see will depend on the time of year – when wild fruits are in season, fewer orang-utans emerge from the forest to seek out the rangers.

Most of the action takes place at a clearing, with seating close by, reached by a short jungle trail from the car park. Don't be surprised if you see the orang-utans roaming around the car park itself – and give them a wide berth if you do. Look out also for orang-utan nests, which they build in the treetops using clumps of leaves and branches, for sleeping. The morning feeding is usually better, and arriving by 8.30am will give you a decent seat.

Annah Rais

Near the mountains that straddle the border with Kalimantan, 60km south of Kuching, the Bidayuh longhouse settlement of **ANNAH RAIS**, while occasionally touristy, makes a decent day-trip from Kuching, particularly if you don't have time to see longhouses elsewhere in Sarawak. It's easy to combine a visit with a trip to Semenggoh if you're driving, and not too hard by bus, though confirm bus times with the tourist office (see p.329).

The settlement of around 1300 feels like a hybrid of **longhouse** and **village** – assorted differently styled wooden "houses" are joined together in two long parallel rows and raised off the ground, with platforms of bamboo slats on planks serving as "streets". This higgledy-piggledy style is in part due to the fact that it is one of the oldest remaining wooden longhouses in Sarawak, with a written history of more than 175 years, and an oral tradition that goes back 500. Behind the facades, individual family quarters open off vast corridors, just as in a regular longhouse, and as ever there's a **river** nearby for bathing (a bridge brings you to a third longhouse). You'll probably be offered a small glass of *tuak* (or Borneo brandy) upon arrival, while depending on the season, you may see the rice harvest or longhouse-made latex sheets being dried. Be sure to pop into the **panggah**, or skull house, where skulls hark back to a martial tradition that only ceased a few generations ago – the villagers claim that they were actually used as part of a ceremony to bring peace.

ARRIVAL AND INFORMATION   ANNAH RAIS

By bus City Public Link bus #K6, which also serves Semenggoh, heads from Kuching to the small town of Kota Padawan (8 daily; 30min) from whose market you can catch a minivan (1hr; RM10) to Annah Rais. The longhouse homestay programme can arrange transfers from/to

Kuching, RM100 for up to four people. or RM140 for up to ten people. Day tours are available from hotels and travel agents in Kuching for RM100-250.

Admission fee RM8, payable at the information booth in front of the longhouse.

6

ACCOMMODATION

★**Annah Rais Homestay Programmes** ☎090 049762, ⓦlonghouseadventure.com Several longhouse homes host homestay programmes, which are for the most part very basic but clean. The English-speaking coordinator, Patrick, lives at #71, in the second longhouse. Packages are available (1/2/3 nights

RM298/398/498); these include food and drink, and activities such as jungle-trekking, hunting with blow-pipes and rafting, as well as cooking, basket-weaving and traditional dancing and music. Activities start at 10am, so you'll need to arrive around 9.30am. 🛜 Full board/person RM100,

Bau and around

Nineteenth-century prospectors were drawn to **BAU**, half an hour's drive southwest of Kuching, by the gold that veined the surrounding countryside, but the modern-day market town is mundane in the extreme, though it does have a picturesque mining lake, **Blue Lake**, on its southwestern edge. Pretty though the lake is, it contains arsenic and is unsafe to swim in; the main reason to come to Bau is to visit the two nearby **caves**, around 4km apart to the west.

Bau caves

Daily 8.30am–5pm • Both caves RM5 • Sarawak Transport Company bus #2 goes from Kuching to Bau (3 daily), from where the Bau Transport Company #2 bus (2 daily) runs to the caves (catch the 11.40am service if you want to return to Kuching by bus; the last service back to Kuching is at 4.30pm) – each cave has its own bus stop on the main road, at least 15min walk from its entrance; there are also taxis from Bau (RM20 each way for Fairy Cave, RM14 for Wind Cave) – get the driver's number for the return.

If you have to pick one of the two **Bau caves** – which you may well have to do if relying on public transport – choose the larger, **Fairy Cave**. Steps inside enable you to wander through the gloom towards a gaping maw at one end of the system, which lets in refreshing breezes and enough light for the cave floor to be blanketed in ferns and moss. The smaller **Wind Cave** is a little less impressive, with two dark tunnels inhabited by a colony of bats –you'll need to make sure you bring a decent torch with you to fully explore it.

ACCOMMODATION AND EATING   BAU

★**Lan e Tuyang** 14km short of Bau and 23km from Kuching on the Batu Kawa Rd, parallel to and north of the main Bau Rd ☎016 816 8525, ⓔjacksonlianngau @gmail.com. This excellent homestay is run by the Kenyah *sape* exponent and artist Mathew Ngau Jau, a mainstay of the Rainforest Music Festival (see box, p.338), who has created a sort of mini-longhouse decorated with Orang Ulu motifs and *sapes* built in his workshop below. He can teach

you the rudiments of the lute-like instrument and how to build one, or you can try your hand at woodcarving. Five simple guest rooms have fans and mosquito nets, with toilets and showers in a separate block; take traditional meals (RM25) in the house or they can give you a lift to the simple restaurants in the Chinese hamlet of Tondong a few minutes' drive away. Arrange ahead for pick-up from Bau town, Kuching or the airport (all RM50/person). 🛜 RM50

Gunung Gading National Park

The main claim to fame of **Gunung Gading National Park**, 75km by road west of Kuching, is that it's home to the parasitic **Rafflesia** plant (see p.586), with its stinky blooms. However, when the buds are maturing the park can go for months without a

6

single *Rafflesia* in flower; if you're coming specifically to see the plants (as the vast majority of visitors are), check with the park in advance.

The park can be visited as a day-trip from Kuching. With an early start, you can tackle the **Waterfall Trail**, on which it takes ninety minutes to reach the end at waterfall 7 – it really is the seventh waterfall en route – where you can have a good, refreshing swim. With more time, you can also climb Gading, one of the park's two hills. It's a full-on hike and a six-hour round trip, though it's a well-marked trail and a guide is not needed.

ARRIVAL AND INFORMATION
GUNUNG GADING NATIONAL PARK

By bus There are eight daily buses from Kuching's regional express bus terminal to the town of Lundu (1hr 30min), from where you can either walk 3km north along the main road to get to the park, or catch a

minivan or taxi which congegate next to the bus station (RM5–10).

Admission fee RM20.

Contact details ☎ 082 735144.

ACCOMMODATION

Gunung Gading National Park accommodation ☎ 082 735144. The park has a campsite, a hostel where four rooms offer dorm beds (or can be let as four-bed

rooms) and a lodge holding six-bed chalets. There's no canteen, but you can cook at the park's kitchens. Camping/person <u>RM5</u>, dorms <u>RM15</u>, doubles <u>RM40</u>, chalets <u>RM150</u>

Tanjung Datu National Park and around

Some 40km west of **Lundu** town, and at the end of the road from Kuching (until the new section of the Pan-Borneo Highway opens), the seaside town of **Semantan** has a long, picturesque beach and reasonably clean almost-yellow sands. However, most foreign visitors are here to visit **Tanjung Datu National Park** (ⓦ sarawakforestry.com), whose beaches are far superior to the wide flat beach in the town.

At the very western tip of Sarawak, this tiny park covers a mountainous region around a coastal spur close to the Kalimantan border. Although it offers splendid rainforest, swift, clean rivers and isolated bays, the main draws are its two dazzling **beaches**, with shallow, unspoilt **coral reefs** perfect for snorkelling only a short distance from the shore, and occasionally frequented by dolphins – bring your own equipment.

The park is also among the few destinations in Sarawak where green **turtles** come to lay eggs (April to October), while the jungle holds six species of primate, seven species of hornbill, elusive clouded leopards and much more easy-to-spot deer and wild boar. There are four marked **trails**, too: the hardest, the Belian Trail, takes around an hour and a half, leading halfway up Mount Melano (542m) to where *Rafflesia* bloom, while the Pasar Antu Laut Trail (also 1hr 30min) leads almost 4km north through the jungle, ending up at the isolated and slightly surreal Golden Sand Beach.

ARRIVAL AND INFORMATION
TANJUNG DATU NATIONAL PARK

By boat At the time of writing, the only independent access to the park was by boat from Sematan (40min; RM600 for up to six people, RM800 for up to eight; Minhad is the best boatman ☎ 012 848 6549). From the Sematan jetty, it's also possible to catch the erratic public boat (often leaving around 10–11am) that takes locals back to the village of Telok Melano (RM50), a 90min walk from the park HQ. However, once the new section of the Pan-Borneo Highway from Sematan to the Indonesian border near Telok Melano is completed (maybe as soon as 2018), all of

this will change, and taxis and minibuses may well ply the route. Getting to Sematan itself is fairly straightforward, with four daily express buses leaving from Kuching's regional express bus terminal, via Lundu (where you may have to change), returning at 7am, 10am, 12.30pm & 4pm.

Package tours You can also come to the park on an over-priced package tour from Kuching, such as from CPH Travel (see p.329), or locally from *Telok Melano Homestay Program* (see opposite).

Admission fee RM20, payable at the Park HQ.

ACCOMMODATION

There are several accommodation options in Sematan, including a couple of resorts along the coast, several homestays signposted from the main road near the bus station, and one grubby but cheap guesthouse.

Tanjung Datu National Park Accommodation
📞 082 248088. Basic accommodation is available at the park HQ, with four fan twin rooms, a six-person, dorm-like forest hut (bedding RM16 extra) and a campsite. There's no canteen, so for food you'll either have to walk to Telok Melano and back or cook your own – cooking equipment can also be rented for RM16/day. Camping/person RM5, jungle huts RM10, twins RM42.50

Telok Melano Homestay Program 📞 082 711101, 🌐 right.sarawak.gov.my. This tiny Malay fishing village of fifty families, around a 90min walk from Park HQ, operates a local homestay programme, with over half the homes here offering rooms. It is used by tour operators (who massivly overcharge for it), though you can contact them directly for one of their packages (starting from RM1150 for up to five people), which includes transport from Sematan, full-board accommodation, cultural shows, park entrance, and other activities. It's also possible to stay on a nightly basis if you are travelling independently. The village has community wi-fi near the only restaurant on the beach. Full board per person RM100,

Batang Ai – the Iban longhouses

The **Iban longhouses** of the Ai headwaters, both 150km due east of Kuching beyond the lake of the Batang Ai hydroelectric dam, and also to the north along the **Lemanak** river system, are the best excuse for anyone travelling between western and central Sarawak not to catch the fast Kuching–Sibu ferry. Despite being on the tourist trail, the longhouses offer a glimpse (if somewhat fake) of what used to the semi-traditional lifestyle in this remote corner of the state, much of which is protected as a **national park** and wildlife sanctuary. Sadly, most locals now prefer to live nearer to the road, and many of the villages and longhouses you'll be taken to are only inhabited while tourists are there – unfortunately, the locals see little of the profits made by the agencies that run tours here, and you may get the impression that they're all rather weary of the whole thing.

Batang Ai dam and lake

Around three and a half hours' drive from Kuching, a couple of kilometres beyond the village of **Jelukong**, a signed 38km turning branches southeast off the main trunk road, passing a few modernish longhouses en route to the small border town of **Lubok Antu**. Some 12km short of that, another small road branches east (left) towards the **Batang Ai dam**, a way station en route to the upper Ai. Built in the 1980s as Sarawak's first hydroelectric venture, the Ai dam created a lake covering 90 square kilometres. Though now dwarfed in scale, generating capacity and controversy by the Bakun dam (see p.358), it's an impressive sight nonetheless and the road up gives good views of the narrow valley downriver.

No parts of the dam are open to tourists, though, and once you get there you'll head to one of the jetties to continue east by boat to an Ai longhouse or the *Aiman Batang Ai Resort & Retreat*.

Batang Ai National Park

Only accessible with an official guide, who can be hired in Lubok Antu; if you're on a tour, you have to pay a tour operator for a day-trip to be added onto a longhouse package • RM20 • 📞 014 718 2342 (manager in Kuching), 🌐 sarawakforestry.com

East of the lakeshore, an hour by boat from the dam, the little-visited **Batang Ai National Park** preserves an important area of rainforest that merges with the Lanjak Entimau Wildlife Sanctuary (LEWS; off-limits to visitors), which itself merges with another protected area across the border in Kalimantan. **Orang-utans** are occasionally spotted on various trails in the national park, but a boat to these trails will set you back RM700–800 from the HQ. The park holds no residential or other facilities, and all visitors must be accompanied by a guide.

Ai River

An hour east from the Batang Ai dam, longhouse-bound boats leave the lake and head up the **Ai River**. As is clear from the tall trees that come right to the water's edge, the

6

initial stretch is still a drowned portion of the river. Further up you'll observe a transition to the true river banks, the vegetation more open and compact. Also visible sporadically to either side are the odd school and clinic in simple metal-roofed timber buildings, and areas of hillslope cleared for traditional rice cultivation. The Iban leave paddies to the jungle once the soil is exhausted and move on to clear new areas. As the river narrows, you also begin to see the occasional **longhouse** lurking in the vegetation. Among those that take tourists are **Nanga Delok** (also called Rumah Ipang, on the Delok, a tributary of the Ai) and the more distant **Nanga Sumpa** (the Sumpa being a tributary of the Delok). Wherever you stay, you will be offered opportunities for additional longboat trips to areas where you can make short treks or local beauty spots such as waterfalls.

THE IBAN

Easily the most numerous of Sarawak's indigenous peoples, the **Iban** make up nearly thirty percent of the state's population. Their language is from the same family as Malay, and any Malay speakers will notice considerable overlap in vocabulary as well as predictable changes in word endings – *datang* (come) and *makan* (eat) in Malay, for example, become *datai* and *makai* in Iban.

ORIGINS AND CONFLICTS

Having outgrown their original home in the Kapuas river basin of west Kalimantan, the Iban migrated to the Lupar River in southwest Sarawak in the sixteenth century, and came into conflict with the Melanau and Malays. With the Brunei sultanate at its height, the Malays pushed the Iban back inland up rivers such as the Rejang, into interior areas dominated by the Kayan. Great battles were waged between the two groups; one source recorded seeing "a mass of boats drifting along the stream, [the combatants] spearing and stabbing each other; decapitated trunks and heads without bodies, scattered about in ghastly profusion". Although such inter-ethnic conflict stopped as migration itself slowed, the Iban were still taking heads as recently as the 1960s during the Konfrontasi, when the Indonesian army came up against Iban who had thrown their lot in with Malaysia.

SOCIETY

The Iban figure prominently in the minds of visitors, thanks to their traditional communal dwelling, the **longhouse** (see opposite). Each has its own *tuai* (headman), who leads more by consensus than by barking orders. Traditionally, young men left the longhouse to go on **bejalai**, the act of joining a warring party – essentially a rite of passage for a youth to establish his independence and social position before marriage. Nowadays, to the extent that *bejalai* has meaning, it may translate into going to university or earning a good wage on offshore oil rigs or in a hotel or factory in Singapore.

Further complicating the *bejalai* tradition is the fact that **women** are now much more socially mobile, and can pursue education and their own careers. Traditionally, however, women had distinct duties, which is cited as a reason why a woman is not permitted to be *tuai*. They never went hunting, but were great weavers – an Iban woman's weaving prowess would once have determined her status in the community. The women are most renowned for their **pua kumbu** (blanket or coverlet) work, a cloth of intricate design and colour. The *pua kumbu* once played an integral part in Iban rituals, hung up prominently during harvest festivals and weddings, or used to cover structures containing charms and offerings to the gods.

DEVELOPMENT AND URBANIZATION

More than half of Sarawak's Iban have moved permanently to the cities and towns in the west of the state, or may spend the working week there and weekends back in their longhouse. Most rural Iban no longer live purely off the land but also undertake seasonal work in the rubber and oil industries. By no small irony, logging – the business that most devastated their traditional lands – also long supplied plentiful and lucrative work; these days oil-palm cultivation and production provide more employment.

LONGHOUSE ARCHITECTURE

Longhouses can be thought of as indoor villages, housing entire communities under one roof. Although several indigenous peoples build dwellings that are sometimes called longhouses, the definitive article is the **Iban** longhouse. This has a long veranda or *tanju* at the front where rice, rubber and other produce can be laid out to dry; it's accessed by steps or sometimes a log into which notches are cut. Behind the front wall, running the entire length of the building, a corridor or *ruai* serves as a sort of main street where the community can socialize. Multiple doors (*pintu*) open on to the *ruai*, behind which lie each family's quarters (*bilik*); locals describe a longhouse not in terms of its length or the number of inhabitants, but by how many *bilik* or *pintu* it has. Above the living quarters, a loft space (*sadau*) is used for storage.

Traditionally longhouses were built of hardwood timber and bamboo, perhaps with ironwood shingles on the roof. Even though most longhouses now feature plenty of unsightly concrete, they still retain their characteristic *ruai* inside, and most continue to be sited close to rivers or streams, where people enjoy bathing even when piped water supplies exist.

Lemanak River

The **Lemanak River** is, like the Batang Ai dam, reached by the Lubok Antu Road, though you turn off earlier to head to the jetties. Several longhouses here regularly host travellers, notably **Ngemah Ulu**, where guests are put up in the longhouse itself, which has been adopted by Diethelm Travel in Kuching (ⓦdiethelmtravel.com). Independent travel here is not easy. Coming on a two-night package offers the option of a great local trek.

ARRIVAL AND DEPARTURE   BATANG AI

By tour Most visitors book with a Kuching or Miri tour operator, which usually includes the road transfers, the journey in and out by longboat, plus all meals.

By travelling independently Roads have reached some longhouses north of the Ai, but since many longhouses aren't signposted, having your own car is little advantage unless you have local friends or hire a guide in Lubok Antu. That said, you can visit by public transport. If you get dropped at Jelukong Junction on the main road by any bus to or from Miri, then it's 39km to Lubok Antu (RM50 taxi, often possible

to share) where there is accommodation and you can ask around to find a guide (around RM100–200/day). To get to the more remote settlements by boat (without hiring a whole one), there are usually "public" boats taking students back for the weekend from the dam; they'll most likely leave Friday afternoon, and return on Sunday afternoon. When leaving, there's no need to backtrack all the way to Kuching; to head on to Sibu and beyond, flag down a bus on the main road. There are at least a couple of buses per hour and tickets can be bought on board.

ACCOMMODATION

Aiman Batang Ai Resort & Retreat Southeastern shore of Batang Ai lake, 40min from the dam ☏1300 889908, ⓦaimanbatangai.com. A 5-star resort is definitely a misfit in this isolated area, but then, so is the dam – so you might as well just enjoy the lake vistas from the hotel terrace. Each block is a timber building with rooms on one side of a long corridor, just as in a longhouse; built in the 1990s, the rooms now look a tad dated. Either drive up and be collected at the dam, or pay RM150 (min 4 people) for shuttle transport from the *Kuching Hilton*. <u>RM380</u>

Nanga Sumpa Ai River, a 90min boat ride from the dam; only bookable as part of a package. This longhouse deserves special mention as the site of an excellent purpose-built tourist lodge, sited at a discreet distance from the longhouse itself across a creek. Rooms have wooden platforms that hold a simple mattress and a mosquito net, but little else, though there's a pleasant open sitting/dining area and modern shared bathrooms. Prices vary; only bookable through tour operators based in Kuching (see p.329).

Central Sarawak

For travellers, central Sarawak offers rather slim pickings compared to Kuching's hinterland and the north of the state. Those visitors who venture here tend to be drawn by the prospect of travelling into the interior along the **Rejang** (also spelled **Rajang**), Malaysia's longest river. All such trips start from the bustling city of **Sibu**, some 50km

6

inland near where another major river, the **Igan**, splits away from the Rejang. Express boats depart daily to zip up the Rejang to **Kapit**, beyond which, through the **Pelagus Rapids** and on to the sleepy town of **Belaga**, eight hours from Sibu, the Rejang becomes wild and unpredictable and the scenery spectacular. There's not much to do in either Kapit or Belaga, and while there are longhouse communities near both, almost all are made from concrete – the last easily accessible traditional wooden longhouse is east of Kapit along the Balui River. Public transport is thin on the ground, so it's best to regard the Rejang journey as an end in itself or else fork out for (pricey) local guides to arrange trips for you.

With Sibu being so far from the sea, and the coast here dominated by mangrove swamp, the main trunk road runs deep inland until it finally hits the coast again at Bintulu. Halfway along, a side road leads off through a chink in the vegetation to the coastal town of **Mukah**, which has an appealing museum-cum-guesthouse nearby. **Bintulu** itself is a nondescript but (thanks to oil and gas) prosperous town, whose main attraction is as a base for **Similajau National Park**, easily reached yet appealingly quiet.

Sibu

From its humble 1850s origins as a tiny Melanau encampment, **SIBU** has grown into Sarawak's third largest city and its biggest port. Nearly half its quarter-million population are ethnic Chinese. Unusually for Malaysia, many are Foochow, descended from migrants from what's now Fuzhou in southeast China. Their diligence is often credited with helping the city become the commercial centre it is today. Its Foochow flavour aside, Sibu is also identified with Sarawak's controversial **logging** industry, which helped the city recover from the Japanese occupation, when many Chinese were forced into slave labour. Sibu subsequently became, for a time, the centre for timber processing in Sarawak and investors, many drawn from long-established Chinese families, made large fortunes as a result.

Having experienced devastating fires in 1889 and 1928, plus serious damage during World War II, Sibu is characterized more by energy than visual appeal. However, boasting a huge **market** and a lively **waterfront**, it has enough sights to keep you occupied for half a day – just as well, as most travellers en route to or from the upper Rejang spend at least a night here.

Waterfront

If you arrive on the boat from Kuching, you'll find yourself on the **waterfront** on the Rejang's right bank, facing rows of dull modern shophouses and commercial buildings. Efforts have been made to landscape and beautify the **Rejang Esplanade** – the tiny riverside recreation area by the ferry terminal – but it's still a fairly humdrum spot. Look out, however, for a riverside marker indicating the Rejang's level during historic floods. Sibu's commercial lifeline is also a scourge; every few years the river overtops this area and inundates the city centre. Efforts are ongoing to tame the Rejang by dredging away sediment, some of which no doubt results from forest clearance.

Tua Pek Kong temple

Eastern end of Jalan Temple • Daily 6.30am–8pm • Free • ☎ 082 312005

A small wooden temple stood on the site of Sibu's Taoist **Tua Pek Kong temple**, at the northern end of the riverfront, as early as 1870. Soon afterwards it was rebuilt on a much grander scale, with a tiled roof, stone block floor and decorative fixtures imported from China. Two large concrete lions guard the entrance. The **statue** of Tua Pek Kong, the temple's most important image, survived both the fire of 1928 and Japanese bombardment. The pagoda at the back is, by contrast, Buddhist, and if you ask for the key you can walk up to enjoy the views from the top.

SIBU

ACCOMMODATION
Kingwood	5
Li Hua	4
The Paramount Hotel	2
Tanahmas	1
Ting Ying Hotel	3

● EATING
The Ark Café	5
Café Café	3
Hai Bing	4
Hock Chu Leu	2
Payung Café	6
Peppers Café	1

Long-Distance Bus Station (2.4km) & Airport (20km)

Rejang Medical Centre

JALAN BUKIT ASSEK

JALAN TONG SANG

JALAN PEDADA

JALAN HOE PING

HARDIN WALA

JALAN TOOCHOW

JALAN TIONG HUA

JALAN MUI HONG

JALAN EMPLAM

JALAN LAI CHEE

JALAN HUA KIEW

PERSIARAN BROOKE

JALAN TUANKU OSMAN

JALAN PERSIARAN/JALAN KAMPUNG NYABOR

Sibu Gateway Monument

JALAN LANANG/PERSIARAN BROOKE

JALAN MASSION

JALAN LANANG/PERSIARAN BROOKE

JALAN LONG BRIDGE

JALAN RAH TING

JALAN MAJU

JALAN TAN SRI

JALAN MAJU

LORONG LANANG 4

LORONG LANANG 2

JALAN MAJU

Rejang Esplanade

Malay Food Stalls

JALAN CHAMBERS

Pasar Malam

JLN BENGKEL

HIGH ST

JALAN CENTRAL

JALAN MARKET

JALAN CHANNEL

Central Market

JALAN KHOO PENG LOONG

Local Bus Station & Taxis

Terminal Penumpang

Police Station

Taxis

Sibu Heritage Centre

CHINATOWN

JALAN WONG NAI SIONG

JALAN CROSS

JALAN TUKANG BESI

Standard Chartered Bank

JALAN MOHSIDI SIDEK

JALAN LANANG/PERSIARAN BROOKE

JALAN CENTRAL

JL CHEW GEOK LIN

JALAN TEMPLE

JALAN BANK

Tua Pek Kong Temple

JALAN WHARF

JALAN PULAU

Batang Rejang

Kuching

Kapit, Song, Belaga & Kanowit

KMMP Pharmacy

Guardian Pharmacy

JALAN CAUSEWAY

Wisma Sanyan

JALAN KAMPUNG NYABOR

JALAN SUKAN

Padang

Warehouses

JALAN BUJANG SUNTONG

0   100
metres

6

6

Central Market

Northern end of the riverside Jalan Khoo Peng Loong • Daily dawn–dusk, hawker stalls upstairs stay open into the evening

Sibu's modern and entertaining **Central Market**, one of the biggest in the country, is housed in a long, curved-roofed building. It's best to turn up on a Saturday, when it's at its busiest and the entire ground floor is taken up with vendors selling items such as bamboo tubes for stewing *ayam pansoh*, live roosters tied up in newspaper, slabs of what look like mummified bats but are in fact smoked fish, and, in the run-up to tribal festivals, gongs – which prospective buyers have no qualms about trying out. Stalls at the edge offer a tasty Sibu speciality, *kongbian*, sometimes called Chinese bagels but more like dainty versions of the sesame-seed breads sold in Turkey and Lebanon. An upstairs **food court** offers a few vantage points overlooking the colourful goings-on below.

Sibu Heritage Centre

Jalan Central • Tues–Sun 9am–5pm • Free • ☎ 084 331315

The **Sibu Heritage Centre** is a fine museum highlighting the city's history and cultural diversity. There's a good discussion of how Chinese pioneers, with the support of Brooke officials, founded the settlement and got it off the ground with crops such as rubber – logging didn't arrive until the 1930s – and of Foochow immigration, which only began in earnest at the start of the twentieth century. Among the basketware, beadwork and so forth you can see a striking nineteenth-century Kayan burial hut (*salong*) atop a 1m-high totem pole.

ARRIVAL AND DEPARTURE   SIBU

By plane Sibu's airport (☎ 084 307770) is 25km east of the centre. While you could walk 10min to the nearest major road junction and flag down a passing bus or yellow-topped van into town (roughly hourly; RM3), it's a lot easier to pay for a taxi (RM32). Heading out to the airport, any bus from the local bus station bound for Sibujaya or Kanowit can drop you at the same junction. MAS/MASwings and AirAsia, have offices at the airport.
Destinations Bintulu (7.20am daily; 35min); Johor Bahru (11.50am daily; 1hr 35min); Kota Kinabalu (2 daily; 1hr 35min); Kuala Lumpur (8 daily; 1hr 55min); Kuching (7 daily; 40min); Miri (2–3 daily; 55min).
By boat Sibu's express-boat terminal on the esplanade, Terminal Penumpang, is used by Bahagia fast boats between here and Kuching via Sarikei downriver; it's

advised to take the more expensive upper-deck seats, which have better views and a/c (11.30am daily; 4–5hr; ☎ 084 319228). There are also more frequent boats upriver to Kanowit (3 daily, last at 8.30am; 30min) and Kapit (18 daily, last 2.30pm; 3hr).
By long-distance bus All express buses use the long-distance bus station, 5km northeast of the centre off Jalan Pahlawan with a taxi to the centre costing around RM15. Hourly Lanang Bus Company services #20 and #21 go to the local bus terminus, which is in front of the express-boat terminal close to the centre.
Destinations Bintulu (every 1–2hr; 4hr); Kuching (7 daily; 8hr); Miri (10 daily, morning and evening only; 7hr 25min); Mukah (around 5 daily, last at 4.30pm; 3hr 30min); Pontianak (Indonesia; at least 2 daily; 18hr).

INFORMATION AND TOURS

Tourist information Knowledgeable and helpful staff at Sibu's central Visitors' Information Centre, at the Sibu Heritage Centre (Mon–Fri 8am–5pm; ☎ 084 340980, ✉ vic-sibu@sarawaktourism.com), also cover the Rejang River towns plus Bintulu and Mukah, which don't have tourist offices. They produce a very good guide to Sibu town and the region with several maps included.

TOUR OPERATORS

Great Holiday First floor Pusat Pedada, eastern end of Jalan Pedada ☎ 084 348196, ⊚ ghtborneo.com. This agency does a one-day Sibu tour (RM160/person), and a

half-day one (RM120) to visit to the Bawang Assan longhouses (see box opposite).
Greatown Travel Behind the Rejang Medical Centre at 6 Lorong Chew Siik Hiong ☎ 084 211243, ⊚ greatown .com. Unusual one-day trips downriver to Sarikei (RM220), where you can do some trekking, see pepper being cultivated and visit a wooden Iban longhouse where you can also add on a homestay (RM100/person full-board). Even more unusually, they can take you down north down the Igan River to Mukah (three days/two nights full board RM900), which includes a visit to Lamin Dana (see p.358). Book a few days in advance.

ACCOMMODATION

Sibu has a couple of decent inexpensive **hotels**, plus loads of choice once you get to mid-range and above. The cheapest guesthouses are around Chinatown, though this area also hosts a couple of loud bars and is also frequented by prostitutes.

Kingwood 12 Lorong Lanang ☏084 335888, ✉kingwood.sibu@yahoo.com.my; map p.349. Incredibly, this huge hotel, with a gleaming extension back from the river, has never seen fit to have a website despite boasting a pool, gym, sauna and other amenities. Prices can be slashed by RM50 when things are quiet, making the place an absolute steal. Rates include breakfast, though you can save yourself RM54 if you get a rate without. ☏ RM170

★**Li Hua** By the river at the junction of Lorong Lanang 2 and Jalan Maju ☏084 324000; map p.349. It's not the place to come for little refinements, and the sound of guests' chatter can echo around the small lobby, but this is a terrific budget hotel, efficiently run, with dated and plain but well-kept en-suite rooms and free wi-fi on quite a few floors. Reserve ahead. ☏ RM65

The Paramount Hotel 3 Lorong, 9A Jalan Kampung Dato ☏084 331122, ✉paramount_hotel@yahoo.com; map p.349. Located a five-minute walk north of the market near the river, this ageing mid-range place is a little careworn but retains a certain style, like a glamourous great-aunt. The rooms are good-value and, while not super modern, are spacious and have nice views of the river. The hotel's restaurant serves local food, including a RM12.90 lunchtime buffet. Avoid staying on the fourth floor as this is where the karaoke room is. ☏ RM141

★**Tanahmas** Off the eastern end of Jalan Chambers ☏084 333188, ⊛tanahmas.com.my; map p.349. This slick mid-range hotel boasts some of the nicest rooms in its class, fairly spacious with elegant modern furnishings, a swimming pool, mini-gym and a popular Chinese restaurant on the second floor. ☏ RM207

Ting Ying Hotel Jalan Channel (directly opposite the market) ☏084 341122; map p.349. By far the best (non-sleazy) budget option, it has small but clean rooms with good bathrooms, and is fairly quiet at night – the market is noisy in the morning, but if you're getting a boat you'll need to be up early anyway. No wi-fi. RM42

EATING AND DRINKING

Local specialities include **Foochow noodles** – steamed and then served in a soy and oyster sauce with spring onions, chilli, garlic and dried fish; and *kang puan mee*, which literally translates as "dry-plate noodles" though it is in fact *mee* fried in lard and garnished with pork slices. Good **bars** are thin on the ground, but not for lack of trying; a few venues, such as along Jalan Tukang Besi, are beautifully done out but lack finesse and descend into karaoke at the slightest opportunity – there is also quite a lot of prostitution.

The Ark Café Rejang Esplanade ☏084 313445; map p.349. It may look like a designer home, but *The Ark* is actually a multi-cuisine restaurant that serves Thai, Western, Chinese, Korean and Malaysian dishes. The food,

---

LONGHOUSES NEAR SIBU

There are very few traditional wooden **longhouses** left along the Rejang, but there are a couple of semi-traditional ones within easy striking distance of Sibu that are excellent and well-established at hosting tourists.

Bawang Assan Sibu Longhouse Homestay Program 14km southwest of Sibu ☏014 582 8105, ⊛rantaukemiding.blogspot.com. Just 40min by road from Sibu (RM50–60 by charter taxi, or RM2 by minivan every two hours from the Central Market), there are nine colourful longhouses here where Iban families (all with English-speaking members) take guests. The longhouses are a mix of traditional and modern, and prices include food, board and a range of activities such as paddy planting and fishing. The tourist office in Sibu can help you make the arrangements. RM110

Rumah Benjamin Angki Rantau Kemiding, 4km southwest of Kanowit, which is a boat stop or a 40min bus ride upriver from Sibu ☏013 882 3076, ⊛rantaukemiding.blogspot.com. Painted bright yellow, this venerable longhouse with more than 64 doors and a correspondingly vast *ruai* dates back to 1936. Being set in an agricultural area just uphill from the Kanowit River, it isn't a full-on outback experience, and is great for families with young children. Guests can stay in a purpose-built modern block with two a/c rooms, or in the longhouse itself, where some of the Iban speak good English. Call Benjamin in advance to discuss prices and some kind of programme as well as to arrange a pick-up from Kanowit; potential activities, all costing extra, include guided walks through the woods, fishing trips and so forth; check website for available packages. Per person, full board in modern block RM65, longhouse without meals RM75 at best, is not bad (try the Emperor Pork Belly), but the contemporary decor compensates, and prices are reasonable (from around RM30/person without alcohol) and rice and noodle dishes are just RM20–25. Several outdoor tables, set around a courtyard that's nicely lit at night, have river views by day. Daily 11am–11pm.

Café Café 8 Jalan Chew Geok Lin ☎084 328101; map p.349. While not as swish as *The Ark*, *Café Café* is for many middle-class locals the place for a smart night out. The food is mostly a mix of Chinese, Malay and Thai dishes (the Thai chicken salad is very popular), served in different portion sizes with rice for around RM18–38, with set lunches for RM12.90–19.90. No credit cards. Tues–Sun noon–4pm & 6–11pm.

Hai Bing 31 Jalan Maju ☎084 321491; map p.349. Well-established, earthy, and often busy Chinese restaurant known for its seafood, such as ginger crab (RM60/kg), though the prawns and other options are a bit cheaper. If you stick with the meaty rice and noodle dishes you can eat for under RM10. Daily 11.30am–1.30pm & 5.30–11.30pm.

Hock Chu Leu Upstairs at 28 Jalan Tukang Besi ☎084 330254; map p.349. *Kopitiams* aside, you'd expect Sibu to have a more formal downtown place offering Foochow cuisine – and this is it, and though it's a little fusty it's certainly Chinese-looking. Come here for classics such as Foochow noodles and *ang chow kai*, chicken that's red from being cooked with the sediment from a certain type of Chinese wine. Around RM20, excluding drinks. Daily 11am–1.30pm & 5–8pm; sometimes closed Tues.

★**Payung Café** Jalan Lanang, ☎016 890 6061; map p.349. This smart and stylish restaurant, smartened up with tribal artefacts and a thatched awning, is one of the quirkiest in Sarawak, with a fusion menu that reflects enthusiasm rather than fancy culinary training. Their cooking often uses local herbs and could feature anything from Indochinese pomelo salad to prawns with starfruit and spaghetti. You can wash down your meal with, say, their brilliant home-made pineapple ginger soda (RM7), or even fresh durian milkshake, if the pongy fruits are in season. Around RM30 with soft drinks. Daily 11.30am–3pm & 6–11.30pm.

Peppers Café Tanahmas Hotel, off eastern end of Jalan Chambers ☎084 333188, ⓦtanahmas.com.my; map p.349. The usual hotel restaurant menu ranging from Western staples – including lamb chop and rump steak (RM28–69) – to Malaysian fried rice and Chinese noodles (under RM25), in plush surroundings and at somewhat elevated prices. It's the best Western grub in town, and not a bad option for a slap-up buffet breakfast (RM31). Daily 6am–1.30am.

DIRECTORY

Hospitals and clinics The Sibu Hospital is a taxi ride away at 5 1/2 mile on Jalan Ulu Oya (☎084 343333); alternatively, try the Rejang Medical Centre, 29 Jalan Pedada (☎084 330733).

Pharmacies Guardian is just outside Wisma Sanyan mall, and KKMP is just inside the mall (both daily 9.30am–10pm).

Police Jalan Kampung Nyabor (☎084 336144).

Up the Batang Rejang

Even though much of the traditional culture and architecture of the region has been lost, a journey to the **upper reaches of the Rejang** should still engender a little frisson of excitement. This area was, after all, once synonymous with remoteness and with mysterious warring tribes. Even a century ago, conflict persisted between the Iban and the Orang Ulu, particularly the Kayan. Things had been much worse before the arrival of the Brookes, who wanted to develop – and therefore subjugate – the interior. To that end, James Brooke bought a section of the Rejang from the Sultan of Brunei in 1853, while his successor, Charles, asserted his authority over the Iban and Kayan tribes and encouraged the Chinese to open up the interior to agriculture and trade.

Thus began the gradual pacification of the Rejang. Even today, despite development and modern communications, it's possible to glimpse something of that pioneer spirit in these upriver towns, while forts at **Kanowit** and **Kapit** hint at the lengths taken by the Brookes to get the region under their thumb. The furthest boats go upriver is the nondescript town of **Belaga**, reached by a thrilling ride through the **Pelagus Rapids**. There is, however, another exciting route into or out of Belaga – by **4WD**, the road connecting up with the main trunk road near Bintulu (see p.360).

Unfortunately **visits to traditional wooden longhouses** can be difficult to pull off. The vast majority are now made of concrete – notable exceptions are Bawang Assan near Sibu, the Rumah Benjamin Angki Longhouse near Kanowit (see box, p.351), the Rumah William Unchat longhouse near Kapit, and a few up the tributaries near Belaga or Kapit – easy enough to get to by "flying coffin" (see opposite).

REJANG BOATS

One explanation for the nickname "flying coffins" – formerly attached jokingly to the **Rejang express boats** – is that they are long and narrow, and feature aircraft-like seating. Otherwise they are serviceable, if not massively comfortable or user-friendly: boarding entails stepping off the jetty onto the boat's rim or gunwale and walking around until you reach the entrance hatch. You may also have to fling your luggage on the roof yourself, although sometimes staff are on hand to help load and unload.

Several companies operate the boats, but look out for people selling **Bahagia** and **Husqvarna** tickets at the boat terminal; both companies stand out for having more comfortable boats that are also more likely to leave on time and to have windows through which you can see clearly – though the jungle views may get monotonous after a while. Otherwise you'll have to be entertained by the onboard DVDs of overly patriotic Chinese and Hollywood action flicks – one of the advantages of going first class is that they often leave the volume down.

SCHEDULES AND FARES

Boats **depart** Sibu at least twice an hour from 6.15am until 11am, then every 45 minutes until 3pm. All go to Kapit (around 3hr), just a couple to Kanowit (45min) and many more serve Song, the stop before Kapit. Downriver boats from Kapit operate to a similar schedule. To get to Belaga, you'll have to change at Kapit, where the connecting boat leaves at 11am, so if you're going to go all the way in one day, you need to ideally leave Sibu before 7.45am. Note that during the dry season, if the river level is low, Belaga boats are cancelled – ask at the jetty or tourist office in Sibu (see p.350) for the latest.

The **fare** from Sibu to Kapit is RM20 (RM5/10 extra for second/first class, which when available offers a bit more legroom and slightly better air conditioning). A Kapit–Belaga ticket costs RM25. You should try and arrive thirty minutes before departure time, and at busy times, say during the run-up to a festival, buy tickets a day or two before.

Kapit

KAPIT is the main commercial centre upriver from Sibu, and it looks it too, trapped in an architectural no-man's-land between the modern town it could become and the rustic backwater it was a generation ago – the place feels like an utter jumble, despite a certain appealing energy. If you do end up here, you may well stay the night – either because you can't face the journey to Belaga in one go or because this is as far as you intend to get – and fortunately it has some good accommodation options. Although there are a couple of **museums** (plus several banks and a couple of internet cafés), there's not much else to do beyond wandering the river bank or having a look around the market.

Fort Sylvia

Tues–Sun 10am–noon & 2–5pm (you may need to wait for the caretaker to show up with the keys) • Free • ☎ 082 239672

Fort Sylvia, the white, low-slung building a couple of minutes' walk upriver from the boat terminal, makes quite a grand first impression. Built in 1880 of tough *belian* (ironwood) timber, it was an attempt to prevent the marauding Iban attacking smaller and more peaceable tribes, and to limit Iban migration along the nearby Balch River, confining them to the Rejang below Kapit; note the diamond-shaped gun holes all along the facade.

The fort is now a small **museum** and conference venue, managed by the people behind Kuching's Tun Jugah Foundation gallery (see p. 327). Evocative photographs depict great moments in the history of the Ulu Rejang, including the 1924 peace-making ceremony in Kapit between Brooke officials and the warring Iban and Kayan tribal representatives. In addition, ceramic jars, *pua kumba* textiles and small cannon are on display.

Civic Centre and Museum

Jalan Hospital • Tues–Sun 8am–5pm • ☎ 084 796003 • Free

Also known by its Malay name, Dewan Suarah, Kapit's **Civic Centre and Museum** holds interesting exhibits on the tribes in the Rejang region, including a well-constructed longhouse and a mural painted by local Iban. Sketches and watercolours of Kapit, Belaga and Song portray a life that is slowly disappearing. The museum also describes the lives of the Hokkien traders who helped put towns like Kapit on the map.

Rumah William Unchat Longhouse

Yong River • Entry, photo permit and community donation for 1–6 people RM65; skull room RM40 extra • Contact Cikgu (teacher) Jega Keling on ☎ 014 881 2906 or ☎ 084 796903 • You can visit using a guide from Kapit, though it's not that difficult to organize yourself; a minivan from Kapit's market square should cost around RM120–130 return (45min) – if the driver speaks English, ask them to come in with you as not many people speak English here

Some 50km southwest from Kapit, the weather-worn **Rumah William Unchat Longhouse** is one of the last remaining traditional wooden longhouses in the region, and one of the few anywhere that still keep the skulls hanging outside the skull room, though most of today's inhabitants now live in the shiny new 34-door longhouse built next door. It's also possible to **stay** here, and although you'll have to bring your own food, they'll help you to cook it.

ARRIVAL AND INFORMATION

By boat Kapit's large boat terminal is used by all boats except Belaga services, which use a pier just a couple of minutes' walk downriver.

Destinations Belaga (1 daily; 5hr); Kanowit (1–2 daily; 2hr); Sibu (18 daily; 2hr 30min).

Guides If you want to visit Rumah William Unchat Longhouse, your accommodation can usually organize an English-speaking guide, which should cost around RM250–300/person from Kapit for an all-inclusive overnight stay, depending on group size. For trips into the jungle, contact Iban guide Jose (☎ 019 485 9190), as well as for destinations such as Nanga Pulang Longhouse (two nights RM595/person) or the remote Horse Mountains (four nights RM1350/person); both minimum 4 people. Make sure all the terms are clearly agreed before you set out.

ACCOMMODATION

Kapit has a few reasonable budget hotels (if the ones listed here are full, you'll easily stumble upon a handful more around town) and two mid-range options, though accommodation tends to be slightly overpriced. There is also the option of staying at the **Rumah William Unchat Longhouse** nearby. If you want to experience staying at one of the longhouses between Kapit and Belaga, or on the less-visited tributary between Kapit and the logging camp at Putai, residents often hang out around the docks looking for tourists.

Ark Hill Inn Jalan Penghulu Gerinang ☎ 084 796168, ✉ arkhill168@gmail.com. Good-value budget place with spartan but quite serviceable and clean en-suite doubles, twins, triples and a couple of "single" rooms that hold a bed large enough for two (RM55). Wi-fi in lobby only. 📶 RM90

Dragon Inn Lot 46, Jalan Teo Chow Beng ☎ 084 796105, ✉ kingsingwong@yahoo.com. It's the first hotel you come to walking up from the jetty, and it has the most economical rooms. Most are a/c, en suite, and bare but clean. The fan rooms on the top floor are more worn, with shared bathrooms, but they're the cheapest in town. Wi-fi in lower floor rooms only. 📶 RM40

★ **Greenland Inn** Jalan Teo Chow Beng ☎ 084 796388. Snug, clean and carpeted en-suite rooms, all with a/c, TV, comfy beds and the best bathrooms in Kapit. It can be noisy at reception, so try to get a room on an upper floor. No breakfast. 📶 RM120

EATING

Eating in Kapit is largely a matter of picking from the numerous **kedai kopis** and ordering from a fairly predictable range of dishes. All eating places – apart from the *Taman Selera Empurau*, the *KFC*, and the *Sugarbuns* – close by 6.30pm.

Taman Selera Empurau One block back from Jalan Teo Cheow Beng, behind the Methodist church. The only decent option after dark, this open-air food market serves inexpensive and delicious Malay food at plastic tables – noodles, fried rice, excellent satay sticks and of course *nasi goreng*. It would be hard to spend more than RM10. Daily 5pm–1am.

6

Belaga

Belaga-bound boats make frequent stops upriver from Kapit, and some passengers decamp to the roof for views of longhouses as the Rejang narrows. Forty minutes from Kapit, the **Pelagus Rapids** is an 800m-long, deceptively shallow stretch of the river where large, submerged stones make the through passage treacherous, and although it might get your adrelalene pumping slightly, remember that the boatmen are well-practiced in traversing them. Further upriver, the population shifts from being largely Iban to featuring a mix of other tribes, including the Kayan and Kenyah.

Five hours beyond Kapit, the boat finally reaches tiny **BELAGA**, 40km west of the confluence of the Rejang and the Balui. The town started life as a small bazaar, and by 1900 pioneering Chinese *towkays* were supplying the tribespeople – both the Kayan and the then-nomadic Punan and Penan – with kerosene, cooking oil and cartridges, in exchange for beadwork and mats, beeswax, ebony and tree gums. The British presence in this region was nominal; Belaga has no crumbling fort to serve as a museum, as no fort was built this far upriver.

The town square and around

The first sight that confronts new arrivals climbing the steps from the river bank is Belaga's slightly shabby tennis and basketball court. Next door a small garden serves as the **town square**, with a hornbill statue atop a traditional-style round pillar bearing tribal motifs. There are just six streets and alleys in the centre, and while quite a few shops sell provisions, there's no market, though Orang Ulu traders may arrive at weekends to sell jungle produce in the streets. In the morning, picturesque mists settle on the Rejang.

Walks around Belaga

Having made it all the way here, the best thing you can do is luxuriate in Belaga's tranquillity, a welcome contrast from Kapit. Short walks lead through the **Malay kampung** just downriver (which includes the shanty town by the river for children

---

THE KAYAN AND KENYAH

The **Kayan** and the **Kenyah** are the most populous and powerful of the Orang Ulu groups who have lived for centuries in the upper Rejang and, in the northern interior, along the River Baram. The Kayan are more numerous, at around forty thousand, while the Kenyah population is around ten thousand (with substantially more Kenyah over the mountains in Kalimantan). Both groups migrated from East Kalimantan into Sarawak roughly six hundred years ago; they were pushed back to the lands they occupy today during the nineteenth century, when Iban migration led to clashes between the groups,

The Kayan and the Kenyah have a fair amount in common: their language, though of the same family as the other Bornean tongues and Malay, has a singsong quality that sounds like Chinese, and they have a well-defined social hierarchy, unlike the Iban or Penan. Traditionally, the **social order** was topped by the **tuai rumah** (chief) of the longhouse, followed by a group of three or four lesser aristocrats or **payin**, lay families and slaves (slavery no longer exists). Both groups take pride in their **longhouses**, which can be massive.

KAYAN ART

Artistic expression plays an important role in longhouse culture. The Kayan especially maintain a wide range of **musical traditions** including the lute-like **sape**, used to accompany long voice epics. **Textiles** are woven by traditional techniques in the upriver longhouses, and Kayan and Kenyah **woodcarvings**, among the most spectacular in Southeast Asia, are produced both for sale and for ceremonial uses. One artist, Tusau Padan, originally from Kalimantan, became much revered. He used mixed media of vibrant colours to create the flowing motifs he applied to painting and textiles – adorning burial poles, longboats and the walls of many Ulu Sarawak chiefs' homes. Some Kayan still drink potent **rice wine**, although now that nearly all the communities have converted to Christianity, alcohol is harder to come by.

from outlying villages attending the school here) or cross the river (boat RM5) and walk two hours along a red paint-marked path through the jungle to the **Sihan** (a semi-nomadic people) village – there are only a handful of sporadic inhabitants now, coming for harvest and festivals only.

ARRIVAL AND DEPARTURE

BELAGA

By bus There is one daily boat to Kapit, which leaves around 7.30am. Boats use the jetty by the basketball court.

By 4WD Most days at least a couple of 4WD vehicles leave for Bintulu from the town square, usually in the early morning (3hr 40min; RM60/person). It costs RM50 to reach the main trunk road, where you can flag down a long-distance bus. Contact Daniel Levoh (see below) for a booking. Alternatively, it's possible for men and groups to hitch the route (just stand by the bridge in Belaga or at the junction on the main road) – you may be asked to pay RM20–60, so clarify whether you're expected to pay before you get in.

INFORMATION AND TOURS

Banks The town has a Bank Simpanan National, with ATM, three streets back from the river.

Tours and longhouse trips About the only person seriously organizing tours in Belaga is Daniel Levoh, who runs trips to the small waterfall 20min away up a tributary (RM90 for one to three people), as well as an all-day tour to the Bakun Dam using 4WD and boat, which stops in various old and new longhouses on the way (RM600; one to four people) – this tour could drop you on the Bintulu–Miri highway. Although his guesthouse is very good value, the tours are pricey. However, if you bargain, prices may come down considerably.

ACCOMMODATION AND EATING

The town's Malay *kedai kopis* cluster on the main street, while there are a couple of decent Chinese places, which serve beer, a few doors down from the *Daniel Levoh Guesthouse*. None of them are bad, but none particularly good, and all close shortly after dark. This is when you can get the best food at the sociable **night food stalls** just north of the centre, which dish up inexpensive Malay foods including outstanding grilled meats and satay.

Belaga Hotel Main St ☎ 086 461244. The oldest of the main street's three all-but-identical hotels (all the same price) and it looks it too, with dated fittings. The simple en-suite rooms have a/c, and – this gives it an edge – there's a café below with wi-fi. ☎ RM40

★**Daniel Levoh Guesthouse** Two blocks behind Main St ☎ 013 848 6351, ✉ daniellevoh@hotmail.com. More like a homestay, with two double rooms and a dorm that open up on to a nice and homely communal area where there is also a small kitchen. Daniel, an ex-history teacher, is a good host, and can tell you stories in the evening about the local area over a glass of *tuak*. ☎ Dorm RM20, doubles RM40

Sing Soon Huat At the end of a lane, just back from the Sing Soon Hing ☎ 086 461307. Sharing management with the nearby *Sing Soon Hing*, these are probably the best rooms in town; bigger and a little quieter than those on the main street, with a/c, TV and better en-suite bathrooms. ☎ RM50

The coast from Sibu to Bintulu

The drive from Sibu to Bintulu is mundane, the roadscape lacking the grandeur of southwest Sarawak's mountains, though there are occasional glimpses of (usually modern) longhouses by the highway. The chief point of interest on this coastal stretch is **Similajau National Park**, a strip of forest with isolated beaches thirty minutes' drive beyond the industrial town of **Bintulu**. With plenty of time, you could also get a dose of the culture of the largely Muslim Melanau people by diverting off the trunk road to the small coastal market town of **Mukah**. While not of huge interest in itself, it's a potential base for the Melanau water village of **Kampung Tellian**, which has a heritage centre, **Lamin Dana**, that you can also stay at.

Kampung Tellian and around

The Melanau water village of **KAMPUNG TELLIAN**, 3km east of **MUKAH**, is a veritable spaghetti junction of ramshackle wooden houses connected by precarious crisscrossing boardwalks and bridges. It's an immensely atmospheric and peaceful spot, the kind of place where you might wish you were born so that you could always go back there.

6

THE BAKUN DAM

The massive **Bakun hydroelectric dam** (ⓦ sarawak-hidro.com), 37km east of Belaga on the Balui tributary of the Rejang, has been dogged by controversy since the project got the go-ahead in the 1990s. The 200m-high dam was designed to generate 2400 megawatts – much more power than Sarawak could use – but construction would flood an area of rainforest the size of Singapore, displacing ten thousand Orang Ulu and destroying many thriving longhouses.

Furious environmentalists and human-rights campaigners asked what was the point, and for years their concerns seemed vindicated as the dam was beset by delays. First, the **Asian economic crisis** of 1997 put the project on hold, but even so the government continued to resettle local communities to Asap, two hours' drive along the logging road connecting Belaga with the coast. When construction resumed it lumbered on until, in mid-2011, the dam finally began operating. However, it still doesn't run at anything near capacity, since there is no obvious market for the **surplus power** (one idea, to lay a submarine cable to Peninsular Malaysia, would be technically challenging and prohibitively expensive). Despite this, yet another dam has been built just upriver on the Rejang at Long Murum – it and another proposed dam on the Baram have seen massive protests and blockades by local people, thanks to which the Baram dam was cancelled in 2015.

Attempts have already begun to create tourist facilities at the Bakun Dam lake, as has been tried with limited success at Batang Ai and Tasik Kenyir in Terengganu, though these have yet to bear fruit, and the hotel there is mostly used to house dam workers. Sibu's tourist office (see p.350) and Daniel Levoh (see opposite) in Belaga (whose family live there) have details of the enormous and quite swanky Kayan and Kenyah **longhouses** at Asap that accept guests (RM50/person), and whose inhabitants have a fishing lodge on the lake itself.

Some of the Melanau residents of its many stilt houses still process sago the traditional way – by pulverizing the pith in large troughs and squeezing the pulp through a sieve, then leaving it to dry.

Lamin Dana

Daily 9am–5pm for non-residents • RM3 • ☎ 019 849 5962, ✉ genistarose@gmail.com

Aside from its picturesque appeal, Tellian's main attraction is its beautiful heritage centre and guesthouse, **Lamin Dana**, built in 1999 in the style of a traditional Melanau tall house, though not quite on the scale of the one at the Sarawak Cultural Village in Santubong (see p.335). Exhibits include a collection of betel-nut jars, once used to store heirlooms, finely woven textiles for ceremonial occasions, musical instruments – including the obligatory gongs – and handicrafts such as hand-woven rattan baskets for which the Melanau are well known. A short walk along the plankway to the front of the tall house reveals a Melanau burial ground, or *bakut*, amid a clump of bare, ancient trees.

ARRIVAL AND DEPARTURE

By plane No buses run between Mukah's airport, 4km northwest of town, and the town itself; a taxi costs around RM15. MASwings flies to both Kuching (2–3 daily; 1hr) and Miri (daily; 1hr 10min).

By bus The bus station in Mukah lies off Jalan Setiaraja, on the southern edge of the old town.

KAMPUNG TELLIAN AND AROUND

Destinations Bintulu (3 daily; 3hr); Miri (1–2 daily; 4hr 20min); Sibu (3 daily; 1hr 30min).

By taxi Taxis from Mukah's bus terminus can take you to Kampung Tellian for RM6–10. Note that all taxi-drivers finish work at around 4 or 5pm.

ACCOMMODATION AND EATING

Lamin Dana Cultural Boutique Lodge Kampung Tellian ☎ 019 849 5962, ⓦ lamindana.com. This recreated tall house is an atmospheric place to stay, with ten variously sized, airy doubles and a couple of family rooms. Bathrooms are shared and there's no a/c. If you come on a package, you'll be taken on a boat trip through the mangroves, do a guided village walk, and see a sago-processing demonstration; contact proprietor Diana Rose for details and to customize an itinerary. ☎ Doubles with breakfast US$40, three-day, two-night full-board package including pick-up from Mukah per person US$250

Sri Umpang Hotel 29 Jalan Lintang, Mukah ☎ 084

872415. Mukah's best choice is a 20min walk from the bus station in the old town, with a bright and appealing foyer and clean, a/c rooms with sizeable bathrooms. Best to book ahead as it's often full; the similar, though slightly more expensive, *Weiming Hotel* is just a few doors down. ☎ RM50

Bintulu

6

Forty years ago, **BINTULU** was little more than a resting point en route between Sibu (220km to the southwest) and Miri (210km northeast). Since large **natural gas** reserves were discovered offshore in the 1960s, however, speedy expansion has seen Bintulu follow in Miri's footsteps as a primary resources boom town. Today some quite prosperous neighbourhoods can be seen on the outskirts, though the old centre remains as unassuming as ever. There are only two reasons why you might want to stop over: to use Bintulu as a base for the excellent **Similajau National Park** or, if you're heading south from Miri, as a springboard for **Belaga** and the Batang Rejang (see p.356). You can also reach **Niah National Park** (see p.368) from here (though it's easier to go on a trip with one of the Miri backpacker lodges), while any express bus to Miri can drop you at **Lambir Hills National Park** (see p.367).

The old centre

You could spend a couple of hours strolling around Bintulu's **old centre**, a grid of streets squashed between the defunct airfield to the east and the wide Kemena River to the west. This is why the town feels so low-key: the centre simply hasn't been able to grow. It looks as though developers and road builders are finally being allowed to chip away at the unaccountably abandoned airfield, however, so the heart of Bintulu is changing rapidly.

The obvious place to start is on Main Bazaar in front of **Tua Pek Kong**, a grand Chinese temple that's really in too good a state of repair to impress. Redevelopment of the **riverfront** has created the open square here, as well as an esplanade and parkland area leading north towards the South China Sea – only 3km away, concealed beyond the Kemena's final bend.

Just downriver are the modern **day market** (*pasar utama*) and the more informal **Tamu Bintulu**, where locals still bring in goods and lay them on rough tables to sell. The jetties behind are a good place to observe life on the river: fishing boats bring their catch in every morning, barges laden with timber or building materials lumber past, while the opposite bank is dotted with rustic kampung houses.

6

BINTULU TO BELAGA BY ROAD

When the water level in the Batang Rejang is too low for boats to reach Belaga, the one sure way to get there – and an interesting drive through remote terrain – is by **4WD** from Bintulu. The four-hour journey involves turning south off the main trunk road, 50km out of Bintulu, on to the road for the Bakun dam (see p.358), 125km southeast.

After 80km, another right turn puts you on a logging road which, while not a classic bone-shaker, is roughish much of the way. The road undulates at first through jungled areas, then climbs steadily, snaking past isolated communities and through areas either already under oil palm or being cleared for it. Eventually there are gorgeous views of lushly forested peaks in the distance; the highest, **Bukit Lumut** at nearly 1000m, is 25km west of Belaga. If you do the return leg in the morning you'll probably see whole valleys blanketed in mist, too. Just as bumping along begins to pall, the road descends quite steeply, and you pull into Belaga.

One or two 4WDs leave Bintulu daily for Belaga, with pick-up from hotels or other central locations by arrangement; a seat costs RM60. You can book the service though Daniel Levoh in Belaga (see p.357).

ARRIVAL AND DEPARTURE

By plane The airport, 5km southwest of town (☎086 331073), holds an AirAsia and a MAS ticket office. It can only be reached by road, detouring east and then south. A taxi into the centre costs RM37 (25min).
Destinations KK (2 daily; 1hr 15min); KL (4 daily; 2hr 5min); Kuching (5 daily; 50min); Miri (1–2 daily; 3hr 50min); Sibu (1 daily; 35min) Singapore (3 weekly; 1hr 50min).
By bus Bintulu's long-distance bus station is 5km northeast of town in the lively suburb of Medan Jaya. You might be able to find an hourly local bus into the centre, but otherwise

you'll have to pay around RM15 for a taxi.
Destinations Kuching (early morning and evening only; 11hr); Miri (13 daily; 4hr); Mukah (3 daily; 3hr); Pontianak (Indonesia; at least 3 daily; 19hr); Sibu (every 1–2hr; 4hr).
By minivan Minivans (which leave when full) ply the highway up to Miri and down to Sibu; the depot is in front of Tamu Bintulu. One route north passes the turning to Similajau National Park (RM5).
By taxi The main taxi rank (☎086 332009) is next to the Tian En Ting temple.

ACCOMMODATION

Central Bintulu holds a number of unexciting **budget hotels**, all with a/c, en-suite rooms. The cheapest are in the red-light district east of Li Hua Plaza, but are a bit unsavoury. Several business-oriented hotels, including some north of the centre towards the seafront, cater to visiting oil-industry executives.

Kemena Plaza 116 Jalan Abang Galau ☎086 335111, ✉kemanaplazahotel@yahoo.com; map p.359. A business-oriented hotel with an opulent lobby, rooftop swimming pool, bar, restaurant (with Western lunches from RM15.90) and café – though the atmosphere can be sterile. Rates include breakfast. RM180
Public Inn 47 Jalan Abang Galau (Main Bazaar) ☎019 815 5510; map p.359. Very clean, safe, quiet and respectable guesthouse with good-value rooms that

have comfortable beds, TV, a/c and wi-fi, as well as friendly staff. There's a food court next door. ☎ RM60
★**Riverfront Inn** 256 Taman Sri Dagang ☎086 333111, ✉riverfrontinn@hotmail.com; map p.359. Both smart (for Bintulu) and homely, and thus deservedly popular even though it lacks the facilities of the Kemena Plaza. Rooms are comfortable and done out in muted colours, and the busy restaurant is open all hours and does room service. ☎ RM110

EATING

Buoyed by oil and gas money and a small expat population, Bintulu boasts several decent restaurants, though many – along with a handful of bars – are in the suburbs. Still, quite a few **central eating places** are worth trying, and for evening snacks you can always try the *pasar malam* in the open space close to the airfield.

★**Famous Mama Café** Jalan Somerville ☎086 336541; map p.359. The closest thing you'll find to a West Malaysian *mamak*-style joint, this excellent Indian *kedai kopi* draws in people of all colours and faiths to socialize and stuff their faces from the great *nasi campur* spread

(eaten with plain or *biriyani* rice) or various *roti* plates – around RM5–12. Daily 6am–11pm.
Popular Corner Food Centre 50 Jalan Abang Galau; map p.359. The size of four or five *kedai kopis* put together, this brilliant food court could hold its own in downtown KL.

An endless range of stalls sell the likes of duck noodles, *yong tau foo* and dim sum, and there's a pastry stall doing custard tarts and local savouries including sweet potato or yam fritters. You can easily eat for RM4–10. Daily 7am–10pm.

Riverfront Inn Café Riverfront Inn, 256 Taman Sri Dagang ☎ 086 333111; map p.359. A mere hotel coffee house it may be, but in Bintulu's centre it counts as posh. Come for the fierce a/c during the day or a late meal if you arrive at an ungodly hour. Choices include Western standards (RM14–42) such fish and chips and spaghetti, or try some of their local specialities such as *Sarawak umai* (chillie and lime-flavoured raw fish), or *rojak Sarawak* (a spicy salad with peanut sauce). Daily 24hr.

DIRECTORY

Hospital Bintulu Jalan Nyabau (☎ 086 255899, ⓦ hbtu.moh.gov.my) is 13km from downtown (a 15min taxi ride at least).
Pharmacies The Park City Mall has branches of Guardian and Watsons.
Police Jalan Somerville ☎ 086 332004.
Visa extensions Immigration Department, 3km north of the centre on Jalan Tun Razak (☎ 086 331441).

Similajau National Park

With its sandy beaches broken only by rocky headlands and freshwater streams, the seventy-square-kilometre **Similajau National Park**, 28km northeast of Bintulu by road, has something of the appeal of the highly popular Bako, near Kuching. Enjoyable trekking makes for a great day-trip, and there's even good accommodation. Though wildlife is not a major highlight, the park is well known for its population of saltwater **crocodiles** (signs along the creeks pointedly warn against swimming), with a few dolphins also sighted each year off the coast outside the rainy season. Birdlife includes black hornbills and, in the mangroves, kingfishers.

The main trail

The first stretch of the 10km **main trail** – which runs northeast, mostly just inland, from the park office – has you crossing a bridge over the mouth of the Likau, more of a large brown creek than a river, and heading into the jungle. Around 1km in, a short side branch leads west to a **viewpoint** – a wooden pavilion perched over a rocky beach, from where you can just spot Bintulu's oil and gas installations at Tanjung Kidurong, 15km north of town. Return to the trail and you eventually come to **Turtle Beach I** (6km along; allow 3hr to reach it), then **Turtle Beach II** (total 7.5km along) and finally **Golden Beach** (10km; 4hr). You can overnight at any of them in the hope of spotting **turtles**, who nest here from March to September, though there are no facilities and you should inform park staff of your intentions. Sadly, **swimming** at these beaches is not advised, because the sea is deep even close to shore and there's a strong undertow, though other smaller stretches of sand en route are okay for a dip.

ARRIVAL AND INFORMATION

SIMILAJAU NATIONAL PARK

By minibus The park lies 9km down an access road off the coastal road to Miri; minibuses heading along the coast road from Bintulu can drop you at the junction from where you can walk or hitch.
By taxi Taxis from Bintulu cost at least RM50–60 one way, and the driver can collect you for the same price.

Park HQ The friendly and helpful staff at the Park HQ (☎ 019 861998, ⓦ sarawakforestry.com), where you pay the admission fee (RM20), can provide a schematic trail map; find you a guide (RM30/hr); book you on a night walk on which you just might see pangolins or wild boar (RM40/person, minimum five people); and arrange boat trips.

GETTING AROUND

By boat Boats are a useful timesaver – instead of trekking in two directions, you can pay RM220 (RM280 return) for a boat for up to five passengers to head out to Golden Beach, or RM180 (RM230 return) to either of the Turtle beaches, then trek back. You can also use boats to reach Batu Mandi ("bath rock" in Malay), a rock formation out at sea with large depressions that regularly fill with sea water (RM150), or do a so-called night cruise along the Likau to spot kingfishers and those notorious crocodiles (RM150, up to six people).

ACCOMMODATION AND EATING

Similajau National Park accommodation ☎ 019 861 0998. The park's generally under-utilized accommodation makes it a relaxing place to spend a night or two and has recently been refurbished. There's quite a range on offer, from two hostels that have rooms rather than dorms, each with one bunk bed and some with a bathroom too, to quite fancy a/c accommodation; check for the latest pricing. A simple canteen serves the usual rice and noodle dishes for RM5–12. Camping RM5, hostel rooms RM40, a/c lodge rooms RM150

The northern coast

North of Bintulu, the scenery along the main trunk road is increasingly dominated by oil-palm estates; if you're driving, the quiet coastal highway is a more scenic option for the 210km drive to **Miri**, Sarawak's second largest city. Though boasting no important sights, Miri is nearly as important a gateway to Sarawak as Kuching, thanks to good flight connections and its location amid the riches of northern Sarawak, mostly deep inland and requiring days to explore properly. A couple of national parks lie close to the coast south of Miri: **Niah** is noted for its formidable **limestone caves**, while **Lambir Hills** offers more predictable jungle trekking.

Sarawak's northern coastal strip is also home to **Lawas**, near the Sabah state boundary. It has an air connection to Ba Kelalan that's useful if you want to see the Kelabit Highlands immediately before or visiting Sabah.

Miri

Before oil was discovered in 1882, **MIRI** was a tiny, unimportant settlement. While production has now shifted offshore, the petroleum industry largely accounts for the thriving city of today, with a population of 300,000. Some of Miri's earliest inhabitants were pioneering **Chinese** merchants who set up shops to trade with the Kayan longhouses southeast along the Baram River, and the city retains a strong Chinese flavour, though the Iban and Malays are also well represented, along with a significant number of Orang Ulu.

Now blandly modern for the most part, Miri makes a surprisingly pleasant base from which to see northern Sarawak; visitors generally wind up staying longer than expected, sometimes in several stints interspersed with trips into the interior. The town is unusually placed within a hairpin bend of the Miri River, with its centre on the east bank close to the river mouth; beyond the west "bank", a mere sliver of land seldom more than 500m wide, lies the South China Sea. In terms of sights, it holds one museum focusing on – guess – the oil industry, plus a few **markets** and a not bad stretch of beach. Where Miri shines is in its great restaurants, accommodation and **air connections**. The hub for MASwings' services to the tiny settlements of the interior (see p.371), Miri also has flights to Kuching, KK, KL and Singapore and a handful of international destinations.

Markets
Daily dawn–dusk

Though eminently walkable and easy to navigate, the centre lacks any obvious focus. It makes sense to start exploring at the clutch of **markets** close to Jalan China and the Padang. The most interesting, the **Tamu Muhibbah** on Jalan Padang, is across from the tourist office. Nothing very unusual is sold in its main building, but the little building at the back is used by indigenous traders selling produce such as *akar bakawali*, spiny twigs boiled up as a high blood pressure cure, and "Bario rice" in various colours (it may in fact be varieties from Bario and grown elsewhere, rather than the genuine article for which the Kelabit Highlands are known). Less positively, you may also spot items that it's no longer legal to sell, such as porcupine quills and other animal-derived products.

Just across the road, in the **Tamu Lama** (also signed **Tamu Kedayan**), Malay traders sell foodstuffs and dried-leaf strips woven into square parcels for cooking *ketupat*, the rice cakes eaten with satay. Just beyond on Jalan Bendahara, next to the Chinese temple, is a lively **fish market**. Most prominent but least interesting of all is the large **Central Market** a couple of minutes' walk east on Jalan Brooke, known to Malays as the *pasar babi* or "pig market", as it's where Chinese meat traders operate. If you're around at the weekend, look out for more jungle produce being sold at a **Sunday market** in the streets to the south of the Tamu Lama (until around 1pm).

Petroleum Museum

Canada Hill (aka Bukit Tenaga); turn off Jalan Miri Pujut opposite Jalan Setia Raja • Tues–Sun 9am–4.30pm • Free • Taxis up cost at least RM15, or it's a stiff 20min climb

From certain points in downtown Miri, for example along Jalan Kingsway, you can catch glimpses of what appears to be a tapering tower on the wooded ridge east of the centre. The tower is the **Grand Old Lady**, Miri's first oil well, drilled in 1910 and now marking Miri's one purpose-built sight, the **Petroleum Museum**. Unfortunately, the displays are – pardon the pun – boring, concentrating on the technical aspects of drilling and refining, with some historical context but no tales of the human impact the nascent industry must surely have had.

The beach

Just over 3km southwest of the Padang • A taxi costs around RM10–15

The coast road out of town (the extension of Jalan Bendahara) holds a stretch of public beach around 500m long. The sands are fairly narrow, but it's a relaxed enough spot and a fine place to watch the sun go down. The beach's proper name is **Tanjung Lobang**, though many locals call it **Taman Selera** as Malay stalls sell seafood at a simple evenings-only food court.

ARRIVAL AND DEPARTURE

MIRI

By plane Miri's airport is 10km south of town (☎085 417315, �𝕨 miriairport.com); AirAsia and MAS/MASwings have ticket offices in the departure lounge. To get a taxi into town, buy a RM25 voucher from the taxi counter.

Destinations Ba Kelalan (3 weekly via Lawas; 1hr 35min); Barlo (2 daily, plus one via Marudi; 40min–1hr 15min); Bintulu (11.15am daily; 35min); Johor Bahru (3 weekly 1hr 55min); Kota Kinabalu (1–2 daily; 50min); Kuala Lumpur (8–9 daily; 2hr 10min); Kuching (6–7 daily; 1hr); Labuan (4 daily; 40min); Lawas (5–6 daily; 45min); Limbang (2 daily; 35min); Long Akah (weekly; 40min; 3 weekly via Marudi; 2hr 30min); Long Banga (2 weekly via Marudi; 1hr 25min); Long Lellang (3 weekly; 45min–1hr 15min); Long Seridan (2 weekly; 45min–1hr); Marudi (3–5 daily; 20min); Mukah (1 daily; 1hr); Mulu (2 daily; 30min); Sibu (2–3 daily; 55min); Singapore (4 weekly; 2hr).

By bus The long-distance bus station is at Pujut Corner, 4km northeast of the centre off Jalan Miri Pujut. Services to Bandar Seri Begawan in Brunei, via Kuala Belait and Seria, are run by PHLS (☎085 407175; daily 8.15am & 3.45pm; 4hr); it's seldom necessary to book tickets in advance, but you must show up 30min before departure, as the conductor gathers passport details for the border crossing. Borneo Express (☎085 430420; daily 8am) and Bintang Jaya (☎085 432 178, ⟨w⟩bintangjayaexpress.com; daily

11.30am) run bus services to Kota Kinabalu, which pass through Brunei but do not call at the capital. Heading all the way to KK is laborious and entails four unpleasant border crossings and thus eight new stamps in your passport, so many people choose to fly direct or via Mulu or Bario. To get into town, you can either walk to the bus stop on the other side of the nearby shopping centre to Jalan Bulan Sabit, wait around for the infrequent #20 bus (every 60–90min) or take a taxi (RM18) or *kereta sapu*, Grab or Uber (RM10–12).

Destinations Bintulu (10 daily; 4hr); Kota Kinabalu (2 daily; 11hr); Kuching (10 daily; 15hr); Lawas (2 daily; 6hr 30min); Limbang (8.30am daily; 4hr); Mukah (1–2 daily; 4hr 20min); Pontianak (Indonesia; at least 3 daily; 24hr); Sibu (10 daily; 7hr 25min).

By kereta sapu Miri is one part of Sarawak where you might want to make use of informal taxis to head into the northern interior – most places can be reached by logging roads, although it will be a long and expensive slog. Some 4WD vehicles leave regularly from the streets close to the tourist office; others will need to be arranged in advance through you accommodation in Miri or Barrio.

Car rental Transworld, second floor, Wisma Pelita Tunku (☎085 422227, ⟨w⟩twtmiri.com.my); Kong Teck, at the airport (☎085 313219, ⟨w⟩ kongteck.com.my).

6

MIRI

Borneo Mainland (50m) & ▲ Borneo Dive Network ▲ Mosque (100m) & ❶ (3km) | Long Distance Bus Station ▲

MALAY KAMPUNG

JALAN SIDA
JLN TRITONIA
JALAN MERPATI
JALAN STAPELIA
Imperial Shopping Mall
✉
JALAN POST
JALAN SYLVIA
Imperial Shopping Mall & Hotel
Air Asia
Bintang Megamall ❸
JALAN CALLANDRIA
JALAN PARRY
JALAN CLIVIA
JALAN TEO CHEW
JALAN MIRI PUJUT
JALAN ROYAL
JALAN MIMOSA
JALAN NORTH YU SENG
JALAN PERMAISURI
JALAN PRINS
JLN ROSS
JALAN HAJI LAMPAM
JALAN RICE MILL
JALAN MERBAU
JALAN SIM CHENG KAY
JALAN SERDANG
♨
❷ ❶ JALAN MERBAU
Miri Handicrafts Centre ❷
JALAN SRI DAGANG
❺
Taxis
Seafood Restaurants
JALAN MERBAU
Mega Inn
Tropical Adventures ★
JALAN MAJU
JLN KORA
JALAN BROOKE
Taman Seroja Malay Stalls
JALAN SETIA RAJA
Multistorey Car Park P
JALAN BENDAHARA
JALAN GARDENIA
PERSIARAN KABOR
JALAN SOUTH YU SENG
JALAN LEE TAK
JALAN GARDENIA
JALAN KWANGTUNG
JALAN HOKKIEN
JLN MAHKODA GAMPAR
JLN LEE TAK
PERSIARAN KABOR
JALAN CYTHULA
JALAN CHIA TZE CHIN
JALAN MIRI PUJUT
❻
JALAN CYTHULA
JALAN CYTHULA
Yu Lan Plaza & Immigration Dept
✚
Police Station
❽
JALAN SRI DAGANG
❶
JALAN BROOKE
JALAN ENTIBA
Central Market
JALAN KINGSWAY
JALAN BEGIA
JALAN RAJA
JALAN ANGSANA
Fish Market
JALAN BENDAHARA
Watson's
HIGH STREET
Taxis
★
RAJA SQUARE
JLN CHINA
Miri River
JLN PADANG
CHINATOWN
JALAN OLEANDER
Wisma Pelita Tunku Shopping Centre
JALAN PADANG
JALAN MELAYU
❶ Local Buses
4WD Taxis
JALAN PADANG
Padang
Tamu Lama
Tamu Muhibbah
JALAN MIRI BINTULU
❼ (8km), Airport (8km) & Main Trunk Road ▲ | ▲ Extension of Jalan Bendahara (1.5km), ❹ (1.7km), Coco Cabana (2.2km) ❺ (2.3km), Beach & Coast Road to Bintulu | ❻ (180m)

Canada Hill (2km) & Petroleum Museum (2km) ▶

● **EATING**
Ang Roasting Fastfood	3
Apollo Seafood Centre	7
Khan's Islamic Restoran	2
Krishna's Fish Head Curry & Banana Leaf	6
Ming Café	5
Puma Sera	4
Summit Café	8
Summer Cafe	1

■ **ACCOMMODATION**
Dillenia	1
Dynasty	8
Miri Marriott and Spa	5
Miri Trail	7
Next Room Homestay	2
Old Town Backpacker	6
ParkCity Everly	4
Silverwood Inn	3

● **SHOPPING**
Borneo Arts	2
Outdoor Life	3
Sarawak Handicrafts	1

N

0 ——— 200
metres

GETTING AROUND

By local bus As Miri's centre is easily walkable, you're very unlikely to catch any of the very limited bus services, which only run to the main hospital.

By bicycle Bicycles (ideal for heading to the beach), can be rented for RM10/day from Hock Sen Hin (☎ 085 412255, ✉ hocksenghin1@gmail.com) on Jalan Rice Mill.

By taxi Miri Taxi Association (☎ 085 432277) and Koperasi Teksi Miri (☎ 085 431000) are both 24hr. Meters are not used, so agree the price beforehand; the minimum fare is RM15. Both Uber and Grab are easily available.

INFORMATION

Tourist office Miri's excellent Visitors' Information Centre, on Jalan Padang at the southern end of downtown (Mon–Fri 8am–5pm, Sat & Sun 9am–3pm; ☎ 085 434181, ✉ vic-miri@sarawaktourism.com), covers all of northern Sarawak as well as Bintulu, and has good maps and leaflets. A Sarawak Forestry desk here (Mon–Fri) has up-to-date information on nearby national parks.

TOUR OPERATORS

A small number of tour operators offer Mulu and Kelabit Highlands packages, as well as, more usefully, genuinely imaginative trips to help you get off the beaten track in the upriver Baram and other parts of the interior. A couple of firms offer **dive trips** at the reefs off Miri's coast, which offer a few wreck dives; practically all sites are within an hour's boat ride.

Borneo Mainland Lot 1081, Jalan Merpati ☎ 085 433511, ⊚ borneomainland.com. One- to three-day birdwatching trips to little-visited Loagan Bunut National Park, as well as packages to the usual Sarawak and Sabah destinations, including the Headhunter's Trail.

Borneo Dive Network (Majestic Leisure & Dive) Lot 1084, First Floor, Jalan Merpati ☎ 085 427751 ⊚ borneotravelnetwork.com. PADI courses plus guided and unguided dives, and other courses up to and including dive master. The same company also does the normal range of Sarawak tours as well as a mammoth five-day deep-sea fishing trip.

Tropical Adventure Across the road from Puma Sera restaurant on Jalan Maju ☎ 085 419337, ⊚ borneotropicaladventures.com. Well-thought-through packages from this excellent outfit include trips to Mulu, the Kelabit Highlands – usually easy four-day packages in and around Bario, and other much longer and more challenging trips of up to fourteen days. They're also good for excursions on the Headhunters' Trail (see p.376).

ACCOMMODATION

Miri's accommodation is mostly used by **business travellers**, or tourists just passing through. It's not cheap, and although there are quite a few budget hotels (RM35–50) in the backstreets around *Mega Hotel* they are pretty bad, with tiny airless (though sometimes a/c) rooms, and the area is a bit of a red-light district.

★ **Dillenia** Jalan Sida ☎ 085 434204, ⊚ sites.google .com/site/dilleniaguesthouse; map opposite. Named after a shrub found all over Malaysia, this guesthouse has a cosy lounge painted green, plus dorms and rooms on two floors, including a family room that sleeps four (RM110). It's very relaxed, but what really sets it apart is that it's impeccably managed by the super-efficient Mrs Lee, who can organize transport to the two nearby national parks and other local destinations (service available to non-guests). ☏ Dorms RM30, doubles RM90

★ **Dynasty** Jalan Miri Pujut ☎ 085 421111, ⊚ dynastyhotelmiri.com.my; map opposite. The good impression given by this hotel's sizeable marbled lobby is reinforced by the spacious, comfortable rooms; some have bathtubs and sea views, too. Facilities include a mini-gym and sauna, though no pool; it's among the best-value places in its class. Breakfast is RM30 extra (note they add the B&B option automatically online). Book ahead. ☏ RM135

Next Room Homestay First Floor, 637 Jalan North Yu Seng ☎ 085 411422, ✉ nextroomhomestay@gmail.

com; map opposite. On its third name change (and owner) in nearly as many years, this guesthouse is still somewhat haphazardly run, though it partly makes amends through its informality and socialiabilty, and the rooms are clean and comfortable enough. However, it's on a busy stretch for bars and restaurants and so the rooms by the street (which includes both dorms) can be very noisy till late. It's also big, with a rooftop area from where you can take in the nightlife below. ☏ Dorms RM32, doubles RM60

Old Town Backpacker 3 Jalan High Street ☎ 085 322507; map opposite. Small, new backpacker place almost slap-bang in the middle of the old town. It's not luxurious, but it does have very keen prices and is kept spotlessly clean – ideal for a typical Miri in-and-out. Rooms are small and windowless, but the eight-bed dorm is okay, and there's a decent communal area with a kitchenette. A/c throughout and simple breakfast included. ☏ Dorms RM25, doubles RM40

ParkCity Everly Jalan Temenggong Datuk Oyong Lawai, 2.5km southwest of Padang ☎ 085 440288,

ⓦ vhhotels.com; map opposite. Unlike the *Marriott*, this seaside hotel has kept its beach and boasts reasonable rates, too. Some of the luxurious, spacious rooms have great views over the lush garden with its pool, and the sands just beyond; sea views cost RM20 extra. **ⓦ** RM208

Silverwood Inn 20A, First Floor, Jalan Bendahara **☎** 085 420577; map p.364. Near the markets in Chinatown, this is a central but quiet budget choice. It's a little run down but the Malay staff are very friendly and the larger-than-average a/c rooms are clean and en suite. The rooms downstairs are a bit dark and pokey, while those upstairs have windows for the same price. Booking through an online booking site will save you around ten percent. **ⓦ** RM55

6

EATING AND DRINKING

Miri's eating scene rivals Kuching's for quality, if not variety – it's a treat to taste genuinely delicious and interesting food after days spent hiking in the northern interior. **North and South Yu Seng roads** hold a particular concentration of restaurants, while along the riverfront you'll find a bunch of not-bad seafood places (no sea views, but occasional sightings of crocodiles in the Miri River). There's also a concentration of more mid-price restaurants and bars at Centrepoint on Jalan Kubu. For inexpensive **stalls**, try the Chinese options at the Central Market (also good for cheap beer) or the Malay outlets on Jalan North Yu Seng and at Taman Seroja, up the road from the *Miri Handicraft Centre*. Unfortunately the **bars** aren't up to much. Apart from a couple of so-so establishments near the *Dillenia* guesthouse, not geared towards backpackers, venues opposite the *Next Room Homestay* on Jalan North Yu Seng are your best bet for a drink in sometimes karaoke-free surroundings.

Ang Roasting Fastfood Lot 304, Jalan Bendahara **☎** 012 805 9799; map p.364. This restaurant in Chinatown serves up Cantonese-style roasted meats – RM5–6 will get you a plate of rice with a choice of roast chicken, duck, crispy pork belly or barbecued pork char siew, or a range of noodle soups such as *laksa*. Add some steamed veggies for an extra RM1. Daily 6.30am–2pm & 5.30–9pm.

Apollo Seafood Centre 4 Jalan South Yu Seng **☎** 085 420813; map p.364. Not much to look at, this old-fashioned Chinese place serves well-regarded standards such as fish-head curry. Around RM25 without drinks, though much more if eating fresh seafood. Daily 10.30am–11pm.

Khan's Islamic Restoran 233 Jalan Maju **☎** 085 418440; map p.364. Though a little dreary, this is a central and well-established *kedai kopis* where the cheap-and-cheerful description really does apply (most dishes RM4–15). Offerings are predictable: *nasi campur,* a range of *biriyani* dishes, curries (veg and non-veg) and tandoori chicken, plus various *roti* and *murtabak* options. Daily 6am–9pm or so.

★**Krishna's Fish Head Curry & Banana Leaf** Centrepoint 2, Jalan Kubu **☎** 085 430095; map p.364. A modern, airy open-air restaurant serving enormous portions of "South Indian" food: order a plain or *biriyani* set plate (RM8–16) and you'll be presented with a mound of rice, and a choice of veg and non-veg curries and dhal soups, with poppadoms, on a metal plate with a token sliver of banana leaf on it. There are also less expensive *dosai*, *nan* and *roti*. Daily 7am–10pm.

★**Ming Café** Corner of Jalan North Yu Seng and Jalan Merbau **☎** 085 422797; map p.364. Probably the most popular bar-restaurant with foreigners, with an a/c indoor section and a prominent, more bar-like area outside with powerful ceiling fans. Separate menus feature Chinese stir-fries (under RM10), Indian curries and sets (RM5–19) and some Western offerings (RM11–30) such as fish and chips and thin crust pizzas, all pretty good if a little overpriced. And it's not a bad place for a drink with a reasonable wine list (from RM15/glass) and a massive selection of imported beers, with seven on draft and around twenty bottled. Happy hour until 7pm daily. Sometimes open later on Fri and Sat. Daily 10am–11pm.

★**Puma Sera** Corner of Jalan Maju and Persiaran Kabor **☎** 085 413468; map p.364. A tiptop Malay/Indonesian *kedai kopis* with a fantastic *nasi campur* spread that might feature *ikan patin* (catfish) curry, *umai* or chilli-fried aubergine. It's also a good place to try the Indonesian dish *lalapan*: *lapan* means "eight" in Malay, so chicken *lalapan*, for example, is a plate of fried chicken, rice, Malay *ulam* (herbal salad) and condiments – eight items in all. Reckon on RM10–15 with a soft drink. Daily 24hr.

Summer Cafe Lot 453, Krokop 9, a small alley between Lian Hua San Ching Tien Temple and Jalan Krocop Utama **☎** 019 885 9923; map p.364. Around 3.5km north of the centre and a little hard to find (check on Google maps), this open and airy garden café-bar-restaurant is worth seeking out for its most agreable atmosphere and mix of local and Western meat and seafood dishes (their burger is mammoth). There's also a wide variety of vegetarian options, including their signature veg sushi (Fri–Sun after 6pm only; RM5–6). Most dishes RM5–15. Daily 8am–9pm.

★**Summit Café** Off Jalan Melayu; head up the lane with Maybank on the corner and you'll see it on the left; map p.364. One of Sarawak's most interesting restaurants: run by a Kenyah woman whose husband is Kelabit, it serves Kelabit food of a sort you may struggle to turn up in Bario. Specialities include *labo senutuk*, smoked shredded pork or wild boar, and *kasam*, a sour/salty fermented combination of wild boar and rice. The latter is in tubs, but you order most dishes from a *nasi campur* spread to be eaten with rice or *nuba laya*, made by pounding rice till smooth and then steaming it wrapped in leaves – under RM10. Closed for   two weeks over the Christmas period. Mon–Sat 7am–4pm.

SHOPPING

Miri's shopping isn't especially distinguished and it's disappointing when it comes to handicrafts, though the malls are lively. The best downtown mall is the **Bintang Megamall** (wbintangmegamall.com) at the corner of Jalan Miri Pujut and Jalan Merbau. With two wings, it houses a branch of the Parkson department store, a Giant supermarket and outlets of several Western fast-food chains. Numerous small shops sell phone chargers, memory cards and the like, while Chinese discount shops here and in the Imperial Mall stock endless camping paraphernalia. Rubber studded shoes ("Kampung Adidas") are sold in the small shops near the Miri Handicrafts Centre, and some also sell mosquito nets and other jungle necessities.

6

Borneo Arts Miri Handicraft Centre, corner of Jalan Brooke and Jalan Merbau ☎085 422373; map p.364. The best of the shops in the handicraft centre is worth a look, with some woodcarving and Kenyah shields on show – the other shops here are a little desultory, and many of their wares are from Kalimantan. All the items in the shops here are overpriced, unfortunately. Daily 8am–6pm.

Outdoor Life Second floor, Bintang Megamall ☎085 425303; map p.364. High quality but expensive torches, sleeping bags, tents and so forth. Daily 10am–9.30pm.
Sarawak Handicraft Block 9, 5B Ground Floor, Lot 96, Jalan Merbau ☎085 430086; map p.364. All the same mass-produced souvinirs you'll find in the Miri Handicrafts Centre but at a fraction of the cost. Daily 10am–6pm.

DIRECTORY

Hospital Miri General Hospital, Jalan Lopeng (☎085 420033).
Laundry Two excellent laundries stand practically side by side a couple of doors along from the *Next Room Homestay* (daily 7am–6pm; RM5/Kg).
Pharmacy Guardian and Watsons are both at Bintang

Megamall.
Police HQ Jalan Kingsway (☎085 433730).
Visa extensions First floor of the Yu Lan Plaza, the tallest building in town, unmissable on Jalan Kingsway (Mon–Fri 8am–5pm; ☎085 442112).

Lambir Hills National Park

Popular with weekend day-trippers, **Lambir Hills National Park**, 35km out of Miri and the closest national park to the city, holds some pleasant trails – though leeches can be annoying – and good accommodation. Mixed dipterocarp forest makes up more than half the park, with giant hardwood trees such as *meranti*, *kapur* and *keruing* creating deep shadows on the forest floor; there's also *kerangas* forest, with its peat soils and scrubby vegetation.

Trails

The park's most popular trail, the short **Latak Trail**, passes three **waterfalls**. The furthest – Latak itself, 1.5km (or 30min) from the park office – is the nicest, its 25m cascade feeding an alluring pool, but is inevitably busy at the weekends. The **Inoue Trail** from the park office joins the **Lepoh–Ridan Trail** half an hour along, which leads after about an hour to three more falls, **Dinding**, **Tengkorong** and **Pancur**; swimming isn't allowed at the last two as their pools are deep. The end of the Lepoh–Ridan Trail marks the start of the trek to the top of **Bukit Lambir** (4–5hr one way from here; set off by 7–8am from the park office to be back by sunset). It's a tough, hot, but rewarding climb with a wonderful view across the park – take snacks and at least two litres of water.

ARRIVAL AND INFORMATION   LAMBIR HILLS NATIONAL PARK

By bus The park lies beside the main trunk road to Bintulu; any long-distance bus en route between Miri and Bintulu can drop you here.
By taxi A taxi from Miri will cost RM70 and can collect you

for the same price.
Admission fee RM20.
Contact details ☎085 471630, wsarawakforestry .com.

ACCOMMODATION

Lambir Hills National Park accommodation ☎085 471630, wsarawakforestry.com. Though accommodation in the park is limited, few people stay so

you shouldn't have trouble overnighting. Choose either a two-bedroom lodge, or take a room within a lodge, sharing facilities. There's also a campsite, and a canteen serving simple Malay and Chinese dishes, that will usually close at 5pm unless there are guests overnighting. Wi-fi available in main building only. Camping RM5, rooms RM40, six-person a/c lodges RM150

Niah National Park

NIAH NATIONAL PARK, 110km south of Miri and 130km from Bintulu, is practically a compulsory visit even if you're already caved out from visiting Mulu. Yes, its main attractions are massive **limestone caves**, but are there any similarity with Mulu ends. Whereas almost all excursions at Mulu are regimented and chaperoned, visitors at Niah simply wander the caves at will, in places stumbling along tunnels – lightless but for your own torch – like questers from *The Lord of the Rings*. Elsewhere the caves are alive, with not just bats but people, who harvest bat guano and swiftlet nests for much of the year. This potent combination of vast caverns, communities at work, the rainforest and Niah's archeological significance – it's famous for prehistoric cave paintings and early human settlement – makes even a day-trip to Niah a wonderful experience. It is indeed possible to see much of Niah in a day: allow two to three hours to get from the park offices to the most distant caves, with breaks along the way.

Niah Archaeological Museum

Tues–Sun 9.30am–4.30pm • Free; no photography

Before becoming a national park in 1974, Niah was made a National Historic Monument in 1958, after Tom Harrisson discovered that early man had been using it as a cemetery. Fragments of human skull, nearly 40,000 years old, were the earliest examples of *homo sapiens* found in Southeast Asia. For a sense of the park's history and archeological importance, spend half an hour at the newly revamped **Niah Archeological Museum** across the stream beyond the park headquarters. Fascinating photos, from a mere half-century ago, but seeming much older, show Harrisson at work, and Iban and other indigenous people engaged in traditional dances or sporting activities, while video and interactive displays help you undestand the geology of the caves.

Caves

Trader's Cave, the nearest cave to the museum, is nearly 3km along a concrete path that soon becomes a jungle boardwalk. En route, you may stumble upon monkeys (including silverleafs and even gibbons), butterflies, snakes, skinks and odd scarlet millipedes. Twenty minutes' walk from the museum, a few traders sell refreshments and souvenirs at the start of a clearly marked path on the left that leads in ten minutes to a small, not all that enthralling, village, **Rumah Patrick Ribau** (often still signed Rumah Chang) where they have a homestay programme at the Sungai Tangap longhouse.

Trader's Cave

A 45-minute walk from the museum, a great metal grille crosses the entire boardwalk, with a small gate below marking the entrance to the cave area. Within a few minutes you reach the **Trader's Cave**, not so much a cave as a long, wedge-shaped gash in the rock, open to the jungle along the entire right-hand side. The wooden platforms here were used as shelters by nest-gatherers, who until the 1970s used to barter their harvests here for goods brought by the townsfolk.

Great Cave and Gan Kira (Moon Cave)

Labelled "Niah Cave" on some maps, the huge, 250m-wide west mouth of the **Great Cave** is not far beyond Trader's Cave. A fenced-off stretch to the left marks the site of Tom Harrisson's groundbreaking archeological **digs** in 1957. The dark, gradually ascending area of cave floor beyond is known thanks to its breadth and flatness as the **Padang**; bear left to begin a path that leads down into the depths of the cave, where you will certainly need your torch. The earthy smell of bat **guano** is pervasive;

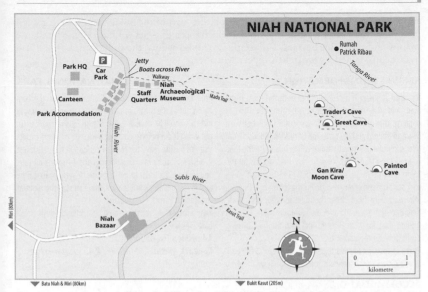

NIAH NATIONAL PARK

Rumah
Patrick Ribau

Tanga River

Park HQ

Car Park

Jetty
Boats across River

Walkway

Niah
Archaeological
Museum

Staff
Quarters

Canteen

Park Accommodation

Niah River

Madu Trail

Trader's Cave

Great Cave

Painted Cave

Gan Kira/
Moon Cave

Subis River

Kasut Trail

Niah Bazaar

Miri (80km)

N

0   1
kilometre

Batu Niah & Miri (80km)   Bukit Kasut (205m)

6

people you may see wandering off-path with sacks on their backs are harvesting it to sell as fertilizer. Between September and March you'll also see **bird's-nest collectors**, who work in groups of three, shinning up bamboo poles and hanging from ropes dangling from the ceiling in search of the edible swiftlet nests so prized by the Chinese. At around 6 or 7pm, you can see the swiftlets fly in and vast numbers of bats stream out for the night, and from much closer up than at Mulu – arrange this with a boatman (see p.370) and remember it takes at least forty minutes to walk back to the river.

The path curls round and then branches, the right-hand track taking you back up and out towards the Padang. Head more or less straight on, past several cave mouths with jungle views on the left, to reach the pitch-black, stuffy tunnel out to Gan Kira at the southern end of the Great Cave system. It takes ten minutes to traverse, though it feels like years.

At the mouth of **Gan Kira**, a delightful spot nearly 4km from the park offices, the boardwalk ends at a shelter bathed in fabulous breezes. A blessed relief after the stuffiness of the preceding tunnel, it offers views of lushly forested hillside beyond.

Painted Cave

A ten-minute walk through the jungle from Gan Kira, and then up some steep stairs, brings you to the mouth of the **Painted Cave**. Early Sarawak communities buried their dead in **boat-shaped coffins**, or "death ships", perched around the cave walls. When Harrisson first entered, the cave had partially collapsed, and the contents were spilled all around. Subsequent dating proved that the caves had been used as a cemetery for tens of thousands of years.

Although the reason visitors plod here is to view the cave's **wall paintings**, they're fenced off and so faded as to be almost impossible to make out – quite at odds with park photos showing bright red boats on a journey, ridden by figures that look to be jumping or dancing.

Trails

It would be tough to squeeze in the park's two trails plus the caves on a day-trip. Splitting off very near the start of the walkway to the caves, the **Jalan Madu Trail** cuts south, across a peat swamp forest, where you see sword-leaved pandanus plants. It

6

crosses the Subis River to end after an hour at the start of the **Bukit Kasut Trail**. It's nearly another hour's walk to the hilltop, which has a fine view of both of the forest canopy and the plains beyond. Park staff may advise against the Bukit Kasut Trail if it has recently rained, as it can be slippery when wet.

ARRIVAL AND INFORMATION · NIAH NATIONAL PARK

By road The park is accessible from both the main trunk road and the coastal highway. All Miri guesthouses organize trips (RM60), or catch any express bus between Miri and Bintulu and get off at the Batu Niah junction from Miri, slightly more from Bintulu), where buses use the food court as a rest stop. Catch a *kereta sapu*, Grab or Uber for the 15km drive to the park entrance (RM25–30/car one way); park staff can summon a vehicle for the return trip. Driving, following signs from either the main road for Batu Niah, Niah Bazaar or the park; after a few minutes take a signed turning east for Niah Bazaar, and then another turning north (left) for the park itself.

Ferry crossings To cross the stream just beyond the park headquarters to the museum and trails, you have to take a

RM1 ferry ride (RM1.50 after 5.30pm). To see the bats flying out at the Great Cave, tell the boatman on your way out that you'll be back at 7.30pm – he finishes work then, but won't leave before you come back if he knows to expect you. It's best to leave the cave by 6.45pm at the very latest – a RM5 gratuity may be apppropriate if you're a bit late. You will need a torch to get back to the jetty at that time and if you get stuck in the park, you can stay the night at the Rumah Patrick Ribau village.

Equipment A reliable torch (flashlight) with fresh batteries is essential.

Admission fee RM20.

Contact details ☏ 085 737454, ⒲ sarawakforestry .com.

ACCOMMODATION

Niah National Park accommodation ☏ 085 737454, ⒲ sarawakforestry.com. Though ageing, Niah's accommodation is in reasonable condition as it's little used – there are no park guides and thus no night walks, so there's little reason to stay except to see the dusk exodus of the bats and to enjoy a little quiet. Options include four-room lodges and fancier rooms with bathroom and a/c,

plus a campsite. A simple canteen serves a limited menu of local food for RM10–15. ☏ Camping RM5, doubles RM40

Sungai Tangap longhouse Patrick Libau village ☏ 013 834 2461. Good homestay at a typical longhouse inside the park itself. Rooms are comfortable but tend to be a little small, and of course have shared bathrooms. Full board for two people ☏ RM100

Lawas

One of the eleven administrative **divisions** into which Sarawak is parcelled is a horseshoe-shaped territory named **Limbang**, whose western arm splits Brunei into two and whose eastern arm slots between Brunei and Sabah. This eastern prong was bought by Charles Brooke from the Sultan of Brunei in 1905 and is home to **LAWAS**, a bustling bazaar town on the Lawas River, with a **tamu** above the river. The only reason to visit is because Lawas has flights to Ba' Kelalan in the Kelabit Highlands, making it possible to reach the Highlands en route to or from Sabah.

ARRIVAL AND DEPARTURE · LAWAS

By plane Lawas's airport is 2km south of town; a taxi into town costs RM10.

Destinations Ba' Kelalan (Mon & Weds; 35min); Kota Kinabalu (Mon & Thurs; 45min); Miri (4–7 daily; 45min).

By bus The bus station is on Jalan Liaw Siew Ann, about 200m from the main junction and just behind the indoor market. The two main companies are Bintang Jaya (☏ 085 283 178, ⒲ bintangjayaexpress.com) and Sipidang Express (☏ 085 284722, ⒲ sipitangexpress.com.my)

Destinations Bandar Seri Begawan, Brunei (1pm daily; 3hr); Kota Kinabalu (1pm & 2.45pm daily; 4hr 30min); Limbang (11.30am & 1pm daily; 1hr 30min); Miri (11.30am & 2.45pm daily; 6hr 30min).

By boat Boats leave from the Customs Wharf beside the old mosque, 300m east of town.

Destinations Labuan (7.30am daily; 2hr 30min); Limbang (9am daily; 2hr).

ACCOMMODATION

Mandarin Lot 466, Jalan Trusan ☏ 085 283222. Centrally located on the main street, and next to the

excellent *Leeya Café*, this place isn't exciting, but the rooms are fairly large, clean, and have nice bathrooms – some even have windows. There is a handful of other budget options nearby. 📶 RM75

Seri Malaysia Jalan Gaya ☎085 283200, 🌐 serimalaysia.com.my. This enormous modern hotel, just over the bridge as you enter town from the airport, is the plushest place to stay – which isn't saying much. There's a coffee house, restaurant and a pool, but the rooms are in need of a bit of TLC. Prices rise by RM20 Fri & Sat and rates include breakfast. 📶 RM170

The northern interior

6

For visitors who take the time and trouble to explore it, Sarawak's **northern interior** often ends up being the most memorable part of their stay. Some of the wildest, most untouched parts of the state are interspersed, sometimes in close proximity, with badly degraded patches, thus putting everything you may have read about the state's environmental problems into sharp relief. The timber industry has been systematically logging here since the 1960s, with tracts of land already under oil palm or being cleared to grow it, yet the rugged terrain still offers fabulous **trekking** – something most visitors only experience at **Gunung Mulu National Park**, with its extensive caves (including one of the largest in the world) and the razor-sharp limestone Pinnacles.

As central Sarawak has the Rejang, so the north has its major river system, the **River Baram** (Batang Baram). There the resemblance ends, for only the lowest part of the Baram – from **Marudi**, 50km southeast of Miri, to the river mouth at **Kuala Baram** near the Brunei border – has anything like a proper boat service, and that stretch is any case devoid of sights. Further upriver, the days of being able to just turn up and find a longboat and someone who can pilot it have long since gone. Much travel is therefore by small **aircraft** (see box below) or **4WD**, using the spider's web of logging roads, which adds to the outback feel. Anyone wanting to get off the beaten track will most likely have to talk to the Miri tour operators (see p.365), who have contacts with boatmen and drivers and can arrange accommodation in towns with hardly any formal places to stay. That said, it is possible to visit remote **Penan settlements** in the upper Baram using a homestay programme called **Picnic with the Penan** (see p.385).

Mulu aside, the highlight is the lush **Kelabit Highlands**, accessible by air and an upgraded logging road, where the pleasant climate is ideal for long treks in the rainforest.

TWIN OTTERS

One entertaining aspect of travel in the northern interior is the chance to fly on **Twin Otters**, nineteen-seater propeller planes. More formally known as the de Havilland DHC-6, the Twin Otter can turn on the proverbial dime and take off from a standing start in seconds, making it ideally suited to the tiny airfields in Sabah and Sarawak. As such, the plane forms the backbone of the Rural Air Services operated by Malaysia Airlines subsidiary **MASwings**, mostly out of Miri (though it's not used for Mulu, where the airport can take larger aircraft).

As the Twin Otter isn't pressurized – you can see daylight around the door rim – it doesn't fly above 3000m, and affords great views of the north's mountain ranges. That MASwings' Twin Otters can be old and a bit shabby (though perfectly serviceable) only adds to the experience; the cabin will be fan-cooled and the cockpit door will be open, letting you see what the pilots are up to.

On a practical note, passengers sit where they like, and luggage is limited to 10kg per person (you may well have to weigh yourself at check-in so staff know the laden weight of the plane). Prices are lower if booked well ahead, rising one week before and three days before travel; the most expensive tickets can be bought at the airport on the day. At some airfields, departing passengers are slapped with a "service fee" of RM10–15 atop the taxes included in ticket prices. Levied by the small private concerns that run the airfields, these fees appear to be condoned by the authorities. Note that the planes get booked solid during public and school holidays and over Christmas and New Year, when you may have to reserve weeks in advance. Flights are seldom cancelled except in very gusty or stormy weather.

6

Of much less significance unless you're an avid birdwatcher is **Loagan Bunut National Park**, some distance off the Miri–Bintulu road and difficult to visit independently.

Gunung Mulu National Park

GUNUNG MULU NATIONAL PARK, Sarawak's premier national park and a UNESCO World Heritage Site, is named after the 2376m mountain at its heart. Modern explorers have been coming here since Spenser St John in the 1850s, who didn't reach the summit but wrote inspiringly about the region in *Life in the Forests of the Far East*. A more successful bid in 1932 saw Edward Shackleton, son of the Antarctic explorer, get to the top during a research trip organized by Tom Harrisson.

The park's best-known features, however, are the mind-bogglingly big **Deer Cave** and, atop another mountain, Mount Api, the dozens of 50m-high razor-sharp limestone spikes known as the **Pinnacles**. Visitors stream into Mulu (as the park is generally known) year-round to catch sight of them – a three-day trek, there and back, from the park offices – and also to see the park's incredible network of **caves**. Mulu contains the largest limestone cave system in the world, formed when surface water eroded vast amounts of material, dividing the limestone belt that runs southwest–northeast across the middle of the park into separate mountains as well as carving cave passages within. Most people see

GUNUNG MULU NATIONAL PARK

Mentawai, Nanga Medamit & Limbang
Kuala Terikan
Terikan River
Headhunters' Trail
BRUNEI
Tiger's Cave
Mount Benarat (1580m)
Medalam River
Camp 5
MELINAU GORGE
PINNACLES
Mount Api (1750m)
Kuala Litut

ACCOMMODATION
D'Cave   1
Mulu Marriott
  Resort and Spa   4
Mulu River Lodge   3
Park Headquarters   2

EATING
Mulu Marriott
  Resort and Spa   2
Park Café   1

Melinau River
Clearwater Cave
Sarawak Chamber
Batu Bungan
Wind Cave
Camp 1
Camp 4
Mount Mulu (2376m)
Lagang Cave
Park HQ
Paku Waterfall
Canopy Skywalk
Camp 3
Tree Top Tower
Lang's Cave
Deer Cave
N
Tutoh River
Long Terawan

0   3
kilometres

some or all four of the dramatic **show caves**, though other caves are accessible on adventure packages and yet more are still being explored (see ⓦ mulucaves.org).

Mulu is unique in Sarawak for having been **privatized**. While the Sarawak Forestry Corporation remains in overall charge, most things to do with tourism, including the accommodation, is now run by Borsarmulu. This means that Mulu feels more like Singapore than Sarawak: **tours** are timetabled and formatted, and you can explore few parts of the park unaccompanied. The tours are well run, the guides are better communicators than at any other Sarawak park, and close supervision has helped prevent the poaching of valuable plants – but if it were possible to make the jungle somehow corporate, this is it. The only way to avoid taking the tours is by having your own registered guide, which enables you to book boat charter and accommodation on the trails separately, though this only makes sense if you are in a group.

6

The caves

The show caves – **Clearwater**, **Wind**, **Lang's** and **Deer** – are a must, though interest can begin to wane if you see all four. If you're doing a Pinnacles trek, the cost will usually include a tour of the Clearwater and Wind caves. If not, and you don't want to spend ages underground, opt for the Lang's and Deer caves – the last is the most impressive of the lot – then hang around for the incredible "**changing of the guard**", when the bats leave Deer Cave at sunset. Tours of these caves fill up quickly, so book as soon as your plans are fixed. It's also possible to do tours of **Lagang Cave**, where obscure cave-dwelling fauna is the highlight, plus more challenging caving trips.

Lang's and Deer caves

3km from the park office • Tours leave park office daily 2pm & 2.30pm • RM35

Lang's Cave, an hour's walk from the park office, is the smallest of the show caves. It makes an unremarkable appetizer for the splendid Deer Cave, though your guide will point out unusual rock formations, most interestingly the curtain stalactites and coral-like growths – helictites – gripping the curved walls.

Deer Cave, a few minutes' walk further, was once inhabited by deer that sheltered in its cavernous reaches. Dim artificial lighting helps you appreciate one of the world's largest cave passages, more than 2km long and up to 174m high, though what's really striking is how scenic it can be: silvery curtains of water plummet from the cave ceiling, while there's at least one chimney-like structure, formed by erosion of a weaker section of limestone, where rainwater jets down as though from a shower head. Elsewhere, your guide will point out the cave's Abraham Lincoln-in-profile rock formation and the entrance to the Garden of Eden.

Once the tour is over, walk back to the park offices unaccompanied or linger with the guide at a viewpoint – the so-called Bat Observatory, with snacks on sale and toilets – near the caves. As it approaches 6pm, swiftlets fly into the caves for the night, which isn't necessarily easy to make out, but what you can't fail to notice is the **bats**. They emerge from various holes in the roof – there are about three million of them – at first in little cloud-like bursts, then in streams that can last for minutes at a time.

Garden of Eden

Tour including Lang's Cave and Deer Cave daily 9.30am (minimum three people) • RM120

A hole at one point in Deer Cave offers a glimpse of lush ferns in the so-called **Garden of Eden**, a veritable "lost world" penned in by the steep cliffs of Mulu's limestone formations. It was discovered by a Royal Geographical Society expedition in 1976 whose leader noted that "even the fish were tame and gathered in shoals around a hand dipped in the water". Today the park offers a trip to the area, reached by wading along a river that flows through a dark passage at Deer Cave. It continues through the jungle to small waterfalls and yet more pools (where you can swim), and ends with lunch in the wilds.

6

ADVENTURE CAVING

Several of Mulu's caves are open for so-called **adventure caving** activities, though only a few count as hard-core, with caving experience compulsory; all require a group of at least three for the trip to go ahead. One advanced trip, the **Clearwater Connection** (RM225/person), takes you through a chamber linking the Clearwater and Wind caves, wading or swimming through the Clearwater River en route. Another, the visit to the **Sarawak Chamber** (RM310), at 9.5 million cubic metres the world's largest known cave chamber – starts at the crack of dawn and lasts an entire day, but there's no descent into the chamber itself, and it's so big that regular torches can't actually reach the walls or ceiling, so all you can experience is turning off the lights and being in the "biggest darkness" – note, they'll need proof of fitness to do this trip, which means doing another adventure caving trip beforehand.

If you just want to try something that isn't a regular trek or cave walk, **Racer Cave** (RM160) is probably best; you spend two hours ascending and descending through tunnels, with guide ropes to help you pull yourself along. More simply, **Lagang Cave** can be visited on a trip in which you search for wildlife, as on the standard "Fast Lane" tour (see below), but in a separate, "off-piste" section (RM160), an escapade that's suitable for families. For details of other caving opportunities and what equipment to bring, speak to the park office (see p.377).

Wind and Clearwater caves

Tours daily 8.45am & 9.15am from the park offices • RM65 including boat transport and a stop at Batu Bungan

As they lie upriver of the starting point for the Pinnacles trek, almost everyone heading to the Pinnacles sees these two caves as well. Most park trips include boat transport and a not-very-interesting stop en route at the Penan settlement of Batu Bungan (see p.374) where you can buy tribal knick-knacks and watch a blowpipe demonstration.

Wind Cave feels rather closed in compared to its much larger siblings, and is home to a great array of golden, contorted rock shapes and pillars, best seen from extended metal stairways. It's five minutes on to the base of **Clearwater Cave**, either by boat along the Melinau River or using a cliffside walkway that passes some "mini-Pinnacles", waist-high limestone shards embedded in the cliff face. Two hundred steps lead up to the cave mouth itself, adorned with curious glossy one-leafed plants unique to Mulu. Inside, the cave certainly impresses with its size – the entire system, probing 150km through Mulu's substratum, is thought to be the longest in Southeast Asia – though it's not all that visually interesting other than for its subterranean river, which joins the Melinau, and for its **notch**, a great horizontal groove in the cave wall running alongside the river. Thirty minutes are set aside for a dip in the chilly Melinau after the tour (there are changing facilities).

Lagang Cave

Lagang "Fast Lane" tours leave daily 2pm from the park office; bring a torch • RM65 including boat rides

Animals rather than geology are the highlight in the **Lagang Cave**. The tour proceeds at a relaxed pace, the guide encouraging people to use their torches to spot the different beasties lurking in the darkness; the blue racer snakes who feed on the bats, the reflective eyes of cave spiders, and the blind white crabs in shallow pools. Of course there are no problems locating the many bats sleeping in little round holes in the ceiling along with mossy-nest swiflet nests (made of a mixture of moss and saliva). Later, as the cave widens, you'll also see some well-lit and interesting rock formations.

Batu Bungan

A stop on boat tours to Wind/Clearwater caves, or a signed 30min walk from the airport in the opposite direction from the park

Just outside the park boundary, a couple of kilometres northwest of the park entrance, is a somewhat desultory collection of concrete houses called **Batu Bungan** which, a worthwhile information display notes, is "probably the most-visited Penan settlement in Sarawak". Tourists indeed visit every morning en route to the caves, and the locals sell souvenirs, but the whole experience is rather artificial. The Penan here perhaps quite haven't got the hang of the whole living-in-houses thing, and the present concrete longhouses are there because previous two wooden ones burned down within ten years.

Canopy skywalk and Tree Top Tower

Six skywalk tours daily; 2hr • RM45; Tree Top Tower free (get key from the park office; RM50 deposit; no guide needed)

Mulu's **canopy skywalk**, 480m long and 20m up in the air, is reached by a side trail off the Deer Cave trail. The skywalk laces around six broad hardwood *kasai*, *betang*, *meranti*, *peran* and *segera* trees and takes around half an hour to complete. Though it's not that different to the canopy walkways at Taman Negara or at Temburong in Brunei, the tours are often full, so book promptly or try spotting birdlife from the elevated hide called the **Tree Top Tower**, just fifteen minutes from the park office.

The Pinnacles

The park charges RM415 for the trek, including accommodation but no food; tour operators offer similar packages, as well as to the Headhunters' Trail north of the Pinnacles (see p.376)

Five million years ago, the splatter of raindrops gradually dissolved Mount Api's limestone and carved out the **Pinnacles** – 50m-high shards, as sharp as samurai swords – from a solid block of rock. Erosion is still continuing, and the entire region is pockmarked with deep shafts penetrating far into the heart of the mountain: one third of Mount Api has already been washed away, and in another ten million years it might all be gone.

The chance to view the Pinnacles draws many visitors to Mulu, and the trek offers exactly that, by heading not to the Pinnacles but to a **ridge** across the way from where you can take everything in. It's a three-day, two-night hike, but only the ascent of the steep final ridge and the awkward descent are genuinely demanding. That said, if you're reasonably fit and suitably equipped, you should cope, and the guides put safety first and make allowances as appropriate for the slower members of their group. With whomever you arrange the trek, book or make enquiries at least a week in advance; base camp, **Camp 5**, sleeps fifty people, so there's a firm ceiling on the number of climbers per day. Considering the tough journey, some people are a little disappointed when they arrive at the Pinnacles, but as with many things in life, the journey is everything, and the views along the way are terrific.

The hike

The itinerary is simple. **Day 1** usually sees trekkers visiting the Wind and Clearwater caves after which the boat takes them down the Melinau to **Kuala Litut**, the start of the 8km trek to Camp 5. Following a rough track of coarse stones embedded in the ground, it's mostly flat and perfectly straightforward, and you can expect to arrive well before sunset.

Camp 5 itself is spruce and homely; all accommodation is dorm-style, and there's a large, reasonably well-equipped kitchen and communal eating area. If you book through the park office, you'll have to bring your own provisions (see p.377) and remember to ask to borrow a free mosquito net at the park HQ. It's close to the **Melinau Gorge**, across which nearby **Mount Api** (1750m) and **Mount Benarat** (1580m) cast long shadows in the fading afternoon light. A bridge straddles the river here, with a path disappearing into the jungle on the far side – the first stage of the Headhunters' Trail. It's possible to explore the gorge instead of tackling the Pinnacles; ask at the park office for details (see p.377).

Day 2 is the only time you are accompanied by a guide, setting off around 7.30am for the ascent. Departure may be delayed in heavy rain; if the weather fails to let up, and the climb has to be called off, you'll get half your money back if you booked through the park office. After two hours, a striking vista opens up: the rainforest stretches below as far as the eye can see, and wispy clouds drift along your line of vision. Eventually the trail reaches **moss forest**, where pitcher plants feed on insects, and ants and squirrels dart in and out among the roots of trees. The last thirty minutes of the climb is especially steep, with ladders and ropes to assist.

Parties usually arrive at the top of the **ridge** that overlooks the Pinnacles in late

6

THE HEADHUNTERS' TRAIL

A wonderful way to start or end a Pinnacles trek, the **Headhunters' Trail** adds just one day to the total duration, but when you consider the itinerary it's clearly all but impossible to make the necessary arrangements independently. The 11km trail – which corresponds to a route once taken by Kenyah and Kayan warring parties – leads north from Camp 5 to **Kuala Terikan**, at the confluence of the Terikan and Medalam rivers on the park's northern boundary. From here it's necessary to find a longboat down the Terikan to reach **Mentawai**, also on the park's edge, where you sign out of the park at a **ranger post** (or sign in if doing the route in reverse). The boat then continues to a longhouse before **Nanga Medamit** where tour operators put visitors up for the night. From here you can drive to the coastal town of **Limbang**, in between the two lumps of Brunei, and pick up a flight to Miri or bus to Kota Kinabalu, Bandar Seri Begawan or Miri.

As a trek, the trail is similar to the path from Kuala Litut to Camp 5, but less well maintained and 3km longer. Some say it's therefore better for exiting the park than entering it, as there's a lot of ground to cover to reach Camp 5 from Nanga Medalan before dark. In practice, people continue to trek in both directions.

To tackle the route, contact a tour operator in Miri or Kuching (the park itself is not currently offering this service). As an example, Tropical Adventure (see p.365) has a five-day excursion from RM1805/person, covering the flight from Miri to Mulu, a night's accommodation at their own lodge near the park, meals, the Pinnacles trek (including the two show caves), and the exit to Limbang via Nanga Medamit.

---

morning. The ridge is itself a pinnacle, sited across a ravine from the main cluster, and if you tap the rocks around you, they reverberate because of the large holes in the limestone underneath. After an hour it's time for the return slog, which can be more awkward on the legs and nerves, and takes longer, especially when the route is slippery. You'll probably arrive back at Camp 5 around 4pm.

On **day 3** trekkers retrace their steps to Kuala Litut for the boat ride back to the park office, usually arriving in plenty of time to catch an afternoon flight out.

Mount Mulu

Expect to pay around RM650/person, including accommodation and a guide, though you'll have to bring provisions and sleeping bags; a porter costs around RM100/day extra

The route to the summit of **Mount Mulu** (2376m) was first discovered in the 1920s by Tama Nilong, a Berawan rhinoceros-hunter. Earlier explorers had failed to find a way around the huge surrounding cliffs, but Nilong followed rhinoceros tracks along the southwest ridge trail, and thus enabled Lord Shackleton to become the first mountaineer to reach the summit in 1932. It's still an arduous climb, a 48km round trip that usually takes four days. Few visitors attempt it, but with enough notice, the park office can usually arrange it for groups of three or more.

Day 1, for most groups, is usually spent heading to **Camp 3** roughly midway along the route, passing Camp 1 en route (there is no Camp 2). The trek takes you from the limestone belt that most tourists associate with Mulu into sandstone terrain that dominates the southeast of the park. On **day 2** you spend the night 1800m up at **Camp 4**. Most climbers set off well before dawn on **day 3** for the hard ninety-minute trek to the **summit**, if possible arriving there at sunrise. Big clumps of pitcher plants dot the final stretch, though it's easy to miss them as by this point you are hauling yourself up by ropes onto the cold, windswept, craggy peak. From here, the view is exhilarating, looking down on Mount Api and, on a clear day, far across the forest to Brunei Bay. Once again you spend the night at Camp 4. **Day 4** is a very full day as the aim is to get right back to the park HQ by nightfall.

ARRIVAL AND DEPARTURE   **GUNUNG MULU NATIONAL PARK**

By plane MASwings flies from Mulu's airport, 1500m from   the park entrance, to Kota Kinabalu (1 daily, sometimes via

Miri; 50min–2hr), Kuching (1 daily; 1hr 30min) and Miri (2 daily; 40min). They're not Twin Otter services, but demand is high, so book a week or two in advance.

GETTING AROUND

By taxi For transport around the Mulu area – for example, to eat somewhere other than where you are staying – contact Edward at the *Sweetwater Café* (see p.377), who drives people around for a few ringgit per trip.

By bicycle Bikes are a useful way of getting to and from the park if you're staying outside. The *Mulu Marriott* (see p.377) rents bikes for RM20/4hr, to non-guests as well.

INFORMATION

Park office The office (daily 8am–6pm) stocks good listings of treks, cave tours and activities, as well as browseable reference books on the park and Borneo.

Discovery Centre The informative displays on cave formation and Mulu's topography and ecology in the excellent Discovery Centre, a small free museum alongside the park office, are worth at least half an hour of your time. The gift shop offers internet access until 8pm at RM5, or you could just ask another tourist for the password.

Entrance fee RM30 for five days.

Contact details ☎085 792300, ⊛ mulupark.com; ⊛ mulucaves.org is also a useful resource.

Equipment Unless you are climbing Mount Mulu itself or doing advanced caving, you will need the same gear that you would bring to other national parks. As people tend to do longer treks here than at most parks, however, items that may seem optional elsewhere become necessities. A poncho (or umbrella) is essential for extended downpours, while rubber shoes come into their own when paths and trails are flooded or waterlogged; carry bandages to deal with any blisters. If you are using regular shoes, they must have a good grip. Ponchos, rubber shoes and food you can cook on multiday treks are sold at the park gift shop, but it's much cheaper to buy these before you arrive.

Money Bring a reasonable amount of cash – there are no ATMs – though this is the one park where you can pay for rooms and tours with plastic, and it's occasionally possible to take cash out on your credit card at the park office, though they often run out of cash (two percent service charge; max advance RM300).

Leeches Leeches are not a problem on trails near the park headquarters, though you might want to take precautions (see p.45) on the Pinnacles climb.

ACCOMMODATION

Accommodation within the park is limited to a hostel – basically a twenty-bed dorm – and much more expensive private rooms and chalets; the dorm fills up, so enquire at least a week in advance. Other places to stay **nearby** range from hostel-type places and homestays (mainly along the road from the airport to the park entrance) to the *Mulu Marriot Resort and Spa*

★**D'Cave** 700m from the airport, at the turning to the park entrance. ☎012 872 9752, ✉ muludcavehomestay@ gmail.com; map p.372. By far the best of the homestays, with a basic ten-person fan dorm and a couple of double rooms, one which has an en-suite (RM80). The friendly family is absolutely lovely, and the rate includes an astonishingly good breakfast served at a long table – they just don't stop bringing out food. ☞ Dorm RM35, doubles RM70

Mulu Marriott Resort and Spa 2km from the park entrance ☎085 792388, ⊛ marriott.com; map p.372. The only upmarket place to stay at Mulu, well known for its swimming pool, which sticks out amid the jungle when viewed from the air, Balinese spa, and its sprawling collection of slick, longhouse-like blocks, raised on stilts. Rooms are spacious, and there's a vaguely smart bar and restaurant – although, unless you're having the buffet, it's quite overpriced (mains around RM35), so many guests go to the cheaper restaurant just across the river. ☞ RM589

Mulu River Lodge Outside the park entrance ☎012 852 7471; map p.372. Friendly guesthouse in a large timber building backing onto the Melinau River, containing a 22-bed dorm and clean bathrooms. When things are quiet they may give you a private room at the back of the *Sweetwater Café* next door, which they also run, at no extra cost. The good-value rates include a simple cooked breakfast. ☞ RM35

Park Headquarters ☎085 792300, ⊛ mulupark.com; map p.372. Clustered around the park office are various chalets and more luxurious bungalows (RM312), some recently built and all with a/c and bathroom, plus its hostel. All rates include breakfast. ☞ Dorms RM55, doubles RM221

EATING

Most people simply **eat** where they're staying, but it can be worth moving around a bit for variety. For the Pinnacles and other long treks, the park gift shop sells sachets of instant pasta, canned beans and curries, biscuits, chocolate and so forth. If you want to save a few ringgit, use the shop for the locals on the way from the park to the *Mulu Marriott*.

6

Park Café Next to park office; map p.372. An airy, modern affair, overlooking the Melinau River and serving pretty decent international food. Their highly spicy and creamy Sarawak *laksa* are their strongest suit (RM17), and they also do a tasty Indian platter (RM13), a limited range of stir-fries to be eaten with rice (including a good Indonesian beef *rendang* for RM21), and the odd dessert such as chocolate cake. They also have some Western options, such as burgers (RM18), and a few vegetarian choices. Beer and wine available too. Around RM15 with a soft drink. Daily 7.30am–9pm.

Mulu Marriott Resort and Spa 2km from park entrance ☎ 085 792388; map p.372. The hotel restaurant's buffet dinner – a grand spread of rice and pasta, salads and stir-fries, and *kuih* for dessert, plus a half-hour tribal dance show at 9pm – will set you back RM88. *Tuak* is available at a RM10 a glass. There's also a bar, which serves reasonably priced light bites at night. Daily 6.30am–10pm.

Loagan Bunut National Park

Some 80km south of Miri as the crow flies, **Loagan Bunut National Park**, best visited on an overnight trip, is a good spot for dedicated birdwatchers, boasting stork-billed kingfishers and hornbills among many other species. Many live around the park's lake, **Tasik Bunut**, tucked away on the upper reaches of the **Teru River**, a tributary of the Tinjar, which in turn flows into the Baram. During prolonged dry spells, when the lake level drops drastically, a peculiar form of fishing, which the local **Berawan** people call *selambau*, is carried out. Just before the lake dries out, fishermen use giant spoon-shaped wooden frames to scoop up any fish that haven't escaped down the lake's two watercourses.

For birds, these dry times are a perfect time to feed too, and in May and June the surrounding peat-swamp forest supports breeding colonies of such species as darters, egrets and bitterns. Initially the lake can appear huge, its edges hard to detect as the sunlight is often hazy; however, it's only around 500m wide and 1km long. Small cabins built on rafts house Berawan fishermen, while around them lies an intricate network of fishing plots, with underwater nets and lines tied to stakes pushed into the lake bed. The best times to drift by boat across the lake are early morning and dusk, when the birds are at their most active.

ARRIVAL AND INFORMATION   LOAGAN BUNUT NATIONAL PARK

By taxi There's no public transport to the park, but cars may head here in the morning from near Miri's tourist office; ask staff there where to wait (3hr; RM350 per car/minibus or RM50/person if you can fill it), though a Grab/Uber will be under RM200. When you want to head back, park staff can usually arrange a vehicle.

By tour Miri tour operators such as Borneo Mainland (see p.365) offer one- to three-day trips to the park.

Admission fee RM20.

Contact details ☎ 019 861 0994, ⊛ sarawakforestry.com.

ACCOMMODATION AND EATING

If you're here on a trip with Borneo Mainland you have the option to stay at a nearby farm with which the company has links. Note that there are some **water** issues at the park accommodation and you should phone ahead to ascertain the situation.

Loagan Bunut National Park accommodation ☎ 019 861 0994, ⊛ sarawakforestry.com. Located near the lake, the in-park accommodation is limited to a hostel and a so-called VIP chalet with two bedrooms, a/c and its own bathroom; a small canteen serves basic meals (RM10–15) and snacks. Dorms RM15, chalet RM150

Kelabit Highlands

Right up against the Kalimantan border, 100km southeast of Mount Mulu, the long, high plateau of the **Kelabit Highlands** has been home to the Kelabit people for hundreds of years. Western explorers had no idea this self-sufficient mountain community existed until the early twentieth century, and the Highlands were literally not put on the map until World War II, when British and Australian commandos, led by Major Tom Harrisson, used Kelabit settlements as bases during a guerrilla war against the occupying Japanese. Before Harrisson's men built an airstrip at Bario, trekking over inhospitable terrain was the only way to get here – it took two weeks from the nearest large town, Marudi, on the opposite side of Mulu. When missionaries arrived and converted the animist Kelabit to Christianity after the war, many traditions, like burial rituals and wild parties called *iraus* (where Chinese jars full of rice wine were consumed) disappeared. Many of the magnificent Kelabit **megaliths** associated with these traditions have been swallowed up by the jungle, but some dolmens, urns, rock carvings and ossuaries used in funeral processes can still be found, so the region draws archeologists and anthropologists from far and wide.

Nowadays the Kelabit (well certainly the males) seem to be the good ol' boys of Asia; cowboy hats are much in evidence and they are very keen on pick-up trucks, country music, hunting, and their dogs. The Kelabit are not the only inhabitants of this part of the state, however; there are also populations of **Penan** and **Lun Bawang** (formerly called the Murut).

Despite logging in the Bario area, the Highlands remain generally unspoiled, with occasional wildlife sightings and a refreshing climate – temperatures are only a few degrees lower than in Miri by day, but in winter at night they can drop to an untropical 15°C (60°F). As such the region is a great target for **walkers**, and it is easily accessible by air, with several villages served by MASwings.

Most visitors head to **Bario** as it has the main airport and well-established formal accommodation, but the real point of being here is to get out into the countryside, doing day-walks or longer treks through the jungle, on which you can be hosted in little settlements or longhouses en route such as at **Pa' Lungan** and **Pa' Dalih**. It's also possible to do more challenging treks up to the peaks of the **Pulong Tau National Park** (which currently has no facilities and no one to collect the entrance fee), notably **Mount Murud**. Another option is the **Picnic with the Penan** scheme (see p.385), further south along the Upper Baram region, which enables you to really get off the beaten track and explore the jungle with the Penan people.

There are **no banks** in the Kelabit Highlands, so bring enough cash to cover board and lodging plus guiding/trekking fees. If you're wondering why the 4WD prices are so high, it's because the region has no mechanics, so if they need repairs one must be flown in once to diagnose, then flown in again with spare parts to finish the job.

6

Bario and around

The short flight from Miri makes a thrilling introduction to this corner of Sarawak, the Twin Otter giving passengers amazing **views** (sit on the left on the way in, on the right on the way back) of serried ranks of blue limestone ridges at Gunung Mulu National Park and then of the double-humped **Batu Lawi** (see p.381) before landing at the settlement of **BARIO**. From the air, it's a sprawling jumble of little paths and houses, as well as fields planted with the rice for which the village is well known. There is a centre of sorts, a grassy space 2km northwest of the airfield, ringed by a few modern buildings housing a few shops, including one selling Penan baskets, uninteresting *kedai kopis* and a small hall with an exhibition on Kelabit culture, but much of the village is scattered around the fields 2km further northwest, along the main road and a couple of minor tracks off or parallel to it.

Between the village centre and the military base stands a **memorial to Tom Harrisson** in the shape of a *sape*, the Orang Ulu lute. Celebrating the enormous contribution Harrisson made to our understanding of Sarawak's history, as curator of the Sarawak Museum in Kuching and as a roving anthropologist and archeologist (notably at Niah), the memorial has an inscription that, besides paying tribute to the military work of Harrisson and his British and Australian comrades, also cites the "sacrifice of the tribal warriors of the Baram and Rejang basins" in helping liberate Sarawak from Japanese occupation.

The village's main street is named Jalan Penghulu Lawai, after the first English-speaking village spokesman appointed by the British in 1948. What the colonial authorities failed to realize, however, was that their appointee had learned English

---

HIGHLANDS TREKS

The well-run and organized **guide association** in Bario (contact Julian from Bario Asal on ☏ 011 2508 1114, visitbario@gmail.com) is the best place to start when planning your trip to the area, and new routes and facilities have recently been developed. Certified, English-speaking guides can be in short supply during the June–August peak season, so you should try and arrange them as far ahead as possible. Guides estimate the fitness of the group and set the pace accordingly. Trips may involve gathering wild vegetables, catching fish and cooking, Kelabit-style, on the campfire, as well as locating dolmens and visiting longhouses.

Guides cost RM120/day for around Bario, RM150/day for jungle trekking, and RM180/day for overnight trips; a **porter** costs around RM150/day. For remote treks, you'll need a minimum of two guides (in case of an accident – one stays with the group and the other goes for help), though if you have a porter, you might be able to forgo the second. These fees generally do not include provisions, which cost around RM40/person/day. Where you overnight in villages, expect to pay RM70–80/person for board and lodging and remember that if you don't return to where you started your trek, you'll have to pay your guide per day for their return journey.

As regards **equipment**, travel light bearing in mind the strict baggage limits on Twin Otters, and slogging through the jungle with more than 10kg is a real drag. On top of what you'd normally bring for a day-trek at a national park, it makes sense to have a thin sleeping bag and poncho, plus warmish clothing if you want to overnight outdoors or do any mountain trekking. A tent can be useful, though it obviously weighs down luggage; guides will usually stop overnight in villages or at shelters, though may have canvas sheets that will suffice for shelter at a pinch. For jungle trekking the best footwear is by far Wellington (rubber) boots as they not only make walking through mud and rivers less hassle but also help keep the leeches off (as does wearing thick, long trousers or anti-leech socks) – all are available in Miri or Lawas.

Leeches are quite common in this region, and although mostly harmless, they are not pleasant to have on you, or worse, biting you. There are a number of ways to discourage them, but they're not fail-safe (see p.45). If all else fails simply do as the locals do and use the sharp pinch and pull technique to get them off, and at least carry some salt, which dissolves them. A good way you deter them is to get some fresh tobacco leaves, grown locally, and rub them into your exposed skin.

while in Marudi Prison, having been imprisoned by them a year earlier for headhunting – Lawai, however, didn't think he'd done anything wrong, so had escaped and walked all the way back to Bario through the jungle.

Situated on a plateau, with very little shade thanks to agriculture, Bario is visually dull in places but scenic in others, with vistas of rice fields and water buffalo against the lush mountains of the **Tama Abu Range** to the north and west. Although there are a few half-day walking opportunities, and a couple of things to look at in the village itself, it is only a taster of what you can experience on longer treks.

6

Bario Asal

While not the sole longhouse in the vicinity, **Bario Asal** is the oldest and close to the northern end of the main road – it was once the only settlement in the area and, technically speaking, they own all of the land in Bario. The unassuming timber building is unusual for effectively having two *ruais* – the second one, at the back, houses a communal kitchen with a long row of individual fireplaces for cooking. As a social venue, it's as important as the main *ruai* at the front. The longhouse also has a special area where travellers can stay (see p.382), and sells Kelabit beadwork, jackets and hats.

Walks around Bario

In addition to the popular trek to Ba' Kelalan and the Batu Lawi trek, the guide association has developed a couple of shorter routes in the area for which you'll need their services. The first, the **Aren Bario Trail**, is a half-day loop west of the village past Pa'Rumapu, via the **Bario Nature Site**, a newly constructed lookout (with café) that offers great views of the surrounding forest – especially of interest to birders. The trail then continues through the jungle and past five waterfalls before heading back to the village. In addition to birds, if you're very lucky you might spot the endangered Bay Cat, a wild feline only found in Borneo.

The overnight **Indigenous Trail** takes you into the jungle to the northwest of Bario, a moderate four to six hour walk to the Batu Buli camp, where there is a basic shelter for sleeping, though a mossy forest and past the 30m-high Batu Buli Waterfall, with a similar return leg the next day. It offers the chance to find the Spider *Rafflesia*, a smaller more arachnoid version of its famous cousin.

Prayer Hill

The best views of Bario are a short hike away up **Prayer Hill**, which will give you a great panorama across the village and to the mountains in the middle distance including Mount Murud. Coming from the village, turn right at Bario Asal and follow the stony path for ten minutes until you reach the end. Here there is a small house up the hill and you should follow the smaller path to the right of it. The path then climbs steeply (with ropes to help haul yourself up) for another twenty minutes until you reach a small wooden church, where services are occasionally held. The summit is another ten minutes up from here, where you'll find a small cross and magnificent views.

Batu Lawi

The most challenging local trek, apart from the one to Murud, is the climb up **Batu Lawi** (2044m), the strange double-horned peak that you may have seen on the flight in. The trek is an attractive prospect as it's less arduous and time-consuming than tackling Mount Murud, though as ever logging roads blight the landscape here and there, making it look as though the forest has been gnawed by rats.

The first day out from Bario (8–10hr) is a fairly easy trek past Pa'Ukat and the **Batu Buli camp**, then the **Batu Narut megalith** and a river sinkhole to where you camp at **Arur Bila Bigan**. On the more taxing second day you scramble to the lower and much blunter of the peak's two "horns" for an amazing view of the other, looking like a huge upright stone pillar, though ruder interpretations are possible. The descent has trekkers camping at **Kubaan camp** near a Penan village, and the fourth day, the descent to Bario. It's also possible to do the trek from Ba' Kelalan; contact Julian at the guide association in Bario (see opposite) or Mr Gukang in Ba' Kelalan (see p.384).

ARRIVAL AND DEPARTURE

BARIO

By land Perhaps the best way to enter the Kelabit Highlands is by using a car, which gives you a real sense of how remote it is, affords some lovely views along the way (despite the logging) and offers the chance to stop off at villages along the way. It's 400km from Miri to Bario via the Lapok Junction (on the Miri–Bintulu highway, and from which you can hitch), from where a decent logging road heads inland through Kiloten, Long Supit (where there are some nice food stalls), Long Kerong, and Pa' Dalih, finally arriving in Bario some 10–20hr later. Every few kilometres there's a muddy bit where you really need a 4WD, and rain will slow you down considerably. A whole car costs around RM1600–2000 to/from Miri, RM600–800 to/from Long Kerong or Long Banga, and RM150 to/from Pa'Lungan.

By plane Passengers arriving by plane are met by Bario's guesthouse owners every morning, so you should be collected if you've booked to stay, and be able to arrange a room if not.

Destinations Marudi (1 daily; 40min); Miri (3 daily, one via Marudi; 50min/3hr 35min).

INFORMATION

Maps & Information For information on Bario check ⓦ barioexperience.com or contact the guide association (see box, p.380). Stephen at *Junglebluesdream* (see below) produces beautifully drawn and useful maps of the area, including several of Bario's limited treks.

Internet The community wi-fi has just opened up, almost next to the military base, and just far enough from village centre that you can't use it in most of the *kedai kopis*. It's free, but you'll need help registering unless you read Malay. Mobile 3G services are likewise currently limited to the area around the military base, and only Celcom has coverage in the region. Plans are afoot for upgrading both, but may take some time.

ACCOMMODATION AND EATING

There are several simple places to **stay** in and around Bario, and although some have 24hr electricity, some only have some solar-powered lighting at night. You may have trouble finding a place to stay over Christmas and New Year – when guesthouses may shut for lack of incoming tourists – and during the annual **Bario Food Festival** in July (ⓦ nukenen.com), when the village centre is transformed into a mini-fair. Rates all include meals, so people usually eat where they stay. Not spicy by Malaysian standards, **Bario cuisine** features ingredients such as wild boar and locally farmed fish such as carp, though guesthouses may not serve traditional staples unless you request them. If you're out for the day, you can request a packed lunch. The Y2K shop on the main road, nearly 10min walk north of the centre, sells drinks and snacks at steepish prices. A full list of accommodation is available at ⓦ barioexperience.com.

★**Bario Asal (Sonarang Homestay)** 4km northwest of the airport ☎019 825 9505. The longhouse has a nice guest area with four homely bedrooms with double beds, one reasonable bathroom (with hot water and washing machine) and a huge lounge area, plus a little balcony where you can take coffee and watch the longhouse's semi-tame hornbill flap around hoping for scraps. Sonarang and her family are excellent hosts, and occasionally host cultural shows. RM70

★**Junglebluesdream** Ulung Palang Longhouse, 3km from centre, reached by a signed path northeast off main road ☎019 884 9892, ⓦjunglebluesdream .weebly.com. Local artist Stephen and his Danish partner Tine offer nice accommodation, with four simple, cosy rooms in their section of a longhouse. Stephen's artwork decorates a lot of the building and his cooking is a treat; everyone eats together on a spacious terrace. They also rent bikes for RM30/day. Price is per-person full-board. RM100

Libal Paradise A 10min walk east of the airport ☎019 807 1640, ✉roachas@hotmail.com. With a couple of relatively private rooms, this Canadian-Kelablit-run place has two lovely little chalets that were made by the owner, Stu, who also runs kayaking trips to and from Pa'Lungan. Rose will keep you well fed and watered, and often incorporates the pineapples that grow in the garden. RM80

Nancy Harriss Next to the military base ☎013-8505850, ✉nancyharriss@yahoo.com. Built next to the old British airstrip (there are the remains of a crashed Australian plane in the garden), this well-run homestay is fairly active, and often busy with groups. The rooms in the main building are pretty standard, but they've just built a row of two- and three-bedroom chalets – the most luxurious accommodation in the village. Rooms per person RM95, chalets RM300.

Pa' Lungan

The lovely, tranquil village of **PA' LUNGAN**, around a four- to five-hour trek (or less by road) north from Bario, is made up of a group of detached houses on stilts built around a large rectangular field for buffalo, with a "new town" slightly higher up past the modern church. While for many it's just an overnight stay on the way to somewhere else, it actually makes a great trekking base as well as being a peaceful place to hang out for a few days. There are several **trails** from here for which you'll need guides: to the 20m-high Arur Waterfall (2hr each way); the Pa' Lungan River loop (three days) though the jungle; the gruelling trek up Mount Murud (see box, p.384); and the easier Kalimantan Loop (four days) via Long Pedit, which involves two nights sleeping in jungle camps and one at a homestay (RM60) in one of the many villages along the way. It is advised that you arrange guides beforehand as the village only has a population of around a forty, and only two licensed guides.

Shorter walks that don't need guides include the two megaliths within a few minutes' walk of the village. One is leaning drunkenly, thanks to some sloppy archeology by Tom Harrisson, and the other has collapsed, damaged by villagers looking for foundation stones. There's also a hill to the north of the village, topped with a tin cross and offering fabulous views – it's a steep forty-minute hike through some nice jungle, but be warned there's little cover at the top. It's unclear as yet what effect the new Bario–Ba'Kelalan road will have on the village, but hopefully the economy will improve and its population will begin to increase.

ACCOMMODATION AND EATING   PA' LUNGAN

★**David and Jenny** ☎019 805 2119. Currently the most active of all the homestays in Pa' Lungan, David is the top English-speaking licensed guide in the village and is your best bet for organizing treks, working closely with Julian in Bario (see p.380). The homestay is in a traditional stilted house, with basic rooms and all the ingredients of your meals are gathered fresh from the jungle daily. Per person full-board RM90

Pa' Lungan to Ba' Kelalan

It's currently possible to walk from **Pa' Lungan to Ba' Kelalan**, either via Mount Murud, which takes five days (see box, p.384) or on the new road (when it's finished in 2018), which for the most part will follow the route of the previous direct trekking path, and should be able to be done in a couple of days. As things may well change significantly when the new road opens, it's best to check the situation first with the guide association in Bario (see box, p.380).

THE BARIO TO PA' LUNGAN TREK

The five-hour **hike** from Bario to Pa'Lungan along the old path is fairly easy for the most part, although it becomes trickier if it's been raining. Otherwise the trail is pretty clear and a guide is not needed, though you will be getting your feet wet at some point. The first stretch involves heading northeast out of town along the main road. About 3km from the centre the road forks; take the left-hand branch to reach, 1km on, the settlement of **Pa'Ukat**– don't follow the obvious path here, but take a right at the church. From here, it passes through a very swampy part, after which it rises into mainly secondary jungle – the really swampy sections are crossed on log or bamboo "bridges" of up to 60m long. Using a stick to stabilize yourself while shuffling forward will make these crossings much easier. Along the way you may come across monkeys and other arboreal mammals, as well as **carvings** on a rock called Batu Narit, an hour out of Pa'Ukat, which shows a masked man and a hornbill, along with more than three hundred notches at the bottom which are thought to represent heads taken. Three or four hours on, you finally arrive at Pa'Lungan.

To save time, some trekkers opt to be taken part of the way to Pa'Lungan (or back) by **boat** (1–2hr; RM250 for four passengers), which Bario guesthouses can usually arrange. The boatman takes you to a point on the river called **Long Palungan**, and can point out the trail to follow uphill from the bank; from the right spot on the hilltop, a clear wide trail takes you on to Pa'Lungan (1hr). At this point you can also arrange kayaking to get back to Bario.

6

MOUNT MURUD

Barring the way between Bario to the south and Ba'Kelalan to the northeast, **Mount Murud** is the highest peak in Sarawak at 2423m, and is part of the Pulong Tau National Park. It presents a challenging but rewarding trek, with spectacular views across the Highlands to Batu Lawi and even Mulu. From Ba'Kelalan, it takes six days there and back; from Bario, allow one day extra.

Leaving Ba'Kelalan, trekkers head to Base Camp 1 at Lepo Bunga (8hr) on the first night, traversing some steep hills. If you need to save a day, you can take 4WD on this leg (RM350/car). On day two the target is **Church Camp** (4–5hr) – a wooden shelter built by local evangelical groups for a three-day Christian meeting held once a year. The next morning sees the haul up to the summit (3hr) via the **Rock Garden**, an exposed area of stunted trees and sharpish boulders. After another night back at Church Camp, you retrace your steps back to Ba'Kelalan.

If you're starting from Bario, the first day is spent reaching **Pa'Lungan**, where you stay the night. The next day brings a trek to a simple shelter at **Long Rapung** (7hr), with about half an hour's worth of climbing en route. On day three, some guides head to Church Camp (7hr), others to the slightly nearer Camp 2 at **Long Belaban**, with hammocks to sleep in (5–6hr), though you have to ford a few streams en route and climb for a couple of hours at the end of the day. If you start from Camp 2, day four is gruelling, the climb up to the summit beginning at dawn (5–6hr); the descent usually means heading to the Rock Garden and Church Camp (4hr). On day five you head back to Camp 2 for the night; it's then possible to get all the way back to Pa'Lungan on day six.

Ba'Kelalan (Bakelalan)

Apart from a few fruit orchards, **Ba'Kelalan** amounts to a mere smattering of houses in five settlements and places selling basic provisions. The chief reason to come here is to trek – you can head to Bario (on the new road, when it's finished, by foot or 4WD), Mount Murud or Batu Lawi, or, less ambitiously, do short walks into Kalimantan and then back within a day, or a four-hour round trip up to the **viewpoint** at Budukteudal. Note that the name is currently changing to Bakelalan, so you may see both spellings.

ARRIVAL AND INFORMATION   BA'KELALAN

By plane The airfield, right next to the village, has flights to Miri (3 weekly; 1hr 35min) via Lawas (3 weekly; 35min).
By 4WD A logging road from Ba'Kelalan to Lawas makes it possible to take a 4WD (6hr; RM70/person), which you can arrange through Mr Gukang.

Guides Guides, along with 4WDs and information, can be arranged via Mr Gukang (☎ 017 855 5048), who speaks good English and can arrange trips to Mount Murud, Bario, Batu Lawi, or Kalimantan (guide RM150–180/day, plus return trip), as well as the viewpoint at Budukteudal (RM80).

ACCOMMODATION AND EATING

Apple Lodge Just across the landing strip from the airport "terminal" ☎ 013 286 5656 & 085 435736. This surprisingly large and well-maintained place has a total of 21 double and triple rooms, some of them en suite (RM10 extra). Breakfast is included in the price, lunch and dinner costs RM12 each, and the food is very good. In the (unlikely) event that it's full, there are a couple of other homestay options nearby. **RM80**

Ulu Baram

The Baram River system so dominates northern Sarawak that you could consider virtually all the interior here, excepting Limbang division, to be the **Ulu Baram** – practically every river, including the Melinau and Tutoh at Mulu, the Tinjar at Loagan Bunut and the Dapur and Kelapang at Bario, ends up flowing into the Baram. The river itself, however, wends its way southwest from the town of **Marudi**, 80km from Miri, occasionally passing confluence towns such as **Long Lama** and **Long San**, before approaching the border with Kalimantan. Here it swings east to peter out beyond **Lio Matoh**, 200km southeast of Miri.

This Ulu Baram, due south of Mulu and southwest of the Kelabit Highlands, is definitely outback territory, rugged and lushly forested, with no specific sights; the reason you might venture here is to **trek** through virgin rainforest and stay in remote settlements as part of a **homestay** programme. The usual **caveats** about Malaysia homestays apply here (see p.38). One key point is that villagers take turns to put up guests, so quite how adept your hosts will be is a matter of luck.

Ulu Baram trekking

It can be hard to get to Ulu Baram, but when you arrive the rewards can be considerable. There are ample chances to **trek** through jungle, using "trails" hacked out by your guide, spending the night perhaps in a hut of the type the Penan erect, or in a shelter that your guide might build using branches. From the Selungo River it's also possible to climb **Mount Murud Kecil** ("Little Murud"; 2112m), at the opposite end of the Tama Abu Range from its more famous sibling, and there are many interesting trips to caves and waterfalls.

Ulu Baram villages

Village life can itself be a highlight in Ulu Baram. Local people can teach crafts, and then there's the simple pleasure of bathing in the river with the villagers, or the spectacle of being at the simple village church on Sunday (many Penan belong to the evangelical Sidang Injil Borneo or SIB movement, which has churches throughout Sarawak); it's great to witness hymns sung in Penan with the village youths showing off their self-taught skills on guitar, keyboards and drums. After the rice is planted (June) or harvested (February), you can even accompany the men as they **hunt** wild pigs, aided by dogs and the odd gun.

ARRIVAL AND INFORMATION   **ULU BARAM**

Picnic with the Penan Though it's possible to visit independently, the best way to visit Penan settlements near Lio Matoh, such as Long Kerong and Ajeng close to the Selungo River, is as part of the Picnic with the Penan scheme (W picnicwiththepenan.org), run with help from Adventure Alternative Borneo (see p.329). The experience is similar to visiting villages in the Kelabit Highlands (see p.378), but much more cut off. It doesn't come cheap, as this area has resisted the logging industry – logging roads and bridges are fewer and further between, so expensive boat charter is required. Currently, the typical trip is five days (four nights; RM350) and starts with a flight to Long

Akah, followed by a two-hour 4WD drive to Long Suit (RM350), where a 30min boat ride (RM250/2 people) gets you to Long Speegan from where you can walk to a jungle camp (45min). Then, a three-day trek takes you through the jungle, staying at camps and homestays, to Long Lellang, from where you can fly out – flights in and out cost RM100–110. Guides cost RM100/day, though have little English so you may want to arrange one through Adventure Alternative Borneo or the Guide Association in Kuching (typically RM200/day; see p.329), while porters cost RM65 – both will also need paying for the return trip.

THE PENAN

For some, the **Penan** have a mystique beyond that of any of Sarawak's many Orang Ulu groups, as a kind of poster child for the ongoing struggle for native peoples' rights. That status is largely thanks to the campaign waged on their behalf by the Swiss activist **Bruno Manser** in the 1980s and 1990s. Manser lived with the Penan for years and became a thorn in the side of the Sarawak government, drawing the world's attention to the destruction of their traditional forest habitat, though his PR successes had little impact on Sarawak's logging industry. The Penan lost their champion when Manser disappeared in 2000, having trekked alone from Bario to meet the Penan in the jungle; he was never seen again, but the campaign he founded soldiers on (W bmf.ch).

Most of Sarawak's twelve thousand Penan live in the upper reaches of the Baram, Tutoh and Belaga rivers, with only two or three hundred still following their nomadic lifestyle. Their language is of the same family as Iban and Malay. Traditionally they were nomadic hunter-gatherers, but these days the majority live in tiny villages – thanks not only to habitat loss but also to the embrace of the outside world and cash economy. Their staple of sago has often been supplanted by rice, which the Penan grow like the Iban, in clearings using shifting cultivation. Many Penan struggle to make ends meet, both in towns where they may be in poorly paid work, and in their villages, where food is in reasonable supply but cash hard to come by. Another problem is the lack of identity documents, without which many Penan cannot access services, education and jobs.

Sabah

KINABATANGAN RIVER

Sabah

Sabah is, in many ways, Malaysia's "Wild East", a state with a frontier feel tinged by the influence of neighbouring Indonesia and the Philippines. It's markedly different to its western neighbour Sarawak, too, despite superficial similarities: both states are largely rural, and both encompass a bewildering number of ethnic groups (see p.578 for more on Sabah's make-up). But whereas Sarawak is prosperous, Sabah is often visibly poor, and – more pertinently for visitors – where Sarawak makes a big thing of its tribal cultures, in Sabah the focus is overwhelmingly on nature. Indeed, this is arguably the very best place in Malaysia for wildlife-spotting, a fact that has kept visitors coming despite the odd security scare (see p.392). Part of the reason for that focus on fauna is the paucity of Sabah's urban heritage; in few other parts of the country do the major cities exude such a sense of rootlessness, due largely to World War II bombing.

The **terrain** of "The Land Below the Wind" – a moniker that has clung to Sabah thanks to Agnes Keith's fine book of the same name (see p.426), although it really means anywhere equatorial outside the typhoon belt – ranges from wild, swampy, mangrove-tangled coastal areas, through the dazzling greens of paddy fields and pristine rainforests, to the substantial Crocker mountain range. It's home to Malaysia's highest peak, **Mount Kinabalu**, whose distinctively craggy summit is visible throughout much of western and central Sabah, and appears on the state flag. A plethora of state parks and forest reserves provide refuges for indigenous animals, although much of eastern Sabah is now given over to oil palm.

The state's most enjoyable city by far is the capital **Kota Kinabalu** (KK) in the northwest. With a fine selection of accommodation, restaurants and markets, it's a springboard for many of Sabah's attractions, notably the **Kinabalu Park** to the northeast and the whitewater rafting and wildlife cruises of the **Klias Peninsula** to the south. Also within reach of here is **Pulau Tiga Park**, for island solitude; the duty-free island of **Labuan**; and the beaches and coconut groves of the **Kudat Peninsula**, whose northernmost point, the **Tip of Borneo**, features windy shorelines and splendid isolation.

Across on the east coast is the mundane city of **Sandakan**, another springboard for major attractions, including the **Sepilok Orang-utan Rehabilitation Centre**, **Bornean Sun Bear Conservation Centre** and **Labuk Bay Proboscis Monkey Sanctuary**. Deeper into the oil-palm plantations of east Sabah lies the protected **Kinabatangan River**, where visitors can take boat trips to see wild proboscis monkeys, elephants and orang-utans.

Highlights

❶ **Tiga Island** With the TV crews long gone, "Survivor Island" remains largely undeveloped with attractive beaches, jungle walks and a natural mud bath for good measure. **See p.408**

❷ **Mount Kinabalu** The climb is arduous and expensive, but still one of the very best experiences in all of Malaysia. **See p.417**

❸ **Sepilok** This rural area outside Sandakan boasts sanctuaries for orang-utans and sun bears, as well as a rainforest park. **See p.431**

❹ **Kinabatangan River** Home to a great diversity of animal life, including proboscis monkeys and the occasional pygmy elephant herd. **See p.434**

❺ **Danum Valley** A stretch of untouched rainforest with plenty of wildlife-spotting possibilities. **See p.439**

❻ **Sipadan and Mabul** Spectacular marine life makes these two islands a must for scuba divers; reefs off other nearby islands are also worth exploring. **See p.441**

❼ **Sapulut** This remote area is home to an excellent community tourism project, offering a dose of nature, Murut culture and the chance to climb limestone pinnacles. **See p.448**

❽ **Maliau Basin** A true taste of virgin jungle, with multi-day treks to take in pretty waterfalls. **See p.449**

HIGHLIGHTS ARE MARKED ON THE MAP ON P.390

SABAH

Zamboanga (Philippines)

THE PHILIPPINES

CELEBES SEA

SULU SEA

Tawi Tawi (Philippines)

Sibutu (Philippines)

Cagayan Sulu (Philippines)

TURTLE ISLANDS PARK

Lankayan

Bandar Sahabat

Pom Pom

Matking

Bum Bum

Tungku

TABIN WILDLIFE RESERVE

Segama River

Darvel Bay

TUN SAKARAN MARINE PARK

Mabul

Sipadan

Kapalai

Mata

Timbun Mata

Kunak

Semporna

Abal

Sukau

Bilit

Lahad Datu

Bukit Piton Reserve

Reserve Entrance

SAPAGAYA FOREST RESERVE

Mount Silam (884m)

Tawau

Sebatik

Nunukan

Tarakan (Indonesia)

TAWAU HILLS STATE PARK

Sandakan

Sepilok

Gomantong Caves

Labuk Bay Proboscis Monkey Sanctuary

Kota Kinabatangan

Batu Putih

DERAMAKOT FOREST RESERVE

DANUM VALLEY CONSERVATION AREA

Kinabatangan River

Imbak Canyon

MALIAU BASIN CONSERVATION AREA

Banggi

Malawali

Karakit

TEN MUSTAPHA PARK

Balambangan

Tip of Borneo

Sikuat

Kudat

Pitas

Kanibongan

Bay

Marudu

Kota

Kampung Bavanggazo

Matunggong

Telupid

Sugut River

Jambongan

KINABALU PARK

Mount Kinabalu (4095m)

Kinabalu Park HQ

Poring

Ranau

Kampung Patau

Kundasang

Tamburan

Mount Tras Madi (2642m)

Batu Punggul

Sapulut

Pensiangan

Mantanani

Mantanani Kecil

Kampung Patau

Penambawan

Tuaran

KOTA KINABALU

Kinatut

CROCKER RANGE PARK

Keningau

Sook

Nabawan

Kota Belud

Papan

Kimanis

Kuala Penyu

Membakut

Beaufort

Padas Gorge

Sipitang

Sindumin

Tenom

Padas River

KALIMANTAN

Mengalum

TUNKU ABDUL RAHMAN PARK

PULAU TIGA PARK

Klias Peninsula

Menumbok

Labuan

Merapok

Lawas

Bangar

BRUNEI

SARAWAK

Murara (Brunei) & Limbang (Sarawak)

N

kilometres

0   50

Those who venture into the state's southeast corner are generally headed to the islands near the town of **Semporna**, which are the jewel in Sabah's crown for divers. **Sipadan Island** offers world-class diving off coral walls, while its neighbour **Mabul Island** is known for its macro marine life. These two are simply the best known, and the area can keep divers and snorkellers enchanted for days. There are also a couple of excellent wildlife reserves here, most notably the **Danum Valley Conservation Area**.

Sabah's remote interior is generally somewhere visitors bypass on a plane between coasts, or else grind through on an express bus, but there are things worth seeing here, too: the forested **Maliau Basin**, where the trekking overshadows the wildlife; and the village of **Sapulut**, home to an excellent community tourism project offering a mix of climbing, caving and trekking.

Brief history

Little is known of Sabah's **early history**, though archeological finds in limestone caves indicate that the northern tip of Borneo has been inhabited for well over ten thousand years. **Chinese merchants** were trading with local settlements by 700 AD, and by the fourteenth century the area was under the sway of the sultans of **Brunei** and **Sulu**.

Colonialism

Europe's superpowers first arrived in 1521, when the ships of **Portuguese** navigator Ferdinand Magellan stopped off at Brunei before sailing northwards. Almost 250 years later, in 1763, colonial settlement began when one Captain Cowley established a short-lived trading post on Balambangan Island, north of Kudat, on behalf of the **British East India Company**. Further colonial involvement came in 1846, when Labuan Island (at the mouth of Brunei Bay) was ceded to the British by the Sultan of Brunei. The 1870s were a pivotal decade: first the Sultan of Brunei signed over what is basically now western Sabah to the British in return for a yearly remittance, and soon after the **Sultan of Sulu** (the archipelago at the southern fringe of what's now the Philippines) struck a similar deal covering eastern Sabah. By 1881 the **British North Borneo Chartered Company** had full sovereignty over northern Borneo.

First steps were then taken towards making the territory pay its way: rubber, tobacco and, after 1885, timber were commercially harvested. By 1905 a **rail line** linked the coastal town of **Jesselton** (later Kota Kinabalu) with the resource-rich interior. When the company introduced taxes, the locals were understandably displeased and some resisted; **Mat Salleh**, the son of a Bajau chief, and his followers sacked the company's settlement on Gaya Island in 1897. Another uprising, in **Rundum** in 1915, resulted in the slaughter of hundreds of Murut tribespeople by British forces.

World War II and independence

On New Year's Day 1942, Japanese imperial forces invaded Labuan Island; Sandakan fell less than three weeks later. By the time the Japanese surrendered on September 9, 1945, little of Jesselton and Sandakan remained standing (although the worst structural damage was inflicted by Allied bombing). Even worse were the hardships endured by civilians and captured Allied troops, the most notorious of which were the Death Marches of 1945 (see p.426).

Unable to finance the postwar rebuilding of North Borneo, the Chartered Company sold the territory to the British Crown in 1946, and Jesselton was declared the new capital of the **Crown Colony of North Borneo**. Within fifteen years, however, plans had been laid for an independent federation consisting of Malaya, Singapore, Sarawak, North Borneo and (it was intended) Brunei. The **Federation** was proclaimed at midnight on September 16, 1963, with North Borneo renamed Sabah.

Modern concerns

Kuala Lumpur feels very remote from Sabah, but federal politics have been gradually imposed ever since independence. Although local and indigenous parties have ruled Sabah in stretches, since 2002 the state has been firmly in the grip of the country's ruling BN coalition. One factor in this is **immigration** – both legal and undocumented – which remains a live issue. Around a quarter of Sabah's population is non-Malaysian, the highest proportion of any state in the federation, and in recent decades there has been a vast influx of largely Muslim migrants from the Philippines and Indonesia. Many indigenous Sabahans view their requests for residency (and in some cases citizenship) with suspicion, seeing them as a creeping way of Islamizing the state, but their opposition has been unfocused and ineffective.

Sabah was, for a time, the poster child for Malaysian tourism. It remains the state with the best environmental track record in the country (although critics might say it could be better managed still) and its wildlife attractions meant visitor numbers boomed in the first decade of the new millennium; for a while, KK even enjoyed direct flights from Australia. Unfortunately things fell off a cliff after a spate of **security incidents** (see box, below). At the time of research the sector was finally looking to be on the mend, despite another sad event, the Mount Kinabalu **earthquake** in 2015 (see p.423).

7

ARRIVAL AND DEPARTURE

By plane Kota Kinabalu, Sandakan and the southeastern town of Tawau all have modern airports, but KK's is the only de facto international gateway, with connections to various Southeast Asian cities. Tawau barely counts as international, with a few short flights to Tarakan in Indonesian Borneo; Sandakan may attract flights from abroad now that a runway extension is complete.

By bus The only overland route into Sabah is from Lawas in Sarawak. Express buses follow this route to KK from Bandar Seri Begawan in Brunei and even from Miri in Sarawak.

By boat Ferries run between Labuan Island and Sipitang, Menumbok and KK; Labuan itself has connections with Limbang and Lawas in Sarawak, plus Brunei. Ferries also sail from Indonesian Borneo to Tawau, and from the Philippines to Sandakan.

GETTING AROUND

The relatively backward state of Sabah's roads can make driving or bus travel a bit of a bore. Four-lane highways are memorable for their rarity, stretching from KK north to around Tuaran and south to Kinarut, and 60km east from Tawau,

---

SECURITY IN SABAH

Certain areas of Sabah are subject to official **travel advisories**, as a result of incidents blamed on Muslim militancy in the southern Philippines. Alarming though this may sound, some perspective is called for: such events are sporadic and, as in other countries that have witnessed random acts of violence of late, ordinary people are going about their lives as normal.

Sabah has witnessed **abductions** on and off over the years, most recently since 2010. Some have involved tourists, seized on the dive islands off Semporna; in Sandakan, two local people were kidnapped and one was subsequently killed, apparently because no ransom was paid. Undoubtedly the most serious event was an **incursion** by armed insurgents near Lahad Datu in 2013, ostensibly to revive the old Sulu Sultanate claim on eastern Sabah; several dozen people, mostly militants, died in the ensuing fighting as the authorities regained control.

In general, however, Sabah remains as calm as any other part of Malaysia, and the travel warnings reflect this. At the time of research, for example, only the islands off the Tip of Borneo and off Semporna were included in a UK warning advising against "all but essential travel", while the US was recommending general caution in eastern Sabah. Things can change for better or worse at any time, of course, so it's best to keep abreast of the latest official advice.

Note that many local people avoid the **water villages** that still exist on the edges of many towns, as they may harbour undocumented migrants – the subtext here being because of petty crime and, perhaps, militancy. Such concerns may be overblown, but in any case most of these settlements aren't really sights (unlike the one in Brunei's capital) – the odd exception is mentioned in the text.

VISITING PARKS AND RESERVES

A range of organizations manage Sabah's wildlife sanctuaries. **Sabah Parks** (☎ 088 523500, ⓦ sabahparks.org.my; see p.398) runs the state's nine **state parks**, six of which are out at sea. There's usually a **conservation fee** to visit (typically RM10–20, although prices may rise in 2018). Note that accommodation and other facilities at the most popular parks – including Kinabalu – are largely privatized and can thus be pricey. Then there are forest **conservation areas** such as Deramakot, which fall under the **Sabah Forestry Department** in Sandakan (entry permits RM15 per day; ☎ 089 242500, ⓦ forest.sabah.gov.my). Some sites are wholly or partly run by other agencies; details are given in the text, along with information on how to sort out a visit, but given the complexities involved it can be preferable to pay one of the many tour operators in KK (see p.398) or Sandakan (see p.429) to sort out the paperwork and transport – in some cases this is the only option.

petering out halfway to Semporna. Highway extension plans seem to drag rather like the two-lane country roads you'll rely on everywhere else. At least there is now a sealed road right through the southern interior to Tawau, and although it can be in a poor state between Sapulut and Maliau Basin, an ordinary car will cope; off the beaten track, you might need to rent a 4WD. It's worth considering internal flights as a timesaver.

By plane MASWings' nineteen-seater Twin Otters (ⓦ maswings.com.my) serve the airfields at Kudat (near the Tip of Borneo) and Lahad Datu on the east coast. For more on these planes, see p.371.

By long-distance bus Long-distance buses provide a fairly comprehensive service but may peter out towards evening, and adherence to timetables can be arbitrary. Fares are reasonable, though; KK to Sandakan (335km) costs around RM45.

By shared minivans/taxis Shared taxis and minivans leave when full on routes of up to 150km, though most

cover distances that are much shorter. Prices are at least twenty percent higher than bus fares for the same distance.

By train Sabah State Railway (☎ 088 262536 or ☎ 088 279300, ⓦ railway.sabah.gov.my) provides a limited service that's of little use to most visitors. The main part of the line runs from the outskirts of KK via several southwestern towns to Beaufort (2 daily; 2hr), where there's a branch line to Tenom in the interior (2 daily; 2hr 30min). It costs only RM7.50 to travel the entire network. Unless timetables change, there are no convenient connections between the two parts of the network at Beaufort, in either direction.

Kota Kinabalu

While first impressions of **KOTA KINABALU** (universally referred to as KK) may be of a glut of functional concrete, it does have a laid-back vibe and plenty of worthwhile amenities. In terms of sights, there's nothing to warrant staying more than a couple of nights – highlights include the **markets** and the islands of the **Tunku Abdul Rahman Park** – but the city's role as a hub for transport and tour operators means you might pass through more than once. Another appealing thing about the place is its manageability: the city centre is a mere 4km strip stretching from the resort area in the southwest to Likas Bay in the northeast, its grid of streets crammed in between the sea and the ridge of Signal Hill.

Brief history

Modern-day KK has its roots in a failed British settlement at Gaya Island, which was burned down in 1897 by followers of the Bajau rebel Mat Salleh. Starting anew, in 1899 the North Borneo Chartered Company founded a new town on a site on the mainland opposite. Named **Jesselton** after Sir Charles Jessel, the company's vice-chairman, the settlement soon prospered as the seaward terminus of the new railway line to Beaufort in the interior, allowing commodities to be brought efficiently to the coast for export.

The Japanese invasion of North Borneo in 1942 marked the start of three and a half years of **military occupation**; little of the old town survived subsequent Allied bombing. Soon after the war, Jesselton replaced Sandakan as Sabah's capital, and in 1968 it acquired its present name – an apt choice considering that on a clear day, Mount Kinabalu is

KOTA KINABALU

ACCOMMODATION		EATING		SHOPPING	
B&B@21	12	Chilli Vanilla	6	The Borneo Store	5
Borneo Backpackers	11	D'Malindo Café	4	Centre Point Mall	8
The Bunk	10	D'Place	12	City Grocer	2
Eden 54	3	El Centro	5	Imago Mall	10
Hashtag 12 Boutique Hotel	15	Fook Yuen	7	Kadaiku/Sri Pelancongan	7
Horizon	8	Grazie	2	Montanic Adventure Begins	3/11
Hyatt Regency	1	Jesselton Point		Mr DIY	12
Jesselton	6	Hawker Centre	1	Outdoor Gear	9
Kinabalu Daya	4	Jothy's Banana Leaf	11	Suria Sabah Mall	1
Klagan	14	October	9	Times Bookstore	4
Le Meridien	9	Sinsuran Night Market	8	Tong Hing	6
Little Gaya	2	Tam Nak Thai	3		
Lucy's Homestay	13	Tavern	13		
Masada Backpacker	16	Welcome Seafood	14		
Maxim	18	Yee Fung	10		
Refarer	17				
Shangri-La		DRINKING AND NIGHTLIFE			
Tanjung Aru Resort	20	999	3		
Sixty3	5	Bed	1		
Step-in Lodge	7	Sharikat Biru-Biru	2		
Sutera Harbour Resort	19				

actually visible from Likas Bay, the airport and elsewhere. Since then KK has grown rapidly, attracting a true cross-section of Sabah's population even though it sits in the Kadazan/Dusun heartland. In 2000 it finally gained official city status, and in terms of property prices, KK is now one of the most expensive cities in East Malaysia.

Gaya Street

There are echoes of the past in the names of the districts in KK's centre: Api-Api was a Bajau fishing village in the area, while Kampung Air ("water village") hints at the land reclamation that was necessary to flesh the centre out to its present size. For more tangible traces of the past, however, head to **Gaya Street** (Jalan Gaya), which still has the feel of a small-town main street even though all the architecture is postwar. The only two buildings of note are the whitewashed former General Post Office, which now houses the main **tourist office**, and the 1954 *Jesselton* hotel metres away, though this packs rather less old-world charm. Signage throughout reveals the presence of Chinese associations, and the odd hardware shop and picture framer can be found clinging on amid fairly obvious gentrification.

One of the very best **street markets** in Malaysia takes place here every Sunday (6am–1pm), when the entire street gets packed out with stalls selling items as varied as tropical fruit trees, hats, basketry and live rabbits. Buskers are usually on hand too.

Australia Place and Signal Hill

A stone's throw south of the tourist office is **Australia Place**, so named because the Australian soldiers made camp here in 1945. From the back of the lane here, called **Lorong Dewan** (also known as Jalan Dewan), two sets of steps lead up the ridge behind KK's centre to **Signal Hill** (Bukit Bendera), which is the highest point in town with a modern **observatory platform** for views over the centre and out to sea.

The oldest surviving structure in the city stands on a hillock just a couple of minutes' walk west of Australia Place: the wooden **Atkinson's Clock Tower**, built in 1903 to commemorate the first district official of Jesselton, Francis George Atkinson, who died of malaria at 28. Practically next door is **Merdeka Field**, where Sabah's independence and simultaneous union with modern Malaysia was declared.

The waterfront

KK's **waterfront** is no grand promenade, but a series of nondescript modern buildings with some overpriced restaurants and bars at the southwestern end (when locals use the term "waterfront", they may mean this area specifically). The real highlights are its markets, most notably the **handicraft market** in the centre of the strip (daily 7am–8pm, though hours may vary). Also known by its old name of the Filipino market, thanks to the ethnicity of some of its traders, it's a veritable warren

7

of stalls mainly selling cheap clothes, with tailors doing alterations at antique sewing machines set up outside.

Next door to the southwest is the **night market**, a photogenic combination of fish market and stalls selling cooked food (see p.402). At the other end of the handicraft market is the large **central market** (daily 6am–6pm), with its own fish market that's at its best first thing in the morning; a few more outdoor food stalls set up in the afternoon and evening just beyond.

Sabah Museum

Jalan Muzium, on a hilltop 2km south of the centre • Daily 9am–5pm • RM15 • ☎ 088 225033, ⦿ museum.sabah.gov.my • Take any Penampang-bound bus from the Marina Court stop; get off once the bus turns into Jalan Penampang, below the museum

Housed in a 1980s hunk of concrete styled to evoke Murut and Rungus longhouses, the **Sabah Museum** isn't the most compelling of its kind, but some worthwhile exhibits make it a decent target, especially on rainy days. One highlight is the **ethnographic collection**, including human skulls dating from the Kadazan/Dusun's head-hunting days, plus examples of traditional crafts, costumes and musical instruments such as the *turali* (nose flute). Elsewhere, there are various Chinese **ceramic jars**, including some sizeable ones used for funerary purposes as in Sarawak, plus **nature dioramas** that impart some fresh insights into rainforest fauna.

Outside the main building is a small gallery of carriages and equipment drawn from modern Sabah's dalliance with railways. Much better is the **Heritage Village** (Kampung Warisan) on the leafy north side of the compound; head down a flight of steps and cross the suspension bridge to reach a lake ringed by wooden, bamboo and palm-thatch dwellings representing the building styles of ethnic groups.

Kota Kinabalu Wetlands

Jalan Bukit Bendera Upper, east of Signal Hill • Tues–Sun 8am–6pm • RM15 • ☎ 088 246955, ⦿ sabahwetlands.org • A 40min walk from the centre up and over Signal Hill; alternatively any bus from Jalan Tunku Abdul Rahman (opposite Merdeka Field) signed "Likas" or "One Borneo" will head to Likas Square, from where it's a short walk south and west

The patch of mangrove forest at **Kota Kinabalu Wetlands** is the only remnant of an extensive system that once covered the coastline. Designated as a bird sanctuary in 1996, it's an important refuge and feeding ground for many species. From marked trails on **boardwalks**, you may catch sight of herons, egrets, sandpipers, pigeons and doves, as well as mudskippers and monitor lizards; for birdlife, it's best to come early in the morning or late in the afternoon. The wetlands are managed by a non-profit conservation group, which does its best to defend them against pollution and fast-encroaching development.

The beaches

Tanjung Aru Beach starts 4km southwest of the centre, and minivans from the Marina Court bus stop can drop you near the start; Likas Bay is only 1km on from the Jesselton Point ferry terminal – take bus #6 northbound from Jalan Tunku Abdul Rahman

They're nothing much to write home about, but the public beaches in KK are out at **Tanjung Aru** and in the opposite direction at **Likas Bay**. The former is preferable, a 2km stretch in three sections – "first beach" near the *Shangri-La* resort the most popular; Likas Bay has nice views but can be a little dirty. Both beaches have basic showers and toilets. Jellyfish are an occasional problem, so it's worth asking the tourist office whether there have been any recent stinging incidents before diving in.

ARRIVAL AND DEPARTURE

BY PLANE

KK International Airport (KKIA) The airport (⦿ kotakinabaluairport.com) is 7km south of the centre in the Kepayan district. A shuttle bus (daily 8am–8.30pm; every 45min; RM5) runs from here to Merdeka Field, although getting a Grab car is a useful alternative if you're travelling with others, as it may work out cheaper per person. Official taxis cost RM30 per trip.

Destinations Bandar Seri Begawan (6 weekly; 40min); Bintulu (2 daily; 1hr 15min); Johor Bahru (1 daily; 2hr 15min); Kota Bharu (3 weekly; 2hr 30min); Kuala Lumpur (at least 12 daily; 2hr 30min); Kuching (4 daily; 1hr 25min); Kudat (3 weekly; 40min); Labuan (4 daily; 30min); Lahad Datu (4 daily; 55min); Lawas (1 daily; 45min); Limbang (3 weekly; 45min); Miri (2–4 daily; 55min); Mulu (4 weekly; 55min); Penang (1–2 daily; 1hr 40min); Sandakan (6–7 daily; 40min); Sibu (2 daily; 1hr 35min); Singapore (2 daily; 2hr 10min); Tawau (6–7 daily; 55min).

BY BUS

City Bus Terminal North (Inanam) In the Inanam suburb 11km east of the centre, this bus terminal is used by buses to the east coast. Note that for Tawau, there are also buses via Keningau and the Interior from Merdeka Field, which are often quicker even with the variable state of the road. Bus #4 (2 hourly; 40min) runs south from the Shangri-La bus stop in the city centre and then east to Inanam (heading into town, it's a short walk south from the terminal to the main road). A taxi there or back will cost at least RM30.

Destinations Lahad Datu (14 daily; 8hr); Sandakan (at least 12 daily; 6hr 30min); Semporna (6 daily; 10hr); Tawau (via the east coast; 7 daily; 11hr); Telupid (frequent; 4hr 30min).

Merdeka Field The Merdeka Field car park right in the city centre is used mainly by shared minivans and taxis, although a handful of buses also operate from here.

Destinations Keningau (frequent; 2hr 30min); Kota Belud (1 daily; 1hr 30min); Kudat (1 daily; 3hr 30min); Tawau (via the interior; 2 daily; at least 10hr); Tenom (4 daily; 3hr).

City Park Bus Terminal Buses for the border town of Menumbok (for Labuan Island ferries) and as far afield as Miri in Sarawak (RM90) depart from close to the City Hall.

There's also a Brunei service from here run by Sipitang Express (w sipitangexpress.com.my).

Destinations Bandar Seri Begawan (Brunei; 1 daily; 8hr 30min); Beaufort (5 daily; 2hr); Menumbok (roughly hourly until 3pm; 2hr 30min); Miri (1 daily; 11hr).

BY MINIVAN AND SHARED TAXI

Minivans and shared taxis serve towns within about 4hr of KK from Merdeka Field, in all directions; signs indicate where each cluster of vehicles is bound. Taxis may fill up more promptly and are quicker generally. The cost with either to travel to Kinabalu Park, for example, is around RM20, although minivans are generally slightly cheaper.

Destinations Beaufort (2hr); Keningau (2hr); Kinabalu Park (2hr); Kota Belud (2hr); Kuala Penyu (for Pulau Tiga Park; 2hr 30min); Kudat (4hr); Menumbok (for Labuan ferries; 3hr); Ranau (3hr); Tambunan (1hr 45min); Tenom (3hr).

BY FERRY

Jesselton Point Ferry Terminal The terminal is at the north end of Jalan Haji Saman. Services to Labuan Island are operated by Double Power (daily 8am & 1.30pm; 3hr 30min; RM40 plus a terminal tax of RM7; ☎ 088 236834). If you're aiming to reach Brunei, the 8am departure will leave you with a mere 2hr wait in Labuan for an onward ferry.

BY TRAIN

Tanjung Aru station The train station is a gleaming new affair just off the highway, 5km southwest of central KK (☎ 088 279300), and provides a limited service. Any bus from Marina Court bound for Kepayan, Petagas or Putatan will pass close by, and they may detour into the station on request.

Destinations Beaufort (2 daily; 2hr); Papar (2 daily; 45min); Kinarut (2 daily; 20min).

GETTING AROUND

By bus or minivan Local buses and minivans are meant to use the Wawasan terminal in the southwest of the centre, but this was closed for long-term rebuilding at the time of research. Until it reopens, you can use the bus stop at the Marina Court condominium on Jalan Tun Fuad Stephens for southbound journeys; for destinations east and north of the city, some routes use the southbound bus stop by the central *Shangri-La* hotel, while others use the northbound stop on Jalan Tunku Abdul Rahman, so check before travelling. Within the centre itself, there are three looping city bus services (#A, #B and #C), though there's little reason to use them

given the compactness of the place. Finally, buses and minivans more often display the suburb where they terminate rather than a route number.

By taxi A journey within the centre should cost RM10–15; taxis park up in little clusters all over the area. Grab cars are generally better value.

By car Companies include Extra Rent A Car, based at the *Sabah Oriental Hotel* off Jalan Kemajuan (☎ 088 251529, w e-erac-online.com); Hertz, at the airport (☎ 088 413326, w hertz.com); and Borneo Kinabalu Elegant Tours, on the ground floor of Wisma Sabah shopping mall (☎ 012 502 0608, w visitmalaysiasabah.com.

INFORMATION

Internet access Check out Gaya Internet Centre, off Gaya Street (daily 9am–2am). KK City Wi-Fi is a free wireless

hotspot available close to City Hall, along the waterfront and possibly elsewhere by the time you read this.

7

Magazines The free *Sabah Malaysian Borneo* magazine (wfacebook.com/smbmagazine), published every two months or so, covers new attractions and upcoming events; Sabah Tourism usually has copies.

Sabah Parks Ground floor, Block H, KK Times Square (Mon–Thurs 8.30am–1pm & 2–5pm, Fri 8.30–11.30am & 2–5pm; ☎088 523500, wsabahparks.org.my). Information on Sabah's state parks, including nitty-gritty details of facilities and so forth.

Sabah Tourism Board 51 Gaya Street (Mon–Fri 8am–5pm, Sat & Sun 9am–4pm; ☎088 212121, wsabahtourism.com). Pick the brains of the knowledgeable, well-organized staff here as much as you can, because Sabah Tourism has no offices in any other towns. Their free tourist map of KK, although sketchy, can be handy for the suburbs.

Tourism Malaysia At the airport (daily 8am–11pm; ☎088 413359, wtourism.gov.my).

ACCOMMODATION

KK has a great selection of hostels and hotels. If it's the latter you're after, it's worth booking at least a couple of weeks in advance as hotels can be unpredictably packed out if there are lots of tour groups or a major conference in town. Note that practically all the **budget hotels** cluster in Kampung Air, a district local people consider seedy and possibly rough at night. It can certainly be rowdy into the small hours, which is as good a reason as any not to stay here, given the poor sound insulation of most cheap hotels. As for hostels, there are two little **backpacker enclaves** abutting the ridge of Signal Hill, at Australia Place and further south in the Bandaran Berjaya neighbourhood, both convenient for Merdeka Field.

HOSTELS

★**B&B@21** 21 Lorong Dewan ☎016 883 3763, ✉bb21@ gmail.com; map p.394. A very cool hostel tucked up against Signal Hill, with a superb garden at the back, a range of dorms and one private room. ☞ Dorms RM35, doubles RM90

Borneo Backpackers 24 Lorong Dewan ☎088 234009, wborneobackpackers.com; map p.394. As well as four double rooms and a number of dorms with up to ten beds, there's a downstairs café here with occasional live music. All rooms have a/c. ☞ Dorms RM25, doubles RM80

The Bunk 113 Gaya Street ☎088 204526, wthebunkborneo.blogspot.com; map p.394. Right in the thick of the Gaya Street action, this is a hostel with designer aspirations: there's a wood-panelled café/lounge

---

KOTA KINABALU TOUR OPERATORS

KK has plenty of handy **tour operators**, many based in Wisma Sabah shopping mall on Jalan Tun Fuad Stephens. Their offerings are usually pricey, but can be worthwhile for destinations that are tricky to arrange independently or if you want to see several places in a short space of time. The companies are also useful for arranging **day-trips** from KK, such as wildlife cruises or firefly-watching at the Klias Peninsula, and rafting on the Padas or Kiulu rivers; a few firms even run their own resorts or attractions.

Adventure Alternative Borneo Orangutan Tattoo Parlour, Lorong Dewan wadventurealternativeborneo .com. Specializes in off-the-beaten-track destinations such as the Deramakot Forest Reserve and Imbak Canyon. You can also try contacting their Kuching office (see p.329)

Bike Borneo Second floor, Block C, City Mall, Damai, 4km southeast of the centre ☎088 484734, wbikeborneo.com. Offers mountain-biking escapades, including a three-day tour of the foothills of Kinabalu and another that combines a riverside ride with rafting.

Borneo Divers Ninth floor, Menara Jubili, 53 Gaya Street ☎088 222226, wborneodivers.info. Diving specialist with its own resort on Mabul (see p.442) and a dive school at the Tunku Abdul Rahman Park – they offer packages at both plus Sipadan Island.

★**Borneo Eco Tours** Kolombong Jaya Industrial Estate, off Jalan Kolombong ☎088 438300, wborneoecotours.com. Inconveniently sited out

towards Inanam, they run the excellent *Sukau Rainforest Lodge* on the Kinabatangan River and a "farmstay" at Kiulu, northeast of KK, where residents can combine trekking with a taste of rice cultivation. Otherwise, they cover all the standard destinations, with birding tours a forte.

Borneo Nature Tours Ground floor, Block D, Sadong Jaya Complex, just west of the centre off Jalan Tunku Abdul Rahman ☎088 267637, wwww .borneonaturetours.com. Runs the luxurious *Borneo Rainforest Lodge* in the Danum Valley (see p.439) and has tours to Maliau Basin.

Borneo Refugia Level 12, Tun Mustapha Tower, far side of Likas Bay ☎088 326317, wborneorefugia .com. Part of the Sabah Foundation, this set-up has package trips to forest reserves under the foundation's stewardship, notably the Danum Valley and Maliau Basin, plus the new *Kawag Danum Rainforest Lodge* near the Danum Valley (see p.439). It can also organize plastered with old photos, and fancy bunk beds with privacy drapes, arranged in one jumbo dorm. A private room is available, too. ☞ Dorms RM30, double RM75

★**Lucy's Homestay** 25 Lorong Dewan ☎ 088 261495, ✉ backpackerkk@yahoo.com; map p.394. A stalwart of the KK hostel scene, launched in the mid-1990s and truly old school. What you get is no-frills accommodation in an unmodernized family home, a slightly cluttered place with both dorms and private rooms. There's no a/c or hot water, but the informality is one compensation. Another is Lucy and her son, both welcoming and knowledgeable hosts, who also run the laundry downstairs. ☞ Dorms RM25, doubles RM65

Masada Backpacker 9 Jalan Masjid Lama, on the edge of Bandaran Berjaya ☎ 088 238494, ⓦ masadabackpacker .com; map p.394. Rooms are clean and comfortable, breakfasts are better than average (including fruit and biscuits), staff are helpful and there's a/c throughout – no wonder it's constantly popular. ☞ Dorms RM35, doubles RM95

Refarer Lorong Berjaya 2, Bandaran Berjaya ☎ 088 257552, ✉ refarer@hotmail.com; map p.394. There's plenty of blond wood at the reception area and in the bunk beds of this quirky, vaguely upmarket hostel, where you can start your day with either a Western breakfast or *nasi lemak*. ☞ Dorms RM40, doubles RM100

★**Step-In Lodge** Block L, Sinsuran Complex ☎ 088 233519, ⓦ stepinlodge.com; map p.394. A homely, buzzing hostel a stone's throw from the waterfront, with an airy lounge and a plant-decked balcony for a bird's-eye view of proceedings below in the bustling Sinsuran district. There's a choice of dorms and private rooms, all with a/c. ☞ Dorms RM50, doubles RM100

HOTELS AND RESORTS

Eden 54 54 Gaya Street ☎ 088 266054, ⓦ eden54.com; map p.394. "Stark opulence" is how staff have styled this place, but forgive them the oxymoron; rooms feature tasteful modern decor and there's a surprisingly large lounge, too. Note that the cheapest rooms, including the singles, are windowless. ☞ RM160

Hashtag 12 Boutique Hotel Jalan Block 3, Api-Api Centre, Lorong Api-Api 2 ☎ 088 313007, ✉ hashtag12hotel@gmail.com; map p.394. Despite its name, this is really a budget hotel that also wants to be a hostel – it has a mixed dorm. Everything's fairly minimalist and a bit sterile, but the place is reasonably soundproofed. Look for the entrance stairway close to the Hong Leong Bank. ☞ Dorms RM50, doubles RM110

Horizon Jalan Tun Razak ☎ 088 518000, ⓦ horizonhotelsabah.com; map p.394. A massive block

expeditions to the little-visited Imbak Canyon (ⓦ imbakcanyon-borneo.com.my).

Borneo Trails First floor, Wisma Sabah ☎ 088 235900, ⓦ borneotrails.com. Has an unusually wide range of day-trips, including mangrove cruises and visits to the Kota Belud Sunday *tamu*, plus standard packages elsewhere.

Borneo Ultimate Ground floor, Wisma Sabah ☎ 088 225188, ⓦ borneoultimate.com.my. Adventurous, extended tours that include longhouse stays, kayaking on the Kinabatangan or mountain biking, to name just a few options.

Nasalis Larvatus Second floor, 56 Lorong Bandaran Berjaya 5 ☎ 088 230534, ⓦ insabah.com. Titled after the scientific name for proboscis monkeys, this firm has its own accommodation at the Kinabatangan River, Sepilok and Libaran Island, and sells a full range of nature tours.

★**River Junkie/Scuba Junkie** Ground floor, Wisma Sabah ☎ 088 277128 & 255816, ⓦ river-junkie.com & ⓦ scuba-junkie.com. Sibling firms with a growing range of eco/nature tours, including the Maliau Basin, Mount Trus Madi climbs and the Sapulut community tourism project, plus rafting trips, and diving and snorkelling off Semporna.

Sabah Divers Ground floor, Wisma Sabah ☎ 088 256483, ⓦ sabahdivers.com. A good range of dive

courses, plus packages at Tunku Abdul Rahman Park, the islands off Semporna, Lankayan Island off Sandakan, and Labuan's waters.

Sticky Rice Travel Third floor, 134 Gaya Street ☎ 088 250177, ⓦ stickyricetravel.com. Ecotourism specialist offering the usual attractions plus lesser-known ones, including the Tabin reserve of eastern Sabah, a multi-day trek in Kinabalu Park, plus climbing and trekking in the Crocker range.

Sutera Sanctuary Lodges Ground floor, Wisma Sabah ☎ 088 287887, ⓦ suterasanctuarylodges .com.my. Offers climbing packages at Kinabalu Park, where they run much of the accommodation; that aside, they operate a resort at the Tunku Abdul Rahman Park.

Travel Rite Tours Tunku Adnan Sports Complex, Likas Bay ☎ 088 421088, ⓦ travelritetours.com. Specializes in rafting trips, including some at the Kadamaian River near Kota Belud, where they run their own homestay; tandem paragliding can be thrown in, too.

Traverse Tours Second floor, Wisma Sabah ☎ 088 260501, ⓦ traversetours.com. Has diving trips to Sepanggar Island just outside the Tunku Abdul Rahman park, where they run their own accommodation, with a similar offering at Mantanani Island much further north (see p.414). They operate the Mari Mari Cultural Village, too, while their Riverbug wing sells the usual rafting packages.

somewhat on its own and hard to miss, but a little disappointing inside, with a charmless lobby and rooms in often gloomy hues, some with old photos blown up across entire walls. The restaurants, gym, spa and sixth-floor pool make the rates half-bearable. 🛜 RM350

★**Hyatt Regency** Jalan Datuk Salleh Sulong ☎088 221234, 🖥 kinabalu.regency.hyatt.com; map p.394. Five-star comforts just metres from the waterfront, boasting oodles of restaurants, a wonderful swimming pool with sunset views and well-appointed rooms. 🛜 RM500

Jesselton 69 Gaya Street ☎088 223333, 🖥 jesseltonhotel.com; map p.394. The oldest hotel in town – not that it means much in a city like KK – with Lady Mountbatten and Muhammad Ali among former guests. The place is reasonably well run but in truth it looks a little frumpy next to newer upstarts. 🛜 RM260

Kinabalu Daya 9 Jalan Pantai ☎088 240000, 🖥 kinabaludayahotel.com; map p.394. A well-established, serviceable affair with snug, en-suite rooms, a ground-floor café and a street-side bar. RM180

Klagan Warisan Square, Jalan Tun Fuad Stephens ☎088 488908, 🖥 theklagan.com; map p.394. This mid-range hotel, part of a small local chain, offers a bit more character than much of the competition. Rooms have big, red designer chairs and swanky bathrooms, and there's also a rooftop restaurant (rates usually include breakfast). 🛜 RM270

Le Meridien Jalan Tun Fuad Stephens ☎088 322222, 🖥 lemeridienkotakinabalu.com; map p.394. A convenient location and sumptuous facilities, including high-spec rooms, pool, spa and gym. 🛜 RM475

★**Little Gaya** 52 Gaya Street ☎088 261838, 🖥 littlegayahotel.com; map p.394. Like its next-door neighbour, *Eden 54*, this just about counts as a boutique hotel and has a range of rooms, the cheaper ones windowless. There's a more spacious feel here, though, as the bathrooms are only half-walled off so the sink area blends into the rest of the room. 🛜 RM150

Maxim Bandaran Berjaya ☎088 262811, 📧 maximhotelkk@gmail.com; map p.394. A small, decent budget option, with blandly modern rooms (ones with windows cost RM10 extra). RM80

Shangri-La Tanjung Aru Resort Tanjung Aru, nearly 4km southwest of the centre ☎088 327888, 🖥 shangri-la.com; map p.394. Perched on the beach at the tip of the headland, this luxury resort has everything you'd expect of a *Shangri-La*: rolling, landscaped grounds, two pools, a gym, tennis courts, water sports, plus several high-class food outlets and bars. There's also the eleven-hole Kinabalu Golf Club just nearby. 🛜 RM1200

Sixty3 63 Gaya Street ☎088 327888, 🖥 shangri-la.com; map p.394. Opposite the tourist office, this newish, rather bland affair has the usual range of rooms around a narrow rectangular atrium, but no restaurant. Good value, so often full. RM240

Sutera Harbour Resort Sutera Harbour, right at the southwest end of the centre ☎088 318888, 🖥 suteraharbour.com; map p.394. This development is so vast it has its own shuttle buses to whiz guests around. Besides a marina and golf course, it features two hotels: the palatial *Magellan* and the comparatively humble five-star *Pacific*; both feature enormous pool complexes, water sports and a spa. 🛜 RM750

EATING

KK has a decent range of **restaurants** and *kopitiams*, although international cuisine is somewhat lagging. Some worthwhile places are tucked away in malls; by contrast, the glitzy ones at the Waterfront development tend to be overpriced and mediocre. Locally run **indie cafés** are popping up all over, but especially at Australia Place (Lorong Dewan), where quite a few have names reflecting the area's past association with the printing industry.

Chilli Vanilla 35 Jalan Haji Saman ☎088 238098; map p.394. A truly eclectic restaurant, with Middle Eastern-ish tiles and a menu that takes in goulash and chicken schnitzel (the owner is Hungarian), tortillas, Moroccan lamb stew, burgers and more. With something for almost everyone, the place is popular with travellers and locals alike. Mains from about RM25; the weekday set lunch is good value at RM20. Mon–Sat 10am–10.30pm, Sun 4.30–10.30pm.

D'Malindo Café 205A, second floor, Wisma Merdeka, Jalan Tun Razak; map p.394. This hidden-away, no-frills place serves a terrific *nasi campur* spread of Malay and some Bornean food – such as "Sabah vegetable", vaguely spinach-like greens more properly called *sayur manis*. Daily 8.30am–4.30pm.

★**D'Place** Second floor, Shell Plaza, 29 Jalan Tunku Abdul Rahman ☎010 228 2381; map p.394. For many years KK lacked a decent place to try indigenous cuisine, but now this marvellous Kadazan/Dusun restaurant has made amends. Come for the terrific buffets (lunch around RM30, dinner RM40 with a cultural show) with dishes like pineapple chicken and samosas filled with *hinava* (raw fish salad). The accompaniments include reddish hill rice and *ambuyat*, the gluey sago staple also beloved in Brunei. Leave space for stodgy desserts such as stewed pumpkin in coconut milk, and perhaps imbibe some *lihing* (a rice brandy) too. If you're feeling really brave, try one of the *butod* (sago grubs; RM5) in the box by the door, either eaten live and whole or baked into their *butod* pizza, in which case the cheese conveniently masks any larval flavours. Daily 11am–10pm.

7

★**El Centro** 32 Jalan Haji Saman ☎014 862 3877; map p.394. This compact restaurant and bar with multicoloured lights on the walls has fast become a favourite hangout for tourists and expats alike. There are ample portions of food from all over (Mondays feature Mexican specials, for example), plus a good selection of well-priced beers, wine and cocktails. Keep an eye out for regular quiz nights. Mains from around RM20; happy hour 5–9pm. Daily 11am–midnight.

★**Fook Yuen** Ground floor, Menara Jubili, 53 Gaya Street ☎088 743406; map p.394. A mini-food court and bakery rolled into one, this cafeteria chain deserves an award for sheer convenience. Noodles, rice, cooked dishes, dim sum, breads and cakes are all laid out at different counters; nearly everything is self-service apart from toast, eggs and drinks, which are made to order (watch for your order number to come up on the screen once you've paid the cashier). Only slightly more expensive than a standard *kedai kopi*. Daily 7am–late.

Grazie Third floor, Suria Sabah Mall ☎019 821 6936; map p.394. Authentic wood-fired, thin-crust pizzas (from RM35), pasta and other dishes, plus a good range of Italian wines and liqueurs. Daily noon–9.30pm.

Jesselton Point Hawker Centre Jesselton Point, Jalan Haji Saman; map p.394. These stalls roar to life in the evenings selling satay, fried fish and other popular dishes. There's even an Aussie steakhouse and the seating is pleasantly alfresco, looking out over the harbour toward the islands. Daily 4–11pm.

Jothy's Banana Leaf G9, Lorong Api-Api 1, Api-Api Centre ☎088 261595, ⊛jothyscurry.com; map p.394. Excellent South Indian establishment serving satisfying *dosai* and a variety of delicious curries, including a classic fish-head variety. Their filleted chicken 65 is also a hit. Daily 11am–10pm.

October 13 Lorong Dewan ☎088 346129; map p.394. This Korean-owned chain is among the best cafés at Australia Place. Go for the house blend (roasted by the boss himself) or a single-origin coffee to accompany one of the scrumptious cakes or (daytime only) snacks such as the Korean omelette

toasted sandwich. Daily 11am–midnight.

★**Sinsuran Night Market** Pasar Sinsuran, Jalan Tun Fuad Stephens; map p.394. Next door to the handicraft market, dozens of stalls set up in the evening, either part of a frenetic seafood market or selling barbecued fish, grilled meat and other delights. You can have a full meal with accompanying rice and vegetables or just grab some chicken on a stick or even a Bajau snack like *koci* (conical rice dumplings). Daily 5–10.30pm.

Tam Nak Thai Third floor, Suria Sabah Mall ☎016 832 9928; map p.394. Fine Thai cuisine and a pleasing ambience (and some tables with a view) make this place popular. The green curry is good, as is the pineapple rice. Around RM30/head, minus drinks. Mon–Sat 11.30am–2.30pm & 6–10.15pm, Sun 6–10.15pm.

★**Tavern** Ground floor, Imago mall, Jalan Coastal ☎012 586 0093, ⊛tavern.com.my; map p.394. With gaudy wall panels and tables spilling out onto the concourse, this bar-restaurant serves an upmarket take on American, Italian and Asian standards – burgers, pasta, fried rice – sometimes fusing them to good effect (stir-fried seafood spaghetti, for instance), with Sabahan ingredients like *tuhau* (wild ginger) in the mix too. They also serve up a mean range of cocktails, mocktails and humongous milkshakes. Happy hours 3–6pm & 10pm–midnight. Daily 10am–midnight.

Welcome Seafood Ground floor, Star City complex, off Jalan Tunku Abdul Rahman ☎088 447866, ⊛wsr.com .my; map p.394. Massive Chinese restaurant that's a little out of the way but is better value than its more prominent rivals in Kampung Air. There are open-air and a/c sections, and plenty of live fish and crustaceans in dozens of tanks, priced by weight. If you eschew the seafood, a slap-up meal could cost as little as RM40/head, minus drinks; otherwise you could easily pay double that. Daily noon–midnight.

Yee Fung 127 Gaya Street ☎088 312042; map p.394. One of several old-school Chinese *kopitiams* here with a devoted following, in this case for their claypot chicken rice and laksa – it's not uncommon to spot people lining up

---

KAAMATAN

Kaamatan is to Sabah's Kadazan/Dusun what *gawai* is to Sarawak's Iban, a rice harvest festival culminating in **public holidays** on 30 and 31 May. As ever people try to return to their longhouses or villages for the event, with much quaffing of the usual rice-based alcoholic drinks; inevitably, malls get into the spirit too, sporting decorations styled after steamed rice cakes and ears of grains. Most importantly, at the Kadazan/Dusun Cultural Assocation (**KDCA**; ⊛kdca.org. my) in the KK suburb of Penampang, there's a gradual build-up in festivities from mid-May, with arm-wrestling and cookery contests, and sometimes even buffalo races. The climax is a two-day jamboree of music and dance, kicking off on 30 May with **sugandoi,** a traditional singing competition. The following day sees the **Unduk Ngadau pageant**, with women in tribal costume vying to be chosen as the individual who embodies the qualities of Huminodun, a mythical figure; smaller versions of it are staged even in longhouses. The KDCA events aren't ticketed, so get the latest details from Sabah Tourism (see p.398) if you'd like to attend.

here at various times of day. Mon–Fri 7am–6pm, Sat & Sun 7am–5pm.

DRINKING AND NIGHTLIFE

Although there are a few good **bars**, KK is not noted for its **nightlife**. Besides the places listed below, the *El Centro* and *Tavern* restaurants are also great watering holes. KK can seem like a cultural desert most of the year, but towards the end of May there are performances for **Kaamatan** (see box, opposite). The city also hosts annual **film** (ⓦ kkiff.com) and **jazz** (ⓦ kkjazzfest.com) festivals; for a list of cinemas, see p.404.

999 Jalan Haji Yaacob ☎ 088 283889; map p.394. The most over-the-top club you'll ever see, in a converted cinema with Corinthian columns and statues of centurions outside. The interior is hangar-like and sometimes hosts live bands in addition to DJs. No dress code, but pricey drinks. Tues–Sun 9pm–late.

BED Waterfront development ☎ 011 2986 8804; map p.394. Best Entertainment Destination, to give its full name, features Philippine bands playing popular standards most nights. Daily 8pm–late.

Sharikat Biru-Biru 24 Lorong Dewan ☎ 011 1412 3490; map p.394. Informal venue with an old-fashioned Malay/Chinese signboard and quirky décor, including an old bicycle stuck to one wall. A good selection of beers and spirits, plus light bites, salsa sessions and acoustic and open-mic nights keep travellers and locals happy. Daily 11am–11pm.

SHOPPING

BOOKS

The Borneo Shop Ground floor, Wisma Merdeka, Jalan Haji Saman ☎ 012 385689; map p.394. Head to this shop for specialist books on Borneo, including titles published by the KK-based National History Publications. Mon–Sat 10am–8pm, Sun 10am–5.30pm.

Times Bookstore Level 2, Suria Sabah Mall ☎ 088 487118; map p.394. For general books and magazines, try this bookstore. Daily 10am–10pm.

CAMPING AND OUTDOOR EQUIPMENT

KK is a good place to stock up for a Kinabalu climb or exploits elsewhere in the country.

Montanic Adventure Begins Basement level, Suria Sabah ☎ 088 274538, ⓦ montanic.com; map p.394. Sells high-end branded rucksacks, anoraks and camping equipment. Also has a branch on the first floor of Imago mall (☎ 088 274699). Daily 10am–10pm.

Mr DIY Level 1, Imago mall; map p.394. Nationwide chain selling household items, also great for head torches, water bottles, cycling gloves and other basics. Daily 10am–10pm.

Outdoor Gear Level 3, Centre Point ☎ 088 260585; map p.394. Cheap but with a limited range of products. Daily 11am–9.30pm.

MALLS

It's not hard to notice there's a glut of malls in KK, which means only a handful are thriving.

Centre Point Mall Jalan Tun Razak; map p.394. The busiest of the Asian-style shopping complexes, housing small stores. Daily 10am–10pm

Imago Mall Just beyond the KK Times Square office complex ⓦ imago.my; map p.394. This enormous, Western-style mall is the very best of the lot, and it's packed with major stores and franchises. Daily 10am–10pm

Suria Sabah Mall Opposite Wisma Sabah ⓦ suriasabah.com.my; map p.394. KK's second best mall, with the usual range of eating outlets and boutiques. Daily 10am–10pm

SOUVENIRS AND CRAFTS

Make a beeline for the Gaya Street Sunday market, offering a host of interesting local products including tribal instruments such as the *sompoton* (like pan pipes stuck to a gourd) and handmade soaps containing unusual ingredients such as seaweed. Items sold at the handicraft market are of variable quality and may originate in the Philippines or Indonesia. Grocery shops on Gaya Street, plus Kadaiku and stalls at the central market, stock edibles made with local produce, including chocolate and Tenom coffee.

The Borneo Shop Ground floor, Wisma Merdeka, Jalan Haji Saman ☎ 012 385689; map p.394. This bookstore also has some textiles and beadwork. Mon–Sat 10am–8pm, Sun 10am–5.30pm.

Kadaiku/Sri Pelancongan Block L, Sinsuran ☎ 088 232121, ⓦ kadaiku.com; map p.394. Kitsch orang-utan and proboscis monkey soft toys infest the wares of Kadaiku/Sri Pelancongan, a Sabah Tourism subsidiary, though they also sell handicrafts, including woven textiles; the tourist office has a small selection of these and other items. Mon–Fri 8am–6pm, Sat 10am–6pm

SUPERMARKETS

City Grocer Third floor, Suria Sabah ☎ 088 488844; map p.394. Has the widest range of local and imported produce, including alcoholic beverages. Daily 10am–10pm.

Tong Hing 55 Gaya Street ☎ 088 230300; map p.394. Specializes in imported products but is expensive, although many swear by its bakery's bread. Daily 8am–10pm.

DIRECTORY

Banks Gaya Street and nearby streets are littered with banks, including HSBC and Maybank. Both Suria Sabah and Imago malls have ATMs.

Cinemas Some films in English are screened at the Growball Cinemax in Centre Point Mall (☎088 256836, ⓦgrowball.com), MBO in Imago Mall (ⓦmbocinemas.com) and Golden Screen Cinemas (ⓦgsc.com.my) at Suria Sabah.

Consulates Indonesia, Lorong Kemajuan, off Jalan Kemajuan in the southwest corner of the centre (☎088 218600).

Hospitals and clinics The state-run Queen Elizabeth Hospital is beyond the Sabah State Museum, on Jalan Penampang (☎088 517555); closer in is the private Gleneagles (☎088 518888), just beyond KK Times Square. For a routine consulation, head to the private Permai

Polyclinics, 4 Jalan Pantai (24hr; ☎088 232100); a doctor will usually see you within 30min.

Laundry Both Bandaran Berjaya and Lorong Dewan have laundries close to the hostels, and coin-operated affairs have popped up in various locations all over the centre.

Pharmacies In addition to the pharmacies in many malls, there's a handy branch of Guardian on Jalan Gaya.

Police The main police station is below Atkinson's Clock Tower (☎088 247111).

Post office The GPO is on Jalan Tun Razak (Mon–Fri 8am–4.30pm, Sat 8am–12.30pm).

Visa extensions Immigration Department, UTC Building, Jalan Belia, off Jalan Tunku Abdul Rahman (Mon–Thurs 8.30am–5pm, Fri 8.30–11.30am & 2–5pm; ☎088 270586); it's a walkable 1.5km from Merdeka Field.

Around Kota Kinabalu

There are a number of attractions and activities available around KK, including **Mari Mari Cultural Village** and **Monsopiad Cultural Village** for a dose of local culture; you could also consider a ride on the pricey **North Borneo railway** (see p.407). Most popular of all, however, are the beaches of **Tunku Abdul Rahman Park** just offshore.

Tunku Abdul Rahman Park

3km west of KK • Conservation fee RM20; diving permit RM50 ⓦsabahparks.gov.my

Named after Malaysia's first prime minister, **Tunku Abdul Rahman Park** contains five islands representing the most westerly ripples of the Crocker mountains. Their forests, beaches and coral reefs lie within 8km of KK, with marine park territory as close as 3km off the mainland; snorkelling, diving, watersports and more unusual **activities** are available. Such is the park's appeal that **Manukan Island** in particular is often overrun. This isn't to say you can't have an enjoyable day-trip either on one island or, as many people do, on one in the morning and another in the afternoon – but don't expect total calm unless you stay the night at one of the park's pricey **resorts**. Manukan aside, only **Sapi** and **Mamutik** islands are served by regular boats.

Manukan Island

Crescent-shaped **Manukan Island** is in the centre of the group. The most developed of the islands, it has become something of a victim of its own success, with tour-group parties hogging stretches of beach and departing day-trippers struggling to make their way through at the little jetty, assuming they can even spot the right boat. Among plus points, the island boasts a lengthy beach and there are upmarket meals, including buffet lunches, to be had at the *Manukan Island Resort*, although many settle for cheap food at the Sabah Parks co-op restaurant next door. If you tire of the beach, you could try the island's **marine education centre** or the brand new **aquarium**, or hike wooded paths signed at the edge of the resort area; one heads up a ridge to the other side of the island, and the other goes 1.5km west along the island's length to Sunset Point.

Mamutik Island

Southeast of Manukan, tiny **Mamutik Island** is a snorkeller's delight. The island is surrounded by coral gardens, with the best stretch off the beach to the southwest, towards the back of where the boat drops you, but to reach it it's necessary either to clamber over rocks or to swim right round. **Borneo Divers** (see p.398) has its own diving school on the island; head out early if you plan to dive, as it's much more cost-effective to do two or three dives than just one.

Sulug Island
Southwest of Manukan, **Sulug Island** is the quietest island in Tunku Abdul Rahman Park: hardly any public boats come, although the dive operators bring their customers here to spot the plentiful marine life, including turtles and moray eels among others, amid healthy corals.

Gaya Island
The largest island in the group is **Gaya Island**, a fifteen-minute boat ride north of Manukan. The site of the British North Borneo Chartered Company's abortive settlement before Jesselton was founded, the island initially seems a mass of jungle and anything but developed, but it actually holds three out of the park's four resorts. Although the closest island to KK, Gaya doesn't feature on standard island-hopping routes; visitors can simply take any boat to neighbouring Sapi and ask to be dropped off across the channel. If you do make it over, you'll find idyllic stretches of sand such as **Police Bay Beach**, as well as jungle **trails** where you might see proboscis monkeys and hornbills.

Sapi Island
Little **Sapi Island**, off the southwest tip of Gaya, has a very decent beach and so draws an equally decent crowd, meaning it has reasonable facilities without feeling quite as packed as Manukan. Beachside outfits offer diving (from RM200 for a taster session) as well as snorkelling gear for rent, and food is generally cheaper here than on Manukan, with a small café for basic meals (daily 8am–4pm). If you head generally rightwards from the jetty, you will come to a very short, gently uphill trail hugging the shore, where you might well see monitor lizards before the track halts at the end-point of the **Coral Flyer** zip line from Gaya (see below).

ARRIVAL AND DEPARTURE   TUNKU ABDUL RAHMAN PARK

By boat A dozen or so operators run boats to Manukan, Mamutik and Sapi from the Jesselton Point Ferry Terminal (departures from around 8.30am, last boat back leaves around 5pm). Try to get there by 9.30am, if not earlier, as the first set of departures sell out quickly and you may not get your preferred outward (or return) slot if you're tardy. Prices vary slightly between operators, but are typically RM23 for one island, RM33 for two or RM43 for all three, plus a RM7.20 terminal tax. The operator should explain the arrangements for island-hopping and returning. You might also be able to charter a boat for around RM35 per person for one island. Some boat firms and other companies at the terminal also arrange activities; rent your snorkelling gear at the terminal if you plan to go to more than one island.

ACTIVITIES

Jetskiing and parasailing Jetskiing (RM175 for 30min) and parasailing (RM110 for 10min) are among the watersports available at Manukan, Sapi and Mamutik islands, through operators like Sea Quest Tours (☎ 088 248 006, ⓦ seaquesttours.net).

Seawalking This peculiar activity has people donning what look like astronaut suits with air piped in from above, in order to spend half an hour wandering the sea floor (around RM270). One operator has an office at the beach on Sapi, and Sea Quest Tours (see above) can arrange this as well.

Snorkelling and diving Snorkelling and, to a lesser extent, diving are worthwhile around the islands, with a decent amount of marine life around though the health of the coral is variable. Beachside outfits rent snorkelling equipment (RM15 for mask, snorkel and fins); diving packages can be arranged in advance with tour operators in KK (see p.398) or on Manukan, Sapi and Mamutik.

Zip lining It's possible to descend, from high above the sea, from Gaya to Sapi using the Coral Flyer zip line, billed as the longest inter-island line of its kind (RM70; seek out the team near the Sapi jetty or enquire on ☎ 011 2984 2023, ⓦ coralflyer.com). The experience is so brief that it works out at RM2/second, but then it's the adrenaline rush you're really forking out for.

ACCOMMODATION

The prices for **resorts** here represent starting prices during high season if booked early, and include breakfast and boat transfers except where stated; discounts of around twenty percent may be available at other times. **Camping** is allowed on Gaya, Mamutik and Sapi (permits RM5.30/person; tents may be available to rent for RM30, but it's better to have your own).

Bungaraya Island Resort Gaya ☎088 380390, ⓦechoresorts.com/bungaraya. Offers luxurious timber villas hidden away within the forest; rooms are spacious and some feature their own jacuzzi or mini-pool. There's a gym and spa, and guests can partake of activities at their sister *Gayana Marine Resort*. RM1400

Gaya Island Resort Gaya ☎018 939 1100, ⓦgayaislandresort.com. A lavish affair blending contemporary design with traditional elements, nestled neatly into a bay on Gaya's north shore. There's a spa, pool, dive shop and several restaurants of course, and the resort also has its own marine conservation centre. Price excludes boat transfers. RM1400

Gayana Marine Resort Gaya ☎088 380390, ⓦechoresorts.com/gayana. This resort has attractive chalets, many built out over the sea, with its own dive shop and marine conservation centre where guests can get involved in simple projects. RM1100

Manukan Island Resort Manukan ☎017 833 5022, ⓦsuterasanctuarylodges.com.my. Features small, somewhat characterless units resembling little houses. Unusually, the beach units are cheaper; the "hillside" ones are fancier and more removed from the noise of day-trippers. Price excludes boat transfers. RM850

Monsopiad Heritage Village

13km south of KK on Jalan Putatan Ramayah, Penampang • Daily 9am–5pm • RM20, or RM55 with tour and cultural show • ☎088 734657, ⓦinfomonsopiadcultu.wixsite.com/monsopiadheritage • Bus #13 (or minivan) south to Donggongon, then a Terawi-bound bus

Themed around the tale of a legendary head-hunter, the **Monsopiad Heritage Village** provides an introduction to the history and traditions of the Kadazan/Dusun people. The star attraction is a hut where Monsopiad's grisly harvest of 42 skulls is displayed, although you can also sample rice wine and test your blowpipe skills. If you've paid for the full experience, knowledgeable guides will explain traditions such as the rituals practised by the *bobohizan* (priestess), and there'll be a dance show to take in too.

Mari Mari Cultural Village

18km east of KK, Kionsom • Compulsory tours daily 10am, 2pm & 6pm (2hr) • Day-trips without transport RM100, or RM110 in the evening; day-trips including transport plus one meal RM180, or RM200 in the evening with an additional fire-breathing show; book through Traverse Tours, which runs the village (see p.399), or other KK tour operators • ⓦmarimariculturalvillage.my

Mari Mari Cultural Village has more of an orchestrated theme park feel than the Monsopiad Heritage Village, and unlike Monsopiad it tries to cover a broad sweep of several of Sabah's ethnic groups, with recreations of their traditional houses on site. It sometimes feels a little phoney, but if you take it in the right spirit, you will come away both entertained and educated. Activities and demonstrations include rice-wine tasting, starting a fire using bamboo, making the lacy sweet fritter *kuih jala* and using a blowpipe; for this option, a buffet lunch, tea or dinner is thrown in too.

The southwest coast

The coast southwest of KK, inhabited in particular by the Bisaya and Kedayan ethnic groups, is a largely mundane area. The **Klias Peninsula** here is prime country for **day-trips** organized by tour operators in KK, whether for rafting or wildlife watching. Offshore is **Tiga Island**, the setting for the first series of the TV show *Survivor*.

KK to the Klias Peninsula

The first town of any size on the coast road is **Kinarut**, with a smattering of factories and a decent beachside resort; it's here, some 20km southwest of KK, that you

---

THROWBACK RAIL JOURNEYS

Sabah's tiny rail network features two contrasting journeys that might be worth considering. One uses a specially built **steam train** running from Tanjung Aru station (see p.397) to the small town of Papar (Wed & Sat at 9.30am; 4hr; RM350 including breakfast and lunch on board; book with ⓦ suteraharbour.com). Billed as the **North Borneo Railway**, this is a semi-luxurious 66km round trip using a wood-burning British Vulcan, plus five carriages constructed to a vintage design in the 1970s. In truth they're the most attractive thing about the trip, as the scenery isn't much to write home about.

The other noteworthy journey involves the branch line between the town of **Beaufort** and agricultural **Tenom** in the southern interior (see p.448). This is an ordinary passenger service (2 daily in each direction; 2hr 30min) distinguished by the antiquated, very basic carriages and the fact that the line shadows the **Padas river valley**; indeed rafting packages often include the train ride as a prelude. With endearingly rural scenes en route, there's something for non-railway buffs as well. Whichever direction you do it in, be aware that there were no sensible connections at Beaufort, so a day-trip will require two bus journeys at either end unless you stay the night (Tenom is far preferable to Beaufort).

7

finally feel you've left the environs of the city behind. The scenery soon turns much more rural until at **Papar**, around 15km further on, you're treated to vistas of paddy fields with the Crocker mountain range constantly looming to the east. An old-fangled railway bridge spanning the Papar River is the most memorable thing about the town itself. Another 15km on, the otherwise scraggly **Kimanis** boasts a gleaming petrochemical facility, processing Sabah's offshore oil and gas, and also marks the start of the road up and over the Crocker range to **Keningau** and the southern interior (see p.446). Within another 15km, the coast starts veering ever further away as the road enters the Klias Peninsula.

ACCOMMODATION   **KK TO THE KLIAS PENINSULA**

Langkah Syabas Kampung Kinarut Laut ☏ 088 752000, ⓦ langkahsyabas.com.my. Appealing, small-scale beachfront resort, managed by an Australian/Malaysian couple and attracting plenty of Antipodean guests. The older chalets are set in a garden and encircle the swimming pool, while the newer ones facing the sea cost fifty percent more. The restaurant does a popular Sunday roast, and they make their own surprisingly good cheese on the premises. Rates include breakfast. 🛜 **RM250**

The Klias Peninsula

The gateway to the **Klias Peninsula** is the forgettable Padas River town of **BEAUFORT**, on the main KK road some 40km southwest of Kimanis and 65km from the border with Sarawak. Named after an early governor of British North Borneo, the town itself is utterly forgettable, distinguished only being the hub of Sabah's puny rail network. The Padas, however, is a fine choice for **whitewater rafting**, arranged through tour operators in KK, while the peninsula offers an excellent chance of spotting **proboscis monkeys** on the Garama or Klias rivers, or at Weston near the mouth of the Padas, with **fireflies** also visible night. Note that although these locations may be signposted nearby, you can't just fetch up and get on a trip, as the boatmen work for the tour companies; however, some firms may offer a discount if you get here under your own steam.

Kuala Penyu

Around an hour northeast of Beaufort, or 45 minutes from Menumbok, at the northern point of the peninsula, **KUALA PENYU** is the departure point for **Pulau Tiga Park**. It's a simple grid of streets with little more than a few basic stores and *kedai kopis*.

7

> **CROSSING INTO SARAWAK**
>
> Note that because Sarawak maintains its own immigration controls, passports will be stamped by the authorities of both Sabah and Sarawak at the **Merapok border post**; the Sarawak stamp entitles visitors to a thirty-day stay. There will be another three border checkpoints to negotiate if Bandar Seri Begawan in Brunei is your final destination – add one more if heading for Miri.

Menumbok

The most westerly settlement on the Klias Peninsula, tiny **MENUMBOK** is notable only for its frequent boat connections with Labuan Island.

ARRIVAL AND DEPARTURE
KLIAS PENINSULA

BEAUFORT

By bus and minivan Buses and minivans park up at a tiny station opposite a yellow-domed mosque less than a 10min walk away from the east bank of the Padas River. There are services to KK (hourly; 2hr) and more sporadic ones to Menumbok and Kuala Penyu (1hr), plus Keningau (at least 2 daily; 2hr 30min).

By train The train station is on the east bank of the river. At the time of research there were no convenient connections between trains on the Tanjung Aru line (2 daily; 2hr) and Tenom line (2 daily; 2hr 30min), whichever direction you're heading in.

MENUMBOK

By bus Buses for KK should leave roughly hourly (2hr 30min), but often delay departures considerably to await arriving ferries. There are also a couple of daily buses for Keningau in the interior (3hr 30min).

By minivan or shared taxi Minivans and shared taxis leave sporadically for KK (3hr), Beaufort (1hr) or Kuala Penyu (45min). If you can't find a vehicle to Kuala Penyu, catch a Beaufort one to the junction (*simpang*) for Kuala Penyu and try to flag down onward transport there.

By boat Speedboats (1–2 hourly; 20min; RM13) and car ferries (5–6 daily between 8am–8.30pm; 1hr 30min; RM5/ person plus RM40/car) travel daily between Menumbok and Labuan Island; note that there's also a ferry terminal tax of RM2–3/person.

KUALA PENYU

By minivan It takes just over 2hr to travel by minivan to KK's Merdeka Field bus stand from Kuala Penyu, or you can get a minivan to Beaufort. These vehicles leave from one block back from the jetty.

Pulau Tiga Park

RM10 conservation fee • A 20min boat ride from Kuala Penyu – the Survivor Lodge provides boats at 10am & 3pm for guests (non-guests can use these for RM100 each way/person if arranged in advance) • ⓦ sabahparks.org.my

Nestled in the South China Sea 12km north of Kuala Penyu, **Pulau Tiga Park** is a beautiful and peaceful place that acquired a degree of fame in 2001 as the paradise location for the first series of the American reality TV show *Survivor*. It used to consist of three islands, one of which has since been reduced to a mere sand bar by wave erosion. Of the remaining two – **Tiga** and **Kalampunian Damit** – only the former holds accommodation; the latter is normally visited as part of a morning snorkelling trip from the *Survivor Lodge*.

Most visitors content themselves with relaxing on the sandy beaches and **snorkelling** or **diving** in the azure sea. It's possible to hike right around the jungle-cloaked island in six hours, but the paths are poorly maintained so it's best to check at the park office which ones are passable. The best is the easy twenty-minute walk to the centre of Tiga, which leads to a couple of **mud volcanoes**.

ACCOMMODATION AND EATING
PULAU TIGA PARK

Two luxury resorts were in the works on Tiga at the time of research, and may be open by the time you read this; meanwhile, the only place to stay is *Survivor Lodge*. Camping is allowed with your own tent (camping permit RM5.30/person).

Survivor Lodge ☏ 088 240584, ⓦ sdclodges.com /pulau-tiga. Also known by its former name, *Pulau Tiga Resort*, this has dozens of twin-bed chalet. It also has its own dive shop and restaurant, and offers kayaking too. Price is for a full-board package, including boat transfer. RM400

Labuan Island

A short distance west of the Klias Peninsula, the 15km-long **LABUAN ISLAND** is surprisingly appealing, with wide, clean streets planted with flowering shrubs and a relaxed pace of life. It's striking how unlike Sabah the place feels, which is half-explained by the fact that it isn't part of Sabah at all, being instead **Federal Territory** – meaning it has the same administrative status as Kuala Lumpur. The rest of the explanation lies in the wealth generated by Labuan's offshore oil and gas, although the island has lately fallen on hard times with the plunge in crude oil prices. For now, Labuan is keeping up appearances, with its eponymous main town still offering decent accommodation, eating, nightlife and **duty-free** shopping. With far fewer oil workers passing through, the authorities are desperate for tourists to keep things going, and in truth the island isn't a bad place to spend a day or two en route between Brunei and Sabah; there are a few minor sights and **beaches**, and **wreck diving** is possible in Labuan's own **marine park**. Most sights outside Labuan Town are a little too far away to walk. Labuan has a basic bus network and taxis, but it's worth considering **cycling** around the island – there are proper cycle lanes on long stretches of the coastal road, and traffic isn't that heavy outside of peak hours. For details of transport and bike rental, see p.411.

7

Labuan Town

The main urban centre, simply called **LABUAN TOWN**, lies on the island's southeastern side. Despite its nondescript modern appearance, the town dates back to the mid-nineteenth century, when the British – having newly prised Labuan from the Brunei Sultanate – established a free port called Victoria here. Centred on the padang, with older quarters to the west, the town is pleasantly walkable, with a couple of museums to visit and a beach not far away to the northeast. Labuan Town is one of Malaysia's duty-free centres, but the selection of goods is rather more limited than at, say, Langkawi. Once you've browsed the imported chocolates, alcohol, perfumes and cigarettes on sale at the ferry terminal there's little to be gained by exploring outlets elsewhere in town.

Labuan Museum

Behind the padang • Daily 8.30am–5pm • Free • ☎ 087 419451, ⓦ www.jmm.gov.my

Although lacking in artefacts, the small, yellow **Labuan Museum** is worthy of an hour's visit. Downstairs, display boards offer a decent account of the island's history and constantly evolving political status: shunted from Brunei to the East India Company, then the British North Borneo Chartered Company, then the Straits Settlements, then Sabah – which it left in the 1980s to become Federal Territory. Displays upstairs outline the customs of Labuan's various ethnic groups including the largest, the Kedayan.

Marine Museum

1.5km east of the centre at Labuan International Sea Sports Complex (Kompleks Sukan Laut), Jalan Tanjung Purun • Daily 8.30am–5pm; fish feeding Sat 10am • Free • ☎ 087 425927 • Bus #1, #3 or #4

Housed in a gleaming modern building at the eastern end of town, the **Marine Museum**

> #### DIVING AROUND TIGA
>
> Tiga's prime dive site is probably **Asmara Point**, close to the Sabah Parks jetty. With a maximum depth of 10m it's a nice, easy dive, albeit sometimes with a slight current, with good coral attracting lionfish, Moorish idols and groupers, plus sometimes sea turtles. Other good sites include **Phukat Point** (where they very occasionally see white-tip sharks) and **Larai Point** (notable for its excellent coral). The dive shop at *Survivor Lodge* charges around RM110 per person for the first dive (minimum of two people), excluding equipment rental, and also does Discover Scuba course (RM210 per person).

7

LABUAN TOWN

ACCOMMODATION
Billion Waterfront 2
Labuan Avenue 1
Palm Beach Resort 3

EATING
Choice 3
Fratini's 4
Mawilla Yacht Club 5
New Sung Hwa 1
Raff 2

DRINKING
Fah Fah 1

Marine Museum (600m), Tanjung Batu beach (1km), ⑤ (1km) & War Cemetery (2km)

Airport (1.5km), Layang-Layangan beach, Peace Park & Chimney Museum

0   100
metres

JALAN TANJUNG BENDERA

JALAN MASJID

JALAN TEMAGA

JALAN OKK ABDULLAH

JALAN TANJUNG PURUN

Wisma Ujana
Kewangan
(Financial Centre)

JALAN MERDEKA

JALAN MAWALAN

Labuan Marina

JALAN TUN MUSTAPHA

JALAN BUNGA ANGGERIK

JALAN BUNGA SEROJA

JALAN BUNGA MAWAR

JALAN BUNGA DAHLIA

JALAN BUNGA KEDUNING

JALAN BUNGA KESUMA

JALAN BERJAYA

LABUAN WALK

Labuan
Museum

Dorsett Grand
Hotel

Police
Station

Padang

JALAN MERDEKA

JATI

JALAN JATI

JALAN KEMAJUAN

JALAN BUNGA MELATI

JALAN BUNGA KENANGA

JALAN BUNGA RAYA

JALAN OKK AWANG BESAR

JALAN BUNGA TANJUNG

JALAN OKK AWANG BISAR

LORONG BUNGA TANJUNG

JALAN MELATI

JALAN TANJUNG

JALAN BUNGA MELOR

JALAN LOKONG BAHASA

Hotel Aifa

Minivan
Terminal

@

Watsons

HSBC

Passenger
Ferry Terminal

JALAN MERDEKA

JALAN DEWAN

JALAN BERKAT

JALAN TUN MUSTAPHA

Car Ferry
Terminal

Chinese
Temple

Utama Jaya
Supermarket

Bus and
Taxi Station

UTC Building
& Central Market

JALAN HUJUNG PASIR

JALAN BUNGA PASIR

JALAN GERSIK

Labuan
Bazar

Boat to
Water
Village

Maybank ATM
Food Stalls

Taxi
Stand

Boats to Brunei, Sabah & Sarawak

LABUAN

0   5
kilometres

Chimney
Museum

Laying-Layangan
Beach &
Peace Park

War
Cemetery

Labuan Town

SEE MAIN MAP
FOR DETAIL

Tanjung Batu
Beach

Papan

Labuan Marine Park

N

contains various displays on coastal and deep-sea ecosystems, plus the environment around Labuan. Its main attraction, however, is its **aquarium**, with more than a dozen tanks plus a touch pool.

Labuan War Cemetery and Memorial

3km northeast of Labuan Town on Jalan Tanjung Batu • Mon–Fri 7am–4.30pm • Free • W cwgc.org • Bus #1

Containing the remains of approximately 3900 Allied soldiers, many of them unidentified, Labuan's **war cemetery** is Malaysia's largest by far (the one at Taiping in Perak is a distant second; see p.133). Many were victims of the Sandakan "death march" (see p.428); hundreds more were transferred here from Kuching, site of an infamous prisoner-of-war camp. Inside the compound, white stone markers are poignantly arrayed on manicured lawns. There's also a red-brick, columned memorial to one side, commemorating the 2300 Australian and other troops who died in Borneo and the Philippines during World War II, and have no known graves.

Chimney Museum

On the northeast tip of the island on Jalan Tanjung Kubong • Daily 8.30am–5pm • Free • T 087 463603, W www.jmm.gov.my • Bus #6

One of the most bizarre museums in the country must be Labuan Island's **Chimney Museum**, which celebrates the mysterious red-brick tower next door. Most of the museum is actually given over to a passable history of **coal-mining** in Labuan – under the British, the northeast of the island was a major centre for this until the early twentieth century. Dioramas and antique equipment attempt to spice up the story, but the great lacuna is just what role the square chimney itself – so heavily restored that you'd swear it was built a few years back, although it's thought to date from 1900 – actually played. Indeed, no one is even sure that the chimney had anything to do with mining at all.

The beaches

There are beaches dotted all around Labuan's coastline, the nearest to Labuan Town being **Tanjung Batu Beach**, 2.5km to the northeast; it's a so-so stretch, let down by brownish sand and views of shipping and the odd oil rig. Rather better are the half a dozen or so beaches dotted all along the northwest coast, which all offer good sunset views. If you only have time for one, make it **Layang-Layangan Beach**, smack in the middle of the stretch and including **Surrender Point**, where Japanese troops acquiesced at the end of World War II. The adjoining **Peace Park**, built in the 1980s with Japanese funds, is a pretty spot to relax.

ARRIVAL AND DEPARTURE   LABUAN ISLAND

By plane Labuan Island's airport is 5km north of Labuan Town, served by all the local minibuses except #1; a taxi into the centre costs RM15.

Destinations KK (6 daily; 30min); Kuala Lumpur (3–5 daily; 2hr 20min); Miri (5 daily; 40min).

By boat Passenger ferries serving Sabah and Sarawak dock at Labuan Town's international ferry terminal on Jalan Merdeka (T 087 581006). Car ferries, which only serve Muara in Brunei

(RM35) and Menumbok in Sabah, leave from a jetty close by to the east. In addition, there are Menumbok speedboats, which use the international terminal (1–2 hourly; RM15). Schedules do change, so check to be sure.

Destinations KK (2 daily; 3hr 15min); Lawas (1 daily; 2hr 15min); Limbang (1–2 daily; 2hr); Menumbok (speedboats hourly; 20–30min; car ferry 5–6 daily; 1hr 30min); Muara (Brunei; 4 daily; 1hr 15min).

GETTING AROUND

By minibus Labuan has six numbered local minibus services operating to an irregular timetable; details are given here where relevant. They leave between dawn

and the early evening from the bus station to the northwest of Labuan Town.

By taxi Taxis park at the bus station and charge around

RM10 for a short ride, rising to RM30 to head right across the island.

By bicycle A counter at the ferry terminal offers bike rental for RM5/hr or RM30/day.

By car If you'd like to rent a car, you can try Hertz at the airport (☏ 087 410740), or LDA Travel & Tour at the ferry terminal (☏ 087 413155).

INFORMATION

Tourist information Tourism Malaysia is at Jalan Merdeka, close to the Labuan Museum (daily 8am–5pm; ☏ 087 423445). The Labuan Corporation, the body that runs the island, also operates an information counter at the airport (Mon–Thurs, Sat & Sun 8am–1pm & 2–5pm, Fri 8–11.30am & 2–5pm; ⓦ pl.gov.my).

Internet access Labuan has a free Wi-Fi service available at facilities like the ferry terminal.

ACCOMMODATION

Hotels in Labuan Town are mostly geared towards **business travellers** and so are struggling somewhat in the face of the local economic slump. Rates here reflect the resulting discounts, but you should expect some volatility. There are no hostels, and the handful of **budget hotels** are usually undone by one thing or another, such as being located close to the noisy nightlife of the Jati district. Elsewhere, there's a beach resort worth considering, and it's also possible to stay on the islands of **Rusukan Besar** (within the marine park, see opposite) and **Papan** (just to the southeast of Labuan Town).

Billion Waterfront Jalan Wawasan, Labuan Town ☏ 087 418111; map p.410. All rooms at this fancy complex are basically the same; prices vary according to location and view. Amenities include a pool, fitness centre, restaurant and – perhaps best of all – a poolside bar where Saturday night buffets are served (RM50). 🛜 RM275

★**Labuan Avenue** Jalan OKK Awang Besar, Labuan Town ☏ 087 427157, ✉ lbn.avenue@yahoo.com; map p.410. This newish budget option is a godsend, as it's quiet, homely and, unlike most of its peers, not bad to look at either,

with a snazzy lobby and pantry where a self-service breakfast is available. Conveniently placed for just about everything in the centre. Rooms with windows cost about ten percent extra, and rates rise by ten percent at weekends. 🛜 RM95

Palm Beach Resort & Spa Jalan Batu Manikar, near the island's northern tip ☏ 087 418700, ⓦ palmbeachresortspa.com; map p.410. A tranquil, likeable affair where the rooms, in modern blocks, are unremarkable, but the leafy grounds and beachside pool really hit the spot. 🛜 RM250

EATING

Labuan Town holds the usual mix of no-frills *kedai kopi*s plus more formal restaurants for Western basics or seafood (as ever, priced by weight).

Choice Restaurant Jalan Okk Awang Besar; map p.410. Spacious, inexpensive a/c place with a long à la carte menu, as well as a good *nasi campur* spread. The *roti* and *dosai* are excellent – try the *ghee masala dosa* for breakfast. Daily 8am–10.30pm.

Fratini's Jalan Bunga Kesuma ☏ 087 417555; map p.410. Outpost of the Bruneian chain known for its reliable thin-crust pizzas. Daily 10am–11pm.

Mawilla Yacht Club Tanjung Batu Beach, just beyond the edge of town ☏ 087 423888; map p.410. An unpretentious affair, despite the grand name, in an open-sided beach bungalow with a fairly standard menu of Chinese stir-fries, plus seafood. Reckon on RM25/head without drinks, or more with seafood. Daily 7am–1am.

New Sung Hwa PCK Building, Jalan Hujong Pasir ☏ 087 411 008; map p.410. Hidden upstairs in a featureless concrete block, but highly popular for its reasonably priced Chinese seafood, including crispy squid. Some tables have views west across the channel to Labuan's two water villages. Daily noon–2pm & 5.30–10.30pm.

★**Raff** Jalan Merdeka, next to Maybank ☏ 019 897 2799; map p.410. This simple restaurant has sea views and a range of Malay food, with a *nasi campur* spread in the morning and à la carte service thereafter. Specialities include *ayam penyet* (pounded, tenderized chicken) and Sarawak *laksa* – the friendly owner hails from Kuching. Dishes cost RM15 or less. Daily 10.30am–10.30pm.

DRINKING

The town was once known for its **nightlife**, with oil-industry workers coming here to unwind. Things have quietened down somewhat, though you might not think so if you're anywhere near the raucous karaoke bars of Jati, with one or two more venues clinging on near the western edge of town – but nowhere is particularly appealing.

VISITING LABUAN'S MARINE PARK

Labuan's **marine park**, 5km southwest of Labuan, encloses three islands, **Kuraman** (the largest by far), **Rusukan Besar** and **Rusukan Kecil**, along with four **wreck dive** sites. With no regular boat service, however, the only way to visit is on a trip organized by an operator in Labuan. It's possible to overnight here, though don't expect resort-style luxury; the only accommodation takes the form of simple A-frame chalets, with a/c and bathroom, on Rusukan Besar. Note there is a RM30 conservation fee.

TOUR OPERATORS

Borneo Wreck Divers Dorsett Grand hotel, Labuan Town ☎013 808 8678. This operator offers a basic diving package to the marine park that costs RM320/person, excluding food and the park conservation fee, while wreck diving starts at RM380; snorkelling and Discover Scuba courses are also available.

Emma Glorious Tours Near the airport ☎087 423688. To explore the marine park without diving, contact Emma Glorious Tours, whose trips feature snorkelling and a fair amount of beach time. Their day-trip to Rusukan Besar includes lunch (RM240); alternatively, see all three islands on a two-day package (RM380), including a night's stay on Rusukan Besar and four meals — one a beach barbecue dinner. Prices are per head and require at least two people; the conservation fee isn't included. The company is located out of town, but can do airport and hotel pickups.

7

Fah Fah Jalan Bunga Mawar ☎087 425 5863; map p.410. With some seating outdoors on a street corner, this slightly desultory place serves *bak kut teh* and a few other dishes, but it can be busy with people enjoying a few beers. In fact, the drinking starts pretty early in the afternoon. Daily 7am–1am.

DIRECTORY

Banks and exchange The ferry terminal has an ATM, while Maybank and HSBC aren't far away on the same street, Jalan Merdeka.
Clinic Permai Polyclinic, Jalan Kemajuan (Mon–Fri & Sun 9am–11pm; ☎087 423100).
Left luggage You'll find this at the ferry terminal for just a few ringgit (daily 7am–5pm).

The northwest coast and Kudat Peninsula

Sabah's northwestern coast is relatively untarnished by oil palm; instead there are views of jewel-bright paddy fields and stilt houses, with Mount Kinabalu looming in the distance. The area tends to be overlooked by visitors, however, partly because it lacks a star attraction, though that could change if the extension of the highway all the way north to the town of **Kudat** gets under way as planned. Until then, the **beaches** of the northernmost **Tip of Borneo** will probably remain off the radar, as will Malaysia's largest marine protected zone, the **Tun Mustapha Park**. Closer to KK, and feasible as a day-trip, are the **Mantanani Islands**.

Kota Belud

Sixty-five kilometres northeast of KK, the main road reaches bustling **KOTA BELUD**, famed for its weekly *tamu*. Early on Sundays, the otherwise indistinguishable town springs to life as hordes of Rungus, Kadazan/Dusan and Bajau people are drawn together at Sabah's largest weekly market. Though a few visitors arrive on tours from KK, you won't see many souvenirs for sale; instead you're far more likely to come across dried dish, chains of yeast beads (used to make rice wine), buffalo and betel nut. If heading here independently from KK, set off by 8am at the latest. In late October, things scale up by an order of magnitude at Kota Belud's annual *tamu besar* (literally "big *tamu*"), which features cultural performances, Bajau men on horseback in traditional finery and handicraft demonstrations. Away from the town, the area is a less common target for proboscis monkey and firefly-spotting cruises run by KK tour operators.

Mantanani Islands

A further 9km drive north and west of Kota Belud is coastal **Kuala Abai**, the departure point for the **Mantanani Islands**, a pair of islands 30km offshore to the north. There's no transport other than that laid on by tour operators who offer it as a long day-trip, including diving (from about RM500) or snorkelling (RM300), but you only get to spend just over four hours on the islands, so it's worth considering a night or two here.

ACCOMMODATION
MANTANANI ISLANDS

Mari Mari Backpacker Lodge c/o Traverse Tours ☎ 088 260501, ⓦ mantananiisland.com. A collection of simple two-person *sulaps* (huts) on stilts, with a hammock and chairs under each one, plus a hostel. Rates given include transfers from KK, breakfast plus one snorkelling session; extra nights cost much less. Dorms RM270, huts RM660

Sumangkap and Bavanggazo

Beyond Kota Belud, it's only half an hour's drive to the start of the road up the **Kudat Peninsula**, which is inhabited by the Rungus people, one of several subgroups of the Kadazan/Dusun and known for their beadwork. The first point of interest, signed some 140km from KK and 42km short of Kudat, is the village of **SUMANGKAP**, where gong-making is a cottage industry. Just about every house seems to be festooned with them, some looking like freakish saucepans, and villagers can be seen (and heard) in their front yards hammering away at them, listening closely to the tones they produce. Hardly anyone can explain their work in English, but that shouldn't prevent you haggling to buy a souvenir gong if you wish. Be sure to check out the field at the back of the village, where one monumental gong is as tall as a two-storey house.

Only a couple of kilometres beyond Sumangkap, a few traditional **Rungus longhouses** have survived the shift to modern housing in the village of **BAVANGGAZO**, where there are a couple where tourists can stay.

ARRIVAL AND DEPARTURE
SUMANGKAP AND BAVANGGAZO

By bus or shared taxi Sumangkap and Bavanggazo are some 140km from KK and 40km short of Kudat; Sumangkap is near the main road, but Bavanggazo lies 2.5km off it. Any bus or shared taxi between KK and Kudat (see below) can drop you at the turning for either village. If you are starting from Kudat and want to charter a taxi, expect to pay up to RM30 one way.

ACCOMMODATION

Bavanggazo Longhouse The second of the two longhouses in Bavanggazo, further in off the main road ☎ 019 842 6990. There are mattresses, each with their own mosquito net, on low sleeping platforms in one of 21 rooms; bathrooms are shared and there's no a/c. Rate here is per person and includes half board and a cultural show. RM95

Kudat

Dreary little **KUDAT** is the jumping-off point for the Tip of Borneo and for Banggi island in the Tun Mustapha Park (see p.416), and that's the best that can be said for it. The town centre sits on a tongue of land jutting into Marudu Bay. The main road in, Jalan Ibrahim Arshad, passes right by an orange-hued **Chinese temple**, with a couple of rows of old timber shophouses just beyond. The road then changes its name to Jalan Lintas, curling past the **harbour** to the southwest, with a new centre – holding a few banks – on its northeast side. The temple, the sea views and the **market** area on Jalan Lintas are the only things worthy of a few minutes of your attention.

By plane MASWings (maswings.com.my) call at Kudat's airfield, 9km northwest of town, on Mondays, Thursdays and Saturdays en route between KK (40min) and Sandakan (50min). A taxi between town and the airport costs about RM10.

By bus Salam Bumimas buses leave from a tiny station near the beginning of Jalan Lintas for KK (daily at 2pm; 3hr 30min) and Sandakan (Tues, Fri & Sun at 9.45am; 5hr).

By boat Ferries to Karakit town on Banggi Island (daily 8.30am, 9.30am & 2.30pm, returning 7.30am, 1.30pm & 2pm; 1hr; RM20; buy tickets on board) leave from an easily spotted jetty In the harbour area.

By taxi Shared taxis serving Kota Belud and KK (RM30) park up northeast of Jalan Ibrahim Arshad in the old part of town.

ACCOMMODATION

Kinabalu Jalan Melor, off Jalan Lintas and opposite KFC 088 612022. This place is good value and well kept for a budget hotel. While rooms are very dated, they do have a/c and private bathrooms. 🛜 RM75

Ria Jalan Ibrahim Arshad 088 622794, riahotel .blogspot.com. This mundane, squarish block towers over other buildings in Kudat and holds the best rooms in the centre. Suites cost more than double the ordinary rate, but they do have their own jacuzzis. 🛜 RM140

EATING AND DRINKING

It speaks volumes that the *KFC* is one of the slickest-looking restaurants in the centre, but many of the drab *kedai kopis* aren't too bad at all for cheap meals.

Bharat Valai Hotel, start of Jalan Lintas 088 621866. With pot-plant-lined parapets and moody lighting at night, this rooftop bar is the closest thing to a proper watering hole in Kudat. Daily noon–10pm.

Hari Hari Seafood Kampung Kelapa complex, Jalan Pasar Awam, off Jalan Lintas 088 623218. Home to more than one restaurant, the Kampung Kelapa complex

is easily spotted north of the market, with what look like giant drums (modelled on Rungus baskets) outside. Inside, under Chinese lanterns, *Hari Hari* has an extensive menu of stir-fries and seafood dishes to choose from (the breakfast selection is limited, though); most dishes cost RM10–15 for a small serving. Daily 6am–11.30pm.

The Tip of Borneo

Chartering a taxi to or from Kudat costs RM50–60

Some 6km short of Kudat, a pair of northbound turnings give access to the triangular cape of the **Tip of Borneo** (Tanjung Simpang Mengayau), which is still fairly rustic and totally bypassed by public transport. The main draws include scenic vistas of azure waters and a good dose of calm, but on the downside, the **beaches** are of variable quality, some pristine, others periodically strewn with detritus.

All roads eventually funnel into the road to the tip itself, which first passes a lovely 2.5km arc of sand – the southern section is **Kosohui Beach**, the northern part **Kalampunian Beach**. At the tip just to the northeast, a small landscaped area is crowned by a globular **monument**, with Balambangan and Banggi islands, part of the Tun Mustapha Park, visible on the eastern horizon.

As for **activities**, mangrove trips, surfing, kayaking, snorkelling and diving are available, although seas can be rough from November to January, and you should be wary of currents at other times. Jungle and coastal walks are possible, for example to **Kelambu Beach** 6km south of Kosohui, where a spit of sand links a forested islet to the mainland, but the lack of bike rental can make for some sweaty treks along shadeless roads.

A handful of places to stay cluster around Kalampunian Beach and the tip itself, with other options scattered all over the area. The most distant of these is noteworthy as it's the only place offering trips to the Tun Mustapha Park. Most of these places have at least a simple kitchen serving breakfast, if not a full restaurant. Wi-fi isn't commonplace, and even a phone signal can be hard to come by.

7

Hibiscus Villa 2.5km southwest of Kosohui Beach on Jalan Marang Parang ☎019 895 0704, Ⓦhibiscusvillaborneo.com. Savour life in your very own seaside mansion at this immaculate two-storey, three-bedroom affair, set in lush gardens and with its own infinity pool. The place sleeps up to nine, with prices depending on group size. If your pockets aren't deep enough, ask about their neighbouring property with just two chalets, each rented separately. Rates include breakfast. 🛜 RM1100

North Borneo Biostation Bak Bak Beach, some 20km southeast of the Tip of Borneo and 8km north of Kudat ☎010 803 7310, Ⓦborneobiostation.com. Part resort, part field station, with unusually spacious A-frame chalets complete with a/c and open-air bathrooms, plus a huge range of activities and trips. Rates include breakfast. RM275

Secret Place Signed off Jalan Marang Parang about 3km south of Kosohui ☎010 414 5291, Ⓦsecretplaceborneo.jimdo.com. A no-frills outfit offering camping on a secluded stretch of sand, with communal toilets and showers as well as a simple restaurant. Two-person tents RM50

★**Tampat Do Aman** Jalan Marang Parang, 2.5km from Kosohui Beach ☎013 880 8395, Ⓦtampatdoaman.com.my. This Rungus/British-run place offers a kind of back-to-basics experience. It's true there are some quite comfortable *sulaps* and chalets, all with bathrooms though no a/c, but many guests go for the basic longhouse rooms with shared showers and composting toilets. A small museum of Rungus culture is a noble feature. The fly in the ointment is the distance from the beach, something several daily free shuttles doesn't quite overcome. Rates exclude meals (only breakfast is served on site – or at their all-day beach restaurant, depending on your taste). Longhouses RM100, chalets RM175

★**TSM Merrimas Villas** Tip of Borneo ☎019 833 2199, Ⓦmerrimasvilla.com. This competently run outfit is set above a secluded cove and has a range of a/c, en-suite chalets on both sides of the road, from very plain ones along a terrace to quite striking bamboo units and substantial timber ones. All have two or even four double beds, apart from the basic chalets (RM180). 🛜 RM275

EATING

Secret Place About 3km south of Kosohui Beach on Jalan Marang Parang ☎010 414 5291, Ⓦsecretplaceborneo.jimdo.com. The restaurant at this beach campsite does simple Malay meals, and best of all they offer evening seafood barbecues on request (minimum charge RM20/person). Daily 9am–6pm.

Tip Top Kosohui Beach. Sister operation to *Tampat Do Aman*, with its own little pizzeria operation as well as a kitchen churning out Western and Asian basics, including

their house special chicken curry and spaghetti bolognese. Pizzas start at RM20, other dishes at RM10; wine and beer available. Daily 8am–9pm.

Tokow Kosohui Beach ☎013 558 9052. Next door to *Tip Top*, this Malay-run place is great for simple, filling rice or noodle variations, with yummy coconut shakes to watch them down. Nothing costs more than RM7. Daily 8am–6pm.

Tun Mustapha Park

No conservation fee or permits at the time of research • Ⓦsabahparks.org.my

The waters north and northeast of the Kudat Peninsula form the **Tun Mustapha Park**, Sabah's newest state park, which was created to try to protect sealife following years of overfishing and general neglect. Covering 9000 square kilometres, the park extends all the way to the Tip of Borneo, encompassing dozens of small islands plus three major ones – none of them have been set up for tourism, however. In principle, it's possible to do a half-day trip by ferry to the largest island, **Banggi**, which is 40km northeast of Kudat. The sights there aren't anything special, though: a **beach** on the northeast coast a couple of hours from the main settlement, **Karakit**, and the 529m **Mount Sinambung,** where the 70m-high **Sinambung Waterfall** nestles in the jungle.

Taxis are the only way to get around independently (at least RM150), so it's far better to visit on a **package trip** run by the *North Borneo Biostation* resort (see opposite). The main draw is, of course, the marine life, but in addition to diving and snorkelling they offer an excursion to **Balambangan Island**, west of Banggi, where there are limestone caves to explore (around RM150 per person).

Kinabalu Park

Main entrance daily 24hr; park office daily 7am–7pm • RM15 conservation fee • ☎ 088 889095, ⓦ sabahparks.org.my

The journey to **Kinabalu Park** is one of the most scenic anywhere in Malaysia, traversing a classic, winding mountain road with views of mist-shrouded valleys and the jagged spectre of its eponymous mountain constantly arresting the eye. The mountain is revered as *aki nabalu* (home of spirits of the dead) by the Kadazan/Dusun, and dominates the park's 750 square kilometres, a UNESCO World Heritage Site renowned for its ecology and geology. All other hikes within the park pale in comparison with the prospect of reaching the summit at Low's Peak (4095m), but climbing slots can be tricky to get, and the climb itself obliges you to **stay** one night on the mountain – an expensive affair, given the logistics of running facilities at altitude.

In view of those downsides, not every visitor is here to tackle the mountain, and the park has other temptations lower down. **Trails** loop the montane forest around the **park headquarters**; for great views, try either the 1082m-long Bukit Burung Trail or the 465m Bundu Tuhan View Trail. There's also the chance to visit **Poring Hot Springs**, reached by another park entrance to the east.

Mount Kinabalu

Climbing permit RM200/person; guide (compulsory) RM230/group of up to five; porter (optional) RM65/10kg up to Panar Laban; summit certificate (optional) RM10.60; insurance (compulsory) RM7; left luggage RM12

Hugh Low, then British colonial secretary on Labuan, made the first recorded ascent of **Mount Kinabalu** in 1851, though he baulked at attempting its highest peak, considering it "inaccessible to any but winged animals". Seven years later, Spenser St John, British consul-general to the native states of Borneo, found his progress blocked by Kadazan/Dusun "shaking their spears and giving us other hostile signs". The peak, subsequently named after Low, was finally climbed in 1888 by John Whitehead.

Things are much easier now, of course, with a **main trail** to follow – actually an exhausting 8.7km-long series of steps and rocky tracks that weaves steeply up through forest on the south side to the bare granite of Low's Peak in the northwest. Its existence is one of the joys of Kinabalu, as **no climbing skills or special equipment** are needed. Indeed, every two years, elite runners **race** from the park HQ to the summit and back down again, with winners covering the 26km in five hours or less (ⓦclimbathon.my).

Even so, Kinabalu deserves respect: conditions can be miserably cold and blowy up top, and you need to watch out for cramping and altitude sickness. Take care as you go, as you really don't want to be stretchered down by porters – which takes hours – because you twisted your ankle high up. At the same time, don't overthink the challenge; this is a mountain that can be climbed by anyone of **reasonable fitness**.

The **Timpohon Trail** is the main route up, and the only one available following the Kinabalu earthquake (see p.423). It's possible to set off for the park from KK on the morning of your climb, but staying the previous night in the area is a lot more restful. Allow half an hour at the park office to register, meet your assigned **guide**, and sort out porters and any luggage you want to store. Note that the guides' main job is to chaperone you up and back down in one piece – consider knowledge of flora and fauna or advanced linguistic skills a bonus.

Timpohon Gate to Panar Laban (around 6km; typically 5–7hr)

The whole climb operates to a timetable, with climbers setting off from the park HQ (1564m) from 8am until about 10.30am; many save time and avoid the tiresome 4.5km trudge up the road to **Timpohon Gate** (1866m) by using park transport (15min; RM17 for up to four people). Beyond the gate, the trail skirts Carson Waterfall around 500m on and, via countless steps, passes six **rest huts**, with toilets

7

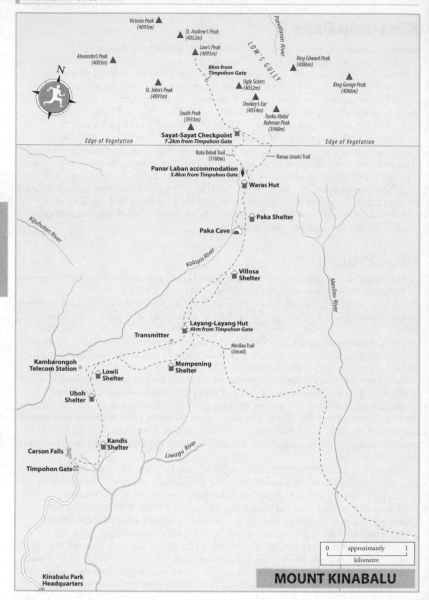

Victoria Peak ▲
(4093m)

St. Andrew's Peak ▲
(4052m)

Low's Peak ▲
(4095m)

Alexandra's Peak ▲
(4003m)

**8km from
Timpohon Gate**

King Edward Peak ▲
(4086m)

Ugly Sisters ▲
(4032m)

King George Peak ▲
(4066m)

St. John's Peak ▲
(4091m)

Donkey's Ear ▲
(4054m)

South Peak
(3933m)

Tunku Abdul
Rahman Peak
(3948m)

**Sayat-Sayat Checkpoint
7.2km from Timpohon Gate**

Edge of Vegetation

Kota Belud Trail
(1100m)

Ranau (main) Trail

Edge of Vegetation

**Panar Laban accommodation
5.8km from Timpohon Gate**

Waras Hut

Kijuhutan River

Paka Shelter

Paka Cave

Kolopis River

**Villosa
Shelter**

Mesilau River

**Layang-Layang Hut
4km from Timpohon Gate**

Transmitter

Mesilau Trail
(closed)

**Kambarongoh
Telecom Station**

**Mempening
Shelter**

**Lowii
Shelter**

**Uboh
Shelter**

**Kandis
Shelter**

Liwagu River

Carson Falls

Timpohon Gate ⊠

0	approximately	1
	kilometre	

MOUNT KINABALU

**Kinabalu Park
Headquarters**

LOW'S GULLY

Panataran River

---

and water supplies, en route to the accommodation at **Panar Laban** (often called
Laban Rata after the accommodation of that name; 3272m). From the outset you're in
montane rainforest, with its delicate ferns, mosses, rhododendrons and orchids, and
it's worth making time to appreciate the vegetation and vistas – the South China Sea
is visible at times – rather than plod on. Many climbers pause for a lunch break at
Layang-Layang hut (2700m), beyond which the vegetation becomes noticeably
sparser, dominated by withered *sayat-sayat* trees occasionally decked with blond

KINABALU PARK HQ

EATING
| Balsam | 1 |
| Panataran Kinabalu | 2 |

ACCOMMODATION
D'Villa Rina Ria Lodge	4
J Residence	3
Kinabalu Mountain Lodge	2
Mile 36 Lodge	5
Nikgold Garden	6
Sutera Sanctuary Lodges	1

strands – a type of lichen. Look out for **pitcher plants**, notably *Nepenthes villosa*, its sizeable pitchers ribbed at the rim. If fatigue hasn't struck yet, it may well bite hard now, turning the last kilometre or so into a grind.

Panar Laban to the summit (2.7km; 2hr 30min–4hr)

After dinner, served from late afternoon, there's time to sleep until 2am (the electricity may be turned off around 8pm), when there's another meal before climbers resume. There's a choice of routes at this point: either the standard **Ranau Trail** or the shorter, steeper **Kota Belud Trail** (the latter must be arranged beforehand at the park HQ). They reunite at the **Sayat-Sayat Checkpoint**, which is 1.2km from Panar Laban via the Ranau Trail. Stragglers must make this checkpoint by 5.30am or will be turned back without reaching the top.

On the Ranau Trail everyone gets bunched together at first like a huge caterpillar, but when the stairs end the faster ones break free to tackle the granite slopes of the mountaintop, with ropes on the steeper sections. The aim is to arrive at Low's Peak shortly before taking in the **sunrise** around 5.40am, to avoid lingering at the exposed summit longer than need be (although you may have to line up to have your picture taken at the summit signboard).

The descent

Heading down in daylight, you can finally take in the breathtaking scenery: the horned **South Peak**, seldom climbed; the curving granite rock face that seems to funnel up towards Low's Peak; and, on a clear day, views of green plains and distant ranges. Back at the Sayat-Sayat Checkpoint, climbers who booked with Mountain

7

CLIMBING KINABALU: KEY POINTS

• The ascent and descent via the main trail takes **two days** in total, with hikers setting off in the morning, staying the night near the summit, and then reaching the top at dawn on day two.
• At the time of research no more than **135 people** were allowed to start the climb daily, although this might return to the pre-quake figure of two hundred once Sabah Parks' new accommodation opens.
• The essential first step is to **book accommodation** up the mountain at Panar Laban (see p.422). You should aim to do so weeks if not months ahead, although last-minute places do pop up if people cancel. If it seems impossible to get a bed for the dates you want, consider paying more for a via ferrata package as *Pendant Hut* is more likely to have spaces (see p.422).
• Only with proof of accommodation can you obtain a **climbing permit** at the park HQ. You should bring adequate **cash** for this and to pay for the guide, transport and everything else; the nearest bank is 5km away in Kundasang.
• If conditions are very wet and/or windy when the final summit push is meant to start, it will be **cancelled**. Rescheduling and partial refunds aren't possible.

WHAT TO PACK

• **Climb as light as you can**, carrying only essentials. It can be worth paying a porter to lug anything else up to Panar Laban, but you should leave those items there for the final ascent.
• **Clothing** is tricky. The daytime hike is warm to mild much of the way, while on the pre-dawn climb temperatures can dip below 10°C and there may be a vicious wind chill; at the same time, the slog will work up a bit of a sweat. A suitable compromise for many people is to don regular clothes for the tropics (trousers, not shorts) and pack a sweater or thermal vest, plus a light to medium jacket and warm headgear. A cheap plastic poncho will keep you dry in the rain and adds warmth. Bring sports gloves, not just for insulation but also to grip the ropes comfortably.
• As for **equipment**, sturdy shoes with a good grip will be especially helpful for the moist, slippery granite at the top. You must have a head torch as the trail is unlit (check the batteries are fresh). Many people also swear by climbing poles to take the pressure off your knees and leg muscles in general. A small water bottle will do, as you can refill it at rest huts along the way. Sugary snacks are handy to refuel.

Torq head off to tackle the **via ferrata** (see p.422); the rest continue down to Panar Laban for a late breakfast and then retrace their steps to Timpohon Gate. The whole descent might take a quarter less time than the climb, although you might be hobbled by aching legs – stairs may be difficult for a couple of days afterwards.

ARRIVAL AND DEPARTURE   MOUNT KINABALU

If you're heading to the park from KK, the best option is to get a shared minivan or taxi from the central Merdeka Field terminal. Returning to KK, however, you may find that these are full, so catching a bus for the inconveniently located Inanam terminal is the better option.

By bus In daylight hours, it's often possible to flag down buses travelling between KK and the east coast, but you may need to be patient as some will be practically full. Also, the fare may be calculated from the last town the bus called at. Destinations KK (frequent; 1hr 30min); Lahad Datu (14 daily; 7–8hr); Sandakan (at least 12 daily; 6hr); Semporna (6 daily; 9–10hr); Tawau (7 daily; 10–11hr); Telupid (frequent; 3hr).

By shared taxi and minivan Shuttling between KK and Kundasang/Ranau, shared taxis and minivans are a convenient way to reach the park. If you intend to set off for the park on the morning of your climb, aim to be at Merdeka Field no later than 7.30am.

INFORMATION

Tourist information Clustered very near the gates are the park HQ (daily 7am–7pm), a Mountain Torq office and a Sutera Sanctuary Lodges counter and shop with a left luggage service. The park office, which is swarming with climbers in the morning, can provide maps and general information, and also find specialist birding guides if contacted in advance.

Internet access Depending on your phone network, you can either get online for much of the mountain trail or not at all. Celcom has 4G coverage at Panar Laban.

THE VIA FERRATA

If the huge trek up to the summit doesn't sound like enough of a challenge, then you might want to book your climb with Mountain Torq (Level 2, MAA Building, Lorong Api-Api 1, KK; ☎088 268126; ⓦmountaintorq.com), who offer two-day full-board packages (from RM1650) and operate the **via ferrata** – pathways of rungs, bridges, rails and planks running along Kinabalu's cliffsides. Their introductory Walk The Torq route is suitable for anyone over 10 (2–3hr), while the alternative Low's Peak Circuit has a minimum age of 17 (4–5hr). It's exhilarating stuff, with some incredible views and the assurance of being tethered or hooked to something all the time; it's also even more tiring as it slots in soon after you've conquered Low's Peak With either route, you will still be back at Timpohon Gate by late afternoon. If that sounds too rushed, consider a longer package, possibly with an **abseiling** course thrown in. In all cases you'll stay in dorms at the firm's own *Pendant Hut* at Panar Laban.

It's also possible to add the via ferrata **last-minute** to an ordinary climbing package: pay on day 1 of your climb (at least RM820 for Walk The Torq; credit cards accepted) at Mountain Torq's office at the Park HQ or at *Pendant Hut*.

7

ACCOMMODATION

Park accommodation at the **HQ** is run by Sutera Sanctuary Lodges (SSL) and is overpriced; there are better deals within 2km of the park entrance. Up the mountain at **Panar Laban**, however, climbers have three outfits to choose from: SSL, Mountain Torq (for via ferrata packages) and Sabah Parks itself. One snag other than sheer demand is that SSL normally steers climbers into buying a three-day package, with the extra night spent at its accommodation at either the park HQ or Poring Hot Springs; the two-day package is on sale only if they have unsold Panar Laban beds with a month to go. The Sabah Parks alternative is **Lemaing Hut**, where foreigners can only get beds if there are vacancies with a few days to go (to register your interest, call the park office or just turn up and ask). The good news, however, is that Sabah Parks' new accommodation at Panar Laban promises to be a game changer and should be open by the time you read this, although no prices were available at the time of research. All the options listed here have their own simple restaurant unless otherwise stated.

PARK HQ AND AROUND

D'Villa Rina Ria Lodge On the main road 750m southeast of the park entrance ☎088 889282, ⓦdvillalodge.com.my; map p.419. This place is not much to look at but isn't a bad choice, with a twelve-bed dorm as well as standard rooms with balconies offering valley views. The restaurant is better than average. Breakfast included. ☎ Dorms RM30, doubles RM120

★**J Residence** 300m west of the park entrance ☎012 869 6969, ⓦjresidence.com; map p.419. Offers eleven rooms spread over six units on the mountainside among the pines, including three in a villa with a kitchen. The design and furnishings are much slicker than most places around here, though there are no mountain views and no meals. Prices leap by half at the weekend. ☎ RM150

Kinabalu Mountain Lodge At the end of a steep, winding 800m road that starts 1.2km west of the park entrance ☎016 208 4909; map p.419. Popular with backpackers, this peaceful wooden building on a spur of the mountain has a lovely view from the terrace, but the trek from it to the park is a drag. Rooms are fairly basic, and en-suite ones cost quite a bit more. Meals aren't included, but don't cost much. Dorms RM35, doubles RM110

Mile 36 Lodge On the main road 1.5km southeast of the park entrance ☎088 888161, ⓦmile36lodge.com;

map p.419. A real hotchpotch of chalets and rooms, ranging from rather bare affairs to genuinely comfy units that are suitable for groups and cost two to three times as much. The best thing about it is the view of Kinabalu from the edge of the sprawling, leafy grounds. Breakfast included. ☎ RM100

Nikgold Garden Signed 1.5km southeast of the park HQ, then another 500m down a steep valley road ☎088 888112; map p.419. An imposing set of two-storey timber buildings staggered up a slope, with spacious modern bedrooms and the mountain towering close by. No meals. RM120

Sutera Sanctuary Lodges On the road to Timpohon Gate ☎017 833 5322, ⓦsuterasanctuarylodges.com. my; map p.419. Sprinkled inside the park north of the HQ are several cosy "lodges", which range from plain-looking chalets to quite plush bungalows and sleep two, four or six people, plus the *Grace Hostel* that has dorms. Rate includes breakfast at the park's *Balsam* restaurant. Dorms RM370, lodges RM520

ON THE MOUNTAIN

Laban Rata Resthouse Panar Laban ☎017 833 5311. It feels like a dated student hostel, but this veteran place is still a welcome refuge on the bitter mountainside.

There are just three private rooms – the rest are dorms. Climbers will find the buffet meals gloriously satisfying, though anything ordered off the menu is pricey – if you're tempted to moan, remember the porters plodding up the trail laden with eggs, melons and other supplies. Those roped into SSL's three-day package will pay RM150–200 more for the extra night's full board down below in a dorm bed. Bookings through SSL in KK. Rates here are for two-day full-board packages, though big discounts are sometimes on offer. Dorms RM980, doubles RM2000

Lemaing Hut Panar Laban. Tiny hostel aimed at Malaysians with two cramped 20-bed dorms and basic bathrooms – it's clean but unmemorable. This is a bargain for foreigners who are able to get a last-minute place – the rates here include meals at *Laban Rata Resthouse*. Book through Sabah Parks (see p.398). Full board per person RM215

EATING

Balsam At the park HQ; map p.419. Run by SSL, the park's restaurant offers predictably expensive yet satisfying buffets with local and Western dishes; breakfast, lunch and dinner cost RM45, RM50 and RM75 respectively. Daily 6.30am–9pm.

Panataran Kinabalu On the main road opposite park turning ☎088 889117; map p.419. Sabah Parks' co-op restaurant is the best spot for inexpensive food close to the park, with a menu of largely Chinese dishes. Many dishes are under RM10. Daily 6.30am–8pm.

Poring Hot Springs

North of Ranau and some 40km east of the main park entrance • Daily 7am–5pm • RM15 including use of outdoor tubs; RM15/hr for indoor tubs; canopy walkway RM5; RM15 conservation fee (not payable if you have visited the park HQ the same day) • ☎088 870102, ⓦsabahparks.org.my

The **Poring Hot Springs** were developed during World War II by the Japanese, who installed wooden tubs that have since been replaced by tiled versions. Don't come expecting natural pools, luxury or solitude, but it can still be a good place to relax aching muscles after descending from Mount Kinabalu. It's least crowded early or late in the day.

There are also a few other attractions within the site, including an orchid garden, a butterfly farm, a **canopy walkway** and a few walking trails. Outside the gates, households occasionally advertise that they have **Rafflesia flowers** to see in their grounds; expect to pay around RM30 to see them.

ARRIVAL AND DEPARTURE

PORING HOT SPRINGS

By bus or minivan Park shuttles run between Poring Hot Springs and the park HQ (1hr; RM18). For long-distance travel, you can hop in a minivan (RM10) from outside the park gates to get to Ranau (see opposite), where you'll find plenty of options for onward transport.

THE 2015 KINABALU EARTHQUAKE

It struck at 7.15am on June 5, 2015 – an unprecedented **magnitude 6 quake** with its epicentre at Kundasang, close to Kinabalu Park. In KK, 50km to the southwest, the tremors sent people scurrying into the stree, but it was on the mountaintop that the impact was terrible. Eighteen people died, including six Singapore schoolchildren on the via ferrata, as well as several guides; in many cases, the victims were crushed by falling rocks.

Mount Kinabalu had been in the **headlines** just days earlier, when a group of foreign climbers partially disrobed for a photo at the summit. Flaunted on social media, the image caused some outrage locally, and when the quake hit some pointed to vengeful spirits. A few of those involved in the stunt were soon charged in court.

Extensive repairs kept the park closed for several months after the quake. The scars are still easy to see, with slopes denuded by landslides and boulders strewn on valley floors; at the summit, Kinabalu's "donkey ears" rock formation is now one ear and a stump. The once-popular **Mesilau Trail**, starting several kilometres east of the main park gate and joining the main trail 2800m up, is out of commission, as is its *Mesilau Nature Resort*, with no date set for their reopening. Signs at the park now warn against "unethical acts (including nude)" and, in the same spirit, notify visitors that **drones** are banned.

ACCOMMODATION

Besides accommodation run by SSL, this part of the park has a campsite (RM50/person) and a great jungle camp.

★ **Lupa Masa** A 40min walk outside the park entrance ✉ lupamasaborneo@gmail.com. This place, whose name means "forget time", has everything you could want in a jungle lodge – so long as you aren't that fussy about creature comforts. There are tents, huts and, fanciest of all, some river-facing chalets. Staff collect guests daily at 3pm in Poring. Rates are for full board. Camping per person RM70, chalets RM200

Sutera Sanctuary Lodges Within the park ☎ 088 878801, ⓦ suterasanctuarylodges.com.my. The official accommodation includes a slick dorm, a handful of mid-range doubles and very pricey lodges sleeping up to six. Breakfast included. Dorms RM180, doubles RM280

EATING

Rainforest Restaurant Just inside the park ☎ 088 877215. The restaurant at *Sutera Sanctuary Lodges* serves buffet lunches and dinners if they have enough guests staying, but otherwise you have to order off the menu and prices are steep. Buffet breakfasts RM45. Daily 7am–10pm.

Round Inn On the main road close to the entrance ☎ 088 879584. This place stands out on the main road, not least for its circular entrance and large drum, which customers are allowed to beat. Decent Chinese meals will set you back around RM15/person. Daily 9am–8.30pm.

Around Kinabalu Park

The area southeast of Kinabalu Park is known for its agriculture, the fruits of which can be glimpsed in tiny **Kundasang**, where simple stalls sell local produce – although the town is also on the tourist trail for its **war memorial**. Further east there's a **tea plantation** with tours and accommodation. In between, the mundane town of **Ranau** is known for paragliding.

Kundasang War Memorial

Just off the main road in Kundasang • Daily 8.30am–5.30pm • RM10 • Buses and minivans stop close to the main junction on the highway, though for onward travel you will have to flag them down

Five kilometres southeast of the main entrance to Kinabalu Park, the **Kundasang War Memorial** commemorates the victims – although no soldiers are buried here – of the Sandakan Death Marches of 1945, when Japanese troops force-marched POWs from Sandakan to Ranau (see p.428). There's an information centre that shows an Australian documentary about the death marches, plus three peaceful and well-tended memorial gardens (Australian, British and Bornean).

ACCOMMODATION   KUNDASANG

Cottage Hotel Off Jalan Kundasang Kaluan, which runs north of the main road through town ☎ 088 888882, ⓦ thecottagehotel.com.my. The rooms here are small and a little dated, though some have lovely views over hills and vegetable farms. There's also a Chinese restaurant specializing in hot pot dishes. Breakfast included. Prices increase by twenty percent on weekends. 🛜 RM115

Ranau and around

RANAU is an undistinguished transport hub, where the main road between the west and east coasts is joined by the interior road for Tambunan and other points east of the Crocker Range. The town hosts a large and lively *tamu* on the first Sunday of the month, based 1km out of town towards Sandakan, and there's also a smaller *tamu* there every Saturday.

Ranau Paragliding Park

6km northeast of Ranau • Daily 10am–4pm • Tandem flight RM220; optional video RM30 extra • ☎ 019 860 8700, ⓦ borneoparagliders.com

The valleys and consistent winds around Mount Kinabalu make the area a good site for **paragliding**, and novices can come here to try a thrilling tandem flight starting at 700m; with an early start, it's feasible as a day-trip from KK. There are multi-day paragliding courses on offer, too.

Sabah Tea Garden

18km east of Ranau in Nalapak • Factory tours RM14 • ☎ 088 440882, ⓦ sabahtea.com.my • Long-distance buses between KK and the east coast will drop passengers here on request; local buses from Ranau can drop you at the start of the turning, from where it's a 15min walk

The **Sabah Tea Garden** is a well-run organic tea plantation and factory that makes a worthwhile place to stay for a night or two, but may also be worth a daytime visit if you're just passing through. Make sure you also ask about getting a **fish massage** at nearby Luanti, where surprisingly large river fish converge to nibble at customers' feet.

7

ARRIVAL AND DEPARTURE RANAU AND AROUND

By bus Long-distance buses stop on the main road beside the turning into town.

Destinations KK (frequent; 2hr); Lahad Datu (14 daily; 7hr); Sandakan (at least 12 daily; 5hr 30min); Semporna (6 daily; 9–10hr); Tawau (7 daily; 10–11hr); Telupid (frequent; 2hr 30min).

By shared minivan and taxi Shared transport parks up at the eastern edge of town and heads to Merdeka Field in KK (2hr) plus the interior town of Tambunan. (1hr 15min)

ACCOMMODATION

Sabah Tea Garden Nalapak, 18km east of Ranau on the road to Sandakan ☎088 440882 or ☎088 876611, ⓦsabahtea.com.my. This plantation has a campsite and longhouses that are popular with student groups, as well as cosy cottages that are equipped with flat-screen TVs and include breakfast. Batik-painting sessions are available, as are organized jungle treks (both RM20/person), although for the latter there must be a minimum of ten people. Camping costs half the price if you bring your own tent. Camping per person **RM30**, longhouses **RM140**, cottages **RM280**

Eastern Sabah

Despite being seemingly engulfed in tracts of oil palm, eastern Sabah is still a superb place for having animal encounters. In the vicinity of the northeastern city of **Sandakan** alone, it's possible to see orang-utans and sun bears in **Sepilok**, proboscis monkeys at **Labuk Bay Proboscis Monkey Sanctuary** and turtles at the **Turtle Islands Park**. Heading further south, the **Kinabatangan River** features prominently and various jungle lodges offer cruises to seek out pygmy elephants, proboscis monkeys and more. Then there's **Danum Valley**, a verdant rainforest area with a majestic canopy walkway, and the equally appealing **Tabin Wildlife Reserve**, both in the southeast. In the same area, the bustling coastal town of **Semporna** is the gateway to superb diving around world-famous **Sipadan**, **Mabul** and numerous other islands.

Sandakan

Situated at the northern edge of Sandakan Bay, facing the Sulu Sea, the town of **SANDAKAN** was all but destroyed during World War II; postwar reconstruction has created a cramped centre of indistinguishable concrete blocks, now plagued by the worst case of inner-city decay anywhere in Malaysia. It is possible to see most of the surrounding wildlife attractions and the **Sandakan Memorial Park** without really setting foot in town, and many visitors do just that, though there's nothing rough or seedy about the centre and it's still worth a visit to see the echoes of the **colonial past** so absent in KK – notably the **Agnes Keith House**, a shrine to the American writer who once brilliantly chronicled Sabah. The town also has a visitable **water village** where you can dine, as well as a sprinkling of tour operators.

Brief history

Although eighteenth-century accounts mention a trading outpost called Sandakan within the Sulu Sultanate, the town's modern history really begins in 1879, when a settlement named **Elopura** got going thanks to the efforts of the Englishman **William Pryer**. By 1884, it was the **capital** of British North Borneo. Its natural harbour and proximity to sources of timber, rattan and edible birds' nests would transform it into a thriving centre, one that lured so many Chinese settlers it was nicknamed "Little Hong Kong". In January 1942 the Japanese seized what was now known as Sandakan, establishing the POW camp from which the **death marches to Ranau** began (see p.428). What Allied bombing failed to destroy, the Japanese burned down, and the end of the war saw Sabah's administration shift to Jesselton (KK). Nevertheless, by the 1950s the rebuilt town was profiting from the **timber boom**, so much so that by the 1970s it was said to have the world's greatest concentration of millionaires. Business then faltered due to the overexploitation of the forests, forcing Sandakan to look to cocoa and **oil palm**; today, tourism aside, much of the town's prosperity hinges on servicing the oil-palm industry.

The old town and waterfront

Sandakan's **old town centre** is squeezed between the sea and Trig Hill (Bukit Bendera) to the north, but has been extended slightly thanks to land reclamation south of Jalan Pryer. The modern **waterfront** area, including a large development called **Harbour Square** to the northeast, has tried its best to breathe some life into the town, but the shops and restaurants are, by and large, a bit mundane. Just beyond here is the sizeable **central market** (daily 6am–8pm), which is unusually tidy and well laid out. The rest of the old centre is lively enough by day but tends to peter out by nightfall, when many of the shops close up.

Sandakan Heritage Museum
Off Lebuh Empat • Daily 9am–5pm • Free • ☎ 089 222679, ⊛ museum.sabah.gov.my

The tiny **Sandakan Heritage Museum** holds the usual mock-ups of tribal houses, but is mostly taken up by vintage photos of the old town. There are also wilder ethnographic-type images, some relating to the exploits of American explorers Martin and Osa Johnson, who spent time in Borneo in the 1920s and 1930s. If you're heading up Trig Hill from here, look out for the small row of monuments on Lebuh Empat itself, one bearing the barely legible name of **William Pryer**, the modern town's founder.

The Agnes Keith House
Jalan Istana, Trig Hill • Daily 9am–5pm • RM15 • ☎ 089 221140, ⊛ museum.sabah.gov.my

In *The Land Below the Wind* (1939), Agnes Keith wrote: "When we sat in that house and looked out through its open doors the harbour of Sandakan with the dark mangrove swamps in the distance became a background to our entire world. I knew then that was where I wanted to live".

Today, Trig Hill – reached by the so-called **hundred steps** leading up from Lebuh Empat – still has the feel of a leafy colonial refuge, and offers views out across the sea to the far side of Sandakan Bay. Its showpiece is the **Agnes Keith House**, a shrine to the American writer whose works (see p.587) introduced many in the West to the peoples of Borneo. The building isn't the actual one Keith wrote about, but a spacious two-storey postwar replacement where she and her husband stayed on their second stint in Sabah. Over-restoration and air conditioning have rendered the museum rather sterile, and the vintage furnishings, including a writing desk that sports a sewing machine, are unconvincing – but if it gets you to seek out Keith's three books, on sale

SANDAKAN

SANDAKAN

0 / 50 metres

Turtle Island Jetty (500m), Sim-Sim Water Village & (2.5km)

(50m) & Agnes Keith House (250m)

Turtle Island Jetty (500m), Sim-Sim Water Village & (2.5km)

Central Market

Maybank

Harbour Mall

Four Points by Sheraton

HARBOUR SQUARE

JALAN BULI SIM-SIM

LEBUH EMPAT

Wisma Khoo Siak Chiew

Masjid Jamek

Wisma Sandakan

LEBUH EMPAT

Wyk Laundry

Police Station

Sandakan Town Council

Public Bank

Sandakan Museum

CIMB Bank

Standard Chartered Bank

Borneo Dispensary

Local Bus Station

Malaysian Navy

Customs

Hundred Steps

Courthouse

JALAN UTARA

Centre Point Mall

Minibuses to Sim-Sim Water Village

Sam Sing Kung Temple

Recreation Club

Padang Bandaran Sandakan

JALAN LEILA

Hokkien Association

St Michael's & All Angels

St Mary Catholic Church

Tun Abdul Razak Memorial Park

SULU SEA

JALAN COASTAL 1

JALAN ELOPURA

JALAN TIGA

JALAN TIGA

JALAN EMPAT

JALAN PRYER

JALAN LIMA

JALAN PELABUHAN LAMA

JALAN COASTAL 1

JALAN SINGAPURA

JALAN PADANG

LEBUH EMPAT

LEBUH TIGA

N

● EATING
7-Heaven Dessert Parlour	2
Ba Lin	6
Borneo Ethnic Cuisine	1
English Tea House	3
My Harbour	8
Nam Choon	5
San Da Gen Café	7
Seafood Sim-Sim 88	4

■ ACCOMMODATION
Four Points By Sheraton	7
Harbourside Backpackers	2
Marine Bay	5
May Fair	3
Nak Hotel	4
Sabah	1
Sandakan Backpackers	6

■ DRINKING
Best Brew	1

● SHOPPING
Borneo in Books	2
Harbour Mall	1

7

Karamunting Jetty (4km)

(1km), (6km), (6.4km), Long-Distance Bus Station, Sandakan Memorial Park (13km) & Sepilok (25km) all over Sabah, it will have done its job.

Around the Padang

Close to the **Padang** are a couple of the oldest buildings in town. On the northern side, the Taoist **Sam Sing Kung Temple** (daily 7am–3pm; free), completed in 1887, is dedicated to three deities – Liu Bei, Guan Yu and Zhang Fei – who were the heroes of the fourteenth-century *Romance of the Three Kingdoms*. On a hilltop west of here and reachable by steps off Jalan Singapura, the Anglican **St Michael's and All Angels Church** (Mon & Wed–Sat 8.30am–4.30pm; RM10) still has something of the feel of an English country church. Although it dates back to 1893, its most notable features are the lurid stained-glass remembrance windows, commemorating Allied war dead, and the POW chapel dotted with regimental plaques.

Sim-Sim Water Village

Jalan Buli Sim-Sim • Look for minibuses signed "Sim-Sim" from Jalan Coastal or take a taxi (around RM15)

The **Sim-Sim Water Village** is split into a sprawling Muslim section starting 1km east of the centre, and a Chinese one 2.5km away; their numbered boardwalks are respectively signed jambatan (bridge) and lorong (lane). Most visitors are here for the seafood served up by several restaurants in the Chinese section (see p.430). The set-up feels not dissimilar to Penang's clan jetties (see p.156), with a grid of boardwalks laid out over the sea, flanked by largely timber houses. If your aim is to wander around and take pictures, be sensitive about residents' privacy, as the lanes take you right past their windows.

Sandakan Memorial Park

Mile 7, 11km west of Sandakan • Daily 9am–5pm • Free • Any bus displaying 7 or higher; taxi from the town centre RM30

Sandakan Memorial Park marks the site of the World War II POW camp where the infamous **death marches** began. In 1942, around 2700 British and Australian soldiers were sent from Singapore to Sandakan and set to work building an airstrip. They were kept in appalling conditions and around three hundred had already died by early 1945, when the decision was made to relocate them to Ranau (260km away through mud and jungle). Around five hundred prisoners died on three forced marches, while many more perished after they arrived in Ranau or – if ill or injured – were left behind to die in Sandakan. In the end only six soldiers, all Australian, survived.

Signboards provide explanations for the few scattered remnants of the camp, while a small but moving museum covers the harsh conditions in the camp and the actual marches. If you are interested in a cycling tour that covers part of the death march route, contact **TYK Adventure Tours** in KK (☏088 232821, ⓦtykadventuretours.com).

ARRIVAL AND DEPARTURE   SANDAKAN

By plane Sandakan's airport is 11km north of town, and a taxi into the centre from here costs about RM30. Buses hardly serve the airport, although occasional shared minivans do set off for the main road into town, where you can pick up onward transport or hop on a minibus bound for Sepilok (any vehicle displaying the number 14 or higher; see p.429).
Destinations KK (6–7 daily; 45min); KL (4 daily; 2hr 45min); Kudat (3 weekly; 50min); Tawau (1 daily; 30min).
By bus The expected transfer of the long-distance bus station to a new terminal at Mile 2 1/2 was several years overdue at the time of research. In the meantime, express buses are using a makeshift car park in the new suburb of Litat Jaya, which is a RM20 taxi ride away from

the centre. Mile 4 buses signed "Taman Mesra" will drop you here on request, but to head back to town you may need to catch an outbound Mile 4 bus, as it will turn around sooner or later.
Destinations Kinabalu Park (at least 12 daily; 5hr); KK (at least 12 daily; 6hr 30min); Kudat (Mon, Thurs & Sat 8.15am; 5hr); Lahad Datu (at least 4 daily; 3hr); Semporna (at least 4 daily; 5hr); Tawau (at least 4 daily; 5hr); Telupid (at least 12 daily; 2hr 30min).
By minivan The only out-of-town service of interest to travellers is a private minivan to Sukau (☏019 536 1889), leaving around 12.30pm from Lorong Satu.
By ferry Aleson Shipping (☏089 216996, ⓦaleson -shipping.com) operates services to the Phillippines

(RM280 economy) from the Karamunting Jetty, 4km southwest of town via any Pasir Putih-bound minivan.

Destinations Zamboanga (Philippines; Tues afternoons; 20hr).

GETTING AROUND

By shared van or minibus Shared vans depart from Lebua Dua, and are much faster than the ageing minibuses that use the bus station on Jalan Pryer. As ever, transport grinds to a halt around dusk.

By taxi It's not hard to find a taxi on the main streets or outside hotels, and you can expect to pay a minimum fare of RM10; a trip to Sepilok will cost you around RM50. Grab cars (ⓦ grab.com/my) are, as ever, better value.

By car If you'd like to rent a car, you can try Borneo Express, which has a base at the airport (ⓣ 016 886 0789, ⓦ borneocar.com).

INFORMATION

Addresses As there's only one main road out of town (Jalan Utara), most suburban addresses include a distance along it – in miles (*batu*). Likewise, the numbers displayed by many minibuses and vans aren't routes, but how far in miles they go up that main road before turning off into one suburb or another. To reach a Mile 6 suburb, you should catch any vehicle numbered six or higher – but make sure you know the right spot on the main road to get off. To avoid what might be a long walk, it's safest to ride only a Mile 6 bus that also displays the name of the suburb you want.

Internet access If you need a reliable spot to check your emails, try Sandakan Cybercafé Wisma Sandakan, Lebuh Empat.

Tourist information The *San Da Gen Café* (see p.430) has an informal information point with leaflets, and staff can also offer basic transport and sightseeing tips. Local travel firms have put together an information app called The Sandakan (Android only at the time of research).

ACCOMMODATION

Central Sandakan has several worthwhile places to stay, although it's feasible to base yourself at Sepilok instead (see p.431) and take a day-trip into town.

★**Four Points By Sheraton** Eastern end of Harbour Square ⓣ 089 244888, ⓦ fourpointssandakan.com; map p.427. Sandakan's most upmarket hotel is a steal – the rooms are undoubtedly plush, there are good wining and dining options, and the view from the rooftop infinity pool over the town and the bay, ringed by green hills, is unrivalled. ⓦ **RM300**

Harbourside Backpackers Harbour Square ⓣ 089 217072, ⓦ harboursidebackpackers.com; map p.427. This is a good-value hostel with sleek bathrooms and dorm beds that all have their own power points. There's also an assortment of private rooms – pay twenty percent more for an en suite. ⓦ Dorms **RM30**, doubles **RM70**

Marine Bay Harbour Square, opposite the Central Market ⓣ 089 203339; map p.427. This is a cheapish hotel with predictably unexciting rooms, but it's clean, well kept and fairly snug. Pay RM20 extra for a sea view. ⓦ **RM110**

May Fair First floor, 24 Jalan Pryer ⓣ 089 219855; map p.427. An old-fashioned cheapie with rather eccentric owners, at least a dozen electrical sockets in each room and a

---

SANDAKAN TOUR OPERATORS

Sandakan's tour operators tend to focus on **packages** involving resorts that they run, notably around the Kinabatangan River (see p.434) or Sepilok (see p.431), but they usually offer other trips, too.

Borneo Sandakan Tours Harbour Square ⓣ 089 215754, ⓦ borneosandakan.com. Offers trips to all the key attractions of eastern Sabah and elsewhere across the state.

Pulau Sipadan Resort and Tours Mile 6, on the main road opposite the Giant supermarket ⓣ 089 673999, ⓦ dive-malaysia.com. Besides the nearby *Sepilok Nature Resort* and the *Lankayan Island Dive Resort* off the coast here, they also run resorts at Sipadan and Kapalai islands off Semporna.

Sepilok Tropical Wildlife Adventure Eastern end of Lebuh Tiga ⓣ 089 271077, ⓦ stwadventure.com. Well-established operator that runs *Bilit Adventure Lodge* on the Kinabatangan River, plus *Sepilok Jungle Resort*.

SI Tours Block Harbour Square ⓣ 089 213502, ⓦ sitoursborneo.com. Runs *Kinabatangan Riverside Lodge* and a second lodge on the Kinabatangan River, as well as offering tours.

Sukau Greenview Block Harbour Square ⓣ 089 212912, ⓦ sukaugreenview.net. Runs the inexpensive *Sukau Greenview B&B* on the Kinabatangan River.

7

vast hoard of DVDs. All rooms are a/c and en suite – try to get one that's well removed from the reception's TV. 📶 RM60

★**Nak Hotel** Jalan Pelabuhan Lama ☎089 272988, ⓦnakhotel.com; map p.427. If there's a glimmer of a revival in the town centre, this wannabe boutique hotel is it – though don't expect Penang-style slickness. There are some vintage Chinese touches such as the colourful chests in the lobby and blue-and-white porcelain sinks in the rooms, and the café and rooftop restaurant are excellent. 📶 RM140

Sabah On the main road, 1.5km north of the centre ☎089 213299, ⓦsabahhotel.com.my; map p.427.

Venerable hotel with restaurants, a swimming pool and various sports facilities, all set within lush grounds spread up a low hill. The walk into town isn't that convenient, though. RM170

★**Sandakan Backpackers** Harbour Square ☎089 211213, ⓦsandakanbackpackershostel.com; map p.427. Snazzy wall art added by past guests aside, the decor here isn't particularly vibrant, though there's a leafy terrace with great bay views, and the owners are friendly and really know their city – you will genuinely feel right at home. Pay a little extra for an en suite or sea view. 📶 Dorms RM35, doubles RM70

EATING

There are a handful of worthwhile restaurants and *kedai kopis* in Sandakan's centre, but it's out in the **suburbs** – especially at Mile 4 and Mile 6 – that you'll find the full range of outlets you'd expect in most large Malaysian towns. There are also a few seafood places out over the water in the Chinese section of the **Sim-Sim Water Village**, east of town, plus two **markets** mainly selling cooked meals and snacks: one in Kim Fung (a Mile 4 neighbourhood; Sat 5–9pm, with a cultural performance by a school group most weeks), the other at Lebuh Dua in the centre (Sun 7am–1pm or so).

7-Heaven Dessert Parlour In the grid of blocks about 200m up Jalan Cicely North, Bandar Indah, Mile 4 ☎089 220326; map p.427. This place isn't worth a special trip unless you have a very sweet tooth, but there's a huge range of ice cream and frozen yoghurts in flavours like green tea, as well as sinful sundaes (around RM10) and cakes. Mon–Thurs & Sun noon–5.30pm & 7–10.30pm, Fri & Sat noon–5.30pm & 7–11.30pm.

★**Ba Lin** Nak Hotel, Jalan Pelahuban Lama ☎089 272988, ⓦbalin-sandakan.com; map p.427. Hearty quantities of inventive Western cuisine in stylish surroundings – this rooftop bar-restaurant ticks all the boxes. The pizzas (from RM25), with unorthodox toppings such as pumpkin and pine nuts or salmon and crab, are terrific, as are the daily specials such as stewed lamb shank (RM60). There's an extensive brunch menu (until 5pm) and a range of cocktails, too. Happy hour 3–7pm. Daily 9am–midnight.

★**Borneo Ethnic Cuisine** Jalan Cicely North, Bandar Indah, Mile 4 ☎010 933 5980, ⓦfacebook .com/borneoethniccuisine; map p.427. This simple restaurant, with walls adorned with woven baskets and hats, is a terrific place to try Kadazan/Dusun cuisine. The extensive menu includes classics like *sup nangka ayam* (chicken soup with chewy young jackfruit), *kerabu pakis* (fern stir-fried with coconut) and the smelly, unripe-mango-like *bambangan*, plus a smattering of Malay and Chinese standards. Wash it all down with the special ginger/lemon grass drink or *tapai* (rice wine). You can eat well for RM20/person. Closed every other Tues. Daily 11.30am–10.30pm.

English Tea House Jalan Istana ☎089 222544, ⓦenglishteahouse.org; map p.427. Sited near the Agnes Keith House and with a lawn crying out for croquet,

this bungalow restaurant majors on English favourites including shepherd's pie and tea for two with sandwiches, scones, jam and cream (RM30). The service can spoil the fantasy. Daily 10am–10pm.

My Harbour Harbour Square ☎016 367 6499; map p.427. One of several inexpensive, so-so places for a waterfront meal, with Chinese noodle options like *watan ho* (flat, white noodles with a gooey, eggy coating), plus seafood and meat stir-fried in any of about two dozen sauces. Most dishes under RM15. Daily 8am–8.30pm.

Nam Choon Northern end of Lebuh Tiga; map p.427. One of not that many surviving old-school *kedai kopis* in the centre, serving four dishes: chicken rice; *nasi paha-paha atas* (the same, with chicken on the bone), *nasi* fish balls and *nasi ikan* (with fish). Each dish is brilliant and costs just a few ringgit. Mon–Sat 6am–3pm.

★**San Da Gen Café** Nak Hotel, Jalan Pelahuban Lama ☎089 272988; map p.427. With its marble tables and pristine floor tiles, *San Da Gen* blends the best of the old *kedai kopis* with modern decor. The menu concentrates on hawker standards with veggie variants (most dishes around RM10). It's also one place to try a Sandakan speciality whose Chinese name literally means "cowdung tart" – more attractively branded here as the UFO tart, with a disc-shaped sponge topped with a "cabin" formed of a meringue ring enclosing custard. Daily 8am–5pm.

Seafood Sim-Sim 88 Lorong 8, Sim-Sim Water Village ☎017 816 2283; map p.427. One of the most popular of the various restaurants in the Sim-Sim Water Village, with lots of open-air tables and colourfully lit tanks of marine creatures awaiting an encounter with the wok. Daily 7.30am–9.30pm.

DRINKING

Best Brew Four Points By Sheraton, Harbour Square ☎089 244602; map p.427. It might be a bit slick for some tastes, but this hotel bar has outside tables for sea views, plus a pool table and electronic darts machines inside. Mon–Thurs & Sun 5pm–midnight, Fri & Sat 5pm–2am.

SHOPPING

Borneo In Books Ground floor, Four Points by Sheraton hotel ☎089 219739; map p.427. Sells not just books but also its own range of locally sourced cultured pearls. Daily 8am–7pm.

Harbour Mall The waterfront; map p.427. This mall is admittedly a bit of a let-down, but has the usual necessities plus a Mr DIY outlet with a few basic camping/outdoor goods. Daily 10am–10pm.

DIRECTORY

Banks Maybank is on Jalan Pryer at the northern end of Harbour Square, and there's a handful of other banks dotted about the centre.
Hospital Try the Duchess of Kent, on the main road 2km north of the centre (☎089 248600).
Laundry Wyk Express at the start of Lebuh Empat is coin-operated and open 24hr.
Pharmacy You can find Guardian and Watsons at Harbour Mall.

Police The main police station is on the main road 1.5 km from town (☎089 211222) with a smaller one on Lebuh Empat.
Post office Off Jalan Leila, just beyond Tun Abdul Razak Memorial Park (Mon–Fri 8am–4.30pm, Sat 8am–12.30pm).
Visa extensions Immigration Department, Wisma Persekutuan, Mile 7 (☎089 668328).

Sepilok

SEPILOK, 22km west up the main road from Sandakan, is a rural, partly forested area that clings on to some of Malaysia's most celebrated **wildlife**, among them rhinoceros hornbills and, famously, orang-utans. A 3km turning south off the main road gives access to three fine attractions: the **Sepilok Orang-utan Rehabilitation Centre** is the most well-known, but also worthwhile are the **Bornean Sun Bear Conservation Centre**, devoted to the world's smallest bear species, and the **Rainforest Discovery Centre**, part very wild town park, part forest reserve. There's also plenty of accommodation in Sepilok, so it's no wonder many visitors base themselves here rather than Sandakan.

Sepilok Orang-utan Rehabilitation Centre

At the end of the Sepilok road • Mon–Thurs, Sat & Sun 9am–noon & 2–4pm, Fri 9–11am & 2–4pm; feeding times 10am & 3pm • RM30; photo pass RM10 • ☎089 531180, ⓦ wildlife.sabah.gov.my

Occupying a 43-square-kilometre patch of lowland rainforest, the **Sepilok Orang-utan Rehabilitation Centre** is one of just a few such sanctuaries and a standard stop on Sabah's tourist trail. Most of the orang-utans here are victims of forest clearance; many have been orphaned, injured or traumatized in the process. Some have been illegally kept as pets, so their survival instincts remain undeveloped. The training the centre gives them in fending for themselves has led to many successful reintroductions to the wild.

There are several chances to observe these animals, designated as critically endangered in 2016: at a glass-fronted viewing gallery as they hone their climbing skills on a rope course; on trails through the trees (where their nests, at least, can be seen) and at the **feeding station** where they are offered only bananas to ensure they keep foraging. Don't be alarmed by a poor turnout: it can point to the health of the forest and its food sources.

Bornean Sun Bear Conservation Centre

Opposite the Orang-utan Rehabilitation Centre • Daily 9am–3.30pm • RM32; photo pass RM10 • ☎089 534491, ⓦ www.bsbcc.org.my

Like orang-utans, sun bears are vulnerable – either because their adorable, teddy-like appearance makes them attractive as pets, or because traditional medicine calls for their body parts – and rescued ones need to relearn life skills. This is where the **Bornean Sun Bear Conservation Centre** comes in, housing some forty animals in woodland enclosures, a small number of which the public can view. The place is the brainchild of Penang biologist Wong Siew Te, who tours the site most days and talks to visitors. Spotting scopes on the elevated boardwalks capture great close-up footage of the bears if you let staff hold your camera up against the eyepiece.

Rainforest Discovery Centre

2km down the Sepilok road and then 700m west along Jalan Fabia • Daily 8am–5pm, site closes 8pm • RM15; Kabili trail permit RM15; night walk RM30 • ☎ 089 533780, ⊛ forest.sabah.gov.my/rdc

At first sight, the **Rainforest Discovery Centre** is a disappointingly landscaped version of the jungle, with an all-too-immaculate lake in the middle. The **canopy walkway** is, however, pretty impressive, a 347m series of substantial aerial bridges from where you might spot brightly coloured trogons and other birds, and perhaps giant squirrels. Take the lake anticlockwise (bear right towards the café from the entrance) to complete the circuit at the nicely air-conditioned visitor building, which has exhibits on rainforest ecology and a mini botanical garden close by. If you sign up for the guided **night walk** (Mon–Fri only), you might just see flying squirrels, slow lorises and (rarely) tarsiers.

It's worth venturing beyond these core sights if you've time. Instead of turning left at the café for the canopy walkway, turn right for a series of signposted trails where the star attraction is the **Sepilok giant**, a 65m *Shorea* tree (allow 40min one-way). A full-scale trek is also possible on the **Kabili trail** (permit required), which terminates 8km from the lake.

ARRIVAL AND DEPARTURE

SEPILOK

By bus Sepilok is at Mile 14 on the Sandakan road, so any bus numbered 14 or higher from town can drop you at the start of the turning; express buses bound for Sandakan will do the same on the north side of the main road. Only the sporadic Mile 14 bus (5–6 daily) travels the full 3km of the Sepilok road. To flag down express buses for the rest of Sabah (routes are as for Sandakan, see p.429), wait at the start of the turning.

By taxi A taxi between Sepilok and Sandakan should cost around RM50.

ACCOMMODATION

Keen competition means Sepilok's accommodation is generally good value. Rates include breakfast except where stated.

Nature Lodge Sepilok 1.5km south of the main road ☎089 535889, ⊛insabah.com/nature-lodge-sepilok. On its own little hillock, this assembly of buildings has surprisingly slick rooms, some with open-air bathrooms at the back opening onto private patches of greenery. There are four-bed dorms, too. ≋ Dorms RM32, doubles RM160

★**Paganakan Dii Tropical Retreat** Taman Hiburan Jalil Alip, a private forest track 2km northwest of the Sepilok turning ☎012 868 1005, ⊛paganakandii.com. A brilliant jungle hilltop haven, this timber and bamboo complex boasts slick chalets with a/c and open-air bathrooms (RM160), plus cheaper longhouse-style fan rooms and dorms. Facilities include an elevated open-air lounge area, a lookout tower and zip line. Breakfast included; other meals from RM15 or so. ≋ Dorms RM32, doubles RM165

★**Sepilok B&B** Jalan Fabia ☎089 534050, ⊛sepilokbednbreakfast.com.my. A friendly place with timber lodges and chalets set in sprawling grounds. The decor isn't the most lavish, but some units come with sizeable living rooms and kitchens that more than compensate. There's also a campsite (own tent required) and dorms (though you'll have to pay a bit extra if you want a/c and hot water). Only campers pay for breakfast. ≋ Camping per person RM20, dorms RM45, doubles RM140

Sepilok Forest Edge Resort 700m up Jalan Rambutan, a turning 2.5km from the main road ☎089 533190, ⊛sepilokforestedgeresort.com. This place has small dorms and a series of appealing chalets, some boasting open-air showers, all dotted around a multilevel landscaped garden with a plunge pool. Their *Nest* restaurant serves up sophisticated takes on local cuisine, plus fusion creations such as lamb shank in a Thai curry sauce; mains from RM20. ≋ Dorms RM45, chalets RM300

Sepilok Jungle Resort 200m up Jalan Rambutan ☎089 533031, ⊛sepilokjungleresort.com. A large complex with its own lake, somewhat dated faux timber dorms and rooms, and a pool (RM35 for non-guests). If you take a double room, a/c will cost you around RM65 extra. ≋ Dorms RM40, doubles RM85

Sepilok Nature Resort Jalan Sepilok, close to the Orang-utan Rehabilitation Centre ☎089 535001, ⊛sepilok.com. The plushest place to stay in Sepilok, with spacious and eco-aware chalets nestled amid lush jungle. The restaurant, looking out on to the resort's lake, is predictably on the pricey side (main courses from RM25). Rates exclude breakfast. 🛜 RM320

Uncle Tan's B&B 300m down the Sepilok road ☎016 824 4749, ⒲uncletan.com. This place has a stream running through the grounds and has long been a favourite with backpackers because its rates include meals. It closed early in 2018, but its owners intend to relaunch accommodation in the near future. They also offer packages at their Kinabatangan River set-up and provide a free shuttle to the Orang-utan Rehabilitation Centre. 🛜 Dorms RM50, doubles RM110

Labuk Bay Proboscis Monkey Sanctuary

Near Samawang, a kampung 15km up a signed turning 30km (i.e. at Mile 19) up the Sandakan road • Daily 9am–5.30pm; feeding times: platform A 9.30am & 2.30pm, platform B 11.30am & 4.30pm • RM60; RM10 camera permit • ☎ 089 672133, ⒲ proboscis.cc • Shuttle minibus (RM20 one way) leaves Sandakan 8am, Sepilok 10.30am, returning at 3pm & 5pm • Taxi from Sandakan RM80 (or RM200 both ways, with a wait)

Set amid mangrove forest and reached via a track through an oil-palm plantation, **Labuk Bay Proboscis Monkey Sanctuary** functions as a companion to the more famous orang-utan sanctuary at Sepilok. Most visitors come on a **day-trip** from Sandakan or Sepilok, which is significantly closer, but it's also possible to stay **overnight**.

Two large observation platforms offer perfect vantage points from which to view the monkeys (see p.457); you might also see silverleaf monkeys scavenge fruit left behind, and there's some fantastic birdlife including hornbills. On a day-trip you could see all four feedings if you like, or even leave after just one, but it's more usual to see one from each platform. Using the shuttle bus makes sense as the site is quite spread out, and it will take you to two feedings and the restaurant at lunchtime.

ACCOMMODATION AND EATING
LABUK BAY

Nipah Resort Labuk Bay ☎089 672133, ⒲labukbay. com.my. Amid the tangle of mangroves of Labuk Bay, with eight chalets sleeping two, a couple of three-bedroom family units and a couple of longer buildings with fan-cooled dorms. Rates include breakfast at the restaurant, which serves fairly standard rice, noodle and stir-fry offerings. Dorms RM35, doubles RM180, chalets RM550

Lankayan Island

Ninety minutes' boat ride north of Sandakan in the Sulu Sea lies the **Sugud Islands Marine Conservation Area**, managed by a Sandakan nonprofit organization called Reef Guardian (⒲reefguardian.com.my). Only one of its three islands, **Lankayan Island**, is visitable, with a delightful resort and an active turtle-hatching programme; that said, **diving** and **snorkelling** are the real pull. Hard and soft corals surround the island and are in very good condition, and the macro life in particular is excellent. Divers may see whale sharks in April and May.

ACCOMMODATION
LANKAYAN ISLAND

Lankayan Island Dive Resort c/o Pulau Sipadan Resort and Tours (see p.429 for details); ☎089 278000, ⒲lankayan-island.com. This is a delightful resort with large, comfortable chalets, helpful staff and a competently run dive shop. The rate shown here is for a two-night package for two, including transfers from Sandakan and the conservation fee – you should add an extra RM1000 to the price if you'd like to try your hand at diving here. RM4100

Turtle Islands Park

Trips operated by Crystal Quest ☎ 089 212711, ✉ cquest1996@gmail.com; enquire for latest prices or book through a travel agent

Peeping out of the Sulu Sea 40km north of Sandakan is the **Turtle Islands Park**, where green and hawksbill turtles haul themselves laboriously above the high-tide mark to bury their clutches of eggs most nights. Although all three of the islands – Selingan,

Bakungan Kecil and Gulisan – hold **hatcheries**, tourists can only visit **Selingan**; full-board overnight packages offer accommodation in 25 double rooms, all en suite and with air conditioning.

Before dark (when a beach curfew kicks in) there's plenty of time for **swimming**, **snorkelling** and **sunbathing**. At night, besides seeing a mother turtle laying her eggs, you can watch as the park wardens release hatchling turtles that waddle, Chaplin-like, into the sea.

Along the Kinabatangan River

Sabah's longest waterway, the 560km **Kinabatangan River**, ends its journey to the Sulu Sea southeast of Sandakan Bay. Whereas logging has had an impact on the river's ecology upstream, the area covered by the **Lower Kinabatangan Wildlife Sanctuary** offers some of the state's best opportunities for seeing wildlife – days of trekking in Sabah's jungle reserves may yield paltry rewards by comparison.

Day-trips from Sandakan and Sepilok are possible with some tour operators (see p.429), but tend to offer just one river trip bookended by meals – it's far better to book at least a one-night package to get an evening and a morning crack at the river or a trek. With a few exceptions, most lodges are located either in or around the villages of **Sukau** or **Bilit**, from either of which you can visit the **Gomantong Caves**, where edible swiftlet nests are harvested. Note that from November to February, rainy-season floods can disrupt trips or close some lodges.

Lower Kinabatangan Wildlife Sanctuary

The last 70km or so of the Kinabatangan River forms the **Lower Kinabatangan Wildlife Sanctuary**, a large forested floodplain, peppered with oxbow lakes and mangrove swamps. The designation of 260 square kilometres of land close to the river as the reserve in 2005 was commendable, but it is still broken up into eleven pockets interspersed with villages of the local **Orang Sungai** (literally "river people") and oil palm plantations. Policing remains a headache: in 2013 a plantation was illegally extended, and there have been sporadic discoveries of dismembered sun bear carcasses, the handiwork of poachers. At least there was one success in 2017 when, following opposition from conservationists – including David Attenborough – the state government scrapped a planned road bridge over the river at Sukau that would, opponents argued, have seriously impeded the movement of animals.

For now, the sanctuary offers visitors a half-decent chance of seeing **mammals** such as pygmy elephants, orang-utans, proboscis monkeys, macaques and gibbons; dolphins are occasionally seen near the river mouth (away from most lodges). The resident **birdlife** is as impressive, including hornbills, brahminy kites, crested serpent eagles, egrets, exquisite blue-banded and stork-billed kingfishers, and oriental darters, which dive for food and then sit on the shore, their wings stretched out to dry. Some lodges offer **night cruises** with opportunities to photograph owls and sleeping birds using floodlights.

Gomantong Caves

Reached by a 4.7km turning off the Sukau road, 19km east of the main road • Daily 8am–6pm • RM30; camera permit RM30 • ☎ 019 882 0759, ⓦ wildlife.sabah.gov.my • Without your own transport, take a Sukau-bound minivan from Sandakan to the start of the turning and walk/hitch the rest of the way.

The **Gomantong Caves** are inhabited by swiftlets whose nests, formed of hardened saliva, are harvested for the bird's-nest-soup trade (usually February to April and July to September). There are nineteen limestone caves in all, and they're also home to a huge number of **bats** that emerge at dusk in sinewy streams – although visits as part of Kinabatangan packages are never timed for this.

Tourists usually visit **Simud Hitam**, the "black cave", which gets its name because it mostly contains dark nests produced by the black-nest swiftlet. It's quite an impressive chamber, and of scientific interest because recent laser- and drone-mapping suggests that the acidic bird and bat guano has substantially enlarged the cave over millennia by speeding erosion. That said, the stinky guano attracts hordes of cockroaches that crunch underfoot or crawl on your feet, so sandals aren't a good idea; some visitors don ponchos, in addition to the helmets provided, to keep extra-clean. The even larger **Simud Putih** beyond, from where the bats emerge, is generally closed to all but nest collectors, who head there for the more valuable constructions of the white-nest swiftlet.

Sukau and Bilit

SUKAU, 134km from Sandakan, was where the first tourist lodges on the Kinabatangan opened. Linked to the main road by its own sealed one, the village sits on the north bank of the river and is a particular target for independent travellers. By dint of its popularity, however, Sukau is not the place to seek solitude, with dozens of boats on this stretch of river at peak times. If this doesn't appeal, **BILIT** lies a little further upriver and remains a quiet place to stay – it can be reached by a turning off the Sukau road.

ARRIVAL AND DEPARTURE

By tour Tour operators generally arrange transport to their respective lodges from Sandakan and Sepilok, as well as boat transfers – sometimes all the way from Sandakan – for lodges on the right bank.

By bus If you're travelling independently or arriving from somewhere other than Sandakan or Sepilok, you can reach Sukau by public transport. Any express bus plying the main east-coast road – en route between KK/Sandakan and Lahad

ALONG THE KINABATANGAN RIVER

Datu and beyond – can drop you at the Sukau turning, 89km from Sandakan, from where Sukau minivans travel the remaining 45km to the village (45min; RM20). For Bilit, arrange with your accommodation to be picked up at the Sukau turning. If you're departing, you'll need to ask around about the best time to be back at the main road, as buses tend to leave in clusters – there's usually a group of southbound buses departing daily between 9 and 9.30am, for example.

ACCOMMODATION

Kinabatangan package accommodation ranges from swanky **timber lodges** with eco-friendly credentials to fairly basic affairs, and this is one part of Malaysia where **homestays** (see p.38) are worth considering. Single-night packages always offer an evening boat ride plus a short trek or a second cruise at dawn the next day, and can be totally satisfying if a bit rushed. Two-night packages may only cost thirty percent more and generally include three boat rides, plus a trek and sometimes the Gomantong Caves. Independent travellers can save money by choosing a B&B or homestay and then adding boat trips (from RM50) and activities as desired. Don't expect cheaper places to serve **alcohol**, and make sure you dress conservatively if you choose a homestay – the local Orang Sungai are largely Muslim. Unless otherwise stated, all **prices** are for two people sharing and include all meals and transport to/from Sandakan.

SUKAU AND AROUND

Borneo Nature Lodge ☎089 210718, ⓦ borneonaturelodge.com.my. This mid-range option, attractively surrounded by tall trees, has its own observation tower and a/c restaurant – a rarity in these parts. RM1950

Kinabatangan Riverside Lodge ☎089 213502, ⓦ www.sitoursborneo.com. A slick timber affair whose bougainvillea-laden decking adds a splash of colour to the river. The two-night package includes trips to see the orang-utans and sun bears in Sepilok and boat transfers to/from Sandakan. RM4500

★**Sukau Greenview B&B** At the end of the Sukau road ☎089 212912, ⓦ sukaugreenview.net. This place is cheap and cheerful and thus popular with independent travellers, although you get what you pay for – boats are a little older and English-speaking guides occasionally have

to be shared between them. Rooms and dorms are unremarkable but all have a/c and bathrooms. What makes this a good deal is that their one-night package squeezes in three boat rides, one by night (RM335 with dorm; RM720 with double). Dorms RM45, doubles RM120

Sukau Rainforest Lodge ☎088 438300, ⓦ sukau .com. This has been a sound choice for many years, as it has its own spa and a range of recreational activities including batik painting. Their boats are some of the speediest, giving them an edge whenever wildlife heaves into view. Two-night packages are the basic option, but given that they are run by birding specialist Borneo Eco Tours, there's also a three-night birdwatching package. 🛜 RM3650

Village View Homestay Various locations ☎013 869 9026, ⓦ sukauhomestay.com. This homestay programme arranges B&B accommodation, to which you can add other meals (RM15 each) and boat trips. B&B RM80

extra/person. Dorms RM400, chalets RM1000

BILIT AND AROUND

Bilit Adventure Lodge ☎089 271077, ⊛stwadventure.com. This was the first lodge to open in Bilit and is still popular, with two dozen fairly simple en-suite rooms, some with a/c. The owners have a sense of humour: if you get bitten by a leech, you'll be awarded a blood donor certificate. Price is for a one-night package including the Gomantong Caves. RM1100

Bilit Homestay Programme Various locations ☎013 891 3078, ⊛bilithomestay.wordpress.com. The usual options, including one boat trip plus a dawn trek if you're on their one-nighter; other activities such as fishing and night treks on request. Prices vary depending on numbers, so call them to discuss. RM350

Kinabatangan Jungle Camp (KJC) ☎089 220299 or ☎016 826 9088, ⊛kinabatanganjunglecamp.com. The rooms here are fairly simple en-suite affairs, minus a/c, but owner Robert Chong offers specialist birding and photographic tours in addition to the usual trips. RM1000

★**Last Frontier** ☎016 676 5922, ⊛thelastfrontierresort.com. This chic guesthouse is set on a jungle-swathed hill, only accessible via 538 steps (ask about porters if you need help with your luggage). There are just four rooms, which all offer excellent views over the surrounding plains. Packages include river trips (only one on the one-night option). Transfers from Sandakan cost extra – RM40/person one way. RM1000

Myne Resort ☎089 278288, ⊛myne.com.my. This place offers an attractive clump of chalets and slightly cheaper longhouse rooms nestled amid the forest, as well as an airy restaurant and a huge-range of add-on activities, including cycling and night walks. Price is for a one-night package including the Sepilok Orang-utan Rehabilitation Centre and the Gomantong Caves. 📶 RM1900

Nature Lodge Kinabatangan On the eastern bank near Bilit ☎088 230534, ⊛naturelodgekinabatangan.com. This good-value option has one wing of dorms and another of quite pleasant chalets, a few with a/c. If you're staying two nights, you can enjoy an optional jungle trek to an oxbow lake an hour away (RM27/person), and you can also do a spot of kayaking (free). Transfers from Sandakan or Sepilok cost RM40

OTHER LOCATIONS

Danau Tanjung Bulat Jungle Camp At the Tanjung Bulat oxbow lake, west of the main road and south of Kota Kinabatangan ☎016 812 0704, ⊛oxbowlakeborneo.simplesite.com. A basic timber lodge with a dorm consisting of mattresses on a raised platform, plus some private rooms. They do the usual two- and three-night deals, with Gomantong Caves as an option, and can pick guests up near the town of Kota Kinabatangan. One-night package per person RM300

★**Miso Walai Homestay/Tungog Rainforest Eco Camp** Mengaris village, near the road bridge over the Kinabatangan ☎089 551064, ⊛misowalaihomestay. com. Also known as *Mescot*, the name of the overall community initiative, this excellent scheme offers a choice of village homestay with activities paid for separately, and basic rainforest camp with the usual boat trips plus a trek, and optional trips to funerary caves nearby. Visitors can also sign up for their volunteer programme, doing anything from building maintenance to tree-planting. Full board, per person: homestay RM70, rainforest camp two-night package RM500

Moido Waloi Homestay Abai, near the rivermouth and 45km from Sandakan ☎014 674 6619, ⊛moidowaloihomestay.com. Besides the usual evening river trip, the basic package here includes a night-time firefly cruise plus either tree-planting or a dawn cruise the next day. During the rainy season there's an optional trip to try to spot river dolphins (RM150 per person). Prices plunge if there are more guests; one night for just two people costs RM1500

Uncle Tan's Wildlife Camp Beside the Lokan River, a Kinabatangan tributary ☎016 824 4749, ⊛uncletan .com. "The camp is not exactly the *Hilton*" is the owners' own description of their camp in the wilds, where the huts are elevated against floods and lack doors and windows. Electricity is by night only. Still, this is as close as you'll get to a back-to-nature experience here, and they also offer morning and evening river trips and treks. Price is for a one-night package per person. RM375

Lahad Datu and around

Tiny **LAHAD DATU** is a bland but pleasant enough seaside town on the northern shore of **Darvel Bay**, 173km from Sandakan by road. The town has been a magnet at times for Indonesian and Filipino migrants, often undocumented, who come to work on plantations and in the construction industry, and in 2013 the place hit headlines when the worst of Sabah's recent security incidents took place (see p.392).

The few visitors who come to Lahad Datu usually pass through en route to the **Danum Valley** and the **Tabin Wildlife Reserve**, though it's often necessary to stay at least one night and the town has a few nice diversions to help pass the time – nearby **Mount**

Silam offers a much cheaper taste of the jungle than its celebrated counterparts, for one.

The waterfront market

The main road through town is Jalan Teratai, one block south of which is the seafront Jalan Pantai and the **waterfront market**, which is divided across three buildings: the *pasar ikan* (fish), *pasar rakyat* (meat and vegetables) and *pasar kain* (cheap clothes and bags). The most entertaining of these is undoubtedly the fish market, where tourists are still something of a novelty for the traders who sit within circular enclosures amid the day's catch.

Kwan Tee Temple

Jalan Dahlia • Daily 6.30am–4.30pm • Free • Look for the police post on Jalan Teratai then head north a short distance from there

It isn't anything grand, but the Chinese **Kwan Tee Temple** is worthy of a brief look for its colourful wall reliefs showing a green-robed figure on horseback. Often seen toting a halberd, this is none other than Kwan Tee, a semi-mythological character who may have lived circa 200 AD. Deified as the Chinese god of war, he takes pride of place on the central altar, with his halberd-bearer immediately to his right.

7

ARRIVAL AND DEPARTURE

By plane Lahad Datu's airport has MASwings flights to KK (4 daily; 55min). It's only 1km or so from Jalan Teratai, the main road – head uphill onto Jalan Kastam Lama from the roundabout at the southern end of the runway, and you will shortly arrive in the centre. A taxi into town costs around RM10.

By long-distance bus By the time you read this, the new express bus station should be open at First Palm City Centre, a development 800m northwest of the centre. For now, buses line up on a lane on the west side of the Fajar neighbourhood, about 1.2km northwest of the centre. Walking around 1.2km east from here will

bring you out onto Jalan Kastam Lama – turn right for the town centre.

Destinations Kinabalu Park (14 daily; 7hr); KK (14 daily; 8hr); Sandakan (4 daily; 3hr); Semporna (3–4 daily; 2hr); Tawau (7 daily; 1hr 30min).

By shared taxi, minivan and local bus Shared taxis and minivans leave from a few points around the centre, although most use a station at the corner of Jalan Pantai and Jalan Bunga Raya, towards the eastern end of the centre, which is also used by slow local buses to Tawau and Sandakan. The only vehicles here you might want to use are for Semporna.

LAHAD DATU AND AROUND

INFORMATION AND TOURS

Danum Valley information Three offices linked with the Danum Valley (see p.439) stand side by side, facing the airport runway. The Danum Valley Field Centre office (closed weekends; ☎089 880441) takes bookings for their accommodation, issues permits and can provide general information on the conservation area. Next door you'll find Borneo Nature Tours (☎089 880207, ⓦ borneonaturetours.com), which runs the *Borneo Rainforest Lodge*, as well as an office representing *Kawag Danum Rainforest Lodge* (see p.439).

Tours Bike and Tours has some distinctive offerings alongside its accommodation (see below), including – as their name suggests – a combination tour and bike ride to Mount Silam (see p.438), plus diving at Darvel Bay. They as well as the owner of *Tabin Lodge* (see p.438) run trips to the Bukit Piton reserve (see p.439), where there's a decent chance of spotting orang-utans. Make bookings in advance as time is needed to secure permits and other necessities.

ACCOMMODATION

Bay Hotel Western end of Jalan Teratai ☎089 882801, ⓔ bayhotelldu@yahoo.com. Offers surprisingly pleasant rooms in an otherwise mundane four-storey block. No breakfast and no lifts. ☏ RM130

★**Bike and Tours B&B** 2km northwest of the centre in Taman Hup Heng, near the northern end of the airport runway ☎089 868109, ⓦ bikeandtours .com. Simply furnished but very comfortable a/c double rooms in the sprawling suburban home of

Swiss/Malaysian couple Simon and Itisha, which has its own little garden pool at the back. The cheapest rooms are on the cosy side and share bathrooms. Free guest pick-ups; breakfast for two costs RM20 extra, with other meals on request. ☏ RM200

House 11 Off the western end of Jalan Teratai, behind and around the corner from Maybank ☎089 881007. A good budget option in what's basically a narrow, modern two-storey house with a/c, en-suite rooms on either side of a central aisle. Avoid the ones at the front, where you'll hear kids playing outside and the reception's TV. 🛜 RM70

Tabin Lodge Jalan Urusetia Kecil, near the eastern end of Jalan Teratai ☎017 892 0158, 🖥tabinlodge .com. This must have been quite a guesthouse in its heyday, but some fittings now look museum pieces. Still, the dorms and rooms are perfectly serviceable and come with optional a/c and en-suite bathrooms, though the latter are sometimes simply half-walled off from the rest of the room. 🛜 Dorms RM22, doubles RM55

EATING

★**Auliah** Down a lane opposite the Executive Hotel on Jalan Teratai, close to the RHB Bank ☎089 880266. Featuring a dazzling selection of inexpensive curries and roti/rice variations, including the bright yellow local speciality *nasi kuning*, this is a classic *mamak* place, busy even late in the evening and popular with the entire cross-section of Sabah society. The upstairs tables have a/c. Daily 24hr.

★**Sakura Seafood** Look for Bismi Catering on Jalan Teratai, then head down the lane opposite ☎013 543 1111. The name is misleading on two counts: this unassuming restaurant isn't Japanese but Chinese, and it does a lot besides seafood, including a highly original sizzling venison (*pasai*) with cheese sauce. The salted egg prawns are also good. Most dishes cost RM10. Mon–Fri 10.30am–3pm & 5–10.30pm, Sat & Sun 10.30am–10.30pm.

Mount Silam

15km southwest of Lahad Datu • Daily 8am–5pm • Forestry permit RM15; guides RM100/day • ☎089 881560 • Any southbound local bus from Lahad Datu or express bus can call here

The tallest peak in the vicinity of Lahad Datu is the 884m **Mount Silam**, within the Sapagaya Forest Reserve. From the entrance on the main road, a 10km lane snakes its way up the mountain; en route is an elevated viewpoint, the 33m **Tower of Heaven** (Menara Kayangan), with terrific vistas out to the islands in Darvel Bay and, in the opposite direction, the jungle centred around the Danum Valley. Besides the lookout tower, there are also several jungle **trails** of varying lengths – you may see sambar deer, Bornean gibbons, pig-tailed macaques, the arboreal loris, pitcher plants, and, if you're very lucky the small and orange-red **silam crab**, unique to this mountain.

Tabin Wildlife Reserve

Some 40km northeast of Lahad Datu • 🖥 wildlife.sabah.gov.my • Take the daily minivan (departs 8am, returns 1.30pm; 1hr 30min) from the resort's office at Lahad Datu airport

Tabin Wildlife Reserve, twice the size of Singapore, combines primary and secondary forest with excellent opportunities to see wildlife. Pygmy elephants, macaques, wild boar and orang-utans can be spotted, as can the rare clouded leopard if you're lucky. Birdwatchers can look out for more than three hundred kinds of birds, with endemic species such as the Bornean bristlehead, blue-headed pitta and all eight local species of hornbills. You can take a walk to a **mud volcano**, used by animals as a mineral lick, or head off on a hike (the longest trail is 2.8km) or a night drive. The reserve also houses Malaysia's last two known **Sumatran rhinos**, cared for by the Borneo Rhino Alliance (🖥borneorhinoalliance.org), although this particular sanctuary isn't open to the public. It's difficult to have a proper taste of Tabin with a one-night stay, so it's worth budgeting for at least two.

ACCOMMODATION   TABIN WILDLIFE RESERVE

Tabin Wildlife Resort ☎088 267266, 🖥tabinwildlife.com.my. This place offers a range of chalets with high ceilings, half of them by a river and the other half spread up a hillside; all of them come with nice private balconies, and buffet meals and transport to/from Lahad Datu are provided in the rates. Price is for two nights. 🛜 RM4800

Danum Valley

About 90min from Lahad Datu by 4WD • Conservation fee RM50; camera permits RM10; vehicle permits RM20 • ☎088 326320 • Reached by a signed turning 15km southwest of Lahad Datu

The **Danum Valley** is "perhaps the last area of primary lowland forest in Southeast Asia which remains truly pristine". That glowing description isn't from a tour operator brochure, but from the South East Asia Rainforest Research Partnership (@searrp.org), an international scientific collaboration that's been based here since the 1980s – and you can meet their biologists if you stay at the field centre. **Wildlife** includes bearded pigs, orang-utans, proboscis monkeys, elephants and more than 320 species of bird, and the area is also home to the world's tallest known rainforest tree, a 94m *Shorea*. Be aware that, as ever, spotting animals in dense jungle is a challenge.

There are just two (very different) places to stay here, located apart from each other. Packages at the slick, pricey **Borneo Rainforest Lodge** include the services of professional guides who accompany you on a 300m canopy walkway, a 3km trek to a burial cliff and a night drive, for example. At the prosaic **Danum Valley Field Centre**, it's possible to trek to waterfalls up to three hours away, and rangers can be hired as guides – though their skills in this area vary (RM32/hr).

ACCOMMODATION DANUM VALLEY

Borneo Rainforest Lodge 77km from the Danum Valley turning. Resort-style accommodation in the heart of the jungle in hardwood chalets, all naturally ventilated rather than with a/c. The more expensive units face the Danum River and have a private outdoor tub or even an infinity pool. Book through Borneo Nature Tours in KK or Lahad Datu. Price is for a two-night package for two including transport. 🛜 RM7000

Danum Valley Field Centre Beside the Segama River, 63km from the Danum Valley turning 📞089 841101. The place where researchers and most travellers stay,

featuring a campsite (tents provided), dorms (bunk beds in cubicles for two), en-suite doubles and two chalets with upmarket doubles. Meals cost an extra RM140/day. The 4WD for the Field Centre leaves the Lahad Datu office at 3pm on Mon, Wed & Fri, and vehicles depart the Field Centre at 8am the same days (RM85 one way). Try to book at least a month in advance – you'll need to call the Field Centre or the Lahad Datu office for the latest email address. 🛜 Camping per person RM80, dorms RM95, doubles RM290, chalets RM400

Semporna

Fringed by water villages on either side, **SEMPORNA** is inhabited largely by the **Bajau Laut** (sometimes dubbed sea gypsies) who once lived nomadically on houseboats (*lepa*) – although only a fifth of those in the area now do. As a prelude to the marine marvels of Sabah's southeastern islands, the town is pretty unappealing. The only tourists who seem to relish being here are the ubiquitous groups from China, who saved the local

RESERVES AROUND THE DANUM VALLEY

The Danum Valley is the brightest star in a constellation of forest reserves covering thousands of square kilometres in southeast Sabah, all belonging to the non-profit **Sabah Foundation**, which uses the proceeds of logging to fund scholarships. There are two nearby reserves, reached via the Danum Valley turning, that are also worth visiting.

Kawag reserve, 36km in from the coast road, offers a "jungle-lite" experience in secondary forest northeast of Danum, which has now been restored after logging. The vegetation is noticeably more open here. Wildlife includes gibbons, pig-tailed macaques, elephants, martens, flying squirrels and the usual range of creepy-crawlies. Visitors stay in fairly plain, en-suite rooms at the *Kawag Danum Rainforest Lodge* (book through Borneo Refugia; see p.398), an upgraded former research station that also offers short treks up to 1.5km, including one to a stream where you can swim and try tubing. A two-night all-inclusive package, with transport to and from Lahad Datu, costs around RM2200 for two.

Further east and quite different is the **Bukit Piton reserve**. The big draw in this badly logged region, which is being slowly reforested, is the orang-utans, which were unfortunately marooned here between oil palm plantations to the north and the Segama River to the south. Day-trips run from Lahad Datu are the only way to visit (see p.437).

dive industry when security scares (see p.393) kept Westerners away – it's worth **booking** dive packages a few weeks in advance whenever there's a holiday in China.

Most visitors avoid the grubby centre and stick to the area around **Bandar Baru** (the "new town"), the tiny grid of modern seafront blocks southeast of the **Ur-Rahman mosque** (look for its silvery dome) and beyond the main market. There's little to see except during the touristy **Regatta Lepa** in April (ⓦsabahtourism.com), a pageant contested by *lepa* with colourful sails.

ARRIVAL AND INFORMATION

SEMPORNA

By plane Tawau airport (see p.445) is the gateway for many visitors to Semporna, and is about 110km away. A taxi between the two costs RM100–120.

By bus The main bus terminal is off the coast road about 50m west of the mosque, although one company, Dyana Express, uses a space 100m inland from here. Most buses leave before 9am or after 6pm.

Destinations KK (6 daily; 10hr); Lahad Datu (3–4 daily; 2hr); Sandakan (at least 4 daily; 5hr); Tawau (5 daily; 1hr 30min).
By minivan Most minivans leave from just beside the main bus terminal, though Tawau services set off from close to *KFC* a little further inland.
Destinations Lahad Datu (daily 7am–5pm); Tawau (RM30; RM20 to airport).

ACCOMMODATION

★**Best Bunk Beds** Northern corner of Bandar Baru ☏019 851 8039, ✉bestbunkbeds@gmail.com; map p.440. The bunk beds are crammed together and the management is somewhat bureaucratic, but the whole place is immaculate. The free breakfast – eggs, noodles, cake, toasted sandwiches – is about as good as it gets for a hostel. 📶 Dorms RM50

★**Cube Bed Station** Bandar Baru ☏089 784000, ⓦcbshostel.com.my; map p.440. Swanky capsule beds

with privacy drapes and a handful of double rooms with beds on wooden platforms, and roughly rendered walls lending an industrial chic touch throughout. An en-suite sea view room costs nearly twice the standard rate. 📶 Dorms RM60, doubles RM160

Scuba Junkie Dive Lodge Bandar Baru ☏089 785372, ⓦscuba-junkie.com; map p.440. This is a functional affair with dorms and double rooms (a few with private bathrooms), but a real bargain if you're

SEMPORNA

■ ACCOMMODATION	
Best Bunk Beds	2
Cube Bed Station	3
Scuba Junkie Dive Lodge	4
Seafest Hotel	1

● EATING	
Ocean Treasure Live Seafood	1
Thien Wang	2

Shopping mall (planned)
Seafest
Dive shops
Dragon Inn Resort
Pacific Inn
BANDAR BARU
Jetty
Guardian
Scubaholics
Watsons
Billabong
Giant Supermarket
Scuba Junkie
Water village
Market
JALAN COASTAL
JALAN KASTAM
Water village
Express Buses
Permai Polyclinics
JALAN HOSPITAL
Dyana Express Buses

0   100
metres

▼ Tawau (106km) & Lahad Datu (135km)

DIVING AND SNORKELLING AROUND SEMPORNA

Many of Semporna's **dive shops** focus on selling packages at their own accommodation on the islands (see below), but also sell diving and snorkelling day-trips from town – count on at least RM225 for two dives, RM275 for three.

★**Scuba Junkie** Bandar Baru ☎089 785372, ⊚scuba-junkie.com. This impeccably organized firm runs courses from Discover Scuba right up to instructor level, and takes a strong conservation-oriented stance. They use their Semporna branch for trips to Tun Sakaran Marine Park and their Mabul one as a base for Sipidan trips.

Scubaholics Bandar Baru, above the Century store ☎019 812 7867, ⊚scuba-holics.com. This is a popular indie operator covering all of the usual diving destinations in the area.

Sipidan Scuba Holiday Dive Inn, Bandar Baru ☎089 919148, ⊚sipidanscuba.com. A little cheaper than Scuba Junkie, with trips to some less-visited spots.

diving or snorkelling with them as accommodation prices halve. 🛜 Dorms RM55, doubles RM170

Seafest Hotel Jalan Kastam Extension ☎089 782333, ⊚seafesthotel.com; map p.440. This is the smartest hotel in town, with a pool and gym plus a new "boutique" wing across the road where rooms are actually around twenty percent cheaper. Buffet breakfast included for the more expensive room types, otherwise it's an extra RM25/person. 🛜 RM160

EATING

Ocean Treasure Live Seafood Northern corner of Bandar Baru ☎016 787 9965; map p.440. The food isn't anything special and is a little overpriced, but this airy place is a hotspot for Western travellers and offers lovely views of boats zipping around the harbour. Mains around RM10. Daily 11.30am–10.30pm.

★**Thien Wang** Bandar Baru ☎019 842 7688; map p.440. This place is deservedly popular among Chinese visitors, who flock here for the excellent fresh seafood. The menu is extensive, with simple one-plate meals such as rice and butter squid (RM8) alongside sizzling tofu, lemon chicken and a dozen noodle variations. Daily 8.30am–9.30pm.

DIRECTORY

Bank There's a Maybank near one of the two filling stations in the centre, just one block back from the mosque.
Clinic Permai Polyclinics is around the corner from the Dyana Express bus depot (24hr; ☎017 763 8393).
Pharmacies Bandar Baru has branches of both Guardian and Watsons.

Islands around Semporna

Two marine parks lie off the coast of southeast Sabah. Most famed is **Sipadan Island**, a park in its own right and the prime destination for experienced divers, although nearby **Mabul Island** and **Kapalai Island** (which don't lie within a park) are also renowned for marine life – all three lie south of Semporna. North and east of the town in Darvel Bay are the eight islands of the **Tun Sakaran Marine Park**.

Sipadan Island

Acclaimed by Jacques Cousteau as "an untouched piece of art", **Sipadan Island** is mindboggling, its waters teeming with turtles, moray eels, sharks, barracuda and vast schools of colourful tropical fish, as well as the occasional dolphin and pilot whale. The diversity of coral found here is also comparable to that of Australia's Great Barrier Reef. Only 120 visitor permits are available for Sipadan daily (RM40), so it's likely you'll spend a day here with your dive operator and then a few around the nearby islands.

Most of the dozen-plus commonly visited dive sites around Sipadan offer the chance to see abundant turtles and white-tip sharks. The most popular spot, **Barracuda Point**, is a drift dive where divers hold onto rocks while shoals of barracuda pass by. Another great site is the **Drop-off**, close to the jetty, where you often find large schools of barracuda, bumphead parrotfish and Napoleon wrasse. Close to here is the entrance to **Turtle Cave**, where you'll find the skeletal remains of turtles that have strayed in and become lost.

Mabul Island

Mabul Island is split between dive accommodation and the shanties of the Bajau Laut. There are beaches on the north shore but refuse is a problem in some areas, and while it's possible to stroll round the entire island in 45 minutes, most visitors focus on the attractions offshore. Visibility is less reliable than at Sipadan, and the **muck diving** – seeking out creatures in the sediment – is famous here. Among the marine life close to the island are many turtles of all sizes, seahorses – including the rare pygmy seahorse – frogfish, cuttlefish, mimic octopuses, lionfish, stonefish and ribbon eels.

Kapalai Island

Really a sandbar, tiny **Kapalai Island** is exquisite and otherworldly. The house reef has five minor wrecks, and divers are drawn by macro life such as pygmy seahorses, harlequin ghost pipefish and mandarinfish. There's one pricey resort, although Kapalai is accessible from Mabul, too.

Tun Sakaran Marine Park
Conservation fee RM20

The most interesting islands at **Tun Sakaran Marine Park** are **Sibuan Island**, with a breathtaking beach, shallow reefs and calm waters, making it suitable for inexperienced divers and learners; and **Mantubuan Island**, where you can dive to see rare black (actually multicoloured) coral, resembling a forest of underwater Christmas trees. Accommodation lies just east of the park on two immaculate little islands, namely **Pom Pom Island** and teardrop-shaped **Mataking Island** – the latter has a wall dive where you might see turtles, rays and sharks.

ACCOMMODATION   ISLANDS AROUND SEMPORNA

All accommodation lies outside the two marine parks (the lion's share of it on Mabul Island), and is mostly sold in **packages** including boat transfers and meals, with diving and snorkelling either charged separately or with a fixed number of dives included. Pricing is often quoted per person – unless noted, **room prices** given here are for two people for one night (though longer stays are better value), excluding diving. Details of booking offices in Semporna are given where relevant.

MABUL

Mabul has resorts and a few basic guesthouses of variable quality; all places on the south shore are on stilts out at sea amid the scruffy water villages, although guests are largely insulated from that by dint of arriving and leaving by boat.

RESORTS

★**Borneo Divers** North shore of Mabul ☎088 222226, ⓦborneodivers.info. A great mid-range choice, with fifteen two-room chalets in well-kept grounds centred around a freeform pool. There's a nice restaurant, a bar and spa, too. Two-night diving package RM3800. 🛜 RM3100

★**Mabul Beach Resort** North shore of Mabul. The perfect middle ground between resort and guesthouse, with dorms as well as en-suite rooms equipped with rain showers and outdoor hammocks (although only some rooms have a/c and hot water). There are decent buffet meals and there's an upstairs bar, too. Given Scuba Junkie's conservation stance, they run a small turtle hatchery and don't serve seafood. You can either book an all-inclusive package or pay for everything separately, in which case you'll get a twenty percent discount on accommodation if you're a diver. The one-night diving package is RM1500; book through Scuba Junkie in Semporna (see p.441). 🛜 Dorms RM210, doubles RM520

Mabul Water Bungalows North shore of Mabul ☎088 486389, ⓦmabulwaterbungalows.com. The ultra-luxurious sibling of the *Sipidan-Mabul Resort*, with Balinese-style chalets perched on stilts over the sea. VIP rooms have glass panels in the floor and jacuzzis. Dive packages from RM9200. 🛜 RM5500

Seaventure Off the north shore of Mabul ☎088 261669, ⓦseaventuresdive.com. It looks like a levitating ship from afar, but this is really a former oil rig with good rooms and buffet meals. Price is for a three-night dive package 🛜 RM6500

Sipadan Water Village North shore of Mabul ☎089 792231 or ☎089 751777, ⓦwww.swvresort.com. A less grand version of *Mabul Water Bungalows* next door, with a range of standalone and two-roomed chalets supposedly built according to Bajau design. Dive package RM7000. 🛜 RM5900

Sipadan-Mabul Resort (aka SMART) Eastern shore of Mabul ☎088 486389, ⓦsipadanmabulresortcom. Taking up much of the southeast of Mabul, this fine resort (also known as SMART) has more than forty wooden en-suite chalets, a pool, a large restaurant and jacuzzis in the grounds. Five nights' stay needed for Sipadan; divers pay RM4500. ⓦ RM3700

GUESTHOUSES

Arung Hayat South shore of Mabul ☎010 968 4566, ⓦarunghayatsemporna.com. Compact, very plain rooms, some with a/c, in a sort of longhouse on stilts. Price is for a one-night diving package (without Sipadan) RM1000

Billabong South shore of Mabul; office in Bandar Baru, Semporna ☎089 781866, ⓦbillabongscuba. com. This is the most visually arresting guesthouse, with chalets lining two boardwalks connected by elevated bridges, to allow boats to enter (RM1400). There are also cheaper longhouse rooms, too. Packages exclude diving, which costs around RM350/person for three dives. Two-night snorkelling package RM1100

Paradise Inn South shore of Mabul ☎089 785399, ⓦbigjohnscuba.com. This substantial wooden lodge doesn't qualify as a resort, but certainly transcends the guesthouse label – rooms come with the option of a private hot-water bathroom and a/c. The upstairs viewing deck is the best feature. Dives are at Mabul and Kapalai. Book through Big John Scuba on Jalan Kastam in Semporna. One-night diving package RM1700

Uncle Chang's Dive Lodge South shore of Mabul ☎089 781002, ⓦucsipadan.com. "Reasonably spartan" is how this veteran backpacker place styles itself, so don't come with high expectations. The centrepiece is the restaurant/lounge with a ping-pong table; dorms and rooms are basic and a bit shabby, but some rooms have a/c. Book through the office on Jalan Kastam, Semporna. Divers pay RM100 less for the first night's accommodation. Dorms RM175, doubles RM380

KAPALAI

Sipadan-Kapalai Resort Kapalai ☎089 765200, ⓦsipadan-kapalai.com. Spectacular chalets built on stilts, surrounded by shallow azure water that's perfect for snorkelling. Boats take divers to Mabul (as well as Sipadan if spare permits become available), and there is good diving around the artificial reef. Price is for a two-night package, on which divers can expect to pay RM1000 more. RM4000

POM POM

Celebes Beach Resort Pom Pom ☎089 758228, ⓦcelebescuba.com. This down-to-earth place has simple but nicely furnished a/c chalets, with slightly cheaper rooms in the garden longhouse. Dive packages include unlimited shore dives as well as three boat dives/day. The one-night diving package costs RM1500 more than the non-diving option. RM1200

Pom Pom Island Resort Pom Pom ☎089 781918, ⓦpompomisland.com. Chalets are either out over the water or on (or behind) the beach at this tip-top resort, which also has its own spa. Diving and snorkelling are charged separately (dives are RM160 if booked in advance, minus gear rental). Book through the office on Jalan Kastam Extension in Semporna. RM1600

MATAKING

Reef Dive Resort Mataking ☎089 770022, ⓦmataking.com. This is a luxury development kept in splendid isolation, with swanky beach villas featuring patios and rear jacuzzis. Dive packages include three boat dives/day and free access to the house reef, where an artificial wreck has an underwater mailbox – for this, you can expect to pay around RM400 more than non-divers. RM2900

Tawau and around

Most travellers bypass **TAWAU** altogether, which now rivals Sandakan in size, although it's not a bad idea to overnight here if you're travelling between interior sights like the Maliau Basin and east coast. There are some pleasingly aged timber shophouses on and around Jalan Chester in what passes for an old town centre, and the breezy seafront promenade has views out to Sebatik Island (which is shared with Indonesia). The only real sight in the vicinity is the **Tawau Hills Park**, half an hour's drive away. Smartish hotels and restaurants tend to cluster in the **Fajar** neighbourhood north of **Jalan Dunlop**, the main street.

Tawau Hills Park

25km north of Tawau • Daily 8am–4.30pm • Conservation fee RM10; climbing permits RM32; guides RM160/day • ☎089 918827, ⓦsabahparks .org.my • Taxi RM50 one way; vehicles back to Tawau can be scarce, so ask for a return price including waiting time or get their mobile number

▲ Tawau Airport (30km) & Semporna (106km)

TAWAU

CELEBES SEA

JALAN KUHARA

JALAN ST PATRICK

St Patrick's
Anglican Church

JALAN PERBANDARAN

Public
Bank

HSBC

Al-Khauthar
Mosque

JALAN PESISIRAN

Long-distance
buses
(Sandakan)

JALAN BELUNU

FAJAR

JALAN HAJI KARIM

JALAN KLINIK

JALAN BARU

JALAN DUNLOP

Sabindo Plaza

JALAN HIEW FOOK

Long-distance
buses
(KK, Keningau)

JALAN PERSATUAN

JALAN MAKHKAMAH

RHB Bank

Maybank

JALAN BUNGA

Fajar
Laundry

JALAN TERATAI

SABINDO

JALAN CHEN FOOK

JALAN MASJID

Guardian
Pharmacy

Watsons
Pharmacy

JALAN THEATRE

Food
Stalls

Clothes
Market

JALAN KLINIK

JALAN HO HWANG KIM

JALAN STEPHEN TAN

JALAN CHESTER

JALAN COLE ADAM

Teo Chew
Association

JALAN NUSANTARA

JALAN SEROJA

Tai Yang
Supermarket

JALAN HABIB SHEIKH

JALAN PESISIRAN

JALAN PAYA

Supermarket &
Department Store

JALAN DOMINIC

Taxis

JALAN PESISIRAN

Taxis

JALAN KELAPA

JALAN ABACA

Local buses
& minivans

Local buses

JALAN CHESTER

JALAN DUNLOP

Shell Petrol
Station

Central Market
& UTC

JALAN PELABUHAN

Ferry
Terminal

Fish
Market

JALAN HABIB HUSSIN

Local buses

N

▲ Tawau Hills Park (20m)
◄ T (20m) & Tawau Hills Park (20m)
◄ (20m) & Tawau Hills Park (20m)
◄ Hospital (600m)

■ ACCOMMODATION	
City Garden	4
LA Hotel	2
Shervinton	3
Tawau Hills Park HQ	1

● EATING	
Banana Leaf	3
Jalan Chen Fook Food Court	4
Roof Garden Lounge	2
Siang Siang	1

0 ___ 100
metres

7

The 280-square-kilometre **Tawau Hills Park** is a stretch of rainforest and cloud forest, with the Tawau River cutting through its centre. The thirty-minute trail up **Bombalai hill** from the park HQ offers some great views; also worthwhile is the hike up **Gelas Hill** to a waterfall that's perfect for swimming (2hr one-way). For the ambitious, there are multi-day treks to mounts Magdelana, Lucia and Maria, all just over 1000m; contact the park or Sabah Parks in KK in advance for more details.

ARRIVAL AND DEPARTURE

By plane Tawau's airport (☎089 950777) is 32km east of the centre. Minibuses run from the airport to town (hourly 7am–8pm; 30min), and the trip in a taxi will cost around RM50. Buses and minivans also run east from here to Semporna.

Destinations Johor Bahru (4 weekly; 2hr 35min); KK (6–7 daily; 50min); Kuala Lumpur (6 daily; 2hr 45min); Sandakan (1 daily; 40min); Tarakan (Indonesia; daily; 40min).

By long-distance bus Tawau has two long-distance bus terminals. The bus park on Jalan Chen Fook has services to KK via both Lahad Datu and the interior (via Keningau). Sandakan-bound buses use the station at the eastern end of Jalan Dunlop.

Destinations Keningau (4 daily; 6hr 30min); KK, via the interior (2 daily; at least 10hr); KK, via the coast (7 daily;

TAWAU AND AROUND

11hr); Lahad Datu (7 daily; 2hr); Sandakan (4 daily; 5hr); Sapulut (4 daily; 4hr 30min); Semporna (5 daily; 1hr 30min).

By shared minivan or local bus Services for Tawau's airport, Lahad Datu and Semporna use the Jalan Dunlop long-distance terminal. Most other local transport uses the station at the west end of Jalan Stephen Tan, although you're unlikely to make use of this.

By ferry Ferries to Nunakan (RM90) and Tarakan (RM145) in Indonesia, run by a variety of companies, use the terminal south of the market. Buy tickets early (the terminal opens at 8am and shuts at night) as counters may close irregularly later in the day.

Destinations Nunakan (around 5 daily; 1hr); Tarakan (Tues, Thurs & Sat 10.30am; 3hr).

ACCOMMODATION

★**City Garden** Jalan Chen Fook ☎089 769991, ⓦcitygardenhotel.net; map p.444. Although new and characterless, this hotel has beautifully maintained and seriously soundproofed rooms. It's well located too, directly opposite the food court and near both of the bus terminals. 📶 **RM100**

LA Hotel Jalan St Patrick ☎089 762299, ⓦlahotel.com. my; map p.444. The slickest hotel in town, with a range of plush rooms, a spa and two restaurants (including one that's superbly perched atop the building). 📶 **RM160**

Shervinton Jalan Bunga ☎089 770000,

ⓦshervintonhotel.com; map p.444. A wannabe business-class hotel with a few stylish flourishes, including all-metal sinks in the bathrooms. There's also a rooftop restaurant and bar. Rates include breakfast. 📶 **RM120**

TAWAU HILLS PARK

Tawau Hills Park HQ 25km north of Tawau ☎089 925719; map p.444. The Park HQ's facilities include a hostel with a choice of a/c (RM80) or fan dorms, as well as chalets. An on-site canteen serves up simple dishes. Dorms **RM25**, chalets **RM250**

EATING

Banana Leaf Jalan Bunga ☎016 459 2786; map p.444. Down-to-earth Indian restaurant with a self-explanatory name serving *biryanis* (RM15), fish-head curries (RM40/ two people) and cheap *rotis* and *thosai* for breakfast. Open from 4pm during Ramadan. Daily 7am–2am

★**Jalan Chen Fook Food Court** Jalan Chen Fook; map p.444. There's no official name for this expansive place, which is dominated by two Chinese seafood restaurants (*Kam Ling* and *Good View*; from around RM25/person) and draws crowds every evening. Also worthwhile is *1st Drink and Food Centre* for cheap noodle and dim sum breakfasts (daily until 1.30pm); for very cheap Malay/Indonesian food, try the stalls at the western end of the site. Daily dawn–late.

★**Roof Garden Lounge** Tenth floor, LA Hotel, Jalan St Patrick ☎089 777557; map p.444. One of the nicest restaurant-bars anywhere in Sabah, this rooftop place offers 360-degree views out to the Tawau Hills Park and the sea – get here before sunset to pick a good table. The extensive menu covers everything from steak to satay (mains from RM20), with Strongbow cider and plenty of cocktails to wash it down. Happy hour until 9pm. Daily 4pm–2am.

Siang Siang Off Jalan Haji Karim ☎016 665 2377; map p.444. A curious combo of Western café – good for comfy seats, hot and cold drinks and cake – and Chinese noodle house. Most dishes cost around RM10. Daily 10am–4am.

7

The interior

The Crocker mountain range marks the start of the transition from the western coastal plains to Sabah's geographical **interior**, which covers a vast swathe of terrain south from here to the Indonesian border. The isolation of this sparsely populated region ended at the start of the twentieth century, when a rail line was built between Jesselton (now KK) and Tenom to transport the raw materials being produced by the region's thriving rubber industry. Today, the region is known for the cultivation of coffee, rice, cocoa and, lately, even avocados. The mountains themselves are a major attraction, largely wrapped up within the **Crocker Range Park** – the notable exception is **Trus Madi**, part of a forest reserve. To the east and southeast, lowland rainforest reasserts itself at the wildlife haven of **Deramakot** and the **Maliau Basin**, where there are superb opportunities for trekking. Another draw is the excellent Murut cultural tourism project at **Sapulut**, where visitors get to scale the limestone pinnacle of **Batu Punggul**. The three main towns – **Tambunan**, **Keningau** and **Tenom** – have little to offer in themselves, but you may find yourself passing through en route to nearby attractions.

7

Crocker Range Park

Main entrance 12km northwest of Keningau • RM20 conservation fee • ☏ 019 862 0404, ⊛ sabahparks.org.my • Transport between KK and Keningau or Tambunan can drop you at or close to the entrances, and can be flagged down for onward travel

Covering 1400 square kilometres, the **Crocker Range Park** is the largest of Sabah's terrestrial state parks with, unusually, a road – between Kimanis on the coast and Keningau – slicing right through it. Largely uncommercialized, the park offers cool mountain air, montane forest, birdlife and occasional sightings of *Rafflesia* flowers. The one part of the park that's easily explored independently is reached via the **main entrance**, close to where the road exits the park on its eastern side – here there's a collection of ferns, an insectarium, a lookout tower and a couple of short forest trails.

Two **substations** – as alternative gates are named – are also worth a visit. The **Mahua** substation, 14km north of Tambunan and reached off the Tambunan–Ranau road, gives access to the chilly waters at the Mahua Falls, 500m from the gate. Even better is the **Alab** substation close to **Mount Alab** (2000m) and some 15km northwest of Tambunan, off the KK road – here the 12km **Minduk Sirung Trail** makes an excellent day trek downhill to Mahua, but you will need a guide and permits (contact the park office for details).

ACCOMMODATION   CROCKER RANGE PARK

Manis Manis Resort 300m from the main park entrance ☏ 019 809 8683, ⊛ manismanisresort.com.my. Pleasant place with slick chalets equipped with four-poster beds, plus much cheaper doubles and dorms (which aren't en suite). Chalet prices include breakfast. Dorms RM65, doubles RM180, chalets RM320

Utan Paradise Where the Kimanus–Keningau road meets the western edge of the park ☏ 019 897 4641, ⊛ utanparadise.com. This rustic camp has a lodge with dorms and A-frames that are comfy for two, all with palm-thatch roofs. There are kitchens, but no meals are included unless you come on a package including trekking and a night walk (RM300/person for one night). Dorms RM30, A-frames RM60, chalets RM320

Tambunan and around

The northernmost of the interior's small towns is **TAMBUNAN**, amusingly billed as "the Switzerland of the East" in tourist leaflets, with Mount Trus Madi looming to the southeast and two entrances to the Crocker Range Park to the north. The best thing about the town itself is its lively *tamu* (Wednesday evening and Thursday morning 7am–1pm).

Tambunan Rafflesia Information Centre

On the main road 20km north of Tambunan • Daily 8am–3pm • RM15; guide RM100 (up to five people) • ☎ 088 899589, ⓦ forest.sabah .gov.my • Tambunan minivans and shared taxis from Merdeka Field in KK pass by

Prospects of seeing a *Rafflesia* (see p.586) in flower are decent at the **Tambunan Rafflesia Information Centre**, a small forest reserve often visited as a day-trip from KK. It's worth calling ahead to find out if there are blooms, but as it can be hard to get hold of staff here, you might just have to chance it. Assuming one is flowering, expect a trek of up to an hour to reach it.

Mount Trus Madi

20km southeast of Tambunan • Entry permit RM15; climbing permit RM80 • ⓦ forest.sabah.gov.my/fmu10

At 2642m, **Mount Trus Madi** is the second tallest mountain in Sabah, but is still totally overshadowed by Kinabalu as far as tourists are concerned. It's a pity: Trus Madi is a good place to find **pitcher plants**, and there are wonderful views of Kinabalu from the summit. Three trails (*wayaan* in local dialect) with different starting points lead up Trus Madi; the easiest is the Kaingaran trail, reached by 4WD from Tambunan, which is a two-day round trip and has basic accommodation halfway up. Several KK tour operators offer the climb, including TYK Adventure Tours which has been doing it longer than most (☎ 088 232821, ⓦ tykadventuretours.com).

ARRIVAL AND DEPARTURE

By shared minivan and taxi Shared transport to and from KK (1hr 30min), Ranau (1hr 15min) and Keningau

TAMBUNAN AND AROUND

(45min) stops in Tambunan's main square.

ACCOMMODATION

Tambunan Rafflesia Hotel Jalan Kampung Lintuhun, near the Petronas filling station ☎ 087 771310, ✉ tambunanrafflesiahotel@gmail.com. This new mid-range hotel has pleasant rooms, some with views of paddy fields and Mount Trus Madi. There's a restaurant too, although breakfast costs extra. 🛜 **RM150**

Tandarason Resort 2km north of Tambunan

☎ 087 774076, ⓦ tandarasonresorttambunan.com. Also known as TVRC (the initials of its old name), this place has a holiday camp feel, and is set around a lake where you can kayak (RM10 for half an hour). There are basic en-suite "motel" rooms, plus fancier chalets costing double, and a campsite (RM30 tent rental). Some rates include breakfast. Camping per person **RM10**, doubles **RM100**

Keningau

Just north of the Pegalan River, **KENINGAU** is the largest of the interior towns, with a mainly Kadazan/Dusun, Murut and Chinese population. It's also a minor transport hub, as it's 1km east of where the main road up the eastern side of the Crocker Range meets the road between Kimanis on the coast and Tawau. The only things to see are the night market, which sells produce and snacks in a hangar-like building off the eastern end of the main street, plus the Sunday morning *tamu* in the centre. All worthwhile shops and facilities, including some decent hotels and restaurants, are on the north side of the main street or a block further north around Jalan OKK Sodomon.

ARRIVAL AND INFORMATION

By long-distance bus The Tung Ma Nui Lok company runs the bulk of the town's bus services from a little depot on Jalan Masjid, the road on the western edge of the centre where the mosque is located. Salam Bumimas buses, which only serve KK, Sapulut and Tawau, call at a car park by the post office and night market.

Destinations Beaufort (2 daily; 2hr 15min); KK (hourly during

KENINGAU

the day; 2hr 30min); Menumbok (2 daily; 3hr 30min); Sapulut (4 daily; 2hr), Tawau (4 daily; 6hr 30min); Tenom (4 daily; 1hr).

By shared taxi and minivan Shared transport uses at least three locations in the centre, so ask around to find the right spot for your destination. Routes of use to tourists are the same as for buses, though it's also possible to find vehicles for Tambunan (45min).

ACCOMMODATION

Juta 100m north of the main street ☎087 337888, ⓦhoteljuta.com. Impossible to miss – it's the tallest building in town – this is the closest thing the town has to a business hotel, with surprisingly modern rooms and a restaurant. Breakfast included. 🛜 RM140

Kristal Northern end of Jalan OKK Sodomon ☎087 338888. The best budget option, with antiquated but sound a/c, en-suite rooms. 🛜 RM60

Mee Woo Resort Off Jalan Bariawa, 1km north of the centre ☎087 337108, ✉mee_woo@yahoo.com. Keningau just isn't the sort of place where a glorified holiday camp like this ought to thrive, but this place's swimming pools and water slides draw weekending families from KK. Rooms galore are stacked up the side of a small valley, and there's a restaurant and a café/bar too. 🛜 Half board; weekdays (add 20 percent at weekends) RM275

EATING

Maimunah Off the main street, close to the Juta hotel. Basic but reliable *mamak* place with a good *nasi campur* selection and the usual roti and noodle favourites. Daily 24hr.

Uncle Pepper Look for the RHB Bank beyond the Kristal hotel, then follow the road round to the north ☎087 337005. Its walls plastered with images of Western celebs, this vaguely hip café is the best place in town for burgers, grills and fish and chips. Mains from RM15. Daily noon–10pm.

Tenom

Named after Ontoros Antanom, a Murut warrior, **TENOM** is a backwater on the north bank of the Padas River, with tasteful wooden shophouses and a blue-domed mosque. The closest most visitors get is Pangi station, 10km to the west, which is the starting point for **rafting** trips booked in KK (see p.398). Locally, Tenom is best known for growing **coffee**, and there are opportunities to taste the local product and to stay on a small plantation. The town's *tamu* takes place on Sunday morning.

Sabah Agriculture Park

On the east bank of the Padas River, 15km northeast of Tenom • Tues–Sun 9am–4.30pm • RM25 • ☎087 737952, ⓦsabah.net.my/agripark • Shared minivan from Tenom to Lagud Seberang, then walk 1km

The **Sabah Agriculture Park** is a crop research station known for its **Orchid Centre**, which has four hundred species, and there's a **Living Crop Museum** with tropical plants. Other attractions include the **Bee Centre**, planned gardens, mini zoo and lakes.

ARRIVAL AND DEPARTURE   TENOM

By train The train station is on the east side of the padang, just off the main Keningau road; for more details on the journey, see box, p.407.
Destinations Beaufort (2 daily; 2hr 30min).

By bus Buses call at the padang, with tickets sold across from the train station.

Destinations Keningau (4 daily; 1hr); KK (4 daily; 3hr 30min).

By shared minivan and taxi Minivans congregate close to the padang – the ones heading north to Keningau generally circle around Tenom, looking for passengers. Shared taxis wait at the southern edge of the padang.
Destinations Beaufort (2hr 30min); Keningau (1hr); KK (3hr).

ACCOMMODATION AND EATING

Sri Perdana Jalan Tun Mustapha ☎087 734001. A reliable budget choice, just west of the padang across the main road. RM60

Teak Wood Cabin Fatt Choi coffee plantation, 1.5km west of town ☎087 735230, ⓦfccoffee.com. The four- and six-person cabins here, based in the hills outside town, come with a/c and en-suite bathrooms. If you need help finding it, ask directions at their *Tenom Fatt Choi (TFC)* café on the main road in the centre, where you can sample their coffee for free. RM100

Sapulut and Batu Punggul

Two hours' drive south of Keningau, **SAPULUT** is a district of hamlets in the heartland of the Murut people. Only 30km from the Indonesian border, the area is also home to one of Sabah's most intriguing challenges, **Batu Punggul**; unlike the limestone pinnacles at Sarawak's Mulu National Park, this is one you can climb. It looms like a misshapen brick above the jungle, and the journey to reach it requires a longboat trip followed by a steep half-hour trek up. From the base, most visitors take around twenty minutes to get to the top of the 100m-high mound, where there are views of pristine forest.

On a physical level, Batu Punggul is something any reasonably fit and agile person can manage, with no rock-climbing experience needed. It's like using a series of ladders, with the limestone fiendishly eroded into jagged pockets, providing hand- and footholds; ropes assist on a few sections. It is psychologically testing, however, in that there are **no safety harnesses**; this is a climb you do **at your own risk**, and there is no shame in skipping it at the last minute. The Murut guides are assiduous about safety and will even drag your hands and feet to the right spots if you're stuck. It's worth wearing trousers as the limestone will cause bad grazes or worse if you briefly miss your footing.

ACTIVITIES   SAPULUT AND BATU PUNGGUL

★ **Orou Sapulut** ☎ 019 227 7077, ⊛ orousapulot.com. Once the logistics of climbing Batu Punggul were as tricky as the feat itself, but now it's the highlight of the multi-day trips organized by this Murut community tourism project. Activities include caving, Murut dancing and a rapids-shooting trip starting near the Indonesian border (only an option on longer stays). Accommodation is in purpose-built longhouses and lodges with shared toilets. Bear in mind that you will stay in a different place every night and that there are some very early starts. Their two-night full-board package, including transport to and from Keningau, costs RM1200/person.

Maliau Basin Conservation Area

Off the Sapulut–Tawau road, reached by a turning 63km east of Sapulut • T088 326320, ⊛ maliaubasin.org

Billed as Sabah's "Lost World", the **Maliau Basin Conservation Area** superficially resembles Danum Valley (see p.439). There's a centre for visiting biologists who come to study, among other things, its impressive roster of large mammals, including the Borneo pygmy elephant, clouded leopard, banteng and sun bear. Unlike at Danum, however, here the aim is to range far and wide, with lower montane, heath and dipterocarp forest to explore on extended **treks**, which could mean covering 12km in a day through dense jungle – needless to say, they shouldn't be attempted lightly. Highlights include several waterfalls, notably the seven-tiered **Maliau Falls**. You'll need to book through a tour operator to visit (expect to pay upwards of RM3000/person for an all-inclusive package). Standard itineraries include only one night at the studies centre, where a canopy walkway and night drive provide diversion; the remaining two to four nights are spent at field stations ranging from basic campsites to wooden lodges with hammocks and proper bathrooms.

Deramakot Forest Reserve

Reached by a rough 70km road starting 20km east of Telupid and 105km from Sandakan • RM15/person, extra RM32/car; guides and night drives RM100/day each • ☎ 089 278800 or ☎ 089 242500, ⊛ deramakot.sabah.gov.my

Cradled by the Kinabatangan River, south off the road between Ranau and the east coast, the 555-square-kilometre **Deramakot Forest Reserve** is heralded by the Forestry Department and conservationists alike. In the heart of Sabah, it is the only one of the state's forests with FSC certification, covering not just logging but also **wildife** – the reserve is a good place to spot sun bears, orang-utans, pygmy elephants, marbled cats and the vulnerable clouded leopard. Treks tend to be short, although new trails are being developed; **night drives** are when much of the action takes place. Although it's possible to visit independently, you're far better off booking with a tour operator in KK or Sandakan, who will take care of transport, meals and perhaps take you on unofficial trails.

ACCOMMODATION   DERAMAKOT FOREST RESERVE

Forestry Department Accommodation Reserve HQ ☎ 089 278800. The reserve's accommodation is fairly new and in good shape, with a/c and bathroom. There's no restaurant, however, so if you aren't here on a package you must arrange catering in advance with the Forestry Department and budget at least an additional RM120/person per day. Dorms RM20, doubles RM160, chalets RM250

Brunei

OMAR ALI SAIFUDDIEN MOSQUE

Brunei

A tiny oil-rich monarchy that seems, superficially, more Middle Eastern than Southeast Asian, the enigmatic country of Brunei often intrigues visitors. Its official title is Negara Brunei Darussalam, Darussalam meaning "Abode of Peace" – and tranquil it certainly is, with little crime and a sense of calm, bordering on ennui, thanks to the income generated by massive offshore oil and gas deposits. The 420,000 inhabitants – two-thirds Malay, almost a tenth Chinese, nearly a quarter expatriates and foreign workers, and just a few percent indigenous peoples – enjoy a cosseted existence. While the genuinely wealthy elite form a select few, there's a large middle class; education and healthcare are free; and houses, cars and even pilgrimages to Mecca are subsidized.

Brunei's sultan, **Hassanal Bolkiah** (see p.455), is famously one of the world's richest people. Ruling as an absolute monarch, he is prime minister, defence minister and finance minister rolled into one, and his extended family, the Bolkiahs, control virtually all government departments and the vast majority of the nation's wealth; it's said that nothing of any real importance is decided without the thumbs-up from a family member.

This is, however, no glitzy Gulf sheikhdom. Brunei is basically low-rise and low-key, feeling not unlike Malaysia's oil-rich state of Terengganu (see p.243), only more torpid and with more discernible signs of wealth. Primary and secondary tropical forest still cover seventy percent of the land area; indeed the country's boundaries are easily discerned from the air, as Sarawak's logging roads and oil-palm plantations halt as if by magic at the border. Most of Brunei is less than 150m above sea level, its rainforest, peat swamp and heath forest running down to sandy beaches and mangrove swamps. The country is divided into four districts: **Muara**, which contains the capital, **Bandar Seri Begawan**; agricultural **Tutong**; oil-rich **Belait**; and **Temburong**, a sparsely populated enclave severed from the rest of Brunei by Sarawak's Limbang district.

For most travellers, Brunei is simply a transit zone on the long bus ride between Miri and Kota Kinabalu. Those who stay seldom do so for more than two or three nights, long enough to glimpse the main sights and the way of life without the cost of living – much higher than in Malaysia – creating too much of a dent in their bank account. Conveniently, the capital is home to many of the key attractions, notably the fascinating **Kampong Ayer**, a rambling collection of houses built over the wide Brunei River, and offers one of the best chances to see **proboscis monkeys** in all of Borneo. The other attraction is the pristine rainforest in **Ulu Temburong National Park** in Temburong, though this is a much more controlled and sanitized experience than any Malaysian national park, with few trails to explore. Otherwise, the sultanate holds some interesting Islamic architecture; a clutch of moderately interesting museums, beaches, small nature parks and modern longhouses; and one solitary nod to Dubai-style excess – a hotel/country club, the *Empire*, that's worth seeing for its ludicrous grandiosity.

Visitors may find aspects of the country – not least its use of Sharia law and *hudud* punishments (see p.456) – uncomfortable and oppressive; it remains hard to see how the Sultan will fulfil his aim of making tourism a major part of the nation's GDP by 2035.

ULU TEMBURONG NATIONAL PARK

Highlights

❶ Kampong Ayer This scenic collection of wooden houses, built out over the Brunei River, offers a glimpse of traditional life. **See p.459**

❷ The Royal Regalia Building One of Brunei's most entertaining museums, housing processional chariots, ceremonial paraphernalia and offbeat official gifts. **See p.460**

❸ Proboscis monkeys Just minutes from downtown by boat, a group of these

curious-looking creatures can usually be seen foraging by the Brunei River. **See p.462**

❹ The Empire Hotel Come to witness how a royal folly with a cavernous marble atrium now functions as a successful hotel, then hang around for a bite to eat. **See p.468**

❺ Ulu Temburong National Park Brunei's premier nature reserve holds a heart-stopping canopy walkway and opportunities for river rafting and tubing. **See p.469**

HIGHLIGHTS ARE MARKED ON THE MAP ON P.454

BRUNEI

HIGHLIGHTS

1. Kampong Ayer
2. The Royal Regalia Building
3. Proboscis monkeys
4. The Empire Hotel
5. Ulu Temburong National Park

SABAH (MALAYSIA)

Kota Kinabalu (152km)

Merapok

Lawas

Batang Lawas

Labuan (50km)

Trusan River

SARAWAK (MALAYSIA)

Trusan

Labu

Senokoh

Bukit Peradayan Forest Reserve

Temburong River

TEMBURONG

Batang Duri

Bangar

ULU TEMBURONG NATIONAL PARK

Muara

Selirong Island

Serasa

Pantai

Meragang

BANDAR SERI BEGAWAN

Brunei International Airport

Brunei Bay

Limbang

Kampung Puni

Limbang River

Nanga Medamit

Limbang River

Mount Mulu (2376m)

Medalam River

MULU NATIONAL PARK

Berakas

Jerudong

Gadong

BRUNEI MUARA

Brunei River

Kampung Parit

Kuala Lurah

Lamunin

Tutong River

Empire Hotel & Country Club

Bukit Shahbandar Forest Recreation Park

SOUTH CHINA SEA

Tutong River

Kampung Abang

Kuala Merimbun

Tasek Merimbun

TUTONG

Tutong

Seri Kenangan

Sungai Liang

SUNGAI LIANG FOREST RESERVE

Penipir River

Keduan River

BELAIT

Labi

Wasai Rampayoh

Luagan Lalak Forest Recreation Park

Mendaram Longhouse

Teraja Longhouse

Marudi

Seria

Belait River

Batang Baram

Kuala Belait

Tutoh River

Sungai Tujoh

Kuala Baram

Lutong

Miri

Bintulu (200km)

N

0   20   kilometres

Brief history

The Brunei of today is just the rump of a vast, powerful sultanate that was gradually gobbled up by the Brookes' regime in Sarawak in the nineteenth century. Trade was the powerhouse behind its growth. Tang and Sung dynasty coins and ceramics, found a few kilometres from Bandar Seri Begawan, suggest that China was trading with Brunei as early as the seventh century. Brunei subsequently benefited from its strategic position on the **trade route** between India, Melaka and China, and exercised a lucrative control over merchant traffic in the South China Sea. As well as being a staging post, where traders could stock up on supplies and off-load cargo, Brunei was commercially active in its own right by the fourteenth century; the *nakhoda*, or Bruneian sea traders, traded local produce such as camphor, rattan and brassware for ceramics, spices, wood and fabrics.

The Brunei Sultanate

Islam had begun to make inroads into Bruneian society by the mid-fifteenth century, a process accelerated when wealthy Muslim merchant families decamped to Brunei after Melaka fell to the Portuguese in 1511. Brunei was certainly an Islamic sultanate by the time its first **European visitors** arrived from Spain in 1521. Commonly acknowledged as the sultanate's golden age, this period saw its territory and influence stretch as far as the modern-day Philippines.

However, things turned sour towards the close of the sixteenth century. Following a sea battle in 1578, Spain took the capital, only to relinquish it days later due to a cholera epidemic. The threat of piracy caused more problems, scaring off passing trade. Worse still, factional struggles loosened the sultan's control at home. With the arrival of **James Brooke** (see p.560) in 1839, the sultanate was to shrink steadily as he siphoned off its territory to neighbouring Sarawak. This trend culminated when Charles Brooke's capture of the Limbang region split Brunei in two. By 1888, the British had declared Brunei a **protected state**, meaning responsibility for its foreign affairs lay with London.

The twentieth century and beyond

The start of the twentieth century was marked by the **discovery of oil**, which drove the British to set up a Residency in 1906. By 1931 the **Seria oil field** was on stream, but the

8

THE SULTAN OF BRUNEI

Brunei's head of state, **Sultan Hassanal Bolkiah** (whose full title is 31 words long), is the 29th in a line stretching back six hundred years. Educated in Malaysia and Britain, he has been sultan since 1967, following the voluntary abdication of his father, Omar.

Hassanal Bolkiah was once deemed the world's richest person, though today a conservative estimate of his net worth, at a mere US$20 billion, would put him only in the top forty of *Forbes'* list of billionaires. Tales of his extravagance are legion – of private jets festooned with gold bathroom fittings, for example. However, the sultan takes pains to live down that persona by cultivating an image of accessibility. Brunei's highly compliant press is full of stories of his majesty's presence at community events – the launching of a new school, say – and for two days a year, at Hari Raya Aidilfitri, the sultan throws open the Istana Nurul Iman to the public, with tens of thousands standing in line for hours to meet him and other members of the royal family. Despite the pious nature of the regime, there have been many accusations of corruption and debauchery within the palace, though these tend to be settled out of court.

The sultan defined the philosophy underlying his rule when, in the 1990s, he introduced an ideology called Melayu Islam Beraja, essentially that the monarchy is founded on the twin pillars of Islam and Malayness. There are few signs of participatory democracy, however. In 2004 the sultan reconvened Brunei's **legislative assembly**, two decades after it was suspended, with sixteen appointed members. They voted to enlarge the assembly to include up to fifteen elected members, but no elections have so far taken place. In 2006 the sultan amended Brunei's constitution to make himself infallible under Bruneian law, and in 2014 he took the controversial step of introducing harsh traditional punishments under Islamic law (see p.456).

Japanese invasion of 1941 temporarily halted Brunei's path to prosperity. As in Sabah, Allied bombing during the occupation that followed left much rebuilding to be done.

While Sabah, Sarawak and Labuan became Crown Colonies in the early postwar years, Brunei remained a British protectorate. The British Residency was finally withdrawn in 1959, and a new constitution established, with provisions for a democratically elected legislative council. At the same time, Sultan Omar Ali Saifuddien (the present sultan's father) was careful to retain British involvement in defence and foreign affairs – a move whose sagacity was made apparent when, in 1962, an attempted coup led by Sheik Azahari's pro-democratic **Brunei People's Party** was crushed by British Army Gurkhas. Ever since the failed coup, which stemmed from Omar's refusal to convene the first sitting of the legislative council, the sultan has ruled by decree in his role as an unelected prime minister, and emergency powers have been in place. Despite showing interest in joining the new Malaysian Federation in 1963, Brunei chose to opt out rather than risk losing its oil wealth and compromising the pre-eminence of its monarchy; not until 1984 did it cease to be a British protectorate and become fully independent.

Little scrutinized by the outside world, modern Brunei charts an unruffled course, though there's no clear sense how the country plans to cope when its oil runs out in a couple of decades, and even fairly well-educated young people find it hard to find jobs. The sultanate retains close ties with the UK and, regionally, especially with Singapore and Malaysia. Following the seventy percent slump in the price of oil since 2013, the country has gradually spiralled into debt (which was around sixteen percent of GDP in 2017), and it seems like Chinese investment (US$6 billion in 2016) is largely propping up the country's economy.

In May 2014, to international and some local consternation, **Islamic hudud punishments** were brought in at the sultan's behest. In theory, the *hudud* penal code could mean people convicted of adulterous or homosexual acts being stoned to death, and thieves having a hand amputated. However, at the time of writing none of these punishments had been carried out; check online for the latest situation before visiting.

Some of the more minor sharia laws have, however, already impacted the country's minority peoples and foreign residents, with celebrating Christmas or Chinese festivals banned in public (a Muslim could get five years in prison if they appear in public in a Santa outfit), and in 2017 an Australian expat faced twelve months in prison for "containment" (being in the same house as a non-related member of the opposite sex), though he was eventually allowed to leave the country after a costly legal case. One injunction it's as well to adhere to is the ban on consuming food and drink (even water) in public during daylight hours throughout **Ramadan** – you could be fined B$300 for not adhering to it. Blasphemy is also a serious crime, so exercise caution over anything you might say about religion in public.

ARRIVAL AND DEPARTURE

By plane Bandar's airport has flights from Kota Kinabalu, Kuala Lumpur, Jakarta and Singapore, and reasonable connections with cities elsewhere in the region and further afield. A departure tax (B$5 to Indonesia, Malaysia and Philippines and B$12 for everywhere else) is payable at the check-in desk on departure.

By bus Reaching Brunei by bus is easy. A couple of daily services run to Bandar from Miri in Sarawak, via the coastal towns of Kuala Belait and Seria, and from Kota Kinabalu in Sabah. Daily buses also run all the way from Pontianak in western Kalimantan.

By boat Muara, Bandar's port, is served by boats from Labuan and from Lawas in Sarawak.

GETTING AROUND

By car Brunei is small enough that you can visit most towns as day-trips from the capital. However, the bus system is indifferent, so renting a car is the ideal way to explore. It's not overly expensive, at B$70–130/day, and fuel is cheap, though you may not be allowed to go to Temburong district as you have to leave the country to do so.

ESSENTIALS

Alcohol, tobacco and drugs Brunei is famously dry, though tourists are permitted to bring two bottles of liquor and twelve cans of beer into the country for private consumption, but this must be declared to customs. The sultan is also very anti-smoking (although he himself smokes cigars); you are only permitted to bring one packet of nineteen cigarettes through customs; smoking is not permitted in any public space and doing so carries a fine of B$300. You will also see many signs in customs making it clear that being found with drugs is an executable offence.

Money The Brunei dollar (B$; also called the ringgit in Malay) has the same value as the Singapore dollar, widely used in Brunei.

Opening hours Brunei has a split weekend as far as government bodies are concerned: Fridays and Sundays are days off. Some private businesses follow government hours, others work Monday to Friday with a half-day on Saturday.

Entry visas Most Western nationalities are allowed to enter visa-free for thirty to ninety days, although for some reason Canadians can only get fourteen days.

Bandar Seri Begawan

BANDAR SERI BEGAWAN (known locally as **Bandar** or **BSB**) feels more like a provincial town than a capital. It is also a newish, largely postwar city, dominated by drab concrete – until comparatively recently, the seat of power and main settlement was Kampong Ayer, the picturesque water village visible from all along Bandar's river bank. The commercial centre, built on reclaimed land after the British Resident arrived in 1906, comprises a mere handful of riverside streets and is surprisingly tranquil, not to say dull; recent development has been concentrated in the suburbs.

Despite its underwhelming air, Bandar packs in a surprising amount for visitors. **Kampong Ayer** is the obvious sight, but perhaps even more memorable are the **proboscis monkeys** that live in a mangrove forest just a twenty-minute boat ride upriver from the centre. Not many tourists glimpse them, though, whereas virtually everyone heads to the **Omar Ali Saifuddien mosque** – an iconic building that turns out not to be all that spectacular up close. At their best, the city's **museums**, whether glorifying the sultanate or documenting local history and culture, are genuinely enlightening.

8

The waterfront

Following the middle-class flight to the suburbs, efforts to bring life back to the centre (thus far not entirely successful) have culminated in the revamp of the city's **waterfront** along Jalan McArthur. The 0.5km esplanade is a good place to get your bearings – from here you can see **Kampong Ayer**; a golden onion dome and white

PROBOSCIS MONKEYS

For many visitors, a trip to Borneo would not be complete without an encounter with a **proboscis monkey**, found only in riverine forests and coastal mangrove swamps. The reddish-brown monkey derives its name from the adult male's enlarged, drooping nose; females and young animals are snub-nosed. The role of the male's oversized member, which seems to straighten out when the animal is issuing its curious honking call, is likely to do with establishing dominance within a group and, by doing so, attracting a mate.

The monkeys specialize in eating hard-to-digest mangrove leaves, an adaptation that has enlarged their stomachs and left them with distinctive pot-bellies – and limited their distribution. Entirely arboreal, they're capable of making spectacular leaps across the river channels that cut through mangrove forests, arms thrown wide to catch foliage on the far side – though, in case they miss, they're also proficient swimmers, with webbed toes.

As well as the Brunei River near Bandar Seri Begawan, good places to spot proboscis monkeys include the Kinabatangan (see p.434) and Labuk Bay (see p.433) sanctuaries of Sabah, and Bako National Park (see p.338) in Sarawak.

BANDAR SERI BEGAWAN

N

● SHOPPING	
Arts and Handicrafts Centre	4
Gadong Mall	2
Times Square Shopping Centre	1
Yayasan Complex	3

Ripas ✚

■ ACCOMMODATION	
Brunei	7
Jubilee	5
K.H. Soon Rest House	6
MSS Mega Rest House (Budget Inn)	8
Pusat Bella (Youth Centre)	4
Radisson Jalan	3
Rizqun International	1
Terrace	2

● EATING	
Choices	6
DeRoy@ile C@fe	7
Excapade	1
Fratini's	9
Gadong Pasar Malam	2
Phongmun	10
Syazwan Café	8
Taman Selera	5
Tarindak d'Seni	11
Thiam Hock	3
TT Blues Café	4

⓫(350m), **❹**(350m), Arts & Handicrafts Centre (350m), Tarindak Seni (350m), Bubungan Duabelas (1km) & Museums (3km) ▲

❶ (3.5km), **❽** (1km), **❷** (3.5km), **❹** (3.8km), **❷** (4m) Sunshine Borneo & Borneo Guide (3.5km),
❷ Times Square Shopping Centre (5.6km) **❷** 400 Gadong (550m)

Kianggeh River

JALAN SUNGAI KIANGGEH

JLN KAMPUNG KIANGGEH

JALAN KAMPUNG BERANGAN

JALAN TASEK LAMA

JALAN BENDAHARA

JALAN SULTAN

Lapau Diraja

Dewan Majlis Legislative Assembly

Tengyun Temple

JALAN ELIZABETH DUA

Intrepid Tours

International Buses

Royal Brunei Airlines

Padang

Malay Teachers' Federation Building

Tamu Kianggeh

Guardian Pharmacy

JALAN CATOR

Wisma

HSBC

JALAN PEMANCHA

JALAN ROBERTS

LRG GERAI TIMOR

Jaya

Freme Travel

Standard Chartered Bank

Glok Tee Building

Kompleks Darussalam

Bolkiah Theatre

Bus Station & taxi rank

JALAN MCARTHUR

Old Custom House

Kianggeh Food Court

JALAN PRETTY

Guardian Pharmacy

Yayasan Complex

Taman Selera

Royal Regalia Building

JALAN STONEY

JALAN JAMES PEARCE

Police Station

JALAN SUMBILING

JALAN TUTONG

Omar Ali Saifuddien Mosque

JLN AN ISTANA DARUSSALAM

Istana Darussalem

EDINBURGH BRIDGE

JALAN HJ BASIR

Kedayan River

Supreme Court

LEBUHRAYA SULTAN HASANIL BOLKIAH

JALAN TUTONG

Abdul Razak Plaza

Royal Mausoleum

Kampung Ayer Water Village

Brunei River

JALAN RESIDENCY

River trips

Bandar & Temburong ▶

Kampung Ayer Tourism & Culture Gallery ▶

Airport (8km) ◀

❶ (6.5km) & Airport (8km) ◀

Jame 'Asr Hassanal Bolkiah Mosque (2.3km), ▲ Gadong (4km), Kiarong (4km) & Airport (8km) ▲
Istana Nurul Iman (3km) ▲

0 — 200 metres

8

saddle-roofed building that forms part of the sultan's palace; and the tower of the **Arts and Handicraft Centre**.

At the heart of the esplanade, the simple **Old Custom House** contains a small museum of the city's development (Mon–Thurs & Sun 8.30am–5pm, Fri 8.30–11.30am & 2–5pm, Sat 9.45am–5pm; free), though labelling is entirely in Malay. Nearby, a couple of smaller buildings with pointed white tent-shaped roofs are home to several attempts at smart **cafés**, but they've still not really become part of the city's fabric and are frequented mainly by foreigners – a charge that could equally be levelled at the waterfront as a whole. At night families arrive for a quick stroll, admiring the myriad lights of Kampong Ayer across the dark river, before scooting off elsewhere for refreshments.

Kampong Ayer Tourism and Culture Gallery

Across the water from the esplanade • Mon–Thurs & Sun 9am–5pm, Fri 9–11.30am & 2.30–5pm, Sat 9.45am–5pm • Free • ☎ 220 0874 • Water taxi from main waterfront (B$1)

The **Kampong Ayer Tourism and Culture Gallery** is the obvious place to start exploring Kampong Ayer. It houses the **tourist office** (see p.463), though its small museum is sadly not as interesting as the 600-year-old history of Kampong Ayer it charts, though there are English captions. A little **observation tower** offers good views over the colourful wooden houses and back towards downtown. From here you can simply head off into the water village via assorted meandering walkways, though the maze-like character of the place and lack of signage make it difficult to identify specific sights. A few homes may have crafts for sale, and you may be lucky enough to chance upon, say, cottage industries involving rattan-weaving.

Omar Ali Saifuddien Mosque

Jalan Masjid Omar Ali Saifuddien • Mon–Wed, Sat & Sun 8.30am–noon, 1.30–3pm & 4.30–5.30pm, Thurs open to Muslims only, Fri 4.30–5pm

Though modest in size, the **Omar Ali Saifuddien Mosque** must have been a marvellous sight when completed in 1958. Topped by a 52m-high dome, it would have dominated what was then very much a small town, and is beautifully located on the edge of a circular lagoon. The decision to plonk the modern Yayasan Complex of shops just southeast has done it no favours, however, and the mosque is now at that awkward

---

KAMPONG AYER

While neighbouring Malaysia still holds a few water villages, notably in Kota Kinabalu, none can match Bandar's **Kampong Ayer** for size. Practically a small town by itself, it snakes downriver for 2km beyond the city centre and upriver for another 1km or so, as well as up the Kedayan tributary of the river to the Edinburgh Bridge. Timber houses built on stilts and piles have occupied this stretch of the Brunei River for hundreds of years, and Kampong Ayer's historical significance cannot be underestimated. A census in 1911 showed that nearly half Brunei's population lived here, including the sultan, whose long-vanished palace was a suitably souped-up wooden affair.

Today the area is home to more than 39,000 inhabitants (almost ten percent of the country's population) in 42 villages with their own shops, clinics, mosques, schools and fire services, minus fire engines, of course. They also have electricity and mains water, but many houses remain unconnected to the sewerage system, which seems not to deter the boys who swim in the river. While residents are content with their lot, insofar as they have stayed put rather than move to dry land, the authorities are intent on tinkering with Kampong Ayer. They have embarked on a project to build several dozen non-timber homes in the area, boasting solar panels and billed as eco-friendly, and they continue to extend sanitation to the villages. There's also talk of action to arrest the decline in village traditions, notably crafts; one plan is to market Kampong Ayer as an "artisanal village" to showcase what trades linger, for example silversmithing and boat-building, though it's not clear when this might be put into effect. Most tour operators (see p.463) offer half-day **boat trips** that include the water village.

in-between age where it looks neither gleaming new nor venerable, merely a bit grimy in places. Still, commissioned by and named after the father of the present sultan, it makes tasteful use of opulent fittings – Italian marble, granite from Shanghai, Arabian and Belgian carpets, and English chandeliers and stained glass. The lagoon holds a replica of a sixteenth-century royal barge, or *mahligai*, used on special religious occasions.

Royal Regalia Building

Jalan Sultan • Mon–Thurs, Sat & Sun 9am–5pm, Fri 9–11.30am & 2.30–5pm • Free • ☎ 224 4545

In addition to a handful of uninteresting museums, downtown Bandar holds one that is simply essential – the **Royal Regalia Building**, easy to pick out as its roof is shaped like a strange domed helmet. While the name might lead you to expect a dry costume collection, it's actually a hilarious collection of regal paraphernalia whose subtext is to serve as a massive paean to the sultan. Perhaps the most significant objects are those used during his coronation, including the *tongkat aja* – a model of a human arm in gold, used to support the royal chin during the ceremony, which took place just across the road in the grand-looking Lapau Diraja building. Most visitors get an even bigger kick out of two massive **chariots**, one used for the coronation, the other for his highness's silver jubilee in 1992, the throng on the day recreated by dozens of mannequins in aristocratic Malay dress. Elsewhere there's an eccentric display of gifts the Brunei royals have been lumbered with, courtesy of blue-blooded intimates and world statesmen – replica temples made of crystal, and the like. Note that outdoor shoes must be removed at the entrance.

Tamu Kianggeh

Jalan Sungai Kianggeh • Daily dawn–dusk • Free • ☎ 224 1909 • Bus #37

The central produce market, **Tamu Kianggeh**, alongside the canalized Kianggeh creek sells everything from machetes to *midin* – nothing you can't see in markets in Sarawak or Sabah, but entertaining all the same. Friday morning is the busiest, and thus the best, time to turn up.

Arts and Handicrafts Centre

Jalan Residency, just over 5min walk east of Tamu Kianggeh • Mon–Thurs, Sat & Sun 8am–5pm, Fri 8–11.30am & 2.30–5pm • Free •
☎ 224 1909 • Bus #39

Bandar's **Arts and Handicrafts Centre** is a substantial complex where young Bruneians are taught traditional skills such as weaving, brass-casting and the crafting of the *kris*, the traditional Malay dagger. Unfortunately classes are not generally open to public view without prior arrangement, so you'll have to make do with browsing the overly pricey **gift shop** (note that it doesn't accept credit cards). The other reason to visit is to enjoy classic Bruneian food at their restaurant, *Tarindak d'Seni* (see p.466).

Kota Batu

It's fitting that Brunei's main **museums** should be a little way east of the centre at **Kota Batu**, the site of the capital when the Brunei sultanate was at its height. The area was excavated in the early 1950s by Tom Harrisson, who was instrumental in uncovering so many aspects of Sarawak's history and culture. A few old walls aside, however, this largely wooded area, close to the river, holds scant signs of former habitation.

Malay Technology Museum

Jalan Kota Batu, 4km east of the centre • Mon–Thurs & Sun 9am–5pm, Fri 9–11.30am & 2.30–5pm, Sat 9.45am–5pm; Ramadan daily
9am–3pm (Fri until noon); closed religious holidays • Free • ☎ 224 4545 • Bus #39

Right by the Brunei River, the endearingly misnamed but surprisingly good **Malay**

Technology Museum focuses not on kampung-built MP3 players but on traditional lifestyles and architecture, with – despite Brunei's tiny population of indigenous tribes – some creditable ethnographic exhibits that are sorely lacking in northern Sarawak. The first hall has a thought-provoking display on different styles of kampung house and their bewildering roof shapes; another is devoted to activities such as fishing using traditional traps. Best of all is the third hall, with scaled-down replicas of a Lun Bawang longhouse, a Penan shelter and a hut for trampling sago pith to make flour, among other tribal structures. If you're interested in ships, you may also want to visit the nearby **Maritime Museum** (same hours), whose badly lit interior displays the recovered contents, mostly ceramics, of a sixteenth-century Chinese trade ship discovered in Brunei waters, as well as models of other historic craft that sailed in the region.

Istana Nurul Iman

By the Brunei River 4km west of the centre, off Jalan Tutong • Open two days a year during the Hari Raya Aidilfitri festival marking the end of Ramadan • Bus #42, #44, #46, #48 or #56

Unless you are in town at the right time of year, the closest you're likely to get to the sultan's palace, the **Istana Nurul Iman**, is on a river trip to spot Bandar's proboscis monkeys. Even viewed from afar, the palace impresses with its scale: it's bigger than London's Buckingham Palace, the main buildings stretching for nearly 0.5km. Needless to say, it's also a monument to sheer self-indulgence (it cost over US$1.5 billion), with nearly eighteen hundred rooms – including 257 toilets – and at least five hundred chandeliers. The design, by Filipino architect Leandro Locsin, tries to incorporate Islamic motifs such as arches and domes, plus a traditional saddle-shaped roof, though many might say it fails on all counts. There's said to be a secret passage connecting the palace with the sultan's former home, the considerably more modest Istana Darul Hana, also by the river about 1km closer to the centre of town.

8

Jame 'Asr Hassanal Bolkiah

3km northwest of the centre, on the northern edge of Kiarong suburb • Mon–Wed, Sat & Sun 8am–noon, 2–3pm & 5–6pm, Thurs & Fri open to Muslims only • Free • Bus #1 or #22

With sky-blue roofs, six golden domes and pleasant grounds with fountains, the **Jame 'Asr Hassanal Bolkiah** is a grander sibling to the Omar Ali Saifuddien mosque downtown. Built in the 1990s to mark the sultan's silver jubilee, it's also the largest mosque in Brunei, though some of the neat mosaic decoration has a slightly plastic appearance. The mosque is conveniently close to the malls and restaurants of the suburb of Gadong, 1km north, but getting there on foot means traversing some fearsome highways. If you happen to pass this way at night, look out for the evocative lighting, which gives the building an air of serenity despite the fast-moving traffic.

Gadong

5km northwest of the centre • Bus #1 or #20 runs along the main drag, right past the Abdul Razak Complex; a taxi from downtown costs B$8–10 (B$12–15 after sunset)

If you spend much time outside the centre while in Bandar, it's likely to be in the most thriving suburb of **Gadong**. The place isn't much to look at: a collection of mundane concrete blocks and traffic-clogged streets surrounding the multiple blocks of the **Abdul Razak Complex**, which includes two hotels and the **Gadong Mall**, where despite the grandiose exterior the shopping is unmemorable. Gadong is, however, a good spot for **eating**, with decent restaurants and a terrific **pasar malam** where they sell all manner of Bruneian Malay goodies (see p.466).

ARRIVAL AND DEPARTURE

By plane Brunei International Airport (☎233 1747) is 8km north of the city; it now has a decent range of facilities following its recent refurbishment. A taxi into town takes 20min and costs around B$25 from the prepaid taxi counter; during daylight hours, buses #11, #23, #24, #36, #38 and #57 (B$2) run to the bus station. Royal Brunei Airlines is in the RBA Plaza on Jalan Sultan (☎221 2222); Haji Ahmad Laksamana Othman Building, the building that holds the *DeRoy@lle C@fe*, houses Malaysia Airlines (☎222 3074) and Singapore Airlines (☎224 4901).

Destinations Kota Kinabalu (14 weekly; 40min); Kuala Lumpur (3–5 daily; 2hr 30min); Singapore (2–3 daily; 2hr).

By bus All domestic buses use the bus station on Jalan Cator, while international services park on Jalan Sungai Kiangggeh by a conspicuous modern glass tower. Buses to Malaysia, operated by PHLS (☎277 1668 or ☎718 3838, ⒲phls38 .com), run to Miri at 7am and 1pm (4hr) while the Jesselton/ Sipitang Express(☎714 5734, ⒲sipitangexpress.com.my) heads to Kota Kinabalu (8hr 30min) via Limbang (1hr 30min), Lawas (3hr), Sipitang (4hr 30min) and Beaufort (5hr 30min) daily at 8am. You seldom need to buy tickets in advance, but

can do so either from bus conductors before departure, or from the *DeRoy@lle C@fe* (see p.464). Indonesian buses run by Damri (book through Tenaga Travels at the main bus station; ☎222 3927) and SJS (Bumi Putera Commercial Centre, 7 Jalan Cato; ☎713 0686) make the massive haul to Pontianak at 3pm (daily) and 2.30pm (Tues, Thurs & Sun) respectively (24– 28hr). Both pass through Sarawak's main cities, but can't set passengers down in Malaysia, for which you will have to catch a bus to Miri and change if you want to continue west. Ticket agents can be found above the bus station and, across the elevated concrete link, on the same level in the building on the north side of Jalan Cator.

Intertown buses Public buses no longer serve Tutong, Seria or Kuala Belait so your only option is the PHLS "express" bus to Miri (7am & 1pm) which can drop you off along the way.

By boat The only boats that serve Bandar itself, to and from Bangar in the Temburong district, use a jetty on Jalan Residency close to the Kiangggeh food court (around hourly 6am–4.30pm; 45min; B$7). All international ferries use the terminal in Muara (see p.467).

GETTING AROUND

Nowhere in Bandar's compact centre is more than a 20min walk from anywhere else, but you'll probably use the city's modest **bus** system to reach outlying attractions and the suburbs.

BY BUS

Bus station On the ground floor of Kompleks Darussalam on Jalan Cator.

Routes Most domestic buses are compact, purple 22-seater vehicles, but there are several other liveries and

they all only run between 6am and 6.30pm. There is a bus map in the tourist office's guide, though it's only slightly useful – a coloured "line" gives a general idea where each bus might be heading, but you must note the route number for your destination and ask around in the bus station. On

---

BRUNEI RIVER TRIPS

Most Bandar tour operators (see opposite) offer guided half-day trips on the Brunei River that take in **Kampong Ayer**. Unfortunately the tours tend to be pricey, starting at B$85/person, and, in Kampong Ayer at least, they show you little that you can't see on your own, though most include tea and cakes at one of the houses. Where such trips come in handy is in combining Kampong Ayer with the chance to see **proboscis monkeys**. If you were in Kuching or Kota Kinabalu, the nearest groups of the monkeys would be a long excursion away in Bako or the Garama River, so it's incredible that here in Bandar they can be found a mere twenty minutes' boat ride upriver from the centre, beyond the royal palace in a sliver of woodland and mangrove hemmed in between a residential neighbourhood and the river. The best time of day to see them is around 8am or 5pm, when it's cooler and the monkeys come out to forage.

It's perfectly possible to arrange a river trip **independently**: village boatmen hang around at the jetty area at the western end of Jalan McArthur, close to *Kaizan Sushi* restaurant, which is also where the tour boats leave from. The boatmen won't proffer life jackets or slick commentary (and may not speak that much English), but they charge much less than a tour company: with some bargaining, reckon on around B$20–30 per hour for one person, and B$5 per person after that for up to eight. Note that it will take at least an hour to have a reasonable go at spotting the monkeys (depending if there's a queue to enter the mangroves) and enjoy a quick spin around Kampong Ayer. Another advantage of arranging your own trip is that you can ask to be let off elsewhere along the river later – after monkey-spotting first thing in the morning, possible places to visit include the Handicrafts Centre (see p.460).

average there are two buses an hour on each route (popular services such as #1A to Gadong and #39 to Muara via the Kota Batu museums might run every 15–20min).

Fares and stops A standard fare of B$1 covers any journey within and even quite far out of Bandar. Outside the city centre, designated stops may be thin on the ground (and some are actually only marked on the ground), but drivers usually halt anywhere convenient.

BY TAXI

Ranks and companies Taxis come into their own at night, when the bus network has shut down, but are relatively rare – most people can afford cars so there are only around forty taxis in the whole country, though Uber and Grab are making inroads. While there are a couple of taxi cooperatives (☎ 222 2214 or ☎ 222 6853), most drivers work independently and can only be summoned by mobile phone; hotels keep lists of favourites. In downtown Bandar, there's a taxi rank outside the Jalan Cator bus station. Taxis show up sporadically at suburban malls too, though they can be so scarce in Gadong that you may have to ask a hotel there to book one.

Fares Taxis aren't always metered, so get an idea of current fares from your hotel; reckon on B$8–25 between the centre and anywhere else within the city. Hourly rates can be negotiated (typically B$40/hr), and prices rise by fifty percent after dark.

BY WATER-TAXI

Routes and access Little speedboats plying the Brunei River, known as water-taxis, are fun for whizzing around the river, but of limited use since most of the few waterside attractions are perfectly walkable. You can attract the attention of a boatman at numerous jetties and steps leading down to the river and Kianggeh canal (by Tamu Kianggeh).

Fares The fare for any journey across the central stretch of the river is B$1.

BY CAR

Car rental Avis, at the *Radisson* hotel (☎ 222 7100); Hertz, at the airport (☎ 233 2983); Qawi in Gadong on Jalan Penghubung Berakas Lambak Kanan (☎ 265 5550).

INFORMATION

Tourist offices Brunei Tourism (ⓦ bruneitourism.travel) run offices at the airport and the Kampong Ayer Tourism and Culture Gallery (both Mon–Thurs & Sat 9am–5pm, Fri 9–11.30am & 2–5pm; closed public holidays and in the afternoon during Ramadan; ☎ 220 0874). Both supply maps and brochures, but little else. Tourism Malaysia (Mon–Thurs & Sun 9am–5pm, Fri 9–11.30am & 2–5pm,

Sat 10am–5pm; ☎ 238 1575) is on the first floor of the *Rizqun International* in Gadong (see p.464).

Newspapers Since the closing of *Brunei Times* in 2016, the only English-language newspaper is the *Borneo Bulletin* (ⓦ borneobulletin.com.bn), inevitably filled with news about the royal family, though it offers useful leads on events and new venues.

TOUR OPERATORS

Although Bandar's expensive tour operators major in rather predictable city tours (B$40–80), Ulu Temburong trips and river excursions to see the monkeys and floating village, they also offer a few destinations that are awkward to visit independently, notably **Selirong Island** in Brunei Bay – a great spot for birding – and the **Bukit Peradayan Forest Reserve** on the eastern edge of Temburong (the latter is also sometimes included in Temburong packages). Brunei is also a good spot for diving – although much more expensive than in Malaysia, there are several worthwhile wreck dives in Brunei waters.

Borneo Guide Unit 5, second floor, Plaza Al-Abrar, Simpang 424a, Gadong ☎242 6923, ⓦborneoguide .com. Fairly standard offerings, with two notable exceptions: the Countryside Tour is a day-trip out to Mukim Amo (3hr; US$55) for a slice of rural Brunei, including a visit to the rice paddies and a bee farm. The other is a longhouse visit near Labi that includes a walk into primary rainforest (7hr; US$165).

Freme Travel 403b Wisma Jaya, Jalan Pemancha ☎ 223 4280, ⓦfreme.com. The usual destinations, plus two-night dedicated bird-watching trips (B$540) and another two-night trip that includes the Seria oil field (see p.470).

Intrepid Tours First floor, Brunei Malay Teachers' Federation Building, Jalan Sungai Kianggeh ☎222 1685, ⓦbruneibay.net. An array of more interesting trips include educational packages and the chance to scuba dive, snorkel and fish in Brunei Bay.

Sunshine Borneo 2 Simpang 146, Jalan Kiarong ☎244 1791, ⓦexploreborneo.com. This veteran company has a comprehensive portfolio of packages, though they can do tailor-made trips such as to Bukit Peradayan Forest Reserve, combined with visits to nearby modern longhouses.

ACCOMMODATION

Brunei not being backpacker territory, Bandar holds few great **budget** options, though the city has an adequate array of hotels, and higher-end Airbnb rooms are also available. Some visitors prefer to stay outside Bandar, commuting in for the sights – certainly feasible, though it won't save you any money and you'll have to head out well before sunset if you're using public

8

transport. The obvious out-of-town place to stay is the lavish *Empire* (see p.468), though it's possible to base yourself in **Seria** or even Bangar in **Temburong** if you have your own transport. A few Air B&B properties are available in Kumpung Ayer.

DOWNTOWN

★**Brunei** 95 Jalan Pemancha ☎224 4828, ⓦthebruneihotel.com; map p.458. The nicest and best-value place in the centre, transformed from a dowdy lump of 1960s concrete into a well-run business-oriented hotel. All rooms have beautiful timber flooring and stylish modern fittings, though there's no discount for singles. Free shuttle transport to and from Gadong for the shops and night market. Rates include breakfast. 📶 B$164

Jubilee Jalan Kampung Kianggeh ☎222 8070, ⓦjubileehotelbrunei.com; map p.458. A dull concrete tower with somewhat cramped rooms and dated, slightly worn furniture. Weirdly, many of the supposedly en-suite bathrooms are actually just outside the rooms they belong to, though some do have bathtubs. Still, with rates including breakfast, it is inexpensive. 📶 B$78

K.H. Soon Rest House Third floor, 140 Jalan Pemanacha ☎222 2052; map p.458. Archetypal Chinese-run flophouse, of a kind that's vanishing elsewhere. Rooms are large and have a/c, but are a bit tatty and bare with rough cement floors, though some are en suite. At least the prices are good. They do actually have a six-bed dorm room, though they don't seem to like telling people. 📶 Dorm B$20, doubles B$39

★**MSS Mega Rest House (Budget Inn)** 27 Jalan Sultan ☎222 2384; map p.458. This new place is probably the best budget option in the country. It's located right at the heart of the city, with clean and bare but comfortable rooms. Reception closes at 10pm. Price includes breakfast. Dorm $20, doubles B$38

Pusat Belia (Youth Centre) Jalan Sultan Kianggeh ☎222 2900; map p.458. Used for student conferences, Bandar's youth centre features various dorms – single-sex, in line with local values – that take travellers. Facilities include a small pool (B$1) but no wi-fi, and cleanliness can be an issue. Awkwardly, reception keeps standard office hours (Mon–Thurs & Sat 8am–noon & 2–4pm); at other times, call the manager using the number on display or hope to bump into a staff member. Dorms B$10

Radisson Jalan Tasek Lama ☎224 4272, ⓦradisson.com; map p.458. Brunei's first top-notch hotel, with a pool, spa, fitness centre and other amenities, and the rooms are modern and clean and the service excellent. Free shuttle-bus service to the shopping malls. 📶 B$165

Terrace Jalan Tasek Lama ☎224 3554, ⓦterracebrunei.com; map p.458. Ageing, like the *Jubilee*, but a slightly better deal, with larger rooms, an outdoor pool, and a fairly cheap multicuisine restaurant (mains B$4.50–7). Their advertising slogan, "Brunei's best value in hospitality", isn't far off. 📶 B$65

GADONG

Rizqun International Southeastern end of Abdul Razak Complex ☎242 3000, ⓦrizquninternational .com; map p.458. The priciest hotel in town, adjoining the Gadong Mall, with an ostentatious lobby featuring lots of marble and gaudy stained glass. Facilities include a pool and gym, and forty percent discount is sometimes available at weekends, including breakfast. 📶 B$320

EATING

In a country where eating and shopping count as the main pastimes, Bandar has a good sprinkling of venues catering to both. There are inexpensive stalls downtown at **Tamu Kianggeh** and a stone's throw away at the so-called **Kianggeh food court** on Jalan Residency, the latter good for river views at dusk – however, both pale in comparison to those at Taman Selera and at **Gadong's pasar malam**. If Brunei has a national dish, it's **nasi katok**. Widely sold for as little as B$1 at stalls and in a few cheap diners, it's a more substantial answer to *nasi lemak* – featuring plain rather than coconut rice, topped with a large joint of chicken or sometimes a helping of beef. Various tales explain the name (meaning "knock rice"), the most common being that hawkers devised it as a breakfast for people working night shifts, and used to knock on workplace doors in the morning to announce its arrival. Malay food doesn't dominate the culinary scene, however – there are plenty of Chinese and a few Indian options as well, plus a smattering serving Japanese and other international cuisines.

DOWNTOWN

Choices Brunei Hotel, 95 Jalan Pemancha ☎224 4828, ⓦthebruneihotel.com; map p.458. The *Brunei Hotel's* coffee house is great for a Western-style breakfast – B$14.95 buys a buffet of chicken sausage, beans, hash browns, cereals and so forth, with eggs and pancakes cooked to order, plus the usual local rice or noodle options. At other times they serve up a mixture of

Western and Malaysian food. Daily 6.30–10am, 11.30am–2.30pm & 6–10pm.

DeRoy@lle C@fe Jalan Sultan ☎223 2519; map p.458. This stands out among several cafés in the area as Bandar's most established hangout, with an extensive menu of so-so food: sub-style sandwiches, burgers and the like, free wi-fi and newspapers, plus two screens with BBC news, HBO movies and international sport. Most dishes B$5.90–15.90.

OPPOSITE EMPIRE HOTEL & COUNTRY CLUB >

Not a bad place for breakfast – egg on French bread plus juice and coffee or tea, for example, only costs B$6.50. Daily 24hr.

★**Fratini's** 44 Jalan Sultan ☎ 223 1467, ⊕ fratinis.com; map p.458. Highly popular, *Fratini's* is an upmarket Italian chain with branches around the country. The food tends to be average rather than great, but the breadth of the menu compensates: the best option is their wide range of pizzas (B$15.75–20.75), but they also have similarly-priced pasta options and more expensive mains such as sea bass with ratatouille in a lemon sauce (B$31). Daily 10am–11pm.

Phongmun Second floor, Teck Guan Plaza, Jalan Sultan ☎222 9561; map p.458. Downtown's best Chinese restaurant, overlooking the river and predictably done out with temple-style red arches and dragons. Cantonese food is the order of the day, including dim sum in the mornings; otherwise the house specialities are braised pork leg eaten with buns (from B$20), and claypot chicken (B$14). The full menu runs to several pages, but you'll probably be given a cut-down version; most dishes cost over B$10. Daily 7am–10.30pm.

★**Syazwan Café** 30a Jalan Sultan ☎233 0727; map p.458. A cut above the area's other Indian Muslim *kedai kopis*, frying a full range of rice or noodle dishes to order (RM3 buys an ample portion), plus a good *nasi campur* spread, *thosai*, *murtabak*, very good *roti* and *nan* bread and even Chinese-style stir-fries. Daily 7.30am–9pm or so.

★**Taman Selera** Off Jalan Tutong, close to the Terrace hotel; map p.458. The most atmospheric downtown place for dinner, bar none, is this open-air food court, where dozens of stalls sell Malay food. *Ayam penyet* – tender barbecued chicken – is especially popular (try stall #7) and a couple of vendors sell satay and *nasi katok* too (around B$2–3.50). For something a little pricier, head to the *Mizu Seafood Village*, where they have live lobster in tubs and other seafood, all sold by weight and cooked to order. Cheaper seafood stir-fries, fried rice and noodles are also available for around B$3.50–6. Sit close to the stall you're ordering from. Daily 5pm–3am.

Tarindak d'Seni Eastern end of the Arts and Handicrafts Centre complex, Jalan Residency ☎ 224 0422; map p.458. Despite the bland modern decor, this buffet restaurant serves a very impressive Malay spread; lunch costs B$15, dinner B$25; on Sundays, breakfast is B$8 and high tea B$12. Tables

groan with dishes such as beef rendang, stir-fried *keladi* (yam greens) and *ikan kicap* (fish stewed in soy sauce), all eaten with plain or *biriyani* rice. They also serve a classic Bruneian staple, *ambuyat* – sago starch, looking and smelling like congealed glue; tease it out of the bowl with chopsticks and eat it with sauces such as *tempoyak* (fermented durian). More palatably, they have Western salads and oodles of local and European cakes. Mon–Sat noon–2.30pm & 7–10pm, Sun 8–11am & 3–5pm.

GADONG

Excapade Sushi First floor, Block C, Abdul Razak Complex, north of the main drag ☎ 244 3012; map p.458. Highly popular sushi chain with many branches in Bandar and around the country, thanks to reasonable prices and a menu that also includes a range of Japanese staples, such as sashimi and bento sets. Look at about B$10–20 and book ahead, especially at weekends. Daily 10am–2.30pm & 6–10.30pm.

Gadong Pasar Malam Just east across the canal from the Rizqun hotel; map p.458. Many tourists trek out to Gadong for this entertaining night market. Besides a section selling fruit and vegetables, it has a few dozen stalls selling all manner of local snacks for B$1–3, including grilled chicken and fish, *kelupis* (glutinous rice, often stuffed with minced beef or prawns and steamed in the leaves of the *irik* plant) and the sweet crêpe *apam balik*. As ever with night markets, though, there's nowhere to sit. Daily 6.30–11pm.

★**Thiam Hock** 5 Yong Siong Hai Building ☎ 244 1679; map p.458. Clean and stylish, and revered by locals for its excellent fish head dishes – curried, cooked in a spicy tamarind sauce, or chopped up with noodles. There's also a wide range of other seafood, plus the usual pork, veg and tofu; mornings are dominated by noodles (B$6), while most other non-seafood dishes start at B$8. To find the building, head south out of the Gadong Mall, for example using the exit by the Guardian pharmacy. Daily 8.30am–10pm.

TT Blues Café 12 Yong Siong Hai Building ☎ 242 4527; map p.458. This informal café-restaurant has big-screen soccer and is good for a cholesterol-raising mixed grill (B$12) and Western snacks, though they also have Malay options ranging from *rojak* to *cendol*, all around B$5–7. Especially busy at lunch and weekends. Tues–Sun 9am–2pm & 5–10pm, Fri 9am–noon & 2–10pm.

SHOPPING

Despite the population's healthy disposable incomes and attachment to shopping, Brunei's **malls** are disappointingly devoid of glitz – plenty of people drive across the border to **Miri** to shop, while the genuinely rich jet off to Singapore or Kuala Lumpur on a regular basis. **Opening hours** are curtailed during Ramadan, and individual shops in shopping centres keep their own hours.

Arts and Handicrafts Centre Jalan Residency ☎ 224 0676; map p.458. The gift shop here is a great place to browse a wide selection of crafts, though anything really worth having – notably silverware and brocade – is priced

in the hundreds of Brunei dollars. Mon–Thurs, Sat & Sun 9am–4.30pm, Fri 9–11.30am & 2.30–4.30pm.

Gadong Mall Abdul Razak development; map p.458. While the sheer size of the Gadong Mall is impressive, its shops, mostly selling trinkets, phone accessories, cheap clothes and so on, are nothing special; the big name, such as it is, is the Utama Grand department store. Otherwise, it's more of a place where young people turn out to see and be seen. The paltry selection of English-language books in the ground-floor magazine shop is the best you can get anywhere close to central Bandar. Daily 10am–10pm.

Yayasan Complex South of Omar Ali Saifuddien mosque; map p.458. A much earlier attempt to revive downtown Bandar than the revamped waterfront, this multi-building mall is rapidly losing ground to its out-of-town rivals and the top floors are deserted. The only outlet worth much of a look is the Hua Ho supermarket, but you can make use of 30 min free wi-fi and there are a few cafés. Daily 10am–9.30pm.

DIRECTORY

Cinemas Your best bet is the The Mall Cineplex at Gadong Mall (☎ 242 2455, ⍟ mall-ticket.com).

Embassies, consulates and high commissions (Note that all embassies are shut from Fri lunchtime or afternoon till Mon morning) Australia, 6F DAR Takaful IBB Utama, Jalan Pemancha (☎ 222 9435, ⍟ hbruneidarussalam. embassy.gov.au); Canada, 5F, McArthur Building, 1 Jalan McArthur (☎ 222 0043); Indonesia, Lot 4498, Simpang 528, Sungai Hanching Baru, Jalan Muara (☎ 233 0180); Malaysia, 61 Simpang 336, Kampong Sungai Akar, Jalan Kebangsaan (☎ 238 1095); Philippines, Simpang 336, Diplomatic Enclave, Jalan Kebangsaan (☎ 224 1465); Singapore, 8 Simpang 74, Jalan Subok (☎ 226 2741); Thailand, 2 Simpang 682, Kampung Bunut, Jalan Tutong

(☎ 265 3108); UK, Unit 2.01, Block D, Kompleks Yayasan Sultan Hassanal Bolkiah (☎ 222 2231, ⍟ hukinbrunei.fco. gov.uk); US, Simpang 336-52-16-9, Jalan Kebangsaan (☎ 238 4616, ⍟ brunei.usembassy.gov).

Hospital The RIPAS Hospital is near the centre on Jalan Tutong (☎ 224 2424). For an ambulance, call ☎ 991.

Pharmacies Guardian Pharmacy has outlets on Jalan Sultan and on the ground floor of Gadong Mall.

Police Central Police Station, Jalan Stoney (☎ 222 2333), or call ☎ 993.

Visa extensions The Immigration Office is out towards the airport on Jalan Menteri Besar (Mon–Thurs & Sat 7.45am–12.15pm & 1.30–4.30pm; ☎ 238 3106, ⍟ immigration.gov.bn; bus #1 or #24).

8

Muara district

As most of Brunei's natural attractions are in Temburong and Tutong, there's little to detain you in the capital's district, **Muara**. However, no visit to Brunei would be complete without checking out two eccentric attractions in **Jerudong** – the **Empire Hotel & Country Club** and the **Jerudong Park Playground**. Also worth a visit is **Muara Beach** and the **Bukit Shahbandar Forest Recreation Park**, a nature reserve with only the most basic facilities for visitors.

Muara

MUARA, Brunei's main port, 25km northeast of Bandar, has nothing else to recommend it other than **Muara Beach** 3km north, which boasts an adequate stretch of sand and a small food court; it's a long hot walk out here unless you want to wait for the erratic local minibus. You can wear your bikini on the beach, so long as it's under all your other clothes – everybody in the sea is fully clothed.

ARRIVAL AND DEPARTURE   MUARA

By ferry Brunei's international Serasa Ferry Terminal, a couple of kilometres south of what passes for the town centre, is served by bus #39 (hourly; 1hr), which stops on the main road at the green mosque, just under 1km from the terminal. The #33 minibus runs from Maura Beach via Maura town centre to the port, but it's request-only for the ferry terminal and so only really useful when departing. The latest boat departure schedules appear daily in the local English press. Ferries only run to Labuan (daily 8am, 8.30am, 9.30am, 1pm, 2.30pm & 4.40pm; at least 1hr

30min, depending on weather; foot passengers B$17, cars B$58–78), and you should arrive at least an hour before your departure. From Labuan, boats run to both Lawas in Sarawak, and Kota Kinabalu in Sabah.

By bus From Bandar, the most reliable buses for Muara are #38, which heads north to the airport and then east to Muara, and #39, which goes east to the Kota Batu museums and then north to Muara. The only bus to the beach is the #33 from Maura town centre. All go round the houses and take around an hour.

Jerudong and around

The fishing village at **JERUDONG**, 15km northwest of Bandar, is a simple place where you can see the fishing boats pulled up on the beach, and sample smoked fresh fish in the wet market. Walking west along the beaches and through the car park will bring you to the **Empire Hotel & Country Club**, the big sight around here, while the **Bukit Shahbandar Park** is across the highway, and the **Jerudong Park Playground** is just 4km southwest.

Empire Hotel & Country Club

Close to Jerudong, 15km northwest of Bandar, off the Muara–Tutong Highway • ☎ 241 8888, ⊛ theempirehotel.com • Bus #57 from Bandar may on request call at the hotel itself; if the driver refuses, get off on the highway and walk in (around 10min), or take a #55 to the fish market at Jerudong and walk in through the back entrance; a taxi from Bandar costs B$30

It might seem odd to traipse out of Bandar just to see a hotel, but then the **Empire Hotel & Country Club** is no ordinary hotel. A personal project in the 1990s of Prince Jefri, the wayward and discredited former finance minister, the complex cost US$1 billion to build and put such a drain on the state's coffers that the government had to take a stake in what had been intended as a private development.

The result, benefiting from the skills of thousands of craftsmen from assorted artistic traditions, is jaw-dropping. Just to stroll through the lofty central atrium with its 25m-high marble columns, is striking enough. Then there's the gold-plated balusters of the lobby staircase, laden with 370 tiger's eye gemstones, and the handrails coated with mother-of-pearl. While the hotel doesn't really throw open its doors as a tourist attraction, it's vast enough that no one minds neatly dressed visitors who come to gawp and then, more often than not, eat at one of the restaurants.

Bukit Shahbandar Forest Recreation Park

Along the Muara–Tutong highway, directly south of the Empire Hotel & Country Club • Free • Bus #57

The **Bukit Shahbandar Forest Recreation Park**, a compact area of acacia, pine and heath forest equipped with trails, carpets a hilly area with lookout points over the *Empire Hotel* complex, Bandar and the South China Sea. Marking the entrance to the park is an information centre with displays on the surrounding terrain. The trails are well signposted and popular with joggers, and there are a few rest huts for shade and shelter.

Jerudong Park Playground

Jerudong, south off the Muara–Tutong highway, 4km southwest of the Empire Hotel & Country Club • Thurs & Fri 4–11pm, Sat & Sun 5-11.30pmt • B$20, family pass B$50, foreigners must bring ID • ☎ 261 2044, ⊛ jerudongpark.com • Bus #57

In its 1990s heyday, the **Jerudong Park Playground** was the wonder of Brunei, almost like the country's answer to the Tivoli Gardens in Copenhagen. Built by the government as an amusement park for the sultan's subjects, it was an essential stopover for visitors, the rides all totally free; famously, Michael Jackson and Whitney Houston played the park's theatre. Like all extravagances the place inevitably became uneconomic to maintain, even with Brunei's oil revenues, and it slowly descended into moribundity. Relaunched in 2014, albeit on a diminished scale, the park is worth a visit if you're in the area – but even the kids might think it a bit dated. It's most atmospheric in the evening; if using public transport, be sure to arrange a taxi in advance to collect you after the buses stop at sunset. Note that all rides close for thirty minutes during prayer times.

ACCOMMODATION AND EATING   JERUDONG AND AROUND

Empire Hotel & Country Club Near Jerudong ☎241 8888, ⊛theempirehotel.com. The great thing about staying here is that while the high-ceilinged rooms, unlike the public areas, aren't exceptional for a five-star-type resort, rates can be very reasonable. Amenities include a golf course, spa, cinema, swimming pools and a private lagoon. 🛜 **B$297**

Li Gong Empire Hotel & Country Club ☎241 7783, ⊛theempirehotel.com. Housed in a separate building – look for the red lanterns outside – this is the best known of the *Empire*'s restaurants, serving halal Cantonese food, with dim sum available at lunchtime over the weekend. From B$20. Tues–Thurs 6–10pm, Fri & Sat 11am–3pm & 6–10pm, Sun 10.30am–2.30pm & 6–10pm.

Temburong district

With a population of just ten thousand, including some Iban and Lun Bawang (Murut), **Temburong district** is the wilds of Brunei. Forested and hilly, it contains Brunei's best-known attraction, the 500-square-kilometre **Ulu Temburong National Park**, with its entrancing canopy walkway. The park has limited possibilities for walks, though, so some people visit on a short day-trip from Bandar, while most opt for two-day packages.

Bangar

The starting point for all Ulu Temburong trips is the district's only town, **BANGAR**, normally reached by speedboat from Bandar. The boats head downriver through narrow mangrove estuaries before shooting off into the open expanse of Brunei Bay and then curling back south to head up the Temburong River. It's also possible to drive here via Limbang in Sarawak, or catch the Kota Kinabalu bus from Bandar, which passes through at about 10am. The town itself is nothing to write home about; its main street, running east from the jetty to the town mosque, holds a handful of *kedai kopis* and general stores. However, it is the nearest town to the Ulu Temburong National Park, with much cheaper accommodation, and tour operators that charge around half of what you'll pay in Bandar to visit it.

ACCOMMODATION
BANGAR

Bangar Government Resthouse Just off Jalan Puni on the road to Batang Duri ☎ 522 1239. A pretty, well-laid-out place two blocks behind the harbour across the main road, the *Resthouse* has just six en-suite singles and doubles as well as more expensive and comfortable chalets (B$80); they give priority to bookings by public-sector staff. B$30

Ulu Temburong National Park

Park HQ daily 8am–6.30pm • Prebooked tours compulsory, park fees included in package price

Contained within the Batu Apoi Forest Reserve, which constitutes a tenth of the area of Brunei, the **Ulu Temburong National Park** undoubtedly impresses as a pristine nature area. There isn't that much to do – the only trails are simple and short – but there are some activities on offer and the park is great for peace and quiet.

Canopy walkway

The park's main attraction, the **canopy walkway**, is reached by an hour-long trek (or longboat ride) taking in two hanging bridges and a plankway, followed by a giddying climb up the stairs around a near-vertical, 60m-high aluminium structure. The view from the top, of Brunei Bay to the north and Sarawak's Gunung Mulu National Park to the south, is breathtaking. At this height (on a good day) you can see hornbills and gibbons in the trees, as well as numerous squirrels and small birds. Fifty species of birds have been sighted on the netting around the walkway, while flying lizards, frogs and snakes feed regularly at ground level.

ARRIVAL AND INFORMATION
ULU TEMBURONG NATIONAL PARK

From Bandar On a standard two-day package (around B$280–330), the first day is spent reaching your accommodation from Bandar, and much of the second day given over to the park before you zip back to Bandar in the late afternoon. Tour operators also offer somewhat rushed day-trips at around B$130–150/person.

From Bangar You may find you pay slightly less if you make your own way to Bangar and join a tour there,

though you still need to book in advance. From Bangar, van transport is laid on to the jetty at Batang Duri, 15km south. The final leg is via longboat, with dense jungle cloaking the hills on either side and birds and monkeys bustling around in the trees. Though lasting less than an hour, the journey sets the tone for the park itself. You can also take day-trips from Bangar for around B$75.

8

Activities Besides the climb up to the canopy walkway, activities in and around the park include night walks, rafting or tubing down the river and treks to a nearby waterfall, each costing B$10–30/person.

ACCOMMODATION

Freme Lodge Batang Duri, 30min by longboat from Temburong National Park ☎ 223 4277, ⓦ freme.com. A substantial, comfortable place (though pretty basic considering the price) with a/c dorms and a large open-air communal dining area. Rates include one night's stay, meals and transfers from Bandar. Two-day package per person B$$240

Sumbiling Eco Village Sumbiling Lama, the penultimate village before Batang Duri ☎ 242 6923, ⓦ borneoguide.com/ecovillage. Run as a joint venture with local Iban, this is a fairly simple jungle encampment with tents and three basic huts (B$20 extra/person), though proper toilets are provided. In keeping with the eco theme, meals are eaten off leaves rather than plastic plates. Packages include a night walk in the vicinity. Rates include one night's stay, meals and transfers. Two-day per person US$138

Ulu-Ulu Resort Beside Ulu Temburong National Park HQ ⓦ uluuluresort.com. The resort is run by tour operator Sunshine Borneo (see p.463) and is the only accommodation within the park. It's quite an upmarket affair, with seventeen en-suite rooms with sleek modern decor, five of which are four-bed dorms (called "standard" rooms). The advantage of staying here, comfort aside, is that only resort guests can get to the canopy walkway at sunrise. Rates include one night's stay, meals and transfers. Two-day package per person, dorm B$275, rooms (minimum two people) B$330

Belait district

West of Muara, beyond the noticeably agricultural Tutong district, is **Belait district**, whose coastal section is oil and gas country, and has been the economic heart of the sultanate ever since the Seria oil field was established in 1931. The oil boom led directly to the rise of the region's two main towns, **Seria** and **Kuala Belait**, both still fairly sleepy, with generally ugly concrete centres that contrast with suburbs that have quite a rural feel. Inland, though, it's a much more rural story: down the 50km-long road to **Labi** are a few modern Iban **longhouses** and forest reserves to visit.

The Labi Road

No public transport, though Bandar tour operators such as Borneo Guide and Sunshine Borneo in Bandar offer trips here

More or less midway between Tutong and Seria, a turning south off the highway marks the start of the Labi Road. Just 500m on, the thick lowland forest of the **Sungai Liang Forest Reserve** can be explored by following various walking trails from the lakes. Twenty kilometres further along, at the **Luagan Lalak Forest Recreation Park**, a freshwater swamp swells into a lake with the onset of the monsoon rains. A little further on and you reach **LABI** itself, a small agricultural settlement where durian and rambutan are cultivated.

The road beyond turns into a laterite track; around 300m along, a trail off to the east leads, after two hours' walk, to **Wasai Rampayoh**, a large waterfall. Continue south on the track to reach **Mendaram Longhouse**, the first of four Iban communities here, and home to a few dozen people. Like most Iban architecture in Brunei, it's a modern structure, with electricity and running water, though it does have an informal homestay programme. From here a well-marked path leads past **Teraja Longhouse** to **Wasai Mendaram**, a tiny waterfall thirty or so minutes' walk away with a rock pool perfect for swimming.

Seria

SERIA, 65km southwest of Bandar, stands at the epicentre of Brunei's oil and gas wealth. Before oil was discovered here at the start of the twentieth century, this was nothing more than a malarial swamp, known locally as Padang Berawa, or "Wild

Pigeon's Field". Once S1, the sultanate's first oil well, began to deliver commercially in 1931, Seria expanded rapidly, with offshore drilling following in the 1950s. As you approach from Tutong, you may see small oil wells called "nodding donkeys" because of their rocking motion. Around the town are numerous bungalows, constructed by petroleum companies for their employees, while on the seafront nearly 2km west of the centre the interlocking arches of the **Billionth Barrel Monument** celebrate the huge productivity of the first well. Bandar's tour operators can organize trips to oil-related sights, including the Oil and Gas Discovery Centre. However, if you have no great interest in oil production, you'll probably want to avoid this soulless town.

Oil and Gas Discovery Centre

750m northwest of the bus station • Tues–Thurs & Sat 8.30am–noon & 1.30-5pm, Fri 8.30–11.30am & 2.30–5pm, Sun 9am-noon & 1.30–6pm • B$16 • ⓦ ogdcbrunei.com • From the bus station, head 500m north up Jalan Sultan Omar Ali, the road running west of the Plaza Seria mall, then 250m west; taxi B$15

Seria's only specific sight is the **Oil and Gas Discovery Centre**, a museum created by Brunei Shell to bolster understanding of technology in general and the petroleum industry in particular. With its hi-tech interactive exhibits, it's marginally more entertaining than the similar museum not far away in Miri, though you still need more than a passing interest in oil extraction to get much out of it. It's somewhere that all Brunei school kids are forced to visit at least once. There is also a small "town" where kids can zoom around in pedal cars, though it would be more apt (and fun) if the cars were petrol-driven.

ARRIVAL AND INFORMATION

SERIA

By bus Seria's bus terminus is diagonally across from the bank, south of the mall.
Destinations Kuala Belait (every 30min–1hr; 45min); Miri (daily, around 9am & 3pm; 2hr).

Services There's a bank, HSBC, at the southern end of the drab Plaza Seria shopping mall, which dominates Seria's small centre.

ACCOMMODATION AND EATING

Hotel Koperasi Jalan Sherif Ali ⓣ322 7589, ⓔhotel_ seria@brunet.bn. A dark green building just a couple of minutes walk up Jalan Bunga Kemantin from the bus terminal, the *Koperasi* is old-fashioned in a somehow restful way, its simple rooms equipped with a/c, TV, fridge and bathroom. ⓦ B$61

My Booney Below the Koperasi hotel, Jalan Sherif Ali ⓣ322 7061. Seria's community hangout offers something for everyone – indeed, the menu runs to eighty pages. With dishes from Chinese to Malay to Western to Indian, there's no shortage of choice, and the seafood is great value – meals B$3–5. Daily 6am–2am.

Singapore

GARDENS BY THE BAY

9

Singapore

Singapore is certainly the handiest city I ever saw, as well planned and carefully executed as though built entirely by one man. It is like a big desk, full of drawers and pigeon-holes, where everything has its place, and can always be found in it.

William Hornaday, 1885

Despite the immense changes wrought upon the tiny island of Singapore, natural historian William Hornaday's appraisal is as valid today as it was in 1885. This absorbing city-state, just one degree north of the Equator and only 720 square kilometres in size – if all the outlying islands are included – has evolved from a colonial port into a slick shrine to wealth and consumerism.

Singapore's rise began in 1819, when Sir Stamford Raffles took advantage of its natural harbour and strategic position on the maritime route between China and India to set up a British trading post. The port thrived from the word go, and remains one of the world's busiest. The country's coffers were boosted by **industrialization** following independence, and when in the 1980s Singapore grew too successful to remain a cheap sweatshop for multinationals, it maintained its competitive edge by developing a super-efficient infrastructure and work ethic, and diversifying into technology and finance.

Lacking any significant welfare system, Singapore appears to be a paragon of capitalism. Yet much of the economy is dominated by conglomerates set up by the state, which retains a controlling interest. Regulations govern everything from flushing public toilets after use to jaywalking, and, less benignly, there's a low tolerance of **dissent**.

This unwritten, paternalistic contract underlies what visitors see today: kampungs and slums have long been cleared, with people resettled in bland though well-planned new towns. Even today the island is dogged by a sense of impermanence, its buildings scarcely bedding down before being replaced by something even grander. But while Singapore is the most westernized of Southeast Asia's cities, it would be unfair to dismiss it as sterile. As with Malaysia, much of Singapore's fascination springs from its **multicultural population**, the main groups being the Chinese (around 75 percent), Malays (13 percent) and Indians (9 percent). This diversity can turn a short walk across town into what seems like a hop from one country to another.

Getting a decent taste of the island requires at least three days. Old Singapore is looking better than ever thanks to belated conservation work, and each of the original ethnic enclaves boasts neatly restored shophouses and its own distinct flavour: **Little India** has its garland-sellers and curry houses, **Chinatown** its calligraphers and fortune-tellers, while **Arab Street** is home to cluttered stores selling fine cloths and curios. At the core of downtown Singapore are historic public buildings and the lofty cathedral of the **Colonial District**. It also has a clutch of fine **museums**, something rarely on offer in Malaysia; the **Chinatown Heritage Centre** evokes the harsh conditions endured by Chinatown's earlier inhabitants, while the **Peranakan Museum** and **Baba House** celebrate Singapore's Baba-Nyonya community – just as important as that of Penang and Melaka.

There's much to enjoy by way of modern and, perhaps surprisingly, nature-oriented

Sir Stamford Raffles p.482	**Singapore addresses and maps** p.527
The Singapore River p.483	**Useful bus routes** p.528
Taking Chinese tea p.505	**Organized tours** p.531
Sentosa's cable cars p.521	**Cookery classes** p.536
Watersports on Sentosa p.524	**Street ice cream** p.541
Transport on Sentosa p.526	**Street theatre** p.547

THE BUDDHA TOOTH RELIC TEMPLE

Highlights

❶ National Gallery Singapore's National Gallery is certainly an architectural showpiece, uniting two of the island's grandest colonial buildings. **See p.481**

❷ Little India Old Singapore's most atmospheric district is a sensory overload of Tamil temples, colourful saris and aromatic spice-grinding shops. **See p.490**

❸ The Buddha Tooth Relic Temple One of the island's newest temples is also one of its grandest, housing thousands of Buddha figurines, a sacred tooth and even its own Buddhist art museum. **See p.497**

❹ The Baba House Singapore's answer to the fine showpiece Peranakan residences of Melaka and Penang. **See p.504**

❺ The Botanic Gardens This distinguished park boasts an immaculate orchid collection and forest walks. **See p.511**

❻ Bukit Timah Nature Reserve A pocket of primary rainforest for a decent taste of the jungle, minus leeches. **See p.513**

❼ S.E.A. Aquarium This gargantuan affair revels in the marine life of Southeast Asia's far-reaching maritime trade routes. **See p.522**

❽ Food Hundreds of restaurants serve up every style of Chinese cuisine, sophisticated fusion fare and more. **See p.536**

❾ The arts scene Get a taste of the best cultural life in the region, with international performers constantly passing through. **See p.546**

HIGHLIGHTS ARE MARKED ON THE MAPS ON P.476 & P.479

attractions too. The wings of reclaimed land at the mouth of the Singapore River, together forming **Marina Bay**, hold the striking **Marina Bay Sands** hotel and casino and the bug-eyed **Theatres on the Bay**. Huge investment in the **arts** means that even on a short visit, you may well catch world-renowned performers in town. North of the city, there's primary rainforest to explore at **Bukit Timah Nature Reserve** and the splendid **Singapore Zoo**, which you can even tour at night. The best offshore day-trip is south to **Sentosa**, the island amusement arcade that features Singapore's other casino resort.

Brief history

Little is known of Singapore's ancient history. Third-century Chinese sailors could have been referring to the place in their account of Pu-Luo-Chung, or "island at the end of a peninsula". In the late thirteenth century, Marco Polo reported seeing a place called Chiamassie, which could also have been Singapore; by then the island was known locally as Temasek and was a minor trading outpost of the Sumatran Srivijaya Empire.

Throughout the fourteenth century, Singapura felt the squeeze as the Ayuthaya and Majapahit empires of Thailand and Java struggled for control of the Malay Peninsula. Around 1390, a Sumatran prince called **Paramesvara** threw off his allegiance to Majapahit and fled to Temasek. There he murdered his host and ruled the island until a Javanese offensive forced him further north, where he and his son, **Iskandar Shah**, subsequently founded the Melaka Sultanate.

The country's present name is derived from one first recorded in the sixteenth century, when a legend recounted in the *Sejarah Melayu* (Malay Annals) told of how a Sumatran prince saw what he thought was a lion while sheltering on the island from a storm. He then founded a city here and named it **Singapura**, Sanskrit for "Lion City".

The British colony takes shape

By the late eighteenth century, with China opening up for trade with the West, the British East India Company felt the need to establish outposts along the Straits of Melaka. Enter **Thomas Stamford Raffles** (see p.482), lieutenant-governor of Bencoolen in Sumatra. In 1819, he alighted on the north bank of the Singapore River accompanied by William Farquhar, former Resident of Melaka. Raffles quickly saw the potential of what was then an inconsequential fishing island to provide a deep-water harbour and struck a deal to establish a British trading station with **Abdul Rahman**, the *temenggong* (chieftain) of Singapore and a subordinate of the Sultan of Johor. The Dutch, however, were furious at this British incursion into what they considered their territory. Realizing that the pro-Dutch sultan would not implement the deal, Raffles simply recognized the sultan's brother, **Hussein**, as the new ruler, then concluded a second treaty with both Hussein and the *temenggong*. The Union Jack was raised, and Singapore's future as a trading post was set.

As early as 1822, Raffles set about drawing up the demarcation lines which can still be perceived in the layout of modern Singapore. The area south of the Singapore River was earmarked for Chinese migrants; Muslims were settled around the sultan's palace in today's Arab Street area. In 1824, Hussein and the *temenggong* were bought out, and Singapore was ceded outright to the British. Three years later, the new port was united with Penang and Melaka to form the **Straits Settlements**, which became a British Crown Colony in 1867.

Singapore consolidates

Thanks to its **strategic position** at the gateway to the South China Sea, Singapore grew meteorically. By 1860 it had eighty thousand inhabitants; Arabs, Indians, Javanese and Bugis all settled here, but most numerous of all were southern Chinese. The opening of the Suez Canal and advent of the steamship consolidated the island's position, a status further enhanced as the British drew all of the Malay Peninsula into their clutches, allowing Singapore to profit from its hinterland's tin- and rubber-based economy.

By the 1920s, Singapore's communities were starting to find their voice: in 1926, the

9

Singapore Malay Union was established; as was the Malayan Communist Party four years later, largely backed by local Chinese. But rumblings concerning greater self-rule were barely audible when an altogether more immediate problem reared its head.

World War II

In December 1941, the **Japanese** bombed Pearl Harbour and invaded the Malay Peninsula; less than two months later they were at the Causeway between Johor and Singapore. On February 15, 1942, the **fall of Singapore** was complete. Winston Churchill called the surrender "the worst disaster and the largest capitulation in British history". Three and a half years of brutal Japanese rule ensued, during which upwards of 25,000 Chinese men were shot dead at Punggol and Changi beaches as enemies of the Japanese, and Europeans were either herded into **Changi Prison** or marched up the Peninsula to work on Thailand's infamous "Death Railway".

Independence

After the war, Singaporeans demanded a say in the island's administration, and in 1957 the British agreed to an elected legislative assembly. Full internal self-government was achieved in 1959, when the **People's Action Party** (PAP) emerged on top in elections. Cambridge law graduate **Lee Kuan Yew**, Singapore's first prime minister, quickly sought security via a merger with newly independent Malaya (now Peninsular Malaysia). In 1963 Singapore joined with Malaya, Sarawak and British North Borneo (Sabah) to form the **Federation of Malaysia**, but within two years it was asked to leave (see p.565). Things looked bleak for the tiny island. But Lee's personal vision and drive transformed Singapore into an Asian economic heavyweight, and enabled his party to utterly dominate Singapore politics to this day. Much of the media was taken under the state's wing and opposition politicians were harassed through the courts or even detained without trial.

New leaders, new maturity

Goh Chok Tong became prime minister in 1990 upon Lee's retirement – though many felt that Lee still called the shots. In 2004, Goh was succeeded by **Lee Hsien Loong**, Lee Kuan Yew's son, and on the very same day the elder Lee was named "minister mentor", a new position that gave him an official high horse from which to influence affairs. However, while the younger Lee has a sternness reminiscent of his father, Singapore was already becoming less uptight before his tenure, with a more open stance towards artistic expression and gay issues, for example, and the trend has continued. Perhaps the most startling expression of this maturing character came in the **2011 polls**, when the opposition won nearly forty percent of the popular vote and six out of 87 elected parliamentary seats – its best showing ever.

Although the PAP rebounded in the 2015 polls – held soon after the republic's **golden jubilee** and the **death of Lee Kuan Yew** – it seems clear that Singapore is capable of greater critical thinking than its media would suggest. Issues that continue to rankle include rising **healthcare** and **housing** costs, and the PAP's open stance on **immigration** – foreign workers on short-term contracts make up a quarter of the population.

Downtown Singapore

Taking up the southern part of the diamond-shaped main island, **downtown Singapore** is essentially the historic city centre. Although it's easy to navigate, given the excellent transport network, individual districts are best explored on foot. You need two days to do justice to the main areas, namely the **Colonial District**, **Chinatown**, **Little India** and the **Arab Quarter**, although you could just about squeeze in a trip to **Marina Bay Sands** too, or go shopping in **Orchard Road**.

DOWNTOWN SINGAPORE

9

HIGHLIGHTS
1 National Gallery
2 Little India
3 The Buddha Tooth Relic Temple
9 The arts scene

● **SHOPPING**
Risis 1

● **EATING**
Candlenut 3
Long Beach Seafood 2
Newton Circus
Hawker Centre 1
Samy's 2

■ **DRINKING AND NIGHTLIFE**
The Rabbit Hole 1

9 The Colonial District

On the north bank of the Singapore River is what might be termed the **Colonial District** – although locals might refer to it as the Civic District or use the names of landmarks, notably the **Padang**. This rectangular green expanse is flanked by dignified reminders of British rule, including the erstwhile Parliament House and City Hall; the surrounding area has a viable claim to be the island's **museum quarter**. The river itself was once the epicentre of Singapore's trade boom, although trendy nightspots now occupy its old warehouses. Come in September, and you'll see crash barriers and fences sprouting in both the Colonial District and Marina Centre next door, as main roads are transformed into the racetrack of Singapore's night-time **Formula One Grand Prix**.

The Padang

City Hall, Esplanade or Raffles Place MRT

The **Padang**, earmarked by Stamford Raffles as a recreation ground shortly after his arrival, is the very essence of colonial Singapore. In many respects it remains much as it was in 1907, when G.M. Reith wrote in his *Handbook to Singapore*: "Cricket, tennis, hockey, football and bowls are played on the plain…beyond the carriage drive on the other side is a strip of green along the sea-wall, with a foot-path which affords a cool and pleasant walk in the early morning and afternoon". Once the last over of the day had been bowled, the Padang assumed a more social role: Singapore's European community would hasten to the corner once known as Scandal Point to catch up on gossip.

THE COLONIAL DISTRICT

The brown-tiled roof, whitewashed walls and green blinds of the **Singapore Cricket Club**, at the southwestern end of the Padang, have a nostalgic charm. Founded in the 1850s, the club was the hub of colonial British society and still operates a "members only" rule. (Eurasians, formerly ineligible for membership due to the prejudices of the time, founded their own establishment in 1883: the **Singapore Recreation Club**, at the opposite end of the Padang.)

National Gallery

St Andrew's Rd (main entrance Coleman St) • Mon–Thurs & Sun 10am–7pm, Fri & Sat 10am–10pm • S$20 • ☎ 6271 7000, ⓦ nationalgallery.sg • City Hall or Raffles Place MRT

Taking up the entire west side of the Padang, Singapore's prestigious new **National Gallery** is redolent with history, formed as it is out of two of the island's most imposing colonial buildings. On the right as seen from the Padang is **City Hall**, with steps backed by grandiose Corinthian columns; it was here that Louis Mountbatten, supreme allied commander in Southeast Asia, announced Japan's surrender in 1945. Fourteen years later, Lee Kuan Yew chose the same spot for his address at a victory rally celebrating self-government for Singapore. On the left, the domed former **Supreme Court** was built in Neoclassical style in the 1930s and served its judicial functions until 2006.

DBS Singapore Gallery

Housed inside the erstwhile City Hall is the three-roomed **DBS Singapore Gallery**, which showcases work by artists who were either born in Singapore or lived here for a time. There's a notable emphasis on the **Nanyang style** (*nanyang* being the Mandarin term for the South China Sea), an umbrella term for art featuring a fusion of Western and Chinese techniques. One exemplar is Georgette Chen, whose elegant *Lotus in a Breeze* bears the hallmarks of Neo-impressionism, yet was only painted in 1970. Look out also for Chua Mia Tee's *Epic Poem of Malaya* and Tan Tee Chie's *On Strike*, both stirring depictions of the restive 1950s and yearnings for independence, and Tan Choh Tee's 1981 *Singapore River*, proof – if any were needed – that today's river is but a shadow of its former fetid self (see p.483).

UOB Southeast Asia Gallery

At the opposite end of the National Gallery, former courtrooms now house the **UOB Southeast Asia Gallery**, which attempts to put a hotchpotch of modern, often conceptual, art from the region into some kind of context. Although the exhibits may not grab you, the architecture probably will: this is the most lovingly conserved part of the National Gallery, retaining its original black-and-white marbled floors and wooden ceilings; an internal domed rotunda still houses a collection of legal books.

The roof garden

It's worth heading up to the National Gallery's **roof garden** for a fine panorama out over the Padang, with *Marina Bay Sands* directly opposite; you can even peer down to City Hall's foyer through the glass-floored decorative pools. Turn around and face west to take in the flying-saucer-like crown of the Norman Foster-designed **New Supreme Court** on North Bridge Road, which opened in 2006.

The parliament buildings

Old Parliament House 1 Old Parliament Lane • Daily 10am–10pm • ☎ 6332 6900, ⓦ theartshouse.sg • New Parliament House 1 Parliament Place • ⓦ parliament.gov.sg • Raffles Place or City Hall MRT

Probably the island's oldest surviving building, the **Old Parliament House** was built in 1827 as the home of a rich merchant, with Singapore's pre-eminent colonial architect, the Irishman George Drumgoole Coleman, as its creator. The bronze elephant at the front was a gift to Singapore from King Rama V of Thailand (upon whose father *The King and I* was based) after his visit in 1871. Relieved of its legislative role in 1999, the

9

building now holds a contemporary arts centre called **The Arts House**. Backing onto it and facing North Bridge Road is the rather soulless new **Parliament House**, where parliamentary business is now conducted.

Victoria Concert Hall and Victoria Theatre

11 Empress Place • ☎ 6908 8810, ⓦ vtvch.com • Raffles Place or City Hall MRT

Opposite the Singapore Cricket Club are two more fine examples of colonial architecture, the **Victoria Theatre** and, to the right, the **Victoria Concert Hall** (also called the Victoria Memorial Hall). The former was completed in 1862 as Singapore's town hall, while the concert hall was added in 1905; both now boast extensive glass panelling after a recent refit.

During the Japanese occupation, the concert hall's clock tower was altered to Tokyo time, while the **statue of Raffles** that stands in front of it narrowly escaped being melted down. It was sent to the National Museum, where the newly installed Japanese curator valued it enough to hide it instead of destroying it. A copy can be seen staring towards the Financial District at Raffles' **landing site**, where the great man apparently took his first steps on Singaporean soil in January 1819.

Asian Civilizations Museum

1 Empress Place, north side of Cavenagh Bridge • Mon–Thurs & Sat 10am–7pm, Fri 10am–9pm • S$8; Fri after 7pm S$4 • ☎ 6332 7798, ⓦ acm.org.sg • Raffles Place or City Hall MRT

A robust Neoclassical structure, the **Empress Place Building** was named after Queen Victoria and completed in 1865. Once government offices, it now houses the fine **Asian Civilizations Museum**, tracing the origins and growth of Asia's many cultures.

The museum's glassy new riverside extension is also its highlight, housing the **Tang Shipwreck Gallery**, a dazzling trove of ninth-century Chinese goods controversially

---

SIR STAMFORD RAFFLES

Fittingly for a man who was to spend his life roaming the globe, Thomas Stamford Raffles was born at sea on July 6, 1781, aboard the *Ann*, whose master was his father Captain Benjamin Raffles. By the age of 14, the young Raffles was working as a clerk for the **East India Company** in London, his schooling curtailed because of his father's debts. Even then, Raffles' ambition and self-motivation were evident: he studied through the night with a hunger for knowledge that would spur him to learn Malay, amass a collection of natural history treasures and write his two-volume *History of Java*.

In 1805 he was chosen to join a team going out to Penang, then being developed as a British entrepôt. Once in Southeast Asia, he enjoyed a meteoric rise and by 1807 he was named chief secretary to Penang's governor. In 1810, Raffles was appointed secretary to the Governor-General in Malaya, then **governor of Java** in 1811. Raffles' rule there was libertarian and compassionate, but short-lived – to his chagrin, Java was handed back to the Dutch in 1816. Transferred to the governorship of **Bencoolen** in Sumatra, he arrived there in 1818 and found time to study its flora and fauna, including the incredible *Rafflesia arnoldii*. By this time, Raffles strongly believed that Britain should establish another base in the Straits of Melaka. In 1819 he sailed to the southern tip of the Malay Peninsula, where he secured Singapore early that year in the face of local and Dutch opposition.

For a man inextricably linked with Singapore, Raffles spent remarkably little time there. His last visit was in 1822; by August 1824, he was back in England. Hoping for a pension from the East India Company, he busied himself founding **London Zoo** and setting up a farm in what is now northwest London. But the new life he had planned never materialized, as days after he heard that the Calcutta bank holding his savings had folded, his pension application was refused; worse still, the Company was demanding he return an overpayment of £22,000. Then on July 4, 1826, the brain tumour that had caused him headaches for several years took his life. He was initially buried with no memorial tablet; only in 1832 was Raffles commemorated, by a statue in Westminster Abbey.

THE SINGAPORE RIVER

Little more than a creek, in the nineteenth century the **Singapore River** became the main artery of Singapore's growing trade, and was clogged with **bumboats** – houseboat-sized vessels with eyes painted on their prows. The boat ferried coffee, sugar and rice to warehouses called **godowns**, where coolies loaded and unloaded sacks. In the 1880s the river itself was so busy it was practically possible to walk from one side to the other without getting your feet wet. Of course, **bridges** were built across it as well, most endearingly old-fangled to look at now, apart from the massive new Esplanade Bridge at the river's mouth.

Walking beside the river today, all sanitized and lined with trendy restaurants and bars, some occupying the few surviving godowns, it is hard to imagine that in the 1970s this was still a working river. It was also filthy, occasioning a massive clean-up campaign that moved the river's commercial traffic west to Pasir Panjang within the space of a few years; it contributed to the river's current status as one of the leading nightlife centres of Singapore.

RIVER TOURS

You can get a view of the city at river level on the **Singapore River Experience**, trips taking in Clarke Quay, Boat Quay and Marina Bay in souped-up versions of bumboats (daily 9am–10.30pm; 3–4 hourly; 40min; buy tickets and board at any of several ticket booths along the route; ☎6336 6111, ⑩rivercruise.com.sg). Tickets cost S$25 except for the 7.30pm and 8.30pm sailings, which cost S$38 and take in the laser light show at Marina Bay (see p.506). More prosaically and much more cheaply, it's also possible to ride the company's **river taxi** service, although you will need an ez-link card for this (see p.528).

salvaged from a sunken Arab dhow discovered off the coast of Sumatra in 1998 (a recreation of the ship can be seen at Sentosa's Maritime Experiential Museum; see p.522). There's a profusion of ceramic bowls, but the few specimens of gold and silverware are the most memorable: cups, dishes decorated with swastikas or birds, and flasks for wine. Upstairs in the main building is an assortment of artefacts, including Muslim gravestones, Sumatran lacquerware and some fine examples of *ikat* dyed textiles from Borneo.

Cavenagh Bridge

Raffles Place or City Hall MRT

Cavenagh Bridge, with its elegant suspension struts, is one of the Singapore River's antiquated bridges, linking the Padang with Boat Quay and Raffles Place in the Financial District. Named after Major General Orfeur Cavenagh, governor of the Straits Settlements from 1859 to 1867, it was built in 1869 by Indian convict labourers using imported Glasgow steel. A sign still maintains: "The use of this bridge is prohibited to any vehicle of which the laden weight exceeds 3cwt and to all cattle and horses" – which is just as well, as nowadays the bridge takes only pedestrians.

St Andrew's Cathedral

11 St Andrew's Rd; Visitor Centre on North Bridge Rd • Mon–Sat 9am–5pm; tours Mon, Tues & Thurs 10.30am, Wed & Fri 3.30pm (20min; free) • ☎6337 6104, ⑩cathedral.org.sg • City Hall or Esplanade MRT

The Anglican **St Andrew's Cathedral** is the most distinguished of a clutch of nineteenth-century churches north of the Padang, their steeples dwarfed by most buildings around them. Built in high-vaulted Neo-Gothic style using Indian convict labour, it was consecrated on January 25, 1862. The exterior walls were plastered using Madras *chunam* – an unlikely composite of eggs, lime, sugar and shredded coconut husks which shines brightly when smoothed – while the small cross behind the pulpit was crafted from two fourteenth-century nails salvaged from the ruins of England's Coventry Cathedral after it was razed during World War II. The middle stained-glass window in the nave was dedicated to Raffles in the 1960s and bears his coat of arms.

9 CHIJMES

30 Victoria St • ⓦ chijmes.com.sg • City Hall, Bras Basah or Esplanade MRT

Two venerable Catholic institutions lie almost immediately north of St Andrew's Cathedral, although one of them no longer serves its original purpose. What was the Convent of the Holy Infant Jesus is now a complex of bars and restaurants named **CHIJMES** (pronounced "chimes"). Its Neo-Gothic husk, complete with courtyards, fountains and a sunken forecourt, appeals particularly to expats and tourists, although it still irks some locals that planners allowed a historic convent school to be repurposed like this. Look out for the **Gate of Hope** on its Victoria Street flank, where foundlings were once taken in by the nuns.

Cathedral of the Good Shepherd

Corner of Queen St and Bras Basah Rd • Mon–Fri 8am–9pm, Sat & Sun 7am–9pm • ☎ 6337 2036, ⓦ cathedral.catholic.sg

Opened on June 6, 1847, the **Cathedral of the Good Shepherd** is more modest in scale than its Anglican rival and yet more refined. Neoclassically styled, the building has regained its lovely chequerboard flooring and white, cream and gold colour scheme, thanks to restoration works that cost S$40 million. Upstairs, the 1912 organ is similarly immaculate, having been completely overhauled by specialists from the Philippines.

War Memorial

Esplanade or City Hall MRT

The open plot north of the Padang is home to four 70m-high white columns. They are nicknamed "the chopsticks" but are actually the **Civilian War Memorial**, commemorating those who died during the Japanese occupation. Beneath it are bodily remains, reinterred from unmarked wartime graves around the island.

Church of St Gregory the Illuminator

60 Hill St • Daily 9am–6pm • ⓦ armeniansinasia.org • City Hall or Bras Basah MRT

A couple of blocks west of the Padang, **Hill Street** holds one of the most delightfully intimate buildings in downtown Singapore. The Armenian **Church of St Gregory the Illuminator** was designed by George Drumgoole Coleman and completed in 1835. The white circular interior, fronted by a marble altar and a painting of the Last Supper, includes a framed photo of the few dozen Armenians who lived in Singapore in 1917, for whom the tiny church would have been room enough. Among the handful of graves in the tranquil garden is the tombstone of Agnes Joaquim – a nineteenth-century Armenian resident of Singapore – after whom the national flower, the delicate, purple *Vanda Miss Joaquim* orchid, is named; she discovered it in her garden and had it registered at the Botanic Gardens.

Central Fire Station

Junction of Coleman and Hill streets • Galleries Tues–Sun 10am–5pm • Free • ☎ 6332 2996 • City Hall or Bras Basah MRT

The splendid red-and-white-striped **Central Fire Station**, built in 1908, sports a central watchtower that was once the tallest structure in the area, a perfect vantage point for spotting blazes early. Today it's partly given over to the **Civil Defence Heritage Galleries**, tracing the history of firefighting in Singapore. Of more interest than the displays – restored vintage fire engines and the like – are the accounts of historic fires in Singapore. At Bukit Ho Swee, in 1961, a blaze ripped through a district of *atap* huts and timber yards, destroying sixteen thousand homes. The disaster led directly to a public housing scheme that would ultimately spawn the island's numerous new towns.

Freemasons' Hall

23A Coleman St, directly behind the Central Fire Station • City Hall or Bras Basah MRT

Recently given a fresh lick of paint, Singapore's compact **Freemasons' Hall** features a proud Palladian facade bearing the masonic compass-and-square motif. The building dates from the 1870s and remains in use. It's worth noting that Stamford Raffles himself was apparently a mason.

Peranakan Museum

39 Armenian St, just west of Hill St • Mon–Thurs & Sat 10am–7pm, Fri 10am–9pm • S$10; Fri after 7pm S$5 • ☎ 6332 7591, ⓦ peranakanmuseum.org.sg • City Hall or Bras Basah MRT

A beautifully ornamented three-storey building that started out in 1910 as the Tao Nan School – Singapore's first school to cater for new arrivals from China's Fujian province – now houses the **Peranakan Museum**. It honours a culture which, in its own way, is to Singapore, Malaysia and Indonesia what Creole culture is to Louisiana. The museum should whet your appetite for not only the Baba House (see p.504) but also the Peranakan heritage of the Katong area (see p.517).

The diversity of the Peranakans comes through in the first gallery, which includes video interviews with members of Melaka's small **Chitty** community, a blend of Tamil, Chinese and Malay. Thereafter the galleries concentrate on the **Baba-Nyonyas**, the Peranakans of Singapore, exploring their possessions – theirs was always largely a material culture – and customs, in particular the traditional twelve-day **wedding**. Memorable displays include the classic entrance into a Peranakan home: a pair of *pintu pagar* (tall swing doors), overhung with lanterns; look out also for artefacts such as beautiful repoussé silverware, including "pillow ends", coaster-like objects used for some reason as end-caps for bolsters.

National Museum of Singapore

93 Stamford Rd • Daily 10am–7pm • S$15 • ☎ 6332 3659, ⓦ nationalmuseum.sg • Bras Basah, Dhoby Ghaut or City Hall MRT

An eye-catching dome on Stamford Road, seemingly coated with silvery fish scales, marks the **National Museum of Singapore**. The museum has been revamped twice this century, most recently to tie in with the island's 50th anniversary of independence celebrations in 2015, and the results are a mixed bag. A lack of significant artefacts is always going to be an issue for such a young country, but the main issue is a lack of academic weight – its scale aside, this feels more like a provincial museum with a parochial mindset.

Level 1

Almost the entire lower level of the museum is taken up by the **Singapore History Gallery**. Look out early on for the mysterious **Singapore Stone**, all that survives of an inscribed monolith which once stood near where the *Fullerton* hotel is today, though more memorable is the beautiful gold **jewellery** excavated at Fort Canning in 1928 and thought to date from the fourteenth century. With the colonial era come **portraits** of Stamford Raffles, his sidekicks and later officials, most notably one of Frank Swettenham, governor of the Straits Settlements in the 1900s, by the American artist John Singer Sargent. There's also a look at the lives of colonial housewives, including an amusing Malay phrasebook for transacting with servants, with phrases such as "I want to inspect the kitchen to-day" and "This meat is tainted!".

A replica Japanese tank heralds what's perhaps the most interesting section for foreigners, dealing with the British collapse during **World War II**, and the massacres of Operation Sook Ching (see p.497). Also interesting are the displays on postwar politics, including the abortive marriage with Malaysia. From today's perspective it seems hard to believe that up until around the early 1970s, much was still up for grabs in Singapore politics, and the museum deserves credit for devoting space to former opposition figures.

Level 2

Upstairs are four galleries of varying quality; the best is the **Modern Colony Gallery**, kitted out in Art Deco style to explore the prosperous Singapore of the 1920s. Also worth a look is **Desire and Danger**, a gallery featuring flora and fauna artworks

9

famously commissioned by William Farquhar – one or two are also on display at the National Gallery (see p.481) – with a few biological specimens on show and even odour-dispensing jars for an even more back-to-nature experience.

Fort Canning Park

Numerous entrances, including steps on Hill St or via the back of the National Museum • Fort Canning, Bras Basah, Dhoby Ghaut or Clarke Quay MRT

When Raffles first caught sight of Singapore, **Fort Canning Park** was known as Bukit Larangan (Forbidden Hill). Malay annals tell of the five ancient sultans of Singapura who ruled the island from this site, and unearthed artefacts prove it was inhabited as early as the fourteenth century. The last of the sultans, Iskandar Shah, reputedly lies here, and it was out of respect for – and fear of – his spirit that the Malays decreed the hill forbidden. Singapore's first Resident, William Farquhar, displayed typical colonial tact by promptly erecting a bungalow on the summit. It was replaced in 1859 by a fort named after Viscount George Canning, Governor-General of India, but only a gateway, guardhouse and adjoining wall remain today. The surprisingly grand building up the slope from the National Museum is the **Fort Canning Centre**, a former British barracks that has hosted arts bodies in the past, although it was disused at the time of research.

Battle Box

Cox Terrace • Compulsory tours Mon 1–5pm, Tues–Sun 9am–5pm; 1hr (schedules online) • S$15 • ☎ 6338 6133, ⓦ battlebox.com.sg

On the right of the Fort Canning Centre, a path leads to the 1939 bunkers from which the Allied war effort in Singapore was masterminded. Now restored and called the **Battle Box**, it holds dioramas bringing to life the events leading up to the British surrender in February 1942.

Raffles Terrace

South side of Fort Canning Park

Just left of the Fort Canning Centre, there is a *keramat* (auspicious place) on the supposed site of Iskandar Shah's grave, which attracts a trickle of local Muslims. Continue round the hill and you'll meet the staircase from Hill Street at **Raffles Terrace**, where there are replicas of a colonial flagstaff and a lighthouse – the hill was the site of a working lighthouse that functioned up until the middle of the last century.

Along River Valley Road

Fort Canning Park's southern boundary is defined by **River Valley Road**, which skirts below the park from Hill Street. At the corner with Hill Street is the **MICA Building**, with shuttered windows in bright colours. Formerly the Hill Street Police Station, it is now home to two government ministries, and its central atrium houses several galleries majoring in Asian artworks.

G-MAX and GX5

Daily 2pm–late • Each ride S$45 • ☎ 6338 1766, ⓦ gmaxgx5.sg • Clarke Quay or Fort Canning MRT

Close to the Coleman Bridge is **G-MAX**, billed as a "reverse bungy jump" though it's really more like a metal cage suspended from steel cables, allowing several screaming passengers to be tossed around in the air. Neither it nor the **GX5** "extreme swing" on the same site are best sampled if you've already indulged at one of the many bars and restaurants nearby.

Clarke Quay

3 River Valley Rd • ⓦ clarkequay.com.sg • Clarke Quay or Fort Canning MRT

Painted in gaudy colours and housing flashy eating and nightlife venues, the nineteenth-century godowns of **Clarke Quay** feel about as authentic as the translucent plastic canopy that shelters them; nearby Boat Quay (see p.503) feels homelier even when at its busiest. Further up River Valley Road is **Robertson Quay**, offering more of the same although generally quieter.

Chettiar Temple

15 Tank Rd • Daily 8.30am–12.30pm & 5.30–8.30pm • Free • ☎ 6737 9393, ⓦ sttemple.com • Fort Canning or Dhoby Ghaut MRT, or bus #143 from Orchard Rd or Chinatown

Just west of Fort Canning Park and close to Robertson Quay is what is still often known as the **Chettiar Temple** (its official name being the **Sri Thendayuthapani Temple**). The shrine, with a large, attractive *gopuram*, was built in 1984 to replace a nineteenth-century temple constructed by Indian *chettiars* (moneylenders) and is dedicated mainly to the Hindu deity Lord Murugan. It's also the destination of every participant in the procession that accompanies the annual Thaipusam Festival (see p.47).

Bras Basah Road to Rochor Road

Bras Basah, City Hall, Dhoby Ghaut or Bencoolen/Rochor (when open) MRT

Bras Basah Road – the main thoroughfare between Orchard Road and what would have been the seafront – is so named because rice arriving on cargo boats used to be brought here to be dried (*beras basah* means "wet rice" in Malay). The zone between it and **Rochor Road** at the edge of Little India has a transitional sort of feel, sitting as it does between the Colonial District and two of Raffles' ethnic enclaves to the northeast. The aptly named Middle Road, running smack through the centre of the grid, was originally meant to mark the Colonial District's northern edge.

Despite modernization, the area still boasts some long-established places of worship and is another focus for the **arts**, home to institutions such as the School of the Arts in a striking new building next to the Cathay cinema, and to several creative organizations occupying distinguished old properties on and around **Waterloo Street**.

Raffles Hotel

1 Beach Rd • ☎ 6337 1886, ⓦ raffles.com/singapore • Esplanade or City Hall MRT

The area's most famous occupant is the legendary **Raffles Hotel**, almost a byword for the colonial era; Somerset Maugham once remarked that it "stood for all the fables of the exotic East". With its gleaming white facade and location by the sea – that is, until land reclamation intervened – it very much recalls its former sister hotel, the *Eastern & Oriental* in George Town (see p.150). Liveried, largely Sikh, doormen still greet arriving guests, and the inner courtyard is a true haven, fringed with palm and frangipani trees. If you're not staying here, the best way to glimpse the place is by dining at one of its restaurants or treating yourself to a Singapore Sling in the *Long Bar* (for the princely sum of around S$40).

History of the hotel

Oddly, the hotel started out as a modest seafront bungalow belonging to an Arab trader. In 1886, the property was bought by the Armenian Sarkies brothers, who had only just launched the *E&O*; the *Raffles* opened the following year, and over the next twenty years it was gradually extended to something approaching its present scale. In 1902, according to an apocryphal tale, the last tiger to be killed on the island was shot inside the building. Bartender Ngiam Tong Boon created another *Raffles* legend, the **Singapore Sling** cocktail, in 1915. Over the years, the hotel has hosted many a politician and film star, but it is proudest of its **literary connections**. Hermann Hesse, Rudyard Kipling, Noël Coward and Günter Grass all stayed here, and Somerset Maugham is said to have written many of his Asian tales under a frangipani tree in the garden.

Following the Japanese conquest in 1942, the hotel became a Japanese officers' quarters, then briefly a transit camp for liberated Allied prisoners in 1945. Postwar decay earned it the affectionate but melancholy soubriquet "the grand old lady of the East",

9

BRAS BASAH ROAD TO ROCHOR ROAD

■ ACCOMMODATION	
Carlton	10
G4 Station	1
Hangout@Mount Emily	4
Hotel G	5
Intercontinental	6
Marriott South Beach	8
Marrison	3
Naumi	7
Raffles	9
South East Asia	2
YMCA	11

● SHOPPING	
Bugis Junction	2
Naiise	4
Sim Lim Square	1
Tealjoy	3

● EATING	
Ah Chew Desserts	2
Artichoke	5
Baker & Cook	4
Chin Chin	6
The Daily Scoop	8
Fatty's Wing Seong	1
Herbivore	3
Tiffin Room	9
Yhingthai Palace	7

■ DRINKING AND NIGHTLIFE	
Atlas	1
The Long Bar	3
Loof	2

and the hotel was little more than a shabby tourist diversion when the government declared it a national monument in its centenary year. An expensive and contentious four-year facelift and extension followed, which restored the air of bygone elegance but also added a mundane shopping arcade on North Bridge Road. Another major refit was under way at the time of research, with the *Raffles* – its name now shared with other hotels in an international chain – due to reopen in the second half of 2018.

Waterloo Street
Bras Basah, Bencoolen or Bugis MRT

Head up Waterloo Street from the Art Museum and you'll almost immediately come to the peach-coloured **Maghain Aboth Synagogue**, which looks like a colonial mansion despite the Stars of David on the facade. The surrounding area was once something of a Jewish enclave – another building midway along nearby Selegie Road bears a prominent Star of David – though the Jewish community, largely of Middle Eastern origin, never numbered more than about a thousand. Dating from the 1870s, the synagogue can be visited by prior arrangement (enquiries on ☎6337 2189).

Sri Krishnan Temple
152 Waterloo St • ☎ 6337 7957

In 1870 the **Sri Krishnan Temple** was nothing more than a thatched hut containing a statue of Lord Krishna under a banyan tree. The present-day shrine is a good example of Southeast Asian religious harmony and syncretism in action, with worshippers from the nearby Buddhist Kwan Im Temple sometimes praying outside.

Kwan Im Temple
178 Waterloo St • Daily 6am–6.30pm • ☎ 6337 3965

The best-known sight on Waterloo Street is the **Kwan Im Temple**, named after the Buddhist goddess of mercy. The current version dates only to the 1980s – hence its rather slick, palatial appearance – and draws thousands of devotees daily; it can be filled to overflowing during festivals. Fortune-tellers and religious artefact shops operate in a little swarm just outside.

Albert Street
Northern end of Waterloo St, close to Rochor Rd • Rochor, Bugis or Jalan Besar MRT

Intersecting Waterloo Street is **Albert Street**, which half a century ago looked quite like Jalan Alor in KL (see p.95), lined with hugely popular street food stalls. All of that is now gone, although the street is still worth a stroll to gaze at the zigzagging glass facades of the **Lasalle College of the Arts** near the street's northern end, or to check out the **market** that stays open into the evening around the junction with Waterloo Street, selling everything from potted plants to mobile phone cases. Albert Street is also the starting point for touristy **trishaw** excursions (see p.531).

Bugis Village and Bugis Junction
Bugis MRT

Bugis Street (pronounced "boogis"), the southern extension of Albert Street, was one of the most notorious places in old Singapore, crawling with rowdy sailors, prostitutes and ladyboys by night. The street was duly cleared, partly to build the Bugis MRT station and partly because it was anathema to the government. In its place today is **Bugis Village**, a bunch of stalls and snack vendors lining a few covered alleyways. It's hardly the Bugis Street of old, though it does recapture something of the bazaar feel that the island's markets once had.

Across Victoria Street from here is another throwback to the past, the **Bugis Junction** development. Entire rows of shophouses have been gutted, scrubbed clean and then encased under glass as part of a modern shopping mall and hotel, the *Intercontinental*.

9

Little India

Little India, Farrer Park or Jalan Besar MRT; note that buses up Serangoon Rd return via Jalan Besar

Of all Singapore's historic quarters, the most charismatic has to be **Little India**. Indian pop music blares out from speakers outside cassette shops; the air is perfumed with incense, curry powder and jasmine garlands; Hindu women parade in bright saris; and a wealth of restaurants serve up excellent, inexpensive curries.

That Little India has kept its identity better than any other old quarter is in no small way down to the migrant Tamil and Bengali men who labour to build new MRT stations, shopping malls and private villas. On Sundays they descend on Little India in their thousands, making the place look like downtown Chennai or Calcutta after a major cricket match. The district's backbone is **Serangoon Road**, one of the island's oldest roadways, dating from 1822; the account here starts from Tekka Market, next to Little India MRT, and then covers the side roads off Serangoon Road in stretches. The best time of year to visit is in the run-up to **Deepavali** (October or November) when much of Serangoon Road is festooned with festive lighting and special markets are set up in the open space beyond the Angullia Mosque (opposite Syed Alwi Road) and on Campbell Lane, which sell decorations, garlands and Indian sweets.

Tekka Market

Southwestern end of Serangoon Rd • Little India MRT

Tekka Market is a must-see, combining many of Little India's commercial elements under one roof. It's best to arrive in the morning when the wet market is at its busiest. Halal butchers push around trolleys piled high with goats' heads, while live crabs, their claws tied together, shuffle in buckets on seafood stalls. Look out also for a couple of stalls selling nothing but banana leaves, used to serve up the curry meals you'll probably enjoy at some point during your stay. Talking of food, the hawker centre here is excellent, and although the same can't be said of the mundane outlets upstairs selling Indian fabrics and household items, there are great views over the wet market to be had from above.

Buffalo Road

Buffalo Road, along the northern side of Tekka Market, sports a few provisions stores with sacks of spices and fresh coconut, ground using primitive machines. Its name, and that of neighbouring Kerbau ("buffalo" in Malay) Road, recall the latter half of the nineteenth century when **cattle and buffalo yards** opened in the area, luring more Indians in search of work and swelling the population.

Kerbau Road

Kerbau Road, like Waterloo Street 1km south, is a designated "arts belt", its shophouses home to a couple of creative organizations. Curiously, the road itself has been split into two by a pedestrianized bit of greenery. At no. 37, you can't miss the gaudily restored **Chinese mansion**, built by one Tan Teng Niah, a confectionery magnate, in 1900 and now used as commercial premises. Look out also for the traditional picture framer at no. 57, packed with images of Hindu deities.

Sri Veeramakaliamman Temple

141 Serangoon Rd, just beyond Belilios Lane • ☎ 6295 4538, ⓦ sriveeramakaliamman.com • Little India MRT

The **Sri Veeramakaliamman Temple** is the most prominent shrine on Serangoon Road and just as worthwhile as the more famous Sri Mariamman Temple in Chinatown. The temple is dedicated to Kali, the Hindu goddess of power or energy, and she occupies the central part of the three-doored sanctum inside the *mandapam* (prayer hall), with her sons, the deities Ganesh and Murugan, to the left and right respectively. One of many other notable deities here is the ten-armed figure to the left of the sanctum, Lord Shiva, shown trampling a moustachioed demon of ignorance.

LITTLE INDIA & ARAB STREET

■ ACCOMMODATION	
Backpackers@SG	5
Bunc@Radius	12
The Daulat	18
Destination	8
Dream Lodge	4
Fisher BnB	6
Fragrance Imperial	7
Haising	15
Hilton Garden Inn	10
The Inn Crowd	16
Mayo Inn	17
Mitraa Inn	3
Moon	14
The Pod	1
Shophouse	2
The Sultan	9
Vintage Inn	11
Wanderlust	13

● SHOPPING	
Dakshani Silks	9
The Heritage Shop	8
Jamal Kazura Aromatics	1
Little Shophouse	2
Malay Art Gallery	4
Mustafa Centre	7
Ratianah	3
Rishi Handicrafts	5
Toko Aljunied	6

● EATING	
Banana Leaf Apolo	12
Blu Jaz Café	7
Bumbu	4
Chye Seng Huat Hardware	8
Gokul	14
Hajjah Maimunah	1
Hillman	10
Islamic Restaurant	2
Kampong Glam Café	5
Komala Villas	15
Madras Woodlands Ganga	13
Rumah Makan Minang	3
Saravanaa Bhavan	11
Tekka Food Centre	16
Tiramisu Hero	9
Zam Zam	6

■ DRINKING AND NIGHTLIFE	
The Countryside Café	1
Prince of Wales	2

9

Hastings Road to Cuff Road

Across Serangoon Road from the Tekka Market, the **Little India Arcade** is a lovingly restored block of shophouses bounded by Hastings Road and Campbell Lane. It's a sort of Little India in microcosm: behind pastel-coloured walls and green shutters you can purchase textiles and tapestries, bangles, religious statuary, Indian sweets, music and Ayurvedic herbal medicines. Exiting the arcade onto **Campbell Lane** places you opposite the riot of colours of the Jothi flower shop, where staff thread jasmine, roses and marigolds into garlands for prayer offerings.

Indian Heritage Centre

5 Campbell Lane • Tues–Thurs 10am–7pm, Fri & Sat 10am–8pm, Sun 10am–4pm • S$6 • ☎ 6291 1601, ⊛ indianheritage.org.sg • Rochor, Little India or Jalan Besar MRT

With its startling honeycombed glass facade, the **Indian Heritage Centre** was launched in 2015 but has yet to hit its stride. The museum is the main draw. Start on the top floor for a broad look at Indian traditions via some impressive statuary and carvings, then descend to the rather mundane sections dealing with themes such as stereotypical occupations once pursued by Indian migrants (rubber tappers, policemen and so on).

Dunlop Street and around

Dunlop Street is defined by the beautiful **Abdul Gaffoor Mosque**, completed in 1907 (Mon–Thurs, Sat & Sun 8am–8pm, Fri 8am–noon & 2.30–8pm). With a green onion dome and cream walls decorated with stars and crescent moons, the mosque includes an unusual 25-pointed sundial bearing the names of the same number of prophets in Arabic script. A couple of streets along is **Cuff Road**, where a traditional spice grinder can still be seen at no. 2, though it's mainly open at weekends.

Rowell and Desker roads

Both Rowell and Desker roads mark a noticeable shift from the South Indian flavour of much of Little India, with Bengali featuring prominently on some shops signs. However, both roads have another claim to fame – or infamy – as they have long been synonymous in Singapore with vice. Along the backs of the shophouses between the two roads is an alleyway where the doorways are illuminated at night. Here gaggles of bored-looking prostitutes sit indoors watching TV, seemingly oblivious to the men gathered outside who mostly appear inclined to merely observe them, as if treating the whole thing as some kind of street entertainment.

Syed Alwi Road to Petain Road

Farrer Park MRT

Little India takes on a more Islamic feel around **Syed Alwi Road**, across from which is the Angullia Mosque at its northern end, but the road is better known for being the hub of the shopping phenomenon that is the **Mustafa Centre**. It's an agglomeration of department store, moneychanger, travel agent, jeweller, fast-food joint and supermarket, mostly open 24 hours. You'll probably find it more appealing than most places on Orchard Road, as you rub shoulders with Indian families seeking flown-in confectionery from Delhi, Chinese and Malay shoppers wanting durian fruit or pots and pans, and even African businessmen buying consumer goods that are hard to find at home.

Sam Leong Road is home to some surviving **Peranakan shophouses** decorated with stags, lotuses and egrets. There's more of the same a few blocks north on **Petain Road**, where the shophouses have elegant ceramic tiles reminiscent of Portuguese *azulejos*.

Sri Srinivasa Perumal Temple

397 Serangoon Rd • Daily 6.30am–noon & 6–9pm, though it may be possible to visit at other times • ☎ 6298 5771, ⊛ sspt.org.sg • Farrer Park MRT

Little India more or less comes to an end at Rangoon and Kitchener roads, but it's worth continuing up Serangoon Road to see two very different temples. Dating from the late nineteenth century, though rebuilt in the 1960s, the **Sri Srinivasa Perumal Temple** has an attractive five-tiered *gopuram* with sculptures of the various manifestations of Lord Vishnu the preserver. On the wall to the right of the front gate, a sculpted elephant trumpets silently, its leg caught in a crocodile's mouth. But the temple's main claim to fame is as the starting point for the annual **Thaipusam** festival (see p.47), when devotees leave the temple in procession, pausing only while a coconut is smashed at their feet for good luck, and parade all the way to the Chettiar Temple on Tank Road (see p.487).

Sakaya Muni Buddha Gaya Temple
366 Race Course Rd • Daily 8am–4.30pm • Farrer Park MRT

Just beyond the Sri Srinivasa Perumal Temple, a small path leads northwest to Race Course Road, where the slightly kitsch **Sakaya Muni Buddha Gaya Temple** betrays a strong Thai influence – which isn't surprising as it was built by a Thai monk. On the left of the temple as you enter is a huge Buddha's footprint, inlaid with mother-of-pearl, and beyond it a 15m-high Buddha ringed by a thousand electric lights. Twenty-five dioramas depicting scenes from the Buddha's life decorate the pedestal on which he sits. It is possible to walk inside the statue, through a door in its back; inside is one more diorama, depicting the Buddha in death. One wall of the temple features a sort of wheel of fortune, decorated with Chinese zodiac signs. To discover your fate, spin it (for a small donation) and take the numbered sheet of paper that corresponds to the number at which the wheel stops.

Arab Street (Kampong Glam)
Bugis or Nicoll Highway MRT

The area of Singapore south of the now canalized Rochor River once held a Malay village known as Kampong Glam, possibly named after the *gelam* tree that grew there. After signing the dubious treaty with his newly installed Johor sultan, Raffles allotted the area to him and designated the land around it as a Muslim settlement. Soon the zone was attracting Malays, Sumatrans and Javanese, as well as Hadhrami Arabs from what's now eastern Yemen. Now the Arab community, descended from those Yemeni traders, is thought to number around 15,000, though they are something of an invisible minority, having intermarried into Singapore society and being resident in no particular area.

Today, the area is still referred to as **Kampong Glam** or just **Arab Street**, and is akin in some ways to London's Brick Lane, part Islamic, part hipster. Gentrification seems to be winning out, though, with slick upstart restaurants, many serving alcohol (to the chagrin of some locals), displacing old textiles stores and curry houses. Nevertheless it's worth spending an hour wandering the area's lanes, with the **Sultan Mosque** and the **Malay Heritage Centre** being the two obvious sights. The little shophouses on Arab Street itself and the surrounding lanes have a cosiness and intimacy that's more George Town than Lion City. Textile and carpet stores are most prominent, and you'll also see leather, basketware, gold, gemstones and jewellery for sale.

Haji Lane and Bali Lane

South of Arab Street, **Haji Lane** and tiny **Bali Lane** – the latter petering out into the wide walkway next to Ophir Road – have traditional shops rubbing up against trendy boutiques; in the evenings and at weekends DJs set up informally to spin dance music on Haji Lane.

Incidentally, it's worth taking a brief look at the **Parkview Square** office building just across from here on North Bridge Road. Though the tower is only a decade old, its styling just screams 1930s Art Deco (à la Gotham City), and there's a stunning ground-floor bar in the same vein, *Atlas* (see p.544). When it was built, the need to

9

ensure good feng shui meant it had to be sited dead between the two razor-blade-like towers of **The Gateway** one block south (designed by the Chinese-American architect I.M. Pei – the man behind the glass pyramid fronting the Louvre in Paris).

Sultan Mosque

3 Muscat St • Mon–Thurs & Sat 9.30am–noon & 2–4pm, Fri 2.30–4pm • Free • ☎ 6293 4405, ⓦ sultanmosque.org.sg • Bugis or Jalan Besar MRT

The **Sultan Mosque** is the beating heart of the Muslim faith in Singapore. An earlier mosque stood on this site, finished in 1825 with the help of a donation from the East India Company. The present building was completed a century later to a design by colonial architects Swan and Maclaren. Look carefully at the base of the main dome and you'll see a dark band that looks like tilework, though it actually consists of the bottoms of thousands of glass bottles. The prayer hall is decked out in green and gold, but non-Muslims must look on from just inside the entrance.

Bussorah Street to the south offers the best view of the mosque, and is also home to some worthwhile souvenir outlets. During the Muslim fasting month, the area around the mosque is thronged with stalls of the **Ramadan bazaar** from mid-afternoon, selling *biriyanis, murtabak*, dates and cakes for consumption by the faithful after dusk.

The Malay Heritage Centre (Istana Kampong Glam)

Sultan Gate • Tues–Sun 10am–6pm • S$4 • ☎ 6391 0450, ⓦ malayheritage.org.sg • Bugis or Nicoll Highway MRT

Between Kandahar and Aliwal streets, the colonially styled **Istana Kampong Glam** was built as the palace of Sultan Ali Iskandar Shah, son of Sultan Hussein who negotiated with Raffles to hand Singapore over to the British. Until just a few years ago the house was still home to the sultan's descendants, though it had fallen into disrepair. Then the government acquired it together with the similar, smaller yellow house in the same grounds, which belonged to the heirs of a wealthy merchant.

The yellow house now hosts an attempt at a posh Malay restaurant, while the istana has mutated into the overly slick **Malay Heritage Centre**, a hit-and-miss museum. The best displays celebrate the rural boat-building and fishing lifestyle of yore, plus Singapore's unjustly overlooked Malay literary and pop-culture scene of the postwar period. But there's a deafening silence on the building of new towns – a mixed blessing for all who experienced upheaval and relocation, especially for the Malays, who saw practically all their kampungs razed and communities broken up.

North of Sultan Mosque

The stretch of **North Bridge Road** between Arab Street and Jalan Sultan has a less touristy feel, and although gentrification is evident here, too, the shops and restaurants tend to be geared more towards locals, stocking items such as alcohol-free perfume and the black, fez-like *songkok* traditionally worn by Malay men.

Several roads run off the western side of North Bridge Road, including Jalan Kubor (literally "Grave Street"), which takes you to an unkempt **Muslim cemetery**, where it's said that Malay royalty are buried. Turn right here up Kallang Road to reach Jalan Sultan and the blue **Malabar Mosque**, built for Muslims from the South Indian state of Kerala and a little cousin of the Sultan Mosque, with similar golden domes. Its traditional styling belies its age – the mosque was completed in the early 1960s.

The Hajjah Fatimah mosque

4001 Beach Rd, just east of the junction with Jalan Sultan • Nicoll Highway or Lavender MRT

Beach Road's chandlers and fishing-gear shops betray its former proximity to the sea, until land reclamation created Nicoll Highway and the Marina Centre district. One quirky sight here is the **Hajjah Fatimah Mosque**, its minaret looking strangely like a steeple (perhaps because its architect was European). The minaret also visibly slants at

OPPOSITE DEEPAVALI MARKET, LITTLE INDIA >

9

six degrees to the vertical – locals call it Singapore's Leaning Tower of Pisa. Completed in 1846, the building is named after a wealthy Melaka businesswoman who, having moved out of her home on this site, funded the mosque's construction.

Chinatown

Chinatown, Telok Ayer, Outram Park, Tanjong Pagar or Clarke Quay MRT; buses run southwest along North and South Bridge roads and New Bridge Rd, returning along Eu Tong Sen St

Bounded roughly by Eu Tong Sen Street to the northwest, Neil and Maxwell roads to the south, Cecil Street to the southeast and the Singapore River to the north, **Chinatown** is somewhat misnamed. Never really an enclave – Singapore has long had a Chinese majority, after all – it was more the focus of Chinese life and culture. Within its two square kilometres, newly arrived migrants found temples, shops with familiar goods and, most importantly, *kongsis* – clan associations that helped them find lodgings and work.

This was one of the most colourful districts of old Singapore, but after independence the government tackled its tumbledown slums by embarking upon a drastic **redevelopment** campaign. Not until the 1980s did surviving shophouses and other period buildings begin to be conserved. Furthermore, gentrification has led to *kongsis* and religious and martial arts associations being turned into boutique hotels, new media firms and bars. Getting a taste of the old ways now often means heading off the main streets into the concrete municipal housing estates.

Even so, as in Little India, the character of the area has had a bit of a shot in the arm of late courtesy of recent immigrants. As regards sights, the **Thian Hock Keng**, **Buddha Tooth Relic** and **Sri Mariamman** temples are especially worthwhile, as is the **Chinatown Heritage Centre** museum, and there's enough shophouse architecture to justify a leisurely wander.

Chinatown Heritage Centre

48 Pagoda St • Daily 9am–8pm; last admission 7pm • S$15 • ☎ 6224 3928, ⊛ chinatownheritagecentre.com.sg • Chinatown MRT

One exit from Chinatown MRT brings you up into the thick of the action on Pagoda Street, where the **Chinatown Heritage Centre** stands in marked contrast to the tacky souvenir stalls. Occupying three whole shophouses, it's a museum enshrining the difficult experiences of Chinatown's inhabitants over the past couple of centuries.

Things kick off with a recreation of a comparatively spacious postwar tailor's shop; note the cloth ring dangling down from the ceiling, meant for holding a baby's cot, as still happens in rural Malaysia. Soon you're into the claustrophic living cubicles, recreating conditions in shophouse slums, where you'd find trishaw drivers, clog-makers and prostitutes living cheek by jowl. Landlords once shoehorned as many as forty tenants into a single floor; if you think it couldn't possibly happen today, spare a thought for the thousands of migrant workers on building sites all over Singapore, many of whom are crammed into very basic dormitories. Other sections revisit the sadly vanished nightlife of postwar Chinatown and, commendably, the area's Indian minorities.

Along South Bridge Road

Head down Pagoda Street from the Chinatown Heritage Centre and you come to **South Bridge Road**, one of Chinatown's main thoroughfares, carrying southbound traffic. At no. 218, on the corner of Mosque Street, stands the pastel green **Jamae Mosque** (also called the Chulia Mosque), established by South Indian Muslims in the 1820s. Its twin minarets appear to contain miniature windows while above the entrance stands what looks like a tiny doorway, all of which makes the upper part of the facade look strangely like a scale model of a much larger building.

One street northeast, at the junction with Upper Cross Street, roadblocks were set up during the Japanese occupation, and Singaporeans were vetted for signs of anti-Japanese sentiment in the infamous Sook Ching campaign. That tragic episode is commemorated by a simple signboard in the Hong Lim Complex, a housing estate whose walkways are lined with herbalists and stores selling dried foodstuffs and so forth.

To top up your blood-sugar level while wandering the area, pop into the **Tong Heng pastry shop** (daily 9am–10pm) at no. 285, which sells custard tarts, lotus-seed-paste biscuits and other Chinese sweet treats.

Sri Mariamman Temple

244 South Bridge Rd • Daily 7am–9pm; main sanctum usually closed noon–6pm • Free; cameras RM3 • ☎ 6223 4064 • Chinatown or Telok Ayer MRT

Singapore's oldest Hindu shrine, the **Sri Mariamman Temple**, has its roots in a wood and palm-thatch hut erected here in 1827 on land belonging to Naraina Pillay, a government clerk who arrived on the same ship as Stamford Raffles on the latter's second trip to Singapore. The present temple was finished around 1843, though it has been extended and overhauled several times since.

Inside, walk around the courtyard to admire the temple's roof friezes depicting a host of Hindu deities. The main sanctum is devoted to Mariamman, a goddess worshipped for her healing powers. Smaller sanctums include one dedicated to the goddess Periachi Amman, portrayed with a queen lying on her lap, whose evil child she has ripped from her womb; it's odd, then, that Periachi Amman is the protector of children, to whom babies are brought when one month old.

Once a year, during the festival of **Thimithi** (October or November), a patch of sand to the left of the main sanctum is covered in red-hot coals that male Hindus run across to prove their faith. The participants, who line up all the way along South Bridge Road waiting for their turn, are supposedly protected from the heat by the power of prayer.

Eu Yan Sang Medical Hall

269 South Bridge Rd • Mon–Sat 8.30am–6pm • ☎ 6225 3211 • Chinatown or Telok Ayer MRT

Across from the Sri Mariamman Temple is the **Eu Yan Sang Medical Hall,** one of the oldest Chinese herbalist practices in the area. The smell is the first thing you'll notice (a little like a compost heap on a hot day); the second is the weird assortment of ingredients on the shelves. Besides the usual herbs and roots favoured by the Chinese, there are various remedies derived from exotic species; blood circulation problems, for instance, can supposedly be eased by mixtures of centipedes and insects crushed into a "rubbing liquor". The shop includes a set of displays extolling the health benefits of that much prized delicacy, the edible **birds' nest**, made of swiftlet saliva and harvested at sites such as the Niah Caves in Sarawak (or from birds reared in bricked-up town-centre shophouses, which is why the swiftlets can be seen wheeling at dawn and dusk over many Malaysian town centres).

Buddha Tooth Relic Temple

288 South Bridge Rd • Daily 7am–7pm • Free • ☎ 6220 0220, ⓦ btrts.org.sg • No shorts, vests or non-vegetarian food • Chinatown or Tanjong Pagar MRT

The imposing **Buddha Tooth Relic Temple** is arguably the most in-your-face of Chinatown's shrines. The place simply clobbers you with its opulence – even the elevators have brocaded walls – and the thousands upon thousands of Buddhist figurines, each with its own serial number, arrayed along various interior surfaces.

With gently curving roofs featuring tiles and other ornaments made in Japan, the temple has its origins in the discovery, in 1980, of what was thought to be a tooth of Buddha inside a collapsed stupa at a Burmese monastery. The monastery's chief abbot visited Singapore in 2002 and decided the island would make a suitable sanctuary for the relic, to be housed in its own temple if there were a chance of building one. A prime site in Chinatown was duly secured, and the temple opened in 2007.

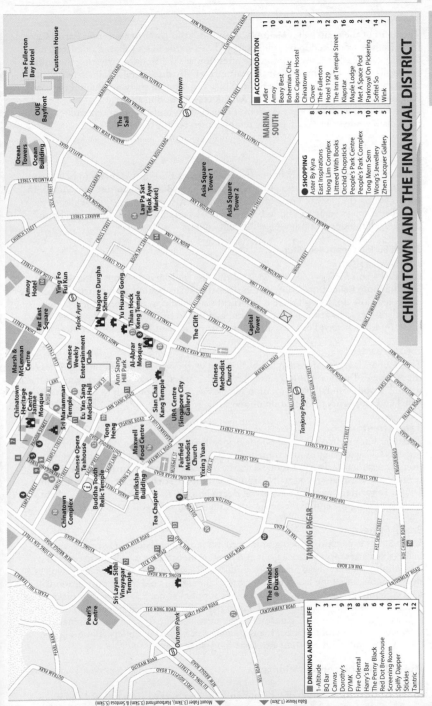

CHINATOWN AND THE FINANCIAL DISTRICT

9

The main hall

The focus of the main hall is **Maitreya**, a Buddha who is yet to appear on Earth. Carved from juniper wood said to be 1000 years old, his statue has a yellow flame-like halo around it. But what really captures the attention are the Buddhas covering the entire side walls. There are a hundred main statuettes, individually crafted, interspersed with thousands more tiny figurines embedded in a vast array of shelving. Behind the main hall, another large hall centres on the **Avalokitesvara Bodhisattva**.

The **mezzanine** affords great views over proceedings and chanting ceremonies in the main hall, while **level 2** contains the temple's own **teahouse**.

Buddhist Culture Museum
Daily 9am–6pm

On **level 3** are some seriously impressive examples of Buddhist **statuary** in brass, wood and stone, plus other artworks. They're all part of the **Buddhist Culture Museum**, with panels telling the story of Gautama Buddha in the first person. At the back, the relic chamber displays what are said to be the cremated remains of Buddha's nose, brain, liver etc, all looking like fish roe in different colours.

Sacred Buddha Tooth Relic Stupa
Daily 9am–noon & 3–6pm

On **level 4** you finally encounter what all the fuss is ultimately about – the **Sacred Buddha Tooth Relic Stupa**. Some 3m in diameter, it sits behind glass panels and can't be inspected close up, though there is a faithful scale model at the front. The Maitreya Buddha is depicted at the front of the stupa, guarded by four lions, with a ring of 35 more Buddhas below; floor tiles around the stupa are said to be made of pure gold.

The roof garden

The temple's lovely **roof garden** has walls lined with twelve thousand tiny figurines of the Amitayus Buddha, but its centrepiece is "the largest cloisonné prayer wheel in the world", around 5m tall. Each rotation (clockwise, should you wish to have a go) dings a bell and represents the recitation of one sutra.

Sago Street

The tight knot of streets west of South Bridge Road between Sago Street and Pagoda Street is Chinatown at its most touristy, packed with souvenir sellers and foreigner-friendly restaurants. But in bygone days these streets formed Chinatown's nucleus, teeming with trishaws, food stalls, brothels and opium dens. Until as recently as the 1950s, **Sago Street** was home to several **death houses**, rudimentary hospices where citizens nearing the end of their lives spent their final hours on rattan beds.

Smith Street

Smith Street is perennially being promoted as Chinatown Food Street, after several half-cocked attempts to repackage it and Trengganu Street as a hub for street eating – ironically, the very thing Singapore abolished decades ago – and the latest involves a slew of phoney-looking hawker "pushcarts". Chinatown's **old trades** can occasionally be seen clinging on for dear life, such as Nam's Supplies at no. 22, where they make shirts, watches, mobile phones and laptops out of paper for burning at funerals, to ensure the deceased don't lack creature comforts in the next life. The ugly, concrete **Chinatown Complex** at the end of the street is a workaday place housing outlets selling silk and household goods, and has some excellent food stalls above.

The Bukit Pasoh conservation area
Outram Park MRT

In the southernmost corner of Chinatown is an area packed with restored shophouses, worth a look for their beautifully painted facades, some in Art Deco style, and tilework. **Clan houses** were once the claim to fame of **Bukit Pasoh Road**, but while some have survived with their character intact, many more have morphed into boutiques or boutique hotels; the Gan Clan's building at 18–20 Bukit Pasoh Rd now rents out space to a posh restaurant. There are clan houses on neighbouring **Keong Saik Road** too, once a notorious red-light area as recounted in Charmaine Leung's memoir, *17A Keong Saik Road* (see p.588).

New Bridge Road and Eu Tong Sen Street

Chinatown's main shopping drag comprises southbound **New Bridge Road** and northbound **Eu Tong Sen Street**, along which are a handful of shopping malls. Try to pop into one of the barbecued-pork vendors around the intersection of Smith, Temple and Pagoda streets with New Bridge Road – as they're cooked, the thin, flat, red squares of *bak kwa*, coated with a sweet marinade, produce a rich, smoky odour that is pure Chinatown. As you chew on your *bak kwa*, check out two striking buildings across the road. On the left is the Art Deco **Majestic Theatre**, built in 1927 as a Chinese opera house by Eu Tong Sen, the wealthy businessman behind the Eu Yan Sang Chinese medicine franchise. Today it has been reduced to housing a few forgettable shops, but five images of figures from Chinese opera still adorn its facade. Just beside it, and built a few years later, stands the former *Great Southern Hotel* (today the Yue Hwa Chinese Products Emporium), which had a fifth-floor nightclub where wealthy locals would drink liquor, smoke opium and pay to dance with so-called "taxi girls".

Ann Siang Hill

Ann Siang Hill is both the name of a little mound and of a lane that leads off South Bridge Road up a slope, where it forks into Club Street on the left and Ann Siang Road, which veers gently right. Despite being only a few paces removed from the hubbub of the main road, the hill is somehow a different realm, a little collection of gentrified shophouses with a distinct village-like feel. Packed with swanky restaurants, cafés and bars, plus the odd boutique, the area typifies the new Chinatown. At the southern end of the road, a short flight of steps leads up to **Ann Siang Hill Park**, a sliver of generic greenery whose only attraction is that it offers a **short cut** to Amoy Street.

Club Street

Scarcely any of the clan associations and guilds whose presence gave **Club Street** its name now remain. Most notable of all is the **Chinese Weekly Entertainment Club** at the end of a side street also called Club Street. Flanked by roaring lion heads, this mansion-like building was constructed in 1891 as a venue where Peranakan tycoons could socialize, and still serves as a private club today.

Singapore City Gallery

URA Centre, 45 Maxwell Rd • Mon–Sat 9am–5pm • Free • ☎ 6321 8321, ⓦ ura.gov.sg/gallery • Tanjong Pagar or Telok Ayer MRT

Town planning may not sound the most fascinating premise for a gallery, but then again, no nation remodels with such ambition as Singapore, whose planners are constantly erasing roads here and replacing one ultramodern complex with an even more souped-up development. The latest grand designs for the island are exhibited west of Ann Siang Hill at the surprisingly absorbing **Singapore City Gallery**, within the government Urban Redevelopment Authority's headquarters.

The URA has rightly been criticized in the past for slighting Singapore's architectural heritage, so it is heartening that the gallery not only explains how shophouses have evolved stylistically but also makes reassuring noises about preserving the ones that remain. But the highlight is the vast and incredibly intricate **scale model** of downtown Singapore, with every row of shophouses, every roof of every building – including some not yet built – fashioned out of plywood.

9

Amoy Street

Amoy Street, together with Telok Ayer Street, was designated a Hokkien enclave in the colony's early days (Amoy being the old name of Xiamen city in China's Fujian province). Long terraces of smartly refurbished shophouses flank the street, all featuring characteristic **five-foot ways**, or covered verandas, so called because they jut five feet out from the house. If you descend here from Ann Siang Hill Park, you'll emerge by the small **Sian Chai Kang Temple** at no. 66. With the customary dragons on the roof, it's dominated by huge urns, full to the brim with ash from untold numbers of burned incense sticks. Two carved stone lions guard the temple; their fancy red neck-ribbons are said to bring good fortune and prosperity.

Telok Ayer Street

One street removed from Amoy Street is **Telok Ayer Street**, its name, meaning "Watery Bay" in Malay, recalling the mid-nineteenth century when the street would have run along the shoreline. Thanks to land reclamation, it's no closer to a beach than Beach Road is, but some of Singapore's oldest buildings cling on between the modern towers – temples and mosques where newly arrived immigrants and sailors thanked their god(s) for their safe passage.

The first building of note you come to if you walk up from the station is the square 1889 **Chinese Methodist Church**, whose design – portholes and windows adorned with white crosses and capped by a Chinese pagoda-style roof – is a pleasing blend of East and West. Just beyond McCallum Street, the blue-and-white **Al-Abrar Mosque** is built on the spot where Chulia worshippers set up a makeshift thatched mosque in 1827.

Thian Hock Keng Temple and around

158 Telok Ayer St · Daily 7.30am–5.30pm · Free · ☎ 6423 4616, ⊛ thianhockkeng.com.sg · Telok Ayer or Chinatown MRT

With ornate dragons stalking its broad, low-slung roofs, the immaculately restored **Thian Hock Keng Temple** feels marooned in a sea of commercialization, and with much of Chinatown's community uprooted, it is something of a museum piece, one that schoolkids are taken to so they can glimpse life in "the old days".

A statue of the goddess Mazu, shipped in from southern China in time for the temple's completion in 1842, stands in the centre of the main hall, flanked by the martial figure of Guan Yu on the right and physician Bao Sheng on the left. Against the left wall, look out for an altar containing the curious figures of General Fan and General Xie. The two are said to have arranged to meet by a river bridge, but Xie was delayed; Fan waited doggedly and drowned in a flash flood, which supposedly accounts for his grimace and dark skin. When Xie finally arrived, he was filled with guilt and hanged himself – hence his depiction, with tongue hanging down to his chest.

Incidentally, the **pagoda** visible to the left from Telok Ayer Street, called **Chongwen Ge**, formed part of an adjacent school, a site that now hosts a Peranakan café and tile shop (see p.539 and p.549). It's also worth walking around to Amoy Street to see the back-wall **mural** by Yip Yew Chong, an accountant who does street art in his spare time; it kicks off on the right with the Chinatown of old in sepia and ends with a full-colour fantasy in which both existing and demolished towers in the Financial District loom over a river still busy with cargo-filled bumboats.

Nagore Durgha Shrine

140 Telok Ayer St · Museum daily 10am–6pm · Free

It's a testament to Singapore's multicultural nature that Thian Hock Keng's next-door neighbour is the charming brown-and-white **Nagore Durgha Shrine** to the Muslim ascetic, Shahul Hamid of Nagore. It was built in the 1820s by Chulias from southern India, as was the Jamae Mosque (see p.496), so it's not surprising that the buildings appear to be cut from the same architectural cloth.

Part of the shrine now houses a fine little **museum** dedicated to the history of Telok Ayer Street. The few simple artefacts and photographs do a good job of unpacking the nuances of Muslim Indian identity in Singapore, a country where Hindu Indians are referred to by the part of India they emigrated from, yet their Muslim counterparts are lumped together under the banner of their faith.

Ying Fo Fui Kun
98 Telok Ayer St, beyond the junction with Cross St • Telok Ayer or Chinatown MRT

Among the smartest of Chinatown's surviving clan houses, the **Ying Fo Fui Kun** was established in 1822 by Hakkas from Guangdong province. It has narrowly avoided being swallowed up by the adjacent Far East Square complex, but in its present orderly state, with an immaculate altar boasting gilt calligraphy and carvings, it's hard to imagine it having been the hub of an entire community. Periodic membership drives try to stop it turning into a senior citizens' club, given that provincial dialects – traditionally used as a marker of identity among the Chinese – have been on the decline since the 1970s following an aggressive state campaign to standardize on Mandarin.

Far East Square

Far East Square is a sort of heritage development, engulfing the shophouses of what would have been the northernmost part of Amoy Street. Also co-opted into the complex, indeed into a hotel, is the **Fuk Tak Chi Street Museum** (76 Telok Ayer St; daily 10am–10pm; free). This was once Singapore's oldest temple, having been founded by Hakka and Cantonese migrants in 1824; now its altar holds a model junk crewed by sailors in blue shorts. A diorama depicts Telok Ayer Street in its waterfront heyday, with a stage set up in front of the temple and opera performers getting ready to strut their stuff.

Hong Lim Park
Between Upper Pickering St and North Canal Rd • Clarke Quay MRT

A few minutes' walk southwest from the Singapore River, **Hong Lim Park** is not much more than a field ringed by trees, but it's of symbolic significance as the home of **Speakers' Corner**, at its northern edge. Since its designation in 2000, citizens have, in theory, been able to speak their minds here, just as people do at its famous exemplar in central London. This being Singapore, regulations require you to register your intention to speak and prohibit discussion of religion or anything that could be deemed to provoke racial discontent. Despite this, the site has regained some of its historic role as a site for political meetings and also hosts the annual gay pride event, Pink Dot.

Boat Quay

Close to the old mouth of the Singapore River, the pedestrianized row of waterfront shophouses known as **Boat Quay** is one of Singapore's most commercially successful bids at urban regeneration. Derelict in the early 1990s, it's since become a thriving hangout, sporting a huge collection of restaurants and bars. The area's historical significance may be easier to appreciate through its street names – Synagogue Street nearby, for example, was the site of the island's first synagogue.

Yueh Hai Ching Temple
30B Philip St

Recently restored, the twin-shrined **Yueh Hai Ching Temple** (also called **Wak Hai Cheng Bio**) feels even more isolated than the Thian Hock Keng, nestling as it does among the towers where Chinatown merges into the Financial District. Completed in the 1850s, it is another of the area's temples built on the old coastline, and was a magnet for newly

9

arrived migrants who, once ashore at Bullock Cart Water (the translation of the Chinese name, used to this day, for what would become Chinatown), would come here to give thanks for their safe arrival. Hai Ching means "calm sea" and an effigy of Tian Hou or Mazu, the queen of heaven and protector of seafarers, is housed in the right-hand shrine. Be sure to look up at the roof, crammed with scenes from Chinese folklore built up using the traditional *jiannian* technique, involving multicoloured porcelain shards.

Tanjong Pagar

Tanjong Pagar or Outram Park MRT

The district of **Tanjong Pagar**, south of Chinatown, was once a veritable sewer of opium dens and brothels. Then it was earmarked as a conservation area and many dozens of shophouses were refurbished as bars, restaurants and shops, notably on Neil Road and Duxton Hill. A grander example of the area's architecture can be found right where South Bridge Road flows into Neil and Tanjong Pagar roads: here you'll easily spot the arches and bricked facade of the **Jinrikisha Building**, constructed at the turn of the last century as a terminus for rickshaws.

Tanjong Pagar's most interesting attraction is the **Baba House**, though as an architectural attention-grabber it's rivalled by the seven interlinked towers of **Pinnacle@ Duxton**, a showpiece municipal housing development on Cantonment Road, dominating Chinatown's southern skyline.

Baba House

157 Neil Rd • Free • ☎ 6227 5731, ⊕ babahouse.nus.edu.sg • Outram Park MRT (Cantonment Rd exit), or bus #174 from Orchard Rd or Bras Basah Rd to its terminus

The **Baba House** is one of Singapore's most impressive museums, partly because it isn't really a museum: what you see is a late nineteenth- or early twentieth-century Peranakan house, meticulously restored to its appearance in the late 1920s, a particularly prosperous time in its history. Like Penang's Cheong Fatt Tze Mansion, the place is easily spotted as it's painted a vivid blue. Note the **phoenixes** and **peonies** on the eaves above the entrance, signifying longevity and wealth respectively and, together, marital bliss. Even more eye-catching is the **pintu pagar**, the swing doors with gilt and mother-of-pearl inlays. Note that taking one of the five weekly tours is compulsory – book at least a week in advance.

The ground floor

Beyond the *pintu pagar*, the altar here, among the last of its kind in Singapore, is backed by an exquisitely carved wood screen behind which the women of the household could eavesdrop on proceedings. Beyond it is the **family hall**, with an air well open to the sky in its midst. Note the original tilework depicting roses and tulips, indicating European influence, and the gilt bats on the walls – bats, *bianfu* in Mandarin, are considered lucky because *fu* is a homonym for the Chinese character meaning "good fortune".

The upper floors

Upstairs at the front end of the house, the centrepiece of the **main bedroom** is an ornate wooden four-poster bed with gilt and red lacquer decorations, bearing carved motifs such as musical instruments and yet more bats. Your guide will almost certainly open up the **peephole** in the floor, exposing a small shaft down to the main hall. The **third storey**, a later addition, is used for temporary exhibitions.

The Financial District

Raffles Place, Telok Ayer or Downtown MRT

If Singapore's **Financial District** (or **Central Business District/CBD**; map p.498) figures in the popular imagination at all, it would be because of the rogue trader Nick

TAKING CHINESE TEA

At two Tanjong Pagar teahouses, visitors can glean something of the deep Chinese connection with tea by taking part in a **workshop** lasting up to an hour. Participants are introduced to different varieties of tea and talked through the history of tea cultivation and the rituals of brewing and appreciating the drink. The water, for example, has to reach an optimum temperature that depends on the type of tea being prepared; experts can tell its heat by the size of the rising bubbles, described variously as "sand eyes", "prawn eyes", "fish eyes", etc. Both venues also stock an extensive range of tea-related accoutrements such as tall "sniffer" cups used to savour the aroma of the brew before it is poured into squat teacups for drinking.

Tea Chapter 9–11 Neil Rd ☏ 6226 1175, ⓦ teachapter.com. Tea appreciation sessions starting at S$45 per head with snacks, or full-blown four-session courses at S$200 per person, for two or more people.

Yixing Yuan Teahouse 78 Tanjong Pagar Rd ☏ 6224 6961, ⓦ yixingxuan-teahouse.com. Hour-long workshops from S$25 per head for a group of at least five.

Leeson, whose antics here brought about the **Barings Bank collapse** of the 1990s. The area, south of the mouth of the Singapore River, has no specific sights but makes a reasonable prelude to nearby Boat Quay (see p.503), Telok Ayer Street (see p.502), the Colonial District (via Cavenagh Bridge; see p.483) or the southern part of Marina Bay (see p.506).

Raffles Place

What is now the Financial District was a swamp until land reclamation in the mid-1820s rendered it fit for building. Within just a few years, it was home to the colony's busiest business address, Commercial Square, boasting the banks, ships' chandlers and warehouses of a burgeoning trading port. The square later became the island's main shopping area until Orchard Road overtook it in the late 1960s; today known as **Raffles Place**, it's the heart of Singapore's high-profile banking sector.

Surfacing from Raffles Place MRT, follow the signs for Raffles Place itself to feel like an ant in a canyon of skyscrapers. To see what things look like from the top of that canyon, the place to head is One Raffles Place, the complex to the west of the square, with truly stunning views from its rooftop bar, *1-Altitude* (see p.545). The three roads that run southwest from Raffles Place – Cecil Street, Robinson Road and Shenton Way – are all chock a block with more high-rise banks and financial houses.

Battery Road

Heading towards the river from Raffles Place, you reach **Battery Road**, its name recalling the days when Fort Fullerton (named after Robert Fullerton, first governor of the Straits Settlements) and its attendant battery of guns stood to the east on the site of the elegant **Fullerton Building** – the main attraction today. This was one of Singapore's tallest buildings when it was constructed in 1928 as the General Post Office, a role it fulfilled until the mid-1990s. These days, it serves as the luxury *Fullerton* hotel; head inside to plunge into the Neoclassical and Art Deco splendour of the atrium, with a Y-shaped marbled staircase surmounting a carp-filled fishpond, and enormous columns reminiscent of Egyptian temples.

Collyer Quay

Collyer Quay runs south along the western shore of Marina Bay from what was the mouth of the Singapore River, linking the Colonial District with Raffles Quay and Shenton Way further south, both of which mark the former line of the seafront. Just east of Collyer Quay, the Merlion Park is home to a cement statue of Singapore's national symbol, the **Merlion**. Half-lion, half-fish and wholly ugly, the creature reflects

9

the island's maritime connections and the old tale concerning the derivation of its present name, derived from the Sanskrit "Singapura", meaning "Lion City".

Clifford Pier
80 Collyer Quay

South of the park, the Art Deco **Clifford Pier** building, long the departure point for boat trips out to Singapore's southern islands, was rendered defunct by the barrage that seals Marina Bay off from the sea. The building, along with the **Customs House** building a minute's walk on, have been transformed into restaurant complexes, run by the firm that owns the *Fullerton* hotel; part of Clifford Pier forms the entrance to the hotel's pricier new sibling, the *Fullerton Bay*.

Lau Pa Sat
18 Raffles Quay

Arguably the best place for refreshments in the Financial District is the charmingly old-world **Lau Pa Sat**, literally meaning "old market" – it was built in 1894 as a place for traders to sell produce. Also known by its original name, **Telok Ayer Market**, Lau Pa Sat has served as a hawker centre since the 1970s, except for a hiatus in the 1980s when tunnelling for the MRT required the octagonal cast-iron structure to be dismantled, then reassembled piece by piece. Aficionados of **satay** should turn up in the evening, when vendors set up in a row outside on Boon Tat Street.

Marina Bay
Bayfront, Downtown or Promenade MRT

It's hard not to be awed by the audacity of **Marina Bay**, the project that has transformed downtown Singapore's seafront over two generations. An exorbitantly ambitious piece of civil engineering, it entailed the creation of three massive expanses of reclaimed land and a barrage to seal off the basins of the Singapore and Kallang rivers from the sea. The result is a seaside freshwater **reservoir** with a crucial role in reducing Singapore's dependence on Malaysian water supplies.

Although the bay's southern "jaw", **Marina South**, now sprouts a host of bank buildings to rival Raffles Place, the area is dominated by the **Marina Bay Sands** casino resort, with its museum and rooftop restaurants; it is inevitably the focus of any visit to the bay, along with the extravagant new **Gardens by the Bay** next door. Close to the Padang, the **Theatres on the Bay arts complex** is worth a detour for its skyline views, with more of the same available from the oversized Ferris wheel of the **Singapore Flyer**.

Marina Bay Sands
10 Bayfront Ave • ☏ 6688 8826, ⓦ marinabaysands.com • Bayfront MRT

Rarely does a building become an icon quite as instantly as the **Marina Bay Sands** hotel and casino, its three 55-floor towers topped and connected by a vast, curved-surfboard-like deck, the SkyPark. Even if you have no interest in the casino – open 24/7, naturally – the complex, which includes a convention centre, a shopping mall, two concert venues, numerous restaurants and its own museum, is well worth exploring. The hotel atrium, often so busy with people gawping that it feels like a train station concourse, is especially striking, the sides of the building sloping into each other overhead to give the impression of being inside a narrow glassy pyramid.

In the evening, a free sound and light show, **Spectra** (daily 8pm & 9pm, Fri & Sat extra show at 10pm; 15min), takes place outside the hotel, with illuminated fountains and lasers. Visible from the Padang and surrounding areas, the display isn't especially captivating unless you're at the hotel itself.

SkyPark

Observation deck Mon–Thurs 9.30am–10pm, Fri–Sun 9.30am–11pm • S$23 • Tickets and access via the basement ticket office of tower 3, at the northern end of the complex

From what would have been an impossible vantage point, high above the sea before the creation of Marina Bay, the SkyPark's observation deck affords superb views over Singapore's Colonial District on one side and the conservatories of **Gardens by the Bay** on the other. Unfortunately tickets are overpriced and don't allow you up close to the most famous feature, the 150m **infinity pool**. On the other hand, there's no charge to visit if you eat or drink at either of the two SkyPark venues, such as *Cé La Vi* (see p.541).

ArtScience Museum

At the northern end of the complex, close to the helix footbridge to the Singapore Flyer and Theatres on the Bay • Daily 10am–7pm • Ticket prices vary depending on the exhibition

The **ArtScience Museum** is easily spotted: its shape is supposed to represent a stylized lotus blossom, though from certain angles it looks more like a stubby-fingered hand. The museum aims to decode the connections between art and science, but in practice it puts on world-class travelling exhibitions, some only tenuously linked to the

9

supposed remit: highlights to date have included items salvaged from the *Titanic* and the self-explanatory Harry Potter: The Exhibition. There's only one permanent gallery, Future World, in which children (and grown-ups) can interact with colourful multimedia installations by, for example, crafting and scanning objects which then pop up in a large-scale animation.

Gardens by the Bay South

18 Marina Gardens Drive • Daily 5am–2am; conservatories 9am–9pm • Free admission; OCBC Skyway S$5; conservatories S$28; last ticket sales at 8pm • ☎ 6420 6848, ⓦ gardensbythebay.com.sg • Bayfront MRT (enter via the Dragonfly Bridge)

Two vast conservatories, roofs arched like the backs of foraging dinosaurs, are the most eye-catching features of the southern section of **Gardens by the Bay**. Intended to be a second botanic garden for Singapore, the gardens are split into three chunks around Marina Bay; the southern area, next to *Marina Bay Sands*, is very much the centrepiece.

One conservatory houses Mediterranean and African flora, the highlight being the stands of bizarrely shaped **baobab** trees. The neighbouring conservatory nurtures **cloud forest** of the kind found on tropical peaks like Kinabalu, and includes a 35m "mountain" covered in ferns, rhododendrons and insect-eating butterworts.

The gardens' other big draw is the **Supertree Grove**, an array of towers resembling gigantic golf tees and sheathed in a sort of red trelliswork, from which climbers, ferns and orchids poke out. More exciting by day is the slightly wobbly **OCBC Skyway**, an aerial walkway connecting the tops of the two tallest supertrees and providing good views. At night, though, the supertrees come into their own when they are illuminated in free **light shows** at 7.45pm and 8.45pm.

Red Dot Design Museum

11 Marina Boulevard • Daily 11am–2am • $6 • ☎ 6514 0111, ⓦ museum.red-dog.sg • Downtown or Bayfront MRT

Housed in a futuristic glass building, the **Red Dot Design Museum** focuses on international product design and the creative use of illustration, following the process from conceptualization all the way through to the realized work – be it a sports car or art installation. It's at its best during the monthly **crafts market**, MAAD, when local artists and designers showcase their work (3–10pm one weekend per month). The gift shop stocks quirky designer items that make good gifts (see p.550).

Marina Centre

Promenade or Esplanade MRT, or City Hall MRT via the subterranean CityLink Mall

The large triangle of reclaimed land east of the Padang and the *Raffles Hotel*, robbing Beach Road of its beach, is officially called **Marina Centre**, though locals invariably invoke the names of the Marina Square or Suntec City malls when referring to it. This is the oldest part of the Marina Bay project, open since the early 1990s, but still feels quite disconnected from the historical neighbourhoods to the west.

Esplanade – Theatres on the Bay

1 Esplanade Drive • Daily 9am–late • Free; tours S$10 (45min; check online for latest schedule) • ☎ 6828 8377, ⓦ esplanade.com

Opinion is split as to whether the two huge, spiked shells that roof the **Esplanade – Theatres on the Bay** project, just east of the Padang, are peerless modernistic architecture or indulgent kitsch. They have variously been compared to hedgehogs and even durians (the preferred description among locals), though two giant insect eyes is perhaps more apt. Facilities include a concert hall, theatres, gallery space and, on the third floor, **library@esplanade**, with a wide range of arts-related books and other resources. It's possible to do a guided tour of the site, but what lures most casual visitors are the **views**, particularly fine at dusk, across the bay to the Financial District and *Marina Bay Sands*.

Singapore Flyer

30 Raffles Ave • Daily 8.30am–10pm • S$33 • ☎ 6333 3311, ⓦ singaporeflyer.com

Standing a lofty 165m high, the **Singapore Flyer** is actually slightly taller than the summit of Bukit Timah, the island's highest natural point, and about 30m taller than the London Eye. The downside is that from its location, the remaining rows of shophouses are largely obscured by clumps of towers; better views can be had from some hotels and rooftop bars, notably *1-Altitude* (see p.545).

The dollar-a-minute ride – billed as a **flight** – initially has you looking east over the Kallang district, home to the new Sports Hub stadium complex. Beyond the shipping lanes, Indonesia's **Riau archipelago** appears very close. Looking north, it's more exciting to pick out the golden domes of the Sultan Mosque and the shophouses of Arab Street beyond the twin Gateway buildings on Beach Road. As your capsule reaches maximum height, you might just make out the low hump of **Bukit Timah**, topped with a couple of radio masts, on the horizon beyond Theatres on the Bay.

The descent affords good views of **Marina Bay Sands** and the **Financial District**. Originally the ride began with these, but the wheel had to be reversed due to feng shui concerns (apparently the old direction was channelling good luck up and away from the area).

Orchard Road and around

It would be hard to conjure an image more at odds with the present reality of **Orchard Road** than historian Mary Turnbull's description of "a country lane lined with bamboo hedges and shrubbery, with trees meeting overhead". In the early part of the last century, merchants taking a constitutional here would have strolled past rows of nutmeg trees, followed at a discreet distance by their manservants. Today, the area is synonymous with **shopping** – huge, often glitzy malls now line the road (see p.548).

Orchard Road begins as the continuation of Tanglin Road and channels traffic east for nearly 3km to Bras Basah and Selegie roads, near the Colonial District. The bucolic allure of the area of old survives 1km beyond Orchard Road's western end, where you'll find Singapore's excellent **Botanic Gardens**.

Dhoby Ghaut

In the **Dhoby Ghaut** area, at the eastern end of Orchard Road, Indian *dhobies* (laundrymen) used to wash clothes in the Stamford Canal, which ran along Orchard and Stamford roads. Those days are long gone, though something of the past survives in the **Cathay building** (ⓦ thecathay.com.sg), home to the company behind one of Singapore's and Malaysia's oldest cinema chains. Boasting a 1939 Art Deco facade, the building houses a multiplex cinema and the **Cathay Gallery** (Mon–Sat 11am–7pm; free), displaying memorabilia – costumes, promotional materials and vintage photos – of eight decades in the movie business, including its 1950s and 1960s heyday, when the company made its own Chinese- and Malay-language films.

The Istana

Istana and grounds only open four or five holidays a year, with a nominal entrance fee (see website for details) • ⓦ istana.gov.sg • Dhoby Ghaut MRT

A short walk west along Orchard Road from Dhoby Ghautz MRT takes you past the **Plaza Singapura** mall, beyond which stern soldiers guard the main gate of Singapore's **Istana**, built in 1869. With ornate cornices, elegant louvred shutters and a high mansard roof, the building was originally the official residence of Singapore's British governors; now it's home to Singapore's president, a ceremonial role for which elections are held nonetheless. The first Sunday of the month sees a **changing of the guard** ceremony at the main gate at 5.45pm.

ORCHARD ROAD

ACCOMMODATION

Emerald Hill

Somerset MRT

A number of architecturally noteworthy houses have survived the bulldozers at **Emerald Hill**, behind the Centrepoint mall and a five-minute walk west of the Istana. Granted to Englishman William Cuppage in 1845, the hill was for some years afterwards the site of a large nutmeg plantation. After his death in 1872, the land was subdivided and sold off, much of it to members of the **Peranakan** community. Walk up Emerald Hill Road today and you'll see exquisite houses from the era, in the so-called **Chinese Baroque** style, typified by the use of coloured ceramic tiles, carved swing doors, shuttered windows and pastel-shaded walls with fine plaster mouldings. Unsurprisingly, quite a few now host trendy restaurants and bars.

ION Orchard

2 Orchard Turn • Orchard MRT

The most striking of the area's malls, **ION Orchard** has a bulging glass frontage vaguely reminiscent of Theatres on the Bay, and is topped by a tower of luxury apartments that also boasts a 55th-floor viewing gallery, ION Sky (S$20).

Goodwood Park Hotel

22 Scotts Rd • Orchard MRT

A few minutes' walk north up **Scotts Road** off Orchard Road stands the impressive **Goodwood Park Hotel**, with gleaming walls and a distinctive squat, steeple-like tower.

DRINKING

Alley Bar	5
Ice Cold Beer	3
Martini Bar	1
No. 5 Emerald Hill	4
Que Pasa	2

EATING

Bistro Du Vin	2
Brunetti	9
Maharajah	4
Marché	8
Min Jiang	1
PS Café	3
Sakae Teppenyaki	5
Spices Café	7
Thai Express	6
Warung M Nasir	10

SHOPPING

313@Somerset	15
Antiques of the Orient	1
C.T. Hoo	6
Charles & Keith	10
Flower Diamond	12
Forum the Shopping Mall	4
The Heeren	8
ION Orchard	11
Kinokuniya	14
Kwok Gallery	5
Ngee Ann City	13
Plaza Singapura	7
Tanglin Shopping Centre	3
Tangs	2
Times Bookstore	9

Having started out in 1900 as the Teutonia Club for German expats, it was commandeered by the British with the outbreak of war across Europe in 1914, and didn't open again until 1918. In 1929 it became a hotel, though by 1942 it and the *Raffles* – designed by the same architect – were lodging Japanese officers. The *Goodwood Park* was later used for war-crimes trials. Today the hotel remains one of the classiest in town and is a well-regarded venue for a British-style tea.

Botanic Gardens

1 Cluny Rd • Daily 5am–midnight • Free, with free weekend tours of some sections plus free concerts • ☎ 6471 7138, ⓦ sbg.org.sg • The Tanglin gate bus #7 from Arab St area or #174 from Chinatown, both via Somerset Rd, next to Orchard Rd; Bukit Timah Rd entrance use Botanic Gardens MRT

Singapore has long made green space an integral part of the island's landscape, but none of its parks come close to matching the refinement of the **Botanic Gardens**, the island's sole UNESCO World Heritage Site. Founded in 1859, the gardens were where the Brazilian seeds that gave rise to the great **rubber plantations** of the Malay Peninsula were first nurtured in 1877. Henry Ridley, named the gardens' director the following year, recognized the financial potential of rubber and spent the next twenty years persuading plantation-owners to convert to this new crop, an obsession that earned him the nickname "Mad" Ridley. In later years the gardens became a centre for the breeding of new **orchid** hybrids. Recent additions have extended the park all the way north to Bukit Timah Road, where the Botanic Gardens MRT station offers a route to the newer, less interesting part of the gardens; the itinerary

9

that follows assumes the classic approach up Tanglin and Napier roads to the **Tanglin gate** at the start of Cluny Road.

Into the gardens

The path from the Tanglin gate, lined with frangipanis, casuarinas and the odd majestic banyan tree, soon reaches the tranquil **Swan Lake**, nearly as old as the gardens themselves. Veer to the left and you reach the newest additions to the gardens, the Walk of Giants (a tree-canopy elevated walkway) with a wetland area at the far end. Both are still bedding down, so it's more interesting to keep to the right side of the lake, following signs for the **ginger garden**, packed with flowering gingers as exotic and gaudy as anything you could hope to see in the tropics.

National Orchid Garden

Daily 8.30am–7pm; last admission 6pm • $$$

A feast of blooms of almost every hue are on show at the **National Orchid Garden**. There's an entire section of orchids named after dignitaries and celebrities who have visited; *Dendrobium Margaret Thatcher* is a severe pink with a couple of petals twisted like pasta spirals, while *Vandaenopsis Nelson Mandela* is a reassuring warm yellowy-brown. Looking slightly out of place is the black-and-white **Burkill Hall**, exemplifying the so-called Tropical Tudor style, few examples of which now survive in Singapore; the gardens' director once lived here. The gift shop at the exit stocks an incredible range of orchid paraphernalia, including blossoms encased in glass paperweights or plated with gold.

Back to the Tanglin gate

Exiting the orchid garden, head up the boardwalk to enter the central **rainforest** with a trail past numbered highlights, including a spectacular banyan tree that's a mass of aerial roots. The trail and forest end above **Symphony Lake**, where occasional concerts are staged.

By now you've seen much of the best of what the gardens have to offer, and there's not that much to be gained by continuing north. Heading back towards the Tanglin gate, look out for the park's loftiest tree, a stunning 47m *jelawai* on the edge of the rainforest tract; this and several other exceptionally tall trees are fitted with lightning conductors. Close by, to the right, is one of the loveliest spots in all of Singapore, a grassy area centred upon a 1930s **bandstand**, encircled by eighteen rain trees for shade.

Head downhill from here through the **sundial garden** to end up back at the lake, or bear left to reach **Holttum Hall** – only a couple of minutes' walk from the Tanglin gate – a 1920s house that hosts a museum of the gardens' history.

North to Bukit Timah Road

Continue northwards from Symphony Lake, and you soon reach the **Visitor Centre** – marooned in the middle of the gardens – with a gift shop and café. Next comes the **Evolution Garden**, where fake petrified trees help to illustrate how plant life has evolved over millennia. From here, it's several minutes' walk through the **bougainvillea and bamboo garden** to reach the MRT station.

Central Catchment Nature Reserve

For a taste of Singapore's wilder side, head to the **Central Catchment Nature Reserve** (informally known as the "Central Nature Reserve"). The lush heart of the island is dominated by **rainforest** and several large **reservoirs**, and there are opportunities for **hikes** up **Bukit Timah**, the island's tallest hill. The interest isn't limited to the jungle though: close to Bukit Timah, the **Former Ford Factory** is a museum housed in the building where the British surrendered to the Japanese, while the northern end of the nature reserve holds Singapore's highly regarded **zoo**, with a separate **Night Safari** section open from dusk, and the zoo's newest offshoot, the **River Safari,** presenting the fauna of rivers as diverse as the Mekong and the Mississippi.

Bukit Timah

Bukit Timah Road shoots northwest from Little India, passing leafy suburbs en route to Johor Bahru (it was the main road to the Causeway until superseded by the Bukit Timah Expressway). Some 9km on from Little India, the road becomes Upper Bukit Timah Road and arrives at **Bukit Timah** itself, often called "Bukit Timah Hill" by locals – a deliberate tautology as the surrounding district is also known as Bukit Timah.

Bukit Timah Nature Reserve

Hindhede Drive • Daily 7am–7pm; exhibition hall 8.30am–5pm • Free • Ⓦ nparks.gov.sg • Beauty World MRT, then a short walk north up Upper Bukit Timah Rd

One of Singapore's last pockets of primary dipterocarp forest can be experienced in the **Bukit Timah Nature Reserve,** established in 1883 by Nathaniel Cantley, then superintendent of the Botanic Gardens. **Wildlife** abounded in this part of Singapore in the mid-nineteenth century, when the natural historian Alfred Russel Wallace came here to do fieldwork; he later observed that "in all my subsequent travels in the East I rarely if ever met with so productive a spot". Wallace also noted the presence of tiger traps, but by the 1930s Singapore's tigers had met their end. **Long-tailed macaques** haven't dwindled, however; some can be seen wandering around the houses at the base of the hill peeking in bins for food.

The trails

Don't expect a full-blown jungle-trekking experience, as the four colour-coded **trails** consist largely of family-friendly boardwalks, steps and stretches of proper road. Three share a very steep start up a sealed road; the exception, the green trail, meanders along the side of the hill before rejoining the others. Most people tackle the red trail (30min), which is the road up to the summit at a paltry 164m; a flight of narrow steps halfway along – the Summit Path – offers a shortcut to the top.

Former Ford Factory

351 Upper Bukit Timah Rd • Mon–Sat 9am–5.30pm, Sun noon–5.30pm • S$3 • Ⓣ 6462 6724, Ⓦ nas.gov.sg/formerfordfactory • Hillview MRT, then backtrack three bus stops on southbound bus #67, #170, #171 or #184

The Art Deco **Former Ford Factory** at Bukit Timah was the first car-making plant of its kind in Southeast Asia when it opened in October 1941. But in early 1942 the Japanese invaded, and on February 15 Lieutenant General Percival, head of the Allied forces in Singapore, surrendered to Japan's General Yamashita in the factory's boardroom. Today the scene is recreated as part of a worthwhile museum focused on the occupation and, less successfully, its aftermath and the beginnings of decolonization. Being run by Singapore's National Archives service, it leans heavily on documents and ephemera – everything from Japanese textbooks and the notorious wartime "banana money" (bananas were depicted on one Japanese-issued banknote) to sketches by POWs at Changi and watercolours commissioned by the occupying administration.

Singapore Zoo

80 Mandai Lake Rd • Ⓣ 6269 3411, Ⓦ zoo.com.sg • Bus #138 from Ang Mo Kio MRT, #927 from Choa Chu Kang MRT or the special Mandai Express bus from Khatib MRT (daily 9am–7pm; every 40min; 1hr; S$1); slightly faster private buses to/from downtown available, details at Ⓦ safarigate.com and Ⓦ saex.com.sg

Singapore's main wildlife attractions cluster in woodland around the tranquil Seletar reservoir: the **Singapore Zoo** and its offshoots, **Night Safari** and **River Safari,** which will

9

be joined in the early 2020s by a rainforest park and resort, as well as the Bird Park being relocated from Jurong. They consistently draw crowds, which is partly down to their "open" policy: many animals are kept in spacious, naturalistic enclosures behind moats, though creatures such as big cats still have to be caged.

The zoo

Daily 8.30am–6pm · S$33 · See ⓦ zoo.com.sg for details of combination tickets including Night Safari, River Safari or Jurong Bird Park

Home to more than 300 species, the **zoo** could easily occupy you for half a day if not longer. A tram ($5) does a one-way circuit of the grounds, but as it won't always be going your way, be prepared for some legwork.

Highlights include the **Fragile Forest** biodome, a magical zone where you can actually walk among ring-tailed lemurs, sloths and fruit bats, and **Frozen Tundra** featuring, naturally enough, polar bears. The **white tigers** are a big draw too, not actually white but resembling Siamese cats in the colour of their fur and eyes. Primates are something of a strong point, too: orang-utans swing through the trees overhead close to the entrance, and at the **Great Rift Valley zone** you can espy the communal life of a hundred Hamadryas baboons, including some rather unchivalrous behaviour on the part of males, who bite females to rein them in. There are animal shows and feeding displays throughout the day, too.

Night Safari

Daily 7.15pm–midnight; shops/restaurants from 6pm; last admission 11pm · S$45 · See ⓦ zoo.com.sg for details of combination tickets including zoo, River Safari or Jurong Bird Park

Many animals are nocturnal, and the **Night Safari** presents them so well that you'll wonder why similar establishments aren't everywhere. It's true that the Borneo-style tribal show at the entrance is tacky, and there can be queues for the free tram tours (40min), but these are mere niggles at what is the most popular strand of the zoo.

The trams take you around two-thirds of the site. You can forgo them and simply walk around the leafy grounds – an atmospheric experience in the muted lighting. But if you do this, you'll miss out on some enclosures, notably those for large mammals such as elephants and hippos, and the **Indo-Malayan trail**, featuring Asiatic black bears and an artificial waterfall. Areas you can only visit on foot include the **Fishing Cat Trail**, with the *binturong*, sometimes called the bearcat (you'll understand why when you see it); and the **Leopard Trail**, where you may spot the clouded leopard and slow loris.

It's worth catching the **Creatures of the Night** show (hourly 7.30–9.30pm, plus Fri & Sat 10.30pm; free), which touches on the importance of conservation and recycling, and stars otters, raccoons, civets and owls, among others.

River Safari

Daily 10am–7pm · S$30; Amazon River Quest and River Safari Cruise each S$5 · See ⓦ zoo.com.sg for details of combination tickets including zoo, Night Safari or Jurong Bird Park

The **River Safari** spans the divide between aquarium and zoo, trying to do justice to the fauna of seven of the world's great rivers and the lands they flow through. There are too many tanks for comfort at the start, presenting badgers, various alligators and crocs, catfish and other creatures of the Congo, Mississippi, Ganges, Nile and Mekong. Much better is the hangar-like **Giant Panda Forest**, housing two giant pandas and the raccoon-like **red panda**, with white ears and a stripy orange tail. The second half of the park is given over almost entirely to what's billed as **Amazonia**, and much of that is taken up by one 10min ride, the so-so **Amazon River Quest**, in which your "boat" is carried along a sluiceway past enclosures of scarlet ibises and spider monkeys, among others. Saved for last is the most humongous tank of all: the **Amazon Flooded Forest**, home to manatees, giant arapaima fish, otters and piranhas.

Kranji and Sungei Buloh

While land reclamation has radically altered the east coast and industrialization the west, the **northern** expanses of the island up to the Straits of Johor still retain pockets of the **rainforest** and mangrove swamp that blanketed Singapore on Raffles' arrival in 1819. Though thickets of state housing blocks are never far away, something of rural Singapore's agricultural past clings on by way of the odd prawn- or poultry-farm or vegetable garden. Two sights make it worth considering coming this far: the **Kranji War Cemetery and Memorial**, and the wetland reserve at **Sungei Buloh**.

Kranji War Cemetery

9 Woodlands Rd • Daily 7am–6.30pm • Free • ⓦ cwgc.org • Kranji MRT then a 10min walk, bus #170 from opposite Little India MRT/Bukit Timah, or #927 from the zoo to the junction of Woodlands and Mandai rds and a 15min walk north

Kranji War Cemetery is the resting place of many Allied troops who died in the defence of Singapore. Row upon row of graves slope up the manicured hill, some identified only as "known unto God". Beyond the simple stone cross that stands over the cemetery is the **memorial**, around which are recorded the names of more than twenty thousand soldiers (including personnel from Britain, Canada, Australia, New Zealand, Malaya and South Asia) who died in this region during World War II. Two unassuming **tombs** stand on the wide lawns below the cemetery, belonging to Yusof bin Ishak and Dr B.H. Sheares, independent Singapore's first two presidents.

Sungei Buloh Wetland Reserve

301 Neo Tiew Crescent • Daily 7am–7pm; guided tours Sat 9.30am • Free • ☎ 6794 1401, ⓦ nparks.gov.sg • Bus #925 from Kranji or Choa Chu Kang MRT to the Kranji reservoir car park, then a 15min walk; on Sun the bus becomes #925C from Kranji MRT and goes direct

A coastal reservoir runs through the western part of Kranji, beyond which is the **Sungei Buloh Wetland Reserve**, the island's only nature park of its kind. Expanses of mangrove and mud flats are crisscrossed by embanked trails and walkways, with views across the strait to Johor Bahru. The vegetation rapidly gets monotonous, but then **birdlife** is the main reason to come. There's a reasonable chance of spotting sandpipers, egrets and kingfishers, and between September and March, migratory birds from around Asia roost and feed here, especially in the early morning. Several **hides** dot the landscape, and you can get an elevated view over the reserve from the tallest of them, the oversized-treehouse-like **Aerie**. It's worth gazing down at the creeks, too, harbouring mudskippers, banded archerfish – which clobber insect prey by squirting water at them with their mouths – and even the occasional saltwater crocodile.

Geylang and Katong

The eastern suburbs of **Geylang** and **Katong** may seem mundane at first sight, but both have deep roots and character of the sort absent from the island's new towns. Malay culture has held sway here since the mid-nineteenth century, when Malays and Indonesians arrived to work first in the local *copra* (dried coconut kernel) processing factory and later on its *serai* (lemon grass) farms. The eastern part of Geylang, called **Geylang Serai**, retains quite a strong Malay feel and is worth checking out for Malay food or merchandise, though there are no specific sights. Katong was once a beachfront district popular with the wealthy, including many Peranakans, who built their villas here in prewar times. That **Peranakan heritage** lives on to some degree, and provides the main lure for visitors. You can sample what both districts have to offer by heading south from Geylang Serai to Katong via **Joo Chiat Road**, as described here.

9

Geylang Serai

Paya Lebar MRT, then a short walk south and east, or bus #2 or #51 (from Chinatown) and #7 (from the Botanic Gardens and Orchard Rd), which pass through Victoria St and will drop you on Sims Ave, the main eastbound drag

Geylang has acquired a certain notoriety as something of a **red-light district**. Arrive by bus, and you'll spot numerous numbered lorongs (lanes) on the way, mainly to the right of Sims Avenue; brothels along them are recognizable by the coloured lights outside. But Geylang is also home to the recently rebuilt **Geylang Serai Market**, which is very much the focus of the area's Malay life. A two-storey complex, it's easily spotted on the side of Sims Avenue, with sloping roofs reminiscent of certain styles of kampung house. The stalls are predominantly Malay, selling textiles, *kuih* (sweetmeats) and snacks such as *rempeyek*, delicious fried flour rounds encrusted with spices and peanuts.

Joo Chiat Road

Languid **Joo Chiat Road** is where Geylang shades into Katong, the latter now a middle-class residential area, though a little of the former's seediness spills over here after dark. The 1.5km stroll southeast into Katong proper at East Coast Road is hardly a chore thanks to several distractions, including some old businesses amid ever fancier shops.

At the northern end of the road, opposite the Geylang Serai market, the **Joo Chiat Complex** has a notable Malay/Islamic feel, the shops selling batik, rugs and silk, Malay music CDs and *jamu* – assorted herbal remedies. Occasionally a stage is set up behind for people to partake of impromptu bouts of old-fangled *joget* dancing.

At no. 252, Chiang Pow Joss Paper Trading produces funerary paraphernalia in one of several nicely restored shophouses on the road, while Nam San at no. 261 makes mackerel *otah-otah*, a kind of dumpling. Just beyond, the immaculate **Peranakan shophouses** on Koon Seng Road (on the left) are the architectural highlight of the area, with their restored multicoloured facades, French windows, eaves and mouldings. At no. 320, peek through the 1960s louvred windows at the workaday Ann Tin Tong Medical Hall, a world away from Chinatown's slick herbalists. Teong Theng, at no. 369, sells attractive rattan furniture and accessories, popular in Singapore homes a generation ago but now almost totally out of favour.

Katong

Bus #12 from Lavender MRT, or #14 from Dhoby Ghaut MRT; both call at Mountbatten MRT en route

From the Koon Seng Road intersection, Joo Chiat Road runs 600m on to **East Coast Road**. The beach hinted at by that name has long since gone – pushed further south by the creation of the East Coast Park on several kilometres of reclaimed land. However, the area is worth visiting thanks to a pocket of outlets celebrating its Peranakan traditions – it's not hard to find places serving Nyonya food, and there's Rumah Bebe at 113 East Coast Rd, selling clothing and jewellery (see p.550).

Katong Antiques House

208 East Coast Rd • Tues–Sun 11am–5pm • Optional tours S$15 per person • ☎ 6345 8544

East of the junction with Joo Chiat Road is the **Katong Antiques House**, whose owner, Peter Wee, is a veteran spokesman for the Peranakan community. He has amassed a treasure trove of artefacts, from wedding costumes to vintage furniture and, more prosaically, old books in Baba Malay, a blend of Malay and Hokkien Chinese. He can give you a tour (book in advance) of the traditionally decorated shophouse, which – as with all such buildings –stretches on for a surprising distance behind the narrow facade.

Changi

Even in the 1970s, eastern Singapore still looked the way the outskirts of some Malaysian towns do today, dotted with kampungs, low-rise housing estates and coconut palms. It's hard to visualize that landscape as you scoot out through new towns like Bedok (once a quiet seaside suburb) on the way to **Changi**, at the eastern tip of the island. The main reason to head this far east is to see **Changi Museum**, commemorating the internment of Allied troops and civilians by the Japanese during World War II. In the Singaporean consciousness, Changi has long embodied a beachside idyll; just a bit further afield from the museum is the **beach**, great for a dip or bask on a hot day.

Changi Museum

1000 Upper Changi Rd North • Daily 9.30am–5pm • Free; audio guides S$8 • ☎ 6214 2451, ⓦ changimuseum.sg • Tanah Merah or Upper Changi MRT, then a 15–20min ride on bus #2

Changi Prison was the site of an infamous World War II POW camp, where Japanese jailers subjected Allied prisoners, civilians included, to the harshest of treatment. Those brutalities are movingly remembered in the **Changi Museum** – which was once housed within the prison itself, but later moved wholesale just up the road when the prison was extended.

Novelist James Clavell drew on his experience of Changi in *King Rat*: "the stench was nauseating… stench from a generation of confined human bodies", he wrote. The museum does a reasonable job of picking over the facts of the Japanese occupation and the conditions prisoners endured. Memorable exhibits include artworks by internees, with pride of place given to reproductions of Stanley Warren's so-called **Changi Murals**, depicting New Testament scenes (the originals are housed within an army camp nearby, where Warren was held). Towards the end, there's a recreation of an improvised theatre where internees put on entertainments to amuse fellow inmates.

9

In the museum courtyard is a simple **wooden chapel**, typical of those erected in Singapore's wartime camps; the brass cross on its altar was crafted from spent ammunition casings. The messages on its board of remembrance are often touching and worth a read (ask staff for pen and notepaper to add your own).

Changi Point and the beach

Bus #2 from Tanah Merah MRT to Changi Point, or #19 from Tampines East MRT to the beach

Beyond Changi Prison, the tower blocks thin out and the landscape becomes a patchwork of fields, often a relic of colonial-era military bases still used by Singapore's forces. Ten minutes on via the #2 bus is the coast at **Changi Point**, with a cluster of eating places and shops called Changi Village, mainly serving the beach-going public.

Just beyond the #2 bus terminus is the **beach**, reached by a footbridge over a canalized inlet. Once you're past a stretch of manicured grass and trees, you'll reach a narrow strip of brownish sand fronting greenish-blue water – actually not uninviting (unless you were expecting something out of coastal Terengganu). The sight of aircraft rumbling in low every few minutes on the Changi flight path soon ceases to be a distraction.

The Southern Ridges and Pasir Panjang

While no less endowed with new towns and industrial estates than the east of the island, western Singapore retains a leafier, more open feel. An unusually verdant example of this is at the **Southern Ridges**, an umbrella term for the coastal ridge that runs 9km northwest from the southern tip of the island. The ridge is lined by parks and greenery, and the whole thing can be walked using a series of ingenious footbridges and walkways.

Two minor attractions en route are **Reflections at Bukit Chandu**, a museum commemorating the wartime defence of that hill by Singapore's Malay Regiment; and **Mount Faber**, with views over downtown Singapore and cable-car rides across to Sentosa Island (see p.521). Down on the coast, **Pasir Panjang**, once a sleepy district of kampungs and still a relatively quiet residential area, is home to the entertainingly tacky Buddhist theme park of **Haw Par Villa**.

The account here takes the Southern Ridges in an easterly direction, ending at Harbourfront MRT beneath Mount Faber – a sensible choice as this avoids a steep climb up the hill and allows you to finish at the massive VivoCity mall, which has plenty of places for refreshment. Haw Par Villa is really an optional extra as far as the walk is concerned. The links between parks on the walk often offer little shade, so be assiduous about **sun protection** and bring a reasonable supply of water.

Haw Par Villa

262 Pasir Panjang Rd • Daily 9am–7pm • Free • ☏ 6872 2780 • Haw Par Villa MRT

Delightfully unmodernized, **Haw Par Villa** is an unexpected star among Singapore's lesser-known sights. Featuring a gaudy parade of statues of people and creatures from Chinese myth and legend, it was once the estate of the brothers Aw, Boon Haw and Boon Par, who made a fortune early in the last century selling Tiger Balm – a cure-all ointment their father devised. The grounds held their villa and private zoo, but when the British wanted to license the owning of large animals the brothers ditched the zoo for statuary; the park then gained a new moniker, a mishmash of the brothers' names.

The main path curls up and around a hill past one kitsch tableau after another. One of the best shows titanic combat as the Eight Immortals of Taoist mythology attack the Dragon King's undersea palace. Elsewhere, look out for a curious folkloric scene in which a deer and a goat, the latter talking into a bakelite telephone, take tea with a rabbit and a rat, who are newlyweds.

The centrepiece, housed in its own tunnel, is the **Ten Courts of Hell**. Here, tax dodgers and late rent-payers are pictured being "pounded with a stone mallet", while prostitutes are drowned in the "filthy blood pool"; in one tableau someone appears to be being gored to death by a giant brush. Finally, the dead are shown having their memories wiped by drinking a cup of "magic tea" prior to reincarnation.

Reflections at Bukit Chandu

31k Pepys Rd • Tues–Sun 9am–5.30pm • Free • ☎ 6375 2510, ⓦ nhb.gov.sg • Pasir Panjang MRT, then a 10min walk north uphill

The defence of Pasir Panjang against the Japanese by the 1st and 2nd Battalion of the Malay Regiment is remembered at the tiny **Reflections at Bukit Chandu** museum. It's housed in a lone colonial building that once served as officer accommodation, though it became a food and munitions store during the war. Here "C" company of the Malay Regiment's second battalion made a brave stand against the Japanese on February 13, 1942 – two days before the British capitulation – and sustained heavy casualties.

There's nothing special about the small collection of artefacts focusing on this event, though the displays do bring home the human toll of the conflict, as well as highlighting British ambivalence about working with the Malays: the regiment was begun as an experiment to see "how the Malays would react to military discipline", and only when they proved themselves were members sent to Singapore for further training.

The canopy walk

Bear left along the ridge from the Reflections at Bukit Chandu for your first taste of the Southern Ridges trail; it also happens to be where the **canopy walk** begins. Soaring above the actual trail, the walkway takes you east through the treetops, with signs pointing out common Singapore trees such as cinnamon and *tembusu*, and views north across rolling grassy landscapes, the odd mansion poking out from within clumps of mature trees. After just a few minutes, the walkway rejoins the trail leading downhill to some nurseries and the west gate of the rather mundane **Hort Park** on Alexandra Road.

From Alexandra Arch to Mount Faber

The Alexandra Road end of Hort Park is very close to one of the huge, purpose-built footbridges on the Southern Ridges trail, the white **Alexandra Arch**, which is meant to resemble a leaf. On the bridge's east side, a long, elevated metal walkway zigzags off into the distance; it's called the **forest walk**, though it passes through nothing denser than mature woodland on its kilometre-long journey east. The walkway zigzags even more as it rises steeply to the top of **Telok Blangah Hill**, whose park offers good views of Mount Faber and Sentosa Island to the southeast.

Proceed downhill, following signs for **Henderson Waves**, and after 750m you will come to a vast footbridge of wooden slats over metal. High up in the air over broad Henderson Road, the bridge has undulating parapets – its "Waves" – containing built-in shelters against the sun or rain.

Mount Faber

On the east side of Henderson Waves and north of the VivoCity mall • Free • ☎ 6377 9688, ⓦ nparks.gov.sg • A stiff walk up from Harbourfront MRT

In bygone years, leafy **Mount Faber**, named in 1845 after government engineer Captain Charles Edward Faber, was a favourite recreation spot for its **views** over downtown. These days, you'll have to look out for breaks in the dense foliage for vistas over Bukit Merah new town to Chinatown and the Financial District, or head to the one of the restaurants at the very summit. The complex is also the departure point for the deluxe **cable car** to the HarbourFront Centre and on to Sentosa Island (see p.521). To descend,

9

follow signs for the **Marang trail**, which eventually leads down a steep flight of steps on the south side of the hill to VivoCity, with the HarbourFront Centre next door.

HarbourFront Centre and VivoCity

Harbourfront MRT

On Telok Blangah Road, the **HarbourFront Centre** is nothing more than a glorified ferry terminal from where boats set off for Indonesia's Riau archipelago (see p.527), as well as a departure point for **cable cars** heading to Mount Faber and Sentosa Island. Much more worthwhile is the **VivoCity** mall, housing three good food courts (in particular *Food Republic* on level 3; see p.543), a slew of restaurants, a cinema and other amenities; from here Sentosa is just a 10min walk away.

Jurong and Tuas

Occupying a sizeable slab of southwestern Singapore, sprawling **Jurong** was notoriously dubbed "Goh's folly" in the 1960s when Goh Keng Swee, then the finance minister, decided it was vital to create a major industrial town here on unpromising swampy terrain. To the surprise of not just the avowed sceptics, the new town took off, and today the area, including neighbouring **Tuas**, boasts a diverse portfolio of industries, including pharmaceuticals and oil refining – in which Singapore is a world leader despite having nary a drop of black gold of its own. Jurong has two significant attractions, the extensive avian zoo that is the **Jurong Bird Park**, plus the **Singapore Science Centre** – but both will move come the early 2020s, when large parts of the town will be remodelled partly to receive the future high-speed rail link with KL.

Jurong Bird Park

2 Jurong Hill (until the early 2020s, when the park will move north to sit alongside the zoo) · Daily 8.30am–6pm · S$29; see website for details of combination tickets including zoo, Night Safari or River Safari · ☎ 6265 0022, Ⓦ birdpark.com.sg · Boon Lay MRT, then bus #194; heading back, catch the bus from the stop where you arrived

Lining Jalan Ahmad Ibrahim, the **Jurong Bird Park** is home to one of the world's biggest bird collections. You'll need at least a couple of hours to have a good look around the grounds, though you can save a little time using the park's trams ($5).

Besides the four expansive walk-in aviaries, described here, the park also has a number of worthwhile smaller enclosures, such as the hugely popular **Penguin Coast** (feeding times 10.30am & 3.30pm). Just inside the entrance, it juxtaposes half a dozen penguin species against the backdrop of a mock Portuguese galleon, designed to evoke the sighting of penguins by explorers such as Vasco da Gama. The park also puts on various bird **shows**, the most exciting being Kings of the Skies (daily 10am & 4pm), in which eagles, hawks, falcons and owls show off their predatory capabilities.

The walk-in aviaries

While not the most impressive of the major aviaries, the **Southeast Asian Birds** section makes seeing local birdlife far easier than overnighting in a hide in Taman Negara; you'll find fairy bluebirds and other small but delightful creatures feasting on papaya slices, with a simulated thunderstorm at midday. Close by are **Jungle Jewels**, featuring South American birdlife in "forest" surroundings, and the **Lory Loft**, a giant aviary under netting, packed with multicoloured, chattering lories and lorikeets amid foliage meant to simulate the Australian bush. At the far end of the park is the **Waterfall Aviary**, long the park's pride. It boasts a 30m cascade and 1500 winged inhabitants, including carmine bee-eaters and South African crowned cranes.

Singapore Science Centre

15 Science Centre Rd; check online for 2020 location • Daily 10am–6pm • S$12 • ☎ 6425 2500, ⓦ science.edu.sg • Jurong East MRT, then a 10min walk or bus #66 or #335

Interactivity is the watchword at the **Singapore Science Centre**, on the eastern edge of the parkland around the artificial Jurong Lake. Galleries here hold hundreds of hands-on displays focusing on genetics, space science and other disciplines, allowing you to understand fire, test your ability to hear high-pitched sounds and be befuddled by optical illusions. It goes down well with the kids on school outings, who sweep around the place in deafening waves.

Omni-Theatre

21 Jurong Town Hall Rd • Films daily noon–8pm; observatory Fri 7.45–10pm • S$14; observatory free • ☎ 6425 2500, ⓦ omnitheatre.com.sg

Just north of the Science Centre but under the same management, the **Omni-Theatre** shows IMAX movies about the natural world, and houses an **observatory** that does free stargazing sessions on Fridays. Being almost on the equator, Singapore enjoys views of both the northern and southern skies, though light pollution and puffy clouds can put a dampener on things.

Tiger Brewery

459 Jalan Ahmad Ibrahim • Tours Mon–Fri 10am–5pm, Sat 1–5pm (see website for tour schedule) • S$20 • ☎ 6860 3005, ⓦ tigerbrewerytour.com.sg • Tuas West Road MRT, then bus #192 or a 10min walk northeast up Tuas Ave 12

Tiger is undoubtedly one of Singapore's best-known brands internationally, brewed here since 1931 as a joint venture between Heineken and a local drinks manufacturer. The German giants Beck's soon set up a brewery to produce a rival, Anchor, but Tiger's parent company acquired the upstart. In 1990 the firm became **Asia Pacific Breweries** and moved into its present plant in Tuas, where it produces Tiger beer as well as Guinness and other beverages. Tours take in a mini museum and let you see the space-age brewing, canning and bottling halls, before you indulge in some free quaffing in the sizeable bar, down out like an old-fashioned pub.

Sentosa Island

S$1 • ☎ 1800 736 8672, ⓦ sentosa.com.sg • Harbourfront MRT, then a 10min walk using the Sentosa Boardwalk footbridge from the VivoCity mall; for more on transport to/on Sentosa, see p.526.

Nearly forty years of rampant development have transformed **Sentosa Island** into the most built-up of Singapore's southern islands, so it's ironic that its name means "tranquil" in Malay. The island has certainly come a long way since World War II, when it was a British military base and known as Pulau Blakang Mati ("Island of Death Behind"). Contrived but enjoyable in parts, Sentosa today is a hybrid of resort island and theme park, with **Resorts World** on its northern shore as the showpiece attraction – incorporating a Universal Studios theme park, a fabulous aquarium and casino. Just about every patch of Sentosa that isn't a beach, hotel, golf course or a home for the

---

SENTOSA'S CABLE CARS

Eight-seater **cable cars**, each with glittering lighting inside and out, shuttle between Mount Faber (see p.519) and Imbiah Lookout on Sentosa Island (daily 8.45am–10pm; S$29, day pass S$39), calling at the HarbourFront Centre en route. The best time for **views** is at dusk, when you see Singapore lighting up from Jurong in the west to the Financial District closer by, to the northeast. The service has recently been complemented by a new branch line within Sentosa, from near the Imbiah station to Siloso Point (for Fort Siloso; same times; S$13 or free with day pass). For more details and prices of tickets valid on both lines, see ⓦ onefabergroup.com.

9

super-rich is a diversion of some kind, ranging from a Merlion replica whose inside you can walk around to a vertical wind tunnel that replicates the sensation of skydiving. The selection here covers a few of the more interesting and sensibly priced offerings.

If you want to visit, avoid the weekends and school breaks unless you don't mind the place being positively overrun, with long waits to get into the main sights. Booking tickets in advance is a good idea, not only to save time lining up but also because discounts may be available and some attractions can sell out on certain days.

Resorts World Sentosa

Close to Waterfront station on the island's north shore • ☎ 6577 8888, ⓦ rwsentosa.com

The **Resorts World Sentosa** casino development looks plastic, like something out of a Silicon Valley corporate headquarters, but it boasts some of Sentosa's biggest attractions.

Universal Studios Singapore

Resorts World Sentosa • Daily 10am–6 or 7pm • S\$74 or S\$100 with S.E.A. Aquarium; many rides have minimum height requirements and may not be suitable for young children

The ersatz character of Resorts World becomes rather entertaining at the **Universal Studios** theme park, where fairy-tale castles and American cityscapes rear bizarrely into view in the sultry heat. The park is divided into seven themed zones, encompassing everything from ancient Egypt – the least convincing of the lot – to DreamWorks' animated hit *Madagascar*. Standard tickets offer unlimited rides, but there's much more to do than get flung around on cutting-edge roller coasters or, in the case of the Jurassic Park Rapids Adventure, on a circular yellow raft. Street performers regularly strut their stuff, and one particularly memorable special-effects show creates an indoor hurricane.

The S.E.A. Aquarium and Maritime Experiential Museum

Resorts World Sentosa • Daily 10am–7pm • S\$38

The wonderful **S.E.A. Aquarium** showcases the marine life of the sea trade route between China, India and the Middle East. Visitors first pass through the **Maritime Experiential Museum**, focused on the history of that very same maritime route. By the time you read this, the museum should be reopen after a secretive revamp, but the highlight should remain the **Jewel of Muscat**, a recreation of a ninth-century Arab dhow. The boat was built without nails (coconut fibre binds the timbers), and was a gift to Singapore from Oman in 2010. Delivery took 68 days – under sail, of course.

The aquarium

Awe-inspiring in its ambition and scale, the **aquarium** has tanks covering ten habitats, arranged in a long loop. If you see it in the intended direction, things begin with a fine evocation of a **shipwreck** swarming with schools of Southeast Asian fish, including mottled honeycomb stingrays. The Southeast Asian theme continues in the next section, with an 8m-tall cylindrical **coral garden**, but both these tanks pale in comparison to the monster **Ocean Gallery** halfway through. Some 36m long, with walls 70cm thick, it's so vast that two restaurants and several hotel suites have their own vistas onto it. Here you can watch mindboggling shoals of tiny, silvery fish moving in unison, while manta rays, goliath groupers and sharks sweep through. Elsewhere, look out for the fabulous collection of **jellyfish**, some glowing as if part of a lava lamp thanks to coloured lighting.

Adventure Cove Waterpark

Resorts World Sentosa, a 2min walk beyond the Maritime Experiential Museum • Daily 10am–6pm • S\$38

The Adventure Cove Waterpark is the best water-themed play park in Singapore, and by no means just for kids. The magic ingredient is actual sea life: **Rainbow Reef** lets you snorkel in the presence of thousands of fish, while at **Adventure River** you float down a channel past

9

surreal marine-themed statues, ending up inside a glass tunnel within an aquarium tank, where the fish gawp at you drifting by. Of the rides and slides, **Riptide Rocket** is the star, a roller coaster which magnetically hoists passengers' dinghies on the upward legs.

Crane Dance

North shore of Resorts World Sentosa, close to the aquarium • Daily 8pm (10min) • Free

Sentosa isn't much of a night-time destination, but if you linger after sunset, you may want to catch either Wings of Time (see opposite) or **Crane Dance**. The latter features the computer-manipulated courtship of two enormous mechanical birds accompanied by fireworks and dazzling lighting and water effects. To help you decide whether to hang around for it, search for the whole shebang on YouTube.

Madame Tussauds

Imbiah Lookout • Mon–Fri 10am–7.30pm (last admission 6pm), Sat & Sun 10am–9pm (last admission 7.30pm) • S$39; book online for discounts • ☎ 6715 4000, ⓦ madametussauds.com/singapore • Imbiah station

Inevitably, the **Madame Tussauds** waxwork franchise has fetched up in Singapore, its seventh opening in Asia. There are a sprinkling of local and East Asian figures, including Malaysian actress Michelle Yeoh, amid the usual cast of celebrities from the worlds of showbiz and sport. Its unique feature, however, is a magical illuminated boat ride down a fake river, past miniaturized Singapore scenes such as Gardens by the Bay, an Indian temple *gopuram* and a Chinese opera. From there, it heads on to **Images of Singapore Live**, which covers Singapore history using a mixture of life-sized dioramas and costumed actors.

Luge and Skyride

Daily 10am–9.30pm • S$23 for two circuits • ☎ 6274 0472, ⓦ skylineluge.com • Beach station for Skyride, Imbiah station for Luge

Surprisingly good fun, the **Skyride**, akin to a ski lift, takes you up the hill behind Siloso Beach, after which you ride your **Luge** – a sort of small, unmotorized go-kart – and coast down one of several curving tracks back to your starting point.

Megazip Adventure Park

A 5min walk west of Imbiah station • Daily 11am–7pm • S$45 for main zip line • ☎ 6884 5602, ⓦ megazip.com.sg

Megazip is a zip-line or flying-fox ride, in which you slide, suspended from a steel cable, from a hilltop down to an islet beyond Siloso Beach. Other offerings include an obstacle course that's all ropes and netting, and a climbing wall.

AJ Hackett Sentosa

Siloso Beach, a 5min walk west of Beach station • Mon–Thurs 11am–7pm, Fri 11am–10pm, Sat 10am–10pm, Sun 10am–7pm • S$200 for bungy jump • ☎ 6911 3070, ⓦ ajhackett.com/sentosa

New Zealand bungy pioneer **A J Hackett** has finally arrived in Singapore with a 50m bungy tower – actually two towers, linked by a narrow bridge meant as a challenge

---

WATERSPORTS ON SENTOSA

Two places at Siloso Beach offer a range of often pricey watersports. Near the start of the beach, **Ola Beach Club** (☎ 6265 5966, ⓦ olabeachclub.com) has everything from kayaking (S$25 per hour) to a water-based jetpack – like something out of a sci-fi movie – that allows you to hover several metres above the sea (S$228). Just 200m on at **Wavehouse** (☎ 6238 1196, ⓦ wavehousesentosa.org), there's surfing on artificial waves in two tanks, one with a flat sheet of water suitable for beginners (daily at least noon–9pm; from S$35 per hour), the other with a barrel-shaped wave for more advanced surfers (Mon, Wed & Fri–Sun; S$30 for 30min).

for people with a fear of heights. You can also pay to stride down the side of one of the towers (harnessed, of course), and there are also two massive swing rides to choose from.

Fort Siloso

At the northwest tip of the island, beyond Siloso Beach • Daily 10am–6pm • Free • ☎ 6736 8672 • Bus A from Beach station

Sentosa's one bona fide historical attraction is the sprawling **Fort Siloso**, which guarded Singapore's western approaches from the 1880s onwards; today, though, only uniformed dummies man the observation posts and gun emplacements. The **Surrender Chambers** are the focus, re-enacting the British and Japanese surrenders of 1942 and 1945, respectively, using waxwork figures. Other chambers offer a deeper analysis of British military failings in the region than anything at the National Museum, although the history can be confused: some panels spin the old story that Singapore's guns were pointing the wrong way as they were meant to deter a naval attack from the south, while others present the revisionist idea that the guns could turn to fire northwards, but were ineffective. Oddly, Japanese labelling is almost ubiquitous, as if sending a none-too-subtle "don't try that again" message.

Wings of Time

At the start of Siloso Beach • Daily 7.40pm & 8.40pm; 25min • S$18 • ⓦ wingsoftime.com.sg • Beach station

The minority of visitors who hang around Sentosa after dusk are either heading to one of the beach bars (see p.545 & p.546) or to **Wings of Time**, a kids' fable cast as a lavish sound-and-light show, featuring pyrotechnics, lasers and live actors. Most of the action takes place on a series of offshore platforms, as well as aerial screens of water and mist, with seating right at the beach to take it all in.

Kidzania

Behind Palawan Beach • Daily 10am–6pm • Adults S$35, children S$58 • ☎ 1800 653 6888, ⓦ kidzania.com.sg

Although pricey, the international **Kidzania** franchise does provides children with terrific role-playing opportunities. Their Singapore set-up is a mini-town in which kids can try "working" in simulations of well-known banks and restaurants, or guide guests around the "Peranakan Museum", among others. There's also a "job information centre" – ironically, something that doesn't exist on the island in real life.

The beaches

The best that can be said about Sentosa's three **beaches**, created with vast quantities of imported beige sand, is that they're decent enough, with blue-green waters, the odd lagoon and facilities for renting canoes, surfboards and aqua bikes. You also get treated to a view of one of the world's busiest shipping lanes – expect a parade of container ships and other vessels all day.

Siloso Beach, extending 1500m northwest of Beach station, is the busiest of the three. **Palawan Beach**, in the opposite direction from Beach station, is meant to be the most family-oriented and boasts a children's play area centred on a mock galleon. It also features a suspension bridge leading out to an islet billed as the "Southernmost Point of Continental Asia" – though a sign concedes that this is so only by virtue of three artificial links, namely the bridge itself, the bridge from HarbourFront to Sentosa, and the Causeway. Beyond Palawan, **Tanjong Beach** tends to be slightly quieter than the other two as it starts a full kilometre from the station.

9

TRANSPORT ON SENTOSA

There are multiple ways to reach the island other than walking, the most popular of which is the **Sentosa Express** monorail. Note that all the options here include the island entry fee in the fare, and that **taxi** journeys to and from the island incur a surcharge of several dollars depending on the time of day.

An **information point** at the end of the Sentosa Boardwalk where you arrive dispenses free **maps** (also available at monorail stations and from Ⓦ sentosa.com.sg), which are especially handy given that new venues and sights seem to replace others every few months. Alternatively, download the **MySentosa app**.

GETTING TO SENTOSA

By monorail The Sentosa Express operates every 5min from level 3 of the VivoCity mall (S$4). See below for details of stops on the island. Note that the ride back to VivoCity is free.
By bus Bus #123 heads to Resorts World from Orchard Rd (passengers do not need to pay the S$1 island admission). At weekends there are one-way night buses #NR1 and #NR6 from Resorts World to Marina Bay, the Colonial District, Clarke Quay and Orchard Rd, with NR#6 continuing to Little India (Fri & Sat 11.30pm–2am; S$4.50).

TRANSPORT ON THE ISLAND

All transport on Sentosa itself is free, with the exception of the newly extended cable car (see box, p.52).
By bus The island has two buses that run on loop routes until midnight, plus a so-called beach tram running the length of the southern beaches; all services are charted on the free island maps.
By monorail The Sentosa Express calls at Waterfront station on the northern shore (for Resorts World), Imbiah station a little further south, and Beach station on the southern shore, for the three beaches.

ARRIVAL AND DEPARTURE
SINGAPORE

Most visitors fly into Changi International Airport, in the east of the island, or arrive by bus via the 1km Causeway that links Johor Bahru to the island (although some buses use the Second Link bridge into Tuas in the west).

BY PLANE

CHANGI INTERNATIONAL AIRPORT

Singapore's airport (☏6542 4422, Ⓦchangiairport.com), at the eastern tip of the island 16km from downtown, is well laid out and runs like clockwork – the country in microcosm. There are four terminals, connected by free Skytrains. Chances are you'll not linger long – baggage comes through so swiftly that you can be heading to the city centre within twenty minutes of arrival. Connections with Malaysia and Brunei include:

Destinations Bandar Seri Begawan (1–2 daily; 2hr); Bintulu (3 weekly; 1hr 50min); Ipoh (2 daily; 1hr 30min); Kota Bharu (4 weekly; 1hr 20min); Kota Kinabalu (1–2 daily; 2hr 30min); Kuala Lumpur (KLIA; hourly; 55min); Kuala Lumpur (Subang; at least 6 daily; 1hr); Kuala Terengganu (3 weekly; 1hr 15min); Kuantan (daily; 50min); Kuching (3–4 daily; 1hr 20min); Langkawi (1–2 daily; 1hr 30min); Miri (4 weekly; 2hr); Penang (at least 8 daily; 1hr 20min).

Onward transport Between 6am–11.15pm, the easiest way to get into the city centre from the airport is on an MRT train (change at Tanah Merah; 30min; S$2.50); the station is beneath terminals 2 and 3. Alternatively, bus #36 (same hours, every 10min; around S$2) heads to the Orchard Rd area via Marina Centre and the Colonial District. Transport desks at each terminal can also book you onto the 24hr airport shuttle buses, which serve most downtown hotels and hostels ($9). A taxi downtown costs at least S$20 and takes up to half an hour; there's an airport surcharge of S$3–5. You can also head straight to Johor Bahru on Transtar buses (daily every 2hrs 8.15am–11.15pm from terminal 2; 1hr 45min; S$10; Ⓦtranstar.travel).

BY TRAIN

Malaysian trains run a shuttle service a dozen times a day between Woodlands station near the Causeway checkpoint and Johor Bahru – a 5min journey. If you arrive at Woodlands station, you can catch bus #170 to Bukit Panjang MRT. For those wanting to head to KL or the east coast by train, it's easier to get a bus to the Causeway and walk through immigration, then continue to JB's train station on foot.

BY BUS

In the absence of a long-distance bus terminal, most buses terminate at, and leave from, the Beach Rd area.

Heading to Malaysia, note that you don't have to buy a ticket from Singapore; it's cheaper to catch a local bus from the Queen St terminal to Johor Bahru's Larkin bus station, where you can pick up the very same buses for much less money (with additional routes to the east coast, too). For details on crossing the Causeway, see p.294.

Golden Mile Complex/Golden Mile Tower Most bus companies serving west coast destinations beyond KL and also Hat Yai in Thailand are based at these two neighbouring shopping/office complexes (5001/6001 Beach Rd), including Konsortium (☎ 6392 3911, ⓦ konsortium.com.sg), Grassland Express (☎ 6292 1166, ⓦ grasslandsg.com), Sri Maju (☎ 6294 8228, ⓦ srimaju.com) and Starmart Express (☎ 6396 5681, ⓦ starmartonline.com). Any westbound bus from outside the complex will take you to City Hall MRT station, while Nicoll Highway station is a 10min walk away.

Destinations Alor Star (2 daily; 12hr 30min); Cameron Highlands (1 daily; 10hr); Gopeng (3 daily; 8hr); Hat Yai (Thailand; 3 daily; 14hr); Ipoh (7 daily; 8hr 30min); Kamunting (for Taiping; 2 daily; 9hr 30min); KLIA (7 daily; 5hr); KLIA2 (4 daily; 5hr); Kuala Kangsar (2 daily; 9hr); Kuala Lumpur (at least hourly; 6hr); Lumut (for Pangkor; 1 daily; 9hr 30min); Melaka (at least 8 daily; 3hr 30min); Penang (5 daily; 10hr 30min); Seremban (9 daily; 5hr); Sungai Petani (1 daily; 11hr); TBS (9 daily; 5hr).

The Plaza Transnasional (☎ 6294 7034, ⓦ transnasional .com.my) operates to both coasts from a basement office on the side of The Plaza (7500A Beach Rd) facing away from Beach Rd itself. Arab St and Bugis MRT are just a few minutes away on foot.

Destinations Kota Bharu (via Merang; 1 daily; 13hr); Kuala Lumpur (at least 6 daily; 6hr); Kuala Terengganu (via Dungun, Kemaman and Marang; 2 daily; 10hr); Kuantan (3 daily; 6hr); Mersing (3 daily; 4hr).

Queen St terminal Johor Bahru buses use this terminal near Bugis MRT, including #170 (daily 5.30am–12.30am; every 15min; 1hr–1hr 30min; S$2)

and two nonstop services, the Singapore–Johor Express (6am–10pm; every 10min; S$3.30) and the Causeway Link #CW2 (6am–11.45pm; 2–4 hourly; same fare; ⓦ causewaylink.com.my). Hang on to your ticket at immigration so you can use it to resume your journey (on the same service, though not necessarily on the same vehicle) once you're through. These buses terminate at JB's Larkin bus station; if you want to reach the town centre, leave the bus at the Causeway. There's also a rank for shared taxis to JB (☎ 6296 7054; S$12). One long-distance bus company, 707-Inc, uses Queen St for services to Melaka (10 daily; 3hr 30min; ☎ 8737 7077, ⓦ 707-inc.com).

City Plaza This is one of a handful of suburban buildings used by bus companies (810 Geylang Rd; use Paya Lebar MRT), in this case Starmart Express and Golden Coach (goldencoach.com.sg).

Destinations Ipoh (2 daily; 8hr 30min); Kuala Lumpur (4 daily; 6hr); Lumut (for Pangkor; 1 daily; 9hr 30min); Melaka (9 daily; 3hr 30min); Seremban (4 daily; 5hr).

BY FERRY

Indonesia Ferries serving Batam, Bintan and Karimun in Indonesia's Riau archipelago (all around S$30 one way in economy class, including taxes) use either the HarbourFront Centre on Telok Blangah Rd ("RFT" in some timetables; HarbourFront MRT) or Tanah Merah ferry terminal in the east of Singapore, linked by bus #35 to Tanah Merah and Bedok MRT stations. For timetables and ferry companies see ⓦ singaporecruise.com.sg.

Malaysia From the Changi Point terminal near Changi Beach, humble bumboats sail when full to Pengerang, just east of Singapore in the Straits of Johor (daily 7am–4pm; 45min; S$15). There are also ferries to Tanjung Belungkor, just northeast of Singapore (Mon–Fri 2 daily, Sat & Sun 4 daily; S$26 one way, S$39 return; ⓦ tanjungbelungkor. com). Both services are used mainly by people bound for the unexciting Johor resort of Desaru. In the unlikely event you arrive on one of these routes, catch bus #2 to pick up the MRT at Tanah Merah station.

SINGAPORE ADDRESSES AND MAPS

Addresses linked to high-rise towers, shopping complexes and other buildings are generally written using two numbers preceded by #, as in #xx-yy. Here xx is the floor (ground level is 01, the next floor up 02, the first basement B01, and so on) while yy is the unit number – thus a restaurant whose address includes #04-08 can be found in unit 8 on the building's fourth storey. All buildings within municipal housing and industrial estates have a **block number** displayed prominently on the side, rather than a number relating to their position on the street.

The usual **online mapping** services cover Singapore pretty well, and they can come in handy as restaurants, shops and even hostels sometimes move their premises because of rent hikes downtown. Two up-to-date, homegrown alternatives are ⓦ streetdirectory.com (available as an app) and the official ⓦ onemap.sg; search by entering a building name, road name, six-digit postal code or, for bus information, a five-digit bus stop number.

GETTING AROUND

Just about all parts of Singapore are accessible by **bus** or the **MRT** (Mass Rapid Transit) metro system. **Fares** are eminently reasonable and usually rise in tiny steps depending on the distance travelled. Two companies run most of the public transport network: **SBS Transit** (☎ 1800 225 5663, ⓦ sbstransit.com.sg) and **SMRT** (☎ 1800 336 8900, ⓦ smrt.com.sg). Their websites can help with journey planning, but more comprehensive advice is available at ⓦ mytransport.sg or via the MyTransport app.

TICKETS

ez-link card Although it's possible to buy tickets for individual train and bus rides, cash is gradually being phased out from the transport system, which makes it all the more sensible to buy a stored-value ez-link card (ⓦ ezlink.com.sg). Aside from offering convenience, it shaves at least twenty percent off the cash fare, with bigger savings the shorter the trip; what's more, the card allows changing between buses and trains, reducing the fare again. You can buy the cards at most MRT stations, post offices and 7-11 stores, with stored credit equal to the purchase price (minus S$5 for the card itself). Hold the card over a reader as you exit an MRT barrier or step off a bus for the fare to be calculated and deducted. The cards, which also work as debit cards in some shops and taxis, can be topped up at ticket offices or using ticket machines, and remain valid for at least five years.

Singapore Tourist Pass For short-stay visitors, the three-day Singapore Tourist Pass is ideal (ⓦ thesingaporetourist pass.com.sg). Sold in visitor centres (see p.531) and a few MRT stations, including the one at the airport, it costs S$10/$16/$20 for 1/2/3 days of unlimited travel (excluding special services such as night buses), plus a S$10 refundable deposit. Once the pass expires, it can be topped up and used like an ez-link card. To reclaim the deposit, be sure to return the card within five days of purchase.

THE MRT

Using Singapore's MRT network (map opposite) is straightforward, although note that you're not allowed to eat, drink or smoke on trains. Signs in the stations appear to ban hedgehogs as well, but actually signify "no durians". Using mobile phones is okay, though – and they even work in the tunnels.

Hours Trains run every five minutes, on average, from 6am until midnight downtown.

Fares From S$1.40 to S$2.50 (S$0.80 to S$2 with an ez-link card).

LRT Three LRT (Light Rail Transit) networks connect suburban estates with the MRT. As a tourist, you're unlikely to make use of any of them.

BUSES

Singapore's bus network is so comprehensive that the sheer profusion of routes can be confusing. Many bus stops do, however, display lists of destinations served by each route.

Hours Buses start running around 6am and wind down from 11.30pm; the very last regular buses leave downtown around 12.30am. Between midnight and 2am a few Night-Rider (prefixed "NR") and Nite Owl (suffixed "N") buses are available; costing around S$4.50, they are one-way services that cross the downtown area and then run as express services to the outlying new towns.

Fares Cash fares range from S$1.30 to S$2.40 (S$0.80 to S$2 with ez-link card). Some buses charge a flat fare while a few don't take cash at all – check signage at the front of the bus. If you're paying cash, drop the fare into the metal chute next to the driver; change isn't given. If you have an ez-link card, you must tap the card on the reader upon entering *and* at the exit door when you get off, or else the maximum fare will be deducted.

USEFUL BUS ROUTES

A few handy **bus routes** are listed below. One-way systems downtown mean that services that use Orchard Road and Bras Basah Road in one direction return via Stamford Road, Penang Road, Somerset Road and Orchard Boulevard; buses up Selegie and Serangoon roads return via Jalan Besar and Bencoolen Street; and services along North and South Bridge roads and New Bridge Road return via Eu Tong Sen Street, Hill Street and Victoria Street.

#7 From the Botanic Gardens to Orchard Road, Bras Basah Road and Victoria Street (for Kampong Glam), then on to Geylang Serai.

#36 Loops between Orchard Road and Changi airport via the Marina Centre and the Singapore Flyer.

#65 Orchard Road to Little India and on up Serangoon Road.

#170 From the Queen Street terminal to Bukit Panjang MRT (shadowing the MRT's Downtown line), then all the way to the Larkin terminal in Johor Bahru. Note that #170A runs the same route but terminates just before the Causeway.

#174 Between the Botanic Gardens and the Baba House in Neil Road, via Orchard Road, the Colonial District, Boat Quay and Chinatown.

THE MRT SYSTEM

KEY

East–West line
North–South line
North–East line
Circle line
Downtown line
Thomson–East coast line
(to open in stages from north to south)
○ Interchange station
● Station
• • Station under development

9

TAXIS

Thousands of taxis roam the streets of Singapore, so you'll seldom have trouble hailing a cab – except late at night or when demand soars during a tropical downpour. All are clearly marked "TAXI". On the whole, drivers are friendly, but their English isn't always good; if you're heading off the beaten track, be aware of a landmark they can aim for. Note that in the downtown area, queuing at a taxi rank is supposed to be compulsory Mon–Sat 7.30am–8pm, though some drivers will ignore this rule to pick up passengers on quieter roads.

Fares All drivers use their meters, the fare starting at S$3–4 for the first kilometre, then rising 25¢ every 400m or so (classier limousine taxis cost 30 percent more). There are annoying surcharges: an extra 25 percent is payable Mon–Fri 6–9.30am & 6pm–midnight, Sat & Sun 6pm–midnight, and 50 percent extra nightly between midnight and 6am. Journeys involving Changi airport or the casinos incur a surcharge of several dollars, as do phone bookings. Fares also factor in road usage tolls on journeys along expressways and within the downtown area. You can pay using your card.

Taxi companies Try Comfort/CityCab ☎ 6552 1111, ⓦ cdgtaxi.com.sg; Premier Taxis ☎ 6363 6888, ⓦ premiertaxi.com; SMRT Taxis ☎ 6555 8888, ⓦ smrt .com.sg. Grab and Uber operate here, too.

RIVER TAXIS

Shuttling between Robertson Quay and Marina Bay, river taxis are pricey but still a lot cheaper than Singapore River cruise trips (Mon–Fri 8am–10am & 5–7pm; every 10min; S$5 via ez-link cards only; ⓦ rivercruise.com.sg).

DRIVING

Car rental Given the excellent public transport, there's hardly any reason to rent a car in Singapore, especially considering it's a pricey business. Major disincentives to driving are in place to combat traffic congestion: a permit just to own a car costs more than many cars themselves. If you were thinking of driving up into Malaysia, rent a car in JB. If you must rent in Singapore itself, contact Avis (ⓦ avis .com.sg) or Hertz (ⓦ hertz.com); both have offices at Changi airport.

INFORMATION

Heritage trails Although targeted at a local audience, leaflets describing Singapore neighbourhoods and a few walking trails can be downloaded from ⓦ ura.gov.sg.

Internet access Internet cafés are fairly thin on the ground. You can still stumble across them in Little India, although the ones here are vanishing too; prices start at S$2/hr. There's also a free wi-fi network, Wireless@SG/ SGx, available in shopping malls and some MRT stations and public buildings. Unfortunately it can be unreliable,

Tolls Drivers have to pay tolls to enter a restricted zone encompassing Chinatown, Orchard Rd and the Financial District, and to use many of the island's expressways. This being Singapore, it's all done in the most hi-tech way using Electronic Road Pricing (ERP) – all cars have a gizmo that reads a stored-value CashCard, from which the toll is deducted as you drive past an ERP gantry.

Parking Generally expensive, though at least many car parks offer the convenience of taking the fee off your CashCard, failing which you have to purchase coupons from a booth, post office or shop.

Driving from Malaysia To drive a Malaysian car into Singapore, you need to buy a stored-value Autopass card and rent a card reader; both are available at the Causeway or Second Link. Thus equipped, you can pay your vehicle entry toll and road tolls in Singapore. For more on this and other matters to do with driving in Singapore, see ⓦ lta .gov.sg.

CYCLING

Despite the clammy heat, tropical downpours and furious traffic, cycling is starting to take off in Singapore, with a handful of bike lanes now in existence and the government publicly committed to making the island more cyclist-friendly in future. Even so, cycling downtown can be tricky unless you have some familiarity with the roads, and bicycles aren't allowed on expressways.

Bike rental Three outfits, Ofo (ⓦ ofo.com), Mobike (ⓦ mobike.com/sg) and local start-up oBike (ⓦ o.bike), have made quite a splash in Singapore. All feature dockless, internally locked bikes which you locate and unlock via their apps; after use, park the bike sensibly at your destination and relock it. A deposit (at least S$40) is payable to use each service; rental is charged at, for example, 50¢ per 15min with oBike.

Parks and beaches Bikes come into their own in recreational areas and nature parks, which are linked by a park connector network; see ⓦ nparks.gov.sg. The East Coast Park, on the southeast shore of the island, has a popular cycle track with rental outlets along the way (expect to pay S$6–8 for a mountain bike, and have some form of ID). You'll also find bike rental at Changi and Siloso beaches (the latter on Sentosa).

and registration requires a password to be sent by text to your phone, which sometimes fails with foreign numbers.

Listings The best of several publications carrying entertainment listings and restaurant reviews is the monthly freebie *SGnow* (ⓦ sg.asia-city.com), available at some malls, museums and restaurants. Also of use to visitors is another free magazine, *The Finder* (ⓦ thefinder. com.sg), geared towards the large expat community.

Malaysia information Tourism Malaysia, 80 Robinson Rd, Financial District (Mon–Fri 9am–5pm; ☎ 6532 6321).
Visitor centres The Singapore Tourism Board (STB; helpline Mon–Fri 9am–6pm ☎ 1800 736 2000, ⓦ visitsingapore.com) bills its tourist offices as visitor centres. Their main downtown location is at 216 Orchard Road (daily 8.30am–9.30pm; Somerset MRT). Much smaller is their counter on the ground floor of the ION Orchard mall (daily 10am–10pm; above Orchard MRT), and their Chinatown office at 2 Banda St, behind the Buddha Tooth Relic Temple (daily 9am–9pm; Chinatown MRT).

ACCOMMODATION

If one thing leaves a nasty taste in the mouth in Singapore, it's the price of **accommodation**; even a lower-mid-range double room now nudges S$140 a night. On the plus side, most accommodation is of a high standard for the price, and rates have been drifting lower in recent years. Budget travellers have a plethora of centrally located **hostels** and **guesthouses** to choose from, often with upmarket decor and fittings; Chinatown and Little India are the best areas for these. Most **hotels** are blandly modern, but there are plenty of **boutique hotels**, usually characterful or quirky affairs in refurbished shophouses. One thing to note is that any hotel advertising hourly or "transit" rates tends to be used by locals for illicit liaisons – normally only obviously seedy hotels stoop to this, though the ubiquitous and otherwise well-managed budget chains *Hotel 81* and *Fragrance* have been tainted by this in the past. Most establishments, even hostels, adjust prices year-round in line with demand, and those that do not will offer **promotional rates** most of the time, except during the Formula One race in the third week of September. The prices here are meant to be typical starting prices, including taxes, if you reserve reasonably early. Besides contacting places directly, you can also book through sites such as ⓦ agoda.com and ⓦ hostelworld.com.

THE COLONIAL DISTRICT

The area immediately north and east of the Singapore River only has a few places to stay, all hotels.

Fort Canning 11 Canning Walk, northern side of Fort Canning Hill ☎ 6559 6770, ⓦ hfcsingapore.com; map p.480. A plush boutique hotel housed in a former British military building; rooms are spacious, immaculately decorated and boast bathtubs that are, curiously, often smack in the middle of the room or out towards the window. There are pools on two levels and lush gardens, too. The one snag: it's a bit of a trek up flights of steps from Dhoby Ghaut MRT and Orchard Rd. 🛜 S$350

Novotel Clarke Quay 177A River Valley Rd ☎ 6338 3333, ⓦ novotelclarkequay.com; map p.480. This dull tower block might seem like just another bland business-oriented hotel, but the wood-panelled lobby and tasteful contemporary furnishings give the boutique hotels a run for their money. The usual four-star amenities include pool and gym. 🛜 S$375

Peninsula Excelsior 5 Coleman St ☎ 6337 2200, ⓦ ytchotels.com.sg; map p.480. Really two hotels fused together – as hinted at by the presence of two swimming pools at either end, one of which abuts the current lobby – and nicely modernized, unlike the 1970s shopping arcades below. 🛜 S$250

Swissôtel The Stamford 2 Stamford Rd ☎ 6338 8585, ⓦ swissotel.com; map p.480. The upper-floor rooms, restaurants and bars aren't for those with vertigo, though the views are as splendid as you'd expect from one of the

---

ORGANIZED TOURS

Singapore is so easy to navigate that there's little reason to do an **organized tour**, which is perhaps why the range of offerings tends to be uninspired. Many seem to feature transport as a key element, whether that be a dedicated tourist bus, a Singapore River boat (see p.483 for more on river trips), a novelty vehicle or the **trishaw**, which at least hearkens back to the island's past.

DuckTours ☎ 6338 6877, ⓦ ducktours.com.sg. Tour the Colonial District and Marina Bay on an amphibious vehicle (daily 10am–6pm; S$37).
The Original Singapore Walks ☎ 6325 1631, ⓦ singaporewalks.com. Guided walks of historic downtown areas and Changi (the latter with a wartime focus), generally lasting 2hr 30min; from around S$35 per person.
Singapore Nature Society ⓦ nss.org.sg. If your stay in Singapore is an extended one, consider taking out annual membership of this conservation group, which conducts guided nature walks, birdwatching trips and so forth.
Trishaw Uncle Booth on Queen St, close to Bugis MRT ☎ 6337 7111, ⓦ trishawuncle.com.sg. This trishaw cooperative charges S$39 for a half-hour ride around the immediate vicinity and Little India, or S$49 for Little India plus Kampong Glam or a one-way ride to Chinatown. Daily 11am–9pm.

9

tallest hotels in the world, with over a thousand rooms. Perhaps even more impressive is the fact it has a MRT station (City Hall) in the basement, and a big sports facility with two pools and several tennis courts. 🛜 S$500

BRAS BASAH ROAD TO ROCHOR ROAD

The grid of streets between Bras Basah Rd and Rochor Rd (and a bit beyond, uphill from Selegie Rd) has been rendered a bit sterile by redevelopment, but remains a good choice if you can afford it; it's within easy walking distance of the Singapore River, Little India and the eastern end of Orchard Rd.

HOSTELS AND GUESTHOUSES

G4 Station 11 Mackenzie Rd ☎6334 5644, ⌨g4station.com; map p.488. An unexciting but well-located hostel, where all residents get a big locker to themselves. Other facilities include a roof terrace and a solitary Wii for gaming. All bathrooms are shared. 🛜 Dorms S$30, doubles S$75

Hangout@Mount Emily 10A Upper Wilkie Rd ☎6438 5588, ⌨hangouthotels.com; map p.488. Owned by the company behind the historic Cathay cinema at the foot of Mount Emily, the *Hangout* is an impressive designer guesthouse with a breezy rooftop terrace that's great for chilling out in the evening, and a convenient self-service laundry. 🛜 Dorms S$45, doubles S$110

HOTELS

Carlton 76 Bras Basah Rd ☎6338 8333, ⌨carltonhotel .sg; map p.488. Boasting a lobby dominated by a spidery glass artwork suspended from the ceiling, this towering four-star hotel has elegant rooms in two wings, plus a pool, spa and gym – and good rates for what's on offer. 🛜 S$320

★Hotel G 200 Middle Rd ☎6809 7988, ⌨hotelgsingapore.com; map p.488. This new hotel occupies a converted office building, which is perhaps why there's a touch of post-industrial chic about the rooms, designated "good", "great" and "greater" in order of size; all are well soundproofed and feature pale wood floors and furniture. The entire ground floor is taken up by two restaurants (breakfast costs extra). 🛜 S$175

Intercontinental 80 Middle Rd ☎6338 7600, ⌨intercontinental.com; map p.488. Like the adjoining Bugis Junction mall, the *Intercontinental* incorporates some of the area's original shophouses, here converted into "heritage rooms" with supposedly Peranakan decor, though this merely amounts to dark wood floors and paintings of tropical fruit. Still, the hotel is luxurious and has all the amenities you could want. 🛜 S$350

Marriott South Beach 30 Beach Rd ☎6818 1888, ⌨marriott.com; map p.488. Dominating the northern Padang skyline, the box-grater-like towers of the South Beach development incorporate some colonial buildings

and this impressive hotel. The lobby – all individually styled chill-out spaces, certainly makes a statement, as do the 600-plus über-chic rooms, the work of French designer Philippe Starck. One of the two pools has glorious views out over the Padang. Nearest stations are Esplanade or City Hall MRT. 🛜 S$500

Marrison 103 Beach Rd ☎6333 9928, ⌨marrisonhotel .com; map p.488. This simple hotel is surprisingly comfortable, the rooms done out in neutral hues. A good deal, and breakfast can be added for very little extra. 🛜 S$125

Naumi 41 Seah St ☎6403 6000, ⌨naumihotel.com; map p.488. The slate-grey exterior with what look like vines creeping up doesn't inspire, but inside is a fine boutique hotel where rooms are kitted out like a slick apartment. The rooftop infinity pool looks out over the *Raffles* hotel, with the Financial District's towers beyond. Rooms on one floor are reserved for women only. 🛜 S$360

Raffles 1 Beach Rd ☎6337 1886, ⌨raffleshotel.com; map p.488. Though the modern extension is a mixed bag, the *Raffles* remains refreshingly low-rise and still has colonial-era charm in spades, especially evident in the opulent lobby and the courtyards fringed by frangipani trees and palms. Amenities include oodles of restaurants and bars, a rooftop pool and a spa. All rooms are suites, and there's a round-the-clock butler service. 🛜 S$800

South East Asia 190 Waterloo St ☎6338 2394, ⌨seahotel.com.sg; map p.488. Behind the yellow and white 1950s facade is a reasonable budget hotel with functional if slightly tired doubles, featuring the usual mod cons. It's practically next door to the lively Kwan Im temple, to boot. Wi-Fi costs extra. 🛜 S$100

LITTLE INDIA, LAVENDER STREET AND ARAB STREET

Little India proper and beyond – the zone extending up to Lavender St, reachable via Farrer Park or Lavender stations – has some decent budget accommodation, although hotels can be hit and miss. Handily for those who end up here, there's an excellent public swimming pool near Farrer Park MRT. The area around Arab St also has some a few places to stay.

HOSTELS AND GUESTHOUSES

Backpackers@SG 1st floor, 111J King George's Ave ☎6683 2924, ⌨bpsg.com.sg; map p.491. Exceptionally plain barring a few snazzy murals, but homelier for it, occupying part of a low-rise residential block. Unlike some, it doesn't have mega-sized dorms – the largest has eight beds. A reasonable choice for a quiet stay, with additional beds in a sister hostel metres away. 🛜 Dorms S$25

Bunc@Radius 15 Upper Weld Rd ☎6262 2862, ⌨bunchostel.com; map p.491. A sprawling, glitzy "flashpacker" hostel with a sleek lobby and a warren of dorms beyond, with individual lighting fixtures and sockets for each custom-built bunk bed. There's a women-only floor as well plus en-suite, wheelchair-accessible private room which anyone can book. 🛜 Dorms S$25, doubles S$125

★**Dream Lodge** 172 Tyrwhitt Rd ☎6816 1036, 🖥 dreamlodge.sg; map p.491. This comfy, superbly run hostel boasts plush capsule beds with privacy drapes and lockers beneath. There's a cosy lounge with a quirky wall drawing of Singapore landmarks by a young student, and bike rental is on offer. Before you leave, you can opt to have your photo turned into a badge and stuck on their wall adorned with the faces of previous guests. 🛜 Dorms S$40

★**Fisher BnB** 127 Tyrwhitt Rd ☎6297 8258, 🖥 fisherbnb.com; map p.491. This unexpectedly smart guesthouse with a twelve-bed women's dorm, a sixteen-bed mixed dorm and a family room for four. The bathrooms are just one area where the decor is right up to date – the management is especially proud of the Japanese-built bidets. 🛜 Dorms S$32, family room S$140

★**The Inn Crowd** 73 Dunlop St ☎6296 9169, 🖥 theinncrowd.com; map p.491. Perennially excellent hostel with some of the cheapest dorms in town plus a range of rooms with, unusually, their own TVs. Shared showers and toilets are kept spotless, and there's a comfy lounge and cheap beer. They run tours too, including a scooter-powered trip around the old quarters and Gardens by the Bay. 🛜 Dorms S$20, doubles S$60

Mitraa Inn 531 Serangoon Rd ☎6396 3317, 🖥 mitraa .com.sg; map p.491. This bills itself as "the friendliest backpacker hostel", and friendly it usually is, as well as organized. Unusually, some dorms are en suite, and there's a range of rooms sleeping two or more. 🛜 Dorms S$25, doubles S$100

★**The Pod** 289 Beach Rd ☎6298 8505, 🖥 thepod.sg; map p.491. Ultra-slick designer place where you check yourself in using an electronic kiosk. Their slogan is "pay for the stay, everything else is free" – and that includes use of their laundry facilities and laptops, plus a cooked breakfast. As the name suggests, all beds are capsule-style, and there are even "suites", rooms with one or two solitary pods. Prices rise by a fifth at weekends. 🛜 Dorms S$40

Shophouse 48 Arab St ☎6298 8721, 🖥 shophousehostel.com; map p.491. The rooftop lounge/terrace is the standout feature at this slick, bustling hostel which, given the location, also has some predictably quasi-Arabic decor. There's a roof terrace, laundry service and a women's floor, too. 🛜 Dorms S$25, doubles S$80

★**Vintage Inn** 60 Race Course Rd ☎6396 8751, 🖥 vintageinn.sg; map p.491. A swanky affair with arrays of capsule-style beds against the wall, each with a privacy curtain. Unusually, there's also a cooked breakfast. 🛜 Dorms S$28

HOTELS

The Daulat 16 Madras St ☎6408 5555, 🖥 thedaulat .com; map p.491. This tiny hotel has an equally tiny rooftop pool, a mere 10m sliver of water. Rooms can be boxy, but some have unusual touches, including upstairs bathrooms in the suites. Rates include breakfast. 🛜 S$140

Destination 700 Beach Rd ☎6679 2000, 🖥 yourdestinationhotel.com; map p.491. A decent mid-range option with bland but nicely soundproofed rooms, in a modern tower. The rooftop pool has good views out towards Marina Bay. 🛜 S$190

Fragrance Imperial 28 Penhas Rd ☎6297 8888, 🖥 fragrancehotel.com; map p.491. Despite the drab yellow exterior, this is a cut above fellow members of the budget chain, with slick if smallish rooms, a café and rooftop swimming pool. Rates include breakfast. 🛜 S$160

Haising 37 Jalan Besar ☎6298 1223, 🖥 haising.com .sg; map p.491. Friendly, secure Chinese-run cheapie offering simple, a/c en-suite rooms with TVs; rather boxy but not bad for the price. 🛜 S$65

Hilton Garden Inn 3 Belilios Rd ☎6491 0500, 🖥 hiltongardeninn3.hilton.com; map p.491. Towering over Little India, this representative of the *Hilton* chain's mid-range brand offers understated contemporary decor, a small outdoor pool and some great vistas out over the surrounding shophouses from rooms higher up. Good value. 🛜 S$225

Mayo Inn 9 Jalan Besar ☎6295 6631, 🖥 mayoinn.com; map p.491. There are just two dozen rooms in this cosy budget hotel, some featuring what's billed as a Japanese-style "bed" – a wooden dais with a mattress on top. Breakfast included. 🛜 S$110

Moon 23 Dickson Rd ☎6827 6666, 🖥 moon.com.sg; map p.491. Aiming to offer a boutique-hotel experience without straining your wallet, the *Moon* has stylishly kitted-out rooms with snazzy wallpaper and strategically placed drapes – to help take your mind off the fact that many are actually windowless. Rates include breakfast. 🛜 S$180

The Sultan 101 Jalan Sultan ☎6723 7101, 🖥 thesultan.com.sg; map p.491. A pleasant, relatively low-key hotel occupying a series of tastefully refurbished shophouses. Take your pick from, among others, a handful of cosy singles plus so-called attic rooms on the top floor, which are a little quieter than the rest. Excellent value, with breakfast included. 🛜 S$150

Wanderlust 2 Dickson Rd ☎6396 3622, 🖥 wanderlusthotel.com; map p.491. Appealingly wacky, *Wanderlust* has an "industrial glam" lobby with barber's chairs, and many rooms are colour-themed, some even with multicoloured lighting you can program. Facilities include a jacuzzi and French restaurant. Rates include breakfast. 🛜 S$240

9

CHINATOWN AND BOAT QUAY

Chinatown runs a close second to Little India and Lavender St in its selection of guesthouses, and also boasts a good many upmarket and boutique hotels. Boat Quay, right on the south bank of the Singapore River, is dominated by restaurants and bars but has a few worthwhile places to stay, one of which is the splendid *Fullerton* hotel.

HOSTELS AND GUESTHOUSES

★**Adler** 259/265 South Bridge Rd ☏6226 0173, ⓦadlerhostel.com; map p.498. What looks like a fancy furniture store from the street is really the lounge of one of the swankiest hostels in town. Its "suite dorms" boast purpose-built capsule beds (including doubles) and the hostel serves an above-average breakfast, including eggs and fruit. Dorms S̲$̲5̲5̲

Beary Best 16 Upper Cross St ☏6422 4957, ⓦbearybesthostel.com; map p.498. A spick-and-span hostel decorated in bright colours and, as the name suggests, bears – ursine stuffed toys litter the place. Beds come with individual reading lights, there's a self-service laundry, and the management offers bike rental and tours. Dorms S̲$̲3̲0̲, doubles S̲$̲9̲0̲

★**Bohemian Chic** 40 Mosque St ☏8380 0500; map p.498. Not truly Bohemian but appealingly quirky, with glittery masks like something from a Baroque-era ball lining one wall in the lounge. No dorm has more than eight beds (choose from capsules or cheaper double-deckers), and breakfast includes sandwiches in additional to the self-service basics. Dorms S̲$̲3̲2̲

Box Capsule Hostel 39 Ann Siang Rd ☏6423 0237, ⓦboxcapsulehostel.com.sg; map p.498. Revels in a good location on chichi Ann Siang Hill, with pod-style beds. There's also a loft space and old-school board games to play. ☏ Dorms S̲$̲4̲0̲

Maple Lodge 66A/B Pagoda St ☏6816 0288, ⓦmaplelodge.com.sg; map p.498. An unexciting but competently run place with ten- or twelve-bed dorms and lots of pastel colours, just footsteps from the MRT station. Good value for Chinatown. Dorms S̲$̲2̲5̲

★**Met A Space Pod** 51A/B Boat Quay ☏6635 2694, ⓦmetaspacepod.com.sg; map p.498. This hostel has high-tech capsule beds which can give you the impression of climbing into a washing machine drum, if not your own personal cylinder on a spaceship. Each bed has a built-in control panel, TV and safe. The kitchen, bathrooms and breakfasts are much more down to earth. Dorms S̲$̲2̲5̲

★**Wink** 8A Mosque St ☏6222 2940, ⓦwinkhostel.com; map p.498. One of the best designer hostels in town, with hi tech capsule beds (including some doubles), each inside flower-themed rooms with colour-coded lighting to match. Facilities include an upstairs kitchen and lounge, and free use of a tablet computer for every guest. Dorms S̲$̲5̲0̲, doubles S̲$̲9̲5̲

HOTELS

Amoy 76 Telok Ayer St ☏6580 2888, ⓦstayfareast.com; map p.498. Entered via the Fuk Tai Chi Museum, this hotel manages to squeeze the best out of every nook and cranny of its shophouse conversion. Rooms are on the small side but feature the odd unusual touch such as slat-floored bathrooms through which water drains away. ☏ S̲$̲2̲7̲5̲

Chinatown 12–16 Teck Lim Rd ☏6225 5166, ⓦchinatownhotel.com; map p.498. Not bad for the price and location, the *Chinatown* has serviceable rooms done out in the usual neutral tones. The bathrooms can be a bit poky, but at least a basic self-service breakfast is included. ☏ S̲$̲1̲5̲0̲

Clover 5 Hongkong St ☏6653 8888, ⓦhotelclover.com; map p.498. Functional, contemporary rooms in a six-storey building crowned by a small rooftop pool. Their sister hotel, round the corner, offers slightly bigger rooms with funky murals and access to the same pool, for about ten percent extra. ☏ S̲$̲1̲7̲5̲

★**The Fullerton** 1 Fullerton Square ☏6733 8388, ⓦfullertonhotels.com; map p.498. Nearly as impressive as the *Raffles*, with a stunning Art Deco atrium; rooms and bathrooms are spacious and feature contemporary styling. Amenities include a gym, spa and pool. ☏ S̲$̲5̲0̲0̲

Hotel 1929 50 Keong Saik Rd ☏6347 1929, ⓦhotel1929.com; map p.498. This shophouse hotel looks genuinely 1929 on the outside, but the interior has been renovated to look like a twenty-first-century version of the early 1960s, all very retro chic. ☏ S̲$̲1̲8̲0̲

The Inn at Temple Street 36 Temple St ☏6221 5333, ⓦtheinn.com.sg; map p.498. This place is packed with old-fangled furniture for a semblance of a period feel, but the rooms are boxy and there's no breakfast. Still, you can't argue with their prices. ☏ S̲$̲1̲2̲5̲

Parkroyal On Pickering 3 Upper Pickering St ☏6809 8888, ⓦparkroyalhotels.com; map p.498. Looming over Hong Lim Park, this is one of Singapore's most architecturally striking hotels since *Marina Bay Sands* and likewise has three towers, linked by curvy-sided rice-terrace-like structures overflowing with vegetation. The use of wood and glass throughout emphasizes the natural theme, in part by allowing plenty of sunlight in. Another garden crops up at the open-sided central tier that serves as a "wellness floor", home to the infinity pool, spa and gym. ☏ S̲$̲4̲5̲0̲

TANJONG PAGAR AND THE FINANCIAL DISTRICT

There are only a few hotels amid the office towers of Tanjong Pagar and the Financial District. Neither area is all that interesting to stay in, but proximity to Chinatown and the Colonial District make them worth considering.

Klapstar 15 Hoe Chiang Rd ☏6533 9000, ⓦklapstar.

com; map p.498. There are just seventeen rooms in this boutique hotel, each with different decor; the suites boast a jacuzzi for good measure. 🛜 **S$250**

★ **Sofitel So** 35 Robinson Rd ☎ 6701 6800, 🖥 sofitel .com; map p.498. Almost lost amid the staid bank buildings, this is a super-cool, Karl Lagerfeld-influenced conversion of two narrow office blocks. The "heritage wing" has decor like a French palace; across the atrium from it is the quirky, eclectic "hip wing", where you might find Russian dolls on the tables or wall-mounted plastic hands for hanging clothes. 🛜 **S$480**

MARINA BAY

Marina Bay accommodation is synonymous with modern four- and five-star affairs, all located at the rather bland Marina Centre district next to Beach Rd, with the obvious exception of *Marina Bay Sands*.

Marina Bay Sands 10 Bayfront Ave ☎ 6688 8868, 🖥 marinabaysands.com; map p.507. Not just one of the island's most famous buildings but also the largest hotel in Singapore, with an astonishing 2500 rooms. Frankly they're no better than those in most of its five-star competitors unless you shell out for, say, one of the Straits suites, with two en-suite bedrooms, a baby grand piano and butler service – costing thousands a night. Otherwise, stay here for the architecture and the infinity pool. 🛜 **S$575**

Ritz-Carlton Millenia 7 Raffles Ave ☎ 6337 8888, 🖥 ritzcarlton.com; map p.507. Arguably king of the pricey hotels in Marina Centre, with magnificent views across to the towers of the Financial District – even from the bathrooms, where butlers will fill the bath for you. 🛜 **S$600**

ORCHARD ROAD

You generally pay a premium to stay in the Orchard Rd shopping area, though it's hardly the most interesting part of downtown, and now that many stores have branches across the city, only the sheer modernity of the district lends it any edge.

Goodwood Park 22 Scotts Rd ☎ 6737 7411, 🖥 goodwoodparkhotel.com; map p.509. Built on a leafy hillock and designed by the architect responsible for the *Raffles*, this is a genuine landmark in a cityscape characterized by transience. It still exudes the refinements of a bygone era and boasts a variety of rooms and suites, plus several highly rated restaurants and two pools. 🛜 **S$375**

Lloyd's Inn 2 Lloyd Rd ☎ 6737 7309, 🖥 lloydsinn.com; map p.509. Less than a 10min walk from Orchard Rd, this low-rise, recently modernized establishment has rooms where the beds are raised on platforms with storage space beneath. Some bathrooms are open to the outside air (with a privacy curtain, of course). There's a garden, too, largely taken up by a water feature intended for foot-dipping.

Breakfast included. 🛜 **S$240**

Mandarin Orchard 333 Orchard Rd ☎ 6737 4411, 🖥 meritushotels.com; map p.509. Female staff at this old favourite wear kitsch quasi-oriental uniforms, but don't let that put you off; this towering hotel with more than 1000 rooms is still at the top of its game, luxurious to a fault, and has its own high-end mini-mall, too. 🛜 **S$375**

★ **The Quincy** 22 Mount Elizabeth ☎ 6738 5888, 🖥 quincy.com.sg; map p.509. One of Singapore's more endearing boutique hotels, melding contemporary aesthetics with comfort. Features include glass-walled bathrooms in some rooms, and a pool near the top of the building. Note that it's a 10min, slightly uphill walk off Orchard Rd. Rate includes breakfast. 🛜 **S$350**

Shangri-La 22 Orange Grove Rd ☎ 6737 3644, 🖥 shangri-la.com; map p.509. A 10min walk west of Orchard Rd, the oldest member of what's now a global hotel chain still epitomizes elegance, with 750 rooms set in oodles of landscaped greenery. Facilities include tennis courts, gym, pool and spa. 🛜 **S$525**

Supreme 15 Kramat Rd ☎ 6737 8333, 🖥 supremeh .com.sg; map p.509. This 1970s concrete box has basic, predictably dated rooms, though they're not too cramped; rates are a steal and include breakfast. 🛜 **S$120**

YMCA 1 Orchard Rd ☎ 6336 6000, 🖥 ymcaih.com.sg; map p.488. This place is predictably staid and the rooms are plain, but nowhere downtown do you get amenities like a pool and gym at the prices charged here (except, as it happens, at the *YWCA* nearby). 🛜 **S$160**

Yotel 366 Orchard Rd ☎ 6336 6000, 🖥 yotel.com; map p.509. This upstart international hotel chain wants to emulate the experience of flying first class, but in reality it's more like a smart home: beds, TV and lighting in your room can be controlled by your phone or tablet, and you can even check yourself in with their app. Everything's ultramodern in the blandest way, and the cheapest rooms are windowless, but a pool and gym are available. 🛜 **S$250**

GEYLANG AND KATONG

With the range of accommodation available downtown, there are few compelling reasons to stay in the suburbs except to save a little money. Katong, with its Peranakan heritage and good restaurants, is as good a choice as any, though note that some of neighbouring Geylang's seediness can spill over into Joo Chiat Rd after dark.

Betel Box 200 Joo Chiat Rd ☎ 6247 7340, 🖥 betelbox .com; map p.516. Styling itself Singapore's socially committed hostel, *Betel Box* tries to highlight the island's heritage by organizing tours of interesting neighbourhoods. A 15min walk from Paya Lebar MRT, or bus #33 from Kallang, Kembangan or Dakota MRT. Dorms **S$20**, doubles **S$80**

Santa Grand East Coast 171 East Coast Rd ☎ 6344 6866, 🖥 santagrand.sg; map p.516. One of the nicer offerings from this mid-priced chain, partly housed in a

9

conservation building. Rooms are more than adequate, and the secluded rooftop pool is a bonus. Bus #14 from Dhoby Ghaut/Mountbatten/Bedok MRT. $\overline{\text{S\$160}}$

SENTOSA

Staying on Sentosa isn't such a bad idea, especially if you have young children. Note that prices can rise by twenty percent over weekends and holidays.

Hotel Michael Resorts World ☏6577 8888, ⓦrwsentosa.com. The main reason to stay at Resorts World is to tap into packages that throw in discounted or free admission to Universal Studios and so forth. *Hotel Michael* is more interesting than the rest, with fittings, wall paintings and other decorative touches by the American architect and designer Michael Graves. ☏ $\overline{\text{S\$350}}$

Le Meridien Sentosa 23 Beach View, near Imbiah station ☏6818 3388, ⓦlemeridiensingaporesentosa .com. A splendid hotel housed partly in former British

barracks dating from 1940. All rooms have elegant contemporary fittings, but the most impressive are the pricey *onsen* suites with their own large outdoor Japanese hot tub. ☏ $\overline{\text{S\$250}}$

Rasa Sentosa Resort Western end of Siloso Beach ☏6275 0100, ⓦshangri-la.com. One of the best pre-casino-era hotels; family-friendly, it boasts a large freeform pool with water slides, a kids' club with purpose-built play areas and activities such as treasure hunts and beach walks, plus a spa. ☏ $\overline{\text{S\$400}}$

Siloso Beach Resort 51 Imbiah Walk ☏6722 3333, ⓦsilosobeachresort.com. The central swimming pool is a stunner, its curvy fringes planted with lush vegetation and featuring a waterfall and slides; it far outshines the slightly tired rooms. Still, the resort is tranquil enough (the music from the nearby beach bars generally stops around 10pm) and rates include breakfast. ☏ $\overline{\text{S\$240}}$

EATING

Along with shopping, **eating** ranks as Singapore's national pastime. Walk along any street downtown and just about every other building seems to be overflowing with food outlets, from restaurants to corner kiosks serving snacks. It's not just local food on offer, of course: the island's restaurants truly run the gamut of Asian and international cuisine. As in Malaysia, food is both a passion and a unifier across ethnic divides. Certain foods are largely or uniquely Singaporean: **chilli crab**, a sweet-spicy dish pioneered at long-gone rural seaside restaurants and now served all over the island; and **bak chor mee**, ribbon noodles with minced pork and chilli vinegar – to name but two. Some Chinese restaurants and *kopitiam*s are popular for **zichar** food – essentially informal, done-to-order cooking that isn't hung up on classical traditions or fancy presentation.

ESSENTIALS

Booking It's worth booking a table at weekends, when many restaurants are packed out – either contact the venue directly, or try ⓦchope.co or the Chope app.

Costs When it comes to costs, by far the cheapest and most fun places to eat are hawker centres/food courts, housed either within shopping malls or in their own open-air premises, where you can eat well for S\$10/person. Old-fangled *kopitiam*s (the same as *kedai kopis* in Malaysia) are also inexpensive, though increasingly rare downtown. Prices at mid-range restaurants start at around S\$20/person, with non-Asian food always noticeably more expensive, although many places do have good-value weekday set lunch specials. As with hotel bills, there's also the matter of the ten percent

service charge and 7 percent tax, levied by all the pricier restaurants and cafés (price indications here include these surcharges).

THE COLONIAL DISTRICT

Although you can eat cheaply in the Colonial District inside malls, the more interesting restaurants tend to be pricey places housed within conservation buildings.

Brussels Sprouts #01–12 The Pier at Robertson Quay, 80 Mohamed Sultan Rd ☏6887 4344, ⓦbrusselssprouts.com.sg; map p.480. This riverside restaurant specializes in – you guessed it – Belgian-inspired mussels and clams. There's a bewildering range of seasonings, from a strongly alcoholic white wine sauce to Thai *tom yam* (S\$50 with fries). You can also choose from a

---

COOKERY CLASSES

There are two venues with half-day courses in the rudiments of Southeast Asian and other cooking. **Food Playground** (24A Sago St, Chinatown; ☏9452 3669; ⓦfoodplayground.sg) is an unusual set-up where senior citizens, among others, get a chance to teach local recipes, including ones for many hawker favourites (S\$120). For a broader culinary palette, try the courses at **Coriander Leaf** (see opposite), run by the restaurant's owner Samia Ahad; she covers Singaporean, Indochinese and Middle Eastern cookery (S\$160).

plethora of fruity Belgian beers, including Leffe on draught. Mon–Thurs 3pm–midnight, Fri 2pm–2am, Sat 11am–2am, Sun 11am–midnight.

★**Cedele** #03–28, Raffles City, above City Hall MRT ☎ 6337 8017, ⓦ cedelegroup.com; map p.480. A café-bakery combo, *Cedele* serves up some of the very best sandwiches in Singapore (S$8) – think, say, honey dijon chicken on rosemary focaccia – and sells a vast variety of specialist breads. Some branches, like this one, also have a restaurant with inventive light meals and all-day breakfasts (all around S$20). Daily 11am–9.30pm.

Coriander Leaf #02-01 CHIJMES, 30 Victoria St ☎ 6837 0142, ⓦ corianderleaf.com; map p.480. Pan-Asian and Mediterranean food in elegant upstairs premises, encompassing everything from Lebanese meze to Vietnamese spring rolls, with a menu of mix-and-match options. They serve an astonishing range of Asian liqueurs and whiskies, too. At least S$40/person without drinks. Mon–Fri noon–2pm & 6.30–10.30pm, Sat 6.30–10.30pm.

Flutes National Museum, 93 Stamford Rd ☎ 6338 8770, ⓦ flutes.com.sg; map p.480. An upmarket choice for modern European and fusion cuisine. It's pricey unless you go for the set lunch (two courses for around S$45) or, even better, the Sunday lunch of roast beef with the usual trimmings, plus dessert (also S$45). Mon–Fri 11.30am–2pm & 6.30–10pm, Sat 10.30am–2pm & 6.30–10pm, Sun 10.30am–4pm.

★**Shiraz** Block A, Clarke Quay #01–06 ☎ 6334 2282, ⓦ shirazfnb.com; map p.480. The best Persian restaurant in town, not that there's much competition, but the many Iranians among the clientele can't be wrong. Portions of tender kebabs and stews, served with mounds of fluffy, aromatic saffron rice, are massive. Not cheap – main courses start at S$35 – but still better value than most places in overpriced Clarke Quay. Belly-dancing some evenings, too, and they do serve alcohol. Mon–Thurs 6.30–11pm, Fri & Sat noon–3pm & 6.30pm–2.30am, Sun 6.30pm–2am.

BRAS BASAH ROAD TO ROCHOR ROAD

The area sandwiched between the Colonial District and Little India features plenty of well-established restaurants, including a good cluster close to *Raffles Hotel*.

Ah Chew Desserts #01–11, 1 Liang Seah St ☎ 6339 8198; map p.488. Taking up two shophouses, *Ah Chew* confronts you with strange local sweets containing beans or other unexpected ingredients. The cashew-nut paste is not bad if you like the sound of a broth made of nut butter; also available are the likes of *pulot hitam*, made with black sticky rice. Cautiously sample a few items by ordering the small servings; most bowls cost S$5 or so. Hours can vary to what's shown. Daily 1.30–11.30pm.

★**Artichoke** 161 Middle Rd ☎ 6336 6949; map p.488. Inspired Middle Eastern-tinged fusion food conceived by the idiosyncratic owner Bjorn Shen. For weekend brunch, there are mains such as the superbly rich lamb shakshouka, lamb shoulder alongside spicy baked eggs; in the evenings, choose from meze and sharing platters, including quirky offerings such as beetroot tzatziki and pork with a coffee and date sauce. The only desserts are their wonderful "neh neh pop" – homemade stick ice creams in flavours such as chocolate baklava. Mains from around S$30; weekend reservations advised. Tues–Fri 6.30–10.30pm, Sat 11.30am–3.30pm & 6.30–10.30pm, Sun 11.30am–3.30pm.

Baker & Cook Intercontinental Hotel, North Bridge Rd ☎ 6825 1502, ⓦ bakerandcook.biz; map p.488. Up-and-coming café chain, Kiwi-run and featuring New Zealand coffee, great croissants and brownies, plus quiches, open sandwiches and salads. Daily 8am–7pm.

Chin Chin 19 Purvis St ☎ 6337 4640; map p.488. This likeably old-fangled Chinese shophouse diner with a cheap and cheerful menu of Hainanese standards like breaded pork chops and more generic faves, including chicken sautéed with cashew nuts and spicy *mapo* beancurd. Around S$20/person, minus drinks. Daily 7am–9pm.

The Daily Scoop School of the Arts, opposite the start of Bras Basah Rd ☎ 6509 4875; map p.488. One of a number of quality ice-cream makers boasting some distinctly Asian flavours such as *cendol* (the coconut milk dessert) or *maoshanwang* (a variety of durian) alongside creations such as lychee Martini. Around S$4 will get you a takeaway cone; if you eat in, you can pair your scoop with waffles, brownies and the like. Mon–Thurs & Sun 11am–10pm, Fri & Sat 11am–10.30pm.

Fatty's Wing Seong #01–31 Burlington Square, 175 Bencoolen St ☎ 6338 1087; map p.488. Run by an avuncular chubby cook in bygone decades, *Fatty's* was an institution on the now-vanished foodie paradise that was Albert St. Today it's a touristy restaurant that maintains the original's no-frills *zichar* approach, and also does standards such as chicken rice. Around S$20/person without drinks. Daily noon–2.30pm & 5.15–10.15pm.

★**Herbivore** #01–13 Fortune Centre, 190 Middle Rd ☎ 6333 1612, ⓦ herbivore.sg; map p.488. There's a cluster of vegetarian restaurants near Waterloo St's Kwan Im Temple, particularly at the Fortune Centre building, where the star is this excellent place serving tasty tempura, "chicken" teriyaki and so forth. Good-value sets (from S$25) with noodles or rice plus accompaniments like soya sashimi, pickle and salad, plus dessert. Daily 11.30am–10pm.

Tiffin Room Raffles Hotel, 1 Beach Rd ☎ 6412 1190; map p.488. High tea at this Anglo-Indian-themed restaurant is a genuinely scrumptious buffet of English scones, pastries, cakes and sandwiches, plus pies with a chicken curry filling and even dim sum – a real treat at

9

S\$70. High tea daily 3–5.30pm. Daily 6.30–10.30am, noon–2pm & 7–10pm.

Yhingthai Palace #01–04, 36 Purvis St ☎ 6337 1161, ⊚ yhingthai.com.sg; map p.488. A smart Chinese-influenced Thai restaurant, where you can't go wrong with the deep-fried pomfret with mango sauce or deboned chicken wings stuffed with asparagus and mushroom. Around S\$40/person, excluding drinks. Daily 11.30am–2pm & 6–10pm.

LITTLE INDIA AND LAVENDER STREET

Little India is paradise if you're after maximum flavour for minimum outlay; the first part of Serangoon Rd and its side streets, as well as Race Course Rd, are packed with inexpensive curry houses specializing in South Indian food, often dished out on banana leaves and with plenty of vegetarian options; some places offer North Indian and Nepali dishes too. The only drawback to eating here is the dearth of worthwhile places that aren't Indian.

★**Banana Leaf Apolo** 54 Race Course Rd ☎ 6293 8682; map p.491. Banana-leaf-type restaurant with a wide selection of Indian dishes, including fish-head curry (from S\$25 depending on size) plus chicken, mutton and prawn curries (S\$15). The lunchtime "South Indian vegetarian meal" is a steal, a huge thali of rice, poppadoms, two main curries and several side ones, plus a dessert, for S\$10. There's another branch in the Little India Arcade nearby. Daily 10am–10pm.

★**Chye Seng Huat Hardware** 150 Tyrwhitt Rd ☎ 6396 0609, ⊚ cshhcoffee.com; map p.491. Part of the slow gentrification that's converting the area's hardware shops into restaurants and hostels, *CSHH* is a hip café-bar with all-day breakfasts and varied mains that include linguine with bacon or Japanese curry rice (around S\$20). Marvellous light bites too, like *soon kueh* (savoury bamboo shoot dumplings) and *cempedak* (a jackfruit relative) crumble, with coffee blended and ground on the premises. In the evening the focus shifts to their craft beer stall in the courtyard. Tues–Thurs & Sun 9am–10pm, Fri & Sat 9am–midnight.

Gokul 19 Upper Dickson Rd ☎ 6396 7769; map p.491. Although they do serve standard Indian vegetarian dishes, *Gokul* also does great meatless versions of local street food classics such as *mee rebus*, the Malay noodle dish with a spicy/tangy gravy. Around S\$15/person. Daily 10.30am–9.30pm.

Hillman 135 Kitchener Rd ☎ 6221 5073, ⊚ hillmanrestaurant.com; map p.491. This little Chinese restaurant is oddly popular with Japanese businessmen, though don't let that put you off. They come, as you should, for the tip-top *zichar* food. The claypot dishes are a particular speciality, ranging from noodles to, for the adventurous, sea cucumber – not a vegetable but a marine relative of starfish. Reckon on S\$35/person excluding

drinks. Daily 11.30am–2.30pm & 5.30–10.30pm.

Komala Villas 76–78 Serangoon Rd ☎ 6293 6980, ⊚ komalavilas.com.sg; map p.491. In business since 1947, this rather cramped vegetarian establishment has more than a dozen variations of *dosai* – what they're best at, although they also have more substantial rice meals – which are just a few dollars each, with fresh coconut water to wash it down. There's another branch at 12–14 Buffalo Rd (☎ 6293 3664). Daily 7am–10.30pm.

Madras Woodlands Ganga 1 Cuff Rd ☎ 6297 1594; map p.491. This simple vegetarian restaurant serves up great-value Indian buffets (Mon–Fri lunchtime S\$10, evenings and weekends S\$12), featuring several curries, rice, *nan* and a dessert, with the option of ordering à la carte as well. Daily 11am–3pm & 6.30–10.30pm.

Saravanaa Bhavan 84 Syed Alwi Rd ☎ 6297 7755, ⊚ saravanabhavan.com; map p.491. A South Indian vegetarian franchise, hailing from Chennai but with branches as far afield as New York. It has all the staples, from *vada* (dhal-flour doughnuts) to *dosai*, plus non-Tamil dishes like *bisabelabeth*, a rice, vegetable and lentil concoction from Karnataka. Also try the Chinese-influenced "Manchurian" dishes – basically sweet-and-sour. Reckon on S\$15/person, minus drinks. Daily 9am–midnight.

★**Tekka Food Centre** Alongside Tekka market at start of Serangoon Rd; map p.491. One of the best old-school hawkers' centres on the island, always steamy, hot and busy. The Indian and Malay stalls are especially good; look out for exceptional Indian *rojak* – assorted fritters with sweet dips. There's a decent selection of Chinese stalls too, but they pale by comparison. Daily 7am–late.

Tiramisu Hero 121 Tyrwhitt Rd ☎ 6292 5271; map p.491. Popular indie café with black-and-white cartoon artwork and three sizes of tiramisu in a multitude of flavours (like matcha green tea, Bailey's and durian). Also loads of waffles, breakfasts and mains such as crayfish pasta (around S\$20). Mon–Thurs & Sun 11am–10pm, Fri & Sat 11am–midnight.

ARAB STREET/KAMPONG GLAM

It seems natural that Arab St should be awash with Middle Eastern and North African restaurants with meze, kebabs and couscous, but many of these places are recent and rather slapdash interlopers; the mainstay of the area's dining has long been Malay and Indonesian food. Note that the more traditional venues don't serve alcohol.

Blu Jaz Café 11 Bali Lane ☎ 9199 0610, ⊚ blujazcafe. net; map p.491. Easily spotted thanks to its gaudy decor, this venue led the gentrification of the area, and now runs two other similarly garish venues close by. The menu combines Turkish, East Asian and European food – anything from chicken kebab to fish and chips – at affordable prices; most mains cost S\$10–15. Live jazz nights, too. Mon–Thurs noon–1am, Fri noon–2am, Sat 4pm–2am.

★**Bumbu** 44 Kandahar St ☎6392 8628, ⓦbumbu .com.sg; map p.491. An entire shophouse festooned with antique Peranakan tiles and carved wooden screens hosts this restaurant serving a terrific mix of Thai and Indonesian cuisine, all fragrantly spiced. Standouts include the inky stir-fried squid, chilli basil chicken and bean sprouts with salted egg yolk, plus traditional desserts such as sago with palm molasses. Eminently affordable at around S$25/person, without drinks. Tues–Sun 11am–3pm & 6–10pm.

★**Hajjah Maimunah** 11 & 15 Jalan Pisang ☎6297 4294, ⓦhjmaimunah.com; map p.491. A tiny branch of the Geylang restaurant that's one of very few places in Singapore for authentic, inexpensive Malay meals; snacks and Malay dessert also available. Closed during Ramadan. Mon–Sat 7am–8pm.

Islamic Restaurant 745 North Bridge Rd ☎6298 7563; map p.491. The modernized premises don't hint at this restaurant's heritage – make sure you check out the photos of functions they catered for in the 1920s. *Biriyanis* are their speciality (S$8) though they also do a huge range of North Indian chicken, mutton, prawn, squid and veg curries, with good-value set meals at around S$10. Mon–Thurs, Sat & Sun 10am–10pm, Fri 10am–1pm & 2pm–10pm.

★**Kampong Glam Café** 17 Bussorah St; map p.491. Fantastic roadside *kopitiam* serving inexpensive Malay rice and noodle dishes, cooked to order, plus curries. Come not just for the food but for a good chinwag with friends over *teh tarik* late into the evening. Closed every other Monday. Daily 8am–3am.

★**Rumah Makan Minang** 18 Kandahar St, ☎9384 4484, ⓦminang.sg; map p.491. A street-corner place serving superb *nasi padang*, including the mildly spiced chicken *balado* and more unusual curries made with *tempeh* (fermented soybean cakes) or offal. For dessert you might get freshly made sweet pancakes stuffed with peanuts and corn – much better than they sound. Just S$10/head for a good feed. Mon–Fri 8.30am–8pm, Sat & Sun 8.30am–5pm.

Zam Zam 697 & 699 North Bridge Rd ☎6298 7011; map p.491. Staff at this venerable Indian Muslim *kopitiam* have the annoying habit of touting for custom even though the place draws crowds, especially on Fridays, with its *murtabak* and *biriyani* offerings (there's even a venison version of the latter). Avoid the house speciality drink, *katira* – it's like one of the local sickly ice desserts, only melted. Daily 8.30am–10pm.

CHINATOWN

Singapore's Chinatown is, of course, no Chinese ghetto and its eating places are thus pretty diverse, although the central Sago, Smith, Terengganu and Pagoda streets tend to be dominated by touristy Chinese restaurants – seldom the best in their class.

Annalakshmi #01–04 Central Square, 20 Havelock Rd ☎6339 9993, ⓦannalakshmi.com.sg; map p.498. Come here for excellent Indian vegetarian buffets served up by volunteers, with no price specified; you pay what you feel the meal was worth. Profits go to an association promoting South Indian culture. Note that they take a dim view of people helping themselves to more than they can finish. Also a more central branch at 104 Amoy St (Mon–Sat 11am–3pm; ☎6223 0809). Mon 11am–3pm, Tues–Sun 11am–3pm & 6.15–9.30pm.

Chinatown Complex Behind the Buddha Tooth Relic Temple; map p.498. The hawkers upstairs are much preferable to anything on the ersatz "food street" of Smith St, and at the time of writing one of their number had shot to fame as one of the island's two Michelin-starred stalls: Liao Fan Hong Kong Soya Sauce Chicken Rice (at #02-126; irregular hours but at least late morning until 3pm). If you don't fancy lining up for half an hour to pay S$2 for a plate, then eat at their pricier, fast-food-style outlet at 78 Smith St (Thurs–Tues until 9pm). Daily 7am–late.

Chongwen Ge Café 168 Telok Ayer St ☎9129 1625; map p.498. Next to Thian Hock Keng, little place has a short, satisfying menu of spicy Peranakan classics like *mee siam* (vermicelli in a tamarind/coconut milk sauce) and *otah* (fish dumplings). You can eat indoors or outside at the base of the pagoda. Nothing costs more than S$12. Daily 10am–6pm.

Indochine Upstairs at 47 Club St ☎6323 0503, ⓦindochine-group.com; map p.498. Classy Vietnamese, Lao and Cambodian cuisine in chic surroundings sums up this chain, and their Club St venue is no exception. The Vietnamese *chao tom* (minced prawn wrapped round sugar cane) and deep-fried spring rolls are mouthwatering starters, while the Lao *larb kai* (chicken in lime juice with salad) is one of many excellent main dishes. Around S$40/person, excluding drinks. Mon–Fri noon–3pm & 6–10.30pm, Sat 6–10.30pm.

★**Kok Sen** 30 & 32 Keong Saik Rd ☎6223 2005; map p.498. Open to the street at the front and back, with the odd pigeon loitering between basic tables, this zichar place serves food as exemplary as the decor is plain: try their *har cheong kai* (fried chicken seasoned in fermented prawn paste), black bean beef *hor fun* noodles, or even the very spicy *kung pao* frog. Note that the English name on their sign is hard to spot. Daily noon–2.30pm & 5–11.30pm.

Lee Tong Kee 278 South Bridge Rd ☎6226 0417, ⓦipohhorfun.com; map p.498. For years the speciality of this retro-styled restaurant, with old-fashioned fans and marble tables, has been Ipoh-style *hor fun* (around S$7), supposedly smoother than equivalent tagliatelli-type rice noodles. Try the signature lime juice too, usually served with a pinch of salt to balance the sugar. Mon 11am–4pm, Wed & Thurs 11am–6pm, Fri–Sun 11am–8pm.

Lime House 2 Jiak Chuan Rd ☎6222 3130, ⓦlimehouse.asia; map p.498. An impressively renovated

9

shophouse where the culinary focus is on the opposite corner of the earth – the Caribbean. The menu includes standards like curried goat, but more interesting are fusiony dishes like the rib-eye steak with a Jamaican Blue Mountain coffee marinade (S$45). Plenty of rum-based cocktails, too, with a bar in the back garden. Tues–Fri 5pm–midnight, Sat 3pm–midnight, Sun 11am–4pm.

Maxwell Food Centre Corner of South Bridge & Maxwell rds; map p.498. One of Singapore's first hawker centres and home to a clutch of popular Chinese stalls, including the well-known *Tian Tian* for Hainanese chicken rice, plus others that are good for satay or *rojak*. Daily roughly 7am–midnight.

My Awesome Café 202 Telok Ayer St ☎ 8428 0102, ⊛ myawesomecafe.com; map p.498. This verging-on-hipster café, in a former Chinese shophouse clinic, constantly draws a crowd with its jumbo salads, sandwiches and wraps (around S$20); sharing platters and a few mains also available. Daily 9.30am–midnight.

★Spring Court 52–56 Upper Cross St ☎ 6449 5030, ⊛ springcourt.com.sg; map p.498. With a pre-war pedigree, *Spring Court* is now a mammoth occupying multiple floors of adjacent shophouses. Its popularity hasn't blunted the quality of the cooking; must-tries include the excellent if expensive *popiah* (steamed spring rolls, hand-wrapped by staff at a counter outside; S$10) and steamed chicken with Chinese ham and greens. Plenty of seafood options plus dim sum, too. At least S$30/person without drinks. Daily 11am–3pm & 6–10.30pm.

★Tak Po 42 Smith St ☎ 6225 0302; map p.498. Compact, competent and inexpensive Cantonese restaurant, refreshingly untouristy considering the location, with a/c inside and some tables out on the street. All the usual dim sum favourites, including *siu mai* dumplings, yam cake and excellent pork ribs with black beans, plus a wide range of *congees* (savoury rice porridges). For afters, try the baked egg tarts, which are spot on, neither too flaky nor oversweet. Around S$20/person without drinks. Daily 7am–10.30pm.

Urban Bites 161 Telok Ayer St ☎ 6327 9460, ⊛ urbanbites.com.sg; map p.498. It's nothing much to look at, but serves excellent Lebanese cuisine, from a tender *kafta khashkhash* (minced lamb kebab) to home-cooking favourites like *mujadara* (rice with lentils and fried onions). You can order mezze-style or individual mains; reckon on S$30/person, minus drinks. Mon–Sat 10.30am–10pm.

Yixin 43 Temple St; map p.498. Workaday vegetarian place turning out dishes such as mock Peking duck (S$8), plus rice and noodle standards like *lor mee* (noodles in a tangy, gloopy sauce). Daily 7.30am–9.30pm.

Zhonghua Bao Ding 241 South Bridge Rd, opposite the Sri Mariamman Temple ☎ 6323 2696; map p.498.

Barely signed in English, the "Explosion Pot Barbecue" (as it styles itself) specializes, unusually for a Chinese restaurant, in grills. Most of the clientele are mainland Chinese, here for spicy mutton and beef kebabs, pork crackling, duck necks and other greasy but tasty delights. Around S$20/person, minus drinks. Daily noon–10pm.

BOAT QUAY TO RIVERSIDE POINT

The south bank of the Singapore River is packed with busy restaurants and bars, at their most atmospheric in the restored shophouses of boisterous Boat Quay, though even the modern complexes can be a more enticing prospect than overpriced Clarke Quay on the north bank. All places reviewed here are right by the river or no more than a couple of streets back from it.

Brewerkz #01–05/06 Riverside Point, 30 Merchant Rd ☎ 6438 7438, ⊛ brewerkz.com; map p.498. Popular for its highly rated beers, brewed on site, and American food, including excellent burgers and sandwiches, plus barbecued ribs, pizzas, nachos and the like. It's on the pricey side though, with burgers starting at S$25, but there is a three-course lunch deal for S$20. Mon–Thurs & Sun noon–midnight, Fri & Sat noon–1am.

Rendezvous #02–72 The Central, 6 Eu Tong Sen St ☎ 6339 7508, ⊛ rendezvous-hlk.com.sg; map p.498. For decades *Rendezvous* has been dishing out its revered *nasi padang*. Its current location in a mediocre mall doesn't suit it at all, but thankfully the curries have stayed the course, in particular the superb chicken korma – a mild curried stew of just the right degree of richness, derived from coconut milk rather than cream or yoghurt. Around S$20/person. Daily 11am–9pm.

Ya Kun Kaya Toast #01–31 The Central, 6 Eu Tong Sen St; map p.498. Now a ubiquitous chain, *Ya Kun* started out in the pre-war years as a Chinatown stall offering classic *kopitiam* breakfast fare – *kaya* toast (the same as *roti kahwin* in Malaysia) plus optional soft-boiled eggs eaten with white pepper and soy sauce. Of course there's strong local coffee too, normally had with condensed or evaporated milk. Daily 7am–10pm.

TANJONG PAGAR AND THE FINANCIAL DISTRICT

You're unlikely to head to these areas for the food alone, but they do boast some excellent restaurants.

Blue Ginger 97 Tanjong Pagar Rd ☎ 6222 3928, ⊛ theblueginger.com; map p.498. In a smartly renovated shophouse, this trendy Nyonya restaurant has become a firm favourite thanks to such dishes as *ikan masal asam gulai* (mackerel in a tamarind and lemon-grass gravy), and that benchmark of Nyonya cuisine, *ayam buah keluak* – chicken braised in soy sauce together with savoury Indonesian black nuts. At least S$25/person, minus drinks. Daily noon–2.30pm & 6.30–10.30pm.

Clifford Pier 80 Collyer Quay ☎ 6597 5266; map p.498. An upmarket restaurant majoring on a sort of nouvelle cuisine take on Southeast Asian street food: *bak chor mee*, *sup kambing* (Malay mutton soup), plus Hokkien *kong bak bao* (soy sauce pork eaten with steamed buns). There's also a posh afternoon tea. Everything costs about four times what you'd pay at a food court, but then food courts don't feature marble floors, a pianist tinkling away and the lofty, arched ceiling of the former boat terminal. Mon–Fri noon–2.30pm, 3.30–5.30pm & 6.30–10pm, Sat & Sun 11am–2pm, 3–5pm, 6.30–10.30pm.

★ **Lau Pa Sat** 18 Raffles Quay; map p.498. The food court at this historic market building offers a real panoply of Singapore hawker food, including satay – vendors set up their barbecues just outside on Boon Tat St in the evenings. Pricier outlets offer cooked-to-order seafood such as chilli crab. Daily 24hr.

Lucha Loco 15 Duxton Hill ☎ 6226 3938, ⓦ luchaloco .com; map p.498. Popular with young expats, this Mexican joint does tacos and burritos at lunchtime, with the burritos dropped in favour of quesadillas and sharing platters in the evenings. Portions are on the small side, but they make amends with a buzzing garden drinking area where you can enjoy their vast range of margaritas. Tues–Fri noon– midnight, Sat 6pm–midnight.

★ **The Populus Café** 146 Neil Rd ☎ 6635 8420, ⓦ thepopuluscafe.com; map p.498. This slick, contemporary café is popular with young professional types for its gourmet coffee blends and fusion meals such as Korean beef with quinoa salad (from S$20). Mon 9am–7pm, Tues 9am–4pm, Wed–Fri 9am–10.30pm, Sat 9.30am–10.30pm, Sun 9.30am–7pm.

MARINA BAY

The malls and fancy hotels scattered around Marina Bay hold some decent restaurants, though few are worth going out of your way for.

Cé La Vi SkyPark at Marina Bay Sands ☎ 6508 2188, ⓦ sg.celavi.com; map p.507. If you find that SkyPark admission charge hard to stomach, you can get round it by eating at this restaurant, serving Asian-influenced fusion food. Best to go for the set lunch (S$45 for two courses) as it can be very pricey otherwise. No shorts or vests in the evenings. Daily noon–3pm & 6–11pm.

Paulaner Bräuhaus #01–01 Millenia Walk, 9 Raffles Boulevard ☎ 6883 2572, ⓦ paulaner.com.sg; map p.507. The cavernous ceiling with a maypole sticking up into it is impressive, as is the menu of Bavarian delights such as the bitty *spätzle* pasta, but the best reason to come is the terrific Sunday brunch spread, including superb pork knuckle, sausages and salads, and desserts like strudel and cheesecake. It's good value at S$68 with unlimited soft drinks, or S$80 with unlimited beer from their microbrewery. Bar daily noon–1am. Mon–Fri noon– 2.30pm & 6.30–10.30pm, Sat 6.30–10.30pm, Sun 11.30am–2.30pm & 6.30–10.30pm.

Pizzeria Mozza #B01–42 Marina Bay Sands mall ☎ 6688 8522, ⓦ singapore.pizzeriamozza.com; map p.507. An excellent range of reasonably priced thin-crust pizzas starting at S$25, with plenty of salads, panini and soups, plus good desserts. Daily noon–11pm.

Singapore Food Treats Beneath the Singapore Flyer; map p.507. Arguably more interesting than the Flyer itself, this retro-style food court evokes Singapore's street-food scene of half a century ago, its stalls mocked up as pushcarts. The food can be retro too – for example satay *bee hoon*, rice vermicelli drenched in the peanut sauce normally eaten with satay, and popular in the 1970s. Nothing costs more than S$10. Daily 11am–11pm.

ORCHARD ROAD AND AROUND

Eating in Singapore's shopping nexus – Orchard Rd, Tanglin Rd and Scotts Rd – is almost completely about restaurants in malls and hotels, though a few venues are housed in refurbished shophouses. Most malls have food courts, and indeed two of the island's slickest are to be found here: *Food Republic* inside 313@Somerset, and *Food Opera* in the basement of ION Orchard.

Bistro Du Vin #01–14 Shaw Centre, 1 Scotts Rd ☎ 6733 7763, ⓦ bistroduvin.com.sg; map p.510. Informal

---

STREET ICE CREAM

A couple of generations ago, ice cream in Singapore often meant stuff sold by hawkers from pushcarts, in **exotic flavours** like sweetcorn, red (aduki) bean and yam. This was so-called *potong* ("cut" in Malay) ice cream because it came in brick shapes and the seller would use a cleaver to slice it into slabs, to be served either between wafers or even rolled up in white bread – giving a new dimension to the term "ice cream sandwich".

The general elimination of street stalls put paid to that trade, but in recent years the ice-cream vendors have made a comeback. They're often to be seen at Cavenagh Bridge, on Orchard Road, outside Bugis MRT and at other downtown locations. The **bread option** complements the ice cream surprisingly well, serving as a sort of neutral sponge cake. As for the **weird flavours**, they're all more than palatable; you can also find red-bean ice cream on a stick in supermarkets and convenience stores, sold under the name "Potong".

9

French restaurant that does an exceptional duck leg confit, plus standards such as escargot and French onion soup – and none of that nouvelle cuisine presentation-over-substance nonsense either. The weekday lunch deals are reasonable value at S$35 for two courses; mains ordered à la carte cost just about as much. Daily noon–2pm & 6.30–10pm.

Brunetti #01–35 Tanglin Mall, 163 Tanglin Rd ☎6733 9088; map p.510. An incredible Australian café with cabinet after cabinet of exquisite macaroons, cakes and ice creams that together come in almost as many colours as you'd find in a paint catalogue. Not too pricey – cheesecake costs S$8 – though the light meals and savoury snacks aren't such good value. Mon–Thurs & Sun 9am–8pm, Fri & Sat 9am–9pm.

Maharajah 39 Cuppage Terrace ☎6732 6331, ⊛maharajah.com.sg; map p.510. Amid the annoyingly touristy options on Cuppace Terrace is this pleasant North Indian restaurant with a tempting menu boasting many tandoori options such as chicken or lamb tikka, plus good snakehead fish curries. Around S$35/person without drinks. Daily 11am–11pm.

★Marché Ground floor and basement, 313@ Somerset, 313 Orchard Rd ☎6834 4041; map p.510. Never mind that Mövenpick's *Marché* restaurants are formulaic when you can have *rösti*, sausages or crêpes cooked to order in front of you, or help yourself to the superb salad bar. Daily lunch specials offer a meal and drink for around S$12, while the bakery counter does takeaway sandwiches (from S$5), bread sticks and Berliners, doughnuts with a range of fillings. Bakery from 7.30am. Daily 11am–11pm.

Min Jiang Goodwood Park Hotel, 22 Scotts Rd ☎6730 1704; map p.510. This stylish affair serves some Cantonese food and lunchtime dim sum, though their spicy Sichuan specialities are the most interesting. Good choices include the prawn fried with dried chillies, and Sichuan smoked duck. Reasonably priced for a top hotel. Daily 11am–2.30pm & 6.30–10.30pm.

Newton Circus Hawker Centre Corner of Clemenceau Ave North and Bukit Timah Rd, near Newton MRT; map p.479. A venerable open-air place with a wide range of hawker food. It's especially noted for its seafood, for which you can end up paying through the nose; prices are on the high side for stalls anyway, as the place is very much on the tourist trail. Late afternoon until the early hours.

★PS Café Level 2, Palais Renaissance, 390 Orchard Rd ☎9834 8232; ⊛pscafe.sg; map p.510. Marvellous though pricey restaurant set in something resembling a glasshouse and offering an inventive, constantly revised menu of fusion fare and great desserts. Mains from S$30. Mon–Fri 11.30am–11pm, Sat & Sun 9.30am–11pm.

Sakae Teppenyaki #B2–52 Plaza Singapura, 68 Orchard Rd ☎6337 5676; map p.510. One of many mini-restaurants squeezed into the shopping mall's basement food court, with tables set around hot griddles all geared up to prepare teppanyaki, Japanese fry-ups of meat or seafood. Choose from various set combinations of ingredients and a chef will cook them with aplomb, and more than a dash of seasoning, in front of you. About S$20/person, excluding drinks. Daily 11.30am–9.30pm.

Spices Café Concorde Hotel, 100 Orchard Rd ☎6739 8370; map p.510. Buffets galore: an evening seafood feast (Mon–Thurs S$62, Fri–Sun S$69), afternoon tea (Sat & Sun noon–4.30pm; S$42), and best of all, a great-value spread of Peranakan and other local cooking for lunch on weekdays (S$42). Daily 6am–11pm.

Thai Express #03–24 Plaza Singapura, 68 Orchard Rd ☎6339 5442, ⊛thaiexpress.com.sg; map p.510. A modern chain with plenty of wood and chrome fittings and where everything is done chop-chop. The menu is packed with Thai rice and noodle standards (from S$12) plus lots of desserts. Daily 11am–10pm.

Warung M Nasir 69 Killiney Rd ☎6734 6228; map p.510. Tiny but well-respected Indonesian *nasi padang* joint, with standards such as fried chicken *balado*, beef and chicken *rendang* and tofu or beans fried with *sambal*. Daily 10am–10pm.

DEMPSEY HILL (AKA TANGLIN VILLAGE)

Dotted with old bungalows and the odd field, the stretch of Holland Rd 1km west of the Botanic Gardens' Tanglin gate and 2km west of the start of Orchard Rd was originally a British army camp, which later housed Singapore's Ministry of Defence. No one quite agrees on what to call the area now, but Dempsey Hill (⊛dempseyhill.com) is worth a look for its jumble of posh restaurants and bars, plus health spas, antique shops and so forth. The venues here are close to the main road and can be reached on foot. Buses #7, #77 and #174 head past here from Orchard Boulevard.

Candlenut Block 17A, Dempsey Rd ☎1800 304 2288; map p.479. It doesn't look especially upmarket, but this restaurant lofts Peranakan food towards haute cuisine, with dishes like barramundi *asam pedas* (with chilli and turmeric). Everything still tastes recognizably Peranakan, just with all the flavours cranked up to eleven. Prices are correspondingly on the high side, too, at around S$40/person minus drinks. Mon–Thurs & Sun noon–3pm & 6–10pm, Fri & Sat noon–3pm & 6–11pm.

Long Beach Seafood Block 25, Dempsey Rd ☎6323 2222, ⊛longbeachseafood.com.sg; map p.479. Once you had to trek to the beaches to find Singapore's best Chinese-style seafood, but no longer, now that this beachside stalwart has set up here. The best dishes really are magic, including treacly crisp baby squid, chunky Alaska crab in a white pepper sauce, steamed *soon hock* (goby) and, of course, chilli crab. An expensive but worthwhile blowout. Daily 11am–3pm & 5pm–1am.

Samy's Block 25, Dempsey Rd ☎6472 2080; map p.479. Housed in a colonial-era hall with ceiling fans whirring overhead, *Samy's* is an institution that's been serving superb banana-leaf meals for decades. Choose from curries of jumbo prawn, fish head, crab or mutton, and either plain rice or the delicate, fluffy *biriyani*. You can eat well for S$20/person excluding drinks. Mon & Wed–Sun 11am–3pm & 6–10pm.

GEYLANG AND KATONG
In line with their heritage, the suburbs of Geylang and Katong hold several inexpensive Nyonya and Malay restaurants.

328 Katong Laksa 51 East Coast Rd, at the corner of Ceylon Rd; map p.516. Just as different parts of Malaysia have their own take on *laksa*, so does Katong: here the noodles are cut into short strands for easy slurping off a spoon. Run by a brother-and-sister team, this café is regarded as one of the original purveyors of the dish, using seafood and without the meat of more modern variations. Daily 8am–10pm.

Guan Hoe Soon 38/40 Joo Chiat Place ☎6344 2761, ⓦ guanhoesoon.com; map p.516. Open in one form or another for more than half a century, this restaurant turns out fine Nyonya cuisine in home-cooked style, including yummy *ngoh hiang*, in which minced prawn is rolled up in a wrapper made from bean curd, and satay *babi* – not a Malay satay, but a sweetish red pork curry. Around S$25/ person. Daily 11am–3pm & 6–9.30pm.

★Hajjah Maimunah 20 Joo Chiat Rd ☎6348 5457, ⓦ hjmaimunah.com; map p.516 Inexpensive Malay diner serving good breakfasts (*nasi lemak* etc) and a fine *nasi campur* spread, featuring the likes of *ayam bakar sunda* (Sundanese-style barbecued chicken), with assorted *kuih* for afters. Tues–Sun 8am–9pm.

Sandwich Saigon 93 East Coast Rd ☎6345 3849, ⓦ sandwichsaigon.com; map p.516. Katong has both gentrified and become a little Vietnam, eating-wise, in recent years. This restaurant stands out for its yummy Vietnamese baguettes, using bread baked on the premises and with fillings such as garlic chicken or pork chop (around S$8). Also well-executed spring rolls and noodle dishes (S$10), plus drip coffee. Mon–Fri 11.30am–2.30pm & 5.30–10pm, Sat & Sun 11.30am–10pm.

SENTOSA AND VIVOCITY
There are few choices for cheap food on Sentosa (one is a simple food court at Palawan Beach), so if you're keen to keep costs down, try the VivoCity mall above HarbourFront MRT.

★Food Republic Level 3 VivoCity. Perhaps the best example of this upmarket food court, where the stalls are "curated" for their culinary calibre and the stalls styled to resemble something out of pre-war Chinatown. Try the scissors-cut curry rice – mixed rice/*nasi campur* but with the hawker slicing up the rice serving with scissors and heaping curry gravy onto it. Avoid at peak times, though, as the place will be rammed. Daily 10am–10pm.

Slappy Cakes Close to Universal Studios ☎6795 0779, ⓦ slappycakes.com.sg. A great place to bring kids: you pick a batter (chocolate or zucchini, say), then something to add to the mix (strawberries or ham, anyone?), and finally prepare pancakes at your table's griddle. It's good fun and if the results aren't up to scratch, well at least you won't have anyone to get cross with other than yourself. One order (S$15) will make enough for two as a snack. Light meals also available. Daily 8am–9.30pm.

★Soup #02–141 VivoCity ☎6376 9969. So-called *samsui* women once sailed from China's Guangdong province to work on Singapore building sites. This fine little restaurant celebrates the cuisine of these redoubtable women, most famously their ginger chicken; steamed, it comes with a gingery dip and iceberg-lettuce leaves to roll it up in. Reckon on S$25/person, excluding drinks. Daily 11.30am–10pm.

Trapizza Siloso Beach ☎6376 2662. *Trapizza* stands out from the many eating places here for its excellent pizzas and pasta dishes starting at S$20. Daily 11.30am–9.30pm.

DRINKING AND NIGHTLIFE

Singapore supports a huge range of watering holes, from elegant colonial chambers through hip rooftop venues with skyline views to slightly tacky joints featuring Chinese karaoke or middling bands covering Western hits. Chinatown is particularly good for **bars**, though anywhere expats hang out won't be short of options. There are also a handful of glitzy **clubs** that spin cutting-edge sounds, all minus – this being Singapore – any assistance from illicit substances. Although the scene has come off the boil in recent years, one or two venues still lure world-leading DJs.

ESSENTIALS
Bars Some surveys deem Singapore one of the world's most expensive cities for drinking, but the reality is more subtle. It's true that a 630ml bottle (1.1 imperial or 1.4 US pints) of Tiger beer at a bar or club typically costs around S$14, but hawker centres charge only half that, and some bars thrive on selling keenly priced drinks. A glass of house wine usually costs much the same as a beer, and spirits a few dollars more. During happy hour, which can last half the evening, you'll either get a considerable discount off drinks or a "one-for-one" deal (two drinks for the price of one), and some bars also have a "house pour", a discounted cocktail, wine or beer on offer all night. Note that some bars close on Sundays, and that more upmarket venues,

9

including hotel bars, often have a "smart casual" dress code: generally no shorts, vests or sandals after 6pm.

Clubs Most clubs have a cover charge, if not all week then at least on Friday and Saturday; the charge almost always includes your first drink or two, and varies between S$15 and S$35 (weekends are pricier, and men pay slightly more than women). Where women get in free on ladies' night (often midweek), they have to pay for their first drink but may get unlimited refills of the "house pour" at certain times.

Drinking laws Following an extraordinary riot in Little India in 2013, which the government saw as fuelled by alcohol (although it was sparked by a fatal road accident involving migrant workers), restrictions were placed on drinking in public. In practice, this means anywhere on the street beyond the premises of restaurants, hawker centres, bars and clubs, plus beaches and parks, and applies nightly from 10.30pm to 7am. Within Little India and Geylang, an additional ban applies throughout the weekend and until 7am on Mondays. Shops and supermarkets are also unable to sell alcohol when the ban is in force.

BARS

THE COLONIAL DISTRICT

Aura Sky Lounge Level 6, National Gallery, St Andrew's Rd ☎6866 1977, ⊛aura.sg; map p.480. Come here for one of the very best views of any bar in Singapore, out over the Padang with *Marina Bay Sands*, Esplanade and the Singapore Flyer beyond; after dark is best. Happy hour Mon–Thurs & Sun 5–8pm. Daily 11.30am–1am.

Tap Craft Beer Bar Ground floor, Capitol Piazza, 15 Stamford Rd ☎6384 7188, ⊛tapthat.com.sg; map p.480. Part of the grand redevelopment of the 1920s Capitol theatre into a mall and luxury hotel, this open-plan venue takes up part of the mall concourse and is especially popular with executive types, who come for its truly eclectic range of imported beers and ciders. Bar bites include spam fries and teriyaki meatballs, and regular promotions help keep costs down. Daily noon–midnight.

BRAS BASAH ROAD TO ROCHOR ROAD

The Long Bar Raffles Hotel, 1 Beach Rd ☎6412 1816; map p.488. It's still just about mandatory to have a Singapore Sling amid the old-fashioned elegance of the bar where Ngiam Tong Boon invented it in 1915. Daily 11am–12.30am.

★**Loof** Top of the Odeon Towers Extension, 391 North Bridge Rd #03–07 ☎6338 8035, ⊛loof.com.sg; map p.488. This rooftop garden bar is an elegant place to chill out, with views into the back of the *Raffles* hotel opposite. There's a strong local flavour too, in the form of cocktails and bar snacks that use lots of Southeast Asian ingredients, plus a nostalgic recreation of an old neighbourhood shop selling knick-knacks. Happy hour weekdays until 8pm. Mon–Thurs 5pm–1am, Fri & Sat 5pm–3am.

LITTLE INDIA AND ARAB ST

★**Atlas** Ground floor, Parkview Square, 600 North Bridge Rd #03–07 ☎6396 4466, ⊛atlasbar.sg; map p.491. Aptly located at the Gotham-esque Parkview Square, *Atlas* is a palatially opulent evocation of Jazz Age glamour, all gilt Art Deco-style fittings. Cabinets stretching to the lofty ceiling hold a veritable library of wines and spirits, including some fiendishly expensive vintages. If you don't feel like indulging, just come for a daytime coffee and a gawp. Mon–Thurs 10am–1am, Fri 10am–2am, Sat 3pm–2am.

The Countryside Café 71 Dunlop St ☎6292 0071; map p.491. A low-key, convivial establishment, with middle-of-the-road oldie sounds and five dozen different bottled beers at reasonable prices. The menu of bar snacks and food – partly Indian, partly Western – is nearly as impressive. Mon 6pm–2am, Tues–Thurs & Sun 10am–2am, Fri & Sat 10am–3am.

Prince of Wales 101 Dunlop St ☎6299 0130, ⊛pow .com.sg; map p.491. This travellers' bar has frequent discount deals on top of already attractive beer and cider prices, plus regular acoustic sets and the occasional quiz night. Mon–Thurs 5pm–late, Fri–Sun 3pm–late.

CHINATOWN, INCLUDING BOAT QUAY & RIVERSIDE POINT

BQ Bar 39 Boat Quay ☎6536 1571, ⊛bqbar.com; map p.498. One of Boat Quay's cooler venues, thanks to the friendly staff, memorable views of the river from upstairs and diverse sounds, anything from dance to rock. Kebabs available too from a nearby outlet run by the same management. Happy hour until 8pm. Mon & Tues 11am–1am, Wed–Fri 11am–3am, Sat 5pm–3am.

Harry's Bar 28 Boat Quay ☎6538 3029, ⊛harrys.com .sg; map p.498. Singapore's most ubiquitous chain of bars started out here, and now has some twenty branches island-wide. Popular with locals as well as foreigners, it does half a dozen draught beers and ciders, plus light meals and snacks; happy hour is until 8pm. Mon–Thurs & Sun 11.30am–1am, Fri & Sat 11.30am–2am.

The Penny Black 26 & 27 Boat Quay ☎6538 2300, ⊛pennyblack.com.sg; map p.498. Hardly a convincing evocation of a "Victorian London pub" but pleasant enough, with one table built around a red pillar box, Strongbow cider on draught, plenty of pub grub – steak pie, ploughman's lunches, etc – and live UK football matches on TV. Mon–Thurs 11.30am–1am, Fri & Sat 11.30am–2am, Sun 11.30am–midnight.

Red Dot Brewhouse 33 & 34 Boat Quay ☎6535 4500, ⊛reddotbewhouse.com.sg; map p.498. Many of Singapore's slicker bars are expat-run, but not the *Red Dot Brewhouse*, the brainchild of one local who got bitten by the homebrew bug many years ago. Among their range of beers and ales, the most radical is the Monster Green Lager, rich in blue-green algae regarded by some as a superfood.

Mon–Thurs noon–midnight, Fri noon–2am, Sat 3pm–1am.

Screening Room 12 Ann Siang Hill ☏6221 1694, ⒲screeningroom.com.sg; map p.498. The unpretentious rooftop bar here is a convivial spot for an evening drink, with the bonus of views of Chinatown's shophouses and modern towers, plus plenty of Mediterranean-influenced snacks. Mon–Thurs 6pm–late, Fri & Sat 6pm–3am.

Spiffy Dapper Upstairs at 73 Amoy St ☏8655 0829, ⒲spiffydapper.com; map p.498. This tiny indie cocktail bar must be the darkest venue in town, its thick drapes keeping out any extraneous lighting. There are at least fifteen standard cocktails on offer (from S$25), and the mixologists can talk through these and other options based on your tastes. Mon–Fri 5pm–late, Sat & Sun 3pm–late.

Stickies 11 Keng Cheow St ☏6221 1694, ⒲stickiesbar .com; map p.498. No fancy decor or fittings here, but the place is often packed with a young, mainly local, crowd thanks to its many discount deals. The most striking offer is hourly pricing on its daily house pour (including beer): they charge S$2 at 2pm, S$3 at 3pm and so on (plus taxes), the idea being to get people to ease off late at night. Daily noon–midnight.

TANJONG PAGAR AND THE FINANCIAL DISTRICT

★**1-Altitude** Levels 61–63, One Raffles Place ☏6438 0410, ⒲1-altitude.com; map p.498. Whether or not this is "the world's highest alfresco bar" as claimed, the views from the roof of the One Raffles Place tower, 282m up, are simply stunning. It's best to drop by towards the end of your stay, when you can make sense of the cityscape and ponder the myriad changes that half a century of rapid development has wrought. Cover charge S$30 (S$35 after 9pm); smart-casual dress only. Hours can vary. Daily 6pm–2am.

Five Oriental 16 Collyer Quay ☏9826 1049, ⒲fivebar sg; map p.498. Thronged with banking staff, this bar bizarrely incorporates two escalators sandwiching the bar area itself and an elevated stage for live music. As befits its name, there's a S$5 deal round the clock, paying for a glass of their house pour spirit or half-pint of Kronenbourg. A full menu of dim sum and other Cantonese food, too. Mon–Fri noon–midnight, Sat 6pm–midnight.

MARINA BAY

Orgo Roof terrace, Esplanade – Theatres on the Bay ☏6336 9366, ⒲orgo.sg; map p.507. They make a big thing of their huge range of cocktails, which emphasize fresh fruit and herbs, but the views of the spires of the Financial District sell themselves. Happy hour until 8pm. Daily 6pm–late.

ORCHARD ROAD AND AROUND

Quite a few of Orchard Rd's most interesting drinking spots occupy restored Peranakan shophouses at the start of Emerald Hill Rd, close to Somerset MRT.

Alley Bar Peranakan Place, corner of Orchard Rd and Emerald Hill Rd ☏6732 6966, ⒲peranakanplace.com; map p.510. Less touristy than its neighbours, *Alley Bar* slots into a narrow, high-ceilinged space and does a good range of cocktails and spirits. The food menu is extensive, too, with lots of sandwiches and more substantial meals. Happy hour until 9pm. Mon–Thurs & Sun 5pm–2am, Fri & Sat 5pm–3am.

Ice Cold Beer 9 Emerald Hill Rd ☏6735 9929, ⒲www .ice-cold-beer.com; map p.510. Noisy, happening place where the beers are kept in ice tanks under the glass-topped bar. Leffe Blond and Fuller's London Pride on tap, among others. Happy hour until 9pm. Shares a kitchen with *No. 5 Emerald Hill*. Happy hour daily 5–9pm. Mon–Thurs & Sun 5pm–2am, Fri & Sat 5pm–3am.

★**No. 5 Emerald Hill** 5 Emerald Hill Rd ☏6732 0818, ⒲emerald-hill.com; map p.510. Set in one of Emerald Hill Rd's restored houses, *No. 5* is not only an opulent feast for the eyes but also offers speciality cocktails plus great chicken wings and thin-crust pizzas. Tetley's on tap, some outdoor seating and a pool table upstairs. Happy hour until 9pm. Mon–Thurs noon–2am, Fri & Sat noon–3am, Sun 5pm–3am.

Martini Bar Grand Hyatt Hotel, 10 Scotts Rd ☏6732 1234; map p.510. Choose from several dozen martini variations at this plush bar, ranging from their trademark lychee martini to options that include local ingredients such as sugar cane. Several are half-price before 9pm, when you can order one for a mere S$17. Mon–Thurs & Sun 5pm–midnight, Fri & Sat 5pm–1am.

Que Pasa 7 Emerald Hill ☏6235 6626, ⒲www .quepasa.com.sg; map p.510. A wine bar with a creaky wooden staircase and plenty of tapas. No happy hour. Mon–Thurs 1.30pm–2am, Fri & Sat 1.30pm–3am, Sun 5.30pm–2am.

DEMPSEY HILL

The Rabbit Hole 39C Harding Rd ☏6473 9965, ⒲thewhiterabbit.com.sg; map p.479. From house of God to gin palace: that's the tale of the *Rabbit Hole*, the marvellous open-air bar at the back of the restored church which now holds the upmarket *White Rabbit* restaurant. There are over twenty types of gin and a dozen gin-based cocktails to navigate your way around, as well as plenty of premium wines. Mon–Thurs & Sun 6pm–11.30pm, Fri & Sat 6pm–12.30am.

SENTOSA

Mambo Beach Club Siloso Beach, opposite the Siloso Beach Resort ☏6276 6270, ⒲mambobeachclub.com .sg. Fancy yet friendly establishment where you can imbibe sundowners at outdoor tables clustered around the freeform pool, with the sea just metres away. Seafood bites and pizzas (from S$20), too. Hours can vary. Daily 11am–9pm.

9

CLUBS

Canvas #B1-06 The Riverwalk, 20 Upper Circular Rd ☎ 6538 2928, ⓦ canvasvenue.sg; map p.498. On the south bank of the Singapore River, *Canvas* spins hip-hop, electronica and other sounds depending on the evening, but Tuesdays sees stand-up comedy rule the roost. Tues 8–11pm, Wed–Sat 8pm–late.

Cé La Vi Marina Bay Sands SkyPark ☎ 6508 2188, ⓦ sg .celavi.com; map p.507. The bar/club at the SkyPark is one way to bypass the 57th-floor admission fee and enjoy fabulous views over downtown Singapore. There's a S$20 entry charge until 9pm, redeemable against food and drink, and a post-midnight cover charge certain days. Daily noon–late.

Tanjong Beach Club Tanjong Beach, Sentosa ☎ 6270 1355, ⓦ tanjongbeachclub.com. If you needed a reason to schlep to the furthest of Sentosa's beaches, this would be it. Styled like a luxury beach bungalow, it boasts an incongruous infinity pool, a pricey restaurant and a bar that hosts weekly beach parties (usually Sun from 2pm). Mon noon–10pm, Tues–Fri 11am–10pm, Sat 10am–10pm, Sun 10am–11pm.

Zouk The Cannery, Clarke Quay, 3C River Valley Rd ☎ 6738 2988, ⓦ zoukclub.com; map p.480. Still going after more than 25 years, *Zouk* is Singapore's pre-eminent club, specializing in house and other dance sounds. Its new home at Clarke Quay, oozing post-industrial chic, is four venues in one, including two bars and its little-sister club *Phuture*, where the emphasis is more on hip-hop and R&B. Wed & Fri 9pm–3am, Sat 9pm–4am,

LGBT VENUES

Singapore's LGBT scene, though modest, is among the best in Southeast Asia, and in recent years the country has seen the annual Pink Dot rally (June or July; ⓦ pinkdot.sg) – an LGBT event, although this being Singapore it's all tame and family-friendly – grow into one of the best-attended mass meetings on the island. That said, attitudes toward homosexuality remain contradictory. The government has declined to repeal colonial-era legislation banning sex between men, though it no longer enforces it either, and in 2017 ordered multinationals to stop sponsoring Pink Dot and banned tourists from participating, suggesting it wants to isolate the domestic social agenda from international trends. So it is that gay venues still keep a low profile, functioning largely unhindered but scarcely using the word "gay" in advertising. The scene centres on Chinatown and Tanjong Pagar, where there are some half a dozen bars and clubs; note that they only really get busy at weekends, and only after 10pm. Two sources of information are the Pelangi Pride Centre (a small gay library project near Commonwealth MRT; ⓦ pelangipridecentre.org) and, for lesbian events, ⓦ facebook.com/twoqueensasia.

Dorothy's 13A Trengganu St; map p.498. Entered through a side door in Temple St (look for the discreetly placed rainbow flag), this tiny bar offers a view over the souvenir stalls of Trengganu St. Daily 6pm–late.

DYMK 41 Neil Rd ☎ 6224 3965; map p.498. Probably the friendliest gay bar in town. They tend to keep the music a tad quieter than elsewhere, making it a good place for a relaxed chat. Most of the crowd are 20- and 30-somethings. Mon–Thurs & Sun 6pm–midnight, Fri 7pm–1am, Sat 8pm–2am.

Tantric 78 Neil Rd ☎ 6423 9232; map p.498. Pleasant enough shophouse bar with a clientele slightly more reflective of Singapore's multi-ethnic make-up than the largely Chinese crowd elsewhere. There's outdoor seating on a slick terrace, and upstairs, a nominally separate bar that's a mini-shrine to the pre-war American Chinese actress Anna May Wong. Daily 8pm–late.

ENTERTAINMENT

Even on a brief visit, it's hard not to notice how much state money has been poured into the **arts**: prime property has been turned over to cultural organizations in areas like the Waterloo St "arts belt", and prestigious venues such as Theatres on the Bay host world-class performers. Cynics might say this cultural push is mainly about keeping Singapore attractive to expats, while others raise the important issue of whether world-class art can bloom where **censorship** is very much alive. Nonetheless, the cultural scene is streets ahead of anything in Malaysia, so it would be a shame not to catch a performance of some kind, whether one drawing on Asian traditions or a gig by a big-name Western band.

ESSENTIALS

Festivals Major cultural festivals include the Singapore International Festival of the Arts (calendar online; ⓦ sifa .sg), running the gamut from concerts to theatre through dance and film; and the Singapore Fringe Festival (Jan or Feb; ⓦ singaporefringe.com), which concentrates on theatre, dance and the visual arts. There's also the annual Singapore Writers' Festival (ⓦ singaporewritersfestival .com), featuring international as well as local writers working in all four of the country's official languages.

Tickets You can buy tickets directly from venues or through the SISTIC ticket agency, with outlets in downtown malls (☎ 6348 5555, ⓦ sistic.com.sg).

FILM

As well as the latest Hollywood blockbusters, Singapore's cinemas show a range of Chinese, Malay and Indian movies, all with English subtitles. Although international cinema features year-round in one-off screenings and mini-film festivals, the main event for cineastes is the Singapore International Film Festival (usually Nov; ⓦ sgiff .com). If you're watching a hot new release, it's worth turning up early or buying tickets in advance. Tickets start at S$10, but can cost two or three times that for blockbuster films or screenings at the fanciest multiplexes. Be prepared for a certain amount of chattering during shows.

MULTIPLEX CHAINS
Cathay Cinemas include: Cineleisure Orchard, 8 Grange Rd (near Somerset MRT); Cathay Cineplex, 2 Handy Rd (near Dhoby Ghaut MRT); ⓦ cathaycineplexes.com.sg.
Golden Village Cinemas include: Level 7, Plaza Singapura, 68 Orchard Rd; Levels 2 & 3, VivoCity, Harbourfront; ⓦ gv.com.sg.
Shaw Cinemas include: Lido 8 Cineplex, Shaw House, 350 Orchard Rd (IMAX-equipped); Bugis Cineplex, Bugis Junction, 200 Victoria St; ⓦ shaw.sg.

INDEPENDENT VENUES
Alliance Française 1 Sarkies Rd ⓦ alliancefrancaise .org.sg. Weekly French-language films with English subtitles. A 10min walk from Newton MRT.
Filmgarde Cineplex Level 5, Bugis+, 201 Victoria St ⓦ fgcineplex.com.sg. Relatively commercial for an indie, with both English- and Chinese-language flicks.
National Museum Cinematheque National Museum, 93 Stamford Rd ⓦ nationalmuseum.org.sg. Intermittent screenings of vintage classics, some free.
★**The Projector** Level 5, Golden Mile Tower, 6001 Beach Rd ☏ 6337 8181, ⓦ theprojector.sg. Lurking within a concrete parking deck is the island's best cinema, an unmodernized 1970s affair lovingly revived with just some fresh coats of paint and cool murals. Devoted to films from around the world, it also sports two bars, one with views of Marina Centre.
The Screening Room 12 Ann Siang Hill ☏ 6221 1694, ⓦ screeningroom.com.sg. This posh restaurant/bar complex incorporates a cinema screening the relatively intellectual end of Hollywood's output.

THEATRE
A surprising number of small drama companies have sprung up over the years, performing works by local playwrights that dare to include a certain amount of social commentary; watch out for productions by The Necessary Stage (ⓦ necessary.org), the Singapore Repertory Theatre (ⓦ srt.com.sg) and Theatreworks (ⓦ theatreworks.org.sg). Foreign companies visit occasionally, too, and a lavish musical is usually staged at least once a year.

CLASSICAL AND TRADITIONAL MUSIC AND DANCE
At the heart of Singapore's healthy Western classical music scene is the Singapore Symphony Orchestra, whose concerts often feature stellar guest soloists, conductors and choirs from around the world. Dance is another thriving art form, with several active local troupes and regular visits by international companies.

COMPANIES AND ORCHESTRAS
Chinese Opera Teahouse 5 Smith St ☏ 6323 4862, ⓦ ctcopera.com.sg. A touristy show of Chinese opera excerpts ($40 with dinner beforehand, or S$25 with just tea and snacks); things kick off Fri & Sat at 7.50pm, or 7pm with dinner included.
Singapore Chinese Orchestra Singapore Conference Hall, 7 Shenton Way, Financial District ☏ 6440 3839, ⓦ sco.com.sg. Traditional Chinese music concerts, with occasional free shows.
Singapore Dance Theatre ☏ 6338 0611, ⓦ singaporedancetheatre.com. Contemporary and classical works at various venues, sometimes by moonlight at Fort Canning Park.
Singapore Lyric Opera ⓦ singaporeopera.com.sg. Western opera and operetta, at various venues.
Singapore Symphony Orchestra ⓦ sso.org.sg. Performances at Esplanade – Theatres on the Bay and the Victoria Concert Hall. Occasional free concerts at the Botanic Gardens and hour-long daytime shows for children.

STREET THEATRE
Walk around Singapore long enough and you're likely to stumble upon some sort of streetside cultural event, most usually a **wayang** – a Malay word used in Singapore to denote **Chinese opera**. Played out on outdoor stages next to temples and markets, or in open spaces in the new towns, *wayangs* are highly dramatic and stylized affairs, in which garishly made-up characters enact popular Chinese legends to the accompaniment of the crashes of cymbals and gongs. They're staged throughout the year, but the best time to catch one is during the **Festival of the Hungry Ghosts**, when they are performed to entertain passing spooks. Another fascinating traditional performance – lion-dancing – takes to the streets during Chinese New Year, and puppet theatres may appear around then, too. Downtown, Chinatown and the Bugis/Waterloo Street area are where you're most likely to stumble upon performances.

9

Siong Leng Musical Association ☎6222 4221, ⓦsiongleng.com. A body dedicated to preserving *nanyin* (literally "southern sound") – the distinctive music and opera of southeast China, sung in dialect. A few shows each year at various locations, sometimes in the exceptional temple surroundings of Thian Hock Keng.

Temple of Fine Arts ☎6535 0509, ⓦtfasg.org. This Indian cultural organization puts on occasional concerts and exhibitions.

POP, ROCK, BLUES AND JAZZ

Singapore is firmly on the East Asian gig circuit for Western stadium-rock outfits as well as indie bands, though some gigs can be a bit staid, with locals wary about letting their hair down. Local bands do exist and some aren't at all bad, but these are more likely to perform in community centres rather than decent venues. Music festivals include Laneway, a satellite of the well-established Australian indie event (Jan; ⓦsingapore.lanewayfestival.com); the Singapore Jazz Festival, which spans world music as well (March/April; ⓦsing-jazz.com) and Baybeats, an Esplanade event focused on Asian indie (dates vary). Canto- and Mando-pop – bland hybrids of Chinese lyrics and Western pop – as well as K-pop are hugely popular, too.

INDEPENDENT VENUES

Blu Jaz Café 11 Bali Lane ☎6292 3800, ⓦblujazcafe.net. Live jazz Wed, Fri & Sat eves. Mon & Fri noon–1.30am, Tues–Thurs noon–12.30am, Sat 4pm–1.30am.

Crazy Elephant #01–03 Block E, Clarke Quay ☎6337 7859, ⓦcrazyelephant.com. Of the hotchpotch of brash venues along Clarke Quay, this bar has a tad more street cred, with live music – blues and rock – practically every night and an open-mike jam session on Sun. Some tables are by the water's edge. Happy hour until 9pm. Mon–Thurs & Sun 5pm–2am, Fri & Sat 5pm–3am.

Timbre The Arts House, 1 Old Parliament Lane ☎6336 3386, ⓦtimbre.com.sg. Sets by local musicians in a high-visibility riverside location. Daily 6pm–midnight.

SHOPPING

Choice and convenience make the Singapore shopping experience a rewarding one, but the island's affluence and strong currency mean most things are priced at Western levels; Kuala Lumpur can be a better hunting ground for bargains. If you're around during the **Great Singapore Sale** (late May to late July; ⓦgreatsingaporesale.com.sg), you may find prices seriously marked down in many stores. **Orchard Road**, of course, is home to the biggest and swankiest malls; more interesting are those in **Chinatown**, which are often like multistorey markets and house more traditional outlets stocking Chinese foodstuffs, medicines, instruments and porcelain. Chinatown also has a few antique and curio shops along South Bridge Rd, and more knick-knacks are on sale around **Arab St**, where you'll also find textiles and batiks, robust basketware and some good deals on jewellery. **Little India** has silk stores and goldsmiths as well as the **Mustafa Centre**, a department store that's known all over the island for being open 24/7. Shopping complexes, malls and department stores are almost all open daily from 10am–9pm, some until 10pm.

ESSENTIALS

Complaints In the unlikely event that you encounter a problem with a retailer that you cannot resolve mutually, you may be able to recover your money by initiating proceedings online with Singapore's Small Claims Tribunal; see ⓦstatecourts.gov.sg for more information.

Tax refunds On leaving the country by air or sea, tourists can claim a refund of Singapore's goods and services tax (GST; seven percent at the time of research) on purchases over S$100, provided the shop in question is a member of one of three tax refund schemes. You will either have to complete a form which must be signed by the retailer, and then present the goods, forms and receipts to the customs authorities when you leave, or else ask the shop to link your purchases to one of your debit or credit cards, in which case you claim the tax back by, for example, scanning a barcode at a booth at the airport. It's a bureaucratic headache; for detailed guidance, have a look at the GST section of ⓦiras.gov.sg, or pick up the appropriate leaflet from a tourist office.

MALLS AND DEPARTMENT STORES
ORCHARD ROAD AND AROUND

313@Somerset 313 Orchard Rd (above Somerset MRT) ⓦ313somerset.com.sg; map p.510. Muji and Zara are the star names here.

Forum the Shopping Mall 583 Orchard Rd ⓦforumtheshoppingmall.com; map p.510. Plenty of items to please the most pampered of children– upmarket kids' clothes, toys and so forth.

The Heeren 260 Orchard Rd; map p.510. There's really only one reason to come here – it's home to the flagship outlet of Robinsons, Singapore's oldest department store.

ION Orchard 2 Orchard Turn (above Orchard MRT) ⓦionorchard.com; map p.510. Despite the impressive hyper-modern facade, 55th-floor viewing gallery and sprinkling of designer names, by far the most popular section of this cavernous mall is *Food Opera*, its excellent food court on basement 4.

Ngee Ann City 391A Orchard Rd ⓦngeeanncity.com.sg; map p.510. A brooding twin-towered complex, home to the Japanese Takashimaya department store and the excellent Kinokuniya bookstore, plus several jewellers.

Plaza Singapura 68 Orchard Rd ⓦplazasingapura .com.sg; map p.510. Veteran mall with a bit of everything: the British Marks & Spencer department store, sports equipment, Yamaha musical instruments and electronic equipment.

Tanglin Shopping Centre 19 Tanglin Rd (next to Orchard Parade hotel) ⓦtanglinsc.com; map p.510. Good for art, antiques and curios.

Tangs Corner of Orchard and Scotts rds ⓦtangs.com; map p.510. Tangs is a department store dating back to the 1950s, and the only one to have its own building on Orchard Rd, topped by a pagoda-style construction occupied by the *Marriott* hotel. The store itself sells a wide range of reasonably priced clothes and accessories.

THE COLONIAL DISTRICT

Raffles City 252 North Bridge Rd (above City Hall MRT) ⓦrafflescity.com; map p.480. Home to a branch of Robinsons department store with a Marks & Spencer within it, plus numerous fashion chains.

BRAS BASAH ROAD TO ROCHOR ROAD

Bugis Junction Victoria St, above Bugis MRT ⓦbugisjunction-mall.com.sg; map p.488. Mall encasing several streets of restored shophouses, and featuring the Japanese/Chinese department store BHG.

Sim Lim Square 1 Rochor Canal Rd ⓦsimlimsquare. com.sg; map p.488. Cameras and electronic goods.

LITTLE INDIA

Mustafa Centre Syed Alwi Rd ⓦmustafa.com.sg; map p.491. Totally different in feel to the malls of Orchard Rd, Mustafa is a phenomenon, selling electronics, fresh food, luggage, you name it – and it never closes. Daily 24hr.

CHINATOWN

Hong Lim Complex 531–531A Upper Cross St; map p.498. One of several Chinatown shopping centres where ordinary people buy ordinary things – dried mushrooms, cuttlefish and crackers from provisions shops, for example.

People's Park Centre 101 Upper Cross St; map p.498. Chinese handicrafts, electronics, silk, jade and gold.

People's Park Complex 1 Park Rd; map p.498. A venerable shopping centre that, like the Hong Lim Complex and adjacent People's Park Centre, is among the most entertaining places to browse in Chinatown because it's so workaday. Also here is the Overseas Emporium on level 4, selling Chinese musical instruments, calligraphy brushes, lacquerwork and jade.

MARINA BAY

The Shoppes at Marina Bay Sands 10 Bayfront Ave; map p.507. Beneath the iconic hotel, this mall actually has its own "canal" for boat rides, as well as the usual designer names.

ELSEWHERE IN SINGAPORE

VivoCity Next to HarbourFront Centre and above HarbourFront MRT ⓦvivocity.com.sg. A humdinger of a mall, containing a branch of Tangs department store, a cinema, three food courts and many restaurants.

ART, ANTIQUES, CURIOS AND SOUVENIRS

Antiques of the Orient #02–40 Tanglin Shopping Centre ☎6734 9351, ⓦaoto.com.sg; map p.510. Antiquarian books and maps, engravings and old photos. Mon–Sat 10am–5.30pm, Sun 11am–3.30pm.

★**Arch** #02-07 Esplanade Mall ☎6338 0161, ⓦarchsingapore.com.sg; map p.507. Their secretive production process works magic on thin slices of wood, transforming them into intricately carved and etched pieces of artwork, often Singapore-themed, that can be framed for your wall or worn as jewellery. A small shophouse facade starts at around S$25, while a 20cm-wide Marina Bay panorama can cost S$250 or more. Daily 11.30am–7.30pm.

Aster By Kyra 168 Telok Ayer St ☎6684 8600, ⓦasterbykyra.sg; map p.498. This little shop sells Peranakan-style scarves and porcelain, but its mainstay is lovely shophouse tiles – Indonesian replicas start at S$12, whereas costs for period ones rescued from old buildings hit three figures if in good condition. Daily 10.30am–6.30pm.

East Inspirations 33 Pagoda St ☎6224 2993; map p.498. The classiest of several antique shops here, offering Asian furniture, porcelain lamps and vases. Daily 10.30am–6.30pm.

The Heritage Shop 93 Jalan Sultan ☎6223 7982, ⓦtheheritageshop.sg; map p.491. An incredible range of bric-a-brac, from antique radios to beautiful enamelware tiffin carriers – little pots for cooked food, stacked and held together within a metal frame for easy carrying. Daily 1.30–8pm.

Jamal Kazura Aromatics 21 Bussorah St ☎6293 3320; map p.491. Veteran maker and seller of alcohol-free perfume, using various essential oils – a small Arabian-style bottle of scent starts at around S$12. Mon–Thurs, Sat & Sun 9.30am–7pm, Fri 9.30am–1pm & 2pm–7pm.

Katong Antiques House 208 East Coast Rd ☎6345 8544; map p.516. Peranakan artefacts and Chinese porcelain (see p.517). Tues–Sun 11am–5pm.

Kwok Gallery #03–01 Far East Shopping Centre, 545 Orchard Rd ☎6235 2516; map p.510. An impressive inventory of traditional Chinese pottery, jade and sculpture.

9

Mon–Sat 11am–6pm.

Little Shophouse 43 Bussorah St, near Sultan Mosque ☎6295 2328; map p.491. Well named, this small outlet boasts some fine but pricey examples of Peranakan beaded slippers (from S$300), plus replica Peranakan crockery. Daily 11am–6pm.

Malay Art Gallery 31 Bussorah St ☎6294 8051, ⓦthemalayartgallery.com; map p.491. Stocks *songket* and *kerises* from Malaysia and Indonesia. Sometimes closed Sundays. Mon–Sat noon–8pm, Sun noon–6pm.

★**Naiise** #B1-08 The Cathay, 2 Handy Rd ⓦnaiise.sg; map p.488. This homeware/stationery shop has a whole section devoted to witty Singapore-themed souvenirs: durian coin bowls, plates bearing recipes for classic hawker dishes, even shophouse-tile Rubik's cubes. Daily noon–10pm.

Orchid Chopsticks 25 Trengganu St ☎6227 0662; map p.498. You'd never have thought chopsticks could be this interesting: here they come in just about every material and hue, some fairly plain, others lustrous and ornamented. Daily 10am–10pm.

Ratianah 23 Bussorah St ☎6392 0323; map p.491. Friendly Malay shop offering Nyonya- style fabrics and blouses, plus bangles and brooches. Mon–Sat 12.30–9pm, Sun 1–5pm.

Red Dot Design Museum 11 Marina Boulevard ☎6514 0111, ⓦmuseum.red-dot.sg; map p.507. A good place for quirky, ergonomically designed items, including household gadgets, plus jewellery and paper artworks for self-assembly. Daily 11am–2am.

Rishi Handicrafts 5 Baghdad St ☎6298 2408; map p.491. Specializes in a range of baskets made from rattan, bamboo and other materials, plus some knick-knacks, too. Mon–Sat 10am–5.30pm, Sun 11am–5.30pm.

Teajoy #01–05 North Bridge Centre, 420 North Bridge Rd ☎6339 3739; map p.488. Close to the National Library, this specializes Chinese Song-dynasty-style tea sets. Daily noon–8pm.

Tong Mern Sern 51 Craig Rd ☎6223 1037, ⓦtmsantiques.com; map p.498. "We buy junk and sell antiques", proclaims the banner outside this great little establishment. The owner is quite a character and can tell you all about the crockery, old furniture and other bric-a-brac he has amassed. Mon–Sat 9am–6pm, Sun 1–6pm.

Zhen Lacquer Gallery 1 Trengganu St ☎6222 2718; map p.498. Specializes in lacquerware boxes and bowls. Daily 10.30am–9pm.

JEWELLERY

C.T. Hoo #01–22 Tanglin Shopping Centre ☎6737 5447; map p.510. Specializes in pearls. Mon–Sat 9.30am–6.30pm.

Flower Diamond #03–02 Ngee Ann City ☎6734 1221, ⓦflowerdiamond.com; map p.510. Contemporary

designs as well as more traditionally styled bling, at sensible prices. Daily 10am–9pm.

Risis National Orchid Garden, Singapore Botanic Gardens ☎6475 5104, ⓦrisis.com; map p.479. Singaporeans tend to view gold-plated orchids – available as brooches, pendants, earrings, even on tie clips – as clichéd, but tourists snap them up here as well as at Changi Airport. Daily 8.45am–6.30pm.

Wong's Jewellery 62 Temple St, Chinatown ☎6323 0236; map p.498. Chinese-style outlet, good for jade, gold and pearls. Daily 10am–7.30pm.

FABRICS AND FASHION

Charles & Keith Several outlets, including #B3–58 ION Orchard ☎6238 1840; map p.510. Singapore's answer to Malaysia's Jimmy Choo, the brothers Charles and Keith Wong design stylish, affordable women's shoes and handbags too. Daily 10.30am–10pm.

Dakshaini Silks 13 Upper Dickson Rd, Little India ☎6291 9969; map p.491. Indian embroidered silk textiles and clothes. Mon–Sat 10am–9pm, Sun 10am–8pm.

Rumah Bebe 113 East Coast Rd, Katong ☎6247 8781, ⓦrumahbebe.com; map p.516. This delightful place sells beaded shoes and handbags, costume jewellery and the traditional garb – *kebaya* and sarong – of Nyonya women. They also offer courses in beading and Nyonya cookery. Tues–Sun 9.30am–6.30pm.

Toko Aljunied 91 Arab St ☎6294 6897; map p.491. Quality batik cloth and *kebaya* – the blouse/sarong combinations traditionally worn by Nyonyas. Bespoke clothes too, by appointment. Mon–Sat 10.30am–7pm, Sun 11.30am–6pm.

BOOKS

Singapore bookshops are reasonably stocked; all the larger ones carry a good selection of Western and local fiction and nonfiction titles, plus a range of magazines. Besides the stores listed here, there's also the mail-order Select Books, with the best selection of specialist titles on Singapore, Malaysia and the rest of East Asia (ⓦselectbooks.com.sg).

Kinokuniya Level 3, Ngee Ann City ☎6339 1790, ⓦkinokuniya.com.sg; map p.510. Singapore's best general bookshop, with titles on every conceivable subject and some foreign-language literature too, plus loads of magazines. Daily 10am–9.30pm.

Littered With Books 20 Duxton Rd ☎6220 6824; map p.498. Despite its name, this indie outlet has a neatly laid out, though somewhat random, selection of literary fiction, thrillers and travel writing. Hours can be irregular, sometimes open longer Fri–Sun. Daily at least noon–8pm.

Times Bookstore #04–05 Plaza Singapura ☎6336 8861, ⓦtimesbookstores.com.sg; map p.510. A well-stocked local chain. Daily 10am–10pm.

DIRECTORY

Banks and exchange There's no shortage of ATMs – practically every MRT station has one, as do all malls. Licensed moneychangers, offering slightly more favourable exchange rates than the banks, aren't hard to find, particularly in Little India (e.g. at Mustafa, see p.492) and on Orchard Rd.

Embassies and consulates The "missions" section of the Singapore Ministry of Foreign Affairs website ⓦ mfa.gov.sg carries a full list.

Emergencies See p.53.

Gyms Fitness First (ⓦ fitnessfirst.com.sg) and Pure Fitness (ⓦ purefitness.com/singapore) operate downtown gyms, though you will need to take out membership to use them.

Hospitals The state-run Singapore General Hospital, Outram Rd (SGH; ☎ 6222 3322; ⓦ sgh.com.sg; Outram Park MRT), has a 24hr casualty/emergency department, as does the privately run Raffles Hospital, 585 North Bridge Rd (☎ 6311 1111, ⓦ rafflesmedicalgroup.com).

Pharmacies Both Guardian and Watsons are ubiquitous downtown, with branches in shopping malls and even in a few MRT stations, though only the largest outlets handle prescriptions.

Phones For details of mobile phone providers, see p.57.

Police In an emergency, dial ☎ 999; otherwise call the police hotline ☎ 1800 225 0000.

Post offices The island has dozens of post offices (typically Mon–Fri 9am–5pm & Sat 9am–1pm), with the one in the basement of City Square Mall, near Farrer Park MRT and Little India, keeping slightly longer hours (Mon–Sat 10am–7pm). For more on the mail system, contact SingPost (☎ 1605, ⓦ singpost.com).

Swimming Singapore has some of the world's best state-run swimming facilities; just about every new town has a well-maintained 50m open-air pool, open from early morning until well into the evening. The best-located downtown pool is the Jalan Besar Swimming Complex on Tyrwhitt Rd, near Lavender and Farrer Park MRT station. Charges are a mere S$1.50 or so; have coins available for the ticket gates and lockers.

Travel agents Try the following for discounted airfares and packages: STA Travel, #B1-46 Singapore Management University Library, 70 Stamford Rd ☎ 6737 7188, ⓦ statravel.com.sg; Chan Brothers, #07-01 Fook Hai Building, 150 South Bridge Rd ☎ 6212 9988, ⓦ chanbrothers.com; and Zuji ⓦ zuji.com.sg.

Vaccinations Tan Tock Seng Hospital, across the road from Novena MRT, has a Travellers' Health & Vaccination Centre (Mon–Fri 8.30am–5pm; ☎ 6357 2222, ⓦ ttsh.com.sg).

Women's helpline AWARE ☎ 1800 774 5935, ⓦ aware .org.sg.

ORANG-UTAN MOTHER AND SON

Contexts

History

The modern-day nations of Malaysia, Singapore and Brunei only became independent in 1963, 1965 and 1984 respectively. Before that, their history was inextricably linked with events in the larger Malay archipelago, from Sumatra across Borneo to the Philippines.

Unfortunately, little hard archeological evidence in the region pertains to the prehistoric period, while events prior to the foundation of Melaka are known only from unreliable accounts written by Chinese and Arab traders. For an understanding of the formative fourteenth and fifteenth centuries, there are two vital sources: the **Suma Oriental** (Treatise of the Orient), by Tomé Pires, a Portuguese emissary who came to Melaka in 1512 and used his observations to write a history of the region, and the seventeenth-century **Sejarah Melayu**, the "Malay Annals", which recount oral historical tales in a poetic style. Portuguese and Dutch **colonists** who arrived in the sixteenth and seventeenth centuries supplied written records, though these tended to concern commercial rather than political or social matters. At least there's a wealth of information from **British colonial** times that, despite an imperialistic bias, gives detailed insights into Malay affairs.

Beginnings

The oldest remains of *Homo sapiens* in the region, discovered in the Niah Caves in Sarawak, are thought to be those of hunter-gatherers, dating back some 40,000 years; other finds in the Peninsular state of Kedah are only 10,000 years old. The variety of **ethnic groups** now found in both east and west Malaysia – from small, dark-skinned Negritos through to paler Austronesian Malays – has led to the theory of a slow filtration of peoples through the Malay archipelago from southern Indochina. That theory is backed by an almost universal belief in animism, celebration of fertility and ancestor worship among the various peoples.

The Malay archipelago acquired a strategic significance thanks largely to the **shipping trade**, which flourished as early as the first century AD. This was engendered by the two major markets of the early world – India and China – and by the richness of its own resources. From the dense jungle of the Peninsula and northern Borneo came aromatic woods, timber and nipah palm thatch, traded by the forest-dwelling Orang Asli with the coastal Malays, who then bartered or sold it on to Arab and Chinese merchants. The region was also rumoured to be rich in **gold**, leading to its being described by contemporary Greek writers as "The Golden Chersonese" (*chersonese* meaning "peninsula"). Although gold was never found in the supposed quantities, ornaments made of the metal helped to develop decorative traditions among craftsmen, and survive today. More significant, however, were the **tin fields** of the Malay Peninsula, mined in early times to provide an alloy used for temple sculptures. Chinese traders were also attracted by the medicinal properties of various sea products, such as sea slugs, collected by the Orang Laut (sea people), as well as by pearls and tortoise shells.

c.35,000 BC	200 AD	7th c.	c.14th c.
Human settlement at Niah in what is now northern Sarawak	Malay Peninsula comes under Indian cultural and religious influence	The Sumatran Sriviyajan empire, encompassing the Malay Peninsula, rises to prominence	Srivijaya is challenged by the Majapahit empire of Java and declines

For their part, the indigenous peoples acquired cloth, pottery, glass and absorbed the beliefs of those with whom they traded. From as early as 200 AD, **Indian traders** brought their Hindu and Buddhist practices, and archeological evidence from later periods, such as the tenth-century temples at Lembah Bujang (see p.171), suggests that the local population not only tolerated these new belief systems, but adapted them to suit their own experiences. Perhaps the most striking contemporary example of such cultural interchange is the traditional entertainment of *wayang kulit* (shadow plays), whose plots are drawn from the Hindu *Ramayana*.

While trade with India developed very early, contact with **China** was initially less pronounced due to the pre-eminence of the Silk Road, further north. Only in the eighth and ninth centuries did Chinese ships first venture into the archipelago. By the time Srivijaya appeared on the scene, a number of states – particularly in the Kelantan and Terengganu areas of the Peninsula – were sending envoys to China.

Srivijaya

The inhabitants of the western Peninsula and eastern Sumatra were quick to realize the geographical advantage afforded by the Strait of Malacca, which provided a refuge where ships could wait for several months for a change in the monsoon winds. From the fifth century onwards, a succession of **entrepôts** (storage ports) were created to cater for the needs of passing vessels. One such entrepôt eventually became the mighty empire of **Srivijaya**, eminent from the start of the seventh century until the end of the thirteenth, and encompassing all the shores and islands surrounding the Strait of Malacca. Its exact location is still a matter for debate, although most sources point to **Palembang** in southern Sumatra. Srivijaya's stable administration attracted commerce when insurrection elsewhere frightened traders away, while its wealth was boosted by extracting tolls and taxes from passing ships. Srivijaya also became an important centre for **Mahayana Buddhism** and learning. When the respected Chinese monk I Ching arrived in 671 AD, he found more than a thousand monks studying the Buddhist scriptures.

Political concepts developed during Srivijayan rule were to form the basis of Malay government in future centuries. Unquestioning **loyalty** among subjects was underpinned by the notion of *daulat*, the divine force of the ruler (called the Maharajah), which would strike down anyone guilty of *derhaka* (treason) – a powerful means of control over a deeply superstitious people.

The decision made around 1080 to shift the capital, for reasons unknown, north from Palembang to a place called **Melayu** seems to have marked the start of Srivijaya's decline. Piracy became almost uncontrollable, and even the Orang Laut, who had previously helped keep it in check, turned against the Srivijayan rulers. Soon both local and foreign traders began to seek safer ports, and the area that's now Kedah was a principal beneficiary. Other regions were soon able to compete by replicating the peaceable conditions and efficient administration that had allowed Srivijaya to thrive.

Srivijaya's fate was sealed when it attracted the eye of foreign rivals. In 1275, the Majapahit empire of Java invaded Melayu and made inroads into many of Srivijaya's peninsular territories. Sumatra and Kedah were raided by the Cholas of India, while the Thai kingdom of Ligor was able to extract **tributes** of gold from Malay vassals, a practice

Early 15th c.	15th c.	1511
Paramesevara, a Srivijayan prince, establishes a kingdom at Melaka, which soon flourishes as a Muslim sultanate	The Brunei Sultanate rises to prominence, exercising power over most of northern Borneo	The Portuguese capture Melaka

that continued until the nineteenth century. Moreover, trading restrictions in China were relaxed from the late twelfth century onwards, making it more lucrative for traders to bypass the once mighty entrepôt and go directly to the source of their desired products. Around the early fourteenth century Srivijaya's name disappears from the records.

The Melaka Sultanate

With the collapse of Srivijaya came the establishment of the **Melaka Sultanate**, the Malay Peninsula's most significant historical period. Both the *Sejarah Melayu* and the *Suma Oriental* document the tale of a Palembang prince named **Paramesvara**, who fled the collapsing empire of Srivijaya to set up his own kingdom, finally settling on the site of present-day Melaka.

As well placed as its Sumatran predecessor, with a deep, sheltered harbour and good riverine access to lucrative jungle produce, Melaka set about establishing itself as an international marketplace. The securing of a special agreement in 1405 with the new Chinese emperor, Yung-lo, guaranteed trade to Melaka and protected it from its main rivals. To further ensure its prosperity, Melaka's second ruler, Paramesvara's son **Iskandar Shah** (1414–24), took the precaution of acknowledging the neighbouring kingdoms of Ayuthaya and Majapahit as overlords. In return Melaka received vital supplies and much-needed immigrants, which bolstered the expansion of the settlement.

Port taxes and market regulations were managed by four **shahbandars** (harbour masters), each in charge of trade with certain territories. Hand in hand with the commodities trade went the exchange of ideas. By the thirteenth century, Arab merchants had begun to frequent Melaka's shores, bringing with them **Islam**, which their Muslim Indian counterparts helped to propagate among the Malays. Melaka's prestige was enhanced both by its conversion to Islam, making it part of a worldwide community with profitable trade links, and by territorial expansion which, by the reign of its last ruler **Sultan Mahmud Shah** (1488–1528), included the west coast of the Peninsula as far as Perak, Pahang, Singapore, and most of east coast Sumatra.

The legacy of **Melaka's golden age** reaches far beyond its material wealth. One significant development, the establishment of a hierarchical **court structure**, was to lay the foundations for a system of government lasting until the nineteenth century. According to Malay royal tradition, the ruler, as head of state, traced his ancestry back through Paramesvara to the maharajahs of ancient Srivijaya; in turn Paramesvara was believed to be descended from Alexander the Great. The ruler also claimed divinity, a belief strengthened by the kingdom's conversion to Islam, which held sultans to be Allah's representatives on earth. To further secure his power, always under threat from the overzealous nobility, the Melaka sultan embarked on a series of measures to emphasize his "otherness": no one but he could wear gold unless it was a royal gift, and yellow garments were forbidden among the general population.

The Melaka Sultanate also allowed the **arts** to flourish; the principal features of the courtly dances and music of this period can still be distinguished in traditional entertainments today. Much more significant, however, was the refinement of **language**, adapting the primitive Malay that had been used in the kingdom of Srivijaya into a language of the elite. Such was Melaka's prestige that all who passed through the entrepôt sought to imitate it, and by the sixteenth century, Malay was the most widely

c.1530	1641	1786
Alauddin Riayat Shah, son of the deposed Melaka sultan, establishes the Johor Sultanate	The Dutch East India Company seizes Melaka from the Portuguese	Francis Light establishes a port at Penang – the first British settlement in the Malay Peninsula

used language in the archipelago. Tellingly, the word *bahasa*, although literally meaning "language", came to signify Malay culture in general.

The Portuguese conquest of Melaka

It wasn't long before Europe set its sights on the prosperous sultanate. At the start of the sixteenth century, the **Portuguese** began to take issue with Venetian control of the Eastern market. They planned instead to establish direct contacts with the commodity brokers of the East by gaining control of crucial regional ports. The key player in the subsequent conquest of Melaka was Portuguese viceroy **Alfonso de Albuquerque**, who led the assault on the entrepôt in 1511, forcing its surrender after less than a month's siege. Aloof and somewhat effete in their high-necked ruffs and stockings, the Portuguese were not well liked, but despite the almost constant attacks from upriver Malays, they controlled Melaka for the next 130 years.

There are few physical reminders of the Portuguese in Melaka, apart from the gateway to their fort, A Famosa, and the small **Eurasian** community, descendants of intermarriage between the Portuguese and local women. The colonizers had more success with religion, however, converting large numbers of locals to **Catholicism**; their churches still dominate the city.

The Dutch in Melaka

Portuguese control over Melaka lasted for well over a century, until it was challenged by the Vereenigde Oostindische Compagnie (VOC), or **Dutch East India Company**, who were already the masters of Indonesia's valuable spice trade. Melaka was the VOC's most potent rival, and the company's bid to seize the colony succeeded in 1641 when, after a five-month siege, the Dutch flag was hoisted over Melaka.

Instead of trying, like the Portuguese, to rule from above, the Dutch cleverly wove their subjects into the fabric of government. Each racial group was represented by a *kapitan*, a respected figure from the community who mediated between his own people and the new administrators – often becoming wealthy and powerful in his own right. The Dutch were also responsible for the rebuilding of Melaka, much of which had turned to rubble during the protracted takeover of the city; many of these structures, in their distinctive Northern European style, still survive today.

By the mid-eighteenth century, conditions for Melaka's trade with China were at their peak: the relaxation of maritime restrictions in China itself had opened up the Strait for their merchants, while Europeans were eager to satisfy the growing demand for tea. The Chinese came to Melaka in droves and soon established themselves as the city's foremost entrepreneurs. Chinese settlement in the area and, in some cases, intermarriage with local Malay women, created a new cultural blend, known as **Peranakan** or Baba-Nyonya – the legacies of which are the opulent mansions and unique cuisine of Melaka, Penang and Singapore.

A number of factors prevented Dutch Melaka from fulfilling its potential, however. Since their VOC salary was hardly bountiful, Dutch administrators found it more lucrative to trade on the black market, taking backhanders from grateful merchants, a situation that severely damaged Melaka's commercial standing. High taxes forced traders to more economical locations such as the newly established British port of

1795	1819	1824
The British East India company captures Dutch possessions in Southeast Asia, including Melaka	Exploiting a succession dispute in Johor, Stamford Raffles negotiates the creation of a British settlement in Singapore	The Anglo-Dutch treaty leaves the British firmly in control of the Malay Peninsula and Singapore

THE BUGIS AND MINANGKABAU

Through the second half of the seventeenth century, a new ethnic group, the **Bugis** – renowned for their martial and commercial skills – trickled into the Peninsula, seeking refuge from the civil wars that wracked their homeland of Sulawesi (in the mid-eastern Indonesian archipelago). By the start of the eighteenth century, they were numerous enough to constitute a powerful court lobby, and in 1721 they took advantage of factional struggles to capture the kingdom of Johor, now based in Riau. Installing a Malay puppet sultan, the Bugis ruled for over sixty years, making Riau an essential port of call on the eastern trade route; they even almost succeeded in capturing Melaka in 1756. But when Riau-Johor made another bid for Melaka in 1784, the Dutch held on with renewed vigour and finally forced a treaty placing all Bugis territory in Dutch hands.

In spiritual terms, the **Minangkabau** (see box, p.267), hailing from western Sumatra, had what the Bugis lacked, being able to claim cultural affinity with ancient Srivijaya. Although this migrant group had been present in the Negeri Sembilan region since the fifteenth century, it was in the second half of the seventeenth century that they arrived in the Malay Peninsula in larger numbers. Despite professing allegiance to their Sumatran ruler, the Minangkabau were prepared to accept Malay overlordship, which in practice gave them a great deal of autonomy. Although the warrior Minangkabau were not natural allies of the Bugis or the Malays, they did occasionally join forces to defeat a common enemy. In fact, over time the distinction between various migrant groups became less obvious as intermarriage blurred clan demarcations, and Malay influence, such as the adoption of Malay titles, became more pronounced.

Penang, whose foundation in 1786 heralded the awakening of British interest in the Straits. In the end, Melaka never stood a chance: the company's attention was distracted by other centres such as Batavia (modern-day Jakarta), the VOC "capital", and by the kingdom of Johor.

Johor and Brunei

When Melaka fell to the Portuguese, the deposed sultan, Mahmud Shah, made for Bintan island in the Riau archipelago, just south of Singapore, where he established the first **court of Johor**. When, in 1526, the Portuguese attacked and razed the settlement, Mahmud fled once again, this time to Sumatra, where he died in 1528. It was left to his son, Alauddin Riayat Shah, to found a new court on the upper reaches of the Johor River, though the kingdom's capital was to shift repeatedly during a century of assaults on Johor territory by Portugal and the Sumatran Sultanate of Aceh.

The **arrival of the Dutch** in Southeast Asia marked a distinct upturn in Johor's fortunes. Hoping for protection from its local enemies, the court aligned itself firmly with the Dutch, and was instrumental in their successful siege of Portuguese Melaka. That loyalty was rewarded with trading privileges and assistance in securing a treaty with Aceh, which at last gave Johor the breathing space to develop. Johor was the supreme Malay kingdom for much of the seventeenth century, but by the 1690s its empire was fraying under the despotic rule of another Sultan Mahmud. Lacking strong leadership, Johor's Orang Laut turned to piracy, scaring off trade, while wars with the Sumatran kingdom of Jambi, one of which resulted in the total destruction of Johor's capital, weakened it still further. No longer able to tolerate his cruel regime, Mahmud's

1826	1841	1846
Singapore joined administratively with Penang and Melaka to form the Straits Settlements	With the Brunei Sultanate in decline, James Brooke is installed as the first rajah of Sarawak	Brunei cedes Labuan island to the British

nobles stabbed him to death in 1699. Not only did this change the nature of power in Malay government – previously, law deemed that the sultan could only be punished by Allah – but it also marked the end of the Melaka dynasty.

During Melaka's meteoric rise, **Brunei** had been busily establishing itself as a trading port of some renown. The Brunei Sultanate's conversion to **Islam**, no doubt precipitated by the arrival of wealthy Muslim merchants fleeing from the Portuguese in Melaka, also helped to increase its international prestige. When geographer **Antonio Pigafetta** visited Brunei with **Ferdinand Magellan**'s expedition of 1521, he found the court brimming with visitors from all over the world. This, indeed, was Brunei's "golden age", with its borders embracing land as far south as present-day Kuching in Sarawak, and as far north as the lower islands of the modern-day Philippines. Brunei's efforts, however, were soon curtailed by Spanish colonization in 1578, which, although lasting only a matter of weeks, enabled the Philippine kingdom of Sulu to gain a hold in the area – and thus put paid to Brunei's early expansionist aims.

The arrival of the British

At the end of the eighteenth century, Dutch control in Southeast Asia was more widespread than ever, and the VOC empire should have been at its height. Instead, it had somehow become **bankrupt**. Defeat in the Fourth Anglo-Dutch War (1781–83) lowered Dutch morale still further, and when the British, in the form of the **East India Company** (EIC), moved in on Melaka and the rest of the Dutch Asian domain in 1795, the VOC barely demurred; it was dissolved five years later.

Initially, the British agreed to a caretaker administration whereby they would assume sovereignty over the entrepôt to prevent it falling under French control, now that Napoleon had conquered Holland. By the time the end of the Napoleonic Wars in Europe put the Dutch in a position to retake Melaka, between 1818 and 1825, the EIC had established the stable port of **Penang** and – under the supervision of **Sir Thomas Stamford Raffles** – founded the new settlement of **Singapore**. The strategic position and free-trade policy of Singapore – backed by the impressive industrial developments of the British at home – threatened the viability of both Melaka and Penang, forcing the Dutch finally to relinquish their hold on Melaka to the British, and leaving Penang to dwindle to a backwater. In the face of such stiff competition, smaller Malay rivals inevitably linked their fortunes to the British.

The British assumption of power was sealed by the **Anglo–Dutch Treaty of 1824**, which apportioned territories between the two powers using the Strait of Malacca and the equator as the dividing lines, thereby splitting the Riau-Johor kingdom as well as putting the brakes on centuries of cultural interchange with Sumatra. This was followed in 1826 when Melaka, Penang and Singapore were unified into one administration, known as the **Straits Settlements**. Singapore replaced Penang as its capital in 1832.

Raffles had at first hoped that **Singapore** would act as a market to sell British goods to traders from all over Southeast Asia, but it soon became clear that **Chinese** merchants, the linchpin of Singapore's trade, were interested only in Malay products such as birds' nests, seaweed and camphor. But passing traders were not the only Chinese to come to the Strait. Although settlers had trickled into the Peninsula since the early days of

1851	1874	1881
Hugh Low makes the first documented ascent of Gunung Kinabalu	Perak becomes the first Malay state to take a British adviser or Resident after the signing of the Pangkor Treaty	The British North Borneo Company takes control over all of what is now Sabah

Melaka, new **plantations** of pepper and gambier (an astringent used in tanning and dyeing), and the rapidly expanding **tin mines**, attracted floods of workers eager to escape a life of poverty in China. By 1845, half of Singapore's population was Chinese, and likewise principal towns along the Peninsula's west coast (site of the world's largest tin field) and, for that matter, Kuching, became predominantly Chinese.

The Pangkor Treaty

Allowed a large degree of commercial independence by both the British and the Malay chiefs, the Chinese formed **kongsis** (clan associations) and triads (secret societies). The **Malays**, too, were hardly immune from factional conflicts, which frequently became intertwined with Chinese squabbles, causing a string of **civil conflicts**: in Penang in 1867, for example, the triads allied themselves with Malay groups in a bloody street battle that lasted several days.

Such lawlessness was detrimental to commerce, giving the British an excuse to increase their involvement in local affairs. A meeting involving the chiefs of the Perak Malays was arranged by the new Straits Governor, Andrew Clarke, on Pulau Pangkor, just off the west coast of the Peninsula. In the meantime, Rajah Abdullah, the man most likely to succeed to the Perak throne, had written to Clarke asking for his position as sultan to be guaranteed; in return, he offered the British the chance to appoint a **Resident**, a senior British civil servant whose main function would be to act as adviser to the local sultan, and who would also oversee the collecting of local taxes. On January 20, 1874, the **Pangkor Treaty** was signed, formalizing British intervention in Malay political affairs.

Perak's first Resident, J.W.W. Birch, was not sympathetic to the ways of the Malays; his centralizing tendencies were opposed by Abdullah when he became sultan. Fearful of a Malay rebellion, senior British officials announced that judicial decisions would from now on be in the hands of the British. This went against the Pangkor Treaty, and furious Malays soon found a vent for their frustration: on November 2, 1875, Birch was killed on an upriver visit. Only with the appointment of the third Resident of Perak, the respected Hugh Low, did the system start to work more smoothly.

Other states soon saw the arrival of a Resident, and agreements along the lines of the Pangkor Treaty were drawn up with Selangor, Negeri Sembilan and Pahang during the 1880s. In 1896, these three and Perak became bracketed together under the title of the **Federated Malay States**, with the increasingly important town of **Kuala Lumpur** as the capital.

British Malaya

By 1888 the name **British Malaya** had come into use – a term that reflected the intention to extend British control over the whole Peninsula. Over subsequent decades, the economic and administrative powers of the Malay sultans were eroded, while the introduction of rubber estates in the first half of the twentieth century made British Malaya one of the world's most productive colonies. The rapidity and extent of the British takeover in the Peninsula was unprecedented, aided by advances in communications.

1887	1890	1890s
Having launched Penang's *Eastern and Oriental* hotel two years earlier, the Sarkies brothers create Singapore's *Raffles*	Charles Brooke, second rajah of Sarawak, captures Limbang from Brunei, splitting the sultanate in two	Henry Ridley, director of Singapore's Botanic Gardens, works out how to tap rubber commercially

The extension of British power brought further unrest, particularly in the east coast states, where the Malays proved just as resentful of British control as in Perak. A set of skirmishes took place in Pahang in the early 1890s, when Malay chiefs protested about the reduction of their privileges. After one powerful chief, Dato' Bahaman, was stripped of his title by Pahang's Resident, Hugh Clifford, the Dato' led a small rebellion that soon became the stuff of legends. One fighter, **Mat Kilau**, earned a place in folklore as a hero who stood up to the British. From this time, Malays would interpret the uprisings as a valiant attempt to safeguard their traditions and autonomy.

By 1909, the northern Malay states of Kedah and Perlis had been brought into the colonial fold. In 1910, Johor accepted a British general-adviser; a 1914 treaty between Britain and Johor made his powers equal to those of Residents elsewhere. Terengganu, which was under Thai control, was the last state to accept a British adviser, in 1919. These four states, together with Kelantan, were sometimes collectively referred to as the **Unfederated Malay States**, though they shared no common administration.

By the outbreak of World War I, British political control was more or less complete. The Peninsula was subdivided into groups of states and regions with the seat of power split between Singapore and Kuala Lumpur.

The expansion of British interests in Borneo

The Anglo-Dutch Treaty did not include **Borneo**, where official expansion was discouraged by the EIC, which preferred to concentrate on expanding its trading contacts rather than territorial control. The benefits of Borneo did not, however, elude the sights of one British explorer, **James Brooke** (1803–68). Finding lawlessness throughout the island, Brooke persuaded the Sultan of Brunei to award him his own area – **Sarawak** – in 1841, becoming the first of a line of "**White Rajahs**" who ruled the state until World War II. Brooke quickly asserted his authority by involving formerly rebellious Malay chiefs in government, although the interior's tribes proved more of a problem. Subsequently Brooke and his successors proved adept at siphoning more land into the familial fiefdom.

Though the association between the British and James Brooke was informal (Brooke was careful not to encourage European contacts that might compromise his hold), trade between Singapore and Sarawak flourished. By the mid-nineteenth century, however, the British attitude had altered; they chose Brooke as their agent in Brunei, and found him a useful deterrent against French and Dutch aspirations towards the valuable trade routes. Eventually, in 1888, Sarawak, North Borneo (Sabah) and Brunei were transformed into **protectorates**, a status that entailed responsibility for their foreign policy being handed over to the British.

The legacy of James Brooke was furthered by his nephew **Charles Brooke** in the second half of the nineteenth century. Like his uncle, Charles ruled Sarawak in paternalistic fashion, recruiting soldiers, lowly officials and boatmen from the ranks of the tribal groups and leaving the Chinese to get on with running commercial enterprises and opening up the interior. **Vyner Brooke**, Charles's eldest son, became rajah in 1917; his reign saw no new territorial acquisitions, though there was a steady development in rubber, pepper and palm-oil production. The tribal peoples mostly continued living a traditional lifestyle in longhouses along the river, while the end of their practice of head-hunting was followed by some degree of integration among the area's varied racial groups.

1896	1917	1933
The Federated Malay States are created, encompassing the four states that have a British Resident, with Kuala Lumpur as capital	Vyner Brooke becomes the third and, as it turns out, last rajah of Sarawak	The first Malay-language feature film, *Laila Majnun*, is made in Singapore

By way of contrast, the **British North Borneo Chartered Company**'s writ in what became Sabah encountered some early obstacles. The company's plans for economic expansion involved clearing the rainforest, planting **rubber** and **tobacco** over large areas, and levying taxes on the tribes. Resistance ensued, with the most vigorous action, in 1897, led by a Bajau chief, **Mat Salleh**, whose men rampaged through the company's outstation on Pulau Gaya. Another rebellion by **Murut** tribespeople in 1915 resulted in a heavy-handed response from British forces, who killed hundreds.

By the start of the twentieth century, the majority of the lands of the once-powerful **Sultanate of Brunei** had been dismembered – the sultanate was now surrounded by Sarawak. But the sultan's fortunes had not completely disappeared and with the discovery of oil, the British thought it prudent to appoint a Resident. Exploitation of the small state's oil fields gathered pace in the 1930s following investment from British companies.

Development and ethnic rivalries

In the first quarter of the twentieth century, the British encouraged hundreds of thousands of **immigrants** from China and India to come to Peninsular Malaysia, Sarawak, North Borneo and Singapore. They arrived to work as tin miners or plantation labourers, and Malaya's population in this period doubled to four million. This bred increasing resentment among the Malays, who believed that they were being denied the economic opportunities advanced to others.

A further deterioration in Malay–Chinese relations followed the success of mainland Chinese revolutionary groups in Malaya. Malayan Chinese joined the **Malayan Communist Party** (MCP) from 1930 onwards and also formed the backbone of postwar Chinese movements that demanded an end to British rule and what they perceived as special privileges extended to the Malays. At the same time, Malay nationalism was gathering its own head of steam. The **Singapore Malay Union**, which held its first conference in 1939, advocated a Malay supremacist line. A year earlier, the first All-Malaya Malays Conference, organized by the Selangor Malays Association, had been held in KL.

The Japanese occupation

Landing in Kelantan in December 1941, Japanese forces took barely two months to sweep down the Peninsula and reach Singapore. The **surrender** of the British forces there in February 1942 ushered in a Japanese regime that brutalized the Chinese, largely because of Japan's history of conflict with China; at least 25,000 people were tortured and killed in the two weeks immediately after the surrender of the island by the British military command. Allied POWs were rounded up into prison camps; many of the troops were subsequently sent to build the infamous "Death Railway" in Burma.

In **Malaya**, towns and buildings were destroyed as the Allies attempted to bomb strategic targets. But with the Japanese firmly in control, the occupiers ingratiated themselves with some of the Malay elite by suggesting that after the war the country would be given independence. Predictably, it was the Chinese activists in the MCP, more than the Malays, who organized resistance during wartime.

December 1941 also saw the Japanese invade **Sarawak**, beginning with the capture of the Miri oil field. Although the Japanese never penetrated the interior, they quickly

Dec 1941	Feb 1942	September 1945	1946
Japan lands forces in Kelantan and captures Miri in Sarawak	Singapore falls to the Japanese	Japanese forces in Southeast Asia formally surrender in Singapore	Britain introduces the Malayan Union, turning Malaya into a full colony rather than a protectorate

established control over the populated towns along the coast. The Chinese in Miri, Sibu and Kuching were the main targets: the Japanese put down rebellions brutally, and there was no organized guerrilla activity until late in the occupation. What resistance there was arose from "Z Force", namely Major **Tom Harrisson** and a team of British and Australian commandos, who in 1945 parachuted into the remote Kelabit Highlands to build a resistance movement.

In **North Borneo**, the Japanese invaded Pulau Labuan on New Year's Day, 1942. Over the next three years the main suburban areas were bombed by the Allies, destroying most of Jesselton (modern-day KK) and Sandakan. Captured troops and civilians suffered enormously – the worst single outrage being the "Death March" in September 1944, when 2400 POWs were forced to walk from Sandakan to Ranau (see p.428).

In September 1945, just prior to a planned Allied invasion to retake Singapore, the **Japanese surrendered** following the dropping of atom bombs on Nagasaki and Hiroshima. The surrender led to a power vacuum in the region, with the British initially having to work with the MCP's armed wing, the **Malayan People's Anti-Japanese Army** (MPAJA), to maintain order in many areas. Violence occurred between the MPAJA and Malays, particularly against those accused of collaborating with the Japanese.

Postwar upheaval

Immediately after the war, the British introduced the **Malayan Union**, in effect turning the Malay States from a protectorate into a colony and removing the sovereignty of the sultans. Another effect was to give the Chinese and Indian inhabitants citizenship and equal rights with the Malays. This quickly aroused opposition from the Malays, the nationalists among whom formed the **United Malays National Organization** (UMNO) in 1946. Its main tenet was that Malays should retain special privileges, largely because they were the first inhabitants, and that the uniquely powerful position of the sultans should not be tampered with.

UMNO's resistance led to the Malayan Union idea being replaced by the **Federation of Malaya**. Established in 1948, this upheld the sultans' power and privileges and brought all the Peninsula's territories together under one government, apart from Chinese-dominated Singapore, whose inclusion would have led to the Malays being in a minority overall. Protests erupted in Singapore at its exclusion, with the **Malayan Democratic Union** (MDU), a multiracial party, calling for integration with Malaya – a position that commanded little support among the Chinese population.

After the Japanese surrender in **Borneo**, the Colonial Office in London made Sarawak and North Borneo **Crown Colonies**, with Vyner Brooke offering no objection. Sarawakians were torn over the change in arrangements, however: while the ruling assembly, the Council Negeri (composed of Malays, Chinese, Iban and British), had voted to transfer power to Britain, some Malays and prominent Iban in Kuching opposed the move. Protests reached a peak with the assassination in Sibu in 1949 of the senior official in the new administration, Governor Duncan Stewart. But on the whole, resentment at the passing of the Brooke era was short-lived as the economy expanded and infrastructure improved. Britain also signed a Treaty of Protection with the Sultan of Brunei, who remained the chief power in the state while Sarawak's high commissioner took on the purely decorative role of governor of Brunei.

1946	1946	1948
Despite local protests, Vyner Brooke cedes Sarawak to the British government, bringing the White Rajahs' dynasty to an end	The British North Borneo Company cedes Sabah to the British government	Malay opposition to the Malayan Union leads to its replacement by the Federation of Malaya, which respects the status of the sultans

The Emergency

Many Chinese in the Peninsula were angered when the country changed status from a colony to a federation, effectively making them second-class citizens. According to the new laws, non-Malays could only qualify as citizens if they had lived in the country for fifteen out of the last twenty-five years, and they also had to prove they spoke Malay or English.

Following the communist takeover in China in 1949, most Malayan Chinese ceased to look to China; the more political among them founded a new political party, the **Malayan Chinese Association** (MCA). Some local Chinese, however, identified with the MCP, which under its new leader, **Chin Peng**, declared its intention of setting up a Malayan republic. Peng fused the MCP with the remains of the MPAJA, and, using arms supplies that the latter had dumped in the forests, from June 1948 he launched sporadic attacks on rubber estates, killing planters and employees as well as spreading fear among rural communities. This civil conflict, which lasted until 1960, was euphemistically called **the Emergency** for insurance purposes; planters would have had their policies cancelled if war had been officially declared. At its peak, around ten thousand of Chin Peng's guerrillas were hiding out in jungle camps, using a support network of Chinese-dominated towns and villages in the interior. In many cases inhabitants were cowed into submission by means of public executions, though many poor rural workers identified with the insurgents' struggle.

Although the Emergency was never fully felt in the main urban areas, British rubber-estate owners would arrive at the *Coliseum Hotel* in KL with harrowing stories of how "communist terrorists" had hacked off the arms of rural Chinese workers who refused to support the cause, and of armed attacks on plantations.

The British were slow to respond to the threat, but once Lieutenant-General Sir Harold Briggs was put in command of police and army forces, Malaya was on a war footing. Briggs' most controversial policy was the **resettlement** of 400,000 rural

THE EMERGENCY AND THE ORANG ASLI

The impact of the Emergency on the **Orang Asli** of the interior was dramatic. All but the most remote tribes were subject to intimidation and brutality, from guerrillas on one side and government forces on the other. In effect, the Orang Asli's centuries-old invisibility had ended; the population of Malaysia was now aware of their presence, and the government of their strategic importance.

The Orang Asli had no choice but to grow food and act as porters for the guerrillas, as well as – most important of all – provide intelligence, warning them of the approach of the enemy. In response, the government implemented a disastrous policy of removing thousands of Orang Asli from the jungle and relocating them in new model villages in the interior, which were no more than dressed-up prison camps. Hundreds died in captivity before the government dismantled these settlements. By then, not surprisingly, active support for the insurgents among the Orang Asli had risen – though allegiances switched to the security forces when it became clear the guerrillas were heading for defeat. Government attempts to control the Orang Asli during the Emergency turned out to be the precursor to initiatives that persist to the present day, drawing the Orang Asli away from their traditional lifestyle and into the embrace of the Malaysian nation-state.

1948	August 1957	1959
The Malayan Community Party launches an insurgency from the jungle, which comes to be called The Emergency	The Federation of Malaya – the Malay Peninsula, minus Singapore – gains independence	Singapore gains full self-government under Lee Kuan Yew, while remaining a British colony

Chinese – mostly squatters who had moved to the jungle fringes to avoid the Japanese during the war – as well as thousands of Orang Asli. Although these forced migrations were successful in breaking down many of the guerrillas' supply networks, they alienated many Chinese and Orang Asli who had previously been sympathetic to the British.

The violence peaked in 1950 with ambushes and attacks near Ipoh, Kuala Kangsar, Kuala Lipis and Raub. The most notorious incident occurred in 1951 on the road to Fraser's Hill, when the British high commissioner to Malaya, **Sir Henry Gurney**, was assassinated. Under his replacement, Sir Gerald Templer, a new policy was introduced to win hearts and minds. "White Areas", perceived as free of guerrilla activity, were established; communities in these regions had food restrictions and curfews lifted, a policy that began to dissipate guerrilla activity over the next three years. The leaders were offered an amnesty in 1956, which was refused, and Chin Peng and most of the remaining cell members fled over the border to Thailand where they received sanctuary.

Towards independence

The Emergency had the effect of speeding up political change prior to independence. UMNO stuck to its "Malays first" policy, though its president, **Tuanku Abdul Rahman** (also the chief minister of Malaya), won the 1955 election by cooperating with the MCA and the Malayan Indian Association. The resulting bloc, the **UMNO Alliance**, swept into power under the rallying cry of **Merdeka** (Freedom). The hope was that ethnic divisions would no longer be a major factor if **independence** was granted.

With British backing, *merdeka* was proclaimed on August 31, 1957 in a ceremony in Kuala Lumpur's padang – promptly renamed Merdeka Square. The British high commissioner signed a treaty that decreed that the **Federation of Malaya** was now independent of the Crown, with Tuanku Abdul Rahman the first prime minister. The new **constitution** allowed for the nine Malay sultans to alternate as king, and established a two-tier **parliament**, comprising a house of elected representatives and a senate with delegates from each state. Under Rahman, the country was fully committed to economic expansion, with foreign investment actively encouraged – a stance that has survived to the present.

Similarly, in **Singapore** the process of gaining independence acquired momentum throughout the 1950s. In 1957, the British gave the go-ahead for the setting up of an elected 51-member assembly, and full **self-government** was attained in 1959, when the People's Action Party (PAP) under **Lee Kuan Yew** won most of the seats. Lee immediately entered into talks with Tuanku Abdul Rahman over the notion that Singapore and Malaya should be joined administratively. Tunku initially agreed, although he feared the influence of the far left in the PAP.

In 1961, Tuanku Abdul Rahman proposed that Sarawak and North Borneo should join Malaya and Singapore in an enlarged federation. Many in Borneo would have preferred the idea of a separate Borneo Federation, although the Konfrontasi (see opposite) was to make clear how vulnerable such a federation would be to attack from Indonesia. Rahman's suggestion was, however, not fuelled by security concerns but by **demographics**: if Singapore were to join the federation, the country would acquire a Chinese majority. This made the two Borneo colonies useful as a counterweight to Singapore's Chinese.

1962	September 1963	August 1965
President Sukarno of Indonesia uses military incursions – the Konfrontasi – to agitate against Sabah and Sarawak joining Malaya	The Federation of Malaya becomes the Federation of Malaysia, augmented by Singapore, Sarawak and Sabah; Brunei opts out	Singapore leaves the Federation and goes it alone as an independent country

Although Abdul Rahman had wanted **Brunei** to join the Malaysian Federation, Sultan Omar refused when he realized Rahman's price – a substantial proportion of Brunei's oil and gas revenues. Brunei remained under nominal British jurisdiction until its **independence** on January 1, 1984.

Federation and the Konfrontasi

In September 1963, North Borneo (quickly renamed Sabah), Sarawak and Singapore joined Malaya in the **Federation of Malaysia** – "Malaysia" being a term coined by the British in the 1950s when the notion of a Greater Malaya had been propounded. Both Indonesia, which laid claim to Sarawak, and the Philippines, which claimed jurisdiction over Sabah as it had originally been part of the Sulu Sultanate, reacted angrily. Border skirmishes with Indonesia known as the **Konfrontasi** ensued, and a wider war was only just averted when Indonesian President Sukarno backed down from taking on British and Gurkha troops brought in to bolster Sarawak's small armed forces.

Within the federation, further differences surfaced in Singapore during this period between Lee Kuan Yew and the Malay-dominated Alliance over the lack of egalitarian policies; many Chinese were concerned that UMNO's overall influence in the federation was too great. Tensions rose on the island and racial incidents developed into full-scale **riots** in 1964, in which several people were killed.

These developments were viewed with great concern by Tuanku Abdul Rahman in Kuala Lumpur, and when the PAP subsequently attempted to enter Peninsular politics, he decided it would be best if Singapore left the federation. This was emphatically not in Singapore's best interests, since it was an island without any obvious natural resources; Lee cried on TV when the expulsion was announced and Singapore acquired full **independence** on August 9, 1965. The severing of the bond between Malaysia and Singapore has led to a kind of sibling rivalry between the two nations ever since.

Racial issues and riots

Singapore's exit from the Malaysian Federation was not enough to quell ethnic tensions. Resentment grew among the Malaysian Chinese over the principle that Malay be the main language taught in schools and over the privileged employment opportunities offered to Malays. After the Alliance lost ground in elections in May 1969, Malays in major cities reacted angrily to a perceived increase in power of the Chinese, who had commemorated their breakthrough with festivities in the streets. Hundreds of people, mostly Chinese, were killed and injured in the **riots** that followed; KL in particular became a war zone with large crowds of youths on the rampage. Rahman kept the country under a state of emergency for nearly two years, during which the draconian **Internal Security Act** (ISA) was used to arrest and imprison activists, as well as many writers and artists, setting a sombre precedent for authoritarian practices still followed today.

Abdul Rahman never recovered full political command and resigned in 1970. That September, the new prime minister, **Tun Abdul Razak Hussein**, initiated a form of state-orchestrated positive discrimination called the **New Economic Policy** (NEP),

May 1969	1971	1981
Deadly race riots scar Kuala Lumpur	The Malaysian government introduces its New Economic Policy, including positive discrimination in favour of Malays	Mahathir Mohamad, to become Malaysia's long-serving prime minister, takes office

THE BUMIPUTRA POLICY

Provisions in the New Economic Policy (NEP), introduced in the wake of the 1969 race riots, became known as the **bumiputra policy** as they were intended to provide a more level economic playing field for Malays, Orang Asli and the indigenous peoples of east Malaysia (*bumiputra* means something like "sons of the soil" in Malay). In terms of wealth, these communities (as well the Indians) were lagging far behind the Chinese. This was partly the result of colonial policy: the immigrant Chinese made strides as businesspeople in the towns, while the Malays were either employed as administrators or left to get on with farming and fishing in rural areas, while the Indians toiled on the railways and the plantations.

The policy has been moderated, renamed and rejigged over the years, but basically awards *bumiputras*, in particular the Malays, privileges such as subsidized housing and easier access to higher education and civil-service jobs. The *bumiputra* policy has undoubtedly achieved a reasonable degree of **wealth redistribution**, though a less laudable consequence has been the creation of a super-rich Malay elite. What's more, the policy is deeply resented by the non-beneficiaries. The Indians are especially aggrieved, having never been wealthy; the Chinese have continued to rely on their own devices in business while shunning the public sector, where they feel the odds have been stacked against them.

Despite the policy's undoubted popularity among Malays, Mahathir and his successors have questioned the wisdom of allowing the system to continue indefinitely, fearing that it has fostered complacency in the very communities it is meant to help. The difficulty for all UMNO leaders is that any meaningful retreat from the policy requires political daring. Only the opposition, which generally wants to reform Malaysian politics in a nonracial mould, has attempted to make progress in this regard, though it is just as risky an enterprise for them.

which gives ethnic Malays and members of Borneo's tribes favoured positions in business and other professions. Also under Razak, a crucial step was taken towards Malaysia's current political map with the formation in 1974 of the **Barisan Nasional** ("National Front", usually abbreviated to **BN**), comprising UMNO plus the main Chinese and Indian parties and – since the 1990s – parties representing indigenous groups in Sabah and Sarawak. This multiethnic coalition has governed the country ever since.

The Mahathir era

The dominant figure in Malaysian politics since independence has been **Dr Mahathir Mohamad**, prime minister from 1981 until 2003. Even Malaysians not generally favourably disposed towards the BN credit him with helping the country attain economic lift-off; under Mahathir, industrialization changed the landscape of regions like the Klang Valley and Johor, manufacturing output eclipsed agriculture in importance, and huge **prestige projects** like the Petronas Towers and KLIA were completed. Mahathir meanwhile kept his supporters happy with a raft of populist pronouncements, including railing against the West for criticizing Malaysia's human-rights record (he claimed that by what he termed "Asian values", prosperity was valued more highly than civil liberties). Less well remembered is the fact that Mahathir's tenure also saw the extensive use of the ISA in what became known as **Operation Lalang** when, in 1987, more than a hundred politicians and activists were

1984	1987	1997	1998
Brunei becomes independent	The Malaysia government launches Operation Lalang, a major crackdown against its critics and sectors of the press	The Asian economic crisis envelopes the region	Anwar Ibrahim, Malaysia's deputy prime minister and finance minister, is sacked by Mahathir and subsequently convicted of corruption and sodomy

detained following tensions between UMNO and Chinese political parties over matters to do with Chinese-language education. These arrests were bad enough, but more durable in its effects was state action to curb press freedom. Especially notable was the government's closure of the pro-MCA English-language *Star* newspaper for several months; when it reopened, many of its senior managers had been replaced.

In 1997, the economy suffered a major setback when Malaysia was sucked into the **Asian economic crisis**, which began in Thailand and Korea. Mahathir took personal charge of getting the economy back on track, sacking his deputy and finance minister **Anwar Ibrahim** in 1998. A former student leader and once an espouser of progressive Islamic policies, Anwar had enjoyed a meteoric rise upon joining UMNO and had been groomed to succeed Mahathir, though relations between the two subsequently soured. The nation was stunned when, within a week of his dismissal, Anwar was arrested on corruption and sexual misconduct charges; a succession of mass demonstrations in his support ensued. Anwar's treatment in detention became the subject of much concern when he appeared in court on the corruption charge sporting a black eye. He was eventually found guilty – leading many observers to question the independence of the judiciary – and sentenced to six years in jail. In 2000, he was also found guilty of sodomizing his driver and sentenced to nine years in prison.

Meanwhile, Anwar's wife, Wan Azizah Wan Ismail, formed a new party, **Keadilan** ("Justice", sometimes also called **PKR**), which has contested subsequent elections in alliance with other opposition parties, including the Chinese-dominated Democratic Action Party (**DAP**) and the Islamist **PAS**.

Malaysia under Abdullah Badawi

Momentously, in 2003, Mahathir resigned and handed power to Anwar's replacement as deputy prime minister, **Abdullah Badawi**. Hailing from Penang, Abdullah (often referred to as Pak Lah) is a genial man, in marked contrast to his abrasive predecessor, and he asserted himself effectively, winning a landslide general election victory in 2004. Soon after, Anwar's sodomy conviction was overturned and he was released, though he remained barred from standing for parliament until 2008 as his corruption conviction was not quashed.

As a relatively new broom, Abdullah enjoyed much goodwill early on; it was hoped he would make good on his promises to sweep cronyism and corruption out of Malaysian politics. But as time wore on, authority seemed to ebb away from his government in the face of crises and scandals.

The most sensational of these was the affair of **Altantuya Shaariibuu**, a Mongolian woman who went missing in the KL area in 2006. Her remains, which had been blown to bits with explosives, were soon discovered, and it transpired that she was an associate of a defence analyst with links to **Najib Tun Razak**, Abdullah's deputy. The case created a stink around the government, and two policemen, members of an elite unit protecting politicians and other senior authority figures, were subsequently sentenced to death for her murder. the bottom of the economic pile.

2003	2004	2004
Abdullah Badawi succeeds Mahathir as Malaysian prime minister	Anwar Ibrahim is freed from jail but only his sodomy conviction is overturned	Lee Hsien Loong, Lee Kuan Yew's son, becomes prime minister of Singapore

The 2008 elections

In February 2008, Abdullah called a **snap general election** for the following month – when Anwar Ibrahim was still barred from standing. If the timing was maximally convenient for Abdullah, the result was anything but: the BN was duly returned to power, but on its **worst showing** since its formation in 1974. This time, the BN failed to win more than two-thirds of seats in parliament, which had hitherto afforded it the right to tinker with the constitution. To make matters worse, the opposition alliance unseated the BN in an unprecedented number of **state assemblies**, not just in largely Malay Kedah, where voters had previously flirted with PAS, but also in cosmopolitan, prosperous Selangor, Penang and Perak.

In the wake of the election, amid euphoria and recrimination, everything in Malaysian politics seemed to be up for grabs. Perhaps the worst news for Abdullah was how badly the BN fared in the Peninsula, home to three-quarters of the population: its majority there was wafer-thin, and it took just one out of eleven seats in KL. Only victories by the BN-allied parties of Sabah and Sarawak had secured the coalition a working majority.

Testing times

Unfortunately for Abdullah, things got no better for the BN in the aftermath of the polls, as the various affairs that had come to light beforehand played themselves out like a tragicomic drama. Against this turbulent backdrop, **Anwar Ibrahim** made a triumphant return to parliament in August 2008, his wife resigning her seat so that he could stand in a by-election. Just prior to all this, however, Anwar was sensationally arrested once again on a charge of sodomy, this time involving a young aide of his. Allowed bail, Anwar took up his new role as leader of the opposition coalition, **Pakatan Rakyat**, while having to make appearances in court. Then in 2009 Abdullah Badawi stepped down, to be replaced by his deputy **Najib Tun Razak**.

In 2012, Anwar was cleared of the second sodomy charge, freeing him to play a frontline role in the impending polls, which took place in May 2013. It proved to be another watershed election, though not quite as the opposition would have liked. For the first time, the combined opposition parties won more than half the popular vote, but the first-past-the-post voting system meant the BN achieved a workable majority in the federal parliament, as well as recapturing the state assemblies in Kedah and Perak. The opposition's next significant move was an attempt to shoehorn Anwar into the chief minister's job in **Selangor**, the most developed state in the Federation and their one true showcase. But that was thwarted when, in March 2014, his acquittal on the second sodomy charge was overturned on a government appeal. In February 2015, the Federal Court – the highest in the land – upheld the government's appeal, and Anwar was sent to prison once again at the age of 67. Under the electoral rules, he was thus removed from front-line politics for an extended period, even though he is likely to be released in mid-2018.

It seems clear that Malaysia is entering ever more uncertain waters. On the one hand, the country remains a working example of a multiethnic, multicultural state. On the other, it is also a collection of little powder kegs, any one of which could spark a conflagration at any time. Scarcely a year seems to go by without some new corruption

Dec 2004	April 2009	May 2013
Penang and Kedah in Malaysia are struck by the Indian Ocean tsunami, though with only modest loss of life	Najib Tun Razak becomes Malaysian prime minister	The Malaysian opposition wins the popular vote in the general election, although the BN coalition remains in power

scandal involving politicians or officials who eventually get off scot-free, and none has been as shocking as the **1MDB affair**, which erupted in 2015 with allegations that prime minister Najib had somehow received billions of ringgit siphoned from 1MDB, a state-owned investment company. The ramifications are wide-ranging, with international criminal investigations ongoing into potential money-laundering, though no one had been called to account at the time of writing. In the US, Najib's stepson has been under scrutiny over whether he used any 1MDB money to fund his film production company, and in 2016 the Department of Justice launched legal proceedings to try to recover some US$1 billion in misappropriated 1MDB funds. Domestically, Malaysia's attorney general was investigating the matter when he was replaced; months later, that replacement gave Najib a clean bill of health, raising eyebrows. There was more scepticism when the head of Malaysian's Anti-Corruption Commission chose to step down early and was replaced with an official who had previously worked for the new attorney general.

Malaysia's official news agency has reported that Saudi donors provided the billions in Najib's bank accounts, an "explanation" that, if true, raises grave questions as to why a politician is in receipt of massive backdoor donations from foreigners. Whatever the eventual fallout of 1MDB, Najib, with his patrician roots – his father was Tun Abdul Razak, Malaysia's second prime minister – has proven an ineffectual, bland leader. Gone are the well-meaning but ultimately fruitless reformist noises of the Abdullah Badawi era. Although Najib has repealed much-hated legislation which provided for detention without trial, he has also done an about-face on a promise to do away with the Sedition Act. This could in principle be used to imprison anyone questioning the country's ethnic or religious policies – though the suspicion is that it will never be used against the Malay Right, and is only being kept on as a thinly veiled threat against non-Malay secularists and intellectuals.

But the **opposition** looks unlikely to capitalize on Najib's weakness, appearing ever more like a marriage of convenience between parties with some sharply contrasting views. So while the rural BN coalition is vulnerable in the Peninsula, it continues to be sustained by rural voters in East Malaysia. Ironically, partly because of the 1MDB affair, Mahathir has now joined the opposition's ranks in a new Malay party, **Pribumi Bersatu**, meaning he is now on the same side as the deputy he fell out with, Anwar.

If Malaysia is sleepwalking towards crisis or stagnation, at least Malaysian democracy is enjoying a small renaissance. The press is less cowed now about reporting the policies of opposition politicians, and civil rights organizations are campaigning ever more vocally, as borne out by several massive **Bersih** (Malay for "clean") demonstrations in KL in recent years, calling for an end to corruption and electoral fraud. Thorny issues around race and religion, long swept under the carpet in the name of economic progress, are being debated with some rancour but also more purposefully, which could ultimately lead to the country taking a more enlightened path.

2014	June 2015	August 2015
Two disasters hit Malaysia Airlines with flight MH370 vanishing and flight MH17 destroyed by a missile	An unprecedented earthquake centred near Mount Kinabalu kills several climbers and guides	Golden jubilee of Singapore independence, months after the death of Lee Kuan Yew

Religion

Islam is a significant force in Malaysia, given that virtually all Malays, who comprise just over half the population, are Muslim; in Singapore, where three-quarters of the population are Chinese, Buddhism is the main religion. There's a smaller, but no less significant, Hindu Indian presence in both countries, while the other chief belief system is animism, adhered to by many of the indigenous peoples of Malaysia. While the colonial period drew Christian missionaries to the region, the British, in a bid to avoid unrest among the Malays, were restrained in their evangelical efforts. Christian missionaries had more success in Borneo than on the Peninsula; indeed, the main tribal group in Sabah, the Kadazan/Dusun, is Christian, as are many or most Kelabit and Iban in Sarawak. That said, Christianity is a significant minority religion in Peninsular Malaysia and Singapore, with a notable following among middle-class Chinese and Indians.

One striking feature of religion here is that it can be a **syncretic** blend of beliefs and influences. In a region where fusion is visible in everything from food to language, it's not hard to come across individuals who profess one faith, yet pray or make offerings to deities of another, in the warm-hearted belief that all religions contain some truth and that it therefore makes sense not to put all your spiritual eggs in one devotional basket.

Animism

Although many of Malaysia's indigenous groups are now nominally Christian or Muslim, many of their old animist beliefs and rites still survive. In the animist world-view, everything in nature – mountains, trees, rocks and lakes – has a controlling soul or spirit (**semangat** in Malay) that has to be mollified. For the Orang Asli groups in the interior of the Peninsula, remaining animist beliefs often centre on healing and funeral ceremonies. A sick person, particularly a child, is believed to be invaded by a bad spirit, and drums are played and incantations performed to persuade the spirit to depart. The death of a member of the family is followed by a complex process of burial and reburial – a procedure that, it is hoped, ensures an easy passage for the person's spirit.

In Sarawak, **birds**, especially the **hornbill**, are of particular significance to the Iban and Kelabit peoples. Many Kelabit depend upon the arrival of migrating flocks to decide when to plant their rice crop, while Iban augury interprets sightings of the hornbill and other birds as good or bad omens. In some accounts of Iban beliefs, two bird spirits are involved in the creation of the Earth and sky, and the Iban themselves are descended from a bird spirit named Sengalang Burong.

Hinduism

Hinduism arrived in Malaysia long before Islam, brought by Indian traders more than a thousand years ago. While almost all of Malaysia's ancient Hindu past has been obliterated, elements live on in the popular arts like *wayang kulit* (shadow plays), the plots of which are drawn from the sacred *Ramayana*.

The central tenet of Hinduism is the belief that life is a series of rebirths and reincarnations that eventually lead to spiritual release. A whole variety of deities are worshipped, which on the surface makes Hinduism appear complex; however, a loose understanding of the *Vedas* – the religion's holy books – is enough for the characters and roles of the main gods to become apparent. The deities you'll come across most often are the three manifestations of the faith's supreme divine being: **Brahma** the creator, **Vishnu** the preserver and **Shiva** the destroyer.

Hinduism returned to the Peninsula in the late nineteenth century when immigrants from southern India arrived to work on the Malayan rubber and oil-palm plantations. The Hindu celebration of Rama's victory – the central theme of the *Ramayana* – in time became the national holiday of **Deepavali** (or Diwali; the festival of lights), while another Hindu festival, **Thaipusam**, when Lord Subramaniam and elephant-headed Ganesh, the sons of Shiva, are worshipped, is marked by some of the region's most prominent religious gatherings.

Step over the threshold of a **Hindu temple** in Malaysia or Singapore and you enter a kaleidoscope world of gods and fanciful creatures. The style is typically Dravidian (South Indian), as befits the largely Tamil population, with a soaring **gopura**, or entrance tower, teeming with sculptures and a central courtyard leading to an inner sanctum housing the presiding deity. In the temple precinct, you'll invariably witness incense being burned, the application of sandalwood paste to the forehead, and *puja* (ritualistic acts of worship).

Islam

Islam gained its first firm foothold in the Malay Peninsula with the conversion of Paramesvara, the ruler of **Melaka**, in the early fifteenth century. The commercial success of Melaka accelerated the spread of Islam; one after another the powerful Malay court rulers took to the religion, adopting the Arabic title "sultan", either because of sincere conversion or because they took a shrewd view of the advantages to be gained by embracing this international faith. On a cultural level, too, Islam had its attractions – its concepts of equality before Allah freed people from the Hindu caste system that had dominated parts of the region. Even after the Melaka Sultanate fell in 1511, the hold of Islam was strengthened by the migration of Muslim merchants to Brunei.

The first wave of Islamic missionaries were mostly **Sufis**, representing the mystical and generally more liberal wing of Islam. In the region Sufism absorbed some animist and Hindu beliefs, including the tradition of pluralist deity worship. However, Sufism's influence declined in the early nineteenth century when the puritanical **Wahhabi** sect of mainstream **Sunni** Islam captured Mecca. The return to the Koran's basic teachings became identified with a more militant approach, leading to jihads in Kedah, Kelantan and Terengganu against the Malay rulers' Siamese overlords and, subsequently, the British.

Islam in Malaysia and Singapore today is a mixture of Sunni and Sufi elements, and its adherents are still largely comprised of Malays, though a minority of the Indian community is Muslim, too. While Islam as practised locally is relatively liberal, the trend away from tacit secularism that has swept the Muslim world in the last two or three decades, has not left the two countries untouched. There's now a better understanding of Islam's tenets – and thus better compliance with them – among Muslims in both countries.

Of course, this drift has its social and political dimensions. In Malaysia, with its history of sometimes awkward race relations, Islam is something of a badge of identity for the Malays; it's significant that the Malaysian **constitution** practically regards being Malay as equivalent to being Muslim. Thus Malaysia has seen an increase in religious programming on TV and in state spending on often ostentatious new mosques, while even in consumerist Singapore, the Malay minority is becoming more actively engaged in religion. Malaysia's religious establishment has also become more vocal, making proclamations to discourage Muslims from practising yoga (because of its supposed Hindu origins) and Muslim women from wearing short hair and trousers (because this would apparently encourage lesbianism). In 2017, there were also instances of Muslim-owned launderettes displaying signs barring non-Muslims from using the facilities; the government, seemingly afraid of confronting part of its support base, merely noted that it disapproved of segregation, and it took intervention from Malaysia's sultans – who normally avoid getting embroiled in politics – to force them to back down, at least for now.

Islam and the law

One striking way in which Islam influences day-to-day affairs is that in certain areas, Muslim and non-Muslim citizens are subject to different **laws**. In Malaysia, for example, while it would be acceptable for an unmarried couple to share a hotel room if neither person is Muslim, it would be illegal (an act known as **khalwat**) if both were Muslim; if only one of them were Muslim, only that person would be committing an illegal act. This legal divide is reflected in the judicial systems of both Malaysia and Singapore, in which **syariah** (sharia) courts interpreting Islamic law exist alongside courts and laws derived from the British legal system.

Both Malaysia and Singapore limit Islamic jurisprudence to matters concerning the family and certain types of behaviour deemed transgressions against Islam, such as *khalwat*, or for a Muslim to consume alcohol in public. In this regard, the *syariah* courts are in many ways subservient to the secular legal framework. This also means the harsher aspects of Islamic justice, such as stoning or the cutting off of a thief's hand, are not deemed permissible; an attempt in the 1990s by the state government of Kelantan, run by the Islamist opposition PAS party, to introduce them within the state was thwarted by Malaysia's federal government. The Islamic standard of proof in a case concerning rape – requiring the victim to be able to produce four witnesses – also does not apply, since rape cases are tried within the secular system.

However, the two juridical systems are experiencing a sort of territorial dispute in the important area of **religious conversion**. It's very difficult for Malaysian Muslims to convert out of Islam as the secular courts are unwilling to uphold their choice without the involvement of the *syariah* court, which might refuse permission or, worse, wish to punish them as apostates. In this Catch-22 situation, any Muslims who take up a new faith or no faith at all can never make their choice official, and for the most part simply keep mum. Controversy has also arisen when one person in a marriage converts to Islam and then wants to use Islamic law to divorce the spouse or change the registered religion of their children, for example. The roles of the two legal systems in these situations ought to be clarified as a matter of urgency, but there has been little progress.

THE BOMOH

An important link between animism and the Islam of today is provided by the Malay **bomoh**, a kind of shaman. While *bomoh*s keep a low profile in these times of greater Islamic orthodoxy – no *bomoh* operates out of an office, and there are no college courses to train *bomoh*s or listings of practitioners in the telephone directory – the fact is that every Malay community can still summon a *bomoh* when it's felt one is needed to cure disease, bring rain during droughts, exorcize spirits from a newly cleared plot before building work starts, or rein in the behaviour of a wayward spouse. A central part of the *bomoh*'s trade is recitation, often of sections of the Koran, while – like his Orang Asli counterparts – he uses techniques such as burning herbs to cure or ease pain and disease.

Mosques

In Malaysia, every town, village and hamlet has its mosque, while the capital city of each state hosts a grandiose **Masjid Negeri** (state mosque). You'll rarely see contemporary mosques varying from the standard square building topped by onion domes and minarets, though the oldest mosques reveal unusual Sumatran or other Southeast Asian influences. Two additional standard features can be found inside the prayer hall, namely the **mihrab**, a niche indicating the direction of Mecca, towards which believers face during prayers (the green *kiblat* arrow on the ceiling of most Malaysian hotel rooms fulfils the same function), and the **mimbar** (pulpit), used by the imam.

One of the five **pillars of Islam** is that the faithful should pray five times a day – at dawn (called the *subuh* prayer in Malay), midday (*zuhur*, or *jumaat* on a Friday), mid-afternoon (*asar*), dusk (*maghrib*) and mid-evening (*isyak*). On **Friday**, the day of the communal *jumaat* prayer, Muslims converge on their nearest mosque around noon to hear the imam deliver a *khutbah* (sermon); all employers allow Muslim staff a three-hour break for the purpose.

Chinese beliefs

The three different strands in Chinese belief ostensibly point in very different directions. **Confucianism** is a philosophy based on piety, loyalty, humanitarianism and familial devotion, a set of principles that permeate every aspect of Chinese life; **Buddhism** is a religion primarily concerned with the attainment of a state of personal enlightenment, nirvana; and **Taoism** propounds unity with nature as its chief tenet.

The Chinese are seldom doctrinaire; someone who claims to be Buddhist, Taoist or Confucianist may be in practice be a mixture of all three. **Ancestor worship** is also common, as is devotion to folk deities such as **Tua Peh** (or **Pek**) **Kong**, sometimes described as the God of Prosperity.

Chinese temples

The rules of **feng shui** are rigorously applied to the construction of Chinese temples, so that each building has a layout and orientation rendering it free from evil influences. Visitors wishing to cross the threshold of a temple have to step over a kerb intended to trip up evil spirits, and walk through doors flanked by fearsome door gods; fronting the doors may be two stone lions, providing yet another defence.

Temples are normally constructed around a framework of huge, lacquered timber beams, adorned with intricately carved warriors, animals and flowers. More figures are moulded onto outer walls, which are dotted with octagonal, hexagonal or round grille-worked windows. Larger temples typically consist of a front entrance hall opening onto a walled-in courtyard, beyond which is the hall of worship, where joss sticks are burned below images of the deities. The most striking element of a Chinese temple is often its **roof** – a grand, multitiered affair with low, overhanging eaves, the ridges alive with dragons, phoenixes and folkloric characters in scenes often assembled using multicoloured pottery shards, an artistic technique known as *jiannian*. In the temple grounds you'll see sizeable ovens, stuffed constantly with paper money, prayer books and other offerings; and possibly a **pagoda** – the presence of which is, once again, a defence against evil spirits. Temples linked to individual clans may also have an **ancestral hall** displaying ranks of upright **ancestral tablets**, each representing a forebear of a clan member.

Peoples

Largely because of their pivotal position on maritime trade routes between the Middle East, India and China, the present-day countries of Malaysia, Singapore and Brunei have always been a cultural melting pot. During the first millennium AD, Malays arrived from Sumatra and Indians from India and Sri Lanka, while later the Chinese migrated from mainland China and Hainan Island. All these traders and settlers arrived to find that the region already held a gamut of indigenous tribes, thought to have migrated around 50,000 years ago from the Philippines, then connected by a land bridge to Borneo and Southeast Asia. The indigenous tribes who still live on the Peninsula are known as the Orang Asli, Malay for "the original people".

Original people they may have been, but their descendants now form a minority of the overall populations of the three countries. Over the last 150 years a massive influx of Chinese and Indian immigrants, escaping poverty, war and revolution, has swelled the population of **Malaysia**, which now stands at over 25 million. Just over half are Malays, while the Chinese make up nearly a quarter of the population, the Indians eight percent, and the various indigenous groups just over a tenth.

Brunei's population of around 380,000 is heavily dominated by Malays, with minorities of Chinese, Indians and indigenous peoples. In **Singapore**, only tiny numbers of indigenes were left on the island when Raffles arrived. They have no modern-day presence in the state, where around three-quarters of the 4.6-million-strong population are of Chinese extraction, around fourteen percent are Malay, and nearly nine percent Indian.

The Malays

The **Malays** are believed to have originated from the meeting of Mainland Southeast Asian, Taiwanese and even Papuan groups over the last 5000 years. Also known as Orang Laut (sea people), they sustained an economy built around fishing, boat-building and, in some communities, piracy. The growth in power of the Malay sultanates from the fifteenth century onwards – coinciding with the arrival of Islam – established Malays as a force to be reckoned with in the Malay Peninsula and Borneo. They developed an aristocratic tradition, courtly rituals and a social hierarchy that have a continued influence today. The rulers of Malaysia's states still wield great influence, reflected in the fact that they elect one of their number to hold the post of Yang di-Pertuan Agong, a pre-eminent sultan who holds the title for a five-year term. Although a purely ceremonial position, the *agong* is seen as the ultimate guardian of Malay Muslim culture and, despite recent legislation to reduce his powers, is still considered to be above the law. The situation is even more pronounced in **Brunei**, to which many Muslim Malay traders fled after the fall of Melaka to the Portuguese in 1511. There, the sultan remains the supreme ruler (as his descendants have been, on and off, for over five hundred years).

Even though Malays have been Muslims since the fifteenth century, the region as a whole is not fundamentalist in character. Only in Brunei is alcohol banned, for instance. Perhaps the most significant recent development affecting Malays in Malaysia has been the introduction of the **bumiputra** policy (see box, p.566).

The Chinese and Straits Chinese

Although **Chinese traders** began visiting the region in the seventh century, the first significant community established itself in Melaka in the fifteenth century. However, the ancestors of most of the Chinese now living in Malaysia – ethnic Hakka, and migrants from Teochew (Chaozhou) and Hokkien (Fujian) – emigrated from southeastern China during the nineteenth century to work in the burgeoning tin-mining industry and, later, rubber and oil plantations. A large number came as labourers, but they swiftly graduated to shopkeeping and business ventures, both in established towns like Melaka and fast-expanding centres like KL, Penang and Kuching. Chinatowns developed throughout the region, even in Malay strongholds like Kota Bharu and Kuala Terengganu, while **Chinese traditions**, religious festivities, theatre and music became an integral part of a wider multiracial culture. On the political level, the Malaysian Chinese are well represented in parliament and occupy around a quarter of current ministerial positions. By way of contrast, **Chinese Bruneians** are not automatically classed as citizens and suffer significant discrimination at the hands of the majority Malay population. **Singapore**'s nineteenth-century trade boom drew many Cantonese, Teochew, Hokkien and Hakka traders and labourers, who established a Chinatown on the south bank of the Singapore River. Today, the Chinese are the most economically successful racial group in Singapore.

One physical reminder of the Chinese presence in major cities is the presence of **kongsi** (literally "company") or **clan halls** (also called clan houses or associations). Each once functioned like a clan or regional club, providing help and protection for newly arrived migrants, who naturally tended to band together with others from the same part of China. At times they could also be a focus for community rivalry, as in the case of the Penang riots (see p.155). Many clan halls are excellent examples of traditional southern Chinese architecture, incorporating courtyards, shrines and sometimes living quarters.

THE BABA-NYONYAS

The **Baba-Nyonyas** are a Chinese subgroup with deep roots in the Malay Peninsula and a distinctive hybrid culture. It's often glibly said that they are the product of Chinese/Malay intermarriage, though this ignores the practical difficulties of marrying into a Muslim family without converting to Islam. What's more likely is that male migrants, arriving from China from at least the sixteenth century onwards, married local women, some Malay, others from the region's various communities such as Orang Asli or ethnic Thais. Eventually their descendants became a community in their own right – the menfolk known as **Babas**, the women **Nyonyas** – although confusingly the terms **Straits Chinese** and **Peranakan** are also used for them as a whole (Peranakan can also refer to other mixed-race groups, such as the Chitties of Melaka).

The Baba-Nyonyas clung on to some aspects of Chinese culture while absorbing influences from the Peninsula, most notably in terms of their dress – Nyonyas wore beautiful Malay-style batik-print clothes – and food (see p.39), but also in their language: many spoke Chinese dialects, notably Hokkien, but they also had their own Malay dialect. With the arrival of the British, they mastered English too, and this was to prove the foundation for a golden era when many Baba-Nyonyas became immensely wealthy. They were the bridge between the Western world and the *sinkeh*, the newly arrived Chinese migrants, who were eager to succeed. Many *sinkeh* married Nyonyas and the resulting family businesses flourished; choice residential areas such as Singapore's Katong were packed with Peranakan mansions.

It wasn't to last. In the interwar years, the British loosened the immigration rules to allow migrants to bring their wives with them, and some members of an older generation of migrants were, by then, giving their children a Western education. The Baba-Nyonyas became far less useful to the new blood from China and were simply outnumbered by them. They were also viewed with disdain by the mainstream community as being not properly Chinese. The Baba-Nyonya identity has now been largely subsumed into a wider Chinese one, though in recent decades their culture has at least been showcased in museums and their culinary heritage, at least, shows no signs of going away.

The Indians

The second largest non-*bumiputra* group in Malaysia, the **Indians**, first arrived as traders more than two thousand years ago, although few settled; only in the early fifteenth century did a small community of Indians (from present-day Tamil Nadu and Sri Lanka) become based in Melaka. Like the majority of Chinese, however, the first large wave of Indians – Tamil labourers – arrived as indentured workers in the nineteenth century, to build the roads and rail lines and work on the European-run rubber estates. An embryonic entrepreneurial class from North India soon followed, and set up businesses in Penang and Singapore; mostly Muslim, these merchants and traders found it easier to assimilate themselves within the existing Malay community than did the Hindu Tamils.

Although Indians comprise under a tenth of the populations of Malaysia and Singapore, their impact is widely felt. The Hindu festival of Thaipusam is celebrated annually at KL's Batu Caves by upwards of a million people (with smaller but still significant celebrations in Singapore and Penang); the festival of Deepavali is a national holiday; and Indians dominate certain professional areas like medicine and law. And then, of course, there's the food – very few Malaysians these days could do without a daily dose of *roti canai*, so much so that this Indian snack has been virtually appropriated by Malay and Chinese cafés and hawkers.

The Orang Asli

Most of the **Orang Asli** – the indigenous peoples of Peninsular Malaysia – belong to three distinct groups, within which various tribes are related by geography, language or physiological features. It's difficult to witness much of Orang Asli life as they largely live off the beaten track, though touristed communities at Taman Negara and the Cameron Highlands can be visited. To learn more about the disappearing Asli culture, the best stop is KL's Orang Asli Museum (see p.109).

Senoi

The largest group, the **Senoi** (the Asli word for "person"), number about forty thousand. They live in the large, still predominantly forested interior, within the states of Perak, Pahang and Kelantan, and divide into two main tribes, the Semiar and the Temiar. These still adhere to a traditional lifestyle, following animist customs in marriage ceremonies and burial rites. On the whole they follow the practice of shifting cultivation (a regular rotation of jungle clearance and crop planting), although government resettlement drives have persuaded many to settle and farm just one area.

Semang

The two thousand or so **Semang** live in the northern areas of the Peninsula. They comprise six distinct, if small, tribes, related to each other in appearance – most are dark-skinned and curly-haired – and traditionally shared a nomadic, hunter-gatherer lifestyle. However, most Semang nowadays live in settled communities and work within the cash economy, either as labourers or selling jungle produce in markets. Perhaps the most frequently seen Semang tribe are the Batek, who live in and around Taman Negara.

Aboriginals

The third group, the so-called **Aboriginal Malays**, live in an area roughly south of the Kuala Lumpur–Kuantan road. Some tribes in this category, like the Jakun and the Semelais who live around the lakes of the southern interior, vigorously retain their animist religion and artistic traditions despite living in permanent villages near Malay communities, and working within the regular economy.

Others
One of Malaysia's other Orang Asli tribes, the Lanoh in Perak are sometimes regarded as Semang, their language is closer to that of the Temiar. Another group, the semi-nomadic Che Wong, of whom just a few hundred survive on the slopes of Gunung Benom in central Pahang, still depend on foraging to survive, and live in temporary huts made from bamboo and rattan. Two more groups, the Jah Hut of Pahang and the Mah Meri of Selangor, are particularly fine carvers, and it's possible to buy their sculptures at regional craft shops.

Indigenous Sarawak: the Dyak
In direct contrast to the Peninsula, indigenous groups make up a larger chunk of the population in **Sarawak**, which stands at 2.8 million. Although the Chinese comprise 29 percent of the state's population and the Malays and Indians around 24 percent together, the remaining 47 percent are made up of various indigenous **Dyak** groups – a word derived from the Malay for "upcountry". Certain general aspects of their culture – for instance, the importance of bronze drums and reburial ceremonies – might indicate that the Dyak arrived in the region from mainland Southeast Asia around 2000 years ago.

The largest Dyak groups are the Iban, Bidayuh, Melanau, Kayan, Kenyah, Kelabit and Penan tribes. They have very distinct cultures as well as a few commonalities. Many live in **longhouses** along the rivers or on hillsides in the mountainous interior, and maintain a proud cultural legacy that draws on animist religion, arts and crafts production and jungle skills.

The Iban
The **Iban** (see p.346) make up nearly thirty percent of Sarawak's population. Originating hundreds of miles south of present-day Sarawak, in the Kapuas Valley in Kalimantan, the Iban migrated north in the sixteenth century, and came into conflict over the next two hundred years with the Kayan and Kenyah tribes and, later, the British. Nowadays, Iban longhouse communities are found in the Batang Ai river system in the southwest and along Batang Rajang and tributaries. These communities are quite accessible, their inhabitants always hospitable and keen to demonstrate such aspects of their culture as traditional dance and textile weaving. In their time, the Iban were infamous head-hunters – some longhouses are still decorated with heads taken in battle long ago.

The Bidayuh
Unlike most Dyak groups, the **Bidayuh** traditionally lived away from the rivers, building their longhouse on the sides of hills. Culturally, the most southerly of Sarawak's indigenous groups are similar to the Iban, although in temperament they are much milder and less gregarious, keeping themselves to themselves in their inaccessible homes on Sarawak's mountainous southern border with Kalimantan.

The Melanau and Kelabit
The **Melanau** are a coastal people, living north of Kuching in a region dominated by mangrove swamps. Many Melanau, however, now live in towns, preferring the kampung-style houses of the Malays to the elegant longhouses of the past. They are expert fishermen and cultivate sago as an alternative to rice. The **Kelabit** people live on the highland plateau separating north Sarawak from Kalimantan. Like the Iban, they live in longhouses and maintain a traditional lifestyle, but differ from some other groups in being Christian.

The Penan
The semi-nomadic **Penan** traditionally live in temporary lean-tos or small huts in the upper Rejang and Limbang areas of Sarawak. They rely, like some Orang Asli groups in

the Peninsula, on hunting and gathering and collecting jungle produce for sale in local markets. In recent years, however, the state government has tried to resettle the Penan in small villages – a controversial policy not entirely unconnected with the advance of logging in traditional Penan land.

The Kenyah and Kayan

Most of the other groups in Sarawak fall into the all-embracing ethnic classification of **Orang Ulu** (people of the interior), who inhabit remote inland areas, further north than the Iban, along the upper Rajang, Balui and Linau rivers. The most numerous, the **Kayan** and the **Kenyah**, are closely related and in the past often teamed up to defend their lands from the invading Iban. But they also have much in common with their traditional enemy, since they are longhouse-dwellers, animists and shifting cultivators.

Indigenous Sabah

Sabah's population of around 3.8 million encompasses remarkable diversity, with forty-plus ethnic groups, some of which are interrelated; between them, they speak over eighty different languages and dialects. The **Kadazan/Dusun** and their various subgroups account for around a third of the population. Traditionally agriculturists (the word Dusun means "orchard", while the "Kadazan" part of the name was originally preferred by those from the Penampang area), they inhabit the western coastal plains and parts of the interior. Other Kadazan/Dusun branches include the Lotud of Tuaran and the Rungus of the Kudat Peninsula, whose longhouses – some characterized by walls that bulge outwards – are all that remain of the group's longhouse-building tradition. Although most Kadazan/Dusun are now Christians, remnants of their animist past are still evident, most obviously in the harvest festival, or **Kaamatan**, when their *bobohizans* (priestesses) perform rituals to honour the *bambaazon*, or rice spirit.

The mainly Muslim **Bajau** tribe, who drifted over from the southern Philippines some two hundred years ago, has overtaken the Chinese as Sabah's second largest ethnic group, accounting for around a tenth of the population. Their penchant for piracy once earned them the sobriquet "sea gypsies", though nowadays they are either fisher-folk or agriculturalists noted for their horsemanship and buffalo rearing. The Bajau live in the northwest of Sabah, where they annually appear on horseback at Kota Belud's market (see p.413), as well as in Semporna and the islands offshore.

Sabah's third sizeable indigenous tribe, the **Murut**, inhabit the area south of Keningau. Their name means "hill people", though some prefer to be known by their individual tribal names, such as Timugon, Tagal and Nabai. The Murut traditionally farm rice and cassava by a system of shifting cultivation. Their head-hunting days are over, but they retain other cultural traditions, such as constructing brightly adorned huts to house the graves and belongings of the dead.

Development and the environment

Malaysia is gradually becoming more environmentally friendly, largely as a result of well-organized and scientifically persuasive organizations within the country, rather than pressures from outside, but the pace of change is slow and huge problems remain. Logging and large-scale development projects, like dams, hog the spotlight, and remain a prime focus for NGOs, but just as pressing are the concerns over oil-palm cultivation and wetlands erosion, as well as the impact of environmental degradation on the lifestyles of indigenous groups.

As a small, highly built-up island, **Singapore** has few wild areas left to spoil. Nevertheless, the country maintains an area of rainforest around its central reservoirs as well as other nature reserves, such the wetland area at Sungai Buloh. Singapore's very compactness dictates that it has to be vigilant on matters of pollution, and thus the island has strict laws on waste emissions and even an island, Semakau, created largely out of ash from incinerated refuse.

The tiny sultanate of **Brunei** has interfered least with its forest, but then, its enormous oil wealth and tiny population ensure it has little need to.

Logging and deforestation

The **sustainable exploitation** of forest products by the indigenous population has always played a vital part in the domestic and export economy of the region – for almost two thousand years, ethnic tribes have bartered products like rattan, wild rubber and forest plants with foreign traders.

Although blamed for much of the deforestation in Sarawak and Sabah, the bulk of indigenous agricultural activity occurs in secondary rather than primary (untouched) forest. Indeed, environmental groups believe that only around one hundred square kilometres of primary forest – a tiny proportion compared to the haul by commercial timber companies – is cleared by the indigenous groups annually. **Logging**, despite having slowed, is still a cause of huge grievances among the indigenous peoples of east Malaysia.

The Peninsula

Peninsular Malaysia's pre-independence economy was not as reliant on timber revenues as those of Sabah and Sarawak. Although one sixth of the region's 120,000 square kilometres of forest, predominantly in Johor, Perak and Negeri Sembilan states, had been cut down by 1957, most of the logging had been done gradually and on a small, localized scale. As in Sabah, it was the demand for rail sleepers during the 1920s' expansion of the Malayan train network that first attracted the commercial logging companies. Wide-scale clearing and conversion to rubber and oil-palm plantations in the more remote areas of Pahang, Perlis, Kedah and Terengganu intensified in the 1960s. By the end of the 1970s, more efficient extraction methods, coupled with a massive increase in foreign investment in the logging industry, had led to over forty percent of the Peninsula's remaining forests being either cleared for plantation purposes or partially logged.

Logging in west Malaysia has, however, slowed significantly in the last few decades, with environmental impact assessments being carried out before logging is allowed to proceed. One positive piece of legislation is the creation, more than a century ago, of

Permanent Forest Reserves. Any logging in these areas must be carried out in a sustainable manner integrating checks and impact assessments.

Sabah

Commercial logging began in **Sabah** in the late nineteenth century, when the British Borneo Trading and Planting Company started to extract timber for use as railway sleepers in China. By World War II, the larger **British Borneo Timber Company** (BBTC) was primarily responsible for the extraction of five million cubic metres of rainforest timber, and Sandakan became one of the world's main timber ports. Areas were logged indiscriminately, and the indigenous tribal groups who lived there became employees of the rubber and tobacco plantations that replaced the forests. By 1970, nearly a third of Sabah's forests had been logged, accounting for over seventy percent of exports.

Since then, oil palm cultivation has taken over much of the logged land, and at the same time Sabah's conservation policies have improved considerably. Half to sixty percent of the state remains under forest cover, and although some of this is previously logged areas, active reforestation programmes are under way. While logging continues, the emphasis is starting to shift towards **plantations** of fast-growing trees like acacias, meaning more forest can be left undisturbed. Cynics might say that Sabah is merely the best of a bad bunch in the context of the whole country, but there is a clearer commitment to sustainable forest use, wildlife protection and transparency here than anywhere else in Malaysia – as exemplified at **Deramakot**, the country's only reserve with international Forest Stewardship Council certification.

Sarawak

In many ways **Sarawak** seems to exemplify Malaysia's environmental policies at their worst. It's here that all the problems come into sharp focus – the forest is either being degraded by commercial logging or felled altogether for oil-palm cultivation, in the process ruining the ancestral lands of native peoples.

Having accelerated in northern Sarawak under Vyner Brooke during the 1930s, timber extraction became a major revenue earner for the state during its short postwar period as a Crown Colony and after independence as part of Malaysia. Accurate figures as to the current state of Sarawak's rainforest are notoriously hard to come by, though perhaps less than thirty percent of the primary forest cover remains, and even that can be so fragmented that it's practically useless from a wildlife conservation point of view.

In principle the indigenous peoples have so-called **native customary rights** over their ancestral forest, and can use them in court to block the government granting logging or other concessions. However, the system is fraught with difficulty, partly because such rights are based on incomplete colonial-era data on tribal agricultural settlement. What's more, in 2016 Malaysia's highest court ruled that existing Sarawak law did not actually recognize two important native customs establishing ties to the land, a situation that can only be corrected with new legislation. Even where tribal people can establish their rights, the demands of the cash economy may mean they are more interested in the jobs and amenities that the logging firms can bring.

Of course, logging, unlike clearing land for oil palm, does not mean the wholesale destruction of the forest: the logging companies are after hardwood trees, which they should try to remove as cleanly as possible. In practice felling may involve collateral damage to other trees, and it's notable that only one timber concession in Sarawak has been certified under the Malaysian Timber Certification Scheme (MTCS) to indicate some compliance with responsible forest management practices.

Meanwhile the state continues to trumpet its target of gazetting 10,000 square kilometres (eight percent of Sarawak's land area) as national parks or wildlife

OIL-PALM CULTIVATION IN MALAYSIA

Anyone who travels around Malaysia immediately notices the ubiquity of the **oil palm**. Native to West Africa, the plant is now widely cultivated on both plantations and smallholdings for its fruit, which yields **palm oil**, used for cooking, in food products and as a biofuel; Malaysia, together with Indonesia, account for at least eighty percent of world production of this valuable commodity. The industry has brought employment to many as well as improved infrastructure, with roads, cellular networks, schools and clinics springing up to serve plantation areas.

Although some cultivation takes place on land long used for agriculture, **forest clearance** for plantations is a huge problem, not just because it threatens many animal species, including the orang-utan. The practice also contributes significantly to global warming, notably via greenhouse gas emissions when fire is used to destroy trees, and can trigger conflict between plantation operators and local people who are forced off their land. Certification schemes exist to try to make palm oil production sustainable, although some critics view the very idea as an oxymoron and mere window-dressing.

While there is some local awareness of oil palm's negative impact, Malaysian media coverage of the issue is largely uncritical; in 2017, European Parliament proposals that could eventually ban the import of any palm oil linked with deforestation or human rights violations were reported with some indignation in Malaysia as a snub to the supposedly well-regulated industry.

reserves that are off-limits to the public, plus a further 60,000 square kilometres as permanent forest reserve. Impressive though these figures may sound, it's notable that many of the newer national parks scarcely function as such, since they are sited in inaccessible areas and have barely any facilities. This haphazard creation of parks might be thought to augment their effectiveness as conservation areas, but there is no such fringe benefit – policing to stop logging or poaching is minimal. It could be argued that the parks are, in fact, a smokescreen for what's happening elsewhere in Sarawak – for example, the intensive logging of the Baram River basin in the north, in areas around the Kelabit Highlands and Mulu National Park. **Dam-building** is another major issue on the Sarawak environmental agenda. Some dams have already been completed, notably the one at Bakun (see p.358), and a couple more are set to be built, all to generate electricity for no obvious market. Overall, the picture in Sarawak does appear bleak, although there is genuine commitment among some government biodiversity managers to try to reform the state's policies.

Air pollution

The environmental issue that has most affected the inhabitants of Peninsular Malaysia and Singapore has been air pollution, specifically dust and smoke caused by sporadic forest fires – dubbed "the **haze**" by the local media. During severe, prolonged episodes in 1997/98 and 2015, things got so bad that respiratory illnesses spiked and schools were closed. Visibility in the Strait of Malacca, one of the world's busiest shipping routes, dropped dramatically.

At one time, the Malaysian government suggested that the agricultural methods of the indigenous peoples – which involve the burning of excess vegetation at the end of growing cycles – were to blame. However, small longhouse communities could not have caused such extensive pollution, and it is now clear that Indonesian plantation companies burning large areas of forest to facilitate the planting of crops such as oil palm and acacia are the culprits. The Indonesian government does not appear to be able to rein in such practices, and the haze must be regarded as a recurrent threat that can plague a visit to Malaysia and Singapore with little warning.

The threat to traditional lifestyles

Although large-scale projects such as the Bakun Dam are the most prevalent threat to indigenous tribes' way of life, **logging**, whether licensed or illicit, represents a constant challenge. The effect on wildlife has an obvious impact on communities' ability to hunt, but the failure to respect native customary rights has also led to the desecration of burial places and sections of rivers used for fishing – notably in the forests around Bintulu, Belaga and Limbang. In southwest Sarawak, the Iban have had some success in challenging logging, however: a historic court case in 2001, Rumah Nor v. Borneo Pulp and Paper, led to a ruling in favour of the longhouse community, after the community's map was accepted as court evidence for ownership of land. Emboldened by this ruling, several communities have filed petitions, but in many cases the courts have not revoked the state-awarded logging concessions.

The **Penan** have arguably been the worst hit by logging, as their traditionally semi-nomadic lifestyle makes it hard for their land rights to be defined and recognized. In addition, the Sarawak state government's avowed policy since the mid-1980s has been to bring the Penan into what it views as the development process (as applied to the more settled Dyak and Orang Ulu groups for many decades), urging them to move to permanent longhouses, work in the cash economy and send their children to school. Very often, the Penan receive no notice that their land has been earmarked for logging until extraction actually begins – examples in remote areas around Belaga have been documented by the environmental group **Sahabat Alam Malaysia** (SAM). Reports from one of the remaining semi-nomadic Penan communities situated in Sarawak's Ulu Baram area reveal that loggers continue to penetrate their last reserves illegally.

Wildlife

Set well inside the tropics and comprising everything from pristine ocean to coastal mangroves, lowland rainforest and mountain moorland, the range of habitats on the Malay Peninsula and Borneo is only matched by the diversity of its fauna – over 700 species of birds and more than 200 kinds of mammals. You don't have to be an ardent nature-spotter to appreciate this: even a brief visit to any of the region's national parks – or just the FRIM forestry reserve on Kuala Lumpur's outskirts – will put you face to face with clouds of butterflies, troops of monkeys, and an incessant background orchestra of insect noise.

Despite being separated by the South China Sea, the wildlife and plant communities of the Peninsula and east Malaysia are similar (the two were joined by a land bridge until after the last Ice Age), though the various regional wildlife reserves offer a range of experiences. On Peninsular Malaysia, **Taman Negara** provides full-on tropical jungle, a good place to see large mammals; **Fraser's Hill**, on the other hand, is better known for its birdlife. Sabah's **Kinabatangan River** and **Bako National Park** in Sarawak are good for estuarine and river forest creatures, while shallow lakes at Sarawak's **Loagan Bunut National Park** are home to many different bird species, as is Brunei's **Ulu Temburong National Park**.

Even though it's now predominantly urban, with little plant or animal life, **Singapore** still holds several remnants of its verdant tropical past, particularly at **Bukit Timah Nature Reserve**, the splendidly manicured Botanic Gardens, and the **Sungai Buloh Nature Wetland Reserve** in the far north of the island. Day-trippers to Pulau Ubin, just off Singapore and easily accessible by boat from the Changi Point ferry terminal, can also see the mangrove flats of **Chek Jawa**.

Poaching and habitation loss due to deforestation mean that the future of the region's wildlife is far from assured. Fortunately, many **not-for-profit organizations**, such as WWF Malaysia (Ⓦwwfmalaysia.org), are campaigning to preserve the species and terrains most under threat.

FORESTS

Coastal mud flats are usually protected by **mangroves**, a diverse family of trees that thrive in brackish water and tend to support themselves on a platform of elevated roots that form an impenetrable barrier to exploration – and refuge for small creatures such as mudskippers, crabs and young fish.

Moving inland, the region's lowland forests are thick with **dipterocarps** (meaning "two-winged fruit"), a diverse group of trees often prized for timber. Other forest species include several palm trees (one of which, the spiky, vine-like rattan palm, is used to make cane furniture and the like); liana vines; massive fig trees (many of which support their huge trunks with buttress roots); 50m-tall *tualang*, Southeast Asia's tallest tree; and wild **fruit trees**, such as durian, mango, guava and rambutan. You'll seldom see flowers though (except fallen petals); so little light reaches the forest floor that trees and climbing plants only flower high up in the canopy. To get around this, a whole group of small plants have become epiphytes – using the trees as perches to get nearer the sunlight – including orchids and a wide range of small ferns, which sometimes cover the upper surface of larger branches.

Montane forest predominates above 1000m, comprising mainly oak and evergreen native conifers with a shrub layer of bamboo and dwarf palm. Above 1500m is **cloud forest**, where trees are often cloaked by swirling mist, and the stunted, damp boughs bear thick growths of mosses and ferns; at elevations of over 1700m, you'll find miniature montane forest of rhododendrons, the boughs heavily laden with dripping mosses, pitcher plants and colourful orchids.

Mammals

Big mammals are exciting to encounter in the wild, and several are unique to the region. Asian **elephant** are found both in Peninsular Malaysia and Borneo, though probably the best chance to see them is at Taman Negara, which is also good for **tapir** – a pony-sized relative of the rhino, with a black-and-white body and vestigial trunk.

Other mammals you might encounter include the **Sunda clouded leopard** – a rare cat species with a pattern of cloud-like markings on the sides of the body – spotted **leopard cat** (around the size of a large domestic cat), and nocturnal **civet**, tree-dwelling creatures that look like a cross between a cat and a weasel. Don't get your hopes up about seeing **tigers**, now thought to number no more than 500 in the Peninsula, or reclusive **sun bears**, marked with a white crescent across their chest – though you do occasionally see their deep claw grooves in tree bark.

Another possibility in undisturbed forest on the Peninsula are seladang, a Malaysian sub-species of **gaur**, a giant type of wild cattle with white leg patches, which look like socks. There are also several species of **deer**: the larger sambar; the muntjac or barking deer, the size of a roe deer; and the lesser and greater mouse deer.

Primates (monkeys and gibbons) are found throughout the Peninsula and Borneo. Most common are the long-tailed and pig-tailed **macaques**, which come to the ground to feed, the latter identified by its shorter tail, brown fur and pinkish-brown face. There are dusky and spectacled **langurs** too, elegant grey monkeys with white patterns that spend most of their time up in the trees – they're also known as leaf-monkeys, after their diet. The region's several gibbon species are entirely arboreal, with specially elongated forearms that allow them to swing athletically through the canopy – they tend to have very loud, wailing calls too, easily recognized. Big-nosed, pot-bellied proboscis monkeys – and Southeast Asia's sole ape, the **orang-utan** – are found only in Borneo.

One of the most unusual smaller mammals to keep eyes peeled for is the **colugo**, a bizarre forest creature that looks like a cross between a fruit bat and a squirrel. It spends the day sleeping in tree hollows, and the night gliding through the forest looking for flowers and fruits.

Birds

One fairly common bird that epitomizes the entire Malay region – and is even a totem to some Dyak tribes – is the **hornbill** (see box, opposite). Its huge size, bold black-and-white markings, large curved beak and noisy, swooshing flight make it easily identifiable, even in thick jungle. Other forest birds include **trogons** (brightly coloured, mid-storey birds); green **fruit pigeons** – strongly coloured but strangely hard to see; **bulbuls**, vocal,

---

HOW TO FIND WILDLIFE

Tropical wildlife is most active at dawn and dusk, though some larger mammals forage through the night. It's surprising how even large animals can be fairly invisible, especially in forest, where low light and random vegetation can break up their otherwise recognizable outlines. Here are some tips for finding creatures, without doing anything dangerous – such as turning over logs to look for snakes:

Listen – aside from calls, many creatures make distinctive noises as they move, from the raucous crashing of active monkey troops, to staccato rustlings of mice and lizards in leaf litter.
Look – many smaller creatures spend the day hidden under leaves and in hollows and crevices in tree trunks. At night, insects – and insect-eating animals – are attracted to lights; check ranger offices, chalets and huts around national park headquarters.
Signs – footprints, scarred bark, mud wallows and flowers, fruit and torn twigs strewn along paths are all signs of animals, some of which might be feeding in the canopy above you.
Eyeshine – if on a guided night trek or drive, use a torch held at or above eye level to reflect eyeshine, either from invertebrates such as crickets and spiders, or nocturnal mammals – anything from tapir to deer, mice and civets.

HORNBILLS

You should have little difficulty in identifying **hornbills**: they are large, black-and-white birds with disproportionately huge bills (often bent downwards), topped with an ornamental **casque** – a generally hollow structure attached to the upper mandible. The function of the casque is unknown; it may play a role in attracting a mate and courtship ceremonies. Ten of the world's 46 species of hornbill are found in Malaysia, many of them endangered or present only in small, isolated populations.

One of the smallest and most commonly seen species, the **pied hornbill**, can be identified by its white abdomen and tail, and white wingtips in flight. Reaching only 75cm in length, it may even be spotted in leafy suburban areas. Also widely seen, the **black hornbill** is only slightly larger and black, save for the white tips of the outer tail feathers (some individuals also show a white patch behind the eye).

Larger species include the **helmeted hornbill** and the **rhinoceros hornbill**, both over 120cm in length, mainly black, but with white tails and bellies. Although it's the symbol of Sarawak, the rhinoceros hornbill is rarely seen there (you may have better luck in Sabah); it has a bright orange rhino-horn-shaped casque, whereas the helmeted hornbill has a bright red head, neck and helmet-shaped casque. The call of the helmeted hornbill is notable for being a remarkable series of "took" notes that start slowly and accelerate to a cackling crescendo.

fruit-eating birds that often flock to feed; **minivets**, slender birds with long, graduated tails and white, yellow or red bands in the wings; and round-winged **babblers**.

Plump and brilliantly coloured, **pitas** are notoriously shy and difficult to approach, though sometimes easily found thanks to their noisy progress through leaf litter on the forest floor. Other ground-dwelling birds to look for include the shy **Malaysian peacock pheasant**, with a blue-green crest and distinctive "eye spots" along its back and long tail; the similar **fireback**; and the 1.7m-long **great argus pheasant**.

The most common birds of prey are kites, buzzards and, along the coast, fish eagles, very large white and grey birds with a wedge-shaped tail. In forest, you might encounter the **crested serpent eagle** and the **changeable hawk eagle**, often spotted soaring over gaps in the forest canopy.

Other species confined to tropical forests are **trogons**, of which five species are present at Taman Negara, and several species of **hornbill** – large, broad-winged, long-tailed forest birds, some of which have huge, almost outlandish bills.

A feature of montane forest bird flocks is the **mixed feeding flock**, which may contain many different species. These pass rapidly through an area of forest searching for insects as they go, and different observers are likely to register entirely different species in the same flock. Look for **racket-tailed drongo**, a black bird with long tail streamers; the **speckled piculet**, a small spotted woodpecker; and the **blue nuthatch**, a small species – blue-black in colour with a white throat and pale eye ring – which runs up and down tree trunks. Several species of brightly coloured **laughing thrushes**, thrush-sized birds that spend time foraging on the ground or in the understorey, also occur in these flocks.

Reptiles

Small lizards – mostly skinks – are probably the commonest **reptiles** in the region; you'll often hear their frantic scuffling among forest-floor leaf litter. Nocturnal geckos have sucker-like pads on their toes that enable them to run up walls (and even glass); they're often seen around lights, stalking any insects that settle nearby. On forest fringes, look for flying lizards, which at rest are small, bony, grey and unimpressive – until they unfold wings and glide between trees like paper darts. Fairly common, even in semi-rural parks, they're easily missed. Around water – and especially near popular picnic spots, where they can pick up scraps – you'll see heavily built **monitor lizards**, the largest of which can approach 2m.

RAFFLESIAS

The *Rafflesia* is a strange plant that parasitizes tree roots, and whose presence can only be detected when its rubbery flowers, up to a metre across, burst into bloom. Its full name, *Rafflesia arnoldii*, recalls its discovery in Sumatra in 1818 by Sir Stamford Raffles (see p.482) and his physician, the naturalist Dr Joseph Arnold, who collected a 7kg specimen and sent a description of it to the Royal Society in London. The blooms, which are the world's largest and stink of rotting meat, are pollinated by carrion flies. Each flower's central "bowl" holds around 7 litres of nectar, while the petals, as Raffles recorded, "are of a brick-red with numerous pustular spots of a lighter colour. The whole substance of the flower is not less than half an inch thick, and of a firm fleshy consistence". The flower buds have been very much in demand by *bomohs* (Malay shamen) and their Chinese *sinseh* counterparts for use in medicine, particularly as an aid to accelerate the shrinking of a woman's womb after she has given birth. There's no specific flowering season, though in any one locality the plants seem to bloom at particular times of the year. As each flower lasts only a few days, however, there's a lot of luck involved in actually seeing one; national park rangers might be able to give likely times.

Snakes – Malaysia and Borneo hold over 200 species, including poisonous cobras, kraits and pit vipers – are another common but seldom-seen creature; they tend to move off as soon as they detect your footfalls. The largest, the reticulated python, is capable of growing 8m long, though you're much more likely to see either harmless **whip snakes** (which eat insects and lizards) and green **tree snakes**.

Saltwater **crocodiles** – the world's largest, heaviest reptile – are now virtually extinct throughout Peninsular Malaysia, though numbers are increasing in Borneo. Scuba divers might encounter several species of marine **turtle**, all of whose populations are declining; certain beaches are also famous as turtle rookeries, where you might see adults coming ashore to lay eggs above the high tide line, or young turtles hatching, digging themselves out of the sand and heading for the sea en masse.

Indian Prairie Public Library
www.ippl.info
630-887-8760

Check out receipt

Date:1/11/2020 11:03:10 AM

2/1/2020
1. The rough guide to Malaysia, Singapore &Brunei
Barcode 31946006496654
Due by 2/1/2020

Current fees: $ 2.50

We are open 24/7!
Did you know you can easily renew
your items &pay any fees through
your account?
catalog.ippl.info

Books

Singapore and, to a lesser extent, Malaysia have healthy English-language publishing scenes, churning out books on local history, politics, society and culture, plus a modest amount of fiction. Besides the major bookshops listed throughout this Guide, a good source for specialist titles is the mail-order-only Select Books (⊕selectbooks.com.sg).

In the reviews that follow, books marked ★ are especially recommended, while o/p signifies a title is out of print. As per Chinese custom, surnames are given first for Chinese authors who don't have Christian names; also, some Malay and Indian authors who do not have surnames are listed under their given name.

TRAVEL AND GENERAL INTEREST

★ *Encyclopedia of Malaysia*. A brilliantly produced series of tomes on different aspects of Malaysia, all beautifully illustrated and – not always the case with locally published material – competently edited. The volumes on the performing arts and architecture are particularly recommended. Available as individual volumes or as a set.

Isabella Bird *The Golden Chersonese*. Delightful epistolary romp through old Southeast Asia, penned by the intrepid Bird, whose adventures in the Malay states in 1879 ranged from strolls through Singapore's streets to elephant-back rides. A free download from various online libraries.

Robin Hanbury-Tenison *Finding Eden*. Forty years after leading the pioneering Royal Geographical Society expedition to the then newly established Mulu National Park, Hanbury-Tenison revisits the experience in this book, much of which dwells on the minutiae of the enterprise, as noted in his diaries. The book is at its best when recounting the discovery of the Garden of Eden and his close bond with the Penan people.

Tom Harrisson *Borneo Jungle* and *World Within*. The abrasive, eccentric polymath Tom Harrisson spent much of his professional life studying Sarawak's Dyak groups, especially the Kayan, Kenyah and Punan, whom he greatly admired. *Borneo Jungle* is a lively account of his first trip during the 1930s; *World Within* the story of how he parachuted into the highlands during World War II to organize Dyak resistance against the Japanese.

Sebastian Hope *Outcasts of the Islands*. Still available as an e-book, this is the 2001 account of the writer's extraordinary attempts to get to know Southeast Asia's itinerant sea peoples, notably Sabah's Bajau Laut at Semporna, at a time when many still lived at sea off Semporna and there were just two resorts at Mabul.

★ **Agnes Keith** *Land Below the Wind*. Bornean memories galore, in this charming account of expat life in prewar Sabah; Keith's true eye and assured voice produce a heartwarming picture of a way of life now long gone. Her naive sketches perfectly complement the childlike wonder of the prose.

Redmond O'Hanlon *Into The Heart of Borneo*. A hugely entertaining yarn recounting O'Hanlon's refreshingly amateurish romp through the jungle to a remote summit on the Sarawak/Kalimantan border, partnered by the English poet James Fenton.

HISTORY AND POLITICS

★ **Munshi Abdullah** *The Hikayat Abdullah*. Raffles' one-time clerk, Melaka-born Abdullah became diarist of some of the most formative years of Southeast Asian history; his firsthand account is crammed with illuminating vignettes and character portraits.

★ **Barbara Watson Andaya and Leonard Andaya** *The History of Malaysia*. Unlike more paternalistic histories penned by former colonists, this newly updated standard text on the region takes a more even-handed view of Malaysia, and finds time for cultural coverage, too.

Farish Noor *What Your Teacher Didn't Tell You*. An enjoyable series of lectures on subjects that remain awkward in Malaysia, from ethnicity to sexual attitudes.

Victoria Glendinning *Raffles and the Golden Opportunity*. An enjoyable, thorough biography of Singapore's founder Sir Stamford Raffles, though occasionally bogged down in the details of his upbringing and domestic life.

★ **Patrick Keith** *Ousted*. Most of the largely young population of Malaysia and Singapore know little of the events that saw Singapore leaving the federation in 1965. But, as this fine memoir by a former Malaysian government adviser demonstrates, many of the issues that led to the rift continue to shape both countries and their mutual ties today – Malaysia is still laden with ethnically based politics, while Singapore remains the fiefdom of the PAP.

★**Sonny Liew** *The Art of Charlie Chan Hock Chye*. This internationally acclaimed graphic novel appears to celebrate an overlooked genius of Singapore comic art. In reality, Liew's "retrospective" on the fictional Mr Chan's satirical work and struggle for recognition is a savage indictment of the autocratic trajectory of postwar Singapore politics – a useful antidote to establishment accounts.

James Minchin *No Man Is An Island* (o/p). This well-researched, and at times critical, study of Lee Kuan Yew refuses to kowtow to Singapore's ex-prime minister and is hence unavailable in Singapore itself.

John Curtis Perry *Singapore: Unlikely Power*. Not quite as critical as it could be, but a highly readable history nonetheless, focusing mainly on development and economic influence rather than society and politics.

★**C.M. Turnbull** *A History of Modern Singapore 1819–2005*. Mary Turnbull had barely completed a major update of this standard work when she died in 2008, and what a fine legacy: the new edition is lucid, thorough, nearly always spot-on in its analysis and utterly readable.

WORLD WAR II

★**Russell Braddon** *The Naked Island* (o/p). Southeast Asia under the Japanese: Braddon's disturbing yet moving first-hand account of the POW camps of Malaya, Singapore and Siam salutes courage in the face of appalling conditions and treatment; worth scouring secondhand stores for.

★**Spencer Chapman** *The Jungle is Neutral*. This riveting firsthand account of being lost, and surviving, in the Malay jungle during World War II reads like a breathless novel.

★**Agnes Keith** *Three Came Home*. Pieced together from scraps of paper secreted in latrines and teddy bears, this is a remarkable story of survival in the face of Japanese attempts to eradicate the "proudery and arrogance" of the West in the World War II prison camps of Borneo.

Eric Lomax *The Railway Man*. Such is the power of Lomax's artless, redemptive and moving story of capture during the fall of Singapore, torture by the Japanese and reconciliation with his tormentor after fifty years, that many reviewers were moved to tears.

★**Lucy Lum** *The Thorn of Lion City*. You might expect a memoir of a wartime childhood in Singapore to be dominated by the savagery of the Japanese, but that's nothing compared to the torment inflicted on the author at the hands of her manipulative and violent mother and grandmother. That it's all told with zero artifice only makes it more compelling.

CULTURE AND SOCIETY

James Harding and Ahmad Sarji *P. Ramlee: The Bright Star*. An uncritical but enjoyable biography of the Malay singer, actor and director sometimes likened to Malaysia's Harry Belafonte. More importantly, it's a window onto what seems like a different era – though little more than half a century ago – when Singapore was the centre of the Malay entertainment universe, and when Malay life was, frankly, more carefree than today.

Michael Heppell *Iban Art: Sexual Selection and Severed Heads* This excellent illustrated volume provides a deeper coverage of Iban art than the pretty pictures might lead you to assume, detailing the motifs and symbolism of traditional clothes, tattoos and carvings.

★**Erik Jensen** *Where Hornbills Fly*. In the 1950s, before he became a British diplomat, the author arrived in Sarawak as a callow young man with idealistic notions of learning about the Iban. He soon wound up living in longhouses in the Lemanak area (near Batang Ai), helping the Iban make the change to a settled existence without imposing upon them as a "superior" foreigner. His memoir is so intricately and tenderly observed you can only wonder why he waited half a century to write up his experiences.

Lat *Kampung Boy* and *Town Boy*. Two comic-strip albums by the country's foremost cartoonist about growing up in Malaysia during the 1950s and 60s; gentle and fun, though without any sentimentality.

Charmaine Leung *17A Keong Saik Road*. This likeable autobiography recounts the author's childhood in a Singapore brothel. The nonlinear narrative spans many decades and can be confusing, but is ultimately rewarding for its insights into how ordinary people kept afloat as Chinatown (and Singapore at large) changed dramatically around them.

★**Paul Malone** *The Peaceful People*. A moving, accessible study of the Penan people of Sarawak and of the enormous upheavals they have been through, transitioning from hunter-gatherers to a largely settled existence in just a few decades. Along the way Malone recounts their run-ins with authority and their ambivalent, unequal relationship with the logging industry eating into their ancestral lands.

Bernard Sellato *Innermost Borneo: Studies in Dayak Cultures*. Anthropologist Sellato spent much of the 1990s with the indigenous Borneo tribes of Kalimantan, who are related to the Sea Dyaks of Sarawak. This excellent ethnographic work contains ravishing images of a traditional, isolated world that will eventually be subsumed into greater Indonesia.

★**Dina Zaman** *I Am Muslim*. A well-observed set of wry essays, with more candour than would be appropriate in this guidebook, on Islam as practised in Malaysia; form without enough substance is, sadly, often the verdict. The section on sexual attitudes is particularly recommended.

FOOD AND COOKERY

Aziza Ali *Aziza's Creative Malay Cuisine; Sambal Days, Kampong Cuisine.* For years, Aziza Ali ran the only worthwhile high-end Malay restaurant in Singapore, and her *Creative Malay Cuisine* cookbook is packed with great recipes, though the emphasis is firmly on southern rather than east coast dishes. *Sambal Days* is quite different, a memoir of a middle-class Malay childhood that soon morphs into a reverie of special foods for just about every occasion.

★**Betty Saw** *Rasa Malaysia: the complete Malaysion cookbook.* A nicely illustrated cookbook that covers dozens of the standard dishes you'll find served at food courts and in homes around the country, including various Chinese and Nyonya recipes, though very little South Indian fare. It's all organized by state, which helps give a feel for regional cuisine, though annoyingly there's no index.

NATURAL HISTORY AND THE ENVIRONMENT

Chin Shui Hiung, Ravi Mandalam and Christopher Chin *East Kinabalu.* Gorgeous photos of montane plants and Mount Kinabalu's incredible vistas, taken on multi-day expeditions in little-visited areas which have since been altered by the 2015 earthquake.

G.W.H. Davison and Chew Yen Fook *A Photographic Guide to Birds of Borneo;* **M. Strange and A. Jeyarajasingam** *A Photographic Guide to Birds of Peninsular Malaysia and Singapore;* **Charles M. Francis** *A Photographic Guide to the Mammals of Southeast Asia.* Well keyed and user-friendly, these slender volumes carry oodles of glossy plates that make positive identifying a breeze.

Junaidi Payne *Wild Malaysia: The Wildlife and Landscapes of Peninsular Malaysia, Sarawak and Sabah.* Coffee-table book, recently reissued, capturing forest and beach vistas of the kind that linger in the mind long after you've left Malaysia.

★**Alfred Russel Wallace** *The Malay Archipelago.* The immensely readable journal of Wallace's 1854–62 expedition to collect natural history specimens in Borneo and Indonesia, during which he independently formulated the theory of evolution by natural selection – prompting Charles Darwin to publish his landmark *On the Origin of Species.*

Lukas Straumann *Money Logging: On the Trail of the Asian Timber Mafia.* An unrelenting exposé of avarice and corruption at the heart of Sarawak's government and timber corporations, by the executive director of the Bruno Manser Fund, which campaigns on behalf of the state's indigenous tribes.

ART AND ARCHITECTURE

Julian Davison and Luca Invernizzi Tettoni *Black & White: The Singapore House;* **Peter and Waveney Jenkins** *The Planter's Bungalow.* Two tomes dealing with colonial "Anglo-Malay" residences, often strange hybrids of mock-Tudor and Southeast Asian elements, and sometimes raised off the ground on posts like a kampung house. Both volumes also examine the lives of those who occupied these houses, not always as wealthy as you might assume.

★**Farish A. Noor and Eddin Khoo** *The Spirit of Wood: The Art of Malay Woodcarving.* Much weightier in tone than your average coffee-table book, this deals not only with the superb woodcarving produced on the east coast of the Peninsula and in southern Thailand, but also with the whole pre-Islamic consciousness that subtly imbues the woodcarver's art. Packed with great photos, too, of gorgeous timber mosques, incredibly detailed *kris* hilts and the like.

★**Kang Ger-Wen** *Decoration & Symbolism in Chinese Architecture.* This beautifully photographed book focuses on temples and clan houses in Singapore, but will come in handy at any Chinese historic building in Malaysia, dissecting the meanings and stories hidden in roofing styles, vegetal motifs, altars and so on.

Peter Lee and Jennifer Chen *The Straits Chinese House.* A beautifully illustrated volume exploring Peranakan domestic artefacts and their now largely vanished traditions; an excellent memento of a visit to the Baba-Nyonya museums of Penang, Meleka and Singapore.

Anthony Ratos and H. Berber *Orang Asli and their Wood Art.* One of few accessible explorations of Orang Asli lifestyles and cultures, though note that only a third of this picture-heavy volume is devoted to their fantastical carvings; the rest of the photos are of Asli settlements and generic, if pretty, jungle scenes.

★**Robert Winzeler** *The Architecture of Life and Death in Borneo.* Highly readable, illustrated study of the traditional architecture of Borneo, looking at the evolution of longhouses over the years and symbolism in building design.

FICTION

Eric Ambler *Passage of Arms.* Recently reissued, this 1959 thriller centres on a lowly Indian rubber-estate clerk who finds a valuable guerrilla arms cache during the Malayan Emergency. Hankering to launch his own bus company, he partners with some wily Chinese businessmen and a naive American in an attempt to peddle the booty. Things go awry, inevitably; the fun is in finding out who comes out on top.

★**Anthony Burgess** *The Long Day Wanes*. Burgess taught at Kuala Kangsar's posh Malay College in the mid-1950s. His Malayan trilogy (*Time for a Tiger*, *The Enemy in the Blanket* and *Beds in the East*), currently available in one volume, provides a witty and acutely observed vision of the country, underscoring the various racial tensions and prejudices during the closing years of colonial rule.

Bernice Chauly *Once We Were There*. Probably the most explicit novel ever written about Malaysia (tellingly, it was published in Singapore), with plenty of sex and drugs as a bunch of Westernized activists in KL graduate from anti-establishment journalism to the messiness of married life and "proper" jobs. The one flaw is the lack of a satisfying resolution to a shocking incident midway through.

James Clavell *King Rat*. Set in Japanese-occupied Singapore, a gripping tale of survival in the notorious Changi Prison.

★**Joseph Conrad** *Lord Jim*. Southeast Asia provides the backdrop to the story of Jim's desertion of an apparently sinking ship and subsequent efforts to redeem himself; modelled upon the sailor A.P. Williams, Jim's character also yields echoes of Rajah Brooke of Sarawak.

★**J.G. Farrell** *The Singapore Grip*. Lengthy novel – Farrell's last – of World War II Singapore in which real and fictitious characters flit from tennis to dinner party as the countdown to the Japanese occupation begins.

Barbara Ismail *Shadow Play*. Lightweight whodunnits seem to be taking off in Malaysia and Singapore: the latter has its Inspector Singh franchise, and now there's Ismail's Kelantan-based Kain Songket Mysteries series. It kicks off with this decent enough novel about a Kota Bharu woman who, not content with selling brocade, turns out to be surprisingly good at solving murders – though not all the allusions to Kelantan's distinctive culture are convincing.

★**W. Somerset Maugham** *Collected Short Stories Volume 4*. Peopled by hoary sailors, bored plantation-dwellers and colonials wearing mutton-chop whiskers and topees, this volume of Maugham's short stories resuscitates the Malaya of the 1900s; quintessential colonial literature graced by an easy style and a ready eye for a story.

Golda Mowe *Iban Dream*. The fabulous saga of a boy raised by apes who has to tackle a series of quests as a rite of passage. Just about every indigenous group in Sarawak makes an appearance at some point in what isn't a bad read once you get used to the mystical-fable style. A sequel, *Iban Journey*, appeared in 2016.

Preeta Samarasan *Evening Is The Whole Day*. Set mostly in 1950s Ipoh, this debut novel ruthlessly dissects the lives of a dysfunctional upper-middle-class Indian family, with precious few laughs to be had in a tale of infidelity, class disparities and violence behind closed doors.

★**Han Suyin** *And The Rain My Drink*. Han is best remembered for her autobiographical novel, which inspired the 1950s Hollywood hit *Love is a Many-Splendored Thing*, but the newly reissued *And The Rain My Drink*, published in 1956, deserves wider attention; there is no better novel of the upheavals of the Communist insurgency and the fag-end of British rule in Malaya, informed by Han's time living in 1950s Johor Bahru.

Tan Twan Eng *The Gift of Rain* and *The Garden of Evening Mists*. By a South Africa-based Malaysian, both these novels are deliberately paced and infused with the author's passion for Japanese culture. The first, set in Penang, focuses on the curious relationship between a Eurasian boy and his family's Japanese tenant as war breaks out, while the second follows a Chinese wartime internee during the subsequent Emergency, when she returns to the Cameron Highlands to confront her ghosts and an old Japanese acquaintance.

Language

Malay, officially referred to as Bahasa Melayu (literally "Malay language"), is the national language of Malaysia, Singapore and Brunei. Part of the Austronesian language family, it's an old tongue that became a regional lingua franca through its use in the ancient kingdom of Srivijaya and during the fifteenth-century Melaka Sultanate. Native speakers of the language are found not just in Peninsular Malaysia and northern Borneo but also in pockets of Indonesia, where a version of Malay has been adopted as the official language.

Malay is only one of many languages used in the three countries covered in this book. In Singapore, English, Mandarin and Tamil are also official tongues, with English pre-eminent as the language of government and business, while Hokkien is the most used regional Chinese dialect. In Malaysia itself, English retains an important position in business, law and government, Tamil is widely spoken among the Indian community, while Mandarin is much used by the Chinese, as are Chinese dialects such as Cantonese (especially in KL and Ipoh) and Hokkien (in Penang and on the east coast).

In practice, **English** is fairly widely understood except in rural areas and in the Malay-dominated east coast and the north of the Peninsula, where it really does pay to pick up a few words of Malay, especially since the basics are simple enough to learn. Besides, it's entertaining to get to grips with a tongue that, like English, is a ready absorber of loan words. The influence of English on modern Malay is apparent to most travellers, and with an awareness of Asian languages, it's not hard to discern the infusion of words from Sanskrit (stemming from the ancient impact of Hinduism on Southeast Asia), such as *jaya* ("success") and *negara* ("country"), as well as from Arabic, which has contributed words like *maaf* ("sorry") and many terms to do with Islam.

To pick up the language, it's best to buy a coursebook that focuses on **vernacular** Malay, as our vocabulary section does, rather than the formal language used in print and broadcasting. A good choice is *A Course in Conversational Malay* by Malcolm W. Mintz (SNP Publishing, Singapore).

Pronunciation

Malay was once written in Arabic script, but over the years this has been almost completely supplanted by a Romanized form. However, the Romanized **spellings** are prone to inconsistencies: for example, *baru*, "new", crops up in variant forms in place names like Johor Bahru and Kota Bharu, while new and old spellings of certain common words still coexist, for example *sungai/sungei, kampung/kampong*, and so forth.

Spelling quirks aside, Bahasa Malaysia is one of the more straightforward languages to pronounce, once you get your head round a few rules. One basic point to remember is that the consonants **k**, **p**, **t** have slightly less force in Malay than in English (to be precise, they aren't aspirated in Malay); if you emulate the sounds at the start of the Spanish words *cuatro*, *pero* and *toro*, you'd be in the right ball park. Other points of difference are listed below.

Syllable stress isn't complicated in Malay, though it can seem unnatural to English speakers. As a general rule, the stress lands on the **penultimate syllable** of a word (or, with words of two syllables, on the first syllable), hence SaRAwak, TerengGAnu. The chief exception concerns two-syllable words whose first syllable contains a short vowel (usually denoted by an "e"); in such cases, the stress sometimes falls on the second syllable – as in *beSAR* (big), *leKAS* (fast), and so forth; unfortunately, this isn't predictable.

MANGLISH AND SINGLISH

Manglish and **Singlish**, the distinctive forms of English widely spoken in Malaysia and Singapore respectively, can be as confusing to the uninitiated as Jamaican patois. They're really two sides of the same coin: in both, conventional English syntax gives way to a word order that's more akin to Malay or Chinese, and tenses and pronouns are discarded. Ask someone if they've ever been abroad, and you might be answered "I ever", while enquiring whether they've just been shopping might yield "Go, come back already". Responses are almost invariably distilled down to single-word replies, often repeated for stress. Request something in a shop and you'll hear "have, have", or "got, got". Other stock manglings of English include:

aidontch-main	"I don't mind"
betayudon(lah)	"You'd better not do that!"
debladigarmen	A contraction of "the bloody government"
is it?	(pronounced *eezeet*?) "Really?"
tingwat?	"What do you think?"
watudu?	"What can we do?", a rhetorical question
yusobadwan	"You're such a bad one!" meaning "that's not very nice!"

Suffixes and **exclamations** drawn from Malay and Hokkien complete this patois, the most notable being the Malay intensifier "lah", which seems to finish off just about every other utterance. In Malaysia you may hear the Malay question marker "kah" at the ends of queries, while Chinese on both sides of the Causeway might apply the suffix "ah", as in "so cheap one ah", which translates as "is it really that cheap?" or "wow, that's cheap" depending on the intonation; "ah" on its own can also mean "yes", especially if accompanied by a nod of the head. If Manglish and Singlish have you baffled, you might try raising your eyes to the heavens and crying either "ayoh" (with a drop of tone on the second syllable) or "alamak", both expressions denoting exasperation or dismay.

While these linguistic quirks often amuse foreigners and locals alike, both countries are worried that an apparent decline in **English standards** could affect their ability to do business globally. During the colonial era, the minority who could speak English tended to have a decent facility for the language. Now all students learn some English in school (in Singapore, English is actually the official language of education), but often they emerge with a weak grasp of the language. In Malaysia, there is an ongoing debate over English, with Malay nationalists wanting to emphasize Malay and other communities wanting English to get more prominence in the school curriculum. For its part, Singapore, a country with a history of preachy state campaigns, has seen the creation of a government-backed Speak Good English movement (Ⓦwww.goodenglish.org.sg).

VOWELS AND DIPHTHONGS

a somewhere in between the vowels of c**a**rp and c**u**p, but changes to a short indeterminate vowel if at the end of a word, as in banan**a**

aa like two "a" vowels separated by the merest pause; thus *maaf* (forgiveness) is rendered *ma + af*

ai as in f**i**ne (written "ei" in older spellings)

au as in h**ow**

e as in h**er**, though in many instances (not predictable) it is like the é of saut**é**, as in *kereta* (car), pronounced *keréta;* in yet others it denotes a short indeterminate vowel

i somewhere between the **i** of t**i**n and the **ee** of t**ee**n

o as in st**o**ne, though shorter and not as rounded as in English

u sometimes short as in p**u**ll, sometimes long (eg, if at the end of a word) as in p**oo**l

ua as in d**oer**

CONSONANTS

c as in **ch**ip (and written "ch" in older spellings), though slightly gentler than in English

d becomes **t** when at the end of a word

g hard, as in **g**irl

h can drop out when flanked by vowels; thus *tahu,* "know", is usually pronounced as though spelt *tau*

k drops out if at the end of the word or if followed by another consonant, becoming a glottal stop (a brief pause); thus *rakyat* (people) is pronounced *ra + yat*

kh as in the Scottish lo**ch**; found in loan words from Arabic

l unlike in English, l is not swallowed if it occurs at the end of a word

ng as in ta**ng** (the "g" is never hard – thus *telinga*, "ear", is *te-ling-a* and not *te-lin-ga*); can occur at the start of a word

ngg as in tango
ny as in canyon; can occur at the start of a word
r is lightly trilled (though in some accents it can be rendered like the French r of Paris); drops out at the ends of words when preceded by a vowel
sy as in shut

Grammar

Word order in Malay is similar to that in English, though note that adjectives usually follow nouns. **Nouns** have no genders and don't require an article, while the **plural** form is constructed either by saying the word twice, if the number of objects is unspecified (thus "book" is *buku*, "books" *buku-buku*, sometimes written *buku2*), or by specifying the number of objects before the singular noun ("three books" is thus *tiga buku*). **Verbs** have no tenses either, the time of the action being indicated either by the context, or by the use of words such as *akan* (functioning like "will") and *sudah* ("already") for the future and past. The verb "to be" seldom appears explicitly, so, for example, *saya lapar* literally means "I [am] hungry". There are two words for **negation**: *bukan*, used before nouns (for example *saya bukan doktor*, "I'm not a doctor"), and *tak* (formally *tidak*), used before verbs and adjectives (as in *saya tak lapar*, "I'm not hungry"; *saya tak makan*, "I've not eaten"). Possessive constructions are achieved simply by putting the "owner" after the thing that's "owned"; thus *kampung saya*, literally "village [of] I", is "my village".

Malay words and phrases

One point to note regarding **pronouns** is that Malay lacks a convenient word for "you", all the options being either too formal or informal. In fact, the normal way to address someone is to use their name to their face, which can seem strange to English-speakers. If you don't know someone's name, then you can use *abang* (brother) or *kak* (sister) to address a person of roughly the same age as you, or *adik* to a child, or *pak cik* or *mak cik* to a much older man or woman respectively.

You'll often see the word Dato' (or Datuk) or Tun placed before the name of a government official or some other worthy. Both are honorific titles of distinction roughly equivalent to the British "Sir". Royalty are always addressed as Tuanku.

PERSONAL PRONOUNS

I/my	saya	**he/she**	dia
we (excludes the person being spoken to) or **kita** (includes the person being spoken to)	kami	**they**	mereka
		Mr	Encik *or* Tuan
		Mrs	Puan
		Miss	Cik
you (formal) or **awak** (informal)	anda		

GREETINGS AND OTHER BASICS

"Selamat" is the all-purpose greeting derived from Arabic, which communicates a general goodwill.

good morning	selamat pagi	**safe journey**	selamat jalan
good afternoon	selamat petang	**welcome**	selamat datang
good midday (used around noon)	selamat tengah hari	**bon appetit**	selamat makan
		how are you?	apa khabar?
good evening	selamat malam	**fine**	baik *or* bagus
good night (literally "peaceful sleep")	selamat tidur	**see you again**	jumpa lagi
goodbye (literally "peaceful stay"; used by someone leaving)	selamat tinggal	**please**	tolong
		thank you	terima kasih
		you're welcome	sama-sama
		sorry/excuse me	maaf

never mind, no matter	tak apalah	husband	suami
yes	ya (sometimes pronounced a bit like "year")	wife	isteri
		friend	kawan
no	tidak	person	orang
this/that	ini/itu	do you speak English?	boleh cakap bahasa inggeris?
here	sini		
there (very nearby), (further away)	situ sana	I (don't) understand	saya (tak) faham
		that's fine/allowed	boleh
what is your name?	siapa nama awak?	can you help me?	boleh tolong saya?
my name is...	nama saya...	can I...?	boleh saya...?
where are you from?	dari mana?	to have, there is/are	ada
I come from...	saya dari...	what?	apa?
...England	...England	what is this/that?	apa ini/itu?
...America	...Amerika	when?	bila?
...Australia	...Australia	where?	di mana?
...Canada	...Kanada	who?	siapa?
...New Zealand	...Zealandia Baru (or just "New Zeelan")	why?	mengapa? or kenapa?
		how?	bagaimana?
...Ireland	...Irlandia	how much/many?	berapa?
...Scotland	...Skotlandia		

USEFUL ADJECTIVES

good	bagus	enough	cukup
a lot	banyak	open/closed	buka/tutup
a little	sikit or sedikit	hungry	lapar
cheap/expensive	murah/mahal	thirsty	haus
hot/cold	panas/sejuk	tired	letih
big/small	besar/kecil	ill	sakit

USEFUL VERBS

come/go	datang/pergi	know (someone)	kenal
do	buat	like	suka
eat/drink	makan/minum	push/pull	tolak/tarik
enter, go in	masuk	see	tengok
give/take	beri/ambil	sit	duduk
have, possess	punya or ada	sleep	tidur
hear	dengar	want	mahu
help	tolong	wish to, intend to	nak
know (something)	tahu		

GETTING AROUND AND DIRECTIONS

where is...?	di mana...?	wait	tunggu
I want to go to...	saya mahu pergi ke...	turn	belok
how do I get there?	bagaimanakah saya boleh ke sana?	left	kiri
		right	kanan
how far?	berapa jauh?	straight on	terus
how long will it take?	berapa lama?	in front	di depan or di hadapan
when will the bus leave?	bila bas berangkat?	behind	di belakang
what time does the train arrive?	jam berapa keretapi sampai?	north	utara
		south	selatan
go up, ride	naik	east	timur
get down, disembark	turun	west	barat
nearby/far away	dekat/jauh	street	jalan
stop	berhenti	airport	lapangan terbang

bus station	stesen bas *or sometimes* hentian bas	ticket	tiket
		fare (adults/children)	tambang (dewasa/kanak-kanak)
train station	stesen keretapi		
jetty	jeti *or* pangkalan	house	rumah
bicycle	baisikal	post office	pejabat pos
boat	bot *or* bot penambang (the latter is used of small passenger-carrying craft)	restaurant	restoran
		church	gereja
		mosque	masjid
longboat	perahu *or* bot panjang	Chinese temple	tokong
car	kereta	museum	muzium
motorcycle	motosikal	park, reserve	taman
plane	kapal terbang	toilet (men/women)	tandas (lelaki/perempuan)
taxi	teksi	entrance	masuk
trishaw	beca	exit	keluar

ACCOMMODATION

hotel	hotel	I need a room	saya perlu satu bilik
guesthouse	rumah tumpangan *or* rumah rehat	I'm staying for... nights	saya mahu tinggal... malam
dorm	asrama	please clean my room	tolong bersih-kan bilik saya
room (double/single)	bilik (untuk dua/satu)		
bed (double/single)	katil (kelamin/bujang)	can I store my luggage here?	boleh titip barang?
fan	kipas		
air-conditioned	berhawa dingin	I want to pay	saya nak bayar
bath, shower	mandi		

BANKING AND SHOPPING

how much is...?	berapa harga...?	market	pasar
I want to buy...	saya mahu beli...	night market	pasar malam
can you reduce the price?	boleh kurang?	supermarket	pasaraya
I'll give you no more than...	saya bayar tidak lebih dari...	bank	bank
I'm just looking	saya hanya lihat-lihat	money	wang *or* duit
shop	kedai	moneychanger	pengurup wang

NUMBERS

0	kosong	10	sepuluh
1	satu (sometimes shortened to the prefix "se-" when used with a noun)	11	sebelas
		12	duabelas
		20	duapuluh
2	dua	21	duapuluh satu
3	tiga	100	seratus
4	empat	121	seratus duapuluh satu
5	lima	200	duaratus
6	enam	1000	seribu
7	tujuh	2000	duaribu
8	lapan	1 million	sejuta
9	sembilan	a half	setengah

TIME AND DAYS OF THE WEEK

what time is it?	pukul jam berapa?	quarter to six ("five three-quarters")	lima tiga suku
time is...	pukul...		
three o'clock	tiga	six-thirty ("six half")	enam setengah
ten past four	empat sepuluh	7am	tujuh pagi
quarter past five	lima suku	8pm	lapan malam

hour	jam	later	nanti
minute	minit	next...	...depan
second	detik	last...	....yang lalu, ...lepas
day	hari	not yet	belum lagi
week	minggu	never	tak pernah
month	bulan	Monday	hari Isnin
year	tahun	Tuesday	hari Selasa
today	hari ini	Wednesday	hari Rabu
tomorrow	esok or besok	Thursday	hari Kamis
yesterday	semalam or on the east coast kelmarin	Friday	hari Jumaat
		Saturday	hari Sabtu
now	sekarang	Sunday	hari Ahad or Minggu

Food and drink glossary

The list below concentrates on Malay terminology, though a few Chinese and Indian terms appear (unfortunately, transliteration of these varies widely), as well as definitions of some culinary words used in local English.

BASICS, INCLUDING COOKING METHODS

Deciphering menus and ordering is sometimes a matter of matching ingredients and cooking methods – for example, to get an approximation of chips or French fries, you'd ask for *kentang goreng*, literally "fried potatoes". If you don't want your food spicy, say *jangan taruh cili* ("don't add chilli") or *saya tak suka pedas* ("I don't like spicy [food]").

bakar baked
bubur porridge
garpu fork
goreng fried
istimewa special (as in "today's special")
kari curry
kedai kek bakery ("cake shop")
kedai kopis a diner ("coffee shop") concentrating on inexpensive rice spreads, noodles and other dishes, while serving some beverages
kering dried
kopitiam Hokkien Chinese term for a *kedai kopis*; commonly used in Singapore
kuah gravy
kukus steamed
layan diri self-service
lemak "fatty"; often denotes use of coconut milk

makanan/minuman food/drink
mangkuk bowl
manis sweet
masam sour
masin salty
medan selera food court
panggang grilled
pedas spicy
pinggan plate
pisau knife
rebus boiled
restoran restaurant
sedap tasty
sudu spoon
sup/sop soup
tumis stir-fried, sautéed
warung stall

MEAT (DAGING) AND POULTRY

ayam chicken
babi pork
burong puyuh quail
char siew Cantonese honey roast pork

daging lembu (sapi in Borneo) beef
itek duck
kambing mutton
lap cheong sweetish, fatty pork sausage (Cantonese)

FISH (IKAN) AND OTHER SEAFOOD

ambal bamboo clams, a Sarawak delicacy
fishball spherical fish dumpling, rubbery in texture, often added to noodles and soups
fishcake fish dumpling in slices, often added to noodles
ikan bawal pomfret

lian bilis anchovy
ikan keli catfish
ikan kembong mackerel
ikan kerapu grouper
ikan kurau threadfin

ikan merah red snapper
ikan pari skate
ikan siakap sea bass
ikan tongkol tuna
ikan yu or jerung shark
kepiting or ketam crab

kerang cockles
keropok lekor tubular fish dumplings (an east coast speciality)
sotong squid, cuttlefish
udang prawn
udang galah lobster

VEGETABLES (SAYUR)

bangkwang a radish-like root (also called *jicama*), used in Chinese *rojak* and in *popiah* fillings
bawang onion
bawang putih garlic
bayam spinach or spinach-like greens
bendi okra, ladies' fingers
bunga kobis cauliflower
bendawan mushroom
chye sim or choy sum brassica greens, similar to *pak choy*
cili chilli
halia ginger
jagung corn
kacang beans, pulses or nuts
kangkung convolvulus greens with narrow leaves and hollow stems; aka water spinach or morning glory
keladi yam

keledek sweet potato
kentang potatoes
kobis cabbage
lada chilli
lobak radish
lobak merah carrot
midin jungle fern, much served in Sarawak
pak choy or pek chye soft-leaved brassica greens with broad stalks
petai beans in large pods from a tree, often sold in bunches
pucuk paku fern tips, eaten as greens
rebung bamboo shoots
tauge beansprouts
terung aubergine
timun cucumber
ubi kayu tapioca

OTHER INGREDIENTS

asam tamarind; also used to indicate a dish flavoured with tamarind
belacan pungent fermented shrimp paste
daun pandan pandanus (screwpine) leaf, imparting a sweet bouquet to foods with which it's cooked; used not only in desserts but also in some rice dishes
garam salt
gula sugar
gula Melaka palm-sugar molasses, used to sweeten *cendol* and other desserts

kaya orange or green curd jam made with egg and coconut; delicious on toast
kicap soy sauce
kicap manis sweet dark soy sauce
mentega butter
minyak oil
tahu tofu (beancurd)
telur egg
tempeh fermented soybean cakes, nutty and slightly sour

NOODLES AND NOODLE DISHES

The three most common types of noodle are *mee* (or *mi*), yellow egg noodles made from wheat flour; *bee hoon* (or *bihun* or *mee hoon*), like vermicelli; and *kuay teow* (or *hor fun*), like tagliatelle.

char kuay teow Chinese fried *kuay teow*, often seasoned with *kicap manis,* and featuring any combination of prawns, Chinese sausage, fishcake, egg, vegetables and chilli
Foochow noodles steamed and served in soy and oyster sauce with spring onions and dried fish
Hokkien fried mee *mee* and *bee hoon* fried with pieces of pork, prawn and vegetables; a variant in KL has the noodles cooked in soy sauce with *tempeh*
kang puan (or kampua) mee a rich Sibu speciality – noodles cooked in lard

kolok mee *mee* served dryish, accompanied by *char siew* slices
laksa basically noodles in a curried soup featuring some seafood and flavoured with the *laksa*-leaf herb (*daun kesom*); variations include Nyonya *laksa* (featuring coconut milk), *asam laksa* (Penang-style, with tamarind) and *laksa Johor* (made with spaghetti)
laksam *kuay teow* rice noodles in a fish sauce made with coconut milk and served with *ulam* (salad); an east coast speciality
mee bandung *mee* served in thickish gravy flavoured with beef and prawn (both of which garnish the dish)

mee goreng Indian or Malay fried noodles; Indian versions are particularly spicy

mee hailam *mee* in an oyster-sauce-based gravy

mee kari noodles in a curried soup

mee pok Teochew dish using ribbon-like yellow noodles, served with fishballs and a chilli dressing

mee rebus boiled *mee*; varies regionally, but one of the best is that sold in Singapore, featuring *mee* in a sweetish sauce made with yellow bean paste, and garnished with boiled egg and tofu

mee siam *bee hoon* cooked in tangy-sweet soup flavoured with tamarind, and garnished with slices of hard-boiled egg and beancurd

mee suah like *bee hoon* but even more threadlike and soft; can be made crispy if fried

sar hor fun flat rice noodles served in a chicken-stock soup, to which prawns, fried shallots and beansprouts are added; a speciality in Ipoh

wan tan mee roast pork, noodles and vegetables, accompanied by pork dumplings

RICE (NASI) DISHES AND SPREADS

char siew fan common one-plate meal, featuring *char siew* and gravy on a bed of steamed rice

claypot rice Chinese dish of rice topped with meat (such as *lap cheong*), cooked in an earthenware pot over a fire to create a smoky taste

daun pisang Malay term for banana-leaf curry, a Southern Indian meal with chutneys and curries, served on a mound of rice, and presented on a banana leaf with poppadums

Hainanese chicken rice Singapore's unofficial national rice dish: steamed or boiled chicken slices served on rice cooked in chicken stock, and accompanied by chicken broth, and a chilli and ginger dip

lemang glutinous rice stuffed into lengths of bamboo

nasi ayam Malay version of Hainanese chicken rice

nasi berlauk simply "rice with dishes"

nasi biryani saffron-flavoured rice cooked with chicken, beef or fish; a North Indian speciality

nasi campur standard term for a rice spread, served with an array of meat, fish and vegetable dishes to choose from

nasi dagang east coast speciality; a slightly glutinous rice steamed with coconut milk, and often brownish in appearance, usually served with fish curry

nasi goreng rice fried with diced meat and vegetables and sometimes a little spice

nasi kandar a spread of rice and curries originating with Indian Muslim caterers in Penang; the rice is often stored in a container made of wood, which is said to give it a distinctive flavour

nasi kerabu blue or green rice traditionally coloured with flower pigments, though these days food colourings may be used; found particularly in Kelantan, it's usually served with a fish curry

nasi kunyit rice given a bright yellow colour by turmeric

nasi lemak a Malay classic, rice cooked with a little coconut milk and served with *ikan bilis*, cucumber, fried peanuts, fried or hard-boiled egg slices and *sambal*

nasi Minang rice spread featuring dishes cooked in the style of the Minang Highlands of western Sumatra; similar to **nasi Padang**

nasi minyak rice cooked with *ghee*

nasi Padang rice spread with the dishes cooked in the style of Padang, Sumatra

nasi putih plain boiled rice

nasi ulam rice containing blanched herbs and greens

pulut glutinous rice

ROTI (BREAD) DISHES

The word *roti* refers both to griddle breads and to Western bread, depending on the context.

murtabak thick griddle bread, usually savoury stuffed with onion, egg and chicken or mutton

murtabak pisang a sweet version of *murtabak*, stuffed with banana.

roti bakar toast, usually served with butter and *kaya*

roti bom an especially greasy *roti canai*, containing a cheesy-tasting margarine

roti canai light, layered griddle bread served with a thin curry sauce

roti John simple Indian dish, a French loaf split and stuffed with an egg, onion and sweet chilli sauce mixture; versions containing meat are occasionally seen

roti kahwin toast spread with butter and *kaya*

roti prata Singapore name for *roti canai*

roti telur *roti canai* with an egg mixed into the dough

roti telur bawang *roti canai* with an egg and chopped onion mixed into the dough

OTHER SPECIALITIES

ayam goreng Malay-style fried chicken

ayam percik barbecued chicken with a creamy coconut sauce; a Kota Bharu speciality

bak kut teh literally "meat bone tea", a Chinese soup

made by boiling up pork ribs with soy sauce, ginger, herbs and spices

chap chye a Nyonya stew of mixed vegetables, fungi and sometimes also glass noodles (aka *tang hoon*, a rather elastic vermicelli)

chee cheong fun Cantonese speciality, vaguely like ravioli, featuring minced shrimp rolled up in rice-flour sheets, steamed and dredged in a sweet-salty red sauce

chye tow kuay also known as "carrot cake", comprising a rice flour/white radish mixture formed into cubes and fried with egg and garlic; a savoury-sweet version with added *kicap manis* is also worth trying

congee watery rice gruel eaten with slices of meat or fish or omelette; sometimes listed on menus as "porridge"

dim sum Chinese meal of titbits – dumplings, pork ribs, etc – steamed or fried and served in bamboo baskets

dosa/dosai/thosai Southern Indian pancake, made from ground rice and lentils, and served with dhal (lentils); *masala dosa* features a potato stuffing, while *rava dosa* has grated carrot in the batter

fish-head curry the head of a red snapper (usually), cooked in a spicy curry sauce with tomatoes and okra

gado-gado Malay/Indonesian salad of lightly cooked vegetables, boiled egg, slices of rice cake and a crunchy peanut sauce

idli South Indian rice-and-lentil cakes, steamed

kari kepala ikan *see* fish-head curry

kongbian Chinese-style bagels, found only in Sibu

kuih pai tee Nyonya dish vaguely resembling fried spring rolls, except that the *pai tee* are shaped like cup cakes; filling is like that for *popiah*

lontong a pairing of a *sayur lodeh*-like curry with rice cakes similar to *ketupat*

oothapam rice-and-lentil pancakes; South Indian

otak-otak mashed fish mixed with coconut milk and chilli paste, then steamed in strips wrapped in banana leaf; a Nyonya dish

popiah spring rolls, consisting of a steamed dough wrapper filled with peanuts, egg, bean shoots, vegetables and a sweet sauce; sometimes known as *lumpia*

rendang dry, highly spiced coconut curry with beef, chicken or mutton

rojak the Chinese version is a salad of greens, beansprouts, pineapple and cucumber in a peanut and prawn-paste sauce; quite different is Indian *rojak*, a variety of fritters with sweet chilli dips

satar similar to *otak-otak* but made in triangular shapes; found on the east coast

satay marinated pieces of meat, skewered on small sticks and cooked over charcoal; served with peanut sauce, cucumber, raw onion and *ketupat* (rice cake)

sayur lodeh mixed vegetables stewed in a curry sauce containing coconut milk

sop ekor Malay oxtail soup

sop kambing spicy Malay mutton soup

sop tulang Malay beef-bone soup

steamboat Chinese fondue: raw meat, fish, veggies and other titbits dunked into a steaming broth until cooked

umai raw fish salad, mixed with shallots and lime, found in east Malaysia and Brunei

umbut kelapa masak lemak young coconut shoots, cooked in coconut milk

vadai South Indian fried lentil patty

yam basket Sarawak speciality: meat, vegetables and soya bean curd in a fried yam crust

yong tau foo bean curd, fishballs and assorted vegetables, poached and served with broth and sweet dipping sauces

SNACKS AND ACCOMPANIMENTS

acar pickle, often sweet and spicy

bak kwa Chinese-style sweet barbecued pork slices, eaten as a snack

budu fermented fish sauce

cempedak goreng *cempedak*, similar to jackfruit, fried in batter, allowing not just the flesh but also the floury stones to be eaten

curry puff also called *karipap* in Malay; a semicircular pastry parcel stuffed with curried meat and vegetables

kerabu not to be confused with *nasi kerabu*, this is a salad of grated unripe fruit, mixed with chilli, grated coconut, cucumber and other ingredients

keropok (goreng) deep-fried prawn or fish crackers, derived from a dough like that used to make *keropok lekor* (see p.597)

ketupat unseasoned rice cubes boiled in packets of woven coconut-leaf strips, served as an accompaniment to satay

pau or **pow** Chinese stuffed bun made with a sweetish dough and steamed; *char siew pau* contains Cantonese honey-roast pork, *kai pau* chicken and egg, while there are also *pau* with sweet fillings include bean paste, dried coconut or *kaya*

rasam sour-spicy South Indian soup flavoured with tamarind and tomato

sambal dip made with pounded or ground chilli; *sambal belacan* is augmented with a little *belacan* for extra depth of flavour

sambar watery South Indian curry served with *dosa*

tempoyak fermented durian paste, a Malay condiment

ulam Malay salad of raw vegetables and herbs

yew char kuay Chinese fried dough sticks, good dunked in coffee; not unlike Spanish *churros* in flavour and texture

DRINKS

When ordering beverages in a *kedai kopis*, there are various standard terms to bear in mind. *Kosong* ("zero") after the name of the drink means you want it black and unsugared; the suffix *-o* (pronounced "oh") means black with sugar, *susu* means with milk (invariably of the sweetened condensed variety), *ais* or *peng* means iced, *tarik* ("pulled") denotes the popular practice of frothing a drink by pouring it repeatedly from one mug to another and back, and *kurang manis* ("lacking sweetness") means to go easy on the sugar or condensed milk. A few places also allow you to order your drink *see* or *si*, meaning with unsweetened evaporated milk. It's quite possible to combine these terms, so in theory you could order *kopi susu tarik kurang manis peng*, which would be a frothy milky coffee, iced and not too sweet. Note that condensed milk is often assumed to be wanted even if you don't say *susu*.

air botol a bottled drink (usually refers to soft drinks)

air kelapa coconut water

air laici tinned lychee juice, very sweet, usually with a couple of lychees in the glass

air minum drinking water

air tebu sugar-cane juice

bandung or **air sirap bandung** a sweet drink, bright pink in colour, made with rose essence and a little milk

bir beer

chrysanthemum tea delicately fragrant tea made from chrysanthemum blossom, and served slightly sweet, either hot or cold

cincau or **chinchow** sweet drink, the colour of cola or stout, made with strips of jelly-like seaweed

jus juice (the word *jus* is usually followed by the name of the fruit in question)

kopi coffee; some *kedai kopis* offer it freshly brewed, others serve instant

kopi jantan coffee that's claimed to be a male tonic, often advertised with posters showing avuncular Malay men apparently endorsing the drink

kopi tongkat Ali similar to *kopi jantan* (tongkat Ali is a herb that Malays believe has aphrodisiac qualities for men)

lassi Indian sweet or salty yoghurt drink

susu milk

teh tea

teh bunga kekwa chrysanthemum

teh limau ais iced lemon tea

tuak rice wine (Borneo)

FRUIT (BUAH)

belimbing starfruit

betik papaya

cempedak similar to jackfruit

duku, duku langsat small round fruits containing bittersweet segments

durian famously stinky large fruit containing rows of seeds coated in sweet creamy flesh

durian belanda soursop

epal apple

jambu batu guava

kelapa coconut

laici lychee

limau lime or lemon

limau bali pomelo

mangga mango

manggis mangosteen

nanas pineapple

nangka jackfruit

nyiur alternative term for coconut

oren orange

pisang banana

rambutan hairy-skinned stone fruit with sweet white flesh

salak teardrop-shaped fruit with scaly brown skin and bitter flesh

tembikai watermelon

DESSERTS

agar-agar seaweed-derived jelly served in squares or diamonds, and often with coconut milk for richness

air batu campur ("ABC") another name for *ais kacang*

ais kacang ice flakes with red beans, cubes of jelly, sweetcorn, rose syrup and evaporated milk

bubur cha cha sweetened coconut milk with pieces of sweet potato, yam and tapioca

cendol coconut milk, palm sugar syrup and pea-flour noodles poured over shaved ice

cheng tng clear, sweet Chinese broth containing fungi and dried fruit

kuih or **kuih-muih** Malay/Nyonya sweetmeats, ranging from something like a Western cake to fudge-like morsels made of mung bean or rice flour

kuih lapis layer cake; either a simple rice-flour confection, or an elaborate wheat-flour sponge comprising numerous very thin layers and unusually rich in egg

pisang goreng bananas or plantains coated in a thin batter and fried

Glossary

adat customary or traditional law

air water

air panas hot springs

air terjun waterfall

ancestral hall building at clan temple housing ancestral tablets

ancestral tablet small upright object representing a departed forebear, venerated in Chinese ancestor worship

atap/attap palm thatch

Baba Straits-born Chinese (male)

bandar town

bandaraya city

bangunan building

banjaran mountain range

batang river system

batik wax and dye technique of cloth decoration

batu rock/stone

bejalai period in an Iban youth's life when he ventures out from the longhouse to experience life in the towns

belian a hardwood traditionally used to construct Sarawak longhouses

belukar secondary rainforest, essentially woodland that regrows in areas where primary forest has been disturbed or cut down

bomoh traditional spiritualist healer

bukit hill

bumbun hide

bumiputra person deemed indigenous to Malaysia ("son of the soil")

bungalow in local English, any detached house

candi temple

Cantonese pertaining to the Guangdong province of southeast China

clan association social club and welfare organization, its members drawn from Chinese migrants from a particular city or area; its premises are called a clan hall/house

coolie colonial-era term for an unskilled labourer

daerah an administrative district

daulat divine force possessed by a ruler that commands unquestioning loyalty

Dayak/Dyak a now largely obsolete umbrella term once used to denote the tribal peoples of Borneo

dipterocarp the predominant family of trees in the rainforest, comprising many types of exceptionally tall trees reaching up to the top of the forest canopy

ekspres express (used of boats and buses)

empangan dam

Foochow pertaining to Fuzhou, a city in Fujian province, southeast China

gasing spinning top

gawai annual festivals celebrated by indigenous groups in Sarawak

gelanggang seni cultural centre

gereja church

godown warehouse

gopuram pyramidal tower decorated with deities and placed over the entrance to a Hindu temple

gua cave

gunung mountain

Hainanese pertaining to Hainan Island, southeast China

halal something permissible in Islam

hill station a settlement or resort at relatively high altitude usually founded in colonial times

Hokkien pertaining to the Fujian province of southeast China, the main dialect of which is more formally called **minnan**

huay guan/kuan another term for clan association

hutan forest

ikat woven fabric

istana palace

jalan road, street

jambatan bridge

kampung/kampong village

kelong a fishing platform extending out to sea from some beaches, acting to lure fish to nets at the far end

kemah campsite

kerangas sparse forest ("poor soil")

khalwat an offence under Islamic law, typically involving an unmarried Muslim couple being together in private

kongsi Chinese clan house/temple; has entered Malay as a word meaning "share"

kota fort

kris wavy-bladed Malay dagger

kuala river confluence or estuary

labu gourd; also used of the gourd-like ceramic bottles made as souvenirs in some parts of the Peninsula

lata waterfall

laut sea

lebuh avenue, street

lebuhraya highway/expressway

lorong lane

mak yong courtly dance-drama

makam grave or tomb

Malaya old name for the area now called Peninsular Malaysia

Mamak Indian Muslim; used particularly of restaurants run by Indian Muslims

mandi Asian method of showering by dousing with water from a tank using a small bucket or dipper

masjid mosque

Mat Salleh Malaysian slang for a white person

Melayu Malay

menara minaret or tower

merdeka freedom, in general; can specifically refer to Malaysian independence

Minangkabau matriarchal people from Sumatra

negara national

nipah a type of palm tree

Nyonya/Nonya Straits-born Chinese (female)

Orang Asli Peninsular Malaysia aborigines ("original people"); also Orang Ulu (upriver people) and Orang Laut (sea people)

padang field/square; usually the main town square

pangkalan jetty or port (literally "base")

pantai beach

parang machete

pasar market

pasar malam night market

pasir sand

pejabat Pos post office

pekan town

pelabuhan port/harbour

penghulu chieftain, leader

Peranakan Straits-born Chinese

perigi well

persekutuan federal

pintu arch/gate/door

pondok hut or shelter

pulau island

rajah prince

Ramadan Muslim fasting month

rebana drum

rotan rattan, and the rattan cane used to inflict corporal punishment

rumah persinggahan lodging house

rumah rehat older guesthouse (literally "resthouse"), now mainly privately run, though once state-owned

rumah tumpangan boarding house

samping songket worn by a man as a short sarong over loose trousers

saree traditional Indian woman's garment, worn in conjunction with a **choli** (short-sleeved blouse)

sarung/sarong cloth worn as a wrap around the lower body

sekolah school

semenanjung Peninsula

seni art or skill

shophouse a two-storey terraced building found mainly in town centres, and often featuring a facade that is recessed at street level, providing a shaded walkway that serves as a pavement

silat Malay art of self-defence

songket brocade

songkok Malay male headgear, a little like a flattish fez, made of black velvet over cardboard

sulap hut (East Malaysia, especially Sabah)

sultan ruler

sungai/sungei river

taman park

tamu market/fair

tanjung/tanjong cape, headland

tasik/tasek lake

telaga freshwater spring or well

teluk/telok bay or inlet

Teochew pertaining to Chaozhou, a city in Fujian province, southeast China

tokong Chinese temple

towkay Chinese merchant

tuai tribal headman (Sarawak)

wasai waterfall or area with a pool (Brunei), Sabah

wau kite

wayang show, ranging from a film screening to Chinese opera

wayang kulit shadow-puppet play (literally "skin show", after the fact that the puppets are made of hide)

wisma building, especially a commercial one

ACRONYMS

BN Barisan Nasional or National Front – the coalition, dominated by UMNO, which has governed Malaysia since 1974

KTM Keretapi Tanah Melayu, the Malaysian national railway company

MAS Malaysia Airlines

MCA Malaysian Chinese Association, the Chinese wing of the governing BN

MCP Malayan Communist Party

MRT Singapore's Mass Rapid Transit system

PAP Singaporean People's Action Party

PAS Parti Islam SeMalaysia, the Pan-Malaysian Islamic Party

PKR Parti Keadilan Rakyat, the Malaysian opposition People's Justice Party (usually called simply Keadilan)

SIA Singapore Airlines

UMNO United Malays National Organization

Small print and index

A ROUGH GUIDE TO ROUGH GUIDES

Published in 1982, the first Rough Guide – to Greece – was a student scheme that became a publishing phenomenon. Mark Ellingham, a recent graduate in English from Bristol University, had been travelling in Greece the previous summer and couldn't find the right guidebook. With a small group of friends he wrote his own guide, combining a contemporary, journalistic style with a thoroughly practical approach to travellers' needs.

The immediate success of the book spawned a series that rapidly covered dozens of destinations. And, in addition to impecunious backpackers, Rough Guides soon acquired a much broader readership that relished the guides' wit and inquisitiveness as much as their enthusiastic, critical approach and value-for-money ethos. These days, Rough Guides include recommendations from budget to luxury and cover more than 120 destinations around the globe, from Amsterdam to Zanzibar, all regularly updated by our team of roaming writers.

Browse all our latest guides, read inspirational features and book your trip at **roughguides.com**.

Rough Guide credits

Editors: Helen Abramson, Emma Gibbs, Joe Staines, Georgia Stephens
Layout: Ankur Guha, Pradeep Thapliyal
Cartography: Katie Bennett, Ed Wright
Picture editor: Marta Bescos Sanchez, Aude Vauconsant

Managing editors: Rachel Lawrence, Andy Turner
Editorial assistant: Aimee White
Cover photo research: Marta Bescos Sanchez
Senior DTP coordinator: Dan May
Managing director: Agnieszka Mizak

Publishing information

This 9th edition published June 2018 by
Rough Guides Ltd

Distribution
UK, Ireland and Europe
Apa Publications (UK) Ltd; sales@roughguides.com
United States and Canada
Ingram Publisher Services; ips@ingramcontent.com
Australia and New Zealand
Woodslane; info@woodslane.com.au
Southeast Asia
Apa Publications (SN) Pte; sales@roughguides.com
Worldwide
Apa Publications (UK) Ltd; sales@roughguides.com
Special sales, content licensing and co-publishing
Rough Guides can be purchased in bulk quantities
at discounted prices. We can create special editions,
personalized jackets and corporate imprints tailored to
your needs. sales@roughguides.com
roughguides.com
Printed in China

Acknowledgements

Marco Ferrarese Thanks to Andy Turner who brought
me on board, Richard Lim for his invaluable help with the
project and Helen Abramson for the careful editing. A
special thanks with hugs goes to my wife Kit Yeng Chan,
who once again was my co-pilot and morale booster
during this umpteenth research trip. And then, thanks to
all the people who helped me out in one way or another
during the different legs of the research: in Penang,
thanks to Gareth Richards and Gerakbudaya Bookshop,
Rebecca Duckett-Wilkinson, Cole Yew at Soundmaker,
Paul Augustin and all the friends who shared information
on George Town's burgeoning art scene. In Taiping,
thanks to Yin and Sojourn Beds & Cafe. In Ipoh, thanks
to CP Lo, Anba Razen and Law Siak Hong. In Tanah Rata,
thanks to Gerard and family. In Lenggong, many thanks
to Hock Seng Ng and Pinky Mok, who adopted me as
a family member. On Pangkor Island, thanks to Mohan,
Bavanni and family at Tiger Rock, and all the staff at Nipah
Guesthouse. In Langkawi, thanks to Kay Mohlman and
Richard Krause for putting me up and the good times.
In Kuala Lipis, thanks to Mister Appu for all the trekking
information. In Jerantut and Taman Negara, thanks to
Auntie Angie and NKS Travel. In Dabong, thanks to Pak Din
and Rose House. And last but not least, thanks to the wild
elephant who, after I'd spent ten years criss-crossing the
peninsula on the East-West Highway without luck, finally
showed up and made my day.

Richard Lim I'd like to thank, in no particular order:
the staff at Sabah Tourism, especially Robin, Diana
and Noredah; Rodzan and Norliza at Sabah Parks; Lucy

and Karen in KK; Anton, C.K., Gert et al. in and around
Sandakan; Itisha, Simon and Suzan in Lahad Datu; Orou
Sapulot; K. Ravi Mandalam; Rory and Kay; Melanie and
Aida; Gavin Bate and Tom; Ann Otegil; James Burns; Cede
Prudente; Surin Suksuwan; Elyrice; Janice Nga; Robin
Hanbury-Tenison; Sophie Grig; Harrison Ngau; Maurice
Balang and Gareth. In Singapore, thanks to the Singapore
Tourism Board, John Gee; Michael Meyer; Quek I-Gek;
and the Bukit Brown posse. Thanks also to my family, plus
David Leffman and Ooi Kee Beng.

Simon Willmore First, thanks to Annabelle for always
understanding my love for Malaysia (I can sincerely say it
is one of the greatest countries in the world) and letting
me go back so many times – I love you. Toine, Philip,
Alberto, Rachel, Andrei: thanks as always for looking after
an old friend. Jazmin and family, Sonny, Justin: thanks for
showing me around. To the whole team at RG HQ and
in particular Andy, Georgia, Joe: it's been an absolute
pleasure working with you, as always.

Charles Young I'd like to thank my wife Qing Qing for
being there on the journey; Emma, Andy and Georgia at
RG; Kester and Anna for their hospitality on the way; Kang,
Zeck and Deen in Kota Bharu, and Awi in Terengganu, for
keeping the backpacker spirit alive; the Sarawak posse
at Mazlan's in Cherating; Antoine and Lolo, the guys at the
forestry office, at the (now nomadic) tourist office, and Paul
at AAB, in Kuching; Julian and family in Bario; and of course
all the Malaysian people we met on the way who were, as
always, so friendly, welcoming and helpful.

ABOUT THE AUTHORS

Marco Ferrarese has lived in Penang since 2009, from where he covers Malaysia, India and the larger Southeast Asian region for a number of international publications, including *Travel + Leisure Southeast Asia*, *The Guardian*, *BBC Travel*, *Air Asia Travel 3Sixty°* and *Nikkei Asian Review*. His debut novel *Nazi Goreng* (2013) was a bestseller in Malaysia until it was banned by the Ministry of Home Affairs in 2015. He has also played guitar in Malaysian hardcore punk bands, earned a PhD in anthropology from Monash University Malaysia, and participated in the country's principal art and literary festivals. He and his Malaysian wife are on the road most of the time. Find out more about him and his books at ⓦmarcoferrarese.com and ⓦmonkeyrockworld.com.

Richard Lim Not to be confused with his Singapore journalist namesake, Richard Lim (ⓖplus.google.com/+RichardLim) has been dabbling on the fringes of travel and science journalism for many years. He lives in London.

Simon Willmore (@SiWillmore), a journalist, author and editor, lived in Kuala Lumpur for three years and loved every minute of it. This is his fourth book for Rough Guides, having also co-authored titles on France, India and Spain, and he has contributed to everything from blogs for *National Geographic Traveller* to a technology column in *Woman* magazine.

Charles Young has been travelling since university and, as well as working on well over a dozen Rough Guide titles, has taught English in Catalunya, run a coffee shop in Hong Kong, been a publican in South Korea and worked in the spice trade in India. He currently lives in deepest, darkest China, but returns to the UK soon.

Help us update

We've gone to a lot of effort to ensure that the 9th edition of **The Rough Guide to Malaysia, Singapore & Brunei** is accurate and up-to-date. However, things change – places get "discovered", opening hours are notoriously fickle, restaurants and rooms raise prices or lower standards. If you feel we've got it wrong or left something out, we'd like to know, and if you can remember the address, the price, the hours, the phone number, so much the better.

Please send your comments with the subject line **"Rough Guide Malaysia, Singapore & Brunei Update"** to mail@uk.roughguides.com. We'll credit all contributions and send a copy of the next edition (or any other Rough Guide if you prefer) for the very best emails.

Readers' updates

Thanks to all the readers who have taken the time to write in with comments and suggestions (and apologies if we've inadvertently omitted or misspelt anyone's name):

Steve Baete, Blaž Cugmas, Val Johnson, Wieteke Kalkema, John Liu, Steve Locke, Monica Mackaness and John Garrett, Maria and Steffen, Nisha Pasha, Tara Scarfe, Veerle Van de Catsye, Damien White.

Photo credits

All photos © Rough Guides, except the following:
(Key: t-top; c-centre; b-bottom; l-left; r-right)

Index

Maps are marked in grey

Map symbols

The symbols below are used on maps throughout the book

	International boundary	ⓘ	Tourist office	⚉	Viewpoint		
	Province boundary	✉	Post office	⚟	Lighthouse		
	Chapter division boundary	⊞	Hospital		Radio Tower		
	Major road	☏	Telephone	⚟	Campsite		
	Minor road	⚏	Public gardens/fountain		Hut/hide		
	Motorway	⚐	Golf course		Park HQ		
	Pedestrian road	⌒	Arch		Mosque		
	Steps	♞	Castle/fort		Buddhist temple		
	Unpaved road	♦	Museum		Hindu/Sikh temple		
	Funicular	⏛	Monument		Chinese temple		
	Railway	⏾	Tower	✡	Synagogue		
	Footpath	⬗	Swimming pool		Snorkelling		
	Ferry route	⊠	Gate/entrance		Church (regional map)		
	River	▲	Peak		Church (town map)		
✈	Airport (international)	⚒	Rock	▭	Market		
✈	Airport (regional)	⌣	Bridge	⬭	Stadium		
Ⓗ	Helipad	☼	Hill	▬	Building		
⊖	MRT station (Singapore)	⌂	Cave		Water village		
★	Transport stop	⋰	Ruin		Park		
▣	Parking	⚘	Marshland		Beach		
⛽	Petrol station	♣	Tree		Christian cemetery		
◆	Point of interest	⚎	Waterfall		Muslim cemetery		
@	Internet access		Gorge				

Listings key

- ■ Accommodation
- ● Eating
- ■ Drinking/nightlife
- ● Shopping